The Fundamentals of
Canadian Income Tax
9th Edition

Vern Krishna, CM, QC, LL.M., LL.D (HON), FRSC,
FCGA
Barrister at Law and Counsel: Borden Ladner Gervais LLP
Professor of Common Law, University of Ottawa

CGA Tax Research Centre
(University of Ottawa)

D0557262

THOMSON
CARSWELL

Library and Archives Canada has catalogued this publication as follows:

   The fundamentals of Canadian income tax.

Irregular.
1985-
ISSN 1204-9050
ISBN 0-459-28028-7 (9ᵗʰ edition)

   1. Income tax — Law and legislation — Canada.   I. Carswell Company

KE5759.K74   343.7105'2   C96-300515-4
KF6370.ZA2F86

THOMSON

CARSWELL

One Corporate Plaza	Customer Relations
2075 Kennedy Road	Toronto 1-416-609-3800
Toronto, Ontario	Elsewhere in Canada/U.S. 1-800-387-5164
M1T 3V4	Fax 1-416-298-5082
	World Wide Web: http://www.carswell.com
	E-mail: carswell.orders@thomson.com

To Savitri, Linda, Nicola,
Sacha and Vivian

PREFACE TO THE 9TH (2006) EDITION

Tax law affects all domestic and international transactions involving the exchange of goods, services and intellectual property. Thus, the subject permeates all commercial and most personal transactions, and its impact as a public policy statute on the lives of individuals is second only to that of constitutional law.

Tax law is complicated and students either endure it with resentment or simply ignore its existence, hoping that it will go away and not contaminate their lives when they become "real lawyers". Law students in tax courses have been known to develop narcotaxis — a medical ailment that, within thirty seconds of hearing their professors begin to explain tax law, causes glassy eyes, loss of bodily feeling, and a shallow coma — which can last for nearly ninety minutes. Fortunately, the condition is not enduring and students recover completely by the end of class.

Although some lawyers manage to fill entire careers without recognizing a tax issue, it is difficult to escape the tentacles of tax law in corporate, commercial, securities, family, property, estates, trusts, and (white-collar) criminal law. Given the ever-increasing bulk and complexity of the law, we need to understand its fundamental principles and underlying policies. Although the *Income Tax Act* is a significant instrument of economic and regulatory policy, it is — first and foremost — a legislative enactment. Hence, we must analyze and interpret it using legal skills and according to the evolving rules of statutory construction.

The purpose of this text is to assist law students and practitioners in understanding the fundamental principles of tax law, the basic structure of the statute and the influence of judicial decisions on the law. It focuses on the principles and basic concepts of income tax law. We superimpose technical detail on the fundamentals only to the extent necessary for a proper and enduring understanding of tax law and practice.

We assume that readers of this text will have no prior knowledge — at least not from a legal perspective — of tax law. Hence, we start with an examination of fundamental concepts. In Chapter 1, in the "Introduction", for example, we look at federal and provincial powers to tax under constitutional doctrines and bilateral agreements. We also look at the key concepts of tax systems and the basic principles of tax policy that influence the structure and politics of the law.

Tax law must make difficult compromises between competing social and economic values, revenue requirements, administrative efficiency, a sense of fair play and the costs of fiscal administration. Although the primary function of tax statutes is to raise revenue, governments also use them to achieve other social and political goals — for example, to dispense benefits, provide economic incentives, hide indirect trade subsidies and, sometimes, even to buy votes.

In this text, we address five fundamental questions that are common to all fiscal statutes:

- Who is taxable?
- What is taxable?

- How much do we tax?
- When is income taxable? and
- What are the processes to ensure compliance and the resolution of disputes?

We answer each of these questions in the context of the underlying policies, statutory and tax treaty authorities, administrative practices and judicial decisions relevant to the federal tax law.

The text is comprehensive but, unlike the multi-volume looseleaf services, it is not exhaustive.

It has been twenty-one years since the appearance of the first edition of this text. The first edition appeared in 1985 just after the Supreme Court of Canada's landmark decision in *Stubart* [1984] 1 S.C.R. 536, the precursor to the General Anti-Avoidance Rule (GAAR) in section 245. The Supreme Court handed down its first decision interpreting GAAR — *Canada Trustco* — on October 19, 2005, twenty-one years after its decision in *Stubart*. It is unclear how much the Supreme Court added to the interpretation of tax avoidance.

The *Income Tax Act* continues to grow and we fully expect it to double in size and complexity during the next generation. The statute is long — approximately 2100 pages — badly drafted, and written in a style that would make our high school teachers of English cringe with embarrassment. Notwithstanding the complexity of tax law, citizens must endure audits, which, like opera, the revenue authorities conduct in a language that few understand and that usually ends in tragedy. Nevertheless, we fervently cling to the doctrine that every person is presumed to know the law and must live according to the dictates of the statute.

Tax law can be a fun course in law school. It provides a better understanding of how society functions. Parliament legislates, and taxpayers — many with limited resources — must assert their rights under difficult rules against increasingly bigger government. How should a student learn tax law in this environment of technical complexity? By understanding the basic structure and topography of the subject. Yes, the tax law has a conceptual foundation, an organized — if not always obvious — structure that sits on a bedrock of economic, political and social policies. To understand the subject one must first place the law in the context of its socio-economic and political dimensions. The *Income Tax Act* is a legislative enactment. Hence, one must read each provision carefully — at least three times — methodically, and in the context of evolving judicial doctrines of statutory interpretation.

I have updated the text for legislative amendments, judicial decisions and administrative pronouncements. The text references relevant statutory provisions, Interpretation Bulletins, Advance Rulings, Information Circulars and significant income tax treaties. These additional references allow the reader to move into greater levels of detail as circumstances warrant. There is also a comprehensive glossary of tax, financial and accounting terms for those unfamiliar with the jargon of business finance.

In writing the various editions of this text, I have always been able to draw upon the assistance of dedicated and diligent research assistants who help me with the project and encourage me to meet deadlines. The revisions to this edition were substantial. I relied on Mr. Gary Donell, B.Comm., Senior Instructor in Advanced Tax and the former Income Tax Rulings Officer with the Canada Revenue Agency. I appreciate his contribution to its improvement and timely production. The text is better for his thoughtful suggestions and contribution. I am also grateful to Marilyn Prince and Mante Molepo at Borden Ladner Gervais LLP for their invaluable assistance in the updating of this edition.

Dr. Johnson said that the only end of writing is to enable readers to enjoy life better or to better endure it. I have always been somewhat skeptical that this text, or, indeed, any text on income tax law, can satisfy his first criterion. I hope, however, that this edition will allow students to better endure their narcotaxis attacks and reduce anxiety in income tax courses. I also hope that it will make it easier for practitioners to adapt to the ever-changing challenges of the operatic world of income tax law.

The law in the text is as of July 30, 2006.

Vern Krishna

Please send your comments by e-mail to *vkrishna@uottawa.ca* or *vkrishna@blgcanada.com*

ACKNOWLEDGEMENT

I wish to acknowledge the generous assistance and support of The Fellows and Life Fellows of the Foundation of Legal Research in the preparation of this text.

*The art of taxation is so to pluck the goose
that the maximum number of feathers are obtained
with the mimimum amount of hissing.*

Jean Colbert (1665)

TABLE OF CONTENTS

Part I — Structure of Tax System

Table of Contents

Part II — Jurisdiction to Tax

CHAPTER 3 — RESIDENCE AND SOURCE 97

Table of Contents

Part IV — Office & Employment Income

CHAPTER 6 — EMPLOYMENT INCOME 219

Table of Contents

Table of Contents

Table of Contents

Table of Contents

Part VII — Other Income & Deductions

Table of Contents

Table of Contents

Table of Contents

Table of Contents

Table of Contents

Table of Contents

Table of Contents

Table of Contents

Table of Contents

Table of Contents

Table of Contents

Table of Contents

Table of Contents

Table of Contents

Part XIII — Mergers & Acquisitions

CHAPTER 29 — AMALGAMATIONS AND WIND-UPS 1219

Table of Contents

Table of Contents

Table of Contents

Table of Contents

Table of Contents

Table of Contents

TABLE OF CASES

Table of Cases

Table of Cases

Table of Cases

Table of Cases

Table of Cases

Table of Cases

Table of Cases

Table of Cases

Table of Cases

Table of Cases

Table of Cases

Table of Cases

Table of Cases

Table of Cases

Table of Cases

Table of Cases

PART I: STRUCTURE OF TAX SYSTEM

CHAPTER 1 — INTRODUCTION

"We are about to consider the unpleasant subject of taxes."

(L. Eisenstein, *The Ideologies of Taxation*)

I. — General Comment

We are about to consider the unpleasant subject of taxes.[1] Income tax is the involuntary expropriation of property without direct compensation — compulsory contributions that the government levies on transactions in goods, services and intellectual property to finance public expenditures that society considers to be for the public good.

Income tax law has a reputation of being a difficult and dry subject. To be sure, tax law is difficult, but it is neither dry nor unpleasant. Yes, tax law is replete with technical detail, difficult — often incomprehensible — sometimes circular, and usually uses obtuse language. Nevertheless, taxpayers must live with the statute as it is and not with the one that they wish to have written. We must comply with the law or face severe sanctions; advisors must advise on uncertain, complex and poorly drafted provisions; and the courts must interpret the legislation in lengthy court battles.

---

[1] Attributed to L. Eisenstein, *The Ideologies of Taxation*.

Ultimately, however, all law is behavioural and tax law more so than any other. At the top end of the rate scale, governments take nearly 46 per cent of all earned income. It is, therefore, understandable that taxpayers expend considerable energy and resources trying to minimize the government's tax bite. At the same time, legislators respond to taxpayer planning by drafting provisions that are ever more complex to reduce tax leakage and revenue loss. The income tax statute and related law takes up 2500 printed pages and grows at the rate of 100-150 pages every year.

To be sure, the raising of revenue is an important, if not imperative, justification of tax law. But governments increasingly use tax law for the purposes of implementing social policies and redistributing income. We see this even in the title of the individual tax return form - "Income Tax and Benefit Return" — and the fact that nearly one-third of Canadians who file tax returns do not pay any income tax at all and file primarily to receive benefits from the government.

Hence, tax law must balance varied needs: adequate funding for public expenditures, economic and regional incentives and equitable redistribution of income. Any statute that serves so many diverse and, often, conflicting purposes is necessarily more complex than a single purpose statute. At the same time, tax law should ensure procedural fairness in administration and reasonable access to the judicial process to resolve disputes.

The drafting of the *Income Tax Act* is poor, which adds to its complexity. The statute violates almost every principle of grammatical construction. The Canadian drafting tradition that each section, no matter its length, should be in a single self-contained sentence does not make the statute easy to read. The comments of a member of the British Parliament speaking about the Irish Home Rule bill in 1889 could just as easily describe the Canadian *Income Tax Act* today:

> . . .it sweats difficulties at every paragraph; every provision breeds a dilemma; every clause ends in a cul-de-sac; dangers lurk in every line; mischiefs abound in every sentence and an air of evil hangs over it all.

Similarly Judge Mogan of the Tax Court of Canada describing the definition of "term preferred share" in *Citibank Canada*:[2]

> The definition of "term preferred share" is prolix in the extreme. The persons who drafted that definition did not practise any economy of words or language. One may well ask how many members of parliament understood the definition when it was made law by amendment to the Act. . . .
>
> It is so detailed, so particularized; so long [the definition extends over 2580 words in a single sentence] and tedious and excessive in its use of language.

---

[2]*Citibank of Canada v. R.*, [2001] 2 C.T.C. 2260 (T.C.C. [General Procedure]); aff'd. [2002] 2 C.T.C. 171 (Fed. C.A.).

Shorn of its technical language, however, all tax law is ultimately policy. The Act is a living document, a mirror that reflects the social, political, economic, and moral values of society at any particular time. Thus, the statute is more than a mere laundry list of provisions; it has a carefully crafted — but not drafted — structure. A reason underlies every provision.

Although the policy of a particular provision may not be obvious on first reading and its language not entirely elegant, its rationale is there for those who search for it. As Justice Frankfurter said:[3]

> Legislation has an aim: it seeks to obviate some mischief, to supply an inadequacy, to effect a change in policy, to formulate a plan of Government. That aim, that policy is not drawn, like nitrogen, out of the air; it is evinced in the language of the statute as read in the light of other external manifestations of purpose.

The focus of tax policy analysis should be to reconcile the language of the statute with the purpose of the provisions. This creates tension in statutory interpretation between applying the plain meaning of words and the purpose of the underlying provision. The courts tell us that they apply the plain meaning of words where the language is clear and unambiguous and look to the purpose of the provision where the language is not so clear but the purpose is.

Ultimately, however, all judges are lawmakers. To be sure, they endeavour to remain inconspicuous in tax law but, in important ways, judges act as policymakers and determine what the law is. The meaning of words in tax law is rarely as plain as its authors anticipated they would be when they drafted the legislation. Thus, judges look at legislative history and engage in purposive analysis when the words are capable of different meanings. Purposive analysis requires an understanding of the underlying principles of tax policy, which allows judges to bring their own policy views to bear in interpreting the statute. Thus, in making the common law, judges often apply their own normative beliefs of the appropriate policy. Hence, it is important in litigation to "know" your judge.

We see judicial lawmaking in the decisions of the tax courts. In *Bailey v. R.*,[4] for example, the taxpayer claimed private elementary school fees as "child care" expenses — which are deductible — and not as education expenses — which are not. The Tax Court in an informal decision looked at the so-called "object and spirit" of the childcare provisions and allowed the deduction saying that any education from the school was merely an *incidental* benefit.

Courts often grope in the technical detail of the statutory language searching for the purpose of the legislation. In *Hewlett-Packard (Canada) Co. v. R.*,[5] for example, the Tax Court had

---

[3]Frankfurter, Felix, "Some Reflections on the Reading of Statutes" (1947) 47 Colum. L. Rev. No. 4, 527 at 538-39.

[4]2005 TCC 305, [2005] 3 C.T.C. 2170 (T.C.C. [Informal Procedure]).

[5]2005 CarswellNat 1765, 2005 TCC 398, 2005 D.T.C. 976, [2005] 4 C.T.C. 2274 (T.C.C. [General Procedure]).

to wrestle with whether the word "lodge" included luxury hotels. If it did, the taxpayer could not deduct expenses to entertain its employees in the particular hotels. The purpose of the rule prohibiting deduction of lodge expenses is to prevent expense account living on the public purse. Although dictionaries sometimes use the word "hotel" to describe "lodge", the Tax Court did not think that most Canadians would describe large resort hotels with a range of modern amenities as "lodges". Hence, the court allowed the taxpayer to deduct its substantial expenses and sideswiped the underlying policy of the provision against the deduction of such expenses.

Thus, although there is no common law taxation, many of the important principles of Canadian tax law come in the form of judge-made common law. Of course, the selection of one method of interpretation over another becomes clear only retrospectively. Bureaucrats write complex laws. Nowhere is this truer than in tax law. Taxpayers must live with the complexity of the statute and pay for professional advisors to comply with it. Ultimately, tax advisors must anticipate whether a court will interpret the "unambiguous words" in the same manner as the advisor. Resolving tax disputes, however, is a slow, arduous and expensive process. Hence, the unpleasant subject of taxes.

1. — Historical Background

The antecedent of most modern income tax systems was the need to finance wars. Prior to World War I, the principal sources of revenue in Canada were customs duties and excise taxes. Sir Robert Borden, Prime Minister of Canada, introduced the federal income tax on business profits in 1916, and a tax on personal income in 1917. Both of these taxes were initially put forward as temporary measures to finance World War I. As Sir Thomas White, Minister of Finance, said when he introduced the *Income War Tax Act*:

> I have placed no time limit upon this measure . . . a year or two after the war is over, the measure should be definitely reviewed.

Louis St. Laurent finally made income taxes permanent on January 1, 1949. The rest is history. The *Income War Tax Act*, which was all of 10 pages, grew through several reincarnations of "tax reform" into the *Income Tax Act* of today. Now it spans over 2500 pages and is growing annually at a healthy pace.[6]

The Canadian income tax system has changed significantly since its introduction in 1917. The *Income War Tax Act* exempted the first $1500 of income — more than $25,000 in 2004 dollars — from any tax whatsoever. The highest rate of 72 per cent applied to $107 million in 2004 dollars. The Act has undergone several reforms and various attempts at simplification. A comprehensive reform of the tax system was undertaken by the *Carter Commission*, which culminated in the present version of the *Income Tax Act* in 1972. Since that time there have been various further attempts at reform and simplification of the statute, all with little

---

[6]Up from 2000 pages since 2004.

success. The Act becomes increasingly complex each year with the addition of hundreds of pages of amendments and regulations. As the Joint Committee on Taxation of the Canadian Bar Association and the Canadian Institute of Chartered Accountants said, in addressing the House of Commons Committee on Finance and Economic Affairs:

> For any taxpayer to pick up some of this legislation we are looking at today and understand how these rules are going to impact on him when he sits down to fill out his tax return is almost impossible.

> There is no quick fix to the complexity issue. It is a very long-term problem, but I fear that the Government's priority for tax simplification has fallen down to the bottom of the various objectives set out for tax reform.

In a similar vein, the Report of the Technical Committee on Business Taxation reported in 1997:[7]

> [I]n a complex society that is part of a world economy, where the form and processes of business activities are increasingly sophisticated, and where the tax system is also used for purposes other than raising revenue, it is unrealistic to expect our tax system to be simple.

Bureaucrats write complex laws. Nowhere is this more true than in tax law. Taxpayers must live with the complexity and pay dearly for professional advice to comply with it. Resolving tax disputes is a slow, arduous and expensive process. Hence, the unpleasant subject of taxes.

2. — The Authority to Tax

(a) — Division of Powers

Under Anglo-Canadian law the government can impose taxes only on the authority of legislation pursuant to the Constitution. This tradition has its origins in the *Magna Carta* (1215).

The Canadian Constitution[8] divides the authority to impose taxes between the federal and provincial governments. The federal Parliament has the power under subsection 91(3) to raise money by *any* mode or system of taxation. The provinces can also impose income taxes but are restricted by subsection 92(2) to *direct* taxation within the province for the purpose of raising revenue for provincial purposes. This division of the taxing power gives the federal government a substantial voice over the national economy and the distribution of wealth amongst the provinces. Neither the Dominion nor a province may delegate to the

---

[7]Report of the Technical Committee on Business Taxation (December 1997), A Report to the Minister of Finance, at 1.2.

[8]*Constitution Act, 1867* (U.K.), 30 & 31 Vict., c. 3.

other its power to legislate on taxation.[9] As we will see in subsequent chapters, this dual authority to levy income taxes results in differential income tax burdens in various regions in the country. The income tax burden on taxpayers in Newfoundland, for example, is substantially higher than the burden in Alberta.

The Act is the primary source of income tax law. *Income Tax Regulations* ("Regulations") are enacted pursuant to the authority of the Act. Unlike the Act, however, which can be amended only by Parliament through a Bill introduced in the House of Commons, Regulations are enacted by an Order-in-Council.

The provincial power to tax is limited. In order for a provincial tax to be valid, the tax must be (1) a direct tax; (2) imposed within the province; and (3) for provincial purposes. The last of these requirements prevents a province from using its taxing power for colourable purposes, for example, to conceal its real objectives.

The constitutional rationale for limiting provincial legislatures to direct taxation is to contain provincial powers within provincial boundaries. In economic terms, we cannot contain provincial taxes if direct taxes are passed on to persons (for example, consumers) outside the province. As a matter of law, however, there is an important distinction between direct and indirect taxation, a distinction formulated by John Stuart Mill in 1848 as follows:[10]

> A direct tax is one which is demanded from the very persons who it is intended or desired should pay it. Indirect taxes are those which are demanded from one person in the expectation and intention that he shall indemnify himself at the expense of another; such as the excise or customs.

We determine the constitutional validity of a tax by its pith and substance or primary purpose.[11] Thus, the crucial inquiry is the object and purpose of the scheme, not simply its formal or superficial characteristics.[12] This contrasts with the categories approach to interpretation, where the courts traditionally regard certain categories of taxes — such as property and income taxes — as direct taxes.[13]

---

[9]*A.G. N.S. v. A.G. Can.* (1950), [1951] S.C.R. 31, 50 D.T.C. 838 (S.C.C.).

[10]See: *Cotton v. The King*, [1914] A.C. 176 at 193 (P.C.); see also *Atlantic Smoke Shops Ltd. v. Conlon*, [1943] C.T.C. 294 (P.C.); see generally La Forest J., "The Allocation of Taxing Power under the Canadian Constitution", *Can. Tax Paper No. 45* (Can. Tax. Foundation, 1967) at 81.

[11]See, for example, the majority of the Supreme Court in *Reference re Questions set out in O.C. 1079/80, Concerning Tax Proposed by Parliament of Canada on Exported Natural Gas* (1982), 136 D.L.R. (3d) 385 (S.C.C.) at 438: "The essential question here is no different than in any other constitutional case: what is the 'pith and substance' of the relevant legislation?"

[12]*Ontario Home Builders' Assn. v. York (Region) Board of Education* (1996), 137 D.L.R. (4th) 449 (S.C.C.).

[13]See *Halifax (City) v. Fairbanks Estate*, [1927] 4 D.L.R. 945 (Nova Scotia P.C.).

The categories approach is appropriate with traditional forms of taxation — such as taxes on land and sales of goods — that existed in 1867. It is not helpful, however, in assessing whether innovative taxation schemes, which could not have been within the reasonable contemplation of the British Legislature when it enacted the *Constitution Act* in 1867, are direct or indirect taxation. As Lord Simonds said in *Atlantic Smoke Shops Ltd. v. Conlon*:[14]

> Their Lordships are of opinion that Lord Cave's reference in his judgment in the Fairbanks' case to "two separate and distinct categories" of taxes, "namely those that are direct and those which cannot be so described", should not be understood as relieving the courts from the obligation of examining the real nature and effect of the particular tax in the present instance, or as justifying the classification of the tax as indirect merely because it is in some sense associated with the purchase of an article.

Hence, we must look at the *legal* incidence of a tax, and not its label, to determine its constitutional validity.[15] This applies equally to traditional taxes, such as those on land.

For example, applying the categories approach, a land tax is usually a direct tax. It can, however, also be an indirect tax under the legal incidence test. As Justice Iacobucci said in *Ontario Home Builders' Association*:[16]

> The hallmarks of a land tax are that the tax is, of course, imposed on land against the owner of the land, and that the tax is assessed as a percentage of the value of the land, or a fixed charge per acre. The tax may be an annual, recurring assessment, or a one-time charge. In some cases, the tax may be enforced through the sale of the land. Although landowners, like everyone, may wish to pass on their tax burden to someone else or otherwise avoid taxation, this desire or ability does not transform the direct nature of the tax into an indirect one. I also accept that the case law reveals that land taxes are generally direct taxes; but I do not believe the case law prevents a tax on land by itself from being treated as an indirect tax.

---

[14][1943] A.C. 550 (Canada P.C.) at 565, quoted with approval by Justice Iacobucci at 492 of *Ontario Home Builders' Assn.*

[15]*Ontario Home Builders' Assn.* at 476:

> Of course, it is the general tendency of the tax that is of concern, rather than the ultimate incidence of the tax in the circumstances of a particular case . . . the test of incidence is based on a legal, rather than an economic distinction . . . When determining the incidence of a tax, it is important to bear in mind the context within which the tax operates as well as the purpose of the tax.

See John Stuart Mill "Principles of Political Economy, Book V", (London: John W. Parker & Son, 1852).

[16]At 478–479.

Thus, Mills' distinction between direct and indirect taxes remains the legal yardstick in constitutional law.[17] In *Eurig Estate, Re*,[18] for example, the taxpayer challenged Ontario's estate probate fees as being an indirect tax beyond the power of the provincial government. Applying Mills' definition, the tax would be indirect if the executor was personally liable for payment of probate fees, as the intention would clearly be that the executor would recover payment from the beneficiaries of the estate. However, the legislation did not make the executor personally liable for the fees. The executor would pay only in his or her representative capacity. The majority of the Supreme Court held that the probate fee was really a direct tax and, therefore, *intra vires* the Province of Ontario.[19]

Most economists consider Mill's definition too narrow and rigid. Indeed, the question as to who actually bears the burden of any tax (the "incidence of taxation") is one of the more unsettled economic issues of our time. The courts, however, still use the test.[20] Given the uncertainty of the incidence of a tax, Mill's definition provides a useful demarcation between direct and indirect taxes for the purposes of constitutional law.[21]

(b) — Restraint on Powers

Section 125 of the *Constitution Act, 1867* provides that no lands or property belonging to Canada or any province shall be liable to taxation. This provision provides inter-governmen-

---

[17]See *Lambe v. North British Mercantile Fire & Life Insurance Co.* (1887), (sub nom. *Bank of Toronto v. Lambe)* L.R. 12 App. Cas. 575, [1917-27] C.T.C. 82 (Quebec P.C.) at 582 per Lord Hobhouse:

> Taxes are either direct or indirect. A direct tax is one which is demanded from the very persons who it is intended or desired should pay it. Indirect taxes are those which are demanded from one person in the expectation and intention that he shall indemnify himself at the expense of another; such are the excise or customs.

> The producer or importer of a commodity is called upon to pay a tax on it, not with the intention to levy a peculiar contribution upon him, but to tax through him the consumers of the commodity, from whom it is supposed that he will recover the amount by means of an advance in price.

[18](1998), 165 D.L.R. (4th) 1, [2000] 1 C.T.C. 284 (S.C.C.).

[19]The court struck down the tax because it violated s. 53 of the *Constitution Act, 1867*. The taxpayer won, but the government amended its legislation and made it retroactive to inception.

[20]See, *Hudson's Bay Co. v. Ontario*, [2000] O.J. No. 2203, 49 O.R. (3d) 455 (Ont. S.C.J.).

[21]*Bank of Toronto v. Lambe* (1887), 12 App. Cas. 575 (P.C.).

tal immunity from taxation in respect of "lands or property" owned by the federal or provincial Crown. The restriction also extends to Crown agents such as Crown corporations.[22]

What is the extent of this protection? The first question we must determine is whether a particular statutory measure is a "taxation" measure or the exercise of regulatory power under some other legislative head, for example, the commerce clause. On its surface, it appears as though section 125 exempts only provincial "lands or property" from federal taxation. The restraint on the federal government is, however, broader: section 125 applies not only to provincial lands or property but also to taxes levied on persons and transactions in respect of Crown property. Thus, section 125 overrides the express powers of taxation contained in subsections 91(3) (the federal power) and 92(2) (the provincial power) of the *Constitution Act, 1867* and provides a constitutional guarantee of immunity from federal taxation of provincial property.[23]The Supreme Court of Canada has stated:[24]

> This immunity would be illusory if it applied to taxes "on property" but not to a tax on the Crown in respect of a transaction affecting its property or on the transaction itself. The immunity would be illusory since, by the simple device of framing a tax as "*in personam*" rather than "*in rem*" one level of government could with impunity tax away the fruits of property owned by the other. The fundamental constitutional protection framed by section 125 cannot depend on subtle nuances of form.

Hence, once we determine that the "pith and substance" of a measure are "taxation", section 125 restrains the federal government from imposing the tax on provincial lands, property, Crown agents, and transactions directly involving provincial property. This appears to be the case whether or not the province is involved in commercial activity. In Professor Hogg's words:[25]

> Section 125 probably covers taxation of all property belonging to Canada or a province, regardless of whether the property is acquired for or employed in a commercial activity or a governmental activity. The section is not limited to non-commercial property.

The determination of whether the substance of legislation constitutes taxation or the exercise of a regulatory power can be a difficult question and, in some cases, produces dubious results.[26]

---

[22]See, e.g., *Nova Scotia Power Inc. v. R.*, 2004 SCC 51 (S.C.C.) (NSPC acting within its purposes as a Crown agent and thus entitled to immunity from legislation, including the *Income Tax Act*, as provided by s. 17 of the *Interpretation Act*).

[23]*Re Exported Natural Gas Tax*, [1982] 1 S.C.R. 1004 (S.C.C.).

[24]*Ibid.*, at 1078.

[25]Hogg, *Constitutional Law of Canada*, loose-leaf (Toronto: Carswell, 1997) at 30–32.

[26]See *British Columbia (A.G.) v. Canada (A.G.)*, [1924] A.C. 222 (P.C.).

(c) — Administrative Responsibility

The Department of Finance determines the policy of financial affairs that fall within the authority of the federal power.[27] The Minister of National Revenue is responsible for administering the *Income Tax Act*.[28] Thus, unlike most other countries, Canada places the responsibility for enacting fiscal legislation and its administration in different ministries.

(d) — Federal-Provincial Agreements

Federal-provincial income tax arrangements are governed by the *Federal-Provincial Fiscal Arrangements Act*.[29]

Prior to 1962, the federal government dominated the field of income taxation. With the exception of Ontario and Quebec, the federal government was allowed to occupy the entire field of individual and corporate income taxation in exchange for agreed-upon "rental" payments to the provinces. The "rental" payments were compensation to the provinces in exchange for giving up their constitutional rights to levy direct taxes.

The structure of the arrangement between the federal and provincial governments was altered by the *Federal-Provincial Fiscal Arrangements Act (1961)*, under which the federal Parliament unilaterally vacated a portion of the income tax field to the provinces. The withdrawal of the federal government allowed the provinces to re-enter the income tax field and impose their own taxes.

The federal government has tax collection agreements (TCAs) with most of the provinces, under which the federal government collects the provincial income tax on behalf of the provinces. To facilitate tax collection and assessment, the agreements require the provinces to levy their tax by reference to a taxable base that is identical to that used for federal income tax purposes.

Prior to 2000, this was accomplished through the "tax on tax" method of income tax collection. Under this method, provincial income tax payable by individuals was calculated as a percentage of their federal tax payable. The disadvantage of this method is that it restricts the provinces' ability to raise revenues and to create tax policies based on their own evolving social and economic priorities.

In response to the provinces' desire for increased control and flexibility in setting tax policy, the federal government agreed to amend the TCAs to change the basis on which the prov-

---

[27] *Financial Administration Act*, R.S.C. 1985, c. F-11.

[28] *Canada Customs and Revenue Agency Act*, S.C. 1999, c. 17.

[29] *Federal-Provincial Fiscal Arrangements Act*, R.S.C. 1985, c. F-8.

inces levy provincial income taxes.[30] Following the amendment, the participating provinces could continue to use the old "tax on tax" method of calculating provincial income taxes or elect to use the new "tax on income" method. The new tax on income method calculates provincial income tax payable by individuals as a percentage of their *taxable income* rather than of their federal tax payable.

The new method allows the provinces to determine their own unique income tax brackets and rates and to create their own distinct block of non-refundable tax credits,[31] which gives the provinces greater flexibility in setting tax policy. However, the provinces must still use the federal definition of "taxable income" in order to ensure a common tax base.

Ensuring a common tax base not only facilitates tax collection and assessment, but also mitigates the problems that can arise where there are significant discrepancies in tax policy from one province to the next. For example, a province may wish to establish a very low tax rate on capital income, compared with other sources of income, in order to attract the highly mobile capital from other provinces. If this was permitted, it could negatively impact the national economy.

The federal government has TCAs with all the provinces and territories except Quebec for the collection of personal income taxes, and with all the provinces and territories except Quebec, Ontario and Alberta for the collection of corporate income taxes. Thus, Quebec is the only province that administers both its corporate and individual income taxes; Ontario and Alberta collect their own corporate taxes but participate with the federal government insofar as individual taxes are concerned. Residents of Quebec receive an abatement of 16.5 per cent from their basic federal tax, but must pay Quebec income tax according to a special scale of rates.

(e) — The Executive Process

The responsibility for fiscal policy and legislation rests with the Minister of Finance. The Department of Finance carries most of the burden of advising the Minister on changes to income tax legislation. The Department also prepares substantive tax policy papers and most of the income tax legislation. The Tax Policy and Legislation Division of the Department reports through an Assistant Deputy Minister to the Deputy Minister of Finance.

The responsibility for administering the *Income Tax Act* lies with the Department of National Revenue, which also has a division concerned with tax policy. The Department of

---

[30]See generally the Department of Finance's *Federal Administration of Provincial Taxes*, October 1998, Report prepared by the Federal-Provincial Committee on Taxation for Presentation to Ministers of Finance, online: *http://www.fin.gc.ca/fapt/fapt3e.html*.

[31]Subject to restrictions on minimums; see *ibid*. at Design and Operation.

Finance and the Canada Revenue Agency (the "CRA")[32] liaise closely on income tax legislation.

(f) — The Legislative Process

Legislation in respect of income tax originates in the House of Commons on the recommendation of the Governor General.[33] Income tax legislation may not be introduced in the Senate, nor is it possible for a private member to introduce a tax Bill in the House of Commons.

(g) — The Budget

As a matter of parliamentary tradition, the Minister of Finance presents a Budget[34] to the House of Commons, following which he tables a Notice of Ways and Means Motions to introduce amendments to the *Income Tax Act*. The Budget allows the government of the day an opportunity to review the state of the economy and to announce policies in respect of economic and fiscal programs. Following the Budget, there is a debate in the House. The debate cannot exceed six sitting days of the House of Commons.

The parliamentary tradition that the Minister of Finance should announce tax changes only in the House of Commons has softened somewhat and some Ministers of Finance now simply announce proposed tax changes by press release.

Some time after the Budget debate, the Minister of Finance introduces amending legislation in the form of a Bill to implement the proposals set out in the Notice of Ways and Means Motions. The Bill is given a first reading in the House to make it a public document and is then debated in principle during second reading. Following second reading, income tax Bills are debated by the Committee of Ways and Means, which is a committee of the whole House.[35] The Bill may also be considered by specialized committees such as the Committee on Finance, Trade and Economic Affairs, where particular provisions of the Bill may be amended. Following detailed examination of the Bill by the Committee of the Whole House, it is given third reading and sent to the Senate.

---

[32]In December 2003, the Canada Customs and Revenue Agency became the Canada Revenue Agency. The Customs program is now part of the new Canada Border Services Agency.

[33]*Constitution Act, 1867* (U.K.), c. 3, ss. 53, 54.

[34]"Budget" (contrary to the understanding of the term by accountants who view it as a financial statement) is a derivation from the old French "bougette", meaning "a little bag". In British parliamentary tradition, the "little bag" was replaced by a "little box" (14 1/2" by 10") made for Gladstone in about 1860. The box was replaced by a new one in 1996.

[35]Unlike bills dealing with non-tax matters, it is the entire House which constitutes the Committee. The public may not make representations directly to the Committee of the Whole House.

The Senate does not have the power to initiate income tax legislation. It does, however, have the constitutional authority to debate tax Bills that have been referred to it by the House of Commons. The Senate Committee on Banking, Trade and Commerce is a particularly influential committee whose deliberations may have a substantial impact on such a Bill. As a practical matter, with the exception of purely technical changes, the Senate does not amend income tax legislation without the approval of the Cabinet.

The Bill is then sent for Royal Assent and becomes law the day that it receives Assent and comes into force. Amendments enacted through a Bill, however, are generally effective as of the date that the legislation stipulates.

II. — Key Concepts

1. — The Meaning of "Tax"

A "tax" is a compulsory contribution that governments levy on individuals, firms or property in order to fund government operations.[36] Thus, the primary purpose of any tax is to raise revenue. A tax system, however, can be used for more than financing public sector goods and services. It can, and is, also used to implement socio-economic and political policies. A levy may in fact be a tax even if it is disguised by a more attractive name. For example, the Canada Pension Plan and Employment Insurance are compulsory transfer payments determined by reference to payroll income. Hence, they are payroll taxes on earned income. Similarly, the airport and other security taxes[37] imposed after September 11, 2001 are in fact user taxes on air travel to finance security needs.

2. — Taxpayers

An income tax system must identify the range of taxpayers that it shall bring within its scope. This seemingly obvious task in fact lies at the root of a good deal of complexity in the tax system. This complexity arises because most business is conducted through artificial entities, some with multiple dimensions. For example, the Canadian income tax system applies to:

- Individuals;

- Corporations;

- Trusts; and

- Partnerships.

---

[36]*Re Eurig Estate*, [1998] 2 S.C.R. 565, [2000] 1 C.T.C. 284 (S.C.C.).

[37]Air Travellers Security Charge.

Each individual is a taxpayer in his or her own right and must file a tax return in respect of tax payable for the year. Corporations, trusts and estates are also taxpayers in their own right and file separate returns from their owners or beneficiaries. A partnership is not a taxpayer in its own right but we determine its income at the partnership level as if it were an entity, and partners then declare their share of income in their individual tax returns. As we will see in subsequent chapters, the tax rules that govern the flow of income between these various types of taxpayers require fairly complex provisions in order to maintain the integrity of the system.

III. — Tax Policy

Income taxation is a transfer of resources from the private to the public sector. The transfer almost always implies reduced economic growth and employment in the private sector. That is the price we pay for the purchase of goods and services for the public good.

Tax policy is concerned with the efficiency with which the transfer occurs and the value and benefit that society derives from the process. Of course, a tax system should raise sufficient revenue to finance government operations. A good tax system, however, is about more than generating sufficient revenue. It is also concerned with the manner in which we collect revenue. A "good" tax system is also:

- Neutral and efficient;
- Fair and equitable;
- Certain; and
- Administratively simple and easy to comply with.

These objectives inevitably require us to consider non-economic values and goals. Thus, tax law is necessarily a compromise of competing economic, social and political values. Tax policy analysis evaluates the effectiveness of these compromises.

1. — Revenue Generation

It is trite to say that income taxes are levied to generate revenues. A tax system must raise sufficient revenues to finance government operations. The amount of revenue that a tax system, or component thereof, raises is determined by a simple mathematical function:

$$\text{Revenue} = \text{Tax Base} \times \text{Tax Rate}$$

Thus, there are really only two variables that directly determine the amount of revenue raised through a tax system. The interplay between these two variables, however, influences the manner in which we achieve the other non-revenue objectives of the system. The size and character of the tax base (what is taxed?) and tax rates affect the fairness of the system, its economic efficiency, its certainty, and administrative simplicity.

We can increase or decrease revenue by enlarging or contracting the tax base, or by increasing or decreasing the tax rate. The smaller the base, the higher the rate required to generate a given amount of revenue. Conversely, the larger the base, the lower the rate needed to generate a pre-determined amount of revenue. Hence, one needs to be careful in international tax comparisons to consider both elements of the equation, tax base and tax rate.

The size of the tax base also has an effect on other aspects of the tax system. A system with a broad base is usually more certain and simpler than a system with a narrowly constrained base. This is because a broad-based system requires fewer lines of demarcation between classifications of income and expenditures than a narrowly based system. A system that taxes all forms of gains, regardless of the types of transactions from which they derive, requires fewer rules to implement than a system that distinguishes between different types of economic gains. For example, a system that distinguishes between income and capital gains is necessarily more complex than one that does not. The same amount of revenue may be generated from a broadly based system as can be generated from a narrowly based system by adjusting tax rates. The trade-off between the two, however, affects the economic efficiency of the system and its complexity, which in turn affects the cost of compliance and tax administration.

The generation of revenues is inextricably and directly linked to the tax base and the tax rate. It is also indirectly linked to the question of *when* tax is payable. The timing of when tax is payable is an important consideration in the collection of taxes. Given the time-value of money, the earlier that taxes are collected, the greater the revenue. From the taxpayer's perspective, however, tax deferral is tax saving.

2. — Neutrality and Efficiency

Neutrality means that a tax system should not draw artificial distinctions between identical transactions merely on the basis of the legal form of transactions or their source. Thus, neutrality implies a level playing field that does not favour or unfairly discriminate against taxpayers merely on the basis of their choice of entities or relationships to structure business and personal transactions. For example, in a perfectly neutral system the tax consequences of a transaction would be the same regardless of whether it was implemented by an individual, a corporation, a partnership or a trust.

In fact, as we will see, the Canadian tax system is far from neutral, and invites behavioural responses from taxpayers who are often motivated purely by tax considerations. This is inevitable. Taxpayers faced with choices respond to the system and attempt to minimise their tax burden. To do otherwise would be irrational. For example, a Canadian corporation pays federal tax at a rate of approximately 13 per cent on the first $300,000 of its business income.[38] In contrast, an individual in the top bracket pays federal tax at approximately 29 per cent on the same income. Since the low rate of tax is not available to businesses conducted by individuals as sole proprietorships, partnerships or trusts, the tax system creates a tax bias in favour of the corporate form of business.[39] This systemic bias is an intrinsic part of the tax system to which taxpayers respond quite rationally. Hence, absent legal prohibition,[40] an individual would almost invariably choose to conduct a profitable Canadian business through a corporation in order to save tax. To do otherwise would invite higher taxes.

Tax efficiency is concerned with the efficient allocation of economic resources to maximize production and economic growth. A tax policy is efficient if it promotes the optimal allocation of capital. A tax system can distort economic efficiency and capital flows by causing persons to make business decisions solely on tax considerations. This is true both in domestic and international markets. Thus, tax measures (for example, tax expenditures[41]) that are intended to stimulate or encourage economic activities should be evaluated on the basis of their cost effectiveness in the light of the objectives of the provision. For example, we can evaluate an investment tax credit based on the increased investment stimulated by the credit against its cost in lost revenues. In other words, one might ask:

- Does the statutory provision deliver the objectives sought in a cost-efficient manner?

- Is the statutory provision target-efficient and taken advantage of only by those persons whom it is intended to benefit?

- Can the same economic objectives be more effectively or efficiently achieved through an alternative non-tax mechanism?

- Does the statutory provision shift economic activity towards tax-saving projects that cause market distortions? and

- Does the statutory provision lead to a non-optimal allocation of resources?

Similarly in the international arena, tax provisions can distort economic decisions and cause a non-optimal allocation of capital. The principle of capital export or international neutrality, for example, suggests that a taxpayer's choice between investing at home or abroad should

---

[38]Subs. 125(2).

[39]See generally subs. 125(1).

[40]Certain professions such as law, accounting, medicine and dentistry are prohibited from practicing in corporate form.

[41]Tax revenues foregone by the government. For example, the reduced rate of corporate tax for manufacturing and processing activities.

not be affected by the pattern of taxation.[42] For example, a Canadian corporate tax rate that is significantly higher than international norms stimulates export of capital and jobs to countries with lower rates in order to enhance domestic after-tax returns. We satisfy capital export neutrality if we tax the foreign and domestic income at the same total rate. For example, if the Royal Bank of Canada is taxed at 45 per cent on its Canadian income and at 40 per cent on its U.K. subsidiary's profits, the Canadian tax system is neutral if it taxes RBC at a net rate (after foreign credits) of 5 per cent on its foreign income.

3. — Fairness and Equity

To be effective, a tax system must be fair. Anything less than a fair system of taxation invites blatant tax avoidance and evasion. Tax equity is concerned with the optimality of distribution. An equitable tax policy is one that treats similarly situated taxpayers in a similar manner (horizontal equity) and promotes a fair distribution of income (vertical equity). That said, however, it is not always easy to settle upon a common measure of fairness. Fairness is a value judgment that incorporates social, political and moral values. Hence, determining whether a tax system is fair (or in tax parlance, "equitable") is contentious.

There is, however, reasonable consensus on the meaning of "fairness" in taxation. First, most people agree that taxpayers in similar financial circumstances should pay similar amounts of tax. At its simplest level, an individual who earns $100,000 from employment should be taxed at the same rate as an individual who earns $100,000 from rental income. We refer to this aspect of fairness as horizontal equity: equal treatment of those with equal ability to pay.

Thus, the accurate measurement of "income" is integral to the fairness of the tax system. This raises contentious issues in the measurement of non-cash benefits. For example, consider the case of two individuals, Jane and Harry, both of whom are in the 50 per cent tax bracket. Jane earns $150,000 as a public servant in government; Harry is employed in the private sector, earns $100,000 in salary, but also gets free accommodation valued at $50,000. The principle of horizontal equity requires that we tax both Jane and Harry in a similar manner because they earn equal amounts of income, albeit in different forms. But what if Jane trades off $10,000 of her salary in exchange for her employer providing on-site child care services that previously cost her $20,000 (after-tax) a year? Should Jane be taxed on $140,000, $150,000, $160,000 or $180,000?

Horizontal equity also requires that we recognize a taxpayer's ability to pay, which may be quite different from the taxpayer's "income" in an accounting sense. Assume, for example, that Harry, a single father with four infant children, looks after his elderly mother who suf-

---

[42]See, for example, P. Musgrave, *United States Taxation of Foreign Investment Income: Issues and Arguments*, 109 (1969); L. Krause & K. Dam, *Federal Tax Treatment of Foreign Income*, 46–52 (1964).

fers from an expensive and chronic disease. Jane is single, in good health, and spends her money on sailing. Horizontal equity requires that we recognize these personal elements in the measure of the taxpayer's "ability to pay".

Second, there is general agreement that individuals with higher incomes should pay "more tax" than individuals with lower incomes. Most people will agree that an individual who earns $100,000 in a year should pay more tax than an individual who earns $30,000. This is the principle of vertical equity. This principle, which is also premised on the theory that a taxpayer should pay according to his or her ability to pay, does not, in itself, provide a ready answer to the more difficult question: *how much more* should the rich pay than the poor? In technical terms, what is the optimum slope of the tax rate curve? Is it sufficient to pay proportionately more, or does the principle compel us to conclude that higher income earners should pay progressively more than lower income earners? And if progressively more, what should be the progressivity rate?

(a) — Proportional Tax Rates

In a proportional rate system all of the taxable base is taxed at a constant or flat rate. For example, if three taxpayers A, B and C with taxable incomes of $20,000, $40,000 and $60,000 respectively are each taxed at a flat rate of 17 per cent, they would pay taxes commensurately proportionate with their income as follows:

Taxpayer	Taxable Income	Tax	Average Rate
A	$20,000	$ 3,400	17%
B	$40,000	$ 6,800	17%
C	$60,000	$ 10,200	17%

The total tax revenue collected would be $20,400.

Thus, in a proportional rate system, higher income levels bear a heavier tax burden. In the above example, C pays three times, and B pays twice, the total tax paid by A. The description "flat tax" refers to the shape of the curve or line when plotted on a graph that displays the tax rate on the vertical axis and income on the horizontal axis. It does not refer to the amount of tax paid. Thus, a true flat tax takes the same percentage of everyone's income — a family with twice the income of another must pay twice the tax.

Sales and consumption taxes (such as the GST) are generally levied as proportional taxes, that is, at a flat rate applied to all sales regardless of the amount expended. The shape of the tax rate curve should not be confused with the incidence of a tax. The GST, for example, is a flat tax on consumption, but has a regressive effect when measured against *income*. It takes a higher percentage of income from lower income levels than it does from higher income levels. *All* flat taxes (for example, gasoline, airline, alcohol, tobacco, entertainment, gaming and fishing, excise, environmental, energy, etc.) on use or consumption have a regressive incidence when measured against income. To state that a flat tax is regressive merely states the obvious. The policy issue is whether the incidence and degree of regressivity of a tax properly reflects the economic and social values of society. If it does not, how can we rectify the situation — rebates or credits?

(b) — Progressive Taxation

There are two classes of people who complain about the tax system: men and women. Most Canadians agree with the principle that individuals with higher incomes should pay more tax than individuals who earn less. The underlying premise is that higher income individuals have a greater ability to pay taxes and, therefore, it is fair that they pay more tax. But how much more is "fair"? The difficulty is that many believe that a tax system is fair if it taxes the other person.

No one seriously argues with the principle that an individual who earns $115,000 should pay more tax than an individual who earns $30,000. However, is it sufficient to pay proportionately more or does the principle compel us to inevitably conclude that higher income earners must also pay progressively more than lower income earners? If higher incomes should pay progressively more taxes, what is the appropriate rate of progression? There are no easy answers to these questions and the debate continues.

Canada taxes individuals on a progressive basis. The adjective "progressive" refers not to the quality of our Byzantine tax law, but to the aspect of our system by which the marginal rate of tax increases at various levels of income. For example, in 2005, the four basic federal rates of tax for individuals were:

   16% on the first $35,595;

   22% on the next $35,595;

   26% on the next $44,549; and

   29% on income over $115,739

Thus, a person who earns $115,000 pays not only more tax in absolute dollars than an individual who earns $30,000, but the rate of federal tax progresses from 16 per cent to 29 per cent as income rises.

We justify progressive taxation on the principle that an individual's ability (though not enthusiasm) to pay tax increases as his or her income rises. This assumption, however, only starts the debate. One-third of Canadian taxpayers (of which there are approximately 22 million) do not pay any income tax at all. The non-payers file tax returns primarily to receive benefits paid out as income redistribution under the GST and child-tax benefits.

That leaves the remaining two-thirds to make up the necessary revenues. In 2002, (the latest year for which data is available), for example, there were 15 million taxable returns, which generated $115 billion in personal federal and provincial income taxes. As the following table shows, the taxable population falls into three broad categories: those who pay less than their proportional numbers; those who pay in proportion; and those who pay proportionately higher than their population numbers.

Income level	Per cent of taxable returns	Per cent of total personal taxes
$1–$40,000	61.6%	20.0%
$40,000–$50,000	12.5%	11.3%
Over $50,000	25.9%	68.6%

Progressivism really kicks in at the $50,000 income level and accelerates thereafter until it peaks at the top federal marginal rate of 29 per cent, which works out to approximately 46 per cent in combined federal and provincial (Ontario) taxes.

In absolute dollar terms, the largest revenue contributors are the middle class, the group between $50,000 and $100,000 income. This group, which comprises only 22 per cent of taxable returns, paid 36 per cent, $41 billion, of personal income taxes.

As we move up the income scale, the numbers of taxpayers drop off dramatically and the percentage of tax collected increases progressively. Contrary to popular myth, Canadian socio-economic demographics are not very egalitarian. In 2002, only 4.3 per cent of the taxable returns showed income of more than $100,000. Further up the ladder, only 161,000 people in all of Canada, or 1.1 per cent of the taxable population, had income levels between $150,000 and $250,000. This group includes professionals (lawyers, doctors, accountants, dentists, architects and federally appointed judges).

At the top of the heap (incomes above $250,000) society becomes even more elitist. Only 97,370 people in all of Canada, 0.4 per cent of the taxable population, qualified for admission into this club. Nevertheless, this group paid $18 billion in taxes, 16 per cent of the total taxes collected, or 40 times their proportional number.

Thus, contrary to popular opinion, the rich in Canada do actually pay substantial taxes. However, there is no consensus, and likely never will be, on the meaning of what is fair in taxation.

(c) — Marginal Tax Rates

As noted above, individual income taxes are progressive so that the rate of tax increases as income rises. The basic federal tax rate for individuals starts out at 16 per cent and rises to 29 per cent. Coupled with surtaxes and provincial tax rates, combined federal-provincial rates start at approximately 22 per cent and increase as income increases. Since provincial rates vary between provinces, the ultimate tax burden is a function of where one resides. The following table shows the top personal marginal income tax rates by province on regular income.

Province/Territory	2005 %	2004 %	2003 %	2001 %	1999 %
British Columbia	43.7	43.7	43.7	45.7	52.3
Alberta	39.0	39.0	39.0	39.0	45.2
Saskatchewan	44.0	44.0	44.0	45.0	50.8
Manitoba	46.4	46.4	46.4	46.4	49.4
Ontario	46.4	46.4	46.4	46.4	49.2
Quebec	48.2	48.2	48.2	48.7	52.2
New Brunswick	46.8	46.8	46.8	46.8	49.7
Nova Scotia	48.3	48.3	47.3	47.3	49.2
P.E.I.	47.4	47.4	47.4	47.4	49.9
Nfld and Labrador	48.6	48.6	48.6	48.6	52.9

Are these rates high or low? Are they overly progressive or not progressive enough? The top Canadian marginal rate in 2005 was 48.6 per cent (Newfoundland), which is about the mid-range of OECD tax rates.

Marginal tax rates play a crucial role in government tax policy analysis and tax planning for private clients. Let us consider a simple example: suppose that your employer offers you a salary increase of $10,000 to match a competitive bid for your services. How much better off will you be after the increase? The answer depends upon your marginal rate of tax. Assuming that you are in the 40 per cent bracket, the salary increase is worth $6,000 after taxes. If, however, you are in a 50 per cent marginal tax bracket, the increase is worth only $5,000 to you.

In a top 50 per cent bracket you would be better off getting a $7,000 non-taxable benefit, which would be a pre-tax equivalent of $14,000. Thus, the benefit of any increase in income or saving in tax payable is a function of the applicable marginal tax rate. The higher the marginal rate of tax, the greater the tax payable, the greater the value of tax savings, and the greater the loss of tax revenue for the government.

Marginal tax rate analysis is also important in tax deduction decisions. A deduction of $500, for example, saves an individual in the 50 per cent bracket $250 and reduces his or her after-tax cost to $250. In contrast, the same deduction for a person in the 40 per cent bracket saves only $200 and leaves an after-tax cost of $300. Thus, the lower income taxpayer has a higher after-tax cost for deductions than a higher marginal rate taxpayer. As we will see later, this inverted effect plays an important role in determining whether we should grant taxpayers deductions or credits for their personal expenditures, such as charitable donations and political contributions.

In contrast with individuals, corporate income taxes are for the most part flat. The basic federal flat rate is 28 per cent. The basic rate, however, is adjusted for certain types of income and corporations. For example, in 2005, a Canadian-controlled private corporation (CCPC) was taxed at a federal rate of approximately 13 per cent on the first $300,000 of its active business income (ABI) and 22 per cent on amounts in excess of $300,000.[43] Thus, the federal marginal rate of tax rises for corporations with more than $300,000 ABI and is flat for corporations with less than $300,000 income. This sudden step-up (or "threshold disaster") in the marginal rate of tax is the reason that CCPCs seek ways to reduce their annual ABI below the $300,000 threshold.

The progressive tax rate structure for individuals (and to a lesser extent corporations) is an incentive for taxpayers to arrange their affairs to reduce their marginal rate. Since every dollar of tax saving is at the top marginal rate of tax, governments are concerned that taxpayers should not artificially siphon off their income to family members with lower marginal tax rates. The attribution rules in section 74.1, for example, prevent income shifting for the purposes of marginal tax rate minimization. Similarly, the low tax rate on corporate business income up to $300,000 makes it attractive to create multiple corporations. Thus, subsection 256(2.1) treats associated corporations as one for the purpose of the low rate of tax.

The more comprehensive the taxable base, the lower the rate required to produce a given amount of revenue. Hence, exclusion of income from the taxable base invariably necessitates a higher tax rate to produce a given amount of revenue. Exclusions of income from the taxable base also distort horizontal equity. For example, the exclusion of gambling gains from taxable income has two separate effects. First, it is unfair because it creates a preference for a particular form of income. Why should a person who derives a million dollars from a lottery ticket be treated more generously than an individual who derives $60,000 from employment? Second, the exclusion means that the tax rate on other forms of income must necessarily be higher to produce a given amount of revenue. Thus, it is important that policy-makers carefully consider exclusions from income and tax preferences (for example, non-taxation of gains on principal residences) both in the light of government revenue requirements and the principles of tax fairness.

High taxes provide social services but can also stagnate economic growth and job creation. They also shift choices away from individuals to governments. Thus, a tax system is more than a mere revenue-generating vehicle for governmental operations: it is a mirror of the social and political values of a society.

(d) — The Relationship Between Horizontal and Vertical Equity

Although we speak of horizontal and vertical equity, the two are not entirely unconnected. Horizontal equity addresses the size of the taxable base. Vertical equity is concerned with the burden imposed by the tax rate. Since total tax revenue (or total tax paid) is the product

---

[43]See Appendix D.2.

of the taxable base and the tax rate, distorting one of the variables usually distorts the other. For example, assume that a government wants to raise $20,000,000 of tax revenue by taxing $100,000,000 of income at a basic rate of 20 per cent. Excluding $10,000,000 of a particular type of income (for example, capital gains) from the tax base inevitably results in a higher rate of tax on what is left in the tax base. The $90,000,000 must be taxed at 22.23 per cent in order to raise the same revenue. This is not to imply that we should not deliberately erode the tax base under the proper circumstances, but merely to emphasize that the benefit that accrues from a narrower base should at least equal the resulting sacrifice of horizontal equity. In other words, if we provide tax preferences to certain groups of taxpayers, there should be at least corresponding countervailing benefits to society at large.

4. — Certainty and Simplicity

A good tax system is one that can be administered economically and should not impose unreasonable compliance costs on taxpayers. The more complex a tax system, the higher the compliance costs. Thus, a good system is one that is certain and simple. There is a danger, however, in overstating these attributes. A tax system must be certain so that taxpayers can plan their affairs and business transactions secure in the knowledge that the consequences that attach to the transactions are as predicted. On the other hand, business transactions in a complex economy are inherently uncertain and some degree of complexity is inevitable.

A tax system should also be simple. This is particularly important in the case of personal taxes, where the majority of individuals should be able to comply with the law without being put to unnecessary professional fees for expert advice.

5. — Compromise of Values

Tax law is a compromise between competing values. Tax policy objectives of revenue generation, neutrality, efficiency, fairness and administrative feasibility pull in different directions. However, at any given required level of revenues, a neutral tax system will generally be less complex than one that has multiple distinctions between classes of taxpayers and types of income. A neutral system, however, will also be less sensitive to the objective of fairness, which implies distinctions based on ability to pay. For example, income taxes are levied both on individuals and on corporations at different rates. This creates two tensions. First, there is an incentive to choose the form of organization that attracts the lowest rate of tax. As previously noted, there is a substantial difference between taxes imposed on Canadian small business and the top marginal rate of tax on individuals. This creates a bias in favour of the corporate form of organization and makes the tax system less neutral. Second, the levy on corporations results in double taxation of income, once at the corporate level and then again at the personal shareholder level when profits, net of tax, are distributed. Double taxation is inefficient and unfair to taxpayers. The mechanism to minimize double taxation through shareholder credits for corporate taxes makes the system fairer but also more complex.

Nor can one entirely ignore the power of the ballot box. Of the 21.9 million individual tax returns filed in 2002, for example, 68 per cent of the population reported total income of less than $35,000.[44] In contrast, only 3 per cent of the tax filing population reported income over $100,000. The percentage of individuals who reported income in excess of $250,000 in 2002 represented 0.4 per cent of the 21.9 million who filed income tax returns.[45] The so-called middle class ($50,000–$100,000) represented 14.9 per cent of the total individual returns filed and 31 per cent of all assessed income. In a one-person, one-vote system, political parties cannot ignore these numbers.

IV. — Fundamental Concepts

Before we embark upon a detailed review of the Canadian income tax system, it may be useful to provide an overview of some of the fundamental concepts of the system. As already noted, we determine a taxpayer's liability for income tax by applying a tax rate to a taxable base.

1. — Tax Base

The tax base for federal purposes is "taxable income". The provinces can elect to use one of two tax bases for the purposes of provincial tax: (a) federal "taxable income", or (b) "federal tax payable".[46] Thus, the provincial tax (except in Quebec) piggybacks on the federal tax base. Hence, any changes to the federal taxable base almost invariably affect provincial revenues.

Taxable income derives from a two-step process. First, we determine gross income and then deduct expenses incurred to earn the income. This process results in the taxpayer's "net income". Next, we deduct other expenditures that may not have been incurred to earn income, but which we allow as a deduction for other policy reasons. For example, in the case of individuals, we permit a limited credit for medical expenses.[47] The residue is the taxpayer's taxable income.

---

[44]Source: CRA, *Income Statistics: 2004 Edition of Interim Statistics* (Ottawa: CRA). See Appendix B for summary.

[45]*Ibid.*

[46]See Chapter 1, Part I, s. 2(d).

[47]Section 118.2.

2. — Tax Rates

The tax structure must identify two essential ingredients in order to estimate or determine the amount of revenue that the state will collect from the system. First, one must identify the tax base, and second, one needs to determine the tax rate that applies to the tax base.

The tax base determines how much is taxable. Thus, manipulation of taxable income by excluding or including special types of income, deductions or credits will affect the amount of tax revenue that the state generates.

One can increase or decrease revenue by enlarging or contracting the tax base. The smaller the base, the higher the rate that one must apply in order to generate a specified amount of revenue. Conversely, the larger the tax base, the lower the rate needed to generate a pre-determined amount of revenue.

A tax system that taxes all forms of income equally will produce a larger tax base than a system that excludes certain forms of income. For example, the Canadian income tax system taxes the full amount of business income but only one-half of capital gains. This means that the tax base is reduced by one-half of the excluded (non-taxable) capital gains.

The second element in determining revenue is the tax rate that one applies to the tax base. In theory, the higher the tax rate, the greater the revenue collected from the tax base. Thus, ignoring tax evasion and avoidance, a tax rate of 40 per cent will produce a greater amount of revenue than a tax rate of 20 per cent.[48]

There are three different aspects to tax rates:

1. marginal tax rates

2. average tax rates

3. effective tax rates.

The marginal tax rate is the level of tax that applies at the top dollar of a taxpayer's income.

Hence, as marginal rates rise, the total tax payable increases by a rate that is more than proportional to the increase in income.

For example, an individual who earns $30,000 taxable income will pay basic federal tax at a federal marginal rate of 16 per cent. In contrast, an individual who earns taxable income of $120,000 will pay at a federal marginal rate of 29 per cent.

We obtain the "average rate" of tax by dividing the total tax payable by the tax base. The average rate reflects the weighted average of all of the marginal tax rates. For example, the average tax rate of the individual who earns $30,000 is $4,800. In this case, the average and

---

[48]This assumes a static model under which human behaviour does not respond to a change in tax rates. In contrast, in a dynamic model, human behaviour will respond to changes in tax rates and produce more or less than the directly proportional mathematical result.

the marginal rates are equal because only one marginal rate applies to all of the income. In the case of an individual who earns $120,000, however, the average rate of tax is 22 per cent, which is 7 per cent lower than the individual's marginal rate of tax.

A taxpayer's "effective rate" of tax is his or her total tax payable divided by *net income* before exclusions and exemptions. In the above example, assume that the individual who has taxable income of $120,000 earned $60,000 of capital gains in the year. By excluding one-half of the capital gains from taxable income, the individual has, in effect, reduced his or her tax base by $30,000. Thus, the individual's effective tax rate is the tax payable divided by "real" net economic income of $150,000. Thus, the effective tax rate is 18 per cent.

Effective tax rates are the only meaningful yardstick for comparing the tax burden in different countries. In international comparisons, marginal and average rates of tax are not particularly helpful because they do not take into account the differences in calculating the taxable base to which one applies the rate. For example, assume that Country A taxes net income at 45 per cent whereas Country B taxes net income at 40 per cent. On the surface, it would appear that Country B has the lower rate of tax on comparable amounts of net income. If, however, Country A allows generous deductions in computing income that Country B does not permit, it is entirely possible that the effective rate of tax in Country A is lower than that on an equivalent business in Country B.[49]

In Canada, few, if any, corporations actually pay tax at the nominal statutory rate. For example, the Mintz Committee found that the average federal effective tax rate for corporations operating in all industries was 16 per cent.[50] Indeed, many profitable companies do not pay any income tax at all for any number of reasons. The companies may be operating in industries that have substantial tax incentives, tax rebates, accelerated expense write-offs or, indeed, even tax holidays.

3. — Provincial Taxes

The provinces can apply tax as a percentage of the federal taxable income or tax payable. A taxpayer's total tax liability is the aggregate of his federal *and* provincial taxes payable. Provincial rate schedules vary between provinces. Hence, Canadian residents face different tax burdens depending upon their province of residence.

---

[49]See, for example, Martin F. Feldstein, James Poterba & Louis Dicks Mireaux, "The Effective Tax Rate and the Pre-Tax Rate of Return" (Working Paper 740) (National Bureau of Economic Research Working Paper Series, August 1981).

[50]Report of the Technical Committee, Note 9 at 4.2.

4. — Taxable Year

Taxpayers pay tax on an *annual* basis. But "annual" means different things to different taxpayers. Employees, for example, must file their tax returns by April 30 on the basis of their income in the previous calendar year. For example, an individual would file his or her 2007 income tax return by April 30, 2008. In contrast, corporate taxpayers must file their tax returns on a "fiscal year" basis. A fiscal year is any 12-month period. For example, a corporation may have a fiscal year that runs from July 1 to June 30. The corporation must file its return within six months of the fiscal year-end.

5. — Retrospective Effect

Constitutional law and tradition dictate that taxes may be imposed and collected only by an Act of Parliament.[51] There is no legal authority to collect taxes before the Budget imposing the tax is enacted and receives Royal Assent. In fact, federal income taxes are usually collected based on the Notice of Ways and Means Motions, sometimes many months before Parliamentary approval is obtained.[52] When enacated, the legislation is retrospective to the Budget date. This process, in effect, whitewashes any potential constitutional illegality of collecting taxes prior to their legislation. Canadian taxpayers and their professional advisers have resigned themselves to this practice with dejected pragmatism. Litigation to establish the constitutional illegality of the practice would end in a pyrrhic victory since most budgets have retrospective effect.[53]

---

[51] See, e.g., *Bowles v. Bank of England*, [1913] 1 Ch. 57.

[52] For example, there was a 16-month delay between the November 1981 budget speech and its eventual legislative enactment.

[53] See, e.g., *Swanick v. M.N.R.*, [1985] 2 C.T.C. 2352, 85 D.T.C. 630 (T.C.C.) (taxpayer filed return on basis of existing law; Minister assessed return on basis of law enacted 14 months later but made retrospective to earlier period; taxpayer not deprived of property without due process of law); see also *Gustavson Drilling (1964) Ltd. v. M.N.R.*, [1977] 1 S.C.R. 271, [1976] C.T.C. 1 (S.C.C.), at 279 *per* Dickson J.:

> First, retrospectivity. The general rule is that statutes are not to be construed as having retrospective operation unless such a construction is expressly or by necessary implication required by the language of the Act. An amending enactment may provide that it shall be deemed to have come into force on a date prior to its enactment or it may provide that it is to be operative with respect to transactions occurring prior to its enactment. In those instances the statute operates retrospectively.

V. — The Administrative Process

The Minister of National Revenue is responsible for the administration of the *Income Tax Act*. The minister's responsibilities are delegated to officials of the CRA.

1. — Income Tax Returns

The Canadian tax regime is a self-assessment system. A taxpayer must calculate his or her income tax liability for a taxation year, complete an income tax return and declare the amount of his or her income tax liability.[54]

Individuals must file an income tax return if they have a taxable capital gain, dispose of capital property or if they have to pay tax for the particular taxation year.[55] Individuals who do not have any tax payable in a taxation year are not required to file income tax returns for the year. An individual may, however, choose to file a tax return even if he or she is not liable for tax in the year so as to trigger the start of the limitation period.

Failure to file a return on time and failure to furnish required information renders a taxpayer liable to penalties.[56] In most cases, individuals file their returns in respect of a calendar year by April 30 of the following year. This date is extended to June 15 for some individuals who earn business income.

In contrast, all corporations (other than registered charities) must file income tax returns on an annual basis, regardless of whether they have tax payable in the year. Corporations must file their return within six months of the end of their fiscal year. The return, accompanied by financial statements and supporting schedules, must be filed whether or not the corporation is taxable.

A trust or estate must file its return in respect of a taxation year for which taxes are payable within 90 days from the end of the year.

A taxpayer does not generally have the statutory right to amend his or her income tax return in respect of a taxation year. As a matter of practice, however, the Minister usually accepts a taxpayer's amended income tax return or supplementary information if he or she provides it within the limitation period during which the return is considered to be open and assessable.

---

[54]Subs. 150(1).

[55]Subs. 150(1.1).

[56]Subs. 162(1)–(3); note, however, that persistent failure to file tax returns, even if done intentionally, does not, *by itself*, constitute wilful evasion.

2. — *Assessment of Returns*

The Minister must examine with all due dispatch all income tax returns filed and to assess the tax thereon according to the law. The CRA does a "quick assessment" of the return to determine if the taxpayer has calculated his or her liability accurately.[57] This assessment is concerned only with obvious mathematical errors. For example, payroll information slips filed by employers are matched with the amount of income declared by employees on their tax returns.

The CRA issues a "quick assessment" between eight and 12 weeks of filing the return. The most important aspect of the Notice of Assessment is that its issuance commences the running of the three or six-year limitation period within which the Minister may reassess the taxpayer.[58]

A taxpayer who receives a Notice of Assessment from the Minister is entitled to object to it if the taxpayer disagrees with the manner in which he or she has been assessed. The objection procedure is initiated by filing a Notice of Objection with the Agency within 90 days of the date of mailing of the Assessment.[59]

For most taxpayers, the "quick assessment" notice is the final communication they will receive from the CRA in respect of a particular year. The Agency does, however, have the authority to reassess a taxpayer if it later determines that its initial assessment was based upon incorrect or inaccurate information.

3. — *Reassessments*

The time period within which the Agency can reassess a taxpayer depends upon the facts leading to the reassessment. Where a taxpayer makes a misrepresentation attributable to neglect, carelessness, wilful default, or fraud, the Agency is not subject to any limitation period and can reassess the taxpayer at any time.[60] Otherwise, the Agency can reassess a taxpayer only within a period of three or, in certain cases, six years (certain types of claims and tax losses) from the day that it mails the taxpayer's initial assessment.[61] The limitation period runs from the date of the mailing of the Notice of Assessment and not from the date that the income tax return is filed. During this three-year period, the Minister may reconsider *any*

---

[57]Subs. 152(1). For the meaning of "assessment" see *Pure Spring Co. v. M.N.R.*, [1946] C.T.C. 169 at 198, 2 D.T.C. 844 at 857 (Ex. Ct.); *Dezura v. M.N.R.*, [1947] C.T.C. 375 at 380, 3 D.T.C. 1101 at 1103 (Ex. Ct.).

[58]Subs. 152(4).

[59]Subs. 165(1).

[60]Subpara. 152(4)(a)(i).

[61]Subs. 152(4).

fact relevant to the calculation of the taxpayer's tax liability, interest or penalties. The limitation period extends to six years in respect of certain types of claims and tax losses.[62]

Special rules apply to corporations. The limitation period during which the Minister can assess a corporation depends upon the nature of the corporation. The "normal reassessment period" for a Canadian-controlled private corporation is three years after the day of mailing of the original Notice of Assessment. For corporations (other than Canadian-controlled private corporations), the limitation period extends to four years from the mailing of the original assessment.[63]

4. — Notice of Objection

A taxpayer who objects to a Notice of Assessment may file a Notice of Objection with the Minister.[64] A properly filed Notice of Objection is the first legal step in the resolution of an income tax dispute. This notice triggers the administrative and legal appeal processes. An individual or a testamentary trust must file the notice in writing within:

- One year of the taxpayer's due date for filing his or her return; or

- 90 days from the date of *mailing* of the Notice of Assessment to which it relates.

All other taxpayers must file the notice within 90 days of the *mailing* of the Notice of Assessment. This Notice of Objection must be filed in writing and delivered to the Chief of Appeals in a CRA district taxation office. The Notice of Objection should set out the reasons for objection.

Failure to file a proper Notice of Objection within the limitation period may leave the taxpayer without any legal recourse against the assessment. Although a taxpayer can apply to the Tax Court to extend the time limit for filing a Notice of Objection, it is not always easy to obtain an extension.[65] In *Savary Beach Lands Ltd. v. M.N.R.*,[66] for example:

> [T]his Board takes the position that the granting of an extension of time under section 167 will be the exception rather than the rule . . . to simply grant such extensions and imply that all applications — where the breach is but a few days — will be granted, is to make a mockery of the period of limitations set down in the Act.

---

[62]Para. 152(4)(b).

[63]Subs. 152(3.1).

[64]Subs. 165(1).

[65]Subs. 166.2(5).

[66]*Savary Beach Lands Ltd. v. M.N.R.*, [1972] C.T.C. 2608 at 2609, 72 D.T.C. 1497 (T.R.B.).

The Minister may also extend the limitation period if the Minister considers it "just and equitable" to do so and in "exceptional circumstances".

The Minister's discretion, however, is circumscribed by the following requirements:[67]

- The application for the extension of time for filing the Notice of Objection must be made no later than one year after the expiry of the original time limit;

- The taxpayer must have been unable to act within the limitation period or had a *bona fide* intention to object to the assessment; and

- The application must be brought as soon as circumstances permit.

5. — Administrative Appeals

An "administrative appeal" involves discussions with, and representations to, the Agency to determine whether the issues in the Notice of Objection can be resolved on an informal basis. At this stage of the dispute, the taxpayer (or his or her representative) generally meets with a designated Appeals Officer of the Agency to present the case for further reconsideration.

In theory, the Appeals Branch of the Agency is "independent" of the auditing and assessing sections of the Agency. The Appeals Branch takes a fresh and independent view of the facts and the law and renders a decision on an objective basis. The review is, however, an internal process in which the auditors of the Agency review the decisions of their colleagues. In the end, the Appeals Branch either confirms or varies the original Assessment or Reassessment.[68]

VI. — The Judicial Process

The responsibility for litigating income tax disputes rests primarily with the Department of Justice. A taxpayer who disagrees with the CRA's assessment of his or her income tax liability may appeal the assessment in the Tax Court of Canada. An appeal or review of a decision of the Tax Court lies with the Federal Court of Appeal and from there, on leave, to the Supreme Court of Canada.

---

[67]Subs. 166.1(7).

[68]Subs. 165(3).

1. — *The Tax Court*

The Tax Court of Canada is the trier of facts in disputes under the *Income Tax Act*. Where the taxpayer fails to resolve his or her dispute at an administrative level, the next step is an appeal to the Tax Court of Canada. Where the Minister confirms the assessment, the taxpayer can appeal the assessment to the Tax Court.[69] The time limit for appeal is 90 days from the date that the Minister mails the Notice of Confirmation to the taxpayer. If the Minister does not respond to the taxpayer's Notice of Objection within 90 days, the taxpayer can appeal at any time.

Appeals to the Tax Court follow one of two procedures — informal or general.

(a) — *Informal Procedure*

The Informal Procedure is the equivalent of a "small claims" process. It is available only if the aggregate of all tax amounts (other than interest or provincial tax) in dispute does not exceed $12,000, the amount of the loss in issue does not exceed $24,000, or the only amount in dispute is the amount of interest assessed under the Act.[70] A taxpayer must make an irrevocable[71] election to use the Informal Procedure. The effect of the election is that the taxpayer gives up his or her right of appeal to an appellate court. The taxpayer may, however, seek judicial review by the Federal Court of Appeal.

The Informal Procedure is simple and requires that:

- The appeal be submitted in writing;
- The taxpayer set out the reasons for the appeal and the relevant facts;
- The Minister submit a reply within 45 days from the time when the Notice of Appeal is filed;
- The appeal be heard within 90 days of the Minister's reply; and
- Judgment be issued within 60 days of the hearing of the appeal.

Thus, the entire Informal Procedure is usually completed within approximately seven months from the date that the taxpayer files his or her Notice of Appeal. The taxpayer can represent him- or herself or be represented by an agent. The Federal Court of Appeal can judicially review the decisions of the Tax Court's informal decisions.

---

[69]S. 169.

[70]*Tax Court of Canada Act*, R.S.C. 1985, T-2, subs. 18(1).

[71]*Bell v. The Queen*, [1993] 2 C.T.C. 2688 (T.C.C.).

(b) — General Procedure

The General Procedure is a formal, full-blown litigation process. It applies to disputes in which federal tax exceeds $12,000. A taxpayer can represent him- or herself or be represented by a lawyer. Non-lawyer agents are not allowed to plead before the Tax Court in a General Procedure appeal. Formal rules of evidence govern the General Procedure and the decisions of the Tax Court following such an appeal are judicial precedents.

In contrast with the Informal Procedure, there is no pre-determined time frame for completion of an appeal in the General Procedure, and the process can take several years. Decisions of the Tax Court under the General Procedure may be appealed to the Federal Court of Appeal, pursuant to the rules of the *Federal Court Act*.[72]

2. — Federal Court of Appeal

The Federal Court of Appeal is the ultimate arbiter of disputes in most tax cases. A taxpayer must institute an appeal to the Federal Court within 30 days from the judgment of the Tax Court. The 30 day limitation excludes the months of July and August.[73] The appeal is commenced by filing a Notice of Appeal with the Federal Court Registry and by serving all parties who are directly affected by the appeal with a true copy of the notice. The Federal Court of Appeal usually hears appeals with a panel of three judges.[74]

3. — Supreme Court of Canada

The Supreme Court of Canada is the ultimate arbiter of income tax matters. Recourse to the Supreme Court, however, is possible only by way of leave to appeal. There is no automatic right of appeal to the Supreme Court. Hence, for all practical purposes, the Federal Court of Appeal is the final appellate tribunal in most income tax cases.

A taxpayer must bring an appeal to the Supreme Court within 60 days from the date that the Court of Appeal hands down its decision. A copy of the Notice of Appeal must be filed with the Registrar of the Supreme Court and all parties directly affected by the appeal must be served with a copy of the notice.

The technical requirements are that:

- The Federal Court of Appeal thinks that the question involved is one that ought to be decided by the Supreme Court; or

---

[72]R.S.C. 1985, c. F-7.

[73]Subs. 27(2), *Federal Courts Act*.

[74]S. 27, *Federal Courts Act* and subs. 180(1), *Income Tax Act*.

- The Supreme Court is of the view that the issue litigated is one of national importance. The dollar value of the dispute does not determine whether leave to appeal is granted.[75]

As a practical matter, the Supreme Court rarely, if ever, grants leave in more than two tax cases in any given year. This effectively restricts the development of jurisprudence in an important area of public law.

4. — Declaration of Taxpayer Rights

The role of taxation in history has not been entirely undramatic. King John's penchant for increasing feudal taxation in England without consultation with his lords precipitated the greatest constitutional document in the common law world, the *Magna Carta*. The underlying grievance of the Peasant's Revolt of 1381 was a poll tax on all males and females over the age of 15. The drama of the event is recorded in Hume's *History of England:*

> The first disorder was raised by a blacksmith in a village of Essex. The tax-gatherers came to this man's shop while he was at work; and they demanded payment for his daughter, who he asserted to be below the age assigned by the statute. One of these fellows offered to produce a very indecent proof to the contrary, and at the same time laid hold of the maid: which the father resenting, immediately knocked out the ruffian's brains with his hammer.

The image of the modern tax collector has improved, but only slightly. The Report of the Conservative Task Force on Revenue Canada (1984) commented on the tax collectors' proclivity towards oppressive conduct and insensitive behaviour. Concerning Revenue Canada's (now the Canada Revenue Agency's) tax collection methods, the Task Force stated:

- What we heard disturbed us deeply. We were distressed by the fear with which ordinary Canadians greet a call from the tax department, a fear that is sometimes cultivated by Revenue Canada.

- Another impression that was deeply instilled in us during our tour was that the tax burden is falling disproportionately on Canadians of modest means, as a result of Revenue Canada's actions.

- The complexity of the many provisions affecting lower income Canadians often causes serious resentment. This is also the group that is most likely to be audited by less-experienced employees who may make serious errors. These taxpayers can least afford the costly professional assistance needed to defend their rights.

- Another factor that undermines the rights of ordinary Canadians is the sweeping powers given to the Department. In some cases, they are even greater than the powers of the police.

---

[75]See, e.g., *The Queen v. Savage,* [1980] C.T.C. 103, 80 D.T.C. 6066; revd. on other grounds [1981] C.T.C. 332, 81 D.T.C. 5258; affd. [1983] C.T.C. 393, 83 D.T.C. 5409 (S.C.C.) (leave to appeal $300 assessment granted).

Later that year, the Conservative Government, by then in power, issued a declaratory statement, impressively entitled the "Declaration of Taxpayer Rights", which addressed some of the Task Force's concerns. However, once elected, the government did not enact the Declaration into law.

Since the *Charter of Rights* does not protect property rights, taxpayers have few constitutional protections against the tax collector. A notable exception is in the area of search and seizures that the government uses to prosecute tax evasion. Apart from this narrow exception, the courts view the *Income Tax Act* as essentially a regulatory statute. Hence, for example, the courts have not overturned the reverse onus clause, which presumes the Minister's assessment to be proper and correct unless the taxpayer proves it is not. Such a presumption would be untenable in most other areas of law, whether regulatory, quasi-criminal or criminal.

VII. — Burden Of Proof

The burden of proof in civil tax cases is the balance of probabilities. In criminal tax cases of tax evasion, the burden is on the Crown to establish its case beyond a reasonable doubt.

1. — *Presumption of Validity*

Subsection 152(8) of the Act sets out the burden in civil cases:

> An assessment shall . . . be *deemed* to be valid and binding notwithstanding any error, defect or omission in the assessment or in any proceeding under this Act relating thereto. [Emphasis added.]

Thus, the taxpayer carries the burden of proof to establish that the factual findings and the assumptions of fact upon which the Minister based the assessment are wrong.[76] The Minister is under an obligation to disclose the findings of fact upon which he or she bases an assessment. He does this in his reply to the notice of appeal. The taxpayer's burden of proof lies in rebutting the facts disclosed by the Minister in the assessment. This burden balances the scale in favour of the Minister. The burden of proof and cost of litigation deprives most taxpayers a judicial remedy in tax cases.

The burden of proof, however, is not immutable. Generally, in civil cases, we place the onus on the party who asserts a proposition or on the person who has particular knowledge of the

---

[76]*Johnston v. M.N.R.*, [1948] C.T.C. 195, 3 D.T.C. 1182 (S.C.C); *R. v. Anderson Logging Co.* (1924), [1925] S.C.R. 45, [1917-27] C.T.C. 198 (S.C.C.).

matter. We then draw inferenes based on the evidence, or lack thereof, that the party produces.[77]

2. — *Reversal of Onus*

Subsection 163(2) of the Act authorizes the Minister to impose a penalty on a person who has either "knowingly" or "under circumstances amounting to gross negligence" made a false statement or omission in an income tax return. In these circumstances, where the Minister imposes a penalty on the basis of the taxpayer's gross negligence, the Act reverses the burden of proof and puts it on the Minister to show the gross negligence on the basis of the particular facts.[78]

Subsection 163(2) requires that the Minister show not only that there has been an act of omission or misstatement by the taxpayer (or his or her agent), but also that the taxpayer (or agent) had a state of mind that justifies a finding of gross negligence. In *Udell v. M.N.R.*,[79] for example, the court stated: "In my view the use of the verb 'made' in the context in which it is used also involves a deliberate and intentional consciousness on the part of the principal to the act done.. . ."

VIII. — Penalties

The Canadian income tax system essentially relies on self-assessment and voluntary compliance. Taxpayers make voluntary disclosure of their income to the Agency in the form of an income tax return. There are, however, several penalty provisions that address failures to comply with the Act.

1. — *Civil Penalties*

Sections 162 and 163 of the Act provide for civil penalties for failing to file income tax returns, failing to provide prescribed information, and for making false statements or omissions.

---

[77]See *Snell v. Farrell*, [1990] 2 S.C.R. 311 (S.C.C.); *Redash Trading Inc. v. R.*, 2004 TCC 446 (T.C.C. [General Procedure]); *Blatch v. Archer* (1774), 98 E.R. 969 (Eng. KB); *Pleet v. Canadian Northern Quebec Railway* (1921), [1923] 4 D.L.R. 112 (S.C.C.).

[78]Subs. 163(3).

[79]*Udell v. M.N.R.*, [1969] C.T.C. 704, 70 D.T.C. 6019 at 6025 (Ex. Ct.) per Cattanach J.

2. — *Criminal Penalties*

In addition to the civil penalties available under the Act, sections 238 and 239 provide for penalties on conviction of a criminal offence under the Act. Subsection 239(1) provides that a person who has made or participated in tax evasion is subject to a fine of not less that 50 per cent, and not more than 200 per cent, of the amount of tax sought to be evaded. In addition to the monetary penalty, a taxpayer convicted of income tax evasion may be imprisoned for a period of up to two years. If the Crown elects to proceed by indictment rather than by way of summary conviction, subsection 239(2) increases the penalties to a fine of not less than 100 per cent and not more than 200 per cent, and imprisonment for no more than five years.

IX. — Remission Orders

A taxpayer's liability for tax under the *Income Tax Act* is a statutory liability and, in most circumstances, the Minister does not have the discretionary power to waive taxes that are payable under the Act. There is, however, some discretionary relief in exceptional circumstances where an obvious injustice is done to a taxpayer. Subsection 23(2) of the *Financial Administration Act*[80] provides that:

> The Governor in Council may, on the recommendation of the appropriate Minister, remit any tax or penalty . . . where the Governor in Council considers the collection of the tax or the enforcement of the penalty is unreasonable or unjust or that it is otherwise in the public interest to remit the tax or penalty.

The Order in Council is made on the basis of a recommendation from the Treasury Board. In fact, however, the request for a remission of taxes is initially made to the Canada Revenue Agency, which sends the request for the remission to the Treasury Board along with its own recommendation. Remission orders are published in the *Canada Gazette* and are reported to the House of Commons in the *Public Accounts*.

X. — Tax Expenditures

A government can achieve its social and economic policies in several ways. It can spend directly on programs by providing grants and subsidies through its annual budget process. Such expenditures are generally referred to as "budgetary expenditures" because their estimates are tabled in Parliament as part of the annual budget process. A government can also pursue its social and economic policies indirectly by using the tax system to provide incentives for particular initiatives or activities. Thus, a government can implement policies by providing an exemption, deduction, credit or deferral through the tax system. We refer to the costs of exemptions, deductions, credits and deferrals as "tax expenditures".

---

[80]R.S.C. 1985, c. F-11.

Tax expenditures, which are an alternative form of government expenditures, are real and substantial. They differ from budgetary expenditures because they are not tabled as direct outgoings and, therefore, do not require parliamentary spending approval. Instead, tax expenditures are approved indirectly through the legislative process that enacts income tax law.

We define tax expenditures as deviations from a "benchmark" tax system. A benchmark tax system refers to a normative system that measures income without reference to special incentives to achieve social, economic, and other policy objectives.

The definition and measurement of income is crucial to the benchmark because any deviation from the benchmark is considered a tax expenditure. For example, the deduction of salaries and wages from income is considered a normal expenditure that is intrinsic to the measurement of *net* business income or "profit". Thus, the deduction of such expenditures in the determination of business income are "normal" and are not tax expenditures.

In contrast, a tax credit for donations to political parties is not intrinsic to the measurement of net income. The Act allows the credit to encourage support for a democratic system of government and to engage Canadians in the political process. Hence, the cost of the political contributions credit is a tax expenditure outside the benchmark tax system. Similarly, a gain on the sale of one's home would normally be "income". We exempt such gains, however, for social and political considerations.

It is useful for a government to disseminate information on its budgetary and tax expenditures. Budgetary expenditures receive closer scrutiny and media attention because it is easier to see the numbers in the budget estimates placed before Parliament. The media understands budget spending. Tax expenditures, which represent equally real costs, are often ignored because they are not clearly visible in the annual estimates. Thus, the cost of tax expenditures buried deep in the detail of the *Income Tax Act* escape public scrutiny.

A tax expenditure represents a loss of revenue that would otherwise be available to the government if it used a benchmark tax system. In 2000, for example, the non-taxation of lottery and gambling winnings was expected to cost the Federal Treasury approximately $1.56 billion in lost revenues. Stated another way, the federal government foregoes $1.56 billion by exempting lottery winnings from taxation, money that it would otherwise have collected if it had a benchmark tax system.

The identification of what constitutes a proper benchmark tax structure is difficult and controversial. A benchmark necessarily implies value judgements that are subjective. The debate is not on the usefulness of tax expenditure analysis, but upon what goes into the list of "tax expenditures" that require analysis. Take, for example, the deduction for child-care expenses. If child-care expenses are viewed as personal and living expenses of parents, the deduction for such expenses in the computation of income is a tax expenditure because they are not part of the normal benchmark for the computation of income. On the other hand, if child-care expenses are viewed as necessary expenditures incurred for, and intrinsic in, the process of earning income, deductions for such expenses are not tax expenditures. In either case, the forgone revenue from the deduction for child-care expenses, whether as part of the benchmark determination of income or as a tax expenditure, represents a financial cost to the public treasury. The controversy is not so much about the fact that child-care expenses cost the federal treasury, but whether we should identify such expenses as "tax expenditures" for analytical purposes.

The definition of income is central to the determination of what is a tax expenditure. Tax provisions that provide for the deduction of normal current costs incurred to earn income are considered to be part of the benchmark system and, therefore, not tax expenditures. Tax provisions that fall outside of what are considered to be "normal" deductions are tax expenditures. The Canadian benchmarks for the personal income tax and corporate income tax systems are as follows:

Personal Income Tax

- Existing tax rates and income tax brackets are taken as given;
- The tax unit is the individual;
- Taxation is imposed on a calendar year basis;
- Nominal income unadjusted for inflation is used to define income; and
- Structural features such as the dividend tax credit to avoid double taxation of corporate income are normal.

Corporate Income Tax

- The existing general tax rate is taken as given;
- The tax unit is the corporation;
- Taxation is imposed on a fiscal year basis;
- Nominal income unadjusted for inflation is used to define income; and
- Structural features such as the non-taxation of inter-corporate dividends are normal.

XI. — Structure Of The Act

All tax systems address five basic questions:

1. Who is taxable?
2. What is taxable?
3. At what rate is tax payable?
4. When is tax payable? and

5. What are the procedures for administrative compliance and judicial review?

The *Income Tax Act* answers each of these questions in a systematic arrangement. The statute is initially divided into Parts, each of which deals with distinct subject matter. The Parts are divided into Divisions; the Divisions into subdivisions, and each subdivision is made up of sections.

Part I contains most of the provisions of the Act. Parts I.1 through XIV deal with special situations and taxes. Parts XV and XVI deal with administration, enforcement and tax evasion. Part XVII is concerned with interpretation and includes most of the general definitions used in the Act.

We said at the outset that tax law is concerned not only with generating sufficient revenues to finance government operations but also seeks to achieve other goals and objectives. Tax policy is concerned with evaluating the effectiveness with which these principles are implemented in the design of the tax structure. Thus, each of the five questions should be evaluated in the context of the objectives of the tax system.

To be sure, the ultimate structure will be a compromise of various competing values and political considerations. It will be improved, however, if it is conducted in the context of tax policy analysis. The following grid sets out the variables that we should consider when we evaluate policy.

A. Tax Policy Objectives of Tax System	A1. Revenue	A2. Fairness	A3. Efficiency	A4. Neutrality	A5. Simplicity
B. Structure of Act					
B1. Who is taxable?					
B2. What is taxable?					
B3. How much is taxed (rate)?					
B4. When is income taxed?					
B5. Administrative controls and compliance?					

XII. — The Time Value Of Money

The fundamental purpose of income tax law is to collect taxes for government expenditures. A taxpayer's obligation for tax arises when he or she earns taxable income. The obligation to pay the tax, however, is determined by a schedule set out in the Act. Thus, the timing of tax payments is key to the effectiveness of the tax system.

Time has value. The value is the effect of time on invested money.

There are two dimensions to value: future and present. Given a sum of money, we can determine its value at some future date if we know the interest rate at which we will invest the money. Conversely, if we know that we are to receive a sum of money in the future, we can determine its value today if we know the rate at which it is, or can be, invested. Thus, money has "time value".

To determine the value of money we need information about the relevant interest rate. *All* assets, tangible and intangible, can be expressed in terms of their future or present value if we can determine the rate at which the asset is invested or discounted. The appropriate rate is usually the market-determined interest or investment rate.

In economic terms, "interest" is the rental cost of borrowing money. As with all rentals, the cost of renting money may be fixed in advance, determinable at a future time, or variable according to specified conditions. Thus, interest and time are inextricably related. An interest rate is relevant if, and only if, it is specified in relation to time.

The concept of the time value of money is relevant to all law. Lawyers deal with assets that have a "time value" in virtually all areas of commercial practice. For example, suppose that a plaintiff's lawyer is offered a choice between a cash settlement of $500,000 or six successive payments of $100,000 payable at the end of each year. Should the lawyer accept the lump-sum settlement or pursue the extended payment plan? Ignoring questions of risk and insolvency, the answer depends upon the prevailing interest rate and income tax considerations associated with the two alternatives. At an interest rate of 10 per cent, the six payments of $100,000 have a present value of only $435,300. Hence, the plaintiff would be better off with the lump-sum settlement. If the interest (discount) rate was 4 per cent, however, the six payments would have a net present value of $524,000 (Table 1-3).

We can arrive at this answer in two ways. First, we can add the present values of each of the payments for six years at 10 per cent. The present values of $1 would be (see Table 1–2):

Year		
	1	0.909
	2	0.826
	3	0.751
	4	0.683
	5	0.620
	6	0.564
		4.353

Hence, the present value of $100,000 payable in six installments would be $435,300.

Alternatively, we arrive at the same answer by looking at Table 1–3. Reading down the 10 per cent column and across the six year row, we see that the present value of an annuity of $1 payable at the end of each year is $4.35. Hence, the present value of a $100,000 annuity would be $435,000 (rounded). At 4 per cent it would be $524,000.

Similarly, the defendant in a lawsuit involving future lost profits of a business enterprise may ask the court to reduce the size of any lump-sum award to the plaintiff to take into account the accelerated value of receiving the money today rather than over an extended period of time. For example, if one can establish that the defendant's actions will cause the plaintiff a loss of $100,000 of business profits annually for a period of five years, should the defendant be required to pay the nominal amount of the damages up front or some lesser discounted amount because of the time value of money? At an interest rate of 12 per cent the annual loss of $100,000 spread over five years is worth only $360,000 today if the payments are receivable at the end of each year (Table 1–3). Ignoring the time value of money would penalize the defendant and provide the plaintiff with a windfall gain. Thus, time value considerations should be taken into account in structuring damage settlements to account for the net present value of related tax costs and savings.

Although most of us are familiar with the calculation of simple and compound interest, we are less intuitive about the concept of the discounted value of future sums of money. This is because we are taught to think intuitively of investing for the future but not of the present value of future sums. Yet, mathematically speaking, future value and present value are mirror images of each other looked at from different perspectives. The primary purpose of determining future and present values is to measure money in comparable terms across time periods by translating future dollars into economically equivalent current dollars, and *vice versa*.

1. — Future Value

We determine the future value of money by reference to the effect of interest on a principal sum. There are two forms of interest, simple and compound. Interest that is paid only on the amount originally invested, but not on any interest that accrues subsequently, is referred to as simple interest. Simple interest is a function of the principal sum (P) multiplied by rate (R) multiplied by time (n):

$$Interest = PRn$$

For example, if one deposits $10,000 in a guaranteed investment certificate (GIC) for a period of one year at 8 per cent, the GIC will be worth $10,800 at the end of the year. The interest earned is $800, or 8 per cent of the principal amount for one year. Thus, if simple interest is paid over (n) periods, the total interest payments and the sum originally invested will grow to:

$$F = P (1 + R)n$$

Where:

F= the future value of money;

P= the present sum of money;

R= net interest rate over a period of time; and

n= the number of periods of time.

Hence, in four years the total sum will equal $13,200.

In contrast, compound interest refers to the process whereby interest is earned not only on the amount originally invested but also on subsequently accrued interest. Compound interest starts out with exactly the same formula as simple interest but extends it to account for the reinvested interest. In other words, the interest on the second and subsequent time periods is calculated not only on the initial principal amount but also on any interest accumulated in preceding time periods.

For example, if one invests $10,000 in a GIC at 8 per cent compounded annually for two years, the GIC is worth $11,664 at the end of the second year. At the end of the first year the principal and the interest are $10,800. But the interest for the second year is calculated as 8 per cent of $10,800, which is $864. We arrive at the same result by looking at Table 1–1, where we see that the future value of $1 invested at 8 per cent for two years is $1.17. In contrast, simple interest for both years would have produced only $11,600. The incremental $64 is due entirely to the fact that the interest in the second year is calculated not only on the initial principal amount but also on the reinvested interest. The $64 is the premium for the compounding of interest. It is the interest on earlier interest.

To generalize, a future amount is determined by the formula:

$$F = P(1 + R)^n$$

Where:

F= the future value of money;

P= the present sum of money;

R= net interest rate over a period of time; and

n= the number of periods of time.

The formula demonstrates that the longer the time horizon for investment and the more frequent the compounding intervals, the greater the future value of a present sum of money. For example, the future value of $1 invested at 8 per cent at the end of years 1 through to 5 is as follows:[81]

Year	1	$1.080
	2	$1.166
	3	$1.260
	4	$1.360
	5	$1.469

If, instead, we compound $10,000 over a period of 8 quarters at 2 per cent per quarter (which nominally appears to be the same thing as 8 per cent per year) we get a future value of $11,717, or $53 more than in the previous example of compounding only once per year. On a $100 million transaction the difference between annual and quarterly compounding is $530,000. The lesson is simple: a lender will benefit from compounding interest as frequently as possible and the borrower will pay more for frequent compounding. Thus, in an open and competitive market, the borrower and the lender must negotiate both the interest rate and compounding intervals.

There is no such negotiation, however, in tax law. The CRA compounds interest on a *daily* basis on outstanding amounts of taxes payable.[82] In the above example, if the $10,000 was the outstanding amount of a tax assessment, daily compounding of the amount at an equivalent of 8 per cent per year would increase the tax payable at the end of two years to $11,735. Hence, it is almost always to a taxpayer's advantage to pay the assessment and then challenge its validity at a later date. It is virtually impossible for a taxpayer to obtain an investment that will yield an equivalent amount of interest for the same risk. Since tax disputes can continue for eight to ten years from the particular taxation year, the daily compounding effect has an enormous impact on the ultimate amount payable if the taxpayer ultimately loses the appeal. For example, an outstanding assessment of $10,000 will grow to $22,240 in 10 years if compounded at 8 per cent on a daily basis.

Compounding allows us to determine the economic equivalence of money across different time periods. For example, if the market rate of interest is 8 per cent, we should be indifferent between paying $1,000 today and $1,469 five years from now because we could invest the $1,000 at 8 per cent today and it would grow to $1,469 in five years on a pre-tax basis. The two sums, $1,000 today and $1,469 in five years, are equivalent returns in economic terms if the prevailing rate of interest is 8 per cent. (See Table 1–1.)

---

[81]See Table 1-1 at the end of this chapter. Note that the Tables are rounded to two decimal places.

[82]Subs. 248(11).

2. — Taxes

Taxes play a significant role in determining future values. Taxes payable on a current basis reduce the amount of interest available for reinvestment (the "R" in the formula) and, hence, reduce the compounding effect on the principal sum. For example, assume that Nicola invests $10,000 in a tax-sheltered investment that earns 10 per cent compounded annually for 10 years. At the end of 10 years, the future value of the investment will be $25,937 (see Table 1–1). The accumulated gain of $15,937 represents the gross compound interest over a period of 10 years. Thus, the money will more than double in 10 years. In contrast, if Nicola pays tax at 40 per cent on her earned interest on a current basis, she will have only 6 per cent to reinvest each year. The future value of $10,000 invested at 6 per cent (net) will be $17,908 at the end of 10 years. Thus, the ultimate value of the currently taxed investment is $8,029 less than the value of the tax-sheltered investment. Therein the attraction of tax shelters and the benefits of tax deferral.

Since taxes decrease the amount that can be reinvested, it generally pays to delay (defer) the payment of taxes (the longer, the better) provided that the CRA is not levying interest on the outstanding amount at the same time. For example, a $1,000 investment compounding at 20 per cent in a tax shelter is worth $1.4 million after 40 years. If the investment is taxed annually at 25 per cent, the net return is 15 per cent and the investment is worth approximately $267,000 in 40 years. If taxed at 40 per cent, the net return is 12 per cent and the investment is worth only $93,000 after 40 years (see Table 1–1).

A simple method to determine how quickly money can double is the rule of 72. The rule provides that if we divide 72 by the interest rate, we obtain the approximate number of years that it will take a sum of money to double with compound interest. For example, at an interest rate of 6 per cent compounded annually, a sum of money will double in approximately 12 years. Table 1–1 tells us that each $1 would be worth $2.01 at the end of 12 years. If taxes reduce the reinvestment rate by 40 per cent to 3.6 per cent, it will take 20 years for the money to double. Thus, reinvestment gross of tax is always preferable to reinvestment net of tax. Compounding for long periods, even at modest rates, leads to explosive growth. At 3 per cent, for example, $1 will grow to $6,874,000,000,000 in 1,000 years!

3. — Present Value

We can approach the time value of money in two ways: the future value of a present sum of money or the present value of a future sum. Although this may seem obtuse, both values are in fact merely different ways of looking at the same thing. The future value is the sum to which an amount, or a series of periodic and equal amounts, will grow at the end of a certain amount of time if compounded at a particular interest rate. The present value is the discounted value at a particular rate of interest of a sum of money to be received in the future. We can restate the compound interest formula as follows:

$$P = \frac{F}{(1 + R)^n}$$

where:

F= the future value of money;

P= the present sum of money;

R= net interest rate over a period of time; and

n= the number of periods of time.

The more distant the time when an amount has to be paid on account of tax, the lower its present value. Hence, it pays to delay or defer the payment of taxes as long as possible so as to minimize the present value of the obligation today.

For example, the present value of $1 invested at 8 per cent at the end of years 1 through to 5 is as follows:[83]

Year	1	$0.926
	2	$0.857
	3	$0.794
	4	$0.735
	5	$0.681

When we say that the interest rate is 8 per cent per year, we mean that we should be able to exchange in the market 93 cents today in return for $1 a year from now and 86 cents in return for $1 two years from now, and so on. Hence, if we can defer the obligation to pay $1,000 in taxes today for five years, the present value of the liability to pay is only $681. Although the face amount of the legal obligation to pay remains the same, namely, $1,000 in five years, its economic value varies depending upon when it is paid. The economic value is only $681 if paid today, $735 if paid a year from now, $794 if paid two years from now, and so on. Stated another way, if we invested $681 in a deposit that compounded tax free at a rate of 8 per cent, we would accumulate $1,000 at the end of five years with which to pay the tax liability. By deferring the tax payable for five years we in effect reduce the tax liability by $319.

To continue with the same example: let us assume that we can defer the tax payable for a period of 50 years. The present value of $1,000 payable in 50 years at a discount rate of 8 per cent is $21. In other words, if we invest $21 today and compound it for 50 years on a net 8 per cent basis, we will have $1,000 at the end of the investment period. The discounted amount shrinks as a function of two factors: time (n) and the discount rate (R). The longer the period of deferral and the higher the interest rate, the lower the discounted present value.

---

[83]See Table 1-2 at the end of this chapter.

Hence, $1,000 payable in 50 years and discounted at 20 per cent has a present value today of (effectively) nil.

In determining present and future values, it is important to specify the assumptions underlying the mathematical calculations. Since time value calculations are premised on an interest rate, an error in estimating the rate can significantly distort results. There is no easy way to minimize this risk other than to rely upon responsible predictions. For example, if one earns 10 per cent (instead of 12 per cent) over 10 years, $10,000 invested in an RRSP would grow to only $25,900 instead of $31,100. The 2 per cent difference in interest rates reduces the investment return by $5,200, a reduction of 16.5 per cent over 10 years. The longer the investment horizon, the greater the risk that inaccurate assumptions will creep into the reinvestment formula. Hence, long-term retirement plans should be based on conservative estimates of future reinvestment rates.

It is also important in time value calculations to take into account the income tax effect of payments. As noted above, reinvestment rates can vary substantially depending upon whether the funds are invested in a tax shelter or in a currently taxable investment. With marginal tax rates of 50 per cent, ignoring taxes can be even more significant than the miscalculation of anticipated inflation.

How realistic are discussions of compounding rates of 10 per cent in present value calculations? The answer depends upon how we choose to invest. According to Ibbotson Associates (a Chicago-based research firm), the Standard & Poors 500 Index (an index that tracks 500 companies and gauges the stock market's performance) provided an annual average rate of return of 10.5 per cent from 1926 to 1995. During the same period, long-term U.S. government bonds provided a rate of return of 5.2 per cent on an annual basis, while short-term U.S. treasury bills earned 3.7 per cent, and inflation averaged 3.1 per cent per year. Eliminating the inflation factor from the returns, the real return on treasury bills was an average of 0.6 per cent, on bonds 2.1 per cent and on stocks 7.4 per cent. Hence, choice of the investment vehicle has a substantial effect upon an investor's rate of return. A 10 per cent nominal rate of return is a realistic objective for long-term investments in equities in a tax-sheltered environment. Outside of a tax shelter, the nominal rate may drop to 6 per cent and the real rate of return after inflation would be lower. Thus, time, risk, inflation and taxes all affect value in financial planning.

XIII. — Conclusion

This chapter highlights the multifaceted nature of the income tax system. Apart from raising revenues for government operations, income tax law also concerns various aspects of government economic and social policies. Since an income tax statute expropriates private property for public purposes, it is almost inevitable that taxpayers will attempt to resist, or at least minimize, the effect of expropriation. The tension between the taxpayer and the tax collector necessitates complex provisions to prevent undue leakage of tax revenues. The scope of coverage and the changing nature of domestic and international economies require frequent changes as taxpayers adapt and adopt new techniques of tax minimization.

At the same time, the line between legitimate and abusive tax avoidance ebbs and flows as the courts develop new approaches to statutory construction of fiscal legislation. The courts have shifted away from interpreting the Act as a penal statute. Nevertheless, we continue with problems of statutory construction. Sometimes we lean towards the "plain meaning" rule and, at other times, in favour of "purposive" interpretation. As we will see in subsequent chapters, this tension in statutory construction leads to uncertainty and legislative complexity in tax law.

Finally, the introduction of the General Anti-Avoidance Rule (GAAR)[84] into our tax law has made the tax system even more uncertain and tax planning more complex. The broad language of section 245 of the *Income Tax Act* stands in contrast to the other detailed provisions of the statute. The effect of GAAR, however, is the same. Every one of its subsections breeds a dilemma and danger lurks in every one of its definitions. To be sure, tax law is difficult, but it is not dry. On the contrary, its influence on human behaviour is probably greater than that of any other statute.

---

[84]See Chapter 24, "Tax Avoidance".

TABLE 1-1

Compound Amount of $1: Amount to Which $1 Now Will Grow by End of Specified Year at Compounded Interest

Year	3%	4%	5%	6%	7%	8%	10%	12%	15%	20%	Year
1	1.03	1.04	1.05	1.06	1.07	1.08	1.10	1.12	1.15	1.20	1
2	1.06	1.08	1.10	1.12	1.14	1.17	1.21	1.25	1.32	1.44	2
3	1.09	1.12	1.16	1.19	1.23	1.26	1.33	1.40	1.52	1.73	3
4	1.13	1.17	1.22	1.26	1.31	1.36	1.46	1.57	1.74	2.07	4
5	1.16	1.22	1.28	1.34	1.40	1.47	1.61	1.76	2.01	2.49	5
6	1.19	1.27	1.34	1.41	1.50	1.59	1.77	1.97	2.31	2.99	6
7	1.23	1.32	1.41	1.50	1.61	1.71	1.94	2.21	2.66	3.58	7
8	1.27	1.37	1.48	1.59	1.72	1.85	2.14	2.48	3.05	4.30	8
9	1.30	1.42	1.55	1.68	1.84	2.00	2.35	2.77	3.52	5.16	9
10	1.34	1.48	1.63	1.79	1.97	2.16	2.59	3.11	4.05	6.19	10
11	1.38	1.54	1.71	1.89	2.10	2.33	2.85	3.48	4.66	7.43	11
12	1.43	1.60	1.80	2.01	2.25	2.52	3.13	3.90	5.30	8.92	12
13	1.47	1.67	1.89	2.13	2.41	2.72	3.45	4.36	6.10	10.7	13
14	1.51	1.73	1.98	2.26	2.58	2.94	3.79	4.89	7.00	12.8	14
15	1.56	1.80	2.08	2.39	2.76	3.17	4.17	5.47	8.13	15.4	15
16	1.60	1.87	2.18	2.54	2.95	3.43	4.59	6.13	9.40	18.5	16
17	1.65	1.95	2.29	2.69	3.16	3.70	5.05	6.87	10.6	22.2	17
18	1.70	2.03	2.41	2.85	3.38	4.00	5.55	7.70	12.5	26.6	18
19	1.75	2.11	2.53	3.02	3.62	4.32	6.11	8.61	14.0	31.9	19
20	1.81	2.19	2.65	3.20	3.87	4.66	6.72	9.65	16.1	38.3	20
25	2.09	2.67	3.39	4.29	5.43	6.85	10.8	17.0	32.9	95.4	25
30	2.43	3.24	4.32	5.74	7.61	10.0	17.4	30.0	66.2	237	30
40	3.26	4.80	7.04	10.3	15.0	21.7	45.3	93.1	267.0	1470	40
50	4.38	7.11	11.5	18.4	29.5	46.9	117	289	1080	9100	50

To read this table, determine the compounding rate for the applicable number of compounding periods. For example, each dollar invested at 8 per cent for five years yields $1.47 if compounding occurs annually at the end of each year. Compounding semi-annually at 4 per cent for 10 time periods yields $1.48.

CHART 1-1

**Compound Amount of $1: Amount to Which $1 Now
Will Grow by End of Specified Year at a
Compounded Interest Rate of 8% per Year**

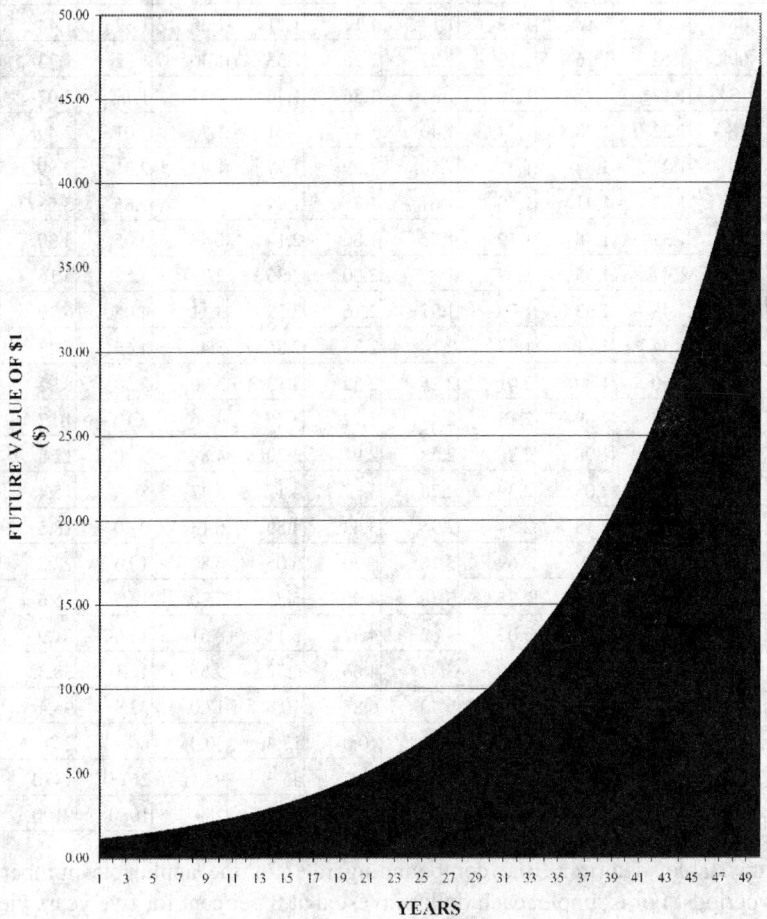

TABLE 1-2

Present Value of $1: What a Dollar at End of Specified Future Year is Worth Today

Year	3%	4%	5%	6%	7%	8%	10%	12%	15%	20%	Year
1	.971	.962	.952	.943	.935	.926	.909	.893	.870	.833	1
2	.943	.925	.907	.890	.873	.857	.826	.797	.756	.694	2
3	.915	.890	.864	.839	.816	.794	.751	.711	.658	.578	3
4	.889	.855	.823	.792	.763	.735	.683	.636	.572	.482	4
5	.863	.823	.784	.747	.713	.681	.620	.567	.497	.402	5
6	.838	.790	.746	.705	.666	.630	.564	.507	.432	.335	6
7	.813	.760	.711	.665	.623	.583	.513	.452	.376	.279	7
8	.789	.731	.677	.627	.582	.540	.466	.404	.326	.233	8
9	.766	.703	.645	.591	.544	.500	.424	.360	.284	.194	9
10	.744	.676	.614	.558	.508	.463	.385	.322	.247	.162	10
11	.722	.650	.585	.526	.475	.429	.350	.287	.215	.134	11
12	.701	.625	.557	.497	.444	.397	.318	.257	.187	.112	12
13	.681	.601	.530	.468	.415	.368	.289	.229	.162	.0935	13
14	.661	.577	.505	.442	.388	.340	.263	.204	.141	.0779	14
15	.642	.555	.481	.417	.362	.315	.239	.183	.122	.0649	15
16	.623	.534	.458	.393	.339	.292	.217	.163	.107	.0541	16
17	.605	.513	.436	.371	.317	.270	.197	.146	.093	.0451	17
18	.587	.494	.416	.350	.296	.250	.179	.130	.0808	.0376	18
19	.570	.475	.396	.330	.277	.232	.163	.116	.0703	.0313	19
20	.554	.456	.377	.311	.258	.215	.148	.104	.0611	.0261	20
25	.478	.375	.295	.232	.184	.146	.0923	.0588	.0304	.0105	25
30	.412	.308	.231	.174	.131	.0994	.0573	.0334	.0151	.00421	30
40	.307	.208	.142	.0972	.067	.0460	.0221	.0107	.00373	.000680	40
50	.228	.141	.087	.0543	.034	.0213	.00852	.00346	.000922	.000109	50

To read this table, determine the discount rate for the applicable number of discounting periods. For example, each dollar receivable in five years is worth only 68 cents today if the discount rate is 8 per cent. If the discount rate is 4 per cent semi-annually, the value of each dollar falls to 67 cents.

CHART 1-2

**Present Value of $1: What a Dollar at End of
Specified Future Year is Worth Today
Assuming an Annual Interest Rate of 8%**

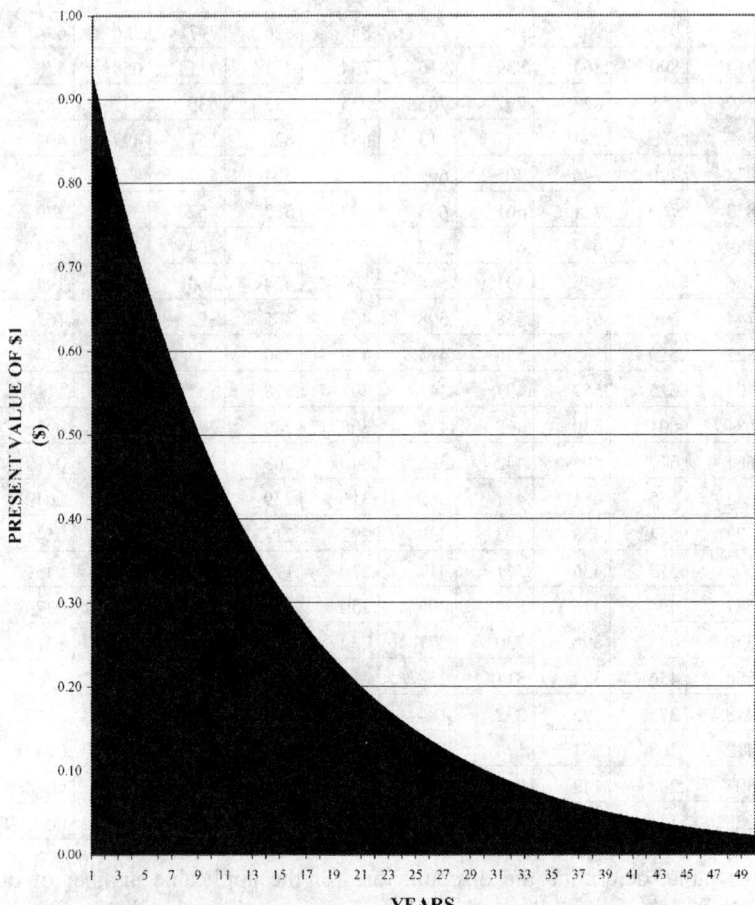

TABLE 1-3

Present Value of Annuity of $1, Received at End of Each Year

Year	3%	4%	5%	6%	7%	8%	10%	12%	15%	20%	Year
1	0.971	0.960	0.952	0.943	0.935	0.926	0.909	0.890	0.870	0.833	1
2	1.91	1.89	1.86	1.83	1.81	1.78	1.73	1.69	1.63	1.53	2
3	2.53	2.78	2.72	2.67	2.62	2.58	2.45	2.40	2.28	2.11	3
4	3.72	3.63	3.55	3.46	3.39	3.31	3.16	3.04	2.86	2.59	4
5	4.58	4.45	4.33	4.21	4.10	3.99	3.79	3.60	3.35	2.99	5
6	5.42	5.24	5.08	4.91	4.77	4.62	4.35	4.11	3.78	3.33	6
7	6.23	6.00	5.79	5.58	5.39	5.21	4.89	4.56	4.16	3.60	7
8	7.02	6.73	6.46	6.20	5.97	5.75	5.33	4.97	4.49	3.84	8
9	7.79	7.44	7.11	6.80	6.52	6.25	5.75	5.33	4.78	4.03	9
10	8.53	8.11	7.72	7.36	7.02	6.71	6.14	5.65	5.02	4.19	10
11	9.25	8.76	8.31	7.88	7.50	7.14	6.49	5.94	5.23	4.33	11
12	9.95	9.39	8.86	8.38	7.94	7.54	6.81	6.19	5.41	4.44	12
13	10.6	9.99	9.39	8.85	8.36	7.90	7.10	6.42	5.65	4.53	13
14	11.3	10.6	9.90	9.29	8.75	8.24	7.36	6.63	5.76	4.61	14
15	11.9	11.1	10.4	9.71	9.11	8.56	7.60	6.81	5.87	4.68	15
16	12.6	11.6	10.8	10.1	9.45	8.85	7.82	6.97	5.96	4.73	16
17	13.2	12.2	11.3	10.4	9.76	9.12	8.02	7.12	6.03	4.77	17
18	13.8	12.7	11.7	10.8	10.1	9.37	8.20	7.25	6.10	4.81	18
19	14.3	13.1	12.1	11.1	10.3	9.60	8.36	7.37	6.17	4.84	19
20	14.9	13.6	12.5	11.4	10.6	9.82	8.51	7.47	6.23	4.87	20
25	17.4	15.6	14.1	12.8	11.7	10.7	9.08	7.84	6.46	4.95	25
30	19.6	17.3	15.4	13.5	12.4	11.3	9.43	8.06	6.57	4.98	30
40	23.1	19.8	17.2	15.0	13.3	11.9	9.78	8.24	6.64	5.00	40
50	25.7	21.5	18.3	15.8	13.8	12.2	9.91	8.30	6.66	5.00	50

This table is a shorthand extension of Table 1–2. It shows the cumulative present value of an annual series of equal payments received at the end of each year. For example, the present value of three annual payments of $1 invested at 8 per cent is equal to $2.58 today. We can arrive at the same result from Table 1–2 by adding together 0.926, 0.857 and 0.794.

CHART 1-3

**Present Value of Annuity of \$1, Received at End of Each Year
Assuming an Interest Rate of 8%**

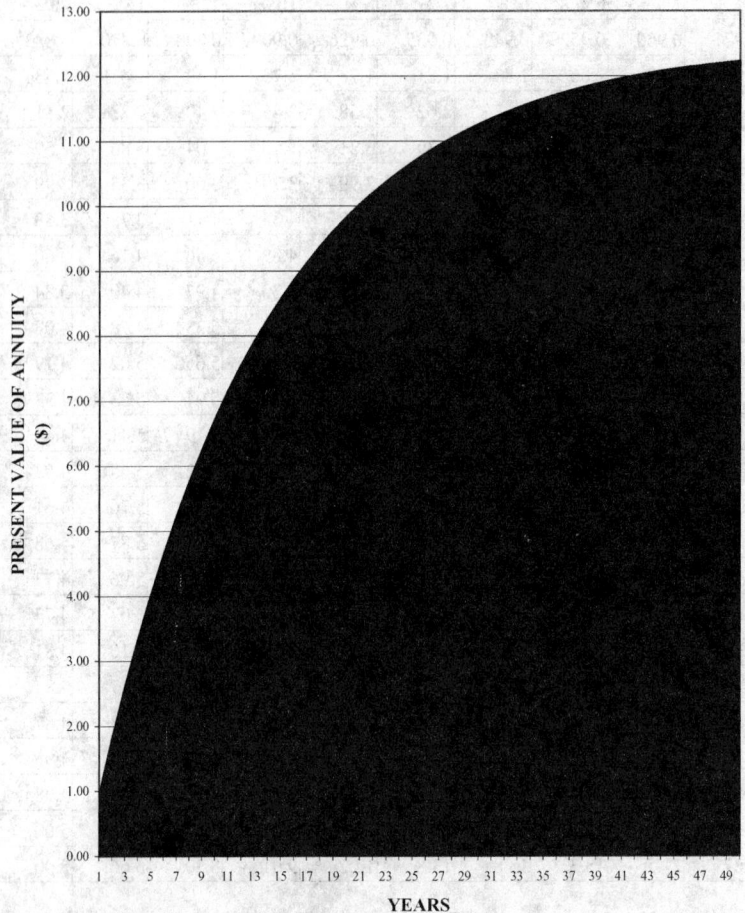

Selected Bibliography to Chapter 1

History

Bale, G., "The Individual and Tax Reform in Canada" (1971) 49 Can. Bar Review 24.

Ballentine, J.G., "Broadening our Approach to Income Tax Reform" (Spring 1986) 5:1 Amer. Journal of Tax Policy 1.

Bittker, B., "A Comprehensive Tax Base as a Goal of Income Tax Reform" (1967) 80 H.L.R. 925.

Blum, W.J., "Federal Income Tax Reform — Twenty Questions" (November 1963) 41 Taxes 672.

Bossons, John, "Tax Reform and International Competitiveness", in *Proceedings of 39th Tax Conf.* 5:1 (Can. Tax Foundation, 1987).

Break, G.F., and J.A. Pechman, *Federal Tax Reform: The Impossible Dream* (Washington: 1975).

Brooks, W. Neil, *The Quest for Tax Reform* (Carswell: Toronto, 1988).

Cohen, Marshall A., and Stephen R. Richardson, "Fifteen Years After Tax Reform: A Retrospective" (1986) Special Lectures LSUC 1.

Dodge, David A., "New Directions in Canadian Tax Policy" (1989) 41 Tax Exec. 111.

Drache, A.B.C., "Introduction to Income Tax Policy Formulation: Canada 1972–76" (1978) 16 Osgoode Hall L.J. 1.

Gibson, "Tax Policy for the Long and Short Run" (1963) 11 Can. Tax J. 58.

Goodman, W.D., "Tax Reform — The Continuing Challenge" (1978) 16 Osgoode Hall L.J. 147.

Grady, Patrick, "Real Effective Corporate Tax Rates in Canada and the United States After Tax Reform" (1989) 37 Can. Tax J. 647.

Harris, "What Should Canada Do with the Carter Report?" (1967) 21 Bull. Int'l. Fisc. Doc. 531.

Head, J.G., "The Carter Legacy: An International Perspective" (1987) 4:2 Australian Tax Forum 143.

Krever, "The Origin of Federal Income Taxation in Canada" (Winter 1981) Can. Tax. 170.

Krishna, Vern, "A Law that Taxes our Understanding" (1986) 10:9 Can. Law

Constitutional Authority for Taxation

Hogg, *Constitutional Law of Canada*, loose-leaf edition. (Toronto: Carswell, 1997).

La Forest, G.V., "The Allocation of Taxing Power under the Canadian Constitution", *Can. Tax Paper No. 45* (Can. Tax Foundation, 1967).

Moull, William D., "Intergovernmental Immunity From Taxation: The Unsolved Issues" (1984) 32 Can. Tax J. 54.

The Legislative Process

Canadian Tax Foundation Committee on the Budget Process, "The Canadian Budget
Process" (1986) 34 Can. Tax J. 989.

The Executive Process

Edwards, S.E., "Drafting Fiscal Legislation" (1984) 32 Can. Tax J. 727.
Jackett, W.R., "Too Much Income Tax Law?", Can. Tax J. 54.

The Income Tax Process

Davidson, "The Reorganization of the Legislation Branch of Revenue Canada Taxa-
tion" (1978) 26 Can. Tax J. 429.
Drache, Arthur B.C., "Income Tax Policy Formulation in Canada, 1972–76" (1978) 16
Osgoode Hall L.J. 1.
Thorson, "Formulation, Enactment and Administration of Tax Changes", in *Proceed-
ings of 24th Tax Conf.* 14 (Can. Tax Foundation, 1972).
Thorsteinsson, P., "How to Settle an Income Tax Controversy, through Litigation and
Before", *1978 Conference Report* (Can. Tax Foundation, 1979).

Tax System Objectives

"Anatomy of a Tax System", in *Proceedings of 20th Tax Conf.* 7 (Can. Tax Founda-
tion, 1967).
Andrews, W.D., "A Consumption Type or Cash Flow Personal Income Tax" (April
1984) 87:6 H.L.R. 1113.
Bale, G., "Temporary Equity in Taxation" (1977) 55 Can. Bar Rev. 1.
Ballantyne, Janet L., "The Tax Burden of the Middle-Class Canadian" (1986) 34 Can.
Tax J. 671–680.
Bird, "Income Redistribution and Ability to Pay", in *Proceedings of 20th Tax Conf.*
242, 256–64 (Can. Tax Foundation, 1967).
Bradford, D.F., "The Case for a Personal Consumption Tax", in *What Would be Taxed:
Income or Expenditure?* (Washington: The Brookings Institution, 1980) at 75–113.
Bruce, Neil, "Ability to Pay and Comprehensive Income Taxation: Annual or Lifetime
Basis?" as found in Brooks, W. Neil, ed., *The Quest for Tax Reform* (Toronto: Cars-
well, 1988) at 157.
Chapman, S.J., "The Utility of Income and Progressive Taxation" (1913), 23 Econ. J.
25.
Crowe, Ian, "Taxation: Uncertain Incentives" (March 1991) 124 CA Magazine 51.
Drache, Arthur B.C., "A Fair Tax System?" (1994) 16 Can. Taxpayer 9.
Drache, Arthur B.C., "Unfairness in Taxation" (1993) 15 Can. Taxpayer 19.

Howard, R., G. Ruggeri and Van D. Wart, "The Progressivity of Provincial Personal Income Taxes in Canada" (1991) 39 Can. Tax J. 288.

Kesselman, Jonathan R., *Rate Structure and Personal Taxation: Flat Rate or Dual Rate?* (Wellington, New Zealand: Victoria University Press for the Institute of Policy Studies, 1990).

Salyzyn, Vladimir, "Canadian Income Tax Policy: An Economic Evaluation" (1987) 66 Can. Bar Rev. 405. *Question of Incidence Analysis* (Department of Economics, University of Western Ontario, 1984).

System Characteristics

Atkeson, T.C., "Tax Simplification from the Viewpoint of a Professor of Taxation", in *Essays on Taxation* (New York: Tax Foundation Inc., 1974) at 93–109.

Audie, Suphan, "Does the Personal Income Tax Discriminate Against Women?" (1981) 1 Pub. Fin. 1.

Cassidy, Michael, "Fairness and Efficiency: Can Tax Reform Do the Job?", in *Proceedings of 39th Tax Conf.* 2:1 (Can. Tax Foundation, 1987).

Daly, Michael J., Jack Jung and Thomas Schweitzer, "Toward a Neutral Capital Income Tax System" (1986) 34 Can. Tax J. 1331.

Drache, Arthur B.C., "Flat Taxes Emerging Again" (1993), 15 Can. Taxpayer 45.

Eustice, James S., "Tax Complexity and the Tax Practitioner" (Fall 1989) 45 The Tax Lawyer 7.

Gillespie, W. Irwin et al., "Tax Incidence in Canada" (1994) 42 Can. Tax J. 348.

Howard, R. et al., "The Redistributional Impact of Taxation in Canada" (1994) 42 Can. Tax J. 417.

Hugget, Donald R., "E Pluribus Unum (The Single Tax)" 18 Can. Tax News 1.

McCaffery, Edward J., "The Holy Grail of Tax Simplification" [1990] 5 Wis. L. Rev. 1267.

Mills, Dennis, *The Single Tax — Fair and Simple for All Canadians* (Toronto: Hemlock Press, 1990).

Mills, W.D., "Tax Simplification from the Viewpoint of the Legislator", in *Essays on Taxation* (New York: Tax Foundation Inc., 1974) at 74–92.

Peterson, C.R., "Tax Simplification From the Viewpoint of the Tax Attorney", in *Essays on Taxation* (New York: Tax Foundation Inc., 1974) at 110–117.

Prebble, John, "Why is Tax Law Incomprehensible?", (1994) British Tax Rev. 380.

Roberts, S.I., et al., "Report on Complexity and the Income Tax" (1971-72), 27 Tax Law Review 325.

Ruggeri, G.C., et al., "The Redistributional Impact of Taxation in Canada" (1994) 42 Can. Tax J. 417.

"Simplification" (Summary of Recommendations of the Commons Standing Committee on Finance and Economic Affairs Report Entitled 'Tax Simplification') (1986) 14 Can. Tax News 25.

Sherbaniuk, D.J., "Tax Simplification — Can Anything Be Done About It?", in *Proceedings of 40th Tax Conf.* 3:1 (Can. Tax Foundation, 1988).

Strain, William J., David A. Dodge and Victor Peters, "Tax Simplification: The Elusive Goal", in *Proceedings of 40th Tax Conf.* 4:1 (Can. Tax Foundation, 1988).

Other

Allen, R.I.G. and D. Savage, "The Case for Inflation Proofing the Personal Income Tax" (1974) Br. Tax Rev. 299.

Alter, Dr. A., "Different Techniques for Adjusting Taxable Income Under Inflationary Conditions" (1986) Br. Tax Rev. 347.

Andrew, W.D., "Personal Deductions in an Ideal Income Tax" (December 1972) 86 H.L.R. 2:309.

Arnold, B.J., *Timing and Income Taxation: The Principles of Income Measurement for Tax Purposes* (Toronto: Can. Tax Foundation, 1983).

Barry, David B., "The Relative Importance of Personal and Corporation Income Tax" (1986) 34 Can. Tax J. 460–67.

Beale, "The Measure for Income Taxation" (1911) 19 Journal of Political Economy 655, 661.

Bird, "The Tax Kaleidoscope" (1970) Can. Tax J. 444.

Blais, André and François Vaillancourt, *The Political Economy of Taxation: The Corporate Income Tax and the Canadian Manufacturing Industry* (Montreal: Université de Montréal, 1986).

Blum, "Tax Lawyers and Tax Policy" (March 1961) Taxes 247.

Bradford, D.F., *Untangling the Income Tax* (Cambridge: Harvard University Press, 1986).

Brean, Donald S., "International Influences on Canadian Tax Policy: The Free Trade Agreement and U.S. Tax Reform" (1988) Corporate Management Tax Conference 13:1.

Broadway and Kitchen, "Canadian Tax Policy", *Can. Tax Paper No. 63* (Can. Tax Foundation, 1980).

Broadway and Kitchen, "Canadian Tax Policy", *Can. Tax Paper No. 76* (Can. Tax Foundation, 1984).

Carver, "The Minimum Sacrifice Theory of Taxation" (1904) 19 Political Science Quarterly 66.

Colley, G.M., "Is Indexing a Necessary Evil/L'indexation: un mal nécessaire?" (1986) 119:9 CA Magazine 52.

Douglas, P.H., "The Problem of Tax Loopholes" (Winter, 1967-68) 37 Amer. Scholar 21.

Drache, Arthur B.C., "Towards a New Tax Philosophy" (1993) 15 Can. Taxpayer 185.

Dulude, Louise, "Taxation of the Spouses: A Comparison of Canadian, American, British, French and Swedish Law" (1985) 23 Osgoode Hall L.J. 67.

Eaton, A.K., "Essays in Taxation", *Can. Tax Paper No. 44* (Can. Tax Foundation, 1966).

Eisenstein, L., "Some Second Thoughts on Tax Ideologies" 20 Tax Law Rev. 453.

Goode, R., *The Individual Income Tax* (Washington: The Brookings Institution, 1976).

Groves, N.M., *Tax Philosophers: Two Hundred Years of Thought in Great Britain and the United States* (Madison: 1974).

Haig, R.M., "The Concept of Income — Economic and Legal Aspects", in *Federal Income Tax* (New York: Columbia University Press, 1921) at 1–28.

Hellerstein, J.R., *Taxes, Loopholes and Morals* (New York: McGraw Hill, 1963).

Heyding, "Legislation by Formula" (1959) Can. Tax J. 366.

Huggett, Donald R., "A Minimum Income Tax", in *Proceedings of 37th Tax Conf.* 10:1 (Can. Tax Foundation, 1985).

Huggett, Donald R., "Dear Mike" (fictitious letter to Minister of Finance Michael Wilson) (1986) 14 Can. Tax News 17.

Johnson, Calvin H., "Why Have Anti-Tax Shelter Legislation? A Response to Professor Zelenak" (February 1989) 67 Texas Law Rev. 591.

Jones, R., *The Nature and First Principles of Taxation* (1914).

Kaldor, N., *An Expenditure Tax* (London: George Allen & Unwin Ltd., 1955).

Klein, W.A., *Policy Analysis of the Federal Income Tax Text and Readings* (New York: The Foundation Press, 1976).

Lahey, Kathleen, "The Tax Unit in Income Tax Theory" in *Women, the Law and the Economy* (Toronto: Butterworths, 1985) at 277–310.

Perry, David B., "Government Reliance on Personal Income Taxes in Canada" (1994), 42 Can. Tax J. 1145.

Perry, David B., "Individual Tax Burdens in the OECD" (1994) 42 Can. Tax J. 288.

Perry, Harvey J., "Taxation in Canada", *Can. Tax Paper No. 74* (Can. Tax Foundation, 1984).

Simons, H.C., *Personal Income Taxation* (Chicago: University of Chicago Press, 1938).

Verchere, Bruce, and Jacques Mernier, "Rights and Freedoms in Tax Matters", in *Proceedings of 38th Tax Conf.* 39 (Can. Tax Foundation, 1986).

CHAPTER 2 — INTERPRETATION OF TAX LAW

"The difficulties of so-called interpretation arise when the Legislature has had no meaning at all; when the question which is raised on the statute never occurred to it; when what the judges have to do is, not to determine what the legislature did mean on a point which was present to its mind, but to guess what it would have intended on a point not present to its mind, if the point had been present."

(John Chipman Gray, *Nature and Sources of the Law: Statutes*, 1921 ed.)

"The law of income tax is sufficiently complicated without unhelpful judicial incursions into the realm of lawmaking."

(Justice Iacobucci, *Canderel Ltd. v. Canada*, [1998] 1 S.C.R. 147)

I. — General Comment

Interpretation is the key to unlocking legislative intent. The interpretational principles of income tax law are a product of the short history of taxation and the long tradition of the common law. Canadian interpretational techniques reflect the influence of the varied principles of English and American tax law. The common bond, however, of all three systems is that government can levy income taxes only under the authority of specific fiscal legislation. Thus, there is no common law power to tax. This principle has been a part of Anglo-Saxon legal tradition since the *Magna Carta* (1215).

Constitutional traditions play an important role in the interpretation of tax law. Tax legislation is the product of elected legislatures. The language of the Act reflects the constitutional will of the people through its elected representatives. Thus, the interpretation of tax law requires careful attention to the words of the statute. In tax law, the courts should confine themselves to judicial interpretation and refrain from judicial rule making.[1]

II. — Constitutional Limits

The Canadian Constitution divides the power to levy taxes between the federal Parliament and provincial Legislatures.[2] The *Income Tax Act* is also subject to the *Canadian Charter of Rights and Freedoms*.[3] Two provisions of the *Charter* are particularly relevant in the context of income tax law: the provision of equal rights and the right to be secure against unreasonable search and seizure. Section 15 of the *Charter* reads:

> 15. (1) Every individual is equal before and under the law and has the right to the equal protection and equal benefit of the law without discrimination and, in particular, without discrimination based on race, national or ethnic origin, colour, religion, sex, age or mental or physical disability.
>
> (2) Subsection (1) does not preclude any law, program or activity that has as its object the amelioration of conditions of disadvantaged individuals or groups including those that are disadvantaged because of race, national or ethnic origin, colour, religion, sex, age or mental or physical disability.

Section 8 of the *Charter* reads:

> Everyone has the right to be secure against unreasonable search or seizure.

A taxpayer whose constitutional rights are violated may apply to a court of competent jurisdiction for appropriate relief. Section 24 of the *Charter* gives the courts broad power to provide relief or remedy for violation of taxpayers' constitutional rights:

> 24. (1) Anyone whose rights or freedoms, as guaranteed by this Charter, have been infringed or denied may apply to a court of competent jurisdiction to obtain such remedy as the court considers appropriate and just in the circumstances.
>
> (2) Where, in proceedings under subsection (1), a court concludes that evidence was obtained in a manner that infringed or denied any rights or freedoms guaranteed by this Charter, the

---

[1] See, *Stewart v. Canada*, [2002] 2 S.C.R. 645, [2002] 3 C.T.C. 439, 2002 D.T.C. 6969 (S.C.C.); *Ludco Enterprises Ltd. v. Canada*, [2001] 2 S.C.R. 1082, [2002] 1 C.T.C. 95, 2001 D.T.C. 5505 (S.C.C.).

[2] *Constitution Act, 1867* (U.K.), 30 & 31 Vict., c. 3, subss. 91(3) and 92(2).

[3] *Canadian Charter of Rights and Freedoms*, Part I of the *Constitution Act, 1982*, being Schedule B to the *Canada Act, 1982* (U.K.), 1982, c. 11, App. II, No. 44.

evidence shall be excluded if it is established that, having regard to all the circumstances, the admission of it in the proceedings would bring the administration of justice into disrepute.

Apart from these specific provisions, it is sometimes argued that courts should use the values of the *Charter* as interpretive aids in statutory construction. However, the courts resort to *Charter* values in limited circumstances and then only to resolve ambiguity in a provision. To do more would be anomalous. As the Supreme Court said in *Symes*:[4]

> . . .to consult the Charter in the absence of such ambiguity is to deprive the Charter of a more powerful purpose, namely, the determination of a statute's constitutional validity. If statutory meanings must be made congruent with the Charter even in the absence of ambiguity, then it would never be possible to apply, rather than simply consult, the values of the Charter. Furthermore, it would never be possible for the government to justify infringements as reasonable limits under s. 1 of the Charter, since the interpretive process would preclude one from finding infringements in the first place.

III. — The Interpretation Act

The construction of the *Income Tax Act* is a question of law. Section 12 of the *Interpretation Act* states:[5]

> Every enactment is deemed remedial, and shall be given such fair, large and liberal construction and interpretation as best ensures the attainment of its objects.

Thus, tax law should be interpreted in such a fair and liberal manner as best ensures the attainment of its purpose as articulated in the statute. The tension of tax law is in interpreting statutory language as expressed by Parliament according to the context and purpose of the underlying provision.

---

[4]*Symes v. Canada*, [1993] 4 S.C.R. 695, [1994] 1 C.T.C. 40, 94 D.T.C. 6001 (S.C.C.) at paras. 99-107.

[5]*Interpretation Act*, R.S.C. 1985, c. I-21, as amended. Section 3 reads:

> (1) Every provision of this Act applies, unless a contrary intention appears, to every enactment, whether enacted before or after the commencement of this Act.

> (2) The provisions of this Act apply to the interpretation of this Act.

> (3) Nothing in this Act excludes the application to an enactment of a rule of construction applicable to that enactment and not inconsistent with this Act.

IV. — General Principles

The general principle of modern statutory construction is to interpret statutes in context, harmony, and within the scheme of the legislation. Dr. Driedger, in the second edition of his work, *Construction of Statutes* (1983), stated the principle as follows (p. 87):[6]

> Today there is only one principle or approach, namely, the words of an Act are to be read in their entire context and in their grammatical and ordinary sense harmoniously with the scheme of the Act, the object of the Act, and the intention of Parliament.. . .Earlier expressions, though in different form, are to the same effect; *Lord Atkinson in Victoria (City) v. Bishop of Vancouver Island*, ([1921] A.C. 384 at p. 387) put it this way:
>
>> In the construction of statutes their words must be interpreted in their ordinary gram-matical sense, unless there be something in the context, or in the object of the statute in which they occur, or in the circumstances with reference to which they are used, to show that they were used in a special sense different from their ordinary grammatical sense.

The Supreme Court of Canada has endorsed this approach repeatedly and, most recently, in *Canada Trustco*[7]: "the words of an Act are to be read in their entire context and in their grammatical and ordinary sense harmoniously with the scheme of the Act the object of the Act and the intention of Parliament."[8]

Thus, courts should read discrete sections of the *Income Tax Act* in light of the other provisions of the Act, the purpose of the legislation and analyze transactions in the context of economic and commercial reality. However, the contextual approach cannot alter the result where the words of the statute are clear and plain and where the legal and practical effect of the transaction is undisputed.[9]

Hence, we should interpret clear and unequivocal words in a statute according to their ordinary, everyday meaning (the plain meaning rule) *unless* the words are specifically assigned different definitions. This rule applies even if the interpretation produces an *unfair* result. It is for Parliament to resolve the unfairness. For example, the requirement that a deduction for support payments be supported by a *written* agreement is strictly enforced even if it produces unforeseen hardship for those who do not reduce their agreement to writing.[10]

---

[6]See also *Canada v. Antosko*, [1994] 2 S.C.R. 312, [1994] 2 C.T.C. 25, 94 D.T.C. 6314 (S.C.C.) at paras. 24–25, 29 and 30.

[7]*Canada Trustco Mortgage Co. v. R.*, [2005] 5 C.T.C. 215 (S.C.C.).

[8]See *65302 British Columbia Ltd.*, [1999] 3 S.C.R. 804 (S.C.C.).

[9]See *Mattabi Mines Ltd. v. Ontario (Minister of Revenue)*, [1988] 2 S.C.R. 175, [1988] 2 C.T.C. 294 (S.C.C.) at 194 [S.C.R.]; *Symes v. Canada*, [1993] 4 S.C.R. 695, [1994] 1 C.T.C. 40, 94 D.T.C. 6001 (S.C.C.).

[10]*Hodson v. The Queen*, [1988] 1 C.T.C. 2, 88 D.T.C. 6001 (F.C.A.).

The meaning of a word or phrase that is capable of diverse interpretation, however, may depend upon the circumstances of its use. Language is not so precise and certain as to always render one, and only one, possible meaning. It is in these circumstances that we encounter the greatest difficulties of statutory construction. As Lord Simon said in *Ransom v. Higgs*:[11]

> The meaning of a word or phrase in an Act of Parliament is a question of law not fact; even though the law may then declare that the word or phrase has no statutory meaning beyond its common acceptance and that is a question of fact whether the circumstances fall within such meaning (*Cozens v. Brutus*, [1973] A.C. 854). But many words and phrases in English have many shades of meaning and are capable of embracing a great diversity of circumstances. So the interpretation of the language of an Act of Parliament often involves declaring that certain conduct must as a matter of law fall within the statutory language (as was the actual decision in *Edwards v. Bairstow*, [1956] A.C. 14, 36 TC 207); that other conduct must as a matter of law fall outside the statutory language; but that whether yet a third category of conduct falls within the statutory language or outside it depends on the evaluation of such conduct by the tribunal of fact. This last question is often appropriately described as one of "fact and degree".

The principle that the *Income Tax Act* should be interpretated textually, contextually and purposively to find a meaning that is harmonious with the Act as a whole is not well established in Canadian tax law. The difficulty lies in reconciling the tension between textual and purposive analysis and determining the harmony of the Act as a whole.

1. — Definitional Structure

Thus, the first step in interpreting the Act is to look at the words of the particular provision to determine their meaning in the context in which they appear.

We determine the meaning of a word or phrase by reference to the definitions of the Act. In the absence of a specific statutory definition, we interpret words and phrases according to their ordinary, everyday meaning.

Subsection 248(1) is a general definition provision that defines terms applicable to the entire Act. There are also divisional definitions that apply only to a particular portion of the Act. For example, the definitions in section 54 apply only to terms used in determining capital gains and losses. Then there are definitions that apply only to a particular section of the Act. For example, the definitions in subsection 125(7) apply specifically to words and phrases used in section 125.

The first rule of statutory interpretation is that the words used in a statute ought to be given their ordinary, everyday meaning *unless* they are defined to have a different meaning. The definitional sections of the Act fall into three broad categories: those that explain the mean-

---

[11]*Ransom v. Higgs*, [1974] S.T.C. 539, [1974] 1 W.L.R. 1594 (H.L.) at 561 [S.T.C.], 1618 [W.L.R.].

ing of a word or phrase, those that merely describe, and those that dictate a particular meaning regardless of all other considerations.

Strictly speaking, a definition is a precise statement of the nature of a thing, the meaning of a word, or the character of an event. Used in this sense, a definition begins by saying that a word or phrase "means" something.[12] The use of the word "means" is usually restrictive; it confines the meaning attributable to the word being defined.

There are many so-called "definitions" that do not define but merely broaden the application of a word or phrase so as to "include" something else.[13] Generally, a provision describing a word to "include" something else tends to enlarge the meaning of the word.[14] There are, however, circumstances in which an "includes" definition is so exhaustive as to be virtually transformed into a "means" definition.[15]

The third category of definitions includes those that *impose* a meaning on a word by deeming it to mean something. A deeming clause can cause a word or phrase to connote something entirely different from that which it would have been understood to mean in the absence of the clause.[16] A deeming provision provides certainty, but can also artificially import into a word or phrase a meaning that it would not otherwise convey. As Beetz J. stated:[17]

> . . . as a rule [a deeming provision] implicitly admits that a thing is not what it is deemed to be but decrees that for some particular purpose it shall be taken as if it were that thing although it

---

[12]See, e.g., subs. 248(1)"prescribed", "regulation", "retiring allowance" and "share".

[13]See, e.g., subs. 248(1)"farming", "shareholder" and "taxpayer".

[14]As Lord Watson observed in *Dilworth v. Stamps Commr.*, [1899] A.C. 99 (P.C.) at 105-106:

> The word "include" is very generally used in interpretation clauses in order to enlarge the meaning of words or phrases occurring in the body of a statute; and when it is so used these words or phrases must be construed as comprehending, not only such things as they signify according to their natural import, but also those things which the interpretation clause declares that they shall include.

See also *C.B.A. Engineering Ltd. v. M.N.R.*, [1971] C.T.C. 504, 71 D.T.C. 5282; affd. [1974] C.T.C. 888 (F.C.A.) (whether engineering firm engaged in farming as public-relations move); *Assoc. Corp. of N. Amer. v. The Queen*, [1980] C.T.C. 80, 80 D.T.C. 6049; affd. [1980] C.T.C. 215, 80 D.T.C. 6140 (F.C.A.) (Minister not permitted to expand meaning of "interest" in tax treaty).

[15]*Dilworth v. Stamps Commr.*, ibid.

[16]*The Queen v. Sutherland*, [1980] 2 S.C.R. 451 (S.C.C.). See, e.g., para. 251(1)(a). A deeming clause is the ultimate manifestation of Parliamentary supremacy and can even defy natural laws.

[17]*The Queen v. Verrette*, [1978] 2 S.C.R. 838 at 845 (S.C.C.). See also *M.N.R. v. People's Thrift & Invt. Co.*, [1959] C.T.C. 185, 59 D.T.C. 1129 (Ex. Ct.) (statute interpreted by "parliamentary expansion", i.e., by reference to subsequent amendments); *Birmount Hldg. Ltd. v. The Queen*, [1978] C.T.C.

is not or there is doubt as to whether it is. A deeming provision artificially imports into a word or an expression an additional meaning which they would not otherwise convey beside the normal meaning which they retain where they are used; it plays a function of enlargement analogous to the word "includes" in certain definitions; however, "includes" would be logically inappropriate and would sound unreal because of the fictional aspect of the provision.

The *Income Tax Act* is replete with deeming provisions, some of which reflect bureaucratic artistry. For example, for certain purposes of the Act, paragraph 55(5)(e) deems a brother and sister not to be related to each other!

2. — Normal Usage

In determining the meaning of a word, the courts prefer its meaning in ordinary speech or usage rather than a technical meaning.[18] A word should be interpreted technically in preference to its ordinary and grammatical meaning only if the statutory context in which it appears justifies such an interpretation.[19] It is, of course, quite possible that a word initially interpreted in its ordinary sense later develops, through judicial reinterpretation, into a word with an unordinary meaning.[20] Where a word has more than one ordinary meaning, we pre-

---

358, 78 D.T.C. 6254 (F.C.A.) (company carrying on business deemed in law to be resident); *Gillespie v. The Queen*, [1982] C.T.C. 378, 82 D.T.C. 6334 (F.C.A.) (statutory assumption, although incorrect, not open to rebuttal).

[18]*Dauphin Plains Credit Union Ltd. v. Xyloid Industries Ltd.*, [1980] C.T.C. 247, 80 D.T.C. 6123 (S.C.C.) (meaning of "liquidation" taken by majority of Court to be wide, usual meaning); *Pfizer Co. v. Dep. M.N.R. (Customs & Excise)*, [1977] 1 S.C.R. 456 (S.C.C.); *Trans-Prairie Pipelines Ltd. v. M.N.R.*, [1970] C.T.C. 537, 70 D.T.C. 6351 (Ex. Ct.) (interest deductible while money employed in business, not for life of loan).

[19]*Canterra Energy Ltd. v. The Queen*, [1987] 1 C.T.C. 89, 87 D.T.C. 5019 (F.C.A.) ("minus" used in its mathematical sense rather than its ordinary and grammatical sense; hence, subtraction could result in a negative number).

[20]See, e.g., *I.R.C. v. Scottish & Newcastle Breweries Ltd.*, [1982] S.T.C. 187 (H.L.), per Lord Wilberforce, on the meaning of the word "plant":

The word "plant" has frequently been used in fiscal and other legislation. It is one of a fairly large category of words as to which no statutory definition is provided ("trade", "office", even "income" are others), so that it is left to the court to interpret them. It naturally happens that as case follows case, and one extension leads to another, the meaning of the word gradually diverges from its natural or dictionary meaning. This is certainly true of "plant". No ordinary man, literate or semi-literate, would think that a horse, a swimming pool, movable partitions or even a dry dock was plant — yet each of these has been held to be so: so why not such equally improbable items as murals or tapestries or chandeliers?

fer the wider, more predominant meaning of the word over a narrow, less common meaning.[21]

3. — Ambiguity

Where statutory language is clear and unambiguous, the plain meaning rule requires courts to apply the language of the statute in its proper context. To do otherwise would have the judiciary usurp the function of the legislature. Where words are ambiguous and capable of various meanings, however, courts should select the interpretation that best promotes the smooth working of the system[22] and avoid interpretations that produce absurd, unjust, anomalous or inconvenient results.[23] In Lord Esher's words:

> If the words of an Act are clear, you must follow them, even though they lead to a manifest absurdity. The court has nothing to do with the question whether the legislature has committed an absurdity. In my opinion, the rule has always been this — if the words of an Act admit of two interpretations, then they are not clear; and if one interpretation leads to an absurdity, and the other does not, the court will conclude that the legislature did not intend to lead to an absurdity, and will adopt the other interpretation.[24]

---

[21]*The Queen v. Continental Air Photo Ltd.*, [1962] C.T.C. 495, 62 D.T.C. 1306 (Ex. Ct.) ("portrait" does not include aerial photography of farms); *M.N.R. v. Ritchie*, [1971] C.T.C. 860, 71 D.T.C. 5503 (F.C.T.D.) (words susceptible both to reasonable and unreasonable interpretation).

[22]*Shannon Realties Ltd. v. Ville de St. Michel*, [1924] A.C. 185 (P.C.).

[23]*The Queen v. Judge of City of London Court*, [1892] 1 Q.B. 273 (C.A.) (whether amount received from employer for completing course constituted a "prize"). See also *Gill v. Donald Humberstone & Co.*, [1963] 1 W.L.R. 929 (H.L.) (roofer not in "working place" when he fell off ladder); *Railton v. Wood* (1890), 15 App. Cas. 363 (P.C.) ("distress for rent" includes holder of bill of sale taking back goods from bailiff); *Fry v. I.R.C.*, [1959] 1 Ch. 86 (C.A.) (estate tax on reversionary interest in possession but not indefeasibly vested); *Arrow Shipping Co. v. Tyne Improvement Commr., The Crystal*, [1894] A.C. 508 (H.L.) (interpretation of "possession" at time of salvage and destruction of vessel); *The Queen v. Overseers of Tonbridge* (1884), 13 Q.B.D. 339 (C.A.) (dispute over jurisdiction to levy rates by opposing burial boards; ordinary meaning conflicted with other Act).

[24]*The Queen v. Judge of City of London Court*, ante, at 290; see also *The Queen v. Savage*, [1980] C.T.C. 103, 80 D.T.C. 6066; revd. on other grounds [1981] C.T.C. 332, 81 D.T.C. 5258; affd. [1983] C.T.C. 393, 83 D.T.C. 5409 (S.C.C.) (whether $500 exemption applicable to "prize" from employer); *Victoria City Corp. v. Bishop of Vancouver Island*, [1921] 2 A.C. 384 (P.C.) (should exemption for house of worship include land upon which building erected); *I.R.C. v. Hinchy*, [1960] A.C. 748 (H.L.) (whether fine of "treble the tax" owed should include surtax); *Cartledge v. E. Jopling & Sons*, [1963] A.C. 758 (H.L.) (statutory limitation period expired before workers aware noxious dust caused injury to lungs); *Mersey Docks & Harbour Bd. v. Henderson Bros.* (1888), 13 App. Cas. 595 (H.L.) (dues in port payable when "trading inwards" or "trading outwards"; interpretation in respect of voyage with several ports); *Clerical, Med. & Gen. Life Ass. Soc. v. Carter* (1889), 22 Q.B.D. 444 (C.A.) (interpretation of "profits or gains" and "interest of money"); *Warburton v. Loveland* (1832), 2 Dow & Cl. 480

The case for avoiding absurd interpretation is easy to make. The more difficult case is resolving ambiguity to promote statutory purpose and harmony. As the Supreme Court said in *Canada Trustco*: "The relative effects of ordinary meaning, context and purpose on the interpretative process may vary, but in all cases the court must seek to read the provisions of an Act as a harmonious whole."[25] Faced with ambiguity courts shift to purposive interpretation to avoid harsh results.[26]

Even the simplest words are susceptible to misunderstanding and should be read in context.[27] Thus, when Justice Holmes was asked to determine whether an aircraft was a "motor vehicle" for the purposes of a motor vehicle theft statute, he disposed of the question as follows:[28]

> No doubt etymologically it is possible to use the word to signify a conveyance working on land, water or air, and sometimes legislation extends the use in that direction.. . . But in everyday speech "vehicle" calls up the picture of a thing moving on land.

Note, however, that the Act takes a page to define "automobile" in subsection 248(1) and specifically excludes taxis.

Harmonious interpretation requires that words and phrases should be interpreted in the context of the statutory provision in which they appear and in the context of the *entire* Act. As Lord Herschell said in *Colquhoun v. Brooks*:[29]

> . . . it is beyond dispute, too, that we are entitled and indeed bound when construing the terms of any provision found in a statute to consider any other parts of the Act which throw light

---

(H.L.); *Corp. d'Administration et de Placements Lté v. Castonguay* (1970), 3 N.B.R. (2d) 278 (Q.B.) (two interpretations of *Creditor's Relief Act*, one avoided injustice).

[25]*Canada Trustco Mortgage Co. v. R.*, [2005] 5 C.T.C. 215 (S.C.C.).

[26]See, for example, *Québec (Communauté urbaine) v. Corporation Notre-Dame de Bon-Secours*, [1994] 3 S.C.R. 3, [1995] 1 C.T.C. 241 (S.C.C.).

[27]As Justice Cardozo explained in *Panama Refining Co. v. Ryan* (1935), 293 U.S. 388 and 433: "The meaning of a statute is to be looked for, not in any single section, but in all the parts together and in their relation to the end in view."

[28]*McBoyle v. U.S.* (1931), 283 U.S. 25 and 26.

[29]*Colquhoun v. Brooks* (1889), 14 App. Cas. 493 at 506 (H.L.); cited with approval by Pratte J. in *The Queen v. Cie Immobilière B.C.N. Ltée*, [1979] C.T.C. 71, 79 D.T.C. 5068 (S.C.C.). See also *Highway Sawmills Ltd. v. M.N.R.*, [1966] C.T.C. 150 at 157-58, 66 D.T.C. 5116 at 5120 (S.C.C.):

> The answer to the question what tax is payable in any given circumstances depends, of course, upon the words of the legislation imposing it. Where the meaning of those words is difficult to ascertain it may be of assistance to consider which of two constructions contended for brings about a result which conforms to the apparent scheme of the legislation.

upon the intention of the legislature and which may serve to show that the particular provision ought not to be construed as it would be if considered alone and apart from the rest of the Act.

But the same word or concept in different statutes does not necessarily bear the same interpretation. Contextual interpretation is particularly important in tax law because of the diversity of policies that the Act promotes. For example, an "investment" for the purposes of legislation regulating investment contracts is not necessarily an investment asset for the purpose of determining whether a gain constitutes a capital gain for tax purposes.[30] A common commercial or financial word should be interpreted in the context of its ordinary commercial or financial usage.[31]

4. — Plain Meaning

At one time, the courts interpreted tax legislation as penal statutes and adopted strict and literal interpretation. This was so even where such interpretation produced hardship or inconvenience. Lord Cairns described the approach in *Partington*:[32]

> I am not at all sure that, in a case of this kind — a fiscal case — form is not amply sufficient; because, as I understand the principle of all fiscal legislation, it is this: if the person sought to be taxed comes within the letter of the law he must be taxed, however great the hardship may appear to the judicial mind to be. On the other hand, if the Crown, seeking to recover the tax, cannot bring the subject within the letter of the law, the subject is free, however apparently within the spirit of the law the case might otherwise appear to be. In other words, if there be admissible, in any statute, what is called equitable construction, certainly such a construction is not admissible in a taxing statute where you simply adhere to the words of the statute.

See also *Can. Sugar Refining Co. v. The Queen*, [1898] A.C. 735 (P.C.) *per* Lord Davey: "Every clause of a statute should be construed with reference to the context and the other clauses of the Act, so as, so far as possible, to make a consistent enactment of the whole statute or series of statutes relating to the subject-matter."; *The Queen v. Cadboro Bay Holdings Ltd.*, [1977] C.T.C. 186, 77 D.T.C. 5115 (F.C.T.D.) ("active business" defined as any quantum of activity giving rise to income); *Noranda Mines Ltd. v. The Queen*, [1982] C.T.C. 226, 82 D.T.C. 6212 (F.C.T.D.) (words claimed to be ineffectual or surplusage).

[30]*First Investors Corp. v. The Queen*, [1987] 1 C.T.C. 285, 87 D.T.C. 5176 (F.C.A.).

[31]*Bank of N.S. v. The Queen*, [1980] C.T.C. 57, 80 D.T.C. 6009; affd. [1981] C.T.C. 162, 81 D.T.C. 5115 (F.C.A.).

[32]*Partington v. A.G.* (1869), 4 L.R. 100 (H.L.).

Thus, courts interpreted the Act literally, regardless of consequences.[33] Similarly, in *Tennant v. Smith*:

> In various cases the principle of construction of a taxing Act has been referred to in various forms, but I believe they may be all reduced to this, that inasmuch as you have no right to assume that there is any governing object which a taxing Act is intended to attain other than which it has expressed by making such and such objects the intended subject for taxation, you must see whether a tax is expressly imposed.
>
> Cases, therefore, under the *Taxing Acts* always resolve themselves into a question of whether or not the words of the Act have reached the alleged subject of taxation.[34]

The doctrine of literal statutory construction worked reasonably well when the tax statute focused primarily on the raising of revenue. Indeed, Canadian courts routinely applied the doctrine despite section 12 of the *Interpretation Act*, which requires every Act to be interpreted in a fair, large and liberal manner *so as to ensure the attainment of its objects*.[35]

The doctrine of strict interpretation works well only if legislative purpose can always be precisely and accurately captured in statutory language. Then, the purpose is implemented simply by applying the words of the act. Experience, however, has taught us that legislation is not susceptible to such precise drafting. As early as 1936, in an era of comparatively

---

[33]In *Pryce v. Monmouthshire Canal & Ry. Co.* (1879), 4 App. Cas. 197 at 202-203 (H.L.), the principle was stated as follows:

> My Lords, the cases which have decided that *Taxing Acts* are to be construed with strictness, and that no payment is to be exacted from the subject which is not clearly and unequivocally required by Act of Parliament to be made, probably meant little more than this, that, inasmuch as there was not a priori liability in a subject to pay any particular tax, nor any antecedent relationship between the taxpayer and the taxing authority, no reasoning founded upon any supposed relationship of the taxpayer and the taxing authority could be brought to bear upon the construction of the Act, and therefore the taxpayer had a right to stand upon a literal construction of the words used, whatever might be the consequence.

[34]*Tennant v. Smith*, [1892] A.C. 150 at 154 (H.L.).

[35]*Interpretation Act*, 1867 (31 Vict.), c. 1, subs. 7(39) (assented to December 21, 1867) read as follows:

> The Preamble of every such Act as aforesaid shall be deemed a part thereof intended to assist in explaining the purport and object of the Act; — And every Act and every provision or enactment thereof shall be deemed remedial, whether its immediate purport be to direct the doing of any thing which Parliament deems to be for the public good or to prevent or punish the doing of any thing which it deems contrary to the public good, — and shall accordingly receive such fair, large and liberal construction and interpretation as will best ensure the attainment of the object of the Act and of such provision or enactment according to their true intent, meaning and spirit.

simple tax legislation, an English codification committee realized the futility of attempting to anticipate every situation with comprehensive legislative drafting:[36]

> The imagination which can draw an income tax statute to cover the myriad transactions of a society like ours, capable of producing the necessary revenue without producing a flood of litigation, has not yet revealed itself.

The doctrine of literal interpretation contributed substantially to the complexity of tax legislation. There is impressionistic evidence to suggest that as the courts interpreted the Act strictly and with increasing stringency, the legislative draftsman responded with ever more complex and comprehensive statutory language in an attempt to provide for, and anticipate, every conceivable factual nuance and circumstance.

The doctrine of literal interpretation does not work as well, however, when tax law is used both to raise revenue *and* promote socio-economic policies. *Stubart Investments Ltd.* marks the first significant breach in the doctrine of strict construction. In that decision, the Supreme Court of Canada rejected six decades of literal interpretation in favour of purposive interpretation.[37] Following *Stubart*, the Supreme Court expanded on more specific aspects of interpretative methodology in *Golden*,[38] *Bronfman Trust*,[39] *Johns-Manville Canada*,[40]

---

[36]*Report of Income Tax Codification Committee*, Cmd. 5131 (England, 1936), at 16–19.

[37]*Stubart Investments Ltd. v. The Queen*, [1984] 1 S.C.R. 536, [1984] C.T.C. 294, 84 D.T.C. 6305. See also: *Irving Oil Ltd. v. The Queen*, [1988] 1 C.T.C. 263, 88 D.T.C. 6138 (F.C.T.D.); affd. [1991] 1 C.T.C. 350, 91 D.T.C. 5106 (F.C.A.); *Indalex Ltd. v. The Queen*, [1986] 2 C.T.C. 482, 86 D.T.C. 6039 (F.C.A.); *Consolidated Bathurst Ltd. v. The Queen*, [1985] 1 C.T.C. 142, 85 D.T.C. 5120 (F.C.T.D.); affd. in part [1987] 1 C.T.C. 55, 87 D.T.C. 5001 (F.C.A.); *Orr v. M.N.R.*, [1989] 2 C.T.C. 2348, 89 D.T.C. 557 (T.C.C.); *Hickman Motors Ltd. v. The Queen*, [1993] 1 C.T.C. 36, 93 D.T.C. 5040 (F.C.T.D.); *Earlscourt Sheet Metal Mechanical Ltd. v. M.N.R.*, [1988] 1 C.T.C. 2045, 88 D.T.C. 1029 (T.C.C.); *Montgomery v. M.N.R.*, [1987] 2 C.T.C. 2023, 87 D.T.C. 355 (T.C.C.); *Vivian v. The Queen*, [1984] C.T.C. 354, (sub nom. *The Queen v. Parsons*) 84 D.T.C. 6447 (F.C.A.); *Bastion Management Ltd. v. M.N.R.*, [1988] 1 C.T.C. 2344, 88 D.T.C. 1245 (T.C.C.); affd. [1994] 2 C.T.C. 70, 94 D.T.C. 6271 (F.C.T.D.); *Daggett v. M.N.R.*, [1992] 2 C.T.C. 2764, 93 D.T.C. 14 (T.C.C.); *454538 Ontario Ltd. v. M.N.R.*, [1993] 1 C.T.C. 2746, 93 D.T.C. 427 (T.C.C.); *Goulard v. M.N.R.*, [1992] 1 C.T.C. 2396, 92 D.T.C. 1244 (T.C.C.).

[38]*The Queen v. Golden*, [1986] 1 S.C.R. 209, [1986] 1 C.T.C. 274, 86 D.T.C. 6138 (S.C.C.).

[39]*Bronfman Trust v. The Queen*, [1987] 1 C.T.C. 117, 87 D.T.C. 5059 (S.C.C.).

[40]*Johns-Manville Can. Inc. v. The Queen*, [1985] 2 S.C.R. 46, [1985] 2 C.T.C. 111, 85 D.T.C. 5373 (S.C.C.).

Antosko,[41] *Corporation Notre-Dame de Bon-Secours*,[42] *Friesen*,[43] *Shell Canada*,[44] *Ludco*,[45] and *Stewart*.[46]

The second significant change in interpretational philosophy after *Stubart* is in the manner of resolving ambiguities by looking to legislative intent and not by applying rigid presumptions.

However, we must be careful of purposive interpretation that puts a gloss on legislative language that was not contemplated by the legislator. In the face of clear and unambiguous language, should the courts attempt to extract legislative purpose or interpret the language as written? If the words of the statute are clear and plain, they should be given their effect and not altered by legislative purpose or object.[47] Purposive interpretation is judicial interpretation and should not be used as judicial rule making. It should not be used to alter the result of commercial transactions where the words of the Act are clear and plain and where the legal and practical effect of the transaction is undisputed. As the Supreme Court said in *Antosko*:[48]

> In the absence of evidence that the transaction was a sham or an abuse of the provisions of the Act, it is not the role of the court to determine whether the transaction in question is one which renders the taxpayer deserving of a deduction. If the terms of the section are met, the taxpayer may rely on it, and it is the option of Parliament specifically to preclude further reliance in such situations.

And:[49]

> Where the words of the section are not ambiguous, it is not for this Court to find that the appellants should be disentitled to a deduction because they do not deserve a "windfall". . . . In the absence of a situation of ambiguity, such that the Court must look to the result of a transaction to assist in ascertaining the intent of Parliament, a normative assessment of the consequences of the application of a given provision is within the ambit of the legislature, not the courts.

---

[41]*Antosko v. The Queen*, [1994] 2 C.T.C. 25, 94 D.T.C. 6314 (S.C.C.).

[42]*Québec (Communauté urbaine) v. Corp. Notre-Dame de Bon-secours*, [1994] 3 S.C.R. 3, [1995] 1 C.T.C. 241 (S.C.C.).

[43]*Friesen v. The Queen*, [1995] 2 C.T.C. 369, 95 D.T.C. 5551 (S.C.C.).

[44]*Shell Canada Ltd. v. Canada* (1999), 99 D.T.C. 5669 (S.C.C.).

[45]2001 S.C.R. 1082, [2002] 1 C.T.C. 95 (S.C.C.).

[46][2002] 2 S.C.R. 645, [2002] 3 C.T.C. 439, 2002 D.T.C. 6969 (S.C.C.).

[47]*Antosko v. The Queen*, [1994] 2 C.T.C. 25, 94 D.T.C. 6314 (S.C.C.).

[48]*Antosko v. The Queen, ibid.*, at 32 [C.T.C.] and 6320 [D.T.C.].

[49]*Antosko v. The Queen, ibid.*, at 33 [C.T.C.] and 6321 [D.T.C.].

And again in *Friesen*:[50]

> The clear language of the *Income Tax Act* takes precedence over a court's view of the object
> and purpose of a provision. . . . The object and purpose of a provision need only be resorted to
> when the statutory language admits of some doubt or ambiguity.

Antosko and *Friesen* draw the line between strict and literal construction and pedantic application of the purposive approach in the face of clear and unambiguous legislative language.
Thus, courts should apply this teleological approach only when the words of the statute are
not clear.[51]

As McLachlin, J. (as she then was) stated in *Shell Canada*:[52]

> Finding unexpressed legislative intentions under the guise of purposive interpretation runs the
> risk of upsetting the balance Parliament has attempted to strike in the Act. . . . The courts' role
> is to interpret and apply the Act as it was adopted by Parliament. *Obiter* statements in earlier
> cases that might be said to support a broader and less certain interpretive principle have there-
> fore been overtaken by our developing tax jurisprudence.

The *Income Tax Act* does not operate in a commercial vacuum, but draws upon the meaning
of words in their broader commercial context. Thus, in applying the plain meaning rule, a
court should interpret words in the context of the general commercial law and settled legal
definitions therein.[53]

The approach to interpreting tax treaties, however, is more expansive and the courts consider
the purpose of provisions even in the absence of ambiguity. The Supreme Court has stated
the rule as follows:

> In interpreting a treaty, the paramount goal is to find the meaning of the words in question.
> This process involves looking to the language used and the intentions of the parties.

To summarize: the purpose rule is not a substitute for the plain meaning rule. It is used
where statutory language is obscure or ambiguous and a court needs assistance in determining legislative intention. Otherwise, unambiguous legislative language is interpreted according to its plain meaning, but not so literally as to produce absurd results. The presumption in
favour of the taxpayer is *residual* in nature and should play only an exceptional part in the

---

[50]*Friesen v. The Queen*, [1995] 2 C.T.C. 369, 95 D.T.C. 5551 (S.C.C.).

[51]See *Québec v. Notre-Dame de Bon-secours*, [1994] 3 S.C.R. 3, [1995] 1 C.T.C. 241 (S.C.C.).

[52]*Shell Canada v. M.N.R.* (1999), 99 D.T.C. 5669 (S.C.C.).

[53]*Will-Kare Paving & Contracting Ltd. v. Canada* (July 20, 2000), [2000] S.C.C. 36 (the word "sale"
has an established meaning that the *Income Tax Act* should not broaden without clear parliamentary
intention). See also: *Rizzo & Rizzo Shoes Ltd., Re*, [1998] 1 S.C.R. 27, 154 D.L.R. (4th) 193 (S.C.C.)
and 65302 *British Columbia Ltd. v. R.*, [1999] 3 S.C.R. 804, [2000] 1 C.T.C. 57 (S.C.C.).

interpretation of tax legislation.[54] Thus, every effort should first be made to determine the meaning of the Act. Only when this proves to be impossible, or produces *bona fide* alternative interpretations, is it legitimate to apply the presumption in favour of the taxpayer. Of course, factual ambiguity in applying penalty provisions should always favour the taxpayer.

5. — No Interpretive Presumptions

The rule that exemptions were to be strictly interpreted against the taxpayer and charging provisions strictly against the state no longer applies. The Supreme Court emphatically rejected any such presumptions in *Corporation Notre-Dame de Bon-Secours*:[55]

> Adhering to the principle that taxation is clearly the rule and exemption the exception no longer corresponds to the reality of present-day tax law.

The purposive approach favours the taxpayer or the revenue authorities depending on the legislative provision in question and *not* on the existence of pre-determined presumptions.[56] The underlying purpose of the provision in question determines whether a strict or liberal interpretation is appropriate in the circumstances and whether the CRA or the taxpayer should be favoured in the particular interpretation.[57] Hence, incentive provisions should be interpreted to enhance their underlying purpose, and anti-avoidance provisions should be read to restrict and circumscribe abusive tax avoidance.

V. — Substance Over Form

In tax law, form generally prevails over substance except in those situations that substance prevails over form. It is trite to suggest that substance should take precedence over form to the extent that it is consistent with the wording and objective of the statute.[58] This chestnut of judicial interpretation is easier to state than it is to apply. Thus, one should ask:

- What does the transaction or arrangement achieve?

- Does it fit within the plain meaning of the provision?

- Does the result fit within the purpose of the statutory provision(s)?

---

[54]*Québec (Communauté urbaine) v. Corporation Notre-Dame de Bon-Secours*, [1994] 2 S.C.R. 3, [1995] 1 C.T.C. 241 (S.C.C.) at 16 [S.C.R.].

[55]*Ibid.* at 14 [S.C.R.].

[56]*Ibid.* at 17 [S.C.R.].

[57]*Ibid.* at 14 [S.C.R.].

[58]*Ibid.* at 17 [S.C.R.].

- If it does not fit within the purpose of the provision(s), should the taxpayer be allowed the benefit of the provision or be subject to the avoidance strictures of the Act?

The difficulty with the substance doctrine is that, despite its intuitive appeal, it does not offer any objective yardstick to measure against particular facts. If applied on an ex-post basis, the doctrine leaves commercial transactions in an uncertain state. It is an unpredictable doctrine of varying reach. Lord Tomlin referred to it disparagingly as the "so-called doctrine" in the *Duke of Westminster*:[59]

> ... it is said that in revenue cases there is a doctrine that the Court may ignore the legal position and regard what is called "the substance of the matter" . . . . This supposed doctrine . . . seems to rest for its support upon a misunderstanding of language used in some earlier cases. The sooner this misunderstanding is dispelled, and the supposed doctrine given its quietus, the better it will be for all concerned, for the doctrine seems to involve substituting "the incertain and crooked cord of discretion" for "the golden and straight metwand of the law". Every man is entitled if he can to order his affairs so as that the tax attaching under the appropriate Acts is less than it otherwise would be.. . . This so-called doctrine of "the substance" seems to me to be nothing more than an attempt to make a man pay and notwithstanding that he has so ordered his affairs that the amount of tax sought from him is not legally claimable.

Notwithstanding these early reservations, the doctrine has had a pervasive, but uncertain, effect in tax law. It was knocked down in *Stubart*,[60] but rose again under the guise of the "commercial reality" test in *Bronfman Trust*,[61] where Chief Justice Dickson stated:[62]

> I acknowledge, however, that just as there has been a recent trend away from strict construction of taxation statutes . . . so too has the recent trend in tax cases been towards attempting to ascertain the *true commercial and practical nature of the taxpayer's transaction*. There has been, in this country and elsewhere, movement away from tests based on the form of transactions and towards tests based on what Lord Pearce has referred to as a "common sense appreciation of all the guiding features" of the events in question. . . This is, I believe, a laudable trend *provided it is consistent* with the text and purposes of the taxation statute. [Emphasis added.]

Thus, for a limited period, we see the pendulum swinging from form towards a looser standard, a common sense appreciation of "commercial reality".

---

[59]*C.I.R. v. The Duke of Westminster*, [1936] A.C. 1 (H.L.) at 3–4.

[60]*Stubart Investments Ltd. v. The Queen*, [1984] 1 S.C.R. 536, [1984] C.T.C. 294 (S.C.C.).

[61]*Bronfman Trust v. The Queen*, [1987] 1 C.T.C. 117, 87 D.T.C. 5059 (S.C.C.).

[62]*Bronfman Trust v. The Queen*, ibid., at 128 [C.T.C.] and 5066–67 [D.T.C.].

However, by 1999 in *Shell Canada*, the Supreme Court once again realigns the doctrine of statutory construction in tax law:[63]

> Unless the Act provides otherwise, a taxpayer is entitled to be taxed on what it actually did, not on what it could have done, and certainly not based on what a less sophisticated taxpayer may have done.

And:[64]

> [I]n the absence of a specific statutory bar to the contrary, taxpayers are entitled to structure their affairs in a manner that reduces the tax payable... An unrestricted application of an "economic effects" approach does indirectly what this Court has consistently held Parliament did not intend the Act to do directly.

What do we mean by the "substance", "commercial reality" or "common sense" view of a transaction? How do we accurately measure the substance of transactions in the context of a tax structure premised upon artificial distinctions of different sources of income? Assume, for example, that a taxpayer requires a capital asset for business use. There are three alternatives. The taxpayer can:

1. Purchase the asset outright and acquire title to it immediately, but pay for it over time;

2. Lease the asset and pay rent for its use, but without acquiring title in the property; or

3. Lease the asset with an option to purchase the property for a token amount of, say, $1 when the lease expires.

In the first case, the taxpayer clearly acquires title and ownership of the property. In the case of depreciable property, for example, the taxpayer can write off the capital cost of the asset as capital cost allowance or tax depreciation.[65]

In the second case, the taxpayer does not acquire title to the property but has a user interest in exchange for rental payments, which may or may not coincide with the amount deductible as capital cost allowance or tax depreciation in the first case. The write-off would depend upon the term of the lease, the underlying cost of financing, etc. But what if the lease is for 99 years? Is the lease transformed into an outright purchase in fee simple? In legal terms, the lease remains a lease with no change in title. In economic terms, however, the lease becomes a sale.

In the third case, the economic substance of the transaction is that the taxpayer purchases the property, but with a delayed transmission of title. The *economic* effect or *commercial reality* of the transaction is identical to an outright purchase of the asset in the first case. As a matter

---

[63] *Shell Canada v. M.N.R.*, [1999] 3 S.C.R. 622, [1999] 4 C.T.C. 313, 99 D.T.C. 5669 (S.C.C.).

[64] *Ibid.*

[65] See Chapter 9, "Deductions from Business and Investment Income".

of *legal* substance, however, the taxpayer is a lessee during the tenure of the lease and acquires legal title only when the lease expires and he or she pays the token sum of $1. Thus, the legal substance of the transaction is that it is a lease until the lessee acquires title to the property by exercising the option.

Although, the general principle is that courts should be sensitive to the economic realities of a particular transaction, rather than being bound to what first appears to be its legal form,[66] the doctrine is subject to at least two important caveats. First, absent a specific provision of the Act to the contrary or a finding that they are a sham, the taxpayer's formal legal relationships should be respected in tax cases. Second, where the provision at issue is clear and unambiguous, its terms must simply be applied.[67]

The Supreme Court has clearly curtailed judicial innovation in tax law. In *Ludco*[68] for example: "this Court has repeatedly stated that in matters of tax law, a court should always be reluctant to engage in judicial innovation and rule making." And in *Canderel*:[69] "[t]he law of income tax is sufficiently complicated without unhelpful judicial incursions into the realm of law making." Thus, courts should not second-guess *bona fide* commercial decisions of the taxpayer.[70]

VI. — Res Judicata

The doctrine of *res judicata* applies in income tax law as it does in other branches of law. A judicial decision determines every right, question, or fact distinctly put in issue by the parties to a dispute and all matters that *ought* to have been brought forward as part of the litigation. Thus, a final judgment conclusively determines all matters in connection with the issues litigated. But the doctrine applies only to facts in dispute in *the particular taxation year*. A judicial determination in respect of a particular issue for a particular year does not bind either the taxpayer or the Agency on the same issue in a subsequent taxation year. For example, a decision that a particular property constitutes inventory in one year does not mean that it, or a similar or identical property, cannot be considered capital property in another year.

---

[66]*Shell Canada Ltd. v. Canada*, [1999] 3 S.C.R. 622, [1999] 4 C.T.C. 313, 99 D.T.C. 5669 (S.C.C.).

[67]*Ibid.*

[68]*Ludco Enterprises Ltd. v. Canada*, [2001] 2 S.C.R. 1082, [2002] 1 C.T.C. 95, 2001 D.T.C. 5505 (S.C.C.) at para 53.

[69]*Canderel Ltd. v. Canada*, [1998] 1 S.C.R. 147, [1998] 2 C.T.C. 35, 98 D.T.C. 6100 (S.C.C.) at para 41.

[70]*Royal Bank of Canada v. Sparrow Electric Corp.*, [1997] 1 S.C.R. 411, 97 D.T.C. 5089 (S.C.C.).

VII. — Estoppel

Taxpayers who rely on the CRA — and government officials generally — for legal interpretations should understand that civil servants cannot make the Crown liable for misstatements of law. The Crown is not estopped by any representation of law made by its officials. A taxpayer who is misled by a statement made by an official of, or a publication by, the CRA cannot generally use the misrepresentation to support his or her position except in limited circumstances.[71]

Three factors give rise to estoppel:

(1) A representation — conduct amounting to a representation — by a person who intends to induce a course of conduct on the part of the person to whom he makes the representation;

(2) An act or omission resulting from the representation, whether actual or by conduct, by the person to whom the representation is made; and

(3) Detriment to such person because of the act or omission.[72]

---

[71]*M.N.R. v. Inland Indust. Ltd.*, [1972] C.T.C. 27, 72 D.T.C. 6013 (S.C.C.) (". . . the Minister cannot be bound by an approval given when the conditions prescribed by the law were not met."); *Wollenberg v. M.N.R.*, [1984] C.T.C. 2043, 84 D.T.C. 1055 (S.C.C.) (estoppel incapable of putting aside or overriding provisions of Act as enacted by Parliament); *Cohen v. The Queen*, [1978] C.T.C. 63, 78 D.T.C. 6099 (T.C.C.); affd [1980] C.T.C. 318, 80 D.T.C. 6250 (F.C.A.) (Minister permitted to renege on earlier arrangement and reassess); *Gauthier v. M.N.R.*, [1978] C.T.C. 2175, 78 D.T.C. 1126 (T.R.B.) (taxpayer followed Minister's advice to her prejudice; Court powerless to remedy situation); *Stickel v. M.N.R.*, [1972] C.T.C. 210, 72 D.T.C. 6178 (F.C.T.D.); revd. on other grounds [1973] C.T.C. 202, 73 D.T.C. 5178 (F.C.A.); affd. [1974] C.T.C. 416, 74 D.T.C. 6268 (S.C.C.) (interpretation bulletin offered incorrect opinion of tax treaty); *Gibbon v. The Queen*, [1977] C.T.C. 334, 77 D.T.C. 5193 (F.C.T.D.) (Minister's erroneous assessment not to be relied upon). But see *The Queen v. Langille*, [1977] C.T.C. 144, 77 D.T.C. 5068 (F.C.T.D.) (first case in which estoppel successfully invoked against Minister). As a matter of administrative practice, the CRA usually considers itself bound by its advance rulings, but only to each taxpayer to whom a ruling is issued; see IC 70-6R2, "Advance Income Tax Rulings" (September 28, 1990). The CRA can, and has, withdrawn rulings which it has given in error; see TR-91 given to Global Strategy Corp. ("Tax world jolted by Revenue's revocation", The Financial Post, Oct. 12, 1985, p. 29).

[72]For example see *Canadian Superior Oil Ltd. v. Paddon-Hughes Development Co.*, [1970] S.C.R. 932 (S.C.C.) at 939-940; *Goldstein v. R.*, (sub nom. *Goldstein v. Canada*) [1995] 2 C.T.C. 2036, 96 D.T.C. 1029 (T.C.C.) at 1033-1034; *Taylor v. R.*, [1995] T.C.J. No. 414, (sub nom. *Taylor v. Canada*) [1995] 2 C.T.C. 2133, 1995 CarswellNat 459 (T.C.C.) at 593-594 [T.C.J.]; ; affirmed [1997] 2 C.T.C. 201 (Fed. C.A.); leave to appeal refused (1997), [1997] S.C.C.A. No. 223 (S.C.C.); and *Moulton v. R.*, [2002] T.C.J. No. 80, [2002] 2 C.T.C. 2395, 2002 CarswellNat 262 (T.C.C. [Informal Procedure]) at para. 11.

Justice Woods of the Tax Court of Canada, in *Von Teichman v. R.* (2003), [2004] 1 C.T.C. 2411 (T.C.C. [General Procedure]), at para.16 described estoppel as follows:

There is, however, an important limitation to the doctrine: Acts of officials and servants of the Crown generally cannot give rise to estoppel on misrepresentations of law.[73] Consequently, rulings of government officials interpreting a statute or advice as to how it applies to particular facts do not generally bind the Crown.[74] The underlying theory is that, regardless of the incompetence of a particular government official, estoppel cannot override the law of the land and the Minister is not bound to misapply the law simply because his officials give him incorrect advice.[75]

Where one person (the "representor") has made a representation to another person ("the representee") in words or by acts or conduct, or (being under a duty to the representee to speak or act) by silence or inaction, with the intention (actual or presumptive), and with the result, of inducing the representee on the faith of such representation to alter his position to his detriment, the representor, in any litigation which may afterwards take place between him and the representee, is estopped, as against the representee, from making, or attempting to establish by evidence, any averment substantially at variance with his former representation, if the representee at the proper time, and in the proper manner, objects thereto.

[73]For example see, *Woon v. Minister of National Revenue* (1950), 50 D.T.C. 871 (Can. Ex. Ct.) at 873-874; *Sturdy Truck Body (1972) Ltd. v. Minister of National Revenue*, [1995] F.C.J. No. 720, 1995 CarswellNat 419, (sub nom. *Sturdy Truck Body (1972) Ltd. v. Canada)*) [1995] 2 C.T.C. 338 (Fed. T.D.), at paras. 7-11; *Alfred v. R.* (2000), [2000] T.C.J. No. 513, 2000 CarswellNat 1774 (T.C.C. [Informal Procedure]) at para. 15; and *R. v. Langille*, [1977] C.T.C. 144, 77 D.T.C. 5086 (Fed. T.D.) at 5089-5090.

[74]*No. 358 v. Minister of National Revenue* (1956), 56 D.T.C. 466 (Can. Tax App. Bd.); *Irving Oil Ltd. v. R.* (1983), [1984] 1 F.C. 281 (Fed. T.D.); affirmed (1985), 11 Admin. L.R. xxxix (Fed. C.A.); *Minister of National Revenue v. Inland Industries Ltd.* (1971), [1974] S.C.R. 514, [1972] C.T.C. 27 (S.C.C.); and see also Holding Revenue Canada to its Word: Estoppel in Tax Law by Glen Loutzenhiser, (1999) 57(2) U.T. Fac. L. Rev 127-164 for a discussion of estoppel and the applicable to advanced tax rulings. See for example *Merriman v. Minister of National Revenue* (1985), 86 D.T.C. 1056, [1986] 1 C.T.C. 2051 (T.C.C.) at 1058 [D.T.C.], estoppel did not apply where the taxpayer relied on an Interpretation Bulletin and an Advance Tax ruling regarding the tax consequences of the forgiveness of employees' obligations under a stock purchase plan; and see also *Greenstone Estate v. Minister of National Revenue*, [1991] T.C.J. No. 402, [1991] 2 C.T.C. 2219, 1991 CarswellNat 581 (T.C.C.) at p. 16.

[75]Justice Sommers in *Gestion Le Montagnais Inc. c. Ministre du Revenu national*, cited with approval at para. 19, *Blackmore v. Minister of National Revenue*, NR 519, where the learned justice stated as follows:

Legally, I am bound to say that notwithstanding any mistake or error or wrong advice on the part of the personnel of the Commission, the Commission is not prevented from seeking to carry out the provisions of the Unemployment Insurance Act, 1971. This has been held repeatedly by umpires in the past. There is the well established principle that an estoppel will not arise when the conditions of a statute are not met. Put tritely, estoppel does not lie against the Crown and, further, estoppels of all kinds are subject to the general rule that they cannot override the law of the land.

However, estoppel against the Crown can arise with respect to representations of fact that officials of the Crown make.[76] As Chief Justice Bowman of the Tax Court of Canada said in *Goldstein v. R.*[77] at 1033-1034:

> It is sometimes said that estoppel does not lie against the Crown. The statement is not accurate and seems to stem from a misapplication of the term estoppel. The principle of estoppel binds the Crown, as do other principles of law. Estoppel in pais, as it applies to the Crown, involves representations of fact made by officials of the Crown and relied and acted on by the subject to his or her detriment. [*Robertson v. Minister of Pensions*, 1 K.B. 227; *The Queen v. Langille*, 77 D.T.C. 5086. The earlier cases are fully reviewed by Cameron J. in *Woon v. M.N.R.*, 50 D.T.C. 871]. The doctrine has no application where a particular interpretation of a statute has been communicated to a subject by an official of the government, relied upon by that subject to his or her detriment and then withdrawn or changed by the government. In such a case a taxpayer sometimes seeks to invoke the doctrine of estoppel. It is inappropriate to do so not because such representations give rise to an estoppel that does not bind the Crown, but rather, because no estoppel can arise where such representations are not in accordance with the law. Although estoppel is now a principle of substantive law it had its origins in the law of evidence and as such relates to representations of fact. It has no role to play where questions of interpretation of the law are involved, because estoppels cannot override the law. [*Maritime Electric Co. v. General Dairies Ltd.*, [1937] A.C. 610 (New Brunswick P.C.); *Minister of National Revenue v. Inland Industries Ltd.* (1971), 72 D.T.C. 6013, [1972] C.T.C. 27 (S.C.C.); *Minister of National Revenue v. Stickel*, 72 D.T.C. 6178, [1972] C.T.C. 210 (Fed. T.D.); reversed [1973] C.T.C. 202 (Fed. C.A.); affirmed [1974] C.T.C. 416 (S.C.C.); *Granger v. Canada (Employment & Immigration Commission)*, [1986] 3 F.C. 70, 69 N.R. 212 (Fed. C.A.); affirmed [1989] 1 S.C.R. 141 (S.C.C.)].[78]

Minister of National Revenue v. Inland Industries Ltd. (1971), [1974] S.C.R. 514, [1972] C.T.C. 27 (S.C.C.); *Louis Sheff (1984) Inc. v. R.* (2003), [2004] 1 C.T.C. 2301, 2003 D.T.C. 1120 (T.C.C. [General Procedure]) at 1131; *Alfred v. R.* (2000), [2000] T.C.J. No. 513, 2000 CarswellNat 1774 (T.C.C. [Informal Procedure]) at para. 13; and *Gibbon v. R.*, 77 D.T.C. 5193, [1977] C.T.C. 334 (Fed. C.A.).

[76] See for example, *Taylor v. R.*, [1995] T.C.J. No. 414, 1995 CarswellNat 459, (sub nom. *Taylor v. Canada*) [1995] 2 C.T.C. 2133 (T.C.C.); affirmed [1997] 2 C.T.C. 201 (Fed. C.A.); leave to appeal refused (1997), [1997] S.C.C.A. No. 223 (S.C.C.); *M.S. Thompson & Associates Holdings Ltd. v. Minister of National Revenue* (1998), [1998] T.C.J. No. 592 (T.C.C.); and *R. v. Langille*, [1977] C.T.C. 144, 77 D.T.C. 5086 (Fed. T.D.) at 5089-5090.

[77] *Goldstein v. R., (sub nom. Goldstein v. Canada)*, [1995] 2 C.T.C. 2036, 96 D.T.C. 1029 (T.C.C.).

[78] *Louis Sheff (1984) Inc. v. R.* (2003), [2004] 1 C.T.C. 2301, 2003 D.T.C. 1120 (T.C.C. [General Procedure]); *Moulton v. R.*, [2002] T.C.J. No. 80, [2002] 2 C.T.C. 2395, 2002 CarswellNat 262 (T.C.C. [Informal Procedure]) at para. 11; *Fisher v. R.*, [2003] T.C.J. No. 87, [2003] 2 C.T.C. 2728, 2003 CarswellNat 309 (T.C.C. [Informal Procedure]), at para. 10; and *Alfred v. R.* (2000), [2000] T.C.J. No. 513, 2000 CarswellNat 1774 (T.C.C. [Informal Procedure]) at para. 14.

In *Rogers v. R.*,[79] for example, a taxpayer enrolled in a course after receiving a representation from a Canada Employment Centre counselor that a portion of the tuition fees paid by the taxpayer would be eligible for the tuition and education credits. The counselor specifically stated that Memorex, was a certified educational institution for the purposes of claiming the credit. The Minister of National Revenue assessed the taxpayer and denied the credit claim on the ground that the taxpayer had not attended a certified educational institution. The Tax Court allowed the taxpayer's appeal of the Minister's reassessment. The Crown was estopped from claiming that the taxpayer was ineligible for credits since the taxpayer had relied on the factual representation of the Crown official that the institution was a certified educational institution. Justice Bowie of the Tax Court of Canada stated:

> . . . estoppel in pais has always applied against the Crown in a proper case. The classic statement of the requirements to raise an estoppel in pais is found in the judgment of the House of Lords in [*Greenwood v. Martins Bank*, [1933] A.C. 51.] and was adopted by the Supreme Court of Canada in [*Canadian Superior Oil v. Hambly*, [1970] S.C.R. 932 at 939-40.] There must be a representation of fact which was intended to induce the party asserting estoppel to act in a particular way, and that party must have acted upon it, to his subsequent detriment. . . . Vital though it is to the operation of the statute, the certification itself is a matter of fact, not of law. But for this representation, the Appellant would have chosen another institution which was certified. His detriment, of course, lies in the reassessment from which this appeal is brought.

In *M.S. Thompson & Associates Holdings Ltd. v. Minister of National Revenue*,[80] a CRA Ruling stated that 11 individuals of Thompson and Associates Holdings Ltd. were not employed in insurable employment. Justice McAuthur held the statement in the Ruling that the 11 individuals were not employed in insurable employment was a representation of fact. Justice McAuthur at para. 9 stated:[81]

> This representation of fact induced the Appellant to organize it's financial affairs to its detriment. It is unconscionable that the Minister be able to renege on the ruling of April 11, 1995 retroactively. The Minister may have been entitled to change positions in November of 1996 for the period after that date presuming that the Appellant would be able to reorganize its finances to meet the new assessment.

VIII. — Retrospective Application

Taxpayers have the right to certainty in tax law, both in respect of legislative changes and administrative interpretation. Retrospective legislation undermines the rule of law. Provisions of the Act that adversely affect taxpayers do not apply retroactively unless such a

---

[79]*Rogers v. R.*, [1998] 2 C.T.C. 3189, 98 D.T.C. 1365 (T.C.C.).

[80]*M.S. Thompson & Associates Holdings Ltd. v. Minister of National Revenue* (1998), [1998] T.C.J. No. 592 (T.C.C.).

[81]*Ibid.*, at para. 9.

construction is very clearly dictated by the statutory language. As Justice Willes said in *Phillips v. Eyre*:[82]

> Retrospective laws are no doubt *prima facie* of questionable policy, and contrary to the general principle that legislation by which the conduct of mankind is to be regulated ought, when introduced for the first time, to deal with future acts, and ought not to change the character of past transactions carried on upon the faith of the then existing law.

Similarly, in *Re Athlumney*:[83]

> Perhaps no rule of construction is more firmly established than this — that a retrospective operation is not to be given to a statute so as to impair an existing right or obligation, otherwise than as regards a matter of procedure, unless that effect cannot be avoided without doing violence to the language of the enactment. If the enactment is expressed in language which is fairly capable of either interpretation, it ought to be construed as prospective only.

The presumption against retrospective application of statutes is, of course, subject to the proviso that the statute itself may deem otherwise. A legislative body can always give retroactive force to statutory provisions:[84]

> The general rule is that statutes are not to be construed as having retrospective operation unless such a construction is expressly or by necessary implication required by the language of the Act. An amending enactment may provide that it shall be deemed to have come into force on a date prior to its enactment or it may provide that it is to be operative with respect to transactions occurring prior to its enactment. In those instances the statute operates retrospectively.

A statutory provision is retrospective if it creates new obligations, imposes new duties, or attaches new disabilities in respect of past events and transactions.[85] The courts should not interpret an Act to impair vested rights unless the language of the amending provision is unambiguous and demands such a construction.[86] Conversely, the enactment of a statutory provision should not be construed as necessarily changing the law that existed prior to the enactment.[87]

---

[82]*Phillips v. Eyre* (1870), 6 L.R. Q.B. 1.

[83]*Re Athlumney*, [1898] 2 Q.B. 547 at 551-2.

[84]*Gustavson Drilling (1964) Ltd. v. M.N.R.*, [1977] 1 S.C.R. 271 at 279, [1976] C.T.C. 1 at 6-7, 75 D.T.C. 5451 at 5454 (S.C.C.), *per* Dickson J.

[85]*Craies on Statute Law*, 7th ed. (London: Sweet & Maxwell, 1971), at 387.

[86]*Spooner Oils Ltd. v. Turner Valley Gas Conservation Bd.*, [1933] S.C.R. 629 (S.C.C.). Note, however, that no person has a vested right to static continuance of the tax law; see *Gustavson Drilling (1964) Ltd. v. M.N.R.*, [1976] C.T.C. 1 at 9, 75 D.T.C. 5451 at 5456 (S.C.C.), specifically, the comments of Dickson J.: ". . . No one has a vested right to continuance of the law as it stood in the past; in tax law it is imperative that legislation conform to changing social needs and governmental policy."

[87]See subs. 45(2) of the *Interpretation Act*, R.S.C. 1985, c. I-21:

IX. — Unconstitutional Law

Constitutional tradition requires that taxes be imposed only under the authority of an Act of Parliament or provincial legislative assembly.[88] Unlike Britain,[89] there is no legal authority in Canada to collect taxes before a Budget bill is enacted and receives Royal Assent. As a matter of practice, Budget bills stipulate an enactment date (usually the date of the Budget speech) for the various motions that are introduced to amend the *Income Tax Act*. The bill, when enacted, is made retrospective to the date specified in the Budget.[90] For example, subsection 96(8), dealing with foreign partnerships, was finally enacted in 1994 but retroactive to December 21, 1992, the date of initial announcement. Similarly, the scope of the general anti-avoidance was enlarged retroactively fifteen years later to apply from the inception of GAAR in 1988.

The subsequent enactment, in effect, whitewashes any constitutional illegality involved in the premature collection of taxes. Litigation to challenge the constitutional illegality of premature tax collection would, at best, result in a pyrrhic victory since the Budget bill would be enacted prior to commencement of the litigation. Once the bill is actually enacted into law, the tax becomes "payable" as of the date set out in the legislation, regardless of the date that the legislation receives Royal Assent.

X. — Territorial Limitations

The Act applies only to persons who have a physical or economic *nexus*, bond or link with Canada.[91] It is a well accepted principle in Anglo-Canadian law that fiscal statutes are not enforced outside the territorial scope of the country responsible for their legislation. Canada does not enforce foreign tax laws, and it will not, even indirectly, assist foreign countries in

---

45. (2) The amendment of an enactment shall not be deemed to be or to involve a declaration that the law under that enactment was or was considered by Parliament or other body or person by whom the enactment was enacted to have been different from the law as it is under the enactment as amended.

[88]*Bowles v. Bank of England*, [1913] 1 Ch. 57.

[89]See the *Provisional Collection of Taxes Act*, 1913 (3 & 4 Geo. 5, c. 3), which allows a resolution adopted by the Committee of Ways and Means the effect of law for a limited period of time.

[90]See, e.g., *Beesley v. M.N.R.*, [1986] 2 C.T.C. 2018, 86 D.T.C. 1498 (T.C.C.) (Parliament constitutionally empowered to enact legislation having retroactive effect).

[91]See generally *Allied Farm Equipment v. M.N.R.*, [1972] C.T.C. 619, 73 D.T.C. 5036 (F.C.A.). See also: *Lea-Don Can. Ltd. v. M.N.R.*, [1969] C.T.C. 85, 69 D.T.C. 5142 (Ex. Ct.); affd. [1970] C.T.C. 346, 70 D.T.C. 6271 (S.C.C.) (CCA not claimable by non-residents unless carrying on business in Canada).

the enforcement of their tax laws in Canadian courts.[92] However, notwithstanding the clear rule, in *R.J.R. Reynolds Tobacco*, Canada unsuccessfully attempted to bypass it by disguising the legal action under a foreign criminal statute — RICO under U.S. law. Under its tax treaties, Canada may be obliged to exchange information and provide administrative assistance to treaty partners.[93]

XI. — French And English Versions

Statutory enactments of the Parliament of Canada must be printed and published in both English and French.[94] The usual practice is to print federal statutes in two columns, one side English and the other side French. Unless one of the versions produces a result or interpretation that is incompatible with the legal system in that particular part of Canada, the general rule of interpretation is to give preference to the version that, according to the true spirit, intent and meaning of the statute, best ensures the attainment of its objects. Thus, a court will look to see which of the versions fits in with the scheme of the statute as a whole and adopt that interpretation which best suits its objects.[95]

XII. — Validity Of Tax Transactions

One of the recurring themes in tax litigation is the extent of taxpayer rights in arranging transactions for tax advantage. Clearly, taxpayers want to maximize their advantage and reduce the amount that they pay in taxes to the public purse. Although the law requires one

---

[92]*Holman v. Johnson* (1775), 98 E.R. 1120 (should individual with knowledge of smuggling scheme be permitted remedy for non-payment of price); *The Queen of Holland v. Drukker*, [1928] 1 Ch. 877 (whether foreign national (Dutch sovereign) permitted to sue in English Courts for revenue claim against Dutch subject). See also, e.g., *U.S. v. Harden*, [1963] C.T.C. 450, 63 D.T.C. 1276 (S.C.C.), where the United States government sought to circumvent this rule, first by obtaining a judgment in the United States court and then by contending that it was seeking to apply, not the United States tax law, but merely the enforceability of a judgment of the United States courts. This was rejected by the Supreme Court of Canada as an indirect attempt to enforce foreign fiscal legislation; *The Attorney General of Canada v. R.J. Reynolds Tobacco Holdings, et al.*, United States District Court (Northern District of New York) (June 30, 2000) (United States Courts will not normally enforce foreign tax judgments).

[93]See, for example, Article 25 *OECD Model Convention*; Article XXVII *Canada-U.S. Tax Treaty*.

[94]*Constitution Act, 1867*, s. 133.

[95]See *The Queen v. Cie Immobilière BCN Lté*, [1979] C.T.C. 71, 79 D.T.C. 5068 (S.C.C.) at 75 [C.T.C.], 5071 [D.T.C.], where Pratte J. rejected the view that the narrower of the two versions should prevail: ". . . the narrower meaning of one of the two versions should not be preferred where such meaning would clearly run contrary to the intent of the legislation and would consequently tend to defeat rather than assist the attainment of its objects."

to pay taxes, there is no law that says one must also leave a tip. Of course, Parliament, which needs to protect the public treasury, has the ultimate advantage in that it writes the rules by which taxpayers must abide and can amend them at will.

The cardinal rule of tax law is that, absent legislative or judicial prohibition, taxpayers can arrange their affairs for the sole purpose of achieving favourable tax results. This principle, more popularly known by its English judicial antecedents as the Westminster principle, applies with equal force in Canada.[96]

The *Income Tax Act* is a complex statute that embodies a myriad of principles and policy objectives. Constitutional tradition dictates that it is for Parliament to write fiscal laws and the courts to interpret them. Thus, the courts provide interpretational guidance when taxpayers engaged in tax reduction arrangements collide with the tax collector. They should not rewrite the law. As Justice Iacobucci said in *Canderel*:[97] "We are a Supreme Court, not a Supreme Legislature."

In the past 20 years or so, the Supreme Court has judiciously balanced the relative roles of the legislator and the courts. In *Shell Canada Limited*,[98] for example:

> This court has consistently held that courts must be cautious before finding within the clear provisions of the act an unexpressed legislative intention [citation submitted]. Finding unexpressed legislative intentions under the guise of purposive interpretation runs the risk of upsetting the balance parliament has attempted to strike in the act.

Hence, a taxpayer is entitled to rely on sophisticated arrangements and transactions if they produce fiscal advantage. It is not the court's role to upset sophisticated arrangements merely because other taxpayers cannot undertake them. Again, in *Shell Canada Limited*:

> ... absent a specific provision to the contrary, it is not the court's role to prevent taxpayers from relying on the sophisticated structure of their transactions, arranged in such a way that the particular provisions of the Act are met, on the basis that it would be inequitable to those taxpayers who have not chosen to structure their transactions that way ... *obiter statements in earlier cases that might be said to support a broader and less certain interpretive principle have therefore been overtaken by our developing tax jurisprudence.* Unless the Act provides otherwise, a taxpayer is entitled to be taxed based on what it actually did, not based on what it

---

[96]See Chapter 24, "Tax Avoidance". See also *Stubart Investments Ltd. v. Canada*, [1984] 1 S.C.R. 536, [1984] C.T.C. 294, 84 D.T.C. 6305 (S.C.C.) at 540 [S.C.R.] *per* Justice Wilson; *Hickman Motors Limited v. Canada*, [1997] 2 S.C.R. 336, [1998] 1 C.T.C. 213, 97 D.T.C. 5363 (S.C.C.) at para. 8 *per* Justice McLaughlin; *Duha Printers (Western) Ltd. v. Canada*, [1998] 1 S.C.R. 795, [1998] 3 C.T.C. 303, 98 D.T.C. 6334 (S.C.C.); *Neuman v. M.N.R.*, [1998] 1 S.C.R. 770, [1998] 3 C.T.C. 177, 98 D.T.C. 6297 (S.C.C.); *Shell Canada Limited v. Canada*, [1999] 3 S.C.R. 622, [1999] 4 C.T.C. 313, 99 D.T.C. 5669 (S.C.C.).

[97]*Canderel Ltd. v. Canada*, [1998] 1 S.C.R. 147, [1998] 2 C.T.C. 35, 98 D.T.C. 6100 (S.C.C.).

[98]*Shell Canada Limited v. Canada*, [1999] 3 S.C.R. 622, [1999] 4 C.T.C. 313, 99 D.T.C. 5669 (S.C.C.).

could have done, and certainly not based on what a less sophisticated taxpayer might have done. [Emphasis added]

Similarly, in *Canada v. Antosko*,[99] Iacobucci J., speaking for a unanimous Court:

> In the absence of evidence that the transaction was a sham or an abuse of the provisions of the Act, it is not the role of the court to determine whether the transaction in question is one which renders the taxpayer deserving of a deduction. If the terms of the section are met, the taxpayer may rely on it, and it is the option of Parliament specifically to preclude further reliance in such situations.

And again in *Continental Bank Leasing Corp. v. Canada*:[100]

> A taxpayer who fully complies with the provisions of the Income Tax Act ought not to be denied the benefit of such provisions simply because the transaction was motivated for tax planning purposes.

Despite the long line of decisions on the role of tax planning and the legitimacy of business arrangements driven by tax considerations, the volume of litigation on the proper interpretation of tax law escalates exponentially at substantial cost to taxpayers.

Paradoxically, despite the volume of litigation, which should provide certainty, tax law generates more legislation annually than any other branch of the law. In addition to new initiatives in annual budgets, government finance departments are quick to legislatively overrule the courts if they disagree with judicial decisions.

Thus, new and lengthy rules quickly emerge to overcome judicial decisions in favour of taxpayers. For example, in less than six months after the Supreme Court found in favour of taxpayers in *Ludco*[101] and *Singleton*[102] — decisions allowing taxpayers to deduct their interest expenses under the terms of the Act — the federal government announced amending provisions to block the judicially approved deductions, stating that the judicial results created uncertainties, were contrary to policy and could lead to "inappropriate" tax results. Of course, one can reasonably expect that the new and enlarged interest deduction rules will become the subject of further interpretational disputes and litigation.

Provincial tax authorities are sometimes even more aggressive in enacting retroactive legislation to preserve their revenue base. For example, in its May 2004 Budget the Ontario government announced an amendment retroactive to 1990 in order to overrule the decision

---

[99] [1994] 2 S.C.R. 312, [1994] 2 C.T.C. 25, 94 D.T.C. 6314 (S.C.C.) at 328 [S.C.R.].

[100] [1998] 2 S.C.R. 298, [1998] 4 C.T.C. 119, 98 D.T.C. 6505 (S.C.C.) at paras. 51-53.

[101] *Ludco Enterprises Ltd. v. Canada*, [2001] 2 S.C.R. 1082, [2002] 1 C.T.C. 95, 2001 D.T.C. 5505 (S.C.C.).

[102] *Singleton v. Canada*, [2001] 2 S.C.R. 1046, [2002] 1 C.T.C. 121, 2001 D.T.C. 5533 (S.C.C.).

of the Ontario Superior Court of Justice in *Toronto Blue Jays Baseball Club, et. al.*[103] Absent protection of property rights in the *Charter*, however, taxpayers must, no matter how unfair, endure retroactive tax legislation under the doctrine of parliamentary supremacy.

Thus, far from being an unpleasant subject, "Basic Tax", as everyone knows, is the only genuinely funny subject in law school (attributed to Martin D. Ginsburg).

---

[103]*Toronto Blue Jays Baseball Club v. Ontario (Minister of Finance)* (April 27, 2004), Doc. 03-CV-248830CM3 (Ont. S.C.J.).

Selected Bibliography to Chapter 2

Statutory Interpretation

Baxt, R., "The New Anti-Avoidance Provisions" N: 9 Aust. Bus. L. Rev. 284.

Beaupré, R.M., *Construing Bilingual Legislation in Canada* (Toronto: Butterworths, 1981).

Brockway, David H., "Interpretation of Tax Treaties and Their Relationship to Statutory Law — A U.S. Perspective", in *Proceedings of 35th Tax Conf.* 619 (Can. Tax Foundation, 1983).

Charles, W.H., "Extrinsic Evidence and Statutory Interpretation: Judicial Discretion in Context" (1983) 7 Dalhousie L.J. 7.

Corn, George, "Rules of Statutory Interpretation" (1985) 2 Can. Current Tax J-95.

Corry, J., "Administrative Law; Interpretation of Statutes" (1939) 1 U.T.L.J. 286.

Corry, J., "The Use of Legislative History in the Interpretation of Statutes" (1954) 32 Can. Bar Rev. 624.

Couzin, Robert, "What Does It Say in French?" (1985) 33 Can. Tax J. 300.

Craies on Statute Law, 7th ed. (Sweet & Maxwell, 1971).

Cross, R., *Statutory Interpretation* (Butterworths, 1976).

Crowe, Ian "Alice in Taxland" (1991) 125 CGA Magazine 3213.

Davis, "Legislative History and the Wheat Board Case" (1953) 31 Can. Bar Rev. 1. (See also, in this article, the letter from Milner (1953) 31 Can. Bar Rev. 228).

Debenham, David Bishop, "The Winds of Taxation" (1986/87) 51 Sask. Law Rev. 292.

Driedger, E.A., "New Approach to Statutory Interpretation" (1951) 29 Can. Bar Rev. 838.

Driedger, E.A., *The Construction of Statutes* (Butterworths, 1974).

Driedger, E.A., "Statutes: The Mischievous Literal Golden Rule" (1981) 59 Can. Bar Rev. 780.

Driedger, E.A., "Statutory Drafting and Interpretation; Canadian Common Law" (1971) 9 Co. I. Dr. Comp. 71.

Edwards, Stanley E., "Drafting Fiscal Legislation" (1984) 32 Can. Tax J. 727.

Falesky, Brian A. and Sandra E. Jack, "Is there Substance to 'Substance Over Form' in Canada?" in *Report of Proceedings of 50th Tax Conf.* (Can. Tax Foundation, 1992).

Frankfurter, Felix, "Some Reflections on the Reading of Statutes" (1947) 47:4 Colum. L. Rev. 527.

Ghosh, I.J., "The Construction of Fiscal Legislation" [1994] British Tax Rev. 126.

Innes, William I., "The Taxation of Indirect Benefits: An Examination of Subsections 56(2) 56(3), 56(4), 245(2), and 245(3) of the *Income Tax Act*", in *Proceedings of 38th Tax Conf.* (Can. Tax Foundation, 1986).

Kernochan, John M., "Statutory Interpretation: An Outline of Method" (1976) 3 Dalhousie L.J. 333.

Kilgour, "The Rule Against the Use of Legislative History: Canon of Construction or Counsel of Caution?" (1952), 30 *Can. Bar Re* v. 769. (See also, in this article, the letters from MacQuarrie (1952), 30 *Can. Bar Re* v. 1087; Milner (1953) 31 Can. Bar Rev. 228).

Krishna, Vern, "The Demise of the Strict Interpretation Rule" (1986) 1 Can. Cur. Tax J-135.

Krishna, Vern, "Federal Court Relaxes Rules on Deductibility of Fines and Penalties" (1987-88), 2 Can. Current Tax J-99.

Krishna, Vern, "Interpreting the *Tax Act*" (1987) 21 CGA Magazine 37.

Krishna, Vern, "New Directions in Tax Interpretation" (1995) 5 Can. Current Law 47.

Krishna, Vern, "Supreme Court Restores Balance in Statutory Interpretation" (1994) Can. Current Tax J-67.

Krishna, Vern, "The Strict Interpretation Rule" (1987) 21 CGA Magazine 33.

Krishna, Vern, "Use of Extrinsic Evidence in Determining the 'Object and Spirit' of Tax Legislation" (1985) 1 Can. Cur. Tax C-117.

Landis, "A Note on Statutory Interpretation'" (1930) 43 Harvard L. Rev. 886.

Levine, Resa E., "Recent Developments in Judicial Interpretation" in *Report of Proceedings of the 50th Tax Conf.* (Can. Tax Foundation, 1992).

Lyman, "The Absurdity and Repugnancy of the Plain Meaning Rule of Interpretation" (1969) 3 Man. L.J. 253.

Maxwell, P.B., *Interpretation of Statutes*, 12th ed. (Sweet & Maxwell, 1969).

McCallum, "Legislative Intent" (1966) 75 Yale L.J. 754.

McDonnell, T.E., "Statutory Interpretation, 'Acceptable' Tax Planning, Court's Role in Filling In the Gaps in Tax Legislation" (1981) 29 Can. Tax J. 188.

McGregor, Gwyneth, "Interpretation of Taxing Statutes: Whither Canada?" (1968) 16 Can. Tax J. 122.

McGregor, Gwyneth, "Literal or Liberal? Trends in the Interpretation of Income Tax Law" (1954) 32 Can. Bar Rev. 281.

McNab, Charles, "Equity in Income Tax Cases" (1980) 28 Can. Tax J. 445.

Minzberg, Samuel, "Income Splitting: Still Alive?", in *Proceedings of 38th Tax Conf.* 35 (Can. Tax Foundation, 1986).

"'Modern' Rules of Statutory Interpretation in the Daily Routine, The" (1990) 44 D.T.C. 7005.

Morgan, Vivien, "Stubart: What the Courts Did Next" (1987) 35 Can. Tax J. 155.

Nadeau, Claude, "The Interpretation of Taxing Statutes Since Stubart", in *Proceedings of 42nd Tax Conf.* 49:1 (Can. Tax Foundation, 1990).

Nathanson, "The Canadian Charter of Rights and Freedoms, Recent Criminal Prosecution Policy, and the Access to *Information Act*", in *Proceedings of 35th Tax Conf.* 636 (Can. Tax Foundation, 1983).

Radin, "Statutory Interpretation" (1930) 43 Harvard L. Rev. 863.

Rand, Clifford and Allan Stitt, *Understanding the Income Tax Act*, 2nd ed. (Toronto: Carswell, 1991).

Sanagan, "The Construction of Taxing Statutes" (1940) 18 Can. Bar Rev. 43.

Schramm, "Taxation, Expenditure Needs and Fiscal Equity" (1968) 16 Can. Tax J. 379.

Sherbaniuk, "Retrospectivity", in *Proceedings of 35th Tax Conf.* 727 (Can. Tax Foundation, 1983).

"'Spirit' of the Tax Act, The" (1988) 10 Can. Taxpayer 89.

"Spirit of the Law, The: "Practical Example" (1988) 10 Can. Taxpayer 110.

Tamaki, "Form and Substance Revisited" (1962) 10 Can. Tax J. 179. Wilberforce, E., *On Statute Law* (Stevens, 1881).

Willis, "Statute Interpretation in a Nutshell" (1938) 16 Can. Bar Rev. 1.

Estoppel

Ainslie, G., "Income Tax Appeals, Administrative and Judicial", *1972 Conference Report* (Can. Tax Foundation, 1973).

Andrews, J., "Estoppel Against Statutes" (1966) 29 M.L.R. 1.

Bentley, D., "Estoppel in Public Law: A Reply" (1975) 125 N.L.J. 379.

Bowett, D., "Estoppel Before International Tribunals and its Relation to Acquiescence" (1957) 33 Brit. Yb. Int. L. 1276.

Dickerson, R., "Estoppel and the Crown", 1977 Conference Report (Can. Tax Foundation, 1978).

Farrer, F., "A Prerogative Fallacy — That the Crown is Not Bound by Estoppel" (1933) Law Quarterly Rev. 511.

Lynn, T., and M. Gerson, "Quasi-Estoppel and Abuse of Discretion as Applied Against the United States in Federal Tax Controversies" (1964) 19 Tax L. Rev. 487.

McDonald, P., "Contradictory Government Action: Estoppel of Statutory Authorities" (1979) 17 Osgoode Hall L.J. 160.

Quigley, "Estoppel Against the Crown: Selected Problems in the Tax Context", LL.M. Thesis [unpublished], Institute of Comparative Law, McGill University (September 1982).

Rider, Cameron, "Estoppel of the Revenue: A Review of Recent Developments" (1994) 23 Aust. Tax Rev. 135

Stikeman, H., *Erosion of Civil Rights under the Income Tax Act — Crown Privilege and Estoppel* (Canadian Bar Association, 1980).

PART II: JURISDICTION TO TAX

CHAPTER 3 — RESIDENCE AND SOURCE

I. — General Comment

The first question we must answer when designing a tax system is: who should be taxable? The answer to this question shapes the substantive and administrative structure of the statute that one devises to raise revenues. Even the most rudimentary tax system based on head count (for example, a poll tax) raises the question as to whose heads one should count for the purposes of tax collection. Thus, we start with the question: On what basis does Canada assert taxable jurisdiction over a person?

We have several choices. We can answer the question by reference to the legal status of the person, the territorial source of income, or the place where the person manages his or her activities. For example, in the case of individuals, we could use citizenship, domicile, or residence to determine whether the person has a taxable nexus with Canada. Similarly, we could use source of income or place of management as connecting factors for artificial entities such as corporations. The choice of taxable nexus is central to the administration of the tax system.

What are the options? We can justify citizenship as a connecting factor on the theory that citizenship confers a legal status that is not constrained by geographical boundaries. One can argue that the citizens of a country should pay their taxes to it regardless of where they reside because they derive benefits from their citizenship. Even non-resident citizens of a state are entitled to its political protection and, therefore, should bear some of the costs to reflect the benefits of citizenship.

However, citizenship, as the sole connecting factor, creates problems. Citizenship is a political nexus between an individual and a country, and has little bearing upon economic activities. There are also administrative difficulties in asserting claims against non-resident citizens and measuring the value of the benefits they derive during their absence from their country of citizenship. Canada decided early on that it would not use citizenship as a connecting factor for tax purposes. Indeed, even those countries (and there are very few[1]) that use citizenship or nationality to establish a taxable nexus usually couple it with other factors such as residence. The United States, for example, asserts full tax liability on the worldwide income of its citizens and aliens who reside in the country.

Domicile is also a form of legal status. Unlike citizenship, however, domicile uses different criteria, namely, physical presence and an intention to reside indefinitely in the country. We premise taxation based upon domicile on the theory that an individual should pay tax commensurate with the individual's economic and social association with the country. Domicile depends upon intention and free choice. Every person has a domicile of origin at birth, usually the father's domicile. An individual may adopt a domicile of choice, which entails physical presence in a country coupled with an intention to reside there indefinitely. Depending as it does on physical presence and intention, domicile is fraught with substantial uncertainty and is not easy to administer for tax purposes. Thus, unlike Britain, Canada does not use domicile for income tax purposes.

Instead, Canada uses residence as the connecting factor to establish taxable nexus. The theory underlying the use of residence is that a person should owe economic allegiance to the country with which he or she is currently most closely connected in economic and social terms. The obligation to pay tax on the basis of residence derives from the principle that persons who benefit from their economic and social affiliation with a country have an obligation to contribute to its public finances. Thus, an intention to reside indefinitely in the country is not necessarily relevant to "residence". Residence as a connecting factor is also administratively practical and convenient. It is generally easy for a country to ensure compliance with its tax laws if the person over whom it asserts the law has close economic links with the country and has assets within its administrative reach.

Taxation based upon source of income is essentially a territorial form of jurisdiction. It is administratively practical and easily enforceable if one can pinpoint the source of income. The use of source of income as the primary connecting factor for taxation is, however, contrary to tax equity because it does not provide an accurate measure of a taxpayer's ability to pay. Corporate taxpayers in particular may derive all the economic, political, and legal benefits of residence in a country and arrange their international transactions so as to source their income in low-tax countries or tax havens. The development of electronic commerce, which can assign the source of transactions to locations that have little bearing on the economic substance of the transactions, are likely to increase the problems of source taxation. Hence,

---

[1]Few countries (United States, Philippines and Korea Vietnam and Eritrea, for example) use citizenship as a basis of personal taxation.

most developed economies (including Canada) use source taxation only as an adjunct to full tax liability based on some other connection, such as citizenship, domicile or residence.

II. — Who Is Taxable?

Canada uses residence as its primary connecting factor to exercise domestic taxable jurisdiction, on the theory that a person who enjoys the legal, political and economic benefits of association with the country should bear the appropriate share of the costs of association. Subsection 2(1) of the Act states the basic rule:

> An income tax shall be paid ... on the taxable income for each taxation year of every person[2] resident in Canada at any time in the year.

The subsection is quite clear: a resident of Canada is taxable on his or her worldwide income. In addition to residence, however, Canada also uses territorial nexus to tax non-resident persons. Thus, subject to tax treaty provisions,[3] Canada also taxes non-residents, but only on their Canadian-source income. Thus, our first task is to distinguish between residents and non-residents.

Canadian residents are taxable on their worldwide income, regardless of where they earn the income. This rule of full tax liability on worldwide income ensures horizontal equity. For example, assume that A and B, both residents of Canada, each earn $100,000, but B earns half of her income from foreign investments. The principle of horizontal equity requires that A and B should pay an equal amount of tax. Since they are Canadian residents, we can apply the principle only if both are fully liable to tax in Canada on their worldwide income. However, to prevent double taxation of B, who might also pay tax at source on her foreign investment income, Canada grants a tax credit on her foreign taxes. As we will see, these decisions as to who should tax particular sources of income require countries to negotiate their taxable jurisdiction through tax treaties.

Canada taxes non-residents only on their Canadian-source income. Subsection 2(3) states that a non-resident is taxable in Canada only if he or she is employed in Canada, carries on business in Canada or derives a capital gain from the disposition of taxable Canadian property. This rule, however, is also subject to Canada's bilateral tax treaties, which can limit the right to tax a non-resident's income.

It is important to note at the outset that the concept of residence for tax purposes is quite different from residence for immigration purposes. A Canadian resident for immigration purposes may be non-resident for tax purposes and *vice versa*. Nor is residence for tax purposes synonymous with physical presence in Canada. Residence for tax purposes refers to the legal and economic *nexus* that an individual has with Canada. Although physical pres-

---

[2]A "person" includes individuals and corporations.

[3]See, for example, Article 7, *OECD Model Convention.*

ence is an important criterion for residence for tax purposes, it is not necessarily conclusive in establishing taxable nexus. A person who is physically present in Canada, for example, a transient visitor, is not necessarily a Canadian resident.[4] Conversely, a person who is absent from Canada for a considerable period (for example, a Canadian diplomat) may be a Canadian resident for income tax purposes.

III. — Individuals

For income tax purposes, an individual may be a resident, non-resident or part-time resident of Canada. Each of these categories marks the boundary of Canada's jurisdiction to tax. A resident of Canada is taxable on his or her worldwide income, regardless of where it is earned.[5] A non-resident is subject to Canadian income tax only if he or she is employed in Canada, carries on business in Canada, or disposes of taxable Canadian property.[6] A part-year resident of Canada is also subject to tax on his or her worldwide income, but only while he or she is resident in Canada.[7]

We determine an individual's residence in one of three ways — under statutory rules, case law rules, or international tax treaty rules. The statutory rules deem individuals with substantial economic connections with Canada to reside in Canada, regardless of their physical presence in the country. The case law rules are essentially facts and circumstances tests that apply in the absence of statutory provisions to determine whether an individual has a taxable nexus with Canada. Tax treaty rules may apply to prevent double taxation of individuals when two countries both claim taxable jurisdiction over the taxpayer.

1. — Statutory Rules

The Act deems an individual to be a resident of Canada if he or she:[8]

- Sojourns in Canada for 183 days or more in a year;

- Is a member of the Canadian Forces;

---

[4]See, however, the 183-day rule in subs. 250(1).

[5]Subs. 2(1). A resident taxpayer is, within limits, entitled to a credit for foreign taxes paid by him or her; see s. 126.

[6]Subs. 2(3).

[7]S. 114.

[8]Subs. 250(1). An individual cannot, however, be deemed to be resident in Canada by virtue of subsection 250(1) if he or she is considered resident in Canada on the basis of the case law rules. In certain circumstances, subs. 250(1)(g) may deem spouses of Canadian diplomats to be resident in Canada if the diplomat marries a non-resident.

- Is a member of the Canadian diplomatic or quasi-diplomatic service;

- Performs services in a foreign country under a prescribed international development assistance program of the Canadian government;

- Is a member of the Canadian Forces school staff; or

- Is a child of a person holding a position referred to in the above categories (other than a sojourner), if he or she is wholly dependent upon that person for support.

A statutory deeming provision is a conclusive presumption of law. Thus, the above deeming rules ensure that individuals who have substantial economic connections with Canada are subject to Canadian tax despite their absence from the country for extended periods of time.

(a) — Sojourners

The Act *deems* an individual who sojourns in Canada for more than 182 days in a year to reside in Canada *throughout the taxation year*.[9] A presence of more than half a year in the country as a sojourner is sufficient economic and social connection with the country to create a taxable nexus. The days need not be consecutive. The term "day" means a 24-hour period or part thereof.[10]

This sojourning rule is the most elusive of the deeming rules in subsection 250(1). The concept of sojourning is not easy to grasp and the term is not defined in the Act. Sojourning implies a temporary stay in a place, as opposed to ordinary residence. As Estey J. said, "One sojourns at a place where he unusually, casually or intermittently visits or stays."[11] "Sojourning", which is something less than establishing a permanent abode in Canada, has the effect of deeming the individual to be resident in Canada throughout the particular taxation year.

Although, the Act *deems* an individual who sojourns in Canada for more than 182 days to be a resident of Canada, the fact that an individual is present in Canada for fewer than 183 days does not, *by itself*, mean that he or she is not a Canadian resident. An individual who is in Canada for fewer than 183 days may be considered a resident under the "facts and circum-

---

[9]Para. 250(1).

[10]See IT-221R3 for similar reference under the *Canada-U.S. Treaty*.

[11]*Thomson v. M.N.R.* (1945), [1946] S.C.R. 209, [1946] C.T.C. 51 at 70, 2 D.T.C. 812 at 813 (S.C.C.).

stances" common law test.[12] Thus, an individual may be considered a Canadian resident for tax purposes even though he or she has only "visitor status" under the immigration rules.[13]

"Sojourning" is different from permanent residence. For example, an individual who ceases to be a Canadian resident after 183 days in the year cannot be deemed to reside in Canada throughout the year by virtue of the sojourning rule. Rather, the individual is a part-time, permanent resident for the particular year and a non-resident thereafter.[14]

(b) — Government Personnel

Subsection 250(1) also deems members of the Canadian Forces, certain development workers, Canadian Forces school staff, and officers and employees of the Government of Canada or a province to be Canadian residents, regardless of where they are posted and the length of time they are out of the country. A person who ceases to hold a position described above is considered to have been resident in Canada for the part of the year during which he or she held that position.[15]

(c) — Prescribed Agencies

Individuals who perform services at any time in the year in a foreign country under a "prescribed international development assistance program of the Government of Canada" are also *deemed* to be resident in Canada during the period of their absence from Canada if they were resident in Canada at any time in the three-month period immediately prior to commencing their service.[16]

---

[12]This rule is subject to treaty provisions to the contrary. See, e.g., Article XV of the *Canada-United States Income Tax Convention*, 1980 re exemption of employment income where an individual spends fewer than 183 days in Canada.

[13]*Lee v. M.N.R.*, [1990] 1 C.T.C. 2082, 90 D.T.C. 1014 (T.C.C.) (individual considered resident prior to obtaining landed immigrant status on basis of marriage to Canadian resident and purchase of matrimonial residence).

[14]The Agency accepts this position in IT-221R3 "Determination of an Individual's Residence Status" (Oct. 4, 2002); but see *Truchon v. M.N.R.* (1970), 70 D.T.C. 1277 (T.A.B.) (incorrectly decided and rule not followed).

[15]Subs. 250(2).

[16]Para. 250(1)(d); Reg. 3400. See *Petersen v. M.N.R.*, [1969] Tax A.B.C. 682, 69 D.T.C. 503; *Bell v. Canada*, [1996] 2 C.T.C. 2191, 97 D.T.C. 484 (T.C.C.) (Shifting of onus to Minister to prove that program qualifies).

2. — "Common Law" Rules

The "common law" rules determine an individual's residence by his or her links with Canada. Where the links are sufficiently strong, we consider the individual to have a nexus with Canada and he or she is a resident for tax purposes.[17] The sufficiency of connecting factors is a question of fact[18] that depends upon multiple criteria, including:

- Nationality and background;

- Physical presence;

- Ownership of property or dwelling in Canada;

- Location of family home;

- Presence of business interests;

- Presence of social interests;

- Mode of life and family ties; and

- Social connections by reason of birth or marriage.

The relative weight that one attaches to these factors is a question of fact in each case.[19] There are, however, certain generally accepted legal propositions:

- A taxpayer must reside somewhere;[20]

- A taxpayer need not have a fixed place of abode to be resident in the jurisdiction;[21]

- Residence requires more than mere physical presence within the jurisdiction;[22]

- Residence does not require constant personal presence;[23]

---

[17]*Weymyss v. Weymyss's Trustees*, [1921] Sess. Cas. 30.

[18]As Lord Buckmaster observed in *I.R.C. v. Lysaght*, [1928] A.C. 234 at 247-248 (H.L.):

> ... it may be true that the word "reside" ... in other Acts may have special meanings but in the *Income Tax Acts* it is, I think, used in its common sense and it is essentially a question of fact whether a man does or does not comply with its meaning ... the matter must be a matter of degree.

[19]See, e.g., *MacLean v. M.N.R.*, [1985] C.T.C. 2207, 85 D.T.C. 169 (T.C.C.) (taxpayer resident on the basis of continued connections with Canada despite the CCRA's waiver of source deductions).

[20]*Rogers v. I.R.C.* (1897), 1 Tax Cas. 225 (Scot. Ct. of Ex.).

[21]*Reid v. I.R.C.* (1926), 10 Tax Cas. 673 (Scot. Ct. of Sess.).

[22]*Levene v. I.R.C.* (1928), 13 Tax Cas. 486 (H.L.).

[23]*Young, Re* (1875), 1 Tax Cas. 57 (Scot. Ct. of Ex.).

- A taxpayer may have more than one residence;[24]

- The number of days that a taxpayer spends within Canada is not determinative;[25]

- Residence may be established by presence within Canada even though the presence is compelled by the authorities, business necessity or otherwise;[26]

- "Residing" and "ordinarily resident" do not have special or technical meanings, and the question whether a person is "residing or ordinarily resident in Canada" is a question of fact;[27] and

- Intention and free choice, which are essential elements in domicile, are not necessary to establish residence; residence is quite different from domicile of choice.[28]

Thus, "residing" is not a term of invariable elements. As Rand J. said in *Thomson v. M.N.R.*:[29]

> ... [it] is quite impossible to give it a precise and inclusive definition. It is highly flexible, and its many shades of meaning vary not only in the contexts of different matters, but also in different aspects of the same matter. In one case it is satisfied by certain elements, in another by others, some common, some new.

The following are the relevant indicia in determining Canadian residence:

- Past and present habits of life;

- Regularity and length of visits to Canada;

- Ties within Canada;

---

[24]*Lloyd v. Sulley* (1884), 2 Tax Cas. 37 (Scot. Ct. of Ex.).

[25]*Reid v. I.R.C., ante.*

[26]*I.R.C. v. Lysaght*, [1928] A.C. 234 (H.L.).

[27]*Ibid.*

[28]*Schujahn v. M.N.R.*, [1962] C.T.C. 364, 62 D.T.C. 1225 (Ex. Ct.) (change of domicile depends on will of individual).

[29]*Thomson v. M.N.R.*, [1945] C.T.C. 63, 2 D.T.C. 684 (Can. Ex. Ct.); affd. (1945), [1946] C.T.C. 51 at 63-64, 2 D.T.C. 812 at 815, [1946] S.C.R. 209 (S.C.C.). See also *Beament v. M.N.R.*, [1952] 2 S.C.R. 486, [1952] C.T.C. 327, 52 D.T.C. 1183 (S.C.C.) (taxpayer not resident where he was physically absent from Canada, did not maintain any dwelling place in Canada, and maintained matrimonial home in U.K.); *Russell v. M.N.R.*, [1949] C.T.C. 13, 49 D.T.C. 536 (Ex. Ct.) (examination of indicia of residence during active service overseas); *Schujahn v. M.N.R.*, [1962] C.T.C. 364, 62 D.T.C. 1225 (Ex. Ct.) (taxpayer not resident though family remained in Canada for purpose of selling home); *Griffiths v. The Queen*, [1978] C.T.C. 372, 78 D.T.C. 6286 (F.C.T.D.) (established residence was yacht in Caribbean despite spouse, assets and income in Canada).

- Ties elsewhere;

- Purpose of stay;

- Ownership of a home in Canada or rental of a dwelling on a long-term basis (for example, a lease for one or more years);

- Residence of spouse, children and other dependent family members in a dwelling that the individual maintains in Canada;

- Memberships with Canadian churches or synagogues, recreational and social clubs, unions and professional organizations;

- Registration and maintenance of automobiles, boats and airplanes in Canada;

- Credit cards issued by Canadian financial institutions and commercial entities, including stores, car rental agencies, etc.;

- Local newspaper subscriptions sent to a Canadian address;

- Rental of a Canadian safety deposit box or post office box;

- Subscriptions for life or general insurance, including health insurance, through a Canadian insurance company;

- Mailing address in Canada;

- Telephone listing in Canada;

- Business cards showing a Canadian address;

- Magazine and other periodical subscriptions sent to a Canadian address;

- Canadian bank accounts other than a non-resident bank account;

- Active securities accounts with Canadian brokers;

- Canadian driver's licence;

- Membership in a Canadian pension plan;

- Frequent visits to Canada for social or business purposes;

- Burial plot in Canada;

- Will prepared in Canada;

- Legal documentation indicating Canadian residence;

- Filing a Canadian income tax return as a Canadian resident;

- Ownership of a Canadian vacation property;

- Active involvement in business activities in Canada;

- Employment in Canada;

- Maintenance or storage in Canada of personal belongings, including clothing, furniture, family pets, etc.;

- Landed immigrant status in Canada; and

- Severing substantially all ties with former country of residence.

3. — Administrative Rules

The Canada Revenue Agency (CRA) discusses its views on the above criteria in its Interpretation Bulletin, "Determination of an Individual's Residence Status". The Agency focuses on three principal factors: (1) dwelling place; (2) family connections; and (3) personal property and social ties.

The most important factors in determining residence for tax purposes is whether the individual maintains a home or dwelling in Canada.[30]

4. — International Treaty Rules

An individual may be a resident of more than one country in the same year. For example, a Canadian resident who is a U.S. citizen is potentially liable to taxation by both Canada and the United States. Similarly, an individual with international investments may be liable to tax in multiple jurisdictions. For example, a U.S. resident who sojourns more than 182 days in the year in Canada and receives dividends from a U.K. corporation would be liable for tax on his or her gross dividend income both in Canada and the United States under the domestic rules of both countries. In addition, the individual would also be liable for any taxes the U.K. government withholds at source on the dividends. Thus, without specific relief, the individual would be potentially liable for tax on the same income in three countries. Multiple taxation of income is unfair and inefficient. Thus, Canada has negotiated numerous bilateral tax treaties to prevent double taxation of income and capital.

Bilateral tax treaties resolve dual residency claims on individuals by two countries by allocating the jurisdiction to tax to one or other of the countries. A treaty allocates taxable jurisdiction by applying a series of tie-breaker rules so that only one of the countries will have the primary right to tax the individual as its resident. The rules determine the degree of attachment that an individual has with a country, and are ranked in descending order of significance as follows:

- Location of permanent home;

---

[30]IT-221R3, "Determination of an Individual's Residence Status" (Oct. 4, 2002).

- Centre of vital interests;

- Habitual abode; and

- Nationality.

Article 4(2) of the *OECD Model Double Taxation Convention on Income and on Capital*, which Canada uses as the model for its treaties, specifies the hierarchy of tie-breakers as follows:

> Where ... an individual is a resident of both Contracting States, then his status shall be determined as follows:
>
> > (a) he shall be deemed to be a resident of the State in which he has a permanent home available to him; if he has a permanent home available to him in both States, he shall be deemed to be a resident of the State with which his personal and economic relations are closer (centre of vital interests);
> >
> > (b) if the State in which he has his centre of vital interests cannot be determined, or if he has not a permanent home available to him in either State, he shall be deemed to be a resident of the State in which he has an habitual abode;
> >
> > (c) if he has an habitual abode in both States or in neither of them, he shall be deemed to be a resident of the State of which he is a national;
> >
> > (d) if he is a national of both States or of neither of them, the competent authorities of the Contracting States shall settle the question by mutual agreement.

If one cannot resolve the issue of dual residency through the application of any of the above criteria, we refer the matter to the revenue authorities of each of the countries concerned for administrative resolution.

(a) — Permanent Home

Treaties typically deem a dual resident individual to reside in the country in which he or she has a permanent home. Permanence implies that the individual must have arranged and retained the home for his or her permanent use or stays of short duration.

A "home" includes any form of residential establishment, for example, a house, apartment, or even rented furnished rooms. It is the permanence of the home, rather than its size or nature of ownership or tenancy, that is the measure of attachment to the country.

(b) — Centre of Vital Interests

Where an individual has a permanent home in both of the countries that consider the individual a resident under their domestic laws, the treaty deems the individual to reside in the country with which he or she has closer personal and economic relations ("centre of vital interests").[31] One determines personal and economic relations by family and social relations, occupation, political and cultural activities, place of business, and the place of administration of property. The OECD Commentary describes the centre of vital interests as follows:[32]

> The circumstances must be examined as a whole, but it is nevertheless obvious that considerations based on the personal acts of the individual must receive special attention. If a person who has a home in one State sets up a second in the other State while retaining the first, the fact that he retains the first in the environment where he has always lived, where he has worked, and where he has his family and possessions, can, together with other elements, go to demonstrate that he has retained his centre of vital interests in the first State.

(c) — Habitual Abode

If one cannot determine an individual's centre of vital interests or if the individual does not have a permanent home in either country, the treaty deems the individual to reside in the country in which he or she maintains an habitual abode. Alternatively, where an individual has a permanent home available to him or her in both countries, an habitual abode in one, rather than in the other, will tip the balance towards the country where he or she stays more frequently.

Where, however, an individual does not have a permanent home in either country, all of his or her stays in the country should be considered without reference to the reason for the stay. For this purpose, it is necessary to determine whether the individual's residence in each of the two countries is sufficiently "habitual" to provide a meaningful answer.

(d) — Nationality

If none of the above criteria are sufficient to break the deadlock, treaties typically deem the individual to reside in the country of which he or she is a national.[33]

(e) — Competent Authorities

Finally, if one cannot resolve dual residency through the application of any of the specific attachment criteria, we refer the matter to the "competent authorities". The CRA is the designated competent authority under Canada's bilateral treaties.

---

[31] Article 4(2), *OECD Model Convention*.

[32] Para. 15, *Commentary on Article 4(2)*.

[33] See, for example, Article IV of the *Canada-U.S. Tax Treaty*.

5. — Part-Year Residents

An individual is a part-year resident if he or she gives up or takes up Canadian residence part way through the year. For example, a Canadian resident may emigrate during the year and take up residence elsewhere. In these circumstances, the individual would be a resident of Canada until his or her departure and a non-resident for the remainder of the year. As a resident, the individual would be taxable on his or her global income. As a non-resident, the individual would be taxable in Canada only if he or she was employed, or carrying on a business, in Canada or if he or she realized a capital gain from taxable Canadian property.[34]

A resident who gives up residence during a taxation year may claim deductions for that year but only on a proportional basis.[35] We determine an individual's non-refundable tax credits for the period of residency based on reasonableness, for example, the number of days of residency. For example, an individual who becomes a Canadian resident on September 1 of a year is liable for Canadian tax on his or her global income earned during the period of September 1 to December 31 of the year. The individual's personal exemptions may be calculated on the basis of 122/365 (122 being the number of days out of the year spent in Canada) of the annual deductions otherwise available. An individual may also claim — subject to annual maximums — additional NRTCs for the period of non-residency if he earns at least 90 per cent of his income for the period of non-residency in Canada.[36]

6. — Giving Up Residence

Generally, to give up Canadian residence, the taxpayer should minimize his or her ties with Canada.[37]It is not easy to relinquish Canadian residence. An individual must produce convincing evidence that he or she has severed ties with Canada on a fairly permanent basis in order to cease residence. The Agency looks at four principal factors to determine whether an individual has given up Canadian residence:

1. Permanence and purpose of stay abroad;

2. Residential ties within Canada;

3. Residential ties elsewhere; and

4. Regularity and length of visits to Canada.

---

[34]Subs. 2(3) and subject to any treaty provisions.

[35]Ss. 114, 118.91.

[36]S. 118.94.

[37]See, e.g., *Ferguson v. M.N.R.*, [1989] 2 C.T.C. 2387, 89 D.T.C. 634 (T.C.C.) (Canadian in Saudi Arabia for five years considered Canadian resident because he retained Ontario driver's license and union membership, and his spouse remained in Canada).

Thus, at the very least, an individual who wishes to give up residence should:

- Sell or lease his or her dwelling in Canada;

- Sell his or her motor vehicle;

- Cancel any lease in respect of a dwelling in Canada that he or she occupies, or sublease the dwelling for the period of his or her absence; and

- Cancel bank accounts, club memberships and similar social and business connections within Canada.

There is no bright-line factual test to determine the minimum length of time that an individual should be out of Canada to claim non-resident status.

7. — Becoming a Resident

It is much easier for an individual to become a Canadian resident than to relinquish residence. An individual who takes up residence in Canada is taxed as a part-year resident for the portion of the year after his or her arrival and as a non-resident prior to his or her arrival.

Thus, it is generally advantageous for an individual to deliberately establish residence in Canada rather than be deemed a "sojourner" in Canada in the year of arrival. The Act deems a sojourner to be a Canadian resident for the *entire year* and taxable on his or her worldwide income.[38] In contrast, an incoming resident is taxable on his or her worldwide income only after arrival in Canada. Thus, timing of immigration is important. An immigrant can minimize tax by splitting income between Canada and the country of departure.

Residence for immigration purposes is different from residence for tax purposes. An individual can establish permanent residence status for immigration purposes without becoming a resident for tax purposes. "Landed immigrant" status is determined on the basis of selection standards that are quite different from those used to determine residence for tax purposes. For immigration purposes, a landed immigrant must spend 183 days in Canada in a *12-month period*. For tax purposes, the Act deems an individual to be a resident of Canada if he or she spends more than 182 days in Canada in a *calendar year*. Thus, an individual can arrange to take up landed immigrant status in Canada in a particular year and maintain non-resident status for income tax purposes.

IV. — Corporations

A corporation is a legal entity, a person, and a taxpayer in its own right, whether or not its shareholders have limited or unlimited liability for its debts. A corporation resident in Can-

---

[38]Para. 250(1)(a); subs. 2(1).

ada is taxable on its worldwide income. Non-resident corporations are taxable in Canada only on their Canadian-source income. As with individuals, we determine the residence of a corporation in one of three ways — under statutory rules, at "common law", or by virtue of international tax treaty provisions.

1. — Statutory Rules

The statutory rule of corporate residence is simple. The Act deems a corporation incorporated in Canada to be resident in Canada for tax purposes.[39] This rule applies to all corporations incorporated in Canada after April 26, 1965, regardless of where they are managed or controlled.[40] The Act also deems a corporation incorporated in Canada prior to April 26, 1965 to be resident in Canada in a taxation year but only if after that date it:[41]

• Becomes resident in Canada at any time under the "common law" rules; or

• Carries on business in Canada.[42]

A corporation incorporated in Canada is also considered a "Canadian corporation".[43] This concept is important because of special incentive provisions that apply only to Canadian corporations.

Finally, the Act deems a corporation that is continued into or outside Canada to have been incorporated in that jurisdiction.[44] Thus, a corporation that is incorporated in Canada and continued outside Canada escapes the deemed residence rules,[45] which are based on the jurisdiction of incorporation. For example, the Act deems a corporation that is initially incorporated in the United States and then continued under federal or provincial corporate law in Canada, but which remains resident in both countries because of the "central management and control" test, to be a resident of Canada. Thus, U.S. corporations continued into Canada

---

[39]Para. 250(4)(a). This deeming provision only applies to corporations incorporated in Canada after April 26, 1965.

[40]Para. 250(4)(a).

[41]Para. 250(4)(c).

[42]See meaning of "carrying on business in Canada" in s. 253.

[43]Subs. 89(1) "Canadian corporation".

[44]Subs. 250(5.1).

[45]Subs. 250(4).

acquire "Canadian corporation" status, even if they are effectively managed from the United States. Such U.S. corporations are eligible for favourable treatment under the Act.[46]

2. — The "Common Law" Rules

The determination of corporate residence at "common law" is essentially a question of fact and circumstances. A corporation is resident where its "central management and control" resides.[47] The test originated in the Court of Exchequer in 1876 in *Calcutta Jute Mills v. Nicholson* (1876), 1 T.C. 83 (Eng. Ex. Div.) and *Cesena Sulphur Co. Ltd. v. Nicholson* (1876), 1 T.C. 88 (Eng. Ex. Div.). The House of Lords adopted the test thirty years later in *De Beers*, now considered the seminal authority on corporate residence. As Lord Loreburn said:[48]

> In applying the conception of residence to a company, we ought, I think, to proceed as nearly as we can upon the analogy of an individual. A company cannot eat or sleep, but it can keep house and do business. We ought, therefore, to see where it really keeps house and does business. ... [A] company resides for purposes of income tax where its real business is carried on. ... I regard that as the true rule, and the real business is carried on where the central management and control actually abides.

We identify central management and control with the control that a company's board of directors has over its business and affairs — generally in the jurisdiction where the board meets. Thus, corporate residence is different from corporate capacity. One determines residence by *de facto* "central management and control"; we determine corporate capacity through the constating documents that created the corporation and the law of the jurisdiction of incorporation.

---

[46]For example, for tax-deferred rollovers on transfers of property to the corporation on a merger with another taxable Canadian corporation.

[47]*De Beers Consolidated Mines Ltd. v. Howe*, [1906] A.C. 455 at 458 (H.L.) (central management and control determined through scrutiny of course of business and trading); *Unit Const. Co. v. Bullock*, [1959] 3 All E.R. 831 (H.L.) (three wholly-owned African subsidiaries of English corporation resident in U.K. because parent corporation exercised *de facto* control of subsidiaries from U.K.). The English common law test of "central management and control" is part of Canadian tax law: see *B.C. Electric Railway v. The Queen*, [1946] C.T.C. 224, 2 D.T.C. 839 (P.C.) (corporation was resident where whole of business carried on, all directors resident, and all shareholders meetings held in Canada). See also *Bedford Overseas Freighters Ltd. v. M.N.R.*, [1970] C.T.C. 69, 70 D.T.C. 6072 (Ex. Ct.) (management and control of business exercised by Canadian directors though instructed by non-resident shareholder owner); *Zehnder & Co. v. M.N.R.*, [1970] C.T.C. 85, 70 D.T.C. 6064 (Ex. Ct.) (management of company and attention to company's interests and affairs exercised in Canada); *Birmount Hldgs. Ltd. v. The Queen*, [1978] C.T.C. 358, 78 D.T.C. 6254 (F.C.A.) (company "keeping house" and "doing business" in Canada; see list of factors considered).

[48]*De Beers Consolidated Mines Ltd. v. Howe, ante* at 458.

(a) — General Propositions

The following propositions apply to corporate residence:

- A corporation can have more than one residence if its central management and control is located in more than one jurisdiction.[49]

- Central management and control refers to the exercise of power and control by the corporation's board of directors and not to the power of the corporation's shareholders. Thus, the residence of shareholders is irrelevant for the purposes of determining corporate residence.[50]

- The residence of a subsidiary corporation, even a wholly-owned subsidiary, is determined independently of its parent corporation — the subsidiary's residence is determined by its central management and control.

- A subsidiary corporation may have the same residence as its parent corporation if the parent exercises effective control over the subsidiary's activities and management.[51]

In corporate law, parent and subsidiary corporations are separate entities each with its own board of directors. Nevertheless, parent corporations will typically influence management of their subsidiaries without effect on the latter's residence. Where, however, the parent's board effectively usurps the subsidiary's management, we determine the residence of the subsidiary by its *de facto* control.

There is no bright-line factual test that determines corporate residence in every case. To determine the central management and control of a corporation one must carefully evaluate all the surrounding factors, including:

- The location of meetings of its directors;

- The degree of independent control exercised by its directors; and

- The relative influence and power that its Canadian directors exercise, as compared with foreign directors (the "rubber stamp" test).

Ultimately, each case depends upon an evaluation of where the corporation is actually managed and controlled.

Conversely, viewed from the opposite perspective, a corporation that desires non-resident status should incorporate outside Canada and conduct all of its board meetings, banking, and

---

[49]*Swedish Central Ry. Co. v. Thompson*, [1925] A.C. 495 (H.L.) (company resident in location of registered office and where controlled and managed); *M.N.R. v. Crossley Carpets (Can.) Ltd.*, [1969] 1 Ex. C.R. 405 (Ex. Ct.) (paramount authority for businesses divided between two countries).

[50]*Gramophone & Typewriter Co. v. Stanley*, [1908] 2 K.B. 89 (C.A.).

[51]*Unit Construction Co. v. Bullock, ante.*

corporate finance outside the country. Where there are several directors, the majority should be non-residents. Annual shareholders meetings should also be held outside Canada.

(b) — Dual Residence

Since different countries use different connecting factors to assert taxable jurisdiction over corporations, a corporation may be considered resident in more than one country. For example, a corporation that is incorporated in the United States and managed and controlled in Canada would be resident in both countries.

The *OECD Model Convention* uses the "place of effective management" as a tie-breaker to determine the residence of persons other than individuals. Article 4(3) of the Convention states:

> Where ... a person other than an individual is a resident of both Contracting States, then it shall be deemed to be a resident of the State in which its place of effective management is situated.

Both Canada and the United States, however, reserve the right to use place of incorporation as the determinative test for corporate residence. Article IV(3) of the *Canada-U.S. Treaty* provides that:

> Where ... a company is a resident of both Contracting States, then if it was created under the laws in force in a Contracting State, it shall be deemed to be a resident of that State.

Some jurisdictions allow local incorporation of an entity that is already organized and incorporated under the laws of another country. Under the *Canada-U.S. Treaty*, however, the determinative factor is the location of the corporation's original creation.[52]

(c) — "Permanent Establishment"

A Canadian resident corporation is taxable in Canada on its worldwide income. A non-resident corporation is taxable in Canada only if it carries on business in Canada.[53]

However, a non-resident enterprise of a country with which Canada has a bilateral tax treaty is taxable only if it carries on business in Canada through a "permanent establishment". Thus, the threshold test for determining source liability for Canadian tax of a non-resident from a treaty country is higher than the simple test of carrying on business in Canada. To be liable for Canadian tax, the non-resident must be carrying on business *through a permanent establishment* in Canada. A "permanent establishment" provides the taxable nexus for source taxation of non-resident corporations.

---

[52]See *Revised Technical Explanation — Canada-U.S. Income Tax Convention 1980* (U.S. Treasury Department).

[53]Subs. 2(3) and s. 253.

The term "permanent establishment" is essentially a tax treaty concept. Canadian tax treaties typically provide that a "permanent establishment" means a "... *fixed* place of business in which the business of the enterprise is wholly or partly carried on."[54] But what does this mean? In *Re Consolidated Premium Iron Ores*, the United States Tax Court said:[55]

> The term "permanent establishment", normally interpreted, suggests something more substantial than a license, a letterhead and isolated activities. It implies the existence of an office, staffed and capable of carrying on the day-to-day business of the corporation and its use for such purpose, or it suggests the existence of a plant or facilities equipped to carry on the ordinary routine of such business activity. The descriptive word "permanent" in the characterization "permanent establishment" is vital in analysing the treaty provisions. ... It indicates permanence and stability.

In determining whether a corporation has "an office" in a particular place, one looks to:

- Presence of permanent physical premises;
- Presence of directors or employees;
- Bank accounts and books of account;
- Telephone listings; and
- Employees or agents established with the general authority to contract for the taxpayer in that jurisdiction.

Consolidated Premium Iron Ores was decided in 1957. It remains to be seen whether the test set out in the decision is entirely relevant in the context of electronic commerce.

(d) — Anti-Treaty Shopping

Corporate taxpayers can quite easily arrange their affairs to take advantage of the rules that determine residence by virtue of specific statutory and treaty provisions. For example, a corporation can be incorporated in a country (for example, the United States) solely to locate its residence in that jurisdiction. This might allow the corporation to take advantage of U.S. bilateral tax treaties that it might not otherwise be able to invoke. There is increasing concern in the international community that treaties should limit, or at least restrain, tax planning motivated solely by tax avoidance through treaty shopping. There is little doubt that the trend in international communities is towards placing greater restrictions on the "improper" use of tax treaties. Thus, just as we see domestic statutory provisions (for example,

---

[54]Article 5, *OECD Model Convention*.

[55]*Re Consolidated Premium Iron Ores* (1957), 28 T.C. 127 at 152, affd. S. (2d) 230 (6th Circuit, 1959).

GAAR[56]) that restrict the application of the *Westminster*[57] principle, so also we are seeing increasing restrictions appearing in bilateral tax treaties that are intended to curtail tax avoidance. Article XXIX(A) of the *Canada-U.S. Treaty*, for example, limits the benefits of the treaty to "qualifying persons", a phrase that the Treaty defines restrictively. The Article also allows the authorities to deny the benefits of the Treaty where taxpayers use it in an abusive manner.

The Commentary on Article 1 of the *OECD Model Convention* considers the improper use of bilateral tax conventions:

> True, taxpayers have the possibility, double tax conventions being left aside, to exploit the differences in tax levels as between States and the tax advantages provided by various country's taxation laws, but it is for the States concerned to adopt provisions in their domestic laws to counter possible manoeuvres. Such States will then wish, in their bilateral double taxation conventions, to preserve the application of provisions of this kind contained in their domestic laws. ... For example, if a person ... acted through a legal entity created in a State essentially to obtain treaty benefits which would not be available directly to such person. Another case would be one of an individual having in a Contracting State both his permanent home and all his economic interests, including a substantial participation in a company of that State, and who, essentially in order to sell the participation and escape taxation in that State on the capital gains from the alienation ... transferred his permanent home to the other Contracting State, where such gains were subject to little or no tax. ... It may be appropriate for Contracting States to agree in bilateral negotiations that any relief from tax should not apply in certain cases, or to agree that the application of the provisions of domestic laws against tax avoidance should not be affected by the Convention.

The Commentary goes on to discuss various approaches that member countries may consider in combatting the problem of tax avoidance through, for example, the use of conduit companies. One approach is to use "look-through" provisions to disallow treaty benefits to corporations that are not owned, directly or indirectly, by residents of the country in which the corporation is a resident. The Commentary suggests the following wording for such a provision:

> A company which is a resident of a Contracting State shall not be entitled to relief from taxation under this Convention with respect to any item of income, gains or profits unless it is neither owned nor controlled directly or through one or more companies, wherever resident, by persons who are not residents of the first-mentioned State.

The use of such provisions in Canadian bilateral tax treaties would prevent residents of third party countries from incorporating in Canada in order to take advantage of Canada's treaty

---

[56]S. 245.

[57]*C.I.R. v. The Duke of Westminster*, [1936] A.C. 1 (H.L.) (taxpayer entitled to order affairs so as to minimize tax payable).

network with other countries. Similar anti-treaty shopping provisions have been negotiated by the United States in all of its treaties.[58]

Canada's anti-treaty shopping rules vary in scope. Article 27(3) of the *Canada-Mexico Income Tax Convention* (1991), for example, states:[59]

> The Convention shall not apply to any company, trust or partnership that is a resident of a Contracting State and is beneficially owned or controlled directly or indirectly by one or more persons who are not residents of that State, if the amount of the tax imposed on the income or capital of the company, trust or partnership by that State is substantially lower than the amount that would be imposed by the State if all of the shares of the capital stock of the company or all of the interests in the trust or partnership, as the case may be, were beneficially owned by one or more individuals who were residents of that State.

In other cases, Canada's treaties state that treaty benefits may not apply to certain corporations established in particular jurisdictions. Article XXX(3) of the *Canada-Barbados Income Tax Agreement*,[60] for example, states that it "... shall not apply to companies entitled to any special tax benefit under the Barbados *International Business Companies (Exemption from Income Tax) Act* ... or to companies entitled to any special tax benefits under any similar law enacted by Barbados in addition to or in place of that law."

V. — Trusts

A trust is a legal relationship that arises when a person (the trustee) is compelled by law to hold property for the benefit of some other person (the beneficiary). The property is to be held in such a manner that the real benefit of the property accrues to the beneficiary, not the trustee.

A trust is *not* a separate legal entity in private law. For tax purposes, however, a trust is taxable as a separate person.[61] The residence of a trust for tax purposes is a question of fact determined according to the common law rules applicable to individuals.

The law considers a trust to reside where its trustee resides.[62] Where a trust has more than one trustee, it is resident where a majority of its trustees reside if the trust instrument permits

---

[58]See, for example, Article 28 of the *U.S.-Germany Treaty* and Article 17 of the *U.S.-Mexico Treaty*.

[59]Article 27(3), *Canada-Mexico Income Tax Convention*, 8 April 1991, [1992] Can. T.S. No. 15.

[60]*Canada-Barbados Income Tax Agreement*, 22 January 1980, [1980] Can. T.S. No. 29.

[61]Subs. 104(2).

[62]*McLeod v. Min. of Customs & Excise*, [1917–27] C.T.C. 290, 1 D.T.C. 85 (S.C.C.) (taxation of accumulated income in hands of trustee); *M.N.R. v. Royal Trust Co.*, [1928–34] C.T.C. 74, 1 D.T.C. 217 (S.C.C.) (trust with non-resident beneficiaries but resident trustee taxable); *M.N.R. v. Holden*, [1928–34] C.T.C. 127, 1 D.T.C. 234; varied on other grounds [1928–34] C.T.C. 129, 1 D.T.C. 243

majority decisions on all matters within the discretion of the trustees.[63] A trust cannot have dual residence. In this respect, trusts are quite unlike individuals and corporations, which can have dual residences.[64]

In the event that a trust has multiple trustees, some of whom are individuals and others corporations, one must determine the residence of each of the trustees according to the common law and statutory rules. For example, we might determine the individual trustee's residence according to the common law tests and the residence of a corporate trustee by reference to its place of incorporation. The determination of a trust's residence is much more complicated if its trustees reside in different jurisdictions, each with bilateral tax treaties with Canada.

Generally, one determines a trust's residence by the residence of its trustees and not by the residence of its beneficiaries or the residence of its settlor. Furthermore, the residence of a trust is not determined by the "central management and control" test because trustees cannot delegate any of their authority to co-trustees. Thus, if a trust is to maintain non-resident status, it should ensure that at least a majority of its trustees are non-residents of Canada. In addition, because of the uncertainty of trust residence, it is prudent to hold trust meetings outside Canada and invest the majority of its assets outside Canada. In the event that the trust has a "protector", the protector should not be a Canadian resident. Further, the protector should not have the unrestricted power to appoint and remove trustees.

VI. — Partnerships

A partnership is the relationship that subsists between persons carrying on business in common with a view to profit.[65] The liability of partners for partnerships may be unlimited (general partnerships) or limited (limited liability partnerships). Whether liability is limited or unlimited, a partnership is *not* a separate legal entity. For tax purposes, however, partnership income is calculated *as if* the partnership were a separate person.[66] A partnership's income is calculated as if the partnership were an entity, and the income is then allocated to the partners according to the terms of the partnership agreement. Thus, a partnership is a

---

(P.C.) (trust taxed on undistributed income whether beneficiaries resident or not); *Williams v. Singer*, [1921] 1 A.C. 65 (H.L.) (trust not taxed on foreign dividends received for non-resident beneficiary); *I.R.C. v. Gull*, [1937] 4 All E.R. 290 (English charitable trust exempt where one trustee non-resident).

[63]*Thibodeau v. The Queen*, [1978] C.T.C. 539, 78 D.T.C. 6376 (F.C.T.D.); see also IT-447, "Residence of a Trust or Estate" (May 30, 1980).

[64]IT-447, "Residence of a Trust or Estate" (May 30, 1980).

[65]*Partnerships Act*, R.S.O. 1990, c. P.5, s. 2.

[66]Para. 96(1)(a).

conduit, and its income flows through to the partners. Individual partners are taxed as individuals; corporate partners are taxed as corporations.

A "Canadian partnership" is a partnership in which all the members are resident in Canada.[67]

VII. — Provincial Residence

A Canadian resident is liable for federal income tax on his or her worldwide income. In addition to federal tax, however, a Canadian resident may also be liable for provincial tax. Provincial income tax liability is generally calculated in a way similar to that of federal income tax liability.

In the case of individuals, we determine provincial income tax liability (except for Quebec) by applying the provincial income tax rates to the individual's "taxable income". "Taxable income" is defined by the federal government and is the tax base used by both levels of government for the calculation of income taxes. For the purpose of determining provincial income tax liability, an individual resides in a province throughout the taxation year if he or she resides in the province on December 31 of the year. For example, an individual who emigrates from Ontario to Alberta on December 30 of a year is taxable on his or her income for the entire year in Alberta. This rule, although somewhat imperfect in its technical accuracy, is easy and convenient for individuals to apply and for the provinces to administer. Thus, the rule trades off some loss of revenue for the province from which the individual emigrates in exchange for administrative simplicity and certainty.

In the case of corporations, the calculation of provincial tax is more complex. A corporation must allocate its Canadian source income to each of the provinces in which it maintains a permanent establishment.[68] The allocation is made in accordance with a formula based on the proportion of revenue and payroll attributable to a province.

VIII. — Non-Residents

Non-residents are taxable in Canada only on their Canadian-source income. Thus, Canada exercises source or territorial jurisdiction over non-residents who earn income in Canada. There are two broad categories of Canadian-source income — active and passive. Active income is taxable under Part I of the Act; passive income is subject to withholding tax under Part XIII. A non-resident person has active Canadian source income if he or she:

- was employed in Canada;

---

[67]Subs. 102(1).

[68]S. 124; *Income Tax Regulation*, C.R.C., c. 945, s. 400.

- carried on business in Canada; or

- disposed of taxable Canadian property

at any time either in the current year or in a previous year.

An individual is considered to be employed in Canada if he or she performs the duties of an office or employment in Canada. This rule applies whether or not the individual's employer resides in Canada.

A non-resident person carries on business in Canada if he or she engages in any business activity, solicits orders, or offers anything for sale in Canada.[69] Subsection 248(1) defines a "business" to include a profession, calling, trade, manufacture or undertaking of any kind whatever, and an adventure or concern in the nature of trade.

Taxable Canadian property includes real property in Canada, shares of resident Canadian corporations (other than public corporations), and capital property used in carrying on a business in Canada.[70]

The liability of a non-resident person for Canadian income tax also depends upon whether the taxpayer resides in a country with which Canada has a tax treaty. A bilateral tax treaty can modify the scope of a non-resident's liability for Canadian tax. The general treaty rule is that business profits earned by a non-resident in Canada are taxable only if the non-resident has a "permanent establishment" in Canada and the profits are attributable to the establishment. A "permanent establishment" (PE) means a "... fixed place of business in which the business of the enterprise is wholly or partly carried on."[71] A PE requires a degree of permanence and stability to the place of business in Canada. The effect of this rule is that the threshold for determining a non-resident's liability for Canadian income tax on business profits is higher in the case of the residents of countries with which Canada has a tax treaty than in the case of non-residents from non-treaty countries.

A non-resident who earns passive Canadian-source income (for example, dividends, interest, or royalties) is liable for Canadian withholding tax under Part XIII of the Act. The general rate of withholding tax is 25 per cent. This rate is reduced, however, in Canada's tax treaties. For example, the withholding rate on interest income is 10 percent under the *Canada-U.S. Treaty*.

---

[69]S. 253.

[70]Subs. 248(1)"taxable Canadian property".

[71]Art. 5, s. 1 of the *OECD Model Convention*.

IX. — Exempt Persons

The Act exempts from tax the following persons who would otherwise be taxable under Part I of the Act:[72]

- Persons holding diplomatic and quasi-diplomatic positions in Canada, members of their families and their servants;

- Municipal authorities;

- Corporations owned by the Crown;

- Registered charities;

- Labour organizations;

- Non-profit clubs, societies or associations ("NPOs");[73]

- Prescribed small business investment corporations;[74]

- Registered pension funds and trusts;

- Trusts created for:

  - Employee profit-sharing plans;

  - Registered supplementary unemployment benefit plans;

  - Registered retirement savings and income plans;

  - Deferred profit-sharing plans; and

  - Registered education savings plans;

  - Retirement compensation arrangements.

These persons are exempt from tax only if they satisfy all of the conditions necessary for attaining exempt status.

---

[72]S. 149. The persons listed in this section are exempt from Part I tax. Subs. 227(14) extends the exemption for taxes under other parts to corporations exempt under s. 149.

[73]An election by an NPO for the purposes of GST legislation does not, in and of itself, adversely affect its tax-exempt status for income tax purposes: Technical Interpretation (August 27, 1990), CRA.

[74]Para. 149(1)(o.3); Reg. 5101(1).

X. — Indians

Indians are subject to all of the responsibilities of Canadian citizens except for those governed by treaties or the *Indian Act*.[75] Thus, Indians resident in Canada are liable for taxes on their worldwide income unless they are specifically exempted from taxation.

The tax status of Indians is determined for the most part by two statutes: the *Indian Act*[76] and the *Income Tax Act*. The principal provision is section 87 of the *Indian Act*, which provides as follows:

> Notwithstanding any other Act of the Parliament of Canada or any Act of the legislature of a province ... the following property is exempt from taxation, namely:
>
> > (a) the interest of an Indian or a band in reserve or surrendered lands; and
>
> > (b) the personal property of an Indian or band situated on a reserve; and no Indian or band is subject to taxation in respect of the ownership, occupation, possession, or use of any property mentioned in paragraph (a) or (b) or is otherwise subject to taxation in respect of any such property. ...

This exemption is recognized by paragraph 81(1)(a), which exempts from taxation "an amount that is declared to be exempt from income tax by any other enactment of the Parliament of Canada." The exemption from taxation is available only if:

- The taxpayer claiming the exemption qualifies as an "Indian or a band";

- The property is either an interest in a reserve or surrendered lands or is personal property; and

- The property is *situated* on a reserve.

Subsection 90(1) of the *Indian Act* deems to be situated on a reserve:

> For the purposes of ss. 87 and 89, personal property that was
>
> > (a) purchased by Her Majesty with Indian monies or monies appropriated by Parliament for the use and benefit of Indians or bands, or
>
> > (b) given to Indians or to a band under a treaty or agreement between a band and Her Majesty,
>
> shall be deemed always to be situated on a reserve.

The exemption of Indians from taxation is rooted in Canadian political history and has no connection whatsoever with income tax policy. Section 87 of the *Indian Act* is more than sufficient authority for the exemption ("Notwithstanding any other Act of the Parliament of Canada. ..."). It does not need to be bolstered by section 81 of the *Income Tax Act*.

---

[75]*Nowegijick v. The Queen*, [1983] 1 S.C.R. 29, [1983] C.T.C. 20, 83 D.T.C. 5041 (S.C.C.).

[76]*Indian Act*, R.S.C. 1985, c. I-5.

The purposes of the exemptions from tax are to preserve the entitlement of Indians to their reserve lands and to ensure that property on their lands is not eroded through taxation or seizure.[77] The exemption is a recognition by the Crown, as expressed in the *Royal Proclamation of 1763*, that Indians should not be dispossessed of their property that they hold *qua* Indians. The exemption is intended to shield Indians from non-natives, who might otherwise be inclined to dispossess Indians of their land base and personal property on their reserves.

The exemption clearly violates the principle of horizontal equity that similarly situated taxpayers should pay similar amounts of tax. Since, however, the exemption is a provision of the *Indian Act*, we should interpret it in the context and policy of that statute, rather than in terms of tax policy. Hence, the exemption must be read in the light of Canadian history, British colonial philosophy, and the intended purposes of protection of Indian reserve lands and personal property situated on such lands.

XI. — Conclusion

The assertion of taxable jurisdiction by Canada depends upon a variety of legal, economic, international, and political concepts. Clearly, the concept of residence as the primary determinant of taxable nexus can create problems of double taxation of income. Although we use residence as the primary basis of asserting jurisdiction to tax, we elaborate the concept of residence through the Act and in bilateral tax treaties for different entities and relationships. Thus, we answer the question — who should be taxable? — in a variety of ways, depending upon the nature of the particular entity or relationship, its economic links with Canada, international trade and treaty considerations, and mindful of principles of fairness and economic efficiency.

---

[77]*Mitchell v. Peguis Indian Band*, [1990] 2 S.C.R. 85 (S.C.C.).

Selected Bibliography to Chapter 3

General

Bale, "The Basis of Taxation", in *Canadian Taxation*, Hansen, Krishna and Rendall, eds., (Toronto: Richard De Boo, 1981).

McGregor, Gwyneth, "Deemed Residence" (1974) 22 Can. Tax J. 381.

Residence — Individuals

Halpern, Jack V., "Residence or Domicile: A State of Mind" (1993) 41 Can. Tax J. 129.

Hansen, "Individual Residence", in *Proceedings of 29th Tax Conf.* 682 (Can. Tax Foundation, 1977).

Jackel, Monte A., "Canadian/U.S. Treaty: Dual Status Aliens Torn Between Two Nations" (March 1989) 47 Advocate 269.

McGregor, "Deemed Residence" (1974) 22 Can. Tax J. 381.

Morris, "Jurisdiction To Tax: An Update", in *Proceedings of 31st Tax Conf.* 414 (Can. Tax Foundation, 1979).

Sherbaniuk, D., et al., "Liability for Tax — Residence, Domicile or Citizenship?", in *Proceedings of 15th Tax Conf.* 325 (Can. Tax Foundation, 1963).

Smart, P. St.J., "Ordinarily Resident" (January 1989) 38 Int. & Comp. L. Q. 175.

Smith, "What Price Residence?" (1961) 9 Can. Tax J. 381.

Wosner, "Ordinary Residence, The Law and Practice" (1983) Br. Tax Rev. 347.

Residence — Corporations

Farnsworth, *The Residence and Domicile of Corporations* (London: Butterworth, 1939).

Flannigan, Robert, "Corporate Residence at Common Law" (1990) 5 Securities and Corporate Regulation Rev. 42.

Ilersic, "Tax Havens and Residence" (1982) 30 Can. Tax J. 52.

Kaufman, "Fiscal Residence of Corporations in Canada" (1984) 14 R.D.U.S. 511.

Lanthier, Allan R., "Corporate Immigration, Emigration and Continuance" (1993) Corp. Mgmt. Tax Conf. 4:1.

Pyrcz, "Corporate Residence" (1973) 21 Can. Tax J. 374.

Raizenne, Robert, "Corporate Residence, Immigration and Emigration", in *Special Seminar on International Tax Issues 1993* (Toronto: Carswell, 1994).

Sarna, "Federal Continued Corporations and the Deemed-Resident Provisions of subsection 250(4) of the *Income Tax Act*" (1979) McGill L.J. 111.

Ward, "Corporate Residence as a Tax Factor", *Corporate Management Tax Conf.* 3 (Can. Tax Foundation, 1961).

Residence — Trusts

Cooper, "Canadian Resident Inter Vivos Trusts with Nonresident Beneficiaries" (1982) 30 Can. Tax J. 422.
Cullity, "Non-Resident Trusts", in *Proceedings of 33rd Tax Conf.* 646 (Can. Tax Foundation, 1983).
Green, "The Residence of Trusts for Income Tax Purposes" (1973) 21 Can. Tax J. 217.

Residence — Partnerships

Witterick, Robert G., "The Partnership as a Modern Business Vehicle", in *Proceedings of 41st Tax Conf.* 21:1 (Can. Tax Foundation, 1989).

PART III: INCOME

CHAPTER 4 — WHAT IS INCOME?

"A word is not a crystal; transparent and unchanged, it is the skin of a living thought and may vary in colour and content according to the circumstances and the time in which it is used."

(Justice Holmes in *Towne v. Eisner*, 245 U.S. 418 and 425, 38 S.Ct. 158 and 159, 62 L.Ed. 372 and 376)

I. — General Comment

The income tax is a tax on income. Thus, we must distinguish income from other potential taxable bases such as capital, wealth, and consumption. The definition of income determines the size of the base and, implicitly, the structure of the tax system. Generally, income is the realized gain from a source. This raises three questions:

1. What constitutes a gain for tax purposes?

2. When do we realize a gain? and

3. What is the source of the gain?

The Act does not define the term "income". Although the Act sometimes speaks of what we include or exclude from income, it neither identifies nor describes the legal characteristics of income.[1] Thus, the initial step in determining whether a receipt is taxable as *income* is to determine its nature and character. We include a receipt in the taxable base if it constitutes income *unless*, even though of an income nature, the Act excludes it by virtue of a specific statutory provision. For example, although salary is usually taxable as income, the Governor General's salary and allowances are exempt from income.[2]

The following figure presents an overview of the Act's characterization of receipts into taxable and non-taxable components.

---

[1]For example, paragraph 6(1)(a) specifies that the value of board and lodging is included in employment income; section 7 deems certain stock option benefits to be employment income; subsection 6(9) deems imputed interest from an interest-free loan to be income, etc. See, e.g., paras. 12(1)(c) (interest), 12(1)(j) (dividends), and 12(1)(m) (benefits from trusts).

[2]Paragraph 81(1)(n).

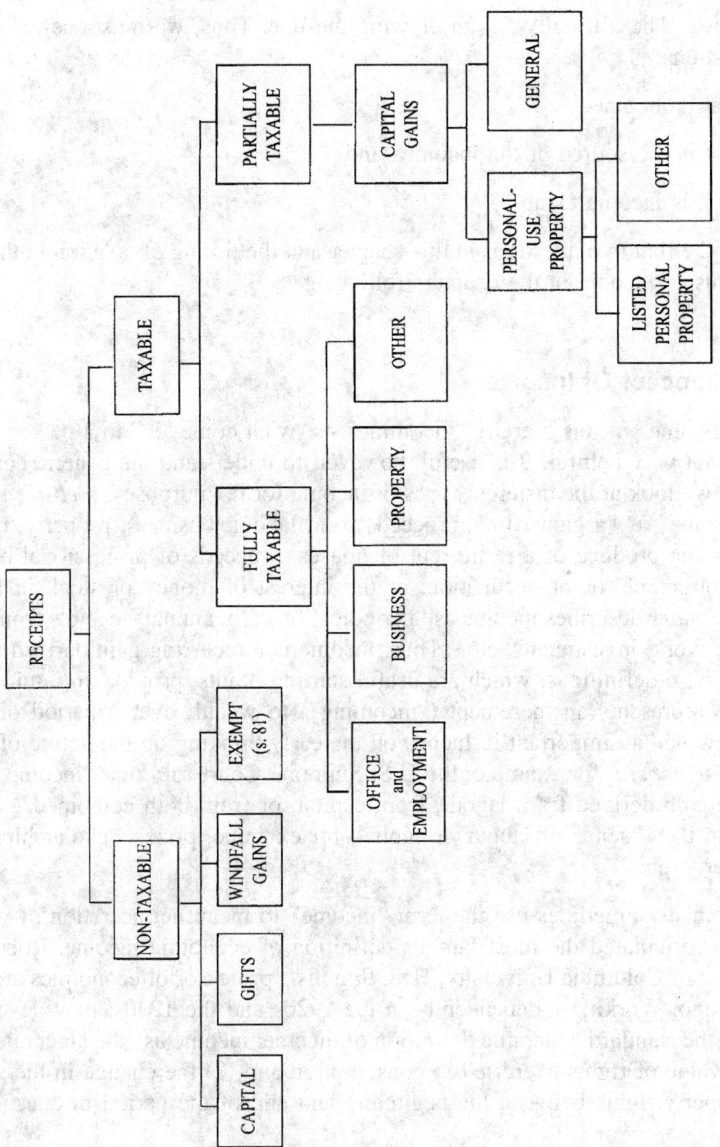

The seemingly simple task of identifying and then characterizing receipts creates considerable difficulty. For example: suppose an employer gives his or her employee $1,000 at Christmas. Is the $1,000 income or a gift to the employee? The distinction is crucial to the employee who will be subject to tax if the $1,000 is remuneration, but will not be taxable if it is a gift. We can determine taxability quite easily after we draw the line between remuner-

ation and gifts. The difficulty lies in drawing the line. Thus, we must answer three fundamental questions:

1. What is income?

2. What is the source of the income? and

3. When is income taxable?

We address the first two questions in this chapter and the timing of taxation in the context of
various forms of income in the chapters following.

II. — The Concept Of Income

The term "income" means literally "incoming" or "what comes in" to a person. This literal
meaning is not very helpful. It is useful, however, to understand the generic concept of the
term before we look at the different types of income for tax purposes. *Webster's Dictionary*
defines "income" as "a gain which proceeds from labour, business, property, or capital of
any kind, as the produce of a farm, rent of houses, proceeds of professional business, the
profits of commerce, or of occupation, or the interest of money or stock in funds." The
Oxford Dictionary describes income as "periodical (usually annual) receipts from one's business, lands, work, investments, etc." Thus, income is a recurring gain derived from labour
or capital. These definitions, which are useful starting points, provide an intuitive response
that income represents an increment ("incoming") to wealth over a period of time. This
intuitive view had an important influence on the early thinking on the nature of income. In
Eisner v. Macomber,[3] for example, the U.S. Supreme Court said that "income may be defined as the gain derived from labour, from capital, or from both combined." But what of
incomings in the absence of labour or capital, for example, prizes, scholarships, damages,
found property, etc.?

Some economists sometimes use the term "income" to mean net accretion of wealth. Two
tax theorists formulated the most famous definition of economic income. Robert M. Haig
was professor of Columbia University; H.C. Simons a professor of economics at the University of Chicago. Working independently in the 1920s and the 1930s, they developed what
has become the standard economic definition of income: income as "the algebraic sum of (1)
the market value of rights exercised in consumption and (2) the change in the value of the
store of property rights between the beginning and end of the period in question."[4] Thus,

---

[3] *Eisner v. Macomber* (1920), 252 U.S. 189.

[4] In Haig's language, income is "the increase or accretion in one's power to satisfy his wants in a given
period in so far as that power consists of (a) money itself or, (b) anything susceptible of valuation in
terms of money." Simons equates personal income with the algebraic sum of consumption and change
in net worth. See "The Concept of Income C Economic and Legal Aspects" in R.M. Haig (ed.), *The
Federal Income Tax* (New York, 1921).

Haig-Simons saw income as the accretion in the *value* of assets on hand at the end of the period over the *value* of assets on hand at the beginning of the period after adjustments for the value of goods consumed. Once again, the concept refers to the increment or "incoming" in the value of wealth over time. Using this approach, if a taxpayer begins a year with $1,000, spends $20,000 on personal expenditures during the year and has $5,000 in assets at the end of the year, his or her income for the year would be $24,000.

Two aspects of the Haig-Simons formulation of income warrant emphasis: (1) the formula does not distinguish between sources of income; and (2) net *accretion* of wealth includes all unrealized gains, imputed income[5] from owner-occupied housing, and even increases in human capital resulting from education or acquired skills. Thus, the Haig-Simons concept of income is broad, all inclusive, and without preferences.

Although the Haig-Simons formulation of income may appear bizarre to the average person, it is generally accepted as gospel among tax theorists and used extensively by economists in the development of tax policy. To be sure, the definition has politically explosive elements. Few politicians would rise to the theory that one should tax imputed income from owner-occupied housing or housework. Nevertheless, tax policymakers view the Haig-Simons formula as the ideal to which we should aspire. Hence, they see any deviation from the definition as inherently unjustifiable. Indeed, the Department of Finance publishes these deviations from the norm in its "tax expenditures" from time to time. The debate intensifies when we come to discuss the capital gains preference that taxes such gains at a lower effective rate.

There are also other definitions of "income". For example:

- R. Haig, "The Concept of Income," in *The Federal Income Tax* 1, 7 (Columbia University, 1921): "Income is the money value of the net accretion to one's economic power between two points of time."

- C. Plehn, "Income as Recurrent, Consumable Receipts," 14 Amer. Econ. Rev. 1, 5 (1924): "Income is essentially wealth available for recurrent consumption, recurrently (or periodically) received. Its three essential characteristics are: receipt, recurrence and expendability."

- W. Hewett, *The Definition of Income and its Application in Federal Taxation*, (1925), pp. 22-23: "Net individual income is the flow of commodities and services accruing to an individual through a period of time and available for disposition after deducting the necessary cost of acquisition."

- R. Posner, *Economic Analysis of Law*, (1973), pp. 231-32: "The broadest definition of income would be all pecuniary and non-pecuniary receipts, including leisure and gifts."

---

[5]We speak of imputed income as the benefit that we derive from consumption or use of our own assets.

- Professor Irving Fisher, of Yale, considered income to be "a flow of benefits during a period of time."[6]

- Professor Ely, of Wisconsin, distinguished between wealth and income:[7] "Wealth refers to the stock of goods on hand at a particular time. Real income, on the other hand, has reference to the satisfaction we derive from the use of material things or personal services during a period of time."

- Sir John Hicks, the Oxford economist and Nobel laureate, defined income as the maximum amount an individual could spend in a period and still expect to be *as well off* at the end of the period as he or she had been at the beginning.

The common feature of these definitions of income is that they are comprehensive and inclusive. The Carter Commission in its report on the Canadian tax system endorsed this comprehensive approach:[8]

> We are completely persuaded that taxes should be allocated according to the changes in the economic power of individuals and families. If a man obtains increased command over goods and services for his personal satisfaction, we do not believe it matters, from the point of view of taxation, whether he earned it through working, made it through operating a business, received it because he held property, made it by selling property, or was given it by a relative. Nor do we believe it matters whether the increased command over goods and services was in cash or in kind. Nor do we believe it matters whether the increase in economic power was expected or unexpected, whether it was a unique or recurrent event, whether the man suffered to get the increase in economic power, or it fell in his lap without effort.

However, the implementation of abstract concepts (such as benefits, utilities, and satisfactions) into a working formula that provides a simple and accurate measure of income is

---

[6]Fisher, Irving, *Elementary Principles of Economics* (New York: The MacMillan Company, 1911) at 34.

[7]Ely, *Outlines of Economics* (New York: The MacMillan Company, 1908) at 98. See also Professor Alfred Marshall, of Cambridge, *Elements of Economics of Industry* (London: MacMillan, 1901) at 51:

> . . . a woman who makes her own clothes, or a man who digs in his own garden or repairs his own house, is earning income just as would the dressmaker, gardener, or carpenter who might be hired to do the work. . . . For scientific purpose, it would be best if the word income when occurring alone should always mean total real income.

[8]*Report of the Royal Commission on Taxation* (Ottawa: Queen's Printer, 1966) (Chair: K.M. Carter), vol. 1, at 9; see also Simons, *Personal Income Taxation: The Definition of Income as a Problem of Fiscal Policy* (Chicago: University of Chicago Press, 1938).

difficult. The concept of income for tax purposes must be one that we can administer at a reasonable cost. As Professor Taussig, of Harvard, said:[9]

> . . . for almost all purposes of economic study, it is best to content ourselves with a statement, and an attempt at measurement, in terms not of utility but of money income. . . . The reason for this rejection of a principle which is in itself sound lies in the conclusion . . . regarding total utility and consumer's surplus: they cannot be measured.

The Haig-Simons formulation of income as the net accretion of wealth between two points in time would be difficult and expensive to administer. The cost, for example, of measuring the "value" of assets at the end of every fiscal year would be prohibitive. In determining whether a taxpayer is "as well off" at the end of a year as he or she was at its beginning, would one measure income in terms of "real" or nominal dollars? Even assuming that it is possible to track one's expenditures accurately for a given period, the periodic valuation of assets would present great difficulties and, in some cases, create considerable uncertainty leading to disputes and litigation.

III. — The Legal Meaning Of Income

As in economic theory, income in tax law is a measure of *gain*. This means that income does not include the realized value of the *source* of the gain itself.[10] For example, if a taxpayer buys goods at a cost of $10 per unit and sells the goods for $30 per unit, his or her income is $20 per unit. The first $10 from the sale merely recovers the capital investment in the goods. As we said earlier, the income tax is a tax on income and not on capital or wealth. *In the absence of specific statutory rules,* "income" means *net* income determined in accordance with ordinary commercial principles. In *Dominion Natural Gas,* for example:[11]

> The generally recognized rule as regards trade expenses is that a deduction is permissible when it is justifiable on business and accountancy principles, but this principle is subject to certain specific statutory provisions which prohibit the allowance of certain expenses as deductions in computing the net profit or gain to be assessed. To the extent that ordinary business and accountancy principles are not invaded by the statute, they prevail.

---

[9]Taussig, *Principles of Economics,* Vol. X (New York: The MacMillan Company, 1916) at 134.

[10]This principle underlies the oft-quoted statement that income is the fruit only and never the tree; see e.g., *Straighten's Independence v. Howbeit*, 213 U.S. 399; *Ryall v. Hoare* (1923), 8 Tax Cas. 521. This principle is modified by statutory provisions in certain circumstances; e.g., para. 12(1)(g) taxes as income any amounts paid that are calculated by reference to production, regardless of whether or not the payment actually represents an instalment of the sale price of the property.

[11]*Dominion Natural Gas Co. v. M.N.R.*, [1940-41] C.T.C. 144 at 147-48, 1 D.T.C. 499-81 at 499-83 (Ex. Ct.); revd. on facts [1940-41] C.T.C. 155, 1 D.T.C. 499-133 (S.C.C.).

Thus, even where the Act does not use the adjective "net" to qualify "income", we read the term as "net income".[12] For example, assume that an individual buys merchandise for $10 per unit and pays $1 per unit on account of freight to have the goods delivered to his or her business premises. The taxpayer then sells the goods for $30 per unit and pays shipping costs of $2 per unit. The taxpayer's *gross* revenue is $30 per unit, but his or her "income" for tax purposes is only $17 per unit, the net *accretion* to the taxpayer's wealth. The taxpayer is entitled to recover his or her capital investment of $10 and expenses of $3 in calculating his or her gain.

The legal concept of income evolves over time. In some countries the evolution is more pronounced than others. In the U.S., for example, the concept of income evolved from the narrow focus in *Eisner v. Macomber* (gains derived from labour or capital) to a more comprehensive and inclusive meaning. In *Glenshaw Glass Co.*,[13] for example, the U.S. Supreme Court held that the entire treble damage award under anti-trust laws was income even though 2/3 of the award was for punitive damages: "Here we have instances of undeniable accessions to wealth, clearly realized, and over which the taxpayers have complete dominion. The mere fact that the payments were extracted from the wrongdoers as punishment for unlawful conduct cannot detract from their character as taxable income to the recipients." As we will see later, however, the source doctrine has held back the development of the concept of income in Canada.

The concept of income for tax purposes is less comprehensive than in economic theory in two important ways: (1) the exclusion of unrealized gains; and (2) the classification of income by source.

1. — Realization

For the purposes of tax law, we recognize income only when we realize or crystallize it in a market transaction such as a sale, exchange or disposition. In contrast, the economist refers to income as an "accretion" to wealth, whether or not the increased value has been realized in a market transaction. For example, assume that an individual purchases shares at a price of $10 per share and the shares increase in value to $25 per share by the end of the year. Under the Haig-Simons concept of income, the individual's income for the year is $15 per share. This amount represents the net accretion in the *value* of the shares and, therefore, measures the increase in his or her wealth. For most tax purposes, however, the taxpayer does not report any income until he or she sells the shares and actually triggers or realizes the gain.[14]

---

[12]See Chapter 7 "The Meaning of Business Income, Investment Income, and Capital Gains".

[13]348 U.S. 426 (1955).

[14]In certain circumstances, the Act deems a disposition even where there has been none. For example, a deceased is *deemed* to have disposed of all his or her property immediately before death: subs. 70(5).

The realization requirement is a compromise between the theoretical purity of the economic concept of income and the administrative feasibility of applying the theory in practice. Taxation on the basis of annual valuations to determine the net *accretion* of one's wealth would be financially inconvenient, create uncertainty, and result in disputes over valuations. Thus, for most purposes, we are content to tax only realized gains. The realization requirement makes the income tax a tax on transactions rather than a tax on income in the economic sense. As well, the realization principle creates other problems, such as the bunching of income in the year of sale. A taxpayer who receives "bunched income" can be bumped up into a higher marginal tax bracket in the year that he or she realizes the investment. As we will see later, however, in some circumstances (for example, death) the Act deems the realization of assets in order to trigger gains and prevent prolonged tax deferral.

The realization requirement raises two issues: (1) when do we realize income? and (2) what are the consequences of not taxing income until we realize it?

Generally, we realize income when we complete a transaction. This means, when we sell or dispose of an asset[15] or complete a service. For example, if A buys shares at a cost of $1,000 and the shares appreciate in value to $3,000, A generates economic income of $2,000, the amount of the appreciation. On paper, A is $2,000 wealthier. For tax purposes, however, the gain is not taxable because he or she has not realized it. In contrast, if B purchases shares at a cost of $10,000 and the shares pay a dividend of $2,000, the dividend is taxable because B realizes it in cash. Thus, although both A and B are wealthier by $2,000, only B is taxable on his or her gain. A defers the tax until he or she disposes of the appreciated shares. The realization rule trades off equity against administrative convenience. Although both A and B are equally able to pay, taxing A on his or her unrealized appreciation would cause a cash flow problem. Of course, A could sell a portion of his or her shares to meet the tax obligations. This would work well with publicly traded shares. It might not be as easy, however, to realize their value in the absence of a public market. The problem of liquidity would be exacerbated if the asset involved was land, for example, instead of shares.

What are the consequences of the realization requirement in tax law? First, we see that the principle of realization converts the tax system from a tax on income to a tax on transactions. This affects the timing of the tax payable on the transaction. Thus, the realization requirement allows us to defer our tax liabilities and, apart from certain events such as death, we can generally control when we will recognize income from appreciated property. The value of the tax deferral depends upon the prevailing interest rate and the length of time that we delay realization. From the taxpayer's perspective, the realization requirement is an opportunity for tax planning. The requirement creates a clear incentive for taxpayers to invest

---

[15]See generally: Shaviro, "An Efficiency Analysis of Realization and Recognition Rules under the Federal Income Tax", 48 Tax L. Rev. 1 (1992); Strand, "Periodicity and Accretion Taxation: Norms and Implementation", 99 Yale L. J. 1817 (1990); Fellows, "A Comprehensive Attack on Tax Deferral", 88 Michigan Rev. 722 (1990); Shakow, "Taxation Without Realization: A Proposal for Accrual Taxation", 134 U. Pa. L. Rev. 1111 (1986).

in shares (which have a greater likelihood of capital gains that we can defer) rather than bonds that pay interest on a current and, therefore, taxable basis. Thus, the system is anything but neutral. From the treasury's perspective, tax deferral is a revenue loss. As between taxpayers who are similarly well off, the requirement allows some to delay paying taxes. The trade-off is a compromise between administrative convenience and equity.

2. — Income by Source

Economic theory is not concerned with the source of income: net accretions of wealth are income, regardless of source. Source is irrelevant as a measure of economic well-being. After all, a taxpayer's ability to pay depends not upon his or her source of income but the measure of his or her enrichment. Equity requires that we tax all gains equally, regardless of their source. The Canadian income tax system, however, rests solidly on the source concept. We calculate income from each source separately and aggregate income according to the rules applicable to that particular source.

The segregation of income by source was first conceived in the United Kingdom in *Addingtons Act*[16] in 1803: taxpayers filed separate tax returns for each source of income so that no single government official would know the total of each person's income. Thus, the source doctrine (known as the schedule system in the U.K.) was originally intended to protect the privacy of taxpayers. The source doctrine developed with a different focus in Canada, however, and its rigid structure is the cause of substantial complexity in the tax system.

There is an important difference between the English schedular system and the Canadian source doctrine. Under the English tax system,[17] a receipt is not taxable as income unless it comes within one of the named schedules, which are mutually exclusive.[18] Thus, the schedules mark the outside boundaries of the tax net.[19]

Under the *Canadian Act*, the named sources of income (office, employment, business, property and capital gains) in section 3 are not exhaustive and income can arise from *any other*

---

[16]1803 (43 Geo. III), c. 122.

[17]*Income and Corporation Taxes Act,* 1970 (Eng.), c. 10.

[18]S. 1. As Lord Radcliffe said in *Mitchell v. Ross*, [1961] 3 All E.R. 49 at 55, 40 Tax Cas. 11:

> Before you can assess a profit to tax you must be sure that you have properly identified its source or other description according to the correct Schedule; but once you have done that, it is obligatory that it should be charged, if at all, under that Schedule and strictly in accordance with the Rules that are there laid down for assessments under it. It is a necessary consequence of this conception that the sources of profit in the different Schedules are mutually exclusive.

[19]There are six schedules, some of which are subdivided into cases. Each schedule deals with a particular type of income.

unnamed source. Thus, income from *any* source inside or outside Canada is taxable.[20] This is justifiable both on the basis of the statutory language and on principle. To the extent that horizontal equity, as measured by the ability to pay, is an important objective of the tax system, all income should be taxable, regardless of its particular source. Thus, the touch-stone of income in law is realized enrichment, regardless of source.

The scope of the source doctrine, however, is far from settled. In *Fries*,[21] for example, the Supreme Court held that strike pay is not income. The Court did not, however, address the fundamental underlying question: was the strike pay not taxable because it was not "income" in the sense of realized enrichment or because it did not flow from a named "source" in section 3?

Fries juxtaposes the situation and source principles. Fries, an employee of the Saskatchewan Liquor Board and a member of the Saskatchewan Government Employees' Union ("Union"), went on strike and received strike pay equal in amount to his normal net take-home pay. The Union's strike fund was formed out of the tax-deductible dues contributed by its members. The usual "strike stipend" paid to members on strike was $10 a week. The Union's provincial executive, however, had the sole right to determine the amount to be paid. They generally authorized strike stipend payments of up to 80 per cent of gross pay. In this case, however, they authorized stipends equal to the full amount of the members' normal take-home pay. The employees of the Liquor Board voted in favour of supporting the strike, and the members knew there would be a recommendation that they would be reimbursed their full loss of pay as a result of the strike support.

The Supreme Court disposed of the appeal in a terse decision that excluded strike pay from income on the basis that the Act does not *specifically* provide for its inclusion in the taxable base:[22]

> The board need express no opinion on the principle involved — whether "strike pay" should or should not be taxable even though that principle was vigorously contested by the parties. It is only required that the Board express an opinion on whether the Act as it now stands provides for the taxation of the amount in question as well as it can be identified and described. *The Act does not provide for such taxation.* [Emphasis added.]

Thus, the Supreme Court bypassed the fundamental issue: should section 3 be read expansively on a global, or narrowly on a schedular, basis. Fries was clearly enriched by his strike pay, which derived from his (and others') deductible contributions to the union.

---

[20]*Income Tax Act*, para. 3(a) requires income "from a source inside or outside Canada" to be included in income.

[21]*Fries v. M.N.R.*, [1990] 2 S.C.R. 1322, [1990] 2 C.T.C. 439, 90 D.T.C. 6662 (S.C.C.).

[22]Adopting the decision of the Tax Review Board, *Fries v. M.N.R.*, [1983] C.T.C. 2124 at 2128, 83 D.T.C. 117 at 121 (T.R.B.).

In *Schwartz*,[23] the Supreme Court once again bypassed the opportunity to fully explore paragraph 3(a). The taxpayer, a lawyer, received damages as compensation for the cancellation of his employment contract. The taxpayer had accepted an offer of employment from a company and, as a consequence thereof, resigned his partnership in a law firm. The parties agreed that the taxpayer would start working only on completion of an interim assignment he had undertaken to perform for the government of Ontario. Before he could complete his assignment, however, the company advised the taxpayer that it would not require his services. The parties reached a settlement under which the company agreed to pay $360,000 as damages plus $40,000 on account of costs. The Supreme Court held that the damages in respect of the intended employment were not taxable as a "retiring allowance" and disposed of the case on that basis. Four of the seven judges maintained in *obiter*, however, that paragraph 3(a) should be read in an expansive manner:

> . . . when Parliament used the words "without restricting the generality of the foregoing," great care was taken to emphasize that the first step in calculating a taxpayer's "income for the year" was to determine the total of all amounts constituting income inside or outside Canada and that the enumeration that followed merely identified examples of such sources. The phrasing adopted by Parliament, in paragraph 3(a) and in the introductory part of subsection 56(1) is probably the strongest that could have been used to express the idea that income from *all* sources, enumerated or not, expressly provided for in subdivision d or not was taxable under the Act.

The *obiter* reflects the underlying policy of paragraph 3(a) and the principle of equity that equates the burden of tax with the ability to pay. We must wait to see whether the principle of horizontal equity is subsumed in the historical development of the source theory. As Major J. noted: "If paragraph 3(a) were applied literally to provide for taxation of income from any source, then again it is arguable the existing jurisprudence would be placed in jeopardy."

IV. — Recovery Of Capital

Income tax is a tax on *net* gains or the increment in realized value. The accurate measurement of gains is essential to a fair and efficient tax system. There are two aspects to the measurement of gain: (1) the recovery of basis (costs), and (2) the matching of income flows against capital.

The net gain from the sale of an asset can be straightforward or complicated, depending upon the number of assets that one holds and the time period over which one acquires the assets. In the simplest case, a gain or loss from the sale of an asset is simply the difference between its selling price and its cost or "basis". For example, where an individual buys 100 shares for $10,000 and later sells the shares for $15,000, the gain on the sale is $5,000. If the

---

[23]*Schwartz v. Canada*, [1996] 1 S.C.R. 254, [1996] 1 C.T.C. 303, 96 D.T.C. 6103 (S.C.C.).

individual also incurs $300 in selling costs, the *net* gain is $4,700. The first $10,000, that is, the cost basis of the shares, is not taxable because it represents the recovery of capital.

The situation is more complicated, however, where an individual acquires several batches of shares over a period of years and then disposes of only a part of his or her shareholding. In these circumstances, we need a method for determining the cost basis of the shares sold so as to obtain a fair and accurate measure of the taxpayer's net gain. We need rules for scheduling the recovery of the capital in the shares. The rules determine whether the taxpayer pays tax on the full amount of his or her economic net gain or on some lesser portion. Assume in the above example that the individual purchases an additional 200 shares at a cost of $30,000 before he or she sells any shares. If the taxpayer then sells 100 shares for $15,000, we must determine the cost basis of his or her shares in order to calculate the gain. There are at least four possibilities. For example, we can assume that the taxpayer sells:

1. The first batch of 100 shares;

2. Half of the second batch of 200 shares;

3. Half from the first batch (50) and half from the second batch (50); or

4. 1/3 from the first batch (33) and 2/3 from the second batch (67).

Each of these assumptions produces a different cost basis to be deducted from the amount realized and, hence, a different net income:

OPTION	COST BASIS*	SALES	NET GAIN
1	$10,000	$15,000	$5,000
2	$15,000	$15,000	NIL
3	$12,500	$15,000	$2,500
4	$13,350	$15,000	$1,650

Notes:

*   Ignoring selling expenses.

There is no absolute yardstick or logic for selecting one basis over the other for tax purposes. The only important point is that each method of cost recovery produces a different result. Each method produces a different allocation between the amount of tax currently payable and the tax deferred. The definitive accounting must wait until a final disposition (for example, on death) of the remaining 200 shares.

A second, and more subtle, aspect of cost recovery arises if we attempt to match income flows against the recovery of capital. Say that in the above example the shares yield an annual dividend of 5 per cent, or $500 on the first batch of 100 shares. Should the shareholder be taxed on the $500 on a current basis or should the shareholder be taxable only after he or she recovers the entire capital cost of the investment (say in 20 years if the dividend rate remains unchanged)? If the current annual dividend is taxable on a current basis, the full recovery of capital is delayed until the shareholder sells his or her shares in 20 years. Under the latter option, the annual dividend would reduce the basis of the capital invested in the shares until such time as it was zero. Of course, when the shares are ultimately disposed of, the net gain would be that much higher because the cost base of the shares would have been reduced to zero. If the shareholder sold his or her shares in 20 years for $40,000, the entire $40,000 would be the realized net gain. Although the ultimate nominal result under both options is the same, the timing of the net gain is significantly different. The net present value of the tax payable under the second option is considerably less than the amount payable under the first. As we will see in subsequent chapters, the Act generally prefers current basis taxation of annual income flows but, in a few rare cases, permits cost basis reduction.

	Original Cost	$10,000
YR1	Dividend received	(500)*
	Cost basis	9,500
YR2	Dividend	(500)
	Cost basis	$9,000
. . .		
	Cost basis	$500
YR20	Dividend	(500)
	Cost basis	0
	Proceeds of sale	40,000
	Capital Gain	$40,000

Notes:

*   The dividend is being used to reduce the cost basis (i.e., being treated as a recovery of capital) rather than being taxed as current income.

V. — Imputed Income

"Imputed income" refers to income that is derived from the personal use of one's own assets and from the performance of services for one's own benefit. For example, assume that Harry, a lawyer, earns $80,000 a year from his law practice. Joseph, a farmer, earns $70,000 from his farming operations and consumes $10,000 of meat and produce that he farms. It is clear that both individuals have the same ability to pay taxes. Each earns the same amount of income, albeit in different forms. Harry earns all his income in the marketplace and must buy his meat and produce in the market. Joseph earns less cash income, but has the advantage that he consumes what he grows or cultivates. Thus, Joseph enhances his economic well-being and his ability to pay by consuming his own produce. The principle of fairness suggests that, other things being equal, the two taxpayers should each pay the same amount of tax.

The Canadian income tax system does not generally impute income to a taxpayer. Consumption of personal services, home repairs, home-grown food, owner-occupied home occupancy, and the like are not taken into account in the measurement of income for tax purposes. There are several reasons for excluding imputed income from the taxable base. First, it is clear that the valuation of goods and services to be imputed would present a substantial problem for taxpayers. One would need to obtain the value of "equivalent market" transactions under comparable circumstances. It would be a nightmare for taxpayers.

Second, the nightmare for taxpayers would soon translate into an administrative nightmare for the Canada Revenue Agency (CRA). The Agency would be faced with innumerable and prolonged debates with taxpayers on the appropriate value to be used in those cases where a taxpayer disclosed the imputed value of goods and services. In many cases, it is more than likely that there would be substantial non-declaration of imputed goods and services. This would ultimately undermine the integrity and credibility of the tax system.

To be sure, the exclusion of imputed income from the taxable base offends the principle of tax neutrality and equity. The exclusion encourages taxpayers to engage in non-market transactions such as home improvements. For example, assume that Jennifer and Lorrie each own homes. Jennifer, an accountant and an accomplished carpenter, regularly does her own home repairs, thereby saving herself $6,000 each year that she would otherwise pay to a professional. In contrast, Lorrie, a hairdresser, is completely incompetent when it comes to home repairs and must pay $6,000 annually to have someone come in and do her home repairs. If both Jennifer and Lorrie also earn $50,000 cash income per year, it is clear that Jennifer has the greater ability to pay taxes. She will also be more inclined toward performing her own home repairs than working longer to earn more income in the marketplace. Lorrie, for example, must first earn her marketplace income, pay tax on that income, and use her after-tax income to pay for her home repairs. If Lorrie has a tax rate of 40 per cent, she must earn an additional $10,000 (in order to have an after-tax amount of $6,000) with which to pay for her home repairs and have the same ability to pay as Jennifer.

The clearest case of the tax advantages inherent in the exclusion of imputed income from the taxable base is home ownership. Assume that two individuals, Martha and Larry, each inherit $200,000 from their parents. Martha invests her $200,000 in a home that she occupies. Larry takes his $200,000 and purchases bonds that yield 8 per cent. Assume further that both individuals have a marginal tax rate of 50 per cent. In these circumstances, Larry earns $16,000 interest income, on which he pays tax of $8,000. He can use his after-tax income of $8,000 to rent a home or an apartment. In contrast, Martha derives the economic benefit of owner-occupancy and uses her $200,000 without any intervention from the tax system. In other words, Martha derives the benefit of pre-tax investment in her home occupancy, while Larry must pay for equivalent accommodation with after-tax dollars. Thus, the tax system clearly makes it advantageous (even ignoring considerations of potential appreciation in property values) for taxpayers to own and occupy their own homes. This bias affects decisions concerning the allocation of resources between rental housing and owner-occupied homes.

VI. — Section 3

Section 3 is the anchor of the Act and contains the basic rules for determining income for a taxation year. Unavoidably, the definition of income in the section is tautological: "The income of a taxpayer for a taxation year . . . is the taxpayer's income for the year. . . ." The section then sets out a sequence for the aggregation of the different sources of income and losses. The sequence is rigid and causes a good deal of complexity in the tax system. The inflexibility of section 3 is also the impetus for tax planning by taxpayers who seek to manoeuvre their transactions from one source of income into another.

Section 3 identifies at least six major categories for the classification of income and losses. Some of the categories (such as capital gains) are further divided into subcategories. The rules in respect of the computation of income and losses from each source are then set out neatly, but not simply, in separate subdivisions of the Act. The rigid scheme by which income and losses are segregated according to source contributes more than any other single factor to the complexity of the tax system. Taxpayers, understandably, make every effort to reclassify income from high-rate sources into income that is either tax-exempt or taxed at a lower rate. One of the basic objectives of tax planning is to convert income that is taxable at a high marginal rate into income that is either tax-exempt or taxable on a deferred basis. Thus, income conversion and tax deferral are two of the cornerstones of tax planning. The distinction between business income and capital gains, for example, has been the subject of hundreds of litigated cases because of the lower effective rate of tax on capital gains. Equally difficult, and sometimes even more subtle, is the distinction between business and investment income, which are also taxed at different rates.

The following is an overview of section 3:

Paragraph		
3(a)	Employment income	$ +
	Business and property income	+
	Other income (excluding taxable capital gains)	+
	ADD	
3(b)	Taxable capital gains	
	(including taxable *net* gains from LPP)*	+
	Exceeds:	
	Allowable capital losses	
	(other than LPP losses) in excess of allowable business investment losses	- +

	EXCEEDS	
3(c)	The remaining subdivision deductions	-
	(negative number is deemed equal to zero)	

	EXCEEDS	
3(d)	Office and employment losses	-
	Business and property losses	
	Allowable business investment losses	-

INCOME FOR THE YEAR

$

(negative number is deemed equal to zero)

Notes:

*   Listed personal property.

Each class of income in section 3 is referred to as "income from a source" and the income from each source must be calculated separately.[24] For example, employment income is a category of income separate and apart from income from business or investments, which, in turn, are different from capital gains. Different rules apply to the computation of income from each of these sources.

We determine the income from each source in the following sequence:

    1. Characterize receipts as being on account of income or capital;

    2. If income, classify the income by source;

    3. Deduct expenses applicable to each source to determine net income; and

    4. Aggregate the various sources of net income in the sequence set out in section 3.

1. — The Named Sources

The named sources of income are as follows:

- Office;

- Employment;

---

[24]Subs. 4(1). The source concept derives from the United Kingdom's tax system under which income is taxable if it falls into one of the Schedules of the *Income and Corporation Taxes Act*, 1970 (Eng.), c. 10.

- Business;

- Property; and

- Capital gains.

These sources do not constitute an exhaustive list. Apart from the named sources, section 3 states that income from *any* other source is also taxable. Thus, the section is intended to bring into income all income on a global basis if it has a source. As we saw earlier in this chapter, however, the meaning of "income" for tax purposes has been narrowly constrained by judicial decisions.

Some of the named sources of income are further divided into subsources. For example, capital gains are divided into personal use property gains, which are further subdivided into listed personal property (LPP) gains. Business investment losses are a subsource of capital losses,[25] etc. Each of these subsources of income is subject to special rules applicable only to the particular source. For example, LPP losses may be offset only against LPP gains and not against any other capital gains. The compartmentalization of income into segregated sources requires a vast number of special rules to prevent the leakage of income and losses from one source into another.

Example

The following data applies to an individual. All amounts shown are net of deductions in each category.

Employment income	$30,000
Business (No. 1) income	12,000
Business (No. 2) loss	(6,000)
Property income	6,000
Taxable capital gains (shares)	1,500
Taxable listed personal property net gain	1,500
Allowable capital losses (*including* allowable business investment losses)	(4,900)
Moving expenses	(800)
Allowable business investment losses	(4,000)

Then the individual's income for the year is as follows:

---

[25]S. 54 "listed personal property" and s. 41, paras. 39(1)(b) and (c); see Chapter 16 "Computation of Tax Payable".

Example		
Paragraph 3(a)		
Employment income		$30,000
Business income		12,000
Property income		6,000
		48,000
ADD Paragraph 3(b)		
Taxable capital gains	$1,500	
Taxable *net* LPP gain	1,500	
	3,000	
Exceeds:		
Allowable capital losses in excess of allowable business		
investment losses ($4,900 - 4,000)	(900)	2,100
		50,100
EXCEEDS Paragraph 3(c)		
Moving expenses		(800)
		49,300
EXCEEDS Paragraph 3(d)		
Business loss	$(6,000)	
Allowable business investment losses	(4,000)	(10,000)
Income for the year		$39,300

2. — Losses by Source

The characterization of losses by source is equally important. Business losses, for example, are fully deductible against any source of income; capital losses are only partially deductible from income and then only against taxable capital gains. Unused business losses may be carried forward for ten years; unused capital losses may be carried forward indefinitely.

Similarly, listed personal property losses are deductible only against gains from listed personal property and not from other types of capital gains, and so on, and on.

We have already seen that income from each source must be calculated separately. A taxpayer must compute income as though *each* source of income was his or her *only* source of income. Deductions from income are similarly limited: a deduction may be taken against a source of income only if it may be regarded as applicable to that source.[26] The following example illustrates the operation of the source doctrine.

Example			
Assume that the following data applies to three corporations:			
		Corporation	
	A	B	C
Business income	$1,000	$2,000	$6,000
Property income	(1,000)	$2,000	—
Taxable capital gains	2,000	(2,000)	(4,000)
Aggregate income	$2,000	$2,000	$2,000
Income for tax purposes is:			
Business income	$1,000	$2,000	$6,000
Property income	—	2,000	—
Taxable capital gains	2,000	—	—
	3,000	4,000	6,000
Exceeds:			
Property or business losses	(1,000)	*	*
Income for the year	$2,000	$4,000	$6,000

Notes:

*   Capital losses may only be offset against capital gains.

---

[26]Subs. 4(1).

VII. — Structure Of The Act

A person may be liable for tax under different Parts of the *Income Tax Act*. For example, residents, and non-residents who are employed or carry on a business in Canada, are taxable under Part I of the Act. Non-residents are also subject to withholding tax on certain forms of passive income (such as dividends, interest) under Part XIII of the Act. There are also special taxes imposed under Part IV on certain types of investment income and under Part II.1 on dividend-like payments. The focus of our present discussion is on Part I of the Act; the other Parts of the Act are discussed later.

A taxpayer's liability for tax under Part I is determined by reference to "taxable income".[27] We then apply the tax rate to taxable income to determine the amount of basic federal tax payable. Tax credits and surcharges are then applied to determine the net *federal* tax payable.

The general scheme for determining tax payable under Part I is as follows:

---

[27]S. 2; Part I, Division C.

TAXATION OF CANADIAN RESIDENTS
Sources of Income
(Division B)

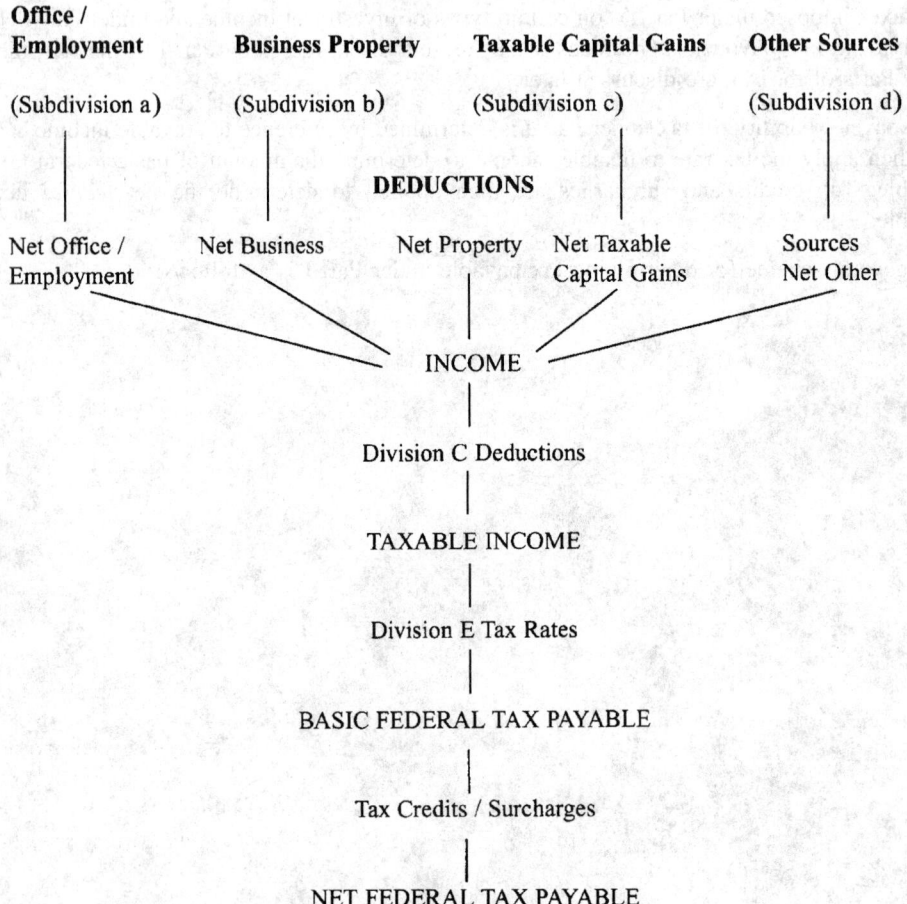

Office /
Employment   **Business Property**   **Taxable Capital Gains**   **Other Sources**

(Subdivision a)   (Subdivision b)   (Subdivision c)   (Subdivision d)

DEDUCTIONS

Net Office /   Net Business   Net Property   Net Taxable   Sources
Employment   Capital Gains   Net Other

INCOME

Division C Deductions

TAXABLE INCOME

Division E Tax Rates

BASIC FEDERAL TAX PAYABLE

Tax Credits / Surcharges

NET FEDERAL TAX PAYABLE

VIII. — Deductions vs. Credits

We said earlier that the income tax is a tax on income *net* of deductions. The amount of tax payable on net income, however, can be further reduced through tax credits, thereby reducing the overall effective rate of tax. The difference between a deduction from income and a tax credit is that a deduction has the effect of reducing income, which indirectly reduces the amount of tax payable, whereas a tax credit directly reduces the amount of tax payable without reducing income.

Example

Assume that an individual with a marginal tax rate of 50 per cent earns $100,000. The following example illustrates the effect of a $20,000 deduction from income compared to a credit of $20,000 against tax.

	Deduction from income	*Tax credit*
Income	$100,000	$100,000
Less: deduction	(20,000)	—
Taxable income	$ 80,000	$100,000
Tax at 50%	$ 40,000	$ 50,000
Tax credit	—	(20,000)
Net payable	$ 40,000	$ 30,000

The above example illustrates that a dollar of tax credit is worth more to a taxpayer than a dollar deduction from income. The reason for this is that a deduction is only worth its face value multiplied by the taxpayer's marginal rate of tax. For instance, a $100 deduction to an individual with a marginal rate of 50 per cent is worth $50 tax savings; at a marginal rate of 25 per cent, the saving is only $25. The value of a deduction increases as the marginal rate rises. In contrast, the value of a tax credit remains constant through all marginal tax rates. This distinction is important in determining the distributional effect of taxes, exemptions and credits.

IX. — Exclusions From Income

1. — General Comment

As we have seen, income for tax purposes is not synonymous with the economist's understanding of income and is a far less comprehensive measure of wealth than that contemplated in economic theory. Economists measure income by reference to the net accretion of wealth between two points in time. The tax measure of income is based on realized gains from sources and a judicial understanding of what constitutes "income", supplemented by numerous *ad hoc* statutory inclusions[28] and exclusions based upon various policy considerations.[29] As Professor Rendall said:[30]

> ... the fact is that our notions of income have been intuitive rather than logical and that our jurisprudence has developed on a case-by-case basis and has often reflected primarily a gut feeling about the characterization of a particular amount. What this means is that "income", for tax purposes, is not at all a single, consistent, concept.

Similarly, as we will see later, income for tax purposes is quite different from income for the purposes of accounting and financial statements.

The most prominent exclusions from income for tax purposes are:

- Gambling gains;
- Gifts and inheritances; and
- Windfall gains.

2. — Gambling Gains

Winnings from casual betting and incidental gambling are not considered income. Some judges have explained this exclusion on the theory that gambling is an irrational activity:[31]

> What is a bet? A bet is merely an irrational agreement that one person should pay another person something on the happening of an event. A agrees to pay B something if C's horse runs quicker than D's or if a coin comes down one side up rather than the other side up. There is no relevance at all between the event and the acquisition of property. The event does not really produce it at all. It rests, as I say, on a mere irrational agreement.

The exclusion of gambling gains from income based on the theory of irrationality is not persuasive. Games of chance are nothing more or less than payouts based on probability distributions. A horse race is hardly more irrational than the trading on commodities futures on a stock exchange. The English courts have said that such gains do not flow from a source and, hence, are not included under any of the U.K. schedules of income. This interpretation,

---

[28]See, e.g., s. 12.

[29]See, e.g., s. 81.

[30]Rendall, "Defining the Tax Base," in Hansen, Krishna, Rendall eds., *Canadian Taxation* (Toronto: DeBoo, 1981).

[31]*Per* Rowlatt, J., in *Graham v. Green (Insp. of Taxes)*, [1925] 2 K.B. 37 at 39-40; *M.N.R. v. Morden*, [1961] C.T.C. 484, 61 D.T.C. 1266 (Ex. Ct.).

however, is not helpful in the Canadian context. It ignores the statutory language of section 3, which includes income from *any* source inside or outside Canada.[32]

We can better justify the exclusion of gambling gains from income on administrative and revenue considerations. Accounting for casual betting for pleasure would impose an unreasonable burden on individuals. One can only speculate how many would voluntarily comply. Any attempt to tax such gains would result in flagrant disregard of the rule and bring the administration of tax into disrepute. Further, if losses were deductible, the net revenue gains would be minimal. Thus, we exclude gambling gains from income where the taxpayer realizes the gain in pursuit of a hobby and is not engaged in the business of gambling.[33] Similarly, losses from gambling are not deductible unless they are incurred in the conduct of a gambling *business*. The exclusion from income, however, applies only to the capital sum of the gambling gain and not to any income earned from its investment. For example, the exclusion does not extend to "cash for life" lotteries.[34]

3. — Gifts and Inheritances

Gifts and inheritances are not income for tax purposes. "Gift" is defined in *Halsbury* as follows:

> A gift *inter vivos* may be defined shortly as the transfer of any property from one person to another gratuitously while the donor is alive and not in expectation of death. . . .

Black's Law Dictionary defines a "gift" as:

> A voluntary transfer of personal property without consideration.. . .
>
> A parting by owner with property without pecuniary consideration.

The *Shorter Oxford Dictionary* defines "giving" as:

> A transfer of property in a thing, voluntarily and without any valuable consideration. . . .

A "gift" is a voluntary and gratuitous transfer of property from one person to another. It may be subject to a pre-condition, but, this apart, it is not revocable or terminable. Thus, a transfer of property qualifies as a gift only if the transfer is both voluntary and made without any expectation of reward or return. A payment that requires a *quid pro quo* is not a gift.

---

[32]See, e.g., *Rumack v. M.N.R.*, [1992] 1 C.T.C. 57 at 59, 92 D.T.C. 6142 at 6144 (F.C.A.).

[33]See, e.g., *M.N.R. v. Walker*, [1951] C.T.C. 334, 52 D.T.C. 1001 (Ex. Ct.) (gambling winnings taxable when achieved by taxpayer who himself owned and raced horses, had inside information, and could not afford to lose).

[34]*Rumack v. M.N.R.*, [1992] 1 C.T.C. 57, 92 D.T.C. 6142 (F.C.A.).

In common law, a gift is a transfer of "capital" from one person to another. A gift represents an accretion to the recipient's wealth and, as such, would be considered income in economic theory. For tax purposes, however, gifts and inheritances are not taxed as income, but are considered capital transfers.[35]

Since Canada does not have gift or inheritance taxes, gifts and inheritances are entirely free of tax. The exclusion of gifts and inheritances from the taxable base clearly impinges on the principle of fairness as measured by ability to pay.

4. — Windfall Gains

The exclusion of "windfall gains" from income is problematic. Windfall gains are clearly accretions to wealth and enhance the taxpayer's ability to pay. Windfalls are not usually capital transfers. The only unusual feature of a windfall is that it is unexpected. If the policy of the income tax is to impose similar taxes on those in similar financial circumstances, there is little merit in distinguishing between increments to wealth on the basis of their source or expectations of return.

It is also difficult to identify what constitutes a "windfall". The phrase generally implies a gain that is unexpected or unplanned and one that we cannot link to one of the named sources (office, employment, business, property, and capital gains) of income. In fact, "windfall gains" represent nothing more than an unarticulated, and irrational, bias against taxing certain types of gains. Thus, the courts say that income can arise only from *expected* returns, and "unexpected" gains are windfalls and are not taxable as income.

In *The Queen v. Cranswick*, for example:[36]

> In the absence of a special statutory definition . . . income from a source will be that which is typically earned by it or which typically flows from it as the expected return.

This harks back to the *Macomber* concept that income is the expected return from labour or capital.

---

[35]The Carter Commission proposed that, subject to a minimum exemption, gifts and inheritances should be included in the income of the recipient; see *Report of the Royal Commission on Taxation* (Ottawa: Queen's Printer, 1966) (Chair: K.M. Carter), vol. III, chapter 17.

[36]*The Queen v. Cranswick*, [1982] C.T.C. 69 at 73, 82 D.T.C. 6073 at 6076 (F.C.A.); leave to appeal to S.C.C. refused 42 N.R. 35; *Frank Beban Logging Limited v. R.*, [1998] 2 C.T.C. 2493, 98 D.T.C. 1393 (T.C.C) (*Ex gratia* payment of $800,000 by government to logging company was windfall as taxpayer did not expect the payment.) See IT-334R2 (February 21, 1992) para. 3.

A windfall gain represents an unexpected and unplanned gain that cannot be directly linked to one of the named sources of income — office, employment, business, property, and capital gains. More specifically, a windfall gain is a gain that

- Does not result from a legally enforceable claim;

- Is not expected, either specifically or customarily;

- Is not likely to recur;

- Is not customarily a source of income for the recipient of the gain;

- Is not given as consideration for services rendered, to garner favour, or anything else provided; and

- Is not earned as a result of an activity or pursuit of gain.

To summarize: a windfall gain is a gain that is unexpected, unplanned, and unrelated to any of the named sources of income.[37]

X. — Barter Transactions

A barter transaction is one in which two or more persons agree to a reciprocal exchange of goods or services without the use of money. In its simplest form, bartering is nothing more nor less than a market transaction where the medium of exchange is goods or services instead of legal tender.[38]

Payments in kind are governed by the same principles applicable to payments in cash. A payment or benefit in kind is an accretion to wealth and enhances the taxpayer's ability to pay. Payments in kind may involve bilateral or multilateral exchanges of property. For example, a lawyer who renders legal services to a farmer may accept a cow in settlement of the account. Alternatively, the lawyer may accept a non-cash credit which can be exchanged in a barter "pool" for other goods and services, e.g., the cow credit may be exchanged for

---

[37]*MacEachern v. M.N.R.*, [1977] C.T.C. 2139, 77 D.T.C. 94 (T.R.B.) (proceeds from sale of gold and silver coins found by three deep-sea divers was income from organized activity that was more than a hobby); *Bell v. The Queen*, [1992] 2 C.T.C. 260, 92 D.T.C. 6472 (F.C.A.) (lump sum payment to corporate taxpayer upon termination of exclusive distributorship agents was income); *Johnson & Johnson Inc. v. Canada*, [1994] 1 C.T.C. 244, 94 D.T.C. 6125 (F.C.A.) (unexpected refund was business income and not windfall when looked at in context); *Federal Farms Ltd. v. M.N.R.*, [1959] C.T.C. 98, 59 D.T.C. 1050 (Ex. Ct.) (voluntary payments to help taxpayer whose farm was flooded during hurricane was gift, not income); *The Queen v. Cranswick*, *ante* (majority shareholder paid minority shareholder sum to avoid controversy over reorganization; unexpected and unusual payment was windfall).

[38]IT-490, "Barter Transactions" (July 5, 1982).

plumbing services. The essence of barter transactions is that they involve a market transaction, whether bilateral or multilateral, of goods and services without the use of money.

Barter transactions raise special valuation problems. Should the payment in kind be valued on the basis of its *value in use* to the recipient or its *value in exchange* for the goods or services sold or rendered? For example, suppose a lawyer renders legal services for which he or she would usually charge $2,000 in exchange for a cow that has a market value of $1,600. How much should the lawyer include in his or her income, $2,000 (value of the services) or $1,600 (value of the exchange)? The Agency takes the view that the recipient's income is increased by the price that he or she would "normally have charged" for the goods or services provided,[39] in this example, $2,000. Where, however, the goods or services given up cannot readily be valued but the goods or services rendered can, the value of the latter can be used to set the price of the transaction.

In multilateral barter schemes with restrictions on exchange of barter credits, the value of consideration received may be considerably less than the "theoretical" value of goods and services sold or rendered. Since barter credits are a substitute medium of exchange, it is the value of the medium that should determine the price to be recognized. In effect, a taxpayer who renders services for credits that have a restricted exchange value, discounts the price normally charged for such services.[40]

XI. — Exempt Income

In addition to the exclusions from income already discussed, the Act specifically exempts certain forms of income from tax. It is important to note the distinction between a taxpayer who is exempt from tax[41] and income that is tax-exempt.[42] In the former case, the recipient is exempt from tax regardless of the nature of the income earned. In the latter case, specific types of income are exempt from tax, regardless of who receives it.

The following list illustrates some of the types of income exempt under the Act:

---

[39]*Ibid.*

[40]*Linett v. M.N.R.*, [1985] 2 C.T.C. 2037, 85 D.T.C. 416 (T.C.C.).

[41]S. 149.

[42]S. 81.

Exempt Income	Statutory Provisions	Comments
Amounts declared by any other federal statute to be exempt from income tax*	para. 81(1)(a)	
Amounts from War Savings Certificates	para. 81(1)(b)	
Income of a non-resident earned in Canada from operation of a ship or aircraft in international traffic	para. 81(1)(c)	only if the individual's country of residence grants a similar exemption
Pension, payment, allowance or compensation received under *Pension Act, Civilian War-related Benefits Act, Gallantry Awards Order* or section 9 of the *Aeronautics Act*	para. 81(1)(d)	
Payments received on account of death or disability incurred in war service from an allied country	para. 81(1)(e)	only if the country grants similar relief with respect to pensions paid in Canada
Any payments with respect to death or injury sustained in the 1917 Halifax explosion	para. 81(1)(f)	
Compensation paid by Federal Republic of Germany to victims of Nazi persecution	para. 81(1)(g)	if amount is exempt from tax by German law
Income or taxable capital gains from property or from disposition of property received as compensation for physical or mental injury	paras. 81(1)(g.1), 81(1)(g.2), 81(5)	if income or gain is earned or received before taxpayer becomes 21; taxpayer may elect deemed disposition of capital property in the year he or she attains age of 21
Receipt of income-tested social assistance payment by taxpayer on behalf of individual other than spouse, common law partner or relative	para. 81(1)(h)	if individual resides in taxpayer's principal residence
Amount for injury, disability or death under *RCMP Pension Continuation Act* or *RCMP Superannuation Act*	para. 81(1)(i)	
Certain payments from an employee profit-sharing plan	para. 81(1)(k); s. 144	

Exempt Income	Statutory Provisions	Comments
Receipts of a share of a corporation by prospector or grubstaker	para. 81(1)(l); s. 35	to extent provided by s. 35
Interest accrued, receivable or received by resident corporation on an obligation received as consideration for the disposition before June 18, 1971 of a business of a public utility or service nature	para. 81(1)(m)	if the obligation is guaranteed by the government or one of its agencies of the country where the business is carried on
Income from the office of Governor General of Canada	para. 81(1)(n)	
Amount paid to an individual as prescribed indemnity under provincial law	para. 81(1)(q); Pt. LXV. Reg. 6501	
Amounts credited to foreign retirement arrangement account	para. 81(1)(r)	
Allowances paid to an elected member of assembly for expenses incidental to the duties of office	subs. 81(2)	to extent that allowance is not more than 1/2 of the maximum of the member's salary
Allowances paid to elected officers of municipal utilities board, commission or corporation; public or separate school board for expenses incidental to the duties of office	subs. 81(3)	to extent that allowance is not more than 1/2 of the officer's salary
Amount received by a part-time employee as an allowance or reimbursement of travelling expenses incurred during a period when he had other employment or carried on a business	subs. 81(3.1)	so long as amounts are reasonable and duties are performed at least 80 kms from his or her principal place of employment or business and residence

Notes:

*   See, e.g., *Indian Act*, R.S.C. 1985, c. I-5; *Foreign Missions and International Organizations Act*, S.C. 1991, c. 41; *Visiting Forces Act*, R.S.C. 1985, c. V-2.

Sample Calculations of Income

Problem

Harry Schmidt is a Canadian resident to whom the following data applies.
INCOME:

Net salary	$ 54,000
Deductions from salary:	
CPP	(445)
EI	(648)
Income tax	(8,000)
Pension plan (registered)	(3,500)
Premiums to group health plan	(50)
Commissions from employment	7,000
Interest on bonds	5,000
Scholarships	3,500
Net rental income	12,000
Taxable capital gain on listed personal property	12,000
Allowable capital loss on listed personal property	13,000
Taxable capital gain	5,500
Allowable capital loss (incl. ABIL)	3,000
Allowable business investment loss (ABIL)	1,500

EXPENSES:

Safety deposit box fees	80
Alimony payments	6,500
Charitable donations	2,000
Tuition fees	1,500
Accounting fees for preparation of personal tax return	500
Legal fees to purchase rental property	1,500
Income tax instalments	5,000

Calculate Mr. Schmidt's income according to section 3.

Solution		
Income determined under section 3:		
para. 3(a):		
Gross salary[*]	$ 66,643	
Commissions from employment	7,000	
Less: pension contributions	(3,500)	
Net employment income		$ 70,143
Income from property:		
Net rental income	$ 12,000	
Interest on bonds	5,000	
Safety deposit box fees	(80)	
		16,920
Scholarships	$ 3,500	
Less: exempt amount	3,000	500
		87,563
para. 3(b):		
Taxable capital gain		5,500
Taxable gain on LPP	$ 12,000	
Allowable loss on LPP	(13,000)	
Net gain on LPP		0
Allowable capital loss (incl. ABIL)	$ 3,000	
Less ABIL	1,500	
		(1,500)
		91,563
para. 3(c):		
Alimony payments		(6,500)
		85,063
para. 3(d):		
Allowable business investment loss		(1,500)
Income		$ 83,563

Note: CPP and EI payments are claimed as tax credits under s. 118.7.

Notes:

* Net salary ($54,000) plus all deductions from salary (CPP, E.I., etc.) added back in.

Problem	
Assume:	
The following data applies to Alesia Ng.	2004
Employment income (gross)	$ 68,000
Registered pension plan contributions	(3,500)
Business income	15,550
Business losses	9,000
Rental income	12,500
Capital gains (gross)	3,000
Taxable listed personal property gain	5,000
Taxable listed personal property loss	7,500
Capital losses (gross) (including BIL)	13,500
Alimony expenses	5,000
Allowable business investment losses (ABIL)	2,000
Calculate Ms. Ng's income according to the section format.	

Solution		
para. 3(a):		
Employment income*	$ 64,500	
Business income	15,550	
Property income (from rental income)	12,500	
		$ 92,550
para. 3(b):		
Taxable capital gains ($3,000 x 50%)	$ 1,500	
Net LPP gains	0	
Net gains	1,500	
Allowable capital losses exceeding ABIL		
[($13,500 × 50%) less $2,000]	4,750	0
		92,550
Exceeds para. 3(c):		
Alimony expenses		(5,000)
		87,550
Exceeds para. 3(d):		
Business losses	$ 9,000	
Allowable Business Investment Losses (ABIL)	2,000	
		(11,000)
Income		$ 76,550

Notes:

*   Employment income less registered pension plan deduction of $3,500.

Problem	**Aggregation of Income Under Section 3**

Assume:

Mr. Turner has provided you with the following information in respect of his income and losses for the tax year:

Income from employment (net)	$ 35,000
Income from property (net)	10,000
Taxable capital gains	20,000
Allowable capital losses (including allowable business investment losses of $35,000)	(45,000)
Loss from business A	(30,000)
Income from business B	40,000
Taxable *net* gains on dispositions of listed personal property (LPP)	16,000
Dividends received from foreign corporations (Canadian dollars)	5,000

Mr. Turner paid fees of $15,000 for professional services to appeal his income tax return. Then, Mr. Turner's income is:

Para. 3(a):

Income from employment (net)	$ 35,000
Income from property (net)	10,000
Income from business B	40,000
Dividends from foreign corporations	5,000
	90,000

Para. 3(b):

Taxable capital gains	$ 20,000
Taxable net gains on LPP	16,000
	36,000

Problem	Aggregation of Income Under Section 3		
	Allowable capital losses minus allowable business investment losses: ($45,000-$35,000)	(10,000)	26,000
			116,000
	Para. 3(c): Legal fees		(15,000)
			101,000
	Para. 3(d): Loss from business A	$ 30,000	
	Allowable business investment losses	35,000	(65,000)
Recall: Income = 3(a) + 3(b) - 3(c) - 3(d)			
INCOME			$ 36,000

XII. — Conclusion

We have seen in this chapter that there is no categorical and definitive definition of income. The measure of income, which is central to the determination of the taxable base, has been substantially influenced by the jurisprudence. Thus, starting with a "pure" economist's concept of income as represented by the Haig-Simons formulation, we have adapted it to more closely accommodate the needs of taxpayers in daily life and commerce. For example, we modify the economic concept of income to include only realized gains and to exclude imputed income completely. The source theory, however, poses difficult questions that need to be addressed. Finally, the list of statutory exclusions in section 81 needs to be re-evaluated to ensure that the policies reflected therein are as valid today as they were when the exemptions were introduced.

Selected Bibliography to Chapter 4

General

Bittker, "Income Tax Reform in Canada: The Report of the Royal Commission on Taxation" (1968) 35 U. Chi. L. Rev. 367.

Bossons, "The Value of a Comprehensive Tax Base Reform Goal" (1970) 13 J. Law & Econ. 327.

Bruce, Neil, "Ability to Pay and Comprehensive Income Taxation: Annual or Lifetime Basis" in *The Quest for Tax Reform: The Royal Commission on Taxation Twenty Years Later* (Toronto: Carswell, 1988) at 157.

Davies, N.H., "Income-Plus-Wealth: In Search of a Better Tax Base" (Summer 1984) 15 Rutgers L. J. 849.

Haig, R.M., ed., *The Federal Income Tax* (New York, 1921).

Knecthel, Ronald C., "Role of Generally Accepted Accounting Principles in Determining Income for Tax Purposes", in *Proceedings of 31st Tax Conf.* 845 (Can. Tax Foundation, 1979).

Koppelman, Stanley A., "Personal Deductions Under an Ideal Income Tax" (1988) 43 The Tax Lawyer 679.

Perry, Harvey, "Federal Individual Income Tax: Some General Concepts" *Tax Paper No. 89* 42 (Can. Tax Foundation, 1990).

Rendall, "Defining the Tax Base", in *Canadian Taxation*, Hansen, Krishna, Rendall eds., (Toronto: De Boo, 1981).

Royal Commission on Taxation, Study No. 19B, pp. 88–157 (1957).

Simons, H.C., *Personal Income Taxation* (Chicago: The University of Chicago Press, 1938).

Stone, "A Comprehensive Income Tax Base for the U.S.?: Implications of the Report of the Royal Commission on Taxation" (1969) 22 Nat. Tax J. 24.

The Meaning of "Income"

"Accounting vs. Tax Income", in *Proceedings of 16th Tax Conf.* 350 (Can. Tax Foundation, 1962).

Ellis, J., "Aggregation of Income and Losses from Various Sources" (1981) Can. Tax. 443.

La Brie, "The Meaning of Income in the Law of Income Tax" (1953) U.T.L.J. 81.

Perry, Harvey, "Federal Individual Income Tax: Some General Concepts", *Tax Paper No. 89* 42 (Can. Tax Foundation, 1990).

Thuronyi, Victor, "The Concept of Income" (1990) 46 Tax L. Rev. 45.

Income from a Source

"Is Polanyi Taxable on his Nobel Prize Money?" (1987) 9:6 Can. Taxpayer 37.

Jones, David P., "Sources of Income", in *Proceedings of 34th Tax Conf.* 911 (Can. Tax Foundation, 1982).

Thuronyi, Victor, "The Concept of Income" (1990) 46 Tax Law Rev. 45.

Exclusions from Income

Barnett, Terry G., "Cash (and Tax?) for Life Lotteries" (1990) 38 Can. Tax J. 675.

Comment, "Taxation of Found Property and Other Windfalls" (1953) 20 U. Chi. L. Rev. 748.

Drache, A.B.C., "Gambling as a Tax Substitute" (1991) XIII Can. Taxpayer 100.

Drache, A.B.C., "Lottery Winner Taxes" (1991) XIV Can. Taxpayer 53.

Drache, A.B.C., "Tax-Free Goodies" (1991) XIV Can. Taxpayer 68.

Duff, David G., "Taxing Inherited Wealth: A Philosophical Argument" (1993) 6 Can. J. of Law and Jurisprudence 3.

Krishna, Vern, "Windfall Gains and Inducement Payments" (1986) 1 Can. Current Tax J-163.

Barter Transactions

Krishna, Vern, "Payments in Kind and Barter C Inclusion in Income C Valuation" (1985) 1:20 Can. Current Tax J-93.

Exempt Income

Drache, A.B.C., "Tax Exempt Expenses for Moonlighting Employees" (1991) XIII Can. Taxpayer 159.

CHAPTER 5 — MEASUREMENT OF INCOME

I. — General Comment

Every tax system needs a method of measuring the base upon which it imposes taxes. Sales taxes, for example, must identify taxable sales of goods and services. Usage taxes, such as highway tolls, must identify the consumer's use of the particular facility. Thus, the key to a good income tax system is the accurate measurement of the taxable base, namely, "income".

We saw in Chapter 4 that "income" is a measure of gain over a period of time. Thus, measuring income requires that we identify the amount of the gain and relate it to the appropriate period when we should recognize the gain for tax purposes. As we will see in this Chapter, both of these aspects of measurement can be uncertain processes influenced by law, economics and accounting. The measurement of income is more art than science.

Accounting is the art of measuring and presenting financial information. As such, accounting is the language of financial transactions. Users of financial information need to understand this language, regardless whether they act for business or represent interests that are adverse to business. Lawyers, for example, must deal with accounting problems in the same way they address other issues, with judgment and analysis. This means that lawyers need to understand accounting to draft financial clauses in contracts to structure negotiated settlements, for advocacy in litigation, for tax purposes, and to negotiate damage awards.

As with all languages, accounting has certain fundamental rules of structure and composition. We refer to these rules as the principles of accounting. Contrary to popular conceptions and, perhaps, most fortunately, accountants did not devise the fundamental structural rules of recording financial data. A Renaissance monk named Pacioli devised the basic process of recording financial data. This process allows us to record information in a methodical manner for analysis and decision-making. It is important to note, however, that the principles of accounting are neither rigid nor uniform. Variations in accounting principles make comparisons of financial information difficult. For present purposes, however, we confine our attention to the basic principles of Canadian accounting.

II. — Accounting Principles

A taxpayer's income for a taxation year from a business or property is his or her *profit* therefrom for the year.[1] The term "profit" means *net* profit, that is, the amount of revenue remaining after the deduction of expenses incurred for the purpose of earning the revenue.[2] Thus, we need a system of principled accounting for measuring profit.

We speak of generally accepted accounting principles ("GAAP") as the principles that underlie the preparation of financial statements for commercial use. We say "generally accepted" because various professional accounting bodies, regulatory agencies, securities commissions, and financial institutions generally accept the principles as appropriate for financial statements. In Canada, the *Canadian Institute of Chartered Accountants ("CICA")* *Handbook* is an authoritative source of GAAP. The *Canada Business Corporations Act* and regulatory statutes recognize it as the benchmark of accounting principles. GAAP, however, encompasses not only the specific recommendations and procedures set out in the *Handbook*, but also broad principles and conventions. Thus, if the *Handbook* does not cover a matter, we use other accounting principles that practitioners accept and that are consistent with the *Handbook*. These accounting principles develop over time and through usage.

When the *Handbook* does not cover a matter, accountants refer to other sources of information. For example, the CICA's Emerging Issues Committee (EIC) Abstracts, International Accounting Standards, standards promulgated by the Financial Accounting Standards Board (FASB) in the U.S., and accounting literature are useful sources. Unfortunately, these sources do not always agree on what constitutes GAAP. The *Handbook* addresses such potential differences by saying, "the relative importance of these various sources is a matter of

---

[1] Subs. 9(1).

[2] *Montreal Light, Heat & Power Consolidated v. M.N.R.*; *Montreal Coke & Mfg. Co. v. M.N.R.*, [1940-41] C.T.C. 217, 2 D.T.C. 506; affd. [1942] C.T.C. 1, 2 D.T.C. 535; affd. [1944] C.T.C. 94, 2 D.T.C. 654 (P.C.).

professional judgment in the circumstances." In practice, the order of importance of these sources is as follows:

- CICA Handbook and EIC Abstracts;
- CICA Accounting guidelines;
- Established Canadian practices;
- Recommendations of the FASB in the U.S.;
- International Accounting standards; and
- Literature.

Since GAAP represent authoritative guidelines for the preparation and presentation of financial statements for commercial purposes, we need to clearly understand their fundamental premises. These assumptions are the bedrock upon which we interpret financial information.

Net income essentially comprises two components, namely, revenue and expenses during a period of time. We calculate net profit or net income according to the formula:

$$NI = R - E$$

where:

NI = Net Income

R = Revenues

E = Expenses

All measurement of income for commercial purposes begins with this basic formula. The essence of the income statement is matching revenues and expenses over a period of time, usually one year.

The first step in the calculation of net profit is to look to accounting and commercial principles. In *Daley v. M.N.R.*, for example:[3]

> ... the first inquiry whether a particular disbursement or expense is deductible should not be whether it is excluded from deduction by [paragraph 18(1)(a) or (b)] but rather whether its

---

[3]*Daley v. M.N.R.*, [1950] C.T.C. 254 at 260, 4 D.T.C. 877 at 880 (Ex. Ct.) (fee for call to Bar not deductible expense as preceding commencement of the practice of law). See also, *The Queen v. Metropolitan Properties Co. Ltd.*, [1985] 1 C.T.C. 169, 85 D.T.C. 5128 (F.C.T.D.) (in absence of specific statutory provisions, generally accepted accounting principles applied); *Imperial Oil Ltd. v. M.N.R.*, [1947] C.T.C. 353, 3 D.T.C. 1090 (Ex. Ct.) (damages paid on negligence settlement incurred as consequence of operations by which business income earned; damages deemed deductible expenses); *Royal Trust Co. v. M.N.R.*, [1957] C.T.C. 32, 57 D.T.C. 1055 (Ex. Ct.) (club fees allowed executives to meet new clients; expenses need not be directly related to income); *M.N.R. v. Frankel*

deduction is permissible by the ordinary principles of commercial trading or accepted business and accounting practice. . . .

See also, *Dom. Taxi Cab Assn. v. M.N.R.*:[4]

> The expression "profit" is not defined in the Act. It has not a technical meaning and whether or not the sum in question constitutes profit must be determined on ordinary commercial principles unless the provisions of the *Income Tax Act* require a departure from such principles.

III. — Accounting Concepts

Three basic concepts underlie the preparation and interpretation of financial statements: (1) historical cost accounting, (2) stable dollar value, and the (3) going concern assumption. As we will see in subsequent chapters, these concepts also determine tax results.

1. — Historical Cost Accounting

We prepare financial statements using historical and original costs to record transactions. Thus, except for the date when we acquire an asset, its cost does not represent the price for which we can replace (replacement cost) or sell it (fair market value). For this reason, historical cost statements, which trade-off relevance for reliability, are of limited value and we use them with caution.

Although accountants generally report assets at either historical or depreciated cost, they adjust some assets, such as temporary investments, for upward and downward swings in market values. In other cases, such as inventories, we write down assets when their historical cost exceeds their realizable or fair market values. The theory underlying such adjustments

---

Corp. Ltd., [1958] C.T.C. 314, 58 D.T.C. 1173 (Ex. Ct.) (sale of capital assets of one of four of taxpayer's businesses not taxable as inventory sales but, oddly, taxable as deemed receipt because of diversion tactics); *C.G.E. Co. v. M.N.R.* (1961), [1962] S.C.R. 3, [1961] C.T.C. 512, 61 D.T.C. 1300 (S.C.C.) (debts decreased due to change in foreign exchange rate; profit apportioned amongst tax years rather than upon actual payment of note); *M.N.R. v. Irwin*, [1964] S.C.R. 662, [1964] C.T.C. 362, 64 D.T.C. 5227 (S.C.C.) (concept of profit for tax purposes clarified); *Quemont Mining Corp. v. M.N.R.*, [1966] C.T.C. 570, 66 D.T.C. 5376 (Ex. Ct.) (disagreement in formula used to calculate mining taxes paid to province); *M.N.R. v. Atlantic Engine Rebuilders Ltd.*, [1967] S.C.R. 477, [1967] C.T.C. 230, 67 D.T.C. 5155 (S.C.C.) (valuation of inventory consistent and coincidentally correct though original basis of evaluation flawed); *Sherritt Gordon Mines Ltd. v. M.N.R.*, [1968] C.T.C. 262, 68 D.T.C. 5180 (Ex. Ct.) (generally accepted business and commercial principles used in respect of capitalization of interest expenses during construction period).

[4]*Dom. Taxi Cab Assn. v. M.N.R.*, [1954] S.C.R. 82, [1954] C.T.C. 34 at 37, 54 D.T.C. 1020 at 1021 (S.C.C.).

is that we expect to realize (sell) inventories in the current term and, therefore, their market value is more relevant than historical cost.

2. — *Stable Dollar Value*

GAAP treats the dollar as a stable unit of measure. Therefore, if a company owns land that it purchased in 1970 for $25,000 and in 2002 it purchased an identical adjacent tract for $500,000, the lands will appear as $525,000 on the balance sheet. This completely overlooks the fact that during the 32-year period the purchasing power of the dollar has substantially declined. Similarly, if the company sold the first plot of land in 2000 for $500,000, we would record a gain of $475,000 on the income statement, even if the $500,000 has no more purchasing power than the $25,000 in 1970. In other words, historical balance sheet values can be meaningless and we need to evaluate them with care. The rationale for continuing to use a constant dollar as a unit of measure is that historical costs are objective. In contrast, financial statements adjusted for changes in purchasing power require subjective judgments in their preparation. This compromises their reliability. Thus, the balance sheet trades off relevance for reliability.

3. — *The Going Concern Assumption*

The going concern assumption means that the entity expects to continue in operation into the indefinite future and, therefore, will realize its assets and discharge its liabilities in the normal course of business. The entity will continue as a "going concern" into the indefinite future. This assumption supports the historical cost basis of accounting. The business can reasonably expect to recoup the cost of its assets during the course of their useful life. If the assumption is not valid, some other model of accounting, for example, the liquidation basis, may be more appropriate. Thus, the basis of valuing assets (historical cost or liquidation value) on the balance sheet must be consistent with expectations for the entity.

IV. — **Accounting Principles And Tax Law**

Having determined the appropriate treatment of a receipt or expenditure according to commercial and accounting practice, the next step is to determine whether the Act or case law prescribes a different treatment for tax purposes. The Minister cannot insist on a taxpayer using a specific method of paying income taxes if the method the taxpayer uses is permissible under well-accepted business principles and is not prohibited by the Act or by some specific rule of law.[5] Although accounting principles are a guide to interpreting tax law, they cannot be used where the Act prescribes otherwise.[6]

Where the Act specifically prohibits the deduction of an expenditure, the statute obviously prevails over commercial and accounting principles and the expenditure is not deductible in computing profit. For example, under generally accepted accounting principles, a taxpayer may deduct depreciation as an expense in calculating income. Depreciation is the allocation of the historical cost of an asset over its useful life. However, since the Act, specifically prohibits the deduction of depreciation, any depreciation calculated for financial statement purposes is not deductible as an expense for tax purposes.[7] Thus, for tax purposes, we add back depreciation to financial net income. As we will see later, the Act allows a taxpayer an alternative deduction to allocate asset costs over their useful life. We refer to this deduction as capital cost allowance.

Similarly, case law may also prohibit the use of a particular method of calculating income that is otherwise acceptable in commercial practice. For example, although the last-in, first-out (LIFO) method of valuing inventory is generally acceptable for financial statement purposes, we cannot use LIFO to calculate income for tax purposes.[8]

The Act can, however, also specifically override a general prohibition against the deduction of a type of an expenditure.[9] For example, interest payable on indebtedness would be a non-deductible payment on account of capital[10] were it not for paragraph 20(1)(c), which specifically allows for its deduction in computing income from a business or property. This simply reflects the rule of statutory construction that a specific rule prevails over a general rule.

[5]*Canderel Ltd. v. Canada*, [1998] 1 S.C.R. 147, [1998] 2 C.T.C. 35, 98 D.T.C. 6100 (S.C.C.).

[6]*The Queen v. Consumers' Gas Co. Ltd.*, [1987] 1 C.T.C. 79, 87 D.T.C. 5008 (F.C.A.).

[7]Para. 18(1)(b).

[8]*M.N.R. v. Anaconda Amer. Brass Ltd.*, [1955] C.T.C. 311, 55 D.T.C. 1220 (P.C.).

[9]See, e.g., the general prohibitions in paras. 18(1)(a) (expenditure must be incurred for the purpose of earning income), 18(1)(b) (expenditure cannot be on account of capital), 18(1)(h) (expenditure cannot be on account of personal or living expenses).

[10]*Can. Safeway Ltd. v. M.N.R.*, [1957] S.C.R. 717, [1957] C.T.C. 335, 57 D.T.C. 1239 (S.C.C.) (use of borrowed money important in characterization of interest expense as business or property; acquisition of shares of subsidiary complicated issue); *Interprovincial Pipeline Co. v. M.N.R.*, [1967] C.T.C. 180, 67 D.T.C. 5125 (Ex. Ct.); affd. [1968] S.C.R. 498, [1968] C.T.C. 156, 68 D.T.C. 5093 (S.C.C.) (tax loophole in treaty cured; incidental interest earned deducted from interest expense to determine loss); *Sherritt Gordon Mines Ltd. v. M.N.R.*, ante.

V. — Measurement And Timing

Measurement and timing of income are actually two different concepts. There is, however, an inextricable relationship between the concepts. For example, suppose a business started up in 1900 and closed down in 2004. There might be a number of difficulties involved in measuring the aggregate income of the enterprise over the 104 years. If all we need to know is the net income figure for the 104 years, there is no issue of timing. Serious problems of timing arise, however, if we need to measure income for 2004 only. Then, we need to match 2004 revenues and expenses. Thus, we need to know when we earn revenues, when we recognize the revenues in our financial statements, and the principles of matching of revenues and expenses.

We can illustrate these problems by examining the accounting concepts of "realization", "recognition", "accrual", "matching", and "conservatism".

1. — Realization

As noted earlier, the measurement of income requires one to calculate gain and relate it to the appropriate time period. Generally, we measure gain at the point of its realization.

A simple definition of "realization" would refer to the point of sale, the time at which X parts with property and receives a real gain in the form of cash. The following examples illustrate the inadequacy of this simple definition. If X sells Black Acre and takes back a mortgage, X realizes a gain that should be recognized for tax purposes. Similarly, we treat an exchange of Black Acre for White Acre, a property of equal value, or for stock in Black Acre Developments Ltd., as a realization. Even if X gives Black Acre away, he or she will realize a gain. In all these cases the rationale is the same: X has parted with his or her investment in Black Acre, and for tax purposes, we treat X as though he or she sold the property for cash.

There is a fundamental question, however, as to *when* we "realize" a gain or loss. Suppose, for example that X buys Black Acre for $50,000. By the end of the year the property is worth $60,000. Does X experience a $10,000 gain? Certainly he or she has a potential gain, a "paper gain", an accrued gain in the Haig-Simons sense. Traditional accounting practice, however, ignores the gain as unrealized.

In the following year, X's property might decline in value to $45,000 or might rise to $70,000. Suppose, in either case, that X then sells the property. According to traditional practice, X is treated as "realizing" a $5,000 loss or a $20,000 gain in the year that the property is sold. In the first case, the $5,000 loss represents a $10,000 paper gain in Year 1 combined with a paper loss of $15,000 in Year 2. In the second case, X had a paper gain of $10,000 in each of the years 1 and 2.

2. — Recognition

The second aspect of measurement is to identify the appropriate period in which we wish to recognize the gain for tax purposes. "Recognition" is the taking into account of an amount in computing income under the Act. Some accounting systems would recognize all the "paper" gains and losses in a year even though they are "unrealized". For the most part, however, the Act does not recognize "unrealized" amounts for tax purposes.

There are good reasons for not recognizing paper gains. Accountants, true to the axiom of their conservatism in estimating income, normally disregard such gains because they may prove illusory if values decline in a subsequent period. From the perspective of a taxpayer, the recognition of unrealized gains could prove a hardship. If X were required to recognize a $10,000 paper gain on Black Acre, and to pay tax on it, X would be required to find the money to pay the tax at the end of Year 1. Attempts in the past to tax unrealized gains on certain corporate shares met with considerable taxpayer resistance and only limited success.[11]

On the other hand, the failure to recognize paper gains, and recognition of the entire gain at the point of realization, gives rise to problems of irregularity and "lumping" of income. Delayed realization also allows taxpayers to defer and, therefore, save tax.

There are some cases in which the Act recognizes unrealized gains. For example, the Act deems a taxpayer who ceases to be a Canadian resident to have disposed of any capital property and realized any accrued gain or loss for tax purposes. In other situations, the Act does not recognize a gain even though it has been realized through an actual disposition. For example, the Act does not recognize realized gains when a person transfers appreciated capital property to his or her spouse. These exceptions reflect other policy considerations in the tax system that override the accurate measurement of income.

Accountants are not as reluctant to recognize unrealized losses as they are to recognize unrealized gains. Consistent with accounting conservatism in estimating income, and depending upon the nature of the asset concerned, it is sometimes considered good accounting practice to recognize a "paper" loss. Understandably, the revenue authorities usually do not agree that this conservatism should be applied to calculations of income for tax purposes. To forestall the possibility of complete accounting doom and gloom in such matters, the Act does not recognize most paper losses for tax purposes.

We have explored, in a very simple way, the concept of realization of gain. There remains a number of slightly more sophisticated problems concerning the time when gains should be recognized.

---

[11]*Proposals for Tax Reform* (Ottawa: Finance Canada, 1969), ss. 1.30 and 3.36.

Suppose that X starts a business of manufacturing and selling widgets. The business cycle can be broken down into the following steps:

1. Acquisition of inventory of raw metal;

2. Fabrication of metal into an inventory of widgets;

3. Sales activity that results in orders for widgets;

4. Delivery of widgets to customers;

5. Invoicing of customers; and

6. Payment of invoices.

An argument could be made for choosing any one of the last five steps as the point at which X's gain should be recognized for the purposes of calculating income. Our earlier discussion would probably suggest that the gain should not be recognized at any point before step 4. Standard accounting would lead to a choice of step 5 as the point at which X should recognize a gain. In any event, as a matter of usual business practice, steps 4 and 5 are merged. Commonly, the invoice accompanies the delivery of widgets. As we shall see below, if X's business adopts a cash basis of accounting, the gain will not be recognized until step 6, when the business actually receives payment.

One of the most important areas of income measurement is revenue recognition. Revenues derive from the sale of products, fees for services, and the use of intellectual property. Thus, the timing of revenues is the first decision in the measurement process. For accounting purposes, we generally recognize revenues at the point when the earning process is substantially complete. The earning process is substantially complete when we pass title to the product to the purchaser, or when we complete the service. At this point, we have sufficient information to measure revenues objectively. The important point to observe here is that revenue does not necessarily relate in the earnings cycle to when we receive cash for the product or service. For example, if a company sells merchandise on credit (payable in 30 days), we recognize the full sales value when we ship the goods to the customer. The fact that the cash may not come in for 30 days or later does not matter. Indeed, in some cases, the customer might even pay in advance for the purchase of the goods. Nevertheless, we recognize revenues only when we ship the goods and title passes from the company to its customer. Until then, we consider the advance to be a debt owing to the customer. At the point of sale, we transform the debt into revenues.

To be sure, this principle of recognizing revenues at the time of sale and shipment does not make a great deal of difference in most cases, except at the end of the accounting cycle. For example, it matters little to a company with a December 31 year-end whether it takes its revenue for July sales into account in July, August, or September when it collects its cash from sales. Since all of the revenue falls in the same accounting period, it matters little for measurement purposes so long as the revenue falls in the current year. The principle, however, is critical at the year-end. It makes a great deal of difference whether revenues from sales for merchandise shipped out in mid-December are taken into the current year's income or in the income of the year following. In this case, the timing of revenues affects the company's bottom-line profit for commercial purposes. Of course, it also affects the company's net income for tax purposes and, therefore, the amount of tax payable in the current year. Thus, we need to match revenues and related expenses in the same period.

3. — Accrual

The principles of accrual accounting are central to the matching of revenues and expenses. Accrual accounting requires that we recognize revenues in the period to which they relate, rather than when we collect the cash. Similarly, we recognize expenses in the period when we incur the expense, rather than when we pay for it. For example, assume we purchase merchandise on December 20 of the current year and pay for it on January 10 of the following year. Accrual accounting requires us to recognize the purchase in the current year, even though we did not pay for it until the following year.

As we will see, recognizing expenses in the appropriate period depends upon the nature of the expense. We recognize time-related expenses such as salaries and wages, utilities, interest, etc. at the end of the accounting period to which they relate. This is so even though we have not paid the expenses. Again, this may not make a great deal of difference to expenses we incur in the middle of an accounting period, but it can be important in terms of year-end accounting. Here also, accounting principles do not rely upon the outgoing of cash to determine when we take the expenditure into account in the financial books. The essential concept is matching the expense with revenues in the period in which we derive the benefit of the expense to earn the revenues.

4. — Matching

So far we have been discussing the appropriate time to recognize gains and losses. In an accounting sense, gains and losses are measured by reflecting expenditures and receipts. "Gains" or "losses" in themselves are net concepts, as is the "income" of a business, since it reflects all expenditures and all receipts.

Accrual and matching are related. The matching principle requires us to deduct expenses (E) in the same period as they contribute to the earning of revenues (R). Hence, if we incur expenses in one time period but the expenses will benefit several periods, we allocate the expense in some reasonable manner between the various periods. This principle lies at the core of the income equation. In other words, the "R" and "E" in the formula must match each other. The "E" must track the "R" so that both match for accounting purposes. For example, assume that a company orders and receives merchandise on December 15, 2004. We allocate the cost of the merchandise to 2004 or beyond depending upon when we sell the goods and pass title. Hence, if we sell the merchandise and recognize revenues in 2004, we also recognize the expenses (cost of goods sold) of the sale in the same year. If, however, the merchandise remains on hand as inventory, we recognize the cost as an asset in the current year. We then recognize the expense when we sell the merchandise in the following year. Thus, expenses are merely consumed assets.

Matching is essentially an allocation process between time periods. We recognize expenses that benefit the current time period in that period. Expenses that will benefit future time periods are "held" in asset accounts. We recognize them in subsequent time periods when we match them against revenues.

Mismatching of revenues and expenses distorts the net income figure and can seriously mislead users of financial statements. Of course, for tax purposes, mismatching leads to tax deferral if we delay recognizing revenues or accelerate recognizing expenses. From a tax perspective, the most extreme scenario is one where the taxpayer delays recognizing revenues and concurrently accelerates the time when he or she charges off the expenses. This might occur, for example, if the taxpayer receives a lump sum for two years' rental that he or she does not recognize until the second year, but recognizes the rental expenses in the first year. Such mismatching would be wrong both for accounting and tax purposes.

The following example illustrates the resolution of the problem of matching.

Assume that City Dairy Ltd. delivers milk door to door and for this purpose requires 100 trucks costing $6,000 each. The trucks will have a useful life of approximately five years and will be disposed of for $1,000 each at the end of that time. Thus, over the course of five years, each truck represents a $5,000 expense of City Dairy's business. If, however, City Dairy bought and expensed 100 trucks in its first business year, it would dramatically distort its income for the year by recognizing the entire cost of $600,000 as an expenditure for that year. This particular problem is resolved by applying the notion of "depreciation" in order to spread the cost that arises from exhaustion of such assets over an appropriate number of years.

Although "matching" is a well-accepted business principle, it is simply an interpretive aid that assists, but is not determinative, in arriving at an accurate picture of the taxpayer's income.[12] We do not need to match if an expenditure does not directly relate to future revenues, or if it relates to future revenues but also refers to benefits realized in the year of expenditure.

---

[12]*Canderel Ltd. v. Canada*, [1998] 1 S.C.R. 147, [1998] 2 C.T.C. 35, 98 D.T.C. 6100 (S.C.C.) (tenant inducement payment paid to secure 10 year lease from key tenant deductible entirely in year paid rather than over the period of the lease since sufficient benefit (preserved reputation, ensured future income stream, satisfied interim financing requirements) realized in first year to match expense); *Ikea Ltd. v. Canada*, [1998] 1 S.C.R. 196, [1998] 2 C.T.C. 61, 98 D.T.C. 6092 (S.C.C.) (tenant inducement payment received for signing a 10 year lease taxable as income entirely in year received); *Toronto College Park Ltd. v. Canada*, [1998] 1 S.C.R. 183, [1998] 2 C.T.C. 78, 98 D.T.C. 6088 (S.C.C.) (tenant inducement payment paid to secure lease deductible entirely in year made since amortization over period of lease would not present a more accurate picture of income).

5. — Conservatism

Conservatism is attitude. Conservatism refers to the accounting profession's approach to measuring profits. Measuring income means allocating costs and values to time periods and then matching revenues and expenses in the periods. Since we do not always know how much to allocate with absolute certainty, measuring profits requires professional judgment. Conservatism requires a cautious approach in allocating values and recognizing revenues and losses. In effect, conservatism means that an enterprise should not recognize revenues before earning them, but should recognize all anticipated losses even before they actually occur. Some call this a pessimistic approach, others say it is merely being prudent. Regardless of the label, conservatism implies caution and prudence. Recognize no gains in advance of realization but recognize all losses at the earliest signal of trouble.

Conservatism and matching can conflict. For example, should we write off research and development costs over time to match revenues through increased sales? The matching principle requires that we recognize research and development as capital costs that we allocate over time as the new products generate revenues. The concept of conservatism, however, dictates prudence. Should we recognize the research expenditures as early as possible without waiting for future revenues that might never materialize? Thus, measuring profit according to accounting principles is fraught with judgment calls that can materially affect an enterprise's bottom line. Indeed, it is entirely possible for two accountants to look at the same set of numbers and arrive at completely different conclusions on net income. Those responsible for the development of tax policy are fully aware of the variances that occur from discretionary judgments. Thus, we see many provisions in the Act that provide for a particular and specific method of measuring profit, regardless of accounting principles. In almost all cases, the Act prescribes a method of measuring profit that is more onerous than that allowed under accounting principles. This is understandable. Given a choice, why would the tax collector prescribe a method of accounting that produces a better result for the taxpayer?

VI. — Accounting Statements

Financial statements provide information about an economic entity's financial performance, economic resources and legal obligations to investors, creditors, management, tax authorities, and other regulators. Thus, we can use financial statements to assess management's performance, predict the entity's ability to generate future cash flows to meet obligations, assess the return to shareholders, and measure tax liabilities.

Accountants prepare four different financial statements:

- The Balance Sheet;
- The Income Statement;
- The Statement of Retained Earnings; and
- The Statement of Changes in Financial Position.

The explanatory notes to financial statements are also an integral part of the statements.

The two most common accounting statements for tax purposes are the balance sheet and the income statement (sometimes called a statement of profit and loss).

A balance sheet reflects, *as at a particular date*, the condition of the business as it may be judged by a statement of what the business owns (assets) and a statement of its obligations (liabilities).

The liabilities side of the balance sheet is divided into two parts: (1) a statement of indebtedness to outsiders, and (2) a statement of the owner's equity. All business financing must come from two sources — capital and debt. The owner may make an initial contribution of capital to the business and the business may borrow money from a bank or purchase goods on credit. The traditional balance sheet equation:

$$A = L + E$$

(assets = liabilities + owner's equity)

is true because owner's equity is a constantly shifting amount that represents the difference between assets and liabilities. Whatever the owner of the business may in fact have contributed, that owner's equity at any time is simply this difference:

$$E = A - L$$

A business is a distinct entity for accounting purposes. This is so regardless of its legal status. City Dairy Ltd., for example, is both an accounting entity and a legal entity separate from its incorporators. Assuming that X Widgets is a sole proprietorship carried on by X, it is not a distinct entity in law. It is, however, in terms of accounting treatment.

An income statement is a summary of the receipts and expenditures of a business *for a stated period of time*.

The two statements, the balance sheet and the income statement, are closely inter-related and must be read together in order to present a complete and meaningful picture of the profitability and solvency of a business.

As an illustration, assume that A and B opened a retail business on January 1, Year 1 with each person contributing $2,500, and a bank loan of $10,000. The opening balance sheet *as at* January 1, Year 1, would appear as follows:

```
                        BALANCE SHEET
                     As at January 1, Year 1

ASSETS                                  LIABILITIES and EQUITY
Cash                      $  15,000     Bank loan                $  10,000
                                        Owner's equity:
                                            Capital A               2,500
                                            Capital B               2,500
                          $  15,000                              $  15,000
```

The first point to observe is that the balance sheet balances: the left side of the statement that lists all the property owned by the business is *exactly equal* to the right side of the statement that lists its sources of financing. In other words, the left side of the statement informs the reader as to *what* the business owns (assets), and the right side discloses *how* the assets were financed (liabilities and equity). Hence, the above balance sheet informs any reader without further explanation of the statement that the business entity (the retail business) owned $15,000 of property (assets) as at January 1, Year 1, and that it held it in the form of cash. Further, it informs the reader that the firm was financed from two sources, one external (bank loan $10,000) and the other internal (owner's equity $5,000).

The following transactions illustrate the operation of the fundamental accounting equation A = L + E:

```
On January 2, Year 1, the business leased office space at an annual rent of $6,000
and pays two months' rent on that date.

                        BALANCE SHEET
                     As at January 2, Year 1

ASSETS                                  LIABILITIES and EQUITY
Cash                      $  14,000     Bank loan                $  10,000
Pre-paid rent                 1,000     Owner's equity:
                                            Capital A               2,500
                                            Capital B               2,500
                          $  15,000                              $  15,000
```

On January 4, Year 1, the business acquired office furniture at a cost of $3,000, paying $1,500 in cash with a promise to pay the balance in 90 days.

BALANCE SHEET
As at January 4, Year 1

ASSETS		LIABILITIES and EQUITY	
Cash	$ 12,500	Accounts payable	$ 1,500
Pre-paid rent	1,000	Bank loan	10,000
Office furniture	3,000	Owner's equity:	
		Capital A	2,500
		Capital B	2,500
	$ 16,500		$ 16,500

On January 15, Year 1, the business hired two employees at a monthly salary of $1,000 each, and paid their salaries on January 31, Year 1.

BALANCE SHEET
As at January 31, Year 1

ASSETS		LIABILITIES and EQUITY	
Cash	$ 11,500	Accounts payable	$ 1,500
Pre-paid rent	500	Bank loan	10,000
Office furniture	3,000	Owner's equity:	
		Capital A	1,750
		Capital B	1,750
	$ 15,000		$ 15,000

During the month of February Year 1, the business sold merchandise and collected $6,000 in cash, again paying its staff $2,000 in salary.

BALANCE SHEET

As at February 28, Year 1

ASSETS		LIABILITIES and EQUITY	
Cash	$ 15,500	Accounts payable	$ 1,500
Office furniture	3,000	Bank loan	10,000
		Owner's equity:	
		Capital A	3,500
		Capital B	3,500
	$ 18,500		$ 18,500

Each of the transactions described has been recorded using the fundamental equation: A = L + E. The reader sees that the business owns property (assets) that cost $18,500, now held in two forms, cash and office furniture, and that the firm is financed, as at February 28, Year 1, by outsiders to the extent of $11,500, with insiders (owner's equity) providing the balance of $7,000. The balance sheet does not, however, disclose any information as to *how* and *why* the owners' interest in the business increased from $5,000 to $7,000 during the two months of operations. Based on the balance sheet alone it would be difficult, if not impossible, for any user to assess the profitability of the business.

Should the owners, A and B, be required to pay income tax on the increase in their equity of $2,000, or on some other amount? We find the answer only in the income statement. The purpose of the income statement is to disclose *how* a business has performed between two successive points in time. In this sense, it is a connecting link between successive balance sheets. Whereas a balance sheet informs a reader *where* a business stands as at a given time, an income statement reveals *how* the business moved from the opening balance sheet to the closing balance sheet.

Continuing with the previous illustration, the income statement reveals the following information:

INCOME STATEMENT

For the *Two Months* ended February 28, Year 1

SALES REVENUE		$ 6,000
EXPENSES		
Wages	$ 3,000	
Rent	1,000	
NET INCOME:		(4,000)
		$ 2,000

ALLOCATION OF NET INCOME

To A at 50% of $2,000 = $1,000

To B at 50% of $2,000 = $1,000

This statement now informs the reader *how* the owner's equity increased by $2,000. Specifically, the business generated revenues of $6,000 and expended $4,000 in the process of generating those revenues, leaving an excess of revenues over expenses (net income) of $2,000. Thus, the purpose of the income statement is to match revenues earned with expenses incurred to generate the revenue. The statement can usually explain the change in the owners' equity between successive points in time. Accounting principles and conventions deal with the methodology behind the task of matching revenues and expenses.

The net income figure derived from the matching process provides a starting point in calculating a taxpayer's income tax liability. One observes this starting point in subsection 9(1) of the *Income Tax Act*: ". . . a taxpayer's income for a taxation year from a business or property is the taxpayer's *profit* from that business or property for that year." The terms "income" and "profit" are often used interchangeably, and it is now well established that in the absence of specific statutory provisions or judicial doctrine, "profit" is to be computed in accordance with commercial principles.

VII. — Accounting Methods

To this point, the term "income" has been used to denote the excess of revenues earned over expenses incurred to generate those revenues. Hence, in one sense income is an increase in net wealth; conversely, a loss is a decrease in net wealth. This definition is terse and obvious but mathematically demonstrable. The essence of the concept is thereby reduced to "gain during an interval of time". Thus, "gain" is the *sine qua non* of income. While this definition satisfies the purpose of conceptual explanation, it is necessary to adapt it for use in the preparation of financial statements.

1. — Time Intervals

As a preliminary matter, it is essential to select the appropriate "interval of time" between successive financial statements. For no other reason than that of administrative convenience, it has been conventionally established that financial statements should be prepared on an annual basis. Thus, annual financial statements for external reporting and tax purposes are now, with limited exceptions, the general statutory rule. It is this statutory requirement of annual reporting that gives rise to several income measurement problems.

2. — Cash vs. Accrual Accounting

The first of these measurement problems is to determine whether financial statements should be prepared on a "cash basis" or on an "accrual basis". The principal distinction between the cash and accrual methods of accounting arises in connection with the treatment of accounts receivable and payable. Accounts receivable from customers and employers are not included in income under the cash method until the taxpayer is actually paid. In contrast, accrual method taxpayers must report their income when services are completed and billed, regardless of when the customer actually pays the account. Thus, the distinction between the two is essentially one of timing.

In cash basis accounting, business transactions are recorded at the time, and in the accounting period, when cash is received or disbursed. Assuming an accounting period of January 1 to December 31 and the sale of merchandise on December 15, YEAR 1 for $3,000 with payment received on January 15, YEAR 2, a cash basis business would record and report the $3,000 revenue earned in YEAR 2. Further assume that the cost of the merchandise to the business was $1,000, paid in cash at time of purchase on December 1, YEAR 1. A cash basis business would record and report the cost of merchandise sold in YEAR 1. The effect of the purchase and sale of merchandise would be reflected in the Income Statements of the business as follows:

(Cash Basis)

	YEAR 1	YEAR 2	COMBINED
Sales Revenue	$ 0	$ 3,000	$ 3,000
Cost of Merchandise Sold	(1,000)	0	(1,000)
Net Income (Loss)	$ (1,000)	$ 3,000	$ 2,000

It is worthy of emphasis that, regardless of the accounting method, the *combined* net income of the business in the circumstances described would always amount to $2,000. The disadvantage of the cash basis method lies, however, in the mismatching in a particular accounting (fiscal) period of revenues earned and expenses incurred to earn those revenues. Thus, YEAR 1 shows a net loss of $1,000 due to the combined effect of early expense recognition and delayed revenue recognition. A year later the statement shows net income of $3,000 by ignoring the earlier expense write-off. Each of years 1 and 2 viewed in isolation would present a distorted result of the underlying business transaction: an economic increase of $2,000 in net wealth.

We saw earlier that net income can only be determined with absolute accuracy when the reporting period for financial statements covers the entire life of a business. The selection of a shorter period of time than the life of the business, changes the task from income determination to estimation of net income. The sacrifice in mathematical accuracy, however, is well justified by the enhanced administrative and business convenience that results from timely financial statements.

The fact that cash basis accounting, in most situations, distorts the financial statements of an entity and more readily conceals the true impact of business transactions has, with very limited exceptions, led to its rejection as an appropriate method of financial reporting. A notable exception is found in the reporting of employment income, which individuals must report on a cash basis. This requirement results from a balancing of the enhanced administrative convenience to the employee, employer, and the Agency, and the minimal distortion that occurs in measuring employment income on a cash basis.

In contrast with the cash basis of accounting, accrual accounting recognizes revenue when it is realized, and expenses are reported in the same time period as the revenues for which they were incurred. The accrual basis is premised on the rationale that reporting revenues earned and expenses incurred in the same accounting period provides a better "matching", and that such "matching" more accurately depicts the underlying business transaction. Using the same figures as in the previous example, an income statement prepared on an accrual basis would disclose the following:

(Accrual Basis)

	YEAR 1	YEAR 2	COMBINED
Sales Revenue	$ 3,000	$ 0	$ 3,000
Cost of Merchandise Sold	(1,000)	0	(1,000)
Net Income (Loss)	$ (2,000)	$ 0	$ 2,000

Although the combined net incomes of the two years is the same in both the cash basis and accrual basis methods of reporting, the latter method more accurately reflects the increase in net wealth in each period. (The outstanding accounts receivable of $3,000 as at December 31, YEAR 1, represented a debt that increased net wealth.)

Regardless of when cash is actually received, accrual accounting requires the reporting of revenue in the fiscal period in which it is realized. The rationale that debt, as much as cash, represents an increase in wealth is one that is particularly appropriate to any modern economy. At the same time, the accrual method requires that expenses incurred to earn revenue be matched with corresponding revenues earned in the same fiscal period. The important task remains to determine the criteria for selection of a given time when revenue may be considered to be realized, and thus recognized as earned, in a particular fiscal period.

The accrual method generally prevents tax deferral. For example, if a person pays five years' worth of lease payments in advance, the lump sum is capitalized and written off over a five-year period. Similarly, the lessor will treat the pre-paid rents as an asset and recognize only 1/5 of the lump sum in each of the five succeeding years. Unfortunately, tax and commercial accounting do not always arrive at the same solution. Tax accounting puts the lessor on the cash method and compels him or her to recognize the full five-year lump sum payment in the year that he or she receives it. The lessee, however, is not entitled to deduct the lump sum in the year that he or she pays it, but must spread it out over five years. This asymmetric policy works to the advantage of the government and against the taxpayer.

3. — Tests for Revenue Recognition

Two tests determine the selection of the appropriate time period for revenue recognition. First, the major economic activity concerned with the earning process must have been substantially completed. Second, there should be some objective measurement available. Thus, revenue should only be recognized when major uncertainties in respect of its measurement have been substantially resolved.

When one examines these criteria it is easy to see the rationale for selection of point of sale as the most usual time of revenue recognition. In most merchandising and service businesses, the point of sale represents completion of the major portion of economic activity. In these situations the point of sale is assumed to be the primary economic event and it provides an objective measurement yardstick, namely, sale price.

At the same time a sale generates a flow of assets that converts inventory into accounts receivable. Concurrently with the objective measurement of revenue, related expenses are determinable with reasonable certainty, and any remaining uncertainty is reduced, for pragmatic purposes, to an acceptable level. Finally, the point of sale is clear and determinable. For all these reasons, time of sale is considered to be the point of revenue recognition in most business transactions.

4. — Accounting Adjustments

Let us assume that X Widgets is preparing its accounting statements for its fiscal year ending October 31, YEAR 1. Some special accounting entries are required to implement the system of accruing expenses incurred and revenue earned, in order to comply with the matching principle. In the preceding section we saw that entries are made when an invoice is received or rendered, even though no cash changes hands. At the year-end, some special entries are required to reflect expense or income that has accrued but as to which no transaction is currently taking place. These entries are designed to adjust the "timing" and recognition of expenses and revenue. A further group of entries may also be made to adjust the "measurement" of revenues or expenses.

(a) — The "Timing" Adjustments

Some transactions that give rise to normal accounting entries represent expense or revenue for a period that straddles the year-end. Assume the following about X Widgets:

1. On July 1, YEAR 1 it paid a $900 premium for insurance for one year to June 30, YEAR 2;

2. Its employees are paid monthly on the 15th of the month and the monthly salary expense is $8,000;

3. It holds a Canada Savings Bond that pays $1,200 interest each November 30;

4. It rents an unused part of the land adjacent to its building to a company that parks its trucks there. The annual rent is $1,200, paid each January 31 and July 31 in advance.

To avoid a misstatement of the expenses and revenues for the year ending October 31, YEAR 1, four adjustments are necessary:

1. A reduction in insurance expense to reflect the fact that 2/3 of the insurance benefit paid for in July still remains;

2. An increase in salary expense to reflect the 1/2 month's labour already enjoyed by the business, but which will not be paid for until November 15;

3. An increase in investment income to reflect the 11/12 of the bond interest accrued to October 31; and

4. A decrease in rental income to reflect the receipt of three months' rent not yet earned.

The following four adjusting entries will be made:

1. Insurance expense will be reduced by $600 and a balance sheet asset, "prepaid expense", will be set up;

2. Salary expense will be increased by $4,000 and a balance sheet liability, "salary expense payable", will be set up;

3. Investment income will be increased by $1,100 and a balance sheet asset, "accrued bond interest", will be set up; and

4. Rental income will be reduced by $300 and a balance sheet liability, "rent received in advance", will be set up.

(b) — The "Measurement" Adjustments

It is consistent with accounting conservatism to recognize, at the year-end, that the value of some of the business assets may be overstated and therefore, that business profitability may be exaggerated.

One of the most obvious adjustments to correct for this danger is an allowance for doubtful debts. If X Widgets shows $20,000 in accounts receivable at the year-end, it may well be realistic to predict that some of the debts will never be collected. On that assumption, the balance sheet asset, "Accounts Receivable", would be reduced by an amount (referred to as an allowance for doubtful accounts) that would also reduce the current year's income.

A business may face many contingencies and hazards which a careful accountant and a prudent business manager would like to provide for by making similar "allowances". All of them will have the effect of reducing the statement of current profitability. It may be obvious that the revenue authorities are not prepared to be as gloomy in their forecasting of business hazards, and that the Act will not permit, for the purpose of reporting income for taxation, all of the allowances that the accountant and the business manager might wish.

One adjustment that must be mentioned is the allowance for depreciation. In our earlier hypothetical situation, City Dairy will experience, over five years, a cost of $500,000 in respect of its fleet of trucks. To allocate this cost appropriately in order to match expense and revenue, it may reflect a depreciation expense of $100,000 at the end of each year. This is essentially a "timing" adjustment designed to spread a large cost over the appropriate accounting periods. There is, however, an element of measurement involved: both the assumed useful life of the trucks and their assumed salvage value are based on estimates.

VIII. — Other Accounting Methods

Some businesses involve such unusual features that the standard accrual basis of accounting fails to achieve an appropriate matching of expenses and revenues. For example, some businesses involve a high volume of sales on terms that call for instalment payments over an extended period of time. Such a business may have significant costs associated with the selling activity but, notionally, a large "profit margin" as judged by the difference between selling price and cost of sales. The incidence of uncollectible accounts in such a business, however, is usually higher than for most other businesses. At best, the accounts are not "receivable" on a current basis, but are going to be received over a much longer period than is usual for businesses generally. This kind of business might adopt the instalment method of accounting which does not recognize the accounts receivable in revenue. In effect, the business uses a hybrid accounting system, which recognizes all expenses except the cost of goods sold on an accrual basis, but recognizes revenue on a cash basis by ignoring its accounts receivable.

Other businesses carry on long-term projects that may involve several years' work to complete. Payment for work completed may be by way of advances or there may be significant delay in receiving payment; and there may be a holdback to satisfy liens or to give the payer a guaranteed opportunity to judge whether the work is satisfactory. Again, because of the difficulty of appropriately matching expenses and revenues, such a business may use a "completed contract" method of accounting.

IX. — Basic Income Tax Accounting

1. — Accounting Period

The division of a business lifetime into arbitrary segments gives rise to problems of accurate income calculation. A taxpayer's lifetime is similarly segmented into annual periods and this segmentation also gives rise to some special problems.

The Act prescribes for individuals a tax year coincident with the calendar year. Corporations are allowed to choose their own fiscal periods for tax purposes.[13]

Businesses carried on in partnership or as a sole proprietorship, although distinct accounting entities, do not have a separate legal personality and are not taxpayers as such. The income from such businesses must be reported by the partners or the proprietor in their personal capacity. The business may, however, use a fiscal period that is different from the calendar year. For example, X Widgets will calculate its income for its fiscal year ending October 31, 2004; that income will be included in X's income for the 2004 taxation year.[14] This means that any income earned in 2004 by X Widgets, after November 1, 2004, need not be reported until X files a 2005 tax return in the spring of 2006.

2. — Accounting Methods

(a) — General Comment

While employees must report their income according to the cash basis of accounting, businesses are generally required to use the accrual method. The accrual method is considered particularly appropriate for a trading business.[15] There are, however, other methods of accounting that may be more appropriate for some businesses, particularly businesses with peculiar or unique cash flow patterns.

---

[13]Subs. 249(1) and 249.1.

[14]S. 11.

[15]*Ken Steeves Sales Ltd. v. M.N.R.*, [1955] C.T.C. 47, 55 D.T.C. 1044 (Ex. Ct.).

(b) — Instalment Sales

As noted above, for tax accounting, a variation of the accrual method may be adopted by certain sales businesses. The instalment method of accounting, for example, is considered appropriate for a taxpayer whose business involves instalment sales requiring a small down payment with the balance due over an extended period.[16]

(c) — Completed Contract

In contrast, the completed contract method of accounting has been rejected for tax purposes although it might be an appropriate accounting method. Under this method, the taxpayer defers recognition of all expenses and all revenues in respect of long-term contracts until the contract is complete.[17]

(d) — Cash

Income from office or employment is usually reported on a cash basis. This is confirmed by the use of the words "received" and "enjoyed" in sections 5 and 6 of the Act.

The decision to allow certain taxpayers to use the cash method of accounting is based primarily on a concern for administrative convenience. It would be quite difficult, if not impossible, for millions of employees to prepare their annual income tax returns on an accrual basis of accounting. The accrual basis requires at least some rudimentary knowledge of accounting principles (realization, timing, etc.) that is beyond the inclination of most non-accountants.

It is also important to remember that accrual basis statements require more careful auditing by the tax authorities. Since employee income tax returns represent approximately 80 per cent of all tax returns filed, mandatory accrual basis returns from all taxpayers would place an intolerable burden on the CRA's resources. The incremental auditing and accounting fees incurred by both taxpayers and the CRA as a result of accrual accounting cannot be justified by the marginal improvement in the accuracy of annual net income calculations.

Having said that, however, it is important to note that the requirement of cash accounting for employees does allow for some modest amount of tax planning. Employees can, within limits, reduce their immediate tax liabilities by accelerating payment of their expenses and delaying receipt of their income.

It is important to note, however, that in determining income for tax purposes under the cash method, an individual must include not only the *cash* that he or she receives in the year, but

---

[16]*M.N.R. v. Publishers Guild of Can. Ltd.*, [1957] C.T.C. 1, 57 D.T.C. 1017 (Ex. Ct.).

[17]*Wilson & Wilson Ltd. v. M.N.R.*, [1960] C.T.C. 1, 60 D.T.C. 1018 (Ex. Ct.).

also any other payments that the individual *constructively* receives in the year. Thus, the cash method of accounting includes in income both actual and constructive receipts. The essence of the constructive receipts doctrine is that an individual cannot postpone recognizing income simply by failing to exercise his or her power to collect it. For example, although an individual can delay actual payment beyond the year-end, he or she cannot avoid including an amount in income merely by waiting until the next year to pick up his or her paycheque.

The distinction between the two situations is subtle but significant. In the first case, the taxpayer does not have the power to cash, or otherwise control, the cheque because he or she does not receive it until after the year-end. In the second case, the taxpayer constructively possesses the cheque, but chooses not to exercise his or her power of possession in order to delay including the amount in income.

These distinctions are particularly important in closely-held corporations. Where an owner-manager of a corporation performs services for the corporation, he or she is entitled to payment for services. Although the owner exercises discretion as to the timing of the payment, the salary is not considered to be paid until the owner has the corporation's cheque in his or her possession. Thus, merely because the owner controls the timing of the cheque does not mean that payment to him or her is accelerated to a point in time before the corporation actually issues the cheque.

To be sure, this allows owner-managers of corporations considerable flexibility in arranging their annual compensation through salary and bonuses. Depending upon the prevailing rates of tax for a particular year, an owner can elect to accelerate or defer salary payments in order to maximize his or her after-tax returns. This form of tax avoidance is a small price to pay for what would otherwise become an impossibly complex accounting system for employees. Similarly, the owner-manager may choose to forego some or all of his or her salary in a year. The amount forgone, however, is not imputed to the individual merely because he or she was entitled to the amount. We do not impute taxable salaries to controlling shareholders.

(e) — Accrual

In contrast with the requirement of cash basis accounting for employment income, business and property income is usually required to be reported on an accrual basis. The Act does not specifically stipulate a particular method for calculating business or property income. Section 9 says only that a taxpayer's income from a business or property is his or her *profit* therefrom. The term "profit", however, has been judicially interpreted to mean profit calculated in accordance with commercial practice, and commercial practice favours accrual accounting for most businesses. Hence, the accrual method is mandated indirectly through the requirement to adhere to generally accepted accounting principles.

(f) — Modified Accrual

There are certain specific departures from the usual rule that business and property income is calculated in accordance with the rules of accrual accounting. First, an important exception is made in the case of farmers and fishers; these two categories of taxpayers are specifically authorized to use the cash basis method of accounting.[18] The theoretical justification for this particular variation is that, in most circumstances, the distortion of net income when using the cash basis method is minimal and, hence, justifiable in that it is easier for these taxpayers to maintain cash basis books of account.

More pragmatically, one recognizes that it would be politically inconvenient to withdraw a tax concession that has been made available to farmers for so long. If anything, the pull is in the opposite direction. Until 1980 only farmers could use the cash basis of accounting; in that year the cash basis of accounting was extended to fishers, a practice that had been administratively tolerated by the CRA for many years.

A second exception from the accrual basis of accounting is found in the "modified accrual method" applicable to professionals. Professionals, like their business counterparts, are required to calculate income on an accrual basis. Professionals can, however, elect to exclude their work-in-progress in calculating net income for tax purposes.[19]

(g) — Holdbacks

We have already stated that, in applying the accrual basis of accounting, the time of sale of goods and services is usually the most convenient time to recognize revenue. The time of sale is not, however, the only time for revenue recognition. Certain businesses may deviate from the norm and recognize revenue at some other time. For example, contractors (persons engaged in the construction of buildings, roads, dams, bridges and similar structures) can, by administrative grace, defer recognition of their income until such time as "holdback payments" become *legally* receivable.[20] This rule varies from the usual accrual accounting test, which does not use legal entitlement as the determining criterion for recognizing revenue. Contractors may, however, also accelerate the recognition of profit by bringing into income amounts that may not be legally receivable by virtue of a mechanics' lien or similar statute.

---

[18] S. 28.

[19] Para. 34(a).

[20] See IT-92R2.

(h) — Net Worth

To this point, we have discussed the more conventional methods of income determination — cash basis, accrual accounting and modified accrual. There remains one other technique for calculating income, which can be particularly painful to a taxpayer and particularly useful to the CRA. This technique is the "net worth" method of calculating income.

A net worth assessment is usually issued by the CRA when a taxpayer does not file a return or, in some cases, when the Agency does not accept the taxpayer's figures.[21] The theoretical principle underlying the calculation of income using the net worth basis is simple: Income is equal to the difference between a taxpayer's wealth at the beginning and at the end of a year, plus any amount consumed by the taxpayer during the year. We saw in Chapter 4 "The Meaning of Income" that this principle derives from the Haig-Simons definition of income.

Algebraically, the principle is stated as follows:

$$Income = (WE - WB) + C$$

where:

    WE = Wealth at end of year,

    WB = Wealth at begining of year, and

    C = Consumption

Note, however, that, unlike the Haig-Simons formulation of income, the formula does not take into account any accrued but unrealized gains in the value of property.

Assume that a taxpayer started out a year owning $100,000 in property, such as a house, car, clothing, furniture, cash, etc. At the end of the year it is estimated that the taxpayer owns $105,000 in property. It is also estimated that the taxpayer spent $45,000 during the year on food, clothing, mortgage payments, vacations, children's education, etc. If the taxpayer has not engaged in any borrowing or repayment of loans, his or her net income for the year is $50,000, i.e., ($105,000 - $100,000) + $45,000. If in fact, the taxpayer borrowed $8,000 during the year, his or her wealth at the end of the year is only $97,000 and his or her income for the year would be only $42,000.

Notice the resemblance between the net worth basis of determining income and the Haig-Simons concept of income.[22] When a taxpayer does not, or cannot, use conventional accounting records to calculate his or her income and the CRA does not have any other way of assessing the delinquent taxpayer's income, the system must rely on fundamental concepts: income is the money value of the net accretion of economic power between two points of time.

---

[21]Subs. 152(7).

[22]See Chapter 4, "The Meaning of Income".

3. — Generally Accepted Accounting Principles

The Act determines income from business or property by reference to subsection 9(1):

> Subject to this Part, a taxpayer's income for a taxation year from a business or property is the taxpayer's profit from that business or property for that year.

At one time there was a tentative proposal to incorporate into the Act a general statement to the effect that business profits should be calculated according to GAAP. The proposal was never implemented because of the difficulty in establishing just what GAAP means in all cases. The absence of a statutory provision requiring the computation of profits according to GAAP did not, however, inhibit the development of a similar doctrine in case law. Indeed, if anything, we have arrived at virtually the same result through judicial decisions.

(a) — Section 9

Although there may be disagreement among accountants concerning the best practice in respect of certain matters, it is now well established that section 9 imports into the Act, at least *as a starting point*, the standard accounting methods used in the business world. Thorson P. dealt with this matter in *Imp. Oil v. M.N.R.*,[23] in *Daley v. M.N.R.*[24] and in *Royal Trust Co. v. M.N.R.*[25] In this last case, dealing with the deductibility of a claimed expenditure, he said:[26]

> ... it may be stated categorically that ... the first matter to be determined ... is whether it was made or incurred by the taxpayer in accordance with the ordinary principles of commercial trading or well accepted principles of business practice.

The important point, however, is that the determination of "net profit" is a question of law and not a matter of generally accepted accounting principles.[27] Although a court may look at the treatment of particular items by reference to GAAP, they are at best only representative of the principles used for preparing financial statements. GAAP may influence the calculation of income only on a case-by-case basis.[28] To be sure, GAAP may well be influential in determining what is deductible, but they are not the operative *legal* criteria. Thus, subsection

---

[23]*Imperial Oil v. M.N.R.*, [1947] C.T.C. 353, 3 D.T.C. 1090 (Ex. Ct.).

[24]*Daley v. M.N.R.*, [1950] C.T.C. 254, 4 D.T.C. 877 (Ex. Ct.).

[25]*Royal Trust Co. v. M.N.R.*, [1957] C.T.C. 32, 57 D.T.C. 1055 (Ex. Ct.); see also *The Queen v. Metropolitan Properties Ltd.*, [1985] 1 C.T.C. 169, 85 D.T.C. 5128 (F.C.T.D.) (GAAP normal rule for measuring income).

[26]*Royal Trust Co. v. M.N.R., ibid.*, at 42 [C.T.C] and 1060 [D.T.C.].

[27]*Symes v. Canada* (1993), [1993] 4 S.C.R. 695, [1994] 1 C.T.C. 40, 94 D.T.C. 6001 (S.C.C.); *Neonex International Ltd. v. The Queen*, [1978] C.T.C. 485, 78 D.T.C. 6339 (F.C.A.).

[28]*Canderel Ltd. v. Canada*, [1998] 1 S.C.R. 147, [1998] 2 C.T.C. 35, 98 D.T.C. 6100 (S.C.C.).

9(1) represents a starting point and normal accounting practices for tax purposes may be overborne by specific statutory provisions, judicial precedent, or commercial practice.[29]

(b) — Tax Profits

What is the relationship between accounting profit and profit as determined for income tax purposes? For tax purposes, the starting point requires an examination of generally accepted commercial practice. Is a particular expenditure deductible in computing income according to the rules of general commercial and accounting practice? Or is a particular receipt included in computing income according to commercial rules? Once these preliminary questions are answered, other factors may come into play in determining the appropriate tax treatment.

Take depreciation as an example.[30] The general commercial and accounting rule is that, in calculating net income, a reasonable amount of depreciation can be deducted from revenues. Indeed, commercial practice recognizes many different methods of calculating depreciation (for example, straight-line, declining balance, sum of the years, etc.). Provided that the method is acceptable and the amount is reasonable, depreciation expense is a deductible expense in determining net income for financial statement purposes.

The Act, however, *specifically* prohibits a deduction for depreciation[31] and, therefore, such an expense cannot be taken into account in calculating net income for tax purposes. In lieu of depreciation, the Act allows a deduction for Capital Cost Allowance ("CCA") in an amount which may or may not be related to accounting depreciation. Thus, tax profits and accounting income may be substantially different.

(c) — Statutory Deviations

The Act deviates from accounting principles in many areas. Three important statutory deviations from standard accounting practice are discussed below.

---

[29]See generally: *Associated Investors of Canada Ltd. v. M.N.R.*, [1967] C.T.C. 138, 67 D.T.C. 5096 (Ex Ct.); *Neonex International Ltd. v. The Queen*, [1978] C.T.C. 485, 78 D.T.C. 6339 (F.C.A.); *The Queen v. Metropolitan Properties Co. Ltd.*, [1985] 1 C.T.C. 169, 85 D.T.C. 5128 (F.C.T.D.); *MHL Holdings Ltd. v. The Queen*, [1988] 2 C.T.C. 42, 88 D.T.C. 6292 (F.C.T.D.); *Coppley Noyes & Randall Ltd. v. The Queen*, [1991] 1 C.T.C. 541, 91 D.T.C. 5291 (F.C.T.D.); and *West Kootenay Power & Light Co. v. The Queen*, [1992] 1 C.T.C. 15, 92 D.T.C. 6023 (F.C.A.).

[30]Numerous other examples may be found in Subdivision b of Division B, Part I of the Act.

[31]Para. 18(1)(b).

(i) — Reserves and Allowances

Accountants sometimes prefer to anticipate certain contingencies by setting up an allowance that has the effect of reducing income in the current period. The Act seriously inhibits this conservative and quite normal accounting practice by denying, as a deduction, "an amount transferred or credited to a reserve, contingent account or sinking fund except as expressly permitted by this Part."[32] Instead, the Act sets out a specific and rigid regime in respect of accounting for reserves. Thus, there can be a significant difference between accounting reserves and tax reserves.

(ii) — Depreciation

At one time, depreciation expense was recognized as a legitimate deduction for tax purposes, subject to showing a sound accounting basis for the deduction. As we have noted, it is indisputable that many capital assets depreciate with use, but the amount of loss in value and the rate at which it occurs are frequently quite speculative. To control the speculations, and to minimize disputes, the Act details a Capital Cost Allowance (CCA) system, which imposes limits on the amount of depreciation deductible in calculating income for tax purposes.

Although, in general, CCA rates are designed to be reasonably realistic, the system is Procrustean. There is no attempt to guarantee that the rates for tax purposes conform to depreciation recognized for accounting purposes. The rates are the same for all taxpayers although their depreciation experience may differ greatly. Further, the CCA system is also used to achieve other socio-economic objectives. It may, for example, be used to stimulate economic activity in depressed regions of the country. Thus, income for tax purposes can differ quite significantly from income reported to shareholders or creditors, and there is nothing unusual or improper in this.

(iii) — Inventory

A major component of the expenses of some businesses, and thus a major factor in determining income, is the cost of goods sold. To calculate the cost of goods sold, a business must establish its inventory of goods on hand at the year-end, and determine its value. There are a number of accounting approaches to inventory valuation. One method that is commonly used by accountants for financial statement purposes, the last-in, first-out ("LIFO"), has been judicially rejected for tax purposes as being inappropriate.[33] Here once again, the use of one method for accounting and another for tax purposes can cause a significant difference in the final net income figure.

---

[32]Para. 18(1)(e).

[33]*M.N.R. v. Anaconda Amer. Brass Ltd.*, [1955] C.T.C. 311, 55 D.T.C. 1220 (P.C.).

4. — *Realization and Recognition of Income*

There are many problems relating to realization and the appropriate time to recognize income for tax purposes. Some of these problems are simply difficulties inherent in the nature of the transaction, but others arise from attempts by taxpayers to apply the realization concept to their best advantage.

Stock options are an example of the inherent difficulty in correctly applying the concepts of realization and revenue recognition in tax law. Suppose that ABC Ltd. gives employee E an option to buy 1,000 shares of its stock at a price of $10/share, exercisable at any time within three years. The option is given in Year 1 at a time when the stock is trading publicly at $12 per share. E exercises the option in Year 2 when the stock is trading at $15 per share. In Year 3, E sells the stock for $16 per share.

Assuming that the transaction gives rise to income in E's hands, two questions arise: (1) how much income? and (2) in what year? It is arguable that E should be treated as having received $2,000 in Year 1; the company conferred on E, in that year, a benefit in the form of an opportunity to buy for $10,000 what a stranger would pay $12,000 to acquire. It is also arguable, however, that E's benefit is purely potential; if the stock drops below $10 and stays down for three years the option will be worthless.

It could be said that the benefit was received in Year 2 when E actually bought the stock at $5,000 below its market value. Our discussion of the conventional approach to paper gains might suggest, however, as a third alternative, that E should not recognize any income until he or she sells the shares or otherwise parts with them. If the shares rise or fall in value before E parts with them, the actual benefit to E will be greater or less, accordingly. Using this reasoning, we would tax E in Year 3 on income of $6,000.

The Act provides an arbitrary, but reasonable, solution to the two problems of timing and quantification. Subsection 7(1) stipulates that E's income will be recognized in the year in which he or she exercises the option or disposes of it. The amount of income is either the difference between the option price and the current value of the shares or the amount received on disposition of the option.[34] Thus, in our hypothetical situation, E would recognize $5,000 of income in Year 2. This solution really involves identifying the option as the source of E's gain. It is consistent with our basic discussion of realization to say that E's gain is only a paper gain so long as E holds the option, but becomes a real gain when he or she parts with the option by exercising it or disposing of it to someone else.

---

[34]Actually, subs. 7(1) is somewhat more complex to provide against artificial dealings through non-arm's length transactions. Further, subs. 7(1.1) provides for different treatment in the case of Canadian-controlled private corporations and subs. 7(8) addresses shares of publicly listed companies.

5. — *Conformity of Accounting Methods*

A taxpayer's income for a taxation year from a business or property is the profit therefrom for the year.[35]

(a) — *Use of GAAP*

The term "profit" means *net* profit. In the absence of any specific proscription, profit is determined according to commercial and generally accepted accounting principles. Hence, absent an express or implicit statutory or judicial proscription against the use of a particular accounting method, a taxpayer may determine income for tax purposes according to any appropriate accounting method. Thorson P. explained the rule in *Publishers Guild of Canada Ltd.*:[36]

> If the law does not prohibit the use of a particular system of accounting then the opinion of accountancy experts that it is an accepted system and is appropriate to the taxpayer's business and most nearly accurately reflects his income position should prevail with the Court if the reasons for the opinion commend themselves to it.

Similarly, in Silverman:[37]

> . . . the statute does not define what is to be taken as the profit from a business, nor does it describe how or by what method such profit is to be computed, though it does contain provisions to which, for income tax purposes, any method is subject . . . the method must be one

---

[35]Subs. 9(1).

[36]*Publishers Guild of Canada v. M.N.R.* (1956), [1957] C.T.C. 1, 57 D.T.C. 1017 at 1026 (Ex. Ct.); see also *The Queen v. Nomad Sand and Gravel Limited*, [1991] 1 C.T.C. 60, 91 D.T.C. 5032 at 5034-5035 (F.C.A.); *Assoc. Investors of Can. Ltd. v. M.N.R.*, [1967] C.T.C. 138, 67 D.T.C. 5096 at 5098-99 (Ex. Ct.); *Maritime Telegraph & Telephone Co. v. The Queen*, [1991] 1 C.T.C. 28, 91 D.T.C. 5038 at 5039 (F.C.T.D.); affd. [1992] 1 C.T.C. 264, 92 D.T.C. 6191 (F.C.A.).

[37]*Silverman v. M.N.R.*, [1960] C.T.C. 262 at 266, 60 D.T.C. 1212 at 1214 (Ex. Ct.); see also, *Bank of Nova Scotia v. The Queen*, [1980] C.T.C. 57 at 62, 80 D.T.C. 6009 at 6013 (F.C.T.D.):

> . . . generally recognized accounting and commercial principles and practices are to be applied to all matters of commercial and taxation accounting unless there is something in the taxing statute which precludes them from coming into play. The legislator, when dealing with financial and commercial matters in any enactment, including of course a taxing statute, is to be presumed at law to be aware of the general financial and commercial principles which are relevant to the subject-matter covered by the legislation. The Act pertains to business and financial matters and is addressed to the general public. It follows that where no particular mention is made as to any variation from common ordinary practice or where the attainment of the objects of the legislation does not necessarily require such variation, then common practice and generally recognized accounting and commercial principles and terminology must be deemed to apply.

which accurately reflects the result of the year's operation, and where two different methods, either of which may be acceptable for business purposes, differ in their results, for income tax purposes the appropriate method is that which most accurately shows the profit from the year's operations.

Ultimately, however, the measure of profit is a question of law.

(b) — Conformity of Methods

A taxpayer can use one generally accepted accounting method for financial statement purposes and another for income tax purposes. In the absence of any statutory requirement that a taxpayer use the same method of accounting to calculate income both for tax and financial statement purposes, a taxpayer can select the most appropriate method of accounting for tax purposes.

The purpose for which income is calculated determines the appropriate method of accounting. An accounting method which is suitable for a particular purpose is not necessarily the appropriate measure of income for tax purposes.[38]

What is appropriate for tax purposes? The general rule is to apply that principle or method which provides the proper picture of net income. In MacGuigan J.'s words:[39]

> ... it would be undesirable to establish an absolute requirement that there must always be conformity between financial statements and tax returns and I am satisfied that the cases do not do so. *The approved principle* is that whichever method presents the "truer picture" of a taxpayer's revenue, which more fairly and accurately portrays income, and which "matches" revenue and expenditure, if one method does, is the one that must be followed. [Emphasis added.]

(c) — A "Truer Picture" of Income?

It is not always easy to apply the rule that a taxpayer may adopt whichever accounting method presents the "truer picture" of revenues and expenses. There are cases where a particular accounting principle presents a "truer picture" for income statement purposes at the expense of some accuracy or relevance in the balance sheet. In other cases, the adoption of a particular accounting method more accurately summarizes a taxpayer's closing balances

---

[38]*Friedberg v. M.N.R.*, [1993] 4 S.C.R. 285, [1993] 2 C.T.C. 306, 93 D.T.C. 5507 (S.C.C.).

[39]*West Kootenay Power & Light Co. v. The Queen*, [1992] 1 C.T.C. 15 at 22, 92 D.T.C. 6023 at 6028 (F.C.A.). See also: *Maritime Telegraph and Telephone Company v. The Queen*, [1992] 1 C.T.C. 264, 92 D.T.C. 6191 (F.C.A.) ("earned method" of reporting income for accounting and tax purposes produced "truer picture" of taxpayer's income).

while sacrificing accuracy on the income statement. *West Kootenay*[40] rightly emphasized a proper matching of revenues and expenses and accuracy of the net income figure for tax purposes. Ultimately, however, the computation of profit for tax purposes is a question of law.[41]

A classic example of the conflict between income statement and balance sheet values is seen in accounting for inventory values. Under the last-in, first-out ("LIFO") method of inventory accounting, the cost of goods most recently purchased or acquired is the cost that is assigned to the cost of goods sold. Hence, the inventory on hand at the end of an accounting period is valued at the cost that was attributed to the inventory at the beginning of the period (first-in, still here). Any increases in quantity during a period are valued at the cost prevailing during the time the accumulations are deemed to have occurred. Any decreases in quantities are considered to have first reduced the most recent accumulations.[42]

Under the first-in, first-out ("FIFO") method, the process is reversed: the cost of goods first acquired is assigned to the first goods sold. The closing inventory comprises the cost of the most recent purchases (last-in, still here).

The use of the FIFO method of accounting for the flow of inventory costs tends to overstate net income during inflationary periods and more accurately reflect the current value of closing inventory on the balance sheet. In contrast, the LIFO method more realistically measures "real" net income, while sacrificing some accuracy in year-end balance sheet values.

Most accountants and business people argue that the use of LIFO for inventory accounting during inflationary periods results in a more meaningful and "truer picture" of business income during inflationary periods. The Privy Council in *Anaconda Brass*,[43] however, rejected the use of the LIFO method of inventory valuation for tax purposes. Their Lordships were concerned that the method would permit the creation of hidden reserves:[44]

> . . . the evidence of expert witnesses, that the LIFO method is generally acceptable, and in this case the most appropriate, method of accountancy, is not conclusive of the question that the Court has to decide. That may be found as a fact by the Exchequer Court and affirmed by the Supreme Court. The question remains whether it conforms to the prescription of the *Income Tax Act*. As already indicated, in their Lordships' opinion it does not.

---

[40]*West Kootenay Power & Light Co. v. The Queen, ante.*

[41]*Canderel Ltd. v. Canada*, [1998] 1 S.C.R. 147, [1998] 2 C.T.C. 35, 98 D.T.C. 6100 (S.C.C.); *Ikea Ltd. v. Canada*, [1998] 1 S.C.R. 196, [1998] 2 C.T.C. 61, 98 D.T.C. 6092 (S.C.C.); *Toronto College Park Ltd. v. Canada*, [1998] 1 S.C.R. 183, [1998] 2 C.T.C. 78, 98 D.T.C. 6088 (S.C.C.).

[42]See *CICA Handbook* §3030.07.

[43]*M.N.R. v. Anaconda Amer. Brass Ltd.*, [1955] C.T.C. 311, 55 D.T.C. 1220 (P.C.).

[44]*M.N.R. v. Anaconda Amer. Brass Ltd., ibid.*, at 321 [C.T.C.] and 1225 [D.T.C.].

The accounting principle for selecting the proper method of inventory valuation is clear: the most suitable method for determining cost is that which results in charging against operations those costs that most fairly match the sales revenue for the period. The *CICA Handbook* states the principle as follows:[45]

> The method selected for determining cost should be one which results in the fairest matching of costs against revenues regardless of whether or not the method corresponds to the physical flow of goods.

Anaconda Brass was an unfortunate decision based upon a misunderstanding of accounting methods. The decision rests on two notions: (1) the physical flow of inventory determines values; and (2) the potential for creation of "hidden" reserves. Both premises are fundamentally flawed. The determination of cost does not depend upon the physical flow of goods but on the fairest matching of revenues and expenses. The "fairest" matching of costs against revenues is, presumably, also the method which presents the "truer picture" of income for tax purposes. Thus, the question is: which method of accounting produces the best and fairest picture of annual profits? Equally, the hidden reserve argument ignores the primary purpose served by the method, namely, the determination of a fair measure of an enterprise's annual income.

6. — Non-Arm's Length Transactions

The Act contains stringent anti-avoidance rules to govern transfers of property between persons who do not deal with each other at arm's length. The purpose of these rules is to discourage taxpayers who have close social, family, or economic relationships with each other from artificially avoiding tax through the manipulation of transaction values.

Related persons are deemed not to deal with each other at arm's length.[46]

It is a question of fact whether unrelated persons deal with each other at arm's length. Parties are not considered to be dealing with each other at arm's length if one person dictates the terms of the bargain on both sides of a transaction.[47]

---

[45]See *CICA Handbook* §3030 and the virtually identical language of *AICPA*, ARB 43, Ch. 4.

[46]S. 251.

[47]*Swiss Bank Corp. v. M.N.R.*, [1971] C.T.C. 427, 71 D.T.C. 5235 (Ex. Ct.); affd. (1972), [1974] S.C.R. 1144, [1972] C.T.C. 614, 72 D.T.C. 6470 (S.C.C.) (parties acted in concert, exerting considerable influence together; money transactions merely moved funds from one pocket to another); *Millward v. The Queen*, [1986] 2 C.T.C. 423, 86 D.T.C. 6538 (F.C.T.D.) (members of law firm who dealt with each other at less than commercial rates of interest not at arm's length); *Noranda Mines Ltd. v. M.N.R.*, [1987] 2 C.T.C. 2089, 87 D.T.C. 379 (T.C.C.) (existence of arm's length relationship excluded where one party has *de facto* control over both parties).

The anti-avoidance rules are as follows:[48]

- Where, in a non-arm's length transaction, a purchaser acquires anything for a price in *excess* of its fair market value, he or she is deemed to have acquired the property at its fair market value. Consequently, notwithstanding that the purchaser actually paid a price higher than fair market value, the purchaser is *deemed* to acquire the property at a cost equal to fair market value.

Example

> A taxpayer buys land from his mother at a cost of $70,000 when, in fact, the land has a fair market value of $50,000 (this may happen if the mother deliberately wants to trigger a higher capital gain to offset unused capital losses). The Act deems the son to have acquired the land at a cost of $50,000. The mother calculates her gain on the basis of her *actual* proceeds of $70,000.

- Where, in a non-arm's length transaction, a vendor has disposed of anything at *less* than its fair market value, the vendor is deemed to have received proceeds equal to fair market value. Thus, notwithstanding that he or she actually received a lower price, the vendor is taxed on the basis of his or her deemed proceeds.

Example

> A taxpayer sells land that has a fair market value of $50,000 to his daughter for $40,000. Paragraph 69(1)(b) *deems* the father to have received $50,000. His daughter, however, acquires the property for her *actual* cost of $40,000, leaving her with the potential of a larger gain when she sells the property.

The overall effect of these rules is that taxpayers can be liable to double taxation in non-arm's length transactions. Section 69 can have a punitive effect. It is structured to discourage non-arm's length parties from dealing with each other at prices other than fair market value.

Example

Assume:	An individual owns a property to which the following applies:

	Cost	$ 1,000
	FMV	$ 5,000

She sells the property to her son for $4,000.

---

[48]S. 69.

Example

Then:

Tax consequences to mother:	
Deemed proceeds of sale	$ 5,000
Cost	(1,000)
Gain	$ 4,000

If the son sells the property at its fair market value of $5,000, he also realizes a gain of $1,000:

Actual proceeds of sale	$ 5,000
Actual cost of property	(4,000)
Gain	$ 1,000
Total gain:	
Realized by mother	$ 4,000
Realized by son	1,000
	$ 5,000

Thus, an asset with an accrued gain of $4,000 triggers an actual gain of $5,000. The $1,000 that is exposed to double taxation represents the shortfall between the fair market value of the property ($5,000) and the price at which it is sold ($4,000).

---

7. — Timing of Income

We saw earlier that employment income is generally taxed on a cash basis. In contrast, with a few important exceptions, business and property income are normally calculated on an accrual basis. Thus, generally speaking, income from business and property are recognized for tax purposes when services are performed or goods are sold, rather than when payment for the goods or services is actually received. In other words, although a taxpayer may have to wait for some time to receive payment for goods sold or services rendered, he or she will be taxed on income in the year in which it is earned.

The accrual method of accounting is the appropriate method of determining profit in most circumstances. It warrants emphasis, however, that this is *not* the only acceptable method for tax purposes. Since subsection 9(1) is silent on the method of accounting that one can use to calculate "profit", a taxpayer is free to use generally accepted accounting principles appropriate to his or her circumstances if the method is not prohibited by the Act or by judicial precedent.[49]

(a) — Payments in Advance

The accrual method is modified by the Act for certain payments. For example, payments received in advance of rendering a service or sale of goods are included in income even though the payments represent unearned amounts that would usually be excluded from income for accounting purposes. Under accounting principles, unearned revenue is considered a liability. For tax purposes, unearned revenue is included in income in the year the payment is received, rather than when the revenue is earned. A taxpayer may, however, claim a reserve for goods and services to be delivered in the future.[50]

(b) — Receivables

A taxpayer is to include in income all amounts *receivable* by the taxpayer in respect of property sold or services rendered in the course of business carried out during the year.[51]

"Receivable" means that the taxpayer has a clearly established *legal right* to enforce payment at the particular time under consideration:[52]

> In the absence of a statutory definition to the contrary, I think it is not enough that the so-called recipient have a precarious right to receive the amount in question, but he must have a clearly legal, though not necessarily immediate, right to receive it.

For example, in the construction industry, it is usual practice, when work is performed under a contract extending over a lengthy period of time, for interim payments to be made to the contractor. These payments, which are based on progress reports, are usually subject to a percentage holdback to ensure satisfactory completion of the project. In these circumstances, holdbacks need not be brought into income as "receivables" until such time as the architect or engineer has issued a final certificate approving the completion of the project.[53]

---

[49]*Oxford Shopping Centres Ltd. v. The Queen*, [1980] C.T.C. 7, 79 D.T.C. 5458 (F.C.T.D.); affd. [1981] C.T.C. 128, 81 D.T.C. 5065 (F.C.A.).

[50]Paras. 12(1)(a) and 20(1)(m).

[51]Para. 12(1)(b).

[52]*M.N.R. v. Colford (J.) Contr. Co.*, [1960] C.T.C. 178 at 187, 60 D.T.C. 1131 at 1135 (Ex. Ct.); affd. without written reasons [1962] S.C.R. viii, [1962] C.T.C. 546, 62 D.T.C. 1338 (S.C.C.).

[53]*M.N.R. v. Colford (J.) Contr. Co.*, [1962] S.C.R. viii, [1962] C.T.C. 546, 62 D.T.C. 1338 (S.C.C.).

An amount is deemed to be receivable on the earlier of the day the account is actually rendered and the day on which it *would have been* rendered had there been "no undue delay" in rendering the account.

(c) — Professionals

(i) — Modified Accrual

The rules in respect of the computation of income of certain professionals (accountants, dentists, lawyers, medical doctors, veterinarians and chiropractors) vary somewhat from the normal accrual basis of accounting. These professional businesses may report income on a so-called modified accrual basis by electing to exclude work in progress in the computation of income.[54] On the sale of the professional business, any work in progress previously excluded is brought into the income of the vendor.[55]

(ii) — Work in Progress

Generally, if a professional elects to exclude work in progress in the computation of income, his or her income is computed on the basis of fees billed, subject to any adjustment for undue delay in billing. The election is binding on the taxpayer for subsequent years unless it is revoked with the consent of the Minister.[56]

(iii) — Advance Payments

Amounts received in advance of performance of services are included in income unless the funds are deposited in a segregated trust account.[57] For example, a lawyer who obtains a retainer that must be returned to the client in the event of non-performance of services may exclude the retainer from income if the funds are deposited in a trust account.[58] The taxpayer may, however, claim a deduction in respect of services that will have to be rendered after the end of the year.[59]

---

[54]Para. 34(a).

[55]Para. 10(5)(a) and s. 23.

[56]Para. 34(b); see IT-457R, "Election by Professionals to Exclude Work-In-Progress from Income" (July 15, 1988).

[57]Para. 12(1)(a).

[58]IT-129R, "Lawyers' Trust Accounts and Disbursements" (November 7, 1986).

[59]Para. 20(1)(m).

(d) — Farmers and Fishers

Income from a farming or fishing *business* may be calculated on a cash basis. Thus, the income of a taxpayer from a farming or fishing business is computed by aggregating amounts *received* in the year and deducting therefrom amounts *paid* in the year. Accounts receivable are included in income only when they are disposed of by the taxpayer.[60]

X. — Reserves And Allowances

1. — Prohibition Against Reserves

The term "reserve" is now in disfavour among accountants because it has been applied so widely as to lose any specific meaning. Nevertheless, the term continues to be employed in commercial jargon. The Act specifically sets its face against "reserves".[61]

The general prohibition in paragraph 18(1)(e) of a deduction for any reserve, "contingent account" or "sinking fund", except as specifically permitted by the Act, not only causes accounting for tax purposes to deviate significantly from accounting for other purposes, but it also produces inconsistencies within the system of income tax accounting.

Whether we refer to "reserve", "allowance", "contingency fund" or some other expression, accountants recognize that a simplistic presentation of accrual basis financial statements fails to estimate profitability accurately. The failure results from overlooking *future* risks or obligations that affect *present* profitability. An obvious example is depreciation of capital assets. It would be foolish, and poor accounting, to fail to recognize an asset's ultimate obsolescence or exhaustion over a period of time. As already noted, the *Income Tax Act* concedes the wisdom of depreciating capital assets and provides for this by way of the capital cost allowance or tax depreciation system.

A clear line must, however, be drawn between depreciation and a decline in the market value of an asset. Although an accountant might think it is prudent for financial statement purposes to recognize a paper loss on investments, the tax system does not allow such an accounting practice for the purpose of determining net income. In *M.N.R. v. Consolidated Glass Ltd.*,[62] for example, the taxpayer attempted to deduct as a capital loss an amount that reflected the decline in value of the shares of its subsidiary company. A majority of the Supreme Court of Canada held that the taxpayer could not claim a loss in respect of assets of a fluctuating value until such time as the assets were sold or became worthless so that the loss was irrevocable.

---

[60]S. 28.

[61]Para. 18(1)(e).

[62]*M.N.R. v. Consolidated Glass Ltd.*, [1957] S.C.R. 167, [1957] C.T.C. 78, 57 D.T.C. 1041 (S.C.C.).

2. — Doubtful and Bad Debts

Accounts receivable is a major balance sheet asset for many businesses. Receivables are normally recorded on the books at face value, i.e., at the value stated on the invoice. As with depreciation, it would be foolish to ignore the obvious risk that all of the accounts of a business are not collected. Every business that sells on credit suffers some credit risk. Although this is the sort of contingent risk that the Act is careful to prevent taxpayers from exploiting, it specifically authorizes a deduction for a reserve for doubtful debts[63] and bad debts.[64]

A taxpayer's doubtful debt reserve may be based on an analysis of the likelihood of collection of individual accounts. Alternatively, it may be stated as a percentage of total accounts receivable. The CRA, however, does not consider percentage based reserves to be reasonable.[65] In either case, the deduction must be reasonable. The mere fact that a debt has remained unpaid for a considerable time is not determinative that it is bad.[66]

The deduction for bad debts is in respect of debts "that are established by the taxpayer to have become bad debts in the year."[67]

3. — Pre-Paid Income

We can make an adjusting entry to reduce current income by setting up a balance sheet liability to reflect the fact that some income received was unearned. For example, X Widgets sets up a liability, "rent received in advance", for the purpose of moving $300, received in its fiscal period ending October 31, into the following accounting period. If the prepayment were a deposit and subject to refund on demand, it could be said that X Widgets had not "realized" the amount and should not recognize it in income at that time.

---

[63]Para. 20(1)(l).

[64]Para. 20(1)(p).

[65]See para. 24 IT-442R.

[66]See *No. 81 v. M.N.R.* (1953), 8 Tax A.B.C. 82, 53 D.T.C. 98 (factors to consider are time element, history of account, finances of client, taxpayer's past experiences with bad debts, business conditions in locality and in country, and relative sales volume); *No. 409 v. M.N.R.* (1957), 16 Tax A.B.C. 409, 57 D.T.C. 136 (delay in payment not sufficient to justify reserve after two months, in circumstances); *Atlas Steels Ltd. v. M.N.R.* (1961), 27 Tax A.B.C. 331, 61 D.T.C. 547 (reserve of 3 per cent of accounts receivable allowed in circumstances despite unfavourable comparison with company's history of collections). See also CRA Rulings doc. 9238377.

[67]Para. 20(1)(p).

Assuming, however, that X Widgets can retain the $300 even if the payer discontinues use of the rented property, it is nevertheless incorrect, from an accrual accounting point of view, to recognize the $300 in the period ending October 31.

There are two ways of expressing the accountant's concern that current income is being overstated. One is to say that revenue is overstated because the $300, though received, has not yet been earned. The other is to say that income is overstated as a result of failure to recognize a business liability in the next accounting period, i.e., the obligation to make the rented property available for three months. Although these two ways of expressing the matching concept boil down to the same thing in accounting terms, they are not at all alike for income tax purposes.

(a) — Inclusion in Income

Paragraph 12(1)(a) reads as follows:

> There shall be included in computing the income of a taxpayer for a taxation year as income from a business or property such of the following amounts as are applicable:
>
> > (a) any amount received by the taxpayer in the year in the course of a business
> >
> > > (i) that is on account of services not rendered or goods not delivered before the end of the year or that, for any other reason, may be regarded as not having been earned in the year or a previous year, or
> > >
> > > (ii) under an arrangement or understanding that it is repayable in whole or in part on the return or resale to the taxpayer of articles in or by means of which goods were delivered to a customer. . . .

Obviously, this requires X Widgets to bring the $300 into income, whether or not it has been earned. The question which then arises is whether X Widgets can make an entry to reflect the overstatement of income. The reference in paragraph 12(1)(a) to amounts "regarded as not having been earned" confirms that the adjustment cannot be made directly to the statement of revenues. In any event, normal accrual accounting practice would recognize the receipt and make the adjustment by setting up the liability (unearned income) to reflect the future obligation to provide the rental property.

(b) — Deduction from Income

This brings us back to paragraph 18(1)(e), which prohibits all reserves except those expressly permitted. Fortunately for X Widgets, subparagraph 20(1)(m)(iii) expressly allows "a reasonable amount as a reserve in respect of . . . periods for which rent or other amounts for the possession or use of land or chattels have been paid in advance."

X Widgets is a simple example of future obligations that affect current income and can easily be accommodated because the future obligation can be precisely quantified and its occurrence can be precisely predicted. Thus, there are no problems of measurement or timing. Other examples may be found in the publishing business, which receive prepaid subscriptions for which the publisher must provide magazines for a determined future period, and the entertainment business, which sells tickets for future performances with each ticket referable to a specified seat on a specified date.

(c) — Uncertainty

In other circumstances, however, businesses may legitimately claim future obligations, but the amount of the obligation may be uncertain both in respect of quantum and timing. Contrast the sale of season tickets to hockey games with the sale by a movie theatre chain of gift books of tickets for cinema performances. In the first case, the hockey club knows the date of each performance for which ticket revenue has been received. Whether or not the seats are occupied, the revenue is earned, and the club's obligation is satisfied on a game-by-game basis as each game is played. In the second case, the theatre company knows neither when the gift tickets will be used, nor how many will go forever unused.

There may be an intermediate situation, in which a business cannot accurately predict the amount of its future obligation, but it can at least predict the timing within reasonable limits. An example would be the dinner-of-the-month arrangement under which a group of restaurants participate in a promotional scheme of selling books of tickets for free dinners at participating restaurants. Each book contains 12 tickets; each ticket is usable at a specified restaurant during a specified month. As each ticket entitles the user to a free meal equal in value to another purchased at the same time by the user's dinner partner, Restaurant A cannot be certain of its maximum obligation. Perhaps it can make a reliable estimate based on past experience. In any event, each month, the obligation for that month is determined, and at the end of 12 months the entire obligation has been quantified and satisfied.

A common business situation, rather like the one just described, is that of the insurance agent or broker who receives commissions in respect of insurance contracts extending into a future period. The broker knows that clients will have to be serviced over the period remaining under each contract, but the extent of the potential obligation in each case is highly speculative. Subsection 32(1) resolves the difficulty arbitrarily by allowing the agent or broker to set up a *pro rata* reserve in respect of unearned commissions.

(d) — Reserve for Future Goods and Services

Paragraph 20(1)(m) authorizes a reserve for a "reasonable amount" for goods or services "that it is reasonably anticipated will have to be delivered [or rendered] after the end of the year."[68] The same provision allows a reasonable reserve for anticipated refunds of deposits

---

[68]Subparas. 20(1)(m)(i) and (ii).

made on containers or other "articles in or by means of which goods were delivered to a customer."[69] The uncertainty involved in determining the amount of these future obligations is apparent from the requirement of the provision that the reserve be a "*reasonable* amount" and that the obligation be "*reasonably* anticipated".

A special problem of future obligations arises from a certain promotional technique used by some retailing businesses. A customer making a purchase at a Canadian Tire Store, for example, receives some "funny money", a form of scrip that can be applied to future purchases at Canadian Tire. Other businesses have used trading stamps that, after a sufficient quantity were accumulated, could be redeemed for merchandise. For a time, some of the major oil companies issued a card in which a hole was punched on the occasion of a purchase from one of the company stations. When the prescribed number of holes had been punched, the card could be redeemed for a set of dishes or cutlery. In all of these cases, the business is being carried on in such a way that current profitability will be overstated unless the future obligation to redeem the scrip, the trading stamps, or the cards is recognized. The problems inherent in any attempt to determine the amount and the timing of future obligations generated by such promotional schemes are, however, very difficult. The proportion of the trading stamps thrown away or lost is probably high, just as it is very likely that the "funny money" will be carried around in the wallets of Canadian Tire customers for years.

In *Dominion Stores Ltd. v. M.N.R.*,[70] the Minister argued that the taxpayer was not entitled to a deduction under paragraph 20(1)(m), which is conditional upon showing that the reserve is in respect of amounts that have been included in the taxpayer's income pursuant to paragraph 12(1)(a). The Minister argued that the "green stamps" given to customers were free, as they were advertised to be, and that the entire payment by the customer was referable to the food and other items being purchased at the time. Accordingly, Dominion Stores had no income in respect of the green stamps and was not entitled to any reserve to recognize the future obligation to redeem them. Cattanach J. held that the price paid at the check-out desk was a combined price for both the goods being purchased and the green stamps that accompanied them. The taxpayer was, therefore, entitled to take a reserve. It is interesting to note that only this narrow legal issue was submitted to the Court. The parties had, by agreement, fixed the appropriate amount of the reserve if the taxpayer was permitted to take it. Obviously, the determination of a "reasonable reserve" would require careful analysis of past experience with green stamp redemptions, and some speculative estimate as to the proportion that would never be redeemed.

---

[69]Subparas. 20(1)(m)(iv) and 12(1)(a)(ii).

[70]*Dominion Stores Ltd. v. M.N.R.*, [1966] C.T.C. 97, 66 D.T.C. 5111 (Ex. Ct.).

XI. — Accounting For Inventory

1. — *Cost of Goods Sold*

The largest single item of expense in a trading or manufacturing business is likely to be the cost of the goods sold. In most businesses that handle a large volume of items that cannot be individually identified, it is neither possible nor desirable to keep a running total of the cost of the goods being sold on a daily basis. The only feasible way to determine the cost of all the goods sold in an accounting period is to add the value of the inventory on hand at the beginning of the period to the cost of inventory purchased during the period and then subtract the value of the inventory on hand at the end of the period. The formula becomes:

Cost of Goods Sold = Opening Inventory + Acquisitions – Closing Inventory

If prices are stable, this formula may give rise to little difficulty. An important problem of valuing opening and closing inventory arises, however, if prices are rising or falling. For example, assume 10,000 units of inventory on hand at the opening of the period, and a current price of $1 per unit;[71] assume 10,000 units on hand at the end of the period and a current price of $4 per unit. Assume also that 100,000 units are traded during the period, the price having risen steadily as the business bought units each month. In many businesses, it will be impossible to say whether the 10,000 units in closing inventory are the same ones as those in the opening inventory, or whether some or none remain from the opening of the period.

If both opening and closing inventory are valued at $10,000, the cost of goods sold will be shown as $30,000 more, and profits will be $30,000 less, than if closing inventory is valued at $40,000.

2. — *Alternative Methods*

The Act permits two general methods of valuing inventory:[72]

    1. Valuation at the *lower* of cost or fair market value for *each* item of inventory; or

    2. Valuation of the entire inventory at fair market value.

---

[71]Note that we are here assuming a price of $1 to the taxpayer and are ignoring the "value" to the taxpayer in the sense of its current resale price. This would obviously add further complexities to the problem of appropriate valuation of inventory.

[72]Subs. 10(1); Reg. 1801. Artists and writers may elect a nil value for their inventory under subs. 10(6).

A taxpayer's inventory at the beginning of the year must be valued at the same amount at which it was valued at the end of the immediately preceding year.[73]

3. — Change of Method

A taxpayer must use the same method of valuation from year to year in the absence of permission from the Minister.[74]

Interpretation Bulletin IT-473R provides:[75]

> A change in the method of valuing inventory will generally be approved by the Minister if it can be shown that, considering the circumstances, the new method:
>
> 1. is a more appropriate way of computing the taxpayer's income;
>
> 2. will be used for financial statement purposes by the taxpayer; and
>
> 3. will be used consistently in subsequent years.

XII. — Conclusion

The arbitrary division of a business lifetime into annual segments produces numerous accounting problems. These problems are greatly exacerbated because of the annual accounting for income tax purposes. Under a progressive rate structure, an individual whose income fluctuates widely over a number of years will pay more tax than another taxpayer with the same aggregate income over the period but with little annual fluctuation.

Further, a serious problem occurs when income falls below zero in some years. Without a system of negative income tax and refunds, there is no automatic solution for a taxpayer with a net loss tax year. Some relief is available in section 111 for the carryover of losses from one tax year to another. Loss carryovers and related issues are discussed in Chapter 16 "Computation of Tax Payable".

The measurement of income or profit, which is the foundation of the taxable base on which we impose taxes, is an imperfect art that involves many estimates, assumptions and judgment calls. To be sure, ultimately, net taxable income is a single number on which we impose taxes. The number itself, however, is at best an educated estimate of properly matched revenues and expenses, accounting principles, judicial doctrines, political and tax policy considerations. To understand the measurement of income one must understand law, economics and accounting principles.

---

[73]Subs. 10(2).

[74]Subs. 10(2.1).

[75]IT-473R, "Inventory Valuation" (December 21, 1998), para. 8.

Selected Bibliography to Chapter 5

Measurement of Income

Arnold, Brian J., "Timing and Income Taxation: The Principles of Income Management for Tax Purposes," in *Proceedings of 35th Tax Conf.* 133 (Can. Tax Foundation, 1983).

Harris, Edwin C., "Measuring Business Income", in *Proceedings of 19th Tax Conf.* 78 (Can. Tax Foundation, 1967).

Drobny, Sheldon, "Inventory and Accounting Methods: Controversy and Paradoxes" (October 1990) 68 Taxes 764.

Kaplow, L. and A.C. Warren, "The Bankruptcy of Conventional Tax Timing Wisdom is Deeper Than Semantics: A Rejoinder to Professors Kaplow and Warren, [Discussion of An Income Tax By Any Other Name — A Reply to Professor Strand]" (1986) 38 Stan. L. Rev. 399.

Robertson, D.A., "Timing is Everything" (1988) 121:3 CA Magazine 32.

Strand, J., "Tax Timing and the Haig-Simons Ideal: A Rejoinder to Professor Popkin [Discussion of Tax Ideals in the Real World: A Comment on Professor Strand's Approach to Tax Fairness]" (1986) 62 Ind. L.J. 73.

White, Robert, "Profits and Prophets — An Accountant's Afterword" (1987) 8 Br. Tax Rev. 292.

Basic Income Tax Accounting

Cooper, Graeme S., "Some Observations of Tax Accounting" (1986) 15 Aust. Tax Rev. 221.

Knight & Knight, "Recent Developments Concerning the Completed Contract Method of Accounting" (1988) 41 Tax Exec. 73.

Roberts, J.R. and William Leiss, "Technological and Accounting Innovation: Can They Mesh?" (1986) 36 Can. Tax Foundation Conf., Report of Proceedings 25:1.

Strand, J., "Tax Timing and the Haig-Simons Ideal: A Rejoinder to Professor Popkin [Discussion of Tax Ideals in the Real World: A Comment on Professor Strand's Approach to Tax Fairness]" (1986) 62 Ind. L.J. 73.

Generally Accepted Accounting Principles

Drobny, Sheldon, "Inventory and Accounting Methods: Controversy and Paradoxes" (October 1990) 68 Taxes 764.

McDonnell, T.E., "Falling Between the GAAP's?" (1991) 39 Can. Tax J. 1313.

Murray, K.J. and Nicole Mondou, "The Relevance of GAAP in Cyprus Anvil Mining Corporation v. The Queen" (1990) 3 Can. Current Tax P5.

Padwe, Gerald W., "The Death of G.A.A.P. Reporting — A Tale from the Folks Who Brought You U.S. Tax Reform", *Corporate Management Tax Conf.* 11:1 (Can. Tax Foundation, 1987).

Strain, William J., "Now You See It, Now You Don't: The Elusive Relevance of G.A.A.P. in Tax Accounting", in *Proceedings of 37th Tax Conf.* 38 (Can. Tax Foundation, 1985).

Realization and Recognition of Income

Callard, Rosalind M., "When to Recognize Revenue" (1986) 119 CA Magazine 67.

Durnford, John W., "If it Is Payable, Is it Due?" Can. Tax Letter, June 3, 1983 (De Boo).

Freedman, Judith, "Profit and Prophets — Law and Accountancy Practice on the Timing of Receipts — Recognition Under the Earnings Basis (Schedule D, Cases 1 and 11)" (1987) Brit. Tax Rev. 61 and 104.

Realization of Income: Timing

Arnold, Brian J., "Timing and Income Taxation: The Principles of Income Management for Tax Purposes", in *Proceedings of 35th Tax Conf.* 133 (Can. Tax Foundation, 1983).

Grower, Kenneth W., "Tax Reform and Farmers", in *Proceedings of 40th Tax Conf.* 24:1 (Can. Tax Foundation, 1988).

McNair, D.K., "The Taxation of Farmers and Farming" (1986) Special Lectures LSUC 77.

McNair, D.K., *Taxation of Farmers and Fishermen* (Toronto: Richard De Boo, 1986).

O'Brien, M.L., "Taxation of Profits Derived From Criminal or Illegal Activities" (1988) 2 Can. Current Tax J-85.

Robertson, D.A., "Timing is Everything" (1988) 121:3 CA Magazine 32.

Tiley, John, "More on Receivability and Receipt" (1986) Br. Tax Rev. 152.

Turner, Paul E., "The Reform Down On The Farm'" (July 1990) 24 CGA Magazine 25.

Turner, Paul E., "Restricted Farm Losses" (December 1990) 24 CGA Magazine 47.

Reserves and Allowances

Cadesky, Michael, "Corporate Losses", in *Proceedings of 42nd Tax Conf.* 19:1 (Can. Tax Foundation, 1990).

Frankovic, Joseph V., "Taxing Times: Foreclosures, Default Sales, Debt Forgiveness, Doubtful and Bad Debts" (1991) 39 Can. Tax J. 889.

Krishna, Vern, "Meaning of Allowance" (1986) 1 Can. Current Tax J-144.

Land, Stephen B., "Contingent Payments are the Time Value of Money" (1987) 40 Tax Lawyer 237.

Lokken, Lawrence, "The Time Value of Money Rules" (1986) 42 Tax Rev. 1.

Accounting for Inventory

Arnold, Brian J., "Conversions of Property To and From Inventory: Tax Consequences" (1976) 24 Can. Tax J. 231.

Arnold, Brian J., "Recent Developments in the Tax Treatment of Inventory", in *Proceedings of 31st Tax Conf.* 865 (Can. Tax Foundation, 1979).

Cadesky, Michael, "Corporate Losses", in *Proceedings of 42nd Tax Conf.* 19:1 (Can. Tax Foundation, 1990).

Innes, William I., "The Tax Treatment of Accrued Gains on Inventory at Death" (1992) 12 Estates and Trust J. 122.

Looney, Steve R., "Using L.I.F.O. to Value Costs Under the Completed Contract Method: A Tale of Two Accounting Methods" (1986) 39 Tax Lawyer 235.

McDonnell, Thomas E., "An Inventory Adventure" (1993) 41 Can. Tax J. 965.

McQuillan, Peter E., "Real Estate Inventory Valuation" (1992) Canada Tax Foundation 5:35.

PART IV: OFFICE & EMPLOYMENT INCOME

CHAPTER 6 — EMPLOYMENT INCOME

"Classification is the beginning of wisdom."

> (Seligman, Double Taxation and International Fiscal Cooperation (1928))

I. — General Comment

One of the distinguishing characteristics of the Canadian income tax system is its insistence on rigid classification of income by source. Section 3 of the *Income Tax Act* sets out the manner and sequence in which income from each source is brought into the computation of income. The section identifies the following sources of income:

- Employment;

- Office;

- Business income;

- Property income;

- Capital gains; and

- Other income.

The rules applicable to each of the sources are different and the Act neatly compartmental-izes them in distinct subdivisions. The segregation of income into distinct sources is respon-sible for a considerable amount of complexity in the statute.

Employment income is the single largest source of revenues, and accounts for the majority of the federal government's total income. Hence, tax revenues from this source play a criti-cal role in government financing. Even a small leak in the employment income system can have substantial revenue consequences to federal and provincial treasuries. At the same time, the employment income rules affect a large number of individuals, each of whom is a potential voter. Thus, tax law must be equally sensitive to the need for government revenues and the fair treatment of individuals.

As we will see, the Act tightly controls inclusions in, and deductions from, employment income. This is as much to protect revenues as to obtain a fair measure of net income.

There are essentially three basic issues in the taxation of employment income:

1. Characterization: what is the nature of the income?

2. Timing: when do we tax it? and

3. Scope: what is taxable?

There are four aspects of employment-source income that distinguish it from other types of income. First, the statute strictly controls deductions from employment income: subsection 8(2) prohibits the deduction of any employment-related expense unless it is specifically au-thorized by the Act.[1] This rule keeps a tight rein on employment deductions. In contrast, we presume that deductions from business or investment income are acceptable if they comply with commercial and accounting principles. The presumption is that business expenses are deductible unless the statute specifically prohibits it.[2] Thus, deducting expenses against bus-iness income is much easier than against employment income. This difference between busi-ness and employment income is a powerful incentive for taxpayers to characterize their in-come as business income.

---

[1] Subs. 8(2).

[2] Subs. 9(1); *Royal Trust Co. v. M.N.R.*, [1957] C.T.C. 32, 57 D.T.C. 1055 (Ex. Ct.) (payment of dues and memberships in community and social clubs on behalf of employees deductible where employees expected to make contacts and generate business); *Dom. Taxicab Assn. v. M.N.R.*, [1954] S.C.R. 82, [1954] C.T.C. 34, 54 D.T.C. 1020 (S.C.C.) (fees to company contracting with taxicab owners not deductible; funds contingently received not income); *Bank of N.S. v. The Queen*, [1980] C.T.C. 57, 80 D.T.C. 6009; affd. [1981] C.T.C. 162, 81 D.T.C. 5115 (F.C.A.) (value of foreign tax credit determined in accordance with ordinary commercial principles, taking weighted rate of exchange at time tax payable).

Second, a taxpayer always calculates employment income on a calendar-year basis.[3] Thus, an employee cannot choose any other fiscal year in respect of employment-source income. In contrast, we determine business income based on a fiscal period. This distinction allows individuals some flexibility in tax planning with business income.

Third, we withhold tax on employment income at source,[4] and hold the tax in trust for the Crown.[5] In contrast, there is no systematic withholding at source on business income. Taxpayers who earn business income must make instalment payments on account of their estimated tax payable.[6]

Fourth, employment income is generally taxable on a cash basis.[7] Business and investment income are taxable on an accrual, or as-earned basis, no matter when the taxpayer receives the income.[8]

Because of these restrictions on the computation of employment income, individuals generally prefer independent contractor status for tax purposes. This distinction causes some tension in the characterization of employment relationships.

We must address six issues:

- Is the taxpayer an employee?

- Does the taxpayer hold an office?

- Has the taxpayer received remuneration or taxable benefits?

- What is the value of the remuneration or benefit?

- When did the taxpayer receive the remuneration or benefit?

- Is the taxpayer entitled to any statutory deductions from employment income?

---

[3] Subs. 5(1) and para. 249(1)(b).

[4] Para. 153(1)(a).

[5] Subs. 227(4). Failure to withhold tax on employment income renders the employer liable to a civil penalty of 10 per cent plus interest at a prescribed rate (subs. 227(8)) and to criminal penalties (subs. 238(1)). Directors of a corporation who fail to withhold and remit taxes may be personally liable (subs. 227.1(1)).

[6] Subs. 156(1).

[7] Subs. 5(1). There is an important exception for "salary deferral arrangements"; see para. 6(1)(i), subs. 248(1)"salary deferral arrangement" and subs. 6(11).

[8] S. 9. See Chapter 5 for a discussion of the cash and accrual methods of reporting income.

II. — Nature Of The Employment Relationship

An employee is an individual in an employment relationship. The term "employee" includes an officer. Thus, the key is to determine whether the parties are in an employment relationship. This is not always an easy question to answer.

"Employment" is defined as the position of an individual in the service of some other person.[9] Employment depends upon a contract of service relationship. Thus, the first step in the characterization of employment income is to determine whether such a relationship exists between the taxpayer and the source of his or her income.

There is a considerable volume of litigation on the employment status of individuals. The structure of the Act is such that employees have little scope to claim deductions. Hence, for most tax purposes, individuals would rather not be employees.

In traditional employer-employee relationships, characterization depends on the degree of control and supervision that a person exercises over another in the provision of services. In an employment relationship, the employee is under the direct control and supervision of the employer and is obliged to obey that person's lawful orders. The employer controls not only what the employee does but also how he or she does it. Hence, older cases refer to a contract of employment as a master-servant relationship.

In an independent contract for services, a person engages another to perform services in order to achieve a prescribed objective. The manner of achieving the objective is not prescribed. An independent contractor offers his or her services for a fee. The distinction between the two types of contracts has been described as follows: "It seems to me that the difference between the relations of master and servant and of principal and his agent is this: a principal has the right to direct what the agent has to do; but a master has not only that right, but also the right to say how it is to be done."[10]

Thus, we must evaluate the elements of a relationship to distinguish a contract of employment from a contract for service. The essential elements are:

• The degree of supervision and control between the parties;

• The method of remuneration for services;

• Arrangements for holidays;

• Provisions for sick leave;

• Opportunities for outside employment;

• Provision of medical coverage;

---

[9]Subs. 248(1).

[10]R. v. Walker (1858), 27 L.J.M.C. 207 at 208 (C.C.R.), Baron Bramwell.

- Compensation for work-related travel; and

- The nature of termination clauses.

Determining an employment relationship is essentially a question of fact. There is no absolute formula or bright-line test by which one conclusively determines whether a person is an employee or an independent contractor. No single test invariably yields a clear answer.[11] Indeed, in some situations, an employee may also provide independent contractor services to his employer outside the scope of his regular employment relationship.[12]

There are several legal tests for determining employment status in different situations. None of the tests, however, is definitive in every circumstance. The law continues to evolve as our economy shifts from conventional "bricks and mortar" commerce to electronic global networks. Thus, the law becomes increasingly uncertain, which leads to increasing disputes and litigation.

1. — Supervision and Control

The classic test to determine whether a person retains another as an employee or as an independent contractor is to look at the degree of control over the service provider. This is the test Baron Bramwell used in 1858[13] and that the Supreme Court of Canada adopted in 1978 in *Hôpital Notre-Dame*.[14] Since then, however, the Supreme Court has shifted to a more flexible approach that looks at the total relationship of the parties.[15]

Traditionally, we evaluate control by four principal criteria:[16]

    1. Power to select the person who renders the service;

---

[11]*671122 Ontario Ltd. v. Sagaz Industries Canada Inc.*, [2001] 2 S.C.R. 983, 2001 SCC 59, [2001] 4 C.T.C. 139 (S.C.C.).

[12]See, for example, *Criterion Capital Corp. v. R.*, [2001] 4 C.T.C. 2844 (T.C.C. [General Procedure]). See also *Wolf v. R.*, [2002] 3 C.T.C. 3, 2002 D.T.C. 6853 (F.C.A.).

[13]*671122 Ontario Ltd. v. Sagaz Industries Canada Inc.*, ante.

[14]*Hôpital Notre-Dame et Théoret v. Laurent*, [1978] 1 S.C.R. 605, 17 N.R. 593 (S.C.C.).

[15]See, for example, *671122 Ontario Ltd. v. Sagaz Industries Canada Inc.*, 2001 SCC 59, [2001] 4 C.T.C. 139 (S.C.C.).

[16]See *Gould v. Minister of National Insurance*, [1951] All E.R. 368, [1951] 1 K.B. 731 (K.B.) (contract for services of a music hall artist contained restrictions and elements of control but only those necessary for proper working of the theatre); *Bell v. M.N.R.* (1952), 52 D.T.C. 8 (T.A.B.) (physician to rural villages contracted to provide services; still maintained private practice); *Fainstein v. M.N.R.* (1952), 52 D.T.C. 102 (T.A.B.) (physician and others setting up health departments). See also: *Hôpital Notre-Dame et Théoret v. Laurent*, [1978] 1 S.C.R. 605 at 613 (S.C.C.) where Pigeon J. quoted with

2. Mode and time of payment;

3. Evaluation of the method and performance of work; and

4. Right to suspend or dismiss the person engaged to perform the work.

In a conventional employment relationship the employer selects his or her employee, sets the amount of wages and benefits and the time of payment, evaluates the employee's performance and the work done, and can terminate the relationship with appropriate notice. Further, depending on the employer's policies, he or she may provide supplementary medical coverage and set out policies in respect of travel, sick leave, disability, outside employment, and vacations.

To be sure, each of these facets of the "control test" is useful in characterizing conventional employment relationships. They are, however, only of limited value in characterizing the working relationships of technical persons and skilled professionals. As MacGuigan J. said in *Wiebe Door Services Ltd.*: "... the test has broken down completely in relation to highly skilled and professional workers, who possess skills far beyond the ability of their employers to direct."[17] Thus, the control test is sometimes supplemented by the "organization and integration" test in the case of professionals.

2. — *Organization and Integration*

Characterizing the working relationships of skilled professionals involves more than merely identifying who has the power to dictate how one is to work. In relationships involving skilled persons, the user of services usually does not have the technical expertise or "know-how" to dictate how the service provider is to work. Hence, any power or control that does exist is more illusory than real. After all, the very reason for hiring a professional person is so he or she can instruct management in the performance of complex and technical tasks that are beyond the competence of the user of the service. We hire a professional to provide expertise, not to tell him or her how to do the job.

Thus, the question becomes: is the person an intrinsic part of the organization or merely an adjunct to it? This question is sometimes described as the organization or integration test. But there is no simple formula or single test that supplies the answer. One looks to the whole

---

approval the following passage from *Traité pratique de la responsabilité civile délictuelle* by André Nadeau (translation):

The essential criterion of employer-employee relations is the right to give orders and instructions to the employee regarding the manner in which to carry out his work.

[17]*Wiebe Door Services Ltd. v. M.N.R.*, [1986] 2 C.T.C. 200 at 203, 87 D.T.C. 5025 (F.C.A.); *671122 Ontario Ltd. v. Sagaz Industries Canada Inc.*, [2001] 2 S.C.R. 983, [2001] 4 C.T.C. 139 (S.C.C.), at para. 33.

scheme of operations to elicit the nature of the relationship between the parties. Here, too, the mode and manner of compensation (vacations, sick leave, disability policies, medical coverage, etc...) provide an indication of the nature of a relationship. The greater the number and value of ancillary benefits, the greater the likelihood of an employment relationship.

3. — Total Relationship Test

Although the control and the organization/integration tests are useful in appropriate situations, they are not determinative in all circumstances. They have an overly narrow focus. The better approach is a more broadly based examination of the "total relationship" between the parties,[18] including:

- Supervision and control;

- Ownership of assets;

- Chance of profit; and

- Risk of loss.

No single test is conclusive.[19]

Although the extent of control may vary from case to case, an employment relationship implies some supervision and control over the employee. Further, in an employment relationship the employer usually owns the assets, carries the risk of the enterprise or working relationship, and derives the benefits of profit.

The intention of the parties to the contract, whilst not determinative, should be given some weight if the evidence supports their view of the relationship.

As in most cases that require characterization of relationships, the extremes of the spectrum are always easy to identify. The bank teller is an employee of the bank and under its stringent supervision and control. A partner in a law firm serves clients, but is not an employee of any client. What of the lawyer with only one large client, who provides all the lawyer's revenue, reimburses all his or her expenses, and permits the lawyer to participate in a bonus arrangement that depends on profits? These are not four separate and independent tests. They are different aspects of the same test. We determine the nature of the relationship of persons on an analysis of the whole scheme of operations.

---

[18]See *Montreal (City) v. Montreal Locomotive Works Ltd.* (1946), [1947] 1 D.L.R. 161 at 169-70 (P.C.), Lord Wright.

[19]For a good synthesis see *Market Investigations Ltd. v. Minister of Social Security*, [1968] 3 All E.R. 732, [1969] 2 Q.B. 173 (Eng. Q.B.); *Lee Ting Sang v. Chung Chi-Keung*, [1990] 2 A.C. 374 (Hong Kong P.C.).

4. — Office

Section 5 brings into income a taxpayer's income from an office or employment. The Act defines the term "office" as a position that entitles an individual to a fixed or ascertainable stipend or remuneration.[20] If the stipend is pre-determined in amount, it is fixed. If it is not pre-determined in amount, but may be determined by reference to some formula, it is ascertainable.

The distinction between an "office" and "employment" is that the former does not require the individual to be in the service of some other person, which would imply an employment relationship. For example, judges, ministers of the Crown, and members of a Legislative Assembly or Parliament are "officers" and are not employees for tax purposes. The distinction between an "officer" and an "employee" is not particularly significant for tax purposes because both categories are taxable on their remuneration and benefits.

5. — The Agency's View

The Agency does not have a general administrative position on employment contracts.[21] Interpretation Bulletin IT-525R, "Performing Artists," considers limited aspects of relationships involving musicians and other performing artists. The bulletin does, however, address the particular problems of persons who have special skills and expertise.[22] For example, it considers an artist is self-employed if he or she:[23]

- Has a chance of profit or risk of loss;

- Provides instruments and other equipment;

- Has a number of engagements with different persons during the course of a year;

- Regularly auditions or makes applications for engagements;

- Retains the services of an agent regularly;

- Selects or hires employees or helpers, fixes their salary, directs them, etc.;

- Arranges the time, place, and nature of performances; or

- Earns remuneration that is directly related to particular rehearsals and performances.. . .

---

[20]Subs. 248(1) "office".

[21]The CRA published guidelines on the employed or self-employed issue in RC4110 available on http://www.cra-arc.gc.ca.

[22]*Ibid.*, at para. 4.

[23]*Ibid.*, at para. 7.

6. — *International Dimensions*

Employment status is also an important issue in international tax treaties. For example, under Article XIV of the *Canada-U.S. Tax Treaty*, Canada has the primary right to tax an independent contractor's income that he earns in the United States. The U.S., however, can also tax the income if the individual has a fixed base in that country. This may result in double taxation for which we provide relief under other provisions.[24]

III. — Timing

We generally calculate employment income on a cash-basis. Thus, we tax an individual on his or her earnings in the year that he or she receives payment[25] and credit any taxes withheld at source. These are rules of administrative convenience that allow employees to comply with the tax system with minimum accounting records.

To be sure, cash-basis accounting allows employees some flexibility in tax planning. For example, an owner-manager of a corporation is taxable on his or her salary in the year that he receives payment, whereas the corporation may deduct the salary payable on an accrual basis.[26] This imbalance between deduction and inclusion permits modest tax deferral. If the corporation accrues the deduction on December 31 of a year and it pays the employee on January 1 of the year following, the employee can defer his or her tax on the income for an entire year. The Act tolerates this minor mismatch of deductions and inclusions in the interests of administrative convenience. It does, however, limit the deferral advantage from mismatching income and expenses to a maximum of 180 days after the end of the employer's fiscal period.[27]

IV. — Salary And Wages

An employee (or a person who holds an office) is taxable on his or her salary, wages, and any other remuneration (including gratuities) that he or she receives in the year.[28] Of course,

---

[24]See Chapter 16.

[25]Subs. 5(1); but see *Blenkarn v. M.N.R.* (1963), 32 Tax A.B.C. 321, 63 D.T.C. 581 (T.A.B.) (voluntary deferment of salary due and payable to employee held to be taxable in year amount due, not when actually received); *Ferszt v. M.N.R.*, [1978] C.T.C. 2860, 78 D.T.C. 1648 (T.R.B.) ($5,000 advance against commissions included in income). Farming and fishing businesses also permitted to use cash method of accounting; see s. 28.

[26]*Earlscourt Sheet Metal Mech. Ltd. v. M.N.R.*, [1988] 1 C.T.C. 2045, 88 D.T.C. 1029 (T.C.C.).

[27]Subs. 78(4).

[28]S. 5.

what constitutes "salary or wages" depends on whether there is an employment relationship between the parties. "Remuneration" is compensation for services from an employment relationship, whether past, present, or future.[29]

V. — Benefits

1. — General Comment

Section 5 brings into a taxpayer's employment income amounts that he or she receives as salary, wages, or other remuneration. It is clear, however, that employment income must also include non-cash benefits in income if the tax system is to be equitable among taxpayers.

Section 6 reinforces the equitable principle in section 5 and brings into income the value of any benefits that the taxpayer receives or enjoys in the year.

A benefit is an economic advantage, measurable in monetary terms, that an employer (or related person) confers on an employee in his or her capacity as an employee. It is not always easy, however, to draw the line between taxable and non-taxable benefits. For example:

- Should a promise to pay in the future be taken into income when the promise is given or when the employer makes the payment?

- Should "bargain purchases" and employee discounts result in income?

- When is an employer-provided benefit (for example, child care services) merely a cost to the employer, and when does it become income to the employee?

Benefits constitute compensation and are taxable because their inclusion in income reflects the taxpayer's ability to pay. We saw in Chapter 1 that the principle of horizontal equity requires taxpayers in comparable financial and personal circumstances to bear comparable burdens of tax. The tax treatment of benefits is important to the principle of fairness in taxation. Exclusion of benefits from income would distort the tax system, undermine its integrity, and erode taxpayer confidence in the self-assessment and voluntary compliance

---

[29]Note that the definition of "salary or wages" in subs. 248(1) does not apply for the purposes of calculating employment income under s. 5. See *Adam v. M.N.R.*, [1985] 2 C.T.C. 2383, 85 D.T.C. 667 (T.C.C.) (mere bookkeeping entries not capable of converting salary into something else, e.g., dividends); *Hochstrasser v. Mayes*, [1959] Ch. 22 at 33 (C.A.); *Brumby v. Milner*, [1976] 3 All E.R. 636 (H.L.); *Tyrer v. Smart (Inspector of Taxes)*, [1979] 1 All E.R. 321, [1979] S.T.C. 34 (H.L.); *Nicoll v. Austin* (1935), 19 Tax Cas. 531 (employer requested continued residence of director in costly manor, but paid stipend to compensate for expenses); *Jaworski v. Inst. of Polish Engr. in Great Britain Ltd.*, [1951] 1 K.B. 768, [1950] 2 All E.R. 1191 (C.A.) (oral contract for foreign national stipulated deductions and taxes borne by "employer"; held to be contract for services).

system. Thus, we need to be particularly careful in considering the effect of excluding bene-fits from income on the tax system.

It is not always easy, however, to determine what is a taxable benefit and how much of it we should tax. Consider, for example, the tax status of three individuals: A works for X com-pany, which pays A $4,000 per month and provides him with low-cost meals in its cafeteria, dental coverage for his entire family, access to a club that provides social and recreational facilities, and discount purchases on its goods. The fringe benefits cost X company $400 per month per employee. B is employed by Y Company, a competitor, and receives $4,400 per month in salary. Y company does not give its employees any fringe benefits. C is paid $4,200 per month to work at Z Company, which also does not pay any fringe benefits, but has a better and a more comfortable working environment than either X Company or Y Company. Z Company's premises have better lighting, air conditioning, and are surrounded by attractive parks and gardens. These environmental facilities cost Z Company an average of $200 per month per employee. Should A, B, and C pay tax only on their cash income or on their cash income and benefits? If they should pay tax on all benefits, which of the bene-fits should we consider "taxable" and which, if any, should we exclude from income? If we consider all the benefits to be "taxable", what value should we attach to the benefits — market value, cost to the employer or value to the employee? What if C suffers from aller-gies that are aggravated by Z Company's environmental surroundings: Should C be taxable on any portion of his or her environmental "benefits"?

(a) — Defining Benefits

Subsection 6(1) is quite clear: a taxpayer must include in his or her income "... the value of board, lodging and other *benefits* of *any* kind whatever received or enjoyed. . ." by the tax-payer in the year in respect of, in the course of, or by virtue of his or her office or employment.

A benefit is an economic advantage or material acquisition, measurable in monetary terms, that one confers on an employee in his or her capacity as an employee. Thus, there are several elements of analysis:

- Did the employee receive or enjoy an economic advantage?

- Is the economic advantage measurable in monetary terms?

- Was the economic advantage for the benefit of the employee or for the benefit of his or her employer? and

- Did the employer confer the economic advantage on the employee in respect of, in the course of, or by virtue of the employment relationship with the employee?

If we answer all these questions in the affirmative, the economic advantage or material acquisition is a taxable benefit from employment *unless* the statute specifically exempts it from tax.[30]

The interpretation of "benefit" is clearly broader under the Canadian statute than under its counterpart in the United Kingdom. In the U.K., a benefit in kind was considered income only if it was readily convertible into cash.[31] For example, rent-free accommodation was considered to be a non-taxable benefit because the employee could not readily convert the accommodation into cash. As the House of Lords said in *Tennant v. Smith*: "A person is chargeable for income tax. . . not on what saves his pocket but what goes into his pocket."[32] Paragraph 6(1)(a) clearly displaces the principle in *Tennant v. Smith* (sometimes described as the "money's worth" principle).

The first question in the analysis is whether the taxpayer derives an economic advantage. Benefits come in all sorts of varieties and guises. Some, such as payment of an individual's personal vacation and living expenses by an employer, are obvious. Others are more subtle: for example, the payment of a grievance settlement to a unionized employee,[33] the discharge of a mortgage upon dismissal from employment,[34] or the issuance of stock options by a person other than the employer.[35]

Canadian tax law has wrestled inconclusively with the concept of economic advantage for several decades. *Ransom*[36] was the first of many decisions to distort the equity of the tax

---

[30]See, *The Queen v. Savage*, [1983] 2 S.C.R. 428, [1983] C.T.C. 393 at 399, 83 D.T.C. 5409 at 5414 (S.C.C.) approving the judgment of Evans, J.A. in *The Queen v. Poynton*, [1972] C.T.C. 411 at 420, 2 D.T.C. 6329 at 6335-56 (F.C.A.):

> I do not believe the language to be restricted to benefits that are related to the office or employment in the sense that they represent a form of remuneration for services rendered. If it is a material acquisition which confers an economic benefit on the taxpayer and does not constitute an exemption, e.g., loan or gift, then it is within the all-embracing definition of s. 3. A gift is a gesture of goodwill and is made without regard to services rendered by the recipient of the gift. For example, if an employer distributes turkeys to all employees at Christmas, the value of the turkey is not considered to be a benefit which must be included in an employee's income.

[31]*Tennant v. Smith*, [1892] A.C. 162 (HL).

[32]The law in the U.K. has been changed by statute, which now requires all payment of expenses, including reimbursements, to be included in income.

[33]*Norman v. M.N.R.*, [1987] 2 C.T.C. 2261, 87 D.T.C. 556 (T.C.C.).

[34]*Galanov v. M.N.R.*, [1987] 2 C.T.C. 2353, 87 D.T.C. 647 (T.C.C.).

[35]*Robertson v. The Queen*, [1988] 1 C.T.C. 111, 88 D.T.C. 6071 (F.C.T.D.); affd. [1990] 1 C.T.C. 114, 90 D.T.C. 6070 (Fed. C.A.); leave to appeal refused (1990), 113 N.R. 319 (note) (S.C.C.).

[36]*Ransom v. M.N.R.*, [1967] C.T.C. 346, 67 D.T.C. 5235 (Ex. Ct.).

system. The taxpayer sold his residence at a loss of approximately $4,000 when his employer relocated him from Sarnia to Montreal. The employer compensated the taxpayer for his loss. The Exchequer Court held that the reimbursement for the loss was not taxable because the taxpayer did not benefit from the payment — it did not put any money in his pocket, but merely saved his pocket. The Court applied the money's worth principle despite the unequivocal language of paragraph 6(1)(a).

Ransom clearly offends the principle of horizontal equity. A taxpayer who receives compensation for his or her capital loss on the sale of a home is clearly better off than an individual who is not so compensated. Nevertheless, many courts applied *Ransom* to relocation expenses. In *Canada (A.G.) v. Hoefele*,[37] for example, the taxpayer, who moved from Calgary to Toronto, purchased a house in Toronto that was more expensive than the one he had left in Calgary. His employer picked up the increased mortgage interest on the differential between the two houses, thereby reducing his personal living expenses. The Federal Court of Appeal held that the mortgage interest subsidy was not taxable because the taxpayer was not enriched, but merely restored to his original position. The Court said:[38]

> If, on the whole of a transaction, an employee's economic position is not improved, that is, if the transaction is a zero-sum situation when viewed in its entirety, a receipt is not a benefit and, therefore, is not taxable under paragraph 6(1)(a).

In contrast, the courts said that compensation for the higher cost of a new home in a new location is a taxable benefit because it increases the taxpayer's net worth. In *Phillips*,[39] for example, the taxpayer moved from Moncton to Winnipeg. His employer paid him $10,000 to compensate for his increased housing costs in Winnipeg. The $10,000 subsidy was a taxable benefit because it "did more than save his pocket — it put money into it." Thus, the Court applied the money's worth principle to arrive at the right decision for the wrong reasons.

It is difficult to rationalize the difference between enhancing one's wealth through employer-subsidized financing[40] and subsidized capital costs.[41] Thus, subsection 6(20) provides special tax treatment for eligible housing losses. Generally, one-half of employer reimbursements in excess of $15,000 in respect of eligible housing losses is taxable as an employment benefit to the taxpayer.[42] The one-half exclusion is an accommodation or com-

---

[37][1996] 1 C.T.C. 131, 95 D.T.C. 5602 (F.C.A.).

[38]See also *Splane v. M.N.R.*, [1992] 2 C.T.C. 224, 91 D.T.C. 5549 (F.C.A.).

[39]94 D.T.C. 6177, [1994] 1 C.T.C. 383 (F.C.A.).

[40]*Canada (A.G.) v. Hoefele*, [1996] 1 C.T.C. 131, 95 D.T.C. 5602 (F.C.A.)

[41]*Phillips v. M.N.R.*, [1994] 1 C.T.C. 383, 94 D.T.C. 6177 (F.C.A.).

[42]Subs. 6(20).

promise for those who move from one city to another and incur a loss as a consequence of their move.

The law on the taxation of reimbursements on relocation is neither clear, consistent, nor rational. In *Gernhart v. M.N.R.*,[43] for example, the Tax Court of Canada refused to extend the reasoning of *Ransom* to reimbursements of income tax to accommodate a differential tax burden between Canada and the United States. The taxpayer, an employee of General Motors, moved from Ohio to Windsor. Her employer compensated her for Canada's higher income tax rates by paying her the tax differential between Canadian and U.S. rates in order to equalize her net after-tax income. The Court rightly characterized the reimbursement as a form of salary compensation. It is difficult in principle to distinguish *Gernhart* from *Hoefele*. In both cases, the taxpayer was not enriched, but merely restored to his or her original position. Nevertheless, the decision in *Gernhart* is preferable, in that the taxpayer was taxed on her benefit based on her enhanced ability to pay.[44]

Thus, the taxability of a benefit depends on the answers to several questions. First, has the taxpayer received or enjoyed an economic advantage? If so, was the economic advantage measurable in monetary terms? We tax an employee on benefits that he or she derives from his or her office but not on the pleasure of pleasant working conditions. Pleasure is not a taxable perk of employment.

Although somewhat dated, Kleinwachter's conundrum illustrates the difficulty with taxing working conditions as income to the employee:

> Let us consider here another of Kleinwachter's conundrums. We are asked to measure the relative incomes of the ordinary officer serving with his troops and a *Flugeladjutant* to the sovereign. Both receive the same nominal pay; but the latter receives quarters in the palace, food at the royal table, servants, and horses for sport. He accompanies the prince to the theatre and opera, and, in general, lives royally at no expense to himself and is able to save generously from his salary. But suppose, as one possible complication, that the *Flugeladjutant* detests opera and hunting.

> The problem is clearly hopeless. To neglect all compensation in kind is obviously inappropriate. On the other hand, to include the perquisites as a major addition to the salary implies that all income should be measured with regard to the relative pleasurableness of different activities — which would be the negation of measurement. There is hardly more reason for imputing additional income to the *Flugeladjutant* on account of his luxurious wardrobe than for bringing into account the prestige and social distinction of a (German) university professor. Fortunately, however, such difficulties in satisfactory measurement of relative incomes do not

---

[43]*Gernhart v. R.* (1997), [1998] 2 C.T.C. 102, 98 D.T.C. 6026 (F.C.A.); affg. [1996] 3 C.T.C. 2369, 96 D.T.C. 1672 (T.C.C.); leave to appeal to S.C.C. refused (July 2, 1998).

[44]See subs. 6(20) for eligible housing losses.

bulk large in modern times; and, again, these elements of unmeasurable psychic income may be presumed to vary in a somewhat continuous manner along the income scale.. . .[45]

Now, substitute for the *Flugeladjutant* an executive assistant to the Governor General or Prime Minister. The third question to consider is whether the economic advantage was for the benefit of the taxpayer or for the benefit of the employer who conferred it. A payment that is primarily for the convenience of the employer is not taxable to the employee. Thus, the key is: who is the *primary* beneficiary of the payment? For example, where an employer requires an employee to take computer courses so that he or she is better trained for his or her job, the cost of the job training is not a taxable benefit to the employee even though he or she becomes a better qualified and more valuable person. The benefit to the employee is ancillary to the benefits that the employer derives.

Similarly, where an employer sends her employee for second language training, the expenses are primarily for the benefit of the employer even though the employee is better trained and marketable. What if the employer sends one of its senior executives on a fully reimbursed basis to Paris for three years? Would it make a difference if the executive was 45 years of age or 70 years?

There is no bright-line test, however, to determine what constitutes a benefit to the employee and convenience-to-the-employer, particularly where there are mutual benefits.[46] The convenience-to-the-employer test does not imply that the employee cannot derive pleasure from the task entrusted to him or her. For example, a hotel manager who is "compelled" to live in a luxury suite in a resort hotel is not taxable on the value of the suite if the manager's job requires him or her to be on the premises.[47]

The final question to consider is whether the economic advantage was conferred in respect of, in the course of, or by virtue of the employment relationship between the taxpayer and his or her employer. Did the employer confer the economic advantage on his or her employee *qua* employee or in his or her personal capacity? The former may be taxable; the latter are not taxable as employment income. A gift to an employee in his or her personal capacity, for example, is not a benefit for tax purposes.[48]

---

[45]H. Simons, Personal Income Taxation 53 (1938).

[46]See, e.g., *Cutmore v. M.N.R.*, [1986] 1 C.T.C. 2230, 86 D.T.C. 1146 (T.C.C.) (employees taxed on fees paid for preparation of personal tax returns despite employer's policy requiring such preparation).

[47]*Benaglia v. Comm'r* (1937), 36 B.T.A. 838.

[48]See, e.g., *Busby v. The Queen*, [1986] 1 C.T.C. 147, 86 D.T.C. 6018 (F.C.T.D.); *Phaneuf Estate v. The Queen*, [1978] C.T.C. 21 at 27, 78 D.T.C. 6001 at 6005 (F.C.T.D.), *per* Thurlow, A.C.J.:

Is the payment made "by way of remuneration for his services" or is it "made to him on personal grounds and not by way of payment for his services"? It may be made to an employee but is it made to him as an employee or simply as a person? Another way of stating it is to say is it received in his capacity as employee, but that appears to me to be the same test. To

The fourth question, characterization of capacity, can be difficult.[49] *Savage*[50] is the classic scenario. The taxpayer, a junior employee of a life insurance company, took three courses offered by the Life Office Management Association that were designed to provide a broad understanding of insurance company operations. She undertook the courses of her own volition and without pressure from her employer. Nevertheless, pursuant to its enlightened corporate policy, which was well known to employees, the employer reimbursed the taxpayer $100 for each course that she successfully completed. The reimbursements were taxable benefits. The phrase "in respect of an office or employment" in paragraph 6(1)(a) has wide

> be received in the capacity of employee it must, as I see it, partake of the character of remuneration for services. That is the effect that, as it seems to me, the words "in respect of, in the course of, or by virtue of an office or employment" in paragraph 6(1)(a) have.

See also *Seymour v. Reed*, [1927] A.C. 554 at 559 (H.L.), where Viscount Cave L.C. expressed the question in the following manner:

> ... the question, therefore, is whether the sum. . . fell within the description, contained in r. 1 of Sch. E. of "salaries, fees, wages, prerequisites or profits whatsoever therefrom" (i.e., from an office or employment of profit) "for the year of assessment", so as to be liable to income tax under that Schedule. These words and the corresponding expressions contained in the earlier statutes (which were not materially different) have been the subject of judicial interpretation in cases which have been cited to your Lordships and it must now (I think) be taken as settled that they include all payments made to the holder of an office or employment as such, that is to say, by way of remuneration for his services, even though such payments may be voluntary, but that they do not include a mere gift or present (such as a testimonial) which is made to him on personal grounds and not by way of payment for services. The question to be answered is, as Rowlatt, J. put it: "Is it in the end a personal gift or is it remuneration?" If the latter, it is subject to the tax; if the former, it is not.

[49]*Ball v. Johnson* (1971), 47 Tax Cas. 155; *Hochstrasser v. Mayes*, [1960] A.C. 376 (H.L.) (Court must be satisfied that the service agreement was *causa causans* and not merely *causa sine qua non* of receipt of benefit); *Bridges v. Hewitt*, [1957] 2 All E.R. 281 (C.A.).

[50]*The Queen v. Savage*, [1980] C.T.C. 103, 80 D.T.C. 6066 (F.C.T.D.); revd. on other grounds [1981] C.T.C. 332, 81 D.T.C. 5258 (F.C.A.); affd. [1983] C.T.C. 393, 83 D.T.C. 5409 (S.C.C.).

scope.[51] Thus, the payments were taxable as benefits from employment because they were paid to the taxpayer in her capacity as an employee and primarily for her advantage.[52]

(b) — Timing

Timing and valuations of benefits are inextricably linked to each other. An employee is taxable on benefits that he or she *receives or enjoys* in the year. The word "enjoy" enlarges the benefit rule beyond actual receipt of the benefit.

Section 6 does not distinguish between cash and "in kind" benefits. To illustrate: assume that on September 1 a corporation confers 100 shares of capital stock on its employee. The shares are trading at $100 per share at the time. On December 31 the shares are trading at $125. The employee sells the shares on March 1 for $160 per share and derives an economic gain of $16,000. This raises two issues: (1) how much should we include in the employee's income in the first year when he or she receives the stock? and (2) what should be the employee's gain when he or she sells the stock? The answer to the first question should be

---

[51]*The Queen v. Savage*, [1983] C.T.C. at 399, 83 D.T.C. at 5414. The Court endorses its earlier decision in *Nowegijick v. The Queen*, [1983] 1 S.C.R. 29, [1983] C.T.C. 20 at 25, 83 D.T.C. 5041 at 5045 (S.C.C.):

> ... the words "in respect of" are, in my opinion words of the widest possible scope. They import such meanings as "in relation to", "with reference to" or "in connection with". The phrase "in respect of" is probably the widest of any expression intended to convey some connection between two related subject matters.

The Court also distinguishes earlier English jurisprudence on benefits:

> Our Act contains the stipulation not found in the English statute referred to, "benefits of any kind whatever. . . in respect of, in the course of, or by virtue of an office or employment". The meaning of "benefit of whatever kind" is clearly quite broad.

See also: *Jex v. The Queen*, [1998] 2 C.T.C. 2688, 98 D.T.C. 1377 (T.C.C.) (CRA employee taxed on reimbursement of professional course fees in the absence of any requirement by employer to take courses); *Faubert v. The Queen*, 98 D.T.C. 1380 (T.C.C.).

[52]Dickson, Ritchie, Lamer and Wilson JJ. specifically addressed the question with reference to para. 6(1)(a)); McIntyre J. left the issue open by excluding payment from income under para. 56(1)(n) and not addressing para. 6(1)(a). According to their Lordships (*The Queen v. Savage, ante,* [1983] C.T.C. at 398, 83 D.T.C. at 5413:

> ... the *Hochstrasser* case and *Ball v. Johnson* are of little assistance. The provisions of s. 156 of the *Income Tax Act, 1952* of England are not unlike s. 5(1) of the Canadian *Income Tax Act* but our Act goes further in s. 6(1)(a). In addition to the salary, wages and other remuneration referred to in s. 5(1), s. 6(1)(a) includes in income the value of benefits "of any kind whatever. . . received or enjoyed. . . in respect of, in the course of, or by virtue of an office or employment".

quite clear. Paragraph 6(1)(a) taxes "in kind" and cash benefits equally in the year of receipt. The only issue is the value of the shares, which in this case we can easily determine. The employee is taxable on $10,000, the market value of the shares. In effect, the shares are the equivalent of a cash bonus. If the taxpayer's marginal tax rate is 50 per cent, he or she must pay tax of $5,000 even though the taxpayer did not receive cash. Thus, the taxpayer must either come up with the $5,000 or sell sufficient shares to raise the cash.

The answer to the second question depends upon the answer to the first. If we tax the employee on the value of the $10,000 benefit in the year that he or she receives the shares, we must allow the employee to bump up the cost basis in the shares from zero to $10,000. Otherwise we would tax him or her twice on the same amount when the employee sells the shares in Year 2. The gain when the employee sells the shares is only $6,000, even though he or she did not pay anything for the shares. Thus, the employee must recognize $10,000 of his or her total economic gain in the first year and can defer recognizing $6,000 until he or she sells the shares.

The difference in timing is important. The present value of the $5,000 tax liability in the first year is $5,000. The present value of the $3,000 tax liability in Year 2 is only $2,778 if we assume an interest rate of 8 per cent. Thus, the employee's decision to delay selling the shares affects not only the timing of the liability but also its present value.

If we assume for a moment that the employee is not taxable in the year that he or she receives the shares but only when he or she sells them, the results are quite different. The employee's income inclusion in the first year is nil and does not trigger any tax. In the subsequent year, however, his or her gain on sale is $16,000, the difference between the cost and selling price. At a tax rate of 50 per cent, he or she is liable to pay $8,000. The present value of the tax at an interest rate of 8 per cent is now only $7,407. Thus, the delay of only one year results in a tax saving of $371. Deferring taxes means saving taxes. This, as we will see, is a repeating concern in tax law.

A benefit is taxable only when it vests in the employee.[53] There are considerable difficulties in determining when rights vest in an employee and, if they have vested, the present value of benefits that are payable in the future. For example, how do we determine when an employee "receives or enjoys" a benefit from his or her employer's contribution to his or her pension plan? Should the employee be taxable on the present value of his or her employer's contribution in the year that the employer contributes it or when it vests in the employee? To circumvent these difficulties of timing and value, the Act specifies a detailed scheme for the taxation of deferred income plans.[54] For example, employer contributions to an employee's

---

[53]*Hogg v. The Queen*, [1987] 2 C.T.C. 257, 87 D.T.C. 5447 (F.C.T.D.).

[54]See Chapter 9, "Deductions from Business and Investment Income".

registered pension plan are not taxable upon payment into the plan, but are taxable when the plan makes pension payments to the employee.[55]

(c) — Valuation

Having determined that a particular "in kind" benefit or "perk" is taxable as employment income, the next question is: what is the taxable amount? Should the employee pay tax on the fair market value of the benefit, the cost of the benefit to the employer, or on its exchange value? For example, suppose an airline allows its employees to travel free of charge on its planes on a space-available basis. Should an employee who takes advantage of the facility be taxable on the equivalent of full-fare, advanced booking fare, or standby fare? What is the value of the trip if the employee is "bumped up" into first class because that is the only available space on the flight?

There is no single formula for the valuation of all benefits. We value some benefits at their cost to the employer,[56] others according to market prices for similar products,[57] and others by their opportunity cost.[58]

The valuation of benefits is almost always a contentious issue between taxpayers and revenue authorities. Thus, in the interests of administration and certainty, the Act prescribes valuation formulas for some of the more contentious benefits such as those from automobiles,

---

[55]Subpara. 6(1)(a)(i) and para. 56(1)(a).

[56]See, e.g., *Rendell v. Went* (1964), 41 Tax Cas. 654 (H.L.) (assumption by employer of costs of employee's criminal defence taxable benefit equal in value to amount of cost assumed); see also IT-470R, "Employees' Fringe Benefits" (April 8, 1988) (cost of subsidized meals).

[57]See, e.g., *Wilkins v. Rogerson* (1961), 39 Tax Cas. 344 (C.A.) (second-hand value, rather than cost, of suits supplied by employer to employees was amount of taxable benefit); *per* Harman L.J.:

> ... the only controversy was whether he was to pay tax on the cost of the prerequisite to his employer, or on the value of it to him. It appears to me that this prerequisite is a taxable subject-matter because it is money's worth. It is money's worth because it can be turned into money, and when turned into money the taxable subject-matter is the value received. I cannot myself see how it is connected directly with the cost to the employer.. ... The taxpayer has to pay on what he gets. Here he has got a suit. He can realize it only for £5. The advantage to him is therefore, £5. The detriment to his employer has been considerably more, but that seems to me to be irrelevant. The validity of the Court's reasoning is dubious. Had His Lordship asked the question "what is the value in use?" instead of "what is the value in exchange?", he may have arrived at a different conclusion.

[58]*Youngman v. The Queen*, [1986] 2 C.T.C. 475, 86 D.T.C. 6584 (F.C.T.D.); revd. [1990] 2 C.T.C. 10, 90 D.T.C. 6322 (Fed. C.A.) (shareholder benefit measured by reference to capital cost of house supplied by corporation rather than by reference to its rental value).

stock options and low-cost loans.[59] In other cases, the Agency simply ignores the value of certain perks. The result is that the tax system is riddled with benefits rules and exceptions that distort comparative tax burdens between similarly situated taxpayers.

As a matter of administrative practice and political expediency, the Agency does not tax a benefit unless it can easily measure the value of the benefit in monetary terms. For example, it does not attribute an amount to an employee who is given free parking on his or her employer's premises if such facilities are available to all employees *and* it is not possible to appraise the value of the benefit. It will, however, attribute tax benefits if the perk is selective and it can value it by commercial standards.

Similar considerations apply to employer-provided child care facilities. These exclusions are premised more on administrative convenience than on principles of tax equity. Why, for example, should we exclude a benefit from income merely because similar benefits are extended to all employees? Why not tax all the employees on the value of the benefit?

2. — Taxable Benefits

Benefits come in various forms and guises. For example, travel rewards are taxable as benefits, but only if the reward mileage was accumulated by virtue of the frequent flyer's employment relationship and paid for by the employer. Reward miles are taxable in the year in which the individual uses the miles for airline travel or other personal expenditures. Thus, the benefit is recognized at the time of utilization and not when the miles are credited to the frequent flyer's account. An individual is taxable on the fair market value of the benefit derived from free (or reduced cost) airline travel.

Other common forms of taxable benefits include:

- Board and lodging furnished at an unreasonably low rate (except for the value of board and lodging at special worksites);

- Rent-free or low-rent housing provided by the employer;

- Personal use of employer's automobile;

- Gifts in cash or in kind, including Christmas gifts (with minor exceptions), if the gift is disguised as remuneration;

- Holiday trips, prizes, and incentive awards in recognition of job performance;

- Premiums paid by an employer under provincial hospitalization and medical care insurance plans, and certain Government of Canada plans;

---

[59]See, e.g., subs. 6(2) (formula for automobile benefits), s. 7 (formula for stock option benefits), s. 80.4 (formula for benefit of low-cost loans).

- Tuition fees paid for, or reimbursed to, employees in respect of their private education;

- Travelling expenses of employee's spouse; and

- Interest-free or low-interest loans.

3. — Excluded Benefits

Paragraph 6(1)(a) excludes as taxable benefits any economic advantage derived from:

- Employer contributions to a registered pension plan, group sickness or accident insurance plan, private health services plan, supplementary unemployment benefit plan, deferred profit-sharing plan, or group term life insurance policy;

- A retirement compensation arrangement, an employee benefit plan, or an employee trust;

- A benefit in respect of the use of an automobile (taxed under other provisions);

- Benefits derived from counselling services; and

- Benefits under a salary deferral arrangement (taxed under other provisions).

These exclusions are justified on varied policy considerations.

Also, as a matter of administrative policy, the Canada Revenue Agency (CRA) does not generally consider the following as taxable benefits:[60]

- Discounts on merchandise for employees of merchandising businesses;

- Subsidized meals to employees, staff lunchrooms, and canteens;

- Uniforms and special protective clothing supplied by employers, including cost of laundry and dry-cleaning;

- Subsidized school services for families of employees in remote areas;

- Transportation to the job in a vehicle supplied by the employer free or for a nominal charge;

- Social or athletic club fees where it is to the employer's advantage for the employee to be a member;

- Moving expenses of an employee paid or reimbursed by the employer;

- Premiums under private health services plans paid on the employee's behalf by the employer; and

---

[60]See IT-470R, Consolidated "Employee Fringe Benefits" (August 11, 1999).

- Contributions by employers to provincial hospitalization and medical care insurance plans to the extent that the employer is required to pay amounts to the plan.

4. — Allowances

A taxpayer must include in his income all amounts that he receives in the year "as an allowance for personal or living expenses or as an allowance for any other purpose.. . ."[61] An "allowance" is a limited and pre-determined sum of money paid to an individual. The amount is at the disposal of the recipient, who is not required to account for it. In contrast, a "reimbursement" is a payment to indemnify an individual against actual expenses and is usually accounted for by providing receipts to substantiate the expenditure.[62] The taxability of allowances and reimbursements is fundamental to the fairness of the tax system.

There is no consistent rationale for the taxation of allowances. Most allowances are taxable as income.[63] There are some, however, that are *specifically* excluded by the Act. For example, salespeople who are employed for the purpose of selling property or negotiating contracts may exclude a reasonable allowance paid for travelling expenses. Employees (other than salespeople) may exclude a reasonable allowance paid to them to cover travelling expenses if the allowance is calculated by reference to time spent by the employee travelling away from the municipality where he or she ordinarily works. Hence, employees in receipt of a *per diem* travelling allowance are not taxable on the allowance if the amount of the allowance is reasonable. Similarly, parliamentary expense allowances are not taxable even though they are paid on a non-accountable basis.

(a) — Personal and Living Expenses

Allowances for personal or living expenses are taxable as income unless the Act specifically excludes them. Reimbursement of personal or living expenses is also taxable as income as a benefit under paragraph 6(1)(a). For example, if an employer reimburses his or her employee's credit card bills for personal travel and entertainment, the amount of the reimbursement constitutes a taxable benefit under paragraph 6(1)(a). If, instead, the employer provides his or her employee with an allowance of $5,000 per month for personal and living expenses, the allowance is taxable under paragraph 6(1)(b). Thus, it makes little difference whether a payment to an employee on account of personal or living expenses is an allow-

---

[61]Para. 6(1)(b).

[62]*Gagnon v. The Queen*, [1986] 1 S.C.R. 264, [1986] 1 C.T.C. 410, 86 D.T.C. 6179 (S.C.C.) ("allowance" linked to spouse's ability to dispose of it for own benefit regardless of restriction that it be applied to particular purpose); *The Queen v. Pascoe*, [1975] C.T.C. 656, 75 D.T.C. 5427 (F.C.A.) (Court defines "allowance" and "payable on periodic basis"; note C.T.C. editorial note at 656).

[63]Para. 6(1)(b).

ance or a reimbursement. In either case, the amount is taxable unless there is an exemption that specifically excludes the allowance from income.

The Act excludes the following allowances for personal and living expenses from income:

- Allowances fixed by an Act of Parliament or by the Treasury Board;

- Travel and separation allowances paid to members of the Canadian Forces;

- Representation or other special allowances paid to diplomats and Canadian officials posted abroad;

- Reasonable allowances for travel expenses paid to an employee who is employed to sell property or negotiate contracts for his or her employer;

- Reasonable allowances for travel expenses paid to an employee where the employee is required to travel away from the municipality where his or her employer's establishment is located; and

- Reasonable allowances for the use of motor vehicles received by an employee from the employer for travelling in the performance of the duties of an office or employment.

(b) — Special Work Sites

Allowances for personal living expenses are usually taxable as employment income. In certain narrowly prescribed circumstances, however, employees who must work in remote locations or must commute long distances are permitted tax-free allowances. This exclusion is justified on the basis of the especially high costs of living in remote locations and to encourage part-time employment. An employee who receives an allowance for transportation, board or lodging at a special work site may exclude the allowance from income if he or she also maintains a principal residence at another location.[64] Thus, only employees who actually maintain two residences, one where they regularly live and the other at the temporary work site, can exclude the allowance. Employees who live in temporary work site residences are fully taxable on their allowances. In effect, the tax system subsidizes the high cost of living and working in remote locations rather than passing on the cost to employers in the form of higher wages.

The cost of commuting to and from a place of employment is considered a personal expense. It follows, then, that commuting expenses are not generally deductible from income. A special rule applies, however, with respect to part-time employees who travel substantial dis-

---

[64]Subs. 6(6).

tances to their part-time jobs. A part-time employee who receives an allowance for, or reimbursement of, travelling expenses may exclude the amount received from income if:[65]

- He or she deals at arm's length with the employer;

- He or she is employed or carries on business elsewhere throughout the period of part-time employment;

- The part-time employment is located not less than 80 kilometres from his or her residence and principal place of employment or business; and

- The amount of the allowance or reimbursement is reasonable and is not on account of other non-travel-related expenses incurred in the performance of the part-time employment.

This rule is intended to encourage individuals to seek part-time employment by reducing their taxable costs.

VI. — Advances And Loans

We saw earlier that employees are taxable on a cash basis on their employment income. Thus, advances against salary are taxable in the year in which the employee *receives* the advance.[66] An "advance" is a payment on account of future salary or wages. Typically, the employee is not expected to repay the advance, but to work off his or her financial obligation by rendering service to the employer.[67] In contrast, a loan is a capital transfer and, therefore, is not income. A loan is a debt with provision for repayment within some reasonable time. Thus, the distinction between an advance and a loan lies not in the fact of repayment but in the mode in which the employee will discharge the obligation.

VII. — Automobiles

1. — General Comment

Employees are generally taxable on the benefit that they derive from employer-supplied automobiles. Taxable benefits from employer-supplied automobiles come in two forms: (1) operating expenses, and (2) standby charges. The Act defines an automobile as a motor

---

[65]Subs. 81(3.1).

[66]*Randall v. M.N.R.*, [1987] 2 C.T.C. 2265, 87 D.T.C. 553 (T.C.C.).

[67]IT-421R2.

vehicle that is designed primarily to carry individuals on highways and that has a maximum seating capacity, including the driver, of nine persons.[68]

2. — *Operating Costs*

An employee is taxable on the value of any personal net operating costs that his employer pays on his or her behalf. Thus, employees must allocate gas, oil, maintenance, and insurance costs to determine their personal component.[69] Payments to an employee to compensate for the operating expenses of a personally owned automobile are also taxable as a benefit.

3. — *Standby Charge*

The purpose of the standby charge is to tax employees on the benefit that they derive from the availability of their employer's car for personal use. The employee must pay the charge if he has access to the car for personal use, regardless whether he actually uses it. The benefit derives from availability, not from use.[70]

The amount of the standby charge is set by formula. The essence of the formula is that the benefit is equal to 2 per cent of the original cost (including GST and PST) of the automobile for every month that it is available to the employee. The word "reasonable" in the phrase "reasonable standby charge" is entirely misleading. The formula is a deeming provision that dictates the *exact* amount to be included in the employee's income. The calculation, which has little to do with the value of the benefit, is precise for administrative convenience and to avoid litigation.

Example
Assume that an employer pays $3,600 toward his employee's *personal*-use operating expenses, for which the employee reimburses the employer $1,600.
Then:
(1) Benefit under para. 6(1)(l) — $ 3,600

---

[68]Subs. 248(1).

[69]Para. 6(1)(l).

[70]*Adams v. The Queen*, [1998] 2 C.T.C. 353, 98 D.T.C. 6266 (F.C.A.) (mere right of usage is sufficient to trigger standby charge).

Example

Amount reimbursed	(1,600)	
Inclusion in income		$ 2,000
(2) Standby charge (see next example)		
2% × $23,000 × 12		5,520
Taxable benefits		$ 7,520

To simplify record keeping, however, an employee who uses his or her automobile primarily (that is, more than 50 per cent) for employment purposes can opt to include an additional one-half of the automobile standby charge in income in lieu of his or her share of operating costs.[71] Hence, the employee could include 3, instead of 2, per cent of the cost of the automobile as a taxable benefit.

The basic standby charge in respect of an employer-owned automobile is equal to:

$$\frac{\text{cost} \times 2\% \times (\text{no. of days available})}{30}$$

The number of days divided by 30 is rounded to the next whole number.

Example

Assume:

Personal use	24,000 kms
Basic cost of automobile	$ 20,000
GST & PST	3,000
Total cost of automobile	$ 23,000
Number of days available	365 days
Expenses reimbursed by employee	NIL

Then, a reasonable standby charge is:

---

[71]Subpara. 6(1)(k)(iv).

Example	
$\dfrac{2\% \times 365 \times \$23{,}000}{30}$	$ \$\ \ 5{,}597$

The standby charge for automobile salespeople is calculated somewhat differently. The rate applicable is 75 per cent of the rate applicable to all other employees.[72] Also, the charge is calculated by reference to the *average* cost of *all* automobiles purchased by the employer in the year.

The benefit from leased automobiles is calculated as two-thirds of the cost of leasing the automobile (excepting any portion related to insurance) for the period that the automobile is made available to the employee. The cost of the automobile, in the formula, is its actual cost and not the cost on which the employer is entitled to depreciate it for tax purposes.[73]

4. — Employee-Owned Cars

Where an employee is compensated for the personal use of his or her own car in the course of employment, the nature and amount of compensation determines the tax treatment of the employee. Generally, an amount paid to reimburse an employee for his or her business use of a personally owned car is not included in income. Similarly, a reasonable allowance from an employer as compensation for the business use of a personal automobile is not taxable. Allowances calculated by reference to something other than kilometres driven are deemed not to be reasonable. Where an employee is reimbursed for expenses in addition to being paid a per-kilometre allowance, the Act deems the allowance to be in excess of a "reasonable amount". In these circumstances, the full amount of the unreasonable allowance is taxable to the employee.[74]

VIII. — Imputed Interest

Another popular employment perk is the low cost loan. The Act taxes employees on the imputed benefit that they derive from low cost loans by virtue of their employment.[75]

---

[72]Subs. 6(2.1).

[73]See Class 10.1, Sch. II, Regulations. The maximum is updated from time to time per Reg. 7307(1)(b).

[74]Subparas. 6(1)(b)(x) and (xi).

[75]Subs. 6(9).

The Act deems a benefit to the employee where it is reasonable to conclude that but for the employment, the loan would not have been made to the employee.[76] Thus, a loan to the employee's spouse is taxable to the employee if he or she obtains it by virtue of his or her employment. The taxable benefit is equal to the interest imputed on the loan[77] at a rate that is determined quarterly. The rate is based on the average Treasury Bill rate of the first month during the preceding quarter.[78]

The value of low-interest loans should not be underestimated as a benefit or perquisite of office. A low-interest loan may produce a taxable benefit, but it is taxable at the marginal rate. Thus, the *effective* after-tax cost of a low-cost loan is considerably lower than the cost of commercial loans.

Example

Assume that a taxpayer with a marginal tax rate of 50 per cent receives an interest-free loan of $100,000 from her employer when the prescribed rate is 8 per cent. The imputed interest is calculated as follows:

Taxable benefit (8% × $100,000)	$ 8,000
Tax thereon (50% × $8,000)	$ 4,000
Effective after-tax cost of loan	
($4,000 / $100,000)	4%

Example

Assume that an individual receives a loan of $150,000 by virtue of her employment. She pays $8,000 interest on the loan and a corporation related to the employer pays $3,000 interest on her behalf. The prescribed rate of interest is 12 per cent and the loan is outstanding throughout the year.

Then:

---

[76]S. 80.4(1.1).

[77]S. 80.4(1).

[78]Reg. 4301.

Example	
Prescribed rate × loan amount	
(12% × $150,000)	$ 18,000
Add amounts paid by third party	3,000
	21,000
Less amounts paid on loan	
($8,000 + $3,000)	(11,000)
Taxable benefit	$ 10,000

1. — Exclusions

The imputed interest rules do not apply if the rate at which an employee borrows from his or her employer is equal to, or greater than, the prevailing commercial rate for parties dealing with each other at arm's length.[79] Thus, an employee who borrows from his or her employer at a commercial market rate is not subject to imputed interest if the commercial rate increases after the loan is taken out, if the other terms and conditions of the loan are no more advantageous than those available in the commercial marketplace.

2. — Deemed Payments

An employee deemed to receive imputed interest is also deemed to have paid an equivalent amount pursuant to a legal obligation.[80] Hence, any interest imputed on a loan or indebtedness used for the purpose of earning income (for example, the purchase of shares) is deductible as interest expense.[81]

3. — Forgiveness of Loan

Where an employer forgives a loan to an employee, the principal amount of the loan is included in the employee's income at the time that the employer forgives the loan.[82] An

---

[79]Subs. 80.4(3).

[80]S. 80.5.

[81]Subpara. 20(1)(c)(i).

[82]Subs. 6(15).

imputed interest benefit is not included in income in the year that the employer forgives the loan.[83]

IX. — Stock Option Plans

1. — General Comment

Stock options are a popular form of compensation for employees and senior executives, particularly for employees in the high technology industries. Companies such as Microsoft and Intel made many secretaries into millionaires through their stock option plans. Stock options are attractive both from the employer's and the employee's perspective. They preserve the corporation's cash for capital investment and link its well-being to the employee's remuneration. This gives the employee an ownership interest in his or her employer.

The taxation of stock options, however, raises special problems of timing and valuation. Suppose, for example, that an employer grants its corporate executive an option to purchase 1,000 shares of its stock at $10 a share at any time in the next three years. The shares trade at $12 on the day that the employer grants the option. The shares are non-transferable. The executive can exercise the options only if he or she is an employee of the corporation when he or she triggers the options. The executive exercises the option in Year 2 when the shares are trading at $50 a share and sells the shares in Year 3 for $60 a share. Clearly, the executive makes an overall profit of $50,000 over the three years.

This gives rise to three questions: (1) should we treat all of the gain as employment compensation? (2) when should we tax the profit? and (3) how much of the profit, if any, should we tax?

We can break down the $50,000 profit into at least three components:

Year 1 profit on the day the option is granted	$2,000
Year 2 profit when the option is exercised	$38,000
Year 3 profit when the shares are sold	$10,000

Clearly, the corporation does not give its executive the option for nothing.[84] The stock option is compensation from employment, which the employer gives in exchange for services and as an incentive for performance.

---

[83]Para. 80.4(3)(b). See also IT-421R2 at para. 11.

[84]*Commissioner v. LoBue* (1956), 351 U.S. 243.

The common law rule is that stock option benefits are taxable in the year in which the option is granted.[85] This is so regardless that the taxpayer has not sold the stock and realized a gain. The option represents compensation for personal service and accretion of wealth, albeit only on paper. Hence, any benefit should be taxable as employment income.

The second question is more troublesome and raises issues of timing and value. To be sure, the executive theoretically increases his or her net wealth in Year 1 when he or she acquires a contractual right of $12,000 value. At that time, however, there are various uncertainties. The options have value but only if the executive continues as an employee with the corporation. The price of the stock may decline before he or she exercises the options. Thus, the common law rule creates several problems. It is difficult to value benefits from unexercised options, particularly where the company restricts the right to dispose of the underlying shares ("golden handcuffs").

Of course, we can tax the employee immediately on the $2,000 gain and then allow for retroactive adjustments for price declines etc., or discount the value of the benefit to take the uncertainties into account. Both of these choices create uncertainty and are prone to valuation disputes. Alternatively, we can delay taxation until the employee exercises the options and crystallises his or her profit of $40,000. There is a trade-off in both solutions. If we delay the tax, the taxpayer defers his or her liability and benefits therefrom. If we tax the employee in Year 1, we must discount the value of the benefits for risk and uncertainty, which will likely stimulate litigation.

The third question raises separate policy issues. Clearly, the final $10,000 gain derives from holding the shares that the taxpayer acquires in Year 2. This portion of the gain derives from the taxpayer's investment decision to hold the shares rather than from his or her employment. Thus, we tax this amount as a gain from the sale of capital assets and not as employment compensation.

2. — The Statutory Scheme

The Act addresses each of the above questions in section 7. The basic stock option rule is simple enough: option benefits are taxable as employment income because they are in effect an alternative to cash compensation. The statutory scheme, however, is more complex, because the rules also serve as an incentive for other economic objectives, such as equity ownership in Canadian corporations and employee equity participation. The statutory rules specify both the method of valuation and the timing of inclusion in income.[86]

We must answer three questions:

(a) Does the option benefit derive from employment?

---

[85] See *Abbott v. Philbin*, [1961] A.C. 352 (H.L.); *Commissioner v. Lobue* (1956), 351 U.S. 243.

[86] S. 7; see generally IT-113R4, "Benefits to Employees — Stock Options" (August 7, 1996).

> (b) When is the benefit taxable?
>
> (c) What is the value of the benefit?

(a) — "By Virtue of Employment"

An employee is taxable on stock option benefits only if he or she derives the benefits by virtue of employment.[87] Subject to tax treaty provisions, non-residents are also taxable on stock options in respect of employment in Canada, regardless of where they exercise the options.[88] Thus, the first question is: does the employee derive the benefit in respect of, in the course of, or by virtue of his or her employment relationship? Stock options issued for other considerations (for example, as a gift or in return for guaranteeing a loan) are not a benefit from employment.[89]

(b) — Timing

The benefit of an option is recognized when shares are acquired at a price less than their value. Thus, timing is the key. We determine the time of acquisition by reference to general principles of commercial practice, as modified by statute. For example, a federal corporation may not issue shares until they are fully paid for in money or in property.[90] Thus, under federal corporate law, a taxpayer cannot acquire shares in a corporation until he or she pays for the shares. In some other jurisdictions, however, shares may be purchased and paid for at different times on an installment basis. In these circumstances, shares are acquired at the time the contract is completed, even though the shares are not paid for until a later date.

(c) — Valuation

The value of the benefit is determined when the shares are acquired or the option exercised.[91] The benefit is equal to the difference between the cost of the option to the employee, any amount paid for the shares, and the value of the shares at the time they are

---

[87]Subs. 7(5).

[88]*Hale v. The Queen*, [1992] 2 C.T.C. 379, 92 D.T.C. 6473 (F.C.A.).

[89]*Busby v. The Queen*, [1986] 1 C.T.C. 147, 86 D.T.C. 6018 (F.C.T.D.) (options granted by virtue of taxpayer's "special" relationship with principal shareholder and for guaranteeing corporation's loans were not taxable as employment income). See also IT-113R4.

[90]*Canada Business Corporations Act*, R.S.C. 1985, c. C-44, subs. 25(3); see also *Business Corporations Act*, R.S.O. 1990, c. B.16, subs. 23(3).

[91]*Steen v. The Queen*, [1988] 1 C.T.C. 256, 88 D.T.C. 6171 (F.C.A.).

acquired from the plan.[92] For example, if an individual acquires 100 shares at a cost of $10 per share when the shares have a value of $15 per share and he or she pays $1 per share for the option, the value of the taxable benefit is $4 per share or $400. At a tax rate of 50 per cent, the net cost of the benefit is $200. The individual would be in the same financial position if the employer paid him or her an additional $400.

"Value" means "fair market value".[93] In the case of publicly traded securities, stock market prices are usually indicative of fair market value. Since listed stock prices inherently reflect the value of minority shareholdings, there is no need to further discount their value for minority interests. The valuation of shares of private corporations is a more difficult matter. Shares of private corporations are generally valued by reference to estimated future cash flows and the adjusted net value of assets. The *pro rata* value of the corporation may be adjusted to reflect a discount for minority interests and lack of liquidity.

3. — Incentive Provisions

The general stock option rule is that option benefits are taxable as employment income. In addition to the general rule, however, there are two special rules. One applies to options issued by Canadian-controlled private corporations ("CCPC") and the other to acquisitions of prescribed equity shares. These rules are essentially incentive provisions to promote equity participation in Canadian corporations.

(a) — Options Issued by CCPCs

The taxable benefit from shares acquired from a CCPC's stock plan in an arm's length transaction is reduced if the taxpayer holds the shares for at least two years.[94] The employee may defer recognition of any benefit that he or she derives from the stock options until he or she disposes of the shares. This rule delays the point of income recognition and defers the tax. The longer the employee holds on to the shares, the greater the value of the tax deferral. Second, when the employee disposes of the shares, he or she is taxable on only 1/2 of the value of the benefit derived.[95] Thus, the employee transfers 1/2 of the benefit into exempt income.

---

[92]Para. 7(1)(a).

[93]See, e.g., *Steen v. The Queen*, [1986] 2 C.T.C. 394, 86 D.T.C. 6498 (F.C.T.D.); affd. [1988] 1 C.T.C. 256, 88 D.T.C. 6171 (F.C.A.).

[94]Subs. 7(1.1) and para. 110(1)(d.1).This is so whether the shares are issued by the employer corporation or by another CCPC with which the employer does not deal at arm's length.

[95]See subs. 7(1.1) and para. 110(1)(d.1).

An employee who disposes of his or her shares in a CCPC within two years from the date that he or she acquires them is usually taxable on the full value of any benefit derived in the year that the employee disposes of the shares.[96] An exchange of options or of shares as a consequence of an amalgamation or a share-for-share exchange is not a disposition for the purposes of the two-year rule.[97]

The Act deems shares that are identical properties to be disposed of in the order they are acquired.[98]

(b) — Options for Prescribed Shares

A less generous rule applies to stock option plans under which an individual acquires pre-scribed equity shares in his or her employer's corporation or in a corporation with which the employer does not deal at arm's length: the employee is taxable on only 1/2 of the value of any benefit derived from such a plan, but the benefit is taxable on a current basis. Thus, the employee cannot defer the tax under such a plan, but may convert 1/2 of his or her benefit into tax-exempt income.[99] This rule applies under the following conditions:[100]

- The shares must be prescribed[101] at the time of their sale or issuance;

- The exercise price plus any amount paid to acquire the stock option must be equal to or greater than the fair market value of the shares at the time that the agreement was made; and

- The employee must have been at arm's length with the employer and the issuing corpo-ration immediately after the agreement was made.

Non-residents are also eligible to claim the benefit of this special treatment.

The purpose of this rule is to encourage corporate employers to draw their employees into common share ownership. The rule promotes employee participation in equity ownership with employers in order to increase economic productivity. Thus, the rule compromises hor-izontal equity in favour of economic incentives.

---

[96]Subpara. 110(1)(d.1)(ii). But see IT-113R4 (para. 19).

[97]Subss. 7(1.4) and 7(1.5).

[98]Subs. 7(1.3).

[99]See note below.

[100]Para. 110(1)(d).

[101]Reg. 6204.

A special election to defer tax within limits is available under subs. 7(8) for publicly traded shares. The maximum amount eligible for deferral is $100,000 annually. Any benefit over the annual limit is taxable in the year that the employee exercises his options.

4. — *Comparison of Option Plans*

The effect of the three different types of stock option plans described above are set out below:

Example

Assume that an employee acquires shares in the following circumstances:

Case (A)   General Rules

    Shares with a fair market value (FMV) of $100 for $76.

Case (B)   CCPC

    Shares with FMV of $100 for $76 from a CCPC and the shares are held for two years.

Case (C)   Prescribed

    Prescribed shares with FMV of $100 for $76 (FMV at time of agreement), which are then sold for $100.

Then:

	(A) General Rules	(B) CCPC	(C) Pre-scribed
Acquisition of shares:			
FMV at acquisition	$ 100	—	$ 100
Cost of acquisition	(76)	$ 76	(76)
Stock option benefit	24	—	24
1/2 deduction	—		(12)
Net inclusion	$ 24		$ 12

Example

Adjusted cost base (ACB) of shares:			
Cost of acquisition	$ 76	$ 76	$ 76
Add:			
stock option benefit	24	—	24
ACB of shares	$ 100	$ 76	$ 100
Disposition of shares:			
Sale price	$ 100	$ 100	$ 100
ACB	(100)	(76)	(100)
Capital gain	—	—	—
Stock option benefit	—	24	—
1/2 deduction	—	(12)	—
Net inclusion		$ 12	
Inclusions in income:			
Upon acquisition	$ 24	$ —	$ 12
Upon disposition	—	12	—
Total	$ 24	$ 12	$ 12

5. — *Disposition of Rights*

The Act deems an employee who disposes of stock option rights to a person in an arm's length transaction to have received a benefit equal to the value of the consideration received for the shares, less any amount paid to acquire the rights.[102] Similarly, any consideration that the employee receives for the surrender of stock option rights is taxable as a benefit from a disposition of the rights, less any amounts paid.[103]

---

[102]Para. 7(1)(b).

[103]*Greiner v. The Queen*, [1984] C.T.C. 92, 84 D.T.C. 6073 (F.C.A.).

6. — Adjusted Cost Base of Shares

The inclusion of stock option benefits in income would lead to double taxation if the full gain was taxed again when the employee disposed of the shares. Hence, in order to prevent double taxation, the full value of any benefit included in the employee's income is added to the cost base of the shares acquired.[104] Thus, any subsequent gain or loss on the disposition of the shares is calculated by reference to the stepped-up cost base of the shares. For example, where an employee of a public company acquires shares at $12 per share when the shares have a market value of $18 per share, the full benefit of $6 is added to the cost base of his shares. Hence, the adjusted cost base of the shares increases to $18. If the employee sells the shares for $30 per share, he will have a capital gain of $12 per share.

7. — Effect on Employer

From the employer's perspective, the opportunity costs associated with a stock option plan are not deductible, because the corporation does not incur any outlay or expense by issuing its shares at less than their market value.[105] The employer corporation merely foregoes capital proceeds that it would have received had it issued the shares at their fair market value. Hence, unless one of the special incentive provisions[106] applies, a corporation that is taxable at full rates may be better off paying its employees an equivalent bonus, which they can then use to purchase shares at full fair market value.

X. — Salary Deferral Arrangements

1. — General Comment

The general rule is that employment income is taxed on a cash basis, that is, when the taxpayer receives payment. This rule opens the door to employees to defer receipt of their salary to suit their personal circumstances. For example, a taxpayer in a high tax bracket might defer receipt of a portion of his or her annual salary until such time as he or she is in a lower tax bracket.

---

[104]Para. 53(1)(j).

[105]Para. 7(3)(b); *The Queen v. Placer Dome Inc.*, [1992] 2 C.T.C. 99, 92 D.T.C. 6402 (F.C.A.).

[106]Subs. 7(1.1) or para. 110(1)(d).

Example

Assume that Levonia Hargreaves defers her bonus of $10,000 payable on January 1 for three years and is credited with the indicated rates of return. Alternatively, the bonus is paid on January 1 and the after-tax amount is invested in a GIC at the indicated rates of return. The income derived from the investment is also reinvested for the remainder of the term at the same rate of return. Levonia has a marginal tax rate of 50 per cent.

	8%	4%
Rate of return		
FV of bonus deferred three years	$12,600	
FV of bonus paid on current basis		$11,200
Tax @ 50%	(6,300)	(5,600)
Net after-tax bonus	$ 6,300	$ 5,600
Percentage increase in after-tax return	12.5%	

To prevent employees from taking advantage of such arrangements, there are special rules that prevent tax deferral and rate shifting by taxing parties to salary deferral agreements on an accrual basis.[107]

A "salary deferral arrangement"[108] ("SDA") is a plan or arrangement (whether funded or not) *one of the main* purposes of which is to permit a taxpayer to postpone tax on his or her salary in a taxation year to a subsequent year. Arrangements that are contingent upon the deferred amount being paid on the occurrence of some event or transaction are also SDAs unless there is a "substantial risk" that the condition will not be satisfied. Thus, a salary deferral arrangement has three components:

- A plan or arrangement;

- A legal right to defer receipt of salary or wages; and

- An intention to defer receipt for tax reasons.

---

[107]See subpara. 6(1)(a)(v), para. 6(1)(i), subss. 6(11)–(14).

[108]Subs. 248(1) "salary deferral arrangement".

At the same time, the employer's deduction of the payment is synchronized with the inclusion of the amount in the employee's income.[109]

2. — Exclusions

The following plans are excluded from salary deferral arrangements:

- Registered pension funds or plans;
- Disability or income-maintenance insurance plans with an insurance corporation;
- Deferred profit-sharing plans;
- Employee profit-sharing plans;
- Employee trusts;
- Group sickness or accident insurance plans;
- Supplementary unemployment benefit plans;
- Vacation pay trusts;
- Education or training plans for employees;
- Plans for deferring salary or wages of professional athletes;
- Plans under which a taxpayer has a right to receive a bonus in respect of services rendered in the taxation year, to be paid within three years following the end of the year;
- Leave-of-absence arrangements,[110] and
- Prescribed plans or arrangements.

An SDA is a plan where tax deferral is *one* of the *main* purposes of the plan or arrangement. Thus, tax deferral does not have to be the only purpose, but it must be one of the *main* purposes. It is difficult to conceive how a plan can have more than one main purpose. If main means "chief" or "principal",[111] is it ever possible to have more than one chief or principal purpose? Can a plan have five *main* purposes?

---

[109]Paras. 18(1)(o.1), 20(1)(oo) and 20(1)(pp).

[110]Reg. 6801.

[111]Oxford Dictionary.

3. — Contingent Arrangements

Contingent plans and deferral arrangements that are at substantial risk that one of the conditions triggering the contingency will not be satisfied are not SDAs. What constitutes a substantial risk of forfeiture sufficient to exclude a plan or arrangement from the definition of SDA? There is a substantial risk of forfeiture if the condition imposes a significant limitation or duty that requires a meaningful effort on the part of the employee to fulfil, and the limitation or duty creates a definite and substantial risk that forfeiture may occur. The Act does not consider the following types of conditions sufficient to exempt a plan or arrangement as an SDA:[112]

- Non-competition clauses following retirement or termination;

- Restraints on the employee's transferring, or encumbering the employee, or the employee's interest in the deferred amount;

- Restraints that make payment contingent on the employee's not being dismissed for cause or the commission of a crime; or

- Receipt of the deferred amount being contingent on the employee's remaining with the employer for a minimum period of time.

4. — Leave of Absence Plans

The Act excludes certain leave of absence plans from salary deferral arrangements. Thus, an employee can use a leave of absence plan to defer tax on income that would otherwise be taxable on a current basis. An employee can self-fund a leave of absence and defer receipt of up to a maximum of 1/3 of his or her regular annual salary. Although the employee defers the tax that would otherwise be payable on the salary, any investment income earned on the deferred salary remains taxable on a current basis.[113]

A leave of absence plan must satisfy the following conditions:[114]

- The arrangement must provide for a leave of absence from employment of not less than six consecutive months (it cannot be used to fund retirement benefits);

- The leave must commence within six years from the beginning of the commencement of the salary deferral;

---

[112]See Department of Finance Technical Notes (Bill C-23) November 7, 1986.

[113]The Department of Finance issued a comfort letter (June 30, 2000) where they agree that any allocated income that is re-contributed to the plan is not taxable.

[114]Reg. 6801; ATR-39 "Self-funded leave of absence".

- The employee must undertake to return to the employer for a further period of employment of at least equal length to that of the leave;

- The amount of salary deferred in any year must not exceed 1/3 of the employee's regular annual salary; and

- During the leave of absence the employee must not receive any salary, other than the deferred amounts, from his or her employer.

Hence, an employee can defer tax on a portion of his or her salary for up to six years and use the accumulated savings to finance a leave of absence from the employer.

Example

Ann Smith earns an annual salary of $70,000. She opts to defer 14 per cent of her annual salary in a leave of absence plan. Assuming an investment rate of 10 per cent and a tax rate of 40 per cent (that is, an after-tax return of 6 per cent), Ms. Smith can accumulate $70,510 in six years.

Annual salary	$ 70,000
Portion deferred (14% × $70,000)	$ 9,800
Monthly deferral (1/12 × $9,800)	$ 816
$816/month compounded at 6% (net of tax for 72 months)	$ 70,510

XI. — Counselling Benefits

Employer-provided counselling services for employees are not taxable as benefits from employment if the counselling is in respect of:[115]

- The employees' (or related individual's) physical or mental health;

- Re-employment for employees whose employment has been terminated; or

- Retirement.

These exclusions from employment income are accommodations for hardship cases and are intended to facilitate re-employment.

---

[115]Subpara. 6(1)(a)(iv).

XII. — Directors' Fees

A director of a corporation holds an "office".[116] Thus, fees received by virtue of a director-ship are taxable as income from an office.[117] Where a director's fees are paid directly to a third party or are turned over by the director to a third party (for example, to a partnership of which he or she is a member), the fees are taxable as the income of the ultimate recipient and not the director.

XIII. — Strike Pay

The taxation of strike pay is a politically contentious issue. As a matter of administrative policy, the Agency exempts certain types of financial assistance paid by unions to their members during the course of a strike.[118]

Political considerations aside, it is not at all clear why strike pay should not be taxable. "Income" in section 3 is the realized accretion to wealth from a source. The concept of income in section 3 is clearly not restricted to the specifically named sources. Income from *any* source inside or outside Canada is taxable under paragraph 3(a) of the *Income Tax Act*. In the only (brief) decision on point, the Supreme Court adopted a narrow concept of income and held that strike pay is not income. Although strike pay is not taxable as income, union dues are deductible as expenses from employment income.[119]

XIV. — Deductions From Employment Income

1. — General Comment

One of the restrictive characteristics of the taxation of employment income is that it is gener-ally taxable on a "gross" basis without deductions. Subsection 8(2) limits the deduction of expenses from employment income to those that the Act specifically authorizes. As we shall see later, business income is much more generously treated and is taxable on a "net" ba-sis — that is, net of deductions. Because of this difference in the treatment of deductions, most individuals would prefer to be considered as independent contractors for tax purposes.

---

[116]Subs. 248(1).

[117]Subs. 5(1) and para. 6(1)(c).

[118]IT-334R2, "Miscellaneous Receipts" (February 21, 1992).

[119]Subpara. 8(1)(i)(iv). See *Fries v. M.N.R.*, [1989] 1 C.T.C. 471, 89 D.T.C. 5240 (F.C.A.); revd. [1990] 2 S.C.R. 1322, [1990] 2 C.T.C. 439, 90 D.T.C. 6662 (S.C.C.).

2. — Salesperson's Expenses

A salesperson may deduct expenses from employment income if he or she is:[120]

- Employed to sell property or negotiate contracts;

- *Required* to pay his or her business expenses;

- *Ordinarily* required to carry out his or her duties away from the employer's regular place of business;

- Remunerated, at least in part, by commissions related to the volume of sales; and

- Not in receipt of a tax-free allowance for travelling expenses that is excluded from income.[121]

The employee must file a prescribed form where the employer certifies that the employee has satisfied the above conditions.[122]

(a) — Limits

The maximum amount of the deduction is limited to the commission income that he or she receives in the year. The employee must file a prescribed form where the employer certifies that the employee has satisfied all the above conditions.[123]

(b) — Capital Cost Allowance

A salesperson may also deduct capital cost allowance ("CCA")[124] and interest expense in respect of a motor vehicle or aircraft that he or she uses in the performance of employment-related duties.[125] The claim for CCA and interest expense is not limited to commission in-

---

[120]Para. 8(1)(f) and subs. 8(9).

[121]Subpara. 6(1)(b)(v). *Cossette v. M.N.R.* (1955), 13 Tax A.B.C. 170, 55 D.T.C. 365 (T.A.B.) (Where the allowance is unreasonably low, the taxpayer may include the allowance in income and deduct his actual expenses.).

[122]Subs. 8(10).

[123]*Laliberté v. M.N.R.* (1953), 9 Tax A.B.C. 145, 53 D.T.C. 370 (T.A.B.) (traveling salesman allowed to deduct rent for sample rooms); *Sherman v. M.N.R.*, [1970] Tax A.B.C. 618, 70 D.T.C. 1409 (T.A.B.) (advertising expenses by securities salesman allowed as deduction).

[124]See Chapter 9, "Deductions from Business and Investment Income" for discussion of CCA.

[125]Para. 8(1)(j); Reg. 1100(1).

come and may be used to reduce income from other sources. Here, as elsewhere in the Act, any expenses claimed must be reasonable in the circumstances.[126]

3. — Travelling Expenses

Employees who:

- Are ordinarily required to carry on their employment duties away from their employer's regular place of business,

- Are required to pay their own travelling expenses, and

- Do not receive a tax-free allowance,

are allowed to deduct their travelling expense[127] to the extent that they are not reimbursed by their employer.[128] In this context, "ordinarily" means as a matter of regular occurrence.[129] The deduction is available to all employees and is not restricted to commissioned salespeople.

A salesperson who claims a deduction for expenses under paragraph 8(1)(f), however, cannot also claim travelling expenses under paragraph 8(1)(h). The salesperson may, however, claim the deduction under whichever of the two provisions is most advantageous to him or her.

(a) — Inadequate Compensation

An employee who is not fully reimbursed for his or her employment-related expenses may be able to claim the shortfall as an expense deduction. For example, an employee who spends 30 cents a kilometre to run a motor vehicle and is reimbursed only 20 cents a kilome-

---

[126]S. 67. *Niessen v. M.N.R.* (1960), 60 D.T.C. 489, 25 Tax A.B.C. 62 (T.A.B.) (claim for CCA on Cadillac disallowed as excessive).

[127]Paras. 8(1)(h) or (h.1).

[128]Subparas. 6(1)(b)(v), (vi), (vii).

[129]*The Queen v. Healy*, [1978] C.T.C. 355, 78 D.T.C. 6239 (F.C.T.D.); revd. [1979] C.T.C. 44, 79 D.T.C. 5060 (F.C.A.) (jockey club employee not "ordinarily" reporting for work at Fort Erie but spending 1/3 of his time there); *The Queen v. Patterson*, [1982] C.T.C. 371, 82 D.T.C. 6326 (F.C.T.D.) (school principal who made 56 trips to other schools "ordinarily" required to carry out duties in different places; expenses deductible).

tre may claim an expense deduction equal to 10 cents per kilometre travelled on the employer's business if he can establish that the allowance was unreasonably low.[130]

(b) — Requirement of Travel

Deductibility of travelling expenses depends upon the employee being required to travel away from his or her employer's place of business. This requirement need not be expressly stated in the employment contract, but may be implied from the surrounding circumstances, such as employer expectations, industry practice, etc.[131] The employer must, however, certify that the employee meets all of the statutory requirements.[132]

(c) — Motor Vehicles and Aircraft

Subject to the restrictions in respect of travelling expenses, an employee may also deduct motor vehicle and aircraft expenses incurred in the course of employment.[133] Any interest paid on money borrowed to purchase, and capital cost allowance resulting from the ownership of, a motor vehicle or aircraft is deductible to the extent that the vehicle or aircraft is used in the course of employment.[134]

(d) — Meals

An employee may claim 50 per cent of meal expenses as part of travel costs if he or she consumes the meal while away for at least 12 hours from the municipality in which his or her employer is located.[135]

---

[130]*Peters v. M.N.R.*, [1986] 2 C.T.C. 2221, 86 D.T.C. 1662 (T.C.C.). But see *Gauvin v. M.N.R.*, [1979] C.T.C. 2812, 79 D.T.C. 696 (T.R.B.) and *Hudema v. The Queen*, [1994] C.T.C. 42, 94 D.T.C. 6287 (Fed. T.D.) and IT-522R.

[131]*Moore v. The Queen*, [1987] 1 C.T.C. 319, 87 D.T.C. 5217 (F.C.T.D.) (principal would have received unfavorable performance reviews had she not attended meetings; expenses allowed); *Rozen v. The Queen*, [1986] 1 C.T.C. 50, 85 D.T.C. 5611 (F.C.T.D.) (requirement to use automobile in course of employment implied term of contract); *The Queen v. Cival*, [1983] C.T.C. 153, 83 D.T.C. 5168 (F.C.A.) (deduction denied where taxpayer not required to use own car under contract of employment).

[132]Subs. 8(10).

[133]Paras. 8(1)(f) and (h).

[134]Para. 8(1)(j) and subs. 8(9).

[135]Subs. 8(4) and s. 67.1.

(e) — Legal Expenses

An employee can deduct legal expenses (to the extent that they are not reimbursed) paid in collecting or establishing a right to an amount that, if received, would be included in his employment income. Legal expenses that the employee subsequently recovers are taxable under para. 6(1)(j) to the extent that they were not previously included in income in collecting or establishing his or her right to a salary from an employer or former employer.[136] Legal expenses associated with establishing a right to a pensions benefit or retiring allowance (including payments for wrongful dismissal) are also deductible.[137]

4. — Musicians

An employed musician who must furnish his or her own musical instruments may deduct amounts that he or she pays on account of the maintenance, insurance or rental of such instruments.[138] Where the musician owns the instrument used in employment, he or she is also entitled to depreciate it at a rate of 20 per cent on a declining balance basis.[139]

5. — Canadian Residents Employed Overseas

As a general rule, Canadian residents are taxable on their global income regardless of where they earn the income.[140] Residence-based taxation ensures that individuals are taxed on an equal basis on their ability to pay tax on income without reference to its geographic source. This promotes horizontal equity. Some residents employed outside Canada, however, are eligible for special tax credits on their overseas employment income. These concessions are provided for "competitive reasons" to allow Canadian employers to compete for international contracts by reducing their net payroll costs. The tax credits put Canadian employers on a competitive footing with foreign companies that receive similar tax subsidies from their governments. Thus, we trade-off some equity for economic competitiveness.

---

[136]Para. 8(1)(b). See, e.g., *Loo v. R.*, [2004] 3 C.T.C. 247, 2004 FCA 249, 2004 D.T.C. 6540 (F.C.A.) (plaintiff one of 55 B.C. lawyers suing their employer, the federal Dept of Justice, because they are paid less than Justice lawyers in Toronto; legal fees deductible; not relevant to determine whether claim is well founded in law or likely to succeed).

[137]Para. 60(o.1). See, e.g., *Atkinson v. R.*, 2004 TCC 445, [2004] 4 C.T.C. 2272 (T.C.C. [Informal Procedure]) (police officer allowed to deduct legal fees of $32,226.49 since he would have lost his job and pension had he not successfully defended the criminal charges made against him.)

[138]Para. 8(1)(p).

[139]Reg. 1100(1)(a)(viii).

[140]Subs. 2(1); s. 3.

The overseas employment tax credit has three constraints. A Canadian resident is entitled to the credit only if:[141]

- He or she is employed by a "specified employer";[142]

- His or her employment-related duties are performed outside Canada for a period of more than six consecutive months; *and*

- The employer is engaged in the construction, exploration, engineering, or agricultural business, or in a *prescribed* activity.

The tax credit is equal to 80 per cent of the employee's net overseas earnings up to a maximum of $80,000 annually. The credit is prorated over the number of days the employee works abroad in a year and is applied against the taxes that he or she would otherwise pay.

6. — Other Deductions

Section 8 also lists other deductions from employment income. Note particularly:

Type of Expense	Statutory Reference
• Legal expenses incurred by employee in collecting or establishing right to his salary or wages.	para. 8(1)(b)
• Value of cleric's residence, or rent paid by cleric	para. 8(1)(c); IT-141R
• Contribution by a teacher to a fund established for the benefit of Commonwealth teachers present in Canada on an exchange program	para. 8(1)(d)
• Expenses of railway company employees employed away from ordinary place of residence	para. 8(1)(e); IC 73-21R8
• Expenses for meals, lodging and travel incurred by a transport business employee while carrying out duties of employment	para. 8(1)(g); IC 73-21R8

---

[141]Subs. 122.3(1).

[142]Para. 122.3(2).

Type of Expense	Statutory Reference
• Annual professional membership dues required to maintain professional status	subpara. 8(1)(i)(i)*
• Dues to a professions board required under provincial law	subpara. 8(1)(i)(vii)
• Trade union or association annual dues	subpara. 8(1)(i)(iv)
• Annual union dues	subpara. 8(1)(i)(v)
• Dues paid to a parity or advisory committee under provincial law	subpara. 8(1)(i)(vi)
• Office rent or salary paid by employee as required by contract of employment	subpara. 8(1)(i)(ii)
• Cost of supplies consumed in the performance of duties of employment	subpara. 8(1)(i)(iii)
• Interest on borrowed money for the purchase of, and capital cost allowance for the use of, a motor vehicle or aircraft used in the performance of duties of employment	subpara. 8(1)(j)(i); Regs. 1100(1)(a)(ix), (x) and (xi)
• Canada Pension Plan contributions and employment insurance premiums paid by an employee to an individual employed as an assistant	para. 8(1)(l.1)
• Employee RCA contributions	para. 8(1)(m.2)
• Amounts paid by employee as reimbursement for amounts paid to the employee as workers' compensation	para. 8(1)(n)
• Amounts forfeited under salary deferral arrangement	para. 8(1)(o)
• Employment expenses of artists	para. 8(1)(q)

Notes:

*   *Lucas v. M.N.R.*, [1987] 2 C.T.C. 23, 87 D.T.C. 5277 (F.C.T.D.).

7. — Limitations on Deductions

(a) — Overall Limitation

For tax purposes, the deductibility of an expense depends on two criteria:

1. Authority for the deduction; and

2. Reasonableness of the amount claimed.[143]

In the context of employment income, subs. 8(2) tells us that the deduction must be specifically authorized. There are no common law deductions from employment income. Further, even otherwise authorized deductions may not be deductible for tax purposes if they are unreasonable in the circumstances. Thus, deductibility depends on both the reasonableness of the amount claimed and the legitimacy of the claim itself.

Whether an expense is reasonable in the circumstances is a question of fact. In the context of salary and bonuses paid to employees, for example, the following factors are relevant in determining whether the amount is reasonable:

* Rank or level within organization;

* Special knowledge, skills or connections;

* Comparable compensation paid to persons in similar businesses with similar responsibilities; and

* Past practices with respect to compensation in the particular business community concerned.

(b) — Food and Entertainment

In addition to the general rule that all expenses must be reasonable in amount, there is an additional restriction for expenses incurred for meals and entertainment. The Act restricts the deduction of these expenditures to 50 per cent of the amount actually paid.[144]

XV. — Conclusion

Although only four sections of the Act deal directly with employment income, the provisions affect millions of employees. Since employment income is the largest source of public revenues, the Department of Finance is ever vigilant to ensure that they bring employment

---

[143] S. 67.

[144] Subs. 67.1(1).

income into the taxable base. We have seen, however, that even this small area of tax law is complex and subject to inconsistent legislation and judicial interpretation. This inconsistency detracts from the equitable treatment of employees. The taxation of relocation benefits, for example, produces inconsistent results for employees who move to new locations. The exemption of non-accountable allowances for legislators, for example, is an obvious distinction in the tax mosaic that differentiates between classes of taxpayers.

The presumption against the non-deductibility of employment expenses is understandable in the interests of administrative convenience. It does, however, place an unfair burden on employees who incur employment-related expenses that are not enumerated in the Act. As we will see in subsequent chapters, the substantial differences between the generous treatment of business expenses and the strict regulation of employment income are a powerful incentive to recharacterize income from one source into the other. Classification may be the beginning of wisdom but it also makes tax law that much more complex.

Selected Bibliography to Chapter 6

General

Atiyah, P.S., *Vicarious Liability in the Law of Torts* (London: Butterworths, 1967).

"Controversy Surrounding the Adjustment of Earnings and Profits for Accrued Tax By a Cash Method Taxpayer (The): How Should the Conflict Be Resolved?" (Spring 1989) 42 The Tax Lawyer 821.

Drache, Arthur B.C., "Employee Compensation" (1986) Special Lectures of the Law Society of Upper Canada 17.

Hansen, Krishna and Rendall, eds., "The Taxation of Employees", *Canadian Taxation* (Toronto: De Boo, 1981) at 187.

Krishna, Vern, "Converting Salary into Management Fees" (1993) 4 Can. Current Tax C-1.

Krishna, Vern, "International Employment Income" (1993) 4 Can. Current Tax C-23.

Krishna, Vern, "The Scope of Employment Benefits" (1994) Can. Current Tax C-55.

McKie, A.B., "Artists and Athletes: Tax Acts" (1990) 3 Can. Current Tax C-17.

Muto, Alexander D., "Same-sex Benefits and the *Income Tax Act*" (1994) 5 Tax. of Executive Compensation and Retirement 854.

The Characterization of Employment Income

Douglas, William O., "Vicarious Liability and the Administration of Risk" (1928-29) 38 Yale L.J. 584.

Drache, A.B.C., "Employee Compensation" (1986) Special Lectures LSUC 17.

Drache, A.B.C. and Goldstein, "The Professional as an Employee", *Tax Planning for Professionals* (Toronto: De Boo, 1979) at 22.

Khan, A.N., "Who is a Servant?" (1979) 53 Austr. L.J. 832.

Noel, Marc, "Contract for Services, Contract of Service — A Tax Perspective and Analysis", in *Proceedings of 29th Tax Conf.* 712 (Can. Tax Foundation, 1977).

Richards, G.M.R., "Employee or Independent Contractor?" (1986) 1 Can. Current Tax J-158.

Robinson, I. Michael, "Personal Service Corporations: New Opportunities and Old Concerns", *Corporate Management Tax Conf.* 165 (Can. Tax Foundation, 1985).

Wilson, Brian J., "Employment Status Under the *Income Tax Act*", *Corporate Management Tax Conf.* 2:1 (Can. Tax Foundation, 1991).

Inclusions in Employment Income

General

Bernstein, Jack, "Fringe Benefits and Equity Participation", *Corporate Management Tax Conf.* 5:1 (Can. Tax Foundation, 1991).

Corn, George, "Expense Reimbursements — Not Taxable as Employee Benefits" (October 1990) 3:10 Can. Current Tax J-49.

Drache, A.B.C., "Tax-Free Goodies" (1991) XIII Can. Taxpayer 68.

"Employee or Shareholder Benefit" (1983) 5 Can. Taxpayer 202.

Krishna, Vern, "Employee Benefits" (1984) 1 Can. Current Tax C7.

Krishna, Vern, "Taxation of Employee Benefits" (1986) 1:35 Can. Current Tax C-173.

Krishna, Vern, "Taxation of Employee Benefits" (August 1987) 21 CGA Magazine 25.

Perry, Harvey, "Federal Individual Income Tax: Income Computation", *Tax Paper No. 89* 42 (Can. Tax Foundation, 1990).

Allowances

Beam, Robert E., and Stanley N. Laiken, "Employee Allowances" (1989) Can. Tax J. 141.

Drache, A.B.C., "Allowances or Reimbursements" (1993) 15 Can. Taxpayer 23.

Drache, A.B.C., "Tax Exempt Expenses for Moonlighting Employees" (1991) 13 Can. Taxpayer 154.

Automobiles

Glover, George, "Effect of Tax Reform on Auto Expenses" (November-December 1987) 61 CMA Magazine 60.

Jason, Robert R., "Personal Use of an Employer-Supplied Automobile" (1983) 116:6 CA Magazine 48.

Keller, Cameron, "The Company Car" (1983) 57 Cost and Management 47.

"Revenue Canada's Framework for Automobile Deductions" (1993) 5 Tax. of Executive Compensation and Retirement 839

Tang & Hyatt, "Business-Use Automobiles: The Complex New Tax Rules" (1988) 36 Can. Tax J. 195.

Imputed Interest on Low Cost Loans

Drache, A.B.C., "Home Purchase Loans" (1983) 5 The Can. Taxpayer 76.

"Revenue Canada Established Policies on Loan-related Benefits" (1991) 2 Tax. of Executive Compensation and Retirement 451.

Stock Option Plans

Atnikov, D., "Stock Options, Stock Purchase Plans and Death Benefits", *Prairie Provinces Tax Conf.* 1 (Can. Tax Foundation, 1980).

Bernstein, Jack, "Fringe Benefits and Equity Participation" (1991) Corp. Mgmt. Tax Conf. 5:1.

Bowman, S.W., "Employment Benefits — Stock Options Not Falling under S. 7" (1990) 38 Can. Tax J. 82.

Dionne, Andre, "Stock Purchase Arrangements can be Structured to Allow Deduction for Employers" (1992) 3 Tax. of Executive Compensation and Retirement 604.

Dunbar, Alisa E., "Sale of Stock Plan Shares may Produce Freely Deductible Loss" (1991) 3 Tax. of Executive Compensation and Retirement 499.

"Employment Benefits C Stock Options Not Falling Under Section 7" (1990) 38 Can. Tax J. 82.

Holmes, William R., "Stock-based Deferred Compensation may be Provided to Employees of Private Corporations" (1990) 2 Tax. of Executive Compensation and Retirement 375.

Krishna, Vern, "Stock Options Exercised after Becoming Non-resident" (1993) 4 Can. Current Tax C-27.

Lee, Julie Y., "Stock-Based Compensation: Selected Regulatory and Taxation Issues", *Corporate Management Tax Conf.* 4:1 (Can. Tax Foundation, 1991).

MacKnight, Robin, "Hidden Problems in Selling Employee Ownership" (1994) 5 Can. Current Tax 7.

MacKnight, Robin, "Planning for Stock Option Benefits: Traps for the Unwary" (1993) 4 Can. Current Tax P-13.

MacKnight, Robin, "Pyrrhic Policy: Fixing the Phantom Loophole in Paragraph 7(3)(b)" (1993) 41 Can. Tax J. 429.

Michaelson, Suzanne, "Employee Stock Options Revisited" (1992) 40 Can. Tax J. 114.

Ramaseder, Brigitte, "Stock Option Benefit Depends on Fair Market Value Determination" (1991) 2 Tax. of Executive Compensation and Retirement 455.

Richards, Gabrielle M.R., "Stock Incentive Plans" (June 1990) 3:6 Can. Current Tax J-31.

Snider, Ken, "Employee Share Purchase Loans and the Predicament of Declining Share Values" (1993) 41 Can. Tax J. 1001.

"Stock Options Plan Involving Foreign Corporations may be Disqualified from Stock Benefit Deduction" (1990) 1 Tax. of Executive Compensation and Retirement 300.

Thomas, Richard B., "Gain Arising from Exercise of stock Option by Shareholder-Director" (1993) 41 Can. Tax J. 505.

Tobias, Norman C., "Employee Stock Options: Taxing Benefits Realized by Former Canadian Residents" (1994) 5 Tax. of Executive Compensation and Retirement 889.

Tunney, Wayne L., "Taking Stock: The Pros and Cons of Stock-Based Compensation", *Corporate Management Tax Conf.* 3:1 (Can. Tax Foundation, 1991).

Wentzell, David, "Stock Purchase Plans: Two Views" (1991) 39 Can. Tax J. 1556.

Reimbursed Legal Expenses

Dunbar, Alisa E., "Legal Services Provided to Employee Results in Tax Benefit" (1991) 2 Tax. of Executive Compensation and Retirement 403.

Krasa, Eva M., "The Income Tax Treatment of Legal Expenses" (1986) 34 Can. Tax J. 757.

Other

Billinger, Jo-anne, "Flexible Benefits a Practical Approach for Employers and Employees in the Cost-conscious '90s" (1993) 4 Tax. of Executive Compensation and Retirement 747.

Boulanger, Claude, "Disability Insurance Plans can be Structured to Avoid Taxable Payout" (1991) 2 Tax. of Executive Compensation and Retirement 435.

Bush, Kathryn M., "Executive Compensation: Supplemental Pension Plans" (1991) 8 Bus. and the Law 46.

Buyers, D.R., and D.E. Harvey, "The Cost of Terminating Employees: Tax and Unemployment Insurance Consequences" (1987) 4 Bus. & L. 9.

Dewling, Alan M., "RCA may be Used to Pre-fund Health and Other Post-Retirement Benefits" (1993) 4 Tax. of Executive Compensation and Remuneration 707.

Dionee, Andre, "RCA Cash Flow Problems may be Alleviated by Filing Early Trust Tax Return" (1990) 2 Tax. of Executive Compensation and Retirement 371.

Drache, A.B.C., "Club Memberships as a Taxable Benefit" (1993) 15 Can. Taxpayer 163.

Drache, A.B.C., "FCA Upholds Revenue Canada on Employee Reimbursement" (1994) 16 Can. Taxpayer 49.

Drache, A.B.C., "Group Life Insurance: New Interpretations" (1980) 17 Can. Taxpayer 152.

Fitzgerald, Brian A.P., "Tax-effectiveness may be Enhanced by Maximizing Ancillary Benefits" (1993) 4 Tax. of Executive Compensation and Retirement 760.

"Home Purchase Loans to Employee/Shareholder may have Extended Term" (1992) 3 Tax. of Executive Compensation and Retirement 552.

Krishna, Vern, "Retiring Allowances" (1994) 4 Can. Current Tax C-53.

Krishna, Vern, "How Will They Tax Frequent Flyer Programs?" (1985) 5:21 Ont. Lawyers Weekly 7.

Laushway, Keith, "Retiring Allowances and Future Employment by Affiliates" (1993) 4 Can. Current Tax P-15.

Maclagan, Bill, "Taxable Benefits on Employer Relocation" (1993) 3 Employment and Labour Law Rev. 25.

McKie, A.B., "Beneficial Occupation" (1994) 4 Can. Current Tax C-49.

Novek, Barbara L., "Employment Benefits may be Tax-free if Provided in Connection with Special Work Site or Remote Location" (1991) 3 Tax. of Executive Compensation and Retirement 505.

Novek, Barbara L., "Retiring Allowances are subject to Administrative Guideline" (1991) 3 Tax. of Executive Compensation and Retirement 523.

Novek, Barbara L. "RCT Expands Unpublished Guidelines in Salary Leave Plans" (1993) 4 Tax. of Executive Compensation and Retirement 715.

"Owner-managers may be Eligible for Tax-free Reimbursement of Medical Expenses" (1990) 1 Tax. of Executive Compensation and Retirement 299.

Pound, R.W., "Fringe Benefits: Management Perks'", *Corporate Management Tax Conf.* 63 (Can. Tax Foundation, 1979).

"Revenue Canada Clarifies Policy on Relocation Assistance" (1992) 3 Tax. of Executive Compensation and Retirement 559.

"Revenue Canada Clarifies Position on Temporary Accommodation" (1992) 3 Tax. of Executive Compensation and Retirement 563.

Roux, Clement, "Current Planning for Fringe Benefits", in *Proceedings of 35th Tax Conf.* 478 (Can. Tax Foundation, 1983).

Schwartz, Alan M., "Tax Considerations on Being Hired and Fired: Some Exotica", *Corporate Management Tax Conf.* 212 (Can. Tax Foundation, 1985).

Simon, Karla W., "Fringe Benefits and Tax Reform: Historical Blunders and a Proposal for Structural Change" (1984) 36 Univ. of Florida Law Rev. 871.

Solursh, John M., "Pension Arrangements can be Funded to Avoid RCA Tax" (1991) 3 Tax. of Executive Compensation and Retirement 469.

Deductions from Employment Income

General

Neville, Ralph T., "Deductibility of Automobiles, Meals and Entertainment and Home Office Expenses After Tax Reform", in *Proceedings of 40th Tax Conf.* 25:1 (Can. Tax Foundation, 1988).

New Rules on Tax Assistance for Retirement Savings (Montreal: Sobeco, 1990).

Perry, Harvey, "Federal Individual Income Tax: Income Computation", *Tax Paper No. 89* 42 (Can. Tax Foundation, 1990).

Teichman, Lyle S., "Deducting Employee Expenses: A Hard Act to Follow" (1994) 5 Tax. of Executive Compensation and Retirement 859.

Templeton, Michael D., "Employee Expenses C A Practical Approach" (1990) 38 Can. Tax J. 666.

Other

Austin, Barbara, "RRSP Implications of the New Foreign Pension Plan Rules" (1993) 1 RRSP Plan. 53.

Boulanger, Claude, "Employee Profit Sharing Plans may Provide Framework for Incentive Payments" (1991) 2 Tax. of Executive Compensation and Retirement 508.

"Can I, as an Employee, Deduct My Home-Office Expenses?" (1990), 44 D.T.C. 7028.

Corn, George, "Expense Reimbursements: Not Taxable as Employee Benefits" (1990) 3 Can. Current Tax J-24.

Expenses of Sales Representatives: Tax Treatment (Toronto: CCH Canadian, 1990).

Kingissepp, Andrew H., "Canadian Officers and Directors can Treat Indemnity Payment as Tax-free Receipt" (1993) 4 Tax. of Executive Compensation and Retirement 763.

Krasa, Eva M., "Recent Developments in Retirement Savings and Deferred Compensation: A Pot Pourri" (1992) Can. Tax Foundation 18:1.

Krishna, Vern, "A Striking Decision" (November 1989) 23 CGA Magazine 43.

Novek, Barbara L., "Part-time and Interrupted Employment Included in Computing Portion of Retiring Allowance Eligible for Rollover to RRSP" (1992) 4 Tax. of Executive Compensation and Retirement 637.

Novek, Barbara L., "Sector Specific Tax Relief for Canadian Residents Working Overseas" (1993) 5 Tax. of Executive Compensation and Retirement 808.

Roberts, David G., "Registered Retirement Savings Plans" (1989) 37 Can. Tax J. 64.

"Sec. 8(1)(f): Is the Frustration Over?" (1990), 44 D.T.C. 7021.

Thomas, Richard B., "No To Nanny Expense Deduction" (1991) 39 Can. Tax J. 950.

"Why Not Work at Home and Deduct the Home-Office Expense?" (1990), 44 D.T.C. 7014.

PART V: BUSINESS & INVESTMENT INCOME

CHAPTER 7 — THE MEANING OF BUSINESS INCOME, INVESTMENT INCOME, AND CAPITAL GAINS

I. — General Comment

We saw in Chapter 4 that income for tax purposes is calculated by determining income from each source separately. Business income and investment income are calculated according to subdivision b of Division B of Part I of the Act. In this chapter we will see how the tax system distinguishes business, investment and capital gains income. The rules that distinguish between the various sources necessarily complicate the Act and cause taxpayers to characterize their transactions for maximum advantage. This in turn leads to anti-avoidance rules to prevent such positioning. Although subdivision b covers both business income and investment income,[1] they are two distinct and separate sources of income. Although most of the rules dealing with these sources of income are common to both, there are important differences in how these sources are taxed. For example:

- The attribution rules in sections 74.1 and 74.2 only apply to investment income and capital gains (losses) and do not apply to income from business;[2] and

- The small business deduction is available only in respect of income from business and does not generally apply to investment income.[3]

Hence, it is important to distinguish between the two sources of income. We determine income or loss for tax purposes in two distinct steps. First, we characterize a receipt or loss as flowing from a particular source that is taxable under section 3 of the Act. Second, we measure the amount of income or loss according to the rules applicable to that particular source.

---

[1]Technically referred to as "income from property".

[2]See Chapter 3, "Residence and Source".

[3]Chapter 20, "Corporate Business Income".

The intrinsic nature of income does not determine its source for tax purposes. The intrinsic nature of income is essentially a question of commercial law, regardless of who receives the income. Interest, rent, royalties or dividends, for example, may be investment income or business income depending upon the degree of activity and effort to earn the income. Thus, in the absence of a deeming rule, the source of income is usually a question of fact.

1. — The Meaning of "Business"

The Act does not define "business", which is a central concept in the income tax system. Subsection 248(1) merely says that "business" *includes* a profession, calling, trade, manufacture or undertaking of any kind whatever, and, for most purposes, also includes an adventure or concern in the nature of trade.[4] This raises the question: When is an "undertaking" a business for tax purposes?

Generally, "business" refers to economic, industrial, commercial, or financial *activity*. The traditional common law definition of business is "anything which occupies the time and attention and labour of a man for the purpose of profit."[5] As the English Court of Appeal said in *Erichsen v. Last*[6]:

> I do not think there is any principle of law which lays down what carrying on of trade is. There are a multitude of incidents which together make the carrying on [of] a trade, but I know of no one distinguishing incident which makes a practice a carrying on of trade, and another practice not a carrying on of trade. If I may use the expression, it is a compound fact made up of a variety of incidents.

A "trade" is the business of selling goods, with a view to profit, that the trader has either manufactured or purchased.[7]

The quintessential characteristics of business are activity, enterprise, entrepreneurship, commercial risk, and the pursuit of profit. How many or how much of each of these characteristics need be present in order for income to be characterized as business income?

---

[4]Subs. 248(1) "business"; see s. 253 for an extended meaning of "carrying on business" as it relates to non-residents.

[5]*Stewart v. Canada*, [2002] 2 S.C.R. 645, [2002] 3 C.T.C. 439, 2002 D.T.C. 6969 (Eng.) (S.C.C.); see also *Smith v. Anderson* (1880), 15 Ch. D. 247 at 258 (Eng. C.A.); *Terminal Dock and Warehouse Co. v. M.N.R.*, [1968] 2 Ex. C.R. 78, [1968] C.T.C. 78, 68 D.T.C. 5060 (Ex. Ct.); affd. 68 D.T.C. 5316, [1968] S.C.R. vi (S.C.C.).

[6](1881), 4 T.C. 422 at 423, 8 Q.B.D. 414, 51 L.J.Q.B. 86, 45 L.T. 703, 46 J.P. 357, 30 W.R. 301 (Eng. C.A.).

[7]*Grainger & Son v. Gough*, [1896] A.C. 325, 3 T.C. 462 (U.K. H.L.).

To be sure, "business" implies activity and profit motive.[8] It is the pursuit of profit that differentiates a trade or business from a hobby or pastime. Thus, the first question to determine is whether the taxpayer undertakes the activity in pursuit of profit or as a personal endeavour or hobby. Pursuit of profit and not its actual realization is the key element in distinguishing between commercial ventures and hobbies.

Paragraph 18(1)(a) merely restates the necessity of the profit motive test: A taxpayer is not entitled to deduct an expense unless he or she incurs the expenditure for the *purpose* of gaining or producing income from a business or property.

The purpose of the pursuit of profit test is simply to distinguish between commercial and personal activities. Hence, one looks to see if there are indicia of commerciality or badges of trade. The test has relevance only if there is some personal or hobby element to the taxpayer's activity. It has no relevance if the activity is clearly commercial. If the activity is clearly commercial, then it is irrelevant whether it actually generates income or loss. It is not for the revenue authorities to determine *ex post* whether the taxpayer had a reasonable expectation of profit in the pursuit of a commercial venture.[9] Thus, one should not evaluate business judgment with hindsight. If the activity is not a personal endeavour or hobby, the next question is whether the source of commercial income is business or property income.[10]

If the venture has both commercial and personal elements, one must determine if the commercial element is sufficient to characterize the income as a source of income for the purposes of the Act.[11] Here one may look to see if there are sufficient commercial indicia such as adequate financing, time devoted to activity, industry norms, etc.

The profit motive test is crucial to the integrity of the tax system. It draws the line between providing limitless tax subsidies for personal pursuits with minimal economic flavour and economic enterprises conducted on a commercial basis for profit. Taxpayers should not expect other taxpayers to subsidize their personal hobbies. On the other hand, the test should not be so stringent that it discourages entrepreneurial activities.

---

[8]See *e.g.*, *Fleming v. M.N.R.*, [1987] 2 C.T.C. 2113, 87 D.T.C. 425 (T.C.C.) (university professors did not have expectation of profit in publishing research); *Shaker v. M.N.R.*, [1987] 2 C.T.C. 2156, 87 D.T.C. 463 (T.C.C.) (keen desire, talent and determination did not necessitate reasonable expectation of profit in an undertaking); *Kusick v. M.N.R.* (1987), [1988] 1 C.T.C. 2052, 88 D.T.C. 1069 (T.C.C.) (taxpayer changed type of business, obviously realized no chance of profits); *Ianson v. M.N.R.* (1987), [1988] 1 C.T.C. 2088, 88 D.T.C. 1074 (T.C.C.) (horse racing carried on as hobby); *Issacharoff v. M.N.R.* (1987), [1988] 1 C.T.C. 2006, 87 D.T.C. 673 (T.C.C.).

[9]As the Supreme Court of Canada said in *Stewart v. Canada*, [2002] 2 S.C.R. 645, [2002] 3 C.T.C. 439, 2002 D.T.C. 6969 (Eng.), 2002 D.T.C. 6983 (Fr.): "With respect, in our view, courts have erred in the past in applying the REOP test to activities such as law practices and restaurants where there exists no such personal element."

[10]See *Stewart v. Canada, ibid.*

[11]*Ibid.*

Prior to the Supreme Court of Canada's decision in *Stewart*[12] the courts applied a "reasonable expectation of profit" test to determine whether a taxpayer's activities were of a commercial or personal nature. In other words, some courts would ask with the benefit of hindsight whether the taxpayer had a reasonable expectation of profits from his or her activities. If the taxpayer had such an expectation, the income was considered to be from a source of business or property.

The term "business" does not equate with the phrase "reasonable expectation of profit". In *Stewart* the Supreme Court effectively overruled the REOP test, saying:

> In our view, the reasonable expectation of profit analysis cannot be maintained as an independent source test. To do so would run contrary to the principle that courts should avoid judicial innovation and rule-making in tax law... . In addition, the reasonable expectation of profit test is imprecise, causing an unfortunate degree of uncertainty for taxpayers. As well, the nature of the test has encouraged a hindsight assessment of the business judgment of taxpayers in order to deny losses incurred in bona fide, albeit unsuccessful, commercial ventures (*per* Iacobucci and Bastarache JJ.).

2. — The Meaning of "Property"

Investment income is the yield from property. For example: shares yield dividends, bonds yield interest, intellectual property yields royalties, real property yields rent, and so on. "Property" includes virtually every type of economic interest:[13]

> "[P]roperty" means property of any kind whatever whether real or personal or corporeal or incorporeal and, without restricting the generality of the foregoing, includes
>
> > (a) a right of any kind whatever, a share or a chose in action,
> >
> > (b) unless a contrary intention is evident, money,
> >
> > (c) a timber resource property, and
> >
> > (d) the work in progress of a business that is a profession.

A right of property includes the right to possess, use, lend, alienate, consume or otherwise possess it to the exclusion of others.[14] Thus, a right of property represents a bundle of dis-

---

[12]*Ibid.*

[13]Subs. 248(1)"property"; see also *Fasken Estate v. M.N.R.*, [1948] C.T.C. 265, 49 D.T.C. 491 (Ex. Ct.); *Jones v. Skinner* (1835), 5 L.J. Ch. 87 at 90: It is well-known, that the word "property" is the most comprehensive of all the terms that can be used, inasmuch as it is indicative and descriptive of every possible interest the party can have. See also *Manrell v. R.*, [2003] 3 C.T.C. 50, 2003 D.T.C. 5225 (Fed. C.A.) (in the context of non-competition payments).

[14]*West. Electric Co. v. M.N.R.*, [1969] C.T.C. 274 at 289, 69 D.T.C. 5204 at 5212 (Ex. Ct.); affd. [1971] S.C.R. vi, [1971] C.T.C. 96, 71 D.T.C. 5068 (S.C.C.) (amounts paid to appellant claimed not to

tinct rights. For example, the right of ownership is a right distinct from the right of posses-sion. One can own without possessing and possess without owning.

There is, however, one particularly important exclusion from property income. "Income from property" does *not* include a capital gain from the property itself. Similarly, "loss from property" does not include a capital loss from the property.[15] Gains and losses from selling a property are a separate source of income to which completely different rules apply.[16]

II. — Characterization Of Income

The first step in computing income is to characterize it according to its source. The Act identifies four specific sources:[17]

    1. Employment income;

    2. Business income;

    3. Investment (property) income; and

    4. Capital gains.

We saw earlier that the Canadian source of income classification system derives from the English schedular system. Since the Act prescribes different rules for each source of income, classification by source is the central nervous system of the tax structure. We need to under-stand this before anything else.

In Chapter 6 "Employment Income" we looked at the distinction between employment in-come and business income. In this chapter we distinguish business income from capital gains, and business income from investment income.

1. — Income vs. Capital Gains

The importance of characterization on account of income or capital is crucial. Capital gains are generally treated preferentially and taxed at lower effective tax rates. In some cases,

---

be rentals, royalties or otherwise for the use of property; Court determined that payments equivalent to royalties under treaty); *The Queen v. St. John Shipbldg. & Dry Dock Co.*, [1980] C.T.C. 352, 80 D.T.C. 6272 (F.C.A.); leave to appeal to S.C.C. refused 34 N.R. 348 (lump sums paid for computer-ized information not related to use, sales or benefit derived; not within classes of property in treaty).

[15]Subs. 9(3).

[16]See subdivision c.

[17]S. 3.

capital gains are completely exempt from tax.[18] In other cases, capital gains are subject to an inflation penalty.

The Act does not define either "capital gain" or "income". The purported definitions in paragraphs 39(1)(a) and (b) of the Act are circular and of minimal practical value. The distinction between "capital gains" and "income" derives essentially from the case law.

In law, the distinction between capital gains and income is deceptively simple. Income derives from trading or the periodic yield of an investment. Capital gains derive from sale or realization of the investment. The distinction is often put in the form of an analogy.[19]

> The fundamental relation of "capital" to "income" has been much discussed by economists, the former being likened to the tree or the land, the latter to the fruit or the crop; the former depicted as a reservoir supplied from springs, the latter as the outlet stream, to be measured by its flow during a period of time.

The tree is the capital that produces a yield (the fruit), and income is the profit that derives when we sell the fruit. A gain from the sale of the tree itself is on account of capital. The answer is always easy when it is obvious. For example:

- A building is capital; rent derived from the building is income;

- Shares are capital; dividends on the shares are income; and

- Bonds are capital; interest payments on the bonds are income.

Thus, an investment in property represents capital, and the flow from the investment represents income.

Capital gains derive from a disposition of investments that constitute "capital property". Income gains derive from a sale of trading assets or as the yield from investments. Thus, the key to determining whether we have an income gain or a capital gain is in identifying whether we have traded assets or sold an investment. Therein lies the difficulty. What is an investment? What if in the above examples, the taxpayer trades in buildings, shares, or bonds?

(a) — The Meaning of "Investment"

To say that a capital gain or loss arises from the disposition of an investment is not very helpful in characterizing capital gains and losses. The fundamental question is: what is an "investment"? How do we recognize investments (the sale of which yields a capital gain)

---

[18]See, for example, the exemption for principal residences and shares of small business corporations.

[19]*Eisner v. Macomber* (1920), 252 U.S. 189; see also Chapter 11, "Computation of Gains and Losses".

and trading assets (the sale of which yields income)? This characterization is more problematic than it first appears. For example, consider the following judicial statement:[20]

> It is quite a well-settled principle that where the owner of an ordinary investment chooses to realize it, and obtains a greater price for it than he originally acquired it at, the enhanced price is not profit. ... But it is equally well established that enhanced values obtained from realisation or conversion of securities may be so assessable, where what is done is not merely a realisation or change of investment, but an act done in what is truly the carrying on, or carrying out, of a business. ...

The statement tells us that the distinction between business income and capital gains depends upon whether the taxpayer is trading or investing. But that merely leads to another question: how do we know when a person is trading or investing?

It is clear that the distinction cannot rest upon the taxpayer's mere desire to make a profit. Everyone wants to make a profit, whether they are trading or investing. Trading implies a profit-making scheme to earn income by buying and selling property. Investment implies acquiring and holding an asset for its potential yield, but with the possibility that the investment may, at some time, be sold for a profit.

In *Sissons*, for example:[21]

> Here the clear indication of "trade" is found in the fact that the acquisition of the securities was a part of a profit-making scheme. The purpose of the operation was not to earn income from the securities but to make a profit on prompt realization. The operation has therefore none of the essential characteristics of an investment; it is essentially a speculation.

The distinction depends upon the taxpayer's intention at the time he or she purchases the property.

To be sure, profit motive is the *sine qua non* of business. But, since both traders and investors search for profit, profit motive by itself is not sufficient to distinguish between business income and capital gains. The distinction rests upon the taxpayer's operative intention at the time he or she acquires the property. Was the taxpayer intending to trade (do business) or invest (hold property)?

(b) — Taxpayer Intention

An "investment" is an asset or property that one acquires with the *intention* of holding or using *to produce* income. Thus, in tax law, an investment is a means to an end. Where a taxpayer acquires property with an intention to trade — that is, to purchase and resell the

---

[20]*Californian Copper Syndicate Ltd. v. Harris* (1904), 5 Tax Cas. 159 at 165-66 (Scot. Ex. Ct. 2nd Div.).

[21]*M.N.R. v. Sissons*, [1969] S.C.R. 507, [1969] C.T.C. 184 at 188, 69 D.T.C. 5152 at 5154 (S.C.C.).

property at a profit — any gain or loss from the trade is business income (loss). Hence, the distinction between an investment and trading inventory depends not upon the nature of the property, but upon the intention with which the taxpayer acquires it.

For example, suppose A registers an Internet domain name for $100 and later sells it to B for $1,000. The characterization of the $900 gain depends upon A's intention at the time A registered the name. If A's regular practice is to acquire and sell domain names, then the gain is business income. If, however, A acquires the name to use for her website and sells it to B when her plans change, the gain is a capital gain.

The taxpayer's intention at the time he acquires the asset is the basic issue in most characterization cases. One determines the character of the gain on the basis of evidence that provides an insight into the taxpayer's state of mind at the relevant time. The taxpayer's conduct, rather than any *ex post facto* declarations, usually provides the key to his or her intention. One may, however, sometimes infer a taxpayer's intention from another taxpayer's conduct. For example, one can attribute the intentions of a person to a spouse where the latter is clearly relying on the knowledge and information of the former.[22]

How do we evaluate a taxpayer's intentions? The only conclusive rule is: *No single factor is conclusively determinative*. We look at the circumstances of the transaction and balance multiple, often conflicting, indicia to determine the taxpayer's intention. As one judge stated: "... a common sense appreciation of *all* the guiding features will provide the ultimate answer."[23] This is not a very helpful statement for taxpayers who must determine the issue, but is one that judges frequently rely upon to make such decisions with the benefit of *ex post* analysis.

In addition to looking at a taxpayer's primary intention for the purpose of characterizing income or gain, the courts sometimes also look to see if the taxpayer had a secondary intention to trade. Where a taxpayer has a *secondary* intention to trade, any gain or loss resulting from the trade is business income (loss).[24] Therefore, a taxpayer who claims that a gain is a

---

[22]See, e.g., *Darch v. Canada*, [1992] 2 C.T.C. 128, 92 D.T.C. 6366 (F.C.T.D.); affd. as Wright in [1994] 2 C.T.C. 1, 98 D.T.C. 6629 (F.C.A.).

[23]*B.P. Australia Ltd. v. Commr. of Taxation of Commonwealth of Australia*, [1966] A.C. 224 at 264 (P.C.), *per* Lord Pearce, approved by the S.C.C. in *Johns-Manville Can. Inc. v. The Queen*, [1985] 2 S.C.R. 46, [1985] 2 C.T.C. 111 at 125, 85 D.T.C. 5373 at 5383 (S.C.C.) (thorough analysis of law; purchase of land to allow expansion of mining pit so that slope could be maintained at safe angle was an operational expense); see also *The Queen v. Canadian General Electric. Co. Ltd.*, [1987] 1 C.T.C. 180, 87 D.T.C. 5070 (F.C.A.) (heavy water production "know-how" and licence sold; amount received was income because sales replaced taxpayer's business); *Paco Corp. v. The Queen*, [1980] C.T.C. 409, 80 D.T.C. 6328 (Eng.) (F.C.T.D.) (losses for demonstration plant constituted operating expense; determined by taxpayer's intention).

[24]*Bayridge Estates Ltd. v. M.N.R.*, [1959] C.T.C. 158, 59 D.T.C. 1098 (Ex. Ct.) (profit one of motives in sale of raw land); *Fogel v. M.N.R.*, [1959] C.T.C. 227, 59 D.T.C. 1182 (Ex. Ct.) (by-laws necessi-

capital gain must show two things: (1) that his or her primary intention at the time of entering into the transaction was to make an investment; and (2) that he or she had no secondary intention at that time to trade in the particular property.

As with intention, secondary intention to trade is also a question of fact and the trier of fact may draw inferences from the taxpayer's conduct.[25] The determination is on a balance of probabilities.[26] Hence, taxpayer credibility is always in issue. The same rules apply to distinguish between business (non-capital) losses and capital losses.[27]

A taxpayer has a secondary intention to trade if the possibility of early resale at a profit was a *motivating* consideration at the time that he or she acquired the property. Thus, the critical times are just before, and the moment that, the taxpayer enters into a binding agreement to purchase the property in question.[28] Although motive to trade or invest is a subjective criterion, we determine its absence or presence by inference from objective evidence — that is, the taxpayer's conduct and the circumstances surrounding the particular transaction.[29]

Mere awareness at the time that one acquires a property that future events might dictate a change of investments does not *necessarily* lead to the inference that the transaction is an adventure in the nature of trade. Nor does sensitivity to the probability of capital apprecia-

---

tated abandonment of building plans; subsequent sale for profit found to have been alternative intention); *Regal Heights Ltd. v. M.N.R.*, [1960] S.C.R. 902, [1960] C.T.C. 384, 60 D.T.C. 1270 (S.C.C.) (plans for shopping centre frustrated and parcels of land sold; profits of highly speculative venture constituted income).

[25]*Reicher v. The Queen*, [1975] C.T.C. 659, 76 D.T.C. 6001 (F.C.A.).

[26]*Factory Carpet Ltd. v. The Queen*, [1985] 2 C.T.C. 267, 85 D.T.C. 5464 (F.C.T.D.).

[27]*M.N.R. v. Freud*, [1969] S.C.R. 75, [1968] C.T.C. 438, 68 D.T.C. 5279 (S.C.C.).

[28]*Dickson v. The Queen*, [1977] C.T.C. 64, 77 D.T.C. 5061 (F.C.A.) (resolution to sell land dated 1964 but agreement dated 1967; purchaser's financial plight at date of signing agreement relevant to intention); *Racine v. M.N.R.*, [1965] C.T.C. 150, 65 D.T.C. 5098 (Ex. Ct.) (to constitute "secondary intention", purchaser must have possibility of reselling as operating motivation for acquisition at moment of purchase).

[29]*Reicher v. The Queen*, [1975] C.T.C. 659 at 664, 76 D.T.C. 6001 at 6004 *per* Le Dain J. A. (F.C.A.):

> The issue on this appeal is whether at the time they acquired the property the appellant ... had a secondary intention, as an operating motivation for such acquisition, to sell the property at a profit should a suitable opportunity present itself.

See also *Hiwako Invt. Ltd. v. The Queen*, [1978] C.T.C. 378, 78 D.T.C. 6281 (F.C.A.) (whether or not onus on taxpayer to disprove Minister's stated assumption that taxpayer primarily motivated by intention to trade); *Kit-Win Hldgs. (1973) Ltd. v. The Queen*, [1981] C.T.C. 43, 81 D.T.C. 5030 (F.C.T.D.) (Minister did not precisely allege exclusive motivation to develop property for profit).

tion necessarily imply a trading intention. Such sensitivity indicates no more than a prudent investment decision.[30]

A gain or loss that results from a taxpayer's response to a changing investment climate is not an adventure in the nature of trade. That is, an intention at the time of acquiring an asset that one will sell the asset if the purchase proves unprofitable merely indicates a prudent investment decision. It does not imply a secondary intention to engage in business or an adventure in the nature of trade.

There is a difference, however, between a taxpayer who responds to a *changing* investment climate and a taxpayer who actively contemplates the potential of profit on resale at the time of investment. Where the potential of profit is a motivating consideration, it suggests a secondary intention to engage in an adventure in the nature of trade:[31]

> ... an intention at the time of acquisition of an investment to sell it in the event that it does not prove profitable does not make the subsequent sale of the investment the completion of an "adventure or concern in the nature of trade". Had the alleged assumption been that there was an expectation on the part of the purchaser, at the time of purchase, that, in the event that the investment did not prove to be profitable, it could be sold at a profit, and that such expectation was one of the factors that induced him to make the purchase, such assumption, if not disproved, might (I do not say that it would) support the assessments based on "trading" if not disproved.

(c) — Criteria Used to Determine Taxpayer Intention

A taxpayer's intention, whether primary or secondary, is always a question of fact. We look objectively at various criteria as aids in determining intention. No single criterion is conclusive. These criteria include: (1) number of similar transactions; (2) nature of the asset; (3) related activity; (4) corporate objects and powers; and (5) degree of organization.

(i) — Number of Similar Transactions

Evidence that a taxpayer engaged in similar transactions to the one at issue provides equivocal, but potentially prejudicial, proof that the taxpayer is a trader and engages in a business. All other things being equal (although they rarely are), the greater the number of similar transactions in the past, the greater the likelihood that the gain or loss in issue is business income or loss. The converse, however, does not apply. Merely because a transaction is an

---

[30]*Hiwako Invt. Ltd. v. The Queen, ante; The Queen v. Bassani*, [1985] 1 C.T.C. 314, 85 D.T.C. 5232 (F.C.T.D.) (mere expectation that price of property would rise did not constitute "secondary intention" without operating motivation).

[31]*Hiwako Investments Ltd. v. The Queen*, [1978] C.T.C. 378, 78 D.T.C. 6281 (F.C.A.) at 383 [C.T.C.] and 6285 [D.T.C.].

isolated event does not mean that it is not business income or loss. As the Exchequer Court stated:[32]

> ... while it is recognized that, as a general rule, an isolated transaction of purchase and sale outside the course of the taxpayer's ordinary business does not constitute the carrying on of a trade or business so as to render the profit therefrom liable to the income tax ... it is also established that the fact that a transaction is an isolated one does not exclude it from the category of trading or business transactions of such a nature as to attract income tax to the profit therefrom.

A gain from an isolated transaction can give rise to business income or loss if the transaction is either closely related to the taxpayer's ordinary business activities or the property disposed of is of a type characterized as a "trading" property.[33] Lord President Clyde put it succinctly:[34]

> A single plunge may be enough provided it is shown to the satisfaction of the Court that the plunge is made in the waters of trade. ...

(ii) — Nature of Asset

The nature of the asset can be important in the characterization of any gain or loss from its disposition. Land, for example, *particularly raw land*, is viewed suspiciously as a trading, rather than an investment, asset. This attitude also extends to the sale of shares of corporations incorporated *solely* for the purpose of holding raw land.[35] In contrast, transactions involving corporate shares are generally seen as on account of capital. As the Supreme Court observed:[36]

> ... a person who puts money into a business enterprise by the purchase of the shares of a company on an isolated occasion, and not as a part of his regular business, cannot be said to have engaged in an adventure in the nature of trade merely because the purchase was speculative in that, at that time, he did not intend to hold the shares indefinitely, but intended, if possible, to sell them at a profit as soon as he reasonably could. I think that there must be

---

[32]*Atlantic Sugar Refineries Ltd. v. M.N.R.*, [1949] S.C.R. 706, [1948] C.T.C. 326 at 333-34, 48 D.T.C. 507 at 511; affd. [1949] C.T.C. 196, 49 D.T.C. 602 (S.C.C.).

[33]*M.N.R. v. Taylor*, [1956] C.T.C. 189, 56 D.T.C. 1125 (Ex. Ct.).

[34]*Balgownie Land Trust Ltd. v. I.R.C.* (1929), 14 Tax Cas. 684 (Scot.).

[35]*Fraser v. M.N.R.*, [1964] S.C.R. 657, [1964] C.T.C. 372, 64 D.T.C. 5224 (S.C.C.); see also *Mould v. The Queen*, [1986] 1 C.T.C. 271, 86 D.T.C. 6087 (F.C.T.D.) (156 acres of land sole asset of corporation: "... the acquisition of the shares was merely a method of obtaining an interest in the land").

[36]*Irrigation Industries Ltd. v. M.N.R.*, [1962] S.C.R. 346, [1962] C.T.C. 215 at 219, 62 D.T.C. 1131 at 1133 (S.C.C.).

clearer indications of "trade" than this before it can be said that there has been an adventure in the nature of trade.

Thus, a purchase of shares with an intention to resell at a profit is not, *by itself*, likely to result in the characterization of any gain or loss from their sale as resulting from an adventure in the nature of trade. An isolated transaction in shares, however, can give rise to business income or loss if there are other factors that indicate an intention to trade.[37] For example, a "quick flip" of shares may suggest a trading intention unless it can be explained on other grounds. An isolated transaction in speculative penny mining shares may well give rise to business income or loss if the taxpayer is acting like a mining promoter. *A fortiori*, speculative and highly leveraged trading in high risk, non-yielding shares and options may be seen as trading in securities.[38]

All investors hope, albeit sometimes unrealistically, that their investments will increase in value. The mere expectation of profit is not, by itself, sufficient to characterize a transaction as an adventure in the nature of trade. Certain types of assets, though, and typically commodities that cannot possibly provide any investment yield, are always suspect as "trading assets". Profits resulting from the sale of these types of assets are summarily classified as business income. As Lord Carmont stated:[39]

> ... this means that, although in certain cases it is important to know whether a venture is isolated or not, that information is really superfluous in many cases where *the commodity itself* stamps the transaction as a trading venture, and the profits and gains are plainly income liable to tax. [Emphasis added.]

In contrast, assets with a *potential, even if a somewhat remote possibility*, of yielding income, are generally seen as "investment assets" and profits resulting from transactions in these types of assets are usually, though not inevitably, characterized as capital gains. Corporate shares in particular enjoy this status. Corporate shares tend to be viewed as investment assets because they have the *potential* to yield dividends. Are corporate shares really

---

[37] *Osler Hammond & Nanton Ltd. v. M.N.R.*, [1963] S.C.R. 432, [1963] C.T.C. 164, 63 D.T.C. 1119 (S.C.C.) (investment dealer sold shares arranged for during underwriting); *Hill-Clarke-Francis Ltd. v. M.N.R.*, [1963] S.C.R. 452, [1963] C.T.C. 337, 63 D.T.C. 1211 (S.C.C.) (lumber dealer purchased all outstanding shares of supplier; Court looked at intention at time of acquisition and sale of shares).

[38] See, e.g., *Oakside Corporation Ltd. v. M.N.R.*, [1991] 1 C.T.C. 2132, 91 D.T.C. 328 (T.C.C.).

[39] *I.R.C. v. Reinhold* (1953), 34 Tax Cas. 389 at 392 (Scot.); see also *Rutledge v. I.R.C.* (1929), 14 Tax Cas. 490 (Scot. Ct. of Sess.) (isolated transaction in toilet paper characterized as adventure in nature of trade); *I.R.C. v. Fraser*, 27 Tax Cas. 502 (Scot.) (isolated transaction in whiskey gave rise to funds taxable as business income); *M.N.R. v. Taylor*, [1956] C.T.C. 189, 56 D.T.C. 1125 (Ex. Ct.) (isolated transaction in lead).

any different from other assets? The Supreme Court thought so in *Irrigation Industries Ltd. v. M.N.R.*:[40]

> ... the nature of the property in question here is shares issued from the treasury of a corporation and we have not been referred to any reported case in which profit from one isolated purchase and sale of shares, by a person not engaged in the business of trading in securities, has been claimed to be taxable. ... *Corporate shares are in a different position because they constitute something the purchase of which is, in itself, an investment.* They are not, in themselves, articles of commerce, but represent an interest in a corporation which is itself created for the purpose of doing business. Their acquisition is a well recognized method of investing capital in a business enterprise. [Emphasis added.]

The Court adopted a more stringent approach, however, in Freud where Pigeon J. stated:[41]

> It is clear that while an acquisition of shares may be an investment ... it may also be a trading operation depending upon circumstances. ...

The converse is equally true. It is generally difficult, but by no means impossible, for a taxpayer to establish that he or she was engaged in a speculative venture or an adventure in the nature of trade in trading shares.[42] Thus, share losses are seen as capital transactions.

Assets other than "trading assets" and "investment assets" fall into some middle ground in which the nature of the asset does not play as important a role as the taxpayer's conduct in relation to the asset. Real estate, other than vacant land, falls into this middle ground.

To summarize:

- *By itself*, nothing conclusive can be determined from the fact that a transaction is an isolated one in the taxpayer's experience;

- If there are other factors indicative of trade, a profit from an isolated transaction will be taxable as ordinary income resulting from an adventure in the nature of trade;

- Even if there are no other business attributes, a transaction may still give rise to business income if the asset traded is of a trading, and not of an investment nature; and

- If the asset in question is an investment asset (e.g., corporate shares), and there are no other factors indicative of trading, the transaction will *usually* (not inevitably) be

---

[40]*Irrigation Indust. Ltd. v. M.N.R.*, *ante* (gain from speculative mining shares purchased with short-term loan on account of capital).

[41]*M.N.R. v. Freud*, [1969] S.C.R. 75 at 80-81, [1968] C.T.C. 438 at 442, 68 D.T.C. 5279 at 5282 (S.C.C.).

[42]*Becker v. The Queen*, [1983] C.T.C. 11, 83 D.T.C. 5032 (F.C.A.) (purchase of shares in business with intention of transforming it into profitable enterprise); *Factory Carpet Ltd. v. The Queen*, [1985] 2 C.T.C. 267, 85 D.T.C. 5464 (F.C.T.D.) (purchase of shares with substantial deductible non-capital losses with intention of revamping and reselling business, therefore trading).

viewed as a capital transaction. This is so even though the investment asset is acquired *for the purpose of resale at a profit.*

(iii) — Related Activity

A taxpayer's profits and losses from transactions that are closely related to his or her other ordinary business activities are usually characterized as business income or losses.[43] It is very difficult for a taxpayer to maintain successfully that a profit arising out of a transaction connected in any manner with ordinary business activity is a capital gain. As Thorson P. stated:[44]

> ... they were transactions in the same commodity as that which it had to purchase for its ordinary purposes. In my view, they were of the same character and nature as trading and business operations as those of its business in its ordinary course, even though they involved a departure from such course.

Therefore, there is a strong presumption that a transaction connected in any way with a taxpayer's usual business is intrinsically part of that business. The presumption is rebuttable. It may be rebutted through evidence that the transaction was not part of the taxpayer's ordinary business, but was an unrelated capital investment. *Actual* use of the property as an

---

[43]See generally: *Smith v. M.N.R.* (1955), 12 Tax A.B.C. 166, 55 D.T.C. 101 (mortgage discounting closely related to taxpayer's business as realtor; treated as trading since so related); *Darius v. M.N.R.*, [1971] Tax A.B.C. 889 (Can. Tax. App. Bd.); affd. by Fed. TD in 74 D.T.C. 6260, [1974] C.T.C. 337 (Fed. T.D.) (shareholder in construction company sold land parcels in her own name to achieve better tax result than company able to achieve); *Morrison v. M.N.R.*, [1917–27] C.T.C. 343, 1 D.T.C. 113 (Ex. Ct.) (taxpayer with skill and knowledge in trade acquired through experience, who then traded privately in the same commodity, was carrying on a business); *McDonough v. M.N.R.*, [1949] C.T.C. 213, 4 D.T.C. 621 (Ex. Ct.) (trading not precluded by mere fact that isolated transaction; prospector became promoter of mines in one trade of over a million shares); *No. 351 v. M.N.R.* (1956), 15 Tax A.B.C. 351, 56 D.T.C. 375 (frequent trading of grain futures); *Boivin v. M.N.R.*, 70 D.T.C. 1364 (a dozen property "flips" by wife on direction of building contractor husband motivated by profit and deemed "trading"); *Kinsella v. M.N.R.* (1963), 34 Tax A.B.C. 196, 64 D.T.C. 56 (frequency of sales and modernization of buildings indicated carefully-planned method of increasing income); *M.N.R. v. Spencer*, [1961] C.T.C. 109, 61 D.T.C. 1079 (Ex. Ct.) (lawyers acted as mortgagees for bonuses; although held to maturity, deemed business and not investments); *Kennedy v. M.N.R.*, [1952] C.T.C. 59, 52 D.T.C. 1070 (Ex. Ct.) (stated intention of taxpayer on purchase only relevant if supported by evidence; see editorial note at C.T.C. 59); *No. 13 v. M.N.R.* (1951), 3 Tax A.B.C. 397, 51 D.T.C. 117 (real estate developer treated one property specially, holding it for 10 years as an investment apart from his ordinary business); *Everlease (Ont.) Ltd. v. M.N.R.*, [1968] Tax A.B.C. 162, 68 D.T.C. 180 (building sold to cover lack of funds was trade due to owner's close association with real estate developers and managers).

[44]*Atlantic Sugar Refineries Ltd. v. M.N.R.*, [1948] C.T.C. 326, 48 D.T.C. 507 at 513; affd. [1949] C.T.C. 196, 49 D.T.C. 602 (S.C.C.).

investment asset over some period of time, or a plausible explanation for selling the investment, may also rebut the presumption.

(iv) — Corporate Objects and Powers

A corporation has the capacity, rights, powers and privileges of a natural person.[45] Thus, unless specifically restricted by its articles of incorporation, a corporation may engage in any business other than those from which it is specifically precluded by statute. A corporation may restrict its scope of business activities by specifying the restrictions in its articles of incorporation or other constating documents.[46]

For tax purposes, characterization of corporate income depends upon the business actually conducted by the corporation and not on any restrictions in its incorporating documents.[47] Thus, corporate income is characterized according to the intention and secondary intention tests and not according to any stipulations in the corporation's constating documents.

(v) — Degree of Organization

Where a taxpayer deals with property in much the same way as a dealer would with similar property, any resulting profit is likely to be characterized as business income. Thus, a transaction, *albeit* isolated and unrelated to the taxpayer's ordinary business activity, may have the stamp of business purpose if it is organized and carried on in the manner of a trader. As Lord Clyde said in *I.R.C. v. Livingston*:[48]

> I think the test, which must be used to determine whether a venture such as we are now considering is, or is not, "in the nature of 'trade'," is whether the operations involved in it are of the same kind, and carried on in the same way, as those which are characteristic of ordinary trading in the line of business in which the venture was made.

For example, a taxpayer who purchases undeveloped land that the taxpayer then subdivides and sells for profit, behaves as a developer would in the normal course of business. In the

---

[45]See, e.g., *Business Corporations Act*, R.S.O. 1990, c. B.16, s. 15.

[46]See, e.g., *Canada Business Corporations Act*, R.S.C. 1985, c. 44, para. 6(1)(f), and Ontario *Business Corporations Act*, R.S.O. 1990, c. B.16, subs. 3(2) and 17(2).

[47]*Sutton Lumber & Trading Co. v. M.N.R.*, [1953] 2 S.C.R. 77, [1953] C.T.C. 237, 53 D.T.C. 1158 (S.C.C.).

[48]*I.R.C. v. Livingston* (1927), 11 Tax Cas. 538 at 542 (Scot.).

absence of a convincing explanation, the taxpayer's profits would constitute income from business.[49]

It is clear that dealing with an asset as a businessperson would deal with similar assets may, by itself, be sufficient to show an intention to trade. It is also clear that a taxpayer's intention at the time of acquisition can be quite different from his or her intention at the time of sale. For example, in *Moluch*,[50] the taxpayer did not originally acquire the lands with an intent to sell them at a profit. The taxpayer's intention to use the land as a capital asset and his actual use as such for an extended period of time were never in question. Nevertheless, the taxpayer's activities subsequent to the acquisition showed that the investment property had been converted into inventory, presumably, on the basis of a change in the taxpayer's intention. The Court said:[51]

> ... even if at the time of acquisition, the intention of turning the lands to account by resale was not present, it does not necessarily follow that profits resulting from sales are not assessable to income tax. If at some subsequent point in time, the appellant embarked upon a business, using the lands as inventory in the business of land subdividing for profit, then clearly the resultant profits would not be merely the realization of an enhancement in value, but rather profits from a business and so assessable to income tax. ...

2. — Electing Capital Gains

To reduce the uncertainty associated with the troublesome question of whether a gain is on account of income or capital, the Act allows taxpayers to elect "guaranteed" capital gains or capital loss treatment on a disposition of certain types of properties.[52] The following rules apply:

- The election is available only upon the disposition of a "Canadian security".

---

[49]See, e.g., *Moluch v. M.N.R.*, [1966] C.T.C. 712, 66 D.T.C. 5463 (Ex. Ct.) at 720 [C.T.C.] and 5468 [D.T.C.] where the Court observed:

> ... moreover I am unable to distinguish what the appellant did after his decision to subdivide had been reached from what a person engaged in the business of land development would do once he had acquired a parcel of property.

See also IT-218R, "Profit, Capital Gains and Losses from the Sale of Real Estate, Including Farmland and Inherited Land and Conversion of Real Estate from Capital Property to Inventory and Vice Versa" (September 16, 1986).

[50]*Moluch v. M.N.R., ibid.*

[51]*Moluch v. M.N.R., ibid.*, at 718 [C.T.C.] and 5466 [D.T.C.]; see also *Hughes v. The Queen*, [1984] C.T.C. 101, 84 D.T.C. 6110 (F.C.T.D.) (apartment building acquired as investment asset; converted into inventory upon application to turn it into condominium).

[52]Subs. 39(4), 39(4.1) and 39(6).

- To qualify as a "Canadian security", the issuer of the security must be a Canadian resident, and the security must be either equity or debt. Warrants and options do not qualify as "Canadian securities".[53]

- Once a taxpayer elects to have a gain deemed a capital gain, all subsequent dispositions of "Canadian securities" by the taxpayer are similarly characterized. Hence, all losses would also be considered capital losses.[54]

- The election is not available to a trader or dealer in securities.[55]

- The election must be made on a prescribed form and filed together with the tax return for the year.

Traders and dealers in securities cannot use the election. Whether a person is a trader or dealer is in itself a question of fact to be determined by the taxpayer's intentions and conduct. A person who participates in the promotion or underwriting of securities is a trader or dealer.[56] The Agency also considers corporate "insiders" who trade for a quick profit to be "traders".

3. — Conversion of Property

Capital property may be converted into inventory and vice versa. The timing of a conversion is a question of fact requiring a clear and unequivocal act implementing such a change of intention as to clearly indicate a change in the character of the property.[57]

4. — Business Income vs. Investment Income

Having drawn a line between "income" and "capital gains", we now further refine the process and distinguish between business income and investment income. The characterization

---

[53]Subs. 39(6); Reg. 6200.

[54]Subs. 39(4).

[55]Subs. 39(5).

[56]IT-479R, "Transactions in Securities" (February 29, 1984).

[57]*Magilb Dev. Corp. v. The Queen*, [1987] 1 C.T.C. 66, 87 D.T.C. 5012 (F.C.T.D.)) (father made plans for development of family farm corporation; actions did not convert farm from a capital to a trading asset); *Cantor v. M.N.R.*, [1985] 1 C.T.C. 2059, 85 D.T.C. 79 (T.C.C.) (townhouses purchased by law partners proved unprofitable and sold as condominiums; no change in character of investment where diversification occurred to dispose of property most profitably).

of income as resulting from business or investments (more technically, income from property) is a question of fact.[58]

Since most businesses use property to generate income, it is not particularly helpful to ask whether the income derives from the *use* of property. The critical question is: does the income flow *from* property or *from* business?[59] It is the subtlety of this distinction that gives rise to difficulties in characterizing the source of income. There is no bright-line test that clearly answers the question.

In many, perhaps most, cases the distinction between business income and property income does not affect the end result. A taxpayer's income for a taxation year from a source that is business *or* property is his or her profit therefrom for the year.[60] We calculate income from both of these sources according to the same commercial and statutory rules. There are, however, circumstances in which the distinction between the two can be important. For example:

- The attribution rules apply only to income from property and do not apply to business income;[61]

- Active business income earned by a Canadian-controlled private corporation is eligible for special tax credits that substantially reduce the effective tax rate on such income;[62]

- Income from property is subject to a different scheme of taxation and at different rates for different sources of such income.

Generally, income from property is the investment yield on an asset. Rent, dividends, interest, and royalties are typical examples. We earn the yield on the investment by a relatively passive process. For example, where an individual invests in land, stocks, bonds, or intangible property,[63] and collects investment income therefrom without doing much more than holding the property, the income is investment income or income *from* property.

In contrast, business income implies activity in the earning process. Business generates from the *use* of property as part of a process that combines labour and capital. For example, a taxpayer may *invest* in bonds and clip the coupons to earn the interest income therefrom;

---

[58]*Cdn. Marconi Co. v. The Queen*, [1986] 2 S.C.R. 522 at 530-31, [1986] 2 C.T.C. 465 at 470, 86 D.T.C. 6526 at 6529 (S.C.C.) *per* Wilson J.: "It is trite law that the characterization of income as income from a business or income from property must be made from an examination of the taxpayer's whole course of conduct viewed in the light of surrounding circumstances."

[59]Para. 3(a); subs. 9(1); see also IT-511R, "Interspousal and Certain other Transfers and Loans of Property", February 21, 1994.

[60]Subs. 9(1).

[61]S. 74.1.

[62]Subs. 125(1); see Chapter 20, "Corporate Business Income".

[63]Such as, copyrights, trademarks, etc.

alternatively, he or she may actively *trade* in bonds to earn a profit from trading activities. In the first case, the earnings derive from a passive process and are investment income; in the second case, the income is from business.[64]

Although the distinction between income from business and investment income is easy to state in general terms, the borderline between the two is unclear. What is the level of activity beyond which a passive holding becomes an active process of earning income?[65] The issue is complicated because of some statements from the Supreme Court that there is a rebuttable presumption that income earned by a corporate taxpayer in the exercise of its duly authorized objects is income from a business.[66]

Traditionally, a corporation carrying on activities described in the objects clause (if any) of its constating documents is presumed to earn income from business. The presumption appears as early as 1880 in *Smith v. Anderson*:[67]

> You cannot acquire gain by means of a company except by carrying on some business or other, and I have no doubt if any one formed a company or association for the purpose of acquiring gain, he must form it for the purpose of carrying on a business by which gain is to be obtained.

---

[64]It is important to note that profits from an isolated trade may be business income. The phrase "adventure in the nature of trade" implies an isolated transaction: see subs. 248(1) "business".

[65]*Cdn. Marconi Co. v. The Queen*, [1986] 2 S.C.R. 522, [1986] 2 C.T.C. 465, 86 D.T.C. 6526 (S.C.C.) ($18 million invested yielded interest that was included in manufacturing and processing profits); *Wertman v. M.N.R.*, [1964] C.T.C. 252, 64 D.T.C. 5158 (Ex. Ct.) (concerning rent from apartment units: "the concepts of income from property and income from business are not mutually exclusive but blend completely"); *Walsh v. M.N.R.*, [1965] C.T.C. 478, 65 D.T.C. 5293 (Ex. Ct.) (ordinary janitorial services did not convert property to business, as would maid, linen, laundry and breakfast services); *Burri v. The Queen*, [1985] 2 C.T.C. 42, 85 D.T.C. 5287 (F.C.T.D.) (services provided by owners incidental to the making of revenue from property through the earning of rent).

[66]*Cdn. Marconi Co. v. The Queen ibid.*, at 529 [S.C.R.], 468 [C.T.C.] and 6528 [D.T.C.]; see also *Supreme Theatres Ltd. v. The Queen*, [1981] C.T.C. 190 at 193, 81 D.T.C. 5136 at 5138 *per* Gibson J. (F.C.T.D.); *Queen & Metcalfe Carpark Ltd v. M.N.R.*, [1973] C.T.C. 810 at 817-18, 74 D.T.C. 6007 at 6011 *per* Sweet D.J. (F.C.T.D.); *Calvin Bullock Ltd. v. M.N.R.*, [1985] 1 C.T.C. 2309 at 2312, 85 D.T.C. 287 at 289 *per* St-Onge T.C.J. (T.C.C.); *No. 585 v. M.N.R.* (1958), 21 Tax A.B.C. 56 at 66, 58 D.T.C. 754 at 759 *per* Mr. Boisvert; *Tenir Ltée v. M.N.R.*, [1968] Tax A.B.C. 772, 68 D.T.C. 589 at 595 *per* Mr. Davis; *SBI Properties Ltd. v. M.N.R.*, [1981] C.T.C. 2288 at 2297, 81 D.T.C. 263 at 270-271 *per* Mr. St-Onge (T.R.B.); *King George Hotels Ltd. et al. v. The Queen*, [1981] C.T.C. 78 at 80 (F.C.T.D.), *per* Smith D.J., affd. [1981] C.T.C. 87, 81 D.T.C. 5082 (F.C.A.).

[67]*Smith v. Anderson* (1880), 15 Ch. D. 247 at 260 (C.A.).

But these judicial statements were born of a foreign tax system with a different structure. It is less clear whether corporations created in jurisdictions that do not require objects clauses should also be subject to this presumption.[68]

One answer is that the rebuttable presumption applies to all corporations, but that it is more readily rebuttable in the case of private corporations that pay the Part IV tax on their investment income.[69] But why should the choice of form of business organization determine the characterization of the source of income?

(a) — Real Estate

The issue in characterizing rental income from real estate is whether the income results from activity and services associated with a commercial enterprise or from passive ownership of the property with only minimal ancillary activity. Income that derives from passive ownership of real estate is investment income. Income that flows from the use of real estate as an asset in a commercial endeavour is business income.[70]

The critical test in distinguishing an investment in real estate from a real estate business is the level of services provided as a supplement to the rental of the real property.[71] The greater the level of services that one provides as an adjunct to the rental of real estate, the greater the likelihood that the income therefrom is business income.[72] The distinction does not rest on any single criterion but upon an assessment of the aggregate level of activity associated with the generation of the income. One factor may outweigh several others, but it is always a facts and circumstances test.

Here, as elsewhere in the law, it is easy to characterize at either extreme of the spectrum. It is clear, for example, that a traditional hotel rents its guests more than a room, whereas a

---

[68]*Smith v. Anderson*, ante, at 530-31.

[69]See Chapter 19, "Corporate Investment Income" for a discussion of the Part IV tax and the statutory scheme in connection therewith.

[70]*Martin v. M.N.R.*, [1948] C.T.C. 189 at 193, 3 D.T.C. 1199 at 1201 (Ex. Ct.).

[71]The phrase "mere [sic] investment" has sometimes been used to describe a passive investment that gives rise to income from property. See, e.g., *Marks v. M.N.R.* (1962), 30 Tax A.B.C. 155, 62 D.T.C. 536.

[72]*Fry v. Salisbury House Estate Ltd.*, [1930] A.C. 432 at 470 (H.L.) (management company operated elevators, provided porters, security guards, heating and cleaning at extra charge; property ownership, not trade); see also *Crofts v. Sywell Aerodrome Ltd.*, [1942] 1 K.B. 317 (C.A.) (activities, though varied and extensive, consisted of exercise and exploitation of property rights of aerodrome); *Malenfant v. M.N.R.*, [1992] 2 C.T.C. 2431, 92 D.T.C. 2065 (T.C.C.) (income from hotel and motel rooms was income from rental property as services provided were only those required to maintain rooms).

tenant in an apartment usually rents only space with minimal services. The distinction is less clear, however, between an apartment that provides extensive ancillary services and a hotel that makes minimal provision beyond accommodation. The provision of maid, linen, laundry and food services, for example, suggests business. In contrast, routine and necessary ancillary services, such as heating, cleaning and snow removal, are seen as mere adjuncts to the ownership of property. In either case, time spent on managing the property is not the determining factor.[73]

(b) — Short-Term Investments

The characterization of income from short-term investments raises more subtle distinctions. The issue is particularly important for Canadian corporations because of the special rules in respect of the small business deduction, the manufacturing and processing credit, and the refundable dividend tax on investment income.

The small business deduction and the manufacturing and processing credit may only be claimed on Canadian "active business" income. Income must first qualify as business income before it can be characterized as "active" business income. The refundable tax on income from property may only be claimed on "investment income" earned by a Canadian-controlled private corporation.[74]

---

[73]See, e.g., the comments of Thurlow J., in *Wertman v. M.N.R.*, [1964] C.T.C. 252 at 267, 64 D.T.C. 5158 at 5167 (Ex. Ct.):

> The nature of the services provided, in my opinion, also has a bearing on the question; some, such as maid service and linen and laundry service, being more indicative of a business operation than the heating of the building which, in my view, is so closely concerned with the property itself as to offer no definite indication one way or the other. Nor do I think that the fact that the management of the property occupies the appellant's time or the fact that he uses his car to go to and from the property indicate that the operation is a business, for, at most, these facts indicate that he renders a service to himself and to the other owners of the building which, so far as charged for, represents a proper outgoing against revenue for the purpose of ascertaining the net profit divisible among the owners regardless of whether the rentals are mere income from property or income from a business.

[74]See Chapter 19, "Corporate Investment Income".

(i) — Integration Test

An "active business" is "... *any* business carried on by the taxpayer *other than* a specified investment business or a personal services business..."[75] and for some purposes "... includes an adventure or concern in the nature of trade."[76]

"Investment income" is "... income for the year from a source ... that is property. ..."

The characterization of a taxpayer's income from short-term investments involves a two-step process:

1. Determine whether the taxpayer's investments are an integral part of his or her business activities. If they are, income from the investments is business income; and

2. If they are not, determine whether the taxpayer's investment activities constitute a separate business. If they do, the income from those activities is business income. If the investment activity does not constitute a separate business, the income from those activities is income from property.

---

[75]Subs. 248(1) "active business".

[76]Subs. 125(7) "active business".

(ii) — "Employed and Risked" Test

A taxpayer's investments are considered to be an integral part of a business if his or her funds are "employed and risked" in the business.[77] Is the making of investments a part of the mode of conducting the business? If the answer is yes, then the income from the investments is part of the income of the business.

Business income from investments represents the fruit derived from a fund "employed and risked" in the taxpayer's business. Thus, the temporary investment of working capital constitutes an intrinsic part of the business.

---

[77]See *Ensite Ltd. v. The Queen*, [1986] 2 S.C.R. 509, [1986] 2 C.T.C. 459, 86 D.T.C. 6521 (S.C.C.), at 529 [S.C.R.], 468 [C.T.C.] and 6528 [D.T.C.]; (property yielding interest must be linked to some "definite obligation or liability of the business"); *Bank Line Ltd. v. I.R.C.* (1974), 49 Tax Cas. 307 (Scot. Ct. of Sess.) (no actual risk or employment of reserve funds in the company's business of owning, operating and replacing ships). In *The Queen v. Marsh & McLennan Ltd.*, [1983] C.T.C. 231, 83 D.T.C. 5180 (F.C.A.), for example, the taxpayer, an insurance broker, temporarily invested its insurance premiums in short-term paper. The taxpayer could do so because of the lag between the time that it received a premium from its customer and the time that it remitted the premium to the customer's insurer. The taxpayer's business involved two dimensions: brokerage and investment. The two activities were so interdependent that its investments were an integral part of its business; hence, its investment income was income from a business and *not* income from property. See also the speech of Lord Mersey in *Liverpool & London & Globe Ins. Co. v. Bennett* (1913), 6 Tax Cas. 327 (H.L.) at 379-80:

> It is said that the dividends in question are derived from investments made ... and that such investments form no part of the "business" of the Company. In my opinion there is no foundation either in fact or in law for this contention. It is well known that in the course of carrying on an insurance business, large sums of money derived from premiums collected and from other sources accumulate in the hands of the insurers, and that one of the most important parts of the profits of the business is derived from the temporary investment of these moneys. These temporary investments are also required for the formation of the reserve fund, a fund created to attract customers and to serve as a standby in the event of sudden claims being made upon the insurers in respect of losses. It is, according to my view, impossible to say that such investments do not form part of this Company's insurance business, or that the returns flowing from them do not form part of its profits. In a commercial sense the directors of the Company owe a duty to their shareholders and to their customers to make such investments, and to receive and distribute in the ordinary course of business, whether in the form of dividends, or in payment of losses, or in the formation of reserves, the moneys collected from them.

(iii) — Separate Business Test

Where a taxpayer's investments are not an integral part of his or her business operations, the question arises whether the investment activities constitute a separate business.[78] The answer to this question depends upon several factors:

- The number and value of transactions;

- The time devoted to investment activities;

- The relationship between the taxpayer's investment income and his or her total income; and

- The relationship between the value of the taxpayer's investment and the total value of his or her assets.

Is the taxpayer merely managing personal investments or carrying on an investment business? The greater the amount of time devoted to, and the greater the value of, investment activities as compared to business activities, the more likely it is that the investment segment constitutes a separate business.

III. — Conclusion

It should be clear by now that the classification of income by source causes enormous complexity in the tax system. Different rules govern each of the sources of income, each of which require strict legislative supervision. Taxpayers, understandably, try to move income into categories that attract lower tax and losses into sources that are taxed at higher rates. Hence, the thousands of disputes that involve capital gains and business income. Conversely, and equally understandably, the Agency is likely to see losses as capital, and not as business losses, in order to protect the tax base. Throughout subsequent chapters, we will see

---

[78]*Cdn. Marconi Co. v. The Queen*, [1986] 2 S.C.R. 522, [1986] 2 C.T.C. 465, 86 D.T.C. 6526 (S.C.C.). The taxpayer, a manufacturer of electronic equipment, divested itself of its broadcasting division and found itself with surplus funds of approximately $20 million. While awaiting a suitable opportunity to invest in another business, the taxpayer invested these surplus funds in short-term, interest-bearing securities. During the period under assessment, the taxpayer earned substantial interest income (approximately $5 million) on which it claimed the manufacturing and processing credit on the basis that its income from its short-term investments represented "business income" and, therefore, "active business income". In deciding in favour of the taxpayer, the Supreme Court applied the presumption that income that a corporate taxpayer earns is business income. The facts fell short of supporting the Minister's contention that he rebutted the presumption. See also *Colonial Realty Services Ltd. v. M.N.R.*, [1987] 1 C.T.C. 2343, 87 D.T.C. 259 (T.C.C.) (excess funds placed in investment certificates; no corporate activity or circumstances converted the yield to active business income).

how the Act seeks to protect the boundaries of each of the sources to prevent leakage between the various categories.

Selected Bibliography to Chapter 7

General

Anderson, William D., "A Potpourri of Elements in Computing Business Income: Part 2", *Corporate Management Tax Conf.* 6:1 (Can. Tax Foundation, 1987).

Carr, Brian R., "A Potpourri of Elements in Computing Business Income: Part 1", *Corporate Management Tax Conf.* 5:1 (Can. Tax Foundation, 1987).

Drache, A.B.C., "A Dog is Not a Horse or a Fish" (1991) XIII Can. Taxpayer 135.

Durnford, John, "The Distinction Between Income From Business and Income From Property and the Concept of Carrying on Business" (1991) 39 Can. Tax J. 1131.

Harris, Edwin C., "Measuring Business Income", in *Proceedings of 19th Tax Conf.* 78 (Can. Tax Foundation, 1967).

Khan, D. and B. Sakich, "Business Income" (1985) 13 Can. Tax News 90.

McGregor, Ian, "Another Look at First Principles" (1962) 10 Can. Tax J. 65.

Roberts, J.R. and William Leiss, "Technology and Accounting Innovation: Can They Mesh?", in *Proceedings of 38th Tax Conf.* 25 (Can. Tax Foundation, 1986).

Characterization of Income

Brayley, C.A.M., "Income or Capital — The Spin of a Coin" (1986) 8 Sup. Ct. L.R. 405.

Boyle, J. Ladson, "What is a Trade or Business?" (1986), 39 The Tax Lawyer 737.

Corn, George, "Interest Income: Business Income or Investment Income" (1992) Can. Current Tax J141.

Corn, George, "Reasonable Expectation of Profit" (1994) Can. Current Tax J61.

Corn, George, "Taxation of Gain on Appreciation of Shares — Capital Gain or Income from an Adventure in the Nature of Trade" (1994) Can. Current Tax J39.

Craig, J.D., "Other than in the Ordinary Course of Business" (1980) 54 Cost and Management 45.

Drache, A.B.C., "Opting to Be a Market Trader" (1991) XIII Can. Taxpayer 175.

Durnford, John W., "Profits on the Sale of Shares: Capital Gains or Business Income — A Fresh Look at Irrigation Industries" (1987) 35 Can. Tax J. 837.

Durnford, John W., "The Distinction Between Income from Business and Income from Property, and the Concept of Carrying on Business" (1991) 39 Can. Tax J. 1131.

Hodgson, John, "What is Income? What is Capital?" (1988) 7 The Philanthropist 24.

Karp, "Rental Income: Property or Business?" (1968) 16 Can. Tax J. 191.

Krishna, Vern, "Characterization of 'Income from Business' and 'Income from Property'" (1984) 1 Can. Current Tax C-37.

Krishna, Vern, "Sale of Franchises: Receipts on Account of Eligible Capital Property or Income from Business?" (1986) 1 Can. Current Tax J-157.

Ladson, Boyle F., "What Is a Trade or Business?" (1986) 39 Tax Lawyer 737.

McDonnell, T.E., "Interest Income: Whether Income from Active Business or Income from Property" (1986) 34 Can. Tax J. 1431.

McGregor, Ian, "Capital Gainsay" (1964) 12 Can. Tax J. 116.

McGregor, Ian, "Secondary Intention" (1961) 9 Can. Tax J. 33.

McKie, A.B., "Properly Taxing Property" (1988) 2 Can. Current Tax C-91.

McLean, Bruce M., "Sourcing of Business Income", *Corporate Management Tax Conf.* 9:1 (Can. Tax Foundation, 1987).

Morris, D. Bernard, "Capital versus Income: Loans and Real Estate" (1992) Can. Tax Foundation 26:1.

Motz, Robert, "Employee vs. Independent Contractor", (November 1990) 64 CMA Magazine 26.

Richards, Gabrielle M.R., "Quick Flips as Adventure in Nature of Trade" (1993) Can. Current Tax J9.

Richardson, Elinore J., "Holding Real Estate for the Production of Income", *Corporate Management Tax Conf.* 1 (Can. Tax Foundation, 1983).

Strother, Robert C., "Income Tax Implications of Personal-Use Real Estate", *Corporate Management Tax Conf.* 59 (Can. Tax Foundation, 1983).

Thomas, Richard B., "Reasonable Expectation of Profit: Are Revenue Canada's and the Court's Expectations Unreasonable?" (1993) 41 Can. Tax J. 1128.

Warnock, Bruce A., "Income or Capital Gains on Dispositions of Property", in *Proceedings of 42nd Tax Conf.* 48:1 (Can. Tax Foundation, 1990).

Measurement of Income

Arnold, Brian J., "Timing and Income Taxation: The Principles of Income Management for Tax Purposes", in *Proceedings of 35th Tax Conf.* 133 (Can. Tax Foundation, 1983).

Harris, Edwin C., "Measuring Business Income", in *Proceedings of 19th Tax Conf.* 78 (Can. Tax Foundation, 1967).

Drobny, Sheldon, "Inventory and Accounting Methods: Controversy and Paradoxes" (October 1990) 68 Taxes 764.

Kaplow, L. and A.C. Warren, "The Bankruptcy of Conventional Tax Timing Wisdom is Deeper Than Semantics: A Rejoinder to Professors Kaplow and Warren, [Discussion of An Income Tax By Any Other Name — A Reply to Professor Strand]" (1986) 38 Stan. L. Rev. 399.

Robertson, D.A., "Timing is Everything" (1988) 121:3 CA Magazine 32.

Strand, J., "Tax Timing and the Haig-Simons Ideal: A Rejoinder to Professor Popkin [Discussion of Tax Ideals in the Real World: A Comment on Professor Strand's Approach to Tax Fairness]" (1986) 62 Ind. L.J. 73.

White, Robert, "Profits and Prophets — An Accountant's Afterword" (1987) 8 Br. Tax Rev. 292.

Other

Beninger, Michael, J., "The Scope and Application of Section 79 of the *Income Tax Act*" (1985) 33 Can. Tax J. 929.

Bernstein, Jack, "Hotels and Motels as Tax Shelters" (1983) 116:10 CA Magazine 1972.

Burke, Harold A., "Real Estate Breakups: Tax, Valuation, and Division Issues", in *Proceedings of 38th Tax Conf.* 43 (Can. Tax Foundation, 1986).

Crawford, R.W., "Sales of Real Estate: Tax Planning for the Seller", *Corporate Management Tax Conf.* 138 (Can. Tax Foundation, 1983).

Curtis, "Isolation, Intention and Income", in *Legal Essays in Honour of Arthur Moxon* 239 (University of Toronto Press, 1953).

"Deferred Compensation: Diabolus Ex Machina", *Can. Tax Letter*, November 25, 1983 (De Boo).

Drache, A.B.C., "Renewed Attack on Management Companies" (1983) 5 Can. Taxpayer 157.

Dwyer, Blair P., "Deductibility of Tenant Inducement Payments" (1987–89) Can. Current Tax C53.

Krishna, Vern, "Does Supreme Court Expand Deductibility of Business Expenses in *Symes*?" (1994) Can. Current Tax J35.

MacInnis, Ian V., "Deduction of Rental Losses Require Reasonable Expectation of Profit" (1990) 7 Business and the Law 39.

O'Brien, Martin L., "Commodity Trading — Convertible Hedges" (1994) Can. Current Tax J31.

Popkin, W.D., "Tax Ideals in the Real World: A Comment on Professor Strand's Approach to Tax Fairness, [Discussion of Taxation of Income from Capital — A Theoretical Reappraisal]" (1986-87) Ind. L.J. 63.

Valliere, Charles E., "Both Deduction and Capitalization Treatment Denied with respect to Real Estate that Produces No Income" (1991) 39 Can. Tax J. 1033.

CHAPTER 8 — INCLUSIONS IN BUSINESS AND INVESTMENT INCOME

I. — General Comment

We saw in Chapter 7 that income from business or property is the "profit" therefrom. Although profit is generally determined according to accounting principles and commercial practice, the *Income Tax Act* does not rely completely upon such principles and practice in the measurement of income for tax purposes. In certain circumstances, the Act specifies the manner in which income is to be calculated for tax purposes. For example, the Act specifies in section 12 that certain amounts are to be included in income for tax purposes, regardless of the manner in which the particular item is treated in accounting practice.

The Act specifies income inclusion in order to:

• Make timing adjustments;

• Modify the common law concept of income; and

• Clarify uncertain issues in accounting practice.

II. — Timing Adjustments

"Profit" from business or property is generally calculated on an accrual basis of accounting. Paragraph 12(1)(b) of the Act reinforces this concept and requires a taxpayer to include in income in a year any receivables on account of goods sold or services rendered in the year, regardless of when the amounts are due or actually collected. An amount is considered "receivable" when the taxpayer completes the sale or service so that his or her right to receive the amount is perfected.

Generally accepted concepts of accrual accounting require inclusion in income only of amounts that have been earned. Unearned revenue is a liability and not income. For tax purposes, however, paragraph 12(1)(a) modifies the general accounting rule: *all* receipts, whether earned or unearned, are included in income for the year. Thus, a taxpayer must include an amount received on account of services to be rendered in the future in income in the year of receipt and not in the year in which he earns the income. The taxpayer may, however, claim a reserve against unearned income.[1]

III. — Modification Of Common Law Rules

1. — Interest Income

"Interest" is defined as the return or material consideration given for the use of money belonging to another person. Interest must be referable to a principal sum of money or an obligation to pay money.[2] Thus:[3]

> ... there must be a sum of money by reference to which the payment which is said to be interest is to be ascertained. A payment cannot be "interest of money" unless there is the requisite "money" for the payment to be said to be "interest of".

Interest may vary with the gross revenues or profits of the borrower.[4] Amounts payable as a percentage of profit are less likely to constitute interest.[5] Profit percentage arrangements are more usually associated with a partnership relationship between the parties.[6]

Payments on account of interest are generally considered to be for the use of money over a period. Thus, in business and commerce, interest is merely the equivalent of a "rental" charge for the use of someone else's money. The courts, however, consider interest as an

---

[1]Para. 20(1)(m).

[2]*Ref. re s. 6 of Farm Security Act 1944 of Sask.*, [1947] S.C.R. 394 at 411; affd. [1949] A.C. 110 (P.C.); *The Queen v. Melford Dev. Inc.*, [1982] 2 S.C.R. 504, [1982] C.T.C. 330, 82 D.T.C. 6281 (S.C.C.); see also, *Halsbury's Laws of England*, 4th ed., vol. 32 (London: Butterworths, 1980) at 53, where "interest" is defined as "... the return or compensation for the use or retention by one person of a sum of money belonging to or owed to another. Interest accrues from day to day even if payable only at intervals. ..." The CRA generally accepts these criteria in defining interest. See IT-533 (October 31, 2003) para. 1.

[3]*Re Euro Hotel (Belgravia)*, [1975] 3 All E.R. 1075 at 1084 *per* Megarry J.

[4]*Pooley v. Driver* (1876), 5 Ch. D. 459 (C.A.); *Cox v. Hickman* (1860), 11 E.R. 431 (H.L.); see *Partnerships Act*, R.S.O. 1990, c. P.5, para. 3(1)(d).

[5]See e.g., *Balaji Apts. Ltd. v. Mfrs. Life Ins. Co.* (1979), 25 O.R. (2d) 275 (Ont. H.C.).

[6]See e.g., *Sedgwick v. M.N.R.*, [1962] C.T.C. 400, 62 D.T.C. 1253 (Ex. Ct.).

expenditure on account of capital. To overcome the judicial characterization of interest as a payment on account of capital, the Act specifically provides for the treatment of interest as an income or expense item.

There are several ways to account for interest income for tax purposes — the cash basis, modified cash basis, receivable basis, accrual basis and modified accrual basis. Different rules apply to individuals, corporations, and partnerships.

For tax purposes, the term "receivable" means *legally* receivable and not "receivable" in the sense that one uses it in accounting.[7] Thus, the word has a narrower meaning for tax purposes than it has in general accounting.

An amount is "receivable" for tax purposes only when the taxpayer has a clear legal right to it. The right must be legally enforceable. For example, assume a taxpayer buys a bond for $1,000 on December 1, and the bond pays interest at a rate of 12 per cent per year payable at the end of May and November of each year. By December 31, the taxpayer will have earned 1/12 of his or her annual interest income. In accrual accounting, the taxpayer is considered to have *earned* $10 in the month of December even though he or she may not have received payment. The $10 would be accrued as a receivable for general accounting purposes. For tax purposes, however, the $10 is not a "receivable" because there is no legal obligation on the issuer of the bond to pay the interest as at December 31. The legal obligation to pay the interest will arise on the date stipulated in the bond contract, namely May 31.

(a) — Consistency

A taxpayer who selects a particular method of reporting interest income for a particular property must conform to that method from year to year. Although a taxpayer is required to account for interest income on a consistent basis from year to year, there is no requirement that the taxpayer follow the same basis for reporting interest income from all sources. For example, a taxpayer may report interest income from Canada Savings Bonds on a cash basis and, in the same year, report interest income from a mortgage on a receivable basis.[8] Paragraph 12(1)(c) merely requires that interest from the *same source* be reported on a consistent basis — that is, interest from the same debtor on the same type of obligation.

---

[7]*M.N.R. v. J. Colford Contr. Co.*, [1962] S.C.R. viii, [1962] C.T.C. 546, 62 D.T.C. 1338 (S.C.C.).

[8]*Indust. Mtge. & Trust Co. v. M.N.R.*, [1958] C.T.C. 106, 58 D.T.C. 1060 (Ex. Ct.); see also IT-396R, "Interest Income" (May 29, 1984).

(b) — Annual Reporting

As a general rule, an individual may report interest income on a cash or accrual basis.[9] Thus, an individual can use cash basis reporting to defer the recognition of income.

There are, however, special restrictions in respect of "investment contracts". Income from "investment contracts" must be reported on an annual basis, regardless of whether or not the income has been paid out in the year.[10] The rule is intended to prevent prolonged deferral of tax on investment income.

An "investment contract" is a debt such as a note, bond, debenture, or guaranteed investment contract. An "investment contract" does not include the following:[11]

- Salary deferral arrangements;
- Income bonds and debentures;
- Retirement compensation arrangements;
- Employee benefit plans;
- Small business development bonds;
- Small business bonds; or
- Debt obligations in respect of which investment income is otherwise included in income at least annually.

(c) — Blended Payments

A taxpayer is *not* obliged to charge interest on money loaned to another.[12] Interest, however, may be blended into principal, in which case it must be segregated and included in income for tax purposes.[13] A blended payment is a single payment in which interest and principal

---

[9]Para. 12(1)(c).

[10]Subs. 12(4).

[11]Subs. 12(11) "investment contract".

[12]*M.N.R. v. Groulx*, [1966] C.T.C. 115, 66 D.T.C. 5126; affd. [1967] C.T.C. 422, 67 D.T.C. 5284 (S.C.C.). Note, however, that the recipient of an interest-free loan may be taxable on the benefit imputed on the loan; see s. 80.4.

[13]Subs. 16(1).

are blended into one amount on repayment of a loan.[14] Whether a payment is blended is a question of fact that depends upon the terms of the contract.

Interest and principal may be blended by issuing a debt instrument at a discount and redeeming it at its face value upon maturity. Government Treasury Bills, for example, do not stipulate any interest rate or amount on their face, but are issued at a discount from their face value. The discount rate is a direct function of the prevailing interest rate, and the substance of the transaction is that the redemption value is, in effect, made up of principal and interest. Thus, the payment on maturity must be broken down into interest and principal components.[15]

Whether an amount represents a blended payment of interest and principal is a question of fact to be determined by the terms of the agreement, the course of the negotiation between the parties and, of particular importance, the price at which the property is sold.

(d) — Discounts

(i) — Rate Adjustments

It is important to distinguish between effective and nominal interest yields. Debt instruments are sometimes issued at a discount to their face value. The discount plus the "coupon rate" (i.e., the nominal rate of interest on the face of the debt instrument) combine to produce the overall "effective" rate of return or "yield" of the instrument. Thus, a debt instrument issued at a discount effectively raises the rate of interest on the debt. For example, if a corporation issues a one year $1,000 bond with a nominal rate of interest of 10 per cent at $960, the effective rate of interest or yield to the bondholder is 14 per cent ($100 interest plus $40 discount). (See example below.) Hence, discounting the issue price of a bond is simply another way of changing the effective rate of interest on the bond.

Example
Assume that S Ltd. issued bonds on April 28, 2006 at a price of $88.38. The bonds have a coupon rate of 6.75 per cent and will mature on June 4, 2020.

---

[14]See generally, IT-265R3 "Payments of Income and Capital Combined" (October 7, 1991) (now archived by the CRA as being out of date).

[15]*O'Neil v. M.N.R.* (1991), 91 D.T.C. 692 (T.C.C.); see also *Beck v. Lord Howard de Walden*, [1940] T.R. 143; *Lomax v. Peter Dixon & Sons Ltd.*, [1943] 1 K.B. 671.

Example			
Then:			
Nominal rate	=	6.75%	($67.50 per $1,000 bond)
Effective rate (yield)	=	8.15%	
Discount on bond	=	$11.62	

The common law, however, does not consider the discount on a bond as interest. Instead, the difference between the issue price and the face value of a bond is considered a capital gain.[16] Hence, the common law rules are an invitation to convert interest income into capital gains. The Minister of Finance described the difficulties of this interpretation in the budget speech of December 20, 1960:

> Unfortunately, increasing use is deliberately being made of a device to pay bondholders the equivalent of interest in a form that is tax-free. If a borrower issues a one-year $100 bond for, say, $96 and the bond bears a coupon rate of 1 per cent, the bondholder will receive $4 more than he paid for it when the bond matures at the end of the year. This excess over purchase price, plus the $1 in interest, will give the lender a 5.2 per cent return on his investment but it has been found difficult to collect tax on more than the $1 designated as interest.

The Act changes the common law rule. The statutory rules in respect of bond discounts vary depending upon the tax status of the issuer of the bond.

(ii) — Tax-Exempt Organizations

Where a tax-exempt organization, a non-resident person not carrying on business in Canada, or a governmental body issues a bond at a "deep discount", the *entire* discount is income in the hands of the first taxable Canadian resident to hold the bond.[17] A bond is considered to have a "deep discount" if the effective rate of interest on the bond exceeds the nominal rate by more than 1/3.

(iii) — Taxable Entities

Where a taxable entity issues a bond at a discount, a purchaser of the bond can treat the difference between the issue price and its par value as a capital gain. If the discount is a "deep discount", the taxable entity issuing the bond can deduct only 1/2 of the discount as interest expense. If the discount is "shallow" (i.e., the effective rate of interest does *not*

---

[16]*Wood v. M.N.R.*, [1969] S.C.R. 330, [1969] C.T.C. 57, 69 D.T.C. 5073 (S.C.C.).

[17]Subs. 16(3).

exceed the nominal rate by more than 1/3 and it is not issued at less than 97 per cent of its maturity value), the taxable entity can deduct the entire discount.[18]

Example

Assume:

A municipality issues bonds with a face value of $1,000 (coupon rate of 4.5 per cent, maturity five years) at a price of $930.

Then:

Nominal rate	4.50 %
Effective rate (yield)	(6.14)
Difference	1.64 %

Since 6.14 per cent is more than 4/3 × 4.50 per cent, the *entire* discount of $70 per bond is income in the hands of the first Canadian resident, taxable owner of the bond.

Example

	Shallow Discount	Deep Discount
Issue price of bond	$ 990	$ 960
Nominal rate of interest	8 %	8 %
Effective rate of interest	10 %	12 %
Discount on bond	10	40
Amount deductible by issuer	$ 10	$ 20

---

[18]Para. 20(1)(f).

IV. — Variations From Accounting Practice

1. — Payments Based on Production or Use of Property

One can determine the selling price of a property in several ways. The price may be fixed at the time the parties enter into the agreement of purchase and sale. Alternatively, the price may be determined by reference to a formula based upon production from, or use of, the property. For example, a taxpayer may sell land containing sand for a fixed amount of $15,000 or on the basis that the purchaser shall pay 5 cents for every ton of sand extracted from the land. The fixed payment of $15,000 may be characterized as an account of capital. In the latter case, the sale price is dependent upon the quantity of sand taken from the land, and the total price is not determined until all of the sand is extracted. The payments would be considered income.

Paragraph 12(1)(g) provides that a taxpayer must include in income all amounts that he or she receives and that depend upon the use of, or production from, property. In the above example, if the purchaser of the land extracts 300,000 tons, he or she will pay $15,000 to the seller, which will be taxed as income. This rule prevents taxpayers from converting what would otherwise be fully taxable rent or royalty income into capital. Subsection 12(9) ensures that any amount includable in income under section is taxable on an accrual basis.

The rationale of the provision is captured in the following analysis by Rowlatt J. in *Jones v. I.R.C.*:[19]

> There is no law of nature or any invariable principle that because it can be said that a certain payment is consideration for the transfer of property it must be looked upon as price in the character of principal. In each case, regard must be had to what the sum is. A man may sell his property for a sum which is to be paid in instalments, and when that is the case the payments to him are not income: *Foley v. Fletcher* (1858), 3 H. & N. 769. Or a man may sell his property for an annuity. In that case the *Income Tax Act* applies. Again, a man may sell his property for what looks like an annuity, but which can be seen to be, not a transmutation of a principal sum into an annuity, but in fact, a principal sum payment which is being spread over a period and is being paid with interest calculated in a way familiar to actuaries — in such a case, income tax is not payable on what is really capital: *Secretary of State [in Council of] India v. Scoble*, [1903] A.C. 299 (H.L.). On the other hand, a man may sell his property nakedly for a share of the profits of the business. In that case the share of the profits of the business would be the price, but it would bear the character of income in the vendor's hands. *Chadwick v. Pearl Life Assurance Co.*, [1905] 2 K.B. 507 and 514, was a case of that kind. In such a case the man bargains to have, not a capital sum but an income secured to him, namely, an income corresponding to the rent which he had before. I think, therefore, that what I have to do is to see what the sum payable in this case really is.

---

[19][1920] 1 K.B. 711.

Examples:

- A sells land containing 300,000 tons of sand for $15,000. The purchase price is payable at a rate of $5,000 per year for three years.

  Paragraph 12(1)(g) does *not* apply to the transaction. The payments are not related to the "use of" or "production from" property.

- B sells land containing sand to X. The sale price is determined at 5 cents per ton of sand extracted over the next three years. X extracts 300,000 tons and pays the vendor $15,000.

  Paragraph 12(1)(g) applies; the $15,000 is income to B.

- C sells land containing sand to Y. The sale price is determined at 5 cents per ton of sand extracted in the next three years, provided that the total price cannot exceed $10,000. Y extracts 300,000 tons and pays C $10,000.

  Paragraph 12(1)(g) applies; the $10,000 is income to C. The payment is based upon production from property.

- D sells land containing sand to Z. The sale price is determined at 5 cents per ton of sand extracted in the next three years but *not to be less than* $10,000. In fact, Y extracts 300,000 tons and pays $15,000.

  Paragraph 12(1)(g) does *not* apply to the $10,000 since this amount is not dependent upon production; $5,000 is included in D's income by paragraph 12(1)(g).

2. — Stock Dividends

Dividends are income from property in the hands of a passive investor and income from business in the hands of a taxpayer who is in the investment business. For tax purposes, a "dividend" includes stock dividends.[20]

For accounting purposes, a stock dividend is simply the capitalization of retained earnings into share capital. It represents the transformation of one type of equity capital (retained earnings) into another type (share capital). A stock dividend does not have any income effect in accounting.

For tax purposes, stock dividends are included in income under section 12. But the tax treatment of dividend income, whether on account of investments or from business, is complicated by the potential of double taxation of such income. Thus, there is a special regime for the taxation of dividends that depends on:

- The status of the recipient;

---

[20]Subs. 248(1) "dividend"

- The source of the dividend; and

- The nature of the payer corporation.

These rules are examined in greater detail in Chapter 19.

3. — Inducement Payments

An "inducement payment" is an economic incentive that is intended to lead or persuade a person to perform a particular action or decision. Examples include government subsidies to business to locate in a particular place, landlord inducements to tenants to sign a lease in a shopping plaza, etc.

An inducement may be on account of capital or on account of income. For tax purposes, however, an inducement receipt, whether from a governmental or private organization, is taxable as income.[21] This is so whether the payment is a grant, subsidy, forgivable loan, deduction from tax, or other allowance. A taxpayer may, however, elect to treat an inducement payment as a reduction in the cost or capital cost of any property that he or she acquires with the payment.[22] The effect of such an election is that it allows the taxpayer to defer recognition of the income until such time as he disposes of the property.

V. — Other Inclusions In Income

Item	Statutory Reference	Comments
Amounts received for goods and services to be rendered in the future	subpara. 12(1)(a)(i)	
Amounts received for deposits on returnable items	subpara. 12(1)(a)(ii)	IT-165R (archived)
Amounts received for property sold or services rendered, due in a future tax year	para. 12(1)(b)	IT-129R, IT-170R
Amounts received as interest (or in lieu of interest) if not previously included	para. 12(1)(c)	IT-396R

---

[21]Para. 12(1)(x).

[22]Subs. 53(2.1) and 13(7.4).

Item	Statutory Reference	Comments
Amount deducted in preceding year as a reserve for doubtful debts	para. 12(1)(d)	IT-442R; authorization for deduction in preceding year: 20(1)(l)
Amounts deducted in preceding year as reserve for guarantee	paras. 12(1)(d.1); 20(1)(l.1)	authorization for deduction: 20(1)(l.1)
Amount deducted in preceding year as a reserve for:	subpara. 12(1)(e)(i)	IT-154R; authorization for deduction in preceding year
• deposits on returnable containers	subpara. 20(1)(m)(iv)	
• goods delivered and services performed after end of year	subparas. 20(1)(m)(i), (ii); subs. 20(6)	
• a manufacturer's warranty	para. 20(1)(m.1)	
• prepaid rent	subpara. 20(1)(m)(iii)	
• policies of an insurer	para. 20(7)(c)	
Amount deducted in preceding year as unpaid amounts	subpara. 12(1)(e)(ii)	IT-154R; authorization for deduction in preceding year: para. 20(1)(n)
Insurance proceeds used to repair depreciable property	para. 12(1)(f)	costs of repairs deductible from income
Amounts received based on production or use of property disposed	para. 12(1)(g) ss. 12(9)	IT-426R, IT-462; exception: sale of agricultural land
Amount deducted in preceding year for quadrennial survey	para. 12(1)(h)	authorization for deduction in preceding year: para. 20(1)(o)
Recovered bad debts, previously deducted	para. 12(1)(i)	IT-442R authorization for deduction in previous years: paras. 20(1)(l), (p), subs. 20(4)
Dividends from corporations resident in Canada and other corporations	paras. 12(1)(j), (k)	IT-67R3, IT-269R3
Income from partnership	para. 12(1)(l)	IT-278R2
Income from trusts	para. 12(1)(m)	
Benefits from profit-sharing plan and employee trust to employer	paras. 12(1)(n)	IT-502

Item	Statutory Reference	Comments
Net amounts received from employee benefit plan	para. 12(1)(n.1)	IT-502
Royalties paid or payable to government authority	para. 12(1)(o) (To be repealed in 2007). See also 12(1)(x.2)	IT-438R2
Amount received under *Western Grain Stabilization Act*	para. 12(1)(p)	deduction of amount: para. 20(1)(ff)
Amount deducted for employment tax	para. 12(1)(q)	inoperative paragraph
Cost of inventory at year-end representing an allowance for depreciation	para. 12(1)(r)	
Reinsurer must include maximum amount which insurer may claim as reserve	para. 12(1)(s)	insurer's reserve: para. 20(7)(c)
Amount deducted as investment tax credit if not previously included	para. 12(1)(t)	IT-210R2, IC 78-4R3
Government of Canada grant for home insulation or energy income conversion	para. 12(1)(u)	for property used principally for earning income from business or property
Forfeited salary deferral amounts	para. 12(1)(n.2)	
Amounts received from retirement compensation arrangement	para. 12(1)(n.3)	
Amount of negative balance arrived at in scientific research deduction	para. 12(1)(v)	IT-151R5; calculation for research made under subs. 37(1)
Benefit received from non-interest bearing or low interest loan by virtue of services performed by corporation carrying on a personal services business	para. 12(1)(w)	IT-421R2; deemed taxable benefit by subs. 80.4(1)

Item	Statutory Reference	Comments
Inducement or assistance payments	para. 12(1)(x); *French Shoes Ltd. v. The Queen*, [1986] 2 C.T.C. 132, 86 D.T.C. 6359 (F.C.T.D.)	all amounts received not already included in income or deducted from the cost of certain property.
Cash bonus on Canada Savings Bonds	s. 12.1	IT-396R
Certain amount in respect of fuel tax rebates under *Excise Tax Act*	para. 12(1)(x.1)	
Automobile provided to partner	para. 12(1)(y)	IT-63R5
Amateur athlete trust payments	para. 12(1)(z)	required by s. 143.1 to be included in income

Selected Bibliography to Chapter 8

General

Freedman, Judith, "Profit and Prophets — Law and Accountancy Practice on the Timing of Receipts — Recognition under the Earnings Basis (Schedule D, Cases I and II)" (1987) Brit. Tax Rev. 61.

Freedman, Judith, "Profit and Prophets — Law and Accountancy Practice on the Timing of Receipts — Recognition Under the Earnings Basis (Schedule D, Cases I and II), Continued" (1987) Brit. Tax Rev. 104.

Harris, Edwin C., "Timing of Income and Expense Items", *Corporate Management Tax Conf.* 84 (Can. Tax Foundation, 1975).

Knechtel, Ronald C., "Role of Generally Accepted Accounting Principles in Determining Income for Tax Purposes", in *Proceedings of 31st Tax Conf.* 845 (Can. Tax Foundation, 1979).

Krishna, Vern, "Conformity of Accounting Methods for Tax and Financial Statement Purposes: A Search for the 'Truer Picture' of Income" (1992) Can. Current Tax C95.

Perry, Harvey, "Federal Individual Income Tax: Taxable Income and Tax", *Tax Paper No. 89* 58 (Can. Tax Foundation, 1990).

Pickford, Barry W., "Tax Accounting for Contract Earnings", in *Proceedings of 31st Tax Conf.* 885 (Can. Tax Foundation, 1979).

Reed, "The Dilemma of Conformity: Tax and Financial Reporting", *Corporate Management Tax Conf.* 20 (Can. Tax Foundation, 1981).

"Timing of Receivables and Expenses for Tax Purposes", *Cana. Tax Letter*, January 3, 1977 (De Boo).

Tremblay, Richard G., "The Meaning of Earned Income in Sub-Paragraph 12(1)(a)(i)" [Case Comment: *Versatile Pacific Shipyards Inc. v. R.*, [1988] 2 C.T.C. 90 (F.C.A.)].

Interest Income

"Discounts, Premiums and Bonuses and the Repeal of IT-114: What Happens Now?" (1994) No. 1181 Tax Topics 1.

"Income Tax Treatment of Interest — What's Happening" (1995) No. 1181 Tax Topics 2.

Kraayeveld, Serena H., "Accrual Basis of Reporting Interest Income", *Prairie Provinces Tax Conf.* 245 (Can. Tax Foundation, 1983).

Razienne, Robert, "Accrual of Interest Income", in *Proceedings of 40th Tax Conf.* 23:1 (Can. Tax Foundation, 1988).

Ulmer, John M., "Taxation of Interest Income", in *Proceedings of 42nd Tax Conf.* 8:1 (Can. Tax Foundation, 1990).

Stock Dividends

Le Rossignol, Dan G., "Stock Dividends and Stock Options" (1979) 112 CA Magazine 67.

Ware, J.G., "Public Corporations — Stock Dividends", *Corporate Management Tax Conf.* 74 (Can. Tax Foundation, 1978).

Inducement Payments

Dwyer, Blair P., "Deductibility of Tenant Inducement Payments (Income Tax)" (1987–89) 2 Can. Current Tax C-53.

Harris, Neil H., "Tax Aspects of Condominium Conversions and Lease Inducement Payments to Recipients" (1986), in *Proceedings of 38th Tax Conf.* 45 (Can. Tax Foundation, 1986).

Ward, David A., and Neil Armstrong, "Corporate Taxation: Lease Inducement Payments" (1986) 5 Legal Alert 98.

Other

Burger, George, "International Aspects of the Taxation of Discounted Securities" (1987) 35 Can. Tax J. 1131.

Haney, M.A., "Payments Dependent on Use or Production: Paragraph 12(1)(g)" (1987) 35 Can. Tax J. 427.

Lawlor, "Income Debentures and Term-Preferred Shares" (1978) 26 Can. Tax J. 200.

Sohmer, David H., "Purchase and Sale of a Closely-Held Business (2)" (1979) 112 CA Magazine 70.

CHAPTER 9 — DEDUCTIONS FROM BUSINESS AND INVESTMENT INCOME

I. — General Comment

Income from business and property is taxable based on *net* profit. Thus, we need to determine which expenses are deductible from revenues in order to calculate net profit for tax purposes.

The calculation of net profit is essentially a question of law governed by legal principles. Nevertheless, we start the process by looking to the taxpayer's financial statements. Thus, we determine net profit according to commercial and accounting principles insofar as they do not conflict with specific statutory provisions or judicial decisions. The Exchequer Court in *Royal Trust* explained the scheme for the deductibility of expenses as follows:

> Thus, it may be stated categorically that in a case under the *Income Tax Act* the first matter to be determined in deciding whether an outlay or expense is outside the prohibition of ... [paragraph 18(1)(a)] of the Act is whether it was made or incurred by the taxpayer in accordance with the ordinary principles of commercial trading or well accepted principles of business practice. If it was not, that is the end of the matter. But if it was, then the outlay or expense is properly deductible unless it falls outside the expressed exception of ... [paragraph 18(1)(a)] and, therefore, within its prohibition. ...[1]

To be deductible from revenue, an expense must satisfy six tests. The expense must:

- Be of an income nature and not a capital expenditure;
- Be reasonable in amount;
- Be incurred for the purpose of earning income;
- Not be a personal expenditure;
- Not be expressly prohibited by the Act; and
- Not constitute "abusive" tax avoidance.

Apart from these, there is no blanket public policy prohibition on deductibility of expenses.[2]

The above criteria serve different purposes from those that generally accepted accounting and commercial principles serve. For example, the requirement that an expenditure should be reasonable in amount is not an accounting rule, but a constraint to protect the government's taxable base. The prohibition against the deductibility of expenses that the statute specifically proscribes allows the legislator to use it to foster socio-economic and public policies. The anti-abusive rule is intended as a broad "catch-all" clause for expenses that the legislator did not proscribe more specifically.

II. — Current Expense Or Capital Expenditure?

1. — General Principles

The income tax is, for most purposes, a tax on realized income. Hence, the starting point is to determine whether an expenditure is on account of income or capital. Only expenditures on account of income are deductible. Expenditures on account of capital are not deductible

---

[1] *Royal Trust Co. v. M.N.R.* (1956), [1957] C.T.C. 32 at 42, 57 D.T.C. 1055 (Ex. Ct.).

[2] *65302 British Columbia Ltd. v. Canada*, [1999] 3 S.C.R. 804, [2000] 1 C.T.C. 57, 99 D.T.C. 5799 (S.C.C.).

for tax purposes.[3] This prohibition reinforces the concept that income represents the excess of revenues over expenses over a specified period.

To be deductible as an expense, an expenditure must satisfy two preliminary tests, purpose and timing: (1) one must incur the expenditure for the purpose of gaining or producing income from a business or property, and (2) the expense must be relevant to the current, and not some future, period. These two requirements are inter-related:[4]

> Since the main purpose of every business undertaking is presumably to make a profit, any expenditure made "for the purpose of gaining or producing income" comes within the terms of [paragraph 18(1)(a)], whether it be classified as an income expense or a capital outlay.

> Once it is determined that a particular expenditure is one made for the purpose of gaining or producing income, in order to compute income tax liability it must next be determined whether such disbursement is an income expense or a capital outlay.

Expenditures that benefit more than one accounting period are generally capital outlays for accounting purposes. For example, expenditures on long-enduring assets, such as goodwill, incorporation fees, patents, and trademarks, are typically expenses of a capital nature. This distinction between current expenses and capital expenditures is central to the measurement of income.[5]

For tax and accounting purposes, we measure income for a finite period of time, usually annually. Thus, we match revenues and expenses during a period. Expenditures that benefit subsequent fiscal periods are not current expenses, but capital outlays. As a statement of principle, this is straightforward enough. But how does one in law distinguish an expenditure that benefits the current period from one that benefits the future?

2. — Mixed Law and Fact

The characterization of expenditures as current expenses or capital outlays is a question of mixed law and fact.[6] The determination of the question depends not upon the nature of

---

[3]Para. 18(1)(b).

[4]*B.C. Electric Ry. v. M.N.R.*, [1958] S.C.R. 133, [1958] C.T.C. 21, 58 D.T.C. 1022 (S.C.C.).

[5]*Canderel Ltd. v. Canada*, [1998] 1 S.C.R. 147, [1998] 2 C.T.C. 35, 98 D.T.C. 6100 (S.C.C.) (Tenant Inducement Payments constituted running expenses that could be deducted entirely in the year in which they were incurred; in attempting to assess a taxpayer's profit for tax purposes, the test is which method of accounting best depicts the reality of the financial situation of the particular taxpayer).

[6]*Johns-Manville Can. Inc. v. The Queen* (1985), [1985] 2 S.C.R. 46, [1985] 2 C.T.C. 111, 85 D.T.C. 5373 (S.C.C.); applied in *Gifford v. R.*, [2004] 1 S.C.R. 411, [2004] 2 C.T.C. 1, 2004 D.T.C. 6120 (Eng.) (S.C.C.) (financial advisor paid departing colleague $100,000 for his client list — i.e. goodwill with clients — and a non-compete agreement; payment on account of capital, thus interest on associated loan not deductible).

property acquired[7] but upon the nature of the expenditure: what did the taxpayer expend the payment for?

There is no single definitive or conclusive test for determining whether an expenditure is of a capital or revenue nature.[8] There are several legal principles that distinguish between capital and revenue expenditures. One applies them flexibly to particular factual situations.[9] A test that may be useful in one set of circumstances may not be relevant in another.[10] One test, however, has general acceptance:[11]

> ... where an expenditure is made, not only once and for all, but with a view to bringing into existence an asset or an advantage for the enduring benefit of a trade, I think that there is very good reason (in the absence of special circumstances leading to an opposite conclusion) for treating such an expenditure as properly attributable not to revenue but to capital.

The primary focus here is on the purpose of the expenditure and not on the physical attributes of the particular property. The *purpose*, rather than the result, of an expenditure determines whether it is a capital outlay or a current expense.[12] Does one incur the expenditure

---

[7]*Golden Horse Shoe (New) Ltd. v. Thurgood*, [1934] 1 K.B. 548 at 563 (C.A.).

[8]*B.P. Australia Ltd. v. Commr. of Taxation of the Commonwealth of Australia, infra.*

[9]*Johns-Manville Can. Inc. v. The Queen, ante*; *B.P. Australia Ltd. v. Commr. of Taxation of the Commonwealth of Australia*, [1966] A.C. 224, [1965] 3 All E.R. 209 (Aust. P.C.) (deductibility of amount paid to gas stations to secure monopoly of station, i.e., that it sell only B.P. gas in furtherance of marketing reorganization plan), approved by the Supreme Court of Canada in *M.N.R. v. Algoma Central Railway*, [1968] S.C.R. 447, [1968] C.T.C. 161, 68 D.T.C. 5096 (S.C.C.) (Court agreed with test enunciated in *B.P. Australia Ltd.*, then decided without reasons); see also *Bowater Power Co. v. M.N.R.*, [1971] C.T.C. 818, 71 D.T.C. 5469 (F.C.T.D.):

> The solution, therefore, depends on what the expenditure is calculated to effect from a practical and business point of view, rather than upon the juristic classification of the legal rights, if any, secured, employed or exhausted in the process. The question of deductibility of expenses, must also, therefore, be considered from the standpoint of the company or its operations, as a practical matter.

[10]*Comm. of Taxes v. Nchanga Consol. Copper Mines Ltd.*, [1964] A.C. 948 at 959, *per* Lord Radcliffe (P.C.).

[11]*Br. Insulated & Helsby Cables v. Atherton*, [1926] A.C. 205 at 213-14 (H.L.).

[12]*Hinton v. Maden & Ireland Ltd.* (1959), 38 Tax Cas. 391 (H.L.) (replacement cost of knives and lasts in shoe manufacturing machinery characterized as capital; equipment essential to functioning of plant); *MacMillan Bloedel (Alberni) Ltd. v. M.N.R.*, [1973] C.T.C. 295, 73 D.T.C. 5264 (F.C.T.D.) (although fan belts and oil were operating costs deductible in maintaining fleet of trucks, tires lasting a year were not; tires comprising 10–15 per cent of value of truck; truck purchased intact not in individual parts); *Oxford Shopping Centres Ltd. v. The Queen*, [1980] C.T.C. 7, 79 D.T.C. 5458 (F.C.T.D.); affd. [1981] C.T.C. 128, (sub nom. *The Queen v. Oxford Shopping Centres Ltd.*) 81 D.T.C. 5065 (F.C.A.) ("once and for all" payment by taxpayer to municipality to assist with road changes deducti-

for the purpose of bringing into existence an asset of enduring value? The physical characteristics of the product of the expenditure do not determine its nature. For example, for General Motors the cost of manufacturing an automobile is an expense if it sells the automobile
in the year (and does not endure), but is on account of capital if it is not sold and remains in
inventory at the end of the year. The recurrence of the expenditure is irrelevant.

Thus, annual expenditures are on account of capital if they are intended to bring into existence assets of enduring value — that is, if the assets have a life longer than a year. Conversely, a one-time expenditure is a current expense if it is intended that one consume the
entire benefit of the expenditure in one fiscal period.

(a) — Enduring Benefit

What is an "enduring benefit"? The test refers to benefits that endure in the sense that some
assets have a life longer than one year. Benefits that accrue from saving payments over a
number of years are not necessarily a capital asset. In *Anglo-Persian Oil Co. Ltd. v. Dale*,
Rowlatt J. explained the distinction as follows:[13]

> ... a benefit which endures, in the way that fixed capital endures; not a benefit that endures in
> the sense that for a good number of years it relieves you of a revenue payment. It means a
> thing which endures in the way that fixed capital endures. It is not always an actual asset, but
> it endures in the way that getting rid of a lease or getting rid of onerous capital assets ...
> endures.

The explanation is not entirely satisfactory. Note that Justice Rowlatt uses the word "en-
dures" seven times to explain "enduring", which suggests the difficulty of defining the
concept.

One can also derive an enduring benefit from discharging a liability as from acquiring an
asset.[14]

> ... the disposition of a source of liability may be equivalent to the acquisition of a source of
> profit — an extension perhaps, but not an exception, to the principle that in some sense or

---

ble); see also *The Queen v. Johns-Manville Can. Inc.*, [1982] C.T.C. 56, 82 D.T.C. 6054 (F.C.A.) in
which the Court stated:

> I recognize that the regular recurrence of the acquisitions is relevant in determining whether
> the outlays for the lots are income or capital in nature. But it is in no way decisive. As Dixon
> J. (as he then was) put it in *Sun Newspapers Limited v. The Federal Commissioner of Taxation*
> (1938), 61 C.L.R. 337 at page 362 ([Aust. HC]), "recurrence is not a test, it is no more than a
> consideration, the weight of which depends upon the nature of the expenditure".

[13]*Anglo-Persian Oil Co. Ltd. v. Dale* (1931), 16 Tax Cas. 253 at 262 (C.A.), approved by Lord Wilberforce in *Tucker v. Granada Motorway Services Ltd.*, [1979] S.T.C. 393 at 396 (H.L.).

[14]*I.R.C. v. Carron Co.* (1968), 45 Tax Cas. 18 at 75 (H.L.).

other an asset of a capital nature, tangible or intangible, positive or negative, must be shown to be acquired.

The "enduring benefit" test is easier to state than it is to apply. To be sure, it provides an answer in self-evident cases. Common sense and accounting principles tell us that a taxpayer who purchases a building for rental cannot write off its entire cost in the year that he or she acquires it, and that the purchase price is a capital expenditure that has enduring benefits over many years. It is equally clear that the costs of heating the building are period costs and should be charged as current expenses against revenues in each year. But what of the in-between cases? Consider the following:

- The taxpayer expends $20,000 on advertising the building for rent;[15]

- The taxpayer spends $40,000 on lobbying against rent control legislation;[16]

- The taxpayer installs a concrete lining in the basement of the building to protect it against an oil nuisance created by a nearby refinery.[17]

Each of these cases involve subtle distinctions that are not as easy to resolve. Some judges are quite candid about the difficulty of characterizing expenditures. As Sir Wilfred Greene M.R. said:[18]

> ... there have been ... many cases where this matter of capital or income has been debated. There have been many cases which fall upon the borderline: indeed, in many cases it is almost true to say that the spin of a coin would decide the matter almost as satisfactorily as an attempt to find reasons. ...

(b) — Direct vs. Indirect Consequences

One must decide each case on its own factual circumstances to determine if the expenditure "brings into existence an asset of enduring value".

In determining whether an expenditure has enduring value, should one look to the direct and immediate consequence of an expenditure, or its ultimate effect on the taxpayer's business?

---

[15]*M.N.R. v. Tower Invt. Inc.*, [1972] C.T.C. 182, 72 D.T.C. 6161 (T.A.B.) (Court allowed deferral of deduction, in effect, matching expense to period when most of the resulting revenue would accrue).

[16]*Morgan v. Tate & Lyle Ltd.*, [1955] A.C. 21, 35 Tax Cas. 367 (H.L.) (expenditure on propaganda campaign to prevent nationalization of sugar refining industry was current expense); *Boarland v. Kramat Pulai Ltd.* (1953), 35 Tax Cas. 1 (cost of pamphlet circulated to shareholders, critical of government policy not wholly on account of trade).

[17]*Midland Empire Packing Co. v. Commr.* (1950), 14 T.C. 635 (U.S.) (concrete lining essentially a repair; deductible as expense).

[18]*I.R.C. v. Br. Salmson Aero Engines Ltd.* (1938), 22 Tax Cas. 29 at 43 (C.A.).

We should not interpret "enduring" literally but in its commercial context. Many current expenses have enduring benefits in the sense that advantages that accrue from the expenditure continue for a long time. For example, a payment to be rid of an incompetent employee is a current expense even though the payment will, hopefully, have enduring beneficial consequences.[19] An oil change is of enduring benefit to the life of an automobile, which would otherwise seize. Nevertheless, routine maintenance is a current expense even though it enhances the long term life of an asset.

(i) — Goodwill

Expenditures on account of the development or acquisition of goodwill are also difficult to classify. In *M.N.R. v. Algoma Central Ry.*,[20] for example, the taxpayer expended funds to obtain a geological survey of the mineral potential of the area through which the railway operated. The expenditure was a once-and-for-all cost intended to stimulate its railway traffic by attracting developers to engage in mining the area. There were two issues: (1) did the expenditures bring into existence an asset of enduring value? and (2) was enduring value to be tested by looking to the immediate or ultimate consequences of the expenditures? The Exchequer Court held that the *direct* consequences of the expenditures did not bring into existence an asset of an enduring nature; the expenses were deductible as a current expense.

Clearly, *purchased* goodwill is an asset of enduring value, and the purchase price is a capital outlay.[21] For example, if one were to purchase the Coca Cola Company, there would be considerable goodwill in the brand name. In contrast, routine institutional advertising by Coca Cola that generates goodwill would be a current deductible expense. In both of these situations, however, we can clearly and directly trace the funds to the end use.

It is the intermediate case, where one expends funds to protect existing goodwill, that presents the most difficulties. In *Canada Starch Co. v. M.N.R.*,[22] for example, the taxpayer spent $80,000 to develop a new brand name, "Viva". When faced with opposition to its registration as a trade mark on the grounds that "Viva" was confusing with another registered trade mark, the taxpayer paid $15,000 in return for withdrawal of the opposition to

---

[19]*Mitchell v. B.W. Noble Ltd.*, [1927] 1 K.B. 719 (C.A.) (payment to get rid of a director was a revenue expense).

[20]*M.N.R. v. Algoma Central Ry., ante.*

[21]See, e.g., *Gifford v. R.*, 2004 SCC 15, [2004] 2 C.T.C. 1, (sub nom. *Gifford v. Canada)* 236 D.L.R. (4th) 1 (S.C.C.).

[22]*Can. Starch Co. v. M.N.R.*, [1968] C.T.C. 466, 68 D.T.C. 5320 (Ex. Ct.); *Border Chem. Co. v. The Queen*, [1987] 2 C.T.C. 183, 87 D.T.C. 5391 (F.C.T.D.) (legal fees to defend a taxpayer's senior officials against criminal prosecution not deductible as expenses if cost incurred to prevent damage to taxpayer's goodwill).

registration. Jackett P. described the difference between acquiring and developing assets as follows:

- An expenditure for the acquisition or creation of a business entity, structure or organization, for the earning of profit, or for an addition to such entity, structure or organization, is an expenditure on account of capital, and

- An expenditure in the process of operation of a profit-making entity, structure or organization is an expenditure on revenue account.

Since the expenditures made *in the course of the taxpayer's operations* that gave rise to the trade mark were current expenses, the $15,000 payment was part of the process of the registration of an asset that already existed. Therefore, the expenditure was deductible as an expense.

On the general question of expenditures on account of promotion, advertising, and goodwill, Jackett P. said:

> [I]n my view, the advertising expenses for launching the new product in this case were expenses on revenue account. I expressed a similar view in *Algoma Central Railway v. M.N.R.* ... a decision that was upheld on appeal. As I indicated there, "According to my understanding of commercial principles ... advertising expenses paid out while a business is operating, and directed to attract customers to a business, are current expenses". Similarly, in my view, expenses of other measures taken by a businessman with a view to introducing particular products to the market — such as market surveys and industrial design studies — are also current expenses. They also are expenses laid out while the business is operating as part of the process of inducing the buying public to buy the goods being sold.

> It remains to consider expenses incurred by a businessman, during the course of introducing new products to the market, to obtain the additional protection for his trade mark that is made available by trade mark legislation. A new mark adopted and used in the course of marketing a product gradually acquires the protection of the laws against passing off (assuming that it is, in fact, distinctive). This is something that is an incidental result of ordinary trading operations. Additional expenditure to acquire the additional protection made available by statute law seems to me to be equally incidental to ordinary trading operations. It follows that, in my view, the fees paid to the trade mark lawyers and to the trade mark office are deductible. In this case, no submission was presented to me as to any principle whereby I should distinguish between the ordinary cost of acquiring trade mark registration and the $15,000 payment that, in this case, was necessary in the judgment of the appellant to obtain registration of the trade mark ... and I have been able to conceive of no such principle.

Although legal fees for commercial purposes are deductible as expenses, legal fees to defend a taxpayer's senior officials against criminal prosecution to prevent damage to the taxpayer's goodwill are not.[23]

---

[23]*Border Chemical Co. v. The Queen, ante.*

(c) — Preservation of Capital Assets

The distinction between a current expense and capital expenditure is even more blurred when the question arises in the context of expenditures to maintain or preserve capital assets already in existence. Is an expenditure that one incurs for the protection or maintenance of a capital asset a capital expenditure? The answer depends more upon the *type* of property on which one incurs the expenditure than on any clear-cut, black-letter rule.

(i) — Legal Expenses

The deductibility of legal expenses for protecting a capital asset is unclear. The weight of the cases is against deductibility. In an early case, *Dom. Natural Gas Co. v. M.N.R.*,[24] for example, the Supreme Court held that legal expenses incurred in successfully protecting the taxpayer's gas franchise were capital outlays and not deductible from income. In reaching his decision, Duff C.J.C. enlarged Lord Cave's test (bringing into existence an asset of enduring benefit to the business) as follows:

> The expenditure was incurred *both* "once and for all" and it was incurred for the purpose and with the effect of procuring for the company "the advantage of an enduring benefit".

In contrast to a decision of the English court in the same year,[25] the court did not accept that the expenses were incidental to the ordinary course of the taxpayer's business. Thus, the Court put up a two-step hurdle to establish that an expenditure is current and deductible.

---

[24][1941] S.C.R. 19, [1940-41] C.T.C. 155, [1920–1940] 1 D.T.C. 499-133 (S.C.C.).

[25]See *Southern v. Borax Consol. Ltd.*, [1940] 4 All E.R. 412 at 416 and 419, *per* Lawrence J.:

> ... In my opinion, the principle which is to be deducted from the cases is that where a sum of money is laid out for the acquisition or the improvement of a fixed capital asset it is attributable to capital, but *if no alteration is made* in the fixed capital asset by the payment, then it is properly attributable to revenue, being in substance a matter of maintenance, the maintenance of the capital structure or the capital assets of the company. ...

> It appears to me that the legal expenses which were incurred ... did not create any new asset at all but were expenses which were incurred in the ordinary course of maintaining the assets of the company, and the fact that it was maintaining the title and not the value of the company's business does not, in my opinion, make it any different. [Emphasis added.]

See also *Mitchell v. B. W. Noble Ltd.* (1927), 11 Tax Cas. 372 at 421:

> The object (of the expenditure) ... was that of preserving the status and reputation of the company which the directors felt might be imperilled ... to avoid that and to preserve the status and divided-earning power of the company seems to me a purpose which is well within the ordinary purpose of the trade.

The stature of *Dom. Natural Gas Co. v. M.N.R.*, however, has been eroded by subsequent decisions. In *M.N.R. v. Kellogg Co. of Can.*,[26] for example, the taxpayer successfully deducted substantial legal fees incurred in defending an allegation of trade mark infringement. The Supreme Court distinguished its earlier decision in *Dom. Natural Gas Co.* on the basis that the trademark action in *Kellogg Co. of Can.* was neither a right of property nor an exclusive right. The Court held the expenses to be ordinary legal expenses and deductible in the ordinary course of business.[27]

In *Evans v. M.N.R.*,[28] the taxpayer, who was entitled to 1/3 of an estate left to her by her husband and by her father, incurred legal fees when her right to the income of the estate was challenged. Once again, the Supreme Court held that the legal fees were a current expense and were not paid on account of capital. Cartwright J., speaking for the majority of the Court, distinguished *Dom. Natural Gas Co.* on the basis that the legal fees in that case were "expenses to preserve a capital asset in a capital aspect." In the Court's opinion, Mrs. Evans's right to the income of the estate was not a capital asset.

Thus, the distinction between a capital expenditure and an expense comes down to whether one incurs the expenditure to preserve a capital asset in a capital aspect or in a revenue aspect. But what is the distinction between "a capital aspect" and "a revenue aspect"?[29] This test does not likely add anything to the other tests. Ultimately, the resolution of the entire

---

[26]*M.N.R. v. Kellogg Co. of Can.*, [1942] C.T.C. 51, 2 D.T.C. 548; affd. [1943] C.T.C. 1, 3 D.T.C. 601 (S.C.C.).

[27]*M.N.R. v. Kellogg Co. of Can.*, *ante*, in which the learned Chief Justice said:

> The right upon which the (taxpayer) relied was not a right of property, or an exclusive right of any description, but the right (in common with all other members of the public) to describe their goods in the manner in which they were described.

[28]*Evans v. M.N.R.*, [1960] S.C.R. 391, [1960] C.T.C. 69, 60 D.T.C. 1047 (S.C.C.); see also *Farmer's Mutual Petroleums Ltd. v. M.N.R.* (1967), [1968] S.C.R. 59, [1966] C.T.C. 283, 66 D.T.C. 5225 (Ex. Ct.); affd. [1967] C.T.C. 396, 67 D.T.C. 5277 (S.C.C.) (legal expenses incurred in defending title to mineral rights were capital outlays); *B.C. Power Corp. v. M.N.R.* (1967), [1968] S.C.R. 17, [1966] C.T.C. 451, 66 D.T.C. 5310; affd. [1967] C.T.C. 406, 67 D.T.C. 5258 (S.C.C.) (legal expenses incurred in preserving right to shares that had purportedly been expropriated by a provincial government were non-deductible capital expenditures).

[29]See, e.g., *The Queen v. Jager Homes Ltd.*, [1988] 1 C.T.C. 215, 88 D.T.C. 6119 (F.C.A.) (legal fees to defend action to wind up company on capital account and not deductible as current expense).

question depends on the facts and circumstances. As the Privy Council said in *B.P. Australia Ltd. v. Commr. of Taxation of Commonwealth of Australia*:[30]

> [T]he solution to the problem is not to be found by any rigid test or description. It has to be derived from many aspects of the whole set of circumstances, some of which may point in one direction, some in the other. One consideration may point so clearly that it dominates other and vaguer indications in the contrary direction. It is a commonsense appreciation of all the guiding features which must provide the ultimate answer.

(ii) — Repairs, Maintenance and Alterations

The dividing line between capital expenditures and current expenses due to routine mainte-nance and repairs is also unclear. Here too, the underlying principle is easy to state, but difficult to apply. An expenditure in one fiscal period that enhances, substantially improves, enlarges, or prolongs the life of an asset beyond the period is a capital outlay. In contrast, an expenditure that merely maintains an asset or restores it to its original condition is a deducti-ble current expense.

Here, as elsewhere in tax law, it is easy to identify the correct answer in polar cases when one does not really need an answer. It is the grey areas in between that cause the problems and litigation. For example, it is clear that the extension of an existing building by adding new floor space is a capital expenditure; it brings into existence an asset of enduring value. It is equally clear that routine maintenance of an existing building, for example, performance of minor repairs, replacement of light bulbs, cleaning, and maintenance of heating and venti-lation systems, are current expenses.

Between these extremes, however, there are cases that cause considerable difficulty. One must distinguish each expenditure *in the context of the taxpayer's activities*. For example, a taxpayer who expends money to restore a decrepit and rundown building incurs capital ex-penditures, even though routine deductible maintenance by the previous owner would have prevented the building from deteriorating to a decrepit state. Similarly, a business that regu-larly expends funds to change the oil in its fleet of automobiles incurs current expenses. Neglecting to change the oil in its automobiles may, at a later date, involve substantial costs by way of engine replacements that would result in capital outlays.[31]

---

[30]*B.P. Australia Ltd. v. Commr. of Taxation of Commonwealth of Australia*, [1965] 3 All E.R. 209, [1966] A.C. 224 at 264 (P.C.), cited with approval by the S.C.C. in *Johns-Manville Can. Inc. v. The Queen*, [1985] 2 C.T.C. 111, 85 D.T.C. 5373 at 5383 (S.C.C.).

[31]*Better Plumbing Co. v. M.N.R.* (1952), 6 Tax A.B.C. 177, 52 D.T.C. 146 (Can. Tax. App. Bd.); see also *Glenco Invt. Corp. v. M.N.R.*, [1967] C.T.C. 243, 67 D.T.C. 5169 (Ex. Ct.) (cost of plumbing and electrical installations in a warehouse acquired and converted into a commercial building suitable for rental was capital outlay).

(iii) — "Repair" vs. "Renewal"

"Repair" and "renew" do not necessarily imply different meanings. "Repair" means, "restoration by renewal or replacement of subsidiary parts of a whole." "Renewal" means, "reconstruction of the entirety, meaning by the entirety, not necessarily of the whole."[32] The Privy Council considered the relationship between repairs and renewals in *Rhodesia Rys. Ltd. v. Bechuanaland Collector of IT*:[33]

> The periodical renewal by sections, of the rails and sleepers of a railway line as they wear out through use, is in no sense a reconstruction of the whole railway and is an ordinary incident of railway administration. The fact that the wear, although continuous, is not and cannot be made good annually, does not render the work of renewal when it comes to being effected, necessarily a capital charge. The expenditure here in question was incurred in consequence of the rails having been worn out in earning the income of the previous years on which tax had been paid without deduction in respect of such wear, and represented the cost of restoring them to a state in which they could continue to earn income. It did not result in the creation of any new asset; it was incurred to maintain the appellant's existing line in a state to earn revenue.

(iv) — Replacements

Renewal costs which go beyond financing the replacement of worn-out parts, and transforming one asset into another, are capital expenditures. In *Highland Rwy. Co. v. Balderston*,[34] the taxpayer was not allowed to deduct the costs of replacing iron rails with steel rails as a current expense. As the Lord President of the Scottish Court of Exchequer put it:

> [T]hen when we come to the question of the alteration of the main line itself, it must be kept in view that this is not a mere relaying of the line after the old fashion; it is not taking away rails that are worn out o[r] partially worn out, and renewing them in whole or in part along with the whole line. That would not alter the character of the line; it would not affect the nature of the heritable property possessed by the Company. But what has been done is to substitute one kind of rail for another, steel rails for iron rails.

In other words, steel rails are a different asset from iron rails, although either may be used for the same purpose — transporting trains.

Whether replacement costs are deductible as a current expense depends on the magnitude of the replacement in the context of the complete unit of which it forms a part. The replacement of small parts in an automobile is routine maintenance; replacement of the entire engine is a capital outlay. The test in each case is: Are the expenditures on account of repair of the

---

[32]*Lurcott v. Wakely*, [1911] 1 K.B. 905 (C.A.).

[33]*Rhodesia Rys. Ltd. v. Bechuanaland Collector of IT*, [1933] A.C. 368 at 374 (P.C.).

[34]*Highland Rwy. Co. v. Balderston* (1889), 2 Tax Cas. 485 at 488; see also *Tank Truck Transport Ltd. v. M.N.R.* (1965), 1965 CarswellNat 140, 38 Tax A.B.C. 332, 65 D.T.C. 405 (Can. Tax. App. Bd.) (replacement of 12 cast iron tanks with stainless steel tanks held to be capital outlay).

larger property by replacement of a component, or on account of replacement of an entire unit, complete in itself?[35] The question is often pragmatically resolved by comparing the cost of replacement with the cost of ordinary repairs in the context of the total unit of which the replacement is a part. The higher the cost of replacement compared to the costs of the total unit, the greater the likelihood that the costs are on account of capital.

(d) — Discharge of Obligations

A payment to eliminate an enduring disadvantage or an onerous obligation may have enduring benefits and constitute a capital expenditure. Here too, the polar cases are clear. A *surrogatum* payment to discharge a revenue expense, for example, a payment to dismiss an unsatisfactory employee, is deductible as a current expense.[36] Similarly, a payment to discharge a capital liability is a capital expenditure.[37] The intermediate cases are not as clear. The emphasis is on the permanency of the advantage secured by discharging the liability.[38]

(e) — Factual Ambiguity

As the above discussion illustrates, the characterization of expenditures is factual in the context of broadly defined legal principles. At the very least, the process is uncertain and am-

---

[35]*M.N.R. v. Vancouver Tugboat Co.*, [1957] C.T.C. 178, 57 D.T.C. 1126 (Ex. Ct.) ($42,000 replacement of tugboat engine held to be replacement of substantial part of the whole, hence capital outlay); *Can. S.S. Lines Ltd. v. M.N.R.*, [1966] C.T.C. 255, 66 D.T.C. 5205 (Ex. Ct.) (cost of replacing boiler in ship held to be capital expenditure).

[36]*Mitchell v. B.W. Noble Ltd.*, [1927] 1 K.B. 719 (C.A.) (payment to secure retirement of director whose conduct likely to damage taxpayer's business was revenue payment).

[37]*Countess Warwick S.S. Co. v. Ogg*, [1924] 2 K.B. 292 (payment to secure cancellation of contract to acquire capital asset was capital expense).

[38]*Whitehead (Inspector of Taxes) v. Tubbs (Elastics) Ltd.*, [1984] S.T.C. 1 at 3 (C.A.) (payment to secure release from onerous term in loan agreement, which significantly limited taxpayer's power to borrow, constituted capital payment), per Oliver L.J.:

> Here the advantage sought to be achieved was one which was permanent in the sense that the company was relieved, for the balance of the loan period, of the disadvantages arising from the restrictions and relieved of restrictions attributable to a non-recurring transaction. One cannot separate the payment made from the origins of the restrictions in respect of which it was made. In effect these restrictions — and whether they were contained in the agreement or the debenture is really immaterial, for they clearly went and were intended to go hand-in-hand — were the price or premium paid by the company for the loan, and the loan, it is not in dispute, was clearly a transaction of a capital nature.

biguous. We resolve factual ambiguity in the taxpayer's favour.[39] As Mr. Justice Estey, speaking for a unanimous Supreme Court, stated:[40]

> Such a determination is, furthermore, consistent with another basic concept in tax law, that where the taxing statute is *not explicit, reasonable uncertainty or factual ambiguity resulting from lack of explicitness in the statute should be resolved in favour of the taxpayer.* This residual principle must be the more readily applicable in this appeal where otherwise, annually recurring expenditures completely connected to the daily business operation of the taxpayer, afford the taxpayer no credit against tax either by way of capital cost or depletion allowance with reference to a capital expenditure, or an expense deduction against revenue. [Emphasis added.]

(f) — Summary

There is no single test that can one can apply to all circumstances. There are, however, three broad criteria that offer a useful starting point in determining whether an expenditure is on account of capital or revenue:

1. The character of the advantage or the duration of the benefit (the more enduring the benefit the more likely that the expenditure is on account of capital);

2. Recurrence and frequency of the expenditure (the more frequent the expenditure the less enduring the benefit); and

3. Identification of the payment as a *surrogatum* for expenditures that would be on account of capital or revenue (a substitute for a capital expenditure is more likely a capital expenditure).

III. — Unreasonable Expenses

A taxpayer cannot deduct an expense except to the extent that it is reasonable in amount. This rule, which relates only to the amount of the expense, prevents taxpayers from artificially reducing their income through unreasonable expenses.

What is "reasonable" is a question of fact. One determines "reasonable" by comparing the expense in question with amounts paid in similar circumstances in comparable businesses. In *Doug Burns Excavation Contractor Ltd. v. M.N.R.*,[41] for example, the Tax Court disallowed the taxpayer's deduction for a bonus of $100,000 that it paid to the president's wife who worked as a clerk in the office.

---

[39]*The Queen v. Johns-Manville Can. Inc.*, [1985] 2 C.T.C. 111, 85 D.T.C. 5373 (S.C.C.).

[40]*Ibid.* at 5384.

[41][1983] C.T.C. 2566, 83 D.T.C. 528 (T.C.C.).

IV. — Levies, Fines, And Penalties

Generally, an expense is deductible if it is incurred for the purposes of gaining or producing income. It is well established that a taxpayer may deduct expenses incurred from illegal acts to the extent that they were incurred to earn income. However, this principle does not extend to the deduction of fines and penalties.

A taxpayer cannot deduct a fine or penalty imposed by law in *any* jurisdiction, including a foreign jurisdiction. The 2004 amendments in effect overturn the decision of the Supreme Court in *65302 B.C. Ltd.*[42] which held that fines and penalties incurred for the purpose of gaining or producing income are deductible expenses under paragraph 18(1)(a).

The rationale behind the prohibition is that allowing the deduction of fines and penalties diminishes their ability to deter taxpayers from engaging in illegal activities, and thus is contrary to public policy objectives. However, the Budget left open the door for the deduction of prescribed fines where it would be inconsistent with public policy to deny their deductibility.[43]

V. — Illegal Payments

Subsection 67.5(1)of the *Income Tax Act* provides that a taxpayer may not deduct certain outlays or expenses that are illegal. The *Corruption of Foreign Public Officials Act*,[44] the *Criminal Code*,[45] and the *Income Tax Act*[46] prohibit the deduction of expenses for bribery, corruption, fraud, and conspiracy. Subsection 67.5(1) removes any possibility that an illegal act, such as a bribe paid to a foreign official, will be allowed as a tax-deductible business expense. In addition, subsection 67.5(2) allows the Minister to reassess *any* taxation year in order to give effect to subsection (1).

---

[42]In *65302 British Columbia Ltd. v. Canada*, [1999] 3 S.C.R. 804, [2000] 1 C.T.C. 57, 99 D.T.C. 5799 (S.C.C.), an over-quota levy imposed on an egg-producing poultry farm by the B.C. Egg Marketing Board an allowable deduction pursuant to subsection 9(1) and paragraph 18(1)(a) of the Act. The levy was incurred as part of the taxpayer's day-to-day operations. Furthermore, the business decision to produce over-quota was a deliberate decision made in order to realize income. Since the fine was imposed to remove the profit of over-quota production, it was allowable as a deductible current expense.

[43]See, for example, Reg. 7309, which prescribes fines under the *Excise Tax Act*.

[44]S.C. 1998, c. 34.

[45]*Criminal Code*, R.S.C. 1985, c. C-46, ss. 119–121, 123–125, 393, 426, or an offence under s. 465 as it relates to an offence described in any of the aforementioned sections

[46]S. 67.5.

VI. — Purpose Of Expenditure

1. — Purpose, Not Result

An expenditure is deductible as an expense in computing income only if one incurs it for the *purpose* of earning income.[47] It is the *purpose*, and not the result, of the expenditure that determines deductibility. Thus, an expense for the purpose of earning income from a business is deductible, regardless of whether it actually produces income. For example, if a taxpayer incurs advertising expenses for the purpose of promoting sales, failure of the advertising program to stimulate sales does *not* disqualify the expenditure as a deductible expense. The Exchequer Court explained the scheme as follows:[48]

> Thus, it may be stated categorically that in a case under the *Income Tax Act* the first matter to be determined in deciding whether an outlay or expense is outside the prohibition of paragraph 18(1)(a) of the Act is whether it was made or incurred by the taxpayer in accordance with the ordinary principles of commercial trading or well accepted principles of business practice. If it was not, that is the end of the matter. But if it was, then the outlay or expense is properly deductible unless it falls outside the expressed exception of paragraph 18(1)(a) and, therefore, within its prohibition. ...

The essential limitation in paragraph 18(1)(a) is that the taxpayer must incur the outlay or expense "for the purpose" of gaining or producing income "from the business". Thus, the purpose must be that of gaining or producing income from the business in which the taxpayer engages. *A fortiori*, the business must exist at the time that the taxpayer incurs the expenditure.

2. — Primary Purpose

What is an income-earning purpose is a question of fact. We can break down expenditures into deductible and non-deductible portions.[49] An expenditure does not have to be wholly

---

[47]Para. 18(1)(a). This rule does little more than reinforce subs. 9(1), which states that the income from a business or property is the profit therefrom. To constitute an "expense", the taxpayer must be under an obligation to pay money to someone. An obligation to do something that may entail an expenditure in the future is *not* an expense; see *The Queen v. Burnco Industries Ltd.*, [1984] C.T.C. 337, 84 D.T.C. 6348 (F.C.A.).

[48]*Royal Trust Co. v. M.N.R.*, [1957] C.T.C. 32 at 42, 44, 57 D.T.C. 1055 at 1060, 1062 (Ex. Ct.); see also *B.C. Electric Ry. v. M.N.R.*, [1958] C.T.C. 21, 58 D.T.C. 1022 (S.C.C.) (payments made by taxpayer to enable it to become more profitable not deductible even though made for purpose of producing income on account of capital; case departing from previous law; see editorial note at [1958] C.T.C. 21).

[49]*Consumer's Gas Co. of Toronto v. M.N.R.* (1955), 13 Tax A.B.C. 429 (T.A.B.) (taxpayer obtained gas export permit to improve business; permit and fees for securing permit capital in nature; remainder of fees referable to particular business difficulties, not assets); *KVP Co. v. M.N.R.*, [1957] C.T.C. 275,

and exclusively expended for business purposes in order to be deductible.[50] The focus is on the *primary* purpose of the expenditure. For example, a lawyer who travels from Toronto to Paris for a business meeting can deduct his or her travel expenses for the trip, even though he or she remains there for the weekend for personal reasons. The lawyer may also deduct any *incremental* expenditures (such as additional hotel and meal charges) associated with the personal portion of his or her visit if the expenses are part of the cost of waiting for meetings to resume on Monday. The personal component is secondary to the primary business purpose of the visit.

VII. — Personal And Living Expenses

1. — General Comment

A taxpayer cannot deduct personal or living expenses in computing income from business or property.[51] To be deductible, an expense must be incurred for the purpose of earning income.[52] The Act allows a taxpayer to deduct expenses incurred "for profit" activities and prohibits the deduction of expenses incurred "for pleasure" activities or on account of capital. The distinction between profit, pleasure and capital expenses involves difficult classification problems in the individual's income tax. Characterization involves drawing a dividing line between categories. The line that divides deductible and non-deductible expenses should provide an accurate measure of income that is both equitable and can be administered easily.

---

57 D.T.C. 1208 (Ex. Ct.) (extensive aerial surveys required by province to preserve timber cutting rights; current expense to the extent of previous average survey expense).

[50]Considerable care should be taken in reading English cases on the deductibility of expenses incurred for business and personal purposes. Under the English statute, an expenditure must be *wholly and exclusively* for business purposes if it is to be deductible; see *Mallalieu v. Drummond*, [1983] 2 A.C. 861 (H.L.).

[51]Para. 18(1)(h) and subs. 248(1) "personal or living expenses". The prohibition does not cover traveling expenses (including the full cost of meals and lodging) incurred on a business trip. "Personal or living expenses" include expenses incurred to maintain a property where the property is not maintained in connection with a business that is being carried on for profit or with a reasonable expectation of profit. They also include expenses incurred for purchasing a life insurance policy, the proceeds of which are payable to the taxpayer, or to a person related to the taxpayer.

[52]Para. 18(1)(h) was originally implemented as para. 2(2)(e) of c. 55, S.C. 1919, which amended s. 3 of the *Income War Tax Act*, 1917. In response to a question in the House regarding the purpose of this section, asked by a questioner who noted that it was already "quite evident that no one has the right to deduct his personal and living expenses from income before he declares it for the purposes of this Act", the Minister of Finance stated that the section was "just to make it clear that deduction must not be made" and to "make it perfectly clear that the full net income must be assessed" (Commons Debates, June 24, 1919).

The distinction between profit and pleasure expenses is blurred and, indeed, sometimes meaningless because it is impossible to quantify profit and pleasure at discreet intervals. Nevertheless, the distinction is important for tax purposes and taxpayers are routinely asked to determine which of the two objectives, profit or pleasure, is the predominant motive for an expenditure. The distinction between the two determines whether a taxpayer pays a dollar or 50 cents on the dollar for a particular expense. The courts are equally uncomfortable with these distinctions and often rely more upon compilations of deductible and non-deductible lists, rather than on principled formulations based upon tax policy.

Expenses can be put on a continuum. At one extreme are those expenses quite obviously of a purely business nature, and there is no serious issue of their deductibility. For example, a taxpayer who pays salaries, rent, utilities and operating expenses on account of his or her business is entitled to deduct the expenditures (subject only to quantum limitations) as routine business expenses.[53] At the other end of the continuum, we find expenses that are of a purely personal nature. Hence, for example, a taxpayer is not generally entitled to deduct his or her personal meals, clothing, cosmetics, personal grooming and the everyday costs of living. The difficulty of determining deductibility, however, lies not at the extremes of the continuum but in the middle where the expenditure is clearly neither one nor the other, but has attributes both of business and personal. It is in this grey area that one must determine which attributes predominate.

Expenditures in the grey zone of deductibility can be broken down into two broad categories: (1) the "special costs" of a person engaged in business, such as, child care and commuting, and (2) "personal gratification costs" that give pleasure in the pursuit of profit or bring about profit in the pursuit of pleasure, for example, travel and entertainment. Tax law deals quite easily with both of these categories of expenditures in the case of employed persons. Employees are simply prohibited from deducting *any* expenses *unless* the deduction is *specifically* authorized by the statute.[54] Thus, we tax employees based on their gross income with minimal deductions. We justify this rule on the basis of administrative simplicity without much concern for an accurate measure of net income.

The problem, however, is not so easily resolved in the case of business expenditures, where the rule is the converse: a taxpayer is entitled to deduct *any* expense incurred for the purpose of earning income *unless* the deduction is *specifically* prohibited. This inverse burden leads to tension between employed persons and those engaged in business and raises the issue of equitable treatment of taxpayers who are similarly situated. Thus, individuals generally prefer independent contractor status for tax purposes and employee status under labour laws. This allows them the best of both worlds, maximum deductions and maximum protection.

---

[53] S. 9.

[54] Subs. 8(2).

2. — *Purpose Test*

We determine the purpose of an expenditure by looking for the predominant reason for which one incurs the expenditure. This is a positive test and quite different from asking the converse: "what would happen if the taxpayer did *not* incur the expense?" Thus, the purpose test is not the "but for" test. The test for deductibility is *not*: "but for this expense, could the taxpayer have earned his income?" Such a broad test would completely obliterate the distinction between business and personal expenses and negate the value of the purpose test.

For example, how should we classify child care expenses, the classic hybrid of "for profit" and "for pleasure" expenditures? In a conventional family setting with infant children, both parents cannot go out to work without some provision for the children. This raises two questions. Are the expenses incurred:

1. Primarily and predominantly for the purpose of allowing the parent (usually the mother) to engage in business? and

2. As a basic function of family life and, hence, of a personal nature?

In *Smith*,[55] for example, the United States Board of Tax Appeals denied the taxpayer a deduction for babysitting expenses on the theory that allowing such a deduction would extend the deduction to all consumption expenditures (such as food, shelter, clothing and recreation) that allow taxpayers to carry on their day-to-day activities. The Board was concerned with opening the floodgates for the deduction of all personal expenditures, however tenuous their connection with the income-earning process.

> The fee to the doctor, but for whose healing service, the earner of the family income could not leave his sickbed; the cost of the labourer's raiment, for how can the world proceed about its business unclothed; the very home which gives us shelter and rest and the food which provides energy, might all by an extension of the same proposition be construed as necessary to the operation of business and to the creation of income. Yet these are the very essence of those "personal" expenses the deductibility of which is expressly denied.

There is, however, an important distinction between expenses incurred primarily for personal purposes and expenses incurred predominantly for the purpose of earning income but which have only incidental and ancillary personal elements. The difficulty lies in drawing the line between the two.

It is clear that certain expenditures are common to everyone, whether they are employed, engaged in a business or unemployed. The basic personal expenditures for food, shelter, clothing and the everyday necessities of life are clearly not deductible, regardless of one's working status. One does not incur such expenditures primarily for the purposes of earning income. Child care expenses, however, pose a different conceptual problem. Child care expenses are a basic family consumption expenditure if we begin from the premise that one parent must stay at home to look after the child. Then, any child care expenses are primarily

---

[55]*Smith v. Commr.* (1939), 40 B.T.A. 1038; 113 F.2d 114 (U.S. 2nd Cir., 1940).

of a personal nature. The business aspect of the expenditure on account of child care arises if, and only if, the previously stay-at-home parent decides to enter the commercial marketplace and engage in business. Thus, one's perspective on child care expenses depends on where one starts the analysis. To be sure, the short answer might well be that the Act has a detailed statutory framework for the deduction of child care expenses and, hence, one cannot deduct such expenses under the general provisions[56] because of the prescribed scheme.[57] But that response merely avoids the difficult question. Apart from specific statutory provisions, the theoretically correct answer is surely that the incremental cost of a hybrid profit/pleasure expenditure is deductible for tax purposes if the *primary and predominant* motive for incurring the expenditure is to earn business income.

The deductibility of child care expenses also raises equity issues if some taxpayers get tax-free child care while others are denied the same treatment. An employer, for example, can deduct the cost of child care that it provides at its facilities if it incurs the expenses for the purposes of earning business income. Since the employer requires and needs the services of all of its employees (some of whom have young children), the cost of providing child care on its premises is directly related to the employees' services. Parents with young children who are being well taken care of on the employer's premises are likely to work longer and with less anxiety than parents who need to dash off to rescue their children at pre-determined hours from day-care services. The same can be said of nanny care.[58] Thus, a person who pays for child care services to get to his or her business is not entitled to deduct the cost, but his or her employer can deduct the same cost to obtain his or her services. The supposed logic of this disparate treatment is that the employer incurs the cost *after* his or her employees are on the business premises, whilst the parent incurs his or her child care expenses to get *to* the employer's premises. This invites arbitrage in salary negotiations. The obvious behavioural response is that one should (if possible) engage in salary arbitrage: Negotiate a lower salary with on-site child care, rather than a higher salary with nanny care paid with after-tax dollars.

The question in *Smith*[59] was essentially whether the differential in child care expenses (or any part thereof) should be allowed as business expenses incurred for the purposes of earning income. The answer, based on the floodgates theory that allowing such expenses would open the door to allowing every other personal expense as a deduction, (the "but for" test as the yardstick for determining deductibility) was not entirely satisfactory. There is a difference between expenses that are incurred, regardless of whether one works or not (basic food, personal clothing, shelter, etc.), and the *incremental* expenses associated only with the process of earning income.

---

[56]S. 9.

[57]S. 63.

[58]See *Symes v. Canada*, [1993] 4 S.C.R. 695, [1994] 1 C.T.C. 40, 94 D.T.C. 6001 (S.C.C.).

[59]*Smith v. Commr.* (1939), 40 B.T.A. 1038; 113 F.2d 114 (U.S. 2nd Cir., 1940).

Scott[60] recognizes this distinction in allowing a "foot and transit courier" to deduct the cost of his incremental food and water required to perform his job. The taxpayer travelled 150 kilometres a day carrying a backpack that weighed between 20–50 pounds. He worked on foot and public transportation 10 hours per day, 5 days per week, 52 weeks per year. He consumed an *extra* meal per day for which he sought to deduct $11 ($8 for extra food and $3 for extra bottled water and juice) as business expenses. Since the taxpayer incurred expenses on account of food and beverages, the Agency denied his deduction for the incremental expenses. The Federal Court, quite rightly, refused to deny the deduction for the expenses simply on the grounds that such expenses have always been considered "personal" and, therefore, must continue to be so.[61] Instead, the Court allowed the taxpayer to deduct his *incremental* food and drink expenses because the extra consumption was the direct result of his efforts to earn income. The incremental food and drink were the equivalent of the incremental gas that a person uses in his automobile for business purposes.[62]

The Court, also quite rightly, rejected arguments that the deduction for food and beverage expenses would open the floodgates to a myriad of claims for deductions for personal expenses. The floodgates argument, always a concern for tax administrators, is an argument of last resort to preserve the status quo. The deduction "... should in no way be interpreted as providing a basis to challenge all traditional prohibitions on the deduction of food and beverages as a business expense under the Act." The deduction for food and beverages is already tightly controlled under subsection 67.1(1) of the Act, which limits the deduction for such expenses to a maximum of 50 per cent of the amount expended, even if one incurs the expense entirely for business purposes. Thus, it is unlikely that the floodgates will open on account of food and beverage expenses incurred for business purposes.

The question remains, however, as to how far the courts will go in permitting the deduction of other personal costs that are incurred solely and incrementally for the purposes of earning

---

[60]*Scott v. Canada*, [1998] 4 C.T.C. 103, 162 D.L.R. (4th) 595, 98 D.T.C. 6530 (Fed. C.A.).

[61]See, for example, Justice Iacobucci's comment in *Symes v. Canada* (1993), [1993] 4 S.C.R. 695, [1994] 1 C.T.C. 40, 94 D.T.C. 6001 (S.C.C.) at 54:

> This appeal presents a particular expense which has been traditionally characterized as personal in nature. If, in coming to a decision, this Court stated that since such expenses have always been personal they must now be personal, the conclusion could be easily and deservedly attacked. For this reason, proper analysis of this question demands that the relationship between child care expenses and business income be examined more critically, in order to determine whether that relationship can be sufficient to justify the former's deductibility.

[62]*Per* Justice McDonald:

> This result takes into account the different methods by which the same job is done and puts all couriers on an equal footing. Arguably, it also recognizes and encourages [rather than discourages as a prohibition on this expense would] new environmentally responsible ways of producing income.

business income. Can the mortician deduct his sombre clothing, the lawyer her navy suit, the accountant his white shirt, the actress her designer clothes, etc.?

To summarize: Characterizing business expenses involves three questions: (1) what is the need that the expense meets? (2) would the need exist apart from the business? and (3) is the need intrinsic to the business? The answers to these questions are essentially questions of fact.[63]

> If a need exists even in the absence of business activity, and irrespective of whether the need was or might have been satisfied by an expenditure to a third party or by the opportunity cost of personal labour, then an expense to meet the need would traditionally be viewed as a personal expense. Expenses which can be identified in this way are expenses which are incurred by a taxpayer in order to relieve the taxpayer from personal duties and to make the taxpayer available to the business.

> Traditionally, expenses that simply make the taxpayer *available* to the business are not considered business expenses since the taxpayer is expected to be available to the business as a *quid pro quo* for business income received.

The needs test based upon primary objective should, in the absence of specific statutory provisions, provide an unequivocal answer. But it does not. The expense must also be *intrinsic* to the business. Why? In *Symes*, for example, the taxpayer's child care expenses met the needs test. The taxpayer could not operate her business without being present on the premises. The Supreme Court, however, said that the expenses merely made her *available* to practice her profession, rather than for any purpose intrinsic to the operation of the business itself. The expenses got her to her business, but they were not an integral part of the business. But having got to her place of business, the expenses would have been deductible *by the business*.

3. — Type of Expenditure

Given the subjective nature of the purpose test, many courts look to the nature of an expenditure to determine its purpose. Is the expenditure of a type that is ordinarily and usually a direct expenditure in the pursuit of business, or one that is primarily personal and only tenuously related to business? Consider the distinction between a businessperson who entertains an out-of-town client at home for $100 and one who takes a client out for dinner to a restaurant for $400. The expenses of entertaining at home are usually personal, even though one devotes the entire discussion to business matters. This is because home entertainment is

---

[63]*Symes v. Canada*, [1993] 4 S.C.R. 695, [1994] 1 C.T.C. 40, 94 D.T.C. 6001 (S.C.C.):

> In another case, the arguments might be differently balanced, since the existence of a business purpose within the meaning of s. 18(1)(a) *is a question of fact*, and that the relative weight to be given to the factors analyzed will vary from case to case. ... It can be difficult to weigh the personal and business elements at play. [Emphasis added.]

ordinarily and usually a personal affair. In contrast, $200 of the cost of the dinner in the restaurant would be deductible as a business expense, even if most of the evening was spent discussing personal affairs. Entertaining in restaurants is ordinarily and usually associated with business, and expenses in respect thereof are usually "business expenses".[64]

The distinction between business and personal expenses sometimes also depends upon the taxpayer's discretionary power to incur the expense. For example, Thorson P. denied a deduction for commuting expenses on the basis that:[65]

> The personal and living expenses referred to ... are those over which the taxpayer has a large amount of personal control, depending upon the scale of living which he may choose. Such expenses would probably not be deductible even if there were no provision in the statute relating to the matter, for if personal and living expenses were deductible from income and only the balance left for taxation purposes, the amount of net or taxable income would depend upon the taxpayer's own choice as to the scale of living that he might adopt and in many cases there would be no taxable income at all. It is obvious that the determination of what the taxable income of a taxpayer shall be cannot depend upon or be left to the taxpayer's own choice as to whether his personal and living expenses shall be up to the extent of his income or not.

---

[64]*Vuicic v. M.N.R.* (1960), 24 Tax A.B.C. 253 (T.A.B.) (tavern keeper not allowed to deduct capital cost allowance in respect of $7,000 boat); *Brown v. M.N.R.* (1950), 1 Tax A.B.C. 373 (T.A.B.) (special clothing required by radio technician posted in north not deductible); *No. 431 v. M.N.R.* (1957), 17 Tax A.B.C. 300 (T.A.B.) (salary paid to physician's housekeeper entirely personal or living expense notwithstanding housekeeper's answering physician's telephone); *Macquistan v. M.N.R.* (1965), 38 Tax A.B.C. 23 (T.A.B.) (babysitter employed by physician in order to permit her to carry on practice was personal expense); *Nadon v. M.N.R.* (1965), 40 Tax A.B.C. 33 (T.A.B.) (housekeeper engaged during illness of taxpayer's wife not deductible); *Lawlor v. M.N.R.*, [1970] Tax A.B.C. 369 (T.A.B.) (lawyer not entitled to deduct cost of babysitters employed to permit business entertaining); *Cree v. M.N.R.*, [1978] C.T.C. 2472, 78 D.T.C. 1352 (T.R.B.) (auto racing not carried on with reasonable expectation of profit; losses not deductible); *Hume v. M.N.R.*, [1980] C.T.C. 2645, 80 D.T.C. 1542 (T.R.B.) ("hobby" investor denied deduction for cost of investment periodicals); *Warden v. M.N.R.*, [1981] C.T.C. 2379, 81 D.T.C. 322 (T.R.B.) (high school principal denied deduction of losses from farming and other operations since no expectation of profit); *Peters v. M.N.R.*, [1981] C.T.C. 2451, 81 D.T.C. 454 (T.R.B.) (bank employee denied deduction of losses from bee keeping and sheep raising); *White v. M.N.R.*, [1981] C.T.C. 2456, 81 D.T.C. 457 (T.R.B.) (taxpayer's losses from breeding and racing quarter horses disallowed for lack of reasonable expectation of profit); *Beyer v. M.N.R.*, [1978] C.T.C. 2026, 78 D.T.C. 1066 (T.R.B.) (car racing losses not deductible); *Payette v. M.N.R.*, [1978] C.T.C. 223, 78 D.T.C. 1181 (T.R.B.) (writing and publication of books without reasonable expectation of profit; outlays not deductible); *Fluet v. M.N.R.*, [1978] C.T.C. 2902, 78 D.T.C. 1657 (T.R.B.) (bank manager's cost and maintenance of guard dog for family protection not deductible); *Merchant v. M.N.R.*, [1980] C.T.C. 2336, 80 D.T.C. 1291 (T.R.B.) (expenses incurred in attempt to secure leadership of Saskatchewan Liberal Party not deductible); *Symes v. Canada*, [1991] 2 C.T.C. 1, 91 D.T.C. 5386 (Fr.) (Fed. C.A.); affirmed (1993), [1993] 4 S.C.R. 695, [1994] 1 C.T.C. 40, 94 D.T.C. 6001 (S.C.C.) (lawyer's nanny expenses not deductible).

[65]*Samson v. M.N.R.*, [1943] C.T.C. 47 at 64, 2 D.T.C. 610 (Can. Ex. Ct.).

The rationale that personal expenses should not be deducted because they are within the discretion of the taxpayer is not persuasive. Most expenses, including business expenses, are ultimately within the taxpayer's discretion. A simpler explanation is sufficient: Personal expenses are not deductible against business income because they are not incurred primarily and predominantly for business purposes and, as such, they are not relevant in determining income from business.

4. — Business versus Personal Expenditures

Expenses are deductible from income only if they are on account of commercial activities, whether from business or property. We saw in Chapter 7 that business income arises from commercial activities generally involving a combination of labour and capital.

We also saw that the concept of source of income is an intrinsic part of the Canadian income tax system.[66] The distinguishing feature of the source concept is the pursuit of profit. In order to determine whether a particular activity constitutes a source of income, the taxpayer must show that he or she carries on the activity in pursuit of profit. Thus, the characterization of income as being from a commercial activity is the first step in determining business or property income.

A hobby for personal pleasure is not a source of income. An amateur photographer, for example, who exhibits his or her works for pleasure but never sells any cannot claim expense deductions for his materials and supplies.

The law presumes that an activity in pursuit of profit that does not involve any personal or hobby element — such as, the practice of law — is a commercial venture and, as such, a source of income.[67] The only question that remains is whether the source is income from business or income from property.

If the activity is clearly commercial, there is no need to further analyze the taxpayer's business decisions even if subsequently they are seen as unsound and unprofitable. After all, many business people make bad commercial decisions. They should not be penalized by the tax system on an ex-post analysis of their commercial decisions. The objective is to determine the commercial nature of the taxpayer's activity and not his or her business acumen with hindsight.[68]

Where there are mixed personal and commercial elements to an activity, one must determine which elements predominate. Does the taxpayer carry on the activity in a sufficiently com-

---

[66]See Chapter 4 and *Stewart v. Canada*, [2002] 2 S.C.R. 645, [2002] 3 C.T.C. 439, 2002 D.T.C. 6969 (S.C.C.), at para. 5.

[67]*Stewart v. Canada, ibid.*, at para. 5.

[68]See *Stewart v. Canada, ibid.*, at para. 55.

mercial manner to constitute a source of income? In these circumstances, one must evaluate the commercial content of the undertaking by looking at the taxpayer's expectation of profit and mode of operation. For example, a serious photographer may conduct his or her activities with the commercial hallmarks of a professional. If on an objective analysis of the evidence it is clear that the taxpayer's predominant intention is to derive profit from his or her activities, the income has a source and expenses to earn the income are deductible if they otherwise satisfy the Act.

Thus, the characterization of income and expenses involves two distinct steps. First, one must determine whether the taxpayer's undertaking is for profit or for personal purposes. If the taxpayer undertakes the activity primarily for profit, it is a source of income. The second step is to determine whether the source of income is from business or from property. The traditional common law definition of "business" is anything that occupies the time, attention and labour of a person for the purpose of profit.[69] Business income generally requires a higher level of taxpayer activity than property income. Nevertheless, regardless of the level of taxpayer activity, any commercial undertaking in pursuit of profit is a source of income, either from business or property.

A commercial activity is one that the taxpayer undertakes for profit. We determine the taxpayer's intention by looking at objective evidence to support his or her intentions. The taxpayer must establish that his or her predominant intention is to make a profit from the activity and that he or she carries on the activity in accordance with objective standards of business behaviour. Thus, one looks at:

1. the taxpayer's profit and loss experience in past years;

2. the taxpayer's training and expertise in the field of his or her activities;

3. the taxpayer's intended course of action; and

4. the financial viability of the venture to show a profit.

This list is not exhaustive and the factors to be taken into account in determining intention will differ according to the facts and circumstances of each case. Thus, having a reasonable expectation in the financial viability of the venture to show a profit is only one factor in evaluating the taxpayer's intention. A reasonable expectation of profit is not the only factor and it is not conclusive.

---

[69] *Smith v. Anderson* (1880), 15 Ch. D. 247 (Eng. C.A.) at 258; *Terminal Dock and Warehouse Co. v. M.N.R.*, [1968] 2 Ex. C.R. 78, [1968] C.T.C. 78, 68 D.T.C. 5060 (Ex. Ct.); affd. 68 D.T.C. 5316, [1968] S.C.R. vi (S.C.C.).

5. — *Statutory Exceptions*

Some expenses that may be, at least in part, personal expenses are, nevertheless, deductible under specific statutory provisions. For example, moving expenses,[70] child care expenses,[71] and tuition fees[72] are all expenditures that are deductible from income or creditable against taxes in narrowly defined circumstances. The justification for the deductibility of these expenses for tax purposes is usually social or economic policy considerations, for example, mobility of labour, access to labour markets, and investment in human capital and resources.

VIII. — General Anti-Avoidance Rule

A taxpayer seeking to deduct expenses from income must be mindful of the general anti-avoidance rule ("GAAR"). GAAR applies to "abusive" income tax avoidance transactions and arrangements. The thrust of the rule is that the CRA can ignore an offensive "avoidance transaction" and redetermine its income tax consequences in certain circumstances.[73]

An "avoidance transaction" is any transaction or series of transactions that gives rise to a tax benefit, unless the transaction is one that is undertaken for *bona fide* purposes other than that of obtaining a tax benefit. The Act defines a "tax benefit" to include, *inter alia*, a transaction to avoid taxes! But even a tax-motivated transaction is not an "avoidance transaction" if it does not misuse the Act Regulations, ITARs, or Tax Treaties.[74]

IX. — Exempt Income

An expense to earn exempt income is not deductible for tax purposes.[75] Generally, "exempt income" is any income that is not included in computing income under Part I of the Act.[76] Thus, one cannot offset expenditures to earn exempt income against other taxable income.

---

[70]S. 62; see Chapter 13, "Other Deductions".

[71]S. 63; see Chapter 13, "Other Deductions".

[72]S. 118.5; see Chapter 16, "Computation of Tax Payable".

[73]S. 245.

[74]Subs. 245(4).

[75]Para. 18(1)(c).

[76]Subs. 248(1) "exempt income".

X. — Specific Deductions

We saw in Chapter 7 that the starting point in computing income from business or property is to determine the *net* profit therefrom according to generally accepted commercial principles. We repeat, however, that the determination of profit is ultimately a question of law governed by legal precepts.

In addition to the deductions allowed according to commercial and accounting principles, the Act also specifically authorizes the deduction of certain expenses. The rationale for this specific list of deductions varies: some of the rules regulate deductions that might otherwise be governed by unclear or flexible accounting principles (e.g., reserves); some (e.g., capital cost allowances) replace accounting rules with more specific and detailed tax rules; some (e.g., restrictions on financing passenger motor vehicles) reflect a concern that the tax system should not subsidize personal expenditures; and some incorporate political and cultural value judgments (e.g., restrictions on advertising in non-Canadian periodicals). There is no single thread that connects these deductions. Each has its own rationale.

XI. — Reserves And Contingent Liabilities

1. — General Scheme

As a general rule, a taxpayer cannot deduct a reserve or a contingent liability.[77] A reserve is an appropriation, rather than an expense that one incurs for the purpose of earning income. As we will see, however, there are many exceptions to the rule.

The term "reserve" has a much broader meaning in tax law than it does in accounting. For accounting purposes, a "reserve" denotes an appropriation of income from retained earnings. Such appropriation may be pursuant to a contractual stipulation (for example, pursuant to a trust indenture) or at the discretion of the taxpayer.[78] For tax purposes, however, a "reserve" generally refers to an amount that one sets aside for future use. One must distinguish between reserves and unpaid liabilities. A "reserve" represents an amount set aside as a provision against a future uncertain event. A liability is a known and existing obligation.[79] Thus, an obligation is a liability for tax purposes only if all of the conditions precedent to create the liability have been satisfied.[80] In contrast, a contingent liability is only a potential liabil-

---

[77]Para. 18(1)(e); IT-215R Archived, "Reserves, Contingent Accounts and Sinking Funds" (January 12, 1981) as amended by Special Release dated November 30, 1989.

[78]*CICA Handbook*, s. 3260.01.

[79]*No. 297 v. M.N.R.* (1955), 14 Tax A.B.C. 100, 55 D.T.C. 611 (Can. Tax. App. Bd.) (amount set aside by taxpayer for employee bonuses not a reserve since liability to pay definite).

[80]*Kerr Farms Ltd. v. M.N.R.*, [1971] Tax A.B.C. 804, 71 D.T.C. 536 (Can. Tax. App. Bd.) (conditions precedent outstanding; accrued employee bonuses not liabilities).

ity that may become actual if, and only if, certain events occur. Thus, contingent liabilities are not real liabilities, but have the potential of becoming real on the happening of some event.

Generally, a taxpayer may claim a reserve in a year only if the Act specifically authorizes the deduction. A reserve that a taxpayer claims in a particular year is added back into his or her income in the following year. The taxpayer may then claim a new reserve according to the terms and conditions of the authorizing provisions. Thus, there is an annual renewal of the reserve on justification for its deduction. One must annually justify the deduction of a reserve.

2. — Deductible Reserves

Deduction allowed for	ITA Reference	To be included in income in following year
Reserve for doubtful debts	20(1)(l)	12(1)(d)
Reserve for goods delivered and services performed after end of year	20(1)(m)(i), (ii)	12(1)(e)(i)
Reserve for deposits on returnable containers	20(1)(m)(iv)	12(1)(e)(i)
Manufacturer's warranty reserve	20(1)(m.1)	12(1)(e)(i)
Reserves for amounts not due on instalment sales contracts	20(1)(n)	12(1)(e)(ii)
Reserve for quadrennial survey	20(1)(o)	12(1)(h)
Prepaid rents	20(1)(m)(iii)	12(1)(e)(i)

(a) — Doubtful Debts

A taxpayer may deduct a reasonable amount for doubtful trade accounts if the amounts receivable in respect of the accounts were included in income, either in the year in which the reserve is sought or in a previous year.

A reserve may also be claimed for doubtful debts arising on loans or lending made in the ordinary course of business where the taxpayer is an insurer or involved in the business of lending money.[81]

---

[81]Para. 20(1)(l); IT-442R, "Bad Debts and Reserve for Doubtful Debts" (September 6, 1991).

A reserve calculated for financial statement purposes is not necessarily the amount deducti-ble for tax purposes. Whether the collectibility of a debt is sufficiently "doubtful" to justify a reserve is a question of fact that must be answered in light of all of the particular circumstan-ces of the relationship between the debtor and creditor. This requires specific analysis of each account. As a matter of practice, however, the CRA does accept reserves calculated as a percentage of doubtful accounts, provided that the taxpayer can support the percentage by reference to his or her actual loss experience. A reserve computed as a simple percentage of the taxpayer's total accounts receivable is not acceptable for tax purposes.

The factors usually taken into account in determining the collectibility of an account receiv-able are as follows:[82]

- History and age of the overdue account;

- The debtor's financial position;

- Past experience in respect of the debtor's bad debts;

- General business conditions;

- Specific business conditions in the debtor's industry;

- Specific business conditions in the debtor's locality; and

- Changes in sales and accounts receivable as compared with previous years.

A taxpayer who claims a reserve for doubtful accounts in one year must include the amount in income in the following year.[83] The taxpayer can then make a fresh evaluation of the collectibility of accounts receivable and deduct a new reserve in the current year. Thus, unlike accounting practice that permits incremental additions to, and subtractions from, the previous year's reserve, we deduct the *entire* amount of the reserve in the year in which we claim it. This amount is then added to income in the following year, a new amount is de-ducted, and so on. This scheme allows the CRA to challenge the entire reserve in the year it is claimed, without any risk that a portion of the reserve is statute-barred. Under accounting practices, it is arguable that only the incremental portion is current. The base of the reserve could be statute-barred.[84]

A taxpayer may also deduct his or her actual bad debts.[85] Thus, the initial claim for a re-serve is a tentative one that is added back to income in the following year. The taxpayer may either collect the amount in a subsequent year or claim a write-off for actual bad debts. An

---

[82]*No. 81 v. M.N.R.* (1953), 8 Tax A.B.C. 82 at 98, 53 D.T.C. 98 (Can. Tax App. Bd.).

[83]Para. 12(1)(d).

[84]Subs. 152(4).

[85]Para. 20(1)(p).

amount written off that is subsequently collected by the taxpayer is brought back into income in the year of collection.[86]

Example

Assume:

Year	Accounts Receivable (year end)	Reserve for Doubtful Debts	Bad Debts Deducted	Bad Debts Recovered
1	$100,000	$10,000	—	—
2	$120,000	$12,000	$6,000	—
3	$150,000	$15,000	$4,000	$5,000

Then, the *net* deduction from income in each year is determined as follows:

Year 1

Reserve for doubtful debts	$10,000
Net deduction (Year 1)	$10,000

Year 2

Reserve for doubtful debts	$12,000
Bad debts deducted	6,000
	18,000
Less: reserve deducted (Year 1)	(10,000)
Net deduction (Year 2)	$ 8,000

Year 3

Reserve for doubtful debts	$15,000
Bad debts deducted	4,000
	19,000
Less: reserve deducted (Year 2)	(12,000)
bad debts recovered	(5,000)
Net deduction (Year 3)	$ 2,000

---

[86]Para. 12(1)(i).

(b) — Goods and Services

Payments on account of goods to be delivered or services to be rendered in the future are included in income in the year the taxpayer receives the payment.[87] This rule overrides the generally accepted accounting principle that we recognize income when it is realized and not when it is received.[88] A taxpayer can, however, deduct a reasonable amount in respect of goods that will be delivered, or services that will be rendered, in a subsequent year.[89] This reserve is available only in computing income from a business and *not* in computing income from property.

A taxpayer can also deduct a reserve for deposits that may be refundable (excluding deposits on bottles), prepaid rent for the use of land or chattels, and for amounts that are receivable but not yet due.[90]

Both paragraphs 20(1)(m) and 20(1)(n) refer to the deduction of a reasonable amount as a reserve. What is "reasonable" is a question of fact depending upon the circumstances. A reasonable reserve is not necessarily equal to the amount included in income under paragraph 12(1)(a). For example, a taxpayer who sells tokens that are redeemable for products must include the proceeds from the tokens in income. If all the tokens have not been redeemed at the end of the taxation year, the taxpayer may claim a reserve equal to the value of the tokens that he or she expects will be redeemed by customers. Where, however, the history of the taxpayer's business indicates that some of the tokens sold will never be redeemed, the reserve must be reduced by the amount of the tokens that are not expected to be redeemed.

(c) — Amounts Not Due

In calculating income from a *business*, a taxpayer may deduct a reserve for the purchase price of property sold that is not due until some time after the end of the year.[91]

---

[87]Paras. 12(1)(a) and (b). This is a variation from accounting principles, which do not recognize income until it is earned. See Chapter 8, "Inclusions in Business and Investment Income".

[88]See Chapter 7, "The Meaning of Business Income, Investment Income, and Capital Gains" under the heading "Measurement and Timing".

[89]Para. 20(1)(m).

[90]Paras. 20(1)(m), (n).

[91]Para. 20(1)(n); *Home Provisioners (Man.) Ltd. v. M.N.R.*, [1958] C.T.C. 334, 58 D.T.C. 1183 (Ex. Ct.) (absolute assignment of right to receive instalment payments precluded right to claim reserve).

(i) — Property Other than Land

Where the subject matter of the sale is property other than land, a taxpayer may claim a reserve only if the proceeds of the sale are not due until a time more than two years after the date of sale. In effect, the taxpayer can allocate his or her profit over an extended period in much the same way as under instalment sales accounting. One calculates the reserve, which must be reasonable, by comparing the amount due as at the end of the taxation year to the gross sales proceeds. This ratio is applied against the gross profit realized on the sale, and the resulting amount is the reserve for that sale for the year.

Example		
Assume:		
Sale price		$ 200,000
Cost		100,000
Gross profit		$ 100,000
Cash received:		
Year 1	$ 125,000	
Year 2	50,000	
Year 3	25,000	
Then:		
Year 1:		
Profit on sale		$ 100,000
Less reserve:	$ 75,000 × $ 100,000	(37,500)
	$ 200,000	
Income (A)		$ 62,500
Year 2:		
Previous year's reserve		$ 37,500
Less reserve:	$ 25,000 × $ 100,000	(12,500)
	$ 200,000	
Income (B)		$ 25,000
Year 3:		
Previous year's reserve		$ 12,500
Less reserve:	0 × $ 100,000	0
	$ 200,000	
Income (C)		$ 12,500

Example	
Total gain included in income	
(A + B + C)	$ 100,000

(ii) — Land

A taxpayer can claim a reserve when he or she sells land if part of the proceeds of sale are payable after the end of the taxation year in which the land is sold.[92]

3. — *Limitations on Reserves*

(a) — *Food, Drink and Transportation*

Where a taxpayer claims a reserve in respect of food, drink or transportation to be delivered or provided after the end of the year, the reserve cannot exceed the revenue from these sources included in income for the year.[93]

Example	
Assume:	
Transportation tickets issued in year	$ 60,000
Tickets unused at the end of the year	$ 10,000
Then:	

The reserve under paragraph 20(1)(m) and subsection 20(6) is $10,000 unless experience indicates that a portion of the tickets will never be redeemed. If experience indicates, for example, that 5 per cent of all tickets issued are never redeemed, a reasonable reserve would be computed as follows:

---

[92]Subpara. 20(1)(n); IT-152R3 "Special Reserves — Sale of Land" (June 18, 1985).

[93]Subs. 20(6).

Example	
Tickets unused at the end of the year	$ 10,000
Tickets that will not be redeemed	
[5% × $60,000]	(3,000)
Reasonable reserve	$ 7,000

(b) — Non-Residents

A taxpayer who gives up his or her Canadian residency and does not carry on business in Canada cannot deduct a reserve in respect of unrealized receivables. Thus, since a reserve that a taxpayer claims in one year is added to his or her income in the following year, the taxpayer cannot avoid tax simply by giving up Canadian residence.[94]

(c) — Guarantees, Indemnities and Warranties

Where a taxpayer sells property or services and provides a guarantee, indemnity or warranty for those goods or services, the cost of the guarantee is usually included in the sale price. The taxpayer cannot claim a reserve in respect of the expected liabilities under the guarantees, indemnities or warranties.[95]

XII. — Interest Expense

1. — General Comment

The cost of financing is one of the more important decisions for businesses and investors. If one starts with the simple financial premise that interest represents the rental cost of the use of money over time, interest expense should be deductible if one incurs it to earn income. Although the Act generally allows a taxpayer to deduct interest on money that he or she borrows to earn income from business or property,[96] there is substantial litigation on interest

---

[94]Subs. 20(8); paras. 20(1)(n) and 12(1)(e).

[95]Subs. 20(7). For obvious reasons, taxpayers computing income on a cash basis are not entitled to claim a reserve under para. 20(1)(m).

[96]Para. 20(1)(c).

deductibility. The disputes arise primarily from source distinctions between types of income and taxpayer attempts to shift their position to minimize taxes.

The trouble began with a Supreme Court decision that held that interest is an expenditure on account of capital. The Court held that a tax deduction for interest on borrowed money would in fairness require a similar deduction for the *imputed* cost of equity capital:[97]

> ... *in the absence of an express statutory allowance*, interest payable on capital indebtedness is not deductible as an income expense. If a company has not the money capital to commence business, why should it be allowed to deduct the interest on borrowed money? The company setting up with its own contributed capital would, on such a principle, be entitled to interest on its capital before taxable income was reached, but the income statutes give no countenance to such a deduction.

The decision in *Canada Safeway* was wrong. Without specific authority, tax law does not allow for the deduction of imputed or notional costs. Nevertheless, the law stands: without specific statutory authority, interest expense is a capital expenditure for tax purposes and, therefore, not deductible.[98]

Paragraph 20(1)(c) is the authority to deduct interest in the pursuit of certain "for profit" activities. The object of section 20(1)(c)(i) is to create an incentive to accumulate income-producing capital by allowing taxpayers to deduct interest costs associated with its acquisition. This is seen as desirable because it creates wealth and increases the income tax base.[99] Parliament formulated this provision specifically to overrule *Canada Safeway's* denial of the deduction of interest as an expense. Thus, the statutory rule is permissive: it allows the deduction for interest as a current expense to earn business and investment income in circumstances that judge-made law would not. Paragraph 20(1)(c) is not an anti-avoidance provision, and one should not interpret it as such without precise and specific language.[100]

2. — Tax Arbitrage

Financing decisions depend upon risk, reward, security and taxes. Two characteristics of the Canadian income tax system have a particularly important influence on financing transactions. First, there are the statutory distinctions between the various sources of income and

---

[97]*Can. Safeway Ltd. v. M.N.R.*, [1957] S.C.R. 717, [1957] C.T.C. 335 at 344, 57 D.T.C. 1239 at 1244 (S.C.C.).

[98]Para. 18(1)(b).

[99]*Ludco Enterprises Ltd. v. Canada*, [2001] 2 S.C.R. 1082, [2002] 2 C.T.C. 95, 2001 D.T.C. 5505 (S.C.C.), at para. 63.

[100]*Neuman v. M.N.R.*, [1998] 1 S.C.R. 770, [1998] 3 C.T.C. 177, 98 D.T.C. 6297 (S.C.C.): "We should not be quick to embellish [a] provision ... when it is open for the legislator to be precise and specific with respect to any mischief to be avoided."

expenses. As we will see, interest on money that one borrows for business and investment purposes is generally deductible for tax purposes. Interest on debt to earn exempt income or capital gains is not deductible.

Second, there is the distinction between debt and equity capital. Debt represents borrowed capital that creates a liability to repay according to a pre-determined schedule. Equity is capital that one invests in exchange for an ownership interest. There is generally no fixed timetable to repay equity capital to the enterprise's owners.[101] Interest on borrowed money is an expense of earning profits. For tax purposes, dividends on shareholder equity are a distribution of profits to the owners *after* they earn the profits. Hence, dividends are not deductible as an expense of obtaining financing. These two features of the tax system, strict segregation of income by source and the distinction between debt and equity capital, materially affect Canadian corporate financing decisions as taxpayers arbitrage to reduce taxes and maximize their economic returns.

Dividend income is double taxed: first, in the corporation that pays tax on the income from which it pays dividends; second, in the hands of the shareholder who receives the dividend. Double taxation is unfair and distorts tax structures — for example, the shift to income trust structures and away from traditional corporations.

Since interest is generally deductible only when one incurs it in the pursuit of "for profit" activities and is not deductible when one uses debt "for pleasure" or for consumption, individuals have an incentive to tax arbitrage, that is, convert non-deductible personal interest into deductible business expenses by arranging transactions to attach the interest to their "for profit" activities. For example, a lawyer with cash savings might borrow an equal amount to invest in the capital of his or her law firm and then use the savings to buy a home.[102]

Even "for profit" activities promote tax arbitrage. For example, one might use loans on which interest is fully deductible to produce income that is taxed at a lower rate. Thus, an investor might deduct interest expense taxed at 46 per cent to earn Canadian-source dividend income taxed at 31 per cent. With only slightly greater sophistication, an investor might borrow to earn business income, which is fully taxable, and convert the end profit into a capital gain, only 1/2 of which is taxable. Tax arbitrage is merely an economic response to a system of segregation of income into categories that we tax at different rates.

---

[101]There may be some exceptions in the case of redeemable preferred shares, etc. These types of shares, however, more closely resemble debt capital with an equity flavor, rather than pure equity capital.

[102]See, for example, *Singleton v. Canada*, [1999] 3 C.T.C. 446, 99 D.T.C. 5362 (F.C.A.); affd. [2001] 2 S.C.R. 1046, [2002] 1 C.T.C. 121, 2001 D.T.C. 5533 (S.C.C.). See also *Ludco Enterprises Ltd. v. Canada*, [2001] 2 S.C.R. 1082, [2002] 2 C.T.C. 95, 2001 D.T.C. 5505 (S.C.C.).

3. — Statutory Requirements

"Interest" is compensation for the use of a sum of money belonging or owed to another.[103] It represents a legal obligation that one calculates by reference to the principal sum owing. The obligation to pay interest may arise from an express agreement, by legal implication, or by statute. Thus, in effect, interest expense represents the rental cost for debt capital.

Paragraph 20(1)(c) allows a taxpayer to deduct interest if the interest:[104]

- Is paid or payable in the year;

- Arises from a legal obligation;

- Is payable on borrowed money that is used for the purpose of earning income (other than exempt income) from a business or property; and

- Is reasonable in amount.

The paragraph clearly overcomes the common law restriction that interest is a capital expenditure. The provision, however, restricts the deductibility of interest to money that one uses in "for profit" activities and denies the deduction for funds used in "for pleasure" activities. Also, it limits the deductibility of interest to money *used for the purpose* of earning income from business or property. Thus, it confines the deduction to specific sources of income. If a payment blends capital and interest, the interest component is deductible if it otherwise satisfies the paragraph.[105] Where an interest rate is established in a market of lenders and borrowers acting at arm's length from each other, it is generally a reasonable rate.[106]

4. — Legal Obligation

The determination of what is interest is essentially a question of law. The main criterion is that interest represents payment for the use of debt capital. Hence, one calculates interest by reference to a principal sum. Some courts have grafted an additional precondition that interest must accrue daily.[107] This requirement, however, serves no particular policy and is an unnecessary appendage. Interest is deductible only if the lender has *legal* rights to enforce payment of the amounts due. Thus, deductibility depends upon an unconditional and legally

---

[103]*Ref re s. 6 of Farm Security Act. 1944 of Sask.*, [1947] S.C.R. 394 at 411; affd. [1949] A.C. 110 (P.C.).

[104]Para. 20(1)(c).

[105]Subs. 16(1).

[106]See *Mohammad v. The Queen*, [1997] 3 C.T.C. 321, 97 D.T.C. 5503 (F.C.A.) at 5509 [D.T.C.]; *Canada v. Irving Oil Ltd.*, [1991] 1 C.T.C. 350, 91 D.T.C. 5106 (F.C.A.) at 359 [C.T.C.].

[107]*Ontario (AG) v. Barfried Enterprises Ltd.*, [1963] S.C.R. 570 (S.C.C.).

enforceable obligation to pay interest. The obligation must be actual and not contingent. If there is no legal obligation to pay the interest, paragraph 18(1)(e) prevents its deduction.

5. — Use of Money

Paragraph 20(1)(c) allows a taxpayer to deduct an amount paid or payable in respect of the year "... pursuant to a legal obligation to pay interest on borrowed money *used for the purpose of* earning income from a business or property ... or a reasonable amount in respect thereof,....." The phrase "... used for the purpose of ..." incorporates two separate tests: use and purpose. One applies these tests to distinguish between "for profit" and "for pleasure" activities.

A taxpayer may deduct interest as an expense only if he or she uses the borrowed money for earning income from a business or investment property. Interest is not deductible for the purposes of earning capital gains, which are a separate source of income.[108] Thus, a taxpayer who borrows to buys shares can deduct interest if he or she reasonably expects that the shares will pay dividends. The *amount* of dividends expected or received is not determinative.[109] However, the taxpayer is not entitled to a deduction if she expects to earn only capital gains when she sells the shares. This distinction causes taxpayers to "hide" the interest, for example, in bond discounts and premiums.

The use test traces the direct flow of funds to determine how one applies the borrowed money. It is the actual, and not the alleged, uses of borrowed money that determines the deductibility of interest payable on the funds.[110] In *Sinha v. M.N.R.*,[111] for example, a student borrowed from the Canada Student Loan Plan at a low rate of interest and reinvested the borrowed funds at a higher rate. The Board rejected the Minister's argument that the purpose of the borrowing was personal and allowed the taxpayer to deduct his interest expense since he *actually* used the borrowed money for investment purposes.

---

[108]See., e.g., *Ludmer v. M.N.R.*, [1993] 1 C.T.C. 2494, 93 D.T.C. 1351 (T.C.C.) (interest on money used to purchase shares not deductible if *income* from shares cannot yield profit); *Ludco Enterprises Ltd. v. Canada*, [1999] 3 C.T.C. 601, 99 D.T.C. 5153 (F.C.A.); *Hastings v. M.N.R.*, [1988] 2 C.T.C. 2001, 88 D.T.C. 1391 (T.C.C.) (interest expense on commodities trades not deductible); *Sterling v. The Queen*, [1985] C.T.C. 275, 85 D.T.C. 5199 (F.C.A.) (interest and safekeeping charges for purchase of gold bullion not deductible in determining capital gain); *The Queen v. Can. Pacific Ltd.*, [1977] C.T.C. 606, 77 D.T.C. 5383 (F.C.A.) (deduction of interest under old subs. 8(3) only allowable where corporation subject to Part I tax); *Birmingham Corp. v. Barnes*, [1935] A.C. 292 (clarification of capital costs for laying tramway lines where expenditure contributed to by another party).

[109]*Ludco Enterprises Ltd. v. Canada*, *ibid.*, at para. 59.

[110]*Bronfman Trust v. The Queen*, [1987] 1 S.C.R. 32, [1987] 1 C.T.C. 117, 87 D.T.C. 5059 (S.C.C.).

[111]*Sinha v. M.N.R.*, [1981] C.T.C. 2599, 81 D.T.C. 465 (T.R.B.).

6. — Purpose of Borrowing

The second test of interest deductibility is that the taxpayer must use the funds for the *purpose* of earning income from business or property. Thus, the taxpayer must have a *bona fide* intention to use the borrowed money for an income-earning purpose. Earning income from business or property need not be the primary or dominant purpose for borrowing. Absent a sham or window dressing, the taxpayer's ancillary purpose to earn income is equally capable of providing the requisite purpose.[112] In addition, whether he or she actually realizes income is irrelevant. The purpose test is concerned solely with intention. The two tests are, however, inter-related:[113]

> Eligibility for the deduction is contingent on the use of borrowed money for the purpose of earning income .... it is not the purpose of the borrowing itself which is relevant. What is relevant, rather, is the taxpayer's purpose in using the borrowed money in a particular manner. ... Consequently, the focus of the inquiry must be centred on *the use to which the taxpayer put the borrowed funds*. [Emphasis added.]

Further, in *Shell Canada*,[114] the Supreme Court said:

> The issue is the use to which the borrowed funds are put. It is irrelevant why the borrowing arrangement was structured the way that it was or, indeed, why the funds were borrowed at all.

For example, a taxpayer who borrows money at a given rate of interest and then lends the money at less than his or her borrowing cost cannot be said to be using the money for the *purpose of* earning income. The absence of an intention to earn income makes the interest non-deductible. There may be limited circumstances, however, where a person borrows money and lends it at a lower rate for the purpose of helping a major customer survive economic hardship. The courts accept the indirect purpose of such transactions.

We determine the purpose of borrowing by tracing the direct and immediate use of the borrowed funds into the income-earning process.[115] The deduction is not available where the link between the borrowed money and an eligible use is merely indirect. Interest is deductible only if there is a sufficiently direct link between the borrowed money and the current eligible use.[116] It also does not necessarily matter if the borrowed funds are commingled with funds used for another purpose, provided that the borrowed funds can in fact be traced

---

[112]*Ludco Enterprises Ltd. v. Canada*, [1999] 3 C.T.C. 601, 99 D.T.C. 5153 (F.C.A.), at para. 51.

[113]*Bronfman Trust v. The Queen*, [1987] 1 S.C.R. 32, [1987] 1 C.T.C. 117, 87 D.T.C. 5059 (S.C.C.) at 125 [C.T.C.] and 5064 [D.T.C.].

[114]*Shell Canada Ltd. v. Canada*, [1999] 3 S.C.R. 622, [1999] 4 C.T.C. 313, 99 D.T.C. 5669 (S.C.C.).

[115]*Singleton v. Canada* (2001), [2001] 2 S.C.R. 1046, [2002] 1 C.T.C. 121, 204 D.L.R. (4th) 564, 2001 D.T.C. 5533 (Eng.) (S.C.C.).

[116]*Tennant v. M.N.R.*, [1996] 1 S.C.R. 305, [1996] 1 C.T.C. 290, 1996 D.T.C. 6121 (S.C.C.).

to a current eligible use.[117] Thus, taxpayers should borrow for income-earning activities and pay for personal consumption through savings. In *Singleton*, for example, the taxpayer, a partner in a law firm, withdrew $300,000 from his capital account in the firm to purchase his home, which he registered in the name of his wife. Later on the same day, he borrowed an identical amount from the bank and replenished his capital account in the firm. The taxpayer could deduct his interest on the bank borrowing because the funds were directly traceable to the business. Tax minimization as a motive is not a bar to the deduction of an expense. Taxpayers can arrange their affairs for the sole purpose of achieving favourable tax results.[118] Tax avoidance is not, *per se*, offensive. Absent statutory language, business transactions do not require an independent business purpose.[119]

Thus, the form of borrowing, not its economic substance, determines the deductibility of interest expense. Interest on debt that only indirectly earns income is not deductible for tax purposes under paragraph 20(1)(c). In *Bronfman Trust*,[120] for example, the settlor created a trust in favour of his daughter under which she would receive 50 per cent of its income and such additional allocations as the trustees in their discretion might decide. The trust invested its capital in income-earning securities.

When the trustees decided to make a capital distribution of $2 million to the beneficiary, they chose to borrow the funds rather than liquidate capital to make the payment. The decision to borrow was based on business reasons. It was financially inexpedient to liquidate any portion of the trust's investments at that time. By borrowing money for the capital distribution, the trustees preserved the income-yielding capacity of the trust's investments. The Supreme Court held that the economic substance of the underlying transactions did not justify deduction of the interest on the borrowing. Chief Justice Dickson said:[121]

> In my view, the text of the Act requires tracing the use of borrowed funds to a specific eligible use, its obviously restricted purpose being the encouragement of taxpayers to augment their income-producing potential. This, in my view, precludes the allowance of a deduction for interest paid on borrowed funds which indirectly preserve income-earning property but which are not directly "used for the purpose of earning income from ... property".

---

[117]*Shell Canada Ltd. v. Canada*, [1999] 3 S.C.R. 622, [1999] 4 C.T.C. 313, 99 D.T.C. 5669 (S.C.C.).

[118]See *Neuman v. M.N.R.*, [1998] 1 S.C.R. 147, [1998] 2 C.T.C. 35, 98 D.T.C. 6297 (S.C.C.): "The ITA has many specific anti-avoidance provisions and rules governing the treatment of non-arm's length transactions. We should not be quick to embellish the provision at issue here when it is open for the legislator to be precise and specific with respect to any mischief to be avoided."

[119]*Stubart Invt. Ltd. v. The Queen*, [1984] 1 S.C.R. 536, [1984] C.T.C. 294, 84 D.T.C. 6305 (S.C.C.); *Neuman v. M.N.R.*, [1998] 1 S.C.R. 147, [1998] 2 C.T.C. 35 (S.C.C.) "Taxpayers can arrange their affairs in a particular way for the sole purpose if deliberately availing themselves of tax reduction devices in the ITA."

[120]*Bronfman Trust v. The Queen*, [1987] 1 S.C.R. 32, [1987] 1 C.T.C. 117, 87 D.T.C. 5059 (S.C.C.).

[121]*Bronfman Trust v. The Queen*, *ibid.*, at 129 [C.T.C.] and 5067 [D.T.C.].

This principle applies equally to all taxpayers, including corporations, trusts and individuals.[122]

However, in *Shell Canada*,[123] the Supreme Court held that while transforming funds into a different currency changed its legal form and relative value, it did not change its substance — it remained money. Hence, there was no change in current use. McLachlin, J. stated:

> The mere fact that an exchange had to occur before usable money was produced is not particularly significant. Except where the borrower is a money trader, borrowed money can rarely itself produce income. It must always be exchanged for something, whether it be machinery or goods, which then produces income. The necessity of such an exchange does not mean the eventual production of income is an indirect use of the borrowed money.

7. — *Expectation of Income*

The deductibility of interest depends upon the intention of the borrower at the time that he or she invests the funds. The investment in business or property must have the potential to yield "income". "Income" in the context of section 20(1)(c)(i) means *gross* income, not *net* income. Thus, it is not necessary to make a taxable profit in order to deduct the interest expense. It is sufficient that the taxpayer had a reasonable expectation at the time the investment was made of earning an amount that would come into income for taxation purposes.[124] Moreover, it is irrelevant whether the invested funds actually produce income.[125] For example, interest on borrowed funds invested in a business venture that loses money is deductible if the taxpayer has a reasonable, albeit frustrated, expectation of earning some income.

In this context, it is important to emphasize that the intention must be to earn income from business or property and *not* from capital gains. Income from capital gains is not income

---

[122]*Bronfman Trust v. The Queen, ibid.*

[123]*Shell Canada Ltd. v. Canada*, [1999] 3 S.C.R. 622, [1999] 4 C.T.C. 313, 99 D.T.C. 5669 (S.C.C.).

[124]*Ludco Enterprises Ltd. v. Canada*, [1999] 3 C.T.C. 601, 99 D.T.C. 5153 (Fed. C.A.), at para. 61.

[125]See: *Lessard v. M.N.R.*, [1993] 1 C.T.C. 2176, 93 D.T.C. 680 (T.C.C.) (interest on funds used to acquire shares deductible even though taxpayer was sole shareholder, because shares constituted a potential source of income).

from property.[126] Thus, interest expenses *solely* to earn capital gains are not deductible in computing income from business or property.[127]

8. — Current Use

It is quite clear that it is the *current*, and not the original, use of funds that determines the deductibility of interest expense. As Jackett P. said in *Trans-Prairie*:[128]

> ... interest should be deductible for the years in which the borrowed capital is employed in the business rather than that it should be deductible for the life of a loan as long as its first use was in the business. ...

Similarly, in *Bronfman Trust*:[129]

> ... a taxpayer who uses or intends to use borrowed money for an ineligible purpose, but later uses the funds to earn non-exempt income from a business or property, ought not to be deprived of the deduction for the current, eligible use.

Hence, change of use can affect deductibility. For example, if a taxpayer initially borrows money to invest in bonds, and later sells the bonds and uses the money to take a vacation, the interest expense ceases to qualify as a deduction from the date of the change of use of the borrowing.[130] Conversely, interest on funds initially borrowed for personal purposes and later used for business purposes qualifies for deduction as of the date of change of use. For example, a taxpayer who borrows money to purchase a residential cottage for personal use, and then sells the cottage and uses the proceeds to buy shares, can deduct the interest on the borrowed funds as of the date of the investment.

---

[126]Subs. 9(3). See: *Ludmer v. M.N.R.*, [1993] 2 C.T.C. 2494, 93 D.T.C. 1351 (T.C.C.); affd. [1994] 1 C.T.C. 368, 94 D.T.C. 6221 (F.C.T.D.); affirmed [1999] 3 C.T.C. 601, 99 D.T.C. 5153 (Eng.) (Fed. C.A.); leave to appeal allowed 2000 Carswell 651, 255 N.R. 200 (note) (S.C.C.); reversed [2002] 1 C.T.C. 95, 2001 D.T.C. 5505 (Eng.) (S.C.C.); *Hugill v. R.*, [1995] 2 C.T.C. 16, 95 D.T.C. 5311 (Fed. C.A.).

[127]*Bronfman Trust v. The Queen, ante.* ("... The fact that the loan may have prevented capital losses cannot assist the taxpayer in obtaining a deduction from income which is limited to use of borrowed money for the purpose of earning income.") See also: *The Queen v. Mandryk*, [1992] 1 C.T.C. 317, 92 D.T.C. 6329 (Fed. C.A.) (taxpayer not entitled to deduct interest expense to honour personal guarantees of corporate indebtedness).

[128]*Trans-Prairie Pipelines Ltd. v. M.N.R.*, [1970] C.T.C. 537 at 541, 70 D.T.C. 6351 at 6354 (Ex. Ct.); approved by S.C.C. in *Bronfman Trust v. The Queen.*

[129]*Bronfman Trust v. The Queen*, [1987] 1 S.C.R. 32, [1987] 1 C.T.C. 117, 87 D.T.C. 5059 (S.C.C.) at 5065 [D.T.C.]

[130]Subpara. 20(1)(c)(i).

9. — Reloaned Funds

As with initial borrowings, where an individual borrows money and then lends the money to his or her corporation, the deductibility of the interest paid by the individual depends upon the *purpose* of the lending. Where an individual borrows at a commercial rate of interest and loans at a lower rate, he or she cannot generally be borrowing for the *purpose* of earning income. Hence, any interest payable on the funds is *prima facie* not deductible. The CRA, does, however allow a deduction to the extent that the individual actually earns income. In certain cases, there is a full deduction of the interest expense even though the individual loans the funds at a lower rate than the cost of his or her borrowing.[131]

10. — Exempt Income

Interest expense is deductible only if one incurs it to earn income from business or property and the income is taxable. Interest expense is not deductible if the taxpayer uses the funds to earn income that is exempt or to acquire a life insurance policy.[132]

11. — Compound Interest

A taxpayer can deduct interest on interest, that is, compound interest, if he or she meets all of the other conditions of deductibility.[133] Compound interest, however, is only deductible when it is paid and not when it is merely payable.

12. — Bond Discounts

A bond is a legal obligation that acknowledges debt. Typically, the debt obligation entitles its owner to periodic payments and, eventually, on a stated date to the repayment of the principal (face value) of the debt. A bond has a nominal interest rate, which is the rate that the contract specifies in relation to the face value of the debt. Assume that a corporation issues bonds each of which has a face value of $1,000. The stated or nominal interest rate is 8 per cent payable annually and the principal is repayable in 25 years. Thus, the purchaser of the bond can expect interest payments of $80 at the end of each year and a lump sum repay-

---

[131]See IT-533, "Interest Deductibility and Related Issues" (October 31, 2003) and *Canadian Helicopters*, [2002] 2 C.T.C. 83, 2002 D.T.C. 6805 (Fed. C.A.).

[132]See para. 20(1)(c). "Exempt income" is defined as property received or acquired by a person in such circumstances that it is, because of any provision in Part I, not included in computing the person's income, but does not include a dividend on a share or a support amount. See para. 248(1) "exempt income".

[133]Para. 20(1)(d).

ment of principal at the end of 25 years. The nominal rate of interest is 8 per cent. If the market rate of interest is also 8 per cent, the present value of the bond is exactly equal to its face value ($1,000).

Present Value of future income stream is:

$80 per year × Present value* of annuity (10.6748)   = $ 854

$1,000 × Present value** of future sum   =   146

Total Present Value of Bond   = $ 1,000

Notes:

*   Present value of a future annuity at 8 per cent for 25 years equals 10.6748.

**   Present value of a future amount at 8 per cent for 25 years equals 0.1460.

The present value of the bond depends upon the annual cash flow ($80), the discount rate (8 per cent), the number of years outstanding (25) and the face value of the principal amount ($1,000) payable at the end of the contract. The price that a rational investor will be willing to pay for the bond today is $1,000, that is, an amount equal to the present value of its future cash flows. This is entirely logical as the nominal contractual interest rate is exactly equal to the market rate of interest.

Now assume that the market rate of interest rises to 10 per cent while the nominal contractual rate of interest remains at 8 per cent. The present value of the bond falls to $818.

Present Value of income stream is:

$80 per year × Present value* of annuity (9.0770)   = $726

$1,000 × Present value** of future sum   =   92

Total Present Value of Bond   = $818

Notes:

*   Present value of a future annuity at 10 per cent for 25 years equals 9.0770.

**   Present value of a future amount at 10 per cent for 25 years equals 0.0923.

If a new investor buys the bond for $818, his or her annual yield is $80/$818 or 9.78 per cent. In addition, the investor will realize a gain of $182, that is, $1,000 minus $818 if he or she holds the bond to maturity. The combination of the interest yield and the gain provides an effective annual yield of 10 per cent over the life of the bond. Thus, the increase in the market rate of interest causes the capital value of the bond to fall, which raises the effective rate of interest to market levels.

It is arguable in law that, for tax purposes, the gain of $182 is an "appreciation gain" that results from holding the asset to maturity. In economic terms, however, what we really have is an increase in the interest income that the bondholder earns to reflect the change in the market rate of interest. It is entirely irrelevant to a bondholder who holds to maturity whether he or she earns 10 per cent annually on a face value of $1,000 or 8 per cent annually on a discounted value of $818 plus a lump sum gain upon maturity. In either case, the bondholder's effective yield to maturity is 10 per cent. This is the inevitable substantive result in efficient capital markets.

A discount is the amount by which the face or nominal value of a debt obligation exceeds its issue or selling price. In the above example, the bond discount is $182. The discount can arise on an initial issuance of the obligation or later in accordance with market fluctuations in interest rates. A corporation can, for example, choose to issue a $1,000 face value bond for $818 in order to increase the effective interest rate for the bondholder. Tax law taxes capital gains at a lower rate than interest income. Thus, applying purely legal principles, form prevails over substance and the bondholder effectively converts $182 of interest income into capital gains if the corporation issues the bond at an initial discount of that amount.

The capital value of a bond also fluctuates with the time remaining to maturity. Continuing with the above example, assume that the $1,000 bond has a nominal rate of 8 per cent and 20 years remaining to maturity. If the market rate of interest is 10 per cent, the bond has a capital value of $830.

Present Value of income stream is:

$80 per year × Present value* of annuity (8.5136)	=	$681
$1,000 × Present value** of future sum (0.1486)	=	149
Total Present Value of Bond	=	$830

Notes:

*   Present value of a future annuity at 10 per cent for 20 years equals 8.5136.

**   Present value of a future amount at 10 per cent for 20 years equals 0.1486.

The value of the bond has increased from $818 to $830 in five years because the bond is that much closer to maturity and the eventual payout of the face value of $1000. At a price of $830 the bond has an effective yield of 10 per cent. Once again, the effective yield comprises two components: the annual interest yield of 80/830 = 9.64 per cent; and the capital gain of $170 over the next 20 years.

The Act recognizes the potential for transforming fully taxable income into capital gains and regulates the treatment of initial issue bond discounts. In effect, the statute looks through the form of the initial issuance of a bond to its economic substance. Discounts on bonds may be deductible in whole or in part in the year paid.[134] Where an issuer floats an obligation at a price of at least 97 per cent of its principal amount and the obligation does not yield an amount in excess of 4/3 of the nominal interest rate, the entire amount of the discount is deductible in computing income. In contrast, where the issuer floats a bond for an amount less than 97 per cent of its face amount, or its yield exceeds 4/3 of its nominal interest rate, only 50 per cent of the discount is deductible in computing income. In the above example, the discounted price of the bond is less than 97 per cent of its face value but the effective yield does not exceed 4/3 of the nominal interest rate.[135] Hence, the issuer can deduct only 50 per cent of the discount as interest expense. A discount on a debt obligation that does not normally stipulate an interest rate (for example, strip coupon bonds) is considered interest if the discount is reasonable in the circumstances.

13. — Refinancing

Where a taxpayer borrows money to repay money that he or she previously borrowed, the Act deems the taxpayer to incur the second borrowing for the same purposes as the original borrowing.[136]

14. — Existence of Source

An essential requirement for the deduction of interest is that the source of income to which the interest expense relates must continue to exist.[137] Thus, interest on borrowed money must be traceable to a current eligible use in order for the expense to be deductible. For example, a taxpayer who finances the purchase of shares may claim any directly related interest expense as a deduction only if he or she continues to hold the original investment or substituted securities. This is so even if the security declines in value or becomes worthless.

---

[134]Para. 20(1)(f).

[135]The effective interest rate of 10 per cent. 4/3 of 8% = 10.67%.

[136]Subs. 20(3); see also ATR-4 "Exchange of Interest Rates" (November 29, 1985) (archived).

[137]*Emerson v. The Queen*, [1986] 1 C.T.C. 422, 86 D.T.C. 6184 (F.C.A.); leave to appeal to S.C.C. refused (1986), 70 N.R. 160 (taxpayer not allowed to deduct interest on money used to purchase shares after selling shares at loss); see also *Deschenes v. M.N.R.*, [1979] C.T.C. 2690, 79 D.T.C. 461 (T.R.B.); *Alexander v. M.N.R.*, [1983] C.T.C. 2516, 83 D.T.C. 459 (T.R.B.); *Lyons v. M.N.R.*, [1984] C.T.C. 2690, 84 D.T.C. 1633 (T.C.C.); *McKay v. M.N.R.*, [1984] C.T.C. 2805, 84 D.T.C. 1699 (T.C.C.); *Botkin v. M.N.R.*, [1989] 2 C.T.C. 2110, 89 D.T.C. 398 (T.C.C.); *The Queen v. Malik*, [1989] 1 C.T.C. 316, 89 D.T.C. 5141 (F.C.T.D.); *Dockman v. M.N.R.*, [1990] 2 C.T.C. 2229, 90 D.T.C. 1804 (T.C.C.); *Kornelow v. M.N.R.*, [1991] 1 C.T.C. 2403, 91 D.T.C. 431 (T.C.C.).

Section 20.1 does, however, allow one to deduct interest in certain circumstances even where borrowed money ceases to be used to earn income because the source of the income no longer exists.[138]

15. — Accrued Interest

The purchaser of a debt obligation (other than an income bond, income debenture, small business development bond, or small business bond) can deduct accrued interest (that is, interest earned but not paid) to the date of the purchase to the extent that he or she includes the amount as interest in computing income for the year. At the same time, the vendor of the debt includes the accrued interest in computing its income.[139]

16. — Financing Costs

A taxpayer can deduct expenses that he or she incurs in issuing shares or in borrowing money for the purpose of earning income from a business or property.[140] Such financing expenses, which typically include legal and accounting fees, printing costs, commissions, etc., would otherwise be caught by the prohibition against deducting expenses not *directly* related to the income-earning process.[141] These expenses are deductible on a rateable basis over a five-year period.

17. — Capitalizing Interest

In certain circumstances, a taxpayer may prefer not to write off interest expense against current operations. For example, there may be little advantage in taking a deduction for interest expense on money borrowed to construct an asset if the asset is not producing income. Where the deduction of interest would merely create a loss that the taxpayer cannot

---

[138]See Department of Finance examples in its technical notes to the section.

[139]Subs. 20(14); IT-410R "Debt Obligations — Accrued Interest on Transfer" (September 4, 1984) (archived). This rule only operates where there has been an assignment or transfer of title; evidence of registration of title would likely be necessary. See: *Hill v. M.N.R.*, [1981] C.T.C. 2120, 81 D.T.C. 167 (T.R.B.) ("bond flip"; interest payment for carrying cost of bonds not deductible); *Smye v. M.N.R.*, [1980] C.T.C. 2372, 80 D.T.C. 1326 (T.R.B.) (purchase of bonds plus accrued interest; upon sale, taxpayer deducted price for accrued interest from investment yield of bond).

[140]Para. 20(1)(e).

[141]*Montreal Light, Heat & Power Consol. v. M.N.R.*, [1944] C.T.C. 94, 2 D.T.C. 654 (P.C.); *The Queen v. Royal Trust Corp. of Can.*, [1983] C.T.C. 159, 83 D.T.C. 5172 (F.C.A.) (whether or not payment constitutes "commission" is a question of fact).

use within the time limits allowed for carryover of losses,[142] the taxpayer may prefer to treat the interest charges as part of the cost of the asset. He or she can then write off the total cost of the asset when it begins to produce income. In other words, the taxpayer may prefer to treat interest costs as a capital expenditure rather than as a current expense.

(a) — Depreciable Property

A taxpayer who acquires depreciable property with borrowed money may elect to capitalize the interest charges.[143] Two points warrant mention. First, the taxpayer may capitalize only those costs that would *otherwise have been deductible* as interest expense or as an expense of borrowing money. Interest expense to earn exempt income is not deductible and cannot be capitalized. Second, the election is available not only in respect of costs the taxpayer incurs in the year that he or she acquires the asset but also costs he or she incurs in the three immediately preceding taxation years. The extension of the election to the three preceding years recognizes that large undertakings extend over many years and that money may be borrowed, and expenses incurred, prior to the period in which the money is actually used for its intended purpose of constructing a capital asset.

(b) — Election

The election must be made for the taxation year in which:

- The depreciable property is *acquired*, or

- The money borrowed has been used for exploration, development, or the acquisition of property.

A taxpayer cannot elect to capitalize interest in anticipation of the acquisition of depreciable property or the use of borrowed money for exploration or development. The taxpayer can elect *only after* acquiring the property or expending the funds. Upon election, however, it becomes effective for the borrowing costs and interest of the current and the three preceding years.

A taxpayer may elect under subsection 21(1) only for the taxation year in which he or she acquires the depreciable property. Where the taxpayer erects a building or other structure, he or she is considered to acquire it at any time to the extent of the construction costs at that

---

[142]See para. 111(1)(a) (limitation period in respect of non-capital losses).

[143]S. 21. Special restrictions on "soft costs" are discussed below; see subs. 18(3.1).

time. Hence, a taxpayer must file a separate election for each taxation year in respect of the interest expense related to that year.[144]

The election does not have to be made in respect of the full amount of the costs of borrowing; a taxpayer may elect to capitalize only part of the interest charges and deduct the remainder as a current expense.

The portion of the interest that the taxpayer capitalizes is added to the capital cost of the depreciable property that he or she acquires. Thus, the capitalized cost will eventually be written off through capital cost allowances. The adjusted cost base of the property will also be increased for the purpose of determining capital gains upon disposition of the property.[145]

(c) — Reassessment

Where the taxpayer elects to capitalize interest charges that would otherwise have been deductible in preceding years, the Minister must reassess the taxpayer for those taxation years. Having made the election, the taxpayer may continue to capitalize interest in succeeding years if in each of those succeeding years, he or she capitalizes the *entire* amount of the interest on the property.

(d) — Compound Interest

A taxpayer can also capitalize compound interest and the expense of raising money. For example, a taxpayer may pay a commitment fee to a financier before it advances the necessary funds. The commitment fee, or standby interest, may be capitalized as part of the cost of borrowed money.[146]

(e) — "Soft Costs"

"Soft costs" (such as interest expense, mortgage fees, property taxes, commitment fees, etc.) incurred in respect of the construction, renovation or alteration of a building, are not deductible as current expenses during construction, and must be added to the cost of the build-

---

[144]This election is explained in the CRA's IT-121R3 "Election to Capitalize Cost of Borrowed Money" (May 6, 1988) (archived).

[145]S. 54 "adjusted cost base".

[146]*Sherritt Gordon Mines Ltd. v. M.N.R.*, [1968] C.T.C. 262, 68 D.T.C. 5180 (Ex. Ct.).

ing.[147] Similarly, "soft costs" in respect of land subjacent to a building under construction must be capitalized. The restriction on the deduction of these expenses only applies in respect of outlays incurred before completion of construction, renovation or alteration of the building.

The scope of the prohibition against writing off soft costs as current expenses is very broad. Included in interest expenses are expenses incurred on borrowed money used to finance working capital if it "*can reasonably be considered*" that the borrowed money freed up other funds for the construction of the building. In other words, "indirect financing" is caught by the prohibition.[148]

18. — Limitations on Deduction

(a) — Real Estate

A taxpayer cannot deduct carrying charges (interest and property taxes) in respect of vacant land to the extent that the expenses exceed income from the land.[149] Thus, carrying charges on land are deductible only to the extent of the taxpayer's net revenues from the land. The purpose of this rule is to discourage speculation in real estate.

Land that one uses in the course of a business is exempt from the limitation in respect of carrying charges for land. However, the exemption from the rule does not apply to property developers whose business is the sale or development of land, or to land that is held, but not used, in a business.

A special rule applies to corporations whose principal business is the leasing, rental, sale or development of real property. Corporations that engage in these businesses may deduct their carrying charges on vacant land. The maximum deduction is equal to the *total* of:[150]

- The income, net of all deductions, from the land, and

- The corporation's "base level deduction" for the year.

---

[147]Subs. 18(3.1). This rule does not apply to capital cost allowance, landscaping costs, disability related modifications to buildings under para. 20(1)(gg) and soft cots deductible under subsection 20(29).

[148]Subs. 18(3.2).

[149]Subs. 18(2).

[150]Subs. 18(2).

A corporation's base level deduction for a taxation year is the amount of interest for the year in respect of $1 million of debt outstanding for the year, computed at the prescribed rate of interest.[151]

For example, assume that a corporation in the land development business has total interest and property taxes of $150,000 on a piece of vacant land. Assume also that the land generates $20,000 of net income for the year and that the prescribed rate of interest is 8 per cent. Then, the maximum deduction for the year is $100,000. The remaining $50,000 is not deductible, but the taxpayer may add the amount to the cost of the land under para. 53(1)(h) (if capital) or subs. 10(1.1) (if inventory).

The base level deduction of a corporation that is a member of an associated group of corporations is determined by reference to a prescribed agreement that each corporation must file. The $1 million to which the prescribed rate is applied must be allocated amongst the associated members of the group.[152] The Minister has the power to allocate the deduction if the corporations do not file their agreements.[153]

XIII. — Capital Cost Allowance

1. — General Comment

We saw earlier that a taxpayer cannot deduct expenditures on account of capital outlays, depreciation, obsolescence, or depletion.[154] The prohibition against the deduction of depreciation and similar expenses flies in the face of accounting principles. The Act does, however, allow for the deduction of capital cost allowance (CCA) in lieu of such expenses. In computing income from a business or property, a taxpayer may deduct[155] "... such part of the capital cost to the taxpayer of property, or such amount in respect of the capital cost to the taxpayer of property, if any, as is allowed by regulation." Thus, a taxpayer cannot deduct depreciation calculated for financial statement purposes, but may claim a deduction for capital cost allowance, according to prescribed rules.

The basic concept underlying the capital cost allowance system is fairly straightforward: CCA is a deduction from income that is intended to allocate the approximate cost of capital assets over their useful lives. Thus, in a sense, the CCA system is nothing more than statu-

---

[151]Subs. 18(2.2); Reg. 4301(c).

[152]Subs. 18(2.3).

[153]Subs. 18(2.4).

[154]Para. 18(1)(b).

[155]Para. 20(1)(a); Regulations Pt. XI (Regs. 1100–1107). The phrase "capital cost allowance" refers to an allowance in respect of the capital cost of depreciable property.

tory depreciation at pre-determined rates. The technical application of the capital cost allowance system is, however, extremely complex. This is a result of the government use of the CCA system as an instrument of social, economic, and political policy. For example, the system sometimes stimulates investment through accelerated capital cost allowance; in other circumstances, the CCA system discourages particular types of investment by denying or restricting the allowance on those investments. For example, prior to 1988, the statute allowed for a rapid write-off of the cost of Canadian films. A taxpayer could claim 100 per cent of the cost of film ownership in one year. This was intended to encourage the development of Canadian culture. In 1988, the CCA rate was reduced to a 30 per cent write-off so as to discourage the use of films as tax shelters by high-income taxpayers. In either case, the CCA rate did not relate to the life of films.

2. — Structure

(a) — Classification

We must answer three basic questions in respect of the capital cost allowance system:

1. Is the capital property depreciable capital property?

2. To which class of assets does the property belong?

3. What is the rate of depreciation applicable to the particular class?

The CCA allows a taxpayer to deduct the actual cost of depreciable assets over a period of time.[156] The statute prescribes the rate at which a taxpayer can claim CCA on an asset. The rate is the same for all taxpayers with similar assets performing similar activities. The rates generally allow for generous write-offs. Thus, the deduction for tax purposes in the early years of an asset's life usually exceed the comparable depreciation allowed on the asset for accounting and financial statement purposes. Thus, in part at least, the capital cost allowance system compensates taxpayers for the effects of inflation on asset replacement costs. It also creates deferred tax accounting problems because of the difference between tax and accounting depreciation.

(b) — Permissive

The deduction of capital cost allowance is permissive: a taxpayer *may* claim capital cost allowance in a particular taxation year. The amount of capital cost allowance that a taxpayer may deduct in any year, however, is subject to prescribed upper limits. Thus, taxpayers have some flexibility in determining the amount of income they will recognize for tax purposes in any year.

---

[156]IT-285R2, "Capital Cost Allowance — General Comments" (March 31, 1994).

An asset is eligible for capital cost allowance only if it is described in one of the classes listed in the Regulations. The classes list most tangible assets that are expected to depreciate over time. The list also includes intangible assets with limited lives (such as patents and limited life franchises).[157]

(c) — General Structure

The general structure of the CCA system is as follows:

- A taxpayer can deduct CCA within the terms of the Statute and the Regulations.

- The Regulations group eligible assets into prescribed classes that have approximately similar lives.

- The balance in each class at any point in time is its undepreciated capital cost (UCC).

- The UCC of each class is increased by acquisitions in that class.

- Each class is subject to a *maximum* percentage rate of capital cost allowance.

- The balance is reduced by dispositions and by the deduction of amounts of capital cost allowance claimed.

- A taxpayer may deduct a portion or all the allowance prescribed, or forgo the claim in a particular year and postpone amortization of the class of assets to later years.

- CCA can be claimed only when assets are available for use.

- The diminishing balance, rather than the straight line,[158] method is used in computing the annual allowance for most classes of assets. Each year, the specified rate is applied to the UCC remaining in the class after deduction of amounts previously allowed.

- The balance remaining to be depreciated diminishes until the taxpayer acquires new assets of the class.

- Proceeds from the disposition of assets reduce the balance of the class, up to a maximum equal to the cost of the asset.

- On disposal of assets, capital cost allowance previously taken is "recaptured" to the extent that the proceeds of disposition exceed the UCC of the group of assets in the particular class.

---

[157]Regs., Part XI (1100–1107); Sched. II.

[158]The straight line method may be used in a few situations, e.g., depreciation of Class 13 leasehold interests.

- The UCC of a class can never be a negative amount. If the proceeds from a disposition of assets exceed the UCC of the class and, therefore, reduce it below zero, the excess amount is immediately recaptured into income.

- Where the proceeds of disposition of an asset exceed its original capital cost, the excess is a capital gain.

- Upon disposal of *all* the assets in a particular class, any remaining balance of UCC for the class is deductible in the year as a "terminal loss".

The following example illustrates these relationships.

Example

Assume:

In Year 1 a taxpayer acquires one tangible asset to which the following data applies:

Capital cost	$ 10,000
Capital cost allowance claimed	$ 2,000

In Year 2 the taxpayer disposes of the asset, which is the only asset in its class. Assume, alternatively, that the taxpayer receives the following amounts:

Example (A)	$ 11,000
Example (B)	$ 9,000
Example (C)	$ 6,000

Then:

	(A)	(B)	(C)
Capital cost	$ 10,000	$ 10,000	$ 10,000
CCA claimed	(2,000)	(2,000)	(2,000)
Undepreciated capital cost	$ 8,000	$ 8,000	$ 8,000
CCA recaptured	$ 2,000	$ 1,000	—
Capital gain	$ 1,000	—	—
Terminal loss	—	—	$ (2,000)

3. — Depreciable Property

Capital cost allowance is claimable only on depreciable property of a prescribed class.[159] "Depreciable property" is defined as "property acquired by the taxpayer in respect of which the taxpayer has been allowed, or ... [is] entitled to, 'capital cost allowance'."[160] This definition is not very helpful.

The Act sets out certain properties that are excluded from the prescribed classes. For example, the following properties are *not* eligible for capital cost allowance:

- Property, the cost of which is *deductible as an* ordinary expense.[161]

- Property that is "described in" or is part of, the taxpayer's inventory.[162]

- Property not acquired for the purpose of gaining or producing income.[163]

- Property for which the taxpayer is entitled to a deduction for scientific research.[164]

- Property that is a yacht, camp, lodge, golf course, or facility if any part of the maintenance costs are not deductible because of subpara. 18(1)(l)(i).[165]

- Certain works of art created by non-residents.[166]

- Land.[167]

- Animals, trees and plants, radium, intangible assets, rights of way.[168]

- Property situated outside of Canada that belongs to a non-resident.[169]

---

[159]Reg. 1100(1)(a).

[160]Subs. 248(1)"depreciable property" and para. 13(21)"depreciable property".

[161]Reg. 1102(1)(a).

[162]Reg. 1102(1)(b). See Chapter 7, "The Meaning of Business Income, Investment Income, and Capital Gains" for distinction between income from business on sale of inventory and capital gains on sale of capital assets. See also IT-128R, "CCA — Depreciable Property" (May 21, 1985) and IT-102R2, "Conversion of Property, Other than Real Property, From or to Inventory" (July 22, 1985).

[163]Reg. 1102(1)(c).

[164]Reg. 1102(1)(d).

[165]Reg. 1102(1)(f).

[166]Reg. 1102(1)(e).

[167]Reg. 1102(2).

[168]Reg., Sched. II, Class 8, subpara. (i).

[169]Reg. 1102(3).

4. — Classes

A taxpayer may claim capital cost allowance on depreciable property of a prescribed class. Schedule II describes the principal classes of property.

The general rule is that similar properties are placed in the same class and, therefore, are subject to the same rate of allowance. For example, all of a taxpayer's automobiles costing $30,000 (prescribed amount effective 2005) or less would be placed in Class 10, and the capital cost allowance claimed at the rate applicable to that class. Similarly, all passenger vehicles costing more than $30,000 each[170] are grouped in Class 10.1.

There are, however, some exceptions to the general rule. Some similar properties are segregated into separate classes. The effect of segregating similar properties into separate classes is that the provisions relating to "recapture" and "terminal loss" are then applied separately to each property rather than to a collective whole. The principal reason for maintaining separate classes is to accelerate the timing of recapture of capital cost allowance that might otherwise be wholly or partially deferred by subsequent acquisitions of similar properties. For example, each rental property having a cost of $50,000 or more constitutes a separate class of property.[171] Hence, it is not possible to defer recapture of capital cost allowance upon a disposition of one property by replacing it with a similar property in the same class and of the same type.[172]

In certain circumstances, a depreciable property may satisfy the requirements of two or more classes. The CRA takes the position that where the description of two or more possible classes includes the words "... property not included in any other class ..." and the property in question fits both classes, the taxpayer is entitled to choose the applicable class.[173] For example, a frame building acquired before 1979 could be included in Class 6; it is also a building for the purposes of Class 3. Since Classes 3 and 6 are both described to include "property not included in any other class", a taxpayer can choose to place the building in either Class 3 or Class 6. Note, however, that a brick building, for example, *must* be included in Class 3 since it is not described in Class 6.

---

[170]Para. 13(7)(g); Reg. 7307(1); Reg. Sched. II, classes 10 and 10.1.

[171]Regs. 1101(5b), 1101(lac).

[172]See "Recapture" section in this chapter.

[173]IT-285R2, "Capital Cost Allowance — General Comments" (March 31, 1994).

5. — *Capital Cost of Property*

(a) — *General Comment*

Capital cost allowance is based on the "capital cost" of an asset. One determines the capital cost of a property by calculating its laid-down acquisition cost.[174] Thus, the capital cost of an asset includes any legal, accounting, engineering, or other fees that the taxpayer incurs to acquire the property.

"Cost" refers to the actual cost of the property to the taxpayer, whether paid in money or some other property. Where the value of the consideration paid is not readily apparent (such as when payment is made by the issuance of shares), the taxpayer should obtain an appraisal to determine the capital cost of the property.[175]

"Cost" means the *entire laid-down cost* of equipment even though certain expensive parts of the equipment might require frequent replacement.[176] The cost of property paid for in foreign currency is its Canadian dollar equivalent as at the date of acquisition.[177]

Where a taxpayer manufactures an asset for personal use, all outlays attributable to the construction of the asset are included in its cost.[178] We determine cost according to generally accepted accounting principles.[179] For example, testing and start-up costs are part of the capital cost of assets.[180] In certain circumstances, a taxpayer may also capitalize interest

---

[174]Para. 20(1)(a); IT-285R2, "Capital Cost Allowance — General Comments" (March 31, 1994), paras. 8–12; see also R. M. Skinner, *Accounting Principles: A Canadian Viewpoint*, CICA (1972), at 5: "The recorded cost of a tangible capital asset should include all costs necessary to put the asset in a position to render service."

[175]*Tuxedo Hldg. Co. v. M.N.R.*, [1959] C.T.C. 172, 59 D.T.C. 1102 (Ex. Ct.); *Craddock v. Zevo Finance Co.*, [1944] 1 All E.R. 566; affd. [1946] 1 All E.R. 523n (H.L.) (price paid by company *prima facie* nominal value of shares but contrary may be established in appropriate cases).

[176]*MacMillan Bloedel (Alberni) Ltd. v. M.N.R.*, [1973] C.T.C. 295, 73 D.T.C. 5264 (F.C.T.D.) (taxpayer claimed cost of tires for logging equipment as current expense; practice held contrary to generally accepted accounting principles); see also *Cockshutt Farm Equip. of Can. Ltd. v. M.N.R.* (1966), 41 Tax A.B.C. 386, 66 D.T.C. 544 ("capital cost to the taxpayer" means actual, factual, or historical cost of depreciable property at time of acquisition).

[177]IT-285R2, "Capital Cost Allowance — General Comments" (March 31, 1994).

[178]See IT-285R2, "Capital Cost Allowance — General Comments" (March 31, 1994).

[179]*B.P. Refinery (Kwinana) Ltd. v. Fed. Commr. of Taxation*, [1961] A.L.R. 52, 12 A.T.D. 204 (H.C.).

[180]*Weinberger v. M.N.R.*, [1964] C.T.C. 103, 64 D.T.C. 5060 (Ex. Ct.).

costs as part of the capital cost of depreciable property, instead of deducting these costs as current expenses.[181]

Where a taxpayer acquires property by way of a gift, he or she is deemed to have acquired it at a cost equal to its fair market value at that time.[182] Inherited assets are also generally deemed to be acquired at a cost equal to their fair market value at the date of the taxpayer's death.[183] This rule is modified when the recipient of the gift or inheritance is the spouse of the donor.[184]

(b) — Foreign Currency Transactions

It is a fundamental principle of tax law that income is measured in local currency. Thus, we convert foreign currency transactions into Canadian dollars. Generally, the translation of foreign currency into Canadian dollars must be at the exchange rate prevailing on the date of the particular transaction. For example, where a taxpayer acquires a capital asset in the United States, the capital cost of the asset will be its purchase price translated into Canadian dollars, plus any duties, taxes, shipping charges, insurance fees, and handling costs.

Assets that are purchased and sold in foreign currencies may trigger a gain or loss in Canadian dollars. It is important to distinguish between the portion of a gain or loss that is attributable to the intrinsic market value of the asset itself and the portion that is attributable to foreign exchange fluctuations between the time of purchase of the asset and the time of its disposition. The foreign exchange gain or loss from holding the asset is to be accounted for separately from the purchase and sale of the asset. The foreign exchange gain or loss is not an adjustment to the cost of the property acquired or sold.

---

[181]Para. 21(1)(b); *Sherritt Gordon Mines Ltd. v. M.N.R.*, [1968] C.T.C. 262 at 283, 68 D.T.C. 5180 at 5193 (Ex. Ct.) it was stated that:

> ... at least where the amount is significant in relation to the business of a company, it is in accordance with generally accepted business and commercial principles to charge, as a cost of construction, payments of interest in respect of the construction period on borrowed money expended by the company for such construction and to write such payments off over a period of years.

See also *Lions Equipment Ltd. v. M.N.R.* (1963), 34 Tax A.B.C. 221, 63 D.T.C. 35 (limitation of deduction to actual source of farming income; hoped-for source excluded); *Ben-Odeco Ltd. v. Powlson* (1978), 52 Tax Cas. 459 (H.L.) (commitment fees and interest charges on loan used to acquire capital asset not included in capital cost despite accord with accounting principles); *S.I.R. v. Eaton Hall (Pty.) Ltd.* (1975), (4) S.A. 953, 37 S.A.T.C. 343 (A.D.).

[182]Para. 69(1)(c).

[183]Subs. 70(5).

[184]Para. 70(6)(c).

Gains and losses on account of foreign exchange transactions are capital gains (losses) or revenue gains (losses) and treated according to the rules applicable to each category. The characterization of foreign exchange gains and losses generally depends upon the nature of the property that gives rise to the gain or loss. Hence, gains and losses on account of inventory transactions are business income (losses); gains and losses on account of capital transactions are capital gains (losses).

Foreign exchange gains and losses on account of income transactions are included in the taxpayer's income according to the general rules.[185] In contrast, the capital gains rules govern foreign exchange gains and losses on account of capital transactions.[186]

(c) — Change of Use of Property

The statute deems a change of use of property to be a disposition. Thus, where a taxpayer changes the use of depreciable property acquired for the purpose of earning income to personal use, he or she is deemed to dispose of the property for proceeds equal to its fair market value. Concurrently, the taxpayer is deemed to reacquire the property at a cost equal to its fair market value.[187] Hence, a change of use can trigger a capital gain, a recapture of capital cost allowance, or a terminal loss.

A change in use of property from personal to business purposes also triggers a deemed disposition of the property. Here, however, the rules are more complicated. The taxpayer's cost of acquisition is determined as follows:

- Where the fair market value at the time of change in use of the property is[188] less than its capital cost, the acquisition is equal to fair market value;

- Where fair market value is more than its capital cost, the acquisition cost is limited to the aggregate of the cost of the property and 1/2 of the excess of fair market value over its cost, to the extent that the taxpayer did not claim a capital gains exemption for that excess.

These rules also apply where there is a split between personal and business usage.

---

[185]S. 9.

[186]Subs. 39(2).

[187]Para. 13(7)(a).

[188]Para. 13(7)(b).

(d) — Non-Arm's Length Transactions

There are special rules for determining the cost of depreciable property acquired in non-arm's length transfers. The following outlines some of the more frequently encountered non-arm's length property acquisitions:

Description	Reference
Depreciable property acquired from person or partnership	para. 13(7)(e)
Bequest of farm property to child	subss. 70(9), (9.1)
Gift of farm property to child	subs. 73(3)
Transfer to corporation from shareholder	subs. 85(1)
Transfer to corporation from partnership	subs. 85(2)
Winding up of partnership	subs. 85(3)
Amalgamation	subs. 87(2)
Winding up of 90 per cent owned Canadian subsidiary	subss. 88(1)–(1.6)
Contribution of property to partnership	subs. 97(2)
Rules applicable where partnership ceases to exist	subss. 98(3), (5)

(e) — Luxury Automobiles

The Act limits the maximum capital cost of passenger vehicles to $30,000, exclusive of provincial sales tax and GST.[189] The capital cost of a passenger vehicle that has an actual cost in excess of $30,000 is deemed to be $30,000. This amount is adjusted periodically to account for inflation and changed circumstances.[190]

Paragraph 13(7)(h) prevents the $30,000 limit on the depreciable capital cost of a passenger vehicle from being circumvented by a transfer of the vehicle between parties not dealing with each other at arm's length. Where a taxpayer acquires a passenger vehicle from a person with whom he does not deal at arm's length, the capital cost of the vehicle to the taxpayer is the least of:

- 30,000;[191]

- The fair market value of the vehicle; and

---

[189]Prescribed amount effective 2005. See para. 13(7)(h) and Reg. 7307(1).

[190]Amounts are prescribed by Regulations and adjusted from time to time; see Reg. 7307(1).

[191]See 7307(1) for current prescribed amount.

- Its undepreciated capital cost to the transferor immediately before the transfer.

(f) — Reduction for Government Assistance

A taxpayer must reduce the capital cost of depreciable property to the extent that he or she deducts federal investment tax credits or receives or is entitled to receive governmental assistance in respect of the property.[192] This rule does not apply to governmental assistance received under an *Appropriation Act* in respect of scientific research and experimental developments ("R&D") expenditures. These items are not deducted from the capital cost of depreciable property, because they reduce the taxpayer's pool of R&D expenditures under subsection 37(1) of the Act.

6. — Exchanges of Property

The capital cost of an asset acquired in a barter transaction is generally equal to the value of the property traded or exchanged. It is the value of the asset used to purchase that determines the cost of the asset purchased. As Jackett P. said:[193]

> ... if A conveys Blackacre to B in exchange for a conveyance by B to A of Whiteacre, the cost of Whiteacre to A is the value of Blackacre (being what he gave up to get Whiteacre) and the cost of Blackacre to B is the value of Whiteacre (being what he gave up in order to get Blackacre). Assuming both parties were equally skillful in their bargaining, there is a probability that the values of the two properties are about the same but this does not mean that A's "cost" is the "value" of what he acquired or that B's "cost" is the "value" of what he acquired.

Of course, in most arm's length transactions one trades property of equal values. Where, however, it is impossible to value the asset given up and the value of the asset acquired is known, it is permissible to use the latter.[194] Ultimately, the question is one of credibility and proof of cost.

7. — Undepreciated Capital Cost

The starting point in calculating capital cost allowance (CCA) is to determine the capital cost of each depreciable property. The Regulations group depreciable properties into classes

---

[192]See subs. 13(7.1).

[193]*D'Auteuil Lumber Co. v. M.N.R.*, [1970] C.T.C. 122 at 128, 70 D.T.C. 6096 at 6099 (Ex. Ct.) (timber cutting rights received from province in exchange for transfer of remaining timber limit; value of former in issue); see also *The Queen v. Can. Pac. Ltd. (No. 1)*, [1977] C.T.C. 606, 77 D.T.C. 5383 (F.C.A.) (interest from subsidiary deemed to be dividends and not deductible by railway company).

[194]See IT-490, "Barter Transactions" (July 5, 1982).

with similar life expectations. When we deduct CCA from the capital cost of property, the residue is the "undepreciated capital cost" ("UCC") of the property.[195] Thus, UCC represents the as yet undepreciated cost of the class of assets. In accounting terms, this is equivalent to the net book value of the asset.

One determines a taxpayer's "undepreciated capital cost" of a class of depreciable property by adding the following:[196]

• The capital cost depreciable property of the class;

• Government assistance repaid by the taxpayer subsequent to the disposition of property in respect of the acquisition of which he or she received assistance;

• Any amount recaptured in respect of the class; and

• Repayment of contributions and allowances the taxpayer received and that were previously deducted from the capital cost of that class;

Next, one deducts the aggregate of:

• The total capital cost allowance and terminal losses that the taxpayer has claimed for property of the class;

• The proceeds of disposition of any property of the class disposed of (the deduction not to exceed the capital cost of the property); and

• Government assistance received, or that the taxpayer is entitled to receive, as well as investment tax credits claimed, subsequent to the disposition by the taxpayer of the property to which such assistance or tax credit related.

For the purpose of calculating CCA in a year an asset is acquired, only 1/2 of the net additions to the class is generally added to the UCC balance.[197] The remaining 1/2 is added to the UCC after calculating CCA for the year of acquisition. The effect of this rule is that CCA on a newly acquired asset may be claimed at only 1/2 of the normal rate in the year of acquisition.

Thus, the UCC of a class can be updated annually by using the following formula:

Undepreciated capital cost of the class at the beginning of the year	$ xxx
Add: purchases during the year	xxx
	xxx

---

[195]Para. 13(21)"undepreciated capital cost"; Reg. 1100(1)(a); see subsections 248(1) and 13(21).

[196]Para. 13(21)"undepreciated capital cost"; Reg. 1100(1)(a).

[197]Reg. 1100(2). There are limited exceptions to this rule.

Deduct: dispositions during the year at the *lesser* of:

•	capital cost	$ xxx	
•	proceeds of disposition	$ xxx	(xxx)

Undepreciated capital cost before adjustment	xxx
Deduct: 1/2 net additions to class	(xxx)
Undepreciated capital cost before CCA	xxx
Deduct: capital cost allowance in the class for the year	(xxx)
Add: 1/2 net additions to class	xxx
Undepreciated capital cost of the class at the end of the year	$ xxx

The UCC of a class can never be a negative amount. If the amount of the inclusions in a class is less than the amount of the deductions in the class, the negative balance becomes income for the year[198] and is then added back into the calculation of UCC of that class.[199] This increases the UCC balance to zero.

Example

Alpha Ltd. acquires one Class 8 asset (depreciable at 20 per cent) for $40,000 in YEAR 1, its first year of operation. In YEAR 2 *Alpha* disposes of the asset for $34,000 and acquires another Class 8 asset for $50,000. Assuming that Alpha claims the maximum CCA in each year, the UCC of the class at the end of YEAR 2 is as follows:

			Class 8
Opening UCC	$ NIL		
Add:			
50% of net additions		20,000	
Balance before CCA			$ 20,000
CCA claimed (YEAR 0)			
($20,000 × 20%)			(4,000)
Balance before adjustment			16,000

---

[198]Subs. 13(1).

[199]Subpara. 13(21)"undepreciated capital cost" B.

Example		
Add:		
	Remaining 50% of net additions	20,000
	UCC at the end of YEAR 1	36,000
Add:		
	Additions in YEAR 2	$ 50,000
	Dispositions in YEAR 2	(34,000)
	Net additions	$ 16,000
	50% × $16,000	8,000
	Balance before CCA	44,000
	CCA claimed (YEAR 2)	
	(20% × $44,000)	(8,800)
	Balance before adjustment	35,200
Add:		
	Remaining 50% of net additions	8,000
	UCC at the end of YEAR 2	$ 43,200

8. — Adjustments on Disposition of Assets

(a) — General Comment

The theory underlying the capital cost allowance system is that the cost of depreciable property can be written off over its useful life by applying pre-determined rates of depreciation. Subsequent events may show, however, that a taxpayer claimed insufficient or excessive capital cost allowance over a period of time. This may occur where the taxpayer voluntarily claims less than the maximum CCA allowable, or where the maximum rate applicable to a class of assets is either too restrictive or too generous.

Thus, the UCC of depreciable property may be higher or lower than its fair market value.

(b) — Terminal Losses

Where a taxpayer disposes of the property of a class for less than its UCC, he or she suffers a shortfall in the depreciation claimed on the particular class. In these circumstances, the taxpayer is entitled to recoup the amount of the shortfall through a claim for a "terminal loss".

A taxpayer can claim a terminal loss only if he or she disposes of all the property of a class and owns no property of the class at the end of the taxation year. Where a taxpayer is eligible for a terminal loss, he or she must claim the loss in the year, or lose it forever. Thus, unlike a claim for CCA, the claim for a terminal loss is not permissive.

Example

Assume:

Beta Ltd. has an undepreciated capital cost (UCC) Class 8 balance of $45,000 at the beginning of YEAR 1. During the year it acquires another Class 8 asset at a cost of $10,000. In YEAR 2, *Beta Ltd.* disposes of all of its Class 8 assets for $38,000. Assuming that it claims the maximum capital cost allowance in each year, *Beta's* terminal loss is determined as follows:

	Opening UCC (YEAR 1)	$ 45,000
Add:		
	50% of net additions	5,000
	Balance before CCA	50,000
	CCA claimed (YEAR 1)(20% × $50,000)	(10,000)
	Balance before adjustment	40,000
Add:		
	Remaining 50% of net additions	5,000
	UCC at the end of YEAR 1	45,000
Subtract:		
	Proceeds of disposition (YEAR 2)	(38,000)
	Balance in class (YEAR 2)	7,000
	Terminal loss claimed (YEAR 2)	(7,000)
	UCC at the end of YEAR 2	NIL

(c) — Automobiles

Special rules apply to terminal losses on passenger vehicles. A taxpayer may not claim a terminal loss in respect of a passenger vehicle costing more than $30,000.[200] The $30,000 limit is subject to periodic adjustments.[201]

(d) — Recapture

Just as a taxpayer may claim too little capital cost allowance on a class of assets, it is also possible that the taxpayer may have been allowed too much capital cost allowance. This may occur, for example, where the rate for a particular class of assets is deliberately set high in order to encourage economic activity in a particular sector. Thus, a sale of the assets of a class at fair market value may show that the assets were "over-depreciated" in the past. The Act "recaptures" any over-depreciated amount into income.[202]

(i) — Negative Balance

As noted earlier, the undepreciated capital cost of a class of assets is calculated by adding certain amounts and deducting others. Where a class has a negative balance *at the end of the year*, the amount of the balance is recaptured into income for that year.[203] Any amount recaptured into income is then added back to the UCC of the class. This brings the asset balance of that particular class back to nil.[204]

In theory, recapture of capital cost allowance represents an adjustment for excessive claims of depreciation in earlier fiscal periods. In most cases, however, one can reduce the amount of CCA subject to recapture in any taxation year by acquiring additional property of the same class during the taxation year. Thus, it is usually possible to manipulate the amount of recapture recognized in a particular year by timing new acquisitions of depreciable capital

---

[200]Subs. 20(16.1); Reg. 7307(1) (prescribed amount). The $30,000 is exclusive of GST and provincial sales tax.

[201]See para. 13(7)(g) and Reg. 7307(1).

[202]Para. 13(21)"undepreciated capital cost"; see also para. 13(21.1)(a); *Malloney's Studio Ltd. v. M.N.R.*, [1979] 2 S.C.R. 326, [1979] C.T.C. 206, 79 D.T.C. 5124 (S.C.C.) (house demolished prior to sale of land; no part of proceeds from sale of land apportionable to demolished building).

[203]Subs. 13(1).

[204]Subpara. 13(21); IT-220R2, "Capital Cost Allowance — Proceeds of Disposition of Depreciable Property" (May 25, 1990).

assets.[205] However, this does not apply to cases where similar properties must be segregated, for example, rental properties that have a cost of $50,000 or more.[206]

(ii) — Limited to Capital Cost

Recapture of CCA is in effect a clawback of excessive depreciation. Thus, the Act limits recapture to the capital cost of the particular depreciable property in the class. Proceeds of disposition in excess of the capital cost of an asset do *not* give rise to recapture of CCA. Rather, the excess of proceeds of disposition over the capital cost of an asset is a capital gain.[207] The distinction is important because recapture of CCA is fully taxable as income, whereas only 1/2 of capital gains are taxable.

Example			
Assume:			
	Capital cost of asset		$ 10,000
	CCA claimed		(5,000)
	UCC of class		$ 5,000
	Proceeds of disposition (net)		$ 8,000
Then:			
	UCC before disposition		$ 5,000
	Deduct *lesser* of:[*]		
	(i) Net proceeds	$ 8,000	
	(ii) Capital cost	$ 10,000	
	Lesser amount		(8,000)
	Recapture of CCA		$ (3,000)

Notes:

*   Subpara. 13(21)"undepreciated capital cost" F.

---

[205]Subpara. 13(21)"undepreciated capital cost".

[206]Reg. 1101(5b) and 1101(1ac).

[207]Subpara. 13(21)"undepreciated capital cost" F. Note: this rule does not apply to timber resource properties.

Example

Assume only one asset in class:

Capital cost	$ 10,000
CCA claimed	(4,000)
UCC	$ 6,000

CASE:	A	B	C	D
Proceeds of disposition:	$ 4,000	$ 6,000	$ 9,000	$ 11,000
UCC	6,000	6,000	6,000	6,000
Terminal loss	$ 2,000	NIL	—	—
Recapture	—	—	$ 3,000	$ 4,000
Capital gain	—	—	—	$ 1,000

(iii) — Deferral

In certain circumstances, a taxpayer can defer the recapture of capital cost allowance. For example, a taxpayer who receives proceeds of disposition by way of insurance compensation for stolen or lost property (or by way of compensation for expropriated property) can elect to defer recognition of any recapture if he or she replaces the property with more expensive property.[208] This election is also available upon disposition of a "former business property".[209]

A "replacement property" is a property that the taxpayer acquires for the same or similar use as the property being replaced. A replacement property need only be a substitute for the original property; it need only be capable of being put to a similar use. It does *not* have to be an identical property.[210]

To obtain the benefit of the deferral, the taxpayer must make an election when filing a return for the year in which he or she acquires the replacement property. Upon election, part of the proceeds of disposition of the former property are, in effect, transferred from the year in which the disposition occurs to the year in which the replacement property is acquired.

---

[208] Subs. 13(4).

[209] Subss. 13(4); 248(1) "former business property".

[210] Subs. 13(4.1).

An election to defer recapture of CCA is also an automatic election to defer any capital gain triggered on the disposition.[211]

9. — First Year Half-Rate Rule

We saw earlier that the Act limits in the first year the capital cost allowance on assets acquired during the year to 1/2 the allowance that is otherwise deductible.[212] This rule prevents tax avoidance by discouraging taxpayers from acquiring property at the end of a year in order to claim the full year's allowance. For example, a taxpayer might otherwise buy an asset on December 31 and claim CCA for the full year.[213]

Thus, the Act excludes from the undepreciated capital cost (UCC) of a class 1/2 of the net additions of property of that class in the year. The 1/2 that is excluded is then added back to the UCC of the class, after one determines the capital cost allowance (CCA) claim.

Example		
Assume:		Class 8 (20%)
UCC beginning of year		$ 10,000
Acquisitions during the year		$ 7,000
Proceeds from dispositions during the year		$ 2,000
Then:		
Opening UCC		$ 10,000
Additions during year	$ 7,000	
Dispositions during year	(2,000)	
Net additions	$ 5,000	

---

[211]Subs. 44(4); IT-259R4, "Exchanges of Property" (Sept. 23, 2003); *Korenowsky v. M.N.R.* (1964), 35 Tax A.B.C. 86 (T.A.B.) (delay beyond specified periods precludes deferral).

[212]Reg. 1100(2). This rule applies only to acquisitions made subsequent to November 12, 1981. For acquisitions made prior to that date, the taxpayer was able to claim the full allowance in the year of acquisition. As to when a taxpayer acquires property, see *M.N.R. v. Wardean Drilling Ltd.*, [1969] C.T.C. 265, 69 D.T.C. 5194 (Ex. Ct.).

[213]*Hewlett Packard (Canada) Ltd. v. R.*, 2004 FCA 240, [2004] 4 C.T.C. 230 (F.C.A.) (each year HP bought a new fleet of cars from Ford to replace the old fleet. In order to maximize its CCA, HP bought the new fleets just before, and sold the old fleets just after, its fiscal year-end. Minister argued HP was doubling up on CCA. Court disagreed and allowed CCA on the old fleet since HP retained both legal and beneficial interest until after fiscal year-end of each year).

Example	
1/2 of net additions	2,500
UCC before allowance	12,500
CCA (20% × $12,500)	(2,500)
	10,000
Add:	
Remaining 1/2 of net additions	2,500
UCC at end of year	$ 12,500

The remaining 1/2 of the net additions, on which CCA is not claimed in the year of acquisition, is added back to the UCC of the class. In effect, the Act defers the capital cost allowance on this half to future years.

The first year half-rate rule does not apply to certain types of properties.[214] Nor does the rule apply to certain business reorganizations in which there is a change in legal title without any effective change in economic ownership.[215]

10. — Available for Use

The Act does not consider a taxpayer to have acquired a property until it becomes available for use, or until 24 months after the actual acquisition of the property.[216] The purpose of the first restriction is to match income and expenses more accurately; the second accommodates long-term construction projects.

The first year half-rate rule applies to the tax year in which the property is considered to have been acquired according to calculations for CCA purposes.

---

[214]Most Class 12 (small items for which a 100 per cent deduction is available in the year); Class 13 (leasehold interests, which are subject to special rules see Reg. 1100(1)(b)); Class 14 (patents and limited period franchises, etc.); Class 15 (timber rights); Classes 24, 27 and 34 (pollution control equipment), and Class 29 properties, are excluded.

[215]Reg. 1100(2.2).

[216]See subss. 13(26)–(32).

11. — Short Taxation Year

The usual rule is that one calculates capital cost allowance on the undepreciated capital cost of assets of a class at the *end* of the taxation year. This rule is subject to the proviso noted above that a taxpayer may claim only 1/2 of the full CCA on an asset in the year that he or she acquires it.

Where the taxpayer's taxation year is less than 12 months, CCA is limited, in certain cases, to a proportional amount. This amount is calculated as follows:

$$\frac{\text{No. of days in the taxation year}^{217}}{365} \times \text{Maximum CCA allowable}$$

This rule applies to all depreciable assets except Classes 14 (limited life intangibles), 15 (wood assets), and industrial mineral mines.[218]

12. — Separate Classes for Similar Properties

Where a taxpayer operates more than one business, he or she must calculate capital cost allowance for *each* business separately.

Similarly, a taxpayer who has income from a business, as well as income from property, must use separate classes for the assets used to derive income from the business and the property.[219] For example, a taxpayer may own a building that he or she uses in business while also owning a rental property. Although the two buildings may be similar in all respects, each of the buildings must be placed into a separate class. This is another illustration of the strict segregation of income by source. Thus, it is quite possible that a taxpayer may trigger a recapture of capital cost allowance on the disposition of one asset when he or she owns a similar property, which, but for this rule, would be included in the same class.

Whether two or more business operations carried out simultaneously are part of the same business depends upon the degree of interconnection or interdependence between the opera-

---

[217]"Number of days in the taxation year" refers to the number of days that the business is in operation, and not the period of ownership of the asset.

[218]Reg. 1100(3).

[219]Reg. 1101(1); IT-206R, "Separate Businesses" (October 29, 1979); see also *Vincent v. M.N.R.*, [1966] S.C.R. 374, [1966] C.T.C. 147, 66 D.T.C. 5123 (S.C.C.) (requirement that taxpayer calculate income from each source separately also applies to calculation of capital cost allowance); *Midwest Hotel Co. v. M.N.R.*, [1972] C.T.C. 534, 72 D.T.C. 6440 (S.C.C.) (taxpayer who sold business then purchased another later in year subject to recapture); *Dupont Canada* (2002), 2002 F.C.A. 464, [2003] 1 C.T.C. 295, 2002 D.T.C. 5001 (separate business concept).

tions of the various units. The CRA sets out its views on "interconnection and interdependence" in IT-206R:[220]

> When determining the degree of interconnection or interdependence between simultaneous business operations, factors to be considered could include, among others, the following:
>
> • The extent to which the two operations have common factors. For example, do the two operations have the same processes, products, customers, services offered to customers, types of inventories, employees, machinery or equipment?
>
> • Whether the operations are carried on in the same premises. For example, if a hardware store and a sporting goods store are operated in two distinct locations, it is possible that they should be looked upon as separate businesses, but if they are in one store, it is almost certain that they are one business.
>
> • One operation may exist primarily to supply the other. An example of this might be the carrying on of market-garden operations chiefly for the purpose of supplying a hotel with fresh produce. In these circumstances, the two operations likely should be regarded as one business, even if a small amount of the market-garden produce is sold elsewhere.
>
> • Whether the operations have differing fiscal year-ends.
>
> • Whether the taxpayer's accounting system records the transactions of both operations as if they were those of one business, or whether separate complete sets of records are maintained throughout the year; if the latter, too much weight should not be given to the possible merging of the results into one statement at the year-end for tax and other reporting purposes.

13. — Rental Buildings Over $50,000

Each rental building that costs $50,000 or more must be placed in a separate class.[221] The rule prevents taxpayers from artificially avoiding recapture of CCA upon the disposition of a rental property by acquiring another similar property of the same class. The rule also applies to rental properties that cost less than $50,000, but to which additions increase the total capital cost above $50,000. In these circumstances, the properties must be transferred into a separate class. Where a taxpayer acquires a rental property consisting of numerous units, the cost of all of the units within the same building must be aggregated to determine whether the total cost exceeds $50,000.

The Act further limits the capital cost allowance claimable on "rental properties" that exceed $50,000 to the *net* of rental incomes and losses for the year from all such properties that the

---

[220]IT-206R, "Separate Businesses" (October 29, 1979), para. 3.

[221]Reg. 1101(1*ac*); IT-304R2, "Condominiums" (June 2, 2000). Rental and non-rental properties must be placed in separate classes: Reg. 1101(1*ae*).

taxpayer owns. Thus, a taxpayer cannot use CCA on this class of assets to create a loss from property and shelter other sources of income.

14. — Transfers of Property Between Classes

A taxpayer can elect to transfer all assets in Classes 2 to 12 that are used in the *same* business into Class 1.[222] Class 1 provides for a lower capital cost allowance rate than any of Classes 2 to 12. Hence, in normal circumstances, it is not to a taxpayer's advantage to transfer assets into Class 1. The transfer rules do, however, allow a taxpayer to establish a terminal loss or defer recapture of capital cost allowance. For example, a taxpayer may have a large UCC in one class but very few assets remaining in the class. The remaining assets may have a very low capital cost. If the taxpayer transferred these items out of the class into another class, he or she could recognize a terminal loss in the class from which he or she transferred the property.

Conversely, the UCC of a class may be low when the market value of the property in the class is high. If the taxpayer sold the property, he or she would have to recognize a recapture of CCA. The taxpayer could, however, transfer the property into another class with a lower rate of capital cost allowance. It would then be possible to defer the recognition of recapture by reducing the UCC of the class into which the taxpayer transferred the property.[223]

Example

Assume the following profile:

Class	UCC	Additions	Disposals	CCA
1	$100,000			$ 4,000
3	35,000		$75,000	(40,000)
8	12,000	$ 3,000		2,700
10	30,000			9,000
				$ (24,300)

---

[222]Reg. 1103(1); The taxpayer must elect the transfer on or before the day on which she is required to file an income tax return for the year (Reg. 1103(3)).

[223]See Regs. 1103(2)–(2)(i) and subsection 13(5), which deals with the rules to transfer the components of classes of depreciable property between classes.

Example

The taxpayer faces a potential recapture of $24,300. He may either purchase a new Class 3 asset or elect to transfer all assets in Classes 3, 8 and 10 to Class 1. If he transfers the assets into Class 1, his CCA profile would appear as:

Class	UCC	Additions	Disposal	Adjustments	CCA	UCC
1	$100,000	$3,000	$75,000	$77,000	$4,200	$100,800

The taxpayer may claim CCA of $4,200 [(100,000 + 3,000 - 75,000 + 77,000) × 4%].

15. — Leaseholds

A taxpayer may deduct capital cost allowance from the cost of certain leasehold improvements (Class 13) in accordance with Schedule III,[224] on the basis of the lesser of:

- 20 per cent of the capital cost of any leasehold improvements, or

- The amount obtained by dividing the capital cost of leasehold improvements by the term of the lease in years, plus the term of the first option to renew, if any (not exceeding 40 years in total).

For example, the cost of a leasehold improvement made under a three-year lease with no option to renew is deductible at 20 per cent of the capital cost per year. If, at the end of the three years, the taxpayer surrenders the lease and owns no other leasehold interests, he or she can deduct a terminal loss. If the lease is for a term of 10 years with an option to renew for five years, the capital cost is deductible in computing income at the rate of 1/15 per year. As we saw earlier, the deductible capital cost allowance in the year that the taxpayer acquires a Class 13 property is limited to 1/2 of the full year amount.[225]

16. — Patents, Franchises, Concessions, or Licences

A taxpayer can deduct CCA on a patent, franchise, concession, or licence if the asset has a limited life.[226] One determines the deductible CCA by prorating the cost of the asset over

---

[224]Reg. 1100(1)(b).

[225]Reg. 1100(1)(b).

[226]Reg. 1100(1)(c); Sched. II, Class 14.

the life of the asset. Alternatively, where the asset is a patent, the taxpayer may claim a deduction that depends on the use of the patent.[227]

Patents also fall into Class 44, which uses a 25 per cent declining balance method. A taxpayer can transfer these properties from Class 44 to Class 14 (see Reg. 1103(2)(h)).

17. — Works of Art

A taxpayer can claim CCA on certain types of works of art created by Canadian artists. These include:[228]

- Prints, etchings, drawings and paintings that cost more than $200; and

- Hand-woven tapestries and carpets that cost more than $215 per square metre.

A taxpayer *cannot* claim CCA on other types of works of art such as:

- Antique furniture more than 100 years old that costs more than $1,000;

- Prints, etchings, drawings, paintings and carpets that are not the work of Canadian artists; and

- Engravings, lithographs, etchings, woodcuts or charts made before 1900.

18. — Capital Cost of Automobiles

We saw earlier that, as a general rule, the capital cost of an asset is its full, laid-down cost. A special rule applies to automobiles. For tax purposes, the maximum cost on which a taxpayer can claim CCA is $30,000. This rule prevents taxpayers from writing off expensive automobiles against business income. The rule does not depend upon the legitimacy of the expenditure. Any amount in excess of the maximum (excluding provincial sales tax and GST) is not eligible for capital cost allowance. Each passenger vehicle that costs more than $30,000 is segregated in a separate class (Class 10.1). Special rules apply to this class. For example, there is no recapture or terminal loss on Class 10.1 passenger vehicles.[229]

---

[227]Reg. 1100(9).

[228]Reg. 1102(1)(e).

[229]Dollar amounts are adjusted by Regulation from time to time; see: para. 13(7)(g) and Reg. 7307(1).

XIV. — Eligible Capital Property

1. — General Comment

The CCA system deals for the most part with capital expenditures for tangible capital property. There is a different regime in respect of capital expenditures on intangible capital assets, such as goodwill, franchises, customer lists, and incorporation fees. We refer to these assets, as "eligible capital property".

Expenditures on account of eligible capital property are deductible in computing business income. The deductibility of such expenditures is, however, subject to stringent limits. Only 3/4 of such expenditures are deductible. The maximum rate of write-off is 7 per cent per year on a declining balance basis. Similarly, the Act includes 75 per cent of the proceeds from the disposition of an eligible property in income, but only for amounts that exceed the taxpayer's "cumulative eligible capital account".[230] Thus, the regime draws on features from both the capital gains and the capital cost allowance systems.

The general tax structure of eligible capital expenditures centres around the operation of a notional account, the "cumulative eligible capital amount". This account functions as follows:

- 75 per cent of outlays on account of eligible capital expenditures are included in the taxpayer's "cumulative eligible capital" account;[231] and

- 75 per cent of the proceeds of disposition from eligible capital properties are credited to the "cumulative eligible capital" account.[232]

The balance in the "cumulative eligible capital" account at the end of the year can be amortized against business income at a maximum rate of 7 per cent per year on a declining balance basis.[233] Any negative balance in the account as at the end of the year is recaptured and included in the taxpayer's income for the year.[234] Thus, the tax structure for eligible capital property is a hybrid between the capital cost allowance rules (declining balance, fixed rate, recapture, etc.) and the capital gains rules.

---

[230]Para. 20(1)(b), s. 14.

[231]Para. 14(5) "cumulative eligible capital".

[232]*Ibid.*

[233]Para. 20(1)(b).

[234]Subs. 14(1).

2. — Cumulative Eligible Capital

"Cumulative eligible capital" (CEC) is the amount by which the aggregate of 75 per cent of the eligible capital expenditures made in respect of the business, and amounts previously included in income under subsection 14(1), exceed:

- Amounts previously deducted in computing income from the business under paragraph 20(1)(b); and

- 75 per cent of the proceeds of sale, less selling expenses from a disposition of eligible capital property.[235]

Example

Assume:

A taxpayer enters into the following transactions in respect of eligible capital properties.

Year	Transaction	Amount
1	Purchase	$53,334
2	—	—
3	Sale	$40,000
4	Sale	$13,334

The taxpayer claims the maximum 7 per cent amortization each year.

Then:

Cumulative Eligible Capital Account

	Year 1	Year 2	Year 3	Year 4
Opening balance	NIL	$ 37,200	$ 34,596	$ 4,274
75% × purchases	$ 40,000	—	—	—
75% × sales	—	—	30,000	10,000
Balance before deduction from account	40,000	37,200	4,596	(5,726)

---

[235]Para. 14(5) "cumulative eligible capital".

Example				
Amortization [7%] (Deducible from business income)	2,800	2,604	322	—
Included in income	—	—	—	5,726
Ending Balance	$ 37,200	$ 34,596	$ 4,274	NIL

3. — Eligible Capital Expenditures

(a) — Meaning

An eligible *capital* expenditure is a capital expenditure of an intangible nature that a taxpayer incurs to earn income from a business, but one that is not deductible under any other provision of the Act. The Act specifically excludes the following expenditures from "eligible capital expenditures":[236]

- An outlay otherwise deductible in computing income or deductible under some provision of the Act, other than paragraph 20(1)(b);

- Outlays made specifically non-deductible by some provision of the Act, other than paragraph 18(1)(b);

- An outlay made to earn exempt income;

- The cost of tangible property or an interest therein, or the right to acquire the same;[237]

- The cost of intangible property that is depreciable property, or an interest therein, for example, leasehold interests, patents and franchises with a limited life, all of which costs would be deductible under the capital cost allowance provisions;

- The cost of property that would otherwise be deductible in computing a taxpayer's business income, or an interest therein, or the right to acquire the same;

- An amount paid to a creditor in settlement of a debt;

- An amount paid to a person in his or her capacity as a shareholder of the corporation;

- The cost, or part of the cost, of an interest in a trust, or a right to acquire the same;

---

[236]Para. 14(5) "eligible capital expenditures".

[237]In most cases, a deduction in respect of tangible property would be available under the capital cost allowance provisions.

- The cost, or part of the cost, of an interest in a partnership, or a right to acquire the same; and

- The cost or part of the cost of a share, bond, etc., or a right to acquire the same.

(b) — "Eligible Capital Amount"

"Eligible capital amount" is 3/4 of the proceeds of the disposition of property (as adjusted by a formula) that would represent an eligible capital expenditure to the purchaser. That is, if the purchaser has made an eligible capital expenditure, the vendor is in receipt of an eligible capital amount equal to 3/4 of that expenditure, less any outlays and expenses incurred on disposition.[238]

(c) — "Eligible Capital Property"

"Eligible capital property" is any property that, if sold, would require the inclusion, in computing the taxpayer's income, of 3/4 of the proceeds under subsection 14(1).

(d) — Characterization of Expenditures and Receipts

Amounts that a taxpayer incurs or receives on the purchase and sale of property are not necessarily characterized as mirror images of each other. In *Samoth*,[239] for example, the taxpayer acquired the exclusive right to sell Century 21 franchises in Canada to licensed real estate brokers. The taxpayer paid $100,000 for this right. The taxpayer acted as a trader in selling the Century 21 franchises, but maintained that the receipts from those sales were on account of eligible capital property. The Federal Court of Appeal held the receipts from the sale of the franchises to be on account of business income and not on account of capital. Hence, not being on account of capital, the receipts could not constitute amounts received on account of eligible capital property. In other words, although the purchase of the franchises might have been on account of eligible capital property, the sale of the franchises did not necessarily require a mirror image characterization of the proceeds of sale. In Justice Mahoney's words:[240]

> In applying the so-called "mirror image rule" ... the face to be seen in the mirror by the [taxpayer] is not that of the actual purchaser of one of its franchises acquiring a capital asset but its own face, that of a trader in franchises.

---

[238]Subpara. 14(5) "cumulative eligible capital"; subs. 14(1).

[239]*Samoth Financial Corp. v. The Queen*, [1986] 2 C.T.C. 107, 86 D.T.C. 6335 (F.C.A.).

[240]*Samoth Financial Corp. v. The Queen*, *ibid.*, at 108 [C.T.C.] and 6335 [D.T.C.].

Example

Assume:

In 2004, A sold her entire business operations to B. B acquired the following assets:

Inventory	$ 10,000
Accounts receivable	15,000
Investments	5,000
Land	20,000
Buildings	25,000
Equipment	6,000
Goodwill	28,000
	$ 109,000

Example

All of the assets listed above, except inventory and accounts receivable, are capital assets. Of the capital assets, only goodwill is an eligible capital expenditure. In computing income for the first year of operations, B can deduct a maximum of $1,307.

The cumulative eligible capital account is as follows:

Opening balance (3/4 of $28,000)	$ 21,000
Amortization — Year 1 [7% × $21,000]	(1,470)
Balance end of Year 1	$ 19,530

If A originally started the business, she would include, as an eligible capital amount, 3/4 of the proceeds of $28,000 in income.

Example	
Assume:	
In year 2, B sells his business assets to C and receives $39,375 for goodwill. B would include $6,720 in income.	
Eligible capital amount	
(3/4 of $39,375)	$ 29,531
Balance of cumulative eligible capital	(19,530)
Income	$ 10,001

Note, 75 per cent of the proceeds from goodwill is considered an eligible capital amount, regardless of its purchase cost. A disposition of eligible capital property cannot give rise to a capital gain.[241]

4. — *Exchanges of Property*

Where a taxpayer disposes of an eligible capital property and acquires a replacement property[242] before the end of the first taxation year following the year of disposition, he or she may elect to defer recognition of any amount that might otherwise be recaptured.[243]

5. — *Goodwill*

"Goodwill" is an asset. It has been described as "... the probability that the old customers will resort to the old place."[244] In other words, it is the advantage that accrues to a person as a result of a reputation. The reputation may rest on honest dealing, hard work or advertising.[245] In financial terms, goodwill means a premium sales price on the disposition of a

---

[241]Subpara. 39(1)(a)(i).

[242]Subs. 14(7).

[243]Subss. 14(1) and (6).

[244]*Cruttwell v. Lye* (1810), 34 E.R. 129 at 134.

[245]*Trego v. Hunt*, [1896] A.C. 7 (H.L.).

business. The premium compensates for the "excess" earning power of the business because of its goodwill. Accountants define goodwill as:[246]

> ... an intangible asset of a business when the business has value in excess of the sum of its net identifiable assets. ... It has been said to fall into the three classes of commercial, industrial, and financial goodwill, which are the consequences of favourable attitudes on the part of customers, employees, and creditors, respectively. As to its value, the most common explanations emphasize the present value of expected future earnings in excess of the return required to induce investment.

"Goodwill" is also defined in terms of excess earning power over the "normal" rate of return of a business. For example, in *Dominion Dairies v. M.N.R.*:[247]

> ... goodwill can be viewed as the purchase of earning power in excess of a normal return on the investment. ... This advantage evidences itself in the form of earnings in an amount greater than that expected in a typical firm in the industry with a similar capital investment.

The determination of the existence of, and the amount attributable to, goodwill is a question of fact; it may result from location,[248] reputation,[249] brand loyalty,[250] competent management, good labour relations and trademarks.[251]

The tax system treats purchased goodwill differently from expenditures incurred in building up goodwill. A taxpayer who expends money on advertising, customer relations, employee relations, etc., may write off the expenditures on a current basis, even though the expenditures cultivate an asset. Where, however, a taxpayer purchases goodwill built up through

---

[246]CICA, *Terminology for Accountants*.

[247]*Dominion Dairies Ltd. v. M.N.R.*, [1966] C.T.C. 1 at 12-13, 66 D.T.C. 5028 at 5033-34 (Ex. Ct.).

[248]*The Queen v. Shok*, [1975] C.T.C. 162, (sub nom. *The Queen. v. Waldorf Hotel (1958) Ltd.*) 75 D.T.C. 5109 (F.C.T.D.) (contract specifying value of goodwill not upheld by court as appraisal differing and vendor was never consulted about allocation); *Saskatoon Drug & Stationery Co. v. M.N.R.*, [1975] C.T.C. 2108, 75 D.T.C. 103 (T.R.B.) (court outlined types of goodwill as well as premium payable to succeed lease of choice location).

[249]*Can. Propane, Gas & Oil Ltd. v. M.N.R.*, [1972] C.T.C. 566, 73 D.T.C. 5019 (F.C.T.D.) (proper assessment of value of goodwill is that amount assigned by opposing parties after hard bargaining); *Pepsi Cola Can. Ltd. v. The Queen*, [1979] C.T.C. 454, 79 D.T.C. 5387 (F.C.A.) (characterization of payment as on account of goodwill not termination of franchise).

[250]*Herb Payne Tpt. Ltd. v. M.N.R.*, [1963] C.T.C. 116, 63 D.T.C. 1075 (Ex. Ct.) (trucking business name part of goodwill; review of law on "goodwill"); *Schacter v. M.N.R.*, [1962] C.T.C. 437, 62 D.T.C. 1271 (Ex. Ct.) (court upheld agreement between taxpayer and vendor of accounting firm, absent contrary evidence of value of goodwill).

[251]*Morin v. M.N.R.*, [1978] C.T.C. 2976, 78 D.T.C. 1693 (T.R.B.) (partnership held to have goodwill, and elements comprising goodwill); *Saskatoon Drug & Stationery Co. v. M.N.R.*, *ante*; *Herb Payne Tpt. Ltd. v. M.N.R.*, *ante*.

such expenditures, the cost is an "eligible capital expenditure", which can only be amortized in the manner described.

6. — Recapture of Negative Balances

(a) — General Rule

Generally speaking, where, at the end of a taxation year the amounts required to be deducted from a taxpayer's pool of expenditures in respect of eligible capital property exceed the amounts required to be added to the pool, the excess ("negative balance") must be included in the taxpayer's income for the year.

(b) — Individuals

Where an individual's cumulative eligible capital has a negative balance at the end of a taxation year, the amount that must be included in income is limited to that portion of the negative balance that represents the recapture of previous deductions claimed in respect of eligible capital property. The remainder of the negative balance is either deemed (in the case of qualified farm property) or electible (in the case of other properties) as capital gains and, therefore, may be eligible for the capital gains exemption (see Chapter 11 "Computation of Gains and Losses").

(c) — Bad Debts

Where a taxpayer has a negative balance in his or her cumulative eligible capital at the end of a taxation year, the negative balance is included in income for the year. This is so, regardless of whether or not the taxpayer has been paid for the disposition of the property that triggered the negative balance. If the amount proves uncollectible, the taxpayer may deduct 3/4 of the amount receivable upon the disposition of an eligible capital property that did not generate a taxable capital gain.[252]

XV. — Home Office Expenses

There are special restrictions on the deductibility of home office expenses incurred on account of "workspace" in a domestic establishment. An individual may not deduct from business income, an amount in respect of an office in his or her home unless it is:

- The principal place of business, or

---

[252]Subs. 20(4.2).

- Used by that person exclusively on a regular and continuous basis for meeting clients, customers or patients.

Home office expenses must be apportioned between business and non-business use when the above conditions are met. We calculate this on a *pro rata* basis, and it is normally based on the amount of floor space used.

Home office expenses may only be deducted to the extent of the taxpayer's income from the business for the year. Thus, an individual may not create a loss on account of such expenses. To the extent that there is a loss, however, it may be carried forward and used in the year immediately following the one in which the loss was incurred. This restriction does not apply to the computation of income from property.[253]

XVI. — Superficial Losses

A taxpayer in the business of lending money in Canada (for example, a financial institution) may not claim a "superficial loss" when it disposes of debt or equity securities used or held by it in its business. This rule is similar to the superficial loss rules applicable to capital properties (see Chapter 11 "Computation of Gains and Losses").

A superficial loss arises where a taxpayer — for example, a money lender — disposes of debt or equity and the taxpayer (or an affiliated person) reacquires the same or identical property within 30 days before and after the disposition. The taxpayer cannot claim the loss. The claim may, however, be revived on the occurrence of certain events.[254]

XVII. — Convention Expenses

1. — General Comment

Taxpayers who are in business or practice a profession may deduct their expenses for attending up to two conventions per year, provided the conventions are in connection with their business or profession. This deduction is subject to several limitations.

---

[253]Subs. 18(12).

[254]Subss. 18(13)–(16).

2. — Territorial Scope

The convention must be at a location that can reasonably be regarded as falling within the territorial scope of the convening organization.[255] The taxpayer does not have to be a member of the sponsoring organization. An organization that is national in character may convene at any location in Canada; an organization that is international in character may convene abroad. A convention held during an ocean cruise is considered to be held outside Canada.

It is the character of the sponsoring organization, and not the nature of the taxpayer's business, that determines what is acceptable in terms of territorial scope.[256] The taxpayer's actual business may, however, reflect on the purpose of the trip.

3. — Primary Purpose

The *primary* purpose of the taxpayer's visit to the convention must be connected to business. Is the taxpayer entitled to enjoy being at the convention? To be sure, provided that such personal enjoyment is incidental to, and not the *raison d'être* of, the trip.

The question of the purpose of attendance at a convention should be determined by the relationship between the taxpayer's business and the subject matter covered at the convention.[257] The closer the relationship between the two, the easier it is to justify the business purpose of the trip. That is not to suggest, however, that a taxpayer who is expanding a business from one field into another is not entitled to attend a convention that discusses the subject matter of the new field.

4. — Blended Purposes

If a taxpayer combines a vacation with attendance at a convention, the personal portion of the trip is not deductible from income. The taxpayer should allocate, on some reasonable basis, the portion of the trip that is considered personal. A reasonable basis could be, for example, the number of days spent at the convention versus the total time spent away from home. The taxpayer is, however, entitled to deduct the entire cost of travel to and from the convention as a business expense. Thus, it is only the portion of the total expenditure that is directly attributable to the vacation portion (apart from travel expenses) that is considered non-deductible for tax purposes.

---

[255]Subs. 20(10).

[256]*Michayluk v. M.N.R.*, [1988] 2 C.T.C. 2236, 88 D.T.C. 1564 (T.C.C.).

[257]*Rovan v. M.N.R.*, [1986] 2 C.T.C. 2337, 86 D.T.C. 1791 (T.C.C.).

Costs incurred for taking the taxpayer's spouse and family to the convention are not usually deductible for tax purposes. Of course, if it can be shown that the presence of the taxpayer's spouse at the convention is *necessary* for business or professional purposes, that portion is also deductible as a business expense. The burden of proving the necessity of the presence of the taxpayer's spouse rests squarely, and heavily, on the taxpayer.

5. — U.S. Conventions

A special rule applies to Canadian businesses and professional organizations that are national in character and that hold conventions in the United States. In these circumstances, the *Canada-U.S. Tax Treaty* provides that expenses incurred for attending the organization's convention in the U.S. are deductible on the same basis as if the convention had been held in Canada. This special provision only applies to organizations that are "national" in character, and does not apply to regional or local organizations.

6. — Intra-Company Meetings: Corporations

The limit of two conventions per year also applies to corporate taxpayers. Thus, where a corporation "attends" a convention through its officers or agents, it is subject to the maximum of two per year. The CRA does accept, however, that where a corporation has diversified business interests (as in the case of an integrated oil company), the limit applies separately to each of its business interests. For example, the corporation may send representatives to attend conventions held on the subjects of administration, accounting, chemistry, geology, etc., and deduct expenses for up to two conventions per subject grouping per year for each of its personnel.

XVIII. — Domain Names

A domain name is an Internet address for electronic communication. The name can be generic or a unique "brand" address. Unlike conventional addresses, however, domain names can uniquely identify the addressee and, therefore, can be valuable business assets. Unlike analog addresses, which merely identify physical location, domain names assume an "identity" unique to the owner. With rare exceptions, such as 24 Sussex Drive or 10 Downing Street, physical addresses do not have commercial value. In contrast, a domain name can be a hallmark of identity with intrinsic commercial value. Thus, the value of domain names such as "Coca-Cola" or "Nike" is the owner's trademark or identity in the product.

Although domain names are as new as the Internet, the market for such names is escalating at a remarkable rate. Never before has the public trading of a property right developed as rapidly as the public market for the underlying asset. Unlike securities markets, however, the marketplace for domain names is free and unregulated. Although most large and well-known businesses have staked their claim to their own name on the Internet address system, the market for generic names is flourishing and likely to expand. Examine the domain names for sale on the Internet at *www.domains.com.* The prices indicate that the market appeals to speculators as eager as penny stock promoters. The most popular generic names available for sale are those that identify common, everyday activities.

How do we account for the cost of domain names bought and sold either in the unregulated public market or in negotiated commercial transactions? Suppose, for example that a business acquires a dot.com compay in its entirety together with its domain name. If the company is not yet a profitable business, the purchase price, presumably, would be largely attributable to its brand identity. How would we account for the cost of the domain name?

The essential test for deducting "expenses" is to determine whether the taxpayer incurs the expenses for the purposes of earning income in the year. If he or she does, the expense is deductible on a current basis. In contrast, a capital expenditure, that is, an expenditure that one incurs to earn income over several years, is not deductible on a current basis. Thus, the distinction between current expenses and capital costs is crucial to taxpayers. It determines the timing and, hence, the economic value of deductions. The distinction is not as easy as it appears. First, one must determine whether the expenditure benefits a single financial period or several years. If the expenditure is capital in nature, we must determine the write-off rate for tax purposes.

The Department of Finance resolves this issue in its draft regulations (July 12, 2005) that contains a definition of "data network infrastructure equipment" that includes, among other things, domain name servers that fall within Class 46 at a rate of 30 per cent instead of the catch-all rate of 20 per cent for Class 8. See Reg. 1104(2).

Should a business that pays a substantial price for a domain name recognize the expenditure as a current expense against its income or as an eligible capital expenditure? There is no ready answer to this seemingly simple question. The law dealing with the intellectual property rights of domain names is in its infancy. It is unclear, for example, whether domain names will become trademarks or trade names. The price of a domain name that has a limited useful life (perhaps under one year) is clearly a current expense deductible against revenues. On the other hand, a domain name can be a valuable capital asset with a long useful life. In these circumstances, the cost of the domain name will likely be an eligible capital expenditure that a business can write off at a maximum rate of 7 per cent.

As with all such problems in tax law, we return to general principles to determine how best we can measure income. To be sure, the well-known brand names are already institutions in the marketplace. In these cases, the domain name has a commercial value that is equivalent to a copyright, patent, trademark or trade name. There are other cases, however, where a domain name has only a limited and transitional value. Given the rapidly expanding nature of electronic commerce and technology, the life of a domain name as we know it today may be transitional. Thus, the write-off for expenditures for limited-life domain names should be commensurately rapid.

Comprehensive Example

Computation of Net Income for Tax Purposes		

Assume:

A taxable Canadian corporation with June 30 as its year-end provides the following statement of income for its 2004 taxation year:

Income Statement — 2004

Revenue		$ 2,000,000
Costs of goods sold:		
Inventory — opening	$ 300,000	
Purchases	800,000	
Cost of goods available	1,100,000	
Inventory — closing	(200,000)	(900,000)
Gross profit		1,100,000
General, administrative and selling expenses:		
Depreciation and amortization	$ 120,000	
Accounting & legal	15,000	
Commission	80,000	
Donations	30,000	
Bad debts	25,000	
Rental	120,000	
Salary, wages and fringe	250,000	
Interest	35,000	
Insurance	5,000	
Travel (airline)	20,000	
Utilities	45,000	
General	100,000	(845,000)
Income before under-noted items		255,000
Other income:		
Dividends	$ 20,000	
Interest	15,000	
Receipt on disposal of investment	50,000	85,000
Income before income tax expense		340,000

Computation of Net Income for Tax Purposes

Current	$ 30,000	
Deferred	140,000	(170,000)
Net income		$ 170,000

Additional information on the above income statement is as follows:

(a) The $50,000 receipt on disposal of investment was the result of the sale of some securities that were acquired in 1974 at a cost of $5,000, resulting in a capital gain of $45,000.

(b) The interest income was derived from the accounts receivable for late payments.

(c) The $20,000 dividends were received from shares that are held for investment purposes.

(d) Included in the general expenses of $100,000 is $5,000 paid as an entrance fee to a social club. In addition, $50,000 was accrued as bonus to be paid to the two senior executives of the company. As of August 10, 2004, the bonus accruals of 2002 and 2003 taxation years of $30,000 and $35,000, respectively, remained unpaid.

(e) Interest expense includes $8,500 of interest paid for late instalments of corporate tax.

(f) The $25,000 bad debts expense was determined for accounting purposes. For income tax purposes, a reserve for bad debts of $35,000 was made at the end of the preceding year; $10,000 was determined to be bad in 2004 and was written off; $4,000 has been collected in 2004 from the accounts written off in previous years; and a reserve for bad debts at the end of the 2004 taxation year was determined to be $50,000.

(g) The maximum capital cost allowance that could be claimed for the year is $100,000. The balance of the cumulative eligible capital account is $64,285 before amortization.

(h) Donations are made up of the following payments:

i) Canadian Red Cross	$10,000
ii) Federal political parties	15,000
iii) United Nations	5,000

Then:

DETERMINATION OF 2004 NET INCOME FOR TAX PURPOSES

Net income per financial statements

$ 170,000

Computation of Net Income for Tax Purposes		
ADD:		
Income tax expense	$ 170,000	
Taxable capital gain	22,500	
Entrance fee	5,000	
Accrued bonus (2003)	35,000	
Interest on late instalment	8,500	
Bad debts	25,000	
Reserve (2003)	35,000	
Bad debts recovered	4,000	
Depreciation & amortization	120,000	
Donations & political contributions	30,000	455,000
		625,000
LESS:		
Gain on investment	$ 50,000	
Bad debts	10,000	
Reserve (2004)	50,000	
CCA	100,000	
CEC deduction at 7%	4,500	(214,500)
Net income for tax purposes		$ 410,500

Selected Bibliography to Chapter 9

General Deductions

Brooks, Neil, "The Principles Underlying the Deduction of Business Expenses", *Canadian Taxation*, Hansen, Krishna, Rendall, eds. (Toronto: Richard De Boo, 1981), chapter 5.

Cruikshank, Allan B., "Business Expenses Under the White Paper on Tax Reform", in *Proceedings of 39th Tax Conf.* 24:1 (Can. Tax Foundation, 1987).

Goodison, Don, "Allowable Business Expenditures" (May 1989) 23 CGA Magazine 14.

Hershfield, J.E., "Recent Trends in the Deduction of Expenses in Computing Income", in *Proceedings of 41st Tax Conf.* 44:1 (Can. Tax Foundation, 1989).

Lawrence J., "Income Receipts and Deductions in the Computations of Income from Employment, Business and Property", in *Proceedings of 31st Tax Conf.* 381 (Can. Tax Foundation, 1979).

Krishna, Vern, "Does Supreme Court Expand Deductibility of Business Expense in Symes?", (1994) Can. Current Tax J. 35.

McCart, Janice, "Deductibility of Business Expenses: Recent Developments", in *Proceedings of 37th Tax Conf.* 41 (Can. Tax Foundation, 1985).

Neville, Ralph T., "Deductibility of Automobiles, Meals and Entertainment and Home Office Expenses After Tax Reform", in *Proceedings of 40th Tax Conf.* 25:1 (Can. Tax Foundation, 1988).

Perry, Harvey, "Federal Individual Income Tax: Taxable Income and Tax", *Tax Paper No. 89* 58 (Can. Tax Foundation, 1990).

Verchere, Bruce, "Deductible Expenses", *Corporate Management Tax Conf.* 55 (Can. Tax Foundation, 1975).

Unreasonable Expenses

McGregor, G., "The 'Reasonable' Test for Business Expenses" (1959) 7 Can. Tax J. 318.

McIntyre, J.M., "The Deduction of Illegal Expenses" (1965) 2 U.B.C.L. Rev. 283.

Personal and Living Expenses

Hershfield, J.E., "Recent Trends in the Deduction of Expenses in Computing Income", in *Proceedings of 41st Tax Conf.* 44:1 (Can. Tax Foundation, 1989).

Perry, Harvey, "Federal Individual Income Tax: Taxable Income and Tax", *Tax Paper No. 89* 58 (Can. Tax Foundation, 1990).

Ramaseder, Brigitte, "Department Continues to Hold Restrictive View on Deductibility of Costs Related to Acquisition of New Residence" (1993) 5 Tax of Executive Compensation and Retirement 844.

Current Expense or Capital Expenditure

Cunningham, Noel B., and Deborah H. Schend, "How to Tax The House That Jack Built" (Spring 1988) 43 Tax Law Review 447.

"Distinguishing Between Capital Expenditures and Ordinary Business Expenses: A Proposal for a Universal Standard" (Spring 1986) 19 U. Mich. J.L. Ref. 711.

Spiro, D.E., "'Genuine Repair Crisis': A Gloss is Added to the Capital 'Improvement' Test for Repair Expenses" (1987) 35 Can. Tax J. 419.

Tremblay, Richard G. and Helen Aston, "The Deductibility of Environmental Clean-Up Costs" (September 1991) 3 Can. Current Tax C77.

Reserves

Champagne, Donald C., "Bad and Doubtful Debts, Mortgage Foreclosures and Conditional Sales Repossessions", in *Proceedings of 27th Tax Conf.* 682 (Can. Tax Foundation, 1975).

Dzau, Vivien, "Reserves: A Tool for Deferring Taxes" (1980) 113 CA Magazine 57.

Krishna, Vern, "Reserves" (1984) 1 Can. Current Tax J-41.

McCullogh, J.D., "Deferred Income Reserves — Improving Cash Flow" (1975) 106 CA Magazine 51.

Merrell, David L., "Bill C-139: New Reserve Provisions and the Forward Averaging Refundable Tax Rules", *Prairie Provinces Tax Conf.* 195 (Can. Tax Foundation, 1983).

Mida, Israel H., "Deductibility of Reserves: Contractors, Maintenance Contracts, Captive Insurance Arrangements", *Corporate Management Tax Conf.* 4:1 (Can. Tax Foundation, 1987).

Nitikman, Bert W., "Reserves", in *Proceedings of 25th Tax Conf.* (Can. Tax Foundation, 1973).

Smyth, "Accounting for Reserves — Tax Relationship and Gross Earnings" (1959) 75 Can. Chartered Accountant 549.

Interest

Arnold, Brian J., and Gordon D. Dixon, "Rubbing Salt into the Wound: The Denial of the Interest Deduction After the Loss of a Source of Income" (1991) 39 Can. Tax. J. 1473.

Atsidis, Elisabeth, "Technical Amendments to the Interest Deductibility Rules in the *Income Tax Act* as Proposed on 20 December 1991" (1993) 2 Dal. J. Leg. Studies 265.

Bale, Gordon, "The Interest Deduction Dilemma" (1973) Can. Tax J. 317.

Bankman, Joseph, and William A. Klein, "Accurate Taxation of Long-Term Debt: Taking Into Account the Term Structure of Interest" (Winter 1989) 44 Tax Law Review 335.

Berger, Sydney H., and Mark Potechin, "When is Interest Expense Deductible?" (1986) 119:5 CA Magazine 54.

Birnie, David A.G., "Consolidation of Corporate Structures", in *Proceedings of 31st Tax Conf.* 177 (Can. Tax Foundation, 1979).

Block, Cheryl D., "The Trouble with Interest: Reflections on Interest Deductions After the *Tax Reform Act* of 1986" (Fall 1988) 40 University of Florida Law Review 689.

Bouman, Donald G.H., "Debt Financing-II", *Corporate Management Tax Conf.* 88 (Can. Tax Foundation, 1974).

"Bronfman Panacea or Pandora's Box" (1990) 44 D.T.C. 7009.

Couzin, Robert, James R. Daman, Michael Hiltz and William R. Lawlor, "Tax Treatment of Interest: Bronfman Trust and the June 2, 1987 Release", *Corporate Management Tax Conf.* 10:1 (Can. Tax Foundation, 1987).

Crawford, William E., "The Deductibility of Interest", in *Proceedings of 42nd Tax Conf.* 4:10 (Can. Tax Foundation, 1990).

Crowe, Ian, "Tax — I'm Tired of Yoghurt" (June 1991) 124 CA Magazine 29.

Damji, Nazee, "Interest and Penalty Charges" (April 1990) 64 CMA Magazine 15.

"Discounts, Premiums and Bonuses and the Repeal of IT-114: What Happens Now" (1994) No. 1181 Tax Topics 1.

Drache, Arthur B.C., "Draft Interest Expense Legislation" (1992) 14 Can. Taxpayer 11.

Drache, Arthur B.C., "Interest Deductibility: Loans to Shareholders and Employees" (1983) 5 Can. Taxpayer 179.

Drache, Arthur B.C., "Interest Deductibility: Planning Still Worthwhile" (1991) 13 Can. Taxpayer 102.

Drache, Arthur B.C., "Interest Deductibility Reviewed" (1991) 13 Can. Taxpayer 189.

Drache, Arthur B.C.,"Mortgage Interest Deductible ... For Now" (1987) 9:4 Can. Taxpayer 29.

Edgar, Tim, and Brian J. Arnold, "Reflections on the Submission of the CBA-CICA Joint Committee on Taxation Concerning the Deductibility of Interest" (1992) 38 Can. Tax J. 847.

Edwards, Stanley E., "Debt Financing-I", *Corporate Management Tax Conf.* 70 (Can. Tax Foundation, 1974).

Ewens, Douglas S., "The Thin Capitalization Restrictions" (1994) Can. Tax J. 954.

Fox-Revett, Melissa G., "Interest Deductibility", (1993) Can. Current Tax P19.

Gagnon, Guy A., "Deducting Shareholder Interest the Hard Way" (1992) 40 Can. Tax J. 1343.

Glover, Paul, "Interest is Deductible — Isn't It?" (July-August 1987) 61 CMA Magazine 28.

Henly, K.S.M., "Late Payment Charges: Interest for the Purpose of Thin Capitalization Rules?" (1987) 35 Can. Tax J. 143.

Hickey, Paul B., "The Proposed New Interest Deductibility Regime: Strategies and Pitfalls" in *Processing of 46th Tax Conference* (Can. Tax Foundation, 1992).

Huggett, Donald R., "A Matter of Interest" (1987) 14 Can. Tax News 105.

Huggett, Donald R. (ed.), "Speculators Beware" (1980) 7 Can. Tax News 114.

"Income Tax Treatment of Interest — What's Happening" (1995) No. 1196 Tax Topics 2.

"Interest Deductibility Revisited" (1990) 44 D.T.C. 7026.

"Interest Expense Detailed" (1992) 4:11 Tax Notes Inter. 513.

Krever, Richard, "'Capital or Current': The Tax Treatment of Expenditures to Preserve a Taxpayer's Title or Interest in Assets" (1986) 12 Monash Univ. L.R. 49.

Krishna, Vern, "Deducting Interest Expenses" (1983) 17:11 CGA Magazine 21.

Krishna, Vern, "Interest Deductibility: More Form Over Substance", (1993) Can. Current Tax C17.

Krishna, Vern, "Interest Expenses" (1983) 17:7 CGA Magazine 39.

Krishna, Vern, "Is There a Choice of Methods in Accounting for Interest Expenses?" (1984) 1 Can. Current Tax C-21.

Krishna, Vern, "More Uncertainty on Deduction of Interest Expenses" [Case Comment: *Attaie v. Canada (M.N.R.)*, T-1319-85(1987) (T.C.)] (1987–89) 2 Can. Current Tax J-59.

Latimer, W.R., "Capitalization of Interest" (1969) 17 Can. Tax J. 331.

Lavelle, P.M., "Deductibility of Interest Costs" (1981) 29 Can. Tax J. 536.

Lawlor, William B., "Interest Deductibility: Where to After Bronfman Trust?", in *Proceedings of 39th Tax Conf.* 19:1 (Can. Tax Foundation, 1987).

Lindsay, Robert F., "Tax Aspects of Real Estate Financing", *Corporate Management Tax Conf.* 258 (Can. Tax Foundation, 1983).

Loveland, Norman C., "Income Tax Aspects of Borrowing and Lending", (1986) Special Lectures LSUC 289.

McDonnell, T.E., "Without a Trace" (1993) 41 Can. Tax J. 134.

McNair, D. Keith, "Restricted Interest Expense" (1987) 35 Can. Tax J. 616.

Mitchell, George, "Current Assessing Trends" (1979) 27 Can. Tax J. 256.

Neville, Ralph T., "Tax Considerations in Real Estate Development and Construction", *Corporate Management Tax Conf.* 7:1 (Can. Tax Foundation, 1989).

Riehl, Gordon W., "Debt Instruments", in *Proceedings of 27th Tax Conf.* 764 (Can. Tax Foundation, 1975).

Shoup, Carl S., "Deduction of Homeowners' Mortgage Interest, Interest on Other Consumer Debt, and Property Taxes Under the Individual Income Tax: The Horizontal Equity Issue" (1979) 27 Can. Tax J. 529.

Smith, David W., "Supreme Court Shakes Up Interest-Deduction Rules" (April 1987) 14:4 Nat. 17.

Smith, Ronald, J., "Sales of Real Estate: Tax Planning for the Buyer", *Corporate Management Tax Conf.* 159 (Can. Tax Foundation, 1983).

Steiss, "Deductibility of Financing Charges", in *Proceedings of 24th Tax Conf.* 126 (Can. Tax Foundation, 1972).

Stikeman, H.H. (ed.), "Interest Deductibility — The Purpose Test", Canada Tax Letter, April 21, 1980 (De Boo).

Stikeman, H.H. (ed.), "The Deduction of Interest and the 'Use' of Money", Canada Tax Letter, July 10, 1974 (De Boo).

Thomas, Douglas, "As a Matter of Interest" (1978) 3 CA Magazine 84.

Ward, David A., "Arm's Length Acquisition Relating to Shares in a Public Corporation", *Corporate Management Tax Conf.* 108 (Can. Tax Foundation, 1978).

Wraggett, Cathy, "Minimizing Your Personal Tax Burden" (March 1990) 64 CMA Magazine 21.

Capital Cost Allowance

Arnold, Brian J., "Conversions of Property to and from Inventory: Tax Consequences" (1976) 24 Can. Tax J. 231.

Arnold, Brian J., "Recent Developments in the Tax Treatment of Inventory", in *Proceedings of 31st Tax Conf.* 865 (Can. Tax Foundation, 1979).

Bird, R.W., and J.R. Williamson, "Capital Cost Allowance" (1981) Can. Taxation 251.

Carter, Ronald W., "CCA and Eligible Capital Property: Tax Reform Implications", in *Proceedings of 40th Tax Conf.* 27:1 (Can. Tax Foundation, 1988).

Colley, Geoffrey M., "More on Capital Cost Allowance" (1976) 109 CA Magazine 62.

Daniels, C. Paul, "Real Estate Investment as a Tax Shelter", in *Proceedings of 28th Tax Conf.* 179 (Can. Tax Foundation, 1976).

"Distinguishing Between Capital Expenditures and Ordinary Business Expenses: A Proposal for a Universal Standard" (Spring 1986) 19 U. Mich. J.L. Ref. 711.

Harris, N.H., "Capital Cost Allowance" (1984) 1 Computer L. 26.

Harris, N.H., "Tax Aspects of Condominium Conversions and Lease Inducement Payments to Recipients", in *Proceedings of 38th Tax Conf.* 45 (Can. Tax Foundation, 1986).

Harris, N.H., "Capital Cost Allowances", in *Proceedings of 21st Tax Conf.* 200 at 231 (Can. Tax Foundation, 1968).

Harris, N.H., "Replacement Property", in *Proceedings of 29th Tax Conf.* 395 (Can. Tax Foundation, 1977).

Huggett, Donald R. (ed.), "Capital Cost Allowances" (1974) 11 Canadian Tax News 71.

Louis, David, *Canada's Best Real Estate Tax Shelters* (Toronto: Hume Pub. Co., 1985).

MacDonald, R.C., "Capital Cost Allowances" (1973) 47 Cost and Management 43.

Matheson, David I., "Acquisition and Disposition of Depreciable Assets" (1969) 17 Can. Tax J. 277.

Milrad, L.H., "Computers and the Law: The Taxation of Computer Systems — An Overview" (1984) 1 Bus. & L. 65.

Revenue Canada Round Table, *Corporate Management Tax Conf.* 601 (Can. Tax Foundation, 1979).

Revenue Canada Round Table, in *Proceedings of 36th Tax Conf.* 834-35 (Can. Tax Foundation, 1984).

Silver, Sheldon "Tax Implications of Different Forms of Holding Real Estate", in *Proceedings of 25th Tax Conf.* 425 (Can. Tax Foundation, 1973).

Sterritt, Deborah, "Partnerships and the Rental Property CCA Restriction: News to Some, Relief to Others", (1987–89) Can. Current Tax P35.

Stikeman, H.H. (ed.), "A Brave New World of Recapture", Canada Tax Letter, September 10, 1976 (De Boo).

Strain, W.J., "Capital Cost Allowances", *Corporate Management Tax Conf.* 26 (Can. Tax Foundation, 1975).

Weyman, C. David, "Manufacturing and Processing, Valuations and Business Deductions Including Capital Cost Allowances", in *Proceedings of 31st Tax Conf.* 254 (Can. Tax Foundation, 1980).

Witterick, Robert G., "Syndicated Acquisitions and Financing of Businesses", *Corporate Management Tax Conf.* 3:1 (Can. Tax Foundation, 1990).

Eligible Capital Property

Carter, Ronald W., "CCA and Eligible Capital Property: Tax Reform Implications", in *Proceedings of 40th Tax Conf.* 27:1 (Can. Tax Foundation, 1988).

Dwyer, Blair P., "Deductibility of Tenant Inducement Payments (Income Tax)" (1987–89) 2 Can. Current Tax C-53.

Grant, Carl T., "The Valuation and Tax Treatment of Goodwill", in *Proceedings of 24th Tax Conf.* 467 (Can. Tax Foundation, 1972).

Huggett, Donald R. (ed.), "Eligible Capital Expenditures" (1974) 11 Can. Tax News 46.

Johnston, Albert N., "All About Nothings" (1977) 110 CA Magazine 47.

Krishna, Vern, "Indirect Payments and Transfers of Income" (1986) 1:28 Can. Current Tax J-137.

Krishna, Vern, "Sale of Franchises: Receipts on Account of Eligible Capital Property or Income from Business?" (1986) 1 Can. Current Tax J-157.

McCallum, J.Thomas, "The Right Rollovers" (October 1991) 25 CGA Magazine 17.

McKay, Russell E., "Income Taxation of a Professional Partnership", in *Proceedings of 24th Tax Conf.* 421 (Can. Tax Foundation, 1972).

Mogan, Murray A., "Recent Developments in Federal Taxation of Income and Deductions", in *Proceedings of 29th Tax Conf.* 59 (Can. Tax Foundation, 1977).

Stikeman, H.H.,"Goodwill or Illwill: When is a Nothing Something?", *Canada Tax Letter*, Feb. 19, 1975 (De Boo).

Stikeman, H.H. (ed.), "Payments for Know-How or Research", Canada Tax Letter, March 31, 1975 (De Boo).

Ward, David A., "Tax Considerations Relating to the Purchase of Assets of a Business", *Corporate Management Tax Conf.* 22 (Can. Tax Foundation, 1972).

Ward, David A. and Neil Armstrong, "Corporate Taxation: Lease Inducement Payments" (1986) 5 Legal Alert 98.

Home Office Expenses

Neville, Ralph T., "Deductibility of Automobiles, Meals and Entertainment and Home Office Expenses After Tax Reform", in *Proceedings of 40th Tax Conf.* 25:1 (Can. Tax Foundation, 1988).

Convention Expenses

Drache, Arthur B.C., "Deductible Convention Expenses" (1992) 13 Can. Taxpayer 7.

Drache, Arthur B.C., "Medical Convention Expenses" (1983) 5 The Can. Taxpayer 124.

Selected Other Deductions

"Automobile Expense Deduction Limits for 1995" (1994) No. 1185 Tax Topics 2.

Bacal, Norman, and Richard Lewin, "Once Bitten, Twice Shy? The Canadian Film Industry Revisited", in *Proceedings of 38th Tax Conf.* 46 (Can. Tax Foundation, 1986).

Colley, Geoffrey M., "Tax Relief for Overseas Employment Income" (1983) 116:11 CA Magazine 71.

Colley, Geoffrey M., "The 3% Inventory Allowance" (1978) 4 CA Magazine 106.

"Company Cars and Automobile Expense" (Toronto: Coopers & Lybrand Canada, 1991).

Corn, G., "Deductibility of Landscaping Costs" (1984) 1 Can. Current Tax J-27.

"Deductible Advertising Expenses" (1995) No. 1195 Tax Topics 3.

Drache, Arthur B.C., "Top Hat Pension Plans: A Rethink" (1983) 5 Can. Taxpayer 155.

Farwell, Peter M., "Scientific Research and Experimental Development", *Corporate Management Tax Conf.* 7:1 (Can. Tax Foundation, 1986).

Gillespie, Thomas S., "Lease Financing: An Update", in *Proceedings of 41st Tax Conf.* 24:1 (Can. Tax Foundation, 1989).

Goldstein, D.L., "Whether a Charitable Donation is Deductible as a Business Expense" [Case Comment: *Impenco Ltd. v. M.N.R.*, [1988] 1 C.T.C. 2339 (T.C.C.)] (1988) 36 Can. Tax J. 695.

Huggett, Donald R. (ed.), "Inventory Allowance" (1980) 7 Can. Tax News 98.

Huggett, Donald R., "Training Costs for Professionals and Other Independent Businessmen" (1980) 8 Canadian Tax News 26.

Krasa, Eva M., "The Income Tax Treatment of Legal Expenses" (1986) 34 Can. Tax J. 757.

Krasa, Eva M., "The Deductibility of Fines, Penalties, Damages and Contract Termination Payments" (1992) 38 Can. Tax Journal 1399.

Krishna, Vern, "Deductibility of Legal and Accounting Fees in Defending Tax Evasion Charges (IT-99R3)" (1986) 1 Can. Current Tax C-129.

Krishna, Vern, "Deducting Fines and Penalties" (September 1988) 22 CGA Magazine 35.

Langlois, Robert, et al., "Mid-Year Amalgamations", *Canada Tax Letter*, Jan. 20, 1978 (De Boo).

McDonnell, T.E., "Issue Costs of Interests in Real Estate Syndicate Deductible" (1992) 40 Can. Tax Journal 710.

Murray, Kenneth J., "The Definition of Scientific Research for Income Tax Purposes", in *Proceedings of 36th Tax Conf.* 563 (Can. Tax Foundation, 1984).

Neville, Ralph T., "Tax Considerations in Real Estate Development and Construction", *Corporate Management Tax Conf.* 7:1 (Can. Tax Foundation, 1989).

Novek, Barbara L., "Deductibility of Financing Expenses", *Corporate Management Tax Conf.* 3:1 (Can. Tax Foundation, 1992).

Pitfield, Ian H., "Prepaid Expenses and Other Deductions — Recent Developments" (1980) 14 CGA Magazine 41.

"Revenue Canada's Framework for Automobile Deductions" (1993) 5 Tax. of Executive Compensation and Retirement 839.

Shafer, Joel, "Income Tax Aspects of Real Estate Financing", *Corporate Management Tax Conf.* 1:1 (Can. Tax Foundation, 1989).

Tremblay, Richard G. and Helen Aston, "The Deductibility of Environmental Clean-up Costs", (1991) Can. Current Tax C77,

Valliere, Charles E., "Both Deduction and Capitalization Treatment Denied for Expenses with Respect to Real Estate that Produces No Income" (1991) 39 Can. Tax J. 1033.

Other

Anthony, Irene, "Franchising" (1983) 116:10 CA Magazine 20.

Beam, R.E., and S.N. Laiken, "Personal Tax Planning — Changes in Use and Non-Arm's Length Transfers of Depreciable Property" (1987) 35 Can. Tax J. 453.

Dean, Jacklyn I., "The January 15, 1987 Draft Amendments Relating to the Acquisition of Gains and Losses", *Corporate Management Tax Conf.* 2:1 (Can. Tax Foundation, 1987).

Drache, Arthur B.C., "Indirect Gifting: The Taxman's Approach" (1980) 2 Can. Taxpayer 167.

Drache, Arthur B.C., "On the Move?" (1979) 1 The Canadian Taxpayer 96.

Fairwell, Peter M., "Debt and Capital Gains Taxation" (1972) 20 Can. Tax J. 101.

Goodison, Donald, "Sex Discrimination and the *Income Tax Act*" (1979) 13 CGA Magazine 20.

O'Brien, Martin L., "Sale of Assets: The Vendor's Position", *Corporate Management Tax Conf.* 1 (Can. Tax Foundation, 1972).

Romano, Dianne L., "Reducing Immediate Tax Liabilities on Asset Disposals" (1979) 53 Cost and Management 44.

Strother, Robert C., "Transfer of Losses and Deduction Between Unrelated Taxpayers" (1987) 2 Can. Current Tax C-19.

Scace, Arthur R.A., and Michael G. Quigley, "Zero Coupon Obligations, Stripped Bonds, and Defeasance — An Update" (1984) 32 Can. Tax J. 689.

Williamson, W. Gordon, "Transfers of Assets to and from a Canadian Corporation", in *Proceedings of 38th Tax Conf.* 12 (Can. Tax Foundation, 1986).

CHAPTER 10 — DAMAGES

I. — General Comment

The only thing that one can say with any certainty about the taxation of damage awards is that some are taxable and others are not. The difficulty lies in properly characterizing the underlying cause of legal action for tax purposes. Are damages income? The answer may depend on what happens at several steps in the litigation process. However, given the speed of our legal system, taxpayers may wait for twenty years for the ultimate resolution of the question.

Broadly speaking, damages in lieu of income that would otherwise have been taxable retain their character as such and are taxable. Thus, in order to determine the nature of damages we need to properly characterize the underlying purpose of the award. The first stage is in framing the cause of action and the claim for damages in the litigation pleadings. Unfortunately, counsel are not usually inclined to consider tax issues at this stage because they are primarily focused on establishing liability. The pleadings can, however, affect the court's assessment of damages.

The second stage is identifying the various parts of the award and the methodology that the trial judge uses for each component. Typically, damage awards breakdown into general damages, special damages, punitive damages (if any), pre-judgement and post-judgement interest. Each of these components can have different tax consequences. Of course, at the end of the long litigation journey, the plaintiff's only real concern is on the amount that he or she eventually gets to keep after all costs, fees and taxes.

The third stage is the actual calculation of the amount of damages. This is the step that is most likely to cause subsequent disputes with the tax authorities. One needs a yardstick to calculate losses and the most obvious choice is to use earnings lost as a result of the wrong done. But that does not mean that the yardstick determines the character of the underlying award. Thus, merely because the trial judge calculates the award by reference to earnings that might otherwise have been taxable does not make the damage award taxable.

In both examples, we determine the *quantum* of capital by capitalizing the *income* that the capital generates. However, the fact that one uses lost profits as the reference point in the calculation of damages does not conclusively determine whether the damages are taxable or non-taxable. It is the actual nature of the settled interest that determines taxability. Thus, just as we can sometimes transform taxable profits into non-taxable capital receipts, we can crystallize an income stream of lost profits into a lump sum non-taxable capital amount.

The taxation of damage awards depends upon the fundamental character of the legal rights that give rise to the litigation. Proper characterization of each component of damages at trial of the action will reduce the uncertainty of subsequent treatment of the damages as income or capital for tax purposes. It will also prevent further prolonged litigation in the tax courts.

The difficulty is in characterizing the underlying nature of the damage award.[1] In *London & Thames Haven Oil Wharves Ltd. v. Attwooll*, for example, the Court said:[2]

> Judges have from time to time been careful to say that no clear and comprehensive rule can be formulated, and no clear line of demarcation can be drawn, by reference to which it can be determined in every case whether the sum received should be regarded as a capital receipt or as a revenue receipt to be taken into account in arriving at the profit or gains of the recipient's trade. Each case must be considered on its own facts.

Therefore, we need to carefully identify the nature of the underlying claim and the cause of action. Additionally, one must determine the character of the damage award: is the award designed to compensate or punish the payer? Finally, if the damage award compensates one must enquire as to the nature of the compensation.

II. — Breach Of Contract

1. — Nature of Claim

Damages for breach of contract are generally decided on the principle of compensation. Thus, contract damages usually restore the plaintiff to the financial position he or she would have enjoyed had the defendant performed the contract.[3] The plaintiff is entitled to the eco-

---

[1]See, for example, the 4:3 split decision of the Supreme Court of Canada in *Tsiaprailis v. R.*, [2005] S.C.J. No. 9, 2005 CarswellNat 431, 2005 CarswellNat 432, [2005] 2 C.T.C. 1 (S.C.C.) February 25, 2005.

[2][1966] 3 All E.R. 145 at 149; revd. [1967] 2 All E.R. 124 (Eng. C.A.) [*London & Thames*].

[3]*Livingstone v. Rawyards Coal Co.* (1880), [1879-80] 5 App. Cas. 25, 28 W.R. 357 (U.K. H.L.) at 39 [App. Cas], Lord Blackburn (damages represent "that sum of money which will put the party who has been injured, or who has suffered, in the same position as he would have been in if he had not sus-

nomic value of his bargain or "expectation interest". Courts rarely award exemplary or punitive damages in contract cases.[4]

2. — The Surrogatum Principle

The general principle is that damages in lieu of receipts that would otherwise have been taxable to the taxpayer are taxable as income. Diplock L.J. stated the principle as follows:[5]

> Where, pursuant to a legal right, a trader receives from another person, compensation for the trader's failure to receive a sum of money which, if it had been received, would have been credited to the amount of profits (if any) arising in any year from the trade carried on by him at the time when the compensation is so received, the compensation is to be treated for income tax purposes in the same way as that sum of money would have been treated if it had been received instead of the compensation. The rule is applicable whatever the source of the legal right of the trader to recover the compensation. It may arise [1] from a primary obligation under a contract, such as a contract of insurance; [2] from a secondary obligation arising out of

---

tained the wrong for which he is now getting his compensation or reparation"); see Street, *Principles of the Law of Damages* (London: Sweet & Maxwell, 1962) at 3; *Yetton v. Eastwoods Froy Ltd.*, [1967] 1 W.L.R. 103, [1966] 3 All E.R. 353 (Eng. Q.B.) at 115 [W.L.R.], Blain J.; Ogus, The Law of Damages (London: Butterworths, 1973) at 17-21, 283-8; *Admiralty Commrs. v. S.S. Susquehanna*, [1926] A.C. 655 (U.K. H.L.) at 661 (loss to damaged ship owners not constituting lost profits from mercantile charter where ship would not have been chartered); *Victoria Laundry (Windsor) Ltd. v. Newman Indust. Ltd.*, [1949] 2 K.B. 528, [1949] 1 All E.R. 997 (Eng. C.A.) at 539 [K.B.], Asquith L.J. (damages for late delivery of boiler deemed foreseeable business losses); *Robinson v. Harman* ((1848), 1 Ex. 850, 154 E.R. 363 (Ex. Ct.) at 855 [Ex.], Parke B. (tenant knew lessee did not have title to property leased; damages assessed at entire amount of loss notwithstanding); *Koufos v. C. Czarnikow Ltd.*, [1969] 1 A.C. 350 (U.K. H.L.) at 400, Lord Morris (sugar cargo depreciated as market price dropped while ship dallying *en route*; shipowner expected to have contemplated such result); *British Westinghouse Electric Mfg. Co. v. Underground Electric Rys. Co. of London*, [1912] A.C. 673, [1911-1913] All E.R. Rep. 63 (U.K. H.L.) at 689 [A.C.], Viscount Haldane L.C. (measure of damages where defective turbines replaced and replacement turbines achieved greater efficiency than the ones in question).

[4]*Addis v. Gramophone Co.*, [1909] A.C. 488, [1908-10] All E.R. Rep. 1 (Eng. H.L.) (although discredited by wrongful dismissal, employee not able to claim compensation for injured feelings or lack of notice); *Dobson v. Winton & Robbins Ltd.*, [1959] S.C.R. 775, 20 D.L.R. (2d) 164 (S.C.C.) (vendor suing on contract of sale of land entitled to specific performance or damages equal to decrease in price eventually received plus interest). See however *Jarvis v. Swan Tours Ltd.* (1972), [1973] 1 Q.B. 233, [1973] 1 All E.R. 71 (Eng. C.A.) (damages awarded against travel agent when plaintiff's holiday failed to meet advertised description).

[5]*London & Thames*, [1967] 2 All E.R. 124 (Eng. C.A.) at 134. See also *Schwartz v. Canada*, [1994] 2 C.T.C. 99, 94 D.T.C. 6249 (F.C.A.); revd. [1996] 1 S.C.R. 254, [1996] 1 C.T.C. 303, 96 D.T.C. 6103 (S.C.C.) (surrogatum principle also applies to employment contracts, whether anticipatory or otherwise).

nonperformance of a contract, such as a right to damages, either liquidated, as under the de-murrage clause in a charter party, or unliquidated; [3] from an obligation to pay damages for tort . . .; [4] from a statutory obligation; [5] or in any other way in which legal obligations arise.

Thus, one must determine whether the receipts, in lieu of which the damages compensate, would have been taxable. Note, however, the characterization of damages as taxable income or non-taxable capital receipts depends upon the nature of the legal right settled and not upon the method used to calculate the award.

3. — *Nature of Legal Rights*

Since damages represent compensation equal to the economic value of the underlying bargain, we usually compute them by reference to the profit lost through non-performance of the contract. However, the fact that one uses lost profits as the reference point to calculate damages does not conclusively determine whether the damages are taxable or non-taxable. It is the nature of the settled interest that determines taxability. Take a simple example. A has a contract with B that will render him a profit of $10,000 per year for the next 15 years. If B does not perform the contract, A will lose $150,000 in profits. Ignoring problems of mitigation, etc., A would usually be entitled to the present value of that amount, which at a discount rate of 8 per cent is $85,595.

Whether the $85,595 is taxable as income depends upon the nature of the contract and not upon the fact that one determines the damages by reference to the annual profits. This is so even if the profits would have been taxable during the normal tenure of the contract. Destruction of an entire business, for example, will invoke compensation for capital even if one determines the capitalized value by discounting future lost profits. Thus, taxable profits may transform into non-taxable capital receipts when we crystallize an income stream into a lump-sum capital amount.

4. — *Global Payments*

A global payment covering several different heads of damages, for example, loss of earnings and payment on account of capital should be broken down and distributed into its taxable and non-taxable segments. The allocation is fairly easy where a court awards damages as a result of litigation and the judgment sets out the various heads of damages. An amount paid in settlement of a cause of action is more difficult to allocate and one should allocate amounts during negotiation of the settlement.

5. — Capital Receipts

Payments on account of capital are not taxable. This is so whether the payment is on account of judicially assessed damages or pursuant to a settlement. For example, a payment to compensate the plaintiff for the destruction of the entire structure of his or her income earning apparatus is a capital receipt.

The distinction between income and capital receipts is easy to state in principle. The difficulty lies in the application of the principle to the particular facts. Are damages for the cancellation of a lucrative service contract, for example, taxable in lieu of the profit that the taxpayer would have earned on the contract? What if the contract is the entire substratum of the business and its cancellation renders the enterprise a hollow shell? The difference between the two cases is essentially one of degree.[6]

6. — Non-Performance

Damages for non-performance of a service contract are usually taxable as income unless non-performance materially and substantially dislocates the taxpayer's business structure. Lord Russell explained the principle as follows:[7]

> The sum received by a commercial firm as compensation for the loss sustained by the cancellation of a trading contract or the premature termination of an agency agreement may, in the recipient's hands, be regarded either as a capital receipt or as a trading receipt forming part of the trading profit. It may be difficult to formulate a general principle by reference to which in all cases the correct decision will be arrived at since in each case the question comes to be one of circumstance and degree. When the rights and advantages surrendered on cancellation are such as to destroy or materially to cripple the whole structure of the recipient's profit-making apparatus, involving the serious dislocation of the normal commercial organisation and resulting perhaps in the cutting down of the staff previously required, the recipient of the compensation may properly affirm that the compensation represents the price paid for the loss or sterilisation of a capital asset and is therefore a capital and not a revenue receipt.

In *Van Den Berghs Ltd. v. Clark*,[8] for example, the taxpayer entered into an agreement with its competitor that provided for, among other things, profit-sharing, joint arrangements, control of supply, and restrictions on entering into other pooling arrangements. The parties ter-

---

[6]See e.g., *Schofield Oil Ltd. v. Canada*, [1992] 1 C.T.C. 8, 92 D.T.C. 6022 (F.C.A.) ($1.37 million payment to release party from remaining 20 months of contractual obligations considered compensation for future profits and taxable as lost income).

[7]*I.R.C. v. Fleming & Co. (Machinery) Ltd.* (1951), 33 Tax Cas. 57 (Scot.) at 63.

[8][1935] A.C. 431, All E.R. Rep. 874 (U.K. H.L.). See also *Transocean Offshore Ltd. v. R.*, 2004 TCC 454, [2004] 5 C.T.C. 2133, 2004 D.T.C. 2915 (T.C.C. [General Procedure]); affirmed [2005] 2 C.T.C. 183 (F.C.A.); leave to appeal refused (2005), 2005 CarswellNat 3125, 2005 CarswellNat 3126 (S.C.C.) (Cdn corporation paid non-resident corporation $40 million in damages to compensate for the repudia-

minated the contract following a dispute between them and the taxpayer received compensation for cancellation of its future rights under the contract. The Court considered the compensation to be on account of a non-taxable capital receipt. In Lord MacMillan's words:[9]

> [T]he cancelled agreements related to the whole structure of the appellants' profit-making apparatus. They regulated the appellants' activities, defined what they might and what they might not do, and affected the whole conduct of their business. I have difficulty in seeing how money laid-out to secure, or money received for the cancellation of, so fundamental an organization of a trader's activities can be regarded as an income disbursement or an income receipt.

III. — Employment Damages

1. — Wrongful Dismissal

(a) — Nature of Claim

Damages for wrongful dismissal are in substance and effect a payment in lieu of notice of termination. Thus, where a contract is terminable on notice, damages for lost earnings are restricted to the amount payable during the period of notice.[10]

(b) — Statutory Rules

The Act treats damages for wrongful dismissal as "retiring allowances"[11] taxable as "other income" and not as employment income.[12] This is so whether the taxpayer receives the damages pursuant to a judgment or in settlement of litigation. In either case, the taxpayer must include the full amount of the payment in his or her income in the year that it is re-

---

tion of a contract. *Surrogatum* principle applies: damages taxable since paid in lieu of rent which would have been taxable under Part XIII, para. 212(1)(d)).

[9]*Van Den Berghs Ltd. v. Clark, ibid.*, at 442 [A.C.]; see also *Barr, Crombie & Co. v. J.R.C.* (1945), 26 Tax Cas. 406 (Scot.) at 411, Lord Normand L.P.:

> In the present case, virtually the whole assets of the appellant company consisted in this agreement. When the agreement was surrendered or abandoned practically nothing remained of the company's business. It was forced to reduce its staff and to transfer into other premises, and it really started a new trading life. Its trading existence as practised up to that time had ceased with the liquidation of the shipping company.

[10]*British Guiana Credit Corp. v. Da Silva*, [1965] 1 W.L.R. 248 (P.C.) at 259.

[11]S. 248(1)"retiring allowance".

[12]Subpara. 56(1)(a)(ii).

ceived. As with employment income, however, the payer must report damage payments and withhold tax at the prescribed rates.[13] Payments to non-residents require withholding tax of 25 per cent of the amount paid.

(c) — Blended Payments

Where the damage award represents compensation for lost earnings during the period for which the employer should have given notice and also for mental suffering, one might argue that the mental suffering component is not taxable as a "retiring allowance" since it is not in respect of loss of office or employment.[14] The better view, however, is that the entire award is *in respect of* a loss of office or employment: The earnings component compensates for lack of notice and the mental anguish component compensates for the manner in which the employee lost his or her office or employment.[15] Thus, one head of the award goes to time, while the other goes to the method, but both arise from the same cause of action. They are *in respect of* improper loss of office or employment.[16]

---

[13]Para. 153(1)(c).

[14]*Specht v. M.N.R.*, [1975] C.T.C. 126, 75 D.T.C. 5069 (F.C.T.D.).

[15]See e.g., the reasoning in *The Queen v. Savage*, [1983] 2 S.C.R. 428, [1983] C.T.C. 393, 83 D.T.C. 5409 (S.C.C.).

[16]*Young v. M.N.R.*, [1986] 2 C.T.C. 2111, 86 D.T.C. 1567 (T.C.C.). As Linden J. said in *Brown v. Waterloo Reg. Bd. of Commr. of Police* (1982), 37 O.R. (2d) 277, 136 D.L.R. (3d) 49 (Ont. H.C) at 288-89 [O.R.]; revd. in part (1983), 43 O.R. (2d) 113, 150 D.L.R. (3d) 729 (Ont. C.A.):

> The aim of aggravated damages is to "soothe a plaintiff whose feelings have been wounded by the quality of the defendant's misbehavior". They are a "balm for mental distress" which is brought about by the wrongful "character of the defendant's wrongdoing". There must be evidence of damage of this type to the plaintiff. Aggravated damages are not meant to punish the defendant. (See Cooper-Stephenson and Saunders, *Personal Injury Damages in Canada* (1981) at 55; *Robitaille et al. v. Vancouver Hockey Club Ltd.* (1979), 19 BCLR 158 at 183, Esson J.; varied 124 D.L.R. (3d) 228, 16 CCLT 225, 30 BCLR 286 (C.A.)) In sum, though based on the quality of the defendant's conduct, aggravated damages are compensatory in purpose.

> Canadian law seems to have recognized the need for something like aggravated damages in contract law by awarding damages, not only for financial losses, but also for any mental suffering incurred by the plaintiff in appropriate cases. (See *Pilon v. Peugeot Canada Ltd.* (1980), 29 OR (2d) 711, 114 D.L.R. (3d) 378, 12 B.L.R. 227, for example.) The purpose behind allowing such damages is to compensate for hurt feelings, anxiety and stress caused by certain types of contractual breach, where they are in contemplation of the parties. Where the conduct of a defendant which violates a contract is particularly callous, the likelihood of mental suffering would be more foreseeable to him.

2. — *Signing Bonuses*

An amount paid to an employee on account of a contractually agreed settlement (such as a "signing bonus") is taxable as income regardless of whether the employer makes the payment pursuant to a legal agreement entered into before, during, or immediately after employment.[17]

3. — *Arbitration Awards*

Arbitration awards for breach of a collective agreement are taxable as employment income if the employer pays the amount as compensation for lost wages or other taxable benefits.[18] The gross amount of the award is income even if the employee receives only the net amount after deductions for income tax, CPP, EI, etc.

4. — *Employment Insurance Benefits [para. 6(1)(f)]*

Insurance payouts for disability benefits are often the product of settlements that combine past and future amount. In *Tsiaprailis*,[19] for example, the insurer settled for a lump-sum payment of $105,000 in lieu of past benefits and 75 per cent of the present value of the insured's future benefits, plus interest, costs and disbursements. The majority of the Supreme Court (per Justice Charron) applied the *surrogatum* principle to the "arrears portion" of the award.

The *surrogatum* principle provides that amounts on account, or in lieu, of otherwise taxable amounts are also taxable. Thus, the determinative issue is: what is the payout intended to replace? Employment and litigation counsel should factor in the tax consequences of negotiated settlements to determine the portion of the "in lieu" amount attributable to past taxable amounts and future non-taxable amounts.

---

[17]Subsec. 6(3); *Greiner v. The Queen*, [1984] C.T.C. 92, 84 D.T.C. 6073 (F.C.A.).

[18]*Vincent v. M.N.R.*, [1988] 2 C.T.C. 2075, 88 D.T.C. 1422 (T.C.C.) (damage award restoring taxpayer to position he would have been in had wages set out in collective agreement for working on day of rest been paid); *Merrins v. M.N.R.*, [1995] 1 C.T.C. 111, 94 D.T.C. 6669 (F.C.T.D.) (amount received on settlement of grievance from lay-off is retiring allowance).

[19][2005] S.C.J. No. 9, 2005 CarswellNat 431, 2005 CarswellNat 432, [2005] 2 C.T.C. 1 (S.C.C.) February 25, 2005.

IV. — Breach Of Warranty Of Authority

1. — Nature of Claim

An agent is liable for breach of warranty of authority for misrepresenting his or her authority to a person who suffers damage by acting on the strength of the misrepresentation. The law imposes the obligation because ". . . a person, professing to contract as an agent for another, impliedly, if not expressly, undertakes to or promises the person who enters into such contract, upon the faith of the professed agent being duly authorized, that the authority which he professes to have does in point of fact exist."[20]

2. — Damage Principles

We determine damages for breach of warranty of authority according to the usual contract rule: Compensate the injured party and restore the person to the position he or she would have enjoyed had the authority claimed by the professed agent truly vested in him or her.[21]

The taxation of damages for breach of warranty of authority also follows the usual *surrogatum* rule: Damages that substitute for amounts that would have been taxable are taxable. Thus, here too, characterization for tax purposes depends upon the anterior determination as to the nature of the receipts that the damage award is intended to replace and not upon the method of calculating the amount.

In *Manley*,[22] for example, the taxpayer received damages of $587,400 in lieu of a finder's fee to which he would have been entitled if the professed agent with whom he was dealing had the authority that he claimed to have. Since the finder's fee would have constituted "profit" from an adventure in the nature of trade, the damages in lieu thereof were also taxable as income from a business:[23]

> In the present case, the [taxpayer] was a trader; he had engaged in an adventure in the nature of trade. The damages for breach of warranty of authority, which he received . . . pursuant to a legal right, were compensation for his failure to receive the finder's fee . . . .. Had the [taxpayer] received that finder's fee it would have been profit from a business required by the *Income Tax Act*, to be included in his income in the year of its receipt. The damages for breach of warranty of authority are to be treated the same way for income tax purposes.

---

[20]*Collen v. Wright* (1857), 8 E. & B. 647 (Ex. Ch.) at 657.

[21]See e.g., *Manley v. Levy* (1974), [1975] 2 S.C.R. 70, 47 D.L.R. (3d) 67 (S.C.C.) (action for commission payment turned on credibility of witnesses); *Re National Coffee Palace Co.* (1883), 24 Ch. D. 367 (Eng. C.A.) (broker purchased shares from wrong company; purchaser repudiated; outstanding purchase price exacted from broker by liquidator).

[22]*Manley v. The Queen*, [1985] 1 C.T.C. 186, 85 D.T.C. 5150 (F.C.A.) [Manley cited to C.T.C.].

[23]*Manley v. The Queen*, *ibid.*, at 191 [C.T.C.].

Thus, at least in contract and agency, tax law considers damages on the *surrogatum* principle. In both cases, it is easy to justify the principle because the law almost invariably relates the damages to an income earning and profit making process.

V. — Tort Damages

1. — General Principles

Tort damages are more complex than damages in contract and agency. Although tort damages are generally taxable on the basis of the same principles that apply to other damages (include compensation for income receipts in income and exclude compensation for capital receipts), there are important differences in the manner in which the courts apply the principle to torts that involve damage to business or investments and torts that concern personal injuries or fatal accidents.

2. — Business or Investments

Compensation for tortious injury to business or property is taxable if the payment compensates for lost profits. Tort compensation is not taxable if made on account of capital receipts.[24] Hence, the taxation of damages depends upon the nature of the hole that the damage award fills. Lord Clyde illustrated the principle as follows:[25]

> Suppose someone who chartered one of the Appellant's vessels breached the charter and exposed himself to a claim of damages . . . there could, I imagine, be no doubt that the damages recovered would properly enter the Appellant's profit and loss account for the year. The reason would be that the breach of the charter was an injury inflicted on the Appellant's trading, making (so to speak) a hole in the Appellant's profits, and damages recovered could not be reasonably or appropriately put . . . to any other purpose than to fill that hole. Suppose on the other hand, that one of the taxpayer's vessels was negligently run down and sunk by a vessel belonging to some other shipowner, and the Appellant recovered as damage the value of the sunken vessel, I imagine that there could be no doubt that the damages so recovered could not enter the Appellant's profit and loss account because the destruction of the vessel would be an injury inflicted, not on the Appellant's trading, but on the capital assets of the Appellant's trade, making (so to speak) a hole in *them*, and the damages could therefore . . . only be used to fill that hole.

Thus, damages for injury to a business resulting in a loss of profits are taxable as income; compensation for destruction of an entire business is a non-taxable capital receipt. This rule

---

[24]*London & Thames Haven Oil Wharves Ltd. v. Attwooll*, [1966] 3 All E.R. 145; revd. [1967] 2 All E.R. 124 (Eng. C.A.).

[25]*Burmah S.S. Co. v. I.R.C.* (1930), 16 Tax Cas. 67 (Scot.) at 71-72 (contract damages for late delivery of ship included in income as being on account of lost profits).

applies regardless of the method that one uses to estimate the loss of profits. As Lord Buck-master said:[26]

> It appears to me to make no difference whether it be regarded as the sale of the asset out and out, or whether it be treated merely as a means of preventing the acquisition of profit which would otherwise be gained. In either case the capital asset of the company to that extent has been sterilized and destroyed, and it is in respect of that action that the sum . . . was paid . . . . It is now well settled that the compensation payable in such circumstances is the full value of the minerals that are left unworked, less the cost of working, and that is of course the profit that would have been obtained were they in fact worked. But there is no relation between the measure that is used for the purpose of calculating a particular result and the quality of the figure that is arrived at by means of the application of that test.

Here too, there is no bright-line test to determine when compensation for lost earnings constitutes income or the capitalized value of earnings. It is a question of fact in each case.

3. — Depreciable Property

The Act includes compensation for damages to depreciable property in the taxpayer's income to the extent that he or she expends the money to repair the damage.[27] In effect, inclusion of the compensation in, and deduction of the repair costs from, income constitute a "wash transaction". This in effect means that the net tax effect is neutral.

4. — Capital Property

Damages for total loss or destruction of capital property are "proceeds of disposition" and go towards determining the capital gain or loss on the disposition of the property.[28] Thus, total loss or destruction of property is equivalent to a sale of the property.

5. — Eligible Capital Property

Compensation for damage to eligible capital property (for example, goodwill) is usually an eligible capital amount. If, however, the damage is so severe as to destroy the substrata of the taxpayer's business, any compensation for such damage is a capital receipt.[29]

---

[26]*Glenboig Union Fireclay Co. v. I.R.C.* (1922), 12 Tax Cas. 427 (U.K. H.L.) at 464.

[27]Para. 12(1)(f).

[28]S. 54"disposition" and "proceeds of disposition".

[29]See Interpretation Bulletin IT-182, "Compensation for Loss of Business Income, or of Property Used in a Business" (October 28, 1974).

6. — Personal Injuries

Income tax considerations are also relevant to damages for torts involving personal injuries. Here, the underlying principles are more elusive. There are two points in time when we can consider the issue of taxability:

(1) At trial when we determine liability and assess damages; and

(2) When the plaintiff receives payment of the award.

(a) — Determination of Settlement

We do not take tax factors into account in determining the amount that a defendant pays to the plaintiff in a personal injury case.[30] The theory is that we are compensating the plaintiff for the loss of his or her earning *capacity* and not for lost earnings. It does not matter that we determine the value of the plaintiff's capacity by direct mathematical reference to lost earnings. We arrive at this result by asserting our conclusion. Dickson J. explained the rule as follows:[31]

> ... an award for prospective income should be calculated with no deduction for tax which might have been attracted had it been earned over the working life of the plaintiff. This results from the fact that it is earning capacity and not lost earnings which is the subject of compensation. For the same reason, no consideration should be taken of the amount by which the income from the award will be reduced by payment of taxes on the interest, dividends, or capital gain. A capital sum is appropriate to replace the lost capital asset of earning capacity. Tax on income is irrelevant either to decrease the sum for taxes the victim would have paid on income from his job, or to increase it for taxes he will now have to pay on income from the award.

Thus, damage awards for personal injuries can be substantial where the tortfeasor renders a person who has a normal life expectancy incapable of working. In these circumstances, we capitalize the plaintiff's pre-tax earnings to determine the value of his or her lost earning capacity.

(b) — Taxation of Settlement

Damages for personal injuries are not taxable to the plaintiff when the judgment amount is received. This is so regardless of whether the amount paid is on account of special damages

---

[30]*Andrews v. Grand & Toy Alta. Ltd.*, [1978] 2 S.C.R. 229, 83 D.L.R. (3d) 452 (S.C.C.) [*Andrews* cited to D.L.R.] (plaintiff awarded $69,981 for prospective loss of earnings determined by discounting at 7 per cent the sum of $564 (monthly earnings) over a period of 30.81 years (estimated working life)).

[31]*Andrews v. Grand & Toy Alta. Ltd.*, *ibid.*, at 474 [D.L.R.].

for loss of earnings up to trial, or general damages for loss of prospective earnings.[32] Here too, the damages compensate for capacity even though one measures them by reference to earnings.[33] Thus, the *surrogatum* principle does not apply in respect of damages for personal injuries.

7. — Fatal Accidents

The theory of tort damages is quite different, however, with respect to fatal accidents. Here, we typically determine damages under fatal accident statutes on a net of tax basis by capitalizing the deceased's net take-home pay. De Grandpré J. explained this rule as follows:[34]

> It seems to me that what the widow and the child have lost in this case is the support payments made by the deceased, support payments which could only come out of funds left after deducting the cost of maintaining the husband, including the amount of tax payable on his income. I cannot see how this pecuniary loss could be evaluated on any other basis than the take-home pay, that is the net pay after deductions on many items, including income tax.

The above rule places the beneficiary in the same financial position that she would have enjoyed had the deceased lived and continued to earn income. It is, however, not possible to reconcile the rule with the theory in non-fatal personal injury settlements. The difference in results is perverse. Nevertheless, the Supreme Court has spoken: the capacity theory does not apply in the context of fatal accident cases.[35]

---

[32]*Cirella v. The Queen*, [1978] C.T.C. 1, 77 D.T.C. 5442 (F.C.T.D.).

[33]See *Graham v. Baker* (1961), 106 C.L.R. 340; see also *Groves v. United Pacific Transport Pty. Ltd.*, [1965] Qd. R. 62 where Gibbs J. observed at 65:

> Although it is usual and convenient in an action for damages for personal injuries to say that an amount is awarded for loss of wages or other earnings, the damages are really awarded for the impairment of the plaintiff's earning capacity that has resulted from his injuries. This is so even if an amount is separately quantified and described as special damages for loss of earnings up to the time of trial. Damages for personal injuries are not rightly described as damages for loss of income.

[34]*Keizer v. Hanna*, [1978] 2 S.C.R. 342, 82 D.L.R. (3d) 449 (S.C.C.) at 371 [S.C.R.]; see also *Andrews v. Grand & Toy Alta. Ltd.*, [1978] 2 S.C.R. 229, 83 D.L.R. (3d) 452 (S.C.C.) at 474 [D.T.C.], Dickson J.:

> In contrast with the situation in personal injury cases, awards under the Fatal Accident Act, R.S.A. 1970, c. 138, should reflect tax considerations, since they are to compensate dependants for the loss of support payments made by the deceased. These support payments could only come out of take-home pay, and the payments from the award will only be received net of taxes.

[35]*Keizer v. Hanna*, [1978] 2 S.C.R. 342, 82 D.L.R. (3d) 449 (S.C.C.) at 372 [S.C.R.], Grandpré J. ("I cannot consider that the deceased here was a capital asset").

8. — *Investment Income*

Interest and dividends on investments acquired with a damage award are generally taxable as income from property.[36] Similarly, taxable capital gains realized on property acquired with the proceeds of a damage award are also included in income. We make an exception, however, for personal injury awards paid to, or on behalf of, persons under the age of 21. Interest and property income received from, or accrued on, the investment of a personal injury award is exempt from tax until the end of the taxation year in which the injured person attains the age of 21. Taxable capital gains from dispositions of property acquired with the proceeds of damage awards or settlements are also exempt from tax if the injured person was less than 21 years of age at any time in the year.[37] Amounts earned from the reinvestment of exempt income are also exempt.[38]

The purpose of this exception is to provide relief for young persons who have suffered personal injuries. It is unclear why the plight of young injured persons warrants preferential treatment over older persons in similar circumstances.

(a) — *Interest on Special Damages*

The law crystallizes tort damages as at the time of the tortious act. In determining the amount of damages it is usual to break down the award into two components: (1) Special damages up to the date of trial; and (2) General damages for future losses. The Department excludes interest on special damages from income.[39]

---

[36]Paras. 12(1)(c) and (k).

[37]Para. 81(1)(g.1). In his 21st year, the injured person can elect to recognize any accrued capital gains; see s. 81(5).

[38]Para. 81(1)(g.2).

[39]See Interpretation Bulletin IT-365R2, "Damages, Settlements and Similar Receipts" (May 8, 1987).

Selected Bibliography

General

Bowman, D.G.H. "Tax Treatment of Payments Made in the Context of Litigation" [1986] Spec. Lect. L.S.U.C. 96.

Corn, George. "Award of Damages — Non-Taxable Capital Receipt or Taxable Reimbursement" (July 1990) 3 Can. Curr. Tax J-85.

Corn, George, "Incorrect Assessment Liability for Damages" (1986) 1 Can. Curr. Tax A-29.

Drache, A.B.C. "Tort Damages and Retiring Allowances" (1991) XIII Can. Taxpayer 79.

Harris, Peter H. "Tax Treatment of Civil Litigation and Damage Awards, Alimony and Maintenance Payments" (1985) 6 Advocates' Q. 346.

Income Tax: *Maintenance, Alimony and Employment Termination Benefits* (Audio Archives of Canada, 1984).

Krishna, Vern. "The Taxation of Damages" (1985) 1 Can. Curr. Tax C-107.

Weir, J.P. "Taxation of Prejudgment Interest: Historical and Current Developments" (1985) 33 CCLT 149.

Employment Damages and Wrongful Dismissal

Brown, Elizabeth and Julie Y. Lee. "Putting Employees on Notice: Tax Treatment of Amounts Paid on Termination of Employment" (1994) 5 Tax. of Executive Compensation and Retirement 908.

Bush, Kathryn and Caroline L. Hilbronner. "Some Tax Considerations Regarding Employment Terminations" (1994) 3 Employment and Labour L. Rev. 111.

Drache, A.B.C. "Legal Expenses in Wrongful Dismissal Not Deductible" (1988) 10 Can. Taxpayer 120.

Hugo, Sharon J. and L. Alan Rautenberg. "Damages and Settlements: Taxation of the Recipient" (1993) 41 Can. Tax J. 1.

Krishna, Vern. "Characterization of Wrongful Dismissal Awards for Income Tax" (1977) 23 McGill L.J. 43.

MacKnight, Robin J. "Termination Payments for Mental Distress and Loss of Reputation" [1993] Can. Curr. Tax P-21.

McDonnell, T.E. "Deductibility of Legal Expenses Incurred to Recover Damages for Wrongful Dismissal" [Case Comment *Lalonde v. M.N.R.*, [1988] 2 C.T.C. 2032 (T.C.C.)] (1988) 36 Can. Tax J. 697.

Morgan, M.A. "Compensatory Payments Made in a Litigation Context: Tax Treatment to the Recipient" [1986] Spec. Lect. L.S.U.C. 109.

O'Brien, M.L. "Litigation Structured Settlements" [1986] Spec. Lect. L.S.U.C. 119.

Olsen, D.C. "Tax Treatment of Damages for Wrongful Dismissal" [1986] Spec. Lect. L.S.U.C. 135.

Trotter, Paul D. "Severance and Downsizing: Ongoing Tax and Benefits Issues" (1992) 5 Can. Petroleum Tax J. 21.

PART VI: CAPITAL GAINS & LOSSES

CHAPTER 11 — CAPITAL GAINS AND LOSSES

I. — General Comment

1. — Structure

Capital gains are a separate and distinct source of income. Thus, we calculate capital gains by reference to a distinct set of rules in subdivision c of Division B. Generally, a taxpayer must include 1/2 of capital gains in income and may deduct therefrom 1/2 of capital losses.[1] Hence, strictly speaking, there is no separate tax on capital gains; capital gains and losses merely expand or contract the taxable base to which tax we apply the normal rates. For analytical purposes, however, we consider capital gains and losses as a separate source of income subject to lower effective tax rates.

It is also important to note that certain taxpayers can claim a complete exemption from tax in respect of certain capital gains. The "capital gains exemption" is a deduction from income

---

[1] S. 38.

in computing taxable income.[2] In effect, the capital gains exemption comes into play in two steps: (1) capital gains are included in income;[3] then, (2) within specified limits, a taxpayer may deduct exempt gains in computing taxable income. In this chapter we look at the rules in respect of including capital gains in, and deducting capital losses from, income. We discuss the capital gains exemption in detail in Chapter 15, "Taxable Income".

Our tax law has consistently "preferred" capital gains over other forms of income. The capital gains preference debate is now long in the tooth, and we are no closer to resolving the issue today than we were when capital gains were first excluded from income. There is little doubt, however, that the lower tax rate on capital gains substantially increases the complexity of the tax statute, the costs of tax planning, compliance and administration. In the United States, the Internal Revenue Service, for example, estimates that determining whether capital gains treatment is appropriate in particular circumstances absorbs more administrative time and effort than any other single feature of the tax statute. It is not unreasonable to assume that the same applies in Canada.

Why should we treat capital gains preferentially? First, there is an intuitive notion that the appreciation of capital is not what we normally consider "income". There is a clear split between the courts and policymakers on this issue. For example, the United States Supreme Court stated in 1872 that "the mere fact that property has advanced in value between the date of its acquisition and sale does not authorize the imposition of the tax on the amount of the advance. Mere advance in value in no sense constitutes the gains, profits, or income. ... It constitutes and can be treated merely as increase of capital."[4] Even as late as 1923, United States Treasury Secretary Andrew Mellon said he "believed it would be sounder taxation policy generally not to recognize either capital gain or capital loss for purposes of income tax." On the other hand, the *Carter Commission* (1967) clearly favoured the theory that "a buck is a buck" regardless of its source. In Canada today one can say that there are no clearly defined objectives of capital gains taxation, and that our policies, both of taxation and preference, are an amalgam of intuition, political ideology, and competitive economic considerations.[5]

A capital gain derives from an increase in the capital value of an asset. This raises two issues: (1) when should we tax the increase? and (2) how much of the increase should we tax? An increase in the value of capital reflects the increase in the discounted future cash income from the underlying investment. In the case of stocks, for example, the increment in stock values is either the enhancement in anticipated future cash flows or a reduction in the

---

[2]See s. 110.6.

[3]Para. 3(b).

[4]*Gray v. Darlington* (1872), 82 U.S. 63. This position was altered by the passage of the 16th Amendment in 1913.

[5]See: Surrey, "Definitional Problems in Capital Gain Taxation" (1956) 69 Har. L. Rev. 985; Blum, "A Handy Summary of the Capital Gains Arguments" (1957) 25 Taxes 247.

discount factor. Since we tax dividends from earnings, we must also tax capital gains to the extent that they represent undistributed earnings. Although there are some similarities between dividends and capital gains, there are also significant differences with respect to timing, bunching, and inflation.

Second, one can justify the capital gains preference as relieving the "bunching" of accrued property appreciation. Capital gains usually result from appreciation that builds up over an extended period. The gain one realizes usually extends beyond one fiscal year. For example, if one buys shares in Year 1 for $20 and sells the shares in Year 5 for $120, the realized gain of $100 reflects the unrealized accrual of gains over five years. Since the personal tax rate structure is progressive,[6] we would penalize the investor with a higher tax rate if we included the entire gain in his or her income in Year 5. This might be unfair to the investor, particularly if we consider that the rule of realization is merely one of administrative convenience. Thus, the capital gains preference of taxing only 1/2 of the normal rate is a rough-and-ready form of mitigating the effect of progressive rates on "bunched" income. The United States Supreme Court recognized this in *Burnet v. Harmel*,[7] where it held that the purpose of the capital gains preference was to "relieve the taxpayer from ... excessive tax burdens on gains resulting from a conversion of capital investments, and to remove the deterrent effect of those burdens on such conversions."

Of course, bunching has no effect at all on an investor whose marginal rate of tax in each of the five preceding years would have been in the top tax bracket even without the capital gain. Such an investor derives a windfall from the preference. Also, one can always relieve against the bunching effect by allowing the investor to spread back the tax on his or her entire gain at the rate that would have applied had the investor accrued the gain annually over the five-year period. This is a more complicated averaging mechanism to the bunching problem. In the end, averaging may, accidentally, yield the same approximate result as simply reducing the overall effective rate. But what is the optimum size of the preference?

Third, the preference mitigates against the "lock-in" effect of the realization rule, and makes it less costly for investors to switch investments when it is in their economic interest to do so. The "lock-in" effect also stems from the realization principle. In the above example, the investor with an unrealized gain of $100 in Year 5 may identify a better economic investment with a higher potential yield. If he or she sells the initial investment, however, the investor will trigger tax at, say, 40 per cent, which would leave him or her with only $60 to reinvest. This effectively reduces the net rate of return on the new investment, and makes it less desirable. Thus, the investor might choose not to sell the original investment and defer the tax that would otherwise be payable. Usually, he or she could defer the tax until the later of the investor's or his or her spouse's death.[8] If the investor can defer the tax for 30 years,

---

[6]See, Chapter 1, "Introduction".

[7](1932), 287 U.S. 103.

[8]Subs. 70(5) and (6).

and the interest rate is 8 per cent, the future value of the $40 tax that would be payable if he or she sells today is $403.[9] Thus, the investor can multiply his or her tax saving 10 times simply by not selling and locking him- or herself into the original investment. Lock-in restricts the mobility of capital and reduces its efficiency to society's overall detriment. To liquidate a poorly performing investment and reinvest in another venture, the return on the new investment must be sufficient to pay for the capital gains tax bite from the initial liquidation. The investor will only liquidate the initial investment if the return on the new opportunity is sufficiently higher to offset the tax bite. Otherwise, it is better to lock in to the initial investment. The capital gains preference reduces the deterrence effect of lock-in and allows capital to flow to its more efficient use.

If the tax on capital gains restricts the mobility of capital, one can remove the problem by allowing the investor a complete rollover of taxes if he or she invests the proceeds in other capital investments. As we will see, we allow many such rollovers for in-kind exchanges of property. The important point to observe is that the capital gains bunching problem derives essentially from the realization principle, which is a rule of administrative convenience. The capital gains preference is a politically convenient, perhaps even optimum, solution to a vexing problem.

That said, however, there is another vexing aspect of capital gains, namely, inflation. Unlike dividends and interest income, which are taxed annually, capital gains are taxable only when we realize them. Suppose you buy a stock for $100 and sell it in a year for $140. If the capital gains tax rate is 40 per cent, the tax on the gain is $16. But the gain of $40 is illusory to the extent that inflation reduces its economic value. If inflation is at 10 per cent, the real economic gain in the year is only $30. This means that the effective tax rate of $16 on the economic gain of $30 is really 53 per cent. Hence, we increase tax rates indirectly in periods of high inflation. This doubly affects the taxpayer. The longer the holding period and the more serious the inflation rate, the higher the effective capital gains tax rate. Thus, at the very least, we should index capital gains so as not to tax illusory gains.

2. — Segregation by Type

We bring capital gains into income according to the rules in section 3. Paragraph 3(b) includes the following gains in income:

- *Net* taxable capital gains from dispositions of property other than listed personal property ("LPP"); and

- Taxable *net* gains from dispositions of LPP.

"Net" refers to the excess of gains over losses. As a rule, capital losses are deductible only against capital gains. One cannot use any excess of capital losses over capital gains to re-

---

[9]Future Value = $40 × 10.063.

duce income from other sources.[10] There is only one exception to this rule: one may apply business investment losses against "ordinary" income.

The scheme of section 3 in respect of capital gains and losses is as follows:

Taxable capital gains from property other than listed personal property	XXX	
Add: taxable *net* gain from listed personal property	XXX	
		XXX
Exceeds:		
The amount, if any, by which allowable capital losses from property other than listed personal property *exceeds* allowable business investment losses	XXX	(XXX)
Amount included in income		(XXX)

The effect of this scheme is to treat capital gains and losses as income from a separate source.

Example
Assume:
The following data applies to Alesia Ng:

Employment income (gross)	$ 64,500
Business income	15,550
Business losses	9,000
Rental income	12,500
Capital gains	4,000
Taxable listed personal property gain	5,000
Taxable listed personal property loss	7,500
Capital losses (includes BIL of $4,000)	18,000
Support payments (deductible)	5,000

---

[10]See paras. 3(d)–(f).

Example		
Allowable business investment losses ("ABIL")		2,000

Then: *paragraph 3(a):*

Employment income	$ 64,500	
Business income	15,550	
Property income	12,500	
		92,550

paragraph 3(b):

Taxable capital gains ($4,000 × 1/2)	$ 2,000	
Net LPP gains	0	
Net gains	$ 2,000	
Allowable capital losses exceeds ABIL*	$ 7,000	0
		92,550

Exceeds paragraph 3(c):

Support payments		(5,000)
		87,550

Exceeds paragraph 3(d):

Business losses	$ 9,000	
ABIL	2,000	
		(11,000)
Income		$ 76,550

Notes:

*   Capital losses times inclusion rate equals allowable capital losses ($18,000 × 1/2 = $9,000); minus ABIL ($2,000).

Business investment losses (BILs) are capital losses.

The excess of allowable capital losses (excluding ABILs) of $7,000 over taxable capital gains is a net capital loss deductible in computing taxable income — see Chapter 15.

II. — Capital Property

A capital gain or loss arises when a taxpayer disposes of capital property. The Act defines "capital property" as property, the disposition of which will give rise to a capital gain or loss.[11] Thus, with the exception of specific items, the characterization of a gain or loss as being on account of income or capital is determined by reference to common law principles.[12]

1. — Exclusions from Capital Gains

The Act specifically excludes the following properties from property that can give rise to a capital gain:[13]

- Property the disposition of which gives rise to income from a business, a property, or an adventure in the nature of trade;[14]

- Eligible capital property;

- Cultural property disposed of pursuant to the *Cultural Property Export and Import Act*;[15]

- Canadian and foreign resource properties, which include mineral, oil and gas rights;

- Insurance policies, including life insurance policies within the meaning of section 138, except for a taxpayer's deemed interest in a related segregated fund trust;

- Timber resource properties; and

- An interest of a beneficiary under a qualifying environmental trust.

Also, dispositions of eligible capital properties, Canadian and foreign resource properties, insurance policies, and depreciable properties do not give rise to a capital loss. They are, *ipso facto*, not capital properties.[16] Note, however, that the disposition of a cultural property can give rise to a capital loss.[17]

To summarize: a capital gain or loss is a gain or loss that arises from the disposition of property *to the extent that* it is not ordinary income or loss and does not arise from the disposition of one of the special types of property listed above. Thus, generally, a capital

---

[11]Para. 54"capital property" (b).

[12]The CRA does not give advance rulings on the characterization of gains — see IC 70-6R5 "Advance Income Tax Ruling" (May 17, 2002).

[13]Para. 39(1)(a).

[14]S. 248(1)"business".

[15]R.S.C. 1985, c. C-51.

[16]Para. 54"capital property" (b).

[17]IT-407R4, "Dispositions of cultural property to designated Canadian institutions" (Consolidated).

gain or loss arises from the disposition of an investment acquired for the purpose of producing income, rather than as a trading asset.[18]

2. — Types of Capital Property

We use the terms "capital gain" and "capital loss" in a broad sense to denote a gain or loss from the disposition of a capital property. There are, however, different types of capital properties, which give rise to different types of capital gains and losses. The Act subdivides capital properties into the following categories:

- Personal-use property;[19]
- Listed personal property;[20]
- "Business investment" property;[21] and
- Other capital properties.

One calculates the gain or loss from each of these subcategories of capital property separately, and according to the rules applicable to each.

3. — Deemed Capital Property

Where a person disposes of *all or substantially all* of the assets used in an active business to a corporation, any shares that he or she receives in consideration for the assets are the capital property of that person.[22] Thus, a disposition of the shares will give rise to a capital gain or loss. For example, a parent corporation may transfer a business to its subsidiary and, subsequently, sell the shares of the subsidiary corporation. Any gain on the sale of the subsidiary's shares is a capital gain. Similarly, an individual might sell his or her business to a newly-formed corporation in exchange for its shares and then dispose of the shares of the corporation. Any gain on the sale of the shares would be a capital gain. This rule provides certainty to taxpayers who engage in business and corporate reorganizations. It is important to note, however, that the rule deems the shares to be capital property only if:

- The taxpayer disposes of "all or substantially all" of the assets of the business; and

---

[18]See Chapter 7, "The Meaning of Business Income, Investment Income, and Capital Gains".

[19]S. 54"personal-use property".

[20]S. 54"listed personal property".

[21]Para. 39(1)(c); IT-484R2, "Business Investment Losses" (November 28, 1996).

[22]S. 54.2.

- The business is an "active" business.

This rule does not apply to dispositions of non-business assets or in circumstances where the corporation disposes of some, but not substantially all, of its assets. Nor does the rule apply to the disposition of assets used in an adventure or concern in the nature of trade. Thus, one cannot use the rule to convert an income gain into a capital gain by exchanging the assets for shares and then selling the shares.

III. — Computation Of Gain Or Loss

A capital gain from a disposition of property is the difference between the "proceeds of disposition" ("POD") that one receives from the property and the sum of its "adjusted cost base" ("ACB") and the expenses of disposition:[23]

$$\text{Capital Gain} = \text{POD} - (\text{ACB} + \text{Expenses})$$

For present purposes, we can assume that "proceeds of disposition" means selling price and "adjusted cost base" means the cost of property. We discuss the technical meaning of these terms later.

Example

Assume:

A taxpayer sells a capital property for $10,000. The asset was purchased for $6,000. He incurs expenses of $800 in selling the property.

Then:

Selling price		$ 10,000
Less: cost (ACB)	$ 6,000	
Selling expenses	800	(6,800)
Capital gain		$ 3,200

The taxpayer's taxable capital gain is $1,600, that is, the capital gain times the inclusion rate ($3,200 × 1/2).

---

[23]Para. 40(1)(a).

A taxpayer's capital loss from a disposition of property is the amount by which the "adjusted cost base" and selling expenses exceed the "proceeds of disposition".[24]

Example

Assume:

T sells a capital property that cost $16,000 for cash proceeds of $2,000; T also incurs $80 as expenses of sale.

Then:

Proceeds of Sale		$ 2,000
Less: Cost (ACB)	$16,000	
Selling expenses	80	(16,080)
Capital loss		$(14,080)

T's allowable capital loss is $7,040, that is, the capital loss times the inclusion rate ($14,080 × 1/2).

---

1. — Reserves

As a rule, the Act recognizes capital gains and losses for tax purposes only when they are realized. The taxable event that gives rise to a gain or loss is the disposition of the property. A taxpayer may, however, dispose of property and not be paid the full sale price upon its sale or exchange. In these circumstances, the taxpayer realizes a capital gain, but does not collect the cash at the time of the transaction. To impose tax on uncollected gains might be a hardship for some taxpayers. The Act provides some relief and allows a taxpayer to defer recognition of some of the gain on uncollected proceeds. There are, however, some restrictions that apply to the amount that the taxpayer can defer.

Where a taxpayer deducts a reserve in one year, he or she must bring the amount deducted into income in the following year. The taxpayer can then claim a further reserve in each of the following years to the extent that part of the proceeds of sale remain outstanding at the end of the year.[25] Where a taxpayer claims a reserve for unpaid proceeds of disposition, it cannot exceed the amount of the reserve claimed in the immediately preceding year in re-

---

[24]Para. 40(1)(b).

[25]Subpara. 40(1)(a)(iii); see also the various restrictions on claiming reserves in subs. 40(2).

spect of the property. Thus, if a taxpayer claims less than the maximum allowed in one year, he or she cannot claim a larger reserve in respect of the same property in the next year.[26]

(a) — Limitations

A taxpayer cannot claim a reserve except as the Act expressly permits.[27] The maximum reserve that a taxpayer may claim in a year is limited to the *lesser* of two amounts:[28]

    1. A "reasonable" amount; and

    2. An amount determined by reference to a formula.

(i) — "A Reasonable Reserve"

What is reasonable is, of course, always a question of fact. The CRA does say, however, that it considers a reserve to be reasonable if it is proportional to the amount that is not payable to the taxpayer until after the end of the taxation year. Thus, one may calculate a reserve as follows:

$$\text{Capital gain} \times \frac{\text{Amount not payable until after the end of the year}}{\text{Total proceeds}}$$

This formula is only one of many ways of calculating a reserve. A taxpayer is free to choose any other "reasonable" method.[29]

Example
Assume:
In Year 1, T sold a capital property in an arm's length transaction. The property, which cost $63,000, was sold for $100,000, payable $20,000 on completion of the sale and $20,000 per year for the next four years. Expenses of selling the property came to $7,000.
Then:
Proceeds of sale $ 100,000

---

[26]Subpara. 40(1)(a)(ii).

[27]Para. 18(1)(e).

[28]Subpara. 40(1)(a)(iii).

[29]*The Queen v. Ennisclare Corp.*, [1984] C.T.C. 286, 84 D.T.C. 6262 (F.C.A.).

Example				
Less: Cost (ACB)			$ 63,000	
Selling expenses			7,000	(70,000)
Capital gain				30,000
Less: Reasonable reserve (see below)				(24,000)
Capital gain recognized in Year 1				$ 6,000

A "reasonable" reserve may be calculated as follows:

Year	Calculation		Reserve	Capital Gain Recognized
Year 1	$30,000	× $\dfrac{\$80,000}{100,000}$ = $24,000		$ 6,000
Year 2	30,000	× $\dfrac{60,000}{100,000}$ = $18,000		$ 6,000
Year 3	30,000	× $\dfrac{40,000}{100,000}$ = $12,000		$ 6,000
Year 4	30,000	× $\dfrac{20,000}{100,000}$ = $ 6,000		$ 6,000
Year 5		NIL		$ 6,000
Total capital gain recognized				$30,000

(ii) — Maximum Reserve

The second limitation restricts the period during which a taxpayer may claim a reserve to a maximum of five years. This limitation ensures that the cumulative amount of capital gain recognized is *not less* than 20 per cent of the total gain times the number of taxation years that have elapsed since the disposition.

Example	
Assume:	

In Year 1, T sells a capital property to which the following data applies:

Proceeds of sale	$90,000
Cost of property (ACB)	$35,000
Selling expenses	$5,000

The property was sold on the basis that the purchase price was payable in five equal instalments commencing in Year 2.

Then in Year 1 the maximum reserve allowed is:

Proceeds of sale		$ 90,000
Less: Cost (ACB)	$35,000	
Selling expenses	5,000	(40,000)
Capital gain		50,000
Maximum reserve ($50,000 × 4/5)		(40,000)
Capital gain recognized		$ 10,000 *

Thus at least 1/5 of the gain is included in income in the year of sale even though the taxpayer did not receive any proceeds in that year. In contrast, a "reasonable reserve" under the first test would be $50,000.

Notes:

* $50,000 × 20% = $10,000

(iii) — Special Reserves

The Act extends the maximum five-year period applicable to general reserves to 10 years if the property that the taxpayer transfers is:[30]

- Land and depreciable property used in a family farm;

---

[30]Subs. 40(1.1).

- A share in a family farm corporation;

- An interest in a family farm partnership; or

- A share in a small business corporation

and the property is transferred to the taxpayer's child.[31]

(b) — Amounts "Not Payable"

A taxpayer may claim a reserve on only the portion of the sale proceeds that are "not payable" to the taxpayer until after the end of the year. Note the distinction between "not payable" and "not collected". Fixed-maturity debt instruments are payable on the date indicated on the face of the instrument, whether or not they are actually paid or collected. A demand note is payable at the time when the note is signed, unless the note is otherwise qualified.[32] Thus, to claim a reserve on a demand note, the note should be made payable a number of days (for example, 10 days) *after* demand for payment.

2. — Selling Expenses

A taxpayer can deduct expenses incurred in disposing of a capital property. Only expenses that one incurs in connection with the *disposition* of capital property are deductible in calculating a capital gain or loss. Expenses that one incurs for the purposes of earning income from a capital property are not deductible in calculating the amount of a capital gain or loss.

Expenses that one incurs in enhancing capital property into a saleable condition, or those connected directly with the disposition of the property, are also deductible from the proceeds of disposition. For example, fixing-up expenses, finder's fees, sales commissions, brokers' fees, surveyor's fees, transfer taxes, title registration fees, and legal expenses that relate to the disposition are deductible.

---

[31]Subs. 252(1).

[32]Subpara. 40(1)(a)(iii); *The Queen v. Derbecker*, [1984] C.T.C. 606, 84 D.T.C. 6549 (F.C.A.). In the words of Parke B. in *Norton v. Ellam* (1837), 2 M & W 461 at 464: "... a promissory note, payable on demand, is a present debt, and is payable without any demand". See also *Pineo v. The Queen*, [1986] 2 C.T.C. 71, 86 D.T.C. 6322 (F.C.T.D.) (demand promissory note secured by share escrow agreement remained present debt).

IV. — Dispositions

1. — *General Comment*

A disposition of capital property is generally the taxable event that gives rise to a capital gain or loss.[33] A taxpayer disposes of the property when the taxpayer legally alienates his or her rights in the property. In certain circumstances, however, the Act deems a taxpayer to dispose of the property even though the taxpayer does not physically or legally alienate his or her property rights.[34]

2. — *"Property"*

The Act defines "property" to include real and personal property (whether corporeal or incorporeal, movable or immovable, tangible or intangible), shares, *choses in action* and timber resource properties. Indeed, the term comprises virtually every possible interest a person may have.[35]

Corporeal properties are substances that one can see or handle. In contrast, incorporeal properties are "merely an idea and abstract contemplation, though their effects and profits may frequently be objects of the bodily senses."[36]

Incorporeal property is a right issuing out of a thing corporate (whether real or personal) or concerning, annexed to or exercisable within the same. It is not the thing corporate itself (such as land, houses or jewels), but something collateral thereto, such as a rent issuing out of the land or houses. Incorporeal property includes such intangibles as reversions, remainders and executory interests in property, life interests, rights-of-way, and rights to sunlight.

3. — *"Disposition"*

The concept of "disposition" is one of the key elements of the capital gains system. The Act does not define the term. There is, however, a fairly comprehensive description of the types of transactions included within its meaning.

---

[33]Subs. 39(1).

[34]See, for example, s. 45 (deemed disposition on change of use of property); subs. 50(1) (deemed disposition of bad debt); subs. 70(5) (deemed disposition on death).

[35]*Re Lunness* (1919), 46 O.L.R. 320 (C.A.). See *Manrell v. R.*, 2003 F.C.A. 128, [2003] 3 C.T.C. 50, 2003 D.T.C. 5225 (Fed. C.A.) for a detailed analysis of the meaning of property in the context of non-competition agreements.

[36]*Re Christmas; Martin v. Lacon* (1886), 33 Ch. D. 332 (C.A.) at 338; *Blackstone's Commentaries on the Laws of England* (1765), vol. 2, at 20.

A "disposition" is any event that is an alienation of property or a loss of ownership. The alienation may occur by a voluntary or involuntary action on the owner's part. In some cases, the Act deems a disposition. Thus, for tax purposes, the word "disposition" has a much broader meaning than "sale".[37] In the simplest case, the proceeds from a disposition of property are equal to the consideration that a taxpayer receives for the property. One determines the value of consideration from the terms of the contract of sale or deed. In some cases, the Act deems the amount.

The Act defines a "disposition"[38] to include any event entitling a taxpayer to "proceeds of disposition," including proceeds from:[39]

- The sale price of property;

- Compensation for stolen property;

- Compensation for property lost or destroyed;

- Compensation for expropriated property (including any interest penalty or damages that are part of the expropriation award);[40]

- Compensation for damaged property (unless funds have been expended in repairing the damage within a reasonable time);

- Mortgage settlements upon foreclosure of mortgaged property (including reductions in the liability of a taxpayer to a mortgagee as a result of the sale of mortgaged property);

- The principal amount of a debtor's claim that has been extinguished as a result of a mortgage foreclosure or conditional sales repossession;[41]

- A winding-up (or redemption) dividend, to the extent that it does not exceed the corporation's pre-1972 capital surplus on hand;

---

[37] *Olympia & York Developments v. M.N.R.*, [1980] C.T.C. 265, 80 D.T.C. 6184 (F.C.T.D.) (instalment contract; transfer of possession but not title constituted "disposition", although no "sale" until later); *M.N.R. v. Imperial General Properties Ltd.*, [1985] 1 C.T.C. 40, 85 D.T.C. 5045 (F.C.A.); leave to appeal refused (1985), 16 D.L.R. (4th) 615 (S.C.C.) (sale complete when conditions precedent satisfied).

[38] Subs. 248(1)"disposition".

[39] S. 54"proceeds of disposition".

[40] *E.R. Fisher Ltd. v. The Queen*, [1986] 2 C.T.C. 114, 86 D.T.C. 6364 (F.C.T.D.) (interest paid pursuant to *Expropriation Act*, as penalty, because Crown's offer inappropriate, constituted "proceeds of disposition"); *Sani Sport Inc. v. The Queen*, [1987] 1 C.T.C. 411, 87 D.T.C. 5253 (F.C.T.D.); affd. [1990] 2 C.T.C. 15, (sub nom. *Sani Sport Inc. v. Can.)* 90 D.T.C. 6230 (F.C.A.)) (amount paid as damages for loss of business opportunity included in proceeds of disposition).

[41] See s. 79.

- Redemptions or cancellations of shares, bonds and other securities;

- Settlements or cancellations of any debt owing to a taxpayer;

- Conversion of shares on an amalgamation;

- Expiry of options to acquire or dispose of property; and

- Transfers of property to or by a trust (including transfers to an RRSP, DPSP, EPSP or RRIF, even if the transfer does not involve a change of beneficial ownership).

A "disposition" does *not* include any of the following:[42]

- Transfers of property to, or by, a creditor for securing or releasing a debt;

- *Issuance* by a corporation of its own bonds or debentures;

- Transfer of property without change in beneficial ownership (except transfer by resident trust to non-resident trust or transfer to a trust governed by RRSP, DPSP, EPSP, RRIF);

- *Issuance* by a corporation of its own shares;

- Amounts that represent a deemed dividend on a winding-up or share redemption; and

- Amounts deemed to be dividends paid to a non-resident person in a non-arm's length sale of shares of one Canadian corporation to another Canadian corporation.

The above list is not exhaustive. A "disposition" includes any event that implies a loss of ownership, whether such loss occurs by voluntary action on the owner's part or the owner suffers it involuntarily. The words "disposed of" embrace every event by which property ceases to be available to the taxpayer for use in producing income, either because the property ceases to be physically accessible to the taxpayer or because it ceases to exist.[43] Thus,

---

[42]S. 54"proceeds of disposition"; subs. 248(1)"disposition".

[43]See, generally, *Victory Hotels Ltd. v. M.N.R.*, [1962] C.T.C. 614, 62 D.T.C. 1378 (Ex. Ct.) (determination of disposition when documentation conflicting); *M.N.R. v. Wardean Drilling Ltd.*, [1969] C.T.C. 265, 69 D.T.C. 5194 (Ex. Ct.) (asset paid for in 1963, delivered in 1964; deductible in 1964, when all incidents of title passed); *The Queen v. Cie immobilìègere BCN Ltée*, [1979] 1 S.C.R. 865, [1979] C.T.C. 71, 79 D.T.C. 5068 (S.C.C.) (meaning of "disposed of"); *Lord Elgin Hotel Ltd. v. M.N.R.* (1964), 36 Tax A.B.C. 268 (T.A.B.); appeal quashed [1969] C.T.C. 24, 69 D.T.C. 5059 (Ex. Ct.) (winding-up of company and distribution of shares constituted "disposition" of hotel); *The Queen v. Malloney's Studio Ltd.*, [1979] 2 S.C.R. 326, [1979] C.T.C. 206, 79 D.T.C. 5124 (S.C.C.) (demolition of building constituted disposition of building even though taxpayer did not receive proceeds of disposition); see also *Rose v. Fed. Commr. of Taxation* (1951), 84 C.L.R. 118 (Aust. H.C.); *Gorton v. Fed. Commr. of Taxation* (1965), 113 C.L.R. 604 (Aust. H.C.); *Henty House Pty. Ltd. v. Fed. Commr. of Taxation* (1953), 88 C.L.R. 141 (Aust. H.C.) at 151, where the Australian High Court commented upon the meaning of the term "disposition" as follows:

for tax purposes "disposition" has a much broader meaning than "sale".[44] There is, however, one important exception: a transfer of legal title of property to a "bare trustee" is not a disposition if there is no change in beneficial ownership.[45]

4. — *Proceeds of Disposition*

In the simplest case, a taxpayer's proceeds from a disposition of property are equal to the consideration that he or she receives for the property. One determines the value of consideration for property from the terms of the contract of sale or deed. For example, assumption or discharge of debt obligations on a transaction can change the face value of proceeds of disposition.[46]

5. — *Changes in Terms of Securities*

A change in the terms or attributes of securities sometimes constitutes a disposition of the security. The determining factor is whether the amended security is in substance the same property as the security that underwent the change. The CRA's position is that any one of the following changes usually constitutes a disposition:[47]

The entire expression "disposed of, lost or destroyed" is apt to embrace every event by which property ceases to be available to the taxpayer for use for the purpose of producing assessable income, either because it ceases to be his, or because it ceases to be physically accessible to him, or because it ceases to exist ... the words "is disposed of" are wide enough to cover all forms of alienation ... and they should be understood as meaning no less than 'becomes alienated from the taxpayer', whether it is by him or by another that the act of alienation is done.

[44]*Olympia & York Dev. Ltd. v. M.N.R.*, [1980] C.T.C. 265, 80 D.T.C. 6184 (F.C.T.D.) (instalment contract; transfer of possession but not title constituted "disposition", although no "sale" until later); *The Queen v. Imp. Gen. Properties Ltd.*, [1985] 1 C.T.C. 40, 85 D.T.C. 5045 (F.C.A.); leave to appeal to S.C.C. refused 16 D.L.R. (4th) 615 (sale complete when conditions precedent satisfied); *Attis v. M.N.R.*, [1984] C.T.C. 3013, 85 D.T.C. 37 (T.C.C.) (Minister entitled to fix proceeds of disposition by reference to sale price).

[45]See ATR-1, "Transfer of Legal Title in Land to Bare Trustee Corporation — Mortgagee's Requirements Sole Reason for Transfer" (November 29, 1985).

[46]*The Queen v. Demers*, [1986] 2 C.T.C. 321, 86 D.T.C. 6411 (F.C.A.) (proceeds reduced by difference between principal amount of debt and its fair market value).

[47]IT-448, "Dispositions — Changes in Terms of Securities" (February 21, 1994), paras. 7 and 14. See also Income Tax Technical News #14 (December 9, 1998).

Debt securities

- An interest-bearing debt becoming non-interest-bearing, or *vice versa*;

- The repayment terms or maturity date being altered significantly;

- The principal amount of the debt being changed;

- The addition, alteration or elimination of a repayment premium;

- A change in the debtor; or

- The conversion of a fixed interest debt into a variable interest debt, or *vice versa*.

Equity securities

- A change in voting rights that results in a change in the control of the corporation;

- The addition or elimination of, or any change in, a preferential right to share in the assets of the corporation upon winding-up;

- The addition or elimination of a right to dividends beyond a fixed preferential rate or amount; or

- The conversion of a cumulative right to dividends into a non-cumulative right, or *vice versa*.

The following changes in the terms of a share are not a disposition of the share:[48]

- The addition of a right to elect a majority of the board of directors, if the class of shares carries sufficient voting power to control the election of the board at that time;

- A change in the number of votes per share, unless the influence of a particular shareholder over the day-to-day operation of the corporation is enhanced or impaired;

- The elimination of contingent voting rights, unless the exercise of such rights would carry control of the corporation;

- A change in transfer restrictions;

- The addition of a right to redeem shares at the option of the corporation;

- A stock split or consolidation;

- The conversion of par value shares to non-par value shares, or *vice versa*;

- A change in ranking or preference features; and

---

[48]*Ibid.* at para. 15.

- A change in the amount or rate of a fixed dividend, other than the addition or deletion of the right itself.

6. — Foreign Currencies

(a) — Characterization

Gains and losses in foreign currency transactions are taxable according to the usual rules, either as income gains (or losses) or as capital gains (or losses). Thus, the first step is to determine whether a gain or loss is on account of income or capital. The characterization of the currency gain or loss usually follows the transaction from which it results.[49] Hence, gains and losses from business transactions are income items; gains and losses from transactions in capital assets are capital gains and losses. A foreign exchange loss is not *per se* an "outlay or expense" for the purposes of determining a capital gain or loss.[50]

(b) — Method of Accounting

The general rule is that a capital gain or loss can occur for income tax purposes only if the taxpayer disposes of property.[51] This rule also applies to capital gains and losses from foreign currency transactions.

A capital gain or loss may result from a fluctuation in the value of a foreign currency relative to the Canadian dollar. Such a gain or loss may arise in respect of a cash balance in a foreign currency or on account of foreign debts. One-half of the *net* amount of such gains and losses is brought into income. To avoid administrative and recordkeeping difficulties, however, the Act allows individuals to exclude the first $200 of any *net* foreign currency capital gain or loss that the individual sustains in a year.[52]

---

[49] *Tip Top Tailors v. M.N.R.*, [1957] S.C.R. 703, [1957] C.T.C. 309, 57 D.T.C. 1232 (S.C.C.).

[50] *Avis Immobilier GMBH v. The Queen*, [1994] 1 C.T.C. 2204, 94 D.T.C. 1039 (T.C.C.); affd. on appeal 97 D.T.C. 5002 (Fr.) (Fed. C.A.); leave to appeal to S.C.C. dismissed (May 22, 1997), Doc. 25749 (S.C.C.).

[51] S. 39.

[52] Subs. 39(2).

Example
Assume:

An individual purchased U.S. shares for $2,000 (U.S.) at a time when the U.S. dollar was worth $0.90 (Cdn.). The shares cost her $1,800 (Cdn.). She sold these shares for $3,000 (U.S.) at a time when the U.S. dollar equalled $1.30 (Cdn.), and received $3,900 (Cdn.).

Then her taxable gain is calculated as follows:

> Regular gain
> ($3,000 U.S. - $2,000 U.S.) @ $0.90 = $900
> Foreign gain
> ($1.30 Cdn - $0.90 Cdn) @ $3,000 U.S. = $1,200
> Total gain
> ($1.30 × $3,000 - 0.90 × $2,000)
>   = $2, 100

Notes:

The CRA takes the position that subsection 39(2) applies only on an *actual* conversion of currency. See also *Rezvankhah*, 2002 D.T.C. 3928 (T.C.C.).

(c) — Determination of Cost

A taxpayer determines the cost of his or her capital property in Canadian dollars as at the date that the taxpayer acquires it, not when he or she disposes of it.[53] This is so even if the taxpayer acquires the asset by payment in foreign currency. Thus, the capital cost of a property to a taxpayer is its actual, factual or historical cost when he or she acquires it.

7. — Purchase of Bonds by Issuer

We saw earlier that a taxpayer generally realizes a capital gain or loss only when the taxpayer disposes of a capital property. Thus, a taxpayer who issues a bond (or similar debt obligation) does not trigger a gain or loss at the time of issuance. A purchase by the issuer of

---

[53]See *Gaynor v. M.N.R.*, [1987] 1 C.T.C. 2359, 87 D.T.C. 279 (T.C.C.); affd. [1988] 2 C.T.C. 163, 88 D.T.C. 6394 (F.C.T.D.) (capital cost of portfolio securities imported into Canada determined as at acquisition date).

its own debt obligation may, however, trigger a capital gain or loss if the purchase is on the open market. The gain or loss is calculated as follows:[54]

Capital gain:	
Issue price	$ 900
Less: purchase price	(600)
Capital gain	$ 300

Capital loss:	
Purchase price	$ 700
Less issue price	(500)
Capital loss	$ 200

Thus, a gain results where the issue price is greater than the purchase price paid by the taxpayer. Conversely, a capital loss arises where the purchase price exceeds the greater of the principal amount and the issue price of the bond, debenture or similar obligation.[55]

8. — Deemed Dispositions

The Act deems certain transactions and events to be dispositions of property. A deemed disposition gives rise to deemed proceeds of disposition. In the following paragraphs we look at some of the more common transactions that give rise to deemed dispositions.

(a) — Change in Use of Property

(i) — Personal to Commercial

A taxpayer who acquires property for personal use is deemed to have disposed of the property for proceeds equal to its fair market value if he or she begins to use the property for commercial purposes.[56] For example, suppose a taxpayer who owns and lives in a house that costs $100,000 begins to rent out the house at a time when its fair market value is $170,000. The act of renting out the house is a change in its use. The Act deems the taxpayer to have disposed of, and immediately reacquired, the house for $170,000. Thus, the taxpayer realizes a capital gain of $70,000 even though he or she does not receive any funds from the change of use.

---

[54]Subs. 39(3); see also ITAR 26(1.1) (obligations outstanding on January 1, 1972).

[55]Para. 39(3)(b).

[56]Para. 45(1)(a).

Where a taxpayer changes the use of property from personal to commercial, he or she may *elect* to ignore the change in use for income tax purposes. The effect of such an election is that the Act deems the taxpayer not to have begun to use the property for commercial purposes.[57] The taxpayer may rescind the election at any time. The taxpayer is deemed to have changed the use of the property on the first day of the year in which he or she rescinds the election.

A change of use can trigger adverse tax consequences. The election allows the taxpayer to defer any capital gain arising by virtue of a change in the use of the property. Thus, the election allows the taxpayer to defer payment of tax until such time as he or she disposes of the property or rescinds the election. Note, however, that during the tenure of the election the taxpayer cannot claim capital cost allowance on the property.[58]

(ii) — Commercial to Personal

The Act also deems a taxpayer who acquires property for commercial purposes to have disposed of the property at its fair market value if he or she begins to use it for personal purposes.[59] In the above example, if the taxpayer changes back the use of the house from commercial to personal use at a time when the fair market value of the house is $200,000, the change of use will trigger a capital gain of $30,000.

This rule does not apply where the taxpayer changes the use of property from commercial use to a principal residence if he or she elects in writing.[60] The deadline for the election is the earlier of two dates:

1. 90 days after the Minister demands the election; or

2. The taxpayer's filing-due date for the taxation year in which the property is actually disposed of by the taxpayer.

---

[57]Subs. 45(2).

[58]Reg. 1102(1)(c) (excludes from depreciable property any property not acquired by taxpayer for the purpose of gaining or producing income).

[59]Para. 45(1)(a); *Woods v. M.N.R.*, [1978] C.T.C. 2802, 78 D.T.C. 1576 (T.R.B.) (capital gain on deemed disposition in respect of taxpayer's dwelling when he occupied it after renting it out for nine years); *Leib v. M.N.R.*, [1984] C.T.C. 2324, 84 D.T.C. 1302 (T.C.C.) (change in use of principal residence deemed to be disposition despite taxpayer not receiving funds).

[60]Subss. 45(3), (4).

(iii) — Mixed Use Property

Where a taxpayer uses a property for both commercial and personal purposes, any change in the *proportion* of use for either of these purposes triggers a deemed disposition.[61] Where the change involves a decrease in the proportion of commercial use of the property, the deemed proceeds of disposition are added to the cost base of the property available for personal use.[62] In other words, the Act deems the taxpayer to reacquire that proportion of the property at a cost equal to its proportion of the fair market value for the entire property. Similarly, where the change involves an increase in the business use of the property, the deemed proceeds of disposition are added to the cost base of the property available for business use.[63] Note that the adjustment to the capital cost of the property under subsection 13(7) is an adjustment made *solely* for the purpose of capital cost allowance and recapture. It is *not* an adjustment for capital gains purposes under subdivision c of Division B. Although the CRA may allow a taxpayer to step up the cost base of the property, the taxpayer does not have statutory authority to insist on the step-up in cost.

Example

Assume:

An individual owns a building that she uses for both business and personal use.

Cost	$ 50,000
Proportion of business use	60%
Proportion of personal use	40%

She takes over an additional 10 per cent of the building for her personal use and decreases the portion occupied for business purposes to 50 per cent. The fair market value at that time is $70,000.

Then, to calculate the capital gain for the 10 per cent change in use:

Deemed proceeds of disposition		
(10% of $70,000)	$	7,000
ACB (10% of $50,000)		(5,000)
Capital gain	$	2,000

---

[61]Para. 45(1)(c).

[62]Subpara. 45(1)(c)(i).

[63]Subpara. 45(1)(c)(ii) (for example, duplex that is partly rented and partly owner-occupied).

Example

Calculation of Revised ACB of Property:

	Business Use	Personal Use	Total
Original ACB	$ 30,000	$ 20,000	$ 50,000
Deemed disposition	(5,000)		(5,000)
Deemed acquisition		7,000	7,000
Revised ACB	$ 25,000	$ 27,000	$ 52,000 *

If immediately thereafter she sells the building at its fair market value of $70,000, the business and personal portions of the resulting capital gain are as follows:

	Business Portion (50%)	Personal Portion (50%)	Total
Proceeds of disposition	$ 35,000	$ 35,000	$ 70,000
Revised ACB	25,000	27,000	52,000
Capital gain	$ 10,000	$ 8,000	$ 18,000
Capital gain previously recognized			2,000
Total capital gain			$ 20,000 **

Notes:

* The revised ACB takes into account the capital gain resulting from the change of use:

Original cost	$50,000
Capital gain	2,000
Revised ACB	$52,000

** Thus, the full amount of the capital gain of $20,000 ($70,000-$50,000) is eventually recognized.

(b) — Leaving Canada

(i) — "Departure Tax"

The Act deems a taxpayer who ceases to be resident in Canada to dispose of his or her property immediately before giving up residence. This deemed disposition may give rise to a capital gain, resulting in a "departure tax" on the taxpayer.[64]

The following properties are not subject to the departure tax:

Description	Reference
• Where the taxpayer is an individual, real or immovable property situated in Canada, a Canadian resource property or a timber resource property.	subpara. 128.1(4)(b)(i)
• Where the taxpayer is an individual, capital property used, eligible capital property in respect of and inventory described in the business carried on by the individual in Canada through a permanent establishment.	subpara. 128.1(4)(b)(ii)
• Where the taxpayer is an individual, an excluded right or interest defined in subs. 128.1(10) as including payments under certain pension plans, deferred income arrangements, retiring allowances, death benefits, unemployment insurance benefits and options under stock option plans;	subpara. 128.1(4)(b)(iii)
• Where the taxpayer is an individual other than a trust and during the preceding 10 years was resident in Canada for a total of 60 months or less, property that the taxpayer owned when he or she last became resident in Canada or that was acquired by the taxpayer by inheritance or bequest after he or she last became resident in Canada;	subpara. 128.1(4)(b)(iv)

Resident taxpayers may, however, elect to defer or trigger accrued gains on their capital property.

(ii) — Election to Dispose

An individual (other than a trust) may elect to be considered to have disposed of real property in Canada, a Canadian resource property, a timber resource property or capital pro-

---

[64]Para. 128.1(4)(b); *Davis v. The Queen*, [1978] C.T.C. 536, 78 D.T.C. 6374 (F.C.T.D.); affd. [1980] C.T.C. 88, 80 D.T.C. 6056 (F.C.A.).

perty used, eligible capital property in respect of and inventory in a business carried on through a PE in Canada at its fair market value and to have reacquired the property at the particular time at a cost equal to those proceeds.[65] This election is useful for departing residents who want to realize accrued capital gains to take advantage of the capital gains exemption.[66]

These two elections are available only to departing residents of Canada. Non-resident taxpayers are liable (subject to tax treaty provisions) for tax on capital gains that they realize upon disposing of their taxable Canadian property.[67]

(c) — Options

(i) — Nature

An option is a contractual right that gives its holder the power to buy or sell property at some time in the future at a fixed or otherwise determinable price.[68] Since an option is a right, it is "property" for income tax purposes.[69] An option right can be sold, exercised or allowed to expire.

(ii) — Characterization on Issuance

The issuance of an option may be an income transaction or a capital transaction.[70] The usual tests in characterizing gains as income gains or capital gains also apply to options. The determination depends upon the taxpayer's intention to invest or trade in the property on which the option is granted.[71] Where the optionor does not grant the option in the course of his or her business, any consideration for the option is a capital gain.

---

[65]Para. 128.1(4)(d).

[66]S. 110.6; see Chapter 15, "Taxable Income".

[67]Para. 2(3)(c).

[68]See, generally, *Day v. M.N.R.*, 71 D.T.C. 723, [1971] Tax A.B.C. 1050 (Can. Tax App. Bd.) for discussion on meaning of option.

[69]Subs. 248(1)"property"; *Day v. M.N.R.*, *ante*.

[70]See, *Western Leaseholds Ltd. v. M.N.R.*, [1960] S.C.R. 10, [1959] C.T.C. 531, 59 D.T.C. 1316 (S.C.C.) (revenues from granting mineral rights options were income); *Hill Clark Francis Ltd. v. M.N.R.*, [1963] S.C.R. 452, [1963] C.T.C. 337, 63 D.T.C. 1211 (S.C.C.).

[71]*Cook v. The Queen*, [1987] 1 C.T.C. 377, 87 D.T.C. 5231 (F.C.T.D.); see also *Day v. M.N.R.*, *ante* (meaning of "option").

(iii) — Granting of Options

As a rule, the Act deems a taxpayer who *grants* an option in respect of a capital property to have disposed of the property at that time.[72] The adjusted cost base of the option is nil. Thus, the issuance of an option for valuable consideration triggers a capital gain in the year in which the taxpayer issues it. This rule does not apply to options to buy or sell a principal residence, options that a corporation issues to acquire its bonds, debentures or equity capital, or options that a trust grants to acquire units of the trust. Special rules apply to employee stock options.[73]

(A) — Call Options

Where a taxpayer grants a call option (an option to purchase property), the granting of the option is a disposition of property. The statute deems the adjusted cost base of the property to be nil. The taxpayer must report the gain on the option in the year that he or she grants it.[74]

If the option is exercised, the granting of the option is retrospectively deemed not to have been a disposition of property.[75] Thus, upon the exercise of the option the earlier transaction is, in effect, retrospectively cancelled for tax purposes. The grantor then includes the price of the option in the proceeds of disposition from the property that he or she sells pursuant to the option.[76] Thus, the price of the option increases the proceeds of disposition. The purchaser includes the cost of the option in the adjusted cost base of the property that he or she acquires.[77] The grantor can retrospectively adjust the tax return for the year in which the grantor issued the option, and recalculate the earlier option gain.[78]

---

[72]Subs. 49(1).

[73]See s. 7; see Chapter 6, "Employment Income" under heading "Stock Option Plans".

[74]Subs. 49(1).

[75]Subs. 49(3).

[76]Para. 49(3)(a).

[77]Para. 49(3)(b).

[78]Subs. 49(4).

Example

Assume:

In Year 1, *Alpha Ltd.* grants T a call option to purchase a parcel of land for $400,000. T pays $15,000 for the option, which T exercises in Year 5. The adjusted cost base ("ACB") of the land is $50,000.

Then:

    1. Effect on *Alpha Ltd.* upon issuance of option:

Proceeds of disposition	$ 15,000
ACB (deemed)	NIL
Capital gain	$ 15,000

    2. Effect on *Alpha Ltd.* upon exercise of option:

Proceeds from sale of land	$ 400,000
Add: proceeds from option	15,000
Total proceeds of disposition	415,000
ACB of land	(50,000)
Capital gain	$ 365,000

Subsequently, *Alpha Ltd.* may file an amended return in Year 5 to retroactively reduce its capital gain in Year 1 to nil.

    3. Adjusted cost base of land to purchaser (T):

Exercise price	$ 400,000
Option price	15,000
ACB	$ 415,000

(B) — Put Options

Where a taxpayer issues a put option (an option to sell property), any consideration that he or she receives for the option is considered as proceeds of disposition in the year of issuance.[79] Where the option is subsequently exercised by the grantee, the Act deems the granting and exercise of the option not to have taken place. Instead, the grantor's and grantee's proceeds of disposition and cost of the property are adjusted for the price of the option.[80]

(d) — Bad Debts

Where a taxpayer establishes that his or her account receivable from a disposition of capital property has become uncollectible, the taxpayer can elect to be deemed to have disposed of the debt.[81] Similarly, a taxpayer who establishes that a corporation in which he or she holds shares has become bankrupt or is subject to a winding-up order can elect to be deemed to have disposed of any shares.[82] The taxpayer can then claim a capital loss even though he or she has not disposed of the shares. Where the taxpayer makes the election, he or she is deemed to have disposed of the bad debt or the shares for nil proceeds at the end of the year, and to have then acquired it for a cost of nil.

(i) — Subsequent Recovery

A taxpayer makes a deduction for bad debts arising from the sale of capital property only when the taxpayer actually establishes the debt to have become bad. The Act does not permit the deduction of a reserve for doubtful accounts in respect of debts created from dispositions of capital property. Since a taxpayer who disposes of a bad debt can elect to do so for nil proceeds and to reacquire it for the same amount, any recovery on account of a debt previously written off will give rise to a capital gain.[83]

(ii) — Insolvent Corporations

Shareholders of a corporation that has ceased to carry on business and is insolvent can elect to be deemed to have disposed of their shares. Therefore, they may be entitled to claim a

---

[79]Subs. 49(1).

[80]Subs. 49(3.1).

[81]Subs. 50(1).

[82]Para. 50(1)(b).

[83]See also subpara. 40(2)(g)(ii).

capital loss. The Act deems a shareholder to have disposed of his or her shares in an insolvent corporation only if:[84]

- The fair market value of the shares is nil;

- It is reasonable to expect that the corporation will be wound up;

- Neither the corporation nor a corporation controlled by it carries on business; and

- The shareholder elects to have the provision apply.

(e) — Death

The Act also deems a taxpayer who dies to have disposed of all his or her capital properties *immediately before* death.[85] The disposition gives rise to deemed proceeds of disposition. The amount of the proceeds depends upon the type of capital property and the date of death.

(i) — Depreciable Capital Property

The Act deems a taxpayer to dispose of his or her depreciable property at its fair market value.[86] Thus, the full amount of any gain accrued on depreciable property is included in the proceeds of disposition.

A beneficiary who inherits property as a consequence of the death of a taxpayer is deemed to acquire the property at an amount equal to the deceased's (deemed) proceeds of disposition (fair market value).[87] A special rule applies, however, if the deceased's capital cost exceeds the beneficiary's deemed acquisition cost. In this circumstance, *for purposes of capital cost allowance and recapture only*, the beneficiary assumes the deceased's original cost, and any difference between this cost and the beneficiary's acquisition cost is deemed to have been claimed as capital cost allowance by the beneficiary.[88] The effect of this special rule is to bump up the beneficiary capital cost, so that the deeming provision does not obscure the true nature of the proceeds of a future disposition by the beneficiary. The bump up in the cost could result in the characterization of proceeds as recapture rather than capital.

---

[84]Subpara. 50(1)(b)(iii).

[85]Para. 70(5)(a).

[86]Para. 70(5)(a).

[87]Para. 70(5)(b).

[88]Para. 70(5)(c).

Example

Assume:

D dies owning a depreciable property that cost $200,000. At the time of his death, the property had a UCC of $120,000 and a fair market value ("FMV") of $320,000.

Then, D's capital gain is $120,000, calculated as follows:

Deemed proceeds	$ 320,000
Original cost	(200,000)
Capital gain	$ 120,000

D is also subject to recapture of capital cost allowance of $80,000.

Example

B inherits depreciable property from D on D's death. The following applies:

Original cost	$	200,000
UCC at death	$	120,000
FMV at death	$	180,000

Then:

Effect on D's Terminal Tax Return:

Deemed proceeds of disposition	$	180,000
UCC at death		(120,000)
Recapture of CCA	$	60,000

Effect on B:

Capital cost for CCA purposes	$	200,000
CCA deemed allowed to B		(20,000)
UCC to B	$	180,000

Example

Subsequent Sale by B for $240,000:		
Deemed capital cost	$	200,000
UCC on sale		(180,000)
Recapture of CCA	$	20,000
Proceeds of disposition	$	240,000
Cost (ACB)		(200,000)
Capital gain	$	40,000

(ii) — Other Capital Property

Capital properties other than depreciable properties are also deemed to be disposed of immediately before death for proceeds equal to the fair market value of the property.[89]

(f) — Trusts

To discourage indefinite accumulations of property in trusts, the Act provides for periodic deemed dispositions of all property held in trust. A trust is deemed to dispose of all of its capital property on the 21st anniversary of the day on which the trust was created.[90]

9. — Involuntary Dispositions

In certain circumstances, a taxpayer may involuntarily dispose of his or her property. For example, the taxpayer's property may be stolen or expropriated. In these circumstances, it can cause hardship to tax a taxpayer on the full value of any proceeds received. To relieve against such hardship, the Act allows a taxpayer who involuntarily disposes of property to elect to defer any capital gain from the disposition,[91] provided that he or she replaces the property with a substitute property before the end of the later end of the second taxation year and 24 months.[92]

---

[89]Para. 70(5)(a).

[90]Subss. 104(4), (5), (5.3)–(5.8).

[91]Subs. 44(1).

[92]IT-259-R4, "Exchanges of Property".

(a) — Election to Defer Gain

The deferral is available in respect of the following types of receipts:[93]

- Compensation for property[94] that has been lost or destroyed;

- Compensation for property that is stolen;

- Compensation for property that is expropriated under statutory authority; or

- Sale proceeds from property sold under the duress of an intention to expropriate under statutory authority.

A taxpayer can defer tax only where he or she acquires a replacement for the property before the end of the later end of the second taxation year and 24 months.[95] The taxpayer must acquire a capital property to replace the former property. A business asset must be replaced with a business asset.

(b) — Proceeds of Disposition

Proceeds of an involuntary disposition are deemed to become receivable on the *earliest* of the following days:[96]

- The day when the taxpayer agrees to an amount as full compensation for property lost, stolen or destroyed;

- Where an appeal or other proceeding has been taken before a court or tribunal, the day on which the taxpayer's compensation for the property is finally determined by the court or tribunal;

- Where no such appeal or other proceeding has been taken before a court or tribunal within two years of the loss, destruction or expropriation of property, the second anniversary day of the loss, destruction or expropriation;

- The day on which the taxpayer ceases to be resident in Canada;

- The day on which the taxpayer dies; or,

---

[93]Subs. 44(1).

[94]*Sani Sport Inc. v. Can.*, [1990] 2 C.T.C. 15, 90 D.T.C. 6230 (F.C.A.) (compensation for property includes damages suffered by business loss).

[95]Para. 44(1)(c).

[96]Subs. 44(2).

- Where the taxpayer is a corporation (other than a taxable Canadian corporation that is 90 per cent owned by another taxable Canadian corporation), immediately before the corporation is wound up.

Example

Assume:

Jones owns a parcel of land to which the following data applies:

ACB of land	$ 80,000
Proceeds upon expropriation	$140,000
Expenses of disposition	$ 2,000
Cost of replacement land (FMV)	$160,000

Then, Jones's capital gain is determined as follows:

Without Election:

Proceeds of disposition		$140,000
Less: ACB of land	$ 80,000	
Expenses of disposition	2,000	(82,000)
Capital gain		$ 58,000

With Election under Section 44:

Capital gain otherwise determined		$ 58,000 *
Proceeds from former property		$140,000
Cost of replacement land	$160,000	
Expenses of disposition	2,000	162,000
Excess of proceeds over replacement cost		NIL **
Deemed capital gain, lesser of * and **		NIL

ACB of Replacement Land After Election:

Cost of replacement land		$160,000
Less excess of:		
Capital gain otherwise determined	$ 58,000	
Excess of proceeds over replacement cost	NIL	(58,000)
ACB of replacement land		$102,000

Example
Note: if Jones immediately sold the replacement land at its FMV of $160,000, she would realize a capital gain of $58,000 ($160,000 less $102,000), which is, in effect, the amount of the capital gain that she deferred.

Thus, in general terms, a taxpayer can defer the entire capital gain that would otherwise be recognized provided that he or she replaces the disposed property with more expensive property. The deferred gain reduces the cost base of the new property.[97] In the above example, the deferred capital gain of $58,000 reduces the cost of the new property from $160,000 to $102,000. Thus, the gain on the sale of the new property will be $58,000 greater than it would otherwise have been.

V. — Adjusted Cost Base

As a general rule, the capital cost of a property is the amount expended for the acquisition of the property, including the amount of any liabilities assumed by the taxpayer. The "adjusted cost base" of a property means:[98]

- Where the property is depreciable property, its capital cost; and

- Where the property is any other property, the cost of the property as adjusted by section 53.

The Act does not define the terms "capital cost" and "cost". Hence, we interpret them according to their commercial usage.

"Cost" refers to the price that the taxpayer gives up in order to acquire the property.[99] It includes incidental acquisition costs such as brokerage, legal, accounting, engineering and valuation fees. Carrying costs (such as interest expense) for the unpaid price of property are not part of the "cost" of the asset for purposes of the capital gains rules.[100]

---

[97]Para. 44(1)(f).

[98]S. 54"adjusted cost base".

[99]*The Queen v. Stirling*, [1985] 1 F.C. 342, [1985] 1 C.T.C. 275, 85 D.T.C. 5199 (F.C.A.) (interest expense on unpaid portion of price of gold bullion, and safe-keeping charges, not part of cost of bullion).

[100]*The Queen v. Stirling*, *ante*, at 343; see also *The Queen v. C.P. Ltd.*, [1977] C.T.C. 606, 77 D.T.C. 5383 (F.C.A.) (taxpayer not entitled to CCA on perishable product or expenditures in respect of property not owned); *The Queen v. Consumer's Gas Co.*, [1984] C.T.C. 83, 84 D.T.C. 6058 (F.C.A.) (taxpayer to add cost of pipelines to UCC without reduction for reimbursement); *Birmingham Corp. v.*

There are special rules for determining the adjusted cost base of properties owned by a taxpayer at the start of the "new system" on January 1, 1972. These rules are set out in the Income Tax Application Rules (ITARs).

1. — Deemed Adjusted Cost Base

Numerous provisions of the Act *deem* the cost of a property to be a certain amount. Note that whenever the Act deems a disposition of property for deemed proceeds, it also deems a reacquisition of the property at a deemed cost base. Thus, every capital property always has an adjusted cost base at any given point in time.

(a) — Change of Use

Where a taxpayer changes the use of a capital property from business to personal use, or *vice versa*, he or she is deemed to have acquired the property for the new purpose at a cost equal to its fair market value at the time of the change in use.[101] Thus, despite the absence of a market transaction, there is a carryover of basis from the business use to the personal use. Similarly, where a taxpayer changes the proportions of business and personal use of a capital property, the taxpayer may be deemed to have acquired the portion of the property, subject to the new use at a cost proportional to its fair market value at that time.[102]

(b) — Identical Properties

The cost of identical properties is their weighted average cost at any time.[103] A new average is to be determined each time another identical property is acquired and added to the pool. The cost of identical capital properties (other than depreciable property or an interest in a partnership) owned by a taxpayer on December 31, 1971, is also the weighted average cost of the properties.[104] Note, however, that this calculation is made separately from the one for identical properties acquired after December 31, 1971. In effect, a taxpayer is required to maintain two separate pools of identical properties: one for pre-1972 properties and the other for post-1971 properties.

Barnes, [1935] A.C. 292 (H.L.) (deductibility of grant received and renewal costs in determination of "actual cost" to build tramway).

[101] S. 45.

[102] Para. 45(1)(c).

[103] S. 47.

[104] ITAR 26(8).

Where a taxpayer issues debt (bonds, debentures, notes, etc.) and equity securities at different times, the securities are considered to be identical to each other if they have the same rights in all respects and differ only in the face value or principal amount of the security.[105]

(c) — Becoming a Canadian Resident

When a taxpayer becomes resident in Canada, the taxpayer is deemed to have acquired each property already owned by him or her at that time, at a cost equal to its fair market value.[106] This rule does not apply to property that would be "taxable Canadian property".[107]

(d) — Options

When a taxpayer exercises an option to acquire property, the adjusted cost base of the property to the purchaser includes the cost of the option.[108] Upon exercise, the option and the property acquired are unified into one cost basis on their joint market values.

(e) — Conversions

Where a taxpayer acquires shares of a corporation in exchange for convertible shares, bonds, debentures or notes issued by the corporation, and the acquisition is made without any cash consideration, the taxpayer's cost of the shares is deemed to be the adjusted cost base of the convertible property immediately before the exchange.[109]

(f) — Non-Arm's Length Transactions

Where a taxpayer acquires property in a non-arm's length transaction at an amount greater than its fair market value, the taxpayer is deemed to have acquired the property at its fair market value at the time of acquisition.[110] If the property is acquired at less than its fair market value, the adjusted cost base of the property is the taxpayer's actual cost.

---

[105]Subs. 248(12).

[106]Para. 128.1(1)(c).

[107]Subs. 248(1) and Para. 128.1(1)(b).

[108]Subs. 49(3).

[109]S. 51.

[110]Para. 69(1)(a).

(g) — Prizes

A taxpayer who wins a prize in a lottery is deemed to acquire the property at a cost equal to its fair market value at the time of winning the prize.[111] Although a lottery prize is exempt from tax, a life annuity in lieu of the prize is *fully* taxable. The recipient may, however, deduct the capital component of the annuity. In effect, the investment earnings component of the annuity is taxable.

(h) — Dividends in Kind

A taxpayer who receives a dividend in kind (other than a stock dividend) is deemed to have acquired the property at its fair market value.[112]

(i) — Stock Dividends

A stock dividend includes any dividend paid by the issuance of shares of any class of a corporation.[113]

The value of a stock dividend is the amount by which the paid-up capital of the corporation paying the dividend is increased by virtue of the payment of the dividend.[114] In the case of a stock dividend that does not qualify as a "dividend", the cost is nil.[115] Note that the cost of stock dividends received by a taxpayer will affect the adjusted cost base of all other identical shares owned by the taxpayer.[116]

A corporation that pays a stock dividend with a low paid-up capital and high fair market value and then repurchases the stock may be liable to a special corporate distributions tax.[117]

---

[111]Subs. 52(4); see *Rumack v. M.N.R.*, [1984] C.T.C. 2382, 84 D.T.C. 1339 (T.C.C.)[1992] 1 C.T.C. 57, 92 D.T.C. 6142 (Fed. C.A.).

[112]Subs. 52(2).

[113]See subs. 248(1)"dividend".

[114]See para. 248(1)(c).

[115]Para. 52(3)(a.1).

[116]S. 47.

[117]Pt. II.1, (ss. 183.1, 183.2).

2. — Adjustments to Cost Base

(a) — General Comment

The cost base of a property is determined by reference to commercial principles and the aforementioned deeming provisions. The cost base may also be adjusted for various events and transactions from time to time. The adjusted cost base of a property is always determined *as of a particular time*, and any adjustments are made up to that time.

There are two types of adjustments to the cost base of property — *additions* to the cost base[118] and *deductions* from the cost base.[119]

Generally, additions to the cost base of property are made when a taxpayer receives an amount that either has previously borne tax or was exempt from tax. Thus, additions to the adjusted cost base of property prevent double taxation of the same amount. For example, where an employee is taxed on a stock option benefit that is included in employment income,[120] the value of the benefit is added to the cost base of the shares.[121] Without this addition, the taxpayer would be taxed again on the same gain when he or she disposed of the shares.

Conversely, deductions from the cost base of property are made when a taxpayer has previously received an amount free of tax. The following is illustrative of some of the adjustments made to the cost base of the more common types of property.

(b) — Acquisition of Land

A taxpayer may not deduct interest on debt relating to the acquisition of vacant land to the extent that the expense exceeds any income from the land.[122] The taxpayer can, however, add the disallowed carrying charges to the cost base of the land.[123]

The phrase "interest on debt relating to the acquisition of land" includes certain interest expenses to finance the acquisition of land by another person with whom the taxpayer does not deal at arm's length.[124] For example, it includes interest on borrowed money that is used

---

[118]Subs. 53(1).

[119]Subs. 53(2).

[120]S. 7; see Chapter 6, "Employment Income" under heading "Stock Option Plans".

[121]Para. 53(1)(j).

[122]Subs. 18(2).

[123]Subpara. 53(1)(h)(i).

[124]Subs. 18(3) "interest on debt relating to the acquisition of land".

to finance the acquisition of land by a corporation of which the taxpayer is a specified share-holder, or by a partnership in which the taxpayer has at least a 10 per cent interest.

(c) — Stock Dividends and Options

Stock dividends have an adjusted cost base equal to the aggregate of the value of the dividend and any amount included in the taxpayer's income as a shareholder benefit.[125]

Where an employee acquires shares of a corporation under an employee stock option plan, the employee is deemed to receive a "stock option" benefit under section 7. The amount of the benefit is added to the adjusted cost base of the shares acquired.[126]

3. — Negative Adjusted Cost Base

As a rule, the adjusted cost base of a property at the time that it is disposed of cannot be less than nil.[127] If at any time the deductions from the cost of property exceed its adjusted cost, the adjusted cost base of the property becomes a negative amount. The Act deems the negative amount to be a capital gain from the disposition of the property. The amount of the deemed gain is then immediately added to the cost of the property, thereby raising its adjusted cost base to nil.[128] The capital gain is eligible for the capital gains exemption under section 110.6.

Example

Assume:

A taxpayer owns a capital property with an adjusted cost base of $2,000. During the year, the cost base is adjusted by subsection 53(1) additions of $300 and subsection 53(2) deductions of $2,700.

---

[125]Subs. 52(3); subs. 15(1.1); subs. 248(l) "stock dividend"; see Chapter 22, "Shareholder Taxation".

[126]Para. 53(1)(j).

[127]Subs. 54"adjusted cost base" (d).

[128]Subs. 40(3).

Example

Then the taxpayer's adjusted cost base is calculated as follows:

Cost of property	$ 2,000
Subsection 53(1) additions	300
	2,300
Subsection 53(2) deductions	(2,700)
Deemed capital gain	(400)
Paragraph 53(1)(a) addition	400
ACB of property	$ NIL

VI. — Part Dispositions

Where a taxpayer disposes of only a part of a capital property, one calculates the adjusted cost base of that part by taking a "reasonable" proportion of the cost base of the part to the whole. The adjusted cost base of the part of the property that was disposed of is then deducted from the adjusted cost base of the whole property.[129] The balance becomes the cost base of the remaining part.[130]

Example

Assume:

A taxpayer disposes of a part of a capital property for its fair market value of $3,000, at a time when the fair market value of the entire property is $14,000. The adjusted cost base of the entire property is $7,000.

Then, (1) the ACB of the disposed property, (2) the taxpayer's capital gain, and (3) the ACB of the remaining property, are calculated as follows:

---

[129]Para. 53(2)(d).

[130]S. 43; there are special rules governing partial dispositions of personal-use property.

Example		
(1)	ACB of portion of property disposed of:	
	$\dfrac{\$\ \ 3,000\ \times\ \$7,000}{\$\ 14,000}$	$ 1,500
(2)	Proceeds of disposition	$ 3,000
	ACB of disposed of portion	(1,500)
	Capital gain	$ 1,500
(3)	ACB of entire property	$ 7,000
	ACB of disposed of portion	(1,500)
	ACB of remaining portion	$ 5,500

VII. — Personal-Use Property

There are special rules for determining capital gains and losses from dispositions of "personal-use property". These special rules serve two purposes. First, they eliminate the need for any record keeping in connection with the purchase and sale of low-value capital assets used primarily for the taxpayer's personal use or enjoyment. Second, they prohibit a deduction for capital losses on the disposition of this particular category of capital property.

Personal-use property includes:[131]

- Property owned by a taxpayer that is used *primarily* for the personal use or enjoyment of:

    - the taxpayer;

    - a person related to the taxpayer; or

    - if the taxpayer is a trust, a beneficiary under the trust or any person related[132] to the beneficiary;

- A debt owing to a taxpayer in respect of the disposition of personal-use property; and

- An option to acquire property that would, if it were acquired, be personal-use property of a taxpayer or a person related to him or her.

---

[131] S. 54 "personal-use property".

[132] See subs. 251(2).

Cars, boats, furniture, clothing, and residences are common examples of personal-use property.

A partnership may also own personal-use property. For example, any partnership property that is used primarily for the personal use or enjoyment of any member of the partnership, or for the personal use or enjoyment of one or more of a group of individuals consisting of a member of the partnership and persons related to him or her, would be personal-use property. Similarly, property owned by a corporation may be personal-use property if the property is primarily for the personal use of a shareholder of the corporation.

1. — Listed Personal Property

"Listed personal property" is a subset of personal-use property that is specifically listed in the Act. Listed personal property includes:[133]

- Prints, etchings, drawings, paintings, sculptures or other similar works of art;

- Jewellery;

- Rare folios, rare manuscripts or rare books;

- Stamps; and

- Coins.

An interest in, or right to, any of these items is also listed personal property. Thus, listed personal property items are assets that one acquires for dual purposes — personal consumption and investment value. Hence, gains from listed personal property are taxable; losses are deductible only against gains from listed personal property.[134]

2. — Computational Rules

To minimize recordkeeping for low-value items of personal-use property, the Act deems the *minimum* adjusted cost base and proceeds of disposition of personal-use property to be $1,000.[135] Consequently, if both the *actual* cost and the *actual* proceeds on disposition of an item of personal-use property are less than $1,000, the transaction does not give rise to any capital gain or capital loss. Thus, taxpayers do not need to keep a detailed record of low-value transactions for income tax purposes.

---

[133]S. 54"listed personal property".

[134]See para. 3(b), which includes *net* LPP gains in income.

[135]Subs. 46(1).

A special rule, however, applies to exclude from the $1,000 minimum any property — typically art — that a taxpayer acquires with the intention of "flipping" to a charity. The purpose of the exclusion is to discourage bogus "art flips" to charities.[136]

Example

A taxpayer purchases and then sells personal-use property for the amounts indicated. The gain or loss in each case is calculated as follows:

	A	B	C
Proceeds of disposition	$ 900*	$ 1,200	$ 2,000
Cost	(600)*	(600)*	(1,500)
Capital gain	$ NIL	$ 200	$ 500

	D	E	F
Proceeds of disposition	$ 400*	$ 800*	$ 1,200
Cost	(60)*	(1,500)	(1,500)
Capital loss**	$ NIL	$ (500)	$ (300)

Notes:

* Deemed to be $1,000

** Capital loss is deemed to be nil unless the personal-use property qualifies as listed personal property.

3. — Bad Debts

Where a taxpayer establishes that a debt owing to him or her from a sale of personal-use property has become a bad debt, the taxpayer may offset any prior capital gain that he or she recognized on the sale of the property by recognizing a capital loss when the debt becomes bad.[137]

---

[136]Subs. 46(5).

[137]Subs. 50(2).

Example

Assume:

A taxpayer sells personal-use property with an ACB of $9,000 for proceeds of $10,000 in Year 1. The taxpayer receives $6,000 cash and accepts a note for $4,000. In Year 3, the debtor defaults on the note and the debt is established to have become bad.

Then:

Year 1 Proceeds of disposition	$ 10,000
ACB of property	(9,000)
Capital gain	$ 1,000
Year 3 Deemed proceeds of debt[*]	$ 3,000
ACB of debt	(4,000)
Capital loss	$ (1,000)

Notes:

*   Calculated as the amount that will give rise to a capital loss equal to the prior capital gain.

4. — Part Dispositions

To prevent taxpayers from taking unfair advantage of the minimum $1,000 adjusted cost base and proceeds of disposition rule by selling sets of property in bits and pieces, a special rule requires that the $1,000 be allocated whenever the various parts of a personal-use property are sold individually or when a set of personal-use property is sold piecemeal. The $1,000 amount is allocated in the following proportion:

$$\$1,000 \times \frac{\text{Adjusted cost base of part disposed}}{\text{Adjusted cost base of the whole property}}$$

The deemed cost and deemed proceeds of disposition rules are then applied in relation to the part of the personal-use property that has been disposed of on the basis of this reduced amount.[138]

---

[138]Subs. 46(2). Note that these allocation rules apply only when a taxpayer disposes of a part of a personal-use property and retains another part. Accordingly, upon the disposition of the final remaining part, no allocation is required, since the taxpayer would not be retaining another part.

The second aspect of this rule applies to dispositions of a set of personal-use properties that have an *aggregate* fair market value in excess of $1,000 and would *ordinarily* be disposed of together. If a set of personal-use properties is sold in more than one transaction to the same person, or to a group of persons who do not deal with each other at arm's length, the set is deemed to be a single property and the $1,000 amount is proportionally reduced.[139]

5. — Capital Losses

Capital losses arising from a disposition of personal-use property (other than listed personal property) are deemed to be nil.[140] An additional rule provides that, where a capital gain is reduced, or a capital loss is increased, on the disposition of a share of a corporation (or an interest in a partnership or trust), and it may reasonably be regarded that the reduction in value of the share results from a decrease in the value of any personal-use property of the corporation (or partnership or trust), then the capital gain or capital loss is adjusted to the amount that it would have been if the particular personal-use property had not decreased in value.[141] This rule applies even if the particular personal-use property is listed personal property.

Finally, there are special rules for calculating losses on listed personal property ("LPP"). The general thrust of these rules is that capital losses on LPP can be offset only against capital gains on LPP. Any remaining balance can be carried back three years and carried forward seven years; in each of those years, the LPP loss can be offset only against LPP gains.[142]

VIII. — Identical Properties

Where a taxpayer acquires a capital property identical to other properties that he or she owns, the cost of each of the properties is calculated by taking the weighted average of their adjusted cost bases. The weighted average cost of properties must be recalculated each time the taxpayer acquires another property identical to property already owned by the taxpayer.[143] The weighted average cost of identical properties is determined by dividing the aggregate of their adjusted cost bases by the number of properties owned.

---

[139]Subs. 46(3).

[140]Subpara. 40(2)(g)(iii).

[141]Subs. 46(4).

[142]Subs. 41(2).

[143]S. 47 and para. 3(b).

Whether property acquired by a taxpayer is "identical" to property already owned by him or her is a question of fact. Corporate shares of the same class and with the same rights are identical properties, notwithstanding that they may be physically identifiable as separate properties by virtue of their serial numbers.

Bonds and debt obligations issued by a corporation are considered similar to other debts issued by the debtor if they are identical in respect of their legal and equitable rights. This is so even if the principal amounts are different.[144]

Land can never be an identical property for tax purposes; this is so even if the lots are adjoining lots and of the same size and quality. Each plot of land is unique.

Example

A taxpayer owns 100 common shares of *XYZ Co.*, which she acquired at a cost of $20 per share. The taxpayer acquires a further 200 shares of the same class and kind of the same corporation at $30 per share.

The weighted average cost of the shares is calculated as follows:

100 shares × $20/share	$ 2,000
200 shares × $30/share	6,000
300	$ 8,000
Weighted Average Cost per Share ($8,000/300)	$ 26.67

Properties owned by a taxpayer as at December 31, 1971, are segregated in a separate pool from identical properties acquired by the taxpayer after that date. In other words, a weighted average cost is calculated for identical properties owned on December 31, 1971, and a separate average cost is calculated for properties acquired subsequently. Note that a disposition of identical properties is always deemed to be made first out of the pre-1972 pool.[145]

To summarize: identical properties are divided into two pools, one pool consisting of the properties on hand at December 31, 1971, and the other group comprising post-1971 acquisitions. The pre-1972 group is deemed to be disposed of first.

---

[144]Subs. 248(12).

[145]ITAR 26(8)–(8.3).

Example

Assume:

Jane Henry, a Canadian resident, has bought and sold shares of *Gamma Ltd.*, a CCPC, as an investment during the past nine years. In Year 9 she liquidated part of her holdings. The following is a history of her transactions:

	Bought		Sold	
	(#)	($)	(#)	($)
Year 1	6,000	18,000		
Year 2	5,000	32,000		
Year 3	7,500	42,000		
Year 4	6,500	35,000		
Year 5			6,500	40,000
Year 6	5,500	28,000		
Year 7	8,000	36,000		
Year 8	6,000	25,000		
Year 9			7,500	45,000

Question: Determine Jane's capital gain for Year 9.

Then:

Acquisitions:

Year 1	$ 18,000	
Year 2	32,000	
Year 3	42,000	
Year 4	35,000	

Total cost of shares to date:	$ 127,000	
Average cost/share:	$5.08	
Year 5 Number of shares sold:	6,500	
Cost of shares sold:		33,020
ACB of remaining shares:		93,980

Example

Acquisitions:

Year 6	$	28,000	
Year 7		36,000	
Year 8		25,000	
		89,000	

Total cost of shares to date		182,980
Average cost/share:	$4.82	

Year 9:	Number of shares sold:	7,500	
	Cost of shares sold:		36,150
	ACB of remaining shares:		146,830

Proceeds of disposition	$	45,000
ACB of shares sold		36,150
Capital gain realized	$	8,850

IX. — Losses Deemed To Be Nil

1. — General Comment

The Act may deem a capital loss to be nil, with the result that the capital loss is not recognized in computing income. The circumstances when the Act deems a capital loss to be nil are varied. The general thrust of these deeming provisions is to prevent a taxpayer from creating or accelerating an "artificial" capital loss by structuring transactions within a group of related economic entities. Sometimes the non-recognition of the capital loss is permanent; at other times the amount of the capital loss that is deemed to be nil is added to the cost base of some other property owned by the taxpayer, so that there will be a corresponding reduction in the capital gain (or increase in the capital loss) on the disposition of the other property.

2. — Dispositions between Affiliated Persons

Section 251.1 — the affiliated person rules — control abusive transactions where taxpayers trigger losses within close economic affiliations. Such transactions, which can be quite complex, usually involve corporate or partnership structures that either inappropriately trigger unrealized losses on certain types of property or move losses from one person to another.

The stop-loss and affiliated person rules deny losses that taxpayers trigger between themselves and their spouses and common-law partners, corporations under common control, partnerships and members of partnerships who, either alone or together with other affiliated persons, are generally entitled to more than half of the partnership's earnings. They also apply to trusts and any beneficiaries who, either alone or together with certain other affiliated persons, are entitled to more than half of the trust's income or capital.

There are essentially three distinct conditions that trigger the rules. First, a person must dispose of a property at a loss. Certain types of dispositions — such as deemed losses that occur as a result of migration from Canada — do not trigger the rules.

Second, the person who disposes of the property or someone affiliated with the person must, within a 61-day window that centres on the date of the disposition, acquire that same property or what is referred to as a substituted property.

Third, the disposing person or a person affiliated with that person must own the property or substituted property in question on the 61st day of that same period.

In these circumstances, the rules apply to deny the loss to the disposing person.[146] There are, however, other consequences depending upon the identity of the disposing person.

If the disposing person is an individual, the loss is added to the tax cost (ACB) of the property or substituted property that is in the hands of the acquirer. In effect the loss can be passed from the individual to another person. If, however, the disposing person is a trust, partnership or corporation, the loss remains with the disposing party and is effectively suspended, thereby preventing such losses from moving from that trust, corporation or partnership to another person. The trust, corporation or partnership may subsequently claim the loss, generally when either the property is subsequently sold to a non-affiliated person or the parties break their affiliated connection.

For example, assume that an individual owns all of the shares of his or her corporation. The individual owns a parcel of land that is capital property. The fair market value of the land is $100,000 but its tax cost or ACB is $275,000. The individual wishes to trigger the loss to offset against his capital gains in the same year. The individual disposes of the land to his or her corporation triggering a capital loss of $175,000. Since the individual and his or her corporation are affiliated persons, the stop loss rules apply. The Act denies the individual the

---

[146]Subpara. 40(2)(g)(i) and para. 40(3.4)(a).

loss and adds it to the ACB of the land, which the corporation now owns.[147] If the corporation subsequently sells the land for $100,000 in a non-affiliated transaction, the corporation can recognize a capital loss of $175,000. In effect, the individual's loss passes to the corporation upon the subsequent sale.

If the corporation had initially owned the land and sold it to its sole shareholder, the corporation could not claim the $175,000 loss.[148] Further, since the disposing person is a corporation, there is no ACB adjustment in this case and the loss is suspended to the corporation. The corporation, however, can claim the loss when the individual sells the land in a non-affiliated transaction. The same rule applies if the disposing person is either a partnership or trust if the individual and the partnership or trust, as the case may be, are affiliated.

There are similar stop-loss rules in the *Income Tax Act* to prevent the early recognition of losses on depreciable and eligible capital property.

3. — Lotteries

A taxpayer who does not win a lottery cannot claim a capital loss in respect of the cost of the ticket.[149]

4. — Superficial Losses

An individual cannot claim a "superficial loss".[150] A superficial loss arises when an individual, or certain affiliated parties,[151] disposes of property and replaces it with "substituted property" within a period of 61 days.[152] This prevents individuals from claiming paper losses for tax purposes. For the purpose of this rule, the 61-day period commences 30 days before, and ends 30 days after, the day of disposition of the property. This rule also applies to property that certain affiliated persons may acquire during the 61 days. For example, it applies to property acquired by the individual, his spouse or common law partner. The rule also applies to controlled corporations.

---

[147]Subpara. 40(2)(g)(i).

[148]Para. 40(3.4)(a).

[149]Para. 40(2)(f).

[150]Subpara. 40(2)(g)(i).

[151]Subs. 251.1(1).

[152]S. 54"superficial loss".

The taxpayer can, however, increase the cost base of the "substituted property" by the amount of his or her superficial loss.[153] Consequently, when the taxpayer disposes of the "substituted property", he or she can reduce any gain on the property. Alternatively, the taxpayer can increase the actual loss by the amount of his or her superficial loss.

The superficial loss rules do not apply in a number of situations where the Act deems a taxpayer to have disposed of property and reacquired certain properties. For example, losses arising from the following deemed dispositions do not give rise to superficial losses:[154]

- Emigration;[155]

- A debt becoming a bad debt;[156]

- Death;[157]

- Change in use of property;[158]

- Realization by a trust under subsection 104(4); and

- An employee's profit-sharing plan as a result of an election made in accordance with subsection 144(4.1) or (4.2).

Also, the superficial loss rules do not apply if the loss results in other circumstances, such as when an option expires.[159]

5. — *Disposition of a Debt*

A capital loss from a disposition, whether actual or deemed, of a debt is deemed to be nil unless the debt was acquired for the purpose of gaining or producing income from a business or property (other than exempt income), or as consideration for the disposition of capital property to an arm's length person.[160]

---

[153]Para. 53(1)(f).

[154]S. 54"superficial loss". Deemed dispositions under subss. 33.1(11), 138(11.3), 149(10) also do not give rise to superficial losses.

[155]S. 128.1.

[156]S. 50.

[157]S. 70.

[158]Subs. 45(1).

[159]Subs. 40(3.4).

[160]Subpara. 40(2)(g)(ii).

6. — Disposition of Personal-Use Property

A taxpayer's loss from a disposition of personal-use property is deemed to be nil unless the property qualifies as listed personal property or is a PUP debt referred to in subsection 50(2).[161] The non-recognition of the loss is permanent.

X. — Principal Residence

As a general rule, a Canadian resident is not taxable on a capital gain from his or her principal residence.[162] The entire amount of the gain is tax exempt, regardless of the value of the property sold. Thus, the principal residence exemption is one of the most generous exemptions in the Act.

1. — Meaning of "Principal Residence"

(a) — Minimum Requirements

There are several requirements to qualify a property as a "principal residence". Generally, these requirements address four separate criteria:[163]

  1. The type of property:

  • the property may consist of a housing unit, a leasehold interest in a housing unit or a share in a co-operative housing corporation;[164]

  2. Owner occupation:

  • the property must be owned by the taxpayer; and

  • the property must be "occupied" by the taxpayer during the year;[165]

---

[161]Subpara. 40(2)(g)(iii).

[162]Para. 40(2)(b).

[163]S. 54"principal residence".

[164]*Flanagan v. M.N.R.*, [1989] 2 C.T.C. 2395, 89 D.T.C. 615 (T.C.C.) (van, trailer or mobile home can qualify as housing unit eligible for exemption).

[165]*Ennist v. M.N.R.*, [1985] 2 C.T.C. 2398, 85 D.T.C. 669 (T.C.C.) (24-hour occupancy of condominium not sufficient to satisfy requirement that residence be "ordinarily inhabited").

3. The period of ownership:

- the property must be ordinarily inhabited at some time during the year by the tax-payer, her spouse, former spouse, common law partner, former common law part-ner or child; or

- if the property was acquired for the purpose of gaining or producing income and the use changes to that of a principal residence, an election can be made under subsection 45(3) to prevent the deemed disposal and reacquisition in subsection 45(1) from operating;

4. Designation on tax return:

- the property must be designated by the taxpayer as his or her sole principal resi-dence for the year.

Note that the residence does not have to be in Canada to be eligible for the exemption.

(b) — Included Land

A principal residence includes the land under and adjacent to the housing unit. Any adjacent land must contribute to the taxpayer's use and enjoyment of the housing unit as a residence. The statute deems land up to 0.5 hectare as part of the principal residence. Where the total area of land exceeds 0.5 hectare,[166] the excess land does not qualify as a principal residence unless the taxpayer can establish that the excess is *necessary* for his or her use and enjoy-ment of the housing unit as a residence.[167] Minimum lot size restrictions and zoning laws can affect the amount of land that is exempt as part of a principal residence.[168] The sever-ability of land is also a relevant factor in determining the value that one assigns to any portion in excess of the exempt amount.

The principal residence exemption is anomalous and clearly regressive. Nevertheless, it is a sacred cow. Given that the Act restricts the exemption by the physical dimensions of the

---

[166]Approx. 1.25 acres.

[167]*The Queen v. Yates*, [1986] 2 C.T.C. 46, 86 D.T.C. 6296 (F.C.A.) (minimum lot size can be used to determine amount of land necessary for use and enjoyment).

[168]*Baird v. M.N.R.*, [1983] C.T.C. 2651, 83 D.T.C. 582 (T.C.C.) (taxpayer cannot make a partial dis-position of principal residence); *The Queen v. Mitosinka*, [1978] C.T.C. 664, 78 D.T.C. 6432 (F.C.T.D.) (each half of duplex separate housing unit); *The Queen v. Yates*, [1983] 2 F.C. 730; affd. [1986] 2 C.T.C. 46, 86 D.T.C. 6296 (F.C.A.) (where taxpayer legally unable to occupy housing unit as residence on less than ten acres, excess portion necessary for taxpayer's use and enjoyment). The *Yates* decision has been accepted by the CRA: see News Release (April 9, 1987) and IT-120R6. See also, *Augart v. M.N.R.*, [1993] 2 C.T.C. 34, 93 D.T.C. 5205 (F.C.A.) ("enjoyment" embraces the exercise of a legal right, one of which is the right of alienation. Taxpayer could not alienate less than 8.99 acres).

residence and land, and not by its value, it is obviously advantageous to own as much land as possible as part of the residence. For example, a residence located on 0.5 hectare of land in, say, Rosedale (Toronto) is obviously much more valuable than one on 0.5 hectare in Moose Jaw (Saskatchewan).

(c) — Designation

Strictly speaking, a property does not qualify as a principal residence for a particular year unless the taxpayer designates it as such in his or her income tax return for the year in which he or she disposes of it. The CRA does not, however, call for the designation unless the taxpayer makes a *taxable* capital gain on the disposition of the principal residence after deducting the exempt portion of the gain.

2. — Exempt Gains

The exempt portion of a capital gain realized on the disposition of a pincipal residence is determined by the following formula:[169]

$$1 \ + \ \frac{\text{Number of taxation years ending after the acquisition date for which the property was the taxpayer's principal residence and during which the taxpayer was resident in Canada}}{\text{Number of taxation years ending after the acquisition date during which the taxpayer owned the property}} \ \times \ \text{Capital gain realized}$$

A taxpayer is eligible for this exemption in respect of a capital gain on the disposition of a property if it was his or her principal residence *at any time* in the year. The effect of the "1 +" in the numerator of the fraction for determining the exempt portion of the capital gain is that a taxpayer may obtain the exemption in respect of the disposition of two principal residences in the same year.

---

[169]Para. 40(2)(b).

Example: Where the taxpayer owns one principal residence

Assume:

A taxpayer purchased a house in Year 1 at a cost of $50,000 and sold it in Year 7 for $200,000 (net of $10,000 selling expenses). He made no capital expenditures on the house while he owned it. He was resident in Canada during the relevant period, and he designated the house as a principal residence for years 1 to 7 inclusive.

Then:

Proceeds of disposition		$ 210,000
Less:		
Adjusted cost base	$50,000	
Expenses of disposition	10,000	(60,000)
Capital gain otherwise determined		150,000
Less:		
Exempt portion of capital gain		
$\dfrac{1 + 6}{7} \times \$150,000$		(150,000)
Capital gain		NIL

Where a taxpayer lives in a residence for only a portion of the period of ownership, the exemption is allocated according to the formula set out above.

Example: Where there is a change in use of residence

Assume the same facts as in the above example, except that the taxpayer lived in the residence only during Years 1 through 3. The rest of the time the building was rented out to a tenant.

Then (ignoring any elections under section 45):

Proceeds of disposition		$ 210,000
Less:		
ACB of property	$50,000	
Selling expenses	10,000	(60,000)
Capital gain otherwise determined		150,000
Less:		
Exempt portion of capital gain		
$\dfrac{1 + 3}{7} \times \$150,000$		(85,714)
Capital gain		$ 64,286

3. — Limits on Exemptions

The general rule is that a family unit living together can together designate only one principal residence per year. For the purpose of this rule, a "family unit" comprises: the taxpayer, his or her spouse, or common-law partner, children under the age of 18 who are not married or living in a common-law partnership.[170]

(a) — Two Exempt Residences

The "1+" in the numerator of the fraction, used to determine the exempt portion of the gain, allows a taxpayer to claim an exemption in respect of two principal residences in the same year. Such a situation typically arises when a taxpayer sells his or her principal residence during the course of the year and purchases another residence in the same year. In these circumstances the taxpayer would own and occupy two residences in the same year, both of which could be eligible for the principal residence exemption.

---

[170]S. 54"principal residence".

Example: Where the taxpayer owns more than one residence

A taxpayer purchased a house in Year 1 and lived in it until he sold it on February 28, Year 4. He purchased a second house on February 1, Year 4, and moved into it on March 1, Year 4, living there until he sold it on October 1, Year 4. He purchased a third house on September 30, Year 4, and moved into it on November 1, Year 4.

First House
Designated as principal residence for Years 1–3
Exempt portion of capital gain on its sale $\dfrac{1 + 3}{4}$
Therefore, any capital gain is exempt.

Second House
Designated as principal residence for Year 4
Exempt portion of capital gain on its sale $\dfrac{1 + 0}{1}$
Hence, any capital gain is also exempt.

If the third house was also sold in Year 4, the taxpayer could not take advantage of the principal residence exemption on both the second and third houses. This is because only one of these houses could be designated as a principal residence for Year 4. In these circumstances, however, the taxpayer may choose which house to designate for exemption. Alternatively, the taxpayer could arrange to have the closing on the third house delayed until January Year 5.

(b) — Extended Family Unit

Where the taxpayer claiming the principal residence exemption is an unmarried person or an individual under 18 years of age, the concept of the family unit is extended to include the taxpayer's mother, father and unmarried brothers and sisters under 18 years of age.[171]

---

[171]S. 54"principal residence" (c).

(c) — "Ordinarily Inhabited"

The principal residence exemption is available only if the residence was ordinarily occupied by the taxpayer, his or her spouse, former spouse, common-law partner, former common-law partner, or child.

The question of whether a residence was "ordinarily inhabited" during the taxation year by the taxpayer (or by certain related persons) is one of fact, and depends upon the circumstances of each case. Generally, the CRA is quite generous in its interpretation of what constitutes habitation of a residence. Thus, the Agency will accept seasonal occupation of a taxpayer's vacation house (such as a cottage or ski chalet) as sufficient to qualify the premises for the principal residence exemption. The Agency goes even further: it will accept a seasonal residence as eligible for the exemption even where the taxpayer rents out the premises for incidental rental income. That is, provided that the rental is not a commercial or business enterprise, the taxpayer may occupy the premises for a limited portion of the season, rent it out for the remainder of the year, and still claim the exemption.

4. — Farm Houses

Special rules apply to taxpayers engaged in a farming business. An individual who disposes of land and a principal residence used by him or her in a farming business is allowed to calculate the exempt portion of the capital gain attributable to the residence in one of two ways.

(a) — Alternative 1

The taxpayer can treat the property as comprising two portions, the first portion being the principal residence and the second the balance of the farmland. Any capital gain realized from the disposition is allocated between these two portions on a reasonable basis.[172] The exempt portion of the capital gain on the principal residence is then determined in accordance with the general rules described above.

---

[172]Subpara. 40(2)(c)(i).

Example

Anne Jones acquired a farm in Year 1 at a cost of $145,000. The purchase price was allocated $25,000 to the farmhouse and $120,000 to the farmland. She sold the property in Year 15 for $250,000 (net of selling expenses), of which $30,000 was allocated to the farmhouse and $220,000 to the farmland. The farmhouse was the taxpayer's principal residence throughout the period. The first method applies automatically.

Gain on farmland ($220,00–120,000)	$ 100,000
Gain on farmhouse ($30,000–25,000)	5,000
Less: Exempt portion	(5,000)
Capital gain	$ 100,000

(b) — Alternative 2

Under the second method, the individual may elect not to allocate his or her proceeds between the residence and the farmland. Instead, the rule is that the exempt portion of the total capital gain realized by the taxpayer is set at $1,000, plus an additional $1,000 for each taxation year ending after the acquisition date for which the property was the taxpayer's principal residence and during which the taxpayer was resident in Canada.[173] This method applies only if the taxpayer elects to use it.

Example

Assume the same facts as in the above example.

Gain on property ($250,00–145,000)		$ 105,000
Less: Exempt portion		
• standard	$ 1,000	
• ($1,000 × 15 years)	15,000	(16,000)
Capital gain		$ 89,000

---

[173]Subpara. 40(2)(c)(ii).

5. — *Change in Use Elections*

(a) — *Personal to Income-Earning Use*

We saw earlier in this chapter that a taxpayer who changes the use of capital property from personal to income-earning use may elect under subsection 45(2) to have the change in use ignored for income tax purposes. The effect of the election is that the taxpayer is deemed not to have changed the use of the property from personal to business and not to have disposed of the property at its fair market value at that time.

(i) — Application to Principal Residence

The "change in use" election is particularly useful in respect of a principal residence. The election has two effects:

> 1. It allows the property to retain its status as a principal residence for four years (or possibly longer in the case of a work relocation) after the year in which the taxpayer moves out of the property;[174] and

> 2. The election deems the taxpayer not to have changed his or her use of the property.

Thus, where an individual elects under subsection 45(3), he or she may designate the property as a principal residence up to four years even though the property is used to earn income. Hence, if the taxpayer changes use of the property again, and resumes habitation of the premises, the second change will not give rise to a deemed disposition; the taxpayer will be considered never to have changed the use of the property in the first place. Thus there will be no income tax consequences when the taxpayer moves back into the property. This is because during the tenure of the election the taxpayer is *deemed* to be using the property for his or her own personal use (whether or not the property still qualifies as a principal residence); when the taxpayer moves back into the property, he or she will actually be using it for his or her own personal use.

(ii) — Timing of Election

An election under subsection 45(2) can be made only in respect of a change of use that occurs when the taxpayer moves out of the property, that is, when the taxpayer changes the use from personal to business. A taxpayer who does not make an election on moving out of the residence cannot avoid the resultant deemed disposition, and related tax consequences, on moving back into the property at a later date.

---

[174]See subs. 45(2), subpara. 54"principal residence"(b)(i) and para. 54"adjusted cost base"(d).

(iii) — Duration

The election continues in effect for up to four years after the year in which the taxpayer moved out or until it is rescinded by the taxpayer, at which time the taxpayer is deemed to have disposed of the property.

(b) — Income-Earning Use to Principal Residence

A taxpayer who converts income property into a principal residence may elect to ignore the change in use if he or she has not claimed capital cost allowance on the property after 1984. This election allows the taxpayer to defer the recognition of any accrued capital gain on the property, but does not allow the taxpayer to defer recapture of capital cost allowance claimed on the property after 1984.[175]

XI. — Shares Of Small Business Corporations

Capital gains from the disposition of shares of a "qualified small business corporation" are exempt from tax up to a maximum of $500,000. A "qualified small business corporation" (QSBC)[176] is defined as a Canadian-controlled private corporation:

> ... that uses all or most of its assets in an active business carried on primarily in Canada and the assets of which, throughout a period of 24 months immediately preceding the disposition of shares, have not been owned by any person other than the individual who claims the exemption, or by a person or partnership related to him or her.

This exemption encourages risk-taking and stimulates investment in small businesses in Canada by providing an economic stimulus to equity participation and the development of Canadian business enterprises. As the Minister of Finance said when he introduced the exemption in 1985, it is intended to "unleash [the] full entrepreneurial dynamism of individual Canadians."[177]

The exemption depends on three factors:

- The taxpayer's residence;

- The type of capital property that gives rise to the gain; and

- The net cumulative amount of investment income and financing expenses in the year in which the gain is realized.

---

[175]Subss. 45(3), (4).

[176]Subs. 125(7)"Canadian-controlled private corporation"; subs. 248(1)"active business", "small business corporation".

[177]Budget speech, *House of Commons Debates* (23 May 1985) at 5014.

The gain is generally restricted to individuals who are resident in Canada.[178] The exemption may not be claimed by a trust, but because a trust is treated as a conduit, it may flow through its capital gains to its beneficiaries by making a special designation.

The exemption applies only to "qualified" small business corporation shares.[179] The qualifications concern the control of the corporation, the fair market value of the assets that are attributable to use in an active business, and the carrying on of the active business primarily in Canada. These restrictions target the exemption to restrict the benefits to activities that are likely to stimulate the Canadian economy.

XII. — Capital Losses

A taxpayer's income for a taxation year is determined by aggregating income from each source on a separate basis. As a general rule, capital losses can be used only to offset capital gains.[180] Unused capital losses may, however, be carried forward indefinitely and applied against capital gains in future years; they may also be carried back three years and applied against capital gains reported in those years.[181]

1. — Current Year Losses

(a) — Listed Personal Property Losses

Capital gains and losses from listed personal property ("LPP") are calculated separately from capital gains and losses on all other types of capital properties. A taxpayer is required to include his or her "taxable *net* gain" for the year from dispositions of LPP with his or her capital gains.[182] Losses from dispositions of LPP are deductible only to the extent of gains for the same year from dispositions of LPP. In other words, if LPP losses exceed LPP gains, the excess cannot be deducted in computing the taxpayer's income for that year, even if he or she has other net taxable capital gains from dispositions of other types of capital property. LPP losses may not be deducted from capital gains on non-LPP.

---

[178]Subs. 110.6(5).

[179]Subs. 110.6(1)"qualified small business corporation share".

[180]Para. 3(b).

[181]Para. 111(1)(b).

[182]Para. 3(b); s. 41.

(b) — Allowable Capital Losses

A taxpayer may also deduct his or her allowable capital losses (net of allowable business investment losses) from dispositions of property for the year to the extent of the taxpayer's taxable capital gains from dispositions of property and his or her taxable *net* gain from dispositions of listed personal property.

The effect of these rules is that a taxpayer may deduct his or her allowable capital losses realized on property (other than LPP) from his or her taxable net gains on listed personal property.

(c) — Allowable Business Investment Losses ("ABIL")

(i) — General Comment

A business investment loss is a special type of capital loss that receives preferential treatment for income tax purposes. A business investment loss arises on the disposition of shares or debt of a "small business corporation".[183] An allowable business investment loss is 50 per cent of a business investment loss.[184]

Unlike ordinary capital losses, which may be deducted only against capital gains, an allowable business investment loss may be deducted against income from any source. Thus, an allowable business investment loss may be deducted from business or property income.

A taxpayer's deduction for business investment losses is restricted if he or she has previously claimed the capital gains exemption.[185]

A business investment loss arises upon the disposition of the shares or debt of a corporation that qualified as a small business corporation *at any time* within the preceding 12 months.[186] The disposition of the shares or debt may be triggered either by an actual disposition (for example, sale or transfer) or through a deemed disposition.[187]

---

[183]Para. 39(1)(c).

[184]Para. 38(c).

[185]Subs. 39(9).

[186]Subs. 248(1)"small business corporation".

[187]See, for example, subs. 50(1).

(ii) — "Small Business Corporation"

A "small business corporation" is a Canadian-controlled private corporation that uses all or substantially all (as measured by fair market value) of its assets in an active business in Canada.[188] A corporation may also qualify as a small business corporation if all, or substantially all, of its assets are invested in shares of another small business corporation with which it is connected.

(iii) — Deemed Disposition

A taxpayer is deemed to have disposed of his or her shares of a small business corporation if:

- The corporation is insolvent or bankrupt, or

- At year end, the corporation is insolvent, the FMV of its shares is nil, the corporation (or any corporation that it controls) does not carry on business and it is reasonable to expect that the corporation will be wound up or dissolved.

The term "insolvent" is not defined, but it is reasonable to expect that it has the usual meaning of insolvency, namely, the inability to pay liabilities as they come due.

2. — Unused Losses

Capital losses that are not deductible in the year in which they are sustained may be "carried over" and deducted in other years. In dealing with capital loss carry-overs, it is important to distinguish between losses from dispositions of listed personal property and losses from dispositions of property other than listed personal property.

(a) — LPP Losses

Where a taxpayer's losses for a year from LPP exceed his or her gains for the year from dispositions of LPP, the excess is the "listed personal property loss" for that year.[189] A listed personal property loss for a particular year can be deducted, in computing the "net gain", only from dispositions of listed personal property for the three preceding and the seven succeeding years.[190]

---

[188]Subs. 248(1)"small business corporation".

[189]Subs. 41(3).

[190]Para. 41(2)(b).

(b) — Net Capital Losses

Allowable capital losses from dispositions of property other than listed personal property which are not deductible in computing a taxpayer's income in the year in which they are sustained, become part of the taxpayer's "net capital loss".[191] A taxpayer's net capital loss for a year may be carried back and deducted in computing his or her *taxable income* for the three preceding years. Also, subject to certain limitations, the loss may be carried forward indefinitely.[192] In either case, net capital losses may be deducted against only the excess of taxable gains over allowable capital losses of other years.

(i) — Change of Corporate Control

A net capital loss from an earlier year cannot be deducted by a corporation if, before the end of the year, control of the corporation changes hands and the corporation is acquired by a person who did not control it at the time when the net capital loss was sustained. This rule does not generally affect the deductibility of capital losses sustained *in the year* in which control is acquired by the new person or persons.[193]

(ii) — Death

Where a taxpayer dies with unclaimed net capital losses, the losses may be applied as follows:[194]

- Against the taxpayer's net taxable capital gains for the year of death, and
- Against the taxpayer's other sources of income in the year of death or in the immediately preceding year, to the extent that the losses exceed the taxpayer's lifetime capital gains exemption.[195]

Thus, exemptions claimed in respect of capital gains during a taxpayer's lifetime reduce the taxpayer's unused net capital losses on death.

---

[191]Subs. 111(8)"net capital loss".

[192]Para. 111(1)(b).

[193]Subs. 111(4).

[194]Subs. 111(2).

[195]The capital gains exemption is discussed in Chapter 15, "Taxable Income".

Example		
Assume:		
Net capital losses carried forward		$ 25,000
Taxable capital gains in year of death		10,000
Allowable capital losses in year of death		4,000
Capital gains exemption claimed during lifetime		15,000
Then, maximum claim in respect of net capital losses in year of death:		
Taxable capital gains		$ 10,000
Less: allowable capital losses		(4,000)
Net taxable capital gains		6,000
Net capital losses	$ 25,000	
Prior year gains exemption	(15,000)	
Terminal year gains exemption	(6,000)	
Excess claimable		4,000
Maximum claim		$ 10,000

XIII. — Transitional Rules

1. — General Comment

With the introduction of the tax on capital gains as of January 1, 1972, it became necessary to ensure that capital gains and capital losses that had accrued prior to 1972 would not be retroactively taxed. Thus, there are transitional rules to ensure smooth passage from the old system to the new. Although the rationale of the transitional rules is simple, the rules are technically complex. The essential purpose of the transitional rules is to provide a taxpayer with either a deemed cost or deemed proceeds of disposition for the capital property that was owned on December 31, 1971, so that, on selling the property, the taxpayer can calculate any gain or loss from that date.

Generally, the transitional rules apply to capital property *actually* owned by a taxpayer on December 31, 1971. In some cases, however, the person to whom the property is disposed of may be *deemed* to have owned it on December 31, 1971, so that the transitional rules will apply to the taxpayer when disposing of the property. The rules can therefore apply to dispositions of property acquired after 1971. Note, however, that the transitional rules do not apply to the property of a taxpayer who becomes resident in Canada after 1971.[196]

2. — Valuation Day

The concept of Valuation Day value is fundamental to the structure of the transitional rules for capital gains. The Valuation Day value of a capital property is its value at the beginning of the new system, when capital gains were first subjected to tax. The "V-Day value" of a property is its fair market value on Valuation Day, which was December 22, 1971, for publicly-traded shares or securities and December 31, 1971, for all other capital property.[197]

The fair market value of publicly-traded securities on Valuation Day is deemed to be the greater of the amount prescribed[198] in respect of the security and the fair market value of the security on December 22, 1971, "as otherwise determined." Any "other determination" of the fair market value of a publicly-traded share or security as at that date must be made by the taxpayer. If this value is greater than the prescribed amount, the taxpayer may use it for the purpose of determining the capital gain or loss realized on the disposition of the security in question.

The Valuation Day value of all other capital properties (i.e., properties other than publicly-traded securities) is their fair market value on December 31, 1971. It is the taxpayer's responsibility to determine this value for the purpose of reporting a capital gain or loss on the disposition of capital property.

3. — Depreciable Property

For depreciable property acquired by a taxpayer before 1972 and owned by him or her continuously since that time, the transitional rules eliminate any capital gain accrued as at December 31, 1971, from the total capital gain realized upon disposition of the property. There is no corresponding rule in respect of a capital loss accrued as at December 31, 1971, because a taxpayer cannot realize a capital loss on depreciable property.[199] Where depreciable property is disposed of in a non-arm's length transaction, the transitional rules preserve the tax-free character of any accrued capital gains.[200]

---

[196]ITAR 26(10).

[197]ITAR 24.

[198]Reg., Sched. VII.

[199]Subpara. 39(1)(b)(i).

[200]ITAR 20(1).

The transitional rules in respect of depreciable property owned on December 31, 1971 operate by deeming the proceeds of disposition of the property to be the amount determined by the following formula:

> Deemed proceeds   = Capital cost + Excess, if any, of actual proceeds of
> of disposition   disposition over fair market value on
>   Valuation Day

The transitional rules do not apply if the actual proceeds of disposition of depreciable property do not exceed the capital cost of that property, since, in this instance, a capital gain could not possibly result.

Example

Capital cost to taxpayer T of a depreciable property
  acquired by him in 1970: $ 10,000
Fair market value of this property on Valuation Day
  (December 31, 1971): $ 12,600
Selling price of the property in 1986: $ 17,200
T's deemed proceeds of disposition:
  $10,000 + ($17,200 - $12,600) $ 14,600
T's capital gain is therefore:
  $14,600 - $10,000 $ 4,600

Arithmetically, the capital gain equals the excess of the actual selling price of the depreciable property over its Valuation Day value, although the gain is not actually computed in this way. The capital gain of $2,600 accrued on the property as at December 31, 1971, is not subject to tax at all but would be added to the pre-1972 capital surplus on hand. In certain circumstances, this amount could be distributed tax-free on a wind-up or dissolution of the corporation. See subs. 88(2.1). Where depreciable property is disposed of after 1971 at a price greater than its original cost but less than its Valuation Day value (e.g., $12,000, in the above illustration), the transitional rules apply in the following manner:

T's deemed proceeds of disposition are:
  $10,000 + ($12,000–$12,600)[*] $ 10,000
T's capital gain is $10,000–$10,000   NIL

Since the depreciable property has been disposed of for less than its Valuation Day value, this is the result one would expect.

Notes:

*   The amount in the brackets cannot be less than zero.

4. — Interest in a Partnership

Transitional rules are also provided for taxpayers who were members of a partnership on December 31, 1971, and have remained so continuously since that date. These rules are provided for the purpose of computing the adjusted cost base of the partnership interest at any time after 1971. These rules affect the amount of the taxable capital gain or allowable capital loss realized by the partner when disposing of the taxpayer's interest.

These transitional rules operate by deeming the partner's cost of the partnership interest to be an amount that is the median[201] of the following three amounts:

1. Its "actual cost" to the partner;

2. His or her share of the partnership's "tax equity", subject to certain adjustments; and

3. The fair market value of the partnership interest, again subject to certain adjustments.

The "actual cost" of a partnership interest and the partnership's "tax equity" are both defined amounts, and all three amounts in this formula are determined as of the particular time when the deemed cost is relevant.[202] If two or more of these amounts are the same, then that amount is the median.

5. — Other Capital Property

There are also transitional rules for the purpose of computing the capital gain or loss of capital property other than the two previous examples. The effect of these rules is to deem a cost to be the taxpayer's adjusted cost base of capital property owned. The capital gain or loss of the property is then computed on the basis of this deemed cost.

There are two distinct methods of determining the deemed cost. The first of these methods is the "median rule" or "tax-free zone" method. This method applies automatically to capital property that was owned on December 31, 1971, by *any taxpayer*. The second method, known as the "Valuation Day value election", is available only to *individuals* (including trusts), and applies only to capital property *actually* owned on December 31, 1971.[203]

---

[201]If two or more of these amounts are the same, that amount is the median.

[202]ITAR 26(9)–(9.4).

[203]The tax-free zone method cannot then be used in respect of any of these properties, although it must still be used in respect of any "other capital property" that the individual taxpayer making the Valua-

For individuals, the two methods for determining the deemed cost of capital property owned on December 31, 1971, are mutually exclusive alternatives. Thus an individual *either* uses the tax-free zone method to determine the deemed cost of *each and every* item of capital property that he or she owned on December 31, 1971, or makes the Valuation Day value election, in which case the taxpayer must use this method to determine the deemed cost of *each and every* item of capital property that he or she actually owned on December 31, 1971.

(a) — Median Rule or Tax-Free Zone Method

The median rule (tax-free zone) method operates by deeming a taxpayer's initial cost of capital property that he or she owned on December 31, 1971, to be the amount that is the median of the following three amounts:[204]

> 1. Its actual cost (or, if the property is an "obligation," its "amortized cost") to him or her on January 1, 1972;

> 2. Its fair market value on Valuation Day; and

> 3. The proceeds of disposition of the property, subject to certain adjustments, which are described below.

If two or more of these amounts are the same, that amount is the median.

If a particular item of capital property has been owned continuously since December 31, 1971, and it is necessary to compute its adjusted cost base at a point in time *before* it is disposed of (in which case there would be no actual proceeds of disposition), the median rule is applied by deeming the proceeds of disposition of the particular property to be its fair market value at that time.[205]

The adjustments to the proceeds of disposition of the property can be summarized as follows:

- *Add* amounts that will be deducted from the deemed cost in computing the adjusted cost base of the particular property.

- *Deduct* amounts that will be added to the deemed cost in computing the adjusted cost base of the particular property.

---

tion Day value election did not actually own on December 31, 1971, but that he is deemed by the Act to have owned on that date.

[204]ITAR 26(3).

[205]ITAR 26(4).

These adjustments are necessary for the purpose of applying the median rule to avoid double-counting of the additions and deductions that are made in computing the adjusted cost base of the property under section 53.

"Proceeds of disposition" in this context means gross proceeds before the deduction of any outlays or expenses incurred for the purpose of making the disposition. Therefore, a capital loss equal to the amount of these outlays and expenses may be realized if the deemed cost of a particular property equals the proceeds of disposition.

Example

Assume:

The actual cost of a capital property that was owned on December 31, 1971 is $4,000. Its Valuation Day value is $8,000. The proceeds of disposition of the property before deducting the sales commission of $800 are $8,000.

Then:

Applying the median rule, the deemed cost of the property is $8,000.

Proceeds of disposition		$ 8,000
Deduct:		
Deemed cost	$ 8,000	
Sales commission	800	(8,800)
Capital loss		$ (800)

(b) — Valuation Day Value Election

As its name implies, the "Valuation Day value" election allows a taxpayer to determine the cost of each capital property (other than depreciable property and partnership interests) *actually* owned by the taxpayer on December 31, 1971, as its value on Valuation Day. This alternative method is administratively convenient: it provides individuals with a deemed cost for every capital property that they actually owned at the start of the new system, and accommodates taxpayers who have not maintained a record of the actual cost of their properties.[206]

---

[206]ITAR 26(7); *Knight v. M.N.R.*, [1984] C.T.C. 2643, 84 D.T.C. 1586 (T.C.C.) (failure to elect V-Day value "in prescribed manner" results in automatic application of median rule).

XIV. — Anti-Avoidance Provisions

There are several anti-avoidance provisions that are intended to prevent or discourage tax-payers from artificially converting fully taxable income into income that is either non-taxable or taxable at a lower rate. Some of these provisions are quite specific and narrow in scope. For example, the rules in respect of "superficial losses" are directed squarely at preventing the creation of capital losses by transferring and reacquiring properties.[207] The following additional provisions should be noted:

Subs. 55(2)	Specific provision to prevent "capital gains strips";
Subs. 110.6(7)	Intended to prevent conversion of taxable capital gains of corporations into exempt capital gains of individuals;
Subss. 110.6(8), (9)	Intended to prevent the conversion of dividend income into exempt capital gains of individuals; and
S. 245	General anti-avoidance provision ("GAAR").
S. 84.1	Designed to pervent surplus stripping.
Part II.1 Tax	Prevent conversion of proceeds of disposition into exempt capital gains.

Comprehensive Examples

Capital Gain or Loss of Listed Personal Properties

Assume:

A taxpayer sells the following listed personal properties in the years (all of which are subsequent to 1971) indicated:

Year	Property	ACB	Proceeds
1	A print	$ 600	$ 4,000
	A coin	1,500	600
2	A rare book	8,000	4,000
	A painting	2,000	2,500
3	Jewellery	500	2,500

---

[207]Subpara. 40(2)(g)(i), s. 54"superficial loss".

Capital Gain or Loss of Listed Personal Properties

Then net gain from the above is as follows:

		Actual	Deemed Subs. 46(1)	
Year 1				
PRINT:				
	Proceeds	$ 4,000	$ 4,000	
	ACB	(600)	(1,000)	
	Gain			$ 3,000
COIN:				
	Proceeds	$ 600	$ 1,000	
	ACB	(1,500)	(1,500)	
	Loss			(500)*
	Gain			$ 2,500
	Loss carryback from Year 2			(2,500)*
NET GAIN				NIL
Year 2				
BOOK:				
	Proceeds	$ 4,000	$ 4,000	
	ACB	(8,000)	(8,000)	
	Loss			$ (4,000)
PAINTING:				
	Proceeds	$ 2,500		
	ACB	(2,000)		
	Gain			500
	Loss			(3,500)
	Loss carryback to Year 1			2,500*
NET GAIN				NIL

Capital Gain or Loss of Listed Personal Properties

Year 3

JEWELLERY:

Proceeds	$ 2,500	$ 2,500	
ACB	(500)	(1,000)	
Gain			$ 1,500
Loss carryforward			(1,000)*
from Year 2			$ 500

NET GAIN

Capital Gain or Loss Where Replacement of Property

Assume:

X Ltd. owns a building to which the following data applies:

Cost	$ 200,000
UCC	$ 50,000

The building is expropriated under statutory authority, and X Ltd. is paid $250,000. In the same taxation year, X Ltd. acquires a substitute building in the same vicinity. The cost of the replacement property is $400,000. X Ltd. makes an election under subsection 13(4).

Then:

(a) *Election under subsection 13(4):*

Proceeds otherwise determined Minus, lesser of:	$ 200,000
(i) $200,000–50,000 = $150,000	
(ii) $400,000	(150,000)
Elected proceeds of disposition	50,000
UCC	(50,000)
Recapture of CCA	NIL
Deemed capital cost of replacement of property	$ 350,000*
Less: Amount of CCA deferred	(150,000)
Deemed UCC of replacement of property	$ 200,000

Capital Gain or Loss Where Replacement of Property	
(b) Election under subsection 44(1):	
Proceeds of disposition	$ 250,000
Less: ACB	(200,000)
(A) Capital gain otherwise determined	$ 50,000
Proceeds of disposition	$ 250,000
Exceeds:	
Capital cost of replacement	400,000
(B) Amount determined	NIL
Capital gain (lesser of (A) and (B))	NIL
(c) Capital cost of replacement property:[*]	
Actual capital cost of replacement property	$ 400,000
Less: capital gain deferred	(50,000)
Deemed capital cost of replacement property	$ 350,000

Notes:

[*]   Paragraph 44(1)(f).

Selected Bibliography to Chapter 11

General

Allan, J.R., et al., "The Effects of Tax Reform and Post Reform Changes in the Federal Personal Income Tax, 1972–75" (1978) 26 Can. Tax J. 1.

Barbacki, Richard, "Use It or Lose It?" (July 1989) 122 CA Magazine 43.

Bernstein, Jack, "Tax Planning for Holding Canadian Real Estate" (1984) 3:8 *Ont. Lawyers Wkly.* 8.

Binavince, E., "The Taxation of Capital Gains and Losses: General Principles," in Hansen, Krishna and Rendall, eds., *Canadian Taxation* (Toronto: De Boo, 1981) p. 297.

Bird, Richard M., "Capital Gains Taxation in Canada: A Review of a Review," in *Proceedings of 31st Tax Conf.* 525 (Can. Tax Foundation, 1980).

Birnie, David A.G., "Shareholders' Buy-Sell Agreements: Some New Opportunities," in *Proceedings of 38th Tax Conf.* 13 (Can. Tax Foundation, 1986).

Boehmer, G.C., "Personal Tax Planning — Small Business Corporations — Capital Gains Planning Opportunities and Pitfalls" (1987) 35 Can. Tax J. 987.

Boehmer, G.C., "Small Business Corporations: Capital Gains Planning Opportunities and Pitfalls" (1987) 35 Can. Tax J. 987.

Bossons, John, "Economic Effects of the Capital Gains Tax" (1981) 29 Can. Tax J. 809.

Bossons, John, "Implementing Capital Gains Reforms" (1979) 27 Can. Tax J. 145.

Broadway, Robin W., and Harry M. Kitchen, "Canadian Tax Policy," *Tax Paper No. 63* (Canadian Tax Foundation, 1980) at 71–77.

Bucovetsky, Meyer W., "Inflation and the Personal Tax Base: The Capital Gains Issue" (1977) 25 Can. Tax J. 77.

Colley, G.M., "Capital Gains Tax — A Perspective" (1981) 14 CA Magazine 63.

Corn, George, "Taxation of Gain on Appreciation of Shares: Capital Gain or Income from an Adventure in the Nature of Trade" (1994) 4 Can. Current Tax J39.

Crawford, R.W., "Sales of Real Estate: Tax Planning for the Seller," *Corporate Management Tax Conf.* 138 (Can. Tax Foundation, 1983).

Cullity, Maurice C., "The Capital Gains Exemption: Implications for Estate Planning," in *Proceedings of 37th Tax Conf.* 18 (Can. Tax Foundation, 1985).

Daly, Michael J., et al., "Toward a Neutral Capital Income Tax System" (1986) 34 Can. Tax J. 1331.

Daly, Michael J., et al., "The Taxation of Income from Capital in Canada: An International Comparison" (1987) 35 Can. Tax J. 88.

Davies, James B., and France St-Hilaire, *Reforming Capital Income Taxation in Canada: Efficiency and Distributional Effects of Alternative Options* (Economic Council of Canada, 1987).

Dean, Jacklyn I., "The January 15, 1987 Draft Amendments Relating to the Acquisition of Gains and Losses," *Corporate Management Tax Conf.* 2:1 (Can. Tax Foundation, 1987).

Drache, A.B.C., "Real Estate Capital Gains Change Raises Strategic Questions" (1992) 14 Can. Taxpayer 21.

Durnford, John W., "Profits on the Sale of Shares: Capital Gains or Business Income? A Fresh Look at Irrigation Industries" (1987) 35 Can. Tax J. 837.

Ewens, Douglas S., "The Capital Gains Exemption and the Butterfly" (1986) 34 Can. Tax J. 914.

James, Larry W., "Capital Gains Exemption, Planning Techniques," in *Proceedings of 38th Tax Conf.* 33 (Can. Tax Foundation, 1986).

James, Larry W., "Disposing of Real Estate", *Corporate Management Tax Conf.* 5:1 (Can. Tax Foundation, 1989).

Jordan, Barbara Ann, "An Economic Evaluation of the Tax Treatment of Capital Gains in Canada" (microform) (Ottawa: National Library of Canada, 1987).

Kellough, Howard J., and K. Travers Pullen, "Planning for the Lifetime Capital Gains Exemption" (1986) 3 Bus. & L. 3.

Kirby, F.P., "The Capital Gains Exemption: Other Than Qualified Small Business Shares," in *Proceedings of 40th Tax Conf.* 30:1 (Can. Tax Foundation, 1988).

Krishna, V., *The Taxation of Capital Gains* (Toronto: Butterworths, 1983).

Kroft, Edwin G., and Bruce W. Aunger, "Some Issues Relating to the Taxation of Insider Trading Transactions — Comments on Interpretation Bulletin IT-479" (1983) 31 Can. Tax J. 763.

Lawlor, William R.G., "Surplus Stripping and Other Planning Opportunities With the New $500,000 Capital Gains Exemption," in *Proceedings of 37th Tax Conf.* 8 (Can. Tax Foundation, 1985).

Maloney, Maureen A., "Capital Gains Taxation: Marching (Oh So Slowly) into the Future" (1988) 17 Man. L. J. 299.

Mayhall, "Capital Gains Taxation — The First One Hundred Years" (1980) 41 L.A. L. Rev. 81.

Messere, Kenneth C., "Capital Gains and Related Taxation in OECD Member Countries," in *Proceedings of 31st Tax Conf.* 505 (Can. Tax Foundation, 1980).

Mida, Israel H., *Capital Gains and the May 1985 Federal Budget* (C.C.H. Can., 1986).

Perry, David B., "Importance of Capital Gains and Losses in the Personal Income Tax System (The)" (1984) 32 Can. Tax J. 178.

Perry, David B., "Selected Statistics on the Evolution of the Personal Income Tax System Since 1970" (1987) 35 Can. Tax J. 207.

Quinton, Cathy, "The Additional Capital Gains Exemption" (December–January 1989) 62 CMA Magazine 47.

Richards, Gabrielle M.R., "Proceeds of Disposition of Property" (1986) 1 Can. Current Tax J-164.

Richards, Gabrielle M.R., "Quick Flips: Capital Gains or Income Treatment?" (1991) 3 Can. Current Tax C57.

Richards, Gabrielle M.R., "The Timing of Dispositions of Property" (1986) 1 Can. Current Tax C-131.

Richardson, Elinore J., "Holding Real Estate for the Production of Income," *Corporate Management Tax Conf.* 1 (Can. Tax Foundation, 1983).

Rotenberg, Charles M., "Making the Deal Work" (1991) 13 Can. Taxpayer 60.

Ruby, Stephen S., "A Glimpse at the Lifetime Capital Gains Exemption (Part I)" (1986) 3:12 Bus. & L. 93.

Ruby, Stephen S., "A Glimpse at the Lifetime Capital Gains Exemption (Part III)" (1987) 4:1 Bus. & L. 6.

Sauve, Marc, *L'imposition des gains en capital et l'égalité fiscale* (Université de Montréal, Faculté de droit, 1987).

Sheppard, Anthony F., "Capital Gains: Twenty Years Later a Buck is Still Not a Buck" in *The Quest for Tax Reform: The Royal Ciommission on Taxation Twenty Years Later* (Toronto: Carswell, 1988).

Silver, Sheldon, "Capital Gains," in *Proceedings of 23rd Tax Conf.* 68 (Can. Tax Foundation, 1971).

Stack, Thomas J., "Capital Gains and Losses on Shares of Private Corporations," in *Proceedings of 39th Tax Conf.* 17:1 (Can. Tax Foundation, 1987).

Tam, Anthony, "Capital Gains Exemption: Small Business Corporations" (1987–89) 2 Can. Current Tax P-5.

Tax Treatment of Real Estate Gains: Working Group Report (Toronto: Fair Tax Commission, 1992).

Thompson, A.E.J., and B.R. Sinclair, "Capital Gains" (1985) 13 Can. Tax News 81.

Walker, Michael A., "Perspectives on Capital Gains Taxation," in *Proceedings of 3lst Tax Conf.* 535 (Can. Tax Foundation, 1980).

Ward, David A., and John M. Ulmer, "Corporate Taxation: Shares Eligible for the Capital Gains Exemption" (1986) 5 Legal Alert 81.

Warnock, Bruce A., "Income or Capital Gains on Dispositions of Property" in *Proceedings of 42nd Tax Conf.* 48:1 (Can. Tax Found., 1990).

Watchuk, Jeanne, "Are Gains on SRTC Debt Flips Capital or Income? Two Opposing Opinions" (1990) 38 Can. Tax J. 380.

Zinn, J.A., "The Taxation of Capital Gains: Selected Topics" (1981) Can. Taxation 363.

Capital Property

Drache, A.B.C., "Real Estate Capital Gains Change Raises Strategic Questions" (1992) 14 Can. Taxpayer 21.

Goodman, Wolfe D., "Charitable Gifts of Appreciated Capital Property" (1986) 8 Estates and Trusts J. 189.

Williamson, W. Gordon, "Transfers of Assets to and from a Canadian Corporation," in *Proceedings of 38th Conf.* 12 (Can. Tax Foundation, 1986).

Computation of Capital Gain or Loss

Corn, G., "Capital Gains — Calculation of Proceeds of Disposition" (1984) 1 Can. Current Tax J-24.

Dzau, Vivien, "Reserves: A Tool for Deferring Taxes" (1980) 113 CA Magazine 57.

Krishna, Vern, "Reserves" (1984) 1 Can. Current Tax J-41.

Nitikman, Bert W.,"Reserves," in *Proceedings of 25th Tax Conf.* 355 (Can. Tax Foundation, 1973).

Rotenberg, Charles M., "Making the Deal Work" (1991) 13 Can. Taxpayer 60.

Stack, Thomas J., "Capital Gains and Losses on Shares of Private Corporations" in *Proceedings of 39th Tax Conf.* 17:1 (Can. Tax Foundation 1987).

Webb, K., "Escalator Clauses, Earn-Outs and Reserves," in *Proceedings of 26th Tax Conf.* 55 (Can. Tax Foundation, 1974).

Dispositions

Alliston, Paul F., "Rental of Real Estate" (1976) 109 CA Magazine 57.

Arnold, Brian J., "An Analysis of the Amendments to the FAPI and Foreign Affiliate Rules" (1983) 31 Can. Tax J. 183.

Arnold, Brian J., "Conversions of Property to and from Inventory: Tax Consequences" (1976) 24 Can. Tax J. 231.

Arnold, Brian J., and David A. Ward, "Dispositions — A Critique of Revenue Canada's Interpretation" (1980) 28 Can. Tax J. 559.

Beam, Robert E., and Stanley N. Laiken, "Personal Tax Planning — Changes in Use and Non-Arm's-Length Transfers of Depreciable Property" (1987) 35 Can. Tax J. 453.

Bittker, "Capital Gains and Losses — The 'Sale' or 'Exchange' Requirements" (1981) 32 Hastings L.J. 743.

Brown, R.D., "Can You Take It With You?" (1972) 20 Can. Tax J. 470.

Chapman, "The Time of Sale Under the Internal Revenue Code" (1964) 22 N.Y.U. Tax Inst. 139.

Corn, George, "Capital Gains — Calculation of Proceeds of Disposition" (1984) Can. Current Tax J-24.

Denega, M.A., "The Migrating Executive: Leaving Canada and Working Abroad", *Corp. Management Tax Conf.* 189 (Can. Tax Foundation, 1979).

Drache, A.B.C., "Foreign Exchange" (1979) 1 Can. Taxpayer 52.

Drache, A.B.C., "Real Estate Capital Gains Change Raises Strategic Questions" (1992) 14 Can. Taxpayer 21.

Ewens, Douglas S., "When Is a 'Disposition'?" in *Proceedings of 26th Tax Conf.* 515 (Can. Tax Foundation, 1974).

Goodison, Don, "Tax Forum — Not a Threat" (1990) 24 CGA Magazine 19.

Kroft, Edwin G., and Bruce W. Aunger, "Disposition of Canadian Securities" (1983) 31 Can. Tax J. 763.

Masson, Guy, et al., "The Expatriate's Departure," *Can. Tax Letter*, August 18, 1980 (De Boo).

Matheson, David I., "Taxation of Investments in Commodities Futures, Precious Metals, Options, Objects of Art, Foreign Exchange and Other Exotica," in *Proceedings of 27th Tax Conf.* 918 (Can. Tax Foundation, 1975).

Middleton, David W., "Tax Implications of Departure From Canada" (1983) 116 CA Magazine 44.

Richards, Gabrielle M.R., "Proceeds of Disposition of Property" (1986) 1 Can. Current Tax J-164.

Richards, Gabrielle M.R., "The Timing of Dispositions of Property" (1986) 1 Can. Current Tax C-131.

Richardson, Elinore, "Currency Swaps — A Canadian Perspective" (1984) 32 Can. Tax J. 345.

Tkachenko, Lorissa V., "Expropriations: The Income Tax Aspects" (1985) 33 Can. Tax J. 1.

White, Michael J., "Isolated Foreign Currency Transactions and Foreign Exchange Contracts," in *Proceedings of 30th Tax Conf.* 490 (Can. Tax Foundation, 1978).

Adjusted Cost Base

Champagne, Donald C., "Bad and Doubtful Debts, Mortgage Foreclosures and Conditional Sales Repossessions," in *Proceedings of 27th Tax Conf.* 682 (Can. Tax Foundation, 1975).

Corn, George, "Computation of Adjusted Cost Base of Shares" (December 1990) 3:12 Can. Current Tax J-59.

Couzin, Robert, "Of Arm's Length and Not Dealing Threat" (1978) 26 Can. Tax J. 271.

Crawford, William E., "Taxation of Land Developers," *Corporate Management Tax Conf.* 75 (Can. Tax Foundation, 1977).

Farwell, Peter M., "Debts and Capital Gains Taxation" (1972) 20 Can. Tax J. 101.

Goldspink, Tom, and David Allgood, "Tax Treatment of Personal Guarantees" (1983) 31 Can. Tax J. 1042.

Hogg, R.D., "Stock Option Benefits in Canadian-Controlled Private Corporations" (1978) 26 Can. Tax J. 85.

Riehl, Gordon W., et al., "Intercompany Non-Arm's Length Transactions — Income Tax Consequences," in *Proceedings of 26th Tax Conf.* 102 (Can. Tax Foundation, 1974).

Smith, David W., "Transferring the Family Business" (1979) 27 Can. Tax J. 1.

Stikeman, H.H., ed. "Stock Dividends," *Can. Tax Letter*, October 30, 1975 (De Boo).

Zinn, John A., "The Taxation of Capital Gains: Selected Topics," in Hansen, Krishna & Rendall, eds. *Canadian Taxation* (Toronto: De Boo, 1981).

Personal-Use Property

Arbuckle, J.E., "Investment in Art — For Pleasure and Profit" (1980) 54 Cost & Mgmt. 46.

Bernstein, J., "Investing in Art and Other Collectibles," in *Proceedings of 35th Tax Conf.* 124 (Can. Tax Foundation, 1983).

Dewling, A.M., "Intergenerational Transfers of Personal-use Property" (1989) 37 Can. Tax J. 1292.

Drache, A.B.C., "Real Estate Capital Gains Change Raises Strategic Questions" (1992) 14 Can. Taxpayer 21.

Edwards, S.E., "Personal Investments," (1986) Special Lectures LSUC 221.

Feingold, Fred, and Marlene F. Schwartz, "Source of Income from Sales of Personal Property" (1987) 35 Can. Tax J. 473.

Rotenberg, Charles M., "Inflation and Personal Property" (1980) 2 Can. Taxpayer 37.

Strother, Robert C., "Income Tax Implications of Personal-Use Real Estate," *Corporate Management Tax Conf.* 59 (Can. Tax Foundation, 1983).

Identical Properties

Lynch, John H., "Income Splitting Among Family Members," in *Proceedings of 32nd Tax Conf.* 752 (Can. Tax Foundation, 1980).

McDonnell, T.E.J., "Capital Gains: Tax Planning for the Individual" (1972) 20 Can. Tax J. 382.

Losses Deemed to be Nil

Brown, Robert D., and Thomas E. McDonnell, "Capital Gains Strips," in *Proceedings of 32nd Tax Conf.* 51 (Can. Tax Foundation, 1980).

Burpee, Thomas R., "Utilization of Tax Losses: A Reasonable Expectation of Profit," in *Proceedings of 37th Tax Conf.* 32:1 (Canadian Tax Foundation, 1985).

Drache, A.B.C., "Superficial Gains" (1980) 2 Can. Taxpayer 17.

Grover, Warren, "Superficial Losses" (1974) 22 Can. Tax J. 253.

Huggett, Donald R. (ed.) "Restrictions on Loss Transfers" (1987) 14:8 Can. Tax News 87.

Income Tax, Capital Gains Strips (Audio Archives of Canada, 1984).

Kirkpatrick, Paul K., "Tax Consequences of a Corporation Dealing in its Own Stock" (1964) 13 Tulane Tax Ins. 85.

Riehl, Gordon W., "Debt Instruments," in *Proceedings of 27th Tax Conf.* 764 (Can. Tax Foundation, 1975).

Stewart, E.C., "Capital Gains Considerations" (1974) 48 Cost & Mgmt. 45.

Sweet, David G., "Capital Losses," in *Proceedings of 24th Tax Conf.* 348 (Can. Tax Foundation, 1972).

Watts, David E., "Recognition of Gain or Loss to a Corporation on a Distribution of Property in Exchange for its own Stock" (1968) 22 Tax Lawyer 161.

Zimmer, Henry B., "Using Your Losses" (1974) 104 CA Magazine 58.

Principal Residence

Bergen, Rodney C., "The Tax Treatment of Principal Residences: An Update" in *Proceedings of 44th Tax Conf.* 12:1 (Can. Tax Found., 1992).

Boivin, Marc, "La 'résidence principale' lors d'un déménagement," *Recueil de fiscalité*, AQPFS, vol. 83-2, 151.

Drache, A.B.C., "The Best Investment" (1991) 13 Can. Taxpayer 134.

Drache, A.B.C., "Buying Your Student a Home" (1991) 13 Can. Taxpayer 115.

Freedman, Martin H., "The Home Owner," in *Proceedings of 25th Tax Conf.* 224 (Can. Tax Foundation, 1973); reprinted and revised in *Butterworth's Canadian Income Tax Revised* 9:5.

Fulton, Patricia, "Tax Preferences for Housing: Is There a Case for Reform?", in Thirsk and Whalley (eds.) "Tax Policy Options in the 1980s", *Tax Paper No. 66* (Can. Tax Foundation, 1982) 73.

Goldstein, D.L., "Capital Gain — Whether the Principle Residence Exemption may be taken on a Gain brought in from a Reserve" (1987) 37 Can. Tax J. 1522.

Goodison, Don, "Tax Forum — Necessary Excess" (1991) 25 CGA Magazine 14.

Gray, W.D., "When Does Land in Excess of One-half Hectare From Part of a Principal Residence?" (1989) 37 Can. Tax J. 113.

Harris, Edwin C., "A Case Study in Tax Reform: The Principal Residence" (1983) 7 Dal. L.J. 169.

Kehler, J.A., "Capitalizing on a Change of Residence or in its Use" (1985) 118 CA Magazine 12:52.

McGregor, G., "Principal Residence: Some Problems" (1973) 21 Can. Tax J. 116.

Moore, D.H., "Does a 'Principal Residence' Include Separate Buildings" (1987) 35 Can. Tax J. 702.

"Personal Tax Planning — The Principal Residence Designation Decision: The New Complexity" (1984) 32 Can. Tax J. 572.

Rotenberg, Charles M., "My Second Home" (1983) 5 Can. Taxpayer 199.

Shead, Richard G., "The Current Status of Real Estate as a Tax Shelter," in *Proceedings of 38th Tax Conf.* 48 (Can. Tax Foundation, 1986).

Simmons, Howard S., *The Family Home and Income Tax* (Toronto: Carswell, 1986).

Strother, Robert C., "Income Tax Implications of Personal-Use Real Estate," *Corporate Management Tax Conf.* 59 (Can. Tax Foundation, 1983).

Thomas, R.B., "Associated Corporations; Principal Residence," in *Proceedings of 35th Tax Conf.* 689 (Can. Tax Foundation, 1983).

William, "Private Residence: Tax Incidence and Exemptions" (1977) 41 Convey. & Prop. Lawyer 389.

Capital Losses

Arnold, Brian J., and D. Keith McNair, "The Stop-Loss Rule in Subsection 97(3): An Analysis" (1980) 28 Can. Tax J. 131.

Burpee, Thomas R., "Utilization of Tax Losses: A Reasonable Expectation of Profit," in *Proceedings of 37th Tax Conf.* 32:1 (Canadian Tax Foundation, 1985).

Cadesky, Michael, "Corporate Losses," in *Proceedings of 42nd Tax Conf.* 19:1 (Can. Tax Foundation, 1990).

Conkwright, Glen E., "The Utilization of Losses in Corporate Groups and Further Relief that Might be Taken," in *Proceedings of 31st Tax Conf.* 316 (Can. Tax Foundation, 1979).

Drache, A.B.C., "Corporate Loss Strategies" (1991) 13 Can. Taxpayer 70.

Drache, A.B.C., "New Treatment for Losses" (1983) 5 Can. Taxpayer 183.

Eaton, K.E., "The Death of the 'Profit Earning Process Test'" (1957) 5 Can. Tax J. 271.

Farwell and Mathew, "The Costs of Corporate Complexity" (1979) 112 CA Magazine 28.

Hirsch, Morley P., "The Corporate Loss Transfer System," in *Proceedings of 37th Tax Conf.* 31:1 (Canadian Tax Foundation, 1985).

Kleinman, Robert A. and Jeffrey Gerstein, "Planning to Maximize the Eligibility and Utilization of Capital Losses for Individuals" (1993) 41 Can. Tax J. 324.

Nowoselski, Barry, "Should You Buy or Sell a Company for Its Tax-Loss Carryovers?" (1983) 116 CA Magazine 64.

Reid, Robert J., "Capital and Non-Capital Losses," in *Proceedings of 42nd Tax Conf.* 20:2 (Can. Tax Foundation, 1990).

Silver, Sheldon, "Utilization of Real Estate Losses," *Corporate Management Tax Conf.* 91 (Can. Tax Foundation, 1983).

Stacey, John A., "The Treatment of Losses," in *Proceedings of 35th Tax Conf.* 29 (Can. Tax Foundation, 1983).

Sweet, David G., "Capital Losses," in *Proceedings of 24th Tax Conf.* 348 (Can. Tax Foundation, 1972).

Wraggett, Cathy, "Accelerated Deduction of Business Losses" (1990) 64 CMA Magazine 33.

Zimmer, Henry B., "Using Your Losses" (1974) 104 CA Magazine 58.

Transitional Rules

Cadesky, Michael, "Corporate Losses," in *Proceedings of 42nd Tax Conf.* 19:1 (Can. Tax Foundation, 1990).

Reid, Robert J., "Capital and Non-Capital Losses," in *Proceedings of 42nd Tax Conf.* 20:2 (Can. Tax Foundation, 1990).

Wise, Richard M., "The V-Day Value of Publicly Traded Shares" (1980) 28 Can. Tax J. 253.

Anti-Avoidance Provisions

Goodison, Don, "Tax Forum — Not a Threat" (1990) 24 CGA Magazine 19.

Lahmer, Craig, "New Measures Against Tax Avoidance Transactions" in *Proceedings of 40th Tax Conf.* 19:1 (Can. Tax Found., 1988).

Templeton, Wendy, "Anti-Avoidance and the Capital Gains Exemption" (1986) 34 Can. Tax J. 203.

Other

Attridge, Ian, "Create Conservation Gains, Not Capital Gains" (1994) 19 Intervenor No. 6 8.

Ballon, Naomi L., "Section 68: Judicial Deference?" (1989) 2 Can. Current Tax P67.

Campbell, Ian R., "Valuation-related Issues: Tax Planning and Post-transaction Follow-up" in *Proceedings of 45th Tax Conf.* 40:1 (Can. Tax Found., 1993).

Drache, A.B.C., "Stock Dividends: Beneficial to the Few" (1981) 3 Can. Taxpayer 99.

Hanson, Suzanee I.R., "Planning for a Share Sale" in *Proceedings of 44th Tax Conf.* 27:1 (Can. Tax Foundation 1992).

Hayos, Gabriel J., "The Capital Gains Exemption: Planning Strategies to Meet the Criterial of a 'Qualified Small Business Corporation'" in *Proceedings of 40th Tax Conf.* 15:1 (Can. Tax Foundation 1988).

Krishna, Vern, "Using the Capital Gains Exemption for Matrimonial Settlement" (1993) 4 Can. Current Tax C5.

Peters, Steven, "Enhancing the Exemption" (1992) 125 CA Mag. No. 5 33.

Potvin, Jean, "The Capital Gains Deduction for Qualified Small Business Corporation Shares Revisited" in *Proceedings of 44th Tax Conf.* 5:50 (Can. Tax Foundation 1992).

Sapona, Ingrid, "Canada's Tax Treaties: A Comparison of the Treatment of Capital Gains" (1992) 40 Can. Tax J. 720.

Silver, Sheldon, "Estate Freezing With Discretion" (1978) 26 Can. Tax J. 705.

Stewart, Donald A.C., "Stock Option Plans: Bright Past, Dim Future" (1972) 20 Can. Tax J. 299.

Tam, Anthony, "Capital Gains Exemption: Small Business Corporations" (1987–89) Can. Current Tax P5.

Wise, Richard M., "Fair Market Determinations — A Few More Requirements" (1983) 31 Can. Tax J. 337.

PART VII: OTHER INCOME & DEDUCTIONS

CHAPTER 12 — OTHER SOURCES OF INCOME

I. — General Comment

To this point, we have examined the rules governing the computation of income from the following specifically identified sources — office, employment, business, property and capital gains. Income and losses from these named sources enter into the computation of total income according to the sequence and manner set out in section 3 of the *Income Tax Act*. There are, however, certain types of income that one cannot conveniently identify as originating from, or relating to, these named sources. These are loosely categorized as "other sources of income", a grouping that comprises various receipts and allowances without a common link or source.

We saw in Chapter 4 that the concept of income for tax purposes is less comprehensive than it is in economic doctrine. In particular, Anglo-Canadian common law insists that income must have a source. The source theory does not, however, conveniently embrace all receipts. We also saw that the Act does not define the concept of income either in the Act or in common law. There are, for example, various exclusions from income, such as gifts, windfall gains, and inheritances.

The taxable base should be broad and inclusive if we use it as the measure of a taxpayer's ability to pay. Thus, section 56 of the Act brings into income a variety of receipts that one may not necessarily include through one of the named sources of income. It is, however, important to note the opening words of section 56: "*Without restricting the generality of section 3*, there *shall* be included in computing the income of a taxpayer for a taxation year.

..." [Emphasis added.] Section 56 is not intended to curtail the scope of section 3. Income from a source inside or outside Canada — that is, income from *any* source regardless of location — is included in section 3. This scope is reinforced in section 3, which provides that the named sources in that section are not to be read as an exhaustive or a restrictive list of the sources of income.

Section 56 contains a long list of items. In this chapter we look at some of the more significant items including the following:

- Pension benefits;

- Death benefits;

- Support payments;

- Indirect payments;

- Retiring allowances;

- Scholarships, bursaries, and fellowships;

- Research grants;

- Prizes; and

- Social assistance payments.

II. — Pension Benefits

Pension income is taxable upon receipt and not upon payment of contributions into the pension plan.

Employer contributions to employee registered pension plans are not taxable as employment-source income.[1] Within specified limits, employees can also deduct contributions to a registered pension fund or plan.[2]

Pension benefits from a pension plan (not including benefits from an employee benefit plan) are taxable upon their withdrawal from the plan and are included in income in the year that the taxpayer receives the payment.[3]

An employee must include all pension benefits in income as he or she receives them. This is so whether the payments are under a formal registered plan, an unregistered plan, lump sum,

---

[1]Subpara. 6(1)(a)(i); subs. 248(1)"superannuation or pension benefit".

[2]Para. 8(1)(m).

[3]Subpara. 56(1)(a)(i); *Muller v. M.N.R.* (1960), 26 Tax A.B.C. 295, 61 D.T.C. 246 (pension does not have to be related to an office or employment to be taxed).

or periodic. Pensions and supplementary pensions received under the *Old Age Security Act* and the *Canada Pension Plan* are also taxable as income.[4]

It is important to observe that one is taxable on all payments made out of a superannuation or pension plan, whether registered or not. Registration is of importance only in determining the deductibility of contributions to a plan; it has no bearing on the taxability of receipts out of a plan.

The source of a pension is also irrelevant to its inclusion in income calculations; all pension income is taxable when received by a taxpayer resident in Canada. Hence, in the absence of special provisions in a tax treaty,[5] a foreign taxpayer who takes up residence in Canada becomes liable to tax on his or her pension income. This is so even though the taxpayer may not have been entitled to a deduction at the time that he or she contributed to the pension plan.[6]

III. — Death Benefits

A payment on account of a death benefit is included in income in the year of receipt. A "death benefit" is a payment made upon the death of an employee in recognition of service in an office or employment. A death benefit to an employee's spouse is tax-free to a maximum of $10,000.[7]

IV. — Support Payments

The statutory provisions in respect of spousal support payments are divided into two segments: (1) receipts are included in income under subdivision d; (2) deductions are permitted under subdivision e. The inclusion and deduction provisions are mirror images of each other.[8] A payment that is deductible by the payer is required to be included in income by the payee. A payment that is taxable to the recipient may be deducted by the payer. These provisions are discussed further in Chapter 13 "Other Deductions".

---

[4]Equivalent payments under Quebec plans are also included in the taxpayer's income.

[5]See, for example, Article XVIII in the *Canada-U.S. Tax Treaty*.

[6]*The Queen v. Herman*, [1978] C.T.C. 442, 78 D.T.C. 6311 (F.C.T.D.).

[7]Subpara. 56(1)(a)(iii), subs. 248(1)"death benefit".

[8]Para. 56(1)(b), s. 56.1; para. 60(b), s. 60.1. See: *Thibaudeau v. Canada*, [1995] 2 S.C.R. 627, [1995] 1 C.T.C. 382, 95 D.T.C. 5273 (S.C.C.) (para. 56(1)(b)) does not impose a burden on recipient so as to attract section 15 of the *Charter*.

V. — Retiring Allowances

In common law, a retiring allowance for the loss of employment is compensation *for the loss of* a source of income, rather than compensation *from* a source of income. If the common law doctrine prevailed, taxpayers could quite easily structure their remuneration to avoid taxation. The Act, however, specifically brings retiring allowances into income.[9]

A "retiring allowance" is a payment in recognition of long service, compensation for loss of an office or employment, or damages for wrongful dismissal.[10]

A payment pursuant to the terms of an employment contract is generally not a retiring allowance; it is remuneration.[11] In exceptional circumstances, a contractual payment to an employee upon termination of employment may be considered a "retiring allowance" if the payment is in recognition of the length of the employee's service to the company. There is generally an element of gratuitousness in the making of the payment, even though it may result from a threat of litigation.

VI. — Scholarships, Bursaries, and Fellowships

Generally, scholarships, fellowships, bursaries, and prizes for achievement are included in income to the extent that the amount received in the year exceeds $3,000.[12] Work-related and business-related awards, prizes and similar payments do not qualify for this exemption.

The terms "scholarship", "fellowship" and "bursary" are often used interchangeably to mean financial assistance to selected students pursuing further education. A "prize for achievement" is an award for accomplishment. The phrase does not necessarily imply an award for victory in a competition or contest.[13] An award is only considered a "prize" if the winner of the prize is aware of the existence of, and enters, the contest.[14]

---

[9]Subpara. 56(1)(a)(ii).

[10]Subs. 248(1)"retiring allowance".

[11]Para. 6(3)(b).

[12]Para. 56(1)(n), subs. 56(3).

[13]*The Queen v. Savage*, [1983] 2 S.C.R. 428, [1983] C.T.C. 393, 83 D.T.C. 5409 (S.C.C.) at 400 [C.T.C.] and 5415 [D.T.C.] *per* Dickson J.

[14]*The Queen v. McLaughlin*, [1978] C.T.C. 602, 78 D.T.C. 6406 (F.C.T.D.).

VII. — Research Grants

A fellowship, scholarship, or bursary should be distinguished from a research grant. A research grant is a sum of money given to a person to defray expenses in connection with a research project. Research grants sometimes include remuneration for the researcher.

"Research" generally involves a critical or scientific inquiry aimed at discovering new facts and exploring the potential for their practical application. Usually, the terms of the grant will establish that the primary purpose of the grant is the carrying out of research.

A research grant is taxable only if received directly by an individual. In other words, a payment of funds to the taxpayer's educational or research institution to finance research by the taxpayer is not taxable to the researcher.[15]

Research-related expenses are deductible from a research grant to the extent of the total value of the grant.

A taxpayer who must travel to conduct his or her research may deduct travelling expenses (including the full amount expended for meals and lodging) incurred in the carrying out of the research. The CRA takes the view, however, that a researcher who resides temporarily in a place while engaged in research is "sojourning" rather than travelling. Amounts paid for meals and lodging while the researcher is sojourning in a place are considered personal and living expenses, and are not deductible from the research grant. It is not clear how long a stay in a place converts a traveller into a sojourner.[16]

VIII. — Prizes

A prize for achievement is an award for accomplishment. Prizes are included in income in the year received[17] if the prize is for an achievement in a field of endeavour ordinarily carried on by the taxpayer. Thus, prizes won in games of chance or for athletic achievement are not taxable.[18] Certain prescribed prizes of recognition by the general public for particularly meritorious endeavours are also excluded from income.[19]

---

[15]Para. 56(1)(o).

[16]Subpara. 56(1)(o)(i) IT-75R4 (June 28, 2003).

[17]Para. 56(1)(n).

[18]*The Queen v. Savage*, [1983] 2 S.C.R. 428, [1983] C.T.C. 393, 83 D.T.C. 5409 (S.C.C.) at 401 [C.T.C.] and 545 [D.T.C.].

[19]Reg. 7700.

IX. — Social Assistance Payments

Most social assistance payments are not taxable. They must, however, be included in income in determining taxable income.[20] The taxpayer may then claim a deduction for the amount included in income.[21] Thus, although the net effect is that social assistance payments are not taxable, the inclusion of social assistance payments in a taxpayer's income may have other consequences. For example, it may reduce the amount of other tax incentives, such as refundable tax credits, to which the taxpayer might otherwise be entitled.

The trend in recent Canadian tax legislation is to shift the tax burden of social welfare payments to the payer of the highest rate of tax in a family. Social assistance payments are taxed to the spouse with the higher marginal tax rate. This ensures that a family's access to any other income-tested tax incentives is determined by reference to the income of the spouse with the higher tax rate.

X. — Other Inclusions

Other Inclusions in Income	Statutory Reference	Comment
Amounts paid for benefit of taxpayer and/or children in taxpayer's custody	56.1	
Unemployment insurance benefits	56(1)(a)(iv)	
Transitional assistance benefit	56(1)(a)(v)	received by employees of automotive industry covered by the 1965 Canada-U.S. pact on automotive products
Prescribed benefit under government assistance program to extent not already included in income	56(1)(a)(vi)	

---

[20]Para. 56(1)(u).

[21]Para. 110(1)(f).

Other Inclusions in Income	Statutory Reference	Comment
Annuity payments	56(1)(d), (d.2)	
Amount received from the disposition of an income-averaging annuity contract	56(1)(e), (f); 61(4) ("income-averaging annuity contract")	
Benefits under a supplementary unemployment benefit plan	56(1)(g); 145	
Benefits received under an RRSP or a RRIF	56(1)(h); 146	
Home buyers' plan	56(1)(h.1); 146.01	
Benefits from a deferred profit-sharing plan	56(1)(i); 147	
Amount received from the disposition of an interest in a life insurance policy	56(1)(j); 148(1), (1.1)	
Legal costs awarded by a court on an appeal for tax assessment, interest or penalties, and costs reimbursed from a decision of the Canada Employment and Immigration Commission or under the *Unemployment Insurance Act, Canada Pension Plan*	56(1)(l)	provided costs of the appeal or decision are deductible under para. 60(o)
Reimbursement of legal expenses paid to collect or establish right to a retiring allowance or pension benefit	56(1)(l.1)	

Other Inclusions in Income	Statutory Reference	Comment
Amount received from an RESP	56(1)(q); 146.1	
Home insulation or conversion grants	56(1)(s); Regs. 5500, 5501	
Benefits from an RRIF	56(1)(t); 146.3	
Worker's compensation	56(1)(v)	
Amounts received from some other person's salary deferral arrangement	56(1)(w)	amount included in income to the extent that it was not included in the other person's income
Proceeds from disposition of an interest in a RCA	56(1)(y)	
Value of benefits received or enjoyed in respect of workshops, seminars, training programs, etc.	56(1)(aa)	received by reason of membership in a registered national arts service organization

Selected Bibliography to Chapter 12

Superannuation or Pension Benefits

Baston, Paul F., "Individual Pension Plans Revisited: Are they Really Worthwhile" (1994) 6 Tax. of Exec. Compensation and Retirement 19.

Bauslaugh, Randy V., "Past Service Enhancement and the Subsection 8503(15) Anti-avoidance Rule" (1994) 5 Tax. of Exec. Compensation and Retirement 899.

Broley, John A., "Overcoming Benefit Limitations for Executives Through Design and Use of Pension and Nonstatutory Arrangements", in *Proceedings of 33rd Tax Conf.* 869 (Can. Tax Foundation, 1981).

Bush, Kathryn M., "Executive Compensation: Supplemental Pension Plans" (1991) 8 Bus. L. 46.

Dutka, Randall J., et al., *Pensions and Retirement Income Planning 1993: Tax Rules and Strategies* (Toronto: CCH Canadian, 1993).

Johnston, William, "Taxation of Non-registered Pension Plans", *Corp. Mgmt. Tax Conf.* 9:1 (Can. Tax Foundation, 1991).

Krasa, Ewa M., "Recent Developments in Retirement Savings and Deferred Compensation: A Potpourri", in *Proceedings of 44th Tax Conf.* 18:1 (Can. Tax Foundation, 1992).

Muto, Alexander D., "Recent Changes to the *Income Tax Regulations* on Retirement Savings" (1994) 5 Tax. of Exec. Compensation and Retirement 942.

Pensions: Significant Issues and Developments (Toronto: Law Society of Upper Canada, Dpt. of Education, 1990).

Solursh, John M. and Jeremy J. Forgie, "Tax-assisted Retirement Savings: An Overview of the New System and its Application to Registered Pension Plans", *Corp. Mgmt Tax Conf.* 7:1 (Can. Tax Foundation, 1991).

Theroux, Marcel and Brad Rowse, "The Individual Pension Plan: A Complete Guide", *Corp. Mgmt. Tax Conf.* 8:1 (Can. Tax Foundation, 1991).

Wolpert, Michael, "Pension Plans and the *Income Tax Act*: The Other Side of the Equation" (1992) 2 Can Corp. Counsel 10.

Death Benefits

Atnikov, D., "Stock Options, Stock Purchase Plans, and Death Benefits", *Prairie Provinces Tax Conf.* 1 (Can. Tax Foundation, 1980).

Support Payments

"Alimony and Maintenance Trusts" (1993) 8 Money and Family Law 81.

"Alimony Insurance could be Tax Deductible" (1992) 7 Money and Family Law 36.

Arnold, Brian J., "Income Tax Consequences of Separation and Divorce", in *Proceedings of 29th Tax Conf.* 193 (Can. Tax Foundation, 1977).

Barnett, Jim, "Alimony and Maintenance Payments" (1979) 112 CA Magazine 65.

Bowman, Stephen W., et al., "The Taxability of Child Support Payments and the Charter of Rights and Freedoms" (1994) Can. Tax J. 907.

Corn, George, "Child Care Expenses — Deductibility as Business Expenses or Personal Living Expenses" (1991) 3 Can. Current Tax J-91.

Douglas, Kristen, "Child Support: Quantum, Enforcement and Taxation" (Ottawa: Library of Parliament, Research Branch, 1994).

Drache, A.B.C., "Reducing Expenses is Not Gaining Income" (1991) 13 Can. Taxpayer 156.

Drache, A.B.C., "Support Payments: All Tax Aspects Should Be Considered" (1991) 13 Can. Taxpayer 160.

Drache, A.B.C., "*Tax Act* Creates Problems in Joint Custody" (1992) 14 Can. Taxpayer 31.

Drache, A.B.C., "Written Separation Agreements" (1991) 13 Can. Taxpayer 61.

Durnford, John W. and Stephen J. Troope, "Spousal Support in Family Law and Alimony in the Law of Taxation" (1994) 42 Can. Tax J. 1.

Freedman, Andrew J., "Arrears Payments: To Tax or Not to Tax?" (1993) 8 Money and Family Law 61.

Goodison, Don, "Tax Forum — Not a Business Expense" (1991) 25 CGA Magazine 17.

Harris, J., "Alimony and Maintenance Payments: Unexpected Results" (1988) 2 Can. Current Tax P-25.

Harris, Peter H., "Tax Treatment of Civil Litigation and Damage Awards, Alimony and Maintenance Payments" (1985) 6 Advocate's Q. 346.

Income Tax and Costs: Setting Aside Separation Agreements: Appeals, Choosing the Right Forum (Audio Archives of Canada, 1984).

Income Tax: Maintenance, Alimony and Employment Termination Benefits (Audio Archives of Canada, 1984).

Klein, William A., "Tax Effects of Nonpayment of Child Support" (1990) 45 Tax Lawyer 259.

Krishna, Vern, "To Love, Honor or Pay" (1990) 24 CGA Magazine 28.

McCallum, J. Thomas, "Deferring the Inevitable" (1990) 24 CGA Magazine 23.

"Post-Marital Trusts" (1984) 6 Can. Taxpayer 15.

Raich, Robert, "Characterization of Income and Third Party Alimony Receipts", in *Proceedings of 32nd Tax Conf.* 238 (Can. Tax Foundation, 1980).

Richards, Gabrielle M.R., "Support Payments: An Update" (1992) 3 Can. Current Tax J-115.

Shillington, Richard and Ellen Zweibel, "Child Support Policy: Income Tax Treatment and Child Support Guidelines" (Toronto: Policy Research Centre on Children, Youth and Families, 1993).

Shultz, Clayton G., "Income Tax Law and Policy Applicable to Periodic Maintenance and Division of Matrimonial Assets" (1987) 1 Can. Fam. L. Q. 293.

"Taxation of Support Payments Received from Non-residents" (1994) 9 Money and
  Family Law 78.
"Taxation of Support Payments Simplified?" (1992) 7 Money and Family Law 75.

Retiring Allowances

Colley, Geofferey, M., "Retirement and Termination" (1980) 113 CA Magazine 57.
Fisher, G.B., "Early Retirement Tax Considerations" (1983) 31 Can. Tax J. 828.
Income Tax: Maintenance, Alimony and Employment Termination Benefits (Audio
  Archives of Canada, 1984).
Levine, Risa, "Retiring Allowances Part 1: How Do You Know if You Have One?"
  (1994) 2 RRSP Plan. 125.
Matheson, D.I., "Termination of Employment", *Corporate Management Tax Conf.* 219
  (Can. Tax Foundation, 1979).
Murill, Raymond F., "Easing the Pain of Severance Pay" (1984) 117 CA Magazine 38.
Novek, Barbara L., "Retiring Allowances are subject to Administrative Guidelines"
  (1991) 3 Tax. of Exec. Compensation and Retirement 523.
Rayside J.W., "Retirement Planning for Owner-Managers" (1982) 30 Can. Tax J. 83.
"Retiring Allowance Reasonableness" (1980) 2 Can. Taxpayer 205.

Other

Duncan, Garry R., "Passing the Hat (The Orderly Succession of a Business to a Worthy
  Heir)" (Jan/Feb 1989) 122 CA Magazine 39.
Finkelstein, David N., "Tax Problems in Estate Planning for the Corporate Executive",
  in *Proceedings of 33rd Tax Conf.* 952 (Can. Tax Foundation, 1981).
Harris, Peter H., "Tax Treatment of Civil Litigation and Damage Awards, Alimony and
  Maintenance Payments" (1985) 6 Advocate's Q. 346.
Wakeling, Audrey A., "Tax Planning with Trusts", in *Proceedings of 42nd Tax Conf.*
  35:1 (Can. Tax Foundation, 1990).

CHAPTER 13 — OTHER DEDUCTIONS

I. — General Comment

Just as the *Income Tax Act* includes in income various miscellaneous receipts that are not directly attributable to a particular source,[1] it also allows for the deduction of certain expenses that are not directly related to a particular source of income. These deductions (described here as "other deductions") constitute an open category of expenses, each with its own rationale. Certain disbursements normally considered to be personal may, however, become deductible by virtue of their intimate connection with a business. For example, meals and entertainment, travelling expenses, and the cost of special wardrobes in specialized professions sometimes take on an aura of business expenditures. These types of expenditures pose difficult problems in the tax system because it is not easy to draw the line between personal and business expenditures. The distinction is not always clear cut, and the connection between the expenditure and the business purposes is sometimes tenuous. Take, for example, the case of personal clothing. A professional lawyer or accountant is expected to dress in an appropriate manner suitable for his or her environment in the business workplace. Thus, the cost of a business suit or business dress is connected with the earning of business income. Nevertheless, expenditures on account of clothing are generally considered to be primarily personal expenses and, hence, not deductible in the computation of income. There comes a point, however, when clothing serves only a limited and specialized purpose, and the expenditure is primarily on account of business. For example: an actor may require special-effects clothing; a doctor or surgeon may require special tunics; an auto mechanic special overalls. In this chapter we examine deductions in respect of the more commonly claimed "mixed purpose" expenditures — support and maintenance payments, child care expenses, and moving expenses.

---

[1]See Chapter 12, "Other Sources of Income".

Note: The *Income Tax Act* uses the term spouse in a broad manner. "Spouse" includes common-law partners and same-sex (homosexual/gay/lesbian) partners. A "common-law partner" is an individual who cohabits with the taxpayer in a conjugal relationship — see subsection 248(1).

II. — Spousal And Child Support

1. — General Comment

The expenses of supporting one's family are clearly personal expenses that one does not incur for the purposes of earning income. Hence, absent statutory authority, one would not be entitled to deduct support payments from income. That said, however, it is entirely tenable from an economic perspective that the recipient should be taxable on support, since such payments are an accretion to wealth.

Note, however, that in law the characterization of receipts does not usually depend on the nature of the expenditure to the payer. The tax consequences to the recipient and the payer are determined independently. For example, where an individual takes his or her family to a restaurant, the cost of the meal is a personal, non-deductible expense. The receipt, however, is taxable to the owner of the restaurant as business income.

There are several reasons for varying from the theoretical norm. We allow a spouse to deduct support payments because we recognize such payments as extraordinary expense that reduce the payer's ability to pay. Indeed, without tax relief, some spouses would find that their tax equalled, or even exceeded, their income after making support payments. Assume, for example, that an individual earns $100,000 and pays support of $35,000. Without a deduction for the support, his or her tax of approximately $36,000 would exceed the support payments. Thus, we justify the deduction for spousal support because it takes into account the taxpayer's ability to pay.

The support provisions significantly affect federal and provincial revenues. Since the payer usually has a higher marginal tax rate than the payee, the deduction for spousal support allows spouses to shift down on the rate schedule. This obviously has revenue consequences. For example, a deduction of $35,000 of spousal support has a net after-tax cost of $17,500 if the payer has a 50 per cent tax rate. The treasury makes up part of the revenue loss by taxing the other spouse on the support. If this spouse has a marginal rate of 25 per cent, however, the tax cost to him or her is only $8,750. Thus, the treasury picks up the net loss of revenue because of the difference in marginal rates.

The statutory provisions in respect of spousal support are mirror images of each other.[2] A payment that is deductible by the payer is taxable to the payee. A payment that is taxable to

---

[2]Para. 56(1)(b); para. 60(b). *Thibaudeau v. M.N.R.*, [1995] 2 S.C.R. 627, [1995] 1 C.T.C. 382, 95 D.T.C. 5273 (S.C.C.) (Para. 56(1)(b) is not unconstitutional under section 15 of the *Canadian Charter*

the recipient is deductible to the payer. Thus, read together, the rules concern the choice of taxable person rather than the definition of income or expense. In effect, one spouse is merely a conduit or pass-through for gross income that legally belongs to the other spouse by virtue of divorce settlement or decree.

An individual who is living separate and apart from his or her spouse or former spouse[3] because of the breakdown of their marriage can deduct spousal support payments if the payments are:[4]

- Pursuant to an order of a competent tribunal or a written agreement;

- In the nature of an allowance;

- Payable on a periodic basis; and

- For the maintenance of the recipient and/or the children.

For tax purposes, the term spouse has a broad meaning. "Spouse" includes a person of the opposite sex who is party to a void or voidable marriage. The term also includes the natural or adoptive unmarried parents of a child of the "spouses".[5] Further, "spouse" includes common-law partners, and same-sex relationships [see subsection 248(1)].

For obvious reasons, the Act limits the deduction to situations where the payer and the payee are living separate and apart from each other. It is a question of fact whether individuals are living separate and apart from each other. In certain circumstances, the law considers persons living under a common roof to be living apart from each other.[6]

---

of Rights and Freedoms, Part I of the *Constitution Act, 1982*, being Schedule B to the *Canada Act 1982* (U.K.), 1982, c. 11); see also, IT-530R, "Support Payments" (July 17, 2003).

[3]See subs. 252(3) for extended meaning of "spouse".

[4]Paras. 60(b) and 56.1(4)"support amount".

[5]Subs. 252(3).

[6]*Sanford*, [2001] 1 C.T.C. 2273, 2001 D.T.D. 12; affd. [2003] 1 C.T.C. 221, 2002 D.T.C. 7442 (F.C.A.). *Rushton v. Rushton* (1968), 66 W.W.R. 764 (B.C.S.C.) ("separate" means having withdrawn from marriage with intent to destroy bond; "apart" means physically separate); *Rousell v. Rousell* (1969), 69 W.W.R. 568 (Sask. Q.B.) (essence of evidence of separation being cessation of marital relationship); *Galbraith v. Galbraith* (1969), 69 W.W.R. 390 (Man. C.A.) (examination of law on cruelty as grounds for separation though couple living in same dwelling); *M.N.R. v. Longchamps*, [1986] 2 C.T.C. 2231 at 2233, 86 D.T.C. 1694 at 1695 (T.C.C.) ("the termination of all rapport between a husband and his wife of the kind evidenced in this appeal is certainly in my opinion within the meaning that must be attributed to the expression, 'living apart'"; "there was no communication between them, no socializing whatsoever, each attending to his or her own affairs without consultation between them"); *Boos v. M.N.R.* (1961), 27 Tax A.B.C. 283, 61 D.T.C. 520 (husband so withdrawn and separated from wife and children as to be in desertion, though still occupying same home).

A payment is spousal support only if the order or agreement clearly identifies it as being *solely* for the support of the spouse or former spouse.[7] Thus, the default rule is that support payments are considered child support and, therefore, are neither deductible nor taxable if the order or agreement is silent as to their character.[8]

2. — Order or Written Agreement

(a) — Payments Prior to Agreement

A payment is deductible only if it is pursuant to an order of a competent tribunal or a written agreement. The Agency does not accept anything less than a decree from a competent tribunal. Amounts that a taxpayer pays *before* the court order requires him or her to do so, or *before* the spouse enters into a written agreement, are deductible[9] only if the order or agreement incorporates the payments. The parties must ensure that they have an order or agreement before the end of the year following the payments.[10]

(b) — Written Agreement

A "written agreement" is a document signed by both parties to the agreement. It is not enough that the parties exchange correspondence with each other or that their lawyers or accountants exchange correspondence and discuss draft agreements.[11] The Agency will not

---

[7]Subs. 56.1(4)"child support amount".

[8]Para. 56(1)(b).

[9]See IT-530R, "Support Payments" (July 17, 2003); *Hardtman v. M.N.R.*, [1977] C.T.C. 358, 77 D.T.C. 5219 (F.C.T.D.) (although Court able to distinguish between sham and equitable maintenance, even prior to any agreement, Court without such equitable jurisdiction); *Pezet v. M.N.R.*, [1974] C.T.C. 2315, 74 D.T.C. 1246 (F.C.T.D.) (no retroactivity of deductibility where payments made prior to agreement, unless legislation provides otherwise); *Gagné v. M.N.R.*, [1976] C.T.C. 2163, 76 D.T.C. 1125 (T.R.B.) (husband's letter listing expenses that he would pay did not constitute "agreement", since no evidence of consent); *Brooks v. M.N.R.*, [1977] C.T.C. 2048, 77 D.T.C. 38 (T.R.B.) (amounts paid prior to agreement and order not deductible; even amount of arrears paid pursuant to order not deductible).

[10]Subs. 60.1(3).

[11]*Feinstein v. The Queen*, [1979] C.T.C. 329, 79 D.T.C. 5236 (F.C.T.D.) (agreement destroyed by fire in attorney's office; payments not deductible in these exceptional circumstances); *Chamberland v. M.N.R.*, [1981] C.T.C. 2302, 81 D.T.C. 288 (T.R.B.) (agreement in principle, signed by one spouse is insufficient even if payments actually made); *Ardley v. M.N.R.*, [1980] C.T.C. 2126, 80 D.T.C. 1106 (T.R.B.) (legal fees for separation agreement paid, but no proof of execution of agreement); *Hardy v. M.N.R.*, [1978] C.T.C. 3120, 78 D.T.C. 1802 (T.R.B.) (and cases cited therein) (payments made pursu-

accept anything less than a clear-cut "written agreement" signed by both parties. An exchange of correspondence may, however, crystallize into a "written agreement" in the same way that one can enter into a contract through an exchange of letters.[12]

(c) — Paid Under an Agreement

A payment is *made under* an order or agreement if it complies with the legal obligation created in the agreement.[13] Thus, only those amounts that are actually set out in the court order or written agreement are deductible by the payer and taxable to the payee. Voluntary payments in excess of the agreed-upon amounts are not "made under" the order or agreement. Conversely, payments that are made under a court order or agreement are taxable as income to the recipient even though the order or agreement might stipulate that the amounts are to be paid on a "tax-free" basis.[14]

3. — "Allowance"

An amount is a pre-determined sum of money that the recipient can use for his or her own benefit. The amount must be:[15]

• Limited and pre-determined;

• Paid on account of maintenance; and

• At the complete discretion of the person to whom it is paid.

In addition, subsection 56.1(4) requires that the amount must be within the complete discretion of the recipient. Amounts over which the recipient does not have discretion do not qualify as spousal support.

---

ant to a written agreement that the payer refused to sign not deductible); *Andrychuck v. M.N.R.*, [1986] 2 C.T.C. 2214, 86 D.T.C. 1667 (T.C.C.) (informal correspondence between spouses does not constitute "written agreement"; wife's letter requesting $300 support per month insufficient); *Jacoby v. M.N.R.*, [1981] C.T.C. 2935, 81 D.T.C. 824 (T.R.B.) (unsigned written agreement insufficient); *Jaskot v. M.N.R.*, [1992] 1 C.T.C. 2145, 92 D.T.C. 1102 (T.C.C.) (increase in support payments not deductible as only written evidence in correspondence of recipient's solicitor).

[12]*Burgess v. M.N.R.*, [1991] 1 C.T.C. 163, 91 D.T.C. 5076 (F.C.T.D.).

[13]*The Queen v. Sills*, [1985] 1 C.T.C. 49, 85 D.T.C. 5096 (F.C.A.).

[14]*The Queen v. Sigglekow*, [1985] 2 C.T.C. 251, 85 D.T.C. 5471; additional reasons at 85 D.T.C. 5594 (F.C.T.D.).

[15]*Gagnon v. The Queen*, [1986] 1 S.C.R. 264, [1986] 1 C.T.C. 410, 86 D.T.C. 6179 (S.C.C.) ($360 paid to spouse pursuant to divorce decree, for purpose of paying two mortgages and interest was "allowance"); *The Queen v. Pascoe*, [1975] C.T.C. 656, 75 D.T.C. 5427 (F.C.A.).

4. — Payable on a Periodic Basis

One of the most troublesome questions in interpreting support agreements is the distinction between support payments and property settlements. Spousal support is deductible by the payer, and taxable to the payee, but only if it is payable on a periodic basis. Thus, the obligation to pay support is an annual charge against one of the spouse's pre-tax income, and entails a redirection of that income to his or her spouse. The amount payable on a periodic basis is deductible even if the payment is a lump sum, whether in arrears or in advance, if all other conditions are satisfied.[16]

The Act confines the deduction to spousal expenses. There is no deduction for property settlements. Property settlements are a division between the husband and wife of the family's after-tax savings. Thus, capital payments to extinguish support are not deductible as an expense.[17] For example, the present value of an agreement to pay 60 monthly payments of $1,000 is equal to a lump sum of $49,272 if we assume an interest rate of 8 per cent. The lump sum and the periodic payments are mathematically equal present-value amounts at that rate. Nevertheless, the lump sum is not deductible for tax purposes because it is the capitalized value of the annual expenses.[18] Thus, form prevails over economic substance in this situation.

"Periodic" means recurring at fixed or regular intervals. The payment must be *payable* on a periodic basis and the periodicity requirement must be in the court order or the written agreement.[19] It is not enough that the taxpayer actually pays on a periodic basis. The statutory requirement is that the payment be *payable* on a periodic basis, not that it actually be paid periodically.[20] Thus, the obligation to pay at periodic intervals must not be left to the discretion of the payer.[21] Although some of the earlier jurisprudence interpreted "periodic" to mean that payments be on at least a monthly basis, the Agency is now more flexible.

---

[16]See *Ostrowski v. Canada*, 2002 FCA 299, [2002] 4 C.T.C. 196, 2002 D.T.C. 7209 (F.C.A.)

[17]There are other provisions that allow for tax-free capital settlements: see, e.g., subs. 73(1).

[18]*M.N.R. v. Armstrong*, [1956] S.C.R. 446, [1956] C.T.C. 93, 56 D.T.C. 1044 (S.C.C.).

[19]Para. 60(b).

[20]*The Queen v. Sills*, [1985] 1 C.T.C. 49, 85 D.T.C. 5096 (F.C.A.) (lump-sum payments for arrears of periodic alimony characterized as periodic notwithstanding tardiness and manner of payment); *James v. The Queen*, [1985] 1 C.T.C. 239, 85 D.T.C. 5173 (F.C.T.D.) (recipient taxable on payments made pursuant to order even though payments were late and amounts less than specified in order).

[21]*Jones v. Ogle* (1872), 8 Ch. App. 192 at 198 (in construction of will, partnership profits did not come within meaning of "periodical payment in the nature of income"); *No. 427 v. M.N.R.* (1957), 57 D.T.C. 291 (T.A.B.) (single $5,000 payment, which was one of several of increasing value to be paid over 12 years, was periodic in nature).

Now, even annual payments sometimes qualify as periodic.[22] It would, however, be quite unusual for payments that recur less frequently than annually to qualify as periodic payments.

The distinguishing characteristics of spousal support and property settlements are usually quite clear. Support is usually paid in cash and recognizes one of the spouse's legal support obligations. It is paid at regular intervals and, in most cases, continues for a stipulated period or until the other spouse's death. Thus, the deduction and inclusion regime is appropriate for spousal support, because the payments are of an income nature and the spouse merely acts as the conduit for his or her legal obligations. In contrast, property settlements are usually executed over a brief period and may include non-cash assets. Property settlements are not contingent upon subsequent events such as remarriage. A spouse is entitled to a share of the marital property, even if he or she remarries immediately after the settlement. The deduction inclusion system is inappropriate for capital settlements.

Difficulties arise because complex and sizable agreements have elements of both spousal support and property settlements. There is also the danger of lump-sum property settlements masquerading as spousal support because of the advantage to the paying spouse (normally the husband), who will usually have the higher marginal rate. Thus, the use of inappropriate language in an agreement can effectively convert spousal support into a property settlement.

An allowance for spousal support is a limited, pre-determined sum of money that one pays to enable the recipient to provide for certain kinds of expenses. Its amount is determined in advance and, once paid, it is at the complete discretion of the recipient. A lump-sum payment also represents a limited, pre-determined sum of money. Thus, the distinction between an allowance and a lump-sum payment blurs if the lump-sum payment is also payable in equal instalments on a periodic basis. The problem is essentially one of formal legal characterization, rather than underlying economic substance. One must distinguish between where support stops and property settlement begins. For example, what is the distinction between spousal support of $1,000 per month, payable for 10 years, despite remarriage and a property settlement, that pays one spouse his or her share of $120,000 at a rate of $1,000 per month over 10 years? What if the spousal support is front-end loaded, that is, one spouse receives an allowance of $1,500 per month for the first five years and only $500 per month for the last five years? What if the front-end load is $1,800 per month for five years and $200 per month for the last five years? At what point does the spousal support convert into a property settlement?

---

[22]*Hanlin v. The Queen*, [1985] 1 C.T.C. 54, 85 D.T.C. 5052 (F.C.T.D.) (three annual payments held to be part of series of payments payable on periodic basis).

(a) — Periodic vs. Lump Sum Payments

The distinction between lump-sum amounts and periodic allowances reflects the underlying difference between income and capital. The *Income Tax Act* taxes income, not capital receipts. Similarly, one may deduct expenses but not capital expenditures. A lump sum payable in instalments is a capital amount and is neither deductible nor taxable. An obligation to pay a lump sum is a finite capital debt. The debt is assignable by the creditor and survives his or her life. Hence, the debt can pass to the estate. The critical element in determining the deductibility of maintenance payments (as opposed to capital settlements) is whether the payments were *payable* on a *periodic* basis. Thus, lump sum payments, whether in arrears or in advance, may be deductible if they are on account of maintenance.[23]

The following criteria are relevant, but not conclusive, in distinguishing between spousal support and property settlements.[24]

Indicia	Spousal support	Property settlement
Frequency of payments	Weekly, Monthly, Annually	More than annually
Ratio of payment in relation to income and living standards	Low Small percentage of annual income of payer	High In excess of annual income of payer
Interest payments prior to due date	None	Yes
Acceleration by payee as penalty on default	No	Yes
Prepayment at option of payer	No	Yes
Amount allows for significant capital accumulation by recipient	No	Yes

---

[23]See, for example, *Ostrowski v. Canada*, 2002 FCA 299, [2002] 4 C.T.C. 196, 2002 D.T.C. 7209 (F.C.A.).

[24]See, generally, *McKimmon v. Can.*, [1990] 1 C.T.C. 109, 90 D.T.C. 6088 (F.C.A.).

Indicia	Spousal support	Property settlement
Liability to pay is for definite and fixed time	No	Yes
Payments for indefinite period or until some identifiable family event (e.g., age of child)	Yes	No
Assignability of payments	No	Yes
Survival of obligation to pay after death of payer	No	Yes
Release from future obligations to pay	No	Yes

(i) — Frequency of Payments

Periodicity implies an obligation to pay at fixed intervals and not at variable times. Moreover, the payments should be payable on a reasonably regular basis, whether weekly, monthly, or quarterly. Payments made at intervals of greater than one year are rarely considered to be allowances on account of maintenance.

(ii) — Amount Paid in Relation to Living Standards

Spousal support is on account of maintenance, and not for the accumulation of capital. Thus, a payment that is a very substantial portion of the payer's income is unlikely an allowance for maintenance. On the other hand, a payment that maintains the recipient's standard of living clearly qualifies as an allowance for maintenance. There is no hard-and-fast rule as to what constitutes maintenance. The answer depends upon the lifestyle of the parties and their standard of living. The courts are fairly strict, and have denied taxpayers deductions for educational expenses, medical expenses, camping expenses, hospital insurance premiums, and life insurance premiums.[25]

---

[25]*Urichuk v. The Queen*, [1993] 1 C.T.C. 226, 93 D.T.C. 5120 (F.C.A.) (characterization in separation agreement of instalment payments as additional maintenance does not prevent a contrary finding); *Golightly v. M.N.R.*, [1979] C.T.C. 2997, [1970] Tax A.B.C. 161, 70 D.T.C. 1120 (various payments, including insurance, university room and board, tuition and medical insurance paid directly to institution pursuant to separation agreement were not "maintenance"); *Ivey v. M.N.R.*, [1982] C.T.C. 2034, 82 D.T.C. 1083 (T.R.B.) (payments of school fees, summer camp fees and medical expenses for child

(iii) — Interest

Maintenance payments do not typically bear interest. Payments that bear interest are more likely lump-sum settlements payable by instalments, rather than a true allowance for maintenance.

(iv) — Acceleration Clauses

Pre-payment and acceleration clauses are generally obligations associated with lump-sum capital settlements. An acceleration clause in a settlement contract suggests that the debt is a non-deductible capital obligation, rather than an amount paid on account of periodic maintenance.

(v) — Accumulation of Capital

The quantum of payments is important: maintenance payments are for the recipient's living costs. They are not intended to allow for an accumulation of capital over a short period of time. It is accepted, however, that modest payments on account of capital accumulation may qualify as maintenance. For example, blended monthly mortgage principal and interest payments allow for a modest accumulation of capital over time. Mortgages are a normal living expense.

(vi) — Term of Payments

Spousal support is either payable for an indefinite or unspecified period of time. Where time is specified, the payments generally relate to a significant event in the life of the parties. For example, spousal support payments may depend upon the coming of age of a child, because one anticipates such an event to cause a material change in the recipient's needs. In contrast, a lump sum generally represents a finite debt between the parties, and payments on account thereof are expected to continue for a fixed and specified term.

---

with cystic fibrosis outside meaning of "maintenance"); *Shaw v. M.N.R.*, [1978] C.T.C. 3230, 79 D.T.C. 26 (T.R.B.) (payment by taxpayer of spouse's income tax on maintenance payments and spouse's moving expenses not "alimony" or "maintenance"); *Evans v. M.N.R.*, [1960] S.C.R. 391, [1960] C.T.C. 69, 60 D.T.C. 1047 (S.C.C.) (car payments made for spouse not "maintenance" although car highly useful).

(vii) — Assignment of Obligation

Maintenance allowances are typically personal and non-assignable. The allowance is not assignable to third parties, and terminates upon the death of the recipient. In contrast, lump sum capital settlements are assignable debts, and form part of the recipient's estate.

(viii) — Release from Future Obligations

An agreement that releases the payer from all future obligations to pay maintenance is a lump-sum settlement and not a payment on account of maintenance. The consideration for the release from future maintenance is the capitalized present value of the payments that would have been made on account of future maintenance. The capital payment may be in cash, or the payer may assume a liability (such as a mortgage) on the recipient's behalf. For example, one spouse may assume a mortgage on the other spouse's property in exchange for his or her release from further liability for maintenance.

(b) — Rollovers

Capital settlements between spouses and ex-spouses are subject to a different tax regime than are periodic payments. Section 73 allows an individual two choices when transferring capital property to his or her spouse or ex-spouse. The spouse may:

1. Rollover the property to the other spouse on a tax-free basis, or

2. Elect to realize any capital gain accrued up to the date of the transfer.

In either case, the recipient takes the property at a cost equal to the transferor's proceeds of disposition. If the transferor elects a rollover, the recipient assumes the property at the transferor's cost; if the transferor realizes a capital gain, the recipient acquires the property at its fair market value.

(c) — Arrears

Payments payable on a periodic basis do not change in character merely because they are not made on time. The test for deductibility is whether the payments are *payable* on a periodic basis and not whether they are actually paid on a periodic schedule.[26] Thus, payments on account of arrears are deductible and taxable if they are identifiable under the terms of the agreement.[27]

---

[26]*The Queen v. Pascoe*, [1975] C.T.C. 656, 75 D.T.C. 5427 (F.C.A.).

[27]*The Queen v. Sills*, [1985] 1 C.T.C. 49, 85 D.T.C. 5096 (F.C.A.).

5. — Child Support

Child support is not deductible by the payer where the payments are made under a written agreement or court order on or after May 1, 1997. Similarly, child support is not taxable to the recipient.[28] Child support means any support the court order or written agreement does not identify as being *solely* for the support of the taxpayer's spouse or former spouse. For example, where an agreement provides for a global support amount for the spouse and children, the entire amount is child support and, therefore, not deductible and not taxable. Similarly, if a court order or written agreement provides for the payment of amounts to a third party, the entire amount is child support if the order or agreement does not clearly specify otherwise.

The term "children" has the same meaning that the term "child" has in other provisions of the Act.[29] For the purposes of paragraphs 56(1)(b) and 60(b), the payer must be the legal parent of a child of the recipient.[30]

Where a payer must make both spousal and child support payments, the presumption is that the payments go first towards child support and then for spousal support. Thus, in the event that the payer defaults, the recipient receives the payments first on a non-taxable basis. The payer cannot deduct any portion on account of spousal support until the payer fully satisfies his or her child support obligations.

6. — Third-Party Payments

It is usual to structure spousal support to make payments tax-deductible to the payer and taxable to the recipient. In most cases, this allows taxpayers to rate-shift and reduce their overall tax obligations. As noted above, payments are deductible if they are paid on a periodic basis by a person to his or her spouse or former spouse. There are circumstances, however, when it is financially prudent to pay some or all of the support payments directly to a third party for the benefit of the spouse or children. Subsection 60.1(1) deems amounts that otherwise qualify for deduction to be deductible even if they are paid directly to a third party. The provision also ensures that the parties can take into account third-party amounts payable for child support in determining the deduction for spousal support.

Third-party support payments are deductible where the payments are:[31]

- Paid pursuant to either a judicial order of a competent tribunal or a written agreement, which stipulates that subsections 56.1(2) and 60.1(2) apply;

---

[28]IT-530R, "Support Payments" (July 17, 2003).

[29]Subs. 252(1).

[30]Subs. 56.1(4)"child support amount".

[31]Subs. 60.1(2).

- For the maintenance of the payer's spouse, former spouse, an individual of the opposite sex who is the legal parent of a child of the taxpayer, and/or children;

- Incurred at a time when the payer and the recipient were living separate and apart; and

- In respect of support expenses incurred either in the year or in the preceding taxation year.

Subsection 60.1(2) deems such payments to be payable on a periodic basis.[32]There are additional requirements if the payment to a third party is in respect of mortgage payments on the family home. In these circumstances a payment is deductible only if:[33]

- The payer does not reside in the family home;

- The payment is not in respect of the purchase of tangible property; and

- The payment for principal and interest is not in excess of 20 per cent of the original amount of the loan incurred to finance the home.

In order for a third-party payment to be deductible, the judicial order or written agreement must *specifically* provide that subsections 60.1(2) and 56.1(2) of the Act apply to the payments. Failure to enumerate the subsections in the terms of settlement disqualifies the payments for deduction. Some courts[34] have blunted the severity of this harsh approach and accepted an oblique reference in the minutes of settlement as sufficient to satisfy the statutory requirement. It is better, however, to specify in the minutes of settlement that the subsections apply.

(a) — Deemed Allowance

The Act *deems* spousal support payments paid to a third party to have been paid as an allowance. Such payments are deductible by the payer and taxable in the hands of the person for whose benefit the payments are made.

Typically, third-party payments are made on account of, for example, medical and dental bills, mortgage payments, tuition fees, household utilities, camp fees and condominium maintenance fees. Of these expenses, mortgage fees, utilities and tangible property associated with medical, dental, or educational requirements can easily be made tax-deductible.

---

[32]See also, IT-530R.

[33]Subs. 60.1(2).

[34]See, e.g., *Cottrell v. M.N.R.*, [1990] 2 C.T.C. 2031, 90 D.T.C. 1581 (T.C.C.) (payments deductible where minutes of settlement referred to payments in issue); *Bishop v. M.N.R.*, [1993] 1 C.T.C. 2333, 93 D.T.C. 333 (T.C.C.) (payment of support arrears to welfare authorities neither taxable nor deductible; payment constituted discharge of indebtedness).

It is less clear, however, whether condominium maintenance expenses (common area charges) paid directly to the condominium corporation are deductible for tax purposes. Expenditures incurred on account of the family home are deductible in respect of the *acquisition* or *improvement* of the home to the extent that they do not exceed 20 per cent of the original cost of financing the home. Condominium fees cannot be considered to qualify as either an acquisition or an improvement cost. Hence, it is generally better to include condominium fees as part of the negotiated allowance that is paid directly to the spouse.

(b) — Prior Payments

Support payments made prior to obtaining a judicial order or entering into a written agreement are also tax-deductible if the order or agreement *specifically* so provides.[35] In effect, the order or agreement can retroactively render the payments deductible even though they were not paid *under* the order or agreement.

III. — Child Care Expenses

Child care is one of the basic functions of family life. Expenses on account of child care have escalated in the last 30 years as more mothers go out of the home to work. Unlike some personal expenses such as food and shelter, which one must incur whether one works or not, child care can have an element of business purpose. If, for example, we assume that the mother is unemployed and cannot work without the child care, then any *incremental* cash outlay for child care that she incurs to work is clearly related to a business purpose. Thus, we can justify the deduction of the incremental expenses of earning a living, as opposed to the basic expenses of just living. This rationale is different from the "but for" test: *but for* the child care expenditure, the parent could not earn income. *Ergo*, the expenditure should be fully deductible for tax purposes. If carried to the extreme, the "but for" line of reasoning extends to justifying virtually any type of personal expenditure as a business expense.

The Act allows a measure of tax relief to parents who incur such expenses so that they may pursue financial gain outside of the home.[36] However, the deduction is strictly controlled. To qualify, the taxpayer must incur the child care expenses to permit one parent (or a supporting person of the child) to pursue employment, business, research or educational activities. The maximum yearly deduction is the least of:

- The amount actually paid for child care;

- 2/3 of the taxpayer's earned income for the year; and

---

[35]Subs. 60.1(3).

[36]S. 63; see also, IT-495R2, "Child Care Expenses" (January 13, 1997).

- $7,000 for each eligible child less than seven years of age and $4,000 for each child between seven and 16 years of age at the end of the year.

In most cases, the deduction for child care expenses is available only to working mothers. Only in extremely rare situations may a father claim a deduction for child care expenses.

1. — Definition of "Child Care Expense"

The Act also defines "child care expense" restrictively. One must satisfy the following additional conditions to qualify an expenditure as a "child care expense":[37]

- The child care services must be provided in Canada;[38]

- The services must be provided by a Canadian resident (other than the child's parents) for whom the taxpayer or his or her spouse does not claim a dependency credit; and

- The person providing the service must not be under 18 years of age if he or she is related to either the taxpayer or his or her spouse.

Advertising expenses, agency placement fees, and transportation expenses to locate, interview or bring to Canada a care-giver also qualify as "child care expenses".

Subsection 63(4) provides another exception to the "in Canada" rule for child care services. Where a taxpayer resides in Canada near the Canada-U.S. border, the child care services may be provided in the United States rather than in Canada. However, the U.S. facility must be closer to the Canadian taxpayer's place of residence by a reasonably accessible route than any place in Canada where such child care services are available. Therefore, assuming these conditions are met, if a Canadian resident pays for child care services at a centre in the U.S. or to an individual in the U.S., the payments are deductible as if the child care was provided in Canada. If the child care is provided by an individual in the U.S., the taxpayer need not provide the individual's social insurance number when claiming the deduction. This exception does not apply to expenses paid for a child to attend a boarding school or camp in the U.S.

---

[37]Subs. 63(3)"child care expense".

[38]However, section 64.1 allows individuals who are absent from Canada, but still resident in Canada for tax purposes, to deduct payments for child care services provided outside of Canada.

2. — Deductible Limits

(a) — Claim by Lower-Income Parent

In two-parent families, child care expenses are generally deductible only by the spouse with the lower income. In exceptional circumstances, the higher-income spouse is entitled to the child care deduction.[39] The parent with the lower income may claim a deduction equal to the lesser of:[40]

- The aggregate of

    - $7,000 multiplied by the number of eligible children under seven years of age (or $10,000 if the child is eligible for disability tax credit) for whom child care expenses have been paid; and

    - $4,000 per other eligible child over 6 and under 16 years of age (or over 15 years of age with physical or mental impairment) for whom child care expenses have been paid; or

- 2/3 of the taxpayer's "earned income" for the year.

(b) — Claim by Higher-Income Parent

The higher-income parent may make a claim for child care expenses, but only if the other parent is:[41]

- In full-time attendance at a designated educational institution;

- Certified in writing by a medical doctor to be either mentally or physically ill and incapable of looking after children;

- Certified in writing by a doctor to be mentally or physically ill to the extent that the person is confined to a bed or wheelchair, or is a patient in a hospital for a period of at least two weeks in the year;

- Imprisoned for at least two weeks in the year; or

- Living apart from the taxpayer for at least 90 days that began in the year by reason of marriage breakdown.

---

[39]Subs. 63(2).

[40]Subs. 63(1).

[41]Para. 63(2)(b).

In these circumstances the amount deductible by the higher-income parent is restricted to the *least* of the following amounts:

- The aggregate of

    - $7,000 per eligible child under seven years of age (or $10,000 if the child is eligible for disability tax credit) for whom child care expenses have been paid; and

    - $4,000 per other eligible child over 6 and under 16 years of age (or over 15 years of age with physical or mental impairment) for whom child care expenses were incurred;

- 2/3 of the taxpayer's "earned income" for the year;

- The number of weeks the taxpayer was eligible to make the claim multiplied by the total periodic child care expenses incurred with respect to an eligible child.

Subsection 63(3) defines "periodic child care expense" to mean 1/40 of the $4,000, $7,000 and $10,000 amounts as $100, $175 and $250 (respectively) weekly.

(c) — Nil Income

In most cases where a husband and wife have child care expenses, the child care expenses are deductible by the spouse with the lower income. The Act deems a taxpayer with no income to have income of zero.[42] This rule effectively prevents the sole breadwinner from claiming child care expenses if only one parent works outside the home.[43]

IV. — Moving Expenses

1. — General Comment

Moving expenses also have a dual flavour of personal and business-related expenditures. In common law, if an employer transferred his or her employee from one location to another and paid the moving expenses, the expenses were deductible to the employer and were not considered income to the employee. An employee could not, however, take a deduction for moving expenses if he or she paid for the move.

---

[42]Para. 3(f).

[43]Para. 3(f) was enacted after court decisions held that where one spouse had no income at all, the spouse with income could deduct the child care expenses since there was only one income. See: *Fiset v. M.N.R.*, [1988] 1 C.T.C. 2335, 88 D.T.C. 1226 (T.C.C.); *McLaren v. M.N.R.*, [1988] 1 C.T.C. 2371, 88 D.T.C. 1259 (T.C.C.); See *Fromstein v. The Queen*, [1993] 2 C.T.C. 2214, 93 D.T.C. 726 (T.C.C.) concerning the same issue, after the enactment of paragraph 3(f).

Mobility of labour is an important and necessary part of the Canadian economy. Labour mobility reduces unemployment and increases productive capacity. Given the size of the country, taxpayers often incur substantial moving expenses in connection with employer-related relocations. The statutory deduction for moving expenses in section 62 recognizes the importance of labour mobility. The deduction also recognizes that employees who pay their own expenses and are not reimbursed by their employers should be placed on an equal footing with self-employed persons who move to a new work location. Thus, the Act generally regards employment-related moving expenses as a cost of earning income and permits the deduction of such expenses, but subject to stringent statutory conditions.

Moving expenses are deductible where the taxpayer:[44]

- Commences employment in Canada;

- Commences business in Canada; or

- Commences full-time studies at a post-secondary educational institution.

Moving expenses may be deducted in the year of the move *or any subsequent year* to the extent that the taxpayer has employment or business income at a new work location against which the moving expenses can be applied.[45]

Moving expenses are not deductible against investment income.[46]

2. — Eligibility for Deduction

An individual who moves to a place in Canada for the purpose of employment or to carry on a business may deduct moving expenses if he or she satisfies three conditions:[47]

1. Both the old residence and the new residence are in Canada;

2. The new residence is at least 40 km closer to the new employment or business location than was the old residence;[48] and

---

[44]See subs. 248(1)"eligible relocation"; see also, IT-178R3, "Moving Expenses" (Consolidated).

[45]*Moodie v. R.*, 2004 TCC 462, [2004] 4 C.T.C. 2329 (T.C.C. [Informal Procedure]).

[46]*Schultz v. The Queen*, [1988] 2 C.T.C. 293, 88 D.T.C. 6468 (F.C.T.D.).

[47]Subs. 62(1); subs. 248(1)"eligible relocation".

[48]*Cameron v. M.N.R.*, [1993] 1 C.T.C. 2745, 93 D.T.C. 437 (T.C.C.) (40 kms is measured "as the crow flies"); *Haines v. M.N.R*, [1984] C.T.C. 2422, 84 D.T.C. 1375 (T.C.C.) (distance to be measured in straight line).

3. The move must be *related to* the commencement of the business, employment or studies.[49]

Students may deduct expenses of moving into or out of Canada. The change in the taxpayer's residence must be by *reason* of the commencement of his or her business, employment, or studies.

3. — Definition of "Moving Expenses"

The Act does not define "moving expenses". Thus, any expenses that fall within the common understanding of "moving expenses" are deductible. One looks at the economic substance of the expenditure to determine whether it constitutes a "moving expense". The following expenditures are specifically included as deductible "moving expenses":[50]

- Travelling costs, including reasonable expenses for meals and lodging, incurred in the course of the move;

- Movers' costs, including storage charges;

- The cost of meals and lodging either near the old residence or near the new residence, for a period not exceeding 15 days;

- The cost of cancelling a lease;

- Selling costs[51] to dispose of the old residence;

- Legal expenses, registration, and land transfer taxes in respect of the acquisition of a new residence in the new location, if the taxpayer sells the old residence;

- Interest, property taxes, insurance premiums, and the cost of heating and utilities in respect of the old residence, to the extent of the lesser of $5,000 and the total of such expenses; and

- The cost of revising legal documents to reflect the address of the new residence, of replacing drivers' licenses and non-commercial vehicle permits, and of connecting or disconnecting utilities.

Expenditures not listed above are also deductible as "moving expenses" if they qualify under the general understanding of that phrase.

---

[49]*Kubryk v. M.N.R.*, [1987] 1 C.T.C. 2125, 87 D.T.C. 75 (T.C.C.).

[50]Subs. 62(3).

[51]*Collin v. M.N.R.*, [1990] 2 C.T.C. 92, 90 D.T.C. 6369 (F.C.T.D.) (lump sum paid by vendor to reduce purchaser's effective mortgage rate constituted "cost of selling property").

The following expenditures are not deductible:[52]

- Expenses reimbursed to the taxpayer by the employer;

- Expenses paid directly by the individual's employer;

- Expenses that are deductible under any other section of the Act;

- Expenses in excess of the individual's income in the year of the move from employment or business at the new location; and

- Where the taxpayer is a student, any expenses in excess of the taxable portion of scholarships, fellowships, bursaries, and research grants.

Moving expenses are generally deductible only in the year in which the move occurs. Expenses in excess of the deductible limit for a year may, however, be carried over and deducted against income in the following year. To be deductible in the year following the move, the expenses must not have been *deductible* in the year in which they were incurred. Thus, deductible moving expenses that are not claimed by the taxpayer in the year of the move are forever lost.[53]

Example

Horace Rumpole graduated from the University of Ottawa in Year 1 and found a job as an accountant in Vancouver. He commenced his job on November 1, Year 1, at a starting salary of $30,000 per year.

As part of his contract of employment, his new employers reimbursed Horace $2,000 to defray the cost of his move to Vancouver.

On October 1, Year 1, Horace moved out of his Ottawa apartment and into a hotel, where he stayed for seven days. As a consequence of his move to Vancouver, Horace incurred the following expenditures:

•	Lease cancellation costs on his apartment in Ottawa	$ 400
•	Hotel and meal expenses in Ottawa and Vancouver 21 days)	2,100
•	Airfare and ground transportation	600

---

[52]Subs. 62(1).

[53]Para. 62(1)(b).

Example

- Movers' charges   3,500
- Storage charges   600
- Legal fees re acquisition of house in Vancouver   1,400
- Airfare for househunting trip in September Year 1 and as-   850
  sociated living costs

Unfortunately for Horace, there was a fire in his mover's premises in Vancouver, where his furniture and belongings were being stored. The storage company did not carry sufficient insurance, and Horace's goods, worth $7,000, were destroyed.

The maximum deduction available to Horace for Year 1 is calculated as follows:

Eligible moving expenses under subsection 62(3):	
Lease cancellation costs	$ 400
15 days hotel and meal expenses	
15/21 × $2,100	1,500
Airfare and ground transportation	600
Movers' charges	3,500
Storage charges	600
	6,600
Reimbursed amount	(2,000)
Net moving expenses	$ 4,600
Income at new job	
2/12 × $30,000	$ 5,000
Maximum deduction	$ 4,600

Note:

1. The legal fees ($1,400) for the acquisition of the new house in Vancouver are not deductible as moving expenses, because the taxpayer did not dispose of a residence at his old location: paragraph 62(3)(f).

2. The "income at new job" limits deductibility of expenses: paragraph 62(1)(c). Horace worked for November and December, Year 1, for 2/12 of his annual salary.

V. — Other Deductions

Other deductions to be found in various sections of the Act or in Income Tax Rulings include the following:

Type of Deduction	Statutory References
Capital element of each annuity payment, if paid under a contract, will or trust	para. 60(a)
Support payments	para. 60(b); IT-530R
Repayment of support payments	para. 60(c.2); IT-530R
Annual interest accruing on succession duties, inheritance taxes or estate taxes	para. 60(d); IT-533
Premium or payment under registered retirement savings plan	para. 60(i); IT-124R6
Transfer of superannuation benefits	para. 60(j); IT-528
Transfer of surplus under a defined benefit provision of a registered pension plan	para. 60(j.01)
Certain payments to registered pension plan	para. 60(j.02)
Repayment under prescribed statutory provision of pension benefits included in income	para. 60(j.03), 60(j.04)
Transfer of retiring allowances	para. 60(j.1); IT-337R4
Transfer to a spousal RRSP	para. 60(j.2)
Transfer of refund of a premium under a registered retirement savings plan	para. 60(l); IT-528
Estate tax applicable to property to which the taxpayer is the successor	para. 60(m)

Type of Deduction	Statutory References
Succession duties payable on property to which the taxpayer is the successor	para. 60(m.1)
Amount of overpayment of pension or benefits received by the taxpayer to the extent repaid by him or her	para. 60(n)
Amount in respect of fees or expenses in the preparation, institution or prosecution of an objection or an appeal regarding certain decisions	para. 60(o); IT-99R5
Amount in respect of legal fees to collect or establish a right to pension benefits	para. 60(o.1); IT-99R5
Refund of income payments in an arm's length transaction	para. 60(q); IT-340R
Repayment in respect of a policy loan under a life insurance policy, to the extent the amount was included in income and not otherwise deductible	para. 60(s)
Certain amount included in income in respect of a retirement compensation arrangement	para. 60(t)
Amount included in income as proceeds from a disposition of an interest in a retirement compensation arrangement	para. 60(u)
Contribution to a provincial pension plan	para. 60(v)
Repayment of unemployment insurance benefit to the extent not otherwise deductible	para. 60(v.1)
Tax on old age security benefits	para. 60(w)
Refund of undeducted additional voluntary contributions to a registered pension plan in respect of services rendered	para. 60.2
Payments made as consideration for an income-averaging annuity contract	subs. 61(1)

Type of Deduction	Statutory References
Moving expenses	s. 62
Child care expenses	s. 63
Disability Supports Deduction	s. 64.1; IT-519R2

Selected Bibliography to Chapter 13

General

Drache, A.B.C., "Charter Offers No Tax Breaks" (1991) 13 Can. Taxpayer 188.

Ross, David W., "Income Tax Consequences of Property Transfers and Payments Made as a Result of Marriage Breakdown and Divorce", in *Proceedings of 41st Tax Conf.* 12:1 (Can. Tax Foundation, 1989).

Support Payments

"Alimony and Maintenance Trusts" (1993) 8 Money and Family Law 81.

Arnold, Brian J., "Income Tax Consequences of Separation and Divorce", in *Proceedings of 29th Tax Conf.* 193 (Can. Tax Foundation, 1977).

Arnold, Brian J., "Tax Aspects of Alimony and Maintenance", 9:7 *Tax Planning and Management of Canadian Income Tax, Revised* (Toronto: Butterworth and Co. (Canada) Ltd., 1975).

Benotto, Mary Lou, "An Income Tax Checklist", (1993) Special Lectures LSUC, 297.

Barnett, Jim, "Alimony and Maintenance Payments" (1979) 112 CA Magazine 65.

Bowman, Stephen W. *et al.*, "The Taxability of Child Support Payments and the Charter of Rights and Freedoms" (1994) 42 Can. Tax J. 907.

Brahmst, Oliver C., "A Definition for the Term 'Spouse': Far-reaching Changes on the Horizons" (1993) 4 Can. Current Tax P1.

Cole, Stephen R. and Andrew J. Freeman, *Property Valuation and Income Tax Implications of Marital Dissolution* (Toronto: Thomson Professional Publishing Canada, 1991).

Coleman, Gene C. and Gary S. Opolsky, "Alimony Insurance Could Be Tax Deductible" (1992) 7 Money and Family Law 36.

Drache, A.B.C., "Post-Marital Trusts" (1984) 6 Can. Taxpayer 15.

Drache, A.B.C., "Reducing Expenses is Not Gaining Income" (1991) 13 Can. Taxpayer 156.

Drache, A.B.C., "Support Payments: All Tax Aspects Should Be Considered" (1991) 13 Can. Taxpayer 160.

Drache, A.B.C., "Tax Act Creates Problems in Joint Custody" (1992) 14 Can. Taxpayer 31.

Durnford, John W. and Stephen J. Trope, "Spousal Support in Family Law and Alimony in the Law of Taxation" (1994) 42 Can. Tax J. 1.

Financial Implications of Child Support Guidelines: Research Report (Ottawa: Department of Justice, Federal/Provincial Territorial Family Law Committee)

Goldstein, D. Lisa, "Until Death Do Us Part" (1991) 39 Can. Tax J. 513.

Goodison, Don, "Taxation of Maintenance Income" (1988) 22 CGA Magazine 18.

Goodison, Don, "Tax Forum — Deduction Denied" (1991) 25 CGA Magazine 17.

Harris, P.H., "Tax Treatment of Civil Litigation and Damage Awards, Alimony and Maintenance Payments" (1985) 6 Advocates' Q. 346.

Income Tax: Maintenance, Alimony and Employment Termination Benefits, Audio Archives of Canada, 1984.

Income Tax and Costs: Setting Aside Separation Agreements: Appeals, Choosing the Right Forum, Audio Archives of Canada, 1984.

Klein, William A., "Tax Effects of Nonpayment of Child Support" (1990) 45 Tax Lawyer 259.

Krishna, V., "Alimony and Maintenance, 'Payable on a Periodic Basis?'; Paragraphs 56(b), (c), (c.1) and 60(b), (c) and (c.1)" (1985), 1 Can. Current Tax J-83.

Krishna, V., "Spousal Payments" (1989) 23 CGA Magazine 44.

Krishna, V., "Structuring Matrimonial Settlements" (1990) 3:3 Can. Current Tax J-19.

Krishna, V., "To Love, Honor or Pay" (1990) 24 CGA Magazine 28.

Krishna, Vern, "Using the Capital Gains Exemption for Matrimonial Settlement" (1993) 4 Can. Current Tax C5.

Kroft, E.G., "Some Income Tax Considerations Relating to Support Payments Made After 1983" (1985) 4 Can. J. Fam. L. 499.

Maisel, Neil and Steve Z. Ranot, "Who Pays the Tax on Tax?" (1992) 7 Money and Family Law 93.

McCue, David J., "Maintenance and Alimony Payments" (1979) 13 CGA Magazine 27.

McGivney, Evelyn L., "Just the Tax Ma'am, Just the Tax!" (1991) 13 Advocates Quarterly 129.

McGregor, Gwyneth, "Alimony and Maintenance Payments" (1983) 5 Can. Taxpayer 169.

Penner, Michael S. and Neil Maisel, "Understanding Capital Gains and the Capital Gains Exemption" (1992) 7 Money and Family Law 9.

Penner, Michael S. and Steve Z. Ranot, "When is Alimony Paid?" (1992) 7 Money and Family Law 65.

Richards, Gabrielle M.R., "Support Payments: An Update" (1992) 3 Can. Current Tax J-115.

Roher, Bruce, "Transferring Shares to a Separated Spouse: Who Pays the Tax?" (1994) 9 Money & Family Law 75.

Sandler, Daniel, "Family Law and the Family Jewels" (1991) 39 Can. Tax J. 513.

Sands, H., and A. Zylberlicht, "The Tax Consequences of Support Payments" (1985) 118:6 CA Magazine 56.

"Second Time Around (The): How Much Does It Cost?", *Can. Tax Letter*, May 10, 1976.

"Sections 60(b) and (c) — A Trap for the Unwary" (1990) 44 D.T.C. 7035.

Sherman, David M., "Till Tax Do Us Part: The New Definition of 'Spouse'" in *Report of Proceedings of 44th Tax Conf.* 20:1 (Canada Tax Foundation, 1992).

Shillington, Robert and Ellen Zweibel, *Child Support Policy: Income Tax Treatment and Child Support Guidelines* (Toronto: Policy Research Centre on Children, Youth and Families, 1993).

Shultz, Clayton G., "Income Tax Law and Policy Applicable to Periodic Maintenance and Division of Matrimonial Assets" (1987) 1 Can. Fam. L.Q. 293.

"Spousal Trust Rollovers" (1990) 44 D.T.C. 7040.

"Taxation of Support Payments Simplified?" (1992) 7 Money and Family Law 75.

"The Written Separation Agreement: Not Quite Dead Yet!" (1993) 18 Money and Family Law 89.

Child Care Expenses

Arnold, B.J., "Section 63: The Deduction for Child Care Expenses" (1973) 21 Can. Tax J. 176.

Bittker, "A Comprehensive Tax Base As A Goal of Income Tax Reform" (1967) 80 Harvard L.R. 925.

Buckley, Melina, "Symes v. The Queen" (1993) 2 National No. 437.

Drache, Arthur B.C., "Child Care Expenses: Planning Leeway" (1983) 5 Can. Taxpayer 3.

Drache, Arthur B.C., "Sexism, Human Rights and Tax" (1979) 1 Can. Taxpayer 114.

Goodison, Don, "Child Care Expenses Deduction" (1988) 22 CGA Magazine 5.

Goodison, Don, "Nanny Means Business" (1989) 23 CGA Magazine 15.

Goodison, Don, "Tax Forum — Not a Business Expense" (1991) 25 CGA Magazine 20.

MacGowan, J.M., "The Tax Consequences of Marriage", in *Proceedings of 26th Tax Conf.* 275 (Can. Tax Foundation, 1974).

McAllister, Debra M., "The Supreme Court in Symes: Two Solitudes" (1994) 4 N.J.C.L. 248.

Young, Claire F.L., "Child Care: A Taxing Issue?" (1994) 39 McGill Law J. 539.

Young, Claire F.L., "Child Care and the Charter: Privileging the Privileged" (1994) 2 Rev. Constit. Studies 20.

Moving Expenses

Finlay, Joe, "Staggered Relocations May Disqualify Moving Expenses" (1991) 49 Advocate 358.

Goodison, Donald, "It's Your Move" (1979) 13 CGA Magazine 16.

Goodison, Donald, "Moving On" (1981) 15 CGA Magazine 37.

Hugget, Donald R., "Moving Employees" (1991) 19 Can. Tax News 44.

"Interest-Free Loans to Employees and Shareholders", Can. Tax Letter, November 10, 1977.

Lemon, K.W., "Tax Considerations Arising from Household Relocation" (1981) 46 Bus. Q. 86.

"On the Move?" (1979) 1 Can. Taxpayer 96.

"Reimbursement of Moving Expenses for Same City Move Could Be Tax Free" (1992) 4 Tax. of Exec. Comp. and Retirement 667.

Schnek, M., "Employee Relocation" (1981) 29 Can. Tax J. 71.

"Student Moving Expenses" (1983) 5 Can. Taxpayer 151.

Thomas, Richard B., "A Hole That You Could Drive a Moving Van Through" (1990) 38 Can. Tax J. 937.

Other Deductions

Beach, Wayne G., "Tax Aspects of Registered Retirement Savings Plans", 9:30 *Tax Planning and Management of Canadian Income Tax, Revised* (Toronto: Butterworth and Co. (Canada) Ltd., 1978).

Boyle, "The Treatment of RRSP Proceeds on Maturity" (1979) 27 Can. Tax J. 68.

Budd, John S., "Two Unlikely Havens from Capital Gains Tax" (1979) 112 CA Magazine 70.

Clare, James L., and Paul F. Della Penna, "Tax Aspects of Employee's Pension Plans", 9:28 *Tax Planning and Management of Canadian Income Tax, Revised* (Toronto: Butterworths and Co. (Canada) Ltd., 1977).

Colley, Geoffrey M., "What's New in Personal Investment" (1977) 110 CA Magazine 63.

Connors, Raymond J., "DPSPs — The Ideal Tax Shelter for Employers and Employees" (1982) 115:2 CA Magazine 50.

Dancey, Kevin J., "Specific Expenditures: Timing and Deductibility", Corp. Mgmt. Tax Conf. 116 (Can. Tax Foundation, 1981).

Drache, Arthur B.C., "Estate Planning: Depreciable Property" (1980) 2 Can. Taxpayer 22.

Drache, Arthur B.C., "Religious School Decision" (1981) 3 Can. Taxpayer 33.

Drache, Arthur B.C., "Single Premium Deferred Annuities" (1981) 3 Can. Taxpayer 27.

Drache, Arthur B.C., "Tax Planning for Higher Education" (1981) 3 Can. Taxpayer 44.

Drache, Arthur B.C., "Tuition Fee Deductibility" (1980) 2 Can. Taxpayer 208.

Eng, Susan, and Goodman, "Education Trusts and Other Provisions for Education Expenses" (1979–81) 5 E. & T.Q. 246.

Farres, Alan E., "RRSPs: The Tax Shelter That Wasn't Meant To Be" (1982) 115:4 CA Magazine 48.

Finkelstein, David N., "Tax Problems in Estate Planning for the Corporate Executive", in *Proceedings of 33rd Tax Conf.* 952 (Can. Tax Foundation, 1981).

Fisher, G.B., "Early Retirement Tax Considerations" (1983) 31 Can. Tax J. 828.

Griffith, Thomas D., "Theories of Personal Deductions in Income Tax" (January 1989) 40 Hastings L. J. 343.

Jarman, Robert E., "Administrative and Tax Problems with Self-Administered RRSP's" (1975) 2 E. & T.Q. 105.

Knechtel, Ronald C., "Federal Income Taxation of Life Insurance Policyholders under the Present Law and under the Current Proposals", in *Proceedings of 29th Tax Conf.* 612 (Can. Tax Foundation, 1977).

Krishna, V., "Registered Retirement Savings Plans (RRSP's) — Availability of Funds for Judgment Creditors" (1984) 1 Can. Current Tax J-43.

Lengvari, George F., "Deferred Annuities as Tax Shelters" (1978) 111 CA Magazine 90.

Le Rossignol, Dan G., "Stock Dividends and Stock Options" (1979) 112 CA Magazine 67.

MacNaughton, Alan, "New Income Tax Rules for Holders of Life Insurance Policies and Annuities" (1983) 31 Can. Tax J. 921.

McGregor, Gwyneth, "Forward Averaging" (1983) 5 Can. Taxpayer 7.

McReynolds, D. Shawn, "Sheltering RRSP Assets from Creditors on Death" (1982–84) 6 E. & T.Q. 106.

Murray, L.C., "Statutory Deferred Income Plans", *Corp. Mgmt. Tax Conf.* Management Tax Conf. 121 (Can. Tax Foundation, 1979).

"1979 Year-End Planning for Individuals", Can. Tax Letter, November 30, 1979.

Rea, Samuel A., "Registered Retirement Savings Plans as a Tax Expenditure" (1980) 28 Can. Tax J. 459.

Schmidt, Rosemary, "Students and Taxation" (1991) 39 Can. Tax J. 673.

Young, Clair F.L., "Deductibility of Entertainment and Home Office Expenses: New Restrictions To Deal with Old Problems?" (1989) 37 Can. Tax J. 227.

PART VIII: INCOME ASSIGNMENT & ATTRIBUTION

CHAPTER 14 — ASSIGNMENT AND ATTRIBUTION OF INCOME

I. — General Comment

Although a taxpayer considers his or her immediate family (spouse and minor children) as an economic unit, the general rule in income tax law is that each individual member of the family is a separate taxpayer. Each individual has an independent status and is liable for tax on his or her personal income. Each spouse and each of their children are responsible for their own taxes.

The Act uses a broad concept of spouse to include common-law partners and same-sex married relationships.[1]

The individual income tax structure is progressive.[2] This means that as an individual receives more income, his or her taxes increase at a progressive rate. Additional increments to income are taxable at higher marginal rates than their predecessors. This means that a family whose income is taxed to only one member (for example, the mother) will pay higher taxes than another family with an identical income that is taxable to two members — say, the father and mother. Thus, high-income taxpayers have an incentive to reduce their taxes by shifting income to members of their family in lower tax brackets. The more that one can sprinkle income amongst family members, the lower the overall family taxes. Thus, two

---

[1] See subs. 248(1)"common-law partner."

[2] See s. 117.

gross incomes of $100,000 each are much more valuable in after-tax terms than one gross income of $200,000.

The following table is an example of the tax payable at various levels of taxable income. The progressive structure of the income tax system shows the tax savings from income splitting. For example, taxable income of $200,000 split equally four ways in a family would reduce the total tax bill by $21,129 for a saving of 28 per cent.

Taxable Income Per Individual	Tax Payable Per Individual	Multiplier (No. of Individuals)	Total Tax Payable	Percentage Saving
$200,000	$74,529	1	$74,529	
$100,000	$31,650	2	$63,300	18%
$ 50,000	$13,350	4	$53,400	28%

Notes:

Assumes: (1) that the federal tax rate is 16% on the first $35,000, 22% on income between $35,000–$70,000, 26% on income between $70,000–$113,804, and 29% above $113,804; and (2) that the provincial rate is approximately 50% of the federal tax payable.

Potential savings of this magnitude are a powerful inducement to shift income from high marginal rate taxpayers to lower marginal rates. For example, a father with income of $200,000 and a marginal tax rate of 50 per cent might transfer part of his portfolio of securities to his minor daughter to reduce his investment income and potential future capital gains. If his daughter's tax rate is only 15 per cent, he saves 35 percentage points of tax. The problem is exacerbated if the father can retrieve the securities at any time from his daughter and have title revert to him.

Professionals and entrepreneurs can also split business income through a corporation. For example, an individual can incorporate a company and have it issue different classes of shares to each member of his or her family. The corporation can then sprinkle dividends amongst the family members according to their financial circumstances. For example:

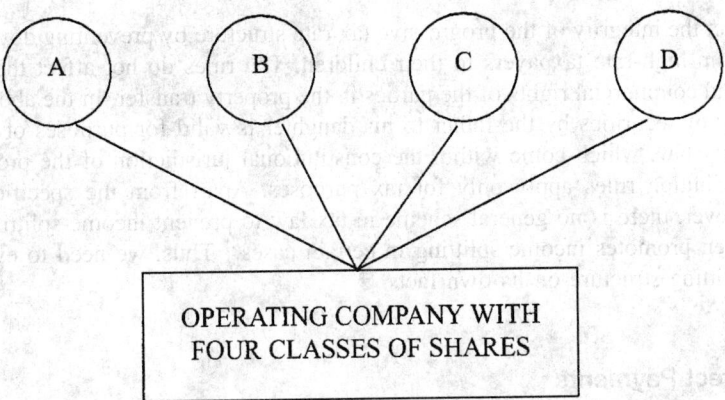

OPERATING COMPANY WITH
FOUR CLASSES OF SHARES

Dividend-sprinkling would reduce each family member's marginal rate of tax and the overall family tax burden.

In a slightly more sophisticated variation one might interpose a trust between the corporation and each member of the family and have the trustee sprinkle the dividends according to each member's financial circumstances. For example:

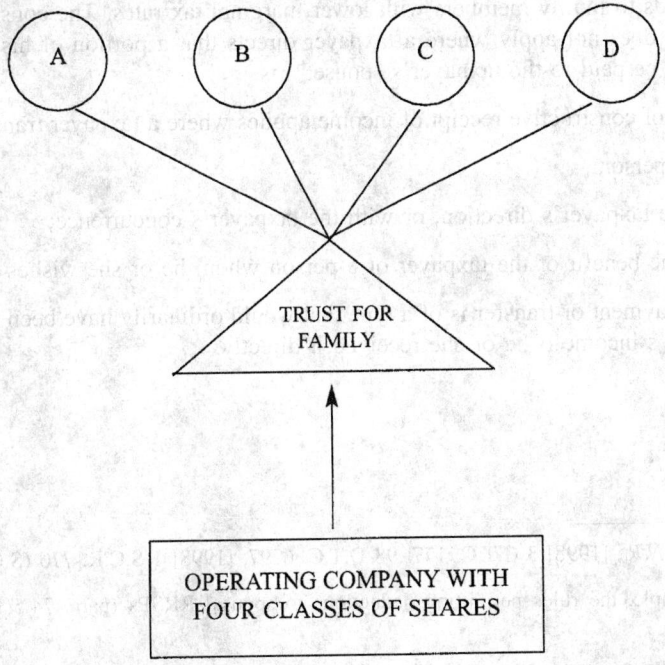

TRUST FOR
FAMILY

OPERATING COMPANY WITH
FOUR CLASSES OF SHARES

The Act contains various specific attribution rules that prevent certain forms of income-splitting amongst the immediate family and in certain non-arm's length relationships. These rules protect the integrity of the progressive tax rate structure by preventing downward rate-shifting from high-rate taxpayers to their children. The rules do not affect the underlying property and commercial rights of the parties in the property transfer. In the above example, the transfer of securities by the father to his daughter is valid for purposes of commercial and property law, which come within the constitutional jurisdiction of the provinces. The federal attribution rules apply only for tax purposes. Apart from the specific attribution rules, however, there is no general scheme in tax law to prevent income-splitting.[3] Indeed, the Act even promotes income-splitting in certain cases.[4] Thus, we need to evaluate each income-splitting structure on its own facts.

II. — Indirect Payments

A taxpayer who transfers income or property to another taxpayer may be deemed to have constructively received the diverted income or property.[5] For example, an individual who directs his employer to deposit his pay cheque directly into his spouse's savings account is liable for tax on the salary, even though the taxpayer relinquishes actual ownership and control over the property. For tax purposes, the taxpayer retains constructive ownership of the property. This rule prevents taxpayers from artificially reducing their taxable income by diverting funds to family members with lower marginal tax rates. The constructive owner-ship doctrine does not apply where a taxpayer directs that a portion of his or her Canada Pension Plan be paid to the taxpayer's spouse.[6]

The doctrine of constructive receipt of income applies where a taxpayer transfers property:[7]

1. To a person;

2. At the taxpayer's direction, or with the taxpayer's concurrence;

3. For the benefit of the taxpayer or a person whom he or she wishes to benefit, *and*

4. The payment or transfer is of a type that would ordinarily have been included in the taxpayer's income if he or she received it directly.

---

[3]*Neuman v. M.N.R.*, [1998] 3 C.T.C. 177, 98 D.T.C. 6297, [1998] 1 S.C.R. 770 (S.C.C.).

[4]See, for example, the rules permitting deductions to spousal RRSPs (para. 74.5(12)(a) and subs. 146(5.1)).

[5]Subs. 56(2); see also IT-335R2, "Indirect Payments" (September 11, 1989).

[6]Including a prescribed provincial pension plan (see regulation 7800).

[7]Subs. 56(2). IT-335R2, "Indirect Payments" (September 11, 1989).

In these circumstances the Act deems the transferor to receive the payment or transfer directly.[8]

The doctrine does not normally apply to corporate dividends. Directors of a corporation who declare a dividend do so in their capacity as directors and fiduciaries. The fourth condition requires that the taxpayer would have received the dividend if it had not been paid to the shareholder of record. An unpaid dividend remains in the corporation's retained earnings if it is not paid to the shareholder of record. Thus, subsection 56(2) cannot apply to dividends if the fourth test is not satisfied.[9] In a closely held family corporation, for example, dividends to the taxpayer's spouse on his or her shareholdings do not come within the doctrine of constructive receipt. This is so even if the taxpayer waives his or her right to receive a dividend, because the waived dividend merely remains in the corporation's retained earnings. The situation is different, however, if the shareholder of record directs the corporation to pay his or her dividend to another person.

---

[8]*Neuman v. M.N.R.*, [1998] 1 S.C.R. 770, [1998] 3 C.T.C. 177, 98 D.T.C. 6297 (S.C.C.); *McClurg v. M.N.R.*, [1990] 3 S.C.R. 1020, [1991] 1 C.T.C. 169, 91 D.T.C. 5001 (S.C.C.) (income not attributed to director of corporation for participating in declaration of corporate dividend); *Boardman v. The Queen*, [1986] 1 C.T.C. 103, 85 D.T.C. 5628 (F.C.T.D.) (shareholder taxable on diversion of corporate assets to settle financial obligations on divorce); *M.N.R. v. Bronfman*, [1965] C.T.C. 378, 65 D.T.C. 5235 (Ex. Ct.) (directors of corporation liable for taxes on account of gifts to relatives in need of financial assistance; combining subss. 15(1) and 56(2)); *Reininger v. M.N.R.*, 58 D.T.C. 608 (corporate loan to wife of principal shareholder taxable to him under subss. 15(2) and 56(2)); *Perrault v. The Queen*, [1978] C.T.C. 395, 78 D.T.C. 6272 (F.C.A.) (waiver of dividend by majority shareholder in favour of minority shareholder was dividend income); *New v. M.N.R.*, [1970] Tax A.B.C. 700, 70 D.T.C. 1415 (T.A.B.) (controlling shareholder in receipt of income for benefit conferred on son through rental of corporate property to son at less than fair market value).

[9]*Neuman v. M.N.R.*, [1998] 1 S.C.R. 770, [1998] 3 C.T.C. 177, 98 D.T.C. 6297 (S.C.C.) (dividends paid to controlling shareholder's spouse not taxable in his hands despite absence of any "contribution" by spouse). *The Queen v. McClurg*, [1988] 1 C.T.C. 75, 88 D.T.C. 6047 (F.C.A.); affd. [1991] 1 C.T.C. 169, 91 D.T.C. 5001 (S.C.C.), *per* Urie J.:

> The language of the subsection [56(2)] creating the essential ingredients required in its application, viewed in light of its purpose, is simply not apt, in my opinion, to encompass the acts of a director when he participates in the declaration of a corporate dividend unless it is read in its most literal sense. To do so ignores the existence of the corporate entity. Only the most explicit language, which is not present in subs. 56(2), would justify the notion that a director acting as such could be seen as directing a corporation to divert a transfer or payment for his own benefit or the benefit of another person, absent bad faith, breach of fiduciary duty or acting beyond the powers conferred by the share structure of the corporation, none of which bases have been alleged here.

See also: Vern Krishna and J. Anthony VanDuzer, "Corporate Share Capital Structures and Income Splitting: *McClurg v. Canada*" (1992-93), 21 Can. Bus. L.J. 335 at 367.

Subsections 56(2), (4) and (4.1) do not apply in respect of amounts included in a minor's split income. Thus, amounts taxed as split income in the hands of a minor child are not also attributable to another person.[10]

1. — Transfers of Rights to Income

The doctrine of constructive receipt also applies where a taxpayer transfers *rights to receive income* (as opposed to the income itself) to another individual.[11] The essence of this type of transfer is that the individual transfers the right to all future income but not the ownership of the income-generating property. Thus, the transferee then owns the *right to all future income or revenues* that the property may yield, but does not own the property itself.

2. — Interest-Free or Low-Interest Loan

A taxpayer can also shift his or her tax burden by loaning money at rates lower than the commercial rate of interest. For example, in the simplest case, an individual can make an interest-free loan. Where the purpose of the loan is to reduce or avoid tax in a non-arm's length transaction, the Act deems the borrower's income from the loan to be the income of the lender.[12] Any income from property substituted for the loan, and income from property purchased with the loan, is also included in the lender's income.

Example
Jane loans $50,000 to her spouse who earns 10 per cent by depositing the money in a GIC. Jane is taxable on the $5,000 interest income for the year.
Mark loans $100,000 to his niece at 5 per cent interest per year. The niece purchases an investment certificate yielding 8 per cent per year. Mark is taxable on the *net* income of $3,000 from the investment certificate.

3. — Transfers/Loans to Spouse

An individual who transfers or loans property, directly or indirectly, to a spouse, or to a person who becomes a spouse after the transfer or loan of property, is taxable on any income from the property or from any property substituted for the transferred property. The Act attributes any income or loss from the property to the transferor during his or her lifetime if

---

[10]Subs. 56(5).

[11]Subs. 56(4).

[12]Subs. 56(4.1).

the transferor resides in Canada and lives with his or her spouse.[13] The transferor is also taxable on any taxable capital gains or allowable capital losses from dispositions of the transferred or loaned property.[14] Thus, in both cases, the Act deems the transferor to have constructively received the transferred income (loss) or taxable gain (loss). These rules apply only to income and losses from *property*, and do not apply to income and losses from a business.[15]

The attribution rules do not apply if the spouses are living separate and apart by reason of a breakdown of their marriage.[16] In the case of capital gains, however, the parties must file a joint election not to have the rules apply. Similarly, the attribution rules in respect of transfers to corporations (other than small business corporations)[17] in which a spouse has a direct or indirect interest generally do not apply to the period during which the spouses are living separate and apart by reason of a breakdown of their marriage.[18]

4. — *Transfers/Loans to Persons Under 18 Years of Age*

An individual who transfers or loans property to a person under 18 years of age who is the transferor's niece or nephew or does not deal at arm's length with the transferor, is taxable

---

[13]Subs. 74.1(1). *The Queen v. Kieboom*, [1992] 2 C.T.C. 59, 92 D.T.C. 6382 (F.C.A.) (income from taxpayer's gift of non-voting shares to wife and children subject to attribution).

[14]Subs. 74.2(1).

[15]See *Robins v. M.N.R.*, [1963] C.T.C. 27, 63 D.T.C. 1012 (Ex. Ct.) where Noel J. had this to say about the predecessor sections to s. 74.1:

> Section 21 as well as Sections 22 and 23 are designed to prevent avoidance of tax by transfer of income producing property to persons who are normally in close relationship with the transferor. But what is deemed to be the income of the transferor, and this is clearly stated, is income from property only. Indeed there is no mention of income from a business such as we have here and, therefore, this section can be of no assistance in determining whether the business profit resulting from a real estate transaction is taxable as income of the appellant or of his wife.

See, also, *Wertman v. M.N.R.*, [1964] C.T.C. 252, 64 D.T.C. 5158 (Ex. Ct.) (spouses' joint investment in building with funds from community property); *M.N.R. v. Minden*, [1963] C.T.C. 364, 63 D.T.C. 1231 (Ex. Ct.) (lawyer advanced money to spouse for investments without documentation, interest or security). For the distinction between income from business and income from property see Chapter 7 "The Meaning of Business Income, Investment Income, and Capital Gains".

[16]Para. 74.5(3)(a).

[17]Para. 74.4(2)(c).

[18]Subs. 74.5(4).

on any income earned on the property.[19] Thus, income and losses realised by the recipient of the transferred property are attributed to the person who transferred or loaned the property.

III. — Non-Arm's Length Loans

The two rules discussed above (loans and transfers to spouses and to certain persons under 18 years of age) prevent taxpayers from engaging in the more blatant forms of income-splitting.

There is, however, an additional rule that is even broader: income from any property (for example, money) loaned to a non-arm's length borrower may be attributed and taxed to the lender if one of the main purposes of the loan is to reduce or avoid tax, for example, by income-splitting.[20] This rule is considerably broader in scope than the more specific attribution rules in that it applies to low-cost or interest-free loans to any individual with whom the lender does not deal at arm's length. This rule does not apply to transfers of property; it only applies to loaned property.

Unlike the more specific attribution rules, the non-arm's length rule applies only if the lender loans the property for the purposes of reducing or avoiding tax on income that he or she would otherwise have earned on the property. There is no attribution of income if the lender does not lend the money for the purposes of tax reduction or avoidance (for example, a loan to a relative or friend for altruistic reasons). Further, the attribution rules do not apply to loans at "commercial" rates of interest if the borrower pays the interest no later than 30 days after the end of the taxation year in which the interest is due.[21]

IV. — Interpretation And Application

The following aspects of the attribution rules warrant particular attention:

- The term "transfer" includes any divestiture of property from one person to another and includes gifts. In *Fasken Estate*, for example, the courts said:[22]

   > ... the word 'transfer' is not a form of art and has not a technical meaning. It is not necessary to a transfer of property from a husband to his wife that it should be made in any particular form or that it should be made directly. All that is required is that the

---

[19]Subs. 74.1(2).

[20]Subs. 56(4.1).

[21]Subs. 56(4.2). The Act prescribes the appropriate rate of interest each quarter according to commercial market rates (Reg. 4301).

[22]*Fasken Estate v. M.N.R.*, [1948] C.T.C. 265 at 279, 49 D.T.C. 491 at 497 (Ex. Ct.); see also *St. Aubyn v. A.G.*, [1952] A.C. 15 at 53 (H.L.), *per* Lord Radcliffe:

husband should so deal with the property as to divest himself of it and vest it in his wife, that is to say, pass the property from himself to her. The means by which he accomplishes this result, whether direct or circuitous, may properly be called a transfer.

- The attribution applies to income and losses from *property*, and not to income and losses from a business.[23]

- The attribution rules do not generally apply to sales at fair market value if the purchaser pays the vendor for the property.[24]

- The attribution rules apply to loans, other than loans that bear a commercial rate of interest. A loan is considered to bear a commercial rate of interest if the rate charged is at least equal to the prescribed rate or the arm's length market rate.[25]

- In the case of a transfer or loan to a person under the age of 18, income attribution continues until the person reaches 18 years of age.

- The attribution rules do not apply to a parent (or other transferor) on amounts that the Act taxes as split income[26] in the hands of a minor child.[27]

If the word "transfer" is taken in its primary sense, a person makes a transfer of property to another person if he does the act or executes the instrument which divests him of the property and at the same time vests it in that other person.

[23]See *Robins v. M.N.R.*, [1963] C.T.C. 27, 63 D.T.C. 1012 (Ex. Ct.) where Noel J. said the following about the predecessor sections to s. 74.1:

Section 21 as well as Sections 22 and 23 are designed to prevent avoidance of tax by transfer of income producing property to persons who are normally in close relationship with the transferor. But what is deemed to be the income of the transferor, and this is clearly stated, is income from property only. Indeed, there is no mention of income from a business such as we have here and, therefore, this section can be of no assistance in determining whether the business profit resulting from a real estate transaction is taxable as income of the appellant or his wife.

See, also, *Wertman v. M.N.R.*, [1964] C.T.C. 252, 64 D.T.C. 5158 (Ex. Ct.) (spouses' joint investment in building with funds from community property); *M.N.R. v. Minden*, [1963] C.T.C. 364, 63 D.T.C. 1231 (Ex. Ct.) (lawyer advanced money to spouse for investments without documentation, interest or security). For the distinction between income from business and income from property see Chapter 7, "The Meaning of Business Income, Investment Income, and Capital Gains".

[24]Subs. 74.5(1).

[25]Subs. 74.5(2).

[26]S. 120.4.

[27]Subs. 74.5(13).

- The liability for tax from the application of the attribution rules is joint and several.[28]

- The income attribution rules apply to spouses only during the period that they are married *and* living together. The rules do not apply upon divorce or separation by reason of matrimonial breakdown.[29]

- There is no attribution of capital gains and losses following divorce or separation pursuant to matrimonial breakdown[30] if the parties file a joint election precluding attribution. The parties may file the election in the year after they begin to live separate and apart.

V. — The "Kiddie Tax"

Although the attribution rules apply to transfers of property to minor children, they do not prevent income-splitting between family members. Since dividends are eligible for the dividend tax credit, minor children could avoid paying tax on approximately $23,000 of any income that they received as dividends. In these circumstances, the dividend tax credit would wipe out any tax payable on the income. Thus, a family with three minor children could, for example, pay no tax on $69,000 of dividend income in the year.

The "kiddie tax" prevents income-splitting with minor children under 18 years of age. The "kiddie tax" is a special 29 per cent tax that applies to certain forms of passive income of individuals under the age of 18 years. Generally, the tax applies to:[31]

- Taxable dividends and other shareholder benefits[32] on unlisted shares of Canadian and foreign companies; and

- Income from a partnership or trust where the partnership or trust derives the income from the business of providing goods or services to a business that a relative of the child carries on or in which the relative participates.

Twenty-nine per cent is the highest rate of federal tax and it applies at a flat rate. This tax prevents some of the more blatant forms of income-splitting.[33] Any income that is taxable as "split income" is deductible from the individual's income from business or property for the

---

[28]Para. 160(1)(d).

[29]Para. 74.5(3)(a).

[30]Para. 74.5(3)(b).

[31]S. 120.4.

[32]See s. 15.

[33]See, for example, *Ferrel v. Canada*, [1999] 2 C.T.C. 101, 99 D.T.C. 5111 (F.C.A.).

year. Hence, the regular income tax does not apply to any portion of the split income. Liability for the tax is joint and several.[34]

The only amounts deductible from the tax are the dividend tax credit and the foreign tax credit in respect of amounts that the minor includes in his or her split income. Thus, the tax has a substantial bite in that it effectively applies to gross income at the highest marginal tax rate.

The "kiddie tax" does not apply to:

- Income paid to individuals over 18 years of age;

- Reasonable remuneration to minors;

- Capital gains; or

- Interest income.

Thus, income-splitting is still permissible unless the Act specifically prohibits it in particular circumstances. For example, income-splitting with spouses is not caught by the above rules.

VI. — Transfers And Loans To Corporations

In certain circumstances, an individual who transfers or loans property to a corporation may be taxable on investment income attributed to the individual on account of the transfer or loan. In the case of equity investments, the Act attributes to the transferor 5/4ths of any dividends that he or she receives on shares issued for the transfer. In the case of a loan, the amount attributed is the amount by which interest at the prescribed rate on the loan exceeds the total of any interest that he or she actually receives on the loan. In both cases, the attribution rules apply only if one of the main purposes of the transfer is to reduce the transferor's income and benefit a person who is his spouse, common-law partner, a related person under 18 years of age, or niece or nephew.[35]

These attribution rules do not apply if the transferee corporation is a small business corporation. This is an important exclusion that allows income-splitting in many cases. A small business corporation[36] is a Canadian-controlled private corporation that uses all or substantially all of its assets in an "active business"[37] that it carries on primarily in Canada. A corporation also qualifies as a small business corporation if a related corporation uses the assets in an active business in Canada.

---

[34]Subs. 160(1.2).

[35]Subs. 74.5(5).

[36]Subs. 248(1)"small business corporation".

[37]Subs. 125(7)"active business carried on by a corporation".

CRA interprets the phrase "all or substantially all" as 90 per cent of the corporation's assets. Hence, if a corporation permanently uses more than 10 per cent of its total assets for investment purposes, it does not qualify as a small business corporation. The Agency also interprets "primarily" as being more than 50 per cent in respect of the business.

VII. — Artificial Transactions

Taxpayers can sometimes structure transactions to take advantage of the attribution rules and "reverse attribution". For example, an individual might guarantee his or her high-income spouse's borrowing from a bank and argue that the income from the borrowed funds is attributable to the individual.[38] Subsection 74.5(11) is an anti-avoidance provision that prevents the attribution rules from applying if "one of the main reasons" for the transfer or loan is to reduce the tax payable on income or gains from loaned or transferred property.

---

[38]See subs. 74.5(7).

Selected Bibliography to Chapter 14

Indirect Payments

Davidson, A. Barrie, "Personal Service and Professional Corporations Incorporating Employment and Professional Income", in *Proceedings of 32nd Tax Conf.* 212 (Can. Tax Foundation, 1980).

Desaulniers, Claude P., "Choix d'une structure du capital", *J. d'études fiscales* 79 (Can. Tax Foundation, 1981).

Drache, A.B.C., "Controlling a Company Without Shares" (1992) 14 Can. Taxpayer 56.

Drache, A.B.C., "Gifting Without a Transfer" (1991) 13 Can. Taxpayer 164.

Drache, A.B.C., "Income Splitting 'Loophole' Closed" (1992) 14 Can. Taxpayer 21.

Drache, A.B.C., "McClurg Obiter Creates Problems" (1992) 14 Can. Taxpayer 47.

Drache, A.B.C., "Technical Hitches Ruin Income Split" (1991) 13 Can. Taxpayer 62.

"Estate Planning Time Bomb" (1983) 5 Can. Taxpayer 42.

Grafton, S., "Income-Splitting" (1985) 13 Can. Tax News 88.

Graschuk, Harry S., "The Professional Corporation in Alberta" (1977) 25 Can. Tax J. 109.

Harris, Neil H., "Tax Aspects of Condominium Conversions and Lease Inducement Payments to Recipients", in *Proceedings of 38th Tax Conf.* 45 (Can. Tax Foundation, 1986).

Innes, William I., "The Taxation of Indirect Benefits: An Examination of Subsections 56(2), 56(3), 56(4), 245(2) and 245(3) of the *Income Tax Act*", in *Proceedings of 38th Tax Conf.* 42 (Can. Tax Foundation, 1986).

Krishna, Vern, "Corporate Share Capital Structures and Income Splitting" (1991) 3 Can. Current Tax C-71.

Krishna, Vern, "Corporate Share Structures and Estate Planning" (1983) 6 E. & T.Q. 168.

Krishna, Vern, "Designing Share Capital Structures for Income Splitting" (1984) 1 Can. Current Tax C-51.

Krishna, Vern, "Indirect Payments and Transfer of Income" (1986) 1 Can. Current Tax J-137.

Kroft, E.G., "Income Splitting" (1983) 17 CGA Magazine 28.

Kwan, Stanley P.W., and Kenneth J. Murray, "Remuneration Planning for the Owner-Manager" (1982) 29 Can. Tax J. 603.

Levine, Risa, "Incorporation and the Taxation of a Private Corporation", *British Columbia Tax Conf.* 1 (Can. Tax Foundation, 1980).

Zaytsoff, J.J., "Accountant's Comment: Innovative Share Capital Structures to Split Income Effectively" (1984) 42 Advocate (Van.) 177.

Non-Arm's Length Loans

Brahmst, Oliver C., "Beware of the Breadth of Subsection 56(4.1)" (1991) 3 Can. Current Tax P-43.

Brahmst, Oliver C., "Subsection 56(4.1) — An Update" (1992) 3 Can. Current Tax P-47.

Drache, A.B.C., "Income Splitting Needs Advance Planning" (1991) 13 Can. Taxpayer 181.

Drache, A.B.C., "Income Splitting Through Lending" (1991) 13 Can. Taxpayer 174.

PART IX: FROM INCOME TO TAX

CHAPTER 15 — TAXABLE INCOME

I. — General Comment

To this point, we have looked at the rules for calculating net income. Now, we look at the rules that determine "taxable income".[1] In the next chapter we will review the computation of tax payable.

A taxpayer is taxable on his or her taxable income. Canadian residents are taxable on their *worldwide taxable income* for the year.[2] Subject to treaty provisions, non-residents are taxable only on their Canadian source taxable income during a taxation year.[3]

There are two particularly controversial issues in designing an appropriate structure to determine the taxable base:

1. What relief, if any, should we provide for individual and personal circumstances?

2. Should the relief take the form of a deduction from income or a credit against taxes payable?

---

[1]Subs. 2(2); Div. C (ss. 110–114.2).

[2]Subs. 2(1).

[3]Subs. 2(3). A non-resident's taxable income is determined by reference to the rules in Div. D (ss. 115-116).

1. — "Taxable Income"

"Taxable income" is simply a mathematical measure of the taxable base. A resident's "taxable income" is his or her net income plus or minus the adjustments and deductions in Division C. Thus, "taxable income" is the mathematical residue of net income adjusted by various items contained in Division C.

We saw in Chapter 4 that income is the measure of a taxpayer's net realized gains attributable to a source recognized in law. Income, which for tax purposes represents the net realized increment to wealth, is not, however, always the most appropriate measure of a taxpayer's ability to pay tax, because it does not take into account personal and individual circumstances. In this chapter we look at some of the adjustments that the tax system makes for individual circumstances. We also see, once again, how we use the system to engineer behaviour by providing incentives for particular behaviour, for example, charitable giving.

Taxable income is a better and fairer measure of a taxpayer's ability to pay tax. In the case of individuals, for example, it is easy to see that taxpayers who have the same amount of net income do not necessarily have equal amounts of disposable income with which to pay their tax. For example, consider two individuals, each of whom earns $50,000: an unmarried person with no dependants and a married person with a family of six, one of whom is seriously ill and requires expensive medication. It is clear that these two individuals have different abilities to pay tax. Should we allow the individual with substantial financial responsibilities a measure of tax relief to ease the burden of his or her responsibilities? Should the amount of relief be related to the taxpayer's income, or should it be determined as a blanket amount regardless of the particular circumstances? If relief is income-tested, should we test by reference to the individual's income or his or her family income? How do we determine "family" for the purposes of income testing? These questions raise difficult and, sometimes, controversial issues for which we do not have absolute answers.

The adjustments in Division C are of three types: (1) those available only to individuals; (2) those available only to corporations; and (3) those available to both individuals and corporations.

2. — Deduction or Credit?

Should we provide relief for persons in different financial circumstances through tax deductions or tax credits? A tax deduction is a deduction from income in computing taxable income. We measure the saving that results from a deduction by multiplying the deduction by the taxpayer's marginal tax rate. For example, a deduction of $1,000 reduces tax by $450 if the taxpayer's marginal rate is 45 per cent, and by $300 if the tax rate is 30 per cent. Thus, the higher the marginal tax rate, the more valuable the deduction to the taxpayer and the greater the revenue loss to the public treasury. We use deductions in the measurement of income to determine the net increment to wealth.

A tax credit also reduces the tax that would otherwise be payable. The savings resulting from a tax credit, however, are constant, regardless of the taxpayer's marginal tax rate. For example, a tax credit of $500 reduces tax by that amount, no matter whether the taxpayer's marginal tax rate is 45 per cent or 30 per cent. Hence, tax credits have a more equal distributive impact. However, generally a tax credit is of value only to those taxpayers who would otherwise have to pay tax. Most tax credits do not assist a taxpayer who does not have any tax payable.[4] We tend to use tax credits to accommodate personal circumstances that might affect a taxpayer's ability to pay tax.

We subtract a tax credit directly from the amount of tax payable, rather than from income. Thus, each individual achieves the same saving regardless of his or her income level or marginal tax rate. For example, the basic tax credit applies to all individuals regardless of their income level. Hence, a person earning $100,000 per year receives the same basic credit as a person earning $8,000 per year.

II. — Charitable Donations

1. — General Comment

The tax system provides financial incentives for taxpayers, particularly high-income taxpayers, who contribute to charitable, philanthropic, and public service organizations. These incentives encourage private financial support of philanthropic activities that are beneficial to the community. We justify the incentives on the basis of social policy, but they have a substantial cost to the federal and provincial treasuries, and, therefore, require strict control.

The nature and extent of the incentives depend upon two criteria: (1) the type of taxpayer, and (2) the dollar amount contributed.

2. — Individuals

An individual can claim a tax credit for charitable donations. The rate at which he or she may claim the credit depends upon the amount donated. The credits are linked to the lowest and highest marginal tax brackets: 16 per cent on the first $200 of gifts; 29 per cent on any excess to a maximum of 75 per cent of net income in the year.[5] For a high-rate taxpayer, the combined provincial-federal rate is equivalent to approximately 46 per cent.

---

[4] However, governments will often create "refundable" tax credits for the purpose of furthering a particular tax policy objective. This type of tax credit will entitle the taxpayer to a tax credit even where no taxes are payable. Hence, a taxpayer could receive money back even when he or she has paid no tax.

[5] Subs. 118.1(3).

3. — Corporations

A corporation is entitled to a *deduction* for its charitable donations. Gifts to charitable and certain other organizations are deductible by a corporation up to an annual maximum of 75 per cent of its income for the year.[6] Crown gifts were not subject to any limitation before 1997, but are now subject to the 75 per cent limit.[7] Donations in excess of 75 per cent of net income may be carried forward for five years and, in any of those years, deducted to the extent that they were not deducted in a previous year.

There are two substantive criteria for determining the deductibility of a donation:

> 1. Does the contribution constitute a gift? and
>
> 2. Was the gift to a registered charity or other public service organization?

(a) — What Constitutes a Gift?

At common law, a gift is a voluntary transfer of property for no consideration or material advantage. As Deane J. said:[8]

> The word "gift" ... is intended to bear the meaning which it bears as a matter of ordinary language. ... [I]t is not to be assumed that its ambit can properly be defined, with a lawyer's or logician's precision, by reference to a number of unqualified propositions or tests. ...

---

[6]Para. 110.1(1)(a).

[7]Para. 110.1(1)(b).

[8]*Leary v. Fed. Commr. of Taxation* (1980), 32 A.L.R. 221 at 241 (F.C.A.).

Generally, a "gift" is a voluntary and gratuitous transfer of property from one person to another; it may be conditional but, once the condition is satisfied, it is not revocable.[9] A transfer of property is a gift where it is made:[10]

- By way of benefaction;[11]

- Without exchange for material reward or advantage; and

- Without contractual obligation.

---

[9]"Gift" is defined in *Halsbury's Laws of England*, 4th ed., Vol. 20, §1 as follows:

A gift *inter vivos* may be defined shortly as the transfer of any property from one person to another gratuitously while the donor is alive and not in expectation of death. ...

In *Black's Law Dictionary*, 4th ed., (1968), "gift" is defined as:

[a] voluntary transfer of personal property without consideration.

and:

[b] parting by owner with property without pecuniary consideration...

The *Shorter Oxford Dictionary* defines "giving" as:

... [a] transfer of property in a thing, voluntarily and without any valuable consideration. ...

See also *Commr. of Taxation (Cth.) v. McPhail* (1968), 41 A.L.R. 346 at 348 (Aust. H.C.), where Owen J. said,

... but it is, I think, clear that to constitute a "gift," it must appear that the property transferred was transferred voluntarily and not as the result of a contractual obligation to transfer it and that no advantage of a material character was received by the transferor by way of return. ...

This definition was approved by the Federal Court in *Canada v. Zandstra*, [1974] C.T.C. 503, 74 D.T.C. 6416 (F.C.T.D.).

[10]*Leary v. Fed. Commr. of Taxation, ante*, at 243 (quoted with approval by the Federal Court of Appeal in *M.N.R. v. McBurney*, [1985] 2 C.T.C. 214, 85 D.T.C. 5433 (F.C.A.); leave to appeal refused (1986), 65 N.R. 320n (S.C.C.)).

[11]*Collector of Imposts (Vic.) v. Cuming Campbell Invt. Pty. Ltd.* (1940), 63 C.L.R. 619 (Aust. H.C.) (transfer by way of benefaction being "essential idea" of gift, *per* Dixon, J. at 642). Some courts speak of a "detached and disinterested generosity"; see, e.g., *Commr. v. Lo Bue* (1956), 351 U.S. 243 at 246 (gift of affection, respect, admiration, charity or like impulses); *Robertson v. U.S.* (1952), 343 U.S. 711 at 714 (U.S., Utah); *C.I.R. v. Duberstein* (1960), 363 U.S. 278 at 285; see also, *Savoy Overseers v. Art Union of London*, [1896] A.C. 296 at 308 and 312 (H.L.) (charitable donation made where donor not looking "for any return in the shape of direct personal advantage," *per* Lord McNaghten); *Collector of Imposts (Vic.) v. Cuming Campbell Investments Pty. Ltd., ante*, at 641.

The essence of a gift is that it is a transfer without *quid pro quo*, a contribution motivated by detached and disinterested generosity.[12]

Subsection 248(30) modifies the common law meaning of "gift" for tax purposes to include donations that confer an advantage[13] on the donor, provided that the value of the donated property exceeds the value of the advantage that the donor receives. Thus, a person does not make a gift if he or she receives valuable consideration equal to his or her "donation".[14] For example, payment for a dinner organized by a charity may involve both charitable and non-charitable elements.[15] Regardless of the form and documentation of the arrangements, it is the substance of the contribution that determines whether the taxpayer makes a gift or a disguised payment for services. But there is no litmus paper test: one looks to the substance of the contribution.[16]

Although a payment pursuant to a contractual obligation to the donee is not a gift, the absence of a contractual obligation does not necessarily imply that the payment is a gift. Note also, a contractual obligation between the donor and a third party does not necessarily deprive a payment of its character as a gift. For example, a contract between A and B that each will contribute an equal amount to a registered charity does not *per se* disqualify their contributions as gifts.

(b) — Blended Payments

Blended contributions should be broken down into their component parts. For example, the admission price to a charity event may cover the costs of goods and services (such as food and entertainment) and a premium intended as a gift.[17] Similarly, a global payment to a

---

[12]*Tite v. M.N.R.*, [1986] 2 C.T.C. 2343, 86 D.T.C. 1788 (T.C.C.).

[13]Para. 248(31)(a)

[14]*Tite v. M.N.R.*, *ante* (taxpayer's claim for charitable donation denied where evidence demonstrated that payment to acquire print equal to value of work).

[15]*Burns v. M.N.R.*, [1988] 1 C.T.C. 201, 88 D.T.C. 6101 (F.C.T.D.) (taxpayer's payments to amateur athletic association not "gifts" because taxpayer expected and received benefit in return for payments).

[16]See, e.g., *C.I.R. v. Duberstein*, *ante*, at 289, *per* Justice Brennan:

> Decision of the issue presented in these cases must be based ultimately on the application of the fact-finding tribunal's experience with the mainsprings of human conduct to the totality of the facts of each case. The nontechnical nature of the statutory standard, the close relationship of it to the data of practical human experience, and the multiplicity of relevant factual elements, with their various combinations, creating the necessity of ascribing the proper force to each, confirm us in our conclusion that primary weight in this area must be given to the conclusions of the trier of fact.

[17]*Aspinall v. M.N.R.*, [1970] Tax A.B.C. 1073, 70 D.T.C. 1669.

charity that offers both religious and secular education might comprise a payment for tuition fees and a gift for charitable purposes. The tuition component is a personal expenditure; the gift for charitable purposes is deductible as a donation. The allocation between the deductible and the non-deductible portions is always a question of fact.[18]

(c) — Eligible Organizations

Donations to the following organizations are deductible to the extent of the annual maximum limit:[19]

- Registered charities;

- Registered Canadian amateur athletic associations;

- Resident housing corporations that provide low-cost housing accommodations for the aged;

- Canadian municipalities;

- The United Nations and its agencies;

- Prescribed foreign universities that admit Canadian students;[20] and

- Certain foreign charitable organizations to which the federal government has contributed in the year or in the preceding year.

The deduction for charitable donations is available only if the taxpayer provides receipts that disclose prescribed information.[21]

(d) — Charities

A "charity" can be either a charitable organization or charitable foundation.[22] A "charitable organization" is an organization that devotes itself to charitable activities[23] and a "charitable

---

[18]*M.N.R. v. McBurney*, [1985] C.T.C. 214, 85 D.T.C. 5433 (F.C.A.).

[19]Para. 110.1(1)(a).

[20]Reg. 3503.

[21]Reg. 3501.

[22]Subs. 149.1(1)"charity".

[23]Subs. 149.1(1)"charitable organization".

foundation" is, more specifically, a trust or corporation that operates exclusively for charitable purposes.[24]

(i) — Charitable Purposes

An organization qualifies as a charity under section 149.1 of the *Income Tax Act* if:[25]

1. Its purposes are charitable, and the purposes define the scope of the activities that it engages in, and

2. It devotes all of its resources to these activities.[26]

The *Pemsel*[27] test determines what is "charitable".[28] Thus, "charity" in its legal sense comprises four divisions:

1. Trusts for the relief of poverty;

2. Trusts for the advancement of education;

3. Trusts for the advancement of religion; and

4. Trusts for other purposes beneficial to the community.

In addition to complying with one or more of these categories, the organization must also have a charitable purpose that is within "the spirit and intendment" of the preamble to the *Charitable Uses Act 1601*.[29]

At first blush, the fourth division appears to be a broad and inclusive category for all sorts of beneficent activities. In fact, it is not that easy to qualify under this division because of the requirement that the charitable purpose must meet the spirit and intendment of the *Charita-*

---

[24]Subs. 149.1(1)"charitable foundation".

[25]*Vancouver Society of Immigrant and Visible Minority Women v. M.N.R.*, [1999] 1 S.C.R. 10, 169 D.L.R. (4th) 34 (S.C.C.).

[26]Unless the organization falls within the specific exemptions of subss. 149.1(6.1) and (6.2).

[27]*Income Tax Special Purposes Commissioners v. Pemsel*, [1891] A.C. 531 at 583 (H.L.). These categories are well accepted in Canadian law; see *Guar. Trust Co. v. M.N.R.*, [1967] S.C.R. 133 at 141, [1966] C.T.C. 755 at 759, 67 D.T.C. 5003 at 5005 (S.C.C.).

[28]*Vancouver Society of Immigrant and Visible Minority Women v. M.N.R.*, [1999] 1 S.C.R. 10, 169 D.L.R. (4th) 34 (S.C.C.).

[29]1601 (43 Eliz. I, c. 4).

ble Uses Act, a statute enacted in 1601. Stated in modern English, but reflecting social perceptions of a bygone era, the statute's list of charitable purposes is as follows:[30]

> The relief of aged, impotent, and poor people; the maintenance of sick and maimed soldiers and mariners, schools of learning, free schools, and scholars in universities; the repair of bridges, ports, havens, causeways, churches, seabanks, and highways; the education and preferment of orphans; the relief, stock, or maintenance of houses of correction; marriage of poor maids; supportation, aid, and help of young tradesmen, handicraftsmen, and persons decayed; the relief or redemption of prisoners or captives; and the aid or ease of any poor inhabitants concerning payment of fifteens, setting out of soldiers, and other taxes.

Only activities that are beneficial to the community *and* that come within the spirit and intendment of the above preamble are recognized as "charitable".[31] Thus, the double-headed aspect of the qualification causes difficulty for organizations that seek registration as a charity.

The Canada Revenue Agency (CRA) typically applies the tests in a rigid and dogmatic manner, without accommodation or adaptation to the nuances of modern Canadian society. But, as Lord Wilberforce said, "the law of charity is a moving subject." The preamble should not be read literally but in the context of contemporary society.[32] As Lord Upjohn put it:[33]

> This so-called fourth class is incapable of further definition and can to-day hardly be regarded as more than a portmanteau to receive those objects which enlightened opinion would regard as qualifying for consideration under the second heading.

It is clear, however, that despite some relaxation of the rules for registration, the basic focus remains: are the activities of a public character or are they "member-oriented"?[34]

---

[30]*Per* Slade J. in *McGovern v. A.G.*, [1982] Ch. 321 at 332 (Eng. Ch. Div.).

[31]See, e.g., *National Anti-Vivisection Soc. v. I.R.C.*, [1948] A.C. 31 (H.L.) (main object political; unclear whether public benefit advanced if such scientific research curtailed); *Re Strakosch*, [1949] Ch. 529 (C.A.) (gift must be beneficial to community in way law regards as charitable).

[32]See, for example, *Native Communications Soc. of B.C. v. M.N.R.*, [1986] 2 C.T.C. 170, [1986] 4 C.N.L.R. 79 (F.C.A.); *Vancouver Regional FreeNet Assn. v. M.N.R.*, [1996] 3 F.C. 880, 137 D.L.R. (4th) 206 (F.C.A.) (non-profit network establishing a free community computer that would provide free access to information on the Internet granted charitable organization status).

[33]*Scottish Burial Reform & Cremation Soc. v. Glasgow Corp.*, [1968] A.C. 138 at 150 (H.C.).

[34]*Nat. Model Railroad Assn. v. M.N.R.*, [1989] 1 C.T.C. 300, 89 D.T.C. 5133, (sub nom. *Seventh Div., Pac. N.W. Region, Nat. Model Railroad Assn. v. M.N.R.)* (F.C.A.).

In *Vancouver Society*,[35] the Supreme Court of Canada set out the test to assess whether an organization's purposes are beneficial in a way the law regards as charitable. In assessing an organization's purposes, one must:

1. Consider the trend of decisions that establish certain objects as charitable under this heading, and determine whether, by reasonable extension or analogy, the facts fits within the earlier decisions;[36]

2. Examine certain accepted anomalies to see whether they fairly cover the objects under consideration; and

3. Ask whether, consistent with the declared objects, the income and property in question can be applied for purposes clearly falling outside the scope of charity.

Under the Pemsel test, an organization is not considered to be charitable if its activities are illegal or contrary to public policy. There must be a definite and somehow officially declared and implemented policy for an activity to be considered "contrary to public policy". An entity will not be denied charitable status on the basis that its objects are merely politically controversial.[37]

(ii) — Tax-Exempt Status

A registered charity is a tax-exempt organization. Thus, the tax subsidy in respect of registered charities is double-barrelled: the charity is tax-exempt and its benefactors obtain a tax deduction or credit.

The tax exemption is justifiable on the basis that it encourages private organizations to engage in philanthropic activities that would otherwise fall to the public sector. The subsidy is expensive. Thus, to control the cost of the subsidy, the tax system has set up stringent registration and annual accounting requirements.

---

[35]*Vancouver Society of Immigrant and Visible Minority Women v. M.N.R.*, [1999] 1 S.C.R. 10, 169 D.L.R. (4th) 34 (S.C.C.).

[36]See, also, *Vancouver Regional FreeNet Assn. v. M.N.R.*, [1996] 3 F.C. 880, 137 D.L.R. (4th) 206, [1996] 3 C.T.C. 102, 96 D.T.C. 6440 (F.C.A.) (the provision of free access to information and to a means of communication was a type of purpose similar to those that had been held to be charitable in previous case law).

[37]*Everywoman's Health Care Society (1988) v. Canada (M.N.R.)*, [1992] 2 F.C. 52, [1991] 2 C.T.C. 320, 92 D.T.C. 6001 (F.C.A.) (abortion counselling and medical services registered as a charity). See also *Canadian Magen David Adom for Israel v. Canada (M.N.R.)*, 2002 FCA 323, [2002] 4 C.T.C. 422, 2002 D.T.C. 7353 (F.C.A.) (medical and ambulance services offered in occupied territory not registered as a charity on other grounds).

(iii) — Political Activities

An organization is not a charity if its main or principal object is political.[38] For example, tenants and ratepayer groups that merely lobby governments to act in support of societal change do not qualify as charitable organizations if their primary focus is political activity.[39] Similarly, anti-pornography groups that are, in effect, "political" organizations lobbying for legislative change under the guise of education do not qualify as charitable organizations.[40]

However, charities that engage in non-partisan political activities that are "ancillary and incidental" to their charitable purposes or activities can maintain registration as tax-exempt organizations.[41] For example, a charity can use mass mailings or media campaigns to influence public opinion or government policy. More active involvement in partisan political activities, however, endangers a charity's registration.[42]

It is not always easy to draw the line between political activity and public education. Generally, there is a reluctance to recognize organizations that merely engage in lobbying for legislative change. The following activities are "political":[43]

* The furthering of the interests of a particular political party;

* The procuring of changes to the laws of the country;

* The procuring of changes to the laws of a foreign country;

---

[38]*Re Patriotic Acre Fund*, [1951] 2 D.L.R. 624 (Sask. C.A.):

> ... the Court has no means of judging whether a proposed change in the law will or will not be for the public benefit and therefore cannot say that a gift to secure the change is a charitable gift.

[39]*N.D.G. Neighbourhood Assn. v. Revenue Can. Taxation Dept.*, [1988] 2 C.T.C. 14, 88 D.T.C. 6279 (F.C.A.) (tenants' association denied registration as charity).

[40]*Positive Action Against Pornography v. M.N.R.*, [1988] 1 C.T.C. 232, 88 D.T.C. 6186 (F.C.A.).

[41]Subs. 149.1(6.1).

[42]Para. 149.1(6.1)(c); *Action des Chrétiens pour l'Abolition de la Torture (L'A.C.A.T.) c. R.*, 2003 FCA 499, [2003] C.T.C. 121, (sub nom. *Action by Christians for the Abolition of Torture (ACAT) v. R.)* 2003 D.T.C. 5394 (Fed. C.A.); leave to appeal refused (2003), 2003 CarswellNat 2040, 2003 CarswellNat 2041 (S.C.C.) (exercise of moral pressure on governments held to be a political rather than charitable purpose); *Alliance for Life v. M.N.R.*, [1999] 3 C.T.C. 1, 99 D.T.C. 5228 (F.C.A.) (pro-life organization did not qualify for exemption under subsection 149.1(6.2) because materials were political and not ancillary and incidental to their charitable activities); *Human Life International in Canada Inc. v. M.N.R.*, [1998] 3 F.C. 202, [1998] 3 C.T.C. 126, 98 D.T.C. 6196 (F.C.A.); leave to appeal refused [1998] S.C.C.A. No. 246 (Minister allowed to revoke organization's charitable status as the organization was primarily concerned with swaying public opinion).

[43]*McGovern v. A.G.*, [1982] Ch. 321, [1982] 2 W.L.R. 222 (Ch. D.).

- The procuring of a reversal of government policy or of particular decisions of governmental authorities in the country; or

- The procuring of a reversal of government policy or of particular decisions of governmental authorities in a foreign country.

(e) — Donations of Capital Property

Where a person donates capital property to a registered charity, he or she can designate the value of the gift at any amount between its fair market value and its adjusted cost base. The designated value then becomes the taxpayer's proceeds of disposition. Thus, a taxpayer has some flexibility in determining the amount of the capital gain on the disposition of the property.[44]

4. — Valuation

(a) — Fair Market Value

Once we determine that a contribution to an eligible organization qualifies as a gift, the next task is to attach a value to it. We generally value gifts at their fair market value at the time that the donor transfers the property to the donee. The fair market value of an asset is its exchange value.[45] Where there is a regular and efficient market for the asset (for example, widely-held shares on a stock exchange), its trading price is probably the best, though not necessarily the only, measure of its fair market value.[46] Where there is no efficient market for the asset, it is necessary to determine fair market value through other criteria, such as, earnings value, liquidation value, replacement value, etc.

The "fair market value" of an asset for tax purposes is the highest price that it "might reasonably be expected to bring if sold by the owner in the normal method applicable to the asset in question, in the ordinary course of business in a market not exposed to any undue stresses, and composed of willing buyers and sellers dealing at arm's length and under no compulsion to buy or sell."[47] Thus, the focus of the determination of fair market value is on an efficient, normal and knowledgeable market.

---

[44]Subs. 110.1(3) and 118.1(6). A non-resident can also make the designation in respect of certain types of real property situated in Canada.

[45]See generally, *Re Mann*, [1972] 5 W.W.R. 23; affd. [1973] 4 W.W.R. 223; affd. [1974] 2 W.W.R. 574 (S.C.C.) [B.C.].

[46]*Re Mann*, ante, at 27.

[47]*Henderson v. M.N.R.*, [1973] C.T.C. 636, 73 D.T.C. 5471 (F.C.T.D.); affd. [1975] C.T.C. 485, 75 D.T.C. 5332 (F.C.A.).

(b) — Expert Evidence

As noted above, the best and usually most accurate measure of a property's value is its fair market value at the time that the taxpayer donates it to the charity. We can determine fair market value with precision if there is an active and open market for the property. For example, one can determine the value of publicly traded shares by reference to the trading price of a share at a particular time on a particular day.

Where there is no active market, however, one must rely upon the opinion of experts to determine the value of the property. A non-arm's length expert opinion can be a reliable guide to value, but only if the expert is truly independent. In recent years, we have seen clever "buy-low, donate-high" arrangements that gave taxpayers a substantial tax benefit for rapid turnover of art.

Valuation is a sophisticated art that calls for the expertise and judgment of people trained in its discipline. It is also an art that is vulnerable to manipulation and one should consider carefully the expert testimony of professional valuators. Expert evidence should, in Lord Wilberforce's words, "... be, and should be seen to be, the independent product of the expert, uninfluenced as to form or content by the exigencies of litigation."[48] Unfortunately, some experts have a propensity for moulding their opinions to identify with, and accommodate, their client's positions. As Adrian Keane says in the *Modern Law of Evidence*:[49]

> ... the danger is particularly acute in the case of opinions expressed by expert witnesses, of whom it has been said, not without some sarcasm, "it is quite often surprising to see with what facility and to what extent, their views can be made to correspond with the wishes or the interests of the parties who call them."

Valuation experts find it equally difficult to distance themselves from the purse-strings that determine their livelihood. As Professor Bonbright said:[50]

> ... few, if any, appraisers can take an unbiased position when they take the witness stand under an engagement from one of the contesting parties ... a court must choose between the tremendous errors implicit in a capitalization of audited reported earnings, and the tremendous errors implicit in a capitalization of prejudiced prophecies.

In *Klotz*,[51] for example, the taxpayer participated in a program called "Art for Education" (AFE). Under the AFE program, the program's sponsors would acquire prints for a modest cost, generally under $50 per print. The sponsors would then sell the prints to individuals for

---

[48]*Whitehouse v. Jordan*, [1981] 1 W.L.R. 246 at 256 (H.L.).

[49]Keane, *Modern Law of Evidence* (London: Butterworths, 1985), at 377.

[50]Bonbright, *Valuation of Property* (New York: McGraw-Hill, 1937), vol. 1, at 251.

[51]*Klotz v. R.*, 2004 TCC 147, [2004] 2 C.T.C. 2892, 2004 D.T.C. 2236 (T.C.C. [General Procedure]); affirmed [2005] 3 C.T.C. 78 (F.C.A.); leave to appeal refused (2006), 2006 CarswellNat 930, 2006 CarswellNat 931 (S.C.C.).

approximately $300 per print. The taxpayer purchased 250 such "limited edition" prints on December 28 and donated them two days later to Florida State University. The taxpayer obtained a charitable donation receipt for $258,400, the alleged market value, supported by the expert valuation of an art dealer and appraiser.

Motive is entirely irrelevant in the determination of value. The taxpayer was entitled to take advantage of the tax law provided that all the transactions were proper and appropriately valued. To be sure, the taxpayer did not appear to be preoccupied with broadening the cultural or intellectual horizons of the students at FSU. Indeed, he donated the prints without ever having seen them or having them in his possession. The Tax Court said: "His sole concern was that he get a charitable receipt." Altruistic motivation, however, is not a prerequisite to a charitable gift.

The expert art dealer and appraiser valued most of the prints at $1,000 each. The valuation was significant because the *Income Tax Act* deems the *minimum* cost and proceeds of personal use property to be $1,000. Thus, if the prints qualified as personal use property, there would be no capital gain on the donation to FSU. This would leave the taxpayer with only the deduction for the charitable gift without any corresponding inclusion in income for the gain realized on the gift.

Klotz is also remarkable in that the Canada Revenue Agency did not call any expert witnesses in a valuation dispute involving millions of dollars. Even so, the Tax Court of Canada did not accept the expert valuation opinions of the taxpayer. To be sure, a court is not bound to accept any expert's opinion and, ultimately, must make its own determination of value on the evidence. Nevertheless, it is an indication of the heavy burden of proof that the taxpayer carries in tax cases that the Minister does not even need to introduce expert testimony in a valuation dispute to win the case.

After a careful and thorough analysis of the expert testimony of the art dealer and appraiser, the Tax Court of Canada rejected the expert's opinion on value. The court said:

> It is one thing serendipitously to pick up for $10 a long lost masterpiece at a garage sale and give it to an art gallery and receive a receipt for its true value. It is another for [the promoter] to buy thousands of prints for $50, create a market at $300 and then hold out the prospect of a tax write-off on the basis of a $1,000 valuation.

Notwithstanding the failure of the tax arrangements in *Klotz*, Finance intends to amend the *Income Tax Act* to limit the value of a gift for charitable donation purposes to the donor's cost of the property if the donor donates the property within three years of acquiring it. The new rules deem the fair market value of a gifted property to be the lesser of its fair market value as otherwise determined and its costs basis if the holding period of the property is less than three years. This is intended to prevent escalating valuations.[52]

---

[52]See subs. 248(35) to (38).

However, the statutory rules go even further and introduce a motive test to determine the value of a gift. Even if the taxpayer holds the gifted property for more than three years, he or she may not be eligible to claim any real enhancement in fair market value if the taxpayer acquired the property initially for the purpose of gifting it. For example, assume that a taxpayer purchases a renowned artist's work, knowing full well that it will appreciate in value and that he or she will ultimately donate it to his or her alma mater some years down the road. In these circumstances, the new rules will restrict the fair market value of the gift to its cost basis.

5. — Registration as Charity

Only registered charities receive the benefits of tax-exempt status. To secure or maintain its registration, a registered charity must operate exclusively for charitable purposes and must not carry on any other unrelated business. Otherwise, the Minister may revoke the registration of the charitable organization.[53] A "related business", however, includes "... a business that is unrelated to the objects of the charity if substantially all of the people employed by the charity in the carrying on of that business are not remunerated for such employment."[54]

Where a charity carries on a business, there are, in effect, two separate tests that must be satisfied in order to acquire or maintain its registration: (1) the taxpayer must operate exclusively for charitable purposes, and (2) the business must be a "related business".

(a) — Related Business

We determine whether a business is related to the charitable organization by looking at the use of the profits of the business. It remains unclear, however, how far we can apply the use of funds test.[55]

In *AIMR*, for example, Heald J., speaking for the majority, said:[56]

> [W]here *all* of the monies received are dedicated to the charitable purposes for which the appellant was incorporated and where the business aspect of the operation is merely incidental

---

[53]Para. 149.1(2)(a).

[54]Subs. 149.1(1)"related business"; see also, *Alta. Inst. on Mental Retardation v. Canada*, [1987] 2 C.T.C. 70, 87 D.T.C. 5306 (F.C.A.); leave to appeal refused 87 N.R. 397.

[55]*Alta. Inst. on Mental Retardation v. Canada*, [1987] 2 C.T.C. 70, 87 D.T.C. 5306 (F.C.A.); leave to appeal refused 87 N.R. 397. See *Br. Launderer's Research Assn. v. Hendon Borough Rating Authority*, [1949] 1 K.B. 462 (Eng. C.A.); followed by Supreme Court of Canada in *Guar. Trust Co. v. M.N.R.*, [1967] S.C.R. 133, [1966] C.T.C. 755, 67 D.T.C. 5003 (S.C.C.).

[56]*Alta. Inst. on Mental Retardation v. Canada*, *ibid.*, at 75 [C.T.C.] and 5310 [D.T.C.].

to the attainment of its charitable objects, the appellant can, indeed, be said to be operating exclusively for charitable purposes.

The majority favoured the destination of funds test as "... the clear intention of Parliament to recognize the contemporary reality insofar as the fundraising activities of modern charitable organizations are concerned."[57] The concept of charity must be kept moving with changing social needs.[58] In Justice Heald's words:[59]

> If the operation of a cafeteria on the premises of an art gallery or the operation of a parking lot adjacent to and on premises owned by a hospital, for example, can be said to be related businesses even though the cafeteria and the parking lot may be operated by concessionaires for profit, then surely an activity such as that of this [taxpayer] must be in the same category.

Thus, charities may carry on any type of business so long as the profits of the business are ultimately diverted to charitable purposes.

III. — Residents Of Remote Regions

Individuals who reside in prescribed isolated posts in the near and far north can claim special deductions when computing taxable income.[60] These deductions subsidize the personal costs of taxpayers who live in remote regions.

Thus, the subsidies also indirectly subsidize northern businesses by reducing labour costs. The deduction is the lesser of:

- 20 per cent of the taxpayer's net income for the year, and

- $7.50 multiplied by the number of days in the year that the individual resided in the area plus an additional $7.50 for each day that the taxpayer maintained a dwelling in the area.

Individuals who work in a prescribed area are also entitled to special deductions in respect of travel expenses. These deductions are of two types: (1) travel for medical purposes, and (2) general travel. Travel for trips to obtain medical services is deductible where such services are not available locally. Employees may claim a deduction for up to two trips per calendar year for other purposes.[61]

---

[57]*Alta. Inst. on Mental Retardation v. Canada, ibid.*, at 77 [C.T.C.] and 5306 [D.T.C.].

[58]*Native Communications Soc. of B.C. v. M.N.R.*, [1986] 2 C.T.C. 170, [1986] 4 C.N.L.R. 79 (F.C.A.).

[59]*Alta. Inst. on Mental Retardation v. Canada*, [1987] 2 C.T.C. 70, 87 D.T.C. 5306 (F.C.A.) at 77 [C.T.C.].

[60]S. 110.7. In certain circumstances, the deduction may apply to residents of any isolated or sparsely populated area of the country.

[61]Para. 110.7(1)(a); subs. 110.7(3).

Only residents of the "prescribed northern zone" can claim the maximum deductions. Residents of the "prescribed intermediate zone" receive only 50 per cent of the deductions.

IV. — Losses

1. — General Comment

We saw in Chapter 5 that we measure income for a period of time. We refer to this period as the fiscal year. The fiscal year is the calendar year for individuals and partnerships and any 53-week period for corporations. The use of the fiscal year as the unit of time to measure income creates problems for taxpayers whose incomes fluctuate between years. For example, a taxpayer who earns income in one year and suffers an equal loss in the next would, in the absence of relieving provisions, face financial hardship as a result of paying tax in the first year without relief in the second. Consider the following alternatives:

Taxpayer	Year 1	Year 2	Year 3	Total
A	$ 120,000	$ (40,000)	$ (80,000)	NIL
B	(80,000)	120,000	(40,000)	NIL
C	(40,000)	(80,000)	120,000	NIL

It is obvious that the economic well-being of all three taxpayers is identical over the three-year period. There are, however, important differences if we tax the three taxpayers on an annual basis. Taxpayer A must pay tax on income of $120,000 in Year 1, Taxpayer B in Year 2, and Taxpayer C in Year 3. Thus, we cannot measure a taxpayer's true economic income until the end of his or her economic existence. On the other hand, a tax system cannot wait until the end of an individual's life or the termination of a business enterprise. Instead, we allow taxpayers to shift their losses between fiscal periods. In the absence of provisions that allow for the shifting of losses from one period to another, taxpayers could end up paying tax on illusory income.

A taxpayer can offset his or her losses from one source against income from other sources in the same year.[62] There are, however, several restrictions. For example, capital losses may be offset only against capital gains; listed personal property losses may be used only against listed personal property gains.[63] Losses from a decline in value of household durables (for example, cars, furniture, etc.) are personal losses. The Act deems such losses to be nil.[64]

---

[62]S. 3.

[63]Para. 3(b); subs. 41(2).

[64]Subpara. 40(2)(g)(iii).

Where a taxpayer does not use his or her losses in the year in which they occur, the taxpayer may, within certain limits, use them to offset income in other years.[65]

2. — Types of Losses

The complexity of the tax loss rules stems from three factors. First, economic losses are forced to fit into the annual accounting requirement. Second, in the absence of consolidated corporate reporting, we must confine losses within corporate entities and contain any spillover between corporations. Third, given the compartmentalized structure of the Act, the characterization of losses is as important as the characterization of income. There are different rules for each type of loss. Some losses (such as non-capital losses) are more valuable to a taxpayer than others (such as capital losses) because the entire loss may be written off against all sources of income. But capital losses have a longer shelf life than non-capital losses. Thus, the first step in determining the tax treatment of a loss is to determine the nature and character of the loss.

There are five major categories of losses:

1. Non-capital losses;

2. Net capital losses;

3. Restricted farm losses;

4. Farm losses; or

5. Limited partnership losses.

We subdivide capital losses into three categories:

1. Personal-use property losses;

2. Listed personal property losses; and

3. Business investment losses.

A taxpayer's loss from a source first offsets other sources of income for the purpose of calculating *income* for the current year. Losses that we cannot use in the current year to reduce income from other sources may be carried back or forward to other years and deducted in computing the taxpayer's *taxable income* for those years. Thus, current year losses are deductible in the computation of net income. Losses carried over to other years (whether prior or subsequent) are deductible only in the computation of taxable income.

---

[65]*Burleigh v. R.*, 2004 TCC 197, [2004] 2 C.T.C. 2797, 2004 D.T.C. 2399 (T.C.C. [General Procedure]) (losses can be carried forward/back whether or not they were reported in an income tax return in the year they were incurred).

(a) — Non-Capital Losses

A non-capital loss (which we loosely refer to as a "business loss") is deductible from income in any of the three taxation years preceding, and the 10 taxation years following, the year in which we incur the loss.[66] Thus, we use non-capital losses to offset income over a period of 14 years: the year of the loss, three years prior to the loss, and 10 years subsequent to the loss.

(i) — Meaning

A taxpayer's non-capital loss includes the following amounts:[67]

- A loss from any business (including losses from a farming or fishing business);
- A loss from the ownership of any property;
- A loss from any office or employment;
- An allowable business investment loss for the year;
- Any used portion of the deduction for Part VI.1 special taxes on dividends;
- An amount deductible by a life insurer in computing taxable income in respect of taxable dividends received from taxable Canadian corporations;[68]
- 1/2 of the amount included in the taxpayer's income as an employee benefit in respect of the exercise or disposition of prescribed shares;[69]
- 1/2 of the amount included in the taxpayer's income as an employee benefit in respect of a stock option plan issued by a Canadian-controlled private corporation;[70]
- 1/2 of the amount included in the taxpayer's income as prospectors' shares;[71]
- An amount deductible by a corporation in computing its taxable income in respect of dividends received from other corporations;[72]

---

[66]Para. 111(1)(a).

[67]Subs. 111(8)"non-capital loss".

[68]Subs. 138(6).

[69]Para. 110(1)(d); increased from 1/4 in Budget 2000.

[70]Para. 110(1)(d.1); increased from 1/4 in Budget 2000.

[71]Para. 110(1)(d.2); increased from 1/4 in Budget 2000.

[72]S. 112; subs. 113(1).

- 1/2 of the amount included in the taxpayer's income in respect of certain deferred profit-sharing benefits;[73]

- An amount deducted from taxable income in respect of a home relocation loan;[74]

- An amount claimed as a capital gains exemption;[75]

- Certain amounts deducted under paragraph 110(1)(f), such as amounts exempt under a tax convention, social assistance payments, and workers' compensation; and

- Amounts added to a corporation's taxable income for foreign tax deductions.[76]

Then, we deduct the following amounts from the aggregate of the above:[77]

- The amount determined under paragraph 3(c);

- The taxpayer's farm loss;

- An amount deducted under subsection 111(10) (fuel tax rebate); and

- The amount by which non-capital loss must be reduced under section 80 (debt forgiveness).

Thus, we initially apply a taxpayer's losses from non-capital sources against income in the *current* year. The residue less any portion that is a farm loss becomes the taxpayer's non-capital loss. There are special rules for farm losses.[78]

A taxpayer cannot increase his or her non-capital loss by the deductions permitted under subdivision e of Division B (sections 60–66.8). These deductions may, however, reduce other income in the year. For example, an individual who suffers a business loss in a particular year cannot increase his or her loss carryforward by including in the non-capital loss amounts paid as support. If, however, the individual was also employed in the same year, he or she could use any support payments to reduce or eliminate his or her employment income and carry forward the business loss.

---

[73]Para. 110(1)(d.3); increased from 1/4 in Budget 2000.

[74]Para. 110(1)(j).

[75]S. 110.6.

[76]S. 110.5.

[77]Subs. 111(8)"non-capital loss".

[78]Para. 111(1)(d).

(ii) — Non-Residents

A non-resident taxpayer may not include as a non-capital loss any losses from businesses that are not carried on in Canada.[79] Also, a resident taxpayer may not deduct non-capital losses incurred while he or she was a non-resident and had no Canadian source of income.[80] Thus, a corporation that becomes resident in Canada cannot import its non-capital losses accumulated while it was a non-resident corporation without any Canadian income source.

Section 111 of the Act also restricts a non-resident from applying a business or property loss incurred in Canada in a preceding year from a treaty-exempt source against taxable income earned in Canada in a subsequent year that is not treaty-exempt. These losses cannot be utilized to offset taxable income.

(iii) — Order of Deductions

A taxpayer must deduct his or her non-capital losses in the order in which the taxpayer incurs them.[81]

(iv) — Transfer of Losses

A loss is generally deductible only by the taxpayer who incurs it. For example, where an individual incurs a non-capital loss, the loss cannot be claimed by another taxpayer to whom the business is sold. Similarly, a sole proprietor cannot transfer the losses of the proprietorship on selling his or her business to a corporation. This is so even if the individual owns all the shares of the corporation that acquires the business.

Since a corporation is a legal entity in its own right, any losses that it incurs belong to it. It is only in very rare circumstances that another corporation can use its losses. Note, however, that even though a corporation owns its losses, a change of control of the corporation may extinguish its non-capital losses.[82]

---

[79]Subs. 111(9).

[80]*Oceanspan Carriers Ltd. v. Canada*, [1987] 1 C.T.C. 210, 87 D.T.C. 5102 (F.C.A.).

[81]Subpara. 111(3)(b)(i).

[82]Subs. 111(5).

(b) — Net Capital Losses

Allowable capital losses may only offset taxable capital gains. Listed personal property losses may be used only to offset gains on listed personal property, and not against other capital property.[83]

A taxpayer's "net capital loss" is made up of:[84]

- The excess of its allowable capital losses over taxable capital gains, and

- Any unutilized allowable business investment losses previously included in its non-capital losses in respect of which the carryover period expired in the year.

Net capital losses may be carried back three years and carried forward indefinitely. Hence, they may have an unlimited life. They may, however, be applied only against capital gains in other years.[85]

(c) — Farm Losses

Unlike losses from other activities, where losses are on account of business or capital, farm losses can be on account of:

1. Business "farm losses";

2. Restricted farm losses; or

3. Hobby farm losses.

The Act controls farming losses strictly because of the propensity of "gentlemen farmers" to use such losses against their professional income. Where a taxpayer in the *business* of farming incurs a "farm loss", the loss is subject to the rules generally applicable to business losses.[86] A taxpayer's "farm loss" is the excess of his or her losses from farming and fishing

---

[83]Para. 3(b).

[84]Subs. 111(8)"net capital loss". The taxpayer's net capital loss is also reduced as required by s. 80 (debt forgiveness). Capital losses that also qualify as "allowable business investment losses" are initially treated as non-capital losses and may be written off against income from any source. If they cannot be used as non-capital losses within the ten year carryforward period, they are added to net capital losses and may be carried forward indefinitely.

[85]Para. 111(1)(b).

[86]Para. 111(1)(d) and subs. 111(8) "farm loss"; *Brown v. M.N.R.*, [1975] C.T.C. 611, 75 D.T.C. 5433 (F.C.T.D.). In both *Kroeker v. Canada*, 2002 FCA 392, 2002 D.T.C. 7436, [2003] 1 C.T.C. 183 (F.C.A.) and *Taylor v. Canada*, 2002 FCA 425, 2002 D.T.C. 7596 farming losses were fully deductible even though taxpayers had full time jobs; sufficient time, labour and capital were devoted to farm.

over any income from these sources.[87] A taxpayer may carry back the farm losses 3 years and forward 10 years and apply the losses against income from any source.[88]

A "restricted farm loss" is a farming loss suffered by a taxpayer who carries on business with an expectation of profit, but whose *chief* source of income is *neither* farming nor a combination of farming and some other source of income.[89]

A taxpayer whose chief source of income is neither farming nor a combination of farming and some other source of income cannot deduct more than $8,750 in any year for "farming losses".[90] Any loss in excess of this limit becomes the taxpayer's "restricted farm loss" for the year. The taxpayer can carry forward his or her restricted farm loss to future years.[91]

A restricted farm loss may be carried back three years and forward 10 years.[92] The amount of a restricted farm loss that is deductible in any year is limited to the amount of the tax-payer's income from farming for the year.[93]

Where a farmer disposes of farmland and has unclaimed restricted farm losses that were not deductible in prior years, the farmer may add the unclaimed losses to the adjusted cost base of the land. Thus, he or she can reduce any capital gain on the eventual disposition of the land by the amount of the unclaimed losses.[94]

---

[87]Subs. 111(8)"farm loss". For the meaning of "farm loss", see *Moldowan v. M.N.R.*, [1978] 1 S.C.R. 480, [1977] C.T.C. 310, 77 D.T.C. 5213 (S.C.C.) (three classes of farmers; tests for "chief source of income"); *Graham v. The Queen*, [1983] C.T.C. 370, 83 D.T.C. 5399 (Fed. T.D.); affd. [1985] 1 C.T.C. 380, (sub nom. *The Queen v. Graham*) 85 D.T.C. 5256 (F.C.A.); leave to appeal refused (1985), 62 N.R. 103 (note) (S.C.C.) (although Hydro employee, taxpayer's main preoccupation farming); *Hadley v. Canada*, [1985] 1 C.T.C. 62, 85 D.T.C. 5058 (F.C.T.D.) (sizeable investment in farming made employment more a source of investment finance; losses allowed); *Bender v. M.N.R.*, [1986] 1 C.T.C. 2437, 86 D.T.C. 1291 (T.C.C.) (four-pronged test for deductibility of farm losses); *Croutch v. M.N.R.*, [1986] 2 C.T.C. 246, 86 D.T.C. 6453 (F.C.T.D.) (no reasonable expectation of profit from horse breeding operation).

[88]Para. 111(1)(d).

[89]*Moldowan v. The Queen*, [1977] C.T.C. 310, 77 D.T.C. 5213 (S.C.C.).

[90]Subs. 31(1).

[91]Subs. 31(1.1).

[92]Para. 111(1)(c).

[93]Para. 111(1)(c).

[94]Para. 53(1)(i).

A hobby farm loss is a loss from a farming operation that is conducted without a profit motive or a reasonable expectation of profit.[95] Hobby farm losses are not deductible at all since they are not income from a source.[96]

(d) — Allowable Business Investment Losses

A "business investment loss" is a hybrid loss,[97] a particular type of capital loss that is deductible from income from *any* source.

(i) — Capital Loss

Characterization of a loss as a capital loss is a necessary precondition to its characterization as a business investment loss. A capital loss that is deemed to be nil (for example, a superficial loss) cannot give rise to a business investment loss.[98]

A "business investment loss" is a loss that a taxpayer incurs on a disposition of capital property under the following conditions:[99]

- The capital property is a share of a "small business corporation" or a debt owed to the taxpayer by such a corporation;

- Where the taxpayer is a corporation and the capital property is a debt, the debtor corporation is at arm's length from the taxpayer; and

- The shares or debt are, unless subsection 50(1) applies, disposed of to a person dealing with the taxpayer at arm's length.

(ii) — Hybrid Nature of Loss

An allowable business investment loss has features of both business and capital losses: it results from a disposition of capital property, but it may be used to offset income from *any*

---

[95]See, generally, Chapter 7, "The Meaning of Business Income, Investment Income, and Capital Gains". *Sobon v. R.*, 2004 TCC 2, [2004] 3 C.T.C. 2347 (T.C.C. [Informal Procedure]); reversed (2006), 2006 CarswellNat 1885 (F.C.A.) (taxpayer not entitled to deduct farm losses in excess of $8,750 per year; ostrich farm sustained losses in all 10 years of its operation and could not generate a profit as it was currently run).

[96]See the guidelines that the Supreme Court set out in the *Stewart* and *Walls* decisions.

[97]Para. 39(1)(c); subs. 111(8)"non-capital loss".

[98]Para. 40(2)(g).

[99]Para. 39(1)(c); see also subs. 248(1)"small business corporation".

source.[100] Any unused portion of an allowable business investment loss is a non-capital loss. Thus, one can apply unused allowable business losses against income from any source.

Since an unused allowable business loss is treated as a non-capital loss, it has a limited life. It may be carried back three years and carried forward for only ten years.[101] In contrast, net capital losses may be carried back three years and carried forward indefinitely.

An allowable business loss that is not used within the ten-year carryforward period applicable to non-capital losses reverts to a net capital loss.[102] Thereafter, it may be carried forward indefinitely but applied only against taxable capital gains.

(e) — Net Capital Losses in Year of Death

A taxpayer's net capital losses may be deducted against net taxable capital gains in the year of death and in the immediately preceding year. Unused capital losses can be carried back and written off against income in the year before the taxpayer's death, but only to the extent that such losses exceed any capital gains exemption claimed by that person in his or her lifetime.[103]

Capital losses in excess of capital gains realized by a deceased's estate within its first taxation year may also be written off *as if* they had been realized by the deceased in the year of death. Thus, the deceased's estate is given credit for the amount of income tax that the deceased would have saved in the year of death if the excess capital losses had been sustained by the deceased rather than by the estate.

This relief is available only where the legal representative of the deceased makes an election and designates the amount of the excess capital losses to be carried back. The amount designated is deemed not to have been a capital loss of the estate.[104] The representative must file an amended return for the deceased taxpayer for the year in which he or she died.

---

[100]S. 3.

[101]Para. 111(1)(a), subs. 111(8)"non-capital loss".

[102]Subs. 111(8)"net capital loss".

[103]Subs. 111(2).

[104]Subs. 164(6).

(f) — Limited Partnership Losses

A taxpayer may carry forward limited partnership losses indefinitely and apply them against income from any source. The Act restricts the deduction for limited partnership losses, however, to the amount that the taxpayer is "at risk" in the partnership in the year.[105]

3. — Change of Corporate Control

(a) — General Comment

The Act discourages taxpayers from trading in "loss companies", that is, corporations with accumulated losses purchased and sold primarily for the sake of tax, rather than business, advantages. It does this by streaming the carryforward of losses when control of a corporation changes hands.[106] In the absence of these rules, a taxpayer could purchase a "loss company", inject a new profitable business into it and shelter the profits of the new business from tax.[107]

(b) — Meaning of "Control"

(i) — De Jure Control

"Control" implies ownership of sufficient shares to carry with them the ability to cast a majority of the votes on election of a board of directors. Thus, at common-law, control means *de jure* and not *de facto* control. As Jackett P. said in *Buckerfield's*:[108]

> [M]any approaches might conceivably be adopted in applying the word "control" in a statute such as the *Income Tax Act*...
>
> It might, for example, refer to control by "management," where management and the Board of Directors are separate, or it might refer to control by the Board of Directors. The kind of control exercised by management officials of the Board of Directors is, however, clearly not intended by [s. 256] when it contemplates control of one corporation by another as well as control of a corporation by individuals. ... The word "control" might conceivably refer to *de facto* control by one or more shareholders whether or not they hold a majority of the shares. I am of the view, however, that in [s. 256 of] the *Income Tax Act*, the word "controlled" con-

---

[105]Para. 111(1)(e).

[106]Subss. 111(4), 111(5).

[107]See also, Chapter 30, "Purchase and Sale of a Business".

[108]*Buckerfield's Ltd. v. M.N.R.*, [1964] C.T.C. 504 at 507, 64 D.T.C. 5301 at 5303 (Ex. Ct.); *Duha Printers (Western) Ltd. v. Canada*, [1998] 1 S.C.R. 795, [1998] 3 C.T.C. 303, 98 D.T.C. 6334 (S.C.C.).

templates the right or control that rests in ownership of such a number of shares as carries with it the right to a majority of the votes in the election of the Board of Directors.

The lack of power to elect a majority of the board of directors, however, does not necessarily imply a lack of control; control can also be determined by other tests, such as the power to wind up the corporation.[109]

(ii) — Statutory Exceptions

There are circumstances, however, in which the Act deems control of a corporation not to have changed. For example, the Act deems a person who acquires shares of a corporation *not* to have acquired control by virtue of the acquisition, redemption or cancellation of shares, if immediately before such transaction he or she was related to the acquired corporation.[110]

(iii) — Restrictions on Losses

In the absence of consolidated corporate reporting for tax purposes, the Act applies stringent restrictions on the use of accumulated losses following a change of corporate control. The general thrust of these rules is to limit transfers of losses between unrelated corporate taxpayers and to discourage business arrangements that are nothing more than "loss-trading" or "loss-offset" transactions. For example, in the typical "loss-trading" transaction, a taxpayer would sell property with an accrued gain and use an intermediary corporation with accumulated losses as a conduit. Any gain from the transaction could then be offset against the intermediary's losses to reduce taxable income. Generally, the loss-transfer rules do not allow for migration of losses between corporations. There are, however, several exceptions.

(iv) — Non-Capital Losses

A corporation may carry forward its non-capital and farm losses following a change of control if it satisfies two conditions: prior year's losses are deductible against income from the *same* business, but only if the corporation that sustained the loss continues to carry on that same business for profit or with a reasonable expectation of profit. The corporation must carry on the acquired business with a reasonable expectation of profit *throughout the year* following the time of its acquisition.[111]

---

[109]*Imperial General Properties Ltd. v. M.N.R.*, [1985] 2 S.C.R. 288, [1985] 2 C.T.C. 299, 85 D.T.C. 5500 (S.C.C.).

[110]Para. 256(7)(a).

[111]Subpara. 111(5)(a)(i).

The acquired business by which the losses were originally sustained must be continuously maintained for profit or with a reasonable expectation of profit. The substitution of a new or similar, but more profitable, business does not satisfy this requirement.

Following a change of control, a corporation may only deduct its non-capital and farm losses from prior years to the extent of the aggregate of:[112]

- Its income for the year from the acquired business; and,

- Any other business income substantially derived from the sale, lease, rental, or development of properties, or the rendering of services, which are similar to those properties sold, leased, rented, or developed or the services rendered, as the case may be, in the course of carrying on the *particular* business in question, prior to the change in control.

(v) — Deemed Year-End

The Act deems a corporation to have a year-end immediately before its control changes hands.[113] Any losses incurred in the year in which control changes are subject to the restrictions on loss carryovers. Thus, a change of corporate control can speed up the timetable for the use of losses.

(vi) — Capital Losses

The restrictions on capital losses are even more stringent than for non-capital losses. Net capital losses for preceding years may not be deducted in computing its income for the year of change of control or in any subsequent year. Further, losses incurred in years subsequent to the change of control cannot be carried back to offset income earned in the years prior to the change of control.[114]

Following a change of corporate control, the Act deems a corporation to have realized any losses accrued on its *non-depreciable* capital properties.[115] Its deemed capital losses then become subject to the restrictions on the carryover of capital losses. The Act also reduces the adjusted cost base of the non-depreciable capital properties by the amount of the capital

---

[112]Subpara. 111(5)(a)(ii); *Yarmouth Indust. Leasing Ltd. v. M.N.R.*, [1985] 2 C.T.C. 67, 85 D.T.C. 5401 (F.C.T.D.) ("control" includes both direct and indirect control).

[113]Subs. 249(4).

[114]Subs. 111(4), see also Chapter 30, "Purchase and Sale of a Business".

[115]Para. 111(4)(d). Other provisions — such as, subs. 111(5.1) — apply to properties such as depreciable property.

loss.[116] The purpose of these rules is to make it less attractive to trade in corporations that are pregnant with capital losses.

V. — Capital Gains Exemption

1. — Purpose

Canada did not tax capital gains until 1972 when it introduced a rule that effectively taxed capital gains at 50 per cent of the tax on ordinary income. Since 1972 we have seen the tax on capital gains climb to effective rate of 75 per cent of the tax on ordinary income and then fall back to 50 per cent in 2001. The capital gains exemption of $500,000 was introduced in 1985. The exemption is intended to encourage risk-taking and to stimulate investment in small businesses while assisting farmers and broadening the participation of individuals in the equity markets. In short, the exemption was intended to "... unleash the full entrepreneurial dynamism of individual Canadians."[117]

Capital gains from dispositions of shares of farm properties and qualified small business corporations are exempt from tax to a maximum of $500,000 during a lifetime. At a tax rate of 50 per cent, the full exemption for taxable capital gains of $250,000 is worth $125,000 in tax savings. Thus, the exemption is generous. The future value of the $125,000 at 8 per cent over 25 years is worth $856,250. Here we see the compromise of competing values. First, we tax capital gains on the theory of fairness ("a buck is a buck"). Then, we exempt some gains for certain taxpayers on the theory of economic incentives.

2. — Structure

The $500,000 lifetime capital gains exemption is available in respect of two categories of capital properties:

1. "Qualified farm property";[118] and

2. Shares of qualified small business corporations.[119]

An individual's exemption depends upon three principal factors:

1. The individual's residence;

---

[116]Para. 53(2)(b.2).

[117]Budget speech, May 23, 1985.

[118]Subs. 110.6(2).

[119]Subs. 110.6(2.1).

2. The type of capital property that gives rise to the gain; and

3. The net cumulative amount of the individual's investment income and financing expenses in the year in which he or she realizes the gain.

These three factors determine who is eligible for the exemption and how much of the gain the individual may shelter from tax in a particular year.

3. — Eligible Taxpayers

(a) — Residents

Only individuals resident in Canada may claim the exemption. An individual can claim the exemption if he or she is resident in Canada:

- *Throughout* the year; or

- For part of the year, if the individual was resident in Canada throughout the year preceding, or the year following, the year in which he or she realized the gain.[120]

A trust cannot claim the exemption. A trust may, however, flow through its capital gain to its beneficiaries by making a special designation.[121]

A spouse trust may claim a deduction in respect of its eligible taxable capital gains in the year in which the spouse dies.[122]

(b) — Deemed Residents

For the purposes of the exemption, the Act deems an individual who was resident in Canada at any time in a taxation year to have been resident in Canada throughout the year if he or she was resident in Canada throughout either the year immediately preceding, or the year immediately following, the taxation year.[123] Thus, a person who becomes a non-resident in a particular year can claim the exemption if he or she was resident in Canada throughout the year immediately preceding it.

An immigrant may claim the exemption on becoming resident in Canada if he or she remains a resident throughout the following year.

---

[120]Subs. 110.6(5).

[121]Subs. 104(21) and 104(21.2).

[122]Subs. 110.6(12), paras. 104(4)(a), (a.1).

[123]Subs. 110.6(5).

4. — Eligible Properties

The exemption is available in respect of a maximum of $500,000 of capital gains from the disposition of shares of a "qualified small business corporation" or "qualified farm property".

5. — Restrictions

Generally, an individual (other than a trust) resident in Canada may claim an exemption equal to the least of the following three amounts:

1. The individual's unused capital gains exemption of $500,000;

2. The individual's annual gains limit for the year; and

3. The individual's cumulative gains limit at the end of the year.

6. — Farm Property

The general purpose of the farm property rules is to limit the exemption to taxpayers who are engaged in the business of farming for a minimum stipulated period of time and to circumstances in which farming constitutes the taxpayer's main source of income.

(a) — "Qualified Farm Property"

A taxpayer is entitled to the exemption in respect of "qualified farm property". The phrase "qualified farm property" refers to farm property held personally or through a partnership or family farm corporation.

More specifically, an individual's "qualified farm property" includes any real property that has been used by:[124]

- The individual;

- His or her spouse or common-law partner;

- His or her child or parent;

- The individual's family farm corporation in which he or she owns shares; or

- A family farm partnership in which he or she has an interest.

---

[124]Subs. 110.6(1)"qualified farm property".

The property must have been used to carry on the business of farming in Canada. The business may be, or may have been, carried on by the individual who owns the farm property, that person's spouse or children, a family farm corporation, or, family farm partnership in which the individual, or the spouse, children, or parents have an interest. For the purposes of these rules, grandchildren qualify as children.[125]

(b) — The Business of Farming

To qualify as farm property eligible for the exemption, the property must be used, or must have been used, in the course of carrying on the business of farming in Canada. What constitutes "the business of farming" is a question of fact.

(c) — Additional Tests

The following two tests must also be met:[126] (1) the property must have been owned by the individual, the spouse, common-law partner, children or parents, a family farm partnership, or a personal trust *throughout* the 24 months immediately preceding its disposition; and (2) during a period of at least two years while the property was so owned, the individual's gross revenue from the property used in farming must have exceeded his or her income from all other sources for the year.

7. — Small Business Corporation Shares

The exemption is also available in respect of capital gains that a taxpayer realizes from the disposition of qualified small business corporation ("QSBC") shares.

The Act defines a "small business corporation" as:[127]

- A Canadian-controlled private corporation in which all or most of the fair market value of the assets is attributable to assets used principally in an active business carried on primarily in Canada; and

- A Canadian-controlled private corporation in which the assets, throughout a period of 24 months immediately preceding the corporation's disposition, have not been owned by any person other than the individual claiming the exemption, or by a person or partnership related to the individual.

---

[125]Para. 110.6(1)"child".

[126]Subs. 110.6(1)"qualified farm property".

[127]Subs. 248(1); see also, subs. 110.6(1)"qualified small business corporation share".

Shareholders of newly incorporated small business corporations can, however, claim the exemption, even where the corporation has existed for less than 24 months. Thus, a sole proprietor can dispose of his or her active business by transferring all of the business to a corporation and then selling the shares of the corporation rather than the assets of the business.

There is a risk that the CRA may attack a quick flip of shares after a rollover to a corporation as an income transaction that is not eligible for the capital gains exemption.[128]

8. — Reporting Requirements

A taxpayer who claims a capital gains exemption must disclose the amount claimed on his or her tax return for the year. In other words, a taxpayer may not simply omit net taxable capital gains from income on the basis that they are not, in effect, subject to tax. Failure to file an income tax return within one year of its due date or failure to report the capital gain in income may nullify the exemption.[129] The Minister can deny the exemption only if it can be established that failure to file the return or to disclose the amount of the capital gain was attributable to the taxpayer's gross negligence or that the taxpayer "knowingly" failed to conform to the reporting requirements.

9. — Anti-Avoidance Rules

The capital gains exemption is a generous tax preference. Thus, taxpayers have an incentive to convert income that is taxable into non-taxable capital gains. There are several anti-avoidance provisions in place in anticipation of such manoeuvres. Some of the provisions are very specific, while others are broad provisions that cast a wide net. Indeed, in some cases, the net has been cast so widely that it is impossible to determine the types of transactions it might catch.

The primary focus of the anti-avoidance provisions, however, is the prevention of three types of tax avoidance:

1. Conversion of capital gains earned by corporations into capital gains earned by individuals ("Type A");

2. Conversion of dividend income into capital gains ("Type B"); and

3. Disproportionate allocations of gains between taxpayers.

---

[128]See, for example, *Fraser v. Minister of National Revenue*, 64 D.T.C. 5224, [1964] S.C.R. 657, [1964] C.T.C. 372 (S.C.C.).

[129]Subs. 110.6(6).

(a) — Type A Conversions

As already noted, only individuals can claim the exemption in respect of capital gains. Consequently, there is every incentive to convert potential corporate capital gains into gains attributable to individual shareholders.

An individual cannot claim the exemption for a gain realized as a consequence of a corporation or partnership's acquisition of property at a price that is significantly less than its fair market value.[130] For example, where a corporation disposes of a property by transferring it to another corporation for less than its fair market value, any capital gain from a sale of the shares of either corporation is not eligible for the exemption if the dispositions of property are part of a series of transactions. This rule applies where the transformed gain *results* from a "series of transactions or events."[131] It is not necessary to establish any intention or purpose on the part of the taxpayer to transform the gain. The sequence of events must, however, be sufficiently connected to constitute a "series of transactions".

(b) — Type B Conversions

The second category of anti-avoidance provisions is concerned with the conversion of dividend income into capital gains. In the simplest case, the value of shares may be enhanced by restricting the dividend payout on the shares. In these circumstances, the taxpayer's claim for an exemption in respect of the gain from a disposition of the shares may be denied.[132]

More specifically, an individual may not claim the capital gains exemption in respect of gains realized on shares where:[133]

- It is reasonable to conclude that a significant part of the gain is attributable to non-payment of dividends on the shares; or

- The dividends paid in the year *or in any preceding taxation year* were less than 90 per cent of the average annual rate of return on the shares for that year.

The individual need not have an intention to convert dividend income into capital gains. It is sufficient that there is a causal connection between significant enhancement in the value of the shares and inadequacy of the payment of dividends. The onus is then on the individual to provide an alternative explanation for the enhanced value of the shares.

---

[130]Para. 110.6(7)(b).

[131]See subs. 248(10) (defining "series of transactions").

[132]Subs. 110.6(8).

[133]*Ibid.*

This rule does not apply to prescribed shares.[134] A "prescribed share" is one that is commonly referred to as a "common share", that is, a share not restricted to a maximum dividend, or to a maximum amount upon winding up of the corporation. Shares issued as part of an estate freeze[135] and shares issued by mutual fund corporations are also prescribed for the purposes of this rule.[136]

The average annual rate of return on a share is the rate of return that a "knowledgeable and prudent investor" would expect to receive on such a share.[137] In determining the rate, any delay, postponement, or failure to pay dividends in respect of the shares should be ignored. Variations in the amount of dividends payable from year to year should also be ignored.

Finally, the return is to be determined on the assumption that the shares may only be disposed of for proceeds equal to their issue price. These assumptions are intended to provide a nearly mechanical formula for determining a rate of return, without regard to all the factual financial nuances that might otherwise influence the return on shares.

VI. — Adjusted Taxable Income

High-income taxpayers may be subject to an "alternative minimum tax" ("AMT"), even though they do not have any taxable income.[138] The federal alternative minimum tax is payable at a flat rate of 16 per cent on "adjusted taxable income". Combined with a provincial tax rate of approximately 50 per cent, the AMT is 24 per cent.

The alternative minimum tax was introduced in 1986 for the purpose of improving tax equity and making the tax system *fairer*. There was a perception that the tax was necessary because many high-income taxpayers were not paying their fair share of taxes.

The alternative minimum tax applies only to individuals and trusts (other than mutual fund trusts); it does not apply to corporations. AMT is an alternative tax. Thus, it applies only if the amount computed under it exceeds the individual's regular tax calculated on regular taxable income. The AMT is a substitute for the regular tax.

Generally, a taxpayer's "adjusted taxable income" for the alternative minimum tax is his or her regular taxable income plus certain add-backs in respect of tax preference items.[139] These tax preference items are deductions that might be used to shelter income. For exam-

---

[134]Reg. 6205.

[135]Reg. 6205(2)(a).

[136]Reg. 6205(2)(b).

[137]Subs. 110.6(9).

[138]Subss. 127.5–127.55.

[139]S. 127.52.

ple, 60 per cent of the exempt portion of capital gains, contributions to registered retirement savings plans, deferred savings plans, registered pension plans, write-offs for resource expenses, Canadian films, multiple-unit residential buildings, and stock option deductions are added back into taxable income.

In computing "adjusted taxable income" for AMT purposes, a taxpayer is entitled to a basic exemption of $40,000.[140]

However, the losses can be used in future years.

---

[140]S. 127.53.

Selected Bibliography to Chapter 15

General

McQuillan, Peter E., "Computation of Income for Tax Purposes", in *Proceedings of 44th Tax Conf.* 5:27 (Canada Tax Foundation, 1992).

Swanson, Julie Anne, "The Alternative Minimum Tax" (Toronto: CCH Canadian, 1991).

Charitable Donations, Medical Expenses, etc.

Anderson, Alec R., "The Statutory Non-charitable Purpose Trust: Estate Planning in the Tax Havens" in *Equity, Fiduciaries and Trusts* (Toronto: Carswell, 1993).

Arbuckle, J.E., "Investment in Art — For Pleasure and Profit" (1980) 54 Cost & Mgt. 46.

Bale, G., "Construing a Taxing Statute or Tilting at Windmills: Charitable Donation Deduction and the Charter of Rights and Freedoms" (1985) 19 E.T.R. 55.

Bromley, E. Blake, "A Response to 'A Better Tax Administration in Support of Charities'" (1991) 10 Philanthrop. No. 3 3.

Bromley, E. Blake, "Parallel Foundations and Crown Foundations" (1993) 11 Philanthrop. No. 4 37.

"Charity Lotteries" (1983) 5 Can. Taxpayer 112.

"Corporate Donations" A Double Winner" (1980) 2 Can. Taxpayer 200.

Dickson, M.L., and Lawrence C. Murray, "Recent Tax Developments" (1985) 5 Philanthrop. 50, 52.

Dickson, M.L., and Laurence C. Murray, "Recent Tax Developments" (1986) 6 Philanthrop. 40, 59.

Dickson, M.L., and Lawrence C. Murray, "Recent Tax Developments (Charitable Organizations)" (1985) 5 Philanthrop. 56.

Dickson, M.L., and Lawrence C. Murray, "Recent Tax Developments" (1991) 10 Philanthrop. 42.

Drache, A.B.C., "Abortion Clinic Recognized as Charitable" (1992) 14 Can. Taxpayer 18.

Drache, A.B.C., *Canadian Tax Treatment of Charities and Charitable Donations* (Toronto: De Boo, 1978).

Drache, A.B.C., *Canadian Taxation of Charities and Donations* (Toronto: Carswell, 1994).

Drache, A.B.C., "Complaints Against 'Charitable Business'" (1992) 14 Can. Taxpayer 20.

Drache, A.B.C., "Residual Gift to Charity Recognized" (1992) 14 Can. Taxpayer 15.

Drache, A.B.C., "Tax Exempt Organizations" (1991) 13 Can. Taxpayer 165.

Erlichman, Harry, "Profitable Donations: What Price Culture?" (1992) Philanthrop. No. 2 3.

Farrow, Trevor C.W., "The Limits of Charity: Redefining the Boundaries of Charitable Trust Law" (1994) 13 Estates and Trusts J. 306.

Finkelstein, David N., "Tax Problems in Estate Planning for the Corporate Executive," in *Proceedings of 33rd Tax Conf.* 952 (Can. Tax Foundation, 1981).

Forster, George V., "Tax-effective Compensation for the Employees of Charitable Organizations" (1986) 6 Philanthrop. 24.

Goldstein, Lisa D., "Non-profit Organization Can Be Profitable" (1993) 41 Can. Tax J. 720.

Goodison, Don, "Tax Deductible Donations" (1988) 22 CGA Magazine 11.

Goodman, Wolfe D., "Charitable Gifts of Appreciated Capital Property" (1986) 8 Estates & Trusts Q. 189.

Goodman, Wolfe D., "The Impact of Taxation on Charitable Giving: Some Very Personal Views" (1984) 4 Philanthrop. 5.

Gotlieb, Maxwell, *Charities and the Tax Man and More* (Toronto: Canadian Bar Association — Ontario, Continuing Legal Education, 1990).

Gotlieb, Maxwell, "Taxation of, and Tax Planning for, Charitable Donations" (1993) 11 Philanthrop. No. 4 3.

Haney, Mary-Anne, "Abortion Too Controversial for Revenue Canada" (1992) 40 Can. Tax J. 171.

Innes, William I., "Gifts of Cultural Property by Artists" (1993) 12 Estates and Trusts J. 219.

Juneau, Carl D., "Some Major Issues Affecting Evaluation of the Charities Tax Incentive" (1990) 9 Philanthrop. No. 4 3.

Krishna, Vern, "Advantages des dons de charité au Canada (Les)" (soc. canadienne du cancer, 1984).

Krishna, Vern, "Charitable Donations: What Constitutes a 'Gift'?" (1985) 1 Can. Current Tax J107.

Krishna, Vern, "Charitable Donations: What is a Charitable Purpose?" (1986) 1 Can. Current Tax C159.

Law, Tax, and Charities: The Legislative and Regulatory Environment for Charitable and Non-profit Organizations (Toronto: The Canadian Centre for Philanthropy, 1990).

Midland, Christina H., "Limitations on Charities Under the *Income Tax Act*" (1992) 44 E.T.R. 111.

Monaco, Joseph C., *Charitable Donations: 'Gifts in Kind'* (Hamilton, Ont.: Thorne Ernst and Whinney, 1989).

"Personal Tax Planning: Charitable Giving" (1987) 35 Can. Tax J. 182.

Pintea, Hans O., "Taxation of Ongoing Partnership Operations," in *Proceedings of 33rd Tax Conf.* 195 (Can. Tax Foundation, 1981).

"Private Religious Schools in Jeopardy" (1980) 2 Can. Taxpayer 203.

"Religious School Problem: Final Resolution" (1982) 4 Can. Taxpayer 83.

Schusheim, Pearl E., "Charities and the Federal Income Tax Provisions: Getting and Staying Registered" (1986) 6 Philanthrop. 11.

Senecal, David, "The Tax Sleepers: Charitable and Nonprofit Organizations" (1975) 107 CA Magazine 52.

"Special Fund-Raising Events" (1983) 5 Can. Taxpayer 196.

Stephen, Peter R., "Charitable Giving" (1987) 35 Can. Tax J. 182.

Tamagno, Edward, "The Medical Expenses Deduction" (1979) 1 Can. Taxation 58.

Watson, Rod, "Charity and the Canadian Income Tax: An Erratic History" (1985) 5 Philanthrop. 3.

Zweibel, Ellen B., "A Truly Canadian Definition of Charity and a Lesson in Drafting Charitable Purposes: A Comment on *Native Communications Society of B.C. v. M.N.R.*" (1987) 26 E.T.R. 41.

Zweibel, Ellen B., "Looking the Gift Horse in the Mouth: An Examination of Charitable Gifts Which Benefit the Donor" (1986) 31 McGill L.J. 417.

Zweibel, Ellen B., "Registration as Charity — Political Activities (case comment on *Scarborough Community Legal Services v. R.*)" (1985) 1 Can. Current Tax A20.

Interest and Dividend Income

Alter, Dr. A., "Different Techniques for Adjusting Taxable Income Under Inflationary Conditions" (1986) Br. Tax Rev. 347.

Birnie, David A.G., "Shareholders' Buy-Sell Agreements: Some New Opportunities" in *Proceedings of the 38th Tax Conf.* 13 (Can. Tax Foundation, 1986).

Boultbee, Jack, "Tax Gimmicks", in *Proceedings of 33rd Tax Conf.* 300 (Can. Tax Foundation, 1981).

Colley, Geoffrey M., "Is Indexing a Necessary Evil?" (1986) 119 CA Magazine 52.

Colley, Geoffrey M., "Personal Tax Planning and You" (1976) 109 CA Magazine 45.

Colley, Geoffrey M., "Planning Ahead for Your Tax Exemption" (1981) 14 CA Magazine 59.

Colley, Geoffrey M., "What's New in Personal Investment?" (1977) 110 CA Magazine 63.

Communications Directorate, Revenue Canada Taxation, "Application for Registration: A Revenue Canada Taxation Perspective" (1986) 6 Philanthrop. 4.

Gould, Lawrence I., and Stanley N. Laiken, "Dividends vs. Capital Gains under Share Redemptions" (1979) 27 Can. Tax J. 161.

Gould, Lawrence I., and Stanley N. Laiken, "Effects of the Investment Income Deduction on Investment Returns" (1982) 30 Can. Tax J. 228.

Guilbault, P., "Individuals" (1985) 13 Can. Tax News 97.

"Interest Deductibility" (1979) 1 Can. Taxpayer 20.

"Juggling Dividends" (1980) 2 Can. Taxpayer 27.

Kennedy, James F., "The Use of Trust in Tax and Estate Planning," in *Proceedings of 33rd Tax Conf.* 577 (Can. Tax Foundation, 1981).

McNair, D. Keith, *Taxation of Farmers and Fishermen* (Toronto: De Boo, 1986).

Pintea, Hans O., "Taxation of Ongoing Partnership Operations," in *Proceedings of 33rd Tax Conf.* 195 (Can. Tax Foundation, 1981).

Pipes, Sally, and Michael Walker, with Douglas Wills, *Tax Facts 5: The Canadian Consumer Tax Index and You* (Vancouver: Fraser Institute, 1986).

Thomas, Douglas, "As A Matter of Interest" (1978) 111 CA Magazine 84.

Miscellaneous Deductible Losses

Amighetti, Leopole, "Income Tax Events Triggered by Death, an Examination of Selected Problems," in *Proceedings of 31st Tax Conf.* 652 (Can. Tax Foundation, 1979).

Blom, J., "Deductions for Personal Expenditures (Subdivision e and Divison C)" (1981) Can. Taxation 473.

Cadesky, Michael, "Corporate Losses," in *Proceedings of 42nd Tax Conf.* (Can. Tax Foundation, 1990).

Burpee, Thomas R., "Utilization of Tax Losses: "A Reasonable Expectation of Profit'," in *Proceedings of 37th Tax Conf.* 32:1 (Can. Tax Foundation, 1985).

Clarkson Gordon Foundation, *Policy Options for the Treatment of Tax Losses in Canada* (Scarborough, Ont.: Clarkson Gordon Foundation, 1991).

Dean, Jacklyn I., "The January 15, 1987 Draft Amendments Relating to the Acquisition of Gains and Losses" (1987) Corporate Management Tax Conf. 2:1.

Dunbar, Alisa E., "Sale of Stock Plan Shares May Produce Freely Deductible Loss" (1991) 3 Tax. of Exec. Compensation and Retirement 499.

Farden, Eric N., "Income Tax for Farmers" (Sask.: E.N. Farden, 1985).

Flynn, Gordon W., "Tax Planning for Corporations with Net Capital and Noncapital Losses," *Corporate Management Tax Conf.* 208 (Can. Tax Foundation, 1981).

Foster, David R., "Restoration of Non-capital Losses" (1992) 3 Can. Current Tax A7.

Hirsch, Morley P., "The Corporate Loss Transfer System", in *Proceedings of 37th Tax Conf.* 31 (Can. Tax Foundation, 1985).

Krishna, Vern, "Farm Losses; Subsection 31(1); 'Chief Source of Income'" (1985) 1 Can. Current Tax J-91.

LePan, Nicholas, "Federal and Provincial Issues in the Corporate Loss Transfer Proposal," in *Proceedings of 37th Tax Conf.* 13 (Can. Tax Foundation, 1985).

Neville, Ralph J., "Acquisition of Control and Corporate Losses" in *Proceedings of 44th Tax Conf.* 25:25 (Can. Tax Foundation, 1992).

"New Treatment for Losses" (1983) 5 Can. Taxpayer 183.

Nowoselski, Barty, "Should You Buy or Sell a Company for Its Tax-Loss Carryovers?" (1983) 116 CA Magazine 64.

Pearson, Hugh, "Farming and the *Income Tax Act*" (1993) 41 Can. Tax J. 1135.

Reid, Robert J., "Capital and Non-capital Losses," in *Proceedings of 42nd Tax Conf.* 20:1 (Can. Tax Foundation, 1990).

Richardson, Stephen R., "A Corporate Loss Transfer System for Canada: Analysis of Proposals," in *Proceedings of 37th Tax Conf.* 12 (Can. Tax Foundation, 1985).

Silver, Sheldon, "Utilization of Real Estate Losses," *Corporate Management Tax Conf.* 91 (Can. Tax Foundation, 1983).

Slutsky, Sam, "Insolvency: A Refresher from a Taxation Perspective" (1982) 30 Can. Tax J. 528.

Swirsky, Benjamin, "Utilization of Losses," *Corporate Management Tax Conf.* 213. (Can. Tax Foundation, 1978).

Thomas, Richard B., "A Farm Loss with a Difference: The Farmer is Successful" (1993) Can. Tax J. 513.

Ward, David A., "Arm's Length Acquisitions Relating to Shares in a Public Corporation," *Corporate Management Tax Conf.* 108 (Can. Tax Foundation, 1978).

Wilson, Michael H., *A Corporate Loss Transfer System for Canada*, Dept. of Finance, Canada, 1985.

Wise, Richard M., "Fair Market Determinations — A Few More Requirements" (1983) 31 Can. Tax J. 337.

Wraggett, Cathy, "Accelerated Deduction of Business Losses" (1990) 64 CMA Magazine 33.

Capital Gains Exemption

Attridge, Ian, "Create Conservation Gains, Not Capital Gains" (1994) 19 Intervenor No. 6 8.

Barbacki, Richard, "Use It or Lose It?" (1989) 122 CA Magazine 43.

Colley, G.M., "What Price the Capital Gains Exemption?" (1985) 118 CA Magazine 10:75.

Cullity, Maurice C., "The Capital Gains Exemption: Implications for Estate Planning," in *Proceedings of 37th Tax Conf.* 18 (Can. Tax Foundation, 1985).

Goodison, Don, "Business Losses" (1987) 21 CGA Magazine 6.

Goodman, S.H., and N.C. Tobias, "The Proposed $500,000 Capital Gains Exemption" (1985) 33 Can. Tax J. 721.

Hayos, Gabriel J., "The Capital Gains Exemption: Planning Strategies to Meet the Criteria of a Qualified Small Business Corporation," in *Proceedings of 40th Tax Conf.* 15:1 (Can. Tax Foundation, 1988).

James, Larry W., "Capital Gains Exemption: Planning Techniques," in *Proceedings of 38th Tax Conf.* 33 (Can. Tax Foundation, 1986).

Kellough, Howard J., and K. Travers Pullen, "Planning for the Lifetime Capital Gains Exemption" (1986) 3 Bus. & L. 3.

Kirby, F.P., "The Capital Gains Exemption: Other Than Qualified Small Business Shares," in *Proceedings of 40th Tax Conf.* 30:1 (Can. Tax Foundation, 1988).

Lawlor, W.R., "Surplus Stripping and Other Planning Opportunities with the New $500,000 Capital Gains Exemption" (1986) 34 Can. Tax J. 49.

Peters, Steven, "Enhancing the Exemption" (1992) 125 CA Magazine No. 5 33.

Potvin, Jean, "The Capital Gains Deduction for Qualified Small Business Corporation Shares Revisited," in *Proceedings of 44th Tax Conf.* (Can. Tax Foundation, 1992).

Quinton, Cathy, "The Additional Capital Gains Exemption" (1989) 62 CMA Magazine 34.

Rotenberg, Charles M., "Making the Deal Work" (1991) 13 Can. Taxpayer 60.

Ruby, Stephen S., "A Glimpse at the Lifetime Capital Gains Exemption (Part I)" (1986) 3 Bus. & L. 93.

Ruby, Stephen S., "A Glimpse at the Lifetime Capital Gains Exemption (Part III)" (1987) 4 Bus. & L. 6.

Stack, Thomas J., "Capital Gains and Losses on Shares of Private Corporations," in *Proceedings of 39th Tax Conf.* 17:1 (Can. Tax Foundation, 1987).

Tam, Anthony, "Capital Gains Exemption: Small Business Corporations" (1987–89) 2 Can. Current Tax P-5.

"Taxation of Corporate Reorganizations (The): New Measures to Restrict Netting of Gains and Shelter" (1987) 35 Can. Tax J. 198.

Templeton, Wendy, "Anti-Avoidance and the Capital Gains Exemption" (1986) 34 Can. Tax J. 203.

Templeton, Wendy, "The Taxation of Corporate Reorganizations: Anti-Avoidance and the Capital Gains Exemption" (1986) 34 Can. Tax J. 203.

Templeton, Wendy, "The Taxation of Corporate Reorganizations: Anti-Avoidance and the Capital Gains Exemptions: Part 2" (1986) 34 Can. Tax J. 446.

CHAPTER 16 — COMPUTATION OF TAX

I. — General Comment

The preceding chapters have focused on the computation of income and taxable income, i.e., determination of the base upon which we calculate the tax payable. We now turn to the second variable in determining a taxpayer's liability for income tax: Application of tax rates to the taxable base.

The setting of an appropriate tax rate is a complex matter that requires us to consider several factors. First, and most obvious, we must set the rate at a level that generates sufficient government revenues. Second, we must harmonize individual, trust, and corporate rates in order that the tax system is reasonably neutral among different forms of organization. For example, if the corporate tax rate is substantially lower than individual rates, there is an incentive to incorporate and accumulate income in the corporation. Third, rates — particularly corporate tax rates — must be competitive in the international marketplace. For example, Canadian corporate tax rates must take into account U.S. rates, or risk losing business and investments if our rates are substantially higher. Fourth, political considerations affect tax rates, particularly if the government is vulnerable in an election year.

The determination of tax payable is a multi-step process and involves more than the application of a single rate to taxable income. Once we determine the basic tax by applying a tax rate to taxable income, we apply various credits, surtaxes, and reductions. Finally, once we determine the tax payable under Part I of the *Income Tax Act*, we may also have to make another calculation under the "alternative minimum tax" regime.

Division E of Part I of the Act dealing with the calculation of tax payable has three parts:

1. Rules applicable to individuals;

2. Rules applicable to corporations; and

3. Rules applicable to all taxpayers.

As we will see, the computation takes into account several tax rates, multiple surtaxes, and tax credits in balancing the competing needs of revenue generation, fairness and equity, economic efficiency, and political considerations.

II. — Individuals

1. — Basic Tax Rate

(a) — General Rates

Section 117 sets out the federal tax rates applicable to individuals. The general basic tax rates for 2004 are as follows:

Taxable Income	Rate
$1–35,000	16%
$35,001–70,000	22%
$70,001–113,804	26%
$113,805 and over	29%

These tax rates are indexed by a formula that is linked to the Consumer Price Index ("CPI").[1]

(b) — Provincial Taxes

The rates in section 117 are the federal rates. In addition to the federal tax, Canadian residents are also liable for provincial income tax. Provinces that have a tax collection agree-

---

[1] S. 117.1. From 1974 to 1985 the indexing formula was, with two exceptions, directly linked to changes in the CPI. The two exceptions were in respect of the years 1983 and 1984, when the federal government introduced a restraint program known as "6 and 5". In 1983, notwithstanding a much higher inflation rate, the Minister of Finance capped the indexing of marginal tax brackets and personal exemptions at 6 per cent; for 1984, indexing was capped at 5 per cent in accordance with the federal government's "6 and 5 program". Although full indexing was resumed in 1985, there was no provision to make up for the reductions in 1983 and 1984. In 1986, the federal government, faced with an ever-increasing deficit, cut back on indexation of tax brackets to reflect only that portion of the increase in CPI over 3 per cent. Since the CPI rate has been below 3 per cent from 1992, there were no indexation adjustments to the tax brackets. Thus, individuals were bumped into higher tax brackets as their income increased with inflation. This phenomenon is known as "bracket creep". The 2002 Budget announced a return to full indexation of the personal income tax system through its "Five-Year Tax Reduction Plan". Full indexation took effect as of January 1, 2000, and in 2004, the final phase of the five year plan increased the tax bracket thresholds to specified amounts that went beyond the inflation index amount.

ment with the federal government ("participating provinces") may elect to calculate their income taxes using one of two methods: the "tax on tax" method or the "tax on income" method. All of the participating provinces have adopted the new tax on income method.

The "tax on tax" method calculates the provincial income tax by applying the provincial rate of tax to the *federal tax payable*. This method is inflexible and limits the ability of the provinces to raise revenues and set provincial income tax policies. In response to the provinces' desire for more control over how their income taxes are levied, the "tax on income" method was introduced.[2]

The "tax on income" method calculates the provincial income tax by reference to taxable *income* rather than to federal tax payable. As such, it allows the provinces to determine their own unique income tax brackets and rates and to create their own distinct block of non-refundable tax credits,[3] which gives the provinces greater flexibility in setting tax policy. However, in order to ensure a common tax base, the provinces and the federal government use a common definition of "taxable income".

Quebec is the only province that does not have a tax collection agreement with the federal government. It also calculates the provincial income tax by reference to "taxable income".

The combined federal and provincial marginal income tax rates (including surtaxes) at the top end of the rate schedule as of June 21, 2004 are set out in Figure 1.

Figure 1 — Federal/Provincial Income Tax Rates (2004)

Non-Resident	42.92%
Resident of:	
Alberta	39.00%
British Columbia	43.70%
Manitoba	46.40%
New Brunswick	46.84%
Newfoundland	48.64%
Nova Scotia	48.25%
Ontario	46.41%
Prince Edward Island	47.37%
Quebec	48.22%
Saskatchewan	44.00%

[2] See generally the Department of Finance's *Federal Administration of Provincial Taxes*, October 1998, Report prepared by the Federal-Provincial Committee on Taxation for presentation to Ministers of Finance, online: <http://www.fin.gc.ca/fapt/fapt3e.html.>

[3] Subject to restrictions on minimums; see *ibid.* at Design and Operation.

Figure 1 — Federal/Provincial Income Tax Rates (2004)

Northwest Territories	42.55%
Yukon Territory	42.40%
Nunavut	40.50%

As Figure 1 shows, individuals pay taxes at different rates depending on where they live. A resident of Newfoundland in the top bracket, for example, paid 48.64 per cent in 2004, compared with 39.00 per cent in Alberta. Thus, the tax burden does not always reflect an individual's ability to pay. A part of the price of federalism is that individuals bear differential tax burdens depending on where they live.

Apart from the indexing of tax brackets, the basic rate schedule is fairly stable; the rates are not usually altered from year to year. Instead, governments increase or decrease taxes by imposing or removing surtaxes, or by allowing for special tax credits.

2. — Surtaxes

The disparity of tax rates does not stop at the basic provincial rate. There are further adjustments to tax rates through surtaxes (often labelled as "temporary") or tax credits. A surtax is a tax calculated by reference to another tax, usually the basic federal tax.

(a) — Basic Surtax

The surtax rate has been adjusted frequently in the past few years. The "temporary" surtax was 3 per cent in 1987 and 1988, increased to 4 per cent in 1989 and 5 per cent in 1990 and 1991, reduced to 4.5 per cent in 1992, and 3 per cent in 1993 and subsequent years. The federal government finally abolished the basic surtax in 2000. However, several provinces still charge a surtax on the provincial income tax.

3. — Tax Credits

Once we determine an individual's tentative tax liability before adjustments, he or she may also be entitled to certain personal and other tax credits. A tax credit reduces the tax that would otherwise be payable by the individual. In general, tax credits depend on:

1. Status;

2. Source of income;

3. Type of expenditure; and

4. Location of source of income.

For example, a taxpayer can claim a credit for:

- Personal tax credits;

- Pension income;

- Dividends from taxable Canadian corporations;

- Tuition and education;

- Medical expenses;

- Charitable donations;

- Eligible children;

- Overseas employment; or

- Foreign taxes.

We calculate these according to a formula that applies a percentage to the aggregate of the claimable amounts. The credits are indexed and, as such, are partially adjusted each year to reflect inflationary increases as measured by the Consumer Price Index.

Some of the credits are refundable — that is, the taxpayer receives a cash refund if the credits exceed his or her income for the year. Others are non-refundable, and the taxpayer loses the credit if he or she cannot deduct it from tax otherwise payable for the year.

Tax credits are available at both the federal and provincial levels. Each province has the flexibility (subject to some restrictions) to choose which tax credits it will offer and to set the amount of those credits. Thus, tax credits vary from province to province. The tax credits discussed below are credits under the federal tax statute.

(a) — Personal Tax Credits

A taxpayer can claim tax credits on account of:

- Single status;

- Spousal and common law partner status;

- Equivalent-to-spouse status;

- Dependants; and

- Age.

These credits are not refundable. References to spouse in this chapter include, where appropriate, common-law partners.

(i) — Method of Calculation

A taxpayer claims a credit by aggregating the dollar value of all the amounts that he or she is entitled to claim, and then multiplying this value by the "appropriate percentage" for the year.[4] The "appropriate percentage" for a taxation year is the *lowest* marginal tax rate applicable in the particular year. The lowest "appropriate percentage" is currently 16 per cent.[5]

Provinces determine their own unique income tax brackets and rates and create their own distinct block of non-refundable tax credits.[6] As a result, provincial tax credits are often different than the federal tax credits. Provinces have the flexibility to supplement federal credits or add any additional unique provincial credits. They are also not required to follow any federal increases in a credit except in the case of expenditure-based credits. For expenditure-based credits (e.g., CPP, EI, tuition fees, medical expenses, charitable donations), provinces may increase credits beyond the level of the gross federal credit, but may not fall below the federal level.

(ii) — Single Status

Every individual is entitled to $8,012 (2004) as their personal claim.[7] This amount is multiplied by the "appropriate percentage." For example, in 2004 the credit for a single person is $1,282, that is, 16 per cent of $8,012.

(iii) — Spousal Status

An individual who supports his or her spouse or a common-law partner can claim an additional amount as a tax credit. In 2004, for example, the additional amount was $6,803. Thus, in the simplest case, an individual is entitled to claim a total of $14,815, which converts to a credit of $2,370, that is, 16 per cent of $14,815.

A person is "married" if he or she undergoes a form of marriage recognized by the laws of Canada and is not a widow or widower, or divorced.[8] Subsection 252(3) expands the mean-

---

[4]Subs. 118(1).

[5]Subs. 248(1)"appropriate percentage"; subs. 117(2).

[6]See generally the Department of *Finance's Federal Administration of Provincial Taxes*, October 1998, Report prepared by the Federal-Provincial Committee on Taxation for presentation to Ministers of Finance, online: <http://www.fin.gc.ca/fapt/fapt3e.html.>

[7]Para. 118(1)(c).

[8]*The Queen v. Scheller*, [1975] C.T.C. 601, 75 D.T.C. 5406 (F.C.T.D.); *McPhee v. M.N.R.*, [1980] C.T.C. 2042, 80 D.T.C. 1034 (T.R.B.); *The Queen v. Taylor*, [1984] C.T.C. 244, 84 D.T.C. 6234 (F.C.T.D.).

ing of "spouse" to include individuals of the opposite sex who are party to a void or voidable marriage.

"Income" means *net* income. The spouse's income for the entire year is taken into account in determining whether the supporting taxpayer is entitled to the claim for spousal status.[9] Thus, a taxpayer who marries, or qualifies as a common law spouse, late in the year may claim a deduction for supporting his or her spouse only if the taxpayer's income for the entire year is less than $7,484. Both spouses may not claim a deduction for each other in the same taxation year.

Where the individual was living apart from his or her spouse at the end of the year by reason of marriage breakdown, the spouse's income for the period during the year in which the parties were not separated is taken into account in determining the claim.[10]

(iv) — Wholly-Dependent Persons

A person who is not entitled to the spousal status credit but who supports a person dependent on him or her can claim the credit for a wholly-dependent person (also referred to as the "equivalent-to-spouse credit").[11] The amount claimable under this provision is equivalent to the amount that a married person whose spouse does not earn more than the total threshold amount can claim.

The equivalent-to-spouse credit is available only to an individual who maintains (either alone or jointly with another person), and lives in, a self-contained domestic establishment and actually supports therein the dependent person. For example, a single parent supporting a child would qualify for the credit under this provision.

There are two additional qualifications for the claim on account of wholly-dependent persons. First, except where the claim is in respect of the taxpayer's child, the credit is available only in respect of dependants who reside in Canada.[12] A taxpayer is not entitled to the credit in respect of foreign resident dependants.

---

[9] *Johnston v. M.N.R.*, [1948] S.C.R. 486, [1948] C.T.C. 195, 3 D.T.C. 1182 (S.C.C.) (husband considered to support his wife if contributing to her support, even though she may supply some money towards meeting expenses of household).

[10] Para. 118(1)(a).

[11] Para. 118(1)(b).

[12] Cl. 118(1)(b)(ii)(A).

Second, except in the case of a claim for a parent or grandparent, a taxpayer cannot claim an amount in respect of a dependant who is 18 years of age or older unless the person's dependency is because of mental or physical infirmity.[13]

(v) — Dependants

A taxpayer may also claim an amount in respect of individuals who depend on him or her for support. The claim depends upon five criteria:[14]

1. Dependency;

2. Relationship between the taxpayer and the individual claimed as a dependant;

3. Residence;

4. Age; and

5. Mental or physical infirmity of dependant.

1. — Dependency

Whether an individual is dependent on a taxpayer is a question of fact in each case. In the event that a person is partially dependent on two or more taxpayers, their aggregate claim in respect of that dependant cannot exceed the maximum amount that would be deductible in respect of a claim by one taxpayer. Where the supporting individuals cannot agree on the portion of the total that each is to deduct, the Minister may allocate the amount between them.

2. — Relationship

The term "dependant" in respect of a taxpayer or his or her spouse means:[15]

- Their children or grandchildren;

- Their nieces or nephews, if resident in Canada;

- Their brothers or sisters, if resident in Canada; and

- Their parents, grandparents, aunts or uncles, if resident in Canada.

---

[13]Cl. 118(1)(b)(ii)(D).

[14]Para. 118(1)(d).

[15]Subs. 118(6).

3. — Residence

Except in respect of a claim for the taxpayer's, or his or her spouse's, children or grandchildren, the dependency deduction is available only for the support of dependants who reside in Canada. This distinction between the various categories of dependants reflects the concerns of the tax authorities with bogus dependency claims.

4. — Age

The infirm dependent deduction is available only in respect of dependants over the age of 18. The amount claimable in 2004 is $3,784 less the excess of the dependant's income over $5,368.

5. — Mental or Physical Infirmity

A taxpayer can claim the dependency deduction for individuals over the age of 18 only if they depend upon him or her because of mental or physical infirmity.[16]

(vi) — Age

An individual who is 65 years of age or older can claim an additional amount.[17] The maximum amount claimable is 16 per cent of $3,912 (2004; indexed).[18]

For individuals whose income exceeds $29,124 (2004; indexed),[19] the maximum amount claimable is reduced by 15 per cent of income over that amount.

(b) — Pension Income

The pension income credits provide some relief from inflation, particularly for individuals who have to live on fixed incomes. The credit depends on two factors: the source of the pension and the recipient's age.

An individual who is 65 years of age or older may claim a credit in respect of pension income. We determine the claim by applying the appropriate percentage (16 per cent in

---

[16]Subpara. 118(1)(d)(ii).

[17]Subs. 118(2).

[18]See 117.1.

[19]*Ibid.*

2004) to the lesser of $1,000 and the pension income in the year.[20] For example, in 2004, the maximum credit in respect of pension income is $160, that is, 16 per cent of $1,000 (not indexed).

The claim of an individual who is under 65 years of age is restricted to a percentage of the lesser of $1,000 and his or her "qualified pension income" for the year.[21] The percentage for the year is 16 per cent. For example, in 2004, the maximum credit is $160, that is, 16 per cent of $1,000 (not indexed).

"Pension income" includes:[22]

- Life annuity payments out of a superannuation or pension fund;

- Annuity payments out of registered retirement savings plans;

- Payments out of registered retirement income funds;

- Payments out of deferred profit-sharing plans; and

- Accrued income on an annuity or life insurance policy included in income.

Lump-sum payments out of pension plans and deferred income plans are not eligible for the pension income credit. We determine the credit by reference to *annuity* payments out of these plans. Pensions under the *Old Age Security Act*, the Canada Pension Plan or the Quebec Pension Plan, retirement allowances, death benefits, exempt income, and payments out of an employee benefit plan, an employee trust, a salary deferral arrangement, or a retirement compensation arrangement do not qualify for the credit.

The concept of "qualified pension income" is much narrower than "pension income." "Qualified pension income" includes:[23]

- Life annuities paid out under a superannuation or pension fund plan; and

- Amounts paid as a consequence of the death of a taxpayer's spouse, on account of registered retirement savings plans, registered retirement income funds, deferred profit-sharing plans, or certain annuity payments.

For example, where an individual takes out a guaranteed term annuity under a registered retirement savings plan and designates his spouse as a beneficiary under the plan, any payments made under the guaranteed term of the plan to the beneficiary on his death are eligible for the pension income credit.

---

[20]Para. 118(3)(a).

[21]Para. 118(3)(b).

[22]Subs. 118(7)"pension income".

[23]Subs. 118(7)"qualified pension income".

(c) — Tuition Fees

Tuition fees on account of education are generally personal and capital expenditures. Tuition fees can also be business expenses where an employer pays the fees for business purposes. Thus, an individual could not, without specific authorization, claim a deduction or a credit for tuition fees. For social policy reasons, however, the tax system allows individuals a tax credit for tuition fees paid to certain educational institutions.

There are two different sets of conditions that regulate the credit for tuition fees: the first deals with students attending educational institutions in Canada, the second with those attending educational institutions outside Canada. The rules in respect of the former category are considerably less stringent than those in respect of the latter.

(i) — Institutions in Canada

A student may claim a credit for fees paid to attend:[24]

- A post-secondary educational institution; or

- An institution certified by the Minister of Human Resources Development to provide courses that furnish or improve occupational skills.

We determine the credit by applying the "appropriate percentage" to the eligible tuition fees paid in the year. The credit is available only if the total fees exceed $100.

(ii) — Deemed Residence

A student who is deemed to be a resident of Canada[25] can claim the credit even if he or she attends an educational institution outside Canada. The credit is available on the same terms and conditions as if the student were attending an institution in Canada.[26]

(iii) — Transfer of Unused Credits

A student can transfer the tuition tax credit to his or her spouse.[27] Where a student is unmarried, or a married student's spouse does not claim a personal tax credit for him or her, the

---

[24]Para. 118.5(1)(a).

[25]S. 250.

[26]Subs. 118.5(2).

[27]S. 118.8.

education and tuition tax credit may be transferred to the student's parents or grandparents.[28]

The maximum amount the student can transfer each year is $5,000 minus the amount he or she uses that year.

(iv) — Fees Paid by Employer

Tuition fees paid by a student's employer are also creditable by the student, but only to the extent that the student includes the fees in income. The employer may deduct the fees as a business expense if the fees are paid for business purposes.[29]

(v) — "Tuition Fees"

Tuition fees include:

- Admission fees;

- Charges for the use of a library, or laboratory fees;

- Exemption fees;

- Examination fees;

- Application fees;

- Confirmation fees;

- Charges for a certificate, diploma or degree;

- Membership or seminar fees specifically related to an academic program and its administration;

- Mandatory computer service fees; and

- Academic fees.

Fees for student activities (whether social or athletic), medical care fees, transportation and parking charges, board and lodging, equipment costs of a capital nature, and initiation or entrance fees to professional organizations are not creditable for tax purposes.

---

[28]S. 118.9.

[29]S. 9.

(vi) — Books

Although the cost of books does not usually qualify as a tuition fee, a student may claim a credit for such costs if he or she is enrolled in a correspondence course and the cost of the books is an integral part of the fee paid for the course.

(vii) — Period Covered by Fees

Only tuition fees paid *in respect of a particular year*[30] are creditable in that year. Fees paid to cover tuition for an academic session that straddles the calendar year are eligible for the tax credit only for the year to which they relate. For example, where the academic year is from September in one year to May of the next year, the tuition tax credit must be allocated so that the portion from September to December is claimable in one year and the portion from January to May is claimable in the subsequent year.

(viii) — Educational Institutions Outside Canada

A full-time student enrolled at a university outside Canada can claim a credit by applying the "appropriate percentage" to the amount of eligible tuition fees paid in respect of the year to the university.[31]

The qualifications to claim the tuition fee credit for attending a university outside Canada are considerably more stringent than those for institutions in Canada. The credit is available only if the student satisfies the following conditions:

- The student attends a course that is of not less than 13 consecutive weeks' duration;

- The program of study leads to a *degree* (not a diploma) from the institution;

- The institution that the student attends is a *university*, not a college or other educational institution; and

- The student attends on a full-time basis.

Students are considered to be in "full-time attendance" at a university if the institution regards them to be full-time students for academic purposes. A certificate from a university stating that a student was in full-time attendance in a particular academic year or semester is acceptable for tax purposes. Hence, a student who holds a full-time job and takes a full course load at a university is considered to be in full-time attendance at the educational institution for tax purposes.

---

[30]Subs. 118.5(1).

[31]Para. 118.5(1)(b).

The Canada Revenue Agency ("CRA") interprets the 13 consecutive weeks' attendance requirement quite liberally. For example, a student satisfies the requirement if he or she drops out of the course before completing the program of studies, the particular academic term falls a little short of 13 weeks, or the term is broken by official holidays.

(ix) — Post-Graduate Studies

A student who enrols in a post-graduate program of studies on a regular basis is considered to be in "full-time attendance" if he or she is registered for the regular academic year. This is so even if the requirements for attendance in class are minimal. For example, a registered post-graduate student who spends most of his or her time in a laboratory or a library engaged in research, whether on or off campus, is usually considered to be in full-time attendance. Similarly, a post-graduate student who holds a full-time job is not necessarily precluded from claiming the tuition tax credit.

(x) — Commuting to United States

A Canadian resident who commutes to a post-secondary level educational institution in the United States can claim the tax credit for tuition fees.[32] This credit is available only to students who reside throughout the year near the Canada-U.S. border.

(d) — Education Credit

In addition to the tuition fee credit, a student can also claim an "education credit" for attendance at a designated educational institution, if he or she enrols in a qualifying educational program at that institution.[33] As with the other tax credits, we determine the education tax credit by applying the "appropriate percentage" for the year to the number of months of full-time attendance at the institution, multiplied by $400. For example, the credit for a student who attended a university for eight months in 2004 is $512, that is $400 x 8 months x 16 per cent.[34] Part-time students may claim an education credit of 16 per cent of $120 per month of part-time attendance. Part-time attendance is defined as attendance at a program lasting at least three consecutive weeks and involving a minimum of 12 hours of courses each month.

---

[32]Para. 118.5(1)(c).

[33]S. 118.6.

[34]Subs. 118.6(2).

(e) — Medical Expenses

Medical expenditures are also personal and, therefore, would usually be non-deductible for tax purposes. The Act does, however, provide some relief for "extraordinary" medical expenses over a minimum threshold limit to reflect the burden of such expenditures on one's ability to pay. The statute attempts, with limited success, to balance the social policy of providing relief for extraordinary medical expenses within stringent revenue constraints.

(i) — Computation of Credit

We determine the medical expense credit by applying the "appropriate percentage" (16 per cent in 2004) to the sum of the taxpayer's medical expenses in excess of a threshold amount.[35] The threshold amount is the lesser of $1,813 (2004) and 3 per cent of the individual's income from the year.

Thus, the first step is to determine the taxpayer's total medical expenses for the year. The second step is to deduct from the total medical expenses the *lesser* of $1,813 (2004) and 3 per cent of the taxpayer's income for the year. The final step is to determine the medical expense credit by applying the appropriate percentage to the amount by which the medical expenses exceed the threshold.

(ii) — Meaning of "Medical Expenses"

A taxpayer may deduct medical expenses incurred on behalf of:[36]

- The taxpayer;

- A spouse;

- Children, or a spouse's children, who depend on the taxpayer for support; or

- A spouse's parent, grandparent, brother, sister, uncle, aunt, niece, or nephew who reside in Canada and depend on the taxpayer for support.

The taxpayer must support his or her claim for the credit by filing receipts with the return for the year.

"Medical expenses" means expenses paid to a medical practitioner, dentist, nurse, public or licensed private hospital. At first glance, the phrase "medical expenses" appears to include any expenditures that an individual may incur as a consequence of disability or illness. In

---

[35]Subs. 118.2(1).

[36]Subss. 118.2(2), 118(6).

fact, the phrase is circumscribed by several restrictive conditions. The list of eligible medical expenses is regularly reviewed and expanded in light of new technologies.

Payments for full-time nursing care in a nursing home or group home and payments for a full-time attendant to look after an individual also qualify as medical expenses if the individual who requires the care is suffering from severe and prolonged mental or physical impairment.[37] A person is considered to be suffering from severe and prolonged impairment if his or her disability markedly restricts daily activities and can be expected to last for a continuous period of at least 12 months.[38] Reasonable expenses can also be claimed that were incurred to train an individual to care for a relative having a physical or mental infirmity. This relative must live with or be dependant on the individual.

Payments for a part-time attendant to look after an individual also qualify as medical expenses to the extent that the total paid does not exceed $10,000 (or $20,000, where the individual died in the year). Therapy administered by a person other than a qualified therapist or medical practitioner (e.g., audiologists and psychologists) to persons who are eligible for the disability tax credit also qualify. Finally, tutoring services that are supplementary to the primary education of persons with learning disabilities is a qualifying medical expense.

The restrictions on eligible medical expenses are long and detailed. It is important to note that an individual must satisfy all of the requirements before he or she can claim the credit. The courts used to be very strict in permitting a claim for medical expenses. They applied the statutory rules rigidly, sometimes excessively so, regardless of the underlying purpose of the deduction.[39] Recently, the courts have become more liberal in their interpretation of the provisions following the Supreme Court of Canada's guidelines that the *Income Tax Act* should be read in context and that *ambiguous* provisions should be interpreted according to the "object and spirit" of the rule.[40] See, for example, Judge Bowman's comments in *Radage*, 96 D.T.C. 1615 (T.C.C.): "The court must, while recognizing the narrowness of the tests . . . construe the provisions liberally, humanely and compassionately and not narrowly and technically."[41]

---

[37]See paras. 118.2(2)(b), (b.1).

[38]Subs. 118.4(1).

[39]See, e.g., *Witthuhn v. M.N.R.* (1959), 17 Tax A.B.C. 33, 57 D.T.C. 174 (T.A.B.) (board denied claim for medical expenses for amounts paid to attendant to look after infirm spouse; taxpayer claimed expenses on basis that spouse was confined to bed or wheelchair; spouse in fact did not own wheelchair, instead sat in a special rocking chair; claim denied as rocking chair not a "wheelchair").

[40]*Stubart Invt. Ltd. v. The Queen*, [1984] 1 S.C.R. 536, [1984] C.T.C. 294, 84 D.T.C. 6305 (S.C.C.); See Chapter 2, "Interpretation of Tax Law."

[41]See also, *Crockart*, 99 D.T.C. 3493, [1999] 2 C.T.C. 2409 (T.C.C.) (meaning of a "hospital bed").

(f) — Mental or Physical Impairment

An individual with a severe and prolonged mental or physical impairment may claim a tax credit.[42] In 2004, the credit is 16 per cent of $6,486 (indexed after 2001). The claim must be supported by a doctor's certificate in prescribed form certifying the impairment. A person is considered to have a "severe and prolonged ... impairment" only if he or she is markedly restricted all or substantially all of the time in the ability to perform a basic activity of daily living and the impairment lasts but for therapy that is essential to sustain a vital function of the individual that is required to be administered at least three times each week for a total period averaging not less than 14 hours per week, or can reasonably be expected to last, for a continuous period of at least 12 months.[43] The Act defines the basic activities of daily living.[44]

4. — Dividend Tax Credit

(a) — Tax Integration

Corporate income is potentially vulnerable to double taxation, once at the corporate level and again at the shareholder level. The statute provides partial relief through the dividend tax credit. An individual who receives a taxable dividend from a taxable Canadian corporation must include 125 per cent of the dollar amount of the dividend in income.[45] In other words, the cash value of the dividend is "grossed-up" by 25 per cent. Thus, initially one calculates the tax payable on the dividend by reference to a figure that is higher than the actual income. In theory, the gross-up reflects the underlying corporate tax (at an assumed rate of 20 per cent) paid by the corporation. The individual may, however, claim a dividend tax credit against the amount of federal tax that the gross-up imputes to the corporation.[46]

This two-step process of "grossing up" taxable dividends, followed by a tax credit, is a structural device that prevents, to a limited extent, double taxation of corporate income. The tax credit integrates the tax paid by Canadian corporations with the tax paid by shareholders on dividends. We discuss this process of "tax integration" in greater detail in Chapter 20, "Corporate Business Income." For present purposes, it is sufficient to state that an individual who receives a dividend from a Canadian corporation can claim a partial credit against tax payable.

---

[42] S. 118.3.

[43] S. 118.4.

[44] Paras. 118.4(1)(c), (d).

[45] Para. 82(1)(b).

[46] S. 121.

(b) — Federal Credit

The dividend tax credit is equal to two-thirds of the value of the dividend gross-up. For example, an individual who receives a dividend of $800 is taxable on $1,000 and may claim a federal dividend tax credit of $133 (2/3 × $200).

(c) — Provincial Credit

Most provinces calculate the provincial dividend tax credit in the same manner as the federal tax credit. The provincial credit is often expressed as a percentage of the taxable amount rather than a percentage of the gross-up. For example, if the provincial credit is 25.5 per cent of the gross-up, the CRA will often refer to the credit as 5.1 per cent of the taxable amount.

Example

Assume that in Year 1 Harry Smith receives $40,000 in dividends from taxable Canadian corporations. The tax payable (ignoring personal credits and surtaxes) on the dividend income is as follows:

Cash dividends		$ 40,000
Gross-up by 25%		10,000
Taxable amount		$ 50,000
Federal tax (Year 1 rates)		
On first $35,000 (@16%)	$ 5,600	
On next $15,000 (@22%)	3,300	
Federal income tax		$ 8,900
Federal dividend tax credit		
(2/3 × $10,000)		(6,667)
Net federal tax		$ 2,233
Provincial tax (Year 1 rates)		
On first $35,000 (@6%)	$ 2,100	
On next $15,000 (@9%)	1,350	

Example		
Provincial income tax		
Provincial dividend tax credit	$ 3,450	
(25.5% × $10,000 or		
5.1% of $50,000)	(2,550)	
Net provincial tax		900
Total tax payable on dividend		$ 3,133

Thus, in the above example the federal dividend tax credit is $6,667 and the provincial dividend tax credit is $2,550 for a combined dividend tax credit of $9,217. The $9,217 credit is meant to approximate the underlying corporate tax ($50,000 × 20%) that we assume the corporation paid. As we will see, this system of tax imputation works perfectly only if the corporation actually pays tax at a rate of 20 per cent.

5. — *Overseas Employment Tax Credit*

As a rule, Canadian residents are liable for tax on their worldwide income.[47] We refer to this as a system of full tax liability. An individual employed on an overseas contract may be entitled to a special tax credit. The credit is available only in limited circumstances, but it is extremely generous. We justify the credit on the basis that it allows Canadian businesses employing Canadian workers to compete in international markets with other countries that offer similar tax relief to their residents.

The credit is available only to an individual who is employed by a *specified* employer, and then only if the employee works overseas for a period of at least six consecutive months in certain *approved* activities. Thus the statute limits the credit in four ways:[48]

• The taxpayer must work for a "specified employer";

• The employer must engage in an approved activity;

• The employee must work abroad for more than six consecutive months; and

• The amount of the credit is subject to a ceiling.

---

[47]Subs. 2(1); see also Chapter 3, "Residence and Source."

[48]Subs. 122.3(1); IT-497R4, "Overseas Employment Tax Credit" (May 14, 2004).

A "specified employer" is generally an employer resident in Canada.[49] The employer must engage in an approved activity such as construction, exploration for, and exploitation of, natural resources, or an agricultural project.

The amount of the credit is subject to a ceiling.[50] The credit is equal to that portion of the tax otherwise payable that the *lesser* of $80,000 and 80 per cent of the employee's net overseas employment income is of his or her total income.

6. — Alternative Minimum Tax

High-income taxpayers may be subject to an "alternative minimum tax" ("AMT"), even though they do not have any taxable income.[51] The federal alternative minimum tax is payable at a flat rate of 16 per cent on "adjusted taxable income." Combined with a provincial tax rate of approximately 40 per cent, the AMT is 22 per cent.

The alternative minimum tax applies only to individuals and to certain trusts; it does not apply to corporations. AMT is an alternative tax. Thus, it applies only if the amount computed under it exceeds the individual's regular tax calculated on regular taxable income. The AMT is a substitute for the regular tax.

Generally, a taxpayer's "adjusted taxable income" for the alternative minimum tax is his or her regular taxable income plus certain addbacks in respect of tax preference items.[52] These tax preference items are deductions that might be used to shelter income. For example, 60 per cent of the exempt portion of capital gains, writeoffs for resource expenses, Canadian films, and a portion of the stock option deductions are added back into taxable income.

In computing "adjusted taxable income" for AMT purposes, a taxpayer is entitled to a basic exemption of $40,000.[53]

III. — Rules: Corporations

The rules that deal with the computation of tax payable by corporations are more detailed and complex than the rules applicable to individuals. This is because corporate taxation depends upon numerous variables: (1) type and size of the corporation; (2) ownership structure; (3) type and source of income; and (4) amount of income earned in a year. In this

---

[49]Subs. 122.3(2)"specified employer".

[50]Paras. 122.3(1)(c), (d).

[51]Subss. 127.5–127.55.

[52]S. 127.52.

[53]S. 127.53.

chapter, we look at the general rules applicable to all corporations. In following chapters[54] we will examine the rules in respect of special types of corporations and specific types of income.

1. — General Tax Rate

The general basic rate of federal tax payable by a corporation is 38 per cent,[55] which is reduced by a general rate reduction. The general rate reduction does not apply to the income upon which a CCPC claims the small business deduction.[56]

2. — Surtax

In addition to the general tax, however, corporations are also liable to pay a surtax of 4 per cent of their basic federal tax. We calculate the surtax on the basis of the federal corporate tax payable before deductions for the small business deduction and the manufacturing and processing deduction,[57] but after deducting the full 10 per cent provincial tax credit or federal abatement.

3. — Tax Adjustments

Few, if any, corporations actually pay tax at the basic rate. The adjustments to the basic corporate tax include the following:

- Provincial tax credit;

- Foreign tax credit;

- Small business deduction;

- Manufacturing and processing profits deduction;

- Logging tax deduction;

- Investment tax credit; and

- Political contributions credit.

---

[54]See Chapters 19, "Corporate Investment Income" and 20, "Corporate Business Income" for the taxation of private corporations.

[55]Para. 123(1)(a).

[56]Subs. 123.4(2).

[57]S. 123.2.

Also, the Act taxes certain types of corporations at special rates because of their special status.[58]

4. — Provincial Tax Credit

A corporation can claim a tax credit of 10 per cent of its taxable income earned in a province.[59] The provincial tax credit vacates part of the tax field to the provinces so that they may levy a corporate tax of their own. Where a province imposes a corporate tax of 10 per cent, the total burden of corporate tax (ignoring special tax adjustments) is 38 per cent, subject to the general rate reduction (see Appendix D). Where, however, a province imposes a provincial corporate tax in excess of 10 per cent, the effective corporate tax burden (ignoring special tax adjustments) exceeds 38 per cent, as adjusted by the general rate reduction.

The provincial tax credit is applicable only to a corporation's "taxable income earned ... in a province." We determine this amount by allocating the corporation's total taxable income to its "permanent establishment[s]" in the provinces.[60] Thus, the calculation of a corporation's provincial tax credit involves four steps:

> 1. Determine whether the corporation has a "permanent establishment" in one or more provinces;
>
> 2. Allocate the taxable income of the corporation to the various provinces in accordance with the prescribed formulae;
>
> 3. Calculate the provincial tax abatement as 10 per cent of the amount of "taxable income earned" in the provinces; and
>
> 4. Deduct the provincial tax abatement from the corporation's "tax otherwise payable."

The Act does not define "tax otherwise payable." It means the tax that is payable after the deduction of *all* permissible deductions.

(a) — "Permanent Establishment"

A "permanent establishment" is a fixed place of business of a corporation. A fixed place of business includes:[61]

* An office;

---

[58]For example, investment corporations are subject to the special rules in s. 130.

[59]S. 124(1).

[60]Regs. 401, 402.

[61]Reg. 400(2).

- A branch;

- A mine;

- An oil well;

- A farm;

- Timberland;

- A factory;

- A workshop; or

- A warehouse.

Where a corporation does not have a fixed place of business, the term "permanent establishment" means the principal place in which the corporation conducts its business.[62]

The Act sometimes deems a corporation to have a permanent establishment in a particular place. For example:

- Where a corporation carries on business in a particular place through an employee (or agent) who has general authority to contract or who has a stock of merchandise owned by his or her employer or principal, from which he or she regularly fills orders, that place is a permanent establishment.[63]

- Where a corporation that *otherwise* has a permanent establishment in Canada also owns land in a province, such land is a permanent establishment.[64]

- Where a corporation uses substantial machinery or equipment in a particular place *at any time in a taxation year*, it has a permanent establishment in that place.[65]

- An insurance corporation registered or licensed to do business in a province has a permanent establishment in that province.[66]

The mere fact, however, that a corporation's subsidiary does business in a particular place does not necessarily mean that the parent corporation has a permanent establishment in that

---

[62]Reg. 400(2)(a).

[63]Reg. 400(2)(b).

[64]Reg. 400(2)(d).

[65]Reg. 400(2)(e).

[66]Reg. 400(2)(c).

same place.[67] Similarly, the maintenance of an office solely for the purchase of merchandise does not *necessarily* imply the presence of a permanent establishment in that location.[68]

(b) — Allocation of Taxable Income

Once we determine that a corporation has one or more permanent establishments, the next step is to allocate its taxable income to the provinces in which it maintains the establishments. The allocation is as follows:[69]

- Where a corporation has only one permanent establishment, we allocate its entire taxable income to the province in which it has that permanent establishment; and

- Where the corporation has a permanent establishment in more than one province, we allocate its taxable income on the basis of the following formula:

$$\frac{1}{2}\left[\frac{\text{Provincial Gross Revenue}}{\text{Total Gross Revenue}} + \frac{\text{Provincial Salary \& Wages}}{\text{Total Salary \& Wages}}\right] \times \text{Taxable Income}$$

The Act *deems* a Canadian resident corporation that has only one permanent establishment in Canada and no other permanent establishment outside Canada to have earned its entire taxable income in that province.[70]

(c) — Computation of Provincial Tax Credit

The final step in the determination of the provincial tax credit is to calculate 10 per cent of its total taxable income allocated to the provinces in which the corporation has permanent establishments. This amount is deducted from the federal tax otherwise payable.

The provincial tax credit applies only to taxable income that a corporation earns in a province. It does not apply to taxable income that it earns in a foreign jurisdiction. Foreign-source income that a corporation earns is taxable at the full corporate tax rate. The corporation may however, claim foreign tax credits.

---

[67]Reg. 400(2)(g).

[68]Reg. 400(2)(f).

[69]Reg. 402. The phrase "gross revenue" is defined in subs. 248(1), and detailed rules are prescribed for determining the gross revenue attributable to a permanent establishment.

[70]Reg. 402(1).

Example

Assume that a corporation has permanent establishments in Nova Scotia, Ontario, British Columbia and the U.S., and that its gross revenues and wages are as follows:

	Gross Reveune	Salaries & Wages
Nova Scotia	$ 500,000	$ 150,000
Ontario	1,300,000	400,000
B.C.	700,000	250,000
U.S.	500,000	200,000
Total	$ 3,000,000	$ 1,000,000

Total Taxable Income (assumed): $500,000

Then the corporation's taxable income is allocated to the *three* provinces in which it has a permanent establishment, in the following manner:

Nova Scotia

$$\frac{1}{2} \left[\frac{\$500,000}{\$3,000,000} + \frac{\$150,000}{\$1,000,000} \right] \times \$500,000 \qquad \$\ 79,167$$

Ontario

$$\frac{1}{2} \left[\frac{\$1,300,000}{\$3,000,000} + \frac{\$400,000}{\$1,000,000} \right] \times \$500,000 \qquad \$208,333$$

B.C.

$$\frac{1}{2} \left[\frac{\$700,000}{\$3,000,000} + \frac{\$250,000}{\$1,000,000} \right] \times \$500,000 \qquad \$120,833$$

Total Taxable Income Allocated to Provinces $ 408,333

Provincial Tax Credit (10% × $ 408,333) $ 40,833

5. — Small Business Deduction

A Canadian-controlled private corporation ("CCPC") that earns active business income in Canada can claim an annual tax credit (the "small business deduction") equal to 16 per cent of the first $300,000 of its active business income.[71] Thus, in effect, a CCPC pays federal tax at a rate of 13.12 per cent on the first $300,000 of its business income.

	%
Basic federal rate	38.00
Less provincial abatement	(10.00)
Federal rate before surtax	28.00
Surtax at 4% (of 28%)	1.12
	29.12
Small business deduction	(16.00)
Total federal tax	13.12

6. — Manufacturing and Processing Credit

The manufacturing and processing credit promotes manufacturing and processing in Canada. The credit is available to corporations that carry on an active business in Canada and derive gross revenue from the sale of goods manufactured or processed in Canada.

Corporations that engage in manufacturing and processing can claim a tax credit in respect of their profits from such activities. The tax credit for manufacturing and processing profits is 7 per cent of manufacturing and processing profits that does not qualify for the small business deduction.[72] This reduces the M&P rate to 22.12 per cent (2004).The credit is not available in respect of income eligible for the small business deduction. The purpose of the credit is to make Canada competitive with other countries that offer similar incentives.

---

[71]S. 125. The 2003 Budget increased the business limit from $200,000 to $300,000; it was phased in as follows: $225,000 for 2003, $250,000 for 2004, and $300,000 for 2005.

[72]Subs. 125.1(1). As to the meaning of "manufacturing and processing", see *Can. Marconi Co. v. The Queen*, [1986] 2 S.C.R. 522, [1986] 2 C.T.C. 465, 86 D.T.C. 6526 (S.C.C.) (investments of funds necessary or ancillary to manufacturing and processing business); *Modern Miss Sportswear Ltd. v. The Queen*, [1980] C.T.C. 521, 80 D.T.C. 6390 (F.C.T.D.) (independent contractors sewing for garment manufacturer; not creditable); *Levi Strauss of Can. Inc. v. The Queen*, [1980] C.T.C. 480, 80 D.T.C. 6345; affd. [1982] C.T.C. 65, 82 D.T.C. 6070 (F.C.A.) (payments made to independent contractor for the making of shirts not part of taxpayer's "cost of labour"; payments ineligible for manufacturing and processing credit); *Louben Sportswear Inc. v. M.N.R.*, [1979] C.T.C. 2526, 79 D.T.C. 531 (T.R.B.) (payments made to independent contractor for labour performed on supplied material not eligible for manufacturing and processing credit).

(a) — Manufacturing and Processing Profits

(i) — Formula

The Regulations set a formula for determining the portion of a corporation's profits that is derived from its manufacturing and processing activities.[73] The formula does not directly determine the amount of manufacturing and processing profits earned by a corporation. Rather, it requires the identification of those activities that are considered to be manufacturing and processing activities, and the identification of the cost of labour and the cost of capital employed in those activities. The formula is then used to allocate the total income of the corporation between "manufacturing and processing" and "other income." However, if a corporation can qualify as a "small manufacturer," its entire "adjusted business income" is deemed to be Canadian manufacturing and processing profits. In these circumstances no formula is required.

The following is the prescribed formula to allocate manufacturing and processing income:[74]

$$MP = ABI \times \frac{(MC + ML)}{C + L}$$

where:

MP = Canadian manufacturing and processing profits

ABI = Adjusted business income

MC = Cost of manufacturing and processing capital

C   = Cost of capital

ML = Cost of manufacturing and processing labour

L   = Cost of labour

To qualify for the manufacturing and processing tax credit, the taxpayer must:

- Be a corporation liable to tax under Part I of the Act;

- Carry on an active business in which it processes or manufactures in Canada goods for sale or lease; and

- Derive at least 10 per cent of its gross revenue in the year from manufacturing or processing in Canada goods for sale or lease by it or others.

---

[73]Regs. 5200–5204.

[74]Reg. 5200.

(ii) — "Manufacturing or Processing"

The first step is to determine whether the activity carried on by a corporation constitutes "manufacturing or processing." The terms "manufacturing" and "processing" are not defined. The Act does, however, specifically exclude the following activities:[75]

- Farming or fishing;

- Logging;

- Construction;

- Operating an oil or gas well or extracting petroleum or natural gas;

- Processing heavy crude oil produced in Canada to a stage not beyond the crude oil stage or its equivalent;

- Extracting minerals from a mineral resource;

- Producing industrial minerals;

- Producing or processing electrical energy or steam for sale;

- Processing ore (other than iron ore or tar sands) from a mineral resource not beyond the prime metal stage;

- Processing iron ore from a mineral resource to the pellet stage.

- Processing tar sands from a mineral resource not beyond the crude oil stage; or

- Processing gas for sale or distribution by a public utility.

Since the terms "manufacturing" and "processing" are not defined, the starting point in interpreting these words is to look at their everyday meaning. The "manufacture" of goods normally involves the creation of an object or the shaping, stamping or forming of an object out of something. The "processing" of goods usually refers to a technique of preparation, handling or other activity designed to effect a physical or chemical change in an article or substance, other than by the process of natural growth.

It is important to note, however, that, even if an activity falls within the general understanding of "manufacture" or "process," the Act specifically excludes from the meaning of the terms any activities the revenue from which constitutes less than 10 per cent of the corporation's gross revenue.

---

[75]Subs. 125.1(3)"manufacturing or processing".

(b) — Small Manufacturers

The Canadian manufacturing and processing profit of a small manufacturer is equal to its "adjusted business income."[76] To qualify as a "small manufacturer," a corporation must satisfy the following requirements:

- Its activities during the year must be *primarily* the manufacturing or processing, in Canada, of goods for sale or lease;

- Its active business income, less its active business losses, plus the net active business income of its associated corporations must not exceed $200,000;

- It must not carry on any active business outside Canada in the year;

- The corporation must not carry on any of the activities specifically excluded from "manufacturing and processing";

- The corporation must not engage in processing of ore (other than iron ore or tar sands) from a mineral resource outside Canada to any stage that is not beyond the prime metal stage;

- The corporation must not engage in the processing of iron ore from a mineral resource outside Canada to any stage that is not beyond the pellet stage; and

- The corporation must not engage in the processing of tar sands located outside Canada to any stage that is not beyond crude oil.

7. — Large Corporations Capital Tax

Large corporations are subject to a special tax on their taxable capital employed in Canada.[77] For 2005, the tax is set at an annual rate of 0.175 per cent of a corporation's taxable capital employed in Canada in excess of its capital deduction for the year. The tax is payable in monthly instalments. The tax applies to all corporations, but the threshold of $50 million effectively exempts small businesses.[78] A portion of the 4 per cent corporate surtax related to taxable capital[79] is deductible from the amount payable.[80]

The 2003 Budget announced the elimination of this federal capital tax over five years. It is scheduled to be completely eliminated by 2008.

---

[76]Reg. 5201.

[77]Part. I.3 (ss. 181–181.7).

[78]S. 181.5

[79]S. 125.3(4) and 181.1(6).

[80]Subs. 181.1(4).

IV. — Rules: All Taxpayers

1. — Foreign Tax Credit

(a) — General Comment

Canadian residents are subject to full tax liability on their worldwide income. Hence, a taxpayer may be subject to double taxation: to a foreign government for income taxed at source, and to Canada on the basis of residence. A resident taxpayer may, however, claim a credit against Canadian tax for taxes paid to a foreign government.[81] The foreign tax credit, which one calculates separately in respect of *each* country, relieves juridical double taxation, but does not provide any relief from double taxation.[82] For example, if company A in Canada owns 5 per cent of company B in the United States, income earned by the U.S. company is taxable there. The foreign tax credit merely provides relief from the tax imposed on any dividends paid to company A, and not on the underlying U.S. corporate tax.

The tax credit is available only in respect of obligatory taxes paid to a foreign government. Discretionary foreign taxes levied by a foreign government that would not have been imposed if the taxpayer were not entitled to a Canadian foreign tax credit are not eligible for credit in Canada.[83] The rationale for this rule is that the Canadian government does not want to finance foreign governments by encouraging them to levy taxes on Canadians resident in their country in the expectation that the taxpayers will receive a rebate for the tax under Canadian tax law.

The foreign tax credit rules deal with three different circumstances:

- Foreign taxes paid by a resident on non-business income;

- Foreign taxes paid by a resident on business income; and

- Taxes paid by non-residents in respect of certain capital gains.

(b) — Non-Business-Income Tax

A resident taxpayer may deduct from "tax otherwise payable" under Part I an amount equal to the non-business-income taxes[84] paid to a foreign jurisdiction. The tax credit cannot ex-

---

[81]S. 126.

[82]Subs. 126(6).

[83]Subs. 126(4).

[84]Subs. 126(7)"non-business-income tax".

ceed the amount of Canadian tax that would have been payable on the foreign income had that income been earned in Canada.[85]

(i) — Definition

"Non-business-income tax" generally means taxes paid to a foreign jurisdiction, whether a foreign country or a subdivision of a foreign country. It does not include:[86]

- Amounts included in calculating the taxpayer's "business income tax" (the credit for business income taxes is calculated separately);[87]

- Taxes in respect of which the taxpayer has already taken a *deduction* in computing income;[88]

- Taxes attributable to income eligible for the overseas employment tax credit;[89]

- Taxes payable to a foreign country based solely on the taxpayer being a citizen of that country if the taxes are attributable to income earned in Canada;[90]

- Taxes relating to an amount that is refunded to any person or partnership;[91]

- Taxes reasonably attributable to a taxable capital gain for which the taxpayer or a spouse has claimed a deduction;[92]

- Taxes reasonably attributable to a loan received or receivable by the taxpayer;[93] and

---

[85]This is the effect of the formula in subs. 126(1).

[86]Subs. 126(7)"non-business-income tax".

[87]Subs. 126(7)"non-business-income tax" (a).

[88]Subs. 20(11) (deduction for tax in excess of 15 per cent paid to foreign government on income from property, other than real property); subs. 20(12) (deduction for tax paid to foreign government in respect of income from business or property, other than, where the taxpayer is a corporation, from shares of a foreign affiliate, to the extent of the "non-business-income" tax paid by taxpayer); subs. 104(22.3) (recalculation of trust's foreign tax); subs. 126(7)"non-business-income tax" (b) & (c).

[89]See subs. 122.3(1).

[90]Subs. 126(7)"non-business-income tax" (d); for example, a United States citizen who pays U.S. tax on employment income earned in Canada is not entitled to the foreign tax credit for the U.S. taxes.

[91]Subs. 126(7)"non-business-income tax" (e); some countries, such as Brazil, refund taxes withheld from payments to foreigners to the local payer; the purpose of these refunds is to subsidize domestic operations and borrowings.

[92]Subs. 126(7)"non-business-income tax" (g); s. 110.6.

[93]Subs. 126(7)"non-business-income tax" (h); subs. 33.1(1).

- Taxes relating to an amount that was exempt by treaty.[94]

The credit is available only for foreign taxes *actually paid* by the taxpayer *for the year.* Hence, tax refunded by a foreign government in a subsequent year because of a loss carryback necessitates a recalculation of the foreign tax credit for the year to which the refund applies.[95]

The credit is available only in respect of "income or profits" taxes paid to a foreign government. A corporate taxpayer cannot claim a credit for foreign taxes on income from a share in a foreign affiliate.[96]

(ii) — Limits

The foreign tax credit is subject to a limit calculated according to the following formula:

$$\frac{\text{Amount of foreign non–business income}}{\text{Income from all sources}} \times \text{Canadian tax otherwise payable}$$

The effect of this formula is that the credit for Canadian income tax purposes cannot exceed a rate that is higher than the rate that would have been payable by the taxpayer had the income been earned in Canada rather than in the foreign jurisdiction.[97]

(iii) — No Carryover

There is no carryover for non-business-income tax. Thus, in the example below the foreign tax of $869 cannot be applied to reduce the Canadian tax payable in other fiscal periods; it may, however, be deducted as an expense in calculating income from business or property.[98]

---

[94]Subs. 126(7)"non-business-income tax" (i); subpara. 110(1)(f)(i).

[95]*Icanda Ltd. v. M.N.R.*, [1972] C.T.C. 163, 72 D.T.C. 6148 (F.C.T.D.).

[96]Para. 126(1)(a).

[97]Para. 126(1)(b).

[98]Subs. 20(12).

Example

Assume Mr. X, a Canadian resident, earned the following amounts in the United States:

Employment income (net of deductions)	$ 15,000
Tax thereon: Federal	(3,600)
State	(250)
	$ 11,150
Interest income	$ 500
Tax thereon	(75)
	$ 425

Non-business-income tax paid (A) = $3,600 + $250 + $75 = $3,925.

He also earned $20,000 of business income in Canada and paid Canadian tax of $7,000. Mr. X's non-business foreign tax credit (U.S.) is calculated as follows:

Non-business-income tax paid	$ 3,925 (A)
Non-business income ($15,000 + $500)	$ 15,500
Income for the year ($20,000 + $15,500)	$ 35,500
Canadian income tax (assumed)	$ 7,000

$$\text{Foreign tax credit limit} = \frac{\text{U.S. income}}{\text{Total income}} \times \text{TOP}^*$$

$$\frac{\$15,500}{\$35,500} \times \$7,000$$

	$ 3,056 (B)
Foreign tax credit for non-business income [lesser of (A) and (B)]	$ 3,056

Notes:

* Tax otherwise payable determined according to subs. 126(7) ("tax for the year otherwise payable under this Part").

(c) — Business-Income Tax

The credit for foreign business income tax is for the benefit of Canadian resident taxpayers who have branch operations in foreign countries.

(i) — Definition

"[B]usiness-income tax" means tax paid by the taxpayer that may reasonably be regarded as a tax in respect of the income of the taxpayer from any business carried on by him in a foreign country.[99]

(ii) — Separate Calculation

As with the tax credit for non-business-income tax, the tax credit for business-income taxes must be calculated separately for each country in which the taxpayer carries on business.

(iii) — Carryover

Business-income taxes paid to a foreign jurisdiction may exceed the amount that the taxpayer can claim as a credit against Canadian taxes. Any excess may be carried forward as an "unused foreign tax credit" for 10 years and carried back for three years.[100] The foreign tax credit in respect of the current year must be claimed before any unused credits from other years.[101]

(iv) — Limits

The credit in respect of business-income tax is limited to the amount of tax that would have been payable on a comparable amount of income earned in Canada.[102] Non-business-income tax credits are to be deducted before business-income tax credits.[103]

---

[99]Subs. 126(7)"business-income tax".

[100]Para. 126(2)(a), subs. 126(7)"unused foreign tax credit".

[101]Subs. 126(2.3).

[102]Para. 126(2)(b), subs. 126(2.1).

[103]Para. 126(2)(c).

(d) — Employees of International Organizations

Employees of international organizations are usually exempt from income tax levied by the country in which they are stationed. Some of these organizations (for example, the United Nations) impose a levy upon their employees for the purpose of defraying the expenses of the organization. The levy is calculated in the same manner as an income tax.

Since a Canadian resident working abroad is subject to Canadian income tax on his or her worldwide income, the imposition of this additional levy constitutes double taxation of the income. To prevent double taxation, Canadian residents employed by international agencies are allowed either a deduction or a credit for foreign income.

An employee of a *prescribed* international organization may deduct his or her employment income in calculating taxable income.[104]

Employees of other international organizations may claim a tax credit for foreign taxes paid to the organization.[105]

2. — Political Contributions Credit

Contributions to political parties and to candidates for political office are not deductible from income for tax purposes.[106] The Act does, however, allow a credit for political contributions *against tax payable*.[107] The purpose of the credit is to encourage taxpayers to support the democratic process.

The credit is available in respect of contributions to a "registered party" or to an "officially nominated candidate" in a federal election. Some of the provinces also allow for a credit against provincial taxes for contributions to provincial political parties and officially nominated candidates in provincial elections.

The amount of the federal credit is restricted: The percentage claimable declines as the amount of the contribution increases (2004):

	Contribution	Tax Credit
On the first	$ 400	75%
On the next	$ 350	50%

---

[104]Subpara. 110(1)(f)(iii).

[105]Subs. 126(3).

[106]Para. 18(1)(n); *Stasiuk v. The Queen*, [1986] 2 C.T.C. 346 (F.C.T.D.) (taxpayer denied deduction for amounts expended on publicizing her political views).

[107]Subs. 127(3).

	Contribution	Tax Credit
On the next	$ 525	33 1/3%
On any excess over	$ 1,275	nil

Thus, the maximum credit is $650 (2004).

A claim for the credit must be supported by filing an official receipt signed by a registered agent of the party or candidate. The receipt must disclose certain prescribed information.[108]

3. — Other Tax Credits

There are other special tax credits available to taxpayers who derive income from particular types of activities.

(a) — Logging Tax Credit

Subsection 127(1) allows a credit for "logging taxes" paid by a taxpayer to a province in respect of logging operations.[109]

(b) — Investment Tax Credit

An investment tax credit is available for most current and capital expenditures on account of research and development carried on in Canada.[110]

The investment tax credit is intended to stimulate investment in certain types of activities and in certain regions of the country.

Generally, the credit is available to a taxpayer in respect of acquisitions of depreciable property used by the taxpayer in Canada primarily for the purpose of:[111]

• Manufacturing or processing of goods for sale or lease;

• Operating an oil or gas well;

---

[108]Reg. 2000.

[109]British Columbia and Quebec impose logging taxes.

[110]Subs. 127(5).

[111]Subs. 127(9)"qualified property".

- Processing heavy crude oil recovered from a natural reservoir in Canada to a stage that is not beyond the crude oil stage or its equivalent;

- Extracting minerals from a resource;

- Processing ore (other than iron or tar sands) to the prime metal stage or its equivalent;

- Exploring or drilling for petroleum or natural gas;

- Prospecting or exploring for, or developing, a mineral resource;

- Logging;

- Farming or fishing;

- Storing grain;

- Producing industrial minerals;

- Canadian field processing;

- Producing or processing electrical energy or steam;

- Harvesting peat;

- Processing iron ore to the pellet stage; or

- Processing tar sands to the crude oil stage.

The amount of the credit depends upon the type of investment made by the taxpayer, the region in which the investment is made, whether the property is "available for use" and, in certain cases, the taxpayer's status.

The investment tax credit is deductible against taxes otherwise payable. Unused credits may be carried back 3 years and carried forward for 10 years.[112]

---

[112]Subs. 127(9)"investment tax credit" (c).

Selected Bibliography to Chapter 16

Individuals

Beam, Robert E., and Karen Wensley, "Personal Tax Planning: Alternative Minimum Tax — The Political Tax" (1986) 34 Can. Tax J. 174.

Dart, Robert J., "A Critique of an Advance Corporate Tax System for Canada" (1990) 38 Can. Tax J. 1245.

Erlichman, Harry, "Profitable Donations: What Price Culture?" (1992) 11 Philanthrop. 3.

Huggett, Donald R., "Alternative Minimum Tax (A Fiscal Albatross)" (1986) 13 Can. Tax News 109.

Huggett, Donald R., "Minimum Income Tax (A)", in *Proceedings of 37th Tax Conf.* 10:1 (Can. Tax Foundation, 1985).

Huggett, Donald R., "Minimum Tax (The)" (1985) 13 Can. Tax News 75.

Jenkins, Glenn P., "The Role and Economic Implications of the Canadian Dividend Tax Credit", *Discussion Paper No. 307* (Ottawa: Economic Council of Canada, June 1986).

Low Income Tax Relief Working Group of Fair Tax Commission, *Working Group Report* (Toronto: Fair Tax Commission, 1992).

Newman, Eric J., "Tax Indexing — What Does It Mean to You?" (1974) 105:5 CA Magazine 54.

Novek, Barbara L., "Sector Specific Tax Relief for Canadian Residents Working Overseas" (1993) 5 Tax. of Exec. Compensation and Retirement 808.

Sherbeniuk, Douglas J., "Future Trends in Tax Policy: Focus on the Alternative Minimum Tax and the Corporate Income Tax Discussion Papers," (1986) Special Lectures L.S.U.C. 425.

Smith, Roger S., "Rates of Personal Income Tax: The Carter Commission Revisited" (1987) 35 Can. Tax J. 1226, and in *The Quest for Tax Reform,* W. Neil Brooks, ed., (Toronto: Carswell, 1988) at 173.

Wilson, Michael H., *A Minimum Tax for Canada*, Dept. of Finance, Canada, 1985.

Rules: Corporations

Blais, A., and F. Vaillancourt, "The Federal Corporate Income Tax: Tax Expenditures and Tax Discrimination in the Canadian Manufacturing Industry, 1972–1981" (1986) 34 Can. Tax J. 1122.

Dale, Michael, "A Comparison of Effective Marginal Tax Rates on Income Capital in Canadian Manufacturing" (1985) 33 Can. Tax J. 1154.

Horne, Barry D. and Tim S. Wach, "Canadian Taxation of Foreign Sourced Income: The Foreign Tax Credit" (1991) 3 Imm. & Cit. 4.

Huggett, Donald R., "Temporary Surtax" (1985) 13 Can. Tax News 97.

Lahmer, Craig, "Recent Developments in Manufacturing and Processing" in *Proceedings of 44th Tax Conf.* (Can. Tax Found., 1992) 52:1.

McDonnell, T.E., "Manufacturing and Processing Profits: Some Interpretive Questions" (1994) 40 Can. Tax J. 929.

Sennema, James R., "Temporary Business Operations as 'Permanent Establishments'" (1992) 5 C.U.B.L.R. 171.

Vytas, Nalaitas, "Large Corporation's Tax" (1990) 64 CMA Magazine 34.

Rules: All Taxpayers

Tremblay, Richard G., "Foreign Tax Credit Planning" (1993) Corp. Mgmt. Tax Conf. 3:1.

PART X: CORPORATIONS & SHAREHOLDERS

CHAPTER 17 — BASIC PRINCIPLES OF CORPORATE TAX

I. — General Comment

To this point, we have looked at the general rules in respect of the computation of taxable income and tax payable. Most of these rules apply to all taxpayers, including individuals, corporations, and trusts. We turn our attention now to the rules that apply specifically to corporations and their shareholders.

In terms of economic relationships, the shareholders of a corporation indirectly own its assets, and corporate profits and losses accrue to their benefit or detriment. Thus, in economic terms, the income and losses of the corporation reflect upon the shareholder's financial stake in the corporation. In corporate law, however, a corporation and its shareholders are separate entities. Thus, shareholders do not have a direct legal interest in the assets of the corporation. Instead, the shareholder's legal interest is in the corporation's equity. Tax law follows the corporate model: a corporation is a separate taxpayer in its own right.[1]

This distinction between the economic and the legal relationships between the shareholders of a corporation and the corporate entity works quite well in corporate law. The corporation, which is a statutory entity, allows shareholders to limit their personal liability for corporate debts. Thus, for most corporate purposes, a creditor of a corporation cannot reach through the corporate veil and attach personal liability to its shareholders. In terms of income tax law, however, the legal distinction between a corporation and its shareholders gives rise to difficult problems. Tax law cannot focus solely on the legal relationship and completely ignore the close economic relationship between a corporation and its shareholders. Thus, although the corporation and its shareholders are separate taxpayers, there are many tax rules that reach through the corporation to its shareholders. For example, a shareholder can-

---

[1] Subs. 248(1)"person", "taxpayer".

not claim the capital gains exemption if it results from the disposition of shares if their value increased primarily because of the non-payment of dividends by the corporation. Thus, the shareholder cannot claim the benefit of the enhanced value of the corporation, even though that value attaches to a separate legal entity. Similarly, there are many rules that attribute a corporation's income to its shareholders even though they are not legally entitled to the income.

For most income tax purposes, we calculate the income of a corporation in a manner similar to that of an individual. Of course, a corporation cannot claim personal tax credits and dependency deductions. But apart from these obvious circumstances, we determine the net income and taxable income of a corporation according to the general rules described in the preceding chapters.

There are, however, a few differences in the taxation of shareholders and corporations. First, most individuals (at least those who are employees) file their income taxes on a cash basis. Corporations may not use the cash basis of accounting and must use the accrual basis. This requirement is implicit in section 9 of the Act. Second, individuals who are employees must report their income on a calendar-year basis.[2] In contrast, corporations may select their fiscal year on any 12-month basis.[3] Apart from these small differences, most of the administrative and legal doctrines that apply to individuals also apply to corporations.

While the computation of net income and taxable income for individuals and corporations is similar, there is a whole body of tax law that applies to transactions between a corporation and its shareholders. We look at these rules in this chapter.

II. — The Corporate Entity

1. — Separate Legal Entity

A corporation is a "person," and therefore a "taxpayer" in its own right.[4] A corporation is also a legal entity distinct from its shareholders. A corporation has been described as:[5]

> ... [an] artificial person established for preserving in perpetual succession certain rights, which being conferred on natural persons only, would fail in process of time. ... The royal charter gives it a legal immortality, and a name by which it acts and becomes known. It has power to make by-laws for its own government, and transacts its business under the authority of a common seal — its hand and mouthpiece; it has neither soul nor tangible form, so it can neither be outlawed nor arrested; it only enjoys a legal entity, sues, and is sued by its corporate name,

---

[2]Para. 249(1)(b).

[3]Para. 249(1)(a) and subs. 249.1(1).

[4]Subs. 248(1)"person", "taxpayer".

[5]*Wharton's Law Lexicon*, 8th. ed. (London: Stevens, 1889): "corporation or body politic".

and holds and enjoys property by such name. The several members of a corporation and their successors constitute but one person in law...

The distinction between corporations and trading partnerships is, that in the first the law sees only the body corporate and knows not the individuals, who are not liable for the contracts of the corporation in their private capacity, their share in the capital only being at stake: but in the latter the law looks not to the partnership, but to the individual members of it, who are therefore answerable for the debts of the firm to the full extent of their assets.

Thus, unlike a partnership, which is a *relationship* between persons carrying on business in common with a view to profit,[6] a corporation has a legal existence separate and apart from its shareholders.

The concept that a corporation is a legal entity separate and distinct from its shareholders gives rise to several difficulties in taxation. Since a corporation is a separate entity, its property, assets, and liabilities belong to, or flow from, the corporation. This is so even if there is only one shareholder of the corporation who owns all of its issued and outstanding shares. The "one person company" is no less a separate legal identity than a publicly-held corporation.

The notion that a corporation is a separate legal entity from its shareholders contrasts with the tax treatment of two other legal entities — trusts and partnerships. A trust is a conduit to the extent that it distributes its income to its beneficiaries. A partnership is also a pass-through relationship, and all its income and losses are taxable in the hands of the member partners. The pass-through is complete and there are no tax consequences to the partnership itself.

2. — The Salomon Doctrine

Salomon[7] is the *locus classicus* upholding the principle that a corporation has a separate legal identity that is distinct from its shareholders. Salomon incorporated a company to which he sold his unincorporated shoe manufacturing business in return for all but six of the issued shares of the company and £10,000 of secured debentures. When the company fell upon hard times and was wound up a year later, the unsecured creditors, alleging that the company was a mere alias or agent of its principal shareholder, claimed that Salomon was personally liable to indemnify their claims. The House of Lords held that the parties had complied with all of the requirements of the corporate statute authorizing the creation of the company, that the corporation was not a sham, and that Salomon had not acted fraudulently.

---

[6]See, e.g., *Partnerships Act*, R.S.O. 1990, c. P.5, s. 2.

[7]*Salomon v. Salomon & Co.*, [1897] A.C. 22 (H.L.).

As a secured creditor of the corporation, Salomon ranked ahead of its unsecured creditors. As Lord Macnaghten said:[8]

> The company attains maturity on its birth. There is no period of minority — no interval of incapacity. ... The company is, at law, a different person altogether from the subscribers to the memorandum; and, though it may be that after incorporation the business is precisely the same as it was before, the same persons are managers, and the same hands receive the profits, the company is not in law the agent of the subscribers or trustee for them. Nor are the subscribers, as members liable, in any shape or form, except to the extent and in the manner provided by the Act.

Hence, a corporation that is created according to the terms of the relevant corporate statute is an entity legally distinct from its shareholders.[9]

3. — Parent and Subsidiary

The principle that a corporation is a legal entity separate from its shareholders also applies to the relationship between a parent company and its subsidiary. Thus, in the absence of a specific statutory provision to the contrary, a parent corporation and its subsidiary are sepa-

---

[8]*Ibid.* at 51. Although Mr. Salomon had not committed any fraud on his creditors, it was found that he had sold his business to his company at an extravagant price. As Lord Macnaghten stated, the price "represented the sanguine expectations of a fond owner rather than anything that can be called a businesslike or reasonable estimate of value" (p. 49).

[9]*Army & Navy Department Store v. M.N.R.*, [1953] S.C.R. 498, [1953] C.T.C. 293 at 308, 53 D.T.C. 1185 at 1193 (S.C.C.), *per* Cartwright J.: "With the greatest of respect for those who hold the contrary view, I do not think that shareholders, either individually or collectively, have any ownership direct or indirect in the property of the company in which they hold shares"; see, generally, *Rielle v. Reid* (1899), 26 O.A.R. 54 (C.A.); *Kodak Ltd. v. Clark*, [1902] 2 K.B. 450; affd. [1903] 1 K.B. 505 (C.A.); *Janson v. Driefontein Consol. Mines Ltd.*, [1902] A.C. 484 at 497, 498, 501 (H.L.); *Rainham Chem. Works Ltd. v. Belvedere Fish Guano Co.*, [1921] 2 A.C. 465 at 475, 476, 501 (H.L.); *Meadow Farm Ltd. v. Imp. Bank of Can.* (1922), 18 Alta. L.R. 335 (C.A.); *British Thomson-Houston Co. v. Sterling Accessories Ltd.*, [1924] 2 Ch. 33; *Assoc. Growers of B.C. Ltd. v. Edmunds*, [1926] 1 W.W.R. 535 (B.C.C.A.); *Export Brewing & Malting Co. v. Dom. Bank*, [1937] 2 W.W.R. 568 (P.C.); *The Queen v. Meilicke*, [1938] 2 W.W.R. 97; leave to appeal to P.C. granted [1938] 2 W.W.R. 424; *Hydro-Elec. Power Comm. of Ont. v. Thorold Township* (1924), 55 O.L.R. 431 at 435 (Ont. C.A.); *Beckow v. Panich* (1940), 69 Que. K.B. 398 (C.A.); *White v. Bank of Toronto*, [1953] O.R. 479 (C.A.); *Bank Voor Handel en Scheepvaart N.V. v. Slatford*, [1953] 1 Q.B. 248 at 269; *Lee v. Lee's Air Farming Ltd.*, [1961] A.C. 12, [1960] 3 All E.R. 420 (P.C.). See also: *Kosmopoulos v. Constitution Ins. Co. of Can.*, [1987] 1 S.C.R. 2 at 10, 36 B.L.R. 233 at 240 (S.C.C.), *per* Wilson, J.: "As a general rule, a corporation is a legal entity distinct from its shareholders".

rate and distinct legal entities. This is so even where the parent owns all the shares of its subsidiary and the two are, in effect, one economic entity.[10]

Since a parent corporation and its subsidiaries are separate entities, one cannot automatically be considered to be an agent of the other. Nor, as a general rule, can a parent corporation be held liable for its subsidiary's debts, or *vice versa*.[11]

4. — Multiple Relationships

An important consequence of the doctrine of separate corporate personality is that an individual can have multiple legal relationships with a corporation.[12] An individual may own shares in the corporation, be employed by it, be its director, or have a debtor/creditor relationship with the corporation. As we saw earlier, each of these relationships give rise to different types of income subject to different rules of computation.

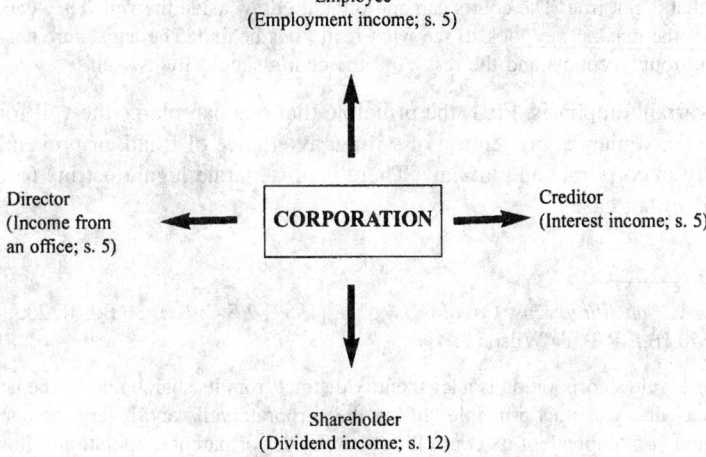

Employee
(Employment income; s. 5)

Director
(Income from an office; s. 5)

CORPORATION

Creditor
(Interest income; s. 5)

Shareholder
(Dividend income; s. 12)

---

[10]*Aluminum Co. of Can. v. Toronto*, [1944] S.C.R. 267 (S.C.C.); *Barnes v. Sask. Co-op. Wheat Producers Ltd.*, [1946] 1 W.W.R. 97 at 113; affd. [1947] S.C.R. 241 (S.C.C. [Sask.]); *Ebbw Vale Urban Dist. Council v. South Wales Traffic Licensing Authority*, [1951] 2 K.B. 366, [1951] 1 All E.R. 806 (C.A.), *per* Cohen L.J. (under ordinary rules of law, parent and wholly-owned subsidiary are distinct legal entities; in absence of agency contract between companies, one cannot be said to be agent of other).

[11]*Hartford Accident & Indemnity Co. v. Millsons Const. Ltd.* (1939), 44 Que. P.R. 170 (S.C.); see *Discount & Loan Corp. v. Supt. of Ins.*, [1938] Ex. C.R. 194; affd. [1939] S.C.R. 285 (S.C.C.) (corporate veil may, of course, be pierced); *Ebbw Vale Urban Dist. Council v. South Wales Traffic Licensing Authority, ante* (statute may deem acts of subsidiary corporation to be acts of its parent corporation).

[12]*Lee v. Lee's Air Farming Ltd.* (1960), [1961] A.C. 12, [1960] 3 All E.R. 420 (P.C.).

5. — *Piercing the Corporate Veil*

In limited circumstances, one can disregard a corporation's separate legal existence and lift its veil to reach through the entity to its individual members. Thus, one can sometimes ignore legal ownership in favour of economic ownership.

(a) — *Common Law Piercing*

Having said that one can pierce the corporate veil, it is not at all easy to identify the circumstances in which a court will do so.[13] The courts usually ignore a corporation's separate legal personality only if one uses it to defeat public convenience, justify wrong, protect fraud, or defend crime.[14] As Lord Denning said in *Littlewoods*:

> The doctrine laid down in *Salomon* has to be watched very carefully. It has often been supposed to cast a veil over the personality of a limited company through which the courts cannot see. But that is not true. The courts can and often do draw aside the veil. They can, and often do pull off the mask. They look to see what really lies behind. The legislature has shown the way with group accounts and the rest. And the courts should follow suit.[15]

Two points warrant emphasis. First, the principle that one can pierce the veil for the protection of public convenience, prevention of wrong, avoidance of fraud, or prevention of crime applies equally in corporate and tax law. There is no separate legal doctrine for piercing the corporate veil in tax cases.[16]

---

[13]*Kosmopoulos v. Constitution Ins. Co. of Can., ante*, [1987] 2 S.C.R. 2, 36 B.L.R. 233 (S.C.C.) at 10 [S.C.R.] and 240 [B.L.R.] *per* Wilson J.:

> As a general rule a corporation is a legal entity distinct from its shareholders. The law on when a court may disregard this principle "lifting the corporate veil" and regard the company as a mere "agent" or "puppet" of its controlling shareholder or parent corporation follows no consistent principle. The best that can be said is that the "separate entities" principle is not enforced when it would yield a result "too flagrantly opposed to justice, convenience or the interests of the Revenue".

[14]See Durnford, "The Corporate Veil in Tax Law" (1979) 27 Can. Tax. J. 282; Feltham, "Lifting the Corporate Veil", [1968] LSUC Lectures 305; see also Wormser, *The Disregard of the Corporate Fiction & Allied Corporate Problems* (1927); Latty, "The Corporate Entity as a Solvent of Legal Problems" (1936) 34 Mich. L. Rev. 597; Horowitz, "Disregarding the Entity of Private Corporations" (1939) 14 Wash L. Rev. 285; *Ballantine on Corporations* (Chicago: Callaghan and Company, 1946) at 292. *Gower's Principles of Modern Company Law*, 4th ed. (London: Stevens, 1979) at 112–38 (English parallel).

[15]*Littlewoods Mail Order Stores v. McGregor*, [1969] 3 All E.R. 855 at 860 (C.A.).

[16]*Consolidated-Bathurst Ltd. v. The Queen*, [1985] 1 C.T.C. 142, 85 D.T.C. 5120 at 5124 (F.C.T.D.); additional reasons at [1985] 1 C.T.C. 351, 85 D.T.C. 5244 (F.C.T.D.); revd. in part [1987] 1 C.T.C. 55, 87 D.T.C. 5001 (F.C.A.).

Second, merely because a court lifts a corporation's veil for a particular purpose does not imply that one can ignore its separate legal personality for all other purposes. One lifts the veil only for the specific purpose of the litigated issue and not for other purposes.[17] Thus, merely because one lifts a corporation's veil for tax purposes does not imply that its shareholders automatically become personally liable for its debts. The corporation's separate personality remains intact for all other purposes, including that of limiting the liability of its shareholders for corporate debts.[18]

(b) — Statutory Piercing

The legislature can also, to use Lord Devlin's phrase, forge a sledgehammer capable of cracking open the corporate shell.[19] Thus, a statute can reach through a corporation and tax its shareholders in their personal capacity, or treat an affiliated group of corporations *as if* they were one legal entity.

---

[17]*Nedco Ltd. v. Clark*, [1973] 6 W.W.R. 425 at 433 (Sask. C.A.) *per* Culliton C.J.S.:

> While the principle laid down in *Salomon* is, and continues to be, a fundamental feature of Canadian law, there are instances in which the court can and should lift the corporate veil, but whether it does so depends upon the facts in each particular case. Moreover, the fact that the court does lift the corporate veil for a specific purpose in no way destroys the recognition of the corporation as an independent and autonomous entity for all other purposes.

[18]See, e.g., *Canada Business Corporations Act*, R.S.C. 1985, c. C-44, subs. 45(1); *Business Corporations Act*, R.S.O. 1990, c. B.16, subs. 92(1).

[19]*Bank Voor Handel en Scheepvaart N.V. v. Slatford*, [1953] 1 Q.B. 248 at 278.

EXAMPLES OF STATUTORY PIERCING		
Statutory Reference	**Item**	**Comment**
Subs. 256(2.1) discretionary anti-avoidance provision	Associated corporations	The Minister has discretionary power to deem two or more corporations to be associated with each other. Associated corporations are, in effect, treated as one corporation for the purpose of certain tax deductions and credits, such as the small business deduction.
S. 227.1	Liability of directors for failure of corporation to remit taxes	Directors may be *personally* liable for certain taxes which the corporation failed to deduct, withhold, remit or pay.
Para. 18(1)(p); subs. 125(7) ("personal services business")	Personal services income	In determining whether a business is a "personal service business," the relationship between the "incorporated employee" and the person to whom services are rendered is examined *as if* the corporation did not exist.
Para. 251.1	Affiliated Persons	To prevent recognition of losses where certain types of property are transferred within an economic group or family-affiliated persons.

6. — *Personal Liability of Shareholders*

We use limited liability companies to attract capital investment without exposing shareholders to unlimited liability for their corporate debts. Although we can pierce the corporate veil to attach personal liability to shareholders, we do so only in clearly convincing cases of fraud, shams, and outrageously offensive conduct. Shareholders can, however, be personally liable for corporate tax. *Algoa Trust*[20] illustrates the potential risks. Algoa paid cash dividends to its shareholders at a time when it had satisfied all of its assessments and was current in respect of its tax liabilities. Some time later, however, the Canada Revenue Agency (CRA) issued reassessments in respect of the corporation's earlier (but not statute barred) taxation years. When the corporation failed to pay its reassessed tax, the Minister assessed the shareholders personally for the unpaid tax. A corporation and its shareholders are jointly and severally liable for tax under section 160 of the *Income Tax Act* even if the shareholders and directors act in good faith.

---

[20]*Algoa Trust et al. v. The Queen*, [1993] 1 C.T.C. 2294, 93 D.T.C. 405 (T.C.C.).

Section 160 prevents a taxpayer from rendering him- or herself judgment-proof by transferring property to persons with whom the taxpayer does not deal at arm's length. The section applies when a corporation pays dividends to a person with whom it does not deal at arm's length (such as an owner/manager or relative) and the corporation at that time is liable for tax. Section 160 is a strict liability provision. It does not require any intent to avoid taxes on the part of the transferor or any knowledge by the transferee that the dividend was paid when the corporation's past tax years were open to potential reassessment.

What is less obvious, however, is that the Minister can apply the section *retroactively* through a subsequent reassessment. This results because the legal obligation to pay tax arises when one *earns* income, not when it is assessed for tax. Since the Minister may reassess a corporation three or four years after its initial assessment, a shareholder's liability for the corporation's tax can be retroactively regenerated when the corporation is subsequently reassessed. Thus, shareholders in receipt of dividends are never free of the potential burden to pay corporate taxes until such time as the corporation's particular taxation year is statute barred.

III. — General Structure Of Corporate Taxation

The rules dealing with corporate taxation are considerably more complex than the rules of individual taxation. There are two principal reasons for the increased complexity: the potential for double taxation of corporate income and the use of corporations to defer personal taxes. For example:

- Since a corporation is a taxpayer separate and distinct from its shareholders, corporate income is potentially subject to double taxation, once at the corporate level and again in the individual shareholder's hands.

- Since each corporation in a related group of corporations (e.g., parent and subsidiary) is a separate taxpayer, dividends among related corporations are subject to double or, indeed, multiple taxation if they are taxed in each of the corporations.

- Since corporations and shareholders are separate taxpayers, individuals can use corporations to defer their personal taxes if corporate income is taxable at a rate that is lower than the individual rate.

- Since corporations and shareholders are separate taxpayers, one can use corporations to park corporate income offshore in low tax countries or tax havens and to defer the domestic tax payable thereon until the repatriation of profits.

The rules that address double taxation and tax deferral are necessarily complex.

Corporate taxation is also complicated because the law manoeuvers between two different contexts: the legal doctrine that a corporation is a separate legal entity and the reality that there is a close economic interest between a corporation and its shareholders. To the extent that the corporation is a separate legal entity, the rate of tax that applies to the corporation is quite independent of any rate that might apply to individuals. Since, however, the corporation and its shareholders are entwined in a close economic relationship, the tax rate that we apply to corporations has a direct beneficial or detrimental bearing on its shareholders. If a corporation is overtaxed, its shareholders suffer economic harm. If a corporation is undertaxed, the shareholders reap the rewards.

The complexity is compounded, particularly in large publicly held corporations, where shares are widely held by a diverse group of individuals, corporations, mutual funds, pension trusts, and tax-exempt entities. Each of these shareholders has its own tax profile and is affected differently by the manner in which the corporation is taxed. For example, a corporation is overtaxed if its shareholders have a lower marginal tax rate and undertaxed if its shareholders have a higher marginal tax rate. When the corporation's income is paid out as a dividend, its shareholders may be overtaxed or undertaxed depending on how we treat the dividend in their hands. If the corporation's income is not paid out but accumulated, its shareholders can dispose of their shares in the corporation. The tax consequences to the shareholder will depend on whether the gain (or loss) is taxable as ordinary income, or capital gains (or losses). Thus, despite corporate legal theory, for tax purposes one cannot ignore the economic interrelationship between a corporation and its shareholders.

1. — Why a Corporate Tax?

Double taxation and deferral of taxes on corporate income result from the taxation of corporations as separate taxable entities. Thus, the first and most obvious question is whether we should have a separate corporate tax. What if we simply attributed income on an annual basis to the corporation's individual shareholders, regardless of whether the income was actually paid out as dividends? Under this scheme, the corporation would merely be a conduit for its shareholders, in much the same way as a partnership is for its partners or a trust is for its beneficiaries. By adjusting the tax rate on dividends, we could raise the same total revenues as we do under the dual regime of corporate and shareholder taxation.

After all is said and done, only individuals bear the burden of tax. Artificial entities do not really "pay" tax — they are merely legal conduits for individuals who ultimately bear the real economic burden of taxation. As the Carter Commission said:[21]

> Equity and neutrality would best be achieved under a tax system in which there were no taxes on organizations as such, and all individuals and families holding interests in organizations were taxed on the accrued net gains from such interests on the same basis as all other net gains. ...

Although theoretically appealing, the concept of *notionally* flowing through corporate income to individual shareholders raises some practical problems. Notional flow-through of

---

[21]*Report of the Royal Commission on Taxation* (Chair: K.M. Carter) (Ottawa: Queen's Printer, 1966) vol. 4 at 4.

corporate income that would be taxed in the hands of individuals could create severe liquidity problems for taxpayers if the corporation did not accompany the flow-through with cash dividends. Shareholders might be compelled to sell portions of their shareholdings to raise the necessary funds to pay their tax liabilities. This could have a significant effect on capital markets.

There would also be difficulties with corporate control if individual shareholders had to sell a portion of their shareholdings in order to raise cash for their tax bills. Corporate control could change from the liquidation of shares, and family-owned businesses in particular would be vulnerable. Private corporations might encounter difficulties in finding a suitable market for their shares, which would need to be valued annually if they were to be sold. Also, non-residents would escape the income tax under Part I of the Act and pay only the substantially lower withholding tax (generally 5–15 per cent) on dividends under Part XIII as modified by Canada's bilateral tax treaties. The Carter Commission recognized these difficulties as sufficient justification for a separate corporate tax:[22]

> Although we can see no grounds in principle for taxing corporations and other organizations, we have reluctantly reached the conclusion that there are good and sufficient reasons for continuing to collect a tax from them. The main reason is the practical difficulty of taxing accrued share gains as required under the ideal approach we have just described. Another reason is the loss in economic benefit to Canada that would result if non-residents holding shares in Canadian corporations were not taxed by Canada on their share of corporate income at approximately the rates that now prevail.

The rationale for the structure of our corporate tax model is clearer if we accept the proposition that corporate income should not flow through and be taxed in the hands of individual shareholders on an annual basis. In the absence of a flow-through of income to shareholders, corporate income must bear its own tax annually if we are to prevent deferral of tax. If corporate income is not taxed at its full rate, there would be incentive to accumulate income in the corporation in order to defer any tax that would otherwise be payable if it were paid out to shareholders. Thus, the prevention of tax deferral is an important reason for levying an annual tax on corporate income.

2. — The Ideal Tax Rate?

If there is to be a separate corporate tax, what is the ideal tax rate? The problem now assumes additional dimensions.

The corporate tax rate determines the extent to which one can defer tax by using the corporate form to conduct business. A corporate tax rate lower than individual rates invites deferral. Assume, for example, that the corporate tax rate is 25 per cent and that the top marginal rate for individuals is 50 per cent. If an individual can shift $200,000 income into his or her

---

[22]*Ibid.*

corporation and invest the tax savings ($50,000) at 8 per cent per year, the tax saved will be worth $233,000 in 20 years. Thus, each dollar of tax savings accumulates to 4.7 times its value in 20 years. If the taxpayer could do this annually for 20 years, the tax savings for each year would accumulate to $2,521,000. If the individual sold his or her shares in the 20th year, the value of the tax savings would transform into a taxable capital gain of $1,260,500.[23] If the capital gains tax rate is 23 per cent, the taxpayer, in addition to the tax deferral advantage, saves 27 per cent of $2,521,000 or $680,670. Thus, the taxpayer can benefit from tax deferral benefit from tax deferral and shifting his or her tax rate to a lower amount.

We could eliminate tax deferral by making the corporate tax rate equal to the highest marginal rate for individuals. If we did, the tax system would be substantially neutral at the top end, and businesses could make their decisions on the basis of nontax criteria. There would be no tax deferral advantage to earning income through a corporation. A corporate rate equal to the top individual tax rate (approximately 50 per cent) would also remove business and economic incentives from those who presently obtain special low rates of taxation, for example small businesses. Thus, any gain in tax neutrality between different types of taxpayers would carry with it the cost of lost tax incentives for certain sectors of the economy. This has significant economic and political implications.

Several factors determine the corporate tax rate, but the desirability of having competitive international tax rates plays a pre-eminent role. Canadian corporations must compete internationally, and the tax rates of our principal trading partners have a significant influence on the structure of Canadian corporate taxation.

There are also other questions: should there be special incentives for domestic investment over foreign investment? Should the corporate tax system favour Canadian corporations that earn income within Canada over Canadian corporations that earn income in foreign countries? Should there be special tax incentives for foreign corporations that come into Canada to do business in Canada? The "ideal" corporate tax rate must take into account competitive tax rates and Canada's obligations under its tax and trade treaties.

3. — Double Taxation

One can argue that in an ideal world corporate tax should be nothing more than a withholding tax for individuals who ultimately bear the real economic burden of taxation. In fact, one of the most acute problems of the corporate tax system is the potential for "double taxation" of corporate income. Corporate income is typically taxed at the corporate level, when it is earned, and is taxed again at the shareholder level, when it is distributed as a dividend.

Where a corporation earns income and distributes it to shareholders who are individuals, both the corporation and the individuals pay tax on the distributed income. The problem of

---

[23] 1/2 × $2,521,000.

"double taxation" is compounded, however, where there is a chain of corporations, and income passes through the chain to the ultimate shareholder. In these circumstances, the double tax problem becomes a multiple taxation problem.

The Canadian corporate tax system is a compromise that attempts to reconcile two different problems. First, corporate income cannot easily be deemed to flow through on a notional basis to shareholders on an annual basis without distorting the capital markets and corporate control. Second, treating the corporation as a separate entity raises the potential of double taxation of corporate income paid out to shareholders and tax deferral of income retained in the corporation. Hence, in the absence of some form of notional flow-through of corporate income to shareholder, corporate income must bear its own tax on an annual basis. Otherwise, there would be an incentive to accumulate income in the corporation in order to defer any tax that would be payable if the income were paid out to shareholders. Thus, the prevention of tax deferral is an important reason for levying a separate annual tax on corporate income.

We could eliminate double taxation of corporate income by levying tax on corporate income at a rate equal to the top marginal rate of tax applicable to individuals and allowing the corporation a deduction for dividends paid to shareholders. Such a system would, in effect, treat the corporation as a conduit for its shareholders and impose a corporate tax only on retained earnings. There would be no tax on distributed earnings. In fact, this is the method applied to the taxation of trusts. This approach, however, does not work as well with corporations. Non-residents own a much larger percentage of corporate shares than trust interests. As noted above, the withholding tax rate on dividend payments to non-residents is determined by Canada's tax treaties and is substantially lower than the rate payable by domestic shareholders. Hence, any such system would create a clear advantage for non-residents over residents or would require complete renegotiation of Canada's treaties, which in itself would have other adverse consequences.

Alternatively, we could tax the corporation only on its income and eliminate the tax on dividends. This would, in effect, eliminate double taxation of corporate income. The problem with this approach, however, is that it would necessitate a corporate tax rate that is at least equal to the top marginal rate of individual taxation. Otherwise, high income taxpayers would pay a lower rate of tax on their corporate income than they would on their personal income. There are two difficulties with this approach: the high tax on corporate income would be unfair to lower-income individuals and tax-exempt shareholders earning corporate income, and the high rate of corporate tax may not be competitive in international markets. A corporate tax rate that is significantly higher than the rate applicable in the United States, for example, would have severe economic repercussions for Canada.

Given the limitations associated with each of the above alternatives, we search for a compromise that relieves double taxation and prevents the tax deferral of corporate income. There is no perfect solution, and each country adopts a method that suits its own economic and political preferences.

The Canadian tax system provides some relief against double/multiple taxation of corporate and shareholder income. The nature of the relief varies depending upon whether the corporate/shareholder relationship is between:

- Corporation and individual;
- Domestic corporation and domestic corporation;
- Domestic corporation and foreign corporation; or
- Individual and foreign corporation.

4. — Integration

Should corporate and individual taxes be fully integrated to prevent double taxation and, if so, how? There are three basic models that countries use to relieve corporate double taxation:

- The classical method;
- The imputation model; or
- The advanced corporate tax model.

(a) — The Classical Method

Under the classical method (for example, the U.S. system), taxable corporations are taxed first at the corporate level and then again at the shareholder level, if and when the corporation's money is distributed to shareholders. This method clearly results in unequivocal double taxation of corporate income. The U.S. provides relief, however, to certain types of corporations (for example, S corporations with fewer than 75 shareholders and limited liability companies) by treating them as conduits for their shareholders. Thus, under this system, depending on the type of corporation, some corporate income is subject to deliberate double taxation and other corporate income is not.

(b) — The Imputation Model

Under the imputation system, corporate income is taxed to the corporation, but the corporation's taxes are subsequently credited or imputed to the shareholder when it pays dividends. Thus, the shareholder obtains relief for the corporation's taxes. In a full imputation system, corporate and individual taxes are "integrated" and income that flows through the corporation to its shareholder is taxed only once.

In this model, an individual who receives a dividend from a corporation "grosses up" the cash value of the dividend to a value that is notionally equivalent to the corporation's pre-tax income. The amount of the gross-up is simply a mathematical function of the underlying corporate tax rate. For example, where a corporation earns $100 of income and pays tax of 50 per cent on the income, it has $50 to distribute to its shareholders. Assuming that the corporation pays a dividend of $50 to an individual shareholder, the shareholder grosses up the dividend by doubling it and includes $100 in income. The amount included is equal to the corporation's pre-tax income. Thus, assuming that the corporation has previously paid 50 per cent tax on its income, the shareholder calculates his or her personal tax liability on the equivalent of the corporation's pre-tax income of $100.

The individual then pays tax on the equivalent of the corporation's *pre-tax* income of $100 and receives a credit for taxes ($50) equal to that paid by the corporation. Thus, the underlying principle of the imputation model is that the corporation's taxes are imputed to its shareholders as if they had paid them, and the shareholders claim a tax credit equal to the gross-up value of the dividends. Figure 2 sets out a full imputation model.

Figure 2 — Imputation Model

Individual's Tax Bracket	26%	39%	44%
Corporate income	$ 100	$ 100	$ 100
Less: Corporate tax @ 50%	(50)	(50)	(50)
Net Income paid as dividend	50	50	50
Add: Dividend gross up of 100%	50	50	50
Taxable amount of dividend	$ 100	$ 100	$ 100
Individual tax	$ 26	$ 39	$ 44
Less: Tax credit	(50)	(50)	(50)
Net refund	24	11	6
Add: Cash dividend	50	50	50
Total cash received by individual	$ 74	$ 61	$ 56

In the example in Figure 2, the corporate tax of $50 that we impute to the individual is fully integrated with the personal tax. The amount that the individual retains is exactly equal to the amount that would have been paid if the individual received the income directly rather than through the corporation. In the top tax bracket of 44 per cent, for example, the shareholder retains $56 net after he or she pays all corporate and personal taxes.

The example in Figure 3 compares the classical, full imputation, and partial imputation models. In each case we assume that the corporate tax rate is 50 per cent, that the shareholder has a personal tax rate of 44 per cent, and that partial imputation is at 50 per cent. Then, assuming that the corporation earns $100 and pays out all of its after-tax income as dividends, the combined cost to the corporation and the shareholder in each case is as follows:

Figure 3 — Classical Method, Full and Partial Imputation Models

Tax	Classical Method	50% Imputation	100% Imputation
Corporate Tax			
Net Income	$ 100	$ 100	$ 100
Less: Corporate tax @ 50%	(50)	(50)	(50)
Net income after tax	$ 50	$ 50	50
Shareholder Tax			
Dividend received	$ 50	$ 50	$ 50
Add: Dividend gross-up	0	25	50
Taxable amount of dividend	$ 50	$ 75	$ 100
Individual Tax @ 44%	$ 22	$ 33	$ 44
Less: Credit for corporate tax	(0)	(25)	(50)
Shareholder tax	$ 22	$ 8	$ (6)
Corporate and shareholder tax	$ 72	$ 58	$ 44

The classical method is clearly the most expensive for taxpayers and results in a combined tax of $72 on income of $100. In contrast, full imputation results in a tax of $44 on $100 of income, which in the example is exactly equal to the tax that would be payable by the shareholder had he or she earned the income directly rather than through a corporation. Hence, other things being equal, one would expect a country with a classical system of corporate taxation (e.g., the United States), to have a lower corporate tax rate than a country with a full imputation system.

Subject to one proviso, the full integration of corporate and personal taxes is equitable, neutral, and eliminates double taxation and tax deferral. In the example given in Figure 3, the shareholder pays 44 per cent tax, whether he or she earns the income through a corporation or personally. A full imputation system integrates the corporate and personal tax. To achieve this result, however, the corporate tax rate must be at least equal to the personal rate, so there is no systemic incentive to defer taxes by retaining income in the corporation. If the corporate tax rate is lower than personal tax rates, there is an incentive to retain earnings in the corporation in order to defer the higher personal tax payable on dividends. Such a bias also creates an ancillary distortion: earnings retained in the corporation will usually cause the value of the corporation's shares to increase, so that, when disposed of, they will give rise to capital gains. Since capital gains are taxable at preferred rates, an additional distortion builds in to the system. Thus, one must structure the imputation model in the context of corporate and personal tax rates and other systemic tax preferences. Since corporate tax rates are substantially influenced by international considerations, it is not always easy to implement an efficient full imputation system.

The imputation model is also not without its conceptual problems. One of the difficulties of the full imputation model is that the shareholder receives a credit for taxes that the corporation notionally pays even though the corporation may not actually have paid any tax on the income in the year. For example, a corporation may earn $100 income but pay no tax on it because it can reduce its taxable income to zero through fast write-offs of expenditures such as capital cost allowance, research and development costs, depletion allowances, or other tax incentives or preferences. The model, however, allows the shareholder a tax credit for the tax supposedly paid by the corporation. Thus, the imputation model is premised on an assumption that may not be, and rarely is, valid.

(c) — The Advance Corporate Tax Model

The Advance Corporate Tax ("ACT") Model is essentially a variation of the imputation model. But unlike the imputation model, which involves a credit for corporate taxes on a notional basis, the ACT model involves tracking the actual taxes and dividends paid by a corporation. Under this model, where a corporation pays taxes, it establishes a "Taxes Payable" account. When it pays a dividend to its shareholders, it withholds tax on behalf of the shareholder and claims the tax withheld from the shareholder as a credit to reduce its Taxes Payable account. The essence of the ACT system is that it relies on a direct dividend tax credit, rather than a notional credit as under the imputation model. The tax withheld on distribution to shareholders is equal to the amount of tax that the corporation paid. The limitation of the system is that it creates an incentive to distribute income. Otherwise, corporate income is double taxed if the corporation does not pay enough dividends to cover its full tax liability. The pressure to pay dividends prevents corporate capital accumulation.

5. — Tax Rates

(a) — General Rates

Canadian corporate tax rates depend on four principal factors:

- The type of corporation,
- The source of its income,
- The timing of its distribution to shareholders, and
- The relationship between the corporation and its shareholders.

The federal corporate tax rate starts at 38 per cent of taxable income.[24] This rate is reduced by 10 per cent of the corporation's taxable income earned in the year in a province.[25] Thus, the general federal corporate rate of tax on taxable income earned in Canada is 28 per cent.

The 10 per cent reduction in the federal corporate tax rate from 38 per cent to 28 per cent in effect vacates an area of the income tax field to the provinces to allow them to levy their own corporate income taxes. The provinces levy corporate taxes at varying rates that generally exceed 10 per cent. We obtain the actual total tax on corporate income by adding the applicable provincial rate to the federal rate. For example, where a province levies corporate tax at 16 per cent, the combined federal-provincial corporate tax is 44 per cent. In fact, the effective rate of federal tax on corporate income depends on various factors that can increase or decrease the nominal rate. For example, some corporations receive tax credits for certain types of income, and surtaxes can raise the effective corporate tax rate above the nominal rate.

(b) — Flat Rate

The basic federal corporate tax is a flat rate, that is, it is applied at a uniform rate to the corporation's taxable income. Because the tax is applied at a flat rate, the average rate of tax paid by a corporation is usually the same as its marginal rate. Thus, with some exceptions, that are discussed below, the rate of tax that a corporation pays on its "top dollar" is the same as the rate that it pays on its first dollar of taxable income. This characteristic of the corporate tax structure is extremely important when considering the interplay between the tax that a corporation pays and the tax that its individual shareholders pay. It might, for example, influence the decision as to how much an owner-manager should extract from a corporation by way of salary (deductible to the corporation) or dividends (not deductible) and taxable to the individual at progressive marginal rates.

(c) — Special Rates

Having said that the Act levies corporate tax at a flat rate, it is important to note that there are, in fact, several different flat rates. The rate applicable to a particular corporation depends upon the type of corporation, the amount that it earns in the year, the source and type of its income, and its shareholdings. Each of these factors plays a role in determining the rate at which a corporation is taxable.[26] For example, the federal tax rate on the first

---

[24]Subs. 123(1).

[25]Subs. 124(1). The basic rate of federal tax is subject to various adjustments in the form of tax credits and surtaxes.

[26]See, e.g., ss. 125, 125.1.

$300,000 of active business income earned by a Canadian-controlled private corporation (CCPC) is approximately 13 per cent.[27]

	%
Basic federal rate	38.00
Federal abatement	(10.00)
	28.00
Federal surtax (4% of 28%)	01.12
	29.12
Small business deduction	(16.00)
Small business rate	13.12
(on income to $300,000)	

6. — *Taxation of Shareholders*

When a corporation pays dividends, its shareholders may also be liable for tax on their dividend income. The taxation of shareholders depends upon the following:

* Type of shareholders (corporate or individual),

* Status (Canadian or foreign) of the payer corporation,

* Size of shareholdings (controlling shareholder or portfolio investor),

* Type of dividend (taxable or capital), and

* Source of income from which the dividend is paid (active or passive).

We saw earlier that a complicating feature of the corporate tax system is the potential for double taxation of income in the corporation and again in the hands of its shareholders. The Act does, however, provide some relief from double taxation. For example, dividends between taxable Canadian corporations flow through on a tax-free basis.[28] Individuals who receive dividends from taxable Canadian corporations can claim a dividend tax credit,[29] which reduces the net tax rate on such income. Whether the relief from double taxation of corporate income is complete or partial depends upon the status of the payer corporation and the source and amount of its income. Generally, the tax system is most generous to share-

---

[27]The 2003 Budget increased the small business limit from $200,000 to $300,000. It was phased in as follows: $225,000 for 2003, $250,000 for 2004, and $300,000 for 2005.

[28]Subs. 112(1).

[29]S. 121.

holders of "small" Canadian corporations that engage in active business. Shareholders of "large" or non-Canadian corporations are subject to some double taxation.

7. — Factors Affecting Corporate Taxation

The corporate tax rate depends upon the following factors:

Type of Corporation:

- Canadian vs. non-Canadian
- Taxable corporation vs. non-taxable corporation
- Public
- Private
    - Canadian-controlled
    - Foreign-controlled
- Other (non-public/non-private)
- Special status
- Exempt

Type of Income:

- Business:
    - Active
    - Manufacturing and processing
    - Personal services
    - Other
- Property:
    - Dividends
    - Interest
    - Specified investment business
    - Other
- Capital gains

Geographic Source of Income:

- Domestic
- Foreign

Nature of Income:

- Active business income
- Passive income

Time of Distribution by Corporation:

- Immediate
- Deferred

Size of Shareholdings:

- Insignificant (under 10 per cent)
- Significant (over 10 per cent)
- Control holding
- Foreign affiliate
  - Controlled foreign affiliate

Size of Capital Base:

- Various levels are significant

Obviously, the permutations and combinations of these factors significantly complicate the corporate tax system.

IV. — Types Of Corporations

1. — Canadian Corporation

A Canadian corporation is a corporation that is resident in *or* incorporated in Canada.[30] There is no requirement that the corporation be owned by Canadian residents or by Canadian citizens.[31]

---

[30]Subs. 89(1)"Canadian corporation".

[31]Para. 250(4)(a).

The Act deems any corporation incorporated in Canada after April 26, 1965 to be resident in Canada.[32] The Act also deems a corporation incorporated in Canada before April 27, 1965, that has either become a resident of Canada or carried on business in Canada after that date to be a resident of Canada.[33]

2. — Taxable Canadian Corporation

A taxable Canadian corporation is a Canadian corporation that is not exempt from Part I tax.[34]

3. — Public Corporations

Generally, public corporations are corporations with widely-dispersed shareholdings that are listed on a stock exchange in Canada.

More specifically, a "public corporation" is a corporation that is resident in Canada that has:[35]

- Its shares listed on a prescribed stock exchange in Canada;[36]

- Elected to become a public corporation and has complied with certain prescribed conditions; or

- Been designated by the Minister to be a public corporation and has complied with certain prescribed conditions.

(a) — Electing Public Corporation Status

Listed corporations are public corporations. To be listed on any of the stock exchanges, a corporation must generally have widely dispersed shareholdings and comply with the rules and regulations of the particular exchange.

---

[32]*Ibid.*

[33]Para. 250(4)(c).

[34]Subs. 89(1)"taxable Canadian corporation".

[35]Subs. 89(1)"public corporation".

[36]Reg. 3200: prescribed stock exchanges include Tiers 1 and 2 of the TSX Venture Exchange (also known as Tiers 1 and 2 of the Canadian Venture Exchange), the Montreal Stock Exchange and the Toronto Stock Exchange. Over-the-counter trading of shares, which is done through Tier 3 of the TSX Venture Exchange, does not qualify a corporation as a public corporation.

A corporation that is not listed on a prescribed[37] stock exchange may elect public corporation status for income tax purposes if it meets certain conditions relating to:[38]

- The number of its shareholders,

- The dispersal of ownership of its shares,

- The public trading of its shares, and

- The size of the corporation.

The conditions are similar to the requirements imposed on corporations listed on stock exchanges. Thus, an unlisted corporation may, by satisfying requirements similar to those imposed on listed corporations, qualify as a public corporation.[39]

A corporation that elects to become a "public corporation" must have:[40]

- At least 150 shareholders (excluding "insiders") holding "equity shares", with each shareholder owning at least one "block of shares" of the class having a total fair market value of not less than $500; or

- At least 300 shareholders (excluding "insiders"), with each shareholder holding at least one "block of shares"[41] of the class having a total fair market value of not less than $500.

An "equity share" is a share with an unrestricted right to share in dividends and the right to participate in the capital of the corporation in the event that the corporation reduces its capital or is wound up; this generally means the common shares of the corporations, but the category can include shares with special rights.[42]

To determine the number of shareholders[43] of a particular class of shares, shareholders owning less than one block of shares with a market value under $500 are arranged so as to form

---

[37]Reg. 3200.

[38]Reg. 4800.

[39]Note that co-operative corporations and credit unions cannot *elect* public corporation status, and can qualify as public corporations only by having their shares listed on a prescribed stock exchange.

[40]Reg. 4800(1).

[41]Reg. 4803(1). A "block of shares" is 100 shares if the fair market value of one share of the class is less than $25, 25 shares if the fair market value of one share of the class is $25 or more but less than $100, and 10 shares if the fair market value of one share of the class is $100 or more.

[42]S. 204"equity share".

[43]Reg. 4800(1). For the purpose of calculating the number of shareholders of a class of shares to determine whether the 150 or 300 minimum numbers are satisfied: each shareholder must hold not less than one "block of shares" of the class; the shares held by each shareholder must have an aggregate

the greatest possible number of groups such that each group owns at least one block of shares with a fair market value of $500 or more; no shareholder is included in more than one group, and each group is considered to be one shareholder for the purpose of meeting the 150 or 300 shareholders requirements.[44]

The class of shares that forms the basis for the election must qualify for distribution to the public. Thus, the corporation must file a prospectus, registration statement or similar document with a public authority, pursuant to the laws of the jurisdiction to which the corporation is subject (such document must have been accepted for filing by the public authority) and there must have been a distribution to the public of that class of shares in accordance with the filed document.[45]

(b) — Ministerial Designation

The Minister may designate a corporation as a public corporation if it complies with all of the conditions that would entitle it to elect public corporation status at the time of the designation.[46] The Minister does so by giving 30 days written notice.

(c) — Electing out of Public Corporation Status

A listed corporation cannot elect out of its public corporation status.

An unlisted public corporation, however, can elect *not* to be a public corporation if it complies with certain conditions. These conditions concern:[47]

- The number of its shareholders,

- The dispersal of ownership of its shares, and

- The public trading of its shares.

The corporation must support the election by an authorization for the election and a statutory declaration by the directors as to compliance with prescribed conditions.

---

fair market value of $500 or more; and insiders must not hold more than 80 per cent of the shares of the class.

[44]Regs. 4803(3), (4).

[45]Reg. 4803(2).

[46]Subs. 89(1)"public corporation" (b)(ii).

[47]Subs. 89(1)"public corporation" (c)(i).

A corporation that elects not to be a public corporation must either have fewer than 50 equity shareholders (excluding insiders) or fewer than 100 shareholders (excluding insiders) if the shares are not equity shares.[48] In addition, insiders must own more than 90 per cent of the shares of the class.

A corporation that elects not to be a public corporation must also establish that at the time of the election it does not have any other class of shares that could form the basis of an election to be a public corporation.

4. — Private Corporations

The Act defines private corporation status by applying a negative test to the definition of a public corporation. A private corporation is a corporation that is:[49]

- Resident in Canada,

- *Not* a public corporation, and

- *Not* controlled by one or more public corporations or prescribed Federal Crown corporations or any combination of the two.[50]

Whether a corporation is controlled by a public corporation is determined on the basis of the *de jure* test.

A corporation that was a private corporation at the commencement of its 1972 taxation year and has continued since then to be a private corporation is deemed to have become a private corporation at the end of its 1971 taxation year.[51]

A corporation incorporated after 1971 that was a private corporation at the time of its incorporation and that has continued without interruption to be a private corporation is deemed to have become a private corporation immediately before its incorporation.[52]

---

[48]Reg. 4800(2). Each shareholder of the class of shares forming the basis of the election must hold not less than one "block of shares" of the class, and the shares must have an aggregate fair market value of $500 or more.

[49]Subs. 89(1)"private corporation".

[50]See section 711 Regulations.

[51]Subs. 89(1)"private corporation" (a).

[52]Subs. 89(1)"private corporation" (b).

5. — Canadian-Controlled Private Corporations

A Canadian-controlled private corporation ("CCPC") is a private "Canadian corporation" that is *not* controlled by non-residents, by a public corporation, or by any combination of non-residents and public corporations.[53] The definition of CCPC does not require control by Canadian residents but lack of control by non-residents. Thus, the Act defines, a CCPC as a private corporation that is not controlled by non-residents. For example, a private corporation that is owned 50 per cent by non-residents and 50 per cent by residents qualifies as a CCPC.

"Control" means both legal and factual control. Thus, one must look at the amount of shareholdings and the *de facto* influence.[54]

The *de jure* (legal) test is essentially numerical. One adds up the shares that non-residents and public corporations own to determine if they exceed 50 per cent.

6. — Other Corporations

A corporation may be *neither* a private corporation nor a public corporation. Thus, the mere fact that a corporation does not qualify as a public corporation does not automatically make it a "private corporation". For example, a resident unlisted subsidiary of a public corporation is neither a public nor a private corporation. In contrast, a resident subsidiary of a non-resident corporation whose shares are widely held may qualify as a private corporation.

7. — Special Status Corporations

Certain types of corporations carrying on business in Canada are subject to special rules under the Act. There are various reasons for granting corporations special status. The Act treats certain investment-type corporations as financial intermediaries for their shareholders and integrates the tax at the corporate and individual levels. In other cases, corporations such as credit unions and co-operative organizations are accommodated by special provisions that take into account the special needs of the businesses that these entities conduct.

---

[53]Subs. 125(7)"Canadian-controlled private corporation".

[54]See subs. 256(5.1); *Mimetix Pharmaceuticals Inc. v. R.* (2001), [2002] 1 C.T.C. 2188 (T.C.C. [General Procedure]); affd. [2003] 3 C.T.C. 72 (Fed. C.A.).

8. — *Exempt Corporations*

Certain corporations are completely exempt from tax. There are two types of exempt corporations:

- Those exempt from tax by virtue of their status per se (e.g., a municipality in Canada or a municipal or public body performing a function of government in Canada);[55] or

- Those exempt from tax by virtue of a particular status *and* additional tests (e.g., a registered charity is exempt from tax on its income if it complies with certain rules in respect of its activities).[56]

---

[55]Paras. 149(1)(c), (d), (d.1) to (d.6) and (e).

[56]Para. 149(1)(f); see, generally, s. 149.1.

Selected Bibliography to Chapter 17

The Corporate Entity

Krishna, Vern, "Blowing Hot and Cold at the Same Time" (1994) 5 Can. Current Tax 7.

Ross, David W., "Incorporation and Capitalization of a Private Corporation," in *Proceedings of 39th Tax Conf.* 11:1 (Can. Tax Foundation, 1987).

Structure of Corporate Taxation

Cumming, Peter, *The Taxation of Business Enterprises* (Toronto: York University, Osgoode Hall Law School, 1992-1993).

Mintz, Jack M., "Alternative Views of the Corporate Tax: A Reassessment of the Carter Report" in *The Quest for Tax Reform: The Royal Commission on Taxation Twenty Years Later* (Toronto: Carswell, 1988).

Mintz, Jack M., "Competitiveness and Tax Policy: How does Canada Play the Game?" in *Proceedings of 43rd Tax Conf.* (Can. Tax Foundation, 1991), 5:1–5:14.

Mintz, Jack M., *An Empirical Estimate of Corporate Tax Refundability and Effective Tax Rates* (Ottawa, Department of Economics, Carleton University, 1987).

Types of Corporations

Beach, Wayne G. and Mark F. Wheeler, "Associated Corporations" in *Proceedings of 40th Tax Conf.* (Can. Tax Foundation, 1988), 10:1.

Cherniak, Janice L.E., "Going Private: Tax Planning Aspects" in *Corporate Structure, Finance and Operations* (Toronto: Carswell, 1990), at 83.

Drache, A.B.C., "Tax Exempt Organizations" (1991) 13 Can. Taxpayer 165.

Dukac, Jules, "An Analysis of the Proposals for the Taxation of Life Insurance Companies," in *Proceedings of 39th Tax Conf.* 35:1 (Can. Tax Foundation, 1987).

MacKight, Robin J., "What's in a Name?: Classifying Partnerships, Associations and Limited Liability Companies for Income Tax Purposes," (1993) Corp. Mgmt. Tax Conf. 21:1.

CHAPTER 18 — CORPORATE FINANCE

I. — General Comment

We can fund a corporation in several ways. The more conventional sources of corporate funding are:

- Share or equity capital,

- Debt capital,

- Retained cash earnings,

- Off-balance-sheet financial instruments (warrants, options, leases, etc.), and

- Government grants and subsidies.

The method that one uses to finance a corporation depends upon the type of corporation, its size, its access to capital markets, and the residence of its shareholders.

Small businesses can generally access debt, share capital, retained earnings, and government grants. Only large, publicly listed corporations with access to sophisticated capital markets issue derivatives such as rights and warrants.

One determines the financial structure of a corporation by two principal factors:

1. Access to funds, and

2. The cost of available funds.

Both market and tax considerations influence the cost of funds. Thus, where a corporation has a choice between alternative sources of funding, its decision to opt for one source over another, or to balance between different sources of funds, may be significantly influenced by income tax considerations. For example, a corporation may determine the ratio of its debt to equity capital by tax considerations such as the residence of shareholders (which determines the withholding tax rate), or the thin capitalization rules,[1] which determine the deductibility of interest.

II. — General Characteristics Of Debt And Share Capital

The capital structure of most small businesses and private corporations essentially comprises two elements: equity and debt. Equity, in turn, comprises two categories: share capital and retained earnings.

1. — Share Capital

Equity or share capital represents an ownership interest in the corporation. The rights, restrictions, terms, and conditions attached to the shares determine the nature of the interest. In the absence of any special provisions, all shares of a corporation are presumed to be equal.[2]

Share capital has two fundamental tax characteristics:

- A corporation can return its paid-up capital of shares to shareholders on a tax-free basis; and

- Dividends are not deductible from income and are paid from after-tax dollars.

These two characteristics determine the corporate financial structure of most enterprises.

2. — Debt Capital

Debt is a sum of money due by agreement, whether express or implied, that includes not only the obligation of the debtor to pay, but also the right of the creditor to receive and enforce payment. Debt generally arises from a contractual obligation whereby one person lends money to another on terms and conditions negotiated between the parties.

The quintessential characteristics of corporate debt are as follows:

- Debt does not represent ownership in a corporation but merely creates a relationship of debtor and creditor between the lender and the corporation;

---

[1] Subs. 18(4).

[2] CBCA, subs. 24(3); OBCA, subs. 22(3).

- Corporate creditors generally rank ahead of shareholders in any claims to the corporation's assets;

- Debt may be secured by corporate assets; and

- Interest on business debt is generally deductible for tax purposes.

3. — Hybrid Financing

Certain financial instruments have characteristics of both debt and share capital. Owing to the significant tax differences in the treatment of debt and equity capital, corporations have an incentive to devise hybrid financial instruments that allow them the best of both worlds. For example: payments on debt are generally deductible for tax purposes; payments can be discretionary and, in this sense resemble dividends on share capital. From the corporation's perspective, it is attractive to issue a hybrid instrument that has all the corporate characteristics of share capital, but that can be classified as debt for tax purposes. The tax authorities are understandably concerned about such instruments and there are complex rules to minimize their use. These rules circumscribe the use of hybrids such as "taxable preferred shares", "term preferred shares", and "income bonds".

III. — Corporate Law Of Equity Financing

We initially determine a corporation's share capital for tax purposes (referred to as "paid-up capital" in the *Income Tax Act*) from its "stated capital" for the purposes of corporate law. Thus, we start with a general discussion of the corporate law applicable to corporate financing through the issuance of shares, and then proceed to a discussion of the income tax consequences of the various forms of corporate financing.

1. — General Comment

The concept of "stated capital" in corporate law serves two distinct interests:

1. Protection of creditors, and

2. Protection of shareholders.

A corporation's creditors have a right to look to its stated capital as a measure of the pool from which the corporation will draw to pay its debts. Hence, creditors have an interest in the capital structure of the corporation to which they loan money. They have a legitimate concern that the corporation does not dissipate its capital through unauthorized corporate distributions.[3]

Stated capital also serves as a measure of limiting shareholder liability for corporate debts. Corporate statutes generally limit a shareholder's exposure for corporate liabilities to the shareholder's contributions to the corporation's stated capital.

Neither the *Canada Business Corporations Act*[4] ("CBCA") nor the *Business Corporations Act* of Ontario[5] ("OBCA") define "capital". Generally, "capital" refers to proceeds from the sale of capital stock and represents money that the purchaser pays for an undivided interest in the assets of a corporation.[6]

The term "capital" can also have other meanings depending upon the context in which one uses it and the adjective by which one modifies it. For example, in accounting we use "working capital" to denote the excess of current assets over current liabilities, "liquid capital" sometimes denotes cash and marketable securities, etc. In corporate law, however, one uses the term "capital" only to describe the share capital of a corporation.

2. — Share Capital

(a) — Nature of Shares

A share represents the proportional financial interest of a shareholder in a corporation. It measures the liability of the shareholder to outside interests and the size of the financial interest in the corporate undertaking.

A share is not a sum of money: it is an interest measured by a sum of money. A share is a chose in action that forms a separate right of personal property.[7] It represents a fractional interest in the capital of the corporation. A share represents the bundle of rights contained in the share contract.[8] Thus, a share is that fraction of the capital of a corporation that confers

---

[3]*Re Inrig Shoe Co.* (1924), 27 O.W.N. 110 (S.C.); see *J.M.P.M. Ent. Ltd. v. Danforth Fabrics (Humbertown) Ltd.*, [1969] 1 O.R. 785 (H.C.) (issuance of additional shares to affect a change in control being "sale or other disposition" of control).

[4]*Canada Business Corporations Act*, R.S.C. 1985, c. C-44.

[5]*Business Corporations Act*, R.S.O. 1990, c. B.16.

[6]*Toronto v. Consumers' Gas Co.*, [1927] 4 D.L.R. 102 (P.C. [Ont.]).

[7]OBCA, s. 41; *Bradbury v. English Sewing Cotton Co.*, [1923] A.C. 744. The term "chose in action" only means that a share does not confer a right to possession of a physical thing; instead, it gives a personal right of property claimable by legal action.

[8]*Borlands Trustee v. Steel Bros. & Co.*, [1901] 1 Ch. 279 at 288 *per* Farwell J.; see also *Re Paulin*, [1935] 1 K.B. 26 (C.A.); *I.R.C. v. Crossman*, [1937] A.C. 26 (H.L.).

on its owner a proportional proprietary interest in the corporation. Shareholders are not part owners of the assets of the undertaking.[9] Instead, they share certain rights, such as the right to participate in profits and capital.

(b) — Rights of Shares

We usually associate three rights to shares:

1. The right to vote,

2. The right to participate in profits by way of dividends, and

3. The right to share in the property of the corporation upon its dissolution.

Under the CBCA, where there is only one class of shares, these three rights attach to each share. Under the OBCA, however, only the right to vote and the right to receive property upon dissolution automatically attach to a single class of shares.[10] Unlike the CBCA, the OBCA does not address the right of a shareholder to receive dividends.

A corporation may issue more than one class of shares. The rights, privileges, restrictions, and conditions that attach to each class of shares must be set out in its articles of incorporation.[11] If a corporation issues more than one class of shares, we must ensure that we attach each of the rights (the right to vote, the right to receive dividends and the right to share in property) to at least one of the classes of shares.[12]

3. — Issuance of Shares

(a) — No Par Value

A corporation must issue its shares in registered form without nominal or par value.[13] Shares are considered to be issued when all the formalities in respect of their issuance are

---

[9]*Short v. Treasury Commrs.*, [1948] 1 K.B. 116. The term "shareholder" merely describes a person who is a holder of shares; it does not mean that that person shares property in common with another.

[10]CBCA, subs. 24(3); OBCA, subs. 22(3). Although there is no statutory right to dividends under the OBCA, all shareholders must be treated equally where there is only one class of shares.

[11]CBCA, subs. 24(4); OBCA, subs. 22(4).

[12]CBCA, para. 24(4)(b).

[13]CBCA, subs. 24(1); OBCA, subs. 22(1).

satisfied.[14] Shares with nominal or par value issued *prior to the enactment of* the CBCA and the OBCA *are deemed to be shares without nominal or par value.*[15]

A corporation issues a share in registered form if it satisfies one of two conditions: it names a person who is entitled to the share such that its transfer may be recorded on a securities register, or it bears a statement that it is in registered form.[16]

(b) — Unlimited Number

In the absence of a specific restriction in its articles of incorporation, a corporation can issue an unlimited number of shares of each class provided for in the articles. A corporation can set an upper limit, however, on the number of shares it will issue, even if the articles specify no such limit.[17]

A corporation that restricts the number of shares it may issue may, at any time, by special resolution, amend its articles of incorporation to remove and or amend the restriction.[18] An amendment to a corporation's authorized capital entitles a shareholder of the corporation to dissent from the change and, if the appropriate procedural steps are followed, the shareholder is entitled to be paid the fair value of the shares.[19]

(c) — Limited Liability

Shares issued by a corporation are non-assessable against its shareholders. Thus, they cannot be called upon to pay additional amounts either to the corporation or to its creditors.[20] Shareholders are not, *qua shareholders*, liable for the acts or default of the corporation.[21]

---

[14]See: *Dale v. Canada*, [1997] 2 C.T.C. 286, 97 D.T.C. 5252 (F.C.A.); *National Westminster Bank v. I.R.C.*, [1994] S.T.C. 184 (C.A.).

[15]CBCA, subs. 24(2); OBCA, subs. 22(2).

[16]CBCA, subs. 48(4); OBCA, subs. 53(1)"registered form".

[17]CBCA, para. 6(1)(c).

[18]CBCA, para. 173(1)(d); OBCA, clause 168(1)(d). "Special resolution" is a defined term and, in effect, means a two-thirds majority; *Trans-Prairie Pipelines Ltd. v. M.N.R.*, [1970] C.T.C. 537, 70 D.T.C. 6351 (Ex. Ct.) (interest on money borrowed used to redeem preferred shares deductible).

[19]CBCA, s. 190; OBCA, s. 185.

[20]CBCA, subs. 25(2); OBCA, subs. 23(2).

[21]CBCA, subs. 45(1); OBCA, subs. 92(1).

(d) — Full Consideration

A corporation may not issue any shares until such time as it receives full consideration in the form of money, property, or past services, in return for the shares. If past services constitute the consideration for issued shares, the fair value of those services must not be less than the money the corporation would have received had the shares been issued for cash.[22]

A corporation may issue shares for non-cash property if the property is no less than equivalent in value to the fair cash consideration the corporation would have received had it issued its shares for money.[23]

The directors of a corporation determine the value of consideration received by the corporation in exchange for its shares (whether in the form of property or past services). They must ensure that this amount is not less than the cash equivalent that it would have otherwise received.[24] In determining what constitutes a fair equivalent value for property or past services, directors may take into account reasonable charges and any expenses of organization that are expected to benefit the corporation.[25] Directors may be personally liable for any shortfall of consideration.[26]

4. — Stated Capital Account

The concept of "stated capital" is particularly important in corporate law. As we shall see, it is also the springboard for determining the "paid-up capital" of a corporation for tax purposes.

Stated capital is the amount of money that a shareholder "commits" to the corporation and, in most cases, represents the shareholder's maximum liability to corporate creditors. Thus, in a sense, it is the financial measure of the limited liability of shareholders and represents to creditors the amount of funds or assets initially invested by shareholders.

---

[22]CBCA, subs. 25(3); OBCA, subs. 23(3).

[23]CBCA, subs. 25(3); OBCA subs. 23(3).

[24]CBCA, subs. 25(3); OBCA, subs. 23(4). The CBCA does not specifically require directors to act on the determination of equivalent fair value. The power of determining share consideration is, however, an incident of the power and duty to manage the affairs of the corporation.

[25]CBCA, subs. 25(4); OBCA, subss. 23(4) and 23(5).

[26]See, for example, CBCA, subs. 118(1) and OBCA, 130(1). Also, CBCA, subs. 25(5) and OBCA, subs. 23(6) generally do not allow a company to issue shares for debt.

(a) — Separate Accounts for Each Class

A corporation must maintain a separate stated capital account for each class and series of shares that it issues.[27] Generally, the stated capital account is credited with the *full* amount of any consideration received in respect of the particular shares issued by the corporation.[28] There are some exceptions (discussed below) to this rule in respect of non-arm's length transactions.

(b) — Shares Issued for Property

A corporation may not issue shares in exchange for any property (or past service) that is valued at less than the amount the corporation would have received had the shares been issued for money.[29] It can, however, issue shares for consideration of greater value than the cash equivalent of property or past services.

(i) — Credit Full Consideration

Generally, the *full* amount of the consideration received must be credited to the stated capital account. A corporation cannot, however, credit to a stated capital account an amount that is greater than the amount of the consideration that it receives for its shares.[30] This rule plays an important role in tax law because a corporation can generally pay back its stated capital without any income tax cost to shareholders.[31]

(ii) — Non-Arm's Length Transactions

There are several exceptions to the general rule that a corporation must credit the full amount of consideration that it receives to its stated capital account. A corporation may add,

---

[27]CBCA, subs. 26(1); OBCA, subs. 24(1).

[28]CBCA, subs. 26(2); OBCA, subss. 24(2), (8) (stated capital account may be maintained in foreign currency).

[29]CBCA, subs. 25(3); OBCA, subs. 23(3).

[30]CBCA, subs. 26(4); OBCA, subs. 24(4).

[31]"Paid-up capital" for tax purposes.

to its stated capital account, an amount that is less than the consideration that it receives for its shares if it issues the shares:[32]

- In exchange for property of a person who, immediately before the exchange, does not deal with the corporation at arm's length;

- In exchange for shares of a body corporate that immediately before the exchange, or because of the exchange, does not deal with the issuing corporation at arm's length;

- Pursuant to an amalgamation with another corporation; or

- Pursuant to an "arrangement" that is, in effect, an amalgamation of the issuing corporation with another corporation.

A corporation may also add an amount less than the fair market value of property to its stated capital account in respect of arm's length transactions if the corporation and all of its shareholders of the particular class consent.[33]

In each of the above circumstances, the corporation may add either all or *some lesser part of* the consideration that it receives for its shares to the appropriate stated capital account. As already noted, it cannot add an amount that is greater than the amount it receives.[34] These exceptions facilitate corporate reorganizations under the *Income Tax Act*.[35]

(c) — Stock Dividends

Where a corporation pays a stock dividend, it must add to the stated capital account of the class of shares on which it pays the dividend, the full financial equivalent of the declared amount of the dividend.[36] In other words, the amount that it capitalizes from retained earnings to share capital for accounting purposes is also the amount that it must credit to the share capital account for corporate law purposes.

---

[32]CBCA, subs. 26(3); OBCA, subs. 24(3). These exceptions all cater to income tax transactions and are intended to facilitate various rollovers under the *Income Tax Act*.

[33]See, for example, CBCA, subpara. 26(3)(a)(iii).

[34]CBCA, subs. 26(4); OBCA, subs. 24(4). Since March 31, 1977 the general rule is that "paid-up capital" for income tax purposes is calculated by reference to the rules of corporate law. In the absence of technical adjustments, we determine the paid-up capital of a class of shares of a corporation by dividing the stated capital account for that class of shares by the number of issued shares of that class.

[35]See Chapter 25, "Transfer of Property to a Corporation".

[36]A stock dividend is a dividend paid by issuing additional fully paid shares of the corporation to existing shareholders; see CBCA, subs. 43(2); OBCA, subs. 38(2).

(d) — Continuances

A corporation continued under either the CBCA or the OBCA may add to its stated capital accounts any consideration that it receives for shares issued prior to its continuance. Also, it may, at any time, add to its stated capital account any amount credited to its retained earnings or other surplus accounts.[37]

(e) — Resolutions

Where a corporation has more than one class of shares outstanding, any addition to the stated capital account of a class or series of shares must be approved by a special resolution if the amount that is to be added was not received as consideration for the issue of shares.[38] An Ontario corporation does not need to pass a special resolution if the amount that it credits to the stated capital account arises by virtue of the payment of a stock dividend.

The OBCA also requires a corporation to conduct a special class vote if an addition to its stated capital account affects the shareholders of one of its classes or series of shares in a manner different from the way in which it affects holders of another of its classes or series of shares. The right to vote separately as a class attaches to the shares whether or not the particular shares would otherwise entitle the holder to vote under normal circumstances.[39]

5. — Reduction of Stated Capital

A corporation's stated capital account serves two important corporate purposes: (1) it serves as a measure of the maximum liability of its shareholders to outsiders; and (2) the amount shown in the account represents the initial investment of its shareholders, which also serves as a measure of security for creditors who loan money to the corporation. Thus, corporate statutes control adjustments, particularly downward adjustments, in these accounts. As we will see, the *Income Tax Act* also stringently controls adjustments to the paid-up capital of corporations.

The general rule is that a corporation may not reduce its stated capital.[40] There are exceptions to this rule, but the exceptions apply only in narrowly circumscribed circumstances.

---

[37]CBCA, subs. 26(6); OBCA, subs. 24(5).

[38]CBCA, subs. 26(5); OBCA, subs. 24(6). Under the CBCA, a special resolution is not required if there are only two classes of shares and all of the issued shares are convertible from one class into the other.

[39]OBCA, subs. 24(7).

[40]CBCA, subs. 26(10); OBCA, subs. 24(9). This prohibition does not apply to mutual funds.

Generally, a corporation may reduce its stated capital only if it satisfies two financial requirements: the reduction must not impair either the solvency or the liquidity of the corporation. Thus, a corporation may reduce its stated capital if it is able to pay its obligations as they fall due and it is able to discharge its obligations to its shareholders and creditors.

The stringency of the financial tests varies with the reason for the reduction of capital and the potential for harm to investors. The less the risk of harm and the lower the potential for abuse, the less stringent the test that the corporation must satisfy to reduce stated capital.

(a) — Acquisition of Corporation's Own Shares

In common law, a corporation could not reduce its capital except with judicial approval. Thus, a corporation could not purchase its own shares, since the purchase of its own shares would be tantamount to a reduction of capital.[41]

The common law rule has been incorporated into both the CBCA and the OBCA, but with substantial exceptions.[42] A corporation may reduce its capital if it protects the financial interests of its investors and creditors.

(i) — Financial Tests

Subject to restrictions in its articles, a corporation may purchase its own shares if it does not have reasonable grounds for believing that the purchase will:[43]

- Render the corporation unable to pay its liabilities as they come due, or

- Cause the realizable value of its assets to be less than the aggregate of its liabilities and the stated capital of all of its classes of shares.

Thus, the corporation must satisfy two financial tests: it must be both liquid *and* solvent after it purchases its shares. The determination of corporate liquidity is fairly clear cut in most cases and can be ascertained from financial statements stated in terms of current market values. Long-term solvency is more difficult to measure.

Directors of a corporation who authorize the purchase of its shares in contravention of the solvency and liquidity tests become jointly and severally liable to the corporation for the

---

[41]*Trevor v. Whitworth* (1887), 12 App. Cas. 409 (H.L.).

[42]CBCA, s. 30; OBCA, s. 28.

[43]CBCA, s. 34; OBCA, s. 30. Note that an Ontario corporation may also purchase its warrants. The financial tests are somewhat less stringent if the purchase of shares is to settle a claim against the corporation, eliminate fractional shares, or fulfil the terms of a non-assignable agreement under which the corporation is obliged to purchase the shares.

amount of the unauthorized disbursement of funds.[44] The CBCA and OBCA absolve from liability a director who dissents from the resolution authorizing the purchase of shares if the director records his or her dissent at the meeting. If the director is not present at the meeting, he or she must notify the secretary of the corporation and record the dissent in the minutes of the meeting.[45]

A director can rely upon reports presented by professionals who are qualified to comment on matters requiring technical expertise. As such, a director who relies upon the report of an accountant, appraiser, or other qualified professional to make valuation judgments is not liable if the purchase of shares subsequently proves to be in contravention of the statutory financial tests.[46]

(ii) — Dissenting Shareholders

A corporation that purchases its own shares to satisfy a dissenting shareholder's claim pursuant to the appraisal remedy faces a less stringent financial test.[47] For example, under a buy-out pursuant to the appraisal remedy, a corporation cannot purchase its own shares from a dissenting shareholder if the purchase would render the corporation unable to pay its obligations as they fall due (the liquidity test), or if the purchase reduces the realizable value of its assets to less than the value of its outstanding liabilities.[48] In these circumstances, the corporation's stated capital is not taken into account in the second prong of the two tests. In other words, a corporation may reduce its stated capital to purchase its own shares if it does not impair its liquidity and solvency insofar as its creditors are concerned.

(iii) — Court Order

A corporation may also purchase its own shares to comply with a court order.[49] In complying with the court order, the corporation does not have to satisfy the liquidity and solvency tests applicable to other purchases.[50] The corporation need only satisfy two tests: (1) that it will be able to pay its liabilities as they become due (the liquidity test); and (2) that the

---

[44]CBCA, subs. 118(2); OBCA, subs. 130(2).

[45]CBCA, s. 123; OBCA, subs. 135(3).

[46]CBCA, subs. 123(4); OBCA, subs. 135(4).

[47]CBCA, para. 35(2)(a); OBCA, cl. 31(2)(a).

[48]CBCA, subs. 190(26); OBCA, subs. 185(30).

[49]CBCA, s. 241; OBCA, s. 248.

[50]CBCA, para. 35(2)(b); OBCA, cl. 31(2)(b).

realizable value of its assets after the purchase does not fall below the aggregate of its liabilities.[51]

(b) — Alternative Acquisition of Corporation's Own Shares

There are three additional circumstances in which a corporation may acquire its own shares by satisfying a somewhat less stringent financial test than those generally applicable. Subject to its articles, a corporation may purchase its own shares to:[52]

1. Settle or compromise debts asserted by or against the corporation;

2. Eliminate fractional shares; or

3. Fulfil the terms of a non-assignable agreement under which the corporation has an option or is obligated to purchase shares owned by a director, officer, or employee of the corporation.

In any of these situations, the corporation may purchase its shares *unless*:[53]

- There are reasonable grounds for believing that the purchase will render the corporation unable to pay its obligations as they fall due; or

- The realizable value of the corporation's assets after the purchase will be less than the aggregate of its liabilities and the amount required to redeem all of its shares the holders of which have the right to be paid *prior* to the holders of the shares to be purchased.

The second prong of the financial tests ensures that a corporation that purchases its own shares does not prejudice the rights of "senior" shareholders who have a higher ranking claim to the assets of the corporation than the holders of the shares purchased. Thus, the corporation cannot prejudice the rights of preferred shareholders by purchasing shares that rank lower in corporate rights.

---

[51]CBCA, subs. 241(6); OBCA, s. 248(6).

[52]CBCA, subs. 35(1); OBCA, subs. 31(1).

[53]CBCA, subs. 35(3); OBCA, subs. 31(3).

(c) — Redemption of Shares

A corporation can redeem its redeemable shares, but it cannot pay an amount in excess of the redemption price stipulated in its articles of incorporation.[54] A "redeemable share" is a share that is redeemable at the option of either the corporation or the shareholder.[55]

A corporation may not redeem its shares unless it satisfies two financial tests. First, a corporation may redeem its shares only if there are reasonable grounds for believing that the redemption will not render the corporation unable to pay its obligations as they fall due.[56] Thus, the corporation must be liquid enough to pay its debts as they mature.

Second, the realizable value of the corporation's assets after the redemption must not be less than the aggregate of its liabilities and the amount required to pay other shareholders who rate equally with or have a higher claim than the holders of the redeemed shares.[57] The concern here is to protect only those who have a claim equal to or higher than the shares redeemed. The financial tests are less stringent because the shares would have been issued on the basis that they were redeemable and this information is available to the public.

(d) — Other Reductions of Stated Capital

A corporation may, by special resolution, reduce its stated capital account at any time and for *any* purpose if it satisfies certain financial tests.[58] Under this general, broad-based power the corporation can proceed only by way of a special resolution of its shareholders. The resolution must identify the particular stated capital accounts that are to be reduced.[59]

(i) — Financial Tests

In addition to the special resolution, the corporation must satisfy two financial tests: liquidity and solvency. These tests are similar, though not identical, to the tests applicable to a purchase or redemption of corporate shares. Thus, a corporation may not reduce its stated

---

[54]CBCA, subs. 36(1); OBCA, subs. 32(1).

[55]CBCA, subs. 2(1)"redeemable share"; OBCA, subs. 1(1)"redeemable share". In financial jargon, a share that is redeemable at the option of the shareholder is referred to as a "retractable share".

[56]CBCA, para. 36(2)(a); OBCA, cl. 32(2)(a).

[57]CBCA, para. 36(2)(b); OBCA, cl. 32(2)(b).

[58]CBCA, subs. 38(1); OBCA, subs. 34(1).

[59]CBCA, subs. 38(2); OBCA, subs. 34(3). A "special resolution" is a resolution passed by a majority of two-thirds of votes cast, or one signed by all of the shareholders entitled to vote on the resolution; see, CBCA, subs. 2(1)"special resolution", OBCA, subs. 1(1)"special resolution".

capital if there are reasonable grounds for believing that the reduction will render the corporation unable to pay its obligations as they fall due.[60]

Second, the stated capital account may not be reduced if there are reasonable grounds for believing that the reduction will cause the realizable value of the corporation's assets to be less than the aggregate of its liabilities.[61] Since the liabilities of a corporation include its contingent liabilities, it may be quite difficult to determine whether the solvency test is satisfied in borderline cases.

Where an Ontario corporation plans to reduce its capital in circumstances in which the reduction will have a different effect on different classes of shares, it must allow a separate class vote for the purposes of obtaining the special resolution from each of the affected classes. The right to a separate class vote does not depend upon whether or not the shares affected would otherwise be entitled to vote.[62]

(ii) — Creditor's Rights

A creditor of a corporation that reduces its stated capital in contravention of either the CBCA or the OBCA is entitled to apply to a court for relief. The court may order the shareholder *or other recipient* who has benefited from the reduction:[63]

- To pay to the corporation an amount equal to any liability of the shareholder that was either extinguished or reduced contrary to the statutory provisions; or

- To deliver to the corporation any money or property paid or distributed to the shareholder or other recipient as a consequence of the improper reduction of capital.

This remedy is in addition to any other remedies that the creditor may have against the directors of the corporation who have authorized an unlawful reduction of capital.[64] There is, however, a limitation period: the creditor must commence action within two years of the

---

[60]CBCA, para. 38(3)(a); OBCA, cl. 34(4)(a). A corporation reducing its stated capital must *always* satisfy the liquidity test so that the rights of creditors are not prejudiced. It is only the solvency test which is more or less stringent depending upon the circumstances surrounding the reduction.

[61]CBCA, para. 38(3)(b); OBCA, cl. 34(4)(b).

[62]OBCA, subs. 34(2).

[63]CBCA, subs. 38(4); OBCA, subs. 34(5).

[64]OBCA, subs. 34(9).

alleged unlawful reduction of capital.[65] Shareholders of Ontario corporations are entitled to apply to bring the suit as a class action.[66]

A shareholder who holds shares as a trustee (or other fiduciary) is not personally liable on an improper reduction of stated capital. Rather, it is the beneficial owner of the shares who assumes all the liabilities flowing from an infringement of the statutory provisions.[67]

6. — Adjustments of Stated Capital Accounts

A corporation must maintain a separate stated capital account for each class and series of shares that it issues.[68] Generally, the corporation must credit the full amount of any consideration that it receives upon issuing shares to the appropriate stated capital account.[69]

(a) — Reduction

When a corporation reduces its share capital, it must adjust the amount shown in its stated capital account. The amount of the adjustment depends upon the manner in which the corporation acquires its own shares. Where the reduction in the share capital of a corporation is pursuant to:

- An acquisition of the corporation's own shares;[70]

- A settlement or compromise of a claim asserted against the corporation;[71]

- A plan to eliminate fractional shares;[72]

---

[65]CBCA, subs. 38(5); see also: section 4, Ontario *Limitations Act*.

[66]OBCA, subs. 34(7).

[67]OBCA, subs. 34(8), subs. 1(1)"personal representative".

[68]CBCA, subs. 26(1); OBCA, subs. 24(1).

[69]CBCA, subs. 26(2); OBCA, subs. 24(2). A lesser amount may be credited to the stated capital account where the shares are issued in exchange for property in a non-arm's length transaction: CBCA, subs. 26(3); OBCA, subs. 24(3). The rationale of this exception is to accommodate income tax planning, particularly under s. 84.1 of the *Income Tax Act*. CBCA, subpara. 26(3)(a)(iii) also permits a corporation to add less than the FMV of property to its stated capital if the corporation and all the shareholders of the particular class consent.

[70]CBCA, s. 34; OBCA, s. 30.

[71]CBCA, para. 35(1)(a); OBCA, cl. 31(1)(a).

[72]CBCA, para. 35(1)(b); OBCA, cl. 31(1)(b).

- The terms of a non-assignable agreement under which the corporation was obliged to purchase shares owned by its directors, officers, or employees;[73]

- A redemption of its shares;[74]

- The enforcement of a lien against its shares;[75]

- A transaction whereby a dissenting shareholder of the corporation exercised appraisal rights;[76] or

- A court order relieving a shareholder from oppression by the corporation,[77]

the amount to be deducted from the stated capital account is calculated according to a formula that reduces the stated capital account by the *average* issue price of all of the shares of the particular class or series.[78]

The formula reduces the stated capital account of the shares in proportion to the amount that was credited to the account when the shares were issued. The premium paid to a shareholder on the redemption of shares in any of the above listed circumstances is not deducted from the stated capital account.[79]

In contrast, if a corporation is required to compensate a shareholder for the purchase price of the shares because of its oppressive conduct, the reduction in the stated capital account is the full amount paid to the shareholder.[80] This amount will not necessarily coincide with the amount credited to the corporation's stated capital account when the shares were initially issued as the shareholder may have purchased the shares from another shareholder at a later date.

Where a corporation reduces its stated capital account pursuant to a special resolution, the amount specified in the resolution as the amount of the reduction is the amount deducted from the appropriate stated capital account.[81] The determination of this amount depends entirely upon the particular circumstances calling for the reduction.

---

[73]CBCA, para. 35(1)(c); OBCA, cl. 31(1)(c).

[74]CBCA, s. 36; OBCA, s. 32.

[75]CBCA, subs. 45(3); OBCA, subs. 40(3).

[76]CBCA, s. 190; OBCA, s. 185.

[77]CBCA, s. 241; OBCA, s. 248.

[78]CBCA, subs. 39(1); OBCA, subs. 35(1).

[79]*Ibid.*

[80]CBCA, subs. 39(2); OBCA, subs. 35(2).

[81]CBCA, subs. 39(3); OBCA, subs. 35(3).

(b) — Conversion or Change of Shares

Where a corporation converts shares from one class into another, it must adjust the stated capital accounts of both of the classes to reflect the conversion. Similarly, when shares are changed from one class or series into shares of another class or series, the stated capital account of both classes or series must be adjusted.[82] In either of these situations, conversion or change, the stated capital account of the class from which the shares are converted is reduced by the amount derived from a formula.

The stated capital account of the shares into which the shares are converted or changed is increased by an equivalent amount *plus* any additional consideration payable on the conversion or change of shares.[83]

Where a corporation has two classes of shares with rights of conversion from one class into the other (that is, interconvertible shares), the adjustment to the stated capital account upon the conversion of a share from one class to the other is equal to the weighted average of the stated capital accounts of both classes of shares.[84]

When shares of one class or series are converted or changed into shares of another class or series, the old shares (that is, the converted or changed shares) are considered to be issued shares of the class or series into which the shares have been converted or changed.[85] Thus, to the extent of the number of shares converted, the issued capital of the old class or series *automatically* becomes issued shares of the new class or series. The automatic conversion of shares from one class into another applies only to the *issued* shares and does not apply to any *unissued* shares. The articles must be amended to convert the unissued shares of the old class into unissued shares of the new class.

7. — Effect of Change of Shares on Authorized Capital

There are circumstances where a corporation may wish to restrict the amount of share capital that it issues.[86] Where a corporation limits the number of shares that it may issue by stipulating a maximum authorized capital, a conversion of shares from one class into another will have the effect of increasing the unissued but authorized shares of the old class by the

---

[82]CBCA, subs. 39(4); OBCA, subs. 35(4). A "conversion" of shares from one class into another occurs pursuant to the terms and conditions of the shares as described in the articles of incorporation. A "change" of shares from one class into another is usually pursuant to a subsequent amendment to the terms and conditions attached to the shares.

[83]CBCA, para. 39(4)(b); OBCA, cl. 35(4)(b).

[84]CBCA, subs. 39(5); OBCA, subs. 35(5).

[85]CBCA, subs. 39(9); OBCA, subs. 35(8).

[86]CBCA, para. 6(1)(c).

number of shares converted or changed into shares of the new class. In other words, the authorized share capital of the old class is restored by the number of shares converted or changed into the new class.[87]

8. — Cancellation of Shares

If its articles of incorporation do not limit the number of shares that a corporation may issue, any shares (or fractions of shares) that the corporation issues and later acquires are automatically cancelled. Where, however, the authorized share capital of a corporation is limited, any of its shares acquired by the corporation are restored to the status of authorized but unissued shares of the particular class.[88] The rationale of these provisions is to prevent the corporation and its senior officials from manipulating the market in the corporation's shares or using corporate assets to acquire, or enhance, voting power.

9. — Corporation Holding Its Own Shares

The common law rule against corporations "trafficking" in their own shares also prohibited a corporation from holding its shares: the retention of cancelled shares would be tantamount to a reduction of capital.[89]

The common law rule is entrenched in both the CBCA and the OBCA.[90] The general rule is that a corporation may not hold shares in itself; nor may it hold shares in its parent corporation. A parent corporation is specifically prohibited from issuing its shares to any of its subsidiaries.[91] Although there are exceptions to these rules, each exception is circumscribed by financial tests which are intended to protect the interests of investors and creditors.

---

[87]CBCA, subs. 39(10); OBCA, subs. 35(8).

[88]CBCA, subs. 39(6); OBCA, subs. 35(6).

[89]*Trevor v. Whitworth* (1887), 12 App. Cas. 409 at 423 (H.L.):

> Paid-up capital may be diminished or lost in the company's trading; that is a result which no legislation can prevent; but persons who deal with, and give credit to a limited company, naturally rely upon the fact that the company is trading with a certain amount of capital already paid, as well as upon the responsibility of its members for the capital remaining at call; and they are entitled to assume that no part of the capital which has been paid into the coffers of the company has been subsequently paid out, except in the legitimate course of its business.

[90]CBCA, subs. 30(1); OBCA, subs. 28(1).

[91]CBCA, subs. 30(2); OBCA, subs. 28(2) (a corporation acquiring a subsidiary that holds its shares must cause the subsidiary to dispose of those shares within five years of its becoming a subsidiary).

IV. — Tax Aspects Of Equity Financing

1. — General Comment

A corporation's share capital represents its permanent capital base. A corporation is generally under no legal obligation to re-purchase its shares and return capital to shareholders. Since, in most cases, the payment of dividends is within the sole discretion of the board of directors, a corporation need not pay dividends when it is not financially secure. Indeed, as already noted, a corporation is prohibited from paying dividends if the payment would impair its financial ability to repay its debts.

One measures a shareholder's ownership of a corporation by the number of shares that is owned. For tax purposes, the paid-up capital of a share represents the owner's interest in the corporation.

Two fundamental aspects of corporate share capital determine the corporate tax structure and tax planning:

1. Dividends are paid from after-tax dollars and are not deductible from income; and

2. The paid-up capital of shares can be returned to shareholders on a tax-free basis.

These two characteristics of the corporate tax system have an enormous influence on the structure of the system and we see their effect in many anti-avoidance rules.

2. — Types of Shares

Unless otherwise stated or provided for in the articles of incorporation, all shares are presumed to be equal in respect of their fundamental rights. These rights include: the right to vote; the right to participate in dividends; and the right to share in any proceeds on liquidation of the corporation.

We can, however, modify the fundamental rights to suit the needs of the corporation and its investors. Thus, we can make shares voting or non-voting, and voting shares can be differently weighted. Similarly, we can grant shares priority in respect of the timing and amount of dividends payable on them. Shares can be redeemable at the option of the corporation and retractable at the option of the shareholder. Shares can be given priority in respect of the return of capital upon liquidation, and so on. These variable attributes permit a very large number of combinations and permutations of share characteristics. Thus, one can craft share conditions to suit the particular purposes for which they are to be used.

The particular terms, conditions, rights and restrictions attached to shares can have a significant effect upon their fair market value and this can be important for the purposes of determining capital gains and losses. For example, the types of share conditions that one uses in an estate freeze are quite different from share conditions in a public offering. In the former case, the objective is to freeze the fair market value of shares so that they do not increase in value; in the latter case, the objective is to facilitate growth in the value of the shares in the public market.

3. — Paid-Up Capital

In corporate law, the concept of stated capital serves two distinct purposes: (1) it is a measure of the cushion upon which creditors may rely for the repayment of their debts, and (2) it is a measure of the limit of shareholder liability. The *Income Tax Act* levies a tax on income, not on capital. Thus, it is necessary to distinguish between a corporation's income and capital for tax purposes.

"Paid-up capital" for tax purposes is analogous to the concept of "stated capital": it measures the amount of capital that a corporation can return to shareholders on a tax-free basis. The Act deems payments to shareholders in excess of the paid-up capital of their shares to be income.[92]

One initially determines the "paid-up capital" of a class of shares under the applicable corporate statute.[93] Hence, the concept of paid-up capital can vary between different corporate jurisdictions in Canada. The paid-up capital of a share is a characteristic of and specific to *the share* — it does not attach to the shareholder. Thus, it does not necessarily change when one sells the share. One always reflects an adjustment to paid-up capital on the corporation's books. In contrast, the adjusted cost base of a share is a feature unique to the shareholder. It does not affect the corporation. An adjustment to the adjusted cost base of a share does not affect the corporation's books.

We determine the paid-up capital of shares as at a point in time. The paid-up capital of a share starts off equal to its stated capital for corporate purposes. For example, where a corporation issues shares for $100 per share, both its stated capital and paid-up capital are $100. The adjusted cost base of the shares to the initial shareholders is also $100.

The two measures of capital can, however, diverge because of subsequent adjustments for tax purposes that do not affect the corporation's financial records. Thus, a corporation's paid-up capital for tax purposes may differ from its stated capital for financial accounting purposes. It will also vary from the cost base of the shares if one sells the shares. In the above example, if the shares are sold for $150, the adjusted cost base of the shares to the purchaser is $150, while their paid-up capital remains $100. Thus, the initial shareholder derives a gain of $50 and the paid-up capital (and stated capital) of the shares remains constant.

---

[92]See, e.g., *Income Tax Act*, s. 84.

[93]Subs. 89(1)"paid-up capital".

Example

Assume:

Holdco is a corporation incorporated under the *Canada Business Corporations Act*. *Holdco* has not issued any shares prior to the transactions described below. Assume also that the shares are issued to, and held by, individual shareholders. *Holdco* is authorized to issue the following classes of shares:

Class	Rights
Class A	Voting, unlimited participation in dividends and on liquidation ("common shares").
Class B	Voting, no dividend entitlement, preferential participation on liquidation to the extent of $100 per share, redeemable and retractable for $100 per share, convertible into Class D on a 1:1 basis.
Class C	Non-voting, no dividend entitlement, preferential participation on liquidation to the extent of $100 per share, retractable for $100 per share.
Class D	Non-voting, unlimited participation in dividends and on liquidation.

Holdco issues one Class A share for $100.

Then:

Stated capital (Class A shares):

Before issuance	$ 0
Increase	100
After issuance	$ 100

Paid-up capital (Class A shares):

Stated capital	$ 100
Adjustment	0
Paid-up capital	$ 100

Hence, paid-up capital equals stated capital of shares.

(a) — Classes of Shares

Corporate statutes presume all shares to be equal and to confer the same rights unless they expressly state otherwise. In order for shares to be considered to belong to different classes, they must, *in substance*, have different rights, conditions, privileges, or restrictions. As Dickson C.J., said in *McClurg*:[94]

> In my view, a precondition to the derogation from the presumption of equality, both with respect to entitlement to dividends and other shareholder entitlements, is the division of shares into different "classes". The rationale for this rule can be traced to the principle that shareholder rights attach to the shares themselves and not to shareholders. The division of shares into separate classes, then, is the means by which shares (as opposed to shareholders) are distinguished, and in turn allows for the derogation from the presumption of equality. ...

One determines the stated capital and paid-up capital of shares of interconvertible classes as if they were combined in one class.[95]

(b) — Capitalizing Retained Earnings

The amount of retained earnings capitalized affects the stated capital and the paid-up capital of the shares and may also trigger a deemed dividend.[96]

Example

Assume:

Holdco capitalizes $50 of its retained earnings to its Class A shares.

Then:

Stated capital (Class A shares):	
Before capitalization	$ 100
Capitalization	50
After capitalization	$ 150
Paid-up capital (Class A shares):	
Stated capital	$ 150
Adjustment	0
Paid-up capital	$ 150

---

[94]*McClurg v. M.N.R.* (1990), [1990] 3 S.C.R. 1020, [1991] 1 C.T.C. 169, 91 D.T.C. 5001 at 5007 (S.C.C.); see also *Int. Power Co. v. McMaster Univ.*, [1946] S.C.R. 178 (S.C.C.) [Que.].

[95]CBCA, subs. 39(5); OBCA, subs. 35(5).

[96]*Income Tax Act*, subs. 84(1).

Example

The Act also deems the shareholder of the Class A shares to have received a dividend to the extent that the paid-up capital of the shares is increased without a corresponding increase in Holdco's net assets — in this example, $50.

(c) — Stock Dividends

A stock dividend is the payment of a dividend in shares. The corporation issues shares to existing shareholders without any additional consideration. Typically, stock dividends are prompted by a desire to ostensibly allocate retained earnings to shareholders, but without distribution of cash. Subsection 43(2) of the CBCA requires the "declared amount" of a stock dividend to be added to the stated capital of the class of shares on which the corporation pays the dividend.[97] The "declared amount" of a dividend is the amount *declared* by the directors in the corporation's resolutions.

Example

Assume:

Holdco declares and pays a dividend in the amount of $10 on its Class A share payable by the issue of one Class B share that has a fair market value of $100.

Then:

Stated capital (Class B shares):	
Before stock dividend	$ 0
Stock dividend	10
After stock dividend	$ 10

Paid-up capital (Class B shares):	
Stated capital	$ 10
Adjustment	0
Paid-up capital	$ 10

---

[97]See also OBCA, subs. 38(2).

Alternatively, and perhaps preferably, pursuant to subsection 26(2) of the CBCA, the "full amount" of the consideration for the stock dividend is the fair value of the dividend — here, $100 per Class B share. This is the amount to be added to the stated and paid-up capital of the shares. This view better accords with the policy of the corporate and tax statutes. It is also in keeping with commercial and accounting practice. For example, as the American Institute of Certified Public Accountants said:[98]

> ... a stock dividend does not, in fact, give rise to any change whatsoever in either the corporation's assets or its respective shareholders' proportionate interests therein. However, it cannot fail to be recognized that, merely as a consequence of the expressed purpose of the transaction and its characterization as a *dividend* in related notices to shareholders and the public at large, many recipients of stock dividends look upon them as distributions of corporate earnings and usually in an amount equivalent to the fair value of the additional shares received. Furthermore, it is to be presumed that such views of recipients are materially strengthened in those instances, which are by far the most numerous, where the issuances are so small in comparison with the shares previously outstanding that they do not have any apparent effect upon the share market price and, consequently, the market value of the shares previously held remains substantially unchanged. The committee, therefore, believes that where these circumstances exist the corporation should, in the public interest, account for the transaction by transferring from earned surplus to the category of permanent capitalization (represented by the capital stock and capital surplus accounts) an amount equal to the fair value of the additional shares issued. ...

(d) — Conversion of Shares

Subsection 39(4) of the CBCA requires stated capital adjustments to be made on a conversion of shares from one class into another class.[99] The stated capital of the class from which one converts the shares is reduced by the appropriate percentage. The stated capital of the class into which the shares are converted is increased by a corresponding amount.

Example	
Holdco's shareholder elects to convert its Class B share into a Class D share.	
Stated capital (Class B shares):	
Before conversion	$ 10
Deduction on conversion	(10)
After conversion	$ 0

---

[98]ARB 43, c. 7 (1953).

[99]See also OBCA, subs. 35(4).

Example

Paid-up capital (Class B shares):	
Stated capital	$ 0
Adjustment	0
Paid-up capital	$ 0

Stated capital (Class D shares):	
Before conversion	$ 0
Increase on conversion	10
After conversion	$ 10

Paid-up capital (Class D shares):	
Stated capital	$ 10
Adjustment	0
Paid-up capital	$ 10

4. — Adjustments to Paid-Up Capital

The paid-up capital of a share starts off equal to its stated capital for corporate purposes. The two measures of capital can, however, diverge because of adjustments that may have to be made for tax purposes. For example, one might adjust the paid-up capital of a class of shares for transactions under any of the following provisions of the *Income Tax Act*:

- Subsections 66.3(2) and (4) (flow-through shares);

- Sections 84.1 and 84.2 (non-arm's length sales);

- Section 85 (transfer of property to a corporation);[100]

- Subsections 87(3) and (9) (amalgamation);

- Subsection 192(4.1) (designation by corporation); and

- Section 212.1 (non-arm's length purchase of shares from non-resident).

Thus, a corporation's paid-up capital for tax purposes may be quite different from its stated capital for financial accounting purposes. The difference between paid-up capital and stated

---

[100]See Chapter 25, "Transfer of Property to a Corporation".

capital can be a trap for anyone who relies solely on the corporation's financial statements to determine the paid-up capital of shares. For example, the Act deems that where a corporation redeems its shares, any amount paid over the paid-up capital of the shares is a dividend to the shareholder.[101] Since paid-up capital may be lower than stated capital for accounting purposes, what appears on the financial statements to be a tax-free return of stated capital, may, for tax purposes, be a taxable dividend in the hands of the shareholder.

To avoid the risk of unexpected deemed dividends, it is desirable to reduce a corporation's stated capital for corporate purposes to accord with its paid-up capital for income tax purposes. This reduces the risk of inadvertently triggering income tax consequences on the basis of corporate share transactions.

5. — Cost of Issuing Shares

(a) — General Comment

The general rules on expense deductions prohibit a corporation from deducting the cost of issuing equity capital. [18(1)(a) and (b)]. However, the Act permits the deduction of certain financing charges, but only according to a specific amortization formula.[102]

(b) — Commissions to Agents

A corporation may deduct certain types of financing expenses associated with the issuance of its shares. For example, deductible expenses include any commissions, fees, or other amounts payable to salespersons, agents, or securities dealers in the course of issuing shares. The deduction is available only to the taxpayer who issues the shares and not to any other person. A parent corporation, for example, may not deduct expenses incurred in respect of shares that its subsidiary issues. The subsidiary may, however, be able to deduct fees that it pays to its parent corporation in respect of the shares issued.

(c) — Commissions to Purchaser

A commission, fee, or bonus paid to the person to whom the shares are sold is not deductible as part of the cost of issuing equity. Such expenses are considered to be a discount of the share price rather than an expense of issuing the shares.

---

[101]*Income Tax Act*, subs. 84(3).

[102]Para. 20(1)(e).

(d) — Deductible Expenses

A corporation may deduct the following expenses when it issues shares:[103]

- Legal fees in connection with the preparation and approval of a prospectus related to the issuance of shares;

- Accounting or auditing fees in connection with the preparation of financial statements, and related data, for inclusion with the prospectus;

- Printing costs for the prospectus, share certificates, etc.;

- Registrars' and transfer agents' fees; and

- Filing fees payable to any regulatory authorities with whom the prospectus must be filed.

Incorporation expenses, which include legal and accounting fees, are not part of the cost of issuing shares and are not deductible expenses for tax purposes. However, such expenses qualify as eligible capital expenditures.[104]

(e) — Amortization of Issuance Expenses

Expenses of issuing securities are deductible in equal portions over a period of five years.[105] Corporations with short taxation years must prorate the deduction for the short year. Where a corporation with an undeducted balance of financing expenses is wound up into, or amalgamated with, another corporation, the parent or new corporation may continue to deduct the expenses over the remainder of the five-year period.

6. — Share Redemptions

Where a corporation redeems shares for an amount in excess of their paid-up capital, the excess is deemed to be a dividend.[106] For example, assume that the stated capital and paid-

---

[103]See also: *International Colin Energy Corp. v. R.* (2002), [2003] 1 C.T.C. 2406, 2002 D.T.C. 2185 (T.C.C. [General Procedure]); *BJ Services Co. Canada v. R.*, [2004] 2 C.T.C. 2169, 2004 D.T.C. 2032 (T.C.C. [General Procedure]) [reviews the meaning of expense "in the course of an issuance or sale of shares of the capital stock of the taxpayer"].

[104]Subs. 14(5)"eligible capital expenditure".

[105]Subpara. 20(1)(e)(iii).

[106]Subs. 84(3); see also Chapter 21, "Corporate Distributions".

up capital of a share are $100, and the shareholder's adjusted cost base is $150. If the corporation redeems the share for $180, the shareholder is deemed to receive a dividend of $80.

Cash paid on redemption	$ 180
Paid-up capital	100
Deemed dividend	$ 80

At the same time, the Act deems the shareholder to dispose of his or her share and to derive proceeds of disposition, which may trigger a capital gain. In order to prevent double taxation, however, the Act reduces the shareholder's proceeds of disposition by the amount of the deemed dividend — that is, $80.

Cash paid on redemption	$ 180
Less: deemed dividend	(80)
Proceeds of disposition	$ 100
Less: adjusted cost base	(150)
Capital loss	$ (50)

Thus, the shareholder is deemed to receive a dividend of $80 and suffers a capital loss of $50, that is an economic net gain of $30. The treatment of the dividend and capital loss for tax purposes, however, is quite different. The shareholder obtains a tax credit on the dividend if the corporation that redeems the share is a Canadian corporation.[107] Only 1/2 of the capital loss of $50 is deductible for tax purposes, and then only against the shareholder's capital gains. If the shareholder does not have any capital gains, the tax bite can exceed the economic gain.

The Act deems the capital loss of $50 to be nil if the taxpayer is affiliated with the corporation immediately after the redemption. In such a case, we add the amount of the denied loss proportionately (based on relative FMV) to the ACB of any other shares that the shareholder owns. The purpose of this stop-loss rule is to prevent the shareholder from recognizing his loss where he remains a part of an economic group of affiliated persons.[108]

7. — Taxable Preferred Shares

(a) — Background

We saw in Chapter 17, "Basic Principles of Corporate Tax" that one of the fundamental structural characteristics of the corporate tax system is that corporations pay dividends with

---

[107]S. 121.

[108]Subs. 40(3.6) and para. 53(2)(f.2).

after-tax earnings. In contrast, interest expense is generally deductible for tax purposes and comes out of pre-tax earnings. On the other side of the coin, dividends generally flow on a tax-free basis between taxable Canadian corporations,[109] whereas interest income is taxable. Thus, the system has a built-in structural bias. A taxable corporation prefers dividend income over interest income, but prefers to pay interest expense instead of dividends on its financings.

Hence, in most cases, the opposing economic interests of creditor and debtor corporations in arm's length relationships will cause the parties to arrive at the most appropriate and market-efficient solution for corporate financing needs. Typically,there is a rate differential between interest charged on debt obligations and dividends on shares. The differential takes into account their disparate income tax treatment. The market model breaks down, however, if one of the parties to the financing transaction is not a taxable entity or has large accumulated losses.

We justify the tax-free flows of inter-corporate dividends on two bases: (1) the dividends are paid out of previously taxed profits to an entity that has an economic interest in the payer; and (2) the dividends will eventually be taxed again when paid out to individual shareholders. Thus, the disparity between dividend and interest income is premised on the prevention of double taxation of the same income within an economic unit of corporations.

The disparate tax treatment of dividend and interest income creates other problems, however, because of hybrid equities with the features and characteristics of both — instruments that look like shares, but that have all the important characteristics of debt, such as a fixed and pre-determined life. These so-called "shares" are usually underwritten by guarantees and have a specific term. Hence, they are known as "term preferred shares".

In substance, term preferred shares are equity instruments with preferences that one usually finds in preferred shares. The difference between ordinary and term preferred shares is that the latter have a limited term and are usually supported by guarantees for repayment. This type of financial instrument is most attractive when the borrower (for example, a taxable corporation) does not need, and cannot use, an interest deduction because it does not have sufficient taxable income to absorb the deduction. (The taxable corporation may not be able to utilize the interest deduction because it has, for example, accumulated losses, low profit margins, or accelerated write-offs.) In these circumstances, the corporation can usually negotiate more favourable borrowing terms on a hybrid, rather than a conventional debt, instrument if the corporation pays the lending institution in the form of tax-free dividends.

Similarly, even if both the lender and the borrower are taxable entities, there can be a tax advantage if the borrower's tax rate is lower than that of the lending institution. The net result of this tax-driven financial arbitrage is that otherwise profitable enterprises (but without taxable income because of available tax write-offs) can transform what are, in effect,

---

[109]See subs. 112(1).

payments on debt-type instruments into tax-free dividends in exchange for a lower borrowing cost.

The financial institutions are frequently the principal beneficiaries of these arrangements and were able to increase their income through tax-free dividends. In 1978, for example, the annual cost to federal and provincial governments of this form of after-tax financing was approximately $500,000,000.[110] In that year, the government introduced new rules to curb the use of after-tax financing. These rules(known as the "term preferred share" rules) are among the most complex provisions in the Act. Basically, they are intended to disallow the manipulation of the inter-corporate dividend deduction by financial institutions. They also ensure that dividends on preferred shares are paid out of a corporation's taxed earnings with after-tax dollars. The rules were substantially amended in 1988 and a new concept, the"taxable preferred share", was introduced into the Act.

(b) — "Taxable Preferred Shares"

(i) — General Scheme

Part VI.1 of the Act levies a special tax to be paid by a corporation that has paid taxable dividends on taxable preferred shares. This tax was introduced in 1988 in a renewed effort to control the use of after-tax financing, which continued to be popular despite the term preferred share rules introduced a decade earlier.

The tax under Part VI.1 is, in effect, a refundable tax on large corporations that use after-tax financing. The tax is imposed at three different rates as follows:[111]

Rate	Application
50%	Taxable dividends (other than excluded dividends) on "short-term" preferred shares in excess of dividend allowance;
40%	Where issuing corporation makes an election at the time of issue and where the terms of the shares so provide; and
25%	In all other cases where taxable dividends are paid on taxable preferred shares.

The rate of 50 per cent is intended to approximate the amount of tax that would be paid on an equivalent amount of interest if we assume a 33.3 per cent rate of corporate tax. The underlying rationale of these rates is to ensure that sufficient income tax is paid at the corpo-

---

[110]See Budget Papers, *Notice of Ways and Means Motions and Supplementary Information*, November 16, 1978.

[111]Subs. 191.1(1)(a) effective from 2003.

rate level to recover the tax benefit given to the recipient corporation for the inter-corporate dividend deduction or to individuals for the dividend tax credit.

(ii) — Meaning of "Taxable Preferred Shares"

The Part VI.1 tax is built around the concept of "taxable preferred shares". Generally, a "taxable preferred share" is a share with a special liquidation or dividend entitlement, or that has a guarantee in respect of its proceeds of sale or return of income. In effect, the definition probably encompasses all preferred and special shares issued after June 18, 1987.

Thus, a share is a taxable preferred share if:

- The shareholder is entitled to a fixed annual dividend, as and when declared by the directors of the issuing corporation,

- The shareholder is entitled to a fixed entitlement on a winding-up or a redemption of the share,

- It has any preference to dividends in relation to any other share, or

- It is convertible into a share that would be a taxable preferred share.

More specifically, a "taxable preferred share" includes a share that can be described in any of the following ways:[112]

- It is a "short-term preferred share" issued after December 15, 1987;

- It may reasonably be considered that the amount of any dividends payable on the share is fixed, limited to a maximum, or established to be not less than a minimum;

- It may reasonably be considered that the amount that a shareholder is entitled to receive for the share upon the dissolution, liquidation, or winding-up of the issuing corporation is fixed, limited to a maximum, or established to be not less than a minimum amount;

- It may reasonably be considered that the amount that a shareholder is entitled to receive upon a redemption, acquisition or cancellation of the share or on a reduction of the paid-up capital of the share is fixed, limited to a maximum, or established not to be less than a minimum amount;

- The share is convertible or exchangeable, unless the share is convertible or exchangeable into something that would not be a taxable preferred share; or

- The share is one the shareholder's investment in which any person (other than the issuing corporation) has undertaken to guarantee.

---

[112]Subs. 248(1)"taxable preferred share".

A "taxable preferred share" does not include prescribed shares or shares issued by a corporation in financial difficulty.[113]

The definition of taxable preferred shares is comprehensive enough to include shares that are considered to be "common shares" in most other circumstances. Given the broad definition of "taxable preferred share", the term encompasses ordinary "common shares" that have rights, conditions, privileges, or restrictions attached to them that fall within the definition. For example, it is not unusual to see so-called "common shares" that may be redeemable at a pre-determined ("fixed")amount. Such a share is caught within the definition of "taxable preferred share" for the purposes of the special taxes.

(c) — Tax on Preferred Shares

The Part VI.1 tax on dividends on taxable preferred shares is, in effect, a refundable tax. The tax is structured to prevent taxable corporations that do not have taxable income from using after-tax financial instruments to pay tax-free dividends to taxable lending institutions.

A corporation pays the tax on its taxable dividends on taxable preferred shares,but can claim a refund of the tax in certain circumstances. The refund is in the form of a deduction from income in an amount equal to three times the tax paid.[114] The tax is fully refundable only if the corporation that pays the dividend has sufficient income against which it can use the deduction. Thus, the payer corporation cannot use its Part VI.1 tax to reduce income if it does not have any income that is subject to tax.

(d) — Exemptions

There are several exemptions from the special tax on taxable preferred shares.

(i) — "Substantial Interest"

There are exemptions in respect of substantial interest shareholdings that are,essentially, dividends received by a related party or those received by a shareholder who owns at least 25 per cent of the votes and of the value of the capital stock of the paying corporation.[115] A

---

[113]The concept of "financial difficulty" is itself defined in paragraph (e) of the definition of "term preferred share" in subsection 248(1).

[114]Para. 110(1)(k).

[115]Subss. 191(1) and (2).

dividend paid to a shareholder with a substantial interest in the corporation is an "excluded dividend" for the purposes of the tax.[116]

(ii) — "Dividend Allowance"

The Part VI.1 tax applies only to dividends paid in excess of the corporation's dividend allowance. The dividend allowance is set at $500,000, which must be shared among associated corporations.[117] The allowance is reduced on a dollar-for-dollar basis by preferred share dividends paid in the preceding year in excess of $1,000,000.[118] Thus, small corporations may issue taxable preferred shares without getting caught by the tax.

(iii) — Financial Intermediaries

There are also some special exemptions in respect of dividends that financial intermediary corporations pay and receive and certain deemed dividends that arise on corporate reorganizations.[119]

(e) — Short-Term Preferred Shares

The tax rate on short-term preferred shares is 50 per cent. This rate reflects the basic 33.3 per cent tax rate plus the effect of the denial of the inter-corporate dividend deduction to the recipient. Thus, in effect, this rate combines the two taxes into one rate and levies it on the issuer of the share, subject to a full refund if the issuer is a taxable corporation. In a sense, then, the tax on taxable preferred shares is the equivalent of an advance corporation tax.

Generally, a short-term preferred share is a share issued after December 15, 1987 that is retractable within five years of its issue, or that is potentially subject to a guarantee of proceeds of disposition that may be effective within five years of the issuance of the shares.[120]

---

[116]Subss. 191(1) and 191.1(1).

[117]Subs. 191.1(3); s. 256(1)"associated corporations".

[118]Subs. 191.1(2).

[119]Subs. 191(1).

[120]Subs. 248(1)"short-term preferred share".

V. — Tax Aspects Of Debt Financing

Debt is often the primary source of capitalization of a small business corporation in the early stages of its life. There are advantages to using debt capital to capitalize a small business corporation. If one structures the loan properly, interest on the debt is deductible for tax purposes. The owner of the business can also secure the debt and rank ahead of other creditors to the extent of the security.[121]

Thus, an individual can start an enterprise with a small amount of share capital and contribute the balance of the capital by way of a secured shareholder loan. External lenders (for example, banks) will, however, usually require the owner/shareholder to provide a personal guarantee for borrowed funds.

There are several factors to be taken into account in selecting an appropriate method of debt financing. One must consider, for example, the cost of capital, its availability, and the risk exposure of the enterprise. No single formula applies to every corporation. Each corporation must take into account the terms and conditions attached to its debt financing in the context of the economic climate at the particular time.

Debt financing falls into one of two broad categories: long-term or short-term debt. One uses long-term debt, typically with a maturity of 15 to 20 years, to finance the purchase of assets that have a long life. Shorter term debt financing is appropriate only for short-term needs.

1. — Discounts and Premiums

Corporations can issue debt obligations at face value, at a discount, or at a premium from their face value. A discount or premium generally reflects economic adjustments to the nominal rate of interest to bring it into line with the effective market rate applicable at the time that the obligation is issued.

A bond's premium or discount may be on account of interest or capital. What is the "true nature" of the discount or premium? Does the debt obligation have a commercial rate of interest? Does the bonus or discount vary with the length of time that the loan funds are outstanding, the extent of capital at risk, and the nature of the financial operation? For example, discounts on financial market instruments, such as treasury bills, bankers' acceptances, and call loans, are in substance interest. The discount is the economic reward for simply holding the principal sum of the instrument for a period of time. For example, a treasury bill that is issued at 95 and matures at par (100) in one year has an effective interest rate of 5.3 per cent.[122]

---

[121]Except against banks and lending institutions.

[122]$5/95 \times 100$.

Discounts on debt obligations are deductible from income.[123] Where an obligation is issued at a price that is equal to at least 97 per cent of its principal amount and it does not yield an amount in excess of 4/3 of the nominal interest rate, the entire amount of the discount is deductible in computing income.

Where, however, a bond is issued for an amount that is less than 97 per cent of its face amount, for a yield in excess of 4/3 of its nominal interest rate, only one-half of the discount is deductible in computing income for tax purposes.

2. — Interest

The Act does not define the term "interest". "Interest" is the return or consideration for the use or retention by one person of a sum of money belonging to or owed to another.[124] It is in effect a payment for the use of property (money). We discussed the treatment of interest expense for tax purposes in Chapter 9 "Deductions from Business and Investment Income".

(a) — Source of Income

One of the requirements for the deduction of interest is the existence of the source of income to which the interest expense relates.[125] For example, a taxpayer who finances the purchase of investment securities may claim any directly related interest expense as a deduction. The deduction is available so long as the taxpayer continues to hold the original investment or substituted securities. This is so even if the security declines in value or becomes worthless.

The deduction may also be claimed, however, in certain circumstances if the investment is sold and the funds are used for another eligible purpose.

---

[123]Para. 20(1)(f).

[124]*Ref. re s. 6 of Farm Security Act, 1944 of Sask.*, [1947] S.C.R. 394 at 411 (S.C.C.); affd. [1949] A.C. 110, (sub nom. *A.G. Sask. v. A.G. Can.*) (P.C.); *Riches v. Westminster Bank Ltd.*, [1947] A.C. 390 (U.K.H.L.); see also Chapter 8 "Inclusions in Business and Investment Income".

[125]*Emerson v. The Queen*, [1986] 1 C.T.C. 422, 86 D.T.C. 6184 (F.C.A.); leave to appeal to S.C.C. refused 70 NR 160 (taxpayer not allowed to deduct interest on money used to purchase shares after shares sold at loss); *The Queen v. Bronfman Trust*, [1987] 1 S.C.R. 32, [1987] 1 C.T.C. 117, 87 D.T.C. 5059 (S.C.C.) (interest not deductible where principal borrowed to make capital distribution to trust beneficiary).

Interest on money used to acquire income earning property may be deductible even if one disposes of the property. The conditions for continued deductibility are:[126]

- The borrowed money must have been used for the purpose of earning income from capital property (other than real or immovable property or depreciable property); and

- The property must have been disposed of at its fair market value.

(b) — Accrued Interest

A taxpayer who purchases a debt obligation (other than an income bond, income debenture, small business development bond, or small business bond) can deduct interest accrued on the debt to the date of the purchase. The deduction is restricted to the extent that the amount is included as interest in computing income for the year. The accrued interest paid to the vendor of the debt obligation is included in computing the vendor's income.[127] Alternatively, the purchasing taxpayer may choose to capitalize the interest.

(c) — Expenses of Issuing Debt

A taxpayer can deduct expenses incurred in borrowing money for the purpose of earning income from a business or property.[128] In the absence of specific authorization, financing expenses (which typically include legal and accounting fees, printing costs, commissions, etc.) would be caught by the prohibition against deducting expenses not directly related to the income-earning process.[129] Financing expenses are deductible on a rateable basis over a five-year period.

---

[126]Subs. 20.1(1).

[127]Subs. 20(14); IT-410R, "Debt Obligations — Accrued Interest on Transfer" (April 23, 1993) archived by CRA. This rule only operates where there has been an assignment or transfer of title. Evidence of registration of title would likely be necessary; see *Hill v. M.N.R.*, [1981] C.T.C. 2120, 81 D.T.C. 167 (T.R.B.); *Smye v. M.N.R.*, [1980] C.T.C. 2372, 80 D.T.C. 1326 (T.R.B.); *Antosko v. Canada*, [1994] 2 S.C.R. 312, [1994] 2 C.T.C. 25, 94 D.T.C. 6314 (S.C.C.).

[128]Para. 20(1)(e).

[129]*Montreal Light, Heat & Power Consol. v. M.N.R.*, [1944] C.T.C. 94, 2 D.T.C. 654 (P.C.); see *The Queen v. Royal Trust Corp. of Can.*, [1983] C.T.C. 159, 83 D.T.C. 5172 (F.C.A.) (payment was commission for services rendered therefore qualified as an eligible capital expenditure).

(d) — Lump Sum Payments

Interest may be paid lump sum at the end of the term of a loan.[130]

3. — Capitalizing Interest

(a) — General Comment

A taxpayer may prefer not to write-off the interest expense against current operations. For example, there may be little advantage in taking a deduction for interest expense on money borrowed to construct an asset if the asset is not currently producing income. The deduction of interest would merely create a loss that the taxpayer may not be able to use within the time limits allowed for carryover of losses.[131] In such circumstances, the taxpayer may prefer to treat the interest expense as part of the capital cost of the asset and write-off the total cost of the asset at a later time when it begins to produce income. In other words, a taxpayer may treat interest costs as a capital expenditure rather than as a current expense.

(b) — Depreciable Property

A taxpayer who acquires depreciable property with borrowed money can elect to capitalize related interest charges.[132] The taxpayer can capitalize only those costs that would *otherwise have been deductible* as interest expense or as an expense of borrowing money. Interest expense to earn exempt income is not deductible and may not be capitalized.

The election is available not only in respect of costs incurred in the year in which one acquires the asset, but also in respect of costs that one incurred in the three immediately preceding taxation years. The extension of the election to the three preceding years recognizes that large undertakings extend over many years and that interest may be incurred on money borrowed prior to the period in which the money is actually used for its intended purpose.

---

[130]*Lomax v. Dixon*, [1943] 1 K.B. 671 (C.A.).

[131]See para. 111(1)(a) (limitation period in respect of non-capital losses).

[132]S. 21. Special restrictions on "soft costs" are discussed below; see subs. 18(3.1).

(c) — Election

(i) — Timing

The taxpayer must make the election for the taxation year in which he or she:

- *Acquires* the depreciable property,[133] or

- Uses the money borrowed for exploration, development, or the acquisition of property.[134]

A taxpayer may not elect to capitalize interest in anticipation of the acquisition of depreciable property or the use of borrowed money for exploration or development. The taxpayer may elect only *after* he or she acquires the property or expends the funds. Once it is made, however, the election is effective for borrowing costs and interest incurred in the year and in the three preceding years.

A taxpayer may elect under subsection 21(1) only for the taxation year in which the depreciable property is acquired. Where a building or other structure is being erected by a taxpayer, it is considered to have been "acquired" at any time to the extent of the construction costs to that time. Hence, a taxpayer must file a separate election for each taxation year in respect of the interest expense related to that year.

(ii) — Amount Capitalized

The election to capitalize interest does not have to be in respect of the full amount of the costs of borrowing. A taxpayer may elect to capitalize only a part of the interest charges and deduct the remainder as a current expense.

The portion of any capitalized interest is added to the capital cost of the depreciable property acquired. Thus, any capitalized interest can be written off through capital cost allowance charges in the future. The adjusted cost base of the property is also increased for the purpose of determining capital gains upon disposition of the property.[135]

(d) — Reassessment

Where a taxpayer elects to capitalize interest charges in respect of prior years, the Minister must reassess the taxpayer's preceding taxation years if the interest would have been other-

---

[133]Subs. 21(1).

[134]Subs. 21(2).

[135]Para. 54"adjusted cost base".

wise deductible in those years. Having made the election, the taxpayer may continue to capitalize interest in succeeding years if, in each of those succeeding years, the taxpayer capitalizes the *entire* amount of the interest on the property.

(e) — Compound Interest

A taxpayer may also capitalize compound interest and the expense of raising money. For example, a taxpayer may pay a commitment fee to a financier before funds are advanced. The taxpayer can capitalize the commitment fee, or standby interest, as part of the cost of borrowed money.[136]

VI. — Hybrid Debt

Just as a corporation can issue hybrid share capital (that is, share capital with substantial debt characteristics), so also can it issue hybrid debt — debt capital with all of the characteristics of equity. There are two advantages of hybrid debt: (1) in the absence of special rules, payments on debt are generally deductible for tax purposes; and (2) payments can be discretionary and, in this sense, resemble dividends on share capital. There are special rules that control the deductibility of interest on hybrid debt capital.

1. — Income Bonds and Debentures

(a) — General Rule

An income bond or debenture is a hybrid that pays interest or dividends only when and to the extent that the issuing corporation makes a profit.[137] This allows its issuer the flexibility of making interest or dividend payments only if it is in a profitable position and able to do so. Thus, an income bond or debenture resembles share capital. In addition, the Act defines an "income bond" or "income debenture" as an instrument that does not, in any circumstances, exceed a term of five years, and is issued:[138]

- As part of a proposal or arrangement with creditors that is approved under the *Bankruptcy Act* and *Insolvency Act*;

- At a time when all or substantially all of its assets were under the control of a receiver, or similar person; or

---

[136]*Sherritt Gordon Mines Ltd. v. M.N.R.*, [1968] C.T.C. 262, 68 D.T.C. 5180 (Ex. Ct.).

[137]Subs. 248(1)"income bond".

[138]*Ibid.*

- At a time when the issuing corporation or a resident non-arm's length corporation was in default, or reasonably expected to be in default, on a debt obligation,

The proceeds of the issue must be used in a business that is carried on immediately before its issue by the issuing corporation, or by a corporation with which it does not deal at arm's length. The Act deems interest or dividends paid by a resident corporation on an income bond or debenture to be dividends[139] and, therefore, not deductible from income for tax purposes.

(b) — Financial Difficulty

Interest on income bonds that a resident corporation issues to afford relief from financial difficulty is deductible and is not deemed to be a dividend.[140]

(c) — Taxable as Dividends

Payments on income bonds or debentures that are deemed to be dividends are taxable as such in the recipient's hands. Thus, in the case of individuals, the dividend is treated as a taxable dividend subject to the usual gross-up and dividend tax credit rules.[141] Where the recipient is a corporation, the dividend may be deductible as an inter-corporate dividend under section 112 of the Act. The dividend may also be subject to the refundable tax under Part IV if the recipient is a private corporation.

2. — Convertible Debt

A convertible debt is debt that is convertible into equity. Convertible debt allows the lender the best of two worlds: the security of debt capital and the growth potential of share capital. The corporation that issues convertible debt also benefits in that it can deduct interest payments on the debt. As a trade-off for the convertibility feature, interest on convertible debt is usually lower than that on conventional debt.

---

[139]Subs. 15(3).

[140]Para. 18(1)(g).

[141]Para. 82(1)(b), s. 121.

(a) — Rollover Into Shares

A holder of convertible debt can roll over the debt into share capital of the issuing corporation without triggering a disposition.[142] Thus, the lender can defer recognition of any accrued capital gain on the conversion of the debt instrument into share capital. This rollover is not elective: it applies automatically if the taxpayer satisfies all of the conditions of the provision.

The rollover is available only if:[143]

- The convertible debt constitutes capital property to the taxpayer;

- The capital property is exchanged for shares in the same corporation; and

- The taxpayer receives no additional consideration for the conversion other than the shares of the corporation.

In these circumstances, the Act deems the taxpayer not to have disposed of the convertible debt and the cost of the debt is rolled over into the cost of the newly acquired shares. Hence, there are no immediate income tax consequences of the conversion.

The rollover is available only in respect of certain types of convertible properties: bonds, debentures, notes, and shares. It does not extend to other debt instruments such as mortgages. The rollover is available only in respect of "capital property" and does not extend to any property, a gain or loss from the disposition of which would constitute a capital gain or loss.

(b) — Indirect Gifts

The rollover is not available where the fair market value of the convertible debt before the exchange exceeds the fair market value of the shares immediately after the exchange *and* it is reasonable to regard the excess of the value of the debt over the value of the shares as a benefit that the taxpayer desires to confer on a related person.[144] Thus, a taxpayer cannot dispose of high valued debt in exchange for lower value shares and have the difference accrue to the benefit of a person related to the taxpayer. In the absence of such a rule, a taxpayer could divest of capital property without triggering a capital gain or loss.

It is not always clear what constitutes a "gift" or benefit in these circumstances. It is not enough that a related taxpayer benefits from the conversion: subsection 51(2) applies only if the taxpayer who converts a debt actually desires to have the benefit conferred on a person

---

[142]Para. 51(1)(c).

[143]Subs. 51(1).

[144]Subs. 51(2).

related to him or her. The test is objective. The taxpayer must have at least some minimum threshold level of intention to benefit a related person.

Subsection 51(2) deems the taxpayer to receive proceeds of disposition for the convertible property equal to the lesser of its fair market value immediately prior to the exchange and the aggregate of its adjusted cost base and the "gift" portion. Thus, the taxpayer defers the capital gain on the conversion, except to the extent that the gain is decreased (or loss increased) as a result of the indirect gift. The Act deems the taxpayer's capital loss from the disposition to be nil.

VII. — Leases

A lease is a contractual arrangement whereby one of the parties (the "lessor") grants to another party ("the lessee") the use, possession and enjoyment of an asset for a period of time in consideration of rental payments. Thus, a lease payment represents rental for the use of property. The terms and conditions of a lease can be tailored to meet the financial needs of the lessor and the lessee. Almost any asset that can be purchased can be leased. The most common forms of leases in business, however, deal with automobiles, furniture, equipment, and real property.

Leasing is "off-balance sheet" financing. The popularity of leasing assets is attributable to the financial advantage of keeping debt off the balance sheet, which allows for a more favourable debt to equity ratio. Also, leasing does not drain the cash flow of an enterprise in the same way as a purchase of assets.

1. — Advantages

The financial advantages of leasing are as follows:

- Since leasing is an "off-balance sheet" form of financing, it does not affect debt/equity ratios, which are often covenants in debt instruments that an enterprise issues.

- Since leases are not reported as liabilities on the balance sheet, they do not reflect adversely on the enterprise's access to the credit markets.

- Small businesses do not usually have easy access to the capital markets in order to purchase substantial amounts of tangible assets. A lease is an alternative to long-term financing to purchase equipment.

- Leasing terms and conditions are flexible and, therefore, can be readily adapted to the particular needs of the business. Lease payments can be linked to the enterprise's profits.

2. — *Disadvantages*

There are also certain disadvantages associated with leases:

- Since the leased asset belongs to the lessor, any appreciation in the value of the asset belongs to the lessor and not to the lessee. This is a significant financial consideration in leases involving real property.

- Leases are fixed term contracts (*albeit* often with options to renew) and during the term of the contract the lessee is committed to the contract. It is not usually easy to exit from the contract without paying a penalty or premium. Thus, unlike the owner of an asset who may be able to dispose of it if circumstances change, a lessee is contractually locked in even when economic circumstances change or become unattractive.

3. — *Tax Treatment*

Leasing brings to the fore the entire form versus substance debate in tax law. This in turn raises difficult issues of whether we should look at legal versus economic substance in determining the character of a "lease". Consider the following situations:

1. X agrees to lease a small office for 55 years. In exchange for the long lease, the landlord gives X a fixed rental price of $10,000 per year. The agreement is clearly a rental for the use of the office for 55 years.

2. Y buys an office for $123,860 (the present value of $10,000 annually over 55 years at 8 per cent) and finances the purchase through a 10-year mortgage at 8 per cent. The agreement is clearly the purchase of real property. Y can claim capital cost allowance on the property and can deduct the mortgage interest for business purposes.

3. Z leases an office for $10,000 per year (as in case 1 above) but also negotiates an option to purchase the property at the end of 55 years for $1. Until that time, the landlord retains full legal title to the property, but Z pays all of the maintenance, taxes, and utilities for the office. The form of the transaction is clearly hybrid. Z does not have title but has all the costs of ownership. The agreement looks like a lease, but, in economic substance, it more closely resembles an outright purchase.

The income tax considerations of leasing depend upon three principal factors:

1. The nature of the agreement;

2. The tax status of the lessee and the lessor; and

3. The type of property leased.

(a) — Nature of Lease

What is a "lease" for tax purposes? The answer to this question is crucial in the context of property acquisitions. The leasing rules apply only to property leases. The capital cost allowance rules apply to purchases of property. Thus, the distinction between a lease and purchase is critical.

In the absence of specific tax rules, the characterization of a contractual arrangement depends upon the law of the jurisdiction that regulates the contract. One determines the nature of an acquisition by reference to the normal incidents of ownership of property: title (actual or constructive), possession, use and risk. In Quebec, the matter is determined by reference to the *Civil Code*.

(b) — Rentals or Instalments

Payments for the use of leased property may represent rental payments or instalments on account of its purchase price. Payments on account of rent are deductible as a current expense in the computation of income.[145] Payments on account of the purchase of depreciable property are capital costs and eligible for capital cost allowance.[146] The distinction between these two types of payments is blurred, however, where the contract provides for a lease with an option to purchase the property. In such cases, one must determine the true nature of the contract: is it, in substance, a lease or an instalment purchase?

There are two different types of lease agreements, operating leases (pure leases with no option to purchase) and financing leases with options to purchase. Financing leases are of two types:

1. A financing arrangement for the purchase of an asset that one will acquire at a later date pursuant to a determinable option price; or

2. A rental agreement for the use of an asset, but which gives the lessee an option to purchase it at a later date.

A lease option agreement that is a pure financing arrangement, is, in effect, a transaction that is a purchase of an asset: the lease is merely the vehicle to finance the purchase. In contrast, a "genuine" lease-option agreement is, in both substance and form, a rental agreement, but one which allows the lessee the privilege of changing his or her mind and purchasing the asset at a later date. There is no bright line test to distinguish between these two types of agreements. Obviously, they both involve the same arrangements, namely, periodic payments with an option to purchase the asset at a later date. The two arrangements, however, have substantially different legal and tax results.

---

[145]S. 9.

[146]Para. 20(1)(a).

The administrative position is that the following factors point toward a sale rather than a lease:[147]

- The lessee *automatically* acquires title to the property after payment of a specified amount in the form of rental payments;

- The lessee *must* buy the property from the lessor during or at the termination of the lease;

- The lessee has the right, during or at the expiration of the lease, to acquire the property at a price which, *at the inception* of the lease, is substantially less than what the probable fair market value of the property will be at the time that the lessee *can* acquire the property; or

- The lessee has the right, during or at the expiration of the lease, to acquire the property at a price, or under terms and conditions which, *at the inception* of the lease, are such that no reasonable person would fail to exercise the option.

The above criteria indicate that the determination of whether a contract is a lease or a purchase of property is almost always a question of fact. One determines the issue by examining the conduct of the parties, the nature of the legal obligation, and, where relevant, past dealings between the parties in similar transactions.

The examination requires more than a superficial enumeration of the relevant criteria. For example, in a "financial lease", it is quite usual for the lessee to assume the responsibility for paying the expenses of the leased property, such as taxes, insurance, maintenance, etc. The obligation to pay these expenses, which are normally associated with the ownership rather than the rental of property, does not, in and by itself, necessarily imply that the transaction is, in substance, a purchase. Such an obligation is only one factor that one evaluates to determine the character of a particular contract. The fact that the lessee assumes the expenses does not necessarily render the contract something other than a true lease.

(i) — Option to Purchase at Fair Market Value

An option agreement that is in substance a purchase agreement is not a genuine "lease". The so-called "lessee" cannot deduct lease payments. Where, however, the lease-option agreement is a genuine lease, the taxpayer can deduct lease payments during the tenure of the lease.

---

[147]IT-233R, "Lease-option Agreements; Sale-leaseback Agreements" (February 11, 1983), para. 3 (IT-233R has been cancelled by Technical News No. 21 (June 14, 2001)).

(ii) — Option to Purchase at Less Than Fair Market Value

A special rule applies to options to purchase property at less than its fair market value. Where a taxpayer purchases an asset at less than its fair market value pursuant to an option, any amounts that had been paid previously to use the property (for example, rent) are considered as amounts previously claimed as capital cost allowance in respect of the property.[148] The effect of this rule is that a subsequent disposition of the property may trigger recapture of capital cost allowance.

More specifically, this rule applies where a taxpayer acquires a depreciable property or real or immovable property in respect of which:

- The taxpayer (or a person with whom the taxpayer was not dealing at arm's length) was entitled to a deduction from income for use (for example, rent) of the property; and

- The capital cost of acquisition is less than the fair market value of the property, determined without reference to the option price.

This rule prevents the taxpayer from receiving the best of both worlds: current deductions of lease payments and capital gains treatment on any gains that the taxpayer realizes when he or she eventually sells the asset. This rule applies only in circumstances in which, *even though the lease-option agreement is a genuine lease*, the option allows the taxpayer to acquire the property at less than its fair market value. The rule does not apply to instalment purchases whereby the purchaser is not, in any event, entitled to a rental deduction.

Subsection 13(5.2) deems a taxpayer who exercises an option to acquire property at less than its fair market value to acquire the property at the *lesser* of:

- Its fair market value at the time that the taxpayer exercises the option; and,

- Its actual cost at that time *plus* all payments that the taxpayer previously paid on account of rent for its use.

If the actual cost of the property to the taxpayer is less than its deemed cost, the Act deems the taxpayer to have previously claimed the difference as capital cost allowance on the property. Thus, the taxpayer may be subject to recapture of capital cost allowance at a later date if he or she sells the property at a profit.

---

[148]Subs. 13(5.2).

Example

Assume:

In 1998, X Ltd. leased some land from T Ltd. at an annual rental of $20,000. The lease allows X Ltd. to purchase the land at the end of five years at an agreed upon price of $80,000, which is a reasonable estimate of its fair market value at that time. In 2003 X Ltd. exercises its option to purchase the land and it is determined at that time that the fair market value of the land is $120,000. X Ltd. sells the land in 2005 for $200,000.

Then:

Upon exercise of the option in 2003

Exercise price of option		$ 80,000 (A)
Lesser of:		
(i) FMV of land		$ 120,000
(ii) Cost of land plus	$ 80,000	
Rental payments	100,000	$ 180,000
Deemed cost of land		120,000 (B)
Depreciation deemed claimed ((B) minus (A))		$ 40,000

Upon sale of the land in 2005

Proceeds of disposition	$ 200,000
ACB + gain taxed under 39(1)(a)	120,000
Capital gain	$ 80,000
Recapture of depreciation	$ 40,000

Subsection 13(5.2) applies to all capital property that is depreciable property or real or immovable property, including land. Thus, in the above example, the Act deems the land to be depreciable property of a separate prescribed class and, therefore, the rental payments (or a portion thereof) on the land are subject to "recapture," and are taxable as income.

To prevent a taxpayer from circumventing this rule by disposing of, instead of exercising, the option to acquire the property, subsection 13(5.3) deems that any difference between the proceeds of disposition of the option itself and its cost, is taxable as "recaptured" income.

4. — Restrictions on After-Tax Financing

We have seen that leasing can be used as an alternative to the more usual methods of financing. The tax advantages of leasing arise because capital cost allowance ("CCA") for leased property often exceeds its actual depreciation, particularly in the early years of a lease. This allows non-taxable lessees to trade off accelerated CCA against reduced rental payments. The Act restricts the use of leases as a form of after-tax financing for tax-exempt entities and taxpayers who are not currently taxable. It does this through the capital cost allowance rules.

(a) — The Lessor's Position

A taxpayer ("the lessor") who leases specified leasing property (other than exempt property) with a fair market value of more than $25,000 to another person for more than one year is restricted in the amount that may be claimed for capital cost allowance on the property.[149] The CCA claimable is limited to the amount that would have been a repayment of principal if the lease had been a loan and the rental payments were considered blended payments that represented principal and interest.[150] Thus, the entire regime depends upon the concept of notional loans and repayments.

The lessor is regarded as having made a loan to the lessee in an amount equal to the fair market value of the leased property, and the rental payments on the lease are considered to be a blend of principal and interest. Generally, the capital cost allowance that may be claimed by the lessor on each property is restricted to the difference between rental income and a notional value for interest.

Regulation 1100(1.1) restricts the capital cost allowance that is deductible by the lessor in respect of such property to the *lesser* of:

- The amount that would be received by the lessor in the year as a return of principal had the lessor made a loan to the lessee at a prescribed rate of interest in an amount equal to the fair market value of the leased property; and

- The amount by which the total capital cost allowance that the lessor could have claimed in respect of the property in the absence of any special leasing rules, over the amount of any capital cost allowance previously claimed by the lessor in respect of the property.

A rate of interest is prescribed for each month.

---

[149]Reg 1100(1.11).

[150]Reg. 1100(1.1).

"Specified leasing property" is depreciable property (other than exempt property) that is used principally to earn leasing revenue from a lease that has a term of more than one year.[151]

"Exempt property" includes automobiles, light trucks and trailers, buildings, home furnishings, appliances, office furniture, office equipment, computers and general-purpose electronic data-processing equipment included in Class 45. The exemption in respect of office furniture, office equipment, and electronic data processing equipment does not apply to individual assets that have a capital cost in excess of $1,000,000.[152]

(b) — The Lessee's Position

Lessees are generally entitled to claim the full amount of lease payments that relate to the use of the property in the year in the normal manner.

A lessee may, however, jointly elect with the lessor to have the lease considered as money borrowed to purchase the asset leased.[153] The lessee is entitled to claim capital cost allowance and deduct the interest portion of the deemed blended payments of principal and interest. Thus, *both* the lessee and the lessor may be able to claim capital cost allowance in certain circumstances.

Where the lessor and lessee *jointly* elect in prescribed form and agree upon the fair market value of the leased property, the lessee is considered to have borrowed an amount equal to the fair market value of the property and to have acquired the property. In these circumstances, rental payments under the lease are not considered to be rent, but are treated as blended payments of principal and interest on the loan.

To the extent that the property is used to earn income, the lessee is able to claim capital cost allowance in respect of the property, and to deduct the interest portion of each rental payment. This rule applies only in computing the income of a lessee who leases property (other than prescribed property) for a term of more than one year from an arm's-length person who is resident in Canada, or who carries on business in Canada through a permanent establishment.

---

[151]Reg. 1100(1.11).

[152]Reg. 1100(1.13).

[153]Subs. 16.1(1).

Example

Assume:

A taxpayer leases an asset with a fair market value of $10,000 in an arm's length transaction. The lease is for a period of five years at an annual rental of $1,314. The capital cost allowance rate applicable in respect of the property is 25 per cent (diminishing balance basis) subject to the half-year rule. Both the lessor and the lessee jointly elect to treat the lease as a loan and purchase for the term of the lease. The prescribed rate in effect at the time of the lease is 10 per cent.

Then:

The lessee may deduct interest expense and capital cost allowance as follows:

Year	Lease Payments	Principal	Interest	CCA	UCC
					$ 10,000
1	$ 1,314	$ 314	$ 1,000	$ 1,250	8,750
2	1,314	345	969	2,188	6,562
3	1,314	380	934	1,641	4,921
4	1,314	418	896	1,230	3,691
5	1,314	460	854	923	2,768
TOTAL	$ 6,570	$ 1,917	$ 4,653	$ 7,232	

At the end of the five-year lease period, the lessee is deemed to have disposed of the property for the remaining principal amount of the deemed loan, that is, $8,083. Assuming that the property was the only property in that class of assets, the lessee is subject to recapture of capital cost allowance of $5,315:

Principal amount of loan	$10,000
Loan (principal) payments	(1,917)
Principal balance outstanding	8,083
Undepreciated capital cost (UCC)	(2,768)
Recapture of CCA	$ 5,315

Thus, the total deductions allowed to the lessee with respect to the property over the term of the lease is $6,570, that is, interest expense of $4,653 and capital cost allowance of $7,232 less the recapture of capital cost allowance of $5,315.

(c) — Anti-Avoidance Rule

Leases that one enters into for less than one year, but which are then extended, are subject to an anti-avoidance rule. The Act deems property that is the subject of a lease to be a lease longer than one year if it is reasonable to conclude that the lessor knew, or ought to have known, that the lessee would lease the property for more than one year. The burden is on the lessor to establish that he or she could not have known that the lessee would extend the term of the lease beyond one year.[154]

Where a taxpayer acquires a lease that has a remaining term of more than one year, with certain exceptions, the taxpayer is treated as having entered into a new lease of the property at that time for a term of more than one year.[155] There is an exception for acquisitions from a non-arm's length person or in the course of certain rollover transactions, for example, an amalgamation of corporations.[156] Apart from these exceptions, however, the acquiring taxpayer steps into the shoes of the vendor in respect of the property covered by the lease.

---

[154]Reg. 1100(1.13)(b).

[155]Reg. 1100(1.15).

[156]Reg. 1100(1.16).

Selected Bibliography to Chapter 18

General

Andison, Douglas, "Categories of Corporations", in *Proceedings of 24th Tax Conf.* 73 (Can. Tax Foundation, 1972).

Ashton, R.K., "Does the Tax System Favour Incorporation?" (1987) Br. Tax Rev. 256.

Bonham, D.H., "Corporations", (1986) Special Lectures LSUC 259.

Darling, C. Brian, "Revenue Canada Perspectives" in *Corp. Management Tax Conf.* (Can. Tax Foundation, 1992).

Edgar, Tim, "The Classification of Corporate Securities for Income Tax Purposes" (1990) 38 Can. Tax J. 1141.

Ewens, Douglas S., "Proposed Amendments Affecting Debt and Equity Reorganizations" (1993) 6 Can. Petro. Tax J. 49.

Novek, Barbara L., "Deductibility of Financing Expenses" in *Corp. Management Tax Conf.* (Canada Tax Foundation, 1992).

Richardson, Stephen R., "New Financial Instruments: A Canadian Tax Perspective" in *Corp. Management Tax Conf.* (Can. Tax Foundation, 1992).

Ruby, Stephen S., "Recent Financing Techniques", in *Proceedings of 41st Tax Conf.* 27:1 (Can. Tax Foundation, 1989).

Shafer, Joel, "Income Tax Aspects of Real Estate Financing", in *Corp. Management Tax Conf.* 1:1 (Can. Tax Foundation, 1989).

Spindler, Robert J., "New Investment Products", in *Proceedings of 44th Tax Conference* 19:1 (Can. Tax Foundation, 1992).

Sullivan, Daniel F., and James P. O'Sullivan, "Recent Developments in Corporate Financing" in *Corp. Management Tax Conf.* (Can. Tax Foundation, 1992).

Teltscher, Lawrence, "Small Business Financing" in *Corp. Management Tax Conference* (Can. Tax Foundation, 1992).

General Characteristics of Debt and Share Capital

Andison, Douglas, "Categories of Corporations", in *Proceedings of 24th Tax Conf.* 73 (Can. Tax Foundation, 1972).

Ashton, R.K., "Does the Tax System Favour Incorporation?" (1987) Br. Tax Rev. 256.

Barry, David B., "The Relative Importance of Personal and Corporation Income Tax" (1986) 34 Can. Tax J. 460.

Bonham, D.H., "Corporations" (1986) Special Lectures LSUC 259.

Dart, Robert J., "An Analysis of the Tax Position of Public, Private and Canadian-Controlled Private Corporations" (1972) 20 Can. Tax J. 523.

Dart, Robert J., "Specific Uses of Companies in Tax Planning", in *Proceedings of 31st Tax Conf.* 117 (Can. Tax Foundation, 1979).

Hariton, David P., "The Taxation of Complex Financial Instruments" (1988) 43 Tax Lawyer 731.

Corporate Law Aspects of Equity Financing

Baillie, William J., "To Incorporate or Not to Incorporate — From an Income Tax Perspective" (1983) 41 Advocate 615.

Barry, David B., "The Relative Importance of Personal and Corporation Income Tax" (1986) 34 Can. Tax J. 460.

Bonham, D.H., "Corporations", (1986) Special Lectures LSUC 259.

Brean, Donald J.S., "The Redemption of Convertible Preferred Shares: The Implications of Terms and Conditions" (1985) 33 Can. Tax J. 957.

Broadway, Robin W., "Reforming the Corporate Tax System", in *Proceedings of 37th Tax Conf.* 5 (Can. Tax Foundation, 1985).

Brown, Robert D., "Corporate Tax Reform: Necessary but not Sufficient", in *Proceedings of 37th Tax Conf.* 5 (Can. Tax Foundation, 1985).

Chanin, Faralee, "Paid-up Capital Pitfalls" (1990) 3 Can. Petroleum Tax J. 117.

Colley, Geoffrey M., "Are Corporate Tax Changes Imminent?" (1986) 119 CA Magazine 60.

Daly, M.J. and P. Mercier, "The Impact of Tax Reform on the Taxation of Income from Investment in the Corporate Sector" (1988) 36 Can. Tax J. 345.

Dart, Robert J., "An Analysis of the Tax Position of Public, Private and Canadian-Controlled Private Corporations" (1972) 20 Can. Tax J. 523.

Dart, Robert J., "Specific Uses of Companies in Tax Planning", in *Proceedings of 31st Tax Conf.* 117 (Can. Tax Foundation, 1979).

Durnford, John W., "Tax Essay — The Corporate Veil in the Tax Law" (1979) 27 Can. Tax J. 282.

"Equity Investment As An Alternative to Stock Incentive Arrangement" (1990) 2 Tax Profile 256.

Hariton, David P., "The Taxation of Complex Financial Instruments" (1988) 43 Tax Lawyer 731.

Hiseler, Gregory R., "Judicial Decisions Relating to the Taxation of Corporations and Their Shareholders", in *Proceedings of 35th Tax Conf.* 429 (Can. Tax Foundation, 1983).

Impact of Income and Other Taxes (The), Audio Archives of Canada, 1984.

Jones, David Phillip, "Corporations, Double Taxation and the Theory of Integration" (1979) 27 Can. Tax J. 405.

Krishna, Vern, "Common Law Piercing of the Corporate Veil to Reach Individual Shareholders" (1985) 1 Can. Current Tax J-10l.

Krishna, Vern, "Corporate Share Capital Structures and Income Splitting", (1991) Can. Current Tax C71.

Krishna, Vern, "Income Splitting Corporate Structures", (1994) Can. Current Tax C45.

Krishna, Vern and Anthony VanDuzer, "Corporate Share Capital Structures and Income Splitting: McClurg v. Canada" (1993) 21 Can. Business Law J. 335.

Marble, Del, and Mark Walsh, "The Emphasis is Misplaced (Exposure Draft on Corporate Income Taxes)" (1989) 122:1 CA Magazine 253.

McIvor, R. Craig, "Canadian Cooperatives and Credit Unions: The Tax Scene Revisited" (1972) 20 Can. Tax J. 32.

McKie, A.B., "Corporations and Shareholders: Tax Reform or Reforming" (1986) 93 Can. Banker 46.

McLure, Charles E., "Rationalizing the Corporate Income Tax: The Recent U.S. Proposals", in *Proceedings of 37th Tax Conf.* 6 (Can. Tax Foundation, 1985).

Morin, Robert et Marc Papillon, *Impôt sur le revenu des particuliers et des corporations* (éditions Merlin, 1985).

Reid, Robert J., *Tax Aspects of Incorporations* (Toronto: Butterworths, 1983).

Richards, Gabrielle M.R., "When are Shares Issued?", (1994) Can. Current Tax J43.

Rixon, F.G., "Lifting the Veil Between Holding and Subsidiary Companies" (1986) 102 L.Q.R. 415.

Roberts, David G., "Some Issues in the Determination of Paid-up Capital" (1992) 40 Can. Tax J. 338.

Schwartz, Alan M., "Income Tax Aspects of Shareholders' Agreements", (1986) Special Lectures LSUC 327.

Thomas, R.B., "Associated Corporations; Principal Residence", in *Proceedings of 35th Tax Conf.* 689 (Can. Tax Foundation, 1983).

Tremblay, Richard, "Contributions to Capital: Cost Basis", (1987–89) Can. Current Tax P1.

Weyman, C. David, "Restructuring the Corporate Income Tax", in *Proceedings of 37th Tax Conf.* (Can. Tax Foundation, 1985).

Wilson, James R., and Stuart F. Bollefer, *Taxation of Corporations and their Shareholders* (Toronto: Carswell, 1986).

Tax Aspects of Equity Financing

Brean, Donald J.S., "The Redemption of Convertible Preferred Shares: The Implications of Terms and Conditions" (1985) 33 Can. Tax J. 957.

Brussa, John A., "Flow-through Share Financing for Oil and Gas Companies: An Update" (1993) 6 Can. Petro. Tax J. 1.

Colley, Geoffrey M., "Tax Affairs Aren't Just an April Filing" (1989) 122 CA Magazine 46.

Couzin, Robert, and Robert J. Dart, "The New Preferred Share Rules", in *Proceedings of 39th Tax Conf.* 18:1 (Can. Tax Foundation, 1987).

Dixon, G.D., and B.J. Arnold, "Rubbing Salt into the Wound: The Denial of the Interest Deduction after the Loss of a Source of Income" (1991) 39 Can. Tax J. 1473.

Dunn, A.W., "The Draft Associated Corporation Rules: New Ways to Skin a Cat" (1988) 2 Can. Current Tax P17.

"Equity Investment As An Alternative to Stock Incentive Arrangement" (1990) 2 Tax Profile 256.

Ewens, Douglas S., "Forced Share Conversions" (1992) 40 Can. Tax J. 1407.

Fiscal Figures — Selected Statistics on the Evolution of the Corporate Income Tax System Since 1965" (1987) 35 Can. Tax J. 502.

Fitchett, Gary A., "Creative Structuring of Equity" (1990) 64 CMA Magazine 22.

Fooladi, Iraj, Patricia A. McGraw, and Gordon S. Roberts, "Preferred Share Rules Freeze Out the Individual Investors" (1988) 121 CA Magazine 38.

Hariton, David P., "The Taxation of Complex Financial Instruments" (1988) 43 Tax Lawyer 731.

Jans, Gord, "Stripping 'Safe Income'" (1991) 65 CMA Magazine 9.

Gradey, Patrick, "The Recent Corporate Income Tax Reform Proposals in Canada and the United States" (1986) 34 Can. Tax J. 111.

Kennedy, Henry A., *Introduction to Business Taxation* (Edmonton: Univ. of Alberta, Dept. of Accounting, 1984).

Malach, David, and Barbara Worndl, "Waltzing Though the Preferred Share Maze" (1988) 121 CA Magazine 47.

Raich, Robert, "Flow-Through Financing — Present and Future", in *Proceedings of 41st Tax Conf.* 43:1 (Can. Tax Foundation, 1989).

Roberts, David G., "Some Issues in the Determination of Paid-up Capital" (1992) 40 Can. Tax J.i 338.

Ruby, Stephen S., "Recent Financing Techniques", in *Proceedings of 41st Tax Conf.* 27:1 (Can. Tax Foundation, 1989).

Sinclair, B.R., "Paid-up Capital" (1986) 34 Can. Tax J. 1483.

Tax Aspects of Debt Financing

Arnold, Brian J., "Canada's Draft Legislation on Deductibility of Interest Expense Detailed" (1992) 4:11 Tax Notes Int. 513.

Arnold, Brian J., "Is Interest a Capital Expense?" (1992) 40 Can. Tax J. 533.

Arnold, Brian J. and Tim Edgar, "The Draft Legislation on Interest Deductibility: A Technical and Policy Analysis" (1992) 40 Can. Tax J. 267.

Bankman, Joseph, and William A. Klein, "Accurate Taxation of Long-Term Debt: Taking Into Account the Term Structure of Interest" (1989) 44 Tax Lawyer 335.

CBA and CICA, Joint Committee on Taxation, "Submission to the Minister of Finance on the Issue of Deductibility of Interest", in Can. Tax Reports, Special Report No. 964 (Toronto: CCH Canadian, August, 1990).

Crowe, Ian, "I'm Tired of Yoghurt" (1991) 124 CA Magazine 29.

Drache, A.B.C., "Draft Interest Expense Legislation" (1992) 14 Can. Taxpayer 11.

Drache, A.B.C., "Interest Deductibility: Planning Still Worthwhile" (1991) 13 Can. Taxpayer 102.

Dunn, A.W., "The Draft Associated Corporation Rules: New Ways to Skin a Cat" (1988) 2 Can. Current Tax P17.

Edgar, Tim, and Brian J. Arnold, "Reflections on the Submission of the CBA-CICA Joint Committee on Taxation Concerning the Deductibility of Interest" (1990) 38 Can. Tax J. 847.

Edgar, Tim, "The Thin Capitalization Rules: Role and Reform" (1992) 40 Can. Tax J. 1.

Ewens, Douglas S., "The Thin Capitalization Restrictions" (1994) 42 Can. Tax J. 954.

Farden, Eric N., *Income Tax for a Small Business* (E.N. Farden, 1985).

Felesky, Brian A. and Sandra E. Jack, "Is there Substance to 'Substance over Form' in Canada?", [1992] Can. Tax Foundation 50:1

"Fiscal Figures — Selected Statistics on the Evolution of the Corporate Income Tax System Since 1965" (1987) 35 Can. Tax J. 502.

Flatters, Michael J., "Assumption of Debt Obligations" (1992) 40 Can. Tax J. 509.

Fox-Revett, Melissa G., "Interest Deductibility", (1993) Can. Current Tax P19.

Gradey, Patrick, "The Recent Corporate Income Tax Reform Proposals in Canada and the United States" (1986) 34 Can. Tax J. 111.

Hariton, David P., "The Taxation of Complex Financial Instruments" (1988) 43 Tax Lawyer 731.

Hickey, Paul B., "The Proposed New Interest Deductibility Regime: Strategies and Pitfalls", [1992] Can. Tax Foundation 23:1.

Hugget, Donald R., "It Certainly Does Make A Difference!" (1990) 17 Can. Tax News 69.

Kennedy, Henry A., *Introduction to Business Taxation* (Edmonton: University of Alberta, Dept. of Accounting, 1984).

Krishna, Vern, "Interest Deductibility: More Form Over Substance", (1993) Can. Current Tax C17.

Loveland, Norman C., "Income Tax Aspects of Borrowing and Lending", (1986) Special Lectures of the LSUC 289.

McDonnell, T.E., "Without a Trace" (1993) 41 Can. Tax J. 134.

McKie, A.B., "Interest: A Taxing Problem" (1987) 35 Can. Banker 20.

McNair, D. Keith, "Restricted Interest Expense" (1987) 35 Can. Tax J. 616.

Richardson, Stephen R., "Current Developments in Debt Financing: A Canadian Perspective", in *Proceedings of 40th Tax Conf.* 22:1 (Can. Tax Foundation, 1988).

Ruby, Stephen S., "Recent Financing Techniques", in *Proceedings of 41st Tax Conf.* 27:1 (Can. Tax Foundation, 1989).

Small Business Taxation (Audio Archives of Canada, 1984).

Ulmer, John M., "Index-linked Debt and Other Derivatives: Canadian Income Tax Implications" (1992) 11 National Banking Law Rev. 65.

Wraggett, Cathy, "Minimizing Your Personal Tax Burden" (1990) 64 CMA Magazine 21.

Hybrid Debt

Burgoyne, Terrence R. and David J. Tetrault, "Distress Preferred Shares: Re-structuring with After-tax Financing (Part 1)" (1992) 9 Nat. Insolvency Rev. 91.

Burgoyne, Terrence R. and David J. Tetrault, "Distress Preferred Shares: Re-structuring with After-tax Financing (Part 2)" (1993) 10 Nat. Insolvency Rev. 1.

Dunn, A.W., "The Draft Associated Corporation Rules: New Ways to Skin a Cat" (1988) 2 Can. Current Tax P17.

Edgar, Tim, "Distress Preferred Shares and Small Business Development Bonds: A Tax Expenditure Analysis" (1994) 42 Can. Tax J. 659.

Ewens, Douglas S., "Amending Grandfathered Preferred Share Conditions" (1994) 42 Can. Tax J. 548.

Ewens, Douglas S., "Convertible Property: Section 51 — Part 1" (1994) 42 Can. Tax J. 1413.

Ewens, Douglas S., "Forced Share Conversions" (1992) 40 Can. Tax J. 1407.

Ewens, Douglas S., "The New Preferred Share Dividend Tax Regime" in *Report of Proceedings of 40th Tax Conference* (Can. Tax Foundation, 1988).

"Fiscal Figures — Selected Statistics on the Evolution of the Corporate Income Tax System Since 1965" (1987) 35 Can. Tax J. 502.

Gradey, Patrick, "The Recent Corporate Income Tax Reform Proposals in Canada and the United States" (1986) 34 Can. Tax J. 111.

Hariton, David P., "The Taxation of Complex Financial Instruments" (1988) 43 Tax Lawyer 731.

Kennedy, Henry A., *Introduction to Business Taxation* (Edmonton: University of Alberta, Dept. of Accounting, 1984).

Loveland, Norman C., "Securities Lending and Repurchase Agreements: Canadian Tax Issues" (1989) 4 Securities and Corp. Regulation Rev. 205.

Meredith, P. Mark, "Securities Lending: Evolving Tax Problems and Issues" (1992) 11 National Banking Law Rev. 18.

Robinson, Chris and Alan White, "Guaranteed Preferred Shares: Debt or Equity" (1986/87) 1 Banking & Finance Law Rev. 211.

Ross, David W., "Equity Preferred Shares" (1992) 40 Can. Tax J.

Sugg, Donald M., "Preferred Share Review: Anomalies and Traps for the Unwary", [1992] Can. Tax Foundation 22:1.

Leases

Athanassakos, George and Margaret Klatt, "Lease or Buy?: How Recent Tax Changes have Affected the Decision" (1993) 41 Can. Tax J. 444.

Atlas, Michael I., "Income Tax Issues in Real Estate Leasing", Corp. Mgmt. Tax Conf. 3:1 (Can. Tax Foundation, 1989).

Bowman, Stephen W., "Equipment Leasing Revisited" (1994) 42 Can. Tax J. 206.

Bowman, Steve, "Lease or Buy? Tax Considerations" (1990) 64 CMA Magazine 22.

Bowman, Steve, "Leasing Rules — Tax Simplification?" (1989) 63 CMA Magazine 18.

Birnie, David A.G., "Shareholders' Buy-sell Agreements: Some New Opportunities", in *Proceedings of 38th Tax Conf.* 13 (Can. Tax Foundation, 1986).

Gillespie, Thomas S., "Lease Financing" in *Corp. Management Tax Conf.* (Canada Tax Foundation, 1992).

Haney, M.A., "Leasing Property — Use in the Year" (1987) 35 Can. Tax J. 970.

Hugget, Donald R., "Leasing Property Rules" (1990) 17 Can. Tax News 70.

McDonnell, Thomas E., "Questions About Leasing" (1993) 41 Can. Tax J. 509.

McKie, A.B., "Corporations and Shareholders: Tax Reform or Reforming" (1986) 93 Can. Banker 46.

Ross, David W., "Corporate Taxation and Tax Avoidance", in *Proceedings of 31st Tax Conf.* 400 (Can. Tax Foundation, 1979).

Templeton, Michael D., "Not a Lease But Not a Sale" (1991) 39 Can Tax J. 288.

Ward, David A., and John M. Ulmer, "Corporate Taxation: 1986 Federal Budget" (1986) 5 Legal Alert 81.

Weyman, C. David, "Restructuring the Corporate Income Tax", in *Proceedings of 37th Tax Conf.* (Can. Tax Foundation, 1985).

Wilson, Michael H., *The Corporate Income Tax System: A Direction for Change*, Dept. of Finance Canada, 1985.

Zinn, John A., "Advancements in Off-balance Sheet Financing (Part 1)" (1994) 13 Nat. Banking L. Review 24.

CHAPTER 19 — CORPORATE INVESTMENT INCOME

I. — General Comment

The taxation of income that a private corporation earns depends upon the source of its income. In general terms, we classify corporate income into two broad categories: "investment" and "business". In this chapter we examine the taxation of investment income. In Chapter 20, "Corporate Business Income", we will look at the taxation of business income.

II. — Tax Objectives

The rules in respect of the taxation of corporate investment income serve two objectives: (1) to "integrate" the amount of tax that a corporation pays on its investment income with the tax that its individual shareholders pay; and (2) to discourage individuals from deferring tax by placing their investments in private holding companies.

"Integration" means that an individual should pay the same amount of tax on investment income, regardless of whether the individual earns the income personally or indirectly through a corporation. We achieve integration by synchronizing the corporate tax rate with the effective rate of tax that an individual pays on investment income through a corporation.

We implement the second objective by initially taxing corporate investment income at a high rate to prevent tax deferral. Thus, we tax investment income (other than taxable dividends) that a Canadian-controlled private corporation earns at the full corporate rate. A portion of this tax is refunded to the corporation when it pays taxable dividends to shareholders. The initial tax has the effect of blunting any tax deferral advantage. The tax refund to the corporation when it pays out dividends reduces the net effective rate of tax to a level that approximately equals to the rate that would be paid on such income if an individual earned it directly.

III. — Types Of Investment Income

There Are three basic categories of investment income:

- Dividends;

- Rent, interest, royalties, etc.; and

- Capital gains.

The following chart sets out some of the more common forms of property in each of these categories:

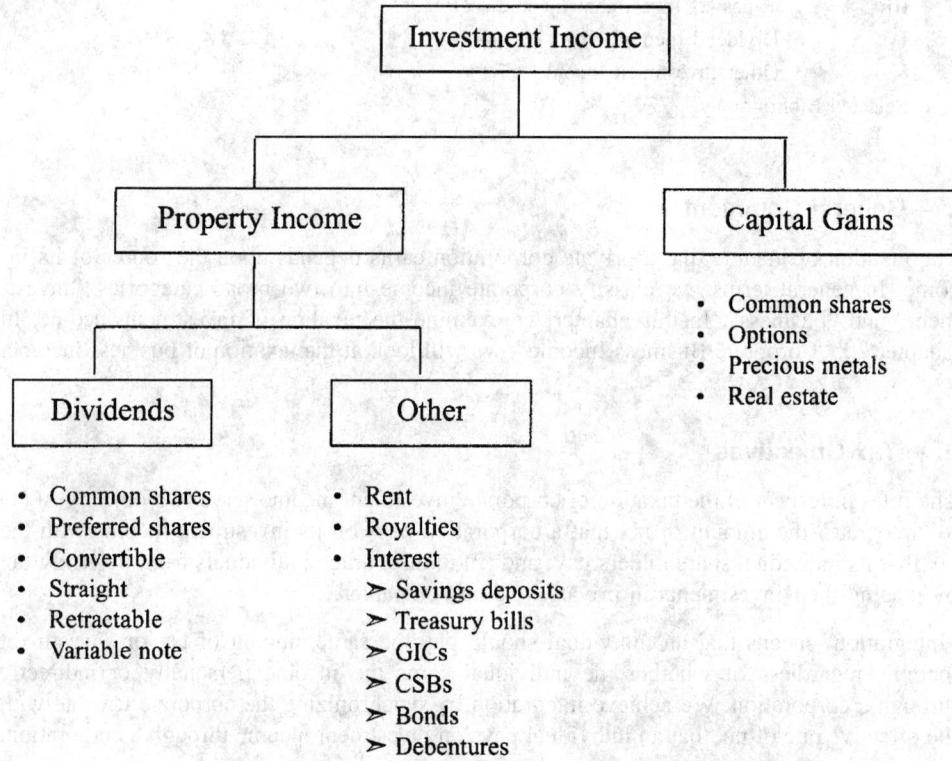

The regime of full taxation followed by a tax refund applies to all three forms of investment income. But since each of the three different forms of investment income is subject to different rules, the mathematical adjustments to integrate each type of investment income are slightly different.

In this chapter we look at models for taxing each of the three types of investment income. Each model is premised on assumptions, which may or may not apply in each case in every province. The important point, however, is to understand the flow-through of corporate income to shareholder and the potential of double taxation of corporate income.

IV. — Dividend Income

All corporate income is potentially subject to double taxation. The Canadian tax system provides some relief by partially imputing corporate taxes to shareholders. But the relief is neither complete nor perfect. The tax rules in respect of inter-corporate dividends between private corporations do, however, substantially eliminate double taxation while preventing tax deferral.

Generally, the tax relief operates as follows. A corporation includes in its income all taxable dividends that it receives from other corporations.[1] In computing its taxable income, however, a corporation may deduct taxable dividends that it has received from:[2]

- A "taxable Canadian corporation"; or

- A resident corporation that it controls.

The effect of this two-step structure is that dividends between Canadian corporations flow through free of Part I tax and are not subject to double taxation.

The basic structure for the taxation of inter-corporate dividends prevents multiple taxation of income passing through several different corporations. Including taxable dividends in income and then deducting these dividends in the computation of taxable income effectively exempts inter-corporate dividends from Part I tax. (It should be noted, however, that increasingly in recent years the Act curtails the mechanism for the tax-free flow-through of inter-corporate dividends. There are now numerous exceptions to the general rule.[3])

Without more control, however, taxpayers could defer taxes because the above structure would permit tax deferral where the corporate tax rate is lower than personal tax rates at the top end of the scale. Individuals in higher tax brackets could leave their dividend income in a holding company and defer personal taxes until the company paid out its income. Thus, a special tax under Part IV of the Act on the dividend income of private corporations prevents tax deferral by high-income individuals. However, the Part IV tax on dividend income is fully refundable to the corporation when it pays taxable dividends to shareholders so that there is no double taxation.[4]

---

[1]Paras. 12(1)(j),(k).

[2]Subs. 112(1); dividends from non-resident investment corporations may *not* be deducted.

[3]See, for example, Chapter 18, "Corporate Finance", for a discussion on "Taxable Preferred Shares".

[4]Subs. 129(1).

1. — Theoretical Model

The underlying scheme of the Part IV tax is to:

1. Prevent tax deferral through the use of holding companies; and

2. "Integrate" the personal and corporate tax on investment income.

We achieve these objectives through a three-part mechanism: (1) a Part IV tax on portfolio dividend income; (2) a dividend refund to the corporation; and (3) a dividend gross-up and tax imputation credit for individuals.

Since inter-corporate dividends flow tax-free, an individual could defer personal taxes by placing the investments in a holding company. The Part IV corporate tax, which is fully refundable, prevents tax deferral.

An individual who receives a dividend from a taxable Canadian corporation is taxable on 125 per cent of the cash value of the dividend. In theory, the 25 per cent "gross-up" accounts for corporate taxes previously paid by the corporation. The individual may claim a federal tax credit equal to 2/3 of the "gross-up" of 25 per cent included in income.[5] The grossing-up of the dividend in income followed by a dividend tax credit "integrates" the total tax paid by the individual with the tax paid by the corporation. The dividend tax credit imputes taxes paid by the corporation to its shareholders. Thus, in theory and under certain assumptions, the combined effect of the Part IV tax and the dividend tax credit should prevent tax deferral and integrate corporate and shareholder taxes. The following example illustrates the theory of integration of corporate and personal taxes on dividend income in a private corporation. Note, the model rests upon at least four assumptions: the corporate tax rate, the dividend gross-up rate, federal-provincial tax rates, and the Part IV refund rate.

Example	
Portfolio Dividends: Theoretical Model	
Assume that Harry Smith owns all the shares of Smith Ltd., which receives a dividend of $10,000 from the Royal Bank of Canada. The corporation flows through the $10,000 as a dividend to Harry Smith. Assume a combined (federal and provincial) tax rate of 40 per cent for both personal and corporate tax.	
Corporate Tax:	
Net income from portfolio dividends	$ 10,000
Less: Inter-corporate dividends (subs. 112(1))	(10,000)

Example	
Taxable income	nil
Part I tax	nil
Part IV tax on dividends @ 33.3%	3,333
Net income after tax	6,667
Refund of Part IV tax on payment of dividend	3,333
Amount available for dividend	$ 10,000
Shareholder Tax:	
Dividend income	$10,000
Gross-up of dividend by 25% (para. 82(1)(b))	2,500
Taxable amount	$ 12,500
Federal/provincial tax @ 40% (Assumed)	$ 5,000
Federal/provincial Dividend tax credit (Assumed)*	2,500
Net tax payable	$ 2,500
Income retained	$ 7,500
Effective Tax Rate on Dividend	25%

Notes:

*   Assuming the federal credit is 2/3 of the gross-up and the provincial credit is 1/3 of the gross-up.

In the model, the Part IV tax washes out when the corporation pays dividends. The net effect of the refundable tax is that an individual who owns portfolio investments through a holding company is in the same position as a person who holds portfolio investments directly. In the above example, Harry Smith, with a combined federal/provincial tax rate of 40 per cent, would end up paying $2,500 tax on a dividend of $10,000, regardless of whether he receives the dividend directly or through a holding corporation. Thus, in theory at least, the tax on portfolio dividends that a private corporation earns integrates with the personal tax system.

2. — Actual Rates

The theoretical model may or may not apply as we move away from the underlying assumptions. For example, the rates of corporate and personal taxes shift from time to time. Also, the provinces can vary their effective rates and move off the model. The example below compares a "pure" integration model with actual rates in Ontario (2004).

Example

Portfolio Dividends: Theory vs. Actual

	Integration Model	Actual Taxes (Ontario-2004)
Corporate Tax:		
Portfolio dividends	$10,000	$ 10,000
Part IV tax payable	3,333	3,333
Net income after tax	$ 6,667	$ 6,667
Refund of tax on payment of dividend	3,333	3,333
Amount available for dividend	$10,000	$ 10,000
Shareholder Tax:		
Dividend income	$10,000	$ 10,000
Gross-up of dividend	2,500	2,500
Taxable amount	$12,500	$ 12,500
Federal/provincial tax @ 40%	$ 5,000	
Dividend tax credit	2,500	
Tax thereon at top marginal rates (31.33% in Ontario)		$ 3,133
Net tax payable	$ 2,500	$ 3,133
Income retained	$ 7,500	$ 6,867
Effective Tax Rate on Dividend	*25%*	*31%*

As federal and provincial taxes fluctuate, the effective tax rate on dividends varies from the theoretical norm. In the above example, the effective rate of tax on dividends in Ontario (2004) is 31 per cent, which closely approximates the amount of the Part IV tax.

3. — Part IV Tax

(a) — Rationale

The Part IV tax is an anti-deferral mechanism. It attempts to place an individual who holds portfolio investments through a holding company in the same position as a person who holds portfolio investments directly. Thus, in theory, the income tax effects of owning portfolio investments are neutral regardless of the vehicle selected to hold the investments.

(b) — Application

The Part IV tax, which is a fully refundable tax, applies to only two types of corporations:[6]

1. Private corporations; and

2. "Subject corporations".

A "subject corporation" is a corporation (*other than* a private corporation) that resides in Canada and is controlled directly or indirectly in any manner by, or for the benefit of, an individual or a related group of individuals.[7] An individual or a related group of individuals is considered to be in control of a corporation if its shares are indirectly controlled by another corporation, partnership, or trust.[8]

(c) — Taxable Dividends

A private corporation is subject to Part IV tax on taxable dividends that it receives from:

- *Non-connected*[9] Canadian corporations resident in Canada, if the dividends are deductible in computing the recipient's taxable income;[10]

- Foreign affiliates;[11] and

---

[6]Para. 186(1)(b).

[7]Subs. 186(3)"subject corporation".

[8]See s. 104, subs. 186(6), para. 251(5)(a) and subs. 256(6.1).

[9]Subs. 186(4).

[10]Subpara. 186(1)(a).

[11]Subss. 186(1) and 186(3)"assessable dividend".

- Connected private corporations in proportion to the dividend refund obtained by the payer corporation.[12]

For the purpose of determining its liability for Part IV tax, a corporation may deduct its non-capital losses and farm losses for the current year[13] and its non-capital and farm loss carry-over.[14] A corporation has the option of deducting its loss carryovers to reduce its Part IV tax or in calculating its taxable income.

(d) — Connected Corporations

The critical factor in determining the liability of a corporation for Part IV tax is its relationship with the corporation from which it receives a dividend (the "payer" corporation). If the payer and recipient corporations are *not* connected with each other, the recipient corporation is liable to Part IV tax on its taxable dividends from the payer. If the corporations are connected, the recipient corporation is liable for Part IV tax, *but only if* the payer corporation gets a dividend refund as a consequence of paying the dividend.

A payer and a recipient corporation are "connected" with each other if:[15]

- The recipient corporation controls the payer; or

- The recipient corporation owns more than 10 per cent of the issued fully-voting shares of the payer and the fair market value of *all* the shares owned by the recipient exceeds 10 per cent of the fair market value of *all* issued shares of the payer.

Thus, a private corporation that receives a taxable dividend is not subject to Part IV tax if it owns more than 10 per cent of the votes and value of the payer corporation, *unless* the payer obtains a dividend refund in respect of the dividend.

---

[12]Para. 186(1)(b). This provision ensures that, until such time as dividends are paid out to individuals or non-connected corporations, the payer corporation's tax refund is matched with the payee corporation's liability to Part IV tax.

[13]Para. 186(1)(c).

[14]Para. 186(1)(d).

[15]Subs. 186(4).

Example

Assume:

R Ltd., a private corporation, owns 60 per cent of the issued and outstanding shares of *P Ltd. P Ltd.* pays a dividend of $150,000 and receives a dividend refund of $30,000.

Total dividend paid by *P Ltd.*	$ 150,000
Dividend received by *R Ltd.*	
(60% of $150,000)	$ 90,000

Then *R Ltd.* is liable for $18,000 Part IV tax calculated as follows:

$$\frac{\text{Taxable dividend}}{\text{Total taxable dividend}} \times \text{(Dividend refund)}$$

$$= \frac{\$ 90,000}{150,000} \times (\$30,000)$$

$$= \$ 18,000$$

The RDTOH on which the dividend refund is based is $30,000.

For the purpose of determining whether one corporation controls another corporation, "control" means the ownership of more than 50 per cent of the issued fully-voting shares of the corporation.[16] Note that, for the purposes of the Part IV tax, one corporation can control another with a direct holding of less than 50 per cent in that corporation. This can occur where one corporation that controls another corporation has an interest in a third corporation. For example:

---

[16]Subs. 186(2). This definition of control does not apply for the purpose of determining whether a corporation is a "subject corporation".

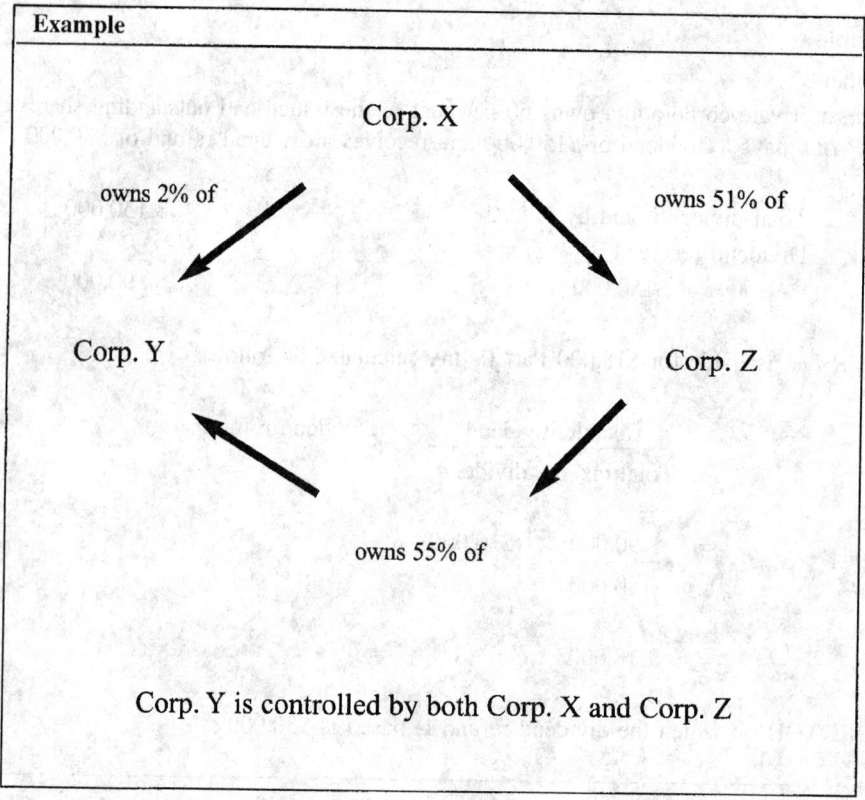

In the above example, Corp. X and Corp. Z are not at arm's length with each other. Since Corp. Z owns more than 50 per cent of Corp. Y, for the purposes of the Part IV tax, Corp. X "controls" Corp. Y.

(e) — Excluded Dividends

We saw earlier that inter-corporate dividends generally flow tax-free between corporations. There are certain dividends, however, that do not flow on a tax-free basis between corporations. For example, subsections 112(2.2) and (2.4) deny the inter-corporate dividend deduction on certain "guaranteed" shares and "collateralized preferred shares" that have security guarantees to protect any loss on the shares. In these circumstances, since the corporation is fully taxable under Part I on the dividends, Part IV does not apply. Paragraph 186(1)(a) also excludes from Part IV tax any taxable dividends received from a *connected* corporation.

The following example illustrates the theoretical operation of the Part IV tax.

Example (Theoretical model)

Assume:

A private corporation receives $1,000 interest income. The corporation pays Part I tax at a rate of 40 per cent and pays a dividend to its sole shareholder, an individual with a marginal tax rate of 40 per cent. The dividend refund is assumed at 33.3 per cent. The "CORP." column shows how the income would be treated if originally earned by a corporation and the "PERSONAL" column shows how it would be treated if originally earned by an individual.

Then:

	CORP.	PERSONAL
Tax effect on corporation:		
Interest income	$ 1,000	
Corporate Part I tax 40%	400	
Net income after tax	600	
Refund of tax on payment of dividend	200	
Available for dividend	$ 800	
Effective corporate tax rate	20%	
Tax effect on individual:		
Interest income earned directly by individual		$ 1,000
Dividend received	$ 800	
Gross-up @ (equal to corporate tax)	200	
Taxable amount	$ 1,000	$ 1,000
Tax thereon:		
Personal tax before dividend tax credit 40%	$ 400	$ 400
Dividend tax credit (equal to corporate tax)	200	
Tax payable	$ 200	$ 400
Net income retained by individual	$ 600	$ 600
Effective individual tax rate	20%	40%
Combined corporate/personal tax rate	40%	40%

V. — Other Investment Income

"Other investment income" describes investment income other than portfolio dividends; it includes taxable capital gains, income from property, and income from a "specified investment business".[17]

1. — Tax Integration

There are similar rules that deal with other forms of investment income, such as interest income, rents, royalties, and taxable capital gains,[18] that also neutralize the use of holding companies. Thus, an individual who places investments in a holding company does not in theory enjoy any tax advantage over an individual who holds his or her investments directly. But in the case of investment income other than dividends, the rules apply only to income that a Canadian-controlled private corporation earns.

The structure for the taxation of investment income earned by a Canadian-controlled private corporation involves four steps:

1. A Canadian-controlled private corporation is initially taxed on its investment income at the full federal corporate tax rate of 38 per cent;

2. When the corporation pays a dividend, it receives a refund for a portion of the taxes that it previously paid on that income;[19]

3. When the dividend is paid to an individual, the "grossed-up" value of the dividend is included in the individual's income;[20]

4. The individual may then claim a dividend tax credit to adjust for the net amount of corporate tax that was notionally paid on the individual's behalf by the corporation.[21]

Once again, the purpose of the structure is to prevent tax deferral and to eliminate double taxation of corporate investment income.

---

[17]Subs. 125(7)"specified investment business".

[18]*Ibid.*

[19]The refund is processed through an account described as the "refundable dividend tax on hand account" ("RDTOH"); subs. 129(3).

[20]Para. 82(1)(b).

[21]S. 121.

2. — "Investment Income"

There are two types of investment income: "aggregate investment income" and "foreign investment income".

(a) — Aggregate Investment Income

"Aggregate investment income" comprises:[22]

- The excess of taxable capital gains over allowable capital losses to the extent that such gains and losses are from sources in Canada that relates to a period that the corporation was a CCPC; and

- Net property income (including income from a "specified investment business") from Canadian sources.

(i) — Presumptions

Investment income does not include income from a business.[23] The distinction between investment income and business income is essentially a question of fact.[24] In the case of corporate taxpayers, however, there is a rebuttable presumption that income earned in the pursuit of the corporation's objects (as stated in its constating documents) is income from a business.[25] Although the question is open,[26] there does not appear to be any compelling reason why the presumption would not also apply to corporations that do not require objects clauses in their constating documents.

Thus, depending upon the rigidity with which the presumption is applied, corporations have some flexibility in characterizing the source of their income as flowing from business or investments. The presumption should not, however, be applied in such a manner as to destroy the legislative scheme distinguishing between active business income and investment income.[27]

---

[22]Subs. 129(4)"aggregate investment income".

[23]See Chapter 20, "Corporate Business Income".

[24]*Can. Marconi Co. v. The Queen*, [1986] 2 S.C.R. 522, [1986] 2 C.T.C. 465, 86 D.T.C. 6526 (S.C.C.) at 470 [C.T.C.] and 6529 [D.T.C.].

[25]*Can. Marconi Co. v. The Queen, ibid.*, at 468 [C.T.C.] and 6528 [D.T.C.].

[26]*Can. Marconi Co. v. The Queen, ibid.*, at 470 [C.T.C.] and 6529 [D.T.C.].

[27]*Ensite Ltd. v. The Queen*, [1986] 2 S.C.R. 509, [1986] 2 C.T.C. 459, 86 D.T.C. 6521 (S.C.C.) at 464 [C.T.C.] and 6524 [D.T.C.].

(ii) — Specified Investment Business

A "specified investment business" is a business whose principal or main purpose is to derive income from property.[28] Such income includes dividends, interest, rents, and royalties. A "specified investment business" does *not* include the business of leasing personal property, but it does include the business of leasing real property. The principal purpose test is an annual test.

There are two important exceptions to the meaning of specified investment business. A business that employs more than five full-time employees throughout the year is not a "specified investment business". Thus, a "specified investment business" includes any business with less than six full-time employees whose principal purpose is to earn income from property or the leasing of real property.

A business that derives income from property can be an active business even if it does not have more than five full-time employees if it derives administrative services from an associated corporation, and it would have employed more than five employees if the associated corporation did not provide the support services.

(b) — Foreign Investment Income

We calculate "foreign investment income" in the same way as "aggregate investment income", except that it takes into account only income earned from non-Canadian sources.[29] "Foreign investment income" does not include any income or loss from property that an active business uses incidentally.[30]

3. — Refund of Tax

The original theoretical model for the refund of taxes on investment income was based on the assumption that the top individual tax rate was 40 per cent. As the provinces increased their tax rates, however, it became attractive to hold investments through a CCPC. To address the disparity between theoretical and actual provincial rates, section 123.3 imposes an additional refundable tax of 6.67 per cent. Thus, the total amount refundable is now 26.67 per cent.

---

[28]Subs. 125(7)"specified investment business".

[29]Subs. 129(4)"foreign investment income".

[30]See *Aqua-Gem Invt. Ltd. v. M.N.R.*, [1986] 1 C.T.C. 2528, 86 D.T.C. 1392 (T.C.C.) (interest from short-term investments was income "incident to" taxpayer's business).

A Canadian-controlled private corporation that earns investment income (other than portfolio dividends) is eligible for a *partial refund* of taxes when it pays out dividends.[31] The effective rate of tax (net of refunds) on investment income (other than portfolio dividends) is in theory approximately 20 per cent. Hence, individual and corporate taxes payable by Canadian-controlled private corporations on investment income are approximately integrated where the individual's combined federal-provincial marginal rate of tax is 46.67 per cent.

The theoretical scheme of the refundable tax is as follows: we assume that a Canadian-controlled private corporation pays tax on its investment income at 46.67 per cent; when it pays out dividends, it receives a refund of 26.67 per cent on its Canadian investment income. (This is the "refundable portion" of its Part I tax.[32]) Also assume that the shareholder includes the grossed-up value (125 per cent) of the cash dividend in income and claims a dividend tax credit equal to the value of the dividend gross-up. Then, corporate and personal taxes are "integrated" if the individual's marginal tax rate is 46.67 per cent. Thus, the tax burden is neutral, whether the shareholder receives the investment income directly or through a holding company.

"Aggregate investment income" also includes the excess of Canadian source taxable capital gains over Canadian source allowable capital losses. The theory in respect of the taxation of capital gains is to integrate the tax payable on corporate capital gains with the tax that would be payable by an individual who receives such income directly.

As with other sources of investment income, interest, or rent, the theory is that a corporation pays Part I tax on its capital gains at 46.67 per cent, but can claim a refund of 26.67 per cent on dividends that it pays out.

There is one significant difference, however, between the tax structure in respect of corporate capital gains and other sources of investment income. Only 50 per cent of capital gains are included in income as taxable capital gains, and only 50 per cent of capital losses are allowed as a deduction from taxable capital gains. The non-taxable portion (50 per cent of the capital gain) goes into a special account called the "Capital Dividend Account",[33] which may be paid out on a tax-free basis to shareholders and does not affect the adjusted cost base of the shares.[34] Thus, capital gains earned through a corporation are treated in a similar manner to gains earned directly by an individual.

---

[31]Subs. 129(1); para. 129(3)(a). Note that the corporation must be a Canadian-controlled private corporation *throughout the taxation year*.

[32]Subs. 129(1); subpara. 129(3)(a)(ii).

[33]Subs. 89(1)"capital dividend account".

[34]Subs. 83(2).

The following example illustrates the flow-through of capital gains through a corporation. (The theoretical model assumes a combined corporate/personal tax of 27 per cent on capital gains.)

Example (Theoretical model)

Assume:

A private corporation earns $1,000 capital gains. The corporation pays a dividend to its sole shareholder, an individual with a marginal tax rate of 40 per cent. The corporation pays Part I tax at a rate of 46.67 per cent. The dividend refund is assumed at 33.3 per cent.

Then:

	CORP.	PERSONAL
Tax effect on corporation:		
Capital gains	$ 1,000	
Tax-free portion of gain (50%)	500	
Taxable capital gain	500	
Corporate Part I tax (46.67%)	233	
Net income after tax	267	
Refund of tax on payment of dividend	133	
Available for dividend	$ 400	
Effective corporate tax rate on gain	10%	
Tax effect on individual:		
Capital gains realized directly by individual		$ 1,000
Taxable dividend received	$ 400	—
Gross-up @ 1/4 (equal to corporate tax)	100	—
Taxable amount	$ 500	$ 500
Tax thereon:		
Personal tax before dividend tax credit (40%)	$ 200	$ 200
Dividend tax credit (equal to corporate tax)	(100)	—
Tax payable	$ 100	$ 200
Capital dividend (tax free)	$ 500	
Net income retained by individual	$ 800	$ 800
Effective personal tax rate	10%	20%
Combined corporate/personal tax rate	20%	20%

4. — Capital Dividends

The non-taxable portion of capital gains is credited to an account called the "Capital Dividend Account".[35] A dividend paid out of the "Capital Dividend Account" is tax-free to the shareholder and does not affect the adjusted cost base of the shares.[36] It is important to track the balance of the capital dividend account. Part III of the Act imposes a 60 per cent tax upon amounts that a taxpayer elects in excess of the CDA balance.

5. — Integration

As the preceding examples illustrate, the tax payable on investment income by an individual is approximately the same whether the individual earns the income directly or through a corporation. The Act integrates personal and corporate taxes through the refund and dividend tax credit mechanism. In each case, the amount taxable in the individual's hands is approximately equal to the corporation's pre-tax income. In addition, the combined federal-provincial dividend tax credit approximately equals the tax that the corporation pays.

Two factors, however, can distort the tax integration model as it applies to investment income: (1) the combined federal-provincial corporate tax rate can shift because of surtaxes and variations in provincial rates; and (2) the amount of the dividend tax credit varies from province to province. Thus, perfect integration of taxes on investment income occurs only when federal corporate tax rates exactly synchronize with provincial tax rates. This rarely happens. If it does, it is entirely by coincidence.

6. — Refundable Dividend Tax On Hand

The "refundable dividend tax on hand" ("RDTOH") account is a notional account used to calculate a corporation's entitlement to a tax refund.

The refundable tax in respect of portfolio dividend income is available to all private corporations. For non-portfolio dividend income, however, the refund is available only in respect of the investment income of a corporation that was a *Canadian-controlled* private corporation *throughout* the taxation year.[37]

---

[35]Subs. 89(1)"capital dividend account".

[36]Subs. 83(2).

[37]Para. 129(3)(a).

The tax refund is equal to 1/3 of taxable dividends paid by the corporation, subject to a maximum equal to the corporation's RDTOH.[38] The refund can be applied against other corporate taxes payable by the corporation.

The balance in the RDTOH account at the end of a particular year is reduced in the following year by the amount of dividend refunds to which the corporation has become entitled as a result of the payment of taxable dividends to its shareholders.[39]

Where a corporation loses its private corporation status, its RDTOH account is erased. The only income credited to the RDTOH of a corporation is its investment income earned after it *last became a private corporation*. Hence, once its RDTOH is erased, the amount is never again available for future refunds of tax.

Where a private corporation has a balance in its refundable dividend tax on hand account, the Minister may, at the time of mailing of the notice of assessment, refund to the corporation an amount equal to the *lesser* of:[40]

- 1/3 of all taxable dividends paid by the corporation in the year; and

- The balance in its RDTOH account at the end of that year.

The Minister must make the refund if the corporation applies for it after the notice of assessment has been mailed three years from the end of the year.[41] The Minister may, however, apply the refund to offset the corporation's existing or prospective income tax liability.

---

[38]Subs. 129(1).

[39]Para. 129(3)(c).

[40]Subs. 129(1).

[41]Paras. 129(1)(b) and 152(4)(a).

Selected Bibliography to Chapter 19

General

Fenwick, "Incorporation of Investment Income", in *Proceedings of 29th Tax Conf.* 141 (Can. Tax Foundation, 1977).

Institute for Fiscal Studies, *Equity for Companies: A Corporation Tax for the 1990's* — A Corporation Tax for the 1990's — A Report of the IFS Capital Taxes Group (London, 1991).

Provenzano, Louis J., "The Impact of Escalating Provincial Tax Rates on an Owner-manager's Decision to Earn Investment and Active Business Income Directly or through a Corporation", in *Proceedings of 45th Tax Conf.* 33:1 (Can. Tax Foundation, 1993).

Dividends

Institute for Fiscal Studies, *Equity for Companies: A Corporation Tax for the 1990's* — A Report of the IFS Capital Taxes Group (London, 1991).

Lanthier, "A Critical Analysis of the Part IV Tax Provisions" (1978) 26 Can. Tax J. 625.

McCallum, J. Thomas, "Taxation of Portfolio Dividends" (1995) 5 Can. Current Tax 67.

Other Investment Income

Broadhurst, David G., "Income Tax Treatment of Investment Corporations and Nonresident-Owned Investment Corporations", in *Proceedings of 37th Tax Conf.* 44 (Can. Tax Foundation, 1985).

McLean, D.S., "Canadian Investment Income — Property Used or Held by a Corporation in the Course of Carrying on a Business" (Comment on *R. v. Ensite Ltd.*, [1983] C.T.C. 296 (F.C.A.); *R. v. Brown Boveri Howden Inc.*, [1983] C.T.C. 301 (F.C.A.)), (1983) 31 Can. Tax J. 1006.

Novis, Derrick, "Tax Incentives: More Good Reasons to Invest" (1987) 120 CA Magazine No. 5, 68.

Other

Birnie, David A.G., "Shareholder's Buy-Sell Agreements: Some New Opportunities", in *Proceedings of 38th Tax Conf.* 13 (Can. Tax Foundation, 1986).

Durnford, John W., "Profits on the Sale of Shares: Capital Gains or Business Income? A Fresh Look at Irrigation Industries" (1987) 35 Can. Tax J. 837.

Farden, Eric N., *Income Tax for a Small Business* (E.N. Farden, 1985).

Potter, Christopher J., "Part IV Tax Implications in Butterfly Transactions" (1992) 40 Can. Tax J. 992.

Small Business Taxation, Audio Archives of Canada, 1984.

Williamson, Gordon, "Transfer of Assets To and From a Canadian Corporation", in *Proceedings of 38th Tax Conf.* 12:1 (Can. Tax Foundation, 1986).

CHAPTER 20 — CORPORATE BUSINESS INCOME

We saw in Chapter 17, "Basic Principles of Corporate Tax" that there are various types of corporations: private, public, exempt, conduit, investment, etc. The scheme of taxation in respect of each of these types of corporations is different and takes into account their special needs and circumstances. In Chapter 19 "Corporate Investment Income" we looked at the rules for the taxation of investment income that private corporations earn. In this chapter we look at the taxation of the business income of private corporations.

I. — The Statutory Scheme

The scheme for the taxation of corporate business income is different from the taxation of investment income because the underlying policies of the two schemes are quite different. The statutory scheme for private corporations reflects three distinct objectives:

1. High income taxpayers should not be able to defer tax on investment income by holding their investments in personal holding corporations;

2. Corporate income should not be taxed more than once; and

3. We should use the income tax system to support "small businesses" through tax incentives.

The taxation of corporate business income depends upon:

1. The type of corporation;

2. The type of income; and

3. The source of income

  • Active business;

  • Personal service business;

  • Specified investment business; or

  • Investment.

Although corporate tax rates vary from year to year, the tax system generally encourages small and family-owned businesses through rate incentives for Canadian-controlled private corporations, which we tax at special low rates on business income. Thus, the Act provides a "small business deduction" to recognize the special financing difficulties and higher capital costs that small businesses face. This is an economic and political choice.

II. — Tax Integration

One objective that is common to both the taxation of investment and business income is the mitigation of double taxation. Thus, the Act integrates corporate and shareholder taxes on business income by imputing corporate taxes to shareholders at the personal level.

"Integration" means that the amount of tax that a taxpayer pays on income should be the same, regardless whether the income is earned through a proprietorship, partnership, or a corporation. We integrate corporate and shareholder taxes through a notional credit or imputation of corporate taxes against shareholder taxes. The shareholder receives a credit at the personal level for taxes previously paid at the corporate level. These two features "integrate" the total amount of tax payable by corporations and their shareholders.

The theoretical tax integration model for business income uses three basic premises:

  • The combined federal and provincial corporate tax is 20 per cent on business income;

  • Dividends to individual shareholders are taxable at a grossed-up value to take into account the corporate tax previously paid; and

  • Individual shareholders pay tax at 40 per cent and receive a tax credit equal to the amount of the tax previously paid by the corporation.

If all of these assumptions apply, the tax payable by the corporation and its shareholder on its business income would be exactly equal to the amount of tax that would have been paid by the individual shareholder if he or she had earned the income directly. In other words, the corporate tax would fully "integrate" with the individual's tax. The following example illustrates the theoretical framework of tax integration.

Example		
THEORETICAL MODEL OF INTEGRATION		

Assume:

Federal corporate tax rate		12%
Provincial corporate tax rate		8%
Combined federal/provincial tax rate		20%
Shareholder federal/provincial marginal rate		40%
Dividend gross-up		25%
Active business income	$	100

Then:

Corporate Tax:

Business income	$	100
Corporate tax		(20)
Net income paid as dividend	$	80

Shareholder Tax:

Dividend received	$	80
Gross-up for corporate tax		20
Amount taxable	$	100

Tax thereon:

Federal/provincial tax	$	40
Credit for corporate taxes		(20)
Net tax payable	$	20
Net cash ($80 dividend less $20 tax)	$	60
Amount retained if income earned personally	$	60
Tax differential		0

1. — Over- and Under-Integration

The underlying theory of the tax integration model is that the corporation pays corporate tax at a rate of 20 per cent (12 per cent federal plus 8 per cent provincial). Another premise is that the shareholder is taxed at a rate of 40 per cent. Both of these assumptions are essential to the model. Any variation from the assumed rates causes over- or under-integration of corporate and individual taxes.

In fact, neither the federal government nor any province fully satisfies the theoretical model. There is always some over- or under-integration of corporate/shareholder taxes.

- The combined rate of the federal/provincial corporate tax is rarely, if ever, exactly equal to 20 per cent in any province. Each province levies tax independently of the federal government and sets its own corporate tax rates, regardless of the federal government's theoretical assumptions.

- Federal and provincial governments sometimes impose surtaxes, which effectively increase the basic tax rates. For example, there is a federal corporate surtax of 4 per cent (2004) payable on top of the basic federal tax. This immediately distorts the underlying assumption that the federal rate is 12 per cent. In addition, provincial surtaxes introduce additional distortions.

- The corporation may have a fiscal year that does not coincide with the calendar year. Thus, assumptions made about corporate tax rates on a fiscal year basis do not necessarily coincide with actual tax rates applicable to individuals who are taxable on a calendar year basis.

- A corporation is taxed at approximately 13 per cent on a maximum of $300,000 of its active business income. Income in excess of $300,000 is taxable at the full federal tax rate of 22.12 per cent.[1] The average provincial rate on income in excess of $300,000 is 12 per cent on top of the federal tax. This raises the "normal" tax rate to approximately 34 per cent plus surtaxes. Thus, although the distortion is small for income levels below $300,000, it increases above that level.

- The combined marginal tax rate of individuals in the top bracket is well in excess of the theoretical 40 per cent. In 2004, for example, the top marginal rate varied from a low of 39 per cent (Alberta) to a high of 49 per cent (Newfoundland & Labrador).

Any of these factors distorts tax integration and results in double taxation of corporate income.

2. — Limits on Integration

The tax incentives for "small business" are an important part of the Canadian tax system. The incentives take two forms: low rates of tax on business income and partial integration of corporate and shareholder taxes. But the incentives have a cost. They are, in effect, "tax expenditures". Hence, the system restricts the incentives to a manageable cost. The low tax

---

[1]See Appendix D.2.

rate is available only to Canadian-controlled private corporations ("CCPCs") on active business income ("ABI") earned in Canada.

The basic rate of federal tax on a CCPC's active business income is 13 per cent on the first $300,000 of income, compared with 22.12% per cent for other corporations. Assuming a provincial tax rate of approximately 5 per cent, the total rate of tax (ignoring surtaxes) on the first $300,000 of income is 18 per cent. This rate of tax is available only to CCPCs that earn active business income in Canada.

The dividend tax credit is premised on the assumption that the corporation paid tax at a rate of 20 per cent. Thus, even in the theoretical model, there is a penalty of double taxation for doing business through a corporation if income exceeds $300,000. The penalty is substantial. As the following examples illustrate, double taxation of corporate income over the maximum threshold amount for the low rate of tax is systemic.

Example

CORPORATE AND SHAREHOLDER EARNINGS IN 2004 — $300,000

	Integration Model		Income Earned by Corporation		Income Earned by Individual	
	Rates	Example	Rates[1]	Example	Rates	Example
Assume						
Federal Tax Rate ($0 - $300,000)[2]	12%		13.12%			
Federal Tax Rate (over $300,000)	12%		22.12%			
Ontario Prov. Rate (up to $400,000)[3]	8%		5.50%			
Ontario Prov. Rate (over $400,000)[4]	8%		14.00%			
Gross Up	25%		25.00%			
Dividend Tax Credit[5] (approx. of actual dividend)		Corp. Tax Paid	23.08%			
Individual Tax Rate (Fed. + Prov.)	40%		18.62%		46.41%	
Corporate Income						
Taxable Income		$ 300,000		$ 300,000		
Corporate Tax (Fed. + Prov.)	20%	60,000	18.62%	55,860		
Net Income After Tax		$ 240,000		$ 244,140		
Dividend Paid		$ 240,000		$ 244,140		
Personal Tax						
Dividend Income		$ 240,000		$ 244,140		
Gross Up	25%	60,000	25.00%	61,035		
Income Earned Directly						$ 300,000
Taxable Income		$ 300,000		$ 305,175		$ 300,000

Example

Tax Thereon

Fed./Prov. Tax	40%	$ 120,000	46.41%	$ 141,632	46.41%	$ 139,230
Fed./Prov. Dividend Tax Credit		Corp. Tax Paid 60,000	23.08%	56,348		
Net Tax Payable		$ 60,000		$ 85,284		$ 139,230
Net Income After Tax		$ 180,000		$ 158,856		$ 160,770

Total Tax Payable

Corporate Tax	$ 60,000	$ 55,860	$ 139,230
Personal Tax	60,000	85,284	139,230
Total Tax	$ 120,000	$ 141,144	$ 139,230

Net Cash to Individual

Income Earned	$ 240,000	$ 244,140	$ 300,000
Personal Tax Paid	60,000	85,284	139,230
Net Cash Received	$ 180,000	$ 158,856	$ 160,770

Notes:

1   See Appendix D to see how the federal tax rates are calculated. Note that these are the general tax rates; Manufacturing & Processing income is usually subject to a different tax rate and does not qualify for the reduced small business tax rate.

2   The small business deduction limit was only $250,000 for 2004. The 2003 Budget increased the small business deduction limit from $200,000 to $300,000; however, the phase in was not complete until 2005.

3   Each province sets its own small business deduction limit and its own dividend tax credit. In 2004, Ontario's "Incentive Deduction for Small Business Corporations" (IDSBC) applied to the first $400,000 of active business income earned by a CCPC.

4   The benefit of Ontario's IDSBC is gradually reduced by a surtax on income exceeding $400,000. The IDSBC benefit is entirely eliminated when the CCPC's income reaches $1,128,519.

5   The federal dividend tax credit (DTC) is 2/3 of the "gross-up" amount (or 16.67% of the dividend). The Ontario DTC is calculated as [(highest provincial tax rate / highest federal tax rate) x federal DTC]. For example, in 2004 the Ontario DTC on a $10,000 dividend was [(11.16% / 29%) × $1666.67] = $641.38 (or 6.41% of the dividend). Thus, the combined federal/provincial tax credit is 23.08% of the dividend (16.67% fed. + 6.41% prov.).

Example

CORPORATE AND SHAREHOLDER EARNINGS IN 2004 — $400,000

	Income Earned by Corporation		Income Earned by Individual	
Assume	Rates[1]	Example	Rates	Example
Federal Tax Rate ($0 - $300,000)[2]	13.12%			
Federal Tax Rate (over $300,000)	22.12%			
Ontario Prov. Rate (up to $400,000)[3]	5.50%			
Ontario Prov. Rate (over $400,000)[4]	14.00%			
Gross Up	25.00%			
Dividend Tax Credit[5]	23.08%			
(approx. of actual dividend)				
Individual Tax Rate (approx.)			46.41%	
Corporate Income				
Taxable Income		$ 400,000		
Corporate Tax (Fed. + Prov.)				
$0 - $300,000	18.62%	$ 55,860		
$300,000 - $400,000	27.62%	27,620		
Corporate Tax		$ 83,480		
Net Income After Tax		$ 316,520		
Dividend Paid		$ 316,520		
Personal Tax				
Dividend Income		$ 316,520		
Gross Up	25.00%	79,130		
Income Earned Directly				
Taxable Income		$ 395,650		$ 400,000
				$ 400,000
Tax Thereon				
Fed/Prov Tax	46.41%	$ 183,621	46.41%	$ 185,640
Fed./Prov. Dividend Tax Credit	23.08%	73,053		
Net Tax Payable		$ 110,568		$ 185,640
Net Income After Tax		$ 205,952		$ 214,360

Example		
Total Tax Payable		
Corporate Tax	$ 83,480	
Personal Tax	110,568	$ 185,640
Total Tax	$ 194,048	$ 185,640
Net Cash to Individual		
Income Earned	$ 316,520	$ 400,000
Personal Tax Paid	110,568	185,640
Net Cash Received	$ 205,952	$ 214,360

Notes:

1   See Appendix D to see how the federal tax rates are calculated. Note that these are the general tax rates; Manufacturing & Processing income is usually subject to a different tax rate and does not qualify for the reduced small business tax rate.

2   The small business deduction limit was only $250,000 for 2004. The 2003 Budget increased the small business deduction limit from $200,000 to $300,000; however, the phase in was not complete until 2005.

3   Each province sets its own small business deduction limit and its own dividend tax credit. In 2004, Ontario's "Incentive Deduction for Small Business Corporations" (IDSBC) applied to the first $400,000 of active business income earned by a CCPC.

4   The benefit of Ontario's IDSBC is gradually reduced by a surtax on income exceeding $400,000. The IDSBC benefit is entirely eliminated when the CCPC's income reaches $1,128,519.

5   The federal dividend tax credit (DTC) is 2/3 of the "gross-up" amount (or 16.67% of the dividend). The Ontario DTC is calculated as [(highest provincial tax rate / highest federal tax rate) x federal DTC]. For example, in 2004 the Ontario DTC on a $10,000 dividend was [(11.16% / 29%) × $1666.67] = $641.38 (or 6.41% of the dividend). Thus, the combined federal/provincial tax credit is 23.08% of the dividend (16.67% fed. + 6.41% prov.).

Example				
CORPORATE AND SHAREHOLDER EARNINGS IN 2004 — $500,000				
	Income Earned by Corporation		Income Earned by: Individual	
	Rates[1]	Example	Rates	Example
Assume				
Federal Tax Rate ($0 - $300,000)[2]	13.12%			
Federal Tax Rate (over $300,000)	22.12%			
Ontario Prov. Rate (up to $400,000)[3]	5.50%			
Ontario Prov. Rate (over $400,000)[4]	14.00%			
Gross Up	25.00%			
Dividend Tax Credit[5]	23.08%			
(approx. of actual dividend)				
Individual Tax Rate (approx.)			46.41%	
Corporate Income				
Taxable Income		$ 500,000		
Corporate Tax (Fed. + Prov.)				
$0 - $300,000	18.62%	$ 55,860		
$300,000 - $400,000	27.62%	27,620		
$400,000 - $500,000[6]	36.12%	36,120		
Corporate Tax		$ 119,600		
Net Income After Tax		$ 380,400		
Dividend Paid		$ 380,400		
Personal Tax				
Dividend Income		$ 380,400		
Gross Up	25.00%	95,100		
Income Earned Directly				
Taxable Income		$ 475,500		$ 500,000
				$ 500,000
Tax Thereon				
Fed/Prov Tax	46.41%	$ 220,680	46.41%	$ 232,050
Fed./Prov. Dividend Tax Credit	23.08%	87,796		
Net Tax Payable		$ 132,884		$ 232,050
Net Income After Tax		$ 247,516		$ 267,950

Example

Total Tax Payable

Corporate Tax	$ 119,600	
Personal Tax	132,884	$ 232,050
Total Tax	$ 252,484	$ 232,050

Net Cash to Individual

Income Earned	$ 380,400	$ 500,000
Personal Tax Paid	132,884	232,050
Net Cash Received	$ 247,516	$ 267,950

Notes:

1   See Appendix D to see how the federal tax rates are calculated. Note that these are the general tax rates; Manufacturing & Processing income is usually subject to a different tax rate and does not qualify for the reduced small business tax rate.

2   The small business deduction limit was only $250,000 for 2004. The 2003 Budget increased the small business deduction limit from $200,000 to $300,000; however, the phase in was not complete until 2005.

3   Each province sets its own small business deduction limit and its own dividend tax credit. In 2004, Ontario's "Incentive Deduction for Small Business Corporations" (IDSBC) applied to the first $400,000 of active business income earned by a CCPC.

4   The benefit of Ontario's IDSBC is gradually reduced by a surtax on income exceeding $400,000. The IDSBC benefit is entirely eliminated when the CCPC's income reaches $1,128,519.

5   The federal dividend tax credit (DTC) is 2/3 of the "gross-up" amount (or 16.67% of the dividend). The Ontario DTC is calculated as [(highest provincial tax rate / highest federal tax rate) x federal DTC]. For example, in 2004 the Ontario DTC on a $10,000 dividend was [(11.16% / 29%) x $1666.67] = $641.38 (or 6.41% of the dividend). Thus, the combined federal/provincial tax credit is 23.08% of the dividend (16.67% fed. + 6.41% prov.).

6   This rate ignores the surtax on income exceeding $400,000, which is imposed to gradually "claw back" the low-rate benefit of the IDSBC. The benefit is entirely eliminated at when the CCPC's income reaches $1,128,519.

The double tax penalty is small at the $300,000 level, but begins to accelerate above this amount. Above $400,000, the combined federal and provincial (Ontario) rate rises to approximately 36 per cent. Thus, at $400,000 the penalty is approximately 14 per cent.

III. — Canadian-Controlled Private Corporations

A Canadian-controlled private corporation ("CCPC") is a private corporation that resides in Canada and that is not controlled, directly or indirectly, by non-resident persons, by public corporations or by any combination of non-residents and public corporations.[2] The definition of CCPC does not require control by Canadian residents. Rather, the Act defines a CCPC as a private corporation that is *not controlled* by non-residents.

Control refers to both legal (*de jure*) and factual (*de facto*) control. Hence, a private corporation that is owned 50 per cent by non-residents and 50 per cent by residents qualifies as a CCPC unless the non-residents exercise *de facto* control.[3] For the purpose of this rule, a corporation does not qualify as a CCPC because it is not actually controlled by non-residents merely because its shares are widely held.

IV. — Active Business Income

The basic federal corporate rate of tax is 28 per cent after a reduction of 10 per cent for the provincial tax abatement. Therefore, all corporations are initially taxable at the federal level at 28 per cent. There are, however, several exceptions to this rate.

An important exception applies to Canadian-controlled private corporations (CCPCs). A corporation that is a CCPC *throughout its taxation year* can claim a special tax credit equal to 16 per cent on its first $300,000 of net Canadian "active business income" that it earns in the year.[4] This tax credit reduces the corporate tax payable by a CCPC on the first $300,000 of its active business income from 28 per cent to 12 per cent. Surtaxes and provincial taxes then raise the effective corporate rate to 18 per cent.

Basic rate	38 %
Provincial abatement	(10)
	28 %

---

[2]Subs. 125(7)"Canadian-controlled private corporation"; IT-458R2, "Canadian-Controlled Private Corporation" (May 31, 2000).

[3]See, for example, *Mimetix Pharmaceuticals v. R.*, [2002] 1 C.T.C. 2188, 2001 D.T.C. 1026 (T.C.C. [General Procedure]); affd. [2003] 3 C.T.C. 72, 2003 D.T.C. 5194 (Fed. C.A.) (non-residents exercised *de facto* control under subs. 256(5.1) — corporation was not a CCPC).

[4]Subs. 125(1). The credit is also commonly known as the "Small Business Deduction".

Federal surtax (4% of 28%)	1
	29 %
Small business deduction	(16)
Total federal	13
Provincial tax	5
Combined federal/provincial	18 %

The low rate allows CCPCs to accumulate more after-tax income for reinvestment and expansion.

"Active business" includes *any business other than* a "specified investment business" or a "personal service business". It also includes income from an adventure or concern in the nature of trade.[5]

"Business" includes "a profession, calling, trade, manufacture or undertaking of any kind whatever."[6] The adjective "active" is expansive. For example, in *Cadboro Bay*:[7]

> [A]ny quantum of business activity that gives rise to income in a taxation year for a private corporation in Canada is sufficient to make mandatory the characterization of such income as income from an "active business carried on in Canada".

1. — Presumptions

There is a *rebuttable* presumption that corporate income derives from business. In *Can. Marconi*,[8] for example, Madam Justice Wilson said:

> It is frequently stated in both the English and Canadian case law that there is in the case of a corporate taxpayer a rebuttable presumption that income received from or generated by an activity done in pursuit of an object set out in the corporation's constating documents is income from a business. ...
>
> The question whether particular income is income from business or property remains a question of fact in every case. However, the fact that a particular taxpayer is a corporation is a very

---

[5]Subs. 125(7)"active business carried on by a corporation".

[6]Subs. 248(1)"business".

[7]*The Queen v. Cadboro Bay Hldg.*, [1977] C.T.C. 186 at 199, 77 D.T.C. 5115 at 5123 (F.C.T.D.).

[8]*Can. Marconi Co. v. The Queen*, [1986] 2 S.C.R. 522, [1986] 2 C.T.C. 465 at 468, 470, 86 D.T.C. 6526 at 6528, 6529 (S.C.C.).

relevant matter to be considered because of the existence of the presumption and its implications in terms of the evidentiary burden resting on the appellant.

The presumption, coupled with the generous judicial interpretation of "active", gives an expansive meaning to the phrase "active business".

The presumption is not ironclad, however, and should be read in the context of the statutory structure for the taxation of corporate income. Business income is taxed quite differently from investment income. The judicial presumption should not negate the statutory scheme for the taxation of business and investment income.

2. — Business vs. Investment Income

The distinction between investment income and business income is essentially a question of fact that depends upon several factors, including:[9]

- Activity associated with the generation of the income;

- Number and value of transactions;

- Relationship between the income in question and total income; and

- Relationship between the value of the assets producing the income in question and total assets.

The greater the volume of activity and the value of transactions, and the closer the relationship between the income earned and the total income and assets of the taxpayer, the greater the likelihood that the income is "business income".

A corporation's business income is almost invariably "active business income", *unless* it derives from a "specified investment business" or a "personal service business".[10] A "specified investment business" is a business that derives its income principally from investments and property. Thus, it includes a business whose principal purpose is to earn income from interest, dividends, royalties, rents, etc.[11]

---

[9]*Can. Marconi Co. v. The Queen, ante.*

[10]Subs. 125(7)"active business carried on by a corporation", "personal services business", "specified investment business".

[11]Subs. 125(7)"specified investment business" and subs. 129(4)"income or loss".

3. — Incidental Business Income

A corporation's active business income includes any incidental income that pertains to the business.[12] For example, cash and short-term liquid investments that are an integral part of a business are business assets. Hence, they generate business income.[13] The critical element is whether the corporation depends and relies upon the investments for the operation of its business.[14] A business that engages in the lending of money under security of mortgages, investing in securities, and the renting of property can qualify as an active business.[15]

Incidental business income, such as income from investment of surplus cash, rental of excess space, interest on accounts receivable, and certain investment income from associated corporations is also active business income.[16] Active business income does not, however, include income from property from a source in Canada.[17]

V. — The Small Business Deduction

The Act limits the small business deduction, which is an incentive to stimulate small and family-owned Canadian businesses, by three parameters:

1. The corporation's active business income;

2. The corporation's Canadian source taxable income; and

3. An overall limit of $300,000.

---

[12]Subs. 125(7)"income of the corporation for the year from an active business".

[13]*Irving Garber Sales Canada Ltd. v. Canada*, [1992] 2 C.T.C. 261, 92 D.T.C. 6498 (F.C.T.D.).

[14]*Majestic Tool & Mold Ltd. v. The Queen*, [1993] 2 C.T.C. 2813, 94 D.T.C. 1220 (T.C.C.) (interest from term deposits was active business income).

[15]*The Queen v. Rockmore Invt. Ltd.*, [1976] C.T.C. 294, 76 D.T.C. 6156 (F.C.A.).

[16]Subs. 125(7) ("income of the corporation for the year from an active business"); *The Queen v. Marsh & McLennan Ltd.*, [1983] C.T.C. 231, 83 D.T.C. 5180 (F.C.A.); leave to appeal to S.C.C. refused 52 NR 231 (meaning of what is ancillary, incidental or subsidiary to active business); *The Queen v. Ensite Ltd.*, [1983] C.T.C. 296, 83 D.T.C. 5315 (F.C.A.); affd. [1986] 2 S.C.R. 509, [1986] 2 C.T.C. 459, 86 D.T.C. 6521 (S.C.C.) (test is whether property employed and risked in business; property used to fulfil a mandatory condition precedent to trade was property used or held in the business); *Alamar Farms Ltd. v. The Queen*, [1993] 1 C.T.C. 2682, 93 D.T.C. 121 (T.C.C.) (rental payments from surface leases and royalty income was incidental to taxpayer's principal activity of farming and, therefore, active business income). See also subs. 129(6) (investment income from associated corporation deemed to be active business income).

[17]Subs. 129(4)"income or loss".

These restrictions ensure that only small corporate businesses with Canadian-source active business income can claim the deduction. The small business deduction is not available to proprietorships and partnerships, regardless of their size.

Subsection 125(1) limits a corporation's small business deduction in any year to 16 per cent of the *least* of its:[18]

- *Net* Canadian active business income for the taxation year;

- Taxable income for the taxation year less 10/3 of its foreign non-business income tax credit and three times its foreign business income tax credit; and

- Business limit, which is $300,000 unless the corporation is associated with another corporation.

These three limiting factors restrict the availability of the small business deduction to the active business income of "small" Canadian corporations.

Each of the three limits to the small business deduction plays a different role. The first confines the deduction to "active business income" and excludes investment income and income from a personal service business.[19]

The second limitation confines the small business deduction to domestic source income. Thus, a CCPC cannot claim the deduction on foreign income that has not been taxed in Canada and on account of which it claims a foreign tax credit.[20]

The corporation's taxable income is reduced by 10/3 of its foreign non-business income tax credit. The factor (10/3) is based on the assumption that the corporation paid a tax of 30 per cent on its foreign non-business income. For example, assume that a corporation earns $100 foreign non-business income on which it pays $30 tax. Then, $10/3 \times \$30 = \$100$, which is the amount that the corporation deducts from its taxable income. Similarly, the multiplication factor of three times assumes that the corporation paid foreign tax at a rate of 33.3 per cent on its foreign business income.

The third restriction limits the *annual* deduction to a maximum of $300,000[21] so as to restrict the deduction to "small" businesses. The overall limit also curtails the revenue loss from the tax expenditure.

---

[18]Subs. 125(1).

[19]Para. 125(1)(a), subs. 125(7)"active business carried on by a corporation".

[20]Para. 125(1)(b).

[21]Para. 125(1)(c); subss. 125(2), (3) (business limit of $200,000 to be allocated among group of associated corporations).

VI. — Corporate Partnerships

We calculate partnership income at the partnership level and allocate it to the partners according to their respective shares. Each partner then includes in income his or her own share of the partnership's income or loss for the fiscal period. For the purposes of the small business deduction, a corporation must include in its income its share of the active business income or loss of any partnership of which it is a member. A corporation does this by including in its income its "specified partnership income" and deducting therefrom its "specified partnership losses".[22]

Since the maximum amount of active business income on which a corporation may claim the small business deduction is $300,000, the Act ensures that corporations cannot multiply the limit by carrying on business in partnerships. Otherwise, corporations carrying on business in partnership could claim a much larger deduction.

Two anti-avoidance rules ensure that the taxpayers do not abuse the $300,000 maximum limit. First, a corporation's "specified partnership income" is the lesser of its share of the partnership's income from active businesses in Canada and the proportion of the $300,000 limit that is its share of the total partnership income.[23] For example, if a partnership of five equal corporate partners earns active business income of $1,500,000, each corporate partner's "specified partnership income" is $300,000 (that is, 1/5 × $1,500,000) for the purpose of calculating its small business deduction.

Second, where a corporation becomes a member of multiple partnerships in order to claim an increased small business deduction, the Minister can disregard the multiple partnerships and reduce the amount of the partnership income that qualifies for the deduction in the hands of the corporate partner.[24]

The Minister can also "look through" several tiers of partnerships. For example, where a corporation is a member of a partnership which in turn is a member of another partnership, the Minister can deem the corporation to be a member of the second tier partnership. The Minister can deem its share of income to be the amount to which it is directly or indirectly entitled through the first and second partnerships.[25] Thus, the corporation's share of the small business deduction may be determined by looking through multiple tiers of partnership to ensure that it does not obtain a larger claim than that to which it would otherwise be entitled.

The small business deduction benefits Canadian-controlled private corporations. To ensure that corporate partnership income is treated in the same manner as if the business were car-

---

[22]Paras. 125(1)(a), (7)"specified partnership income" and "specified partnership loss".

[23]Subs. 125(7)"specified partnership income".

[24]Subs. 125(6).

[25]Subs. 125(6.1).

ried on directly by the corporation, income of a partnership that is controlled, *directly or indirectly, in any matter whatever,* by non-resident persons or public corporations does not qualify for the small business deduction.[26] Hence, an otherwise non-qualifying corporation cannot claim the small business deduction by structuring its affairs through a partnership.

VII. — Associated Corporations

The small business deduction is an obvious incentive for taxpayers to set up multiple corporations solely for the purpose of multiplying the deduction. Thus, a special set of rules controls artificial multiplication of the deduction by restricting the maximum amount that a group of associated corporations can claim.[27] Corporations can be associated with each other because of inter-related shareholdings[28] or through Ministerial discretion.[29]

Where two or more Canadian-controlled private corporations are "associated" with each other, the maximum of their aggregate claim is $300,000. Income subject to this preferential tax rate will be allocated between associated corporations based on their allocation of the business limit. The group must file an agreement allocating the annual business limit among the associated corporations. They must file the agreement annually with the Minister.[30] The allocation may be in any amount that the group agrees upon.[31]

Where a corporation in an associated group fails to sign and file the prescribed form allocating its annual business limit, the Minister is required, after 30 days and proper notice, to assess the corporation on the basis of the Minister's own allocation.[32]

1. — Inter-Related Shareholdings

Corporations are associated with each other if they are subject to common control and common ownership of shares by a person or a related group of persons. The central element underlying "association" is control, whether *de jure* or *de facto*. There are five basic rules to determine corporate association and several anti-avoidance rules to prevent taxpayers from circumventing the basic rules.

---

[26]Subs. 125(6.3).

[27]Subs. 125(2).

[28]Subs. 256(1).

[29]Subs. 256(2.1); See generally IT-64R4, "Corporations: Association and Control" (August 14, 2001).

[30]Subs. 125(3).

[31]Subs. 125(3).

[32]Subs. 125(4).

(a) — Control of One Corporation by Another

Two corporations are associated with each other in a taxation year if, at any time in the year, one of the corporations controls (directly, indirectly *or in any manner whatever*) the other.[33]

Example

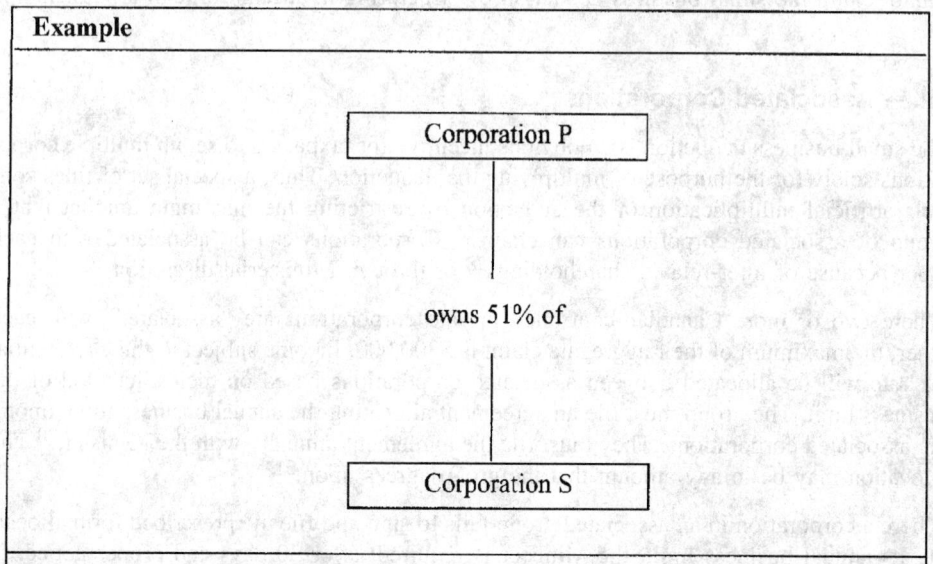

Since Corporation P controls Corporation S, the two corporations are associated with each other.*

* Subs. 256(1.4) expands the meaning of "control" set out in, e.g., *Buckerfield's Ltd. v. M.N.R.*, [1964] C.T.C. 504, 64 D.T.C. 5301 (Ex. Ct.) (corporations associated due to common ownership of shares by third party); see also *Dworkin Furs (Pembroke) Ltd. v. M.N.R.*, [1967] S.C.R. 223, [1967] C.T.C. 50, 67 D.T.C. 5035 (S.C.C.) (absence of majority votes in election of board of directors indicated that one corporation was not controlled by the other); *Br. Amer. Tobacco Co. v. I.R.C.*, [1943] 1 All E.R. 13 (H.L.) (owners of majority of voting power in a company are persons who are in effective control of its affairs and fortunes, *per* Viscount Simon LC at15).

De Jure control is generally manifested through voting rights. Thus, 51 per cent of voting power is usually sufficient to secure control for most corporate purposes. Control may, however, also exist by virtue of other factors. For example, the power to wind up a corporation and appropriate the majority of its assets may be effective control.[34]

---

[33]Para. 256(1)(a).

[34]*The Queen v. Imp. Gen. Properties Ltd.*, [1985] 2 S.C.R. 288, [1985] 2 C.T.C. 299 at 302, 85 D.T.C. 5500 at 5503 (S.C.C.) (in interpreting subs. 256(1), "the court is not limited to a highly technical and narrow interpretation of the legal rights attached to the shares of a corporation").

(b) — *Control of Corporations by Same Person*

A corporation is associated with another corporation in a taxation year, if at any time in the year, the same person or group of persons control both corporations.[35]

Example

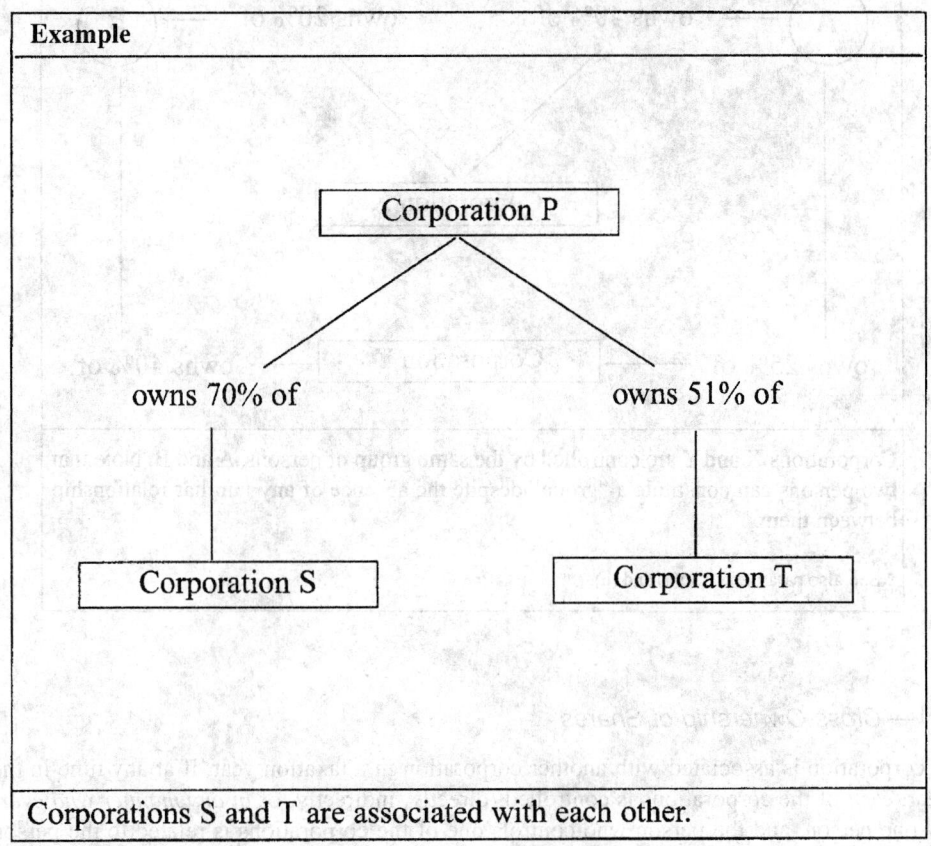

Corporations S and T are associated with each other.

---

[35]Para. 256(1)(b).

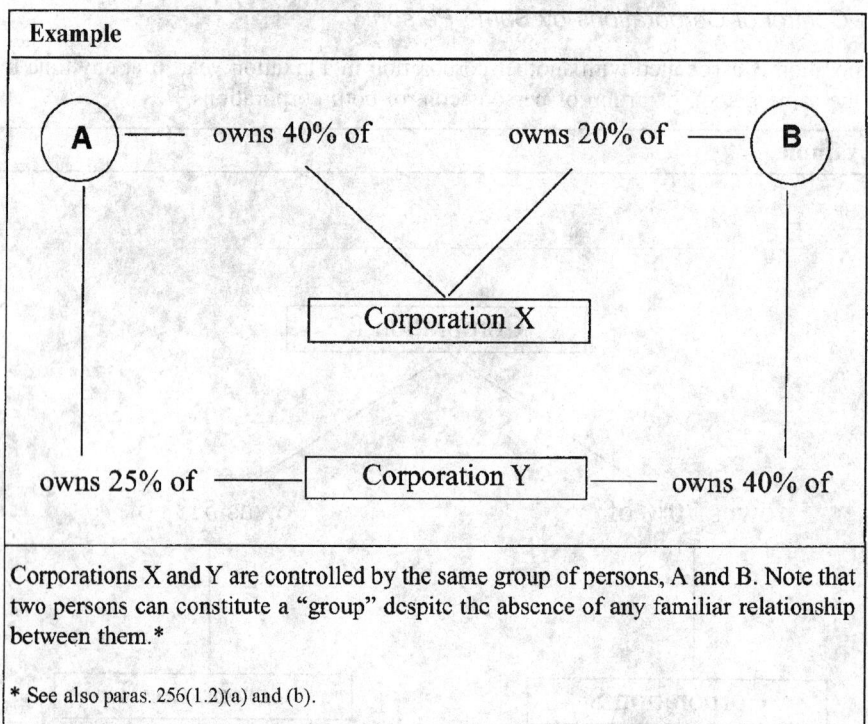

Example

A — owns 40% of   owns 20% of — B

Corporation X

owns 25% of ——— Corporation Y ——— owns 40% of

Corporations X and Y are controlled by the same group of persons, A and B. Note that two persons can constitute a "group" despite the absence of any familiar relationship between them.*

* See also paras. 256(1.2)(a) and (b).

(c) — Cross-Ownership of Shares

A corporation is associated with another corporation in a taxation year, if at any time in the year, each of the corporations is controlled (directly, indirectly, or *in any manner whatever*) by one person, and the person who controls one of the corporations is related to the person who controls the other, and *either one* of those persons owns, in respect of each corporation, not less than 25 per cent of the issued shares of any class (other than a specified class) of the capital stock thereof.[36]

---

[36]Para. 256(1)(c).

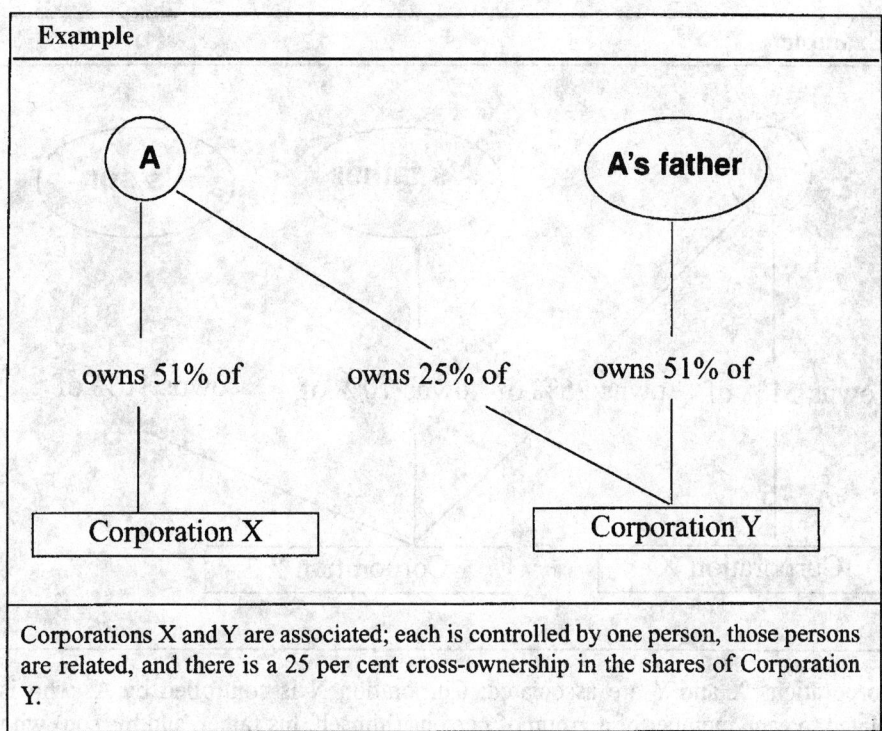

Example

owns 51% of   owns 25% of   owns 51% of

Corporations X and Y are associated; each is controlled by one person, those persons are related, and there is a 25 per cent cross-ownership in the shares of Corporation Y.

(d) — Group Control and Cross-Ownership

A corporation is associated with another corporation in a taxation year if, at any time in the year, one of the corporations is controlled (directly, indirectly, or *in any manner whatever*) by one person and that person is related to each member of a group of persons that controls the other corporation, and that person owns not less than 25 per cent of the issued shares of any class (other than a specified class) of the capital stock of the other corporation.[37]

---

[37]Para. 256(1)(d).

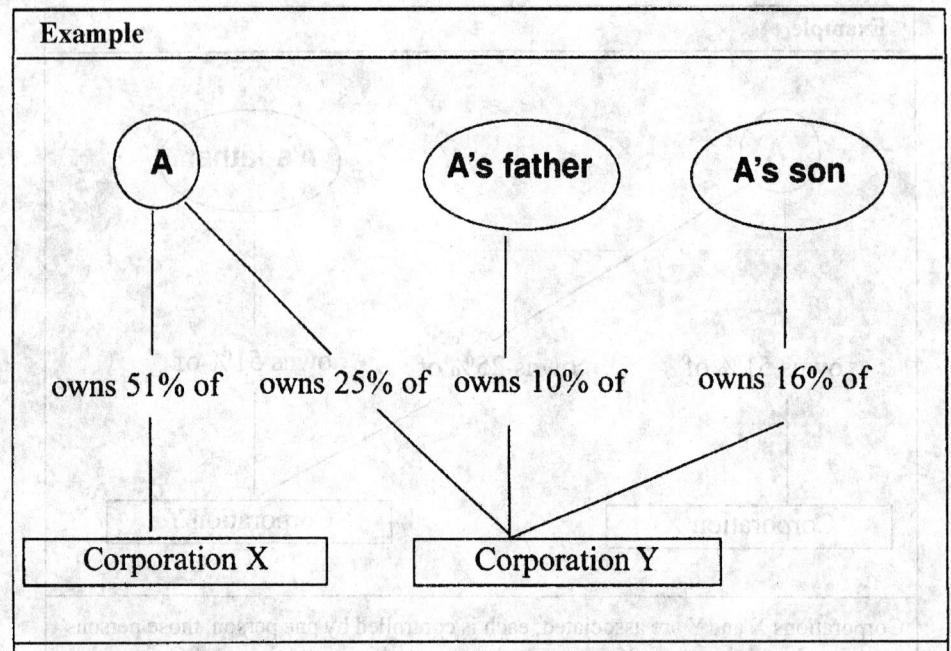

Corporations X and Y are associated; Corporation X is controlled by A, who is related to each member of a group of persons (himself, his father, and his son) who together control Corporation Y. In addition, A has cross-ownership of 25 per cent of Corporation Y.

(e) — Control by Related Group and Cross-Ownership

A corporation is associated with another corporation in a taxation year if, at any time in the year, each of the corporations is controlled (directly, indirectly, *or in any manner whatever*) by a related group and each of the members of one of the related groups is related to *all* of the members of the other related group, and one or more persons who are members of both related groups owns not less than 25 per cent of the issued shares of any class (other than a specified class) of the capital stock of each corporation.[38]

---

[38]Para. 256(1)(e).

Example

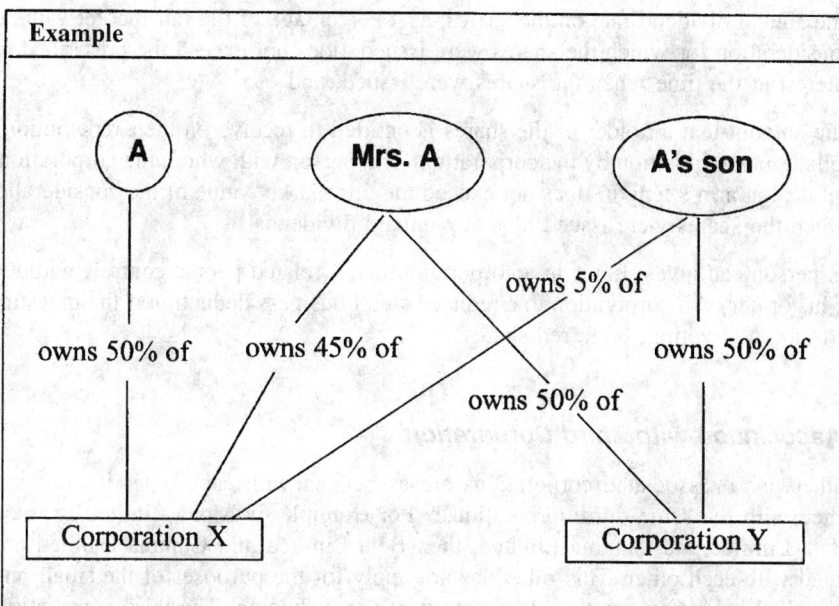

A and Mrs. A are a related group in control of Corporation X. Mrs. A and her son are a related group in control of Corporation Y. Each member of the group in control of Corporation X is related to each member of the group in control of Corporation Y. The related group in control of Corporation Y (Mrs. A and her son) own 25 per cent or more of Corporation X. Therefore, Corporations X and Y are associated.

2. — *Specified Class of Shares*

The 25 per cent cross-ownership rules do not apply to shares of a "specified class". "Specified shares" are generally non-voting preferred shares that confer minimal shareholder power.

More specifically, a class of shares is a "specified class" if:[39]

- The shares are neither convertible nor exchangeable;

- The shares are non-voting;

- Dividends payable on the shares are fixed in amount or rate;

---

[39]Subs. 256(1.1).

- The annual dividend rate on the shares, as a percentage of the fair market value of the consideration for which the shares were issued, does not exceed the prescribed rate of interest at the time when the shares were issued; and

- The amount that a holder of the shares is entitled to receive on their redemption, cancellation or acquisition by the corporation (or a person with whom the corporation does not deal at arm's length) does not exceed the fair market value of the consideration for which the shares were issued plus any unpaid dividends.

Thus, a person can invest funds in a corporation that a related person controls without subjecting his or her own corporation to a reduced small business deduction if the investment is in fixed-rate, non-voting, preferred shares.

3. — Association with Third Corporation

Two otherwise unassociated corporations are associated with each other if they are both associated with the same third corporation.[40] For example, if Alpha Limited is associated with Beta Limited and Gamma Limited, then Beta Limited and Gamma Limited are also associated with each other. This rule does not apply for the purposes of the small business deduction if the third corporation does not claim the deduction. The third corporation may not claim the deduction either because it explicitly elects not to do so or because it does not qualify for the deduction because it is not a "Canadian-controlled private corporation".

VIII. — Corporate Control

There are two forms of corporate control: *de jure* and *de facto*. The word "control" without any qualifier means *de jure* control. The Act uses the phrase "controlled, directly or indirectly in any manner whatever" to describe *de facto* control. Either form can result in corporations being associated with each other.

1. — De Jure Control

(a) — Voting Power

Generally, *de jure* corporate control means the ownership of a sufficient number of shares to be able to elect a majority of the board of directors of a corporation.[41] Thus, *de jure* control

---

[40]Subs. 256(2).

[41]*Buckerfields' Ltd. v. M.N.R.*, [1964] C.T.C. 504, 64 D.T.C. 5301 (Ex. Ct.).

is the legal power to manage a corporation's affairs and the power to exercise corporate control in the long run.[42]

This test does not always provide a clear answer. For example, where a corporation's share-holdings are divided equally between two shareholders, neither has the power to elect a majority of the directors, and the corporation may not be legally controlled by either person.

(b) — Appropriation of Assets

The lack of power to elect a majority of the board of directors is not always determinative of *de jure* corporate control. Control may be inferred from some other form of corporate power, for example, the power to wind up a corporation and appropriate its assets.[43]

(c) — "Group of Persons"

For the purposes of determining whether a corporation is controlled by a group of persons, "group" means *any* two or more persons each of whom owns the corporation's shares.[44]

The existence of a group of persons does not depend upon common links between the persons, the size of the collectivity, or a common intention to obtain a tax benefit. Ownership of shares in the corporation by two or more persons is sufficient to constitute a group.

(d) — Control by Two Groups

A corporation may be controlled by a person or a particular group of persons notwithstanding that it is also controlled by another person or group of persons.[45] Hence, it is possible for a corporation to be controlled by several persons or groups of persons.

Where a group of persons owns shares of the capital stock of a corporation, the fact that an individual member of the group owns, by him- or herself, enough shares to control the corporation does not alter the fact that the group also controls the corporation. Hence, a corporation may be controlled by different persons or groups of persons at the same time. This can

---

[42]*Donald Applicators Ltd. v. M.N.R.*, [1969] C.T.C. 98, 69 D.T.C. 5122 (Ex. Ct.); affd. [1971] S.C.R. v, [1971] C.T.C. 402, 71 D.T.C. 5202 (S.C.C.).

[43]*The Queen v. Imp. Gen. Properties Ltd.*, [1985] 2 S.C.R. 288, [1985] 2 C.T.C. 299, 85 D.T.C. 5500 (S.C.C.).

[44]Para. 256(1.2)(a).

[45]Subpara. 256(1.2)(b)(ii).

cause it to be associated with several corporations each of which may otherwise be unconnected with each other.

(e) — Market Value Control

A corporation may be controlled by virtue of a person owning more than 50 per cent of the
fair market value of its shares, even though the shares do not represent majority voting
power in the corporation.

A corporation is deemed to be controlled by another corporation, person or a group of persons where the "controller" owns:[46]

- Shares that represent more than 50 per cent of the fair market value of *all* of the corporation's issued and outstanding shares; or

- Common shares that represent more than 50 per cent of the fair market value of all of
  the corporation's issued and outstanding common shares.

This test is based on the premise that the fair market value of an individual's shareholdings
in a corporation may be as relevant an indication of real power as a test based on the legal
ability of shareholders to elect a majority of the corporation's board of directors.

The market value test does, however, raise very difficult valuation issues, particularly in the
context of corporations that have complex share capital structures. Hence, in certain circumstances, access to the small business deduction may be uncertain and subject to challenge on
the basis of a share valuation conducted after the claim for the deduction has been made.

The fair market value of shares must be determined without regard to the voting attributes of
the shares of the capital stock of the corporation.[47] Hence, it is quite possible that the control
of a corporation may shift between different groups as the value attributable to the shares of
the corporation changes over time. Since the value of a corporation is usually attributable to
the capitalized value of its earnings, common shares valued without voting rights may not
have any value where the corporation does not have a history of established earnings. This
rule is particularly difficult to apply in the context of common shares of a newly-created
corporation.

Since the common shares of a new enterprise may not have any substantial market value if
they are valued on the basis that they are non-voting shares with no evidence of established
earning power, it is possible that such a corporation may be associated with another corporation on the basis of its issued preferred shares. Similarly, the control of a corporation may
shift when the corporation is in financial difficulty, because the common shares will presum-

---

[46]Para. 256(1.2)(c).

[47]Para. 256(1.2)(g).

ably reflect those difficulties and diminish in value. Hence, it is entirely possible for a corporation to be denied access to the full small business deduction and low tax rate at the very time when it is most likely in need of financial assistance.

(f) — Holding Corporations

A shareholder of a holding corporation that has a subsidiary is considered to have an equity ownership in the subsidiary corporation.[48] The Act "looks through" the holding corporation and attributes ownership of the subsidiary's shares directly to the shareholder of the holding corporation. The attributed ownership of the shares is in the proportion that the fair market value of the holding corporation's shares owned by the shareholder is to the fair market value of all of the issued and outstanding shares of the holding corporation at that time. The fair market value of the shares is determined on the assumption that all of the outstanding shares are non-voting.[49]

(g) — Partnerships

A similar "look through" rule also applies to shares owned by a partnership. A member of a partnership that owns shares of a corporation is considered to directly own the proportionate interest in those shares.[50] Where the income and loss of the partnership for its fiscal period is nil, the proportion is calculated on the assumption that the partnership's income is $1,000,000 in that period.

(h) — Trusts

Under trust law, a trustee is the legal owner of shares held in trust by the trustee. For tax purposes, corporate shares owned by a trust are considered to be owned by the beneficiaries of the trust and, in some cases, by the person from whom the trust property was received.[51]

(i) — Testamentary Trusts

Where, in a testamentary trust, some of the beneficiaries are entitled to all of the income of the trust prior to the death of one of them or all of them, and no other person is entitled to

---

[48]Para. 256(1.2)(d).

[49]Para. 256(1.2)(g).

[50]Para. 256(1.2)(e).

[51]Para. 256(1.2)(f).

any capital of the trust before that time, the shares are deemed to be owned by the beneficiaries before that time.[52] If the trust is a discretionary trust, all of the discretionary beneficiaries are deemed to own the shares.[53]

(ii) — Other Trusts

Where the trust is not a testamentary trust, each beneficiary is deemed to own a proportion of the shares based upon the fair market value of the interest in the trust.[54] If the trust is a discretionary trust, all of the discretionary beneficiaries are deemed to own the shares.[55]

(iii) — Reversionary Trusts

Where a trust is a "reversionary" trust, the person from whom the trust receives the property is also deemed to own the shares.[56] The result of these rules is that it is entirely possible that the Act can deem more than one person to own the same shares at the same time.

(i) — Attribution Rules

Where the shares of a corporation are owned (or deemed to be owned) by a child who is under 18 years of age, the shares are considered to be owned by the child's parents.[57] This rule does not apply if the child manages the business and affairs of the corporation without significant influence by the parents. The shares may be attributed to either parent, depending upon the purpose of the determination.

(j) — Options and Rights

A person who has an option or a right to acquire or to control the voting rights of shares is treated as if he or she owned those shares.[58] This rule does not apply where the option or right is not exercisable until the death, bankruptcy, or permanent disability of a designated

---

[52]Cl. 256(1.2)(f)(i)(B).

[53]Cl. 256(1.2)(f)(i)(A).

[54]Subpara. 256(1.2)(f)(iii).

[55]Subpara. 256(1.2)(f)(ii).

[56]Subpara. 256(1.2)(f)(iv).

[57]Subs. 256(1.3).

[58]Para. 256(1.4)(a).

individual. Thus, an option or right that is triggered under a shareholders' agreement may be exempt from the deeming provision, provided that the option or right is exercisable only upon the death, bankruptcy, or permanent disability of the individual designated in the agreement.

Similarly, where a person has a right to cause a corporation to redeem, acquire or cancel its shares owned by *other shareholders*, he or she is deemed to be in the same position in relation to the control of the incorporation and ownership of its shares *as if* the shares had already been redeemed, acquired, or cancelled by the corporation.[59]

(k) — Tax Avoidance

The Act also contains a special anti-avoidance rule to catch cases that may escape through the net of the specific rules described above.

Two or more corporations may be associated with each other where *one* of the main reasons for the separate existence of the corporations in a taxation year is to reduce the amount of tax that would otherwise have to be paid.[60] For example, where two parts of what could reasonably be considered to be one business (for example, manufacturing and sales of a single product line) are carried out by two corporations each of which is controlled by different persons, the two separate corporations may be deemed to be associated with each other for the purposes of the small business deduction. If they are associated, the two corporations may claim only one small business deduction in respect of the income generated by both businesses.

To avoid association under this rule, it is necessary for the taxpayer to establish, in effect, that *none* of the main reasons for the existence of multiple corporations is to reduce the amount of tax that would otherwise be payable.[61] The intention of the corporations is to be inferred from those by whom it is managed and controlled. The taxpayer must establish that the separate existence of the corporations was dictated *solely* by business expediency and not by tax considerations.[62]

---

[59]Para. 256(1.4)(b).

[60]Subs. 256(2.1).

[61]See *Maritime Forwarding Ltd. v. The Queen*, [1988] 1 C.T.C. 186, 88 D.T.C. 6114 (F.C.T.D.) (incorporating to reduce leasing costs not sustainable as main reason for creation of multiple corporations); *Kencar Ent. Ltd. v. M.N.R.*, [1987] 2 C.T.C. 246, 87 D.T.C. 5450, (sub nom. *Kencar Ent. Ltd. v. The Queen*) (F.C.T.D.) ("Minister's direction could only be challenged by establishing that none of the main reasons for the separate existence of the corporations was to reduce the amount of tax payable").

[62]*Doris Trucking Co. v. M.N.R.*, [1968] C.T.C. 303, 68 D.T.C. 5204 (Ex. Ct.).

2. — De Facto Control

The *de facto* test focuses on the influence, as opposed to the power, that a person or group of persons may have on a corporation. It is premised on the theory that there is more to control than mere legal power as expressed in voting rights.

Although the purpose of the *de facto* test is to prevent artificial manipulation of the associated corporation rules, it does not provide any greater certainty than the more traditional common law doctrines. Thus, the *de facto* test merely substitutes statutory uncertainty for judicial uncertainty.[63]

(a) — "Directly or Indirectly in Any Manner Whatever"

A corporation is associated with another corporation if the two corporations are controlled "directly or indirectly in any manner whatever" by the same person or by persons with common and related interests.[64] A corporation is considered to be "controlled, directly or indirectly in any manner whatever" by a person where the person has any "*direct or indirect influence*" that, *if exercised*, would result in control in fact of the corporation.[65]

The critical test in each case is to determine whether a person or group of persons ("the controller") has the requisite direct or indirect influence over the affairs of a corporation. The controlling person may be another corporation, an individual or a group of persons. For example, a corporation may be controlled by a person who owns less than 50 per cent of the voting shares of the corporation if the remaining shares are widely distributed among other persons (such as employees) who could reasonably be considered to be amenable to the wishes of the person with "influence".

(i) — Influence

The test does not require the "controller" to have any legally-enforceable right or power over the corporation. It is sufficient that the controller have *influence*, whether direct or indirect, over the affairs of the corporation.

---

[63]See generally: *Multiview Inc. v. R.*, [1997] 3 C.T.C. 2962, 97 D.T.C. 1489 (T.C.C.) (relevance of absence of casting vote); *Silicon Graphics Ltd. v. R.*, [2002] 3 C.T.C. 527, 2002 D.T.C. 7112 (Fed. C.A.) (*de facto* control and power to effect significant change in board of directors); *Mimetix Pharmaceuticals v. R.*, [2003] 3 C.T.C. 72, 2003 D.T.C. 5194 (Fed. C.A.) (non-residents had significant power — hence, *de facto* control.

[64]Subs. 256(5.1).

[65]Subs. 256(5.1).

(ii) — Potential Influence

The test is predicated upon the presence of potential influence, and not upon the actual exercise of influence in a particular case. In other words, the "controller" does not have to actually exercise influence over the affairs of the corporation; the controller merely has to have sufficient influence that, *if exercised*, could result in control in fact of the corporation. The taxpayer faces a difficult task to discharge his or her burden of proof. The taxpayer must prove a negative proposition, namely, that he or she does not have influence over the corporation.

(iii) — Exceptions

A person may have influence over another by virtue of a legal arrangement between them that governs the manner in which a business is carried on by a corporation. Provided that the corporation and the "controller" are dealing with each other at arm's length, the *de facto* control test does not apply where the controller's influence derives only from an agreement or arrangement the main purpose of which is to govern the business relationship between the corporation and the controller. For example, where a franchise agreement or lease gives the franchisor or lessor some power to regulate the products sold by the corporation or the hours during which it conducts its business, the power does not, *in and of itself*, result in the franchisor or lessor having *de facto* control over the corporation.

IX. — Personal Services Business Income

Employment income is taxed at progressive marginal rates.[66] Corporate income is taxed at a flat rate.[67] Since the corporate tax rate on active business income that a Canadian-controlled private corporation earns is approximately 18 percent (combined federal and provincial rates), there is a considerable advantage in converting employment income (which is taxed at close to 50 percent at the high end) into business income. One common technique of converting employment income into business income was to use a corporation to render personal services. In *Sazio*,[68] for example, the taxpayer, a football coach, had his football club hire his personal corporation to provide the club with coaching services, which he had previously provided directly to the club. The fees paid to the corporation were then taxed as business, instead of employment, income.

The Act now taxes "personal services business income" ("PSBI") on a gross income basis, with only minimal deductions. Thus, the Act taxes PSBI on the same basis as employment

---

[66]S. 117; see also Chapters 6, "Employment Income" and 16, "Computation of Tax Payable".

[67]S. 123.

[68]*Sazio v. M.N.R.*, [1968] C.T.C. 579, 69 D.T.C. 5001 (Ex. Ct.).

income. Neither is eligible for the small business deduction. PSBI is taxable at the full federal corporate rate of 28 per cent without any refund of tax on dividends.

A personal services business is a business in which a major shareholder of a corporation provides services through the corporation in circumstances where the shareholder would normally provide the services as an employee. Thus, in effect, the shareholder is an "incorporated employee".

More specifically, a "personal services business" is a business that a corporation carries on where the services are performed on behalf of the corporation by an individual (or any person related to the individual) who is a specified shareholder of the corporation, and the individual can "reasonably be regarded" as an officer or employee of the entity *to which* he or she provides the services.[69] Thus, the test is: if one notionally ignores the existence of the "incorporated employee's" corporation, is the relationship between the individual and the person to whom he or she renders services in substance an employment relationship?[70] If so, the income is PSBI.

There is no clear cut answer in every case to determine whether corporate income is active business income or PSBI. For example, the Canada Revenue Agency (CRA) accepts that self-employed real estate agents who incorporate to provide real estate services are independent contractors and not "incorporated employees". Thus, their income is eligible for the small business deduction. In contrast, the Agency will not extend independent contractor status to corporate directors who provide management services on an exclusive contract basis.

1. — Specified Shareholder

A "specified shareholder" of a corporation is a person who owns, directly or indirectly, 10 per cent or more of the issued shares of *any* class of the capital stock of the corporation or a related corporation.[71] The Act deems a taxpayer to own each share of the capital stock of a corporation that is owned by a person with whom the taxpayer does not deal at arm's length. Hence, for example, where a taxpayer's spouse owns 10 per cent or more of the issued shares of a corporation, the taxpayer is also a "specified shareholder" of the corporation.

Each beneficiary of a trust is deemed to own his or her proportion of all the shares owned by the trust. The proportion is determined by reference to the total fair market value of the beneficial interests at the particular time. Similarly, each member of a partnership is deemed to own his or her proportionate share of all the shares owned by the partnership.

---

[69]Subs. 125(7)"personal services business".

[70]See, generally, *Wiebe Door Services Ltd. v. M.N.R.*, [1986] 2 C.T.C. 200, 87 D.T.C. 5025 (F.C.A.). For the meaning of "employment relationship," see Chapter 6, "Employment Income".

[71]Subs. 248(1)"specified shareholder"; s. 251.

PSBI does not include:[72]

    1. The income of a corporation that throughout the year employs more than five full-time employees;[73] or

    2. Amounts that a corporation receives from its associated corporation.

2. — Deductions

In computing PSBI, a corporation generally can deduct only salaries and benefits paid to the "incorporated employee".[74] In effect, PSBI is taxed on a gross income basis, which puts it on the same footing as employment income.

X. — Small Business Corporations

An individual can claim a capital gains exemption of $500,000 for gains on the sale of shares of a qualified small business corporation ("QSBC").[75] The exemption applies to small business corporation's ("SBC") shares, but only if the shares "qualify" by satisfying asset use and minimum share ownership tests. Thus, an individual who disposes of QSBC shares may claim a capital gains exemption in respect of the disposition up to a maximum amount of $250,000 of *taxable* capital gains.

The general rule is that a corporation must use more than 50 per cent of the fair market value of its assets directly in an active business carried on primarily in Canada throughout the required holding period.

A "small business corporation" is a Canadian-controlled private corporation where all or substantially all of the fair market value of its assets is attributable to assets that are:[76]

- Used in an active business carried on primarily in Canada;

- Shares or debt of one or more small business corporations connected with it; or

- Used in a combination of the above.

---

[72]Subs. 125(7)"personal services business"(c), (d).

[73]*Hughes & Co Holdings Ltd. v. M.N.R.*, [1994] 2 C.T.C. 170, 94 D.T.C. 6511 (F.C.T.D.) (more than five employees means at least six employees). The employees must be full-time employees.

[74]Para. 18(1)(p).

[75]Subs. 110.6(2.1).

[76]Subs. 248(1)"small business corporation".

Thus, a holding company or an operating company can qualify as a "small business corporation".

The Act does not define the phrase "all or substantially all". The CRA's view is that "substantially all" means that the corporation uses at least 90 per cent of its assets in a qualifying activity.

There are two additional holding period tests to claim the exemption:[77]

- An individual who claims the exemption (or a person or partnership related to the individual) must have owned the shares throughout the period of 24 months immediately prior to their disposition; and

- Throughout the minimum holding period of 24 months preceding the disposition of the shares, more than 50 per cent of the fair market value of the corporation's assets must be attributable to assets used directly or indirectly in an active business.

Where a corporation holds shares or debt of connected corporations, the shares or debt also qualify as active business assets of the corporation if they satisfy two conditions: a holding period test and an active business test. These conditions are similar to those that apply to shares of the corporation held directly by an individual.

1. — New Corporations

Shares issued from a corporation's treasury must also be held for the full 24-month holding period if the shareholder intends to claim the capital gains exemption. The 24-month holding period restriction does not apply, however, to new issues of treasury shares if the shares are issued:[78]

- As consideration for other shares;

- On a transfer of all or substantially all of the assets used in active business;

- On a transfer of certain active partnership interests; or

- As payment of a stock dividend.

Thus, shareholders of newly-incorporated small business corporations may claim the exemption for QSBC shares even though the corporation has been in existence for less than 24 months. For example, a sole proprietor can transfer an active business carried on in Canada

---

[77]Subs. 110.6(1)"qualified small business corporation share".

[78]Para. 110.6(14)(f).

to a corporation in exchange for its shares and then dispose of the shares to claim the capital gains exemption.[79]

2. — Purifying a Small Business Corporation

The exemption in respect of QSBC shares is generous, and it is important that Canadian-controlled private corporations not go offside by holding non-qualifying assets. There are various ways to purify a corporation that might not otherwise qualify as a "small business corporation". For example, an offside corporation can:

- Distribute its non-qualifying assets to its shareholders as a taxable dividend prior to the disposition of its shares;

- Distribute non-qualifying assets as a dividend on a tax-free basis to the extent of its capital dividend account (a dividend out of the capital dividend account is tax-free without any adjustment to the adjusted cost base of the shares);

- Dispose of its non-qualifying assets to another corporation through a "butterfly" reorganization; or

- Transfer its shares to a holding company, with an election under section 85 to realize sufficient gains to fully absorb the $500,000 exemption. The exemption is then locked into the cost base of the holding company's shares.

XI. — Professional Corporations

Under various provincial corporate statutes (for example, the *Business Corporations Act* of Ontario (OBCA)), lawyers, accountants and doctors can incorporate their practices in professional corporations (PCs) and obtain significant tax advantages. However, shareholders of PCs cannot limit their liability for negligence or malpractice and remain jointly and severally liable for all professional liability claims against them. This makes the choice of form of practice an important decision. Large law and accounting partnerships are better off practising as limited liability partnerships (LLPs) in order to limit personal malpractice exposure. On the other hand, sole proprietors and smaller partnerships of two to four partners may be better off practising as PCs for the tax advantages.

The difference between the tax payable by incorporated and unincorporated law and accounting practices is significant. Since individuals pay tax on their business income at progressive marginal tax rates, the top tax rate in 2004 is about 46 per cent in Ontario starting at an income level of approximately $114,000. In contrast, the federal corporate rate of tax is about 13 per cent (approximately 18 per cent combined federal and provincial rates) on the

---

[79]S. 54.2.

first $300,000 of professional income. The 28 percentage point spread allows professionals to defer tax if they leave their income in the corporation. Since partners must share the $300,000 limit between themselves, the real benefits of incorporation will accrue only to sole practitioners and small partnerships.

Tax deferral is a real and substantial tax saving, which can accumulate into very significant amounts in the end.[80] The magnitude of any deferral depends upon the reinvestment rate and the length of time that the entity accumulates its income. Thus, professionals can use tax deferral as a surrogate pension plan. Assume, for example, that Nancy, age 35, manages to save $1,000 annually for 30 years in her PC, which, after tax, the corporation invests in securities that generate 10 per cent per year. After 30 years, Nancy extracts all of the corporation's accumulated investment profits and pays personal tax on the dividends at her top marginal rate (assume 46 per cent) at that time. If her net rate of tax after the dividend tax credit is 30 per cent, she will earn $4,026 more through her corporation than she would have earned personally without her PC. If she can save $50,000 each year in the PC, the comparative advantage of incorporation grows to $201,000.

A PC cannot carry on any business other than the practice of the profession of its shareholders. *All* of the shareholders of the PC must be members of the same profession: lawyers in the case of law firms, accountants in the case of accounting firms, etc. There can be no multi-disciplinary practices in a PC. A PC may, however, carry on any ancillary activities and can invest its surplus funds, including any cash saved from its deferred tax.

Since tax deferral is the key to planning with a PC, one should clearly understand the mathematics of the time value of money and discount rates in advising clients on corporate structures. Without tax deferral, there is no advantage to a PC. Indeed, there are distinct disadvantages in the form of higher costs in maintaining and operating a corporation.

Professionals with incomes above $300,000 pay corporate tax at a federal rate of approximately 22 per cent. Thus, in most cases, taxpayers should ensure that they do not leave more than $300,000 in the PC in the year. Although the tax system completely integrates corporate and personal taxes up to the $300,000, it penalizes income above that level by double taxing the income. Hence, professionals earning more than $300,000 per year are better off leaving no more than that amount taxable in the corporation. This will require considerable care. It will not be easy to simply bonus down the PC's net income as accountants sometimes do with regular business corporations. To bonus down the PC's income, the professional lawyer will have to be both a shareholder and employee of the corporation, which requires contortionist skills in a solo practice.

Professionals can also probably use a holding company (Holdco) to own the shares of a PC and siphon off professional earnings to the holding company through tax-free dividends. This will reduce shareholder risk in the PC and allow the saved cash to accumulate in Holdco. Unfortunately, the regulations to the OBCA are not entirely clear. Nevertheless,

---

[80]See Chapter 1 at Part XII for discussion of "The Time Value of Money".

both on policy and interpretational grounds, one can justify using a holding company to structure a PC. To be sure, there is no real risk in leaving surplus funds to be reinvested in the PC itself if the professional shareholder is fully and adequately insured against negligence. A Holdco, however, adds greater certainty to the structure.

Selected Bibliography to Chapter 20

General

Andersson, Krista, "Implications of Integrating Corporate and Shareholder Taxes" (1991) 50 Tax Notes 1523.

Birnie, David A.G., "Capping the Small Business Deduction", in *Proceedings of 35th Tax Conf.* 13 (Can. Tax Foundation, 1983).

Brookes, Geoff, and Vinneau, "Taxation: Downside Protection" (1992) 125 CA Magazine 53.

Couzin, Robert, "Business and Property Income", *Corp. Mgmt. Tax Conf.* 41 (Can. Tax Foundation, 1981).

Cranston, Ann M., "Bill C-17 and the Small Business Deduction" (1980) 54 Cost and Mgmt. 46.

Dent, Douglas Edward, *The Small Business Deduction and a Canadian Tax on Unreasonable Accumulations* (Vancouver: University of British Columbia, 1985).

Doane, H. Lawrence, "Income Tax Treatment of Specified Investment Business Income, Capital Gains Rollovers for Small Businesses and Business Investment Losses Under Bill C-17", in *Proceedings of 31st Tax Conf.* 106 (Can. Tax Foundation, 1979).

Farden, Eric N., *Income Tax for a Small Business* (E.N. Farden, 1985).

"Getting the Needle" (1981) 3 Can. Taxpayer 23.

Gillix, Marlene, "The New Small Business Tax Rules" (1984), 117:6 CA Magazine 72.

Graham, Douglas D., "Taxation of a Private Corporation", *B.C. Tax Conf.* 66 (Can. Tax Foundation, 1980).

Institute for Fiscal Studies, *Equity for Companies: A Corporation Tax for the 1990's — A Report of the IFS Capital Taxes Group* (London: Institute for Fiscal Studies, 1991).

Jones, David Phillip, "Further Reflections on Integration: The Modified Small Business Deduction, Non-qualifying Businesses, Specified Investment Income, Corporate Partnerships, and Personal Service Corporations" (1982) 30 Can. Tax J. 1.

Kennedy, Henry, "Tax Integration" (May 1990) 123 CA Magazine 43.

Larter, Ronald W., "The Small Business Deduction, Corporate Partnerships, Personal and Facility Corporations and Other Related Matters", *B.C. Tax Conf.* 101 (Can. Tax Foundation, 1981).

Louis, David, *How to Make More Money Out of Your Company With Less Tax* (Toronto: Hume, 1984).

McQuillan, Peter, "Investment Income and Active Business Income Earned by an Individual and Through a Corporation: A Comparative Analysis, 1987-1988", in *Proceedings of 39th Tax Conf.* 12:1 (Can. Tax Foundation, 1987).

O'Brien, Martin L., "Carrying on Business in Canada" (1985) 1 Can. Current Tax J-111.

"Round Table Discussion — Tax Problems of Small Business", in *Proceedings of 33rd Tax Conf.* 342 (Can. Tax Foundation, 1981).

Shead, Richard G., "The 1978 Tax Changes Affecting Family Farms and Small Businesses", in *Proceedings of 30th Tax Conf.* 275 (Can. Tax Foundation, 1978).

Shinder, Bernard, "The Taxation of Small Business: An Historical and Technical Overview" (1984) 32 Can. Tax J. 1.

"Simplifying Tax for Small Business", Budget Papers (1984), Department of Finance, Canada.

Small Business Taxation, Audio Archives of Canada, 1984.

Strain, William J., "Integration Revisited", in *Proceedings of 38th Tax Conf.* 9:1 (Can. Tax Foundation, 1986).

Taxation of a Private Corporation (Deloitte, Haskins & Sells, 1981).

Tax Minimization Strategies for Small Business (Toronto: Insight Educational Services, 1983).

Yin, George K., "A Different Approach to the Taxation of Corporate Distributions: Theory and Implementation of a Uniform Corporate — Level Distributions Tax" (1990) 78 Georgetown L.J. 1837.

Canadian-Controlled Private Corporations

"Active Business Income: A Retroactive Break!" (1980) 2 Can. Taxpayer 83.

Andersson, Krista, "Implications of Integrating Corporate and Shareholder Taxes" (1991) 50 Tax Notes 1523.

Beach, Wayne G., and Mark F. Wheeler, "Associated Corporations", in *Proceedings of 40th Tax Conf.* 10:1 (Can. Tax Foundation, 1988).

Berand, Daniel, "Corporations associées — Les nouvelles r;agegles de jeu" (1989) 37 Can. Tax J. 37.

Bowden, Gregory T.W., "Associated Corporations — A New Test?" (1986) 44 Advocate (Van.) 391.

Bowden, Gregory T.W., "Associated Corporations: Recent Developments", in *Proceedings of 38th Tax Conf.* 40:1 (Can. Tax Foundation, 1986).

Brookes, Geoff, and Vinneau, "Taxation: Downside Protection" (1992) 125 CA Magazine 53.

Colley, Geoffrey, "Small Business Deduction Rules Revisited" (1981) 114:12 CA Magazine 46.

Drache, A.B.C., "Pre-Mortem Planning" (1991) 13 Can. Taxpayer 86.

Glover, Paul, "CCPC's May Lose Low Tax Rate" (April 1988) 62 CMA Magazine 46.

Hierlihy, Thomas G., "Planning to Maximize the Tax Saving from the Small Business Deduction", in *Proceedings of 32nd Tax Conf.* 174 (Can. Tax Foundation, 1980).

Hogg, R.D., "Stock Option Benefits in Canadian-Controlled Private Corporations" (1978) 26 Can. Tax J. 85.

Hugget, Donald R., "The $500,000 Exemption — Fact or Fiction" (1990) 17 Can. Tax News 79.

Lemon, K.W., "Small Business Deduction" (1979) 44 Bus. Q. 18, 85.

Lewin, Richard, "Income Tax Planning and the Rules of Association", in *Proceedings of 39th Tax Conf.* 32:1 (Can. Tax Foundation, 1987).

Mandel, Jeffrey, "New Life for the Small Business Deduction — The Dividend Straddle" (1981) 3 Can. Taxpayer 129.

McCallum, J. Thomas, "Choosing the Right End" (1991) 25 CGA Magazine 20.

Nathason, David C., "Active Versus Passive Once Again: Active Business Income and Investment Income of Canadian-Controlled Private Corporations", in *Proceedings of 33rd Tax Conf.* 908 (Can. Tax Foundation, 1981).

Nolke, David G., "All in the (Corporate) Family" (1991) 25 CGA Magazine 16.

Nolke, David G., *Income Taxes and the CCPC* (Vancouver: CGA Canada, 1993).

Quinton, Cathy, "The Additional Capital Gains Exemption" (December — January 1989) 62 CMA Magazine 47.

Stack, Thomas J., "Capital Gains and Losses on Shares of Private Corporations", in *Proceedings of 39th Tax Conf.* 17:1 (Can. Tax Foundation, 1987).

Strain, W.J., "The Small Business Rules: 'O What a Tangled Web...!'", in *Proceedings of 34th Tax Conf.* 53 (Can. Tax Foundation, 1982).

Tremblay, Richard G., "Active Business Income" (1992) 3 Can. Current Tax 47.

Ulmer, John M., "Family Members as Shareholders of a Small Business Corporation", in *Proceedings of 38th Tax Conf.* 14:1 (Can. Tax Foundation, 1986).

Yin, George K., "A Different Approach to the Taxation of Corporate Distributions: Theory and Implementation of a Uniform Corporate-Level Distributions Tax" (1990) 78 Georgetown L.J. 1837.

Corporate Control

Chyfetz, Bill and Don Jakubowicz, *Associated Corporations in Canada* (Toronto: CCH Canadian, 1992).

Corn, George, "Control — De Jure or De Facto?" (August 1990) 3:8 Can. Current Tax J-43.

"Corporate Control: A Judicially Enacted De Facto Test?" (1990) 44 D.T.C. 7023.

Drache, A.B.C., "Controlling a Company Without Shares" (1992) 14 Can. Taxpayer 56.

Eng, Susan, "The Arm's Length Rules", in *Proceedings of 40th Tax Conf.* 13:1 (Can. Tax Foundation, 1988).

Glover, Paul, "Changes in Control — Corporate Taxpayers Beware" (1988) 62 CMA Magazine 42.

Halpern, Jack V., "Determination of Control for the Purposes of Being a 'CCPC'" (1990) 38 Can. Tax J. 942.

Hiseler, Gregory R., "Corporate Control", in *Proceedings of 40th Tax Conf.* 12:1 (Can. Tax Foundation, 1988).

Hugget, Donald R., "$500,000 Exemption (The) — Fact or Fiction" (1990) 17 Can. Tax News 79.

Hugget, Donald R., "Guilt By Association" (1990) 14 Can. Tax News 103.

Jerrold, J., "How to Assess the Value of Deferral" (1989) 67 Taxes 384.

Krishna, Vern, "The Power of Influence" (February 1990) 24 CGA Magazine 48.

Moskowitz, Evelyn P., "Dealing at Arm's Length: A Question of Fact", in *Proceedings of 39th Tax Conf.* 33:1 (Can. Tax Foundation, 1987).

Sheffield, Jeffrey T., "Holding Company Formations" (1986) 64 Taxes 846.

Wikenfeld, David, "Taxation: Tenuous Connections" (1991) 124 CA Magazine 32.

Personal Services Business Income

Batten, L.J. Dick, "Personal Services Business", *Prairie Provinces Tax Conf.* 101 (Can. Tax Foundation, 1983).

Krishna, Vern, "Personal Services Business Income" (1983) 17:10 CGA Magazine 31.

Small Business Corporations

Boehmer, G.C., "Small Business Corporations: Capital Gains Planning Opportunities and Pitfalls" (1987) 35 Can. Tax J. 987.

Durnford, John W., "Profits on the Sale of Shares: Capital Gains or Business Income — A Fresh Look at Irrigation Industries" (1987) 35 Can. Tax J. 837.

Hayos, Gabriel J., "The Capital Gains Exemption: Planning Strategies to Meet the Criterion of a 'Qualified Small Business Corporation'", in *Proceedings of 40th Tax Conf.* 15:1 (Can. Tax Foundation, 1988).

Howick, Wallace M., "Assets Versus Shares: An Approach to the Alternatives", *Corp. Mgmt. Tax Conf.* 1:1 (Can. Tax Foundation, 1990).

Hugget, Donald R., "The $500,000 Exemption — Fact or Fiction" (1990) 17 Can. Tax News 79.

"Personal Tax Planning — Small Business Corporations — Capital Gains Planning Opportunities and Pitfalls" (1987) 35 Can. Tax J. 987.

Quinton, Cathy, "The Additional Capital Gains Exemption" (December — January 1989) 62 CMA Magazine 47.

Sider, Vance A., "Corporate Restructuring Issues: Public Corporations", *Corp. Mgmt. Tax Conf.* 6:1 (Can. Tax Foundation, 1990).

Stack, Thomas J., "Capital Gains and Losses on Shares of Private Corporations", in *Proceedings of 39th Tax Conf.* 17:1 (Can. Tax Foundation, 1987).

Tam, Anthony, "Capital Gains Exemption: Small Business Corporations" (1987–89) 2 Can. Current Tax P-5.

Truster, Perry, "The Capital Gains Exemption", in *Proceedings of 41st Tax Conf.* 12:1 (Can. Tax Foundation, 1989).

Ward, David A., and John M. Ulmer, "Corporate Taxation: Shares Eligible for the Capital Gains Exemption" (1986) 5 Legal Alert 81.

"Workshop: Capital Gains Exemption and Small Business Corporation Shares", in *Proceedings of 41st Tax Conf.* 46:1 (Can. Tax Foundation, 1989).

Other

Anderson, Eric W., "Owner-Manager Remuneration", in *Proceedings of the 38th Tax Conf.* 11 (Can. Tax Foundation, 1986).

Barbacki, Richard, "Estate Freezing in the Light of Recent Income Tax Changes", in *Proceedings of 38th Tax Conf.* 36 (Can. Tax Foundation, 1986).

Beith, Robert M., Scott Brown, Claude McDonald and George Venner, "Revenue Canada Round Table/Table ronde de Revenu Canada", in *Proceedings of 38th Tax Conf.* 51 (Can. Tax Foundation, 1986).

Bernstein, Jack, "Family Succession", in *Proceedings of the 38th Tax Conf.* (Can. Tax Foundation, 1986).

Birnie, David A.G., "Consolidation of Corporate Structures", in *Proceedings of 31st Tax Conf.* 177 (Can. Tax Foundation, 1979).

Boultbee, J.A., "Minimizing the Taxation Effects of Dividends", in *Proceedings of 37th Tax Conf.* 7 (Can. Tax Foundation, 1985).

Brender, Mark, "The De Minimis Dividend Test under Subsection 110.6(8) — Part 1" (1993) 41 Can. Tax J. 808.

Brender, Mark, "The De Minimis Dividend Test under Subsection 110.6(8) — Part 2" (1993) 41 Can. Tax J. 1034.

Brown, Catharine A., "Spouse Trusts", in *Proceedings of 38th Tax Conf.* 37 (Can. Tax Foundation, 1986).

Corn, George, "Interest Income — Foreign Accrual Property Income or Income from an Active Business", (1990-2) Can. Current Tax J141.

Cullity, Maurice C., "The Capital Gains Exemption: Implications for Estate Planning", in *Proceedings of 37th Tax Conf.* 18 (Can. Tax Foundation, 1985).

Dulude, Louise, "Taxation of the Spouses: A Comparison of Canadian, American, British, French, and Swedish Law" (1985) 23 Osgoode Hall L.J. 67.

Halpern, Jeffrey N., "The Last Word on Management Companies... Or Is It?" (1984) 6 Can. Taxpayer 25.

Minzberg, Samuel, "Income Splitting Still Alive?", in *Proceedings of 38th Tax Conf.* 35 (Can. Tax Foundation, 1986).

Peters, Steven, "Enhancing the Exemption" (1992) 125 CA Magazine 33.

Potvin, Jean, "The Capital Gains Deduction for Qualified Small Business Corporation Shares Revisited", in *Proceedings of 44th Tax Conference* 5:50 (Can. Tax Foundation, 1992).

Provenzano, Louis J., "The Impact of Escalating Provincial Individual Income Tax Rates on an Owner-manager's Decision to Earn Income Directly or through a Corporation", in *Proceedings of 45th Tax Conference* 33:1 (Can. Tax Foundation, 1993).

Reid, R.J., "Tax Implications of a Change in Control" (1984) Income Tax Aspects 84.

Ross, David W., "Incorporation and Capitalization of a Private Corporation", in *Proceedings of 39th Tax Conf.* 11:1 (Can. Tax Foundation, 1987).

Ruby, Stephen S., "A Glimpse at the Lifetime Capital Gains Exemption (Part I)" (1986) 3:12 Bus. & L. 93.

Ruby; Stephen S., "A Glimpse at the Lifetime Capital Gains Exemption (Part III)" (1987) 4:1 Bus. & L. 6.

Stack, T.J., "Corporate Partnerships: Non-Qualifying Business and Related Topics", *Prairie Provinces Tax Conf.* 189 (Can. Tax Foundation, 1981).

Tremblay, Richard, "Active Business Income," (1990-2) Can. Current Tax P45.

"The Taxation of Corporate Reorganizations — The New Part II.1 Tax" (1987) 35 Can. Tax J. 1292.

Weyman, C. David, "Manufacturing and Processing, Valuations and Business Deductions Including Capital Cost Allowances", in *Proceedings of 32nd Tax Conf.* 254 (Can. Tax Foundation, 1980).

Wilson, Brian, "Buy-Sell Agreements", in *Proceedings of 39th Tax Conf.* 16:1 (Can. Tax Foundation, 1987).

CHAPTER 21 — CORPORATE DISTRIBUTIONS

I. — General Comment

The tax system tightly regulates corporate distributions to ensure that there is no leakage of taxes. Generally, most corporate income is taxed twice: first, at the corporate level and then again in the hands of shareholders. Corporate capital, however, can be returned to shareholders on a tax-free basis.

A corporation can distribute its property to the owners and managers of the business through:

- Wages and salary;

- Employee loans;

- Dividends;

- Capital distributions;

- Shareholder benefits; or

- Shareholder loans.

Wages, salary, and employee loans are taxable as employment source income (see Chapter 6, "Employment Income"). In this chapter we look at the other two methods of distributing corporate profits: dividends and capital distributions. Shareholder benefits and loans are taxable under special rules discussed in Chapter 22, "Shareholder Taxation".

II. — Dividends

There are two competing tax policy interests: (1) distributions from corporate income should be taxable in the shareholder's hands; and (2) income should not be subject to double taxation. The resolution of these two competing policy objectives poses a particularly vexing problem in the context of corporate and shareholder taxation. Since a corporation is a legal entity for tax purposes, it is taxable in its own right separate and apart from any tax payable by its shareholders on distributed income. In economic terms, however, the principle of tax neutrality requires us to consider both the form and substance of shareholder interests.

Take a simple case: *Opco*, a wholly-owned subsidiary of *Holdco*, earns $100 on which it pays tax at 45 per cent; it then pays a dividend of $55 to *Holdco*. Should *Holdco* pay tax at 45 per cent on its dividend income of $55? Suppose that *Holdco* distributes its income to its sole shareholder, an individual. Should the shareholder pay tax again at 45 per cent on its dividend income of $55? How many times should we tax the income as it passes through a chain of corporations all owned by the same ultimate owners?

How do we reconcile the principle that we tax corporations as independent entities with the principle that we want to avoid double taxation of income? There are different approaches to this problem. At one extreme, a corporation is a completely separate entity without any regard to its shareholdings. In this model we tax corporations and their shareholders on their respective income without any consideration for their inter-linked economic interests. Under this model (the "classical system"), the principle of full taxation of income overcomes the principle of avoiding double taxation.

But even classical system countries usually accommodate closely-held corporations.[1] The rationale of these exceptions is to encourage commercial enterprises by permitting them to enjoy the benefits of limited liability without suffering double taxation of profits. For example, the United States, which follows the classical system, allows for a flow-through of income for its Subchapter S corporations. These corporations are fiscally transparent and the Code treats them, in effect, on the same basis as partnerships.

At the other extreme, we have the full imputation system, which treats a corporation as a fiscal transparency and all income taxes that it pays are creditable to its shareholders when it distributes its profits as dividends. Thus, under this theory, for tax purposes, a corporation is a conduit for its shareholders. Of course, the corporation remains a separate legal entity for business and commercial purposes.

Then there is the third alternative, a compromise that lies between the two extremes of the classical and full imputation systems. Canada, not unpredictably, adopts the compromise. Canada uses a notional imputation system that allows shareholders a credit for corporate taxes, but in fixed amounts.

---

[1] For example, the United States.

The following example illustrates the theoretical differences between the classical system, full imputation of corporate profits at the shareholder level, and a partial imputation of corporate taxes to shareholders.

Example			
Assume:			
Corporate tax rate:	45%		
Shareholder's marginal tax rate:	40%		
Corporate net income for tax purposes:	$1,000		
Shareholder credit for corporate tax:	0%	100%	50%
Then:	Classical System	Full Imputation	Part Imputation
Taxation of Corporations:	$	$	$
Net income	1000	1000	1000
Corporate tax	450	450	450
Net income after tax	550	550	550
Taxation of Shareholder:			
Dividend received (Gross)	550	550	550
Credit for corporate tax paid	0	450	225
Taxable amount	550	1000	775
Shareholder tax	220	400	310
Net Amount to Shareholder	330	600	465
Total Corporate/Shareholder Tax	670	400	535

This example illustrates how punitive the classical system can be and why countries that adopt such a system provide for some form of relief for closely-held corporations. The above comparison assumes that the corporate tax rate is the same in all three systems. In fact, it is quite unlikely that a full imputation system will levy corporate tax at the same rate as under a classical system. Countries that use a classical system of taxation typically have a lower rate of corporate tax to accommodate the burden of double taxation for shareholders. Thus, they indirectly lower the burden of double taxation.

Canada uses a partial imputation system of corporate taxation that takes into account four factors in the taxation of dividends:

- Type of shareholder;

- Status of the payer corporation;

- Source of the underlying income from which the corporation pays the dividend; and

- Type of share on which the dividend is paid.

OVERVIEW OF TAXATION OF DIVIDEND INCOME RECIPIENT			
PAYING CORPORATION	**RESIDENT INDIVIDUAL**	**RESIDENT CORPORATION**	**NON-RESIDENT TAXPAYER**
TAXABLE CANADIAN CORPORATION	Grossed-up value of dividend included in income. Individual entitled to dividend tax credit. Para. 82(1)(b), s. 121	Dividend included in income [para. 12(1)(j)] and then deducted in computing taxable income [subs. 112(1)].	25% withholding tax on taxable dividends and capital gains. Rate may be reduced by treaty. Subs. 212(2)
NON-RESIDENT CORPORATION THAT IS NOT A FOREIGN AFFILIATE	Dividend received included in income: s. 90. Credit for foreign taxes paid: subs. 126(1).	Dividend received included in income: s. 90. See also subs. 15(4) and 93(1)	N/A
FOREIGN AFFILIATE	Dividend received included in income: s. 90; deduction for portion of dividend paid out of taxable surplus — subs. 91(5). Foreign tax credit.	Divided received included in income: s. 90; deduction for dividends paid out of taxable surplus: subs. 91(5) and exempt surplus: s. 113(1)	N/A

The source of income (business or investment) from which a corporation pays a dividend is also an important determinant, particularly in the case of dividends from a foreign affiliate. The focus of this chapter is on dividends that resident corporations pay to resident shareholders. We discuss foreign source income in Chapter 31.

1. — Meaning of "Dividend"

The Act does not define the term "dividend".[2] In common law, a dividend is a share of profits that a corporation allocates to its shareholders.[3] Dividends may be paid in cash, shares, or other kinds of property.[4]

2. — Types of Dividends

A dividend is an appropriation of corporate assets pursuant to a resolution of the corporation's board of directors or a shareholders' agreement. The declaration and payment of a dividend creates legal rights and obligations, both under corporate law and tax law.

Whether a payment constitutes a dividend is a question of fact and law. A corporation cannot simply recharacterize its payments. For example, where a corporation pays salary to a shareholder, it cannot retroactively "convert" the salary into a dividend through bookkeeping journal entries.[5]

(a) — Cash

A cash dividend is usually paid by a cheque drawn upon the corporation. The face amount of the dividend is the amount used to compute the shareholder's income.

(b) — Stock

A stock dividend is a *pro rata* distribution of additional shares by a corporation to its shareholders without any additional subscription of cash or other property for the shares.[6] Stock dividends are usually paid to shareholders in lieu of cash dividends when the corporation has its cash invested in or earmarked for business operations.

---

[2]Subs. 248(1)"dividend" (definition merely restricts meaning of word in certain circumstances).

[3]The legality of a dividend is a mixed question of fact and law; see, e.g., *Canada Business Corporations Act*, R.S.C. 1985, c. C-44, s. 42.

[4]See, e.g., *Canada Business Corporations Act* ("CBCA"), subs. 43(1).

[5]*Adam v. M.N.R.*, [1985] 2 C.T.C. 2383, 85 D.T.C. 667 (T.C.C.).

[6]See *Income Tax Act*, subs. 248(1)"stock dividend".

(c) — In Kind

Dividends may also be paid in kind.[7] A dividend paid in property (other than cash or a stock dividend) is valued at the fair market value of the property.[8]

III. — Resident Individuals

The taxation of dividends paid to resident individuals depends upon two factors: (1) status of the payer corporation; and (2) source of the underlying income from which the dividend is paid. Depending on these factors, dividends may be taxable or non-taxable to shareholders. Dividends paid out of a corporation's income are taxable to individual shareholders. Dividends paid out of the "capital dividend account" are generally not taxable to shareholders.

1. — From Taxable Canadian Corporations

A "taxable dividend" is any dividend other than a tax-exempt or tax-deferred dividend.[9]

(a) — Imputation of Corporate Taxes

We saw earlier that Canada uses a partial imputation system to prevent double taxation of corporate taxes. An individual who receives a taxable dividend from a taxable Canadian corporation must include 125 per cent of the amount received in his or her income.[10] For example, an individual who receives $80 as a dividend must include $100 in income. The extra 25 per cent included in income is referred to as the dividend "gross-up".

The gross-up is a *notional* amount that in theory represents the tax (or part thereof) that the corporation previously paid. The gross-up is included in the individual's income, so that in theory the individual is taxable on some *pre-tax* equivalent of the corporation's income. A gross-up rate of 25 per cent implies that the corporation paid 20 per cent in taxes.

The individual then pays tax on the grossed-up amount of the dividend at his or her personal tax rate, but claims a credit for taxes that the corporation paid.[11] The federal "dividend tax credit" is equal to 2/3 of the federal gross-up — that is, 2/3 of 25 per cent. The average provincial dividend tax credit is about 1/3 of the federal gross-up — that is, 1/3 of 25 per

---

[7]See, e.g., CBCA, subs. 43(1); see also *Income Tax Act*, subs. 248(1)"property".

[8]*Income Tax Act*, subs. 52(2).

[9]Subs. 89(1)"taxable dividend".

[10]Paras. 12(1)(j), 82(1)(b).

[11]S. 121.

cent.[12] Therefore, where the provincial dividend tax credit is at least 1/3 of the federal gross-up, the combined federal-provincial dividend tax credit is effectively worth the full amount of the gross-up. Thus, the gross-up and the dividend tax credit impute the corporation's taxes to the shareholder, who is then credited with the taxes. This mechanism alleviates double taxation and integrates corporate and shareholder taxes. The following example illustrates the theoretical model of tax integration.

Example

Assume:

Federal corporate tax rate	12.00%
Provincial corporate tax rate	8.00 %
Combined federal/provincial tax rate	20.00%
Shareholder federal/provincial marginal rate	40.00%
Dividend gross-up	25.00%
Active business income	$100

Then:

Corporate Tax:

Active business income	$	100
Corporate tax (federal/provincial)		20
Net income after tax (paid as dividend)	$	80

Shareholder tax:

Dividend received	$	80
Gross-up @ 25%		20
Taxable grossed-up amount	$	100

Tax thereon:

Combined federal/provincial tax	$	40
Dividend tax credit (combined)		(20)
Net tax payable	$	20

---

[12]See Appendix I.

Example

Net cash retained	$	60
Amount retained if dividend earned personally	$	60
Tax saving		0

Under a full imputation model, an individual would pay the same amount of tax, whether the individual received the income directly or indirectly through a corporation. Thus, the theoretical model provides full imputation, but only if the underlying assumptions apply.

The federal dividend tax credit is a constant percentage (2/3) of the gross-up. Therefore, the value of the dividend tax credit increases as the marginal rate of tax decreases. In the following example, the federal dividend tax credit is a constant $167 in each case, whatever the federal tax rate. Hence, the *effective* rate of tax on dividends drops at a faster rate than the marginal rate of tax.

Example

Assume:

An individual receives a dividend of $1,000 from a taxable Canadian corporation.
The individual is taxable at a federal marginal rate in

Case A @	29%
Case B @	26%
Case C @	22%
Case D @	16%

Assume also:

The provincial tax rate is half of the federal tax rate.
The provincial dividend tax credit (DTC) is 1/3 of the federal gross-up.

Then (ignoring provincial surtaxes) the tax payable on the dividend in each case is as follows:

	Case A	Case B	Case C	Case D
Dividend received	$ 1,000	$ 1,000	$ 1,000	$ 1,000
Gross-up @ 25%	250	250	250	250
Taxable amount	$ 1,250	$ 1,250	$ 1,250	$ 1,250

Example				
Tax thereon:				
Federal marginal rate	29%	26%	22%	16%
Federal tax (before fed. DTC)	$ 363	$ 325	$ 275	$ 200
Federal DTC	(167)	(167)	(167)	(167)
Basic federal tax	$ 196	$ 158	$ 108	$ 33
Provincial tax (before prov. DTC)	$ 181	$ 162	$ 137	$ 100
Provincial DTC	(83)	(83)	(83)	(83)
Provincial tax	$ 98	$ 79	$ 54	$ 17
Combined fed./prov. taxes	$ 294	$ 237	$ 162	$ 50
Effective tax rate on dividend income	29%	24%	16%	5%

2. — From Non-Resident Corporations

The structure of taxation of dividends from non-resident corporations is quite different from that which applies to dividends from taxable Canadian corporations. Dividends from non-resident corporations are included in income.[13] There is a less compelling case, however, to integrate the tax paid by a non-resident corporation with the tax payable by its resident shareholders. After all, the tax paid by the corporation is paid to a foreign government.

The principal purpose of the structure in respect of foreign source dividends is to prevent double taxation rather than to integrate corporate and shareholder taxes. Thus, the Act allows resident shareholders a credit for foreign taxes that they pay on foreign dividends.[14] But the foreign tax credit cannot exceed the rate of Canadian tax that would have been payable on the foreign income had a resident taxpayer earned the income in Canada. Thus, Canada does not subsidize foreign governments by allowing Canadian residents to claim a credit for foreign taxes levied at a rate higher than that prevailing in Canada at the relevant time.

The taxation of dividends from non-resident corporations that qualify as foreign affiliates is more complicated. For present purposes, it is sufficient to note that an individual who receives a dividend from a foreign affiliate must include the dividend in income, but may claim a deduction to the extent that the dividend is paid out of the affiliate's "taxable sur-

---

[13]Para. 12(1)(k), s. 90.

[14]S. 126.

plus". The individual may also claim a credit for foreign taxes withheld at source from the dividend.[15]

IV. — Inter-Corporate Dividends

1. — General Comment

Three factors determine the taxation of inter-corporate dividends:

   1. Status of the payer corporation;

   2. Type of share on which the dividend is paid; and

   3. Source of income from which the dividend is paid.

Inter-corporate dividends on common shares paid by a taxable Canadian corporation to a resident corporation are tax-free.[16] This rule prevents multiple taxation of income. Absent this rule, inter-corporate dividends that pass through a chain of corporations would be taxed in each corporation. Thus, the Act restricts the exemption from tax to taxable dividends.

2. — "Taxable Dividend"

"Taxable dividends" includes dividends *other than*:[17]

   • Exempt dividends in respect of which the paying corporation has made an election;[18] or

   • Qualifying dividends[19] paid by public corporations to certain shareholders.

3. — Deduction for Taxable Dividends

Dividends on common shares are not taxable under Part I. The exemption from tax results from two separate provisions: (1) taxable dividends are initially included in calculating *net* income; and (2) the corporation can then deduct the amount of the dividend in calculating its

---

[15]See Chapter 16, "Computation of Tax Payable".

[16]Paras. 12(1)(j), 112(1)(a).

[17]Subs. 89(1)"taxable dividend".

[18]Subs. 83(2).

[19]Subs. 83(1).

taxable income. The combined effect of the two provisions is that inter-corporate taxable dividends from Canadian corporations are not taxable under Part I of the Act.

Example

Assume:

A resident corporation receives taxable dividends of $20,000 from taxable Canadian corporations. The corporation has net business income of $100,000 from other sources, and makes a charitable donation of $90,000.

Ignoring other deductions, the corporation's taxable income is calculated as follows:

Income from business	$ 100,000
Add: Taxable dividends	20,000
Net income	120,000
Deduct:	
Charitable donations	
(Max. deduction [75% x $120,000])	(90,000)
Inter-corporate dividends	(20,000)
Taxable income	$ 10,000

This two-step process can have important implications. Although inter-corporate taxable dividends are, in effect, exempt from Part I tax, the inclusion of such dividends in net income can affect the computation of other deductions, e.g., charitable donations. In the above example, the ceiling for deductible charitable donations rises from $75,000 to $90,000 as a result of including $20,000 of taxable dividends in income.[20]

The deduction for inter-corporate taxable dividends applies only in respect of dividends from a "taxable Canadian corporation" or resident corporations that it controls.

A "taxable Canadian corporation" is a corporation that:[21]

• Resides in Canada;

---

[20]Para. 110.1(1)(a) (annual ceiling of 75 per cent of income for charitable donations made by corporations).

[21]Subs. 89(1)"Canadian corporation", "taxable Canadian corporation".

- Was incorporated in Canada;[22] and
- Is not exempt from Part I tax.[23]

4. — Restrictions on Deduction for Dividends

(a) — Policy Background

The policy underlying the rule that dividends between Canadian corporations should flow through on a tax-free basis is to avoid multiple taxation of income as it passes through a chain of corporations. Thus, the payer corporation pays the dividend with after-tax dollars and the payee corporation is exempted from tax on dividends that it receives from taxable Canadian corporations. In contrast, interest expense on debt obligations is deductible for tax purposes and must be included in the income of the recipient. This rule applies whether the taxpayer is an individual or a corporation.

The exemption of inter-corporate dividends from taxation can, however, also be used to reduce corporate tax. For example, for many years Canadian corporations found it attractive to invest in treasury shares of corporations with accumulated tax losses and unused deductions. The shares were usually preferred shares and came with a "guarantee" to pay a specified investment yield. Typically, the "loss corporation" would invest the money that it received on the issuance of its shares in Canadian treasury bills or similar interest-bearing securities. The accumulated losses and deductions would shelter the corporation's investment income from tax, and the *gross* income would be paid out as an inter-corporate dividend on a tax-free basis. In effect, the loss corporation's tax deductions were transferred indirectly to the profitable corporation through the use of secured preferred shares. These shares (which came to be known as "collateralized preferred shares") were, in effect, more like debt securities with a guaranteed return than equity investments.

(b) — Dividends on Collateralized Preferred Shares

Subsection 112(2.4) prohibits the inter-corporate dividend deduction for dividends on collateralized preferred shares. Generally, subsection 112(2.4) denies the inter-corporate dividend deduction when:

- The issuance of the shares is part of a series of transactions that reduces the tax payable by a corporation on its investment income;

---

[22]If incorporated abroad, has been resident in Canada continuously since June 18, 1971.

[23]Except for para. 149(1)(t).

- The proceeds obtained from the issuance of the shares are used to earn passive property income; and

- The financing transaction and the issuance of shares are structured in such a way that the profitable (investor) corporation's equity interest in the loss corporation is secured.

Subsection 112(2.4) is an anti-avoidance rule: it applies only where preferred shares are structured so that they resemble secured debt with a guaranteed return and where the purpose of the transaction is to reduce the tax that would otherwise be payable on passive investment income such as interest income.[24]

(c) — Term Preferred Shares

We saw in Chapter 18, "Corporate Finance", that preferred shares are sometimes used as a form of after-tax financing by certain issuers. The attraction of term preferred shares also stems from the different treatment of dividends and interest under the Canadian income tax system.

Generally, a corporate debtor can deduct its interest expense and the creditor pays tax on its interest income. In contrast, a corporation pays dividends with after-tax dollars. The tax system, however, provides special relief for dividends paid by taxable Canadian corporations. This system works well as long as the assumptions upon which the system is based are valid. Thus, the system functions efficiently if the corporation that pays the dividend has, in fact, paid corporate tax on the income from which it pays the dividend. In these circumstances, the dividend tax credit for individuals reflects previously paid corporate taxes.

There are, however, significant advantages at the expense of the tax system if the payer corporation has not paid tax on its income. Many taxable corporations that are quite profitable do not pay tax because they take advantage of tax incentives and deductions. These corporations can use preferred shares as a form of after-tax financing.

The following example illustrates the advantage of after-tax financing using preferred shares. Assume that a corporation with a tax rate of 40 per cent borrows $1,000 from another corporation and pays interest at the rate of 10 per cent per year. The interest expense is deductible for income tax purposes, and the borrower's aftertax cost of the interest payment is only $60. The lending corporation earns $100 of interest income, on which it pays tax of $40. Thus, the lending corporation's net after-tax income is $60. Since the $100 interest income exactly matches the $100 interest expense deduction, the tax system is neutral.

If, however, we restructure the $1,000 financing as equity financing instead of debt financing, the borrower might be able to reduce its cost of funds to, say, $80 of dividends, and forgo the greater tax deduction associated with an interest payment. This option would be

---

[24]See also: subs. 112(2.5).

particularly attractive if the borrower was not a taxable corporation. Since inter-corporate dividends are deductible in computing taxable income, the recipient's after-tax return would be $80. Thus, both parties benefit from the arrangement: the borrower's net cost of funds is reduced by $20 and the recipient's after-tax return is increased by $20. Only the public treasury suffers.

This is accomplished through the substitution of so-called "equity financing" for debt financing. The system is even more attractive to the lending corporation if the equity that it receives for its funds contains guarantees that, in effect, give the share capital all of the security of debt capital. The corporation will then benefit, from both the security of debt financing and the tax advantages of equity capital.

The Act contains several different provisions that prevent after-tax financing through the use of preferred shares. The provisions ensure that dividends are paid, at least indirectly, from tax-paid earnings. The Act achieves this result by levying a special tax on the issuer of dividends paid on taxable preferred shares and a special tax on certain shareholders who receive dividends on such shares.[25]

In addition to the special taxes paid on taxable preferred share dividends, the Act also denies the deduction for inter-corporate dividends to "specified financial institutions" that receive dividends on "term preferred shares".[26] The effect of this rule is that dividends that a specified financial institution receives on term preferred shares are taxable at normal corporate rates.

Generally, a share is a "term preferred share" if the holder of the share has the right to require *anyone* to redeem, acquire, cancel, or reduce the paid-up capital of the share, or if anyone provides a guarantee, security, or covenant with respect to the share.[27] This rule effectively taxes dividends in the same way as interest payments. The important difference, however, is that the amount paid to the "specified financial institution" is not considered to be "interest" and, as such, the amount is not deductible to the payer corporation.

A "specified financial institution" includes:[28]

- Banks;

- Corporations licensed to carry on business as trustees (trust corporations);

- Credit unions;

---

[25]Subs. 248(1)"taxable preferred share".

[26]See subs. 112(2.1).

[27]Subs. 248(1)"term preferred share".

[28]Subs. 248(1)"specified financial institution".

- Corporations whose principal business is the lending of money or the purchasing of debt obligations, and insurance corporations; and

- Corporations controlled by, or related to, any of the above.

V. — Stock Dividends And Stock Splits

A stock dividend involves a capitalization of corporate retained earnings into share capital.[29] A corporation can pay stock dividends by issuing shares of the same class as the shares on which the dividend is paid, or by issuing shares of another class. For example, a corporation can pay a stock dividend on its Class A shares by issuing more Class A shares on a *pro rata* basis to existing shareholders of that class or by issuing Class B shares.

In contrast, a stock split is merely a reduction in the *nominal* value of outstanding shares, accompanied by a *pro rata* increase in the number of shares issued. A stock split does not involve any capitalization of retained earnings. For example, a corporation with 100,000 outstanding shares trading at $200 per share may split each share into four, so that there will be 400,000 shares (worth approximately $50 per share) outstanding after the split. A stock split neither involves any substantive financial change in the corporation's position, nor does it generate any income tax consequences for the corporation or its shareholders.

1. — Accounting

A stock dividend does not alter the *total* equity of the corporation; it involves a transformation of one form of equity capital (retained earnings) into another (paid-up capital).[30] Although the CICA has not made any recommendation on the value to be assigned to a stock dividend, the preferred accounting treatment is to capitalize the market value of the dividend from retained earnings into stated capital. The Accounting Research Board in the U.S. supports this treatment.[31]

> The Committee therefore believes that where these circumstances exist the corporation should in the public interest account for the transaction by transferring from earned surplus to the category of permanent capitalization (represented by the capital stock and capital surplus accounts) an amount equal to the fair value of the additional shares issued.

Thus, in accounting terms, a corporation with 1,000,000 issued Class A shares (current market value of $50 per share) that declares a stock dividend of 20 per cent on its shares, should

---

[29]Subs. 248(1)"dividend", "stock dividend".

[30]Subs. 248(1)"amount".

[31]ARB No. 43, c. 7.

transfer $10,000,000 (that is, 20% × 1,000,000 × $50) from its retained earnings to the paid-up capital account of Class A.

2. — Taxable as Dividends

In financial terms, there is not really much difference between stock dividends and stock splits. Neither involves any substantive change in the financial equity of the corporation. In tax terms, however, stock dividends involve a capitalization of retained earnings into capital. Since capital can be distributed tax free, stock dividends are taxable in the same manner as cash dividends.[32] Otherwise, corporations could distribute their retained earnings indirectly without tax. Individuals must include the grossed-up value of the dividend in income, and may claim a tax credit.

3. — Cost Base of Shares

Stock dividends are taxed to shareholders in the same way as cash dividends. The cost of a stock dividend is equal to:[33]

- Its share of the amount capitalized from retained earnings into paid-up capital;[34] and

- Any amount included in the taxpayer's income as a benefit.[35]

The cost of the stock dividend is taken into account in calculating the average cost of identical shares held by the shareholder.[36]

VI. — Part II.1 Tax Of Corporate Distributions

1. — Anti-Avoidance Tax

A special anti-avoidance tax under Part II.1 applies only to publicly traded corporations.[37] The tax is intended to prevent individuals from converting dividend income into tax-free capital gains.

---

[32]Subs. 82(1); subs. 248(1)"dividend".

[33]Subs. 52(3).

[34]Subs. 248(1)"amount".

[35]Subs. 15(1.1).

[36]S. 47.

[37]See Part II.1 of the *Income Tax Act*.

Generally, where a corporation purchases its own shares from its shareholders, the shareholder is considered to have received a dividend to the extent the purchase price of the shares exceeds their paid-up capital. If, however, a shareholder sells shares to someone other than the corporation, the shareholder can realize a capital gain to the extent of the difference between the proceeds of disposition and the adjusted cost of the shares. This rule allows one to convert dividends into capital gains. For example, some public corporations issued stock dividends in redeemable preference shares instead of paying a cash dividend. The shares would have a nominal paid-up capital and a high redemption value. Thus, individuals were required to recognize only a very small taxable dividend. However, the shares had a substantial redemption price in excess of their paid-up capital and could be disposed of in the open market for a substantial capital gain. Consequently, individuals were effectively able to convert taxable dividends into tax-free capital gains.

The Part II.1 tax applies where it may reasonably be considered that proceeds of disposition have been paid by a corporation (or a person with whom it does not deal at arm's length) as a substitute for dividends that would otherwise have been paid in the normal course of the corporation's activities. In these circumstances, the corporation must pay a special tax of 45 per cent of the amount that can reasonably be considered to be a substitute for the dividends it would normally have paid.[38] The 45 per cent rate approximates the 29 per cent maximum federal rate of tax payable by individuals on dividend income.

The factors that determine whether the corporation would have paid a dividend in the "normal course" of its operations are:

- The corporation's past dividend policy;

- The amount of dividends paid for the current year; and

- Evidence of the corporation's intention to pay out other amounts instead of dividends.

2. — Stock Dividends

Subsection 183.1(3) provides a special rule for stock dividends that a corporation issues at fair market value. Where, as part of a transaction or series of transactions or events, a corporation purchases such shares, directly or indirectly, for an amount in excess of their paid-up capital, the excess is considered a "substitute for dividends" that would otherwise have been paid in the normal course of events by the corporation. Thus, any excess redemption value is taxed at an equivalent rate to that which would have been paid on a cash dividend.

---

[38]S. 183.1.

VII. — Dividends From Non-Resident Corporations

Dividends from non-resident corporations are generally taxable as income from property.[39] A resident corporation may, however, deduct a portion of dividends received from a non-resident corporation (other than a foreign affiliate), if:[40]

- The non-resident corporation has been carrying on a business in Canada continuously from June 18, 1971, to the date that the dividend is received; and
- The non-resident conducts its business through a permanent establishment in Canada.

This provision exempts from tax the portion of dividends paid to a resident corporation out of a non-resident's Canadian-source income that has borne Canadian tax.

The proportion of the dividend deductible by the resident corporate taxpayer in computing its taxable income is determined as follows:

$$\text{Total dividends received} \quad \times \quad \frac{\text{Payer's taxable income in Canada in preceding year}}{\substack{\text{Payer's worldwide taxable income in preceding year} \\ \text{if payer had been resident in Canada}}}$$

Example

In 2005, *ABC Ltd.*, a resident corporation, received a dividend of $10,000 from *NR Ltd.*, a non-resident corporation with a permanent establishment in Canada. In 2004, *NR Ltd.* derived $50,000 of its taxable income from carrying on business in Canada and earned worldwide taxable income of $200,000. The deductible portion of the dividend to *ABC Ltd.* is $2,500, determined as follows:

$$\$10,000 \quad \times \quad \frac{\$50,000}{\$200,000} \quad = \quad \$2,500$$

The definition of "permanent establishment" for the purpose of this subsection differs from the definition of "permanent establishment" in some of Canada's tax treaties. Therefore, it is possible that a non-resident corporation that has not paid Canadian income tax by virtue of

---

[39]Para. 12(1)(k).

[40]Subs. 112(2).

not having a permanent establishment in Canada can pay a dividend that qualifies for the inter-corporate dividend deduction.[41]

VIII. — Return Of Capital

1. — *Paid-Up Capital*

The paid-up capital (PUC) of shares is not taxable and can be returned to a shareholder on a tax-free basis. Thus, PUC is a shareholder's friend: it represents the maximum amount that can be returned on a tax-free basis as a return of capital. A return of capital in excess of the paid-up capital of shares triggers a deemed dividend and affects the adjusted cost base of the shares.[42]

The Act contains several rules that ensure that shareholders do not abuse the rule allowing for a tax-free return of capital. The rationale for these rules is to prevent a corporation from converting what would otherwise be taxable dividend income into a tax-free return of PUC.

The Act *deems* a resident corporation to have paid a dividend if the corporation:[43]

- Increases the paid-up capital of a class of its shares without a corresponding decrease in the paid-up capital of another class of its shares, an increase in its net assets or a decrease in its liabilities;

- Distributes property on its winding up, its discontinuance or the reorganization of its business in excess of the paid-up capital of its shares;

- Redeems, acquires, or cancels any of its shares and pays an amount in excess of the paid-up capital of its shares; or

- Reduces the paid-up capital of its shares by means other than the redemption or cancellation of its shares.

(a) — *Corporate Law*

We generally determine the paid-up capital of a class of shares according to the corporate law concept of stated capital.[44] In corporate law, stated capital is the amount of money that a shareholder commits to the corporation, which, in most cases, also represents the share-

---

[41]Reg. 8201.

[42]See, e.g., para. 53(2)(a).

[43]S. 84.

[44]Subs. 89(1)"paid-up capital".

holder's maximum financial exposure to creditors. Thus, in a sense, it is the financial measure of the limited liability of shareholders. Stated capital represents to creditors the amount
of funds or assets invested by shareholders.

For tax purposes, we use paid-up capital to measure the maximum share capital that a corporation can return tax-free to shareholders.[45] Except where specific statutory adjustments apply,[46] one determines paid-up capital according to the relevant corporate law.[47]

(b) — Separate Accounts

A corporation must maintain a separate stated capital account for each class and series of
shares it issues.[48] This account is to be credited with the *full* amount of any consideration
received in respect of the particular shares issued by the corporation.[49] Shares must be without nominal or par value.[50]

(c) — Exchange of Property

A corporation may not issue shares in exchange for property (or past services) valued at less
than the cash equivalent the corporation would have received had the shares been issued for
money.[51] The corporation may, however, issue shares for consideration in excess of the cash
equivalent of property or past services.

(d) — Consideration

Generally, the *full* amount of any consideration received for shares must be credited to its
stated capital account.[52] There are a few exceptions to this rule. A corporation may add to its

---

[45]See, generally, s. 84.

[46]Subs. 89(1)"paid-up capital" (b)(iii) (setting out statutory adjustments).

[47]IT-463R2, "Paid-up Capital" (September 8, 1995).

[48]See, e.g., CBCA, subs. 26(1); *Business Corporations Act*, R.S.O. 1990, c. B.16, subs. 24(1).

[49]CBCA, subs. 26(2); Ontario *Business Corporations Act* ("OBCA"), subs. 24(2); see subs. 24(8)
(stated capital account may be maintained in foreign currency).

[50]CBCA, subss. 24(1), (2); OBCA, subss. 22(1), (2). Par value shares tended to be misleading, and the
determination of par value in any case was quite arbitrary. Par value also gave rise to difficult accounting and disclosure problems.

[51]See, for example, CBCA, subs. 25(3) and OBCA, subs. 23(3).

[52]CBCA, subs. 26(2); OBCA, subs. 24(2).

stated capital account an amount that is *less* than the consideration received for its shares, if the shares are issued:[53]

- In exchange for the property of a person who, immediately before the exchange, does not deal with the corporation at arm's length;

- In exchange for shares of a body corporate that, immediately prior to the exchange, or because of the exchange, does not deal with the issuing corporation at arm's length;

- Pursuant to an amalgamation with another corporation; or

- Pursuant to an "arrangement" that is, in effect, an amalgamation of the issuing corporation with another corporation.

Paragraph 26(3)(a) CBCA does allow a corporation to include a lesser amount in stated capital if the person and the corporation are at arm's length but only if all of the shareholders of the particular class consent.

In each of these cases, the corporation may add either all or a part of the consideration that it receives for its shares to the appropriate stated capital account. It may not, however, add to its stated capital account an amount that is greater than the amount received.[54]

(e) — Adjusted Cost Base

It is important to distinguish between the "paid-up capital" and the "adjusted cost base" of a share. The paid-up capital of a share refers to the amount *the corporation* received from the shareholder as consideration for the shares. The paid-up capital is a characteristic of the share.

The adjusted cost base of a share refers to the *shareholder's* cost of acquiring the share. Thus, the adjusted cost base of a share is unique to its shareholder. The adjusted cost base of a share will usually equal its paid-up capital only when it is *initially* issued by the corporation. That is, when the shareholder purchases his or her shares directly from the corporation. Subsequent transactions and corporate events will cause the adjusted cost base of the share to vary from its paid-up capital.

Suppose, for example, that a new corporation, *A Ltd.*, is formed and that it issues its shares for $10 per share. Suppose further, that B acquires 100 shares. Then, the paid-up capital and adjusted cost base of the shares to B is then $10 per share. If, five years later, B sells shares to C for $200 per share, the paid-up capital of the shares (assuming no adjustments of the type discussed below) remains $10 per share. The adjusted cost base of the shares *to C*, however, is now $200 per share.

---

[53]CBCA, subs. 26(3); OBCA, subs. 24(3).

[54]CBCA, subs. 26(4); OBCA, subs. 24(4).

2. — Increases in Paid-Up Capital

(a) — Deemed Dividend

The Act deems a resident corporation that increases the paid-up capital of its shares to have paid a dividend, *unless* the increase results from:[55]

- The payment of a stock dividend;

- An issuance of shares for net assets of equal value;

- An issuance of shares to reduce a liability of equal value; or

- A transaction which correspondingly reduces the paid-up capital of some other class of shares of the corporation by an equivalent amount.

In other words, a resident corporation is deemed to have paid a dividend to the extent that it increases its paid-up capital without increasing its *net* assets, reducing its liabilities, or making an equivalent adjustment in the paid-up capital of other classes of its shares. The purpose of this rule is to prevent a corporation from capitalizing its retained earnings and then distributing its PUC on a tax-free basis to its shareholders.

(b) — Inadequate Consideration

Where a corporation issues shares with a paid-up capital in excess of the consideration it received for the shares, the Act deems *all* of the shareholders of that particular class to have received a proportional dividend.[56]

(c) — Cost Base

Where an adjustment to PUC triggers a deemed dividend, the dividend is added to the cost base of the shareholder's shares.[57] Thus, the amount taxed as a dividend is not included again in income in the calculation of the capital gain or loss upon disposition of the shares.

---

[55]*Income Tax Act*, subs. 84(1).

[56]Subs. 84(1).

[57]Para. 53(1)(b).

(d) — Stock Dividends

An increase in the paid-up capital of a corporation as a consequence of the declaration of a stock dividend does not give rise to a deemed dividend.[58] The shareholder must include his or her *pro rata* share of the dividend in income. Concurrently, the shareholder increases the adjusted cost base of the shares on which the dividend is paid by the amount included in income.[59]

Example

Assume:

A corporation increases its paid-up capital by capitalizing $50,000 of its retained earnings.

	Equity Structure	
	Before	After
1,000 Class A shares	$50,000	$100,000
1,000 Class B shares	10,000	10,000
Retained earnings	100,000	50,000
	$160,000	$160,000

The Act deems the Class A shareholders to receive a dividend of $50 for each share held. The adjusted cost base of *each* Class A share is increased by $50.

(e) — Pro Rata Dividend

A dividend that is deemed to have been paid on shares as a result of a PUC adjustment is also deemed to have been received by each shareholder of the class on a *pro rata* basis. This is so regardless of the shareholder's actual involvement in the particular transaction.

---

[58]Para. 84(1)(a).

[59]Subs. 52(3).

Example

Assume:
A corporation has the following balance sheet:

ASSETS	$ 100,000
Liabilities	$ 20,000
1,000 Class A shares	50,000
Retained earnings	30,000
LIABILITIES AND EQUITY	$ 100,000

In exchange for land valued at $25,000, the corporation issues an additional 500 shares to X, its principal shareholder, and increases its stated capital by $40,000. Another shareholder, T, owns 80 Class A shares, purchased for $50 per share at the inception of the corporation.

Balance Sheet After Share Issue

ASSETS	$ 125,000
Liabilities	$ 20,000
1,500 Class A shares	90,000
Retained earnings	15,000
LIABILITIES AND EQUITY	$ 125,000

In effect, the corporation has "watered" its stock by $15,000.
Then:

Increase in PUC of class	$ 40,000
Increase in net assets	(25,000)
Deemed dividend (subs. 84(1))	$ 15,000
Number of shares outstanding	1,500
Deemed dividend/share	$ 10
Total dividend to T ($10 × 80)	$ 800
ACB of T's share before transaction (per share basis)	$ 50
Add: deemed dividend	10
ACB of T's share after transaction	$ 60

(f) — Conversion of Shares

Where corporate shares are converted from one class into another, the amount paid on the conversion is equal to the increase in the paid-up capital of the new share issued.

Example

Assume:

A corporation's equity structure at the end of its fiscal year is as follows:

1,000 Convertible Class A shares	$ 5,000
1,000 Class B shares	20,000
	$ 25,000

The Class A shares are convertible into Class B shares on a one-for-one basis. If 1/2 of the Class A shares are converted into Class B shares, the revised equity structure would appear as follows:

500 Convertible Class A shares	$ 2,500
1,500 Class B shares	22,500
	$ 25,000

Since the amount paid on conversion ($2,500) is equal to the paid-up capital of the Class A shares that were converted, the transaction does not give a rise to a deemed dividend.

---

3. — Liquidating Distributions

In common law, payments to shareholders upon the liquidation of a corporation are considered to be on account of capital. Thus, absent a special rule for tax purposes, liquidation payments paid out of a corporation's *pre-liquidation* earnings transform income into capital.

(a) — Deemed Dividends

The Act modifies the common law rule and deems a resident corporation that distributes its property to its shareholders upon winding-up, discontinuance, or the reorganization of its business to have paid a dividend.

The dividend is equal to the amount by which the value of the property distributed exceeds the amount by which the paid-up capital of the corporation is reduced through the distribution.[60] The Act also deems shareholders of the class affected by the distribution to receive a dividend equal to their *pro rata* shareholding.

(b) — Reduction in Proceeds

The amount of the deemed dividend is excluded from the proceeds of disposition of the shares cancelled upon winding-up.[61]

The effect of these rules is that an amount distributed by a corporation to its shareholders upon winding-up, discontinuance, or the reorganization of its business may be divided into two portions: (1) the amount paid in excess of the reduction in paid-up capital is deemed to be a dividend, and is taxed as income; and (2) the remaining portion (the amount that represents the reduction in paid-up capital) is returned to the shareholder as a payment on account of capital, which reduces the adjusted cost base of the shares.[62]

Example

A resident corporation has a paid-up capital of $5,000 divided into 5,000 Class A shares with a paid-up capital of $1 per share. The corporation discontinues its business, makes a cash distribution of $3 per share, and reduces its paid-up capital to nil. The tax consequences to an individual shareholder who owns 500 of the issued Class A shares purchased at $1 per share are as follows:

1. Dividend deemed paid by corporation:

Cash distribution	$ 15,000
Less: reduction in paid-up capital	(5,000)
Dividend deemed by subs. 84(2)	$ 10,000

2. Dividend deemed received by individual:

$$\frac{500}{5,000} \times \$10,000 \qquad \$ \ 1,000$$

---

[60]Subs. 84(2); *RMM Canadian Enterprises v. Canada* (1997), 3 C.T.C. 2103, 97 D.T.C. 420 (T.C.C.).

[61]S. 54"proceeds of disposition" (j).

[62]Subpara. 53(2)(a)(iv).

Example

3. Adjustment to cost base of shares:

ACB of shares before payment (assumed)	$ 500
Less: *pro rata* (10%) reduction in paid-up capital	(500)
ACB of shares after payment	$ NIL

4. Summary:

Deemed dividend	
$2/share × 500 shares	$ 1,000
Return of capital	
$1/share × 500 shares	500
Total	$ 1,500

4. — Redemption, Acquisition or Cancellation of Shares

(a) — Deemed Dividend

The Act deems a resident corporation that redeems, acquires, or cancels any of its shares (except on its winding-up or discontinuance or a reorganization of its business, or on the open market) to have paid a dividend on the redeemed, acquired, or cancelled shares.

The dividend is equal to the excess of the amount paid by the corporation to its shareholders over the paid-up capital of the shares cancelled. At the same time, the Act deems the shareholder to have received a dividend that is directly proportionate to the number of shares cancelled over the total number of shares cancelled.[63]

(b) — Reduction in Proceeds

The deemed dividend is *not* included in the shareholder's proceeds from the disposition of the shares.[64] The purpose of this provision is to ensure that all amounts paid by a resident corporation to acquire its own shares are taxable to the shareholder, except to the extent that

---

[63]Subs. 84(3). A corporation that redeems or otherwise acquires its own shares is deemed to have cancelled them as a matter of corporate law: see, e.g., CBCA, subs. 30(1); OBCA, subs. 28(1).

[64]*Income Tax Act*, s. 54"proceeds of disposition"(j).

the amount paid represents a return of paid-up capital. Thus, the payment is not taxed as a deemed dividend and a capital gain when the shareholder disposes of the shares.

(c) — Capital Gain

In addition to any amount deemed to be a dividend, a shareholder may also realize a capital gain or loss from the acquisition of shares. Payments to a shareholder on account of a redemption of shares do *not* give rise to a shareholder benefit.[65] Subsection 84(3) does not apply where a corporation purchases its own shares on the open market in a normal stock market transaction.[66]

Example

Assume:

An individual owns 100 redeemable shares. Consider the following alternatives:

		Case A	Case B
PUC		$ 100	$ 100
ACB		$ 100	$ 300
FMV		$ 500	$ 500

The shares are redeemed at their fair market value in a private (non-market) transaction. Then:

		Case A	Case B
(i)	Redemption price	$ 500	$ 500
	PUC	(100)	(100)
	Deemed dividend	$ 400	$ 400
(ii)	Cash received	$ 500	$ 500
	Less: deemed dividend	(400)	(400)
	Proceeds of disposition	100	100
	ACB	(100)	(300)
Capital gain (loss)		NIL	$ (200)*

---

[65]Para. 15(1)(a).

[66]Para. 84(6)(b).

Notes:

*   The capital loss may be caught by the stop-loss rule in subs. 40(3.6).

5. — *Reduction of Paid-Up Capital*

(a) — *Deemed Dividend*

A corporation may return its share capital to its shareholders on a tax-free basis. It cannot, however, convert taxable earnings into a tax-free return of capital. The Act deems a resident corporation that reduces its paid-up capital[67] and makes a payment to its shareholders in excess of the reduction, to have paid a dividend equal to the amount by which the payment exceeds the reduction in the paid-up capital of its shares.[68]

(b) — *Pro Rata Distribution*

The Act deems a shareholder who holds shares of the class that has had its paid-up capital reduced to receive a *pro rata* share of the dividend that is deemed to have been paid by the corporation.[69] At the same time, the adjusted cost base of the shares is reduced by deducting the *pro rata* portion of the reduction in paid-up capital.[70]

(c) — *Public Corporations*

The Act deems an amount paid by a public corporation on a reduction of its paid-up capital to be a dividend *unless* the reduction takes place on a redemption, acquisition or cancellation of its shares, on a winding-up, or as part of a reorganization of capital.[71]

6. — *Eliminating Double Taxation*

In situations where more than one of the deemed dividend sections may apply, there are special rules to eliminate the possibility of double taxation. For example, subsection 84(4)

---

[67]Other than by a transaction covered by subs. 84(2).

[68]Subs. 84(4).

[69]Para. 84(4)(b).

[70]Subpara. 53(2)(a)(ii).

[71]Subs. 84(4.1).

does not apply in respect of a reduction in the paid-up capital of a corporation if the transaction leading to the reduction can fit under either subsection 84(2) or 84(4.1).

Similarly, a deemed dividend described in subsections 84(2) and (3) does not arise to the extent that the transaction falls within subsection 84(1); nor is there a subsection 84(3) deemed dividend if the transaction can fit under subsection 84(2). These rules prevent overlapping or double taxation of the same transaction.[72] Where a portion of a dividend deemed to be paid under any of subsections 84(2), (3) or (4) consists of shares of the corporation paying the dividend, for the purposes of determining the amount of the dividend, the shares are valued at their paid-up capital.[73] As a result of this rule, there is no deemed dividend to the extent of the paid-up capital of the shares.

IX. — Capital Dividends

1. — Policy Objectives

A key policy objective in the taxation of investment income earned by private corporations is to "integrate" the tax payable by the corporation with the tax payable by its shareholders. In other words, the tax system tries to ensure that individuals (particularly those in the top bracket) pay the same amount of tax on investment income, whether it is earned personally or indirectly through a corporation. In respect of capital gains, this objective is implemented through the combined structure of the refundable dividend tax on hand (RDTOH) and the capital dividend account (CDA).

The capital dividend account represents the non-taxable portion of capital gains and certain other non-taxable receipts. A dividend paid out of the corporation's capital dividend account is not subject to tax in the hands of shareholders.

2. — Integration of Capital Gains

The integration of capital gains earned by a private corporation works as follows:

- Initially, a private corporation is taxed at full corporate rates[74] on 1/2 of its capital gains;

---

[72]Para. 84(6)(a).

[73]Subs. 84(5).

[74]S. 123.

- The remaining 1/2 of its capital gains is credited to a special account called the "capital dividend account";[75]

- 26 2/3 per cent of its net taxable gains goes into the corporation's RDTOH account;[76]

- Upon payment of a taxable dividend, the corporation receives a refund of 1/3 of the amount of the dividend, up to a maximum of the balance in its RDTOH account;[77]

- An amount paid by the corporation as a taxable dividend to an individual is grossed up by 1/4, and the individual can claim a dividend tax credit;[78] and

- An amount paid to an individual out of the corporation's capital dividend account is not included in the individual's income and does not reduce the adjusted cost base of the shares on which the dividend is paid.[79]

3. — The Capital Dividend Account

A "capital dividend" is one that is paid out of a private corporation's capital dividend account and for which the corporation has made the necessary election.[80]

A private corporation's capital dividend account includes:

- The untaxed 1/2 of its capital gains,

- The untaxed portion of the proceeds of goodwill, and

- Capital dividends from other private corporations.[81]

Capital gains and losses on property which *accrued* during any period when the property was held by a corporation that was not a private corporation are excluded from the capital dividend account.[82]

---

[75]Subs. 89(1)"capital dividend account".

[76]Subpara. 129(3)(a)(i), subs. (4)"aggregate investment income".

[77]Subs. 129(1).

[78]Para. 82(1)(b); s. 121.

[79]Para. 83(2)(b); subpara. 53(2)(a)(i).

[80]Subs. 83(2).

[81]Subs. 89(1)"capital dividend account".

[82]Subs. 89(1)"capital dividend account" (a)(i)(A) and (a)(i)(B).

4. — The Election

A dividend qualifies as a "capital dividend" only if the corporation that pays the dividend elects in prescribed form and manner.[83]

The election must be for the *full* amount of the dividend paid. The election must be filed no later than the date on which the dividend becomes payable or is paid, whichever is earlier.[84]

The election must be accompanied by certified copies of the board of directors' resolution authorizing the election.

Duplicate copies of schedules showing the calculation must also be filed with the election.

(a) — Private Corporation Status

An election to pay a capital dividend is available only to a corporation that is a private corporation *at the time* when the dividend is payable. A capital dividend cannot be paid by a public corporation, even though the corporation may at an earlier time have been a private corporation with a capital dividend account balance. Thus, the tax-free status of a private corporation's capital dividend account is preserved only during the time when it remains a private corporation.[85] For this reason, a private corporation should be sure to empty its capital dividend account before changing its status to a public corporation.

(b) — Late-Filed Election

Subject to certain penalties, a corporation may file a capital dividend election after the dividend has been paid. An election filed after a dividend has been paid will retroactively qualify the payment as a capital dividend if the following requirements are satisfied:[86]

- The election is made in prescribed manner and form;

- The election is supported by an authorization from the board of directors; and

- The estimated penalty tax is paid at the time when the election is made.

---

[83]Reg. 2101.

[84]Reg. 2101; subs. 83(2).

[85]Subs. 83(2).

[86]Subs. 83(3).

(c) — Penalty for Late Filing

The penalty for a late-filed election is the lesser of 1 per cent per year for the amount of the dividend or $41.67 per month (to an annual maximum of $500).[87] Upon receipt of the late-filed election, the Minister will assess the corporation on the exact amount of the penalty payable, and the corporation is then required to pay any balance outstanding.[88]

(d) — Excessive Elections

A corporation that elects an amount in excess of its capital dividend account balance is liable to pay a penalty tax on the excess portion of the election. The penalty is levied at a rate of 60 per cent of the excess portion of the dividend.[89] Further, since the penalty tax is due at the time when the election is made, any outstanding balance carries interest at the prescribed rate.

A corporation may avoid the penalty tax by electing to treat the excess portion (i.e., the amount in excess of the balance of its capital dividend account) as a separate taxable dividend.[90] This election, which must be made in prescribed manner within 90 days of the mailing of the notice of assessment, is available only if it is made with the concurrence of *all* the shareholders of the corporation whose addresses are known to the corporation.

5. — Capital Dividend Transfers

The capital dividend account of a private corporation is a very valuable asset from which non-taxable income may be withdrawn by resident shareholders. The attractiveness of the capital dividend account is also an incentive to transfer such accounts between corporations in order to reduce the tax that might otherwise be payable on taxable distributions to domestic shareholders.

For example, a private corporation controlled by non-residents (who are taxable on capital dividends) may be prepared to sell its shares to a domestic corporation and transfer its capital dividend account in order to permit the domestic corporation to reduce the tax payable on distributions to its domestic shareholders.

There are several anti-avoidance rules to prevent this type of trafficking in capital dividends accounts. Where a capital dividend is paid on a share that was acquired by the holder in a

---

[87]Subs. 83(4).

[88]Subs. 83(5).

[89]Subs. 184(2).

[90]Subs. 184(3).

transaction or as part of a series of transactions, and *one* of the main purposes of the transaction or series of transactions is to receive a capital dividend, the capital dividend is treated as a taxable dividend.[91] In these circumstances, the dividend must be included in computing the shareholder's income, and is taxable according to the normal rules in respect of such dividends.

Note, however, that the capital dividend account retains its character as a capital dividend for purposes of determining the corporation's tax in respect of excessive elections, and for purposes of calculating its capital dividend account.

X. — Directors' Liability

1. — *Legality of Dividends*

The corporate law of the jurisdiction in which the corporation is incorporated determines the legality of dividends paid by a corporation. Generally,[92] we determine the legality of a dividend by a two-pronged test: the dividend must not impair either the liquidity or the solvency of the corporation.

A corporation may not declare or pay a dividend if there are reasonable grounds for believing that:[93]

- The corporation is, or, after the payment, would be, unable to pay its liabilities as they become due; *or*

- The realizable value of the corporation's assets would thereby be less than the aggregate of its liabilities and stated capital of all classes of shares.

Similarly, a corporation may redeem its shares only if it satisfies two financial tests: (1) the corporation must be sufficiently liquid to pay its debts as they mature; and (2) the realizable value of its assets after the redemption cannot be less than the aggregate of its liabilities and the amount required to pay other shareholders who rate equally with or have a higher claim than the holders of the shares being redeemed.[94]

The rationale for these rules is to protect corporate creditors and shareholders. Hence, the two-pronged test: the liquidity test protects corporate creditors and the solvency test protects both creditors and shareholders.

---

[91] Subs. 83(2.1).

[92] See, e.g., *Canada Business Corporations Act*, R.S.C. 1985, c. C-44 ("CBCA"); Ontario *Business Corporations Act*, R.S.O. 1990, c. B.16 ("OBCA").

[93] CBCA, s. 42; OBCA, subs. 38(3).

[94] CBCA, subs. 36(2); OBCA, subs. 32(2).

2. — Personal Liability of Directors

Directors of a corporation who authorize the payment of a dividend or the redemption of shares in contravention of these two tests may be jointly and severally liable to the corporation for the amount of the unauthorized disbursement of funds.[95]

A director who dissents from the resolution authorizing the improper payment of a dividend or improper redemption of shares is not liable provided that the director records his or her dissent at the directors' meeting or, if not present at the meeting, the director notifies the secretary of the corporation and causes a dissent to be recorded in the minutes of the meeting.[96]

A director of a corporation is entitled to rely upon a professional opinion on matters requiring technical expertise.[97] For example, a director may rely upon the opinion of an accountant, appraiser, or valuation specialist to value assets to declare a dividend. In these circumstances, the director is not liable if it is subsequently determined that the valuation was incorrect.

3. — Power of Court

In addition to rendering corporate directors personally liable for improper corporate distributions, most corporate statutes also give the courts wide discretionary powers to remedy improperly declared dividends. For example, where a court is satisfied that the payment of a dividend is "unfairly prejudicial" to the shareholders or creditors of the corporation, it may, upon application by a complainant, make *any order it thinks fit* to rectify the conduct which was the subject of complaint.[98]

4. — Complainant

(a) — Proper Complainant

"Complainant" is defined broadly to include shareholders, directors, officers, and *any other person* who, in the discretion of the court, is a proper person to seek relief against improper corporate conduct.[99]

---

[95]CBCA, subs. 118(2); OBCA, subs. 130(2).

[96]CBCA, s. 123; OBCA, s. 135.

[97]CBCA, subs. 123(4); OBCA, subs. 135(4).

[98]CBCA, subs. 241(2); OBCA, subs. 248(2).

[99]CBCA, s. 238"complainant"; OBCA, s. 245"complainant".

The Minister of National Revenue can be a "complainant" to seek an order against any corporate distribution that might be considered prejudicial to the Minister's interest.[100] To obtain redress, the Minister must show that the impugned dividend was paid in contravention of the appropriate corporate statute.

(b) — Time of Complaint

A taxpayer's obligation for income taxes arises as soon as income is earned income, not when the Agency assesses the taxpayer. In *Simard-Beaudry*,[101], Noel A.C.J.F.C. said:

> The general scheme of the *Income Tax Act* indicates that the taxpayer's debt is created by his taxable income, not by an assessment or re-assessment. ... In principle, the debt comes into existence the moment the income is earned, and even if the assessment is made one or more years after the taxable income is earned, the debt is supposed to originate at that point. ... Indeed, in my opinion, the assessment does not create the debt but is at most a confirmation of its existence.

Thus, the Minister has the status of a "complainant" where a corporation earns income on which tax is payable and outstanding. Since a corporation may be reassessed several years after it earns income, the Minister's status as a "complainant" may be resurrected many years after a taxable event.[102]

---

[100]*The Queen v. Sands Motor Hotel Ltd.*, [1984] C.T.C. 612, 84 D.T.C. 6464 (Sask. Q.B.).

[101]*The Queen v. Simard-Beaudry Inc.* (1971), 71 D.T.C. 5511 (F.C.T.D.) at 5515.

[102]*The Queen v. Sands Motor Hotel Ltd.*, ante.

Selected Bibliography to Chapter 21

General

Colley, Geoffrey M., "Are Corporate Tax Changes Imminent?" (1986) 119 CA Magazine 60.

Hiltz, Michael, "Subsection 247(1) and the 1985 Amendments to the *Income Tax Act*", in *Proceedings of 38th Tax Conf.* 7:1 (Can. Tax Foundation, 1986).

Kellough, Howard J., "Some Current Issues in Corporate Tax" in *Proceedings of 44th Tax Conf.* 21:1 (Can. Tax Found. 1992).

Dividends

Allgood, David R., "Tax Planning for Private Corporations and Their Shareholders: Implications of Recent Changes on the Use of Holding Companies", in *Proceedings of the 38th Tax Conf.* 10 (Can. Tax Foundation, 1986).

Ballantyne, Janet L., "The Alternative Minimum Tax and Dividends" (1986) 34 Can. Tax J. 242.

Boultbee, J.A., "Minimizing the Taxation Effects of Dividends", in *Proceedings of 37th Tax Conf.* 7:1 (Can. Tax Foundation, 1985).

Brean, Donald J.S., "The Redemption of Convertible Preferred Shares: The Implications of Terms and Conditions" (1985) 33 Can. Tax J. 957.

Couzin, Robert, "Inter-corporate Distributions", in *Proceedings of 34th Tax Conf.* 311 (Can. Tax Foundation, 1982).

Drache, Arthur B.C., "A Primer on Dividend Gross-ups" (1986) 3 Bus. and L. 78.

Ewens, Dpuglas S., "Amending Grandfathered Preferred Share Conditions" (1994) 42 Can. Tax J. 548.

Meredith, P. Mark, "Securities Lending: Evolving Tax Problems and Issues" (1992) 11 Nat. Banking L. Rev. 18.

Patterson, David, "Flow-Through Shares: Tax Shelter Financing and Investing" (1986) 1 SCRR 4.

Pullen, K.T., and Howard J. Kellough, "Tax Treatment of Inter-corporate Dividends, Grandfather Provisions and the Use of Press Releases" (1987) Current Dev. in Measuring Bus. Income for Tax Purposes 3.

Skingle, Ken S., "A Guide Through the Preferred Share Maze" (1994) 7 Can. Petro. Tax J. 79.

Strain, William J., "Integration Revisited" in *Proceedings of 38th Tax Conf.* 9:1 (Can. Tax Foundation, 1986).

Sugg, Donald M., "Preferred Share Review: Anomalies and Traps for the Unwary" in *Proceedings of 44th Tax Conf.* 22:1 (Can. Tax Found., 1992).

"Taxation of Corporate Reorganizations (The) — Collateralized Preferred Shares" (1987) 35 Can. Tax J. 467.

"Taxation of Corporate Reorganizations (The) — Impact of Tax Reform on Preferred Share Financing" (1987) 35 Can. Tax J. 1004.

Part II.1 Tax

Boultbee, J.A., "Minimizing the Taxation Effects of Dividends", in *Proceedings of 37th Tax Conf.* 7:1 (Can. Tax Foundation, 1985).

Cronkwright, Dart and Lindsay, "Corporate Distributions and the 1977 Tax Changes", in *Proceedings of 29th Tax Conf.* 279 (Can. Tax Foundation, 1977).

Hogg, Roy D., "Corporate Distributions: The Proposed Part II.1 Tax", in *Proceedings of 39th Tax Conf.* 31:1 (Can. Tax Foundation, 1987).

Return of Capital

Ashton, Raymond, "Cost of Capital and Raising Venture Capital in a Tax Efficient Manner" (1986) Brit. Tax Rev. 176.

Ballantyne, Janet L., "The Alternative Minimum Tax and Dividends" (1986) 34 Can. Tax J. 242.

Boultbee, J.A., "Minimizing the Taxation Effects of Dividends", in *Proceedings of 37th Tax Conf.* 7:1 (Can. Tax Foundation, 1985).

Cronkwright, Dart and Lindsay, "Corporate Distributions and the 1977 Tax Changes", in *Proceedings of 29th Tax Conf.* 279 (Can. Tax Foundation, 1977).

Ewens, Douglas S., "The New Preferred Share Dividend Tax Regime", in *Proceedings of 40th Tax Conf.* 21:1 (Can. Tax Foundation, 1988).

Hirsch, Morley P., "The Corporate Loss Transfer System", in *Proceedings of 37th Tax Conf.* 31 (Can. Tax Foundation, 1985).

Jackson, Brian, "Thin Capitalisation" (1990) 30 European Taxation 319.

Richardson, Stephen R., "A Corporate Loss Transfer System for Canada: Analysis of Proposals", in *Proceedings of 37th Tax Conf.* 12 (Can. Tax Foundation, 1985).

Ross, David W., "Reducing Paid-Up Capital" (1985) 33 Can. Tax J. 591.

Simpson, Muriel A., "Planning Around the New Paid-Up Capital Restrictions" (1986) 34 Can. Tax J. 631.

Skingle, Leslie E., "Carve-Outs and Flow-Through Shares", in *Proceedings of 38th Tax Conf.* 50 (Can. Tax Foundation, 1986).

Sinclair, B.R., "Paid-Up Capital", (1984) 34 Can. Tax J. 1483.

Strain, H. Larry, "Integration Revisited" in *Proceedings of 38th Tax Conf.* 9 (Can. Tax Foundation, 1986).

Tremblay, Richard, "Contributions to Capital: Cost Basis (Practice Note)" (1987–89) 2 Can. Current Tax 1.

Turner, Graham, and Mary Turner, "Making Sense of Corporate Share Capital: Part 1" (1985) 118 CA Magazine 52.

"Use of Low Paid-up Capital Shares in Estate Freezes (The)" (1985) 33 Can. Tax J. 1028.

Capital Dividends

Ballantyne, Janet L., "The Alternative Minimum Tax and Dividends" (1986) 34 Can. Tax J. 242.

Boultbee, J.A., "Minimizing the Taxation Effects of Dividends", in *Proceedings of 37th Tax Conf.* 7:1 (Can. Tax Foundation, 1985).

Cronkwright, Dart and Lindsay, "Corporate Distributions and the 1977 Tax Changes", in *Proceedings of 29th Tax Conf.* 279 (Can. Tax Foundation, 1977).

Ewens, Douglas S., "Meaning of Corporate 'Capital' and Distribution of Post-1971 Surplus as Capital Gains", in *Corporate Management Tax Conf.* 1978, 49 (Canadian Tax Foundation, 1978).

Smith, David W., "Wilson's Minimum-Tax Proposals Treat Dividends Unfairly" (1986) 13 Nat (CBA), 22.

Ward, David A., and Neal Armstrong, "Corporate Taxation: Erroneous Capital Dividend Elections" (1986) 5 Legal Alert 97.

Directors' Liability

Campbell, R. Lynn, "The Fiduciary Duties of Corporate Directors: Exploring New Avenues" (1988) 36 Can. Tax J. 912.

Krishna, Vern, "Improper Corporate Distribution: Liability for Income Tax" (1984) 1 Can. Current Tax J61.

Kroft, Edwin G., "The Liability of Directors for Unpaid Canadian Taxes", in *Proceedings of 37th Tax Conf.* 30:1 (Can. Tax Foundation, 1985).

CHAPTER 22 — SHAREHOLDER TAXATION

Corporate income is subject to double taxation: (1) at the corporate level; and (2) at the shareholder level, when distributed as a dividend.[1] A corporation can also distribute its income in other ways. For example, it can confer indirect benefits upon, or make loans to, its shareholders. In this chapter we examine the taxation of indirect payments and benefits.

I. — Benefits

A "shareholder" of a corporation is the person registered on its books, whether or not the shareholder is the beneficial owner of the shares.[2]

A shareholder is generally taxable on the value of any benefits conferred upon him or her by the corporation in the capacity as shareholder. This is so whether or not the corporation that confers the benefit resides, or carries on business, in Canada. This rule prevents corporate shareholders from indirectly appropriating a corporation's property on a tax-free basis.

---

[1]See Chapter 21, "Corporate Distributions".

[2]*Reininger v. M.N.R.* (1958), 20 Tax A.B.C. 242, 58 D.T.C. 608.

The rule is broad. As Cattanach J. said in *M.N.R. v. Pillsbury Holdings*:[3]

> [The rule] is aimed at payments, distributions, benefits and advantages flowing from a corporation to a shareholder. ... While the subsection does not say so explicitly, it is fair to infer that Parliament intended ... to sweep in payments, distributions, and advantages that flow from a corporation to a shareholder by some route other than the dividend route and that might be expected to reach the shareholder by the more orthodox dividend route if the corporation and the shareholder were dealing at arm's length.

Thus, where a corporation appropriates its property for, or confers a benefit upon, a shareholder, the shareholder must include the value of the benefit or the amount appropriated in income for the year.[4]

Whether something constitutes a shareholder benefit is a mixed question of fact and law and we must answer each case on its own merits. This raises three questions:

1. Does the particular appropriation of property constitute a "benefit"?

2. Was the payment or appropriation of property made to the shareholder in his or her capacity as a shareholder? and

3. What is the amount to be included in the shareholder's income for the year?

1. — Purpose

Whether an appropriation of property to a shareholder constitutes a benefit depends on the purpose for which the payment is made. For whose benefit was the payment made? Was the payment to benefit the corporation in its operations, or for the benefit of the recipient? Thus, the corporation's intention in making the payment or appropriating the property is a key determinant in the characterization of benefits. In *Pillsbury Holdings*, for example, the Exchequer Court said:[5]

> Even where a corporation has resolved formally to give a special privilege or status to shareholders, it is a question of fact whether the corporation's purpose was to confer a benefit or advantage on the shareholders or some other purpose having to do with the corporation's business such as in inducing the shareholders to patronize the corporation.

Payments to shareholders are taxable as shareholder benefits only if they are made outside the ordinary course of business. Thus, a payment to a shareholder in the ordinary course of,

---

[3]*M.N.R. v. Pillsbury Hldg. Ltd.*, [1964] C.T.C. 294, 64 D.T.C. 5184 (Ex. Ct.) at 299 [C.T.C.] and 5186 [D.T.C.].

[4]Subs. 15(1).

[5]*M.N.R. v. Pillsbury Hldg. Ltd.*, [1964] C.T.C. 294, 64 D.T.C. 5184 (Ex. Ct.) at 298 [C.T.C.] and 5187 [D.T.C.].

and pursuant to, a *bona fide* business transaction does not trigger a benefit under this rule. Such payments are taken into account in the normal accounting for profit.[6] For example, a person who rents a building to a corporation of which he or she is a shareholder does not necessarily receive a shareholder benefit in respect of the rental. If the shareholder rents in his or her capacity as a landlord and charges a fair rental value for the building, the shareholder is taxable on the rental income. The payment to the shareholder is made to him or her not *qua* shareholder, but *qua* landlord.

Although the tax consequences of shareholder benefits have the undesireable effect of raising the individual's tax payable, this must be balanced against the tax implications for the corporation. Shareholder benefits may be deductible, effectively lowering the taxable income of the corporation.

2. — Income

Shareholder benefits are fully taxable as ordinary income, and not as dividends.[7] Hence, amounts included in income as shareholder benefits are not eligible for the dividend tax credit.

3. — Prospective Shareholders

A benefit conferred on a person in contemplation of becoming a shareholder is also taxable as income.

4. — Capacity in Which Benefit is Conferred

Section 15 is directed towards benefits conferred on a shareholder in his or her capacity as shareholder. It is not concerned with benefits conferred on a taxpayer in his or her capacity as an employee,[8] which is covered by paragraph 6(1)(a). For most purposes, it makes little difference to the recipient of the benefit whether an amount is included in income as an employment benefit or as a shareholder benefit, the issue is important to the corporation that pays the benefit. Employee benefits are generally deductible to the payer corporation as a

---

[6]See, e.g., subs. 9(1).

[7]Except to the extent that the amount is taxable as a deemed dividend on a corporate distribution.

[8]*Singing Skies Farms Ltd. v. M.N.R.*, [1986] 2 C.T.C. 2146, 86 D.T.C. 1586 (T.C.C.) (home supplied by corporation to principal shareholder deductible by corporation as expense; conferred as employee benefit).

cost of doing business. Shareholder benefits are not deductible to the corporation, even though they are taxable to the shareholder.[9]

One should note, however, that employment benefits increase "earned income", whereas shareholder benefits do not. This can be important, for example, for contribution limits into RRSPs.[10]

II. — Exempt Benefits

The following transactions do not give rise to shareholder benefits:[11]

- Reduction of paid-up capital;

- Redemption, cancellation or acquisition by a corporation of its own shares;

- Winding-up or discontinuance of a corporation or reorganization of its business;

- Payment of a dividend or stock dividend;

- Common shareholder's rights offering;

- Conversion of an insurance corporation's or bank's contributed surplus into paid-up capital; or

- A transaction that results in a deemed dividend.[12]

The above transactions are covered by specific provisions of the *Income Tax Act*.

The exemption for stock dividends is not available where one of the purposes of the payment is to significantly alter the value of a specified[13] shareholder's interest in the corporation.[14] This rule prevents the use of stock dividends to affect a change in shareholder interests so as to shift capital gains from one person to another. In these circumstances, the fair

---

[9]*Broitman v. M.N.R.*, [1986] 2 C.T.C. 2283, 86 D.T.C. 1711 (T.C.C.) (payment by corporation to sole shareholder's spouse as part of divorce settlement not deductible as business expense); *Spicy Sports Inc. v. Canada*, 2004 TCC 463 (T.C.C.) (sports equipment rental company reimbursed its president (majority shareholder) for knee operation; court found expense was not incurred for the purpose of earning income from a business or property but rather to confer a benefit on its president *qua* shareholder; expenses not deductible.

[10]See *Prosnick v. R.* (2004), 2004 1 C.T.C. 2534, 2003 D.T.C. 1416 (T.C.C. [Informal Procedure]).

[11]Subs. 15(1). Also excluded are certain shareholder loans under subs. 15(2).

[12]S. 84.

[13]Subs. 248(1)"specified shareholder".

[14]Subs. 15(1.1).

market value of the stock dividend is included in the recipient shareholder's income except to the extent that it has otherwise been included in income as a taxable dividend.

III. — Taxable Benefits

Shareholder benefits can be conferred in a multitude of ways. For example:

- A transfer of property by a shareholder to the corporation at a price in excess of its fair market value;[15]

- A sale of property by a corporation to its shareholder at a price less than fair market value;[16]

- Funds embezzled by a shareholder;

- Excessive expense claims reimbursed to a shareholder;[17]

- Supply of services to a shareholder without fair payment;[18] or

- Forgiveness of a debt owed by a shareholder to the corporation.[19]

---

[15]See, e.g., *Losey v. M.N.R.*, [1957] C.T.C. 146, 57 D.T.C. 1098 (Ex. Ct.) (distinction between accounting and tax law definitions of "goodwill"); *Neuls v. M.N.R.*, [1975] C.T.C. 2215, 75 D.T.C. 170 (T.R.B.) (valuation of goodwill/salary/other in sale of business).

[16]See, e.g., *No. 403 v. M.N.R.* (1957), 16 Tax A.B.C. 387, 57 D.T.C. 120 (residence sold to president-general manager *cum* shareholder below fair market value); *No. 513 v. M.N.R.* (1958), 19 Tax A.B.C. 243, 58 D.T.C. 301 (valuation of shares of private corporation); *Seeley v. M.N.R.* (1959), 22 Tax A.B.C. 97, 59 D.T.C. 283 (automobile bought by private company, then sold at loss to shareholder); *Carlile v. M.N.R.* (1959), 22 Tax A.B.C. 407, 59 D.T.C. 479 (purchase of underwritten shares by brokers in-house); *Guilder News Co. (1963) v. M.N.R.*, [1973] C.T.C. 1, 73 D.T.C. 5048 (F.C.A.) (benefit conferred; value of benefit not a dividend eligible for dividend tax credit).

[17]See, e.g., *Zakoor v. M.N.R.* (1971), 71 D.T.C. 745 (T.A.B.) (travelling expenses to Florida for shareholder and family in conjunction with citrus fruit business); *Byke Estate v. M.N.R.*, [1974] C.T.C. 763, 74 D.T.C. 6585 (F.C.T.D.) (company subsidized interest and principal on shareholder's loans).

[18]See, e.g., *Cakebread v. M.N.R.* (1968), 68 D.T.C. 424 (T.A.B.) (expenses of maintaining horses sold to company for promotional advantages); *Gibson Bros. Industries Ltd. v. M.N.R.*, [1972] C.T.C. 221, 72 D.T.C. 6190 (F.C.T.D.) (ship sold through wholly-owned subsidiary in sham transaction for personal benefit of customer).

[19]See, e.g., *Perrault v. The Queen*, [1978] C.T.C. 395, 78 D.T.C. 6272 (F.C.A.) (shareholder not able to overcome effect of agreement to extinguish debt to corporation); *No. 523 v. M.N.R.* (1958), 58 D.T.C. 379 (T.A.B.) (benefit taxable, no matter how minuscule).

IV. — Valuation Of Benefits

One of the more troublesome issues that arises in the context of shareholder benefits is the value to be placed on the benefit. The valuation of shareholder benefits raises subtle issues and is a fertile source of tax litigation.[20]

The amount to be included in the shareholder's income as a benefit is the "value" of the benefit to the shareholder, not its cost to the corporation. "Value" generally means "fair market value". However, it is not always clear how fair market value is determined.

1. — Inadequate Consideration

Where a corporation transfers property to its shareholders for inadequate consideration, the Act deems it to have sold the property at its fair market value.[21] Thus, the shareholder may be taxed on the full value of the benefit conferred, while the corporation is taxed on the basis of a deemed sale of its property.

For example, suppose a corporation purchases a painting for $10,000, then gives it to its shareholder when the work is worth $25,000. The shareholder is taxable on the value received — $25,000; the corporation realizes a gain of $15,000.

2. — Excessive Consideration

A corporation may confer a benefit on its shareholder by paying an excessive price for services or goods. In these circumstances, the corporation is not entitled to an expense deduction for the excess portion of the payment.[22] The excessive portion of the payment comes out of after-tax dollars, but the shareholder must include the *entire* amount received in income.

---

[20]See, e.g., *The Queen v. Houle*, [1983] C.T.C. 406, 83 D.T.C. 5430 (F.C.T.D.); *Woods v. M.N.R.*, [1985] 2 C.T.C. 2118, 85 D.T.C. 479 (T.C.C.); *Check v. M.N.R.*, [1987] 1 C.T.C. 2114, 87 D.T.C. 73 (T.C.C.); *Mid-West Feed Ltd. v. M.N.R.*, [1987] 2 C.T.C. 2101, 87 D.T.C. 394 (T.C.C.); *Soper v. M.N.R.*, [1987] 2 C.T.C. 2199, 87 D.T.C. 522 (T.C.C.); *Dudelzak v. M.N.R.*, [1987] 2 C.T.C. 2195, 87 D.T.C. 525 (T.C.C.); *Gendron v. M.N.R.*, [1989] 2 C.T.C. 2378, 89 D.T.C. 575 (T.C.C.).

[21]Subs. 69(4).

[22]S. 67.

3. — Non-Arm's Length Transactions

The Act deems a corporation that disposes of property for less than its fair value in a non-arm's length transaction to have disposed of the property at its fair market value.[23] Where the property is acquired by a shareholder of the corporation, the Act deems the shareholder to receive a benefit.

Where the property is capital property, the shareholder may add the amount of any benefit included in income to the cost base of the property.[24] Note, however, that, notwithstanding the step-up on the cost base of the capital property, a portion of the payment is subject to double taxation.

Example
Assume:

A corporation owns a capital property with an adjusted cost base of $20,000. The corporation sells the property (which has a fair market value of $80,000) to its controlling shareholder for $60,000.

Then:

1. Tax consequences to corporation

Deemed proceeds of disposition	$ 80,000
Adjusted cost base of property	(20,000)
Capital gain	$ 60,000
Taxable capital gain	$ 30,000

2. Tax consequences to shareholder

Fair market value	$ 80,000
Purchase price of property	60,000
Shareholder benefit	$ 20,000

3. Cost of property to shareholder

Purchase price of property	$ 60,000
Add: shareholder benefit	20,000
Cost of property	$ 80,000

---

[23]Para. 69(1)(b).

[24]Subs. 52(1).

In the above example, the disposition of a capital property with an accrued taxable capital gain of $30,000 results in $50,000 being included in income, namely, the taxable capital gain plus the shareholder benefit of $20,000. Thus, the amount taxable is more than the economic value of the gain. In contrast, had the shareholder personally acquired and disposed of the property, only $30,000 would have been subject to tax as a taxable capital gain.

4. — Repayment of Benefits

Where a shareholder repays a benefit previously included in income, he or she is not entitled to deduct the repayment. Hence, where a corporation confers a benefit on a shareholder in one year and the benefit is repaid in a subsequent year, the shareholder must include the benefit in income in the year when the shareholder receives it, but is not allowed to deduct the amount repaid.[25] In contrast, a shareholder loan that is taxable in one year is deductible in the year that it is repaid.[26]

5. — Fair Market Value

(a) — Opportunity Costs

"Value" generally means "fair market value", but market prices do not invariably represent fair market value. Opportunity costs and savings are sometimes used to measure the value of benefits.[27]

(b) — Rental Value

The benefit from a property may be measured by reference to its rental value. But rental value may depend upon the purpose for which the property was acquired. In *Soper*,[28] for example, the taxpayer was the controlling shareholder of a corporation that operated a nursing home. The corporation owned several properties in Florida, which were not used for rental or business purposes. The taxpayer and her family used one of the houses for several weeks each year and allowed certain staff members to use it for their holidays. The taxpayer was taxable on the benefit of her personal use of the property, determined by reference to the

---

[25]*Crosbie v. M.N.R.* (1960), 23 Tax A.B.C. 432, 60 D.T.C. 147.

[26]Para. 20(1)(j).

[27]*Youngman v. The Queen*, [1986] 2 C.T.C. 475, 86 D.T.C. 6584 (F.C.T.D.); revd. 90 D.T.C. 6322, [1990] 2 C.T.C. 10 (Fed. C.A.) (benefit measured by reference to investment value of corporate equity in shareholder's residence).

[28]*Soper v. M.N.R.*, [1987] 2 C.T.C. 2199, 87 D.T.C. 522 (T.C.C.).

annual fair market rental value of the properties. The court rejected the taxpayer's assertion that the benefit should be measured by reference to the time that she actually used the property. Since the properties were not acquired for business purposes and were available for the taxpayer's personal use throughout the year, she was taxable on the *annual* rental value of the property rather than on a lesser percentage based upon actual use.

(c) — Imputed Value

The value of a shareholder benefit may depend upon the corporation's purpose in acquiring the asset. In *Hinkson*,[29] for example, a corporation acquired and maintained a cottage, which its major shareholder used personally for approximately 60 days per year. Since the corporation did not acquire the cottage for business purposes, the benefit was calculated on the imputed value of the savings to the taxpayer. The value of the benefit was the taxpayer's saving of the capital cost that he would otherwise have had to incur to purchase the property.[30]

V. — Deemed Dividends

Where a shareholder transfers property to a corporation, a shortfall in the consideration received may give rise to both a dividend and a shareholder benefit. The portion taxable as a dividend is excluded from the portion taxable as the shareholder's benefit.[31]

Example

Assume:

An individual transfers land worth $20,000 to a corporation in return for shares with a paid-up capital of $40,000 and cash in the amount of $30,000.

Then:

(1) Increase in paid-up capital of corporation		$ 40,000
Increase in net assets of corporation ($20,000 - $30,000)		NIL
Deemed dividend (subs. 84(1))		$ 40,000

---

[29]*Hinkson v. M.N.R.*, [1988] 1 C.T.C. 2263, 88 D.T.C. 1119 (T.C.C.).

[30]See also *Youngman v. The Queen, ante.*

[31]Subs. 15(1).

Example

(2) Fair market value of asset transferred		$ 20,000
Total consideration received		70,000
Excess consideration		50,000
Deemed dividend (subs. 84(1))		(40,000)
Shareholder benefit (subs. 15(1))		$ 10,000
Total inclusion in income		$ 50,000

VI. — Appropriations

Corporate property appropriated to, or for the benefit of, a shareholder gives rise to a taxable benefit unless the appropriation occurs as a result of a reduction of paid-up capital, redemption of shares, or the winding-up, discontinuance, or reorganization of business of the corporation.[32]

The term "appropriation" includes payment for a *quid pro quo* (consideration), a gift, a voluntary or gratuitous division of capital, or any act by which a corporation confers a benefit on a shareholder in respect of any of its property. Indeed, in certain circumstances, corporate property may be appropriated to a shareholder even though its ownership does not change. All that is required is that the corporation's property be appropriated for the shareholder's benefit.[33]

1. — Inadequate Consideration

Where a shareholder purchases property from a corporation at less than its fair market value, the excess of the property value over the amount paid is a shareholder benefit. Where a shareholder sells property to a resident corporation and receives excessive share consideration, the amount of the shareholder benefit is calculated in two steps:

1. The Act deems the amount by which the paid-up capital of the newly-issued shares exceeds the value of the property sold to be a dividend to the shareholder;[34] and

---

[32]Subs. 15(1).

[33]*Reid v. M.N.R.* (1961), 26 Tax A.B.C. 321, 61 D.T.C. 263 (shareholders sold contents of hotel to private company at inflated price; amount of price increase included in income); *Olan v. M.N.R.* (1952), 6 Tax A.B.C. 126, 52 D.T.C. 127 (payment of personal and living expenses of shareholder was income to shareholder).

[34]Subs. 84(1).

2. The amount of the shareholder benefit is the difference between the value of the property sold and the amount paid by the corporation less the amount deemed to be a dividend.[35]

Example

Assume:

An individual sells a capital property worth $50,000 to a corporation in exchange for redeemable shares that have a paid-up capital ("PUC") of $60,000 and a fair market value of $100,000.

Then:

	PUC of shares	$ 60,000
	Net increase in assets	50,000
(1)	Deemed dividend	$ 10,000
	Payment to shareholder	$100,000
	Value of asset sold	(50,000)
	Excess consideration	50,000
	Less: deemed dividend	(10,000)
(2)	Shareholder benefit	$ 40,000

In the above example, the individual includes (ignoring gross-up of the dividend) $50,000 in income, which is equal to the excess of the fair market value of the consideration received over the value of the property conveyed. The corporation can redeem the shares for $60,000 without any tax consequences to the shareholder. If the corporation redeems the shares at an amount in excess of their paid-up capital, the Act deems the shareholder to receive the excess amount as a dividend.[36]

Where corporate assets are transferred to shareholders for inadequate consideration, the Act deems the assets to have been sold at their fair market value.[37] Thus, a corporation cannot artificially reduce its income by disposing of property to its shareholders for less than fair

---

[35]Subs. 15(1).

[36]Subs. 84(3).

[37]Subs. 69(4).

market value. This rule applies to all transactions between corporations and their shareholders, whether at arm's length or otherwise.[38] In addition, the shareholder is also taxed on the amount of his or her benefit.[39]

2. — *Cost of Property*

The Act does not provide a generic formula for determining the cost of property acquired by a shareholder. The cost of a property is simply the amount paid for it. Thus, a shareholder who acquires any property at less than its market value cannot step up its cost amount. A shareholder is, however, entitled to step up the cost base of property by the amount included in income as a shareholder benefit.[40]

3. — *Winding-Up*

The Act deems corporate property appropriated to, or for the benefit of, a shareholder upon the winding-up of a corporation to have been sold at its fair market value immediately before the winding-up.[41] The corporation must calculate its income, gains, and losses in much the same way as if it had disposed of the property in an ordinary commercial transaction. The Act deems the shareholder to acquire the property at a cost equal to its fair market value at that time.[42]

An appropriation of corporate property on the winding-up of a corporation does not give rise to a shareholder benefit.[43] A shareholder who receives property on the winding-up of a corporation may, however, be deemed to receive a taxable dividend to the extent that the value of property appropriated to the shareholder exceeds the reduction in the paid-up capital of the shares in respect of which the appropriation is made.[44]

---

[38]Subs. 69(4) is considerably broader in scope than subs. 69(1).

[39]Subs. 15(1).

[40]Subss. 52(1), (1.1).

[41]Subs. 69(5).

[42]Para. 69(5)(b).

[43]Subs. 15(1).

[44]Subs. 84(2).

VII. — Shareholder Loans

The shareholder loan rules are stringent[45] and intended to discourage corporations from using loans as an indirect means of conferring untaxed economic advantages on shareholders. We have seen that corporate income paid out as dividends is taxable as income.[46] Long-term loans are an indirect way of withdrawing corporate funds and, therefore, are subject to tax.

The rules apply to loans and any other form of indebtedness from any source. The lending corporation does not have to be a resident of Canada or be carrying on business in Canada. Thus, a Canadian resident shareholder who borrows from a non-resident corporation may be taxable on the loan. The rules do not, however, apply in respect of indebtedness between non-resident persons.[47]

An individual who is indebted, in his or her capacity as a shareholder, to a corporation is generally taxable on the amount of the indebtedness. A "connected shareholder" is also taxable on the same basis.[48] A corresponding deduction is available upon repayment of the loan or indebtedness.[49] Thus, in the simplest case, *the principal sum* of a loan by a corporation to its shareholder is included in income in the year in which the loan is made.[50]

---

[45]Subs. 15(2); *Kwong v. The Queen*, [1993] 2 C.T.C. 2056, 93 D.T.C. 588 (T.C.C.); IT-119R4, "Debts of Shareholders and Certain Persons Connected with Shareholders" (August 7, 1998); IT-421R2, "Benefits to Individuals, Corporations and Shareholders from Loans or Debt" (September 9, 1992); see, generally, John W. Durnford, "Loans to Shareholders" (1988), 36 Can. Tax J. 1411.

[46]*Silver v. M.N.R.*, [1976] C.T.C. 2043 at 2046, 76 D.T.C. 1039 (T.R.B.), *per* Cardin (corporation "received", as compared to "derived", income from dividends); *Olson v. M.N.R.*, [1984] C.T.C. 3029 at 3031, 84 D.T.C. 1826 at 1828 (T.C.C.), *per* Taylor J. (amounts of shareholder loans not reported as income in year or repaid within one year, etc.); *Cerny v. M.N.R.* (1952), 6 Tax A.B.C. 385 at 388, 52 D.T.C. 259 at 261, *Cerny v. M.N.R.*, [1954] C.T.C. 40, 54 D.T.C. 1025 (Can. Ex. Ct.); affd. 61 D.T.C. 1092 (S.C.C.) (burden of proof as to income on hand where loan not incidental to company's business); *Ramsay v. M.N.R.* (1961), 26 Tax A.B.C. 193 at 194, 61 D.T.C. 191 at 192, *per* Panneton (funds used to pay back corporate debts; no proof of deceit or fraud); *Zatzman v. M.N.R* (1959), 23 Tax A.B.C. 193 at 195-96, 59 D.T.C. 635 at 637 *per* Boisvert (purpose of section is to prevent distribution of profits under guise of loan).

[47]Subs. 15(2.2).

[48]Subs. 15(2.1); IT-119R4, "Debts of Shareholders and Certain Persons Connected with Shareholders" (August 7, 1998).

[49]Para. 20(1)(j).

[50]See *Tick v. M.N.R.*, [1972] C.T.C. 137, 72 D.T.C. 6135 (F.C.T.D.) (meaning of "loan").

1. — *Application*

The shareholder loan rules apply to:

- Shareholders (other than resident corporations) of the lending corporation;

- Shareholders who are connected[51] to shareholders of the lending corporation; and

- Members of partnerships and beneficiaries of trusts that are shareholders of the lending corporation.

The shareholder loan rules apply whether the loan is made by the corporation in which the borrower holds shares, by any other corporation related to it, or by a partnership in which the corporation or a corporation related to it is a member.

2. — *Inter-Corporate Loans*

Inter-corporate loans to resident corporations are not subject to taxation. Inter-corporate dividends are tax-free and, therefore, inter-corporate loans do not require special regulation.

3. — *Criteria for Taxability*

Three factors determine whether a loan (or other indebtedness) is included in income:

1. The relationship between the borrower and the lender;

2. The purpose of the indebtedness; and

3. Repayment arrangements.

A shareholder loan (or other indebtedness) is not taxable where the loan is made:

- By a lending institution in the ordinary course of its business;[52]

- To an employee of the lender or to the employee's spouse to enable the employee to acquire residential accommodation;[53]

- To assist an employee of the lender to purchase its shares or the shares of a related corporation;[54] or

---

[51]See subs. 15(2.1) (meaning of "connected").

[52]Subs. 15(2.3).

[53]Para. 15(2.4)(b).

[54]Para. 15(2.4)(c).

- To an employee of the lender to assist the employee in purchasing an automobile that is to be used in the performance of employment duties.[55]

These exclusions are, however, all contingent upon *bona fide* arrangements for repayment of the debt within a reasonable time.

Thus, there are three distinct tests:

1. The loan must be *bona fide*,

2. The arrangements for repayment must be *bona fide*, and

3. Repayment must be required within a reasonable period of time.

(a) — Repayment

A shareholder loan (or other indebtedness) that is repaid within one year after the end of the lender's taxation year is not taxable as income, provided that the repayment is not part of a series of loans and repayments.[56] Where the loan is not repaid within one year, the principal sum of the loan is taxable in the year in which the loan was made.[57]

In contrast, with the rules in respect of shareholder benefits, however, an amount repaid on a loan previously included in the shareholder's income is deductible from income in the year in which the loan is repaid if the repayment is not part of a series of loans and repayments.[58]

Subsections 15(2.3) to 15(2.5) require only that *bona fide* arrangements be made for repayment of the loan within a reasonable time. There is no requirement that actual repayment be made within a reasonable time. Failure to repay a loan within a reasonable time may call into question the *bona fides* of the arrangement, particularly where no effort is made to collect the loan.[59] A demand loan may not constitute a *bona fide* arrangement for repayment.[60]

---

[55]Para. 15(2.4)(d).

[56]Subs. 15(2.6).

[57]*Olson v. M.N.R.*, [1984] C.T.C. 3029, 84 D.T.C. 1826 (T.C.C.).

[58]Para. 20(1)(j).

[59]*The Queen v. Silden*, [1993] 2 C.T.C. 123, 93 D.T.C. 5362 (F.C.A.).

[60]*Perlingieri v. M.N.R.*, [1993] 1 C.T.C. 2137, 93 D.T.C. 158 (T.C.C.).

4. — Excluded Loans

Shareholder loans and indebtedness are not taxable as income if they are made in, or arise from, the ordinary course of business and the lending of money is part of the corporation's ordinary business.[61] Thus, there are two requirements:

1. The loan must be made in the *ordinary* course of business; and

2. The lending of money must be part of the *ordinary* business of the lending corporation.

Corporate loans to employees or to spouses of employees are excluded from income if the loan is to assist the employee or spouse to acquire a dwelling.[62]

The term "dwelling" includes normal residential accommodation, a summer cottage, or a self-contained suite in an apartment building. The exemption applies only to loans used to acquire a dwelling for habitation by the employee. A change in circumstances after the loan is made, however, which prevents the employee from inhabiting the dwelling does not disqualify a loan that would otherwise be exempt.

Corporate loans to assist employees to purchase fully-paid shares of the employer corporation (or shares of a related corporation) are not taxable provided that the shares are held for the employee's own benefit.[63] The important point to observe here is that the loan is exempt from inclusion in income only if the shares are purchased *directly* from the corporation. Open market purchases from other shareholders do not qualify for exemption.

These rules apply to all loans that are required to be included in income as a shareholder benefit. Thus, apart from the exceptions noted, the *principal sum* of a loan to a shareholder is included in income even if it is borrowed at the prevailing market rate of interest.

VIII. — Imputed Interest On Loans

A shareholder[64] may be taxable on the interest imputed on a loan. Three factors determine the taxability of imputed interest:

1. The relationship between the borrower and the lending corporation;

2. The rate of interest payable on the loan; and

---

[61]Subs. 15(2.3); *Duquette v. M.N.R.*, [1984] C.T.C. 3008, 84 D.T.C. 1820 (T.C.C.).

[62]Para. 15(2.4)(b).

[63]Para. 15(2.4)(c).

[64]And certain persons related to the shareholder.

3. The prescribed rate of interest at the time when the loan was taken out or the indebtedness was incurred.

In the simplest case, a shareholder[65] of a corporation who, in his or her capacity as a shareholder, obtains a low-interest loan from the corporation is taxable on the benefit from the loan. The value of the benefit is the difference between the shareholder's actual interest cost and the prescribed rate of interest at that time.[66] The prescribed rate of interest is determined quarterly, based on the average interest rate for 90-day treasury bills during the first month of the preceding quarter.[67]

1. — *Relationship Between Parties*

The taxability of imputed interest on corporate loans depends upon the relationship between the borrower and the corporation. Where a shareholder of a corporation, a person who does not deal at arm's length[68] with the shareholder, or a person who is a member of a partnership or a beneficiary of a trust that is a shareholder of the corporation is indebted to the corporation, a related corporation, or a partnership to which that corporation is related, the Act deems the shareholder to have received a benefit in the year in which the loan or indebtedness is incurred.[69] The imputed interest provisions do not apply to inter-corporate loans to corporate shareholders resident in Canada.

2. — *Value of Benefit*

The imputed benefit from indebtedness is the difference between the amount that would have been payable in the year on the indebtedness if interest were calculated at the prescribed rate and the interest actually paid on the debt during the year, or within 30 days after the end of the taxation year, by the debtor.

---

[65]Other than a resident corporate shareholder.

[66]Subs. 80.4(2).

[67]Reg. 4301.

[68]Para. 80.4(2)(b); subs. 80.4(8); s. 251.

[69]Subs. 80.4(2).

Example

Assume:

A Ltd. lends $100,000 at 5% to its shareholder at a time when the prescribed rate of interest is 11%. The loan is outstanding all year.

Then:

Imputed interest (11% × $100,000)	$ 11,000
Less:	
Interest paid (5% × $100,000)	(5,000)
Shareholder benefit included in income	$ 6,000

3. — Exclusions

(a) — Commercial Rate Loans

The imputed interest rules do not apply in certain circumstances where the rate of interest payable on the debt is equal to or greater than the rate of interest that would have been payable in an arm's length transaction *at the time when the loan was taken out or the obligation was incurred.*[70]

For example, interest is not imputed on indebtedness where:

- The shareholder is not indebted by virtue of the shareholding;

- The creditor is in the business of lending money; and

- The debt is repaid by the shareholder and not by any other person on the shareholder's behalf.

The essential issue is to determine the rate that a particular person could negotiate if he borrows arm's length from a bank.

---

[70]Subs. 80.4(3).

(b) — Principal Sum Taxed

A shareholder is not taxable on imputed interest on indebtedness if the principal sum of the debt is included in income.[71]

IX. — Automobile Standby Charge

Where a corporation provides its shareholder (or a person related to the shareholder) with an automobile, the shareholder may be taxable on the benefit derived from the automobile. The shareholder may also be taxable for any operating costs paid by the corporation. The shareholder is taxable on a "standby charge" if the shareholder (or a person related to the shareholder) is supplied with an automobile by the corporation or by any person related to the corporation.[72]

X. — Non-Resident Shareholders And Corporations

For the purpose of calculating a resident shareholder's income, the shareholder benefit provisions apply whether or not the corporation or creditor is resident in Canada or carries on business in Canada.[73] Thus, a Canadian resident who borrows from a non-resident corporation may be liable for tax if the loan does not qualify as an "exempt loan".[74]

A loan by a resident corporation to a non-resident shareholder is not subject to the shareholder benefit provisions. The amount of the benefit that *would have* been included in income if the borrower were a resident is deemed to be a dividend to the non-resident shareholder and is subject to withholding tax.[75]

XI. — Shareholders' Agreements

1. — General Comment

A shareholders' agreement is a contract among shareholders setting out the terms, conditions and obligations agreed upon between the shareholders. The main purpose of a shareholders'

---

[71]Para. 80.4(3)(b).

[72]Subs. 15(5); see Chapter 4, "What Is Income?".

[73]Subs. 15(7).

[74]See the exceptions in subss. 15(2.2)–15(2.7).

[75]Para. 214(3)(a).

agreement is to govern relations between shareholders and to provide a mechanism for the transfer of shares between shareholders.

Why are shareholders' agreements necessary? The best way to answer this question is to consider what would happen absent such an agreement.

The general rule of corporate law is that the business and affairs of a corporation are to be governed by its board of directors. Thus, in the absence of an agreement, most business policies, acquisitions, mergers, dividend payouts, share issues, and repurchases are in the discretion of the board of directors. Obviously, the person who controls the board of directors controls the corporation. Minority shareholders generally do not have enough votes to have representation on the board of directors, and so are vulnerable to corporate actions taken by the majority shareholders.

Where two shareholders have an equal holding of 50 per cent each, the danger lies, not in dominance of one over the other, but in corporate deadlock. The provision of a casting vote to one of the shareholders does not resolve the problem. Such a provision would effectively transform an equal shareholding into absolute control for the person who carries the third vote.

A shareholders' agreement is typically used between shareholders of a closely-held corporation to deal with matters such as:

- Control and management of the corporation;

- Protection of minority shareholders;

- Purchase and sale of its shares;

- Options to acquire additional shares issued by the corporation;

- Expenses that exceed pre-determined limits;

- Valuation of the corporation's shares;

- Sale of a substantial part of the corporation's assets; and

- Amalgamation and liquidation.

A shareholders' agreement is particularly valuable in situations where a corporation is closely held and operates, in effect, as a partnership. For example, a shareholders' agreement can be useful in the following types of situations:

- Where there are two shareholders and each of them has a 50 per cent shareholding in the corporation. This situation is analogous to a two-person partnership, and the shareholders' agreement between the shareholders will usually cover many of the same topics found in a typical partnership agreement. The focus of the agreement may be to prevent deadlock.

- Where there are two or more shareholders and one of the shareholders has a controlling interest. In this type of situation the agreement is generally drafted to protect the minority shareholders, who might otherwise be vulnerable to the controlling shareholder's domination.

- Where there are more than two shareholders and none of them has a majority position, so that no single person can control the corporation. In these circumstances the agreement can provide for the smooth and efficient operation of the corporation despite the absence of control in one person.

2. — Inter Vivos Agreements

Shareholders' agreements fall into two broad categories: (1) *inter vivos* agreements, and (2) agreements that are operative only upon the death of one or more of the shareholders.

A shareholders' agreement is a contract. There are no hard and fast rules as to what should be included in contracts. Typically, such agreements address areas that are of major concern to the parties to the agreement. For example:

- The right to elect members of the board of directors;

- The right to appoint officers of the corporation;

- The right to restrict the powers normally conferred upon directors, particularly powers dealing with corporate borrowing, guarantee of obligations to third parties, and the power to enter into long-term obligations and contracts over a specified value;

- The right of shareholders to enter into competing businesses;

- Dividend policies;

- Pre-emptive rights of shareholders to acquire new issues of shares;

- Restrictions or prohibitions on the right to transfer shares and the obligation to take up shares offered for sale;

- The right or obligation of other shareholders to purchase shares under certain conditions, such as the death or permanent disability of the shareholder;

- The method of share valuation in the event of compulsory acquisition of the shares or where there is a right of first refusal;

- The provision of adequate funding to ensure that there are sufficient funds to finance any compulsory acquisitions under the agreement;

- Dispute resolution mechanisms; and

- Provisions for the alteration and/or termination of the shareholders' agreement to accommodate new and changed circumstances.

A shareholders' agreement should be comprehensive if it is to adequately address each of the issues listed above.

Some of the provisions that address these concerns can have important income tax consequences which should be taken into account at the time when the agreement is drafted. Others have no income tax consequences and are simply a matter of corporate or contract law.

(a) — Control

One of the matters frequently addressed in a shareholders' agreement is the allocation of corporate control. For example, provisions that deal with voting power, options to acquire shares, rights of first refusal, etc., may affect control of the corporation, which in turn can cause the corporation to become associated with other corporations.[76]

The concept of "control" is also important in the following situations:

- Determination of "private corporation" and "Canadian-controlled private corporation" status;

- Availability of the small business deduction;

- Qualification as a "small business corporation" for purposes of the capital gains exemption;

- Limitations on the carryover of capital and non-capital losses;

- Liability for Part IV tax; and

- Allocation of the small business deduction between corporate partnerships and associated corporations.

(b) — Associated Corporations

The Act contains various provisions dealing with "associated corporations". Generally, associated corporations must allocate the small business deduction (maximum $300,000 per year) among themselves. Thus, a group of associated corporations is limited in the amount that it may claim in any year on account of the small business deduction.

Section 256 sets out the rules for determining whether two or more corporations are associated with each other. Two or more corporations are considered to be associated with each other if one of the corporations controls the other or the corporations are controlled by a common person. Thus, in the simplest case, if Corporation A controls Corporation B, then

---

[76]See, for example, subss. 256(6) and (7).

corporations A and B are associated with each other. Similarly, if *Redco* controls *Blackco* and *Whiteco*, then *Blackco* and *Whiteco* are associated with each other.[77]

(i) — Option to Acquire Shares

A person who has a right to acquire shares in a corporation or who can control the voting rights of shares is considered to be in the same position as if he or she actually owned the shares.

Hence, the use of a buy-sell option (usually inserted for the purpose of ensuring a market for the shares) can inadvertently result in two or more corporations becoming associated with each other for tax purposes.Options granted to non-residents and public corporations to acquire shares in a private Canadian corporation can cause a shift of control and disqualify the corporation from having status as a Canadian-controlled private corporation.

Similarly, a person who has a right to cause a corporation to redeem, acquire, or cancel its shares is considered to be in the same position in relation to the control of the corporation as if the shares had been redeemed, cancelled, or acquired by the corporation. Hence, the mere right to acquire shares or the right to redeem or cancel shares can cause a person to be considered in control of a corporation.

The above rules apply, however, only when the right to acquire shares or control the voting rights of shares is exercisable during the lifetime of the shareholders. They do not apply when the right is triggered by the death of a designated shareholder or by the bankruptcy or permanent disability of an individual designated in the shareholders' agreement.

(ii) — Right of Refusal

Is a right of first refusal also a buy-sell option for the purposes of the above rule? The better view is that a right of first refusal is not a right to acquire shares, but only a right to have the first bid on the shares in the event that the shares are, if ever, offered for sale to a third party. The CRA's position is that subsection 256(1.4) of the Act does not normally apply to a right of first refusal.

The scope of subparagraph 251(5)(b)(ii) is also uncertain. The provision reads as follows:

> (b) a person [who] has a right under a contract, in equity or otherwise, either immediately or in the future and either absolutely or contingently
>
>> (ii) to cause a corporation to redeem, acquire or cancel any shares of its capital stock owned by other shareholders of the corporation shall ... be deemed to have the same

---

[77]See Chapter 20, "Corporate Business Income".

position in relation to the control of the corporation as if the shares were so redeemed, acquired or cancelled by the corporation. ...

Under corporate law, the directors of a corporation have the power to exercise their discretion to redeem, acquire, or cancel any shares of capital stock that are issued and outstanding in the hands of shareholders. It would be absurd to interpret this provision to mean that the control of the corporation should be determined *as if* the shares that were issued and outstanding had already been redeemed, acquired, or cancelled by the corporation. The better interpretation is that this provision applies only to shareholders who, in their capacity as shareholders, have such a right by virtue of a contract, such as a shareholders' agreement.

(c) — Market for Shares

One of the important reasons for a shareholders' agreement is to ensure a market for the shares of a closely-held corporation. A shareholders' agreement sets out the events that allow for a transfer of shares between shareholders and the manner in which the transfer is to be executed.

The following mechanisms are frequently used to ensure that there is a market for the shares.

(i) — Right of First Refusal

A right of first refusal obliges a shareholder who wishes to dispose of shares to offer the shares to the other shareholders before they are offered to outside parties. The offer to the current shareholders must be on the same terms and conditions as any offer to the non-shareholders.

Right of refusal also exists to protect current shareholders from the dilution of their ownership interest in the event the company decides to issue new stock from treasury.

(ii) — Shotgun Clause

A shotgun clause provides that a shareholder can give notice to the other shareholders of the shareholder's intention to acquire all of the shares belonging to the other shareholders. The notice specifies the purchase price of the shares as well as the other terms and conditions of the offer. The recipient of the notice must either sell his or her shares to the offeror, or acquire all of the offeror's shares under the same terms and conditions. A shotgun clause can be particularly useful when shareholders reach an impasse, but it can have unpredictable consequences and should be used only when shareholders have equal bargaining power and financial resources.

(iii) — Private Auction

A private auction operates in a similar manner to a shotgun clause: all of the shareholders must offer their shares for sale to the highest bidder at a private auction that is attended only by the shareholders. A private auction offers a little more flexibility than a shotgun clause, because it allows the offeror to increase the offer during the course of the proceedings.

(iv) — Compulsory Offer

A compulsory offer clause obliges a shareholder to offer his or her shares to the other shareholders or to buy the shares of the other shareholders. The clause will set out the circumstances in which the obligation arises. Typically, a compulsory offer clause is triggered in the following circumstances:

- Death of a shareholder;
- Retirement of a shareholder;
- Disability of a shareholder;
- Bankruptcy or insolvency of a shareholder;
- Theft, fraud or embezzlement by a shareholder against the company;
- Termination of a shareholder's employment;
- Competition by a shareholder with the company; or
- Non-observance of the shareholders' agreement.

The clause should set out the price for the shares or a method for establishing the price of the shares. The clause should also specify the manner in which the shares are to be paid for by the purchaser.

(v) — Piggyback Clause

A piggyback clause obliges the minority shareholders to sell their shares when the shares of the majority shareholder are sold to a third party. A piggyback clause allows minority shareholders to avail themselves of terms and conditions that they might not otherwise be able to negotiate for themselves.

Each of these methods of purchase and sale raises two questions: (1) how will the funds be generated to provide for the purchase and sale of the shares? and (2) what are the tax consequences to the purchaser and vendor of the shares?

(d) — Funding the Agreement

There are several ways to fund a shareholders' buy-sell agreement. The best method depends upon the particular structure of the agreement, the financial capabilities of the parties concerned and, where applicable, the insurability of the parties to the agreement.

(i) — Corporation Party to Agreement

Where the corporation itself is a party to the agreement (for example, an "unanimous shareholders' agreement" under the *Canada Business Corporations Act*)[78] and is required to purchase any shares that are offered for sale, the easiest method of financing the purchase is to provide for a reserve or contingency fund to satisfy the terms of the agreement. In most cases, however, closely-held corporations do not segregate their funds for such purposes, and the presence of an accounting reserve on the books does not ensure that liquid funds will be available at the appropriate time to finance the purchase of shares that come onto the market.

A corporation can use a sinking fund to finance the purchase, but this route is rarely followed. A sinking fund is an actual reserve of cash or near-cash assets.

If the corporation must borrow money to finance the repurchase of shares, interest paid may be deductible as an expense in computing income.

(ii) — Corporation Not Party to Agreement

The problem of financing the agreement becomes more complicated if the corporation is not a party to the agreement and the other shareholders are required to take up any shares offered for sale. The purchaser may borrow the necessary funds to purchase the shares. In these circumstances, any interest paid on the borrowed money will generally be deductible in computing income for tax purposes. The use of disability insurance is convenient to finance the purchase of shares that are offered for sale as the result of a shareholder's long term disability.

(e) — Capital Gains

A shareholder may realize a capital gain or capital loss upon the disposition of shares to other shareholders. If the shares sold are the shares of a "qualified small business corporation", the vendor may shelter up to $500,000 of capital gains from tax.[79]

---

[78]R.S.C. 1985, c. C-44, subs. 146(2).

[79]See Chapter 20, "Corporate Business Income".

The capital gains exemption is subject to several special anti-avoidance rules. One of these rules prevents an individual from claiming the capital gains exemption in circumstances where the gain is, in effect, generated by converting dividend income into a capital gain.[80] In other words, this rule applies where the value of corporate shares is enhanced by the non-payment or restrictive payment of dividends. This rule can have important consequences for a shareholder who is a party to a shareholders' agreement, because such agreements quite typically provide for restricted dividend payments. Thus, although a clause restricting dividends may be financially desirable, it may also prove to be expensive from an income tax perspective.

3. — Death

(a) — Market for Shares

One of the principal attractions of a shareholders' agreement is that it provides a market for the shares of a private corporation. Private corporations typically restrict the transfer of their shares. Such restrictions are usually desirable from a business point of view, but they can seriously inhibit the market for minority shareholders. A shareholders' agreement can overcome this disadvantage by providing for an alternative share transfer mechanism and for the orderly settlement of an estate.

Typically, a private corporation's articles of incorporation will state that the corporation's shares may not be transferred without:

- The approval of the directors of the corporation; or

- The approval of the holders of at least a majority of the common shares of the corporation.

These restrictions do not pose a problem for majority shareholders, but can be difficult for the minority.

A shareholders' agreement is a mechanism for arranging shareholder approval in advance of an event. For example, the agreement can provide that, in the event of a shareholder's death, the surviving shareholders shall purchase, or have the *option* to purchase, the deceased's shares. In the first case, the agreement must provide a mechanism to determine the price at which the shares will be purchased and the appropriate procedural mechanism for an orderly transfer. In the second case, the mechanism for price determination may be left open until the time when the option is put to the purchaser. In either case, the formula for determination of the price may have important tax consequences.

---

[80]See subs. 110.6(8).

(b) — Deemed Disposition

Subsection 70(5) of the Act provides that a shareholder is "deemed to have disposed, immediately before his death, of each property owned by him at that time". The deemed disposition does not, by itself, create a market for the shares; it simply triggers income tax consequences as *if* the taxpayer had actually disposed of the shares.

The actual transfer of the shares occurs pursuant to principles of succession law, provisions in the corporation's articles of incorporation, and the terms of the shareholders' agreement. Thus, it is important to ensure that the deemed proceeds of disposition for tax purposes are at least equal to the price received for the shares. Otherwise, tax will be payable on an amount that is higher than the cash actually received for the shares.

(c) — Funding

In addition to ensuring the marketability of shares and the determination of the price of shares, it is also important that the parties provide for a method of funding the purchase and sale of the corporation's shares. After all, it serves little purpose to have a contractual obligation that provides for a mandatory purchase of shares without providing for some method to ensure that the purchaser has the necessary funds to fulfil his or her contractual obligations.

Thus, a shareholders' agreement may incorporate funding provisions to ensure the availability of funds at the appropriate time to finance the share purchase and sale transaction. This is particularly important in the case of mandatory share purchase agreements. The method of funding also has income tax consequences.

(d) — Mandatory Purchases

An agreement may provide that the deceased shareholder's estate is entitled to "put" the deceased's shares to the surviving shareholders and that they are *obliged* to purchase the shares according to the method and formula provided in the agreement. In these circumstances, the surviving shareholders do not have any choice in their decision to purchase the shares, nor is there very much choice as to the price of the shares transferred. The price is determined according to the formula prescribed in the agreement.

Such a clause is generally advantageous to the deceased's estate: it assures a market for the shares at the earliest possible opportunity and with the greatest certainty in respect of the transaction price. A "put" option may, however, place an onerous financial burden on the purchasers by requiring them to purchase the shares at an inopportune time.

(e) — Valuation

Paragraph 70(5)(a) of the Act deems a deceased taxpayer to have disposed of each non-depreciable capital property owned by the taxpayer immediately before death, for proceeds equal to its fair market value. The Act also deems the person who acquires the property to do so at an amount equal to the fair market value of the property. Where there is a shareholders' agreement, the deemed proceeds of disposition may depend upon the relationship of the parties to the agreement.

(i) — Arm's Length Relationships

One of the more troublesome questions in respect of shareholder buy-sell agreements is the value to be attached to shares that are the subject of a "put" clause. Where the deceased and the surviving shareholders deal with each other at arm's length, the contract price provided for in the shareholders' agreement will usually be close to the fair market value of the property at the relevant time. It would be unusual for parties who are at arm's length with each other to arrange for a purchase and sale of property at any price other than its fair market value.

It is, however, possible that the stipulated contract price is out of date and does not fully reflect share values at the time of death. It is also possible that the parties may have drafted the transfer price incorrectly or without much thought.[81] In either case, the CRA is not bound by an improper valuation, even if the parties were at arm's length. Fair market value is to be determined objectively.

(ii) — Non-Arm's Length Relationships

Where the parties were not at arm's length with each other, it is quite possible for the fair market value of the transferred property to be different from the transfer price resulting from the agreement. The Agency takes the view that, where the deceased and the surviving shareholders did not deal with each other at arm's length, the fair market value of the shares must be determined *without reference* to the shareholders' agreement.[82]

(iii) — Insurance

The effect of corporate-owned life insurance may also affect the value of the deceased's shares. Subsection 70(5.3) requires that the cash surrender value of any corporate-owned insurance on the life of the deceased be taken into account in determining the value of the

---

[81]See, e.g., *Carrol v. McArthur* (1983), 25 B.L.R. 132 (Ont. Co. Ct.).

[82]IT-140R3, "Buy-Sell Agreements" (April 14, 1989).

deceased's shares immediately before death. The face value of the policy is irrelevant for this purpose.

Since term life insurance does not generate a cash surrender value, this rule really applies only to whole life policies. The specific rule in subsection 70(5.3) precludes, in effect, the application of any general valuation principle that the discounted expectancy of a term policy should be taken into account in valuing shares immediately before death.[83]

The deceased's estate is deemed to acquire the shares that are deemed to have been disposed of *immediately before death* at an amount equal to the deemed proceeds of disposition. Thus, the cost of the shares to the estate is determined by reference to the value of the shares, which includes the *pro rata* share of the cash surrender value of any whole life policy on the life of the deceased.

It is, however, arguable that the value of the shares to the estate increases *after the death* of the deceased, because the corporation is now actually entitled to the full face value of the whole life policy. In other words, where there is a substantial disparity between the cash surrender value and the face value of a policy, the value of the shares may be enhanced by the corporation's *pro rata* share of the difference between the two values. In these circumstances, the estate may have a gain on the transfer of the shares to the surviving shareholders' pursuant to the shareholders' agreement.

(f) — Right of First Refusal

A right of first refusal clause usually provides that the deceased's estate is obliged to offer the shares to the surviving shareholders but that they are not obliged to purchase the shares offered. A right of first refusal operates to the advantage of the surviving shareholders, but does not provide the deceased's estate with an assured market for the shares. Thus, a right of first refusal may not be the most appropriate transfer mechanism to use if marketability and liquidity of the estate are the primary concerns.

A right of first refusal does simplify many other aspects of share transfers. It is generally considerably easier to provide for a valuation mechanism as part of a right of first refusal than in the case of a mandatory buy-sell agreement. For example, it is not unusual to provide that the surviving shareholders have a right of first refusal to be exercised within a period of time (say, 30 days), after which the deceased's estate is entitled to offer the shares to any other interested party.

From an income tax perspective, however, the problem of valuation may become more complicated. Where the shareholders' buy-sell agreement does not provide for a formula to value the shares, their fair market value must be determined according to general principles

---

[83]See, e.g., *The Queen v. Mastronardi*, [1977] C.T.C. 355, 77 D.T.C. 5217 (F.C.A.).

of share valuation. This can be difficult even in the most routine circumstances, and can be a substantial burden, in both financial and administrative terms, for the estate.

Selected Bibliography to Chapter 22

Benefits

Allgood, David R., "Tax Planning for Private Corporations and Their Shareholders: Implications of Recent Changes on the Use of Holding Companies", in *Proceedings of 38th Tax Conf.* 10:1 (Can. Tax Foundation, 1986).

Beam, Robert E. and Stanley N. Laiken, "Benefits under Subsection 15(1)" (1994) 42 Can. Tax J. 477.

Bernstein, Jack, "Family Tax Planning", in *Proceedings of 37th Tax Conf.* 46 (Can. Tax Foundation, 1985).

Bernstein, Jack, "Fringe Benefits and Equity Participation", *Corp. Mgmt. Tax Conf.* 5:1 (Can. Tax Foundation, 1991).

Birnie, David A.G., "Shareholders' Buy-Sell Agreements: Some New Opportunities", in *Proceedings of 38th Tax Conf.* 13:1 (Can. Tax Foundation, 1986).

Campbell, Ian R., "Valuation-related Issues: Tax Planning and Post-transaction Followup", in *Proceedings of 45th Tax Conf.* 25:1 (Can. Tax Foundation, 1993).

Corn, George, "Indirect Payments and Shareholder Loans as Income Inclusions" (1993) 4 Can. Current Tax J23.

Dan, Robert J., and David W. Smith, "Estate Planning: A New Era" (1986) 34 Can. Tax J. 1.

Drache, A.B.C., "Employee or Shareholder Benefit" (1983) 5 Can. Taxpayer 202.

Dunbar, Alisa, "Use of Holding Corporation may Elude Shareholder Benefit Provisions" (1992) 3 Tax. of Exec. Compensation and Retirement 606.

Durnford, John W., "Benefits and Advantages Conferred on Shareholders" (1984) 32 Can. Tax J. 455.

Goldstein, D.L., "Court Places No 'Ceiling' on Shareholder Benefit Valuation" (1990) 38 Can. Tax J. 669.

Hickey, Pat, "The New Rules for Intergenerational Transfers of Family Assets" (1985) 33 Can. Tax J. 360.

Hoey, D. Graham, "Shareholder-manager Compensation" in *Proceedings of 42nd Tax Conf.* 6:1 (Can. Tax Foundation, 1990).

Hogg, Roy D., "A Canadian Tax Overview of Transfer Pricing" (1983) 116 CA Magazine 54.

"Home Purchase Loans to Employee/Shareholders may have Extended Term" (1992) 3 Tax. of Exec. Compensation and Retirement 552.

Innes, William I., "The Taxation of Indirect Benefits: An Examination of Subsections 56(2), 56(3), 56(4), 245(2) and 245(3) of the *Income Tax Act*", in *Proceedings of 38th Tax Conf.* 42:1 (Can. Tax Foundation, 1986).

Jaskolka, Norman, "Employee and Shareholder Loans — Are They a Benefit?" (1983) 116 CA Magazine 51.

Jones, D. Alan, "Business Equity Valuations and Real Estate Appraisals in Revenue Canada", in *Proceedings of 45th Tax Conf.* 26:1 (Can. Tax Foundation, 1993).

Krishna, Vern, "Shareholder Benefits" (1990) 3 Can. Current Tax C33.

Krishna, Vern, "Who Benefits?" (1991) 5 CGA Magazine 45.

Lee, Julie Y., "Stock-Based Compensation: Selected Regulatory and Taxation Issues", *Corp. Mgmt. Tax Conf.* 4:1 (Can. Tax Foundation, 1991).

McCrodan, Andrew, "Tackling Tax-related Troubles" (1993) 126 CA Magazine No. 4 45.

Montgomery, Anne, "Developments in Executive Compensation" (1992) 3 Can. Current Tax T-21.

"Redemption or Repurchase of Shares (The)", *Can. Tax Letter*, February 22, 1982 (De Boo).

"Revenue Canada Round Table", in *Proceedings of 33rd Tax Conf.* 726 (Can. Tax Foundation, 1981).

Richards, Gabrielle M.R., "A Trap for the Unwary: Subsection 15(2) of the *Income Tax Act*" (1993) 4 Can. Current Tax J27.

"Shareholders Benefits — Vacation Properties" (1988) 15 Can. Tax News 121.

Sklar, Murray, "Don't Get Trapped by the New Income Attribution Rules" (1987) 120 CA Magazine 42.

Smith, David W., "New Income Attribution Rules 'Muddified' *Income Tax Act*" (1986) 13 Nat. (CBA) 12.

Smith, David W., "Wilson's Minimum-Tax Proposals Treat Dividends Unfairly" (1986) 13 Nat. (CBA) 2.

Strain, William J., "Life-insured Share Redemption Provides Advantages Over Outright Buyback" (1993) 5 Tax. of Exec. Compensation and Retirement 811.

Stubbs, Larry, and Don Goodison, "Planning Ahead" (1990) 4 CGA Magazine 42.

Templeton, Michael D., "Loan Made to Shareholder-Employee *qua* Employee Liable to Tax under Subsection 15(2)" (1994) 42 Can. Tax J. 201.

Tunney, Wayne L., "Taking Stock: The Pros and Cons of Stock-Based Compensation", *Corp. Mgmt. Tax Conf.* 3:1 (Can. Tax Foundation, 1991).

Ulmer, John M., "Family Members as Shareholders of a Small Business Corporation", in *Proceedings of 38th Tax Conf.* 14:1 (Can. Tax Foundation, 1986).

Ward, David A., and John M. Ulmer, "Corporate Taxation: Shares Eligible for the Capital Gains Exemption" (1986) 5 Legal Alert 81.

Zien, Randolph B., "Remuneration of Shareholders and Executives: Selected Problems", *British Columbia Tax Conf.* 149 (Can. Tax Foundation, 1980).

Indirect Benefits

Desaulniers, Claude P., "Choix d'une structure du capital", *J. d'études fiscales* 79 (Can. Tax Foundation, 1982).

Drache, A.B.C., "Estate Planning Time Bomb" (1983) 5 Can. Taxpayer 42.

Graschuk, Harry S., "The Professional Corporation in Alberta" (1977) 5 Can. Tax J. 109.

Katz, Robert L., "Income Splitting: The Labyrinth of Attribution", *B.C. Tax Conf.* 93 (Can. Tax Foundation, 1980).

Kellough, Howard J., "Selecting an Appropriate Share Capital Structure for Private Corporations", in *Proceedings of 33rd Tax Conf.* 49 (Can. Tax Foundation, 1981).

Krishna, V., "Corporate Share Structures and Estate Planning" (1983) 6 E. & T.Q. 168.

Kroft, E.G., "Income Splitting" (1983) 17 CGA Magazine 28.

Kwan, Stanley P.W., and Kenneth J. Murray, "Remuneration Planning for the Owner-Manager" (1981) 9 Can. Tax J. 603.

Leuser, John, "Income Splitting Within the Family" (1981) 55 Cost & Mgmt. 47.

McKenzie, H.G., "Recent Developments in Income Splitting", *Prairie Provinces Tax Conf.* 413 (Can. Tax Foundation, 1981).

Morris, J.S.D., "Freezing Family Business Interests — Inflation and Other Concerns" (1981) 9 Can. Tax J.11.

Promislow, Norm, "Estate Planning and Income Splitting: Recent Developments", *Prairie Prov. Tax Conf.* 371 (Can. Tax Foundation, 1983).

Shinerock, Stanley, "Tax Planning for the Canadian-Controlled Private Corporation" (1980) 14 CGA Magazine 32.

Zaystoll, J.J., "Accountant's Comment: Innovative Share Capital Structures to Split Income Effectively" (1984) 42 Advocate (Van.) 177.

Deemed Dividends

Boultbee, J.A., "Minimizing the Taxation Effects of Dividends", in *Proceedings of 37th Tax Conf.* 7 (Can. Tax Foundation, 1985).

Carten, Michael A., "Income Tax Considerations in the Capitalization of a Corporation", *Corp. Mgmt. Tax Conf.* 50 (Can. Tax Foundation, 1980).

Gould, Lawrence I., and Stanley N. Laiken, "Dividends vs. Capital Gains under Share Redemptions" (1979) 7 Can. Tax J. 161.

Hart, Stephen D., "Estate Freezes, Part: Income Splitting" (1982) 115 CA Magazine 60.

Hogg, R.D., "Stock Option Benefits in Canadian Controlled Private Corporations" (1978) 6 Can. Tax J. 85.

Kellough, Howard J., "Formation, Operation, and Disposition of Closely Held Corporations", in *Proceedings of 30th Tax Conf.* 703 (Can. Tax Foundation, 1978).

"Revenue Canada Round Table", in *Proceedings of 33rd Tax Conf.* 726 (Can. Tax Foundation, 1981).

Sohmer, David H., "Purchase and Sale of a Closely-Held Business (2)" (1979) 112 CA Magazine 70.

Spindler, Herbert O., "Article X: Dividends", in *Proceedings of 32nd Tax Conf.* 405 (Can. Tax Foundation, 1980).

Imputed Interest on Loans

Drache, A.B.C., "Reduction of Tax at Source" (1983) 5 Can. Taxpayer 130.

Hamill, James R., "Tax Consequences of Corporation-Shareholder Loans" (1989) 67 Taxes 608.

Hugget, Donald R., "Obfusclarity" (1992) 9 Can. Tax News 57.

Jaskolka, Norman, "Employee and Shareholder Loans — Are They a Benefit?" (1983) 116 CA Magazine 51.

Kar, William J., "The Onus of Shareholder Loans" (1993) 126 CA Magazine 34.

Novek, Barbara L., "Taxable Benefit from Interest Free Loan may Reduce Capital Gains Exemption" (1992) 3 Tax. of Exec. Compensation and Retirement 572.

Shareholder Agreements

Hugget, Donald R., "Shareholder Agreements" (1991) 19 Can. Tax News 24.

Krishna, Vern, "Buy-Sell Shareholders' Agreements" (1988) 2 CGA Magazine 39.

Krishna, Vern, "Shareholder Agreements" (1988) 2 CGA Magazine 21.

Magee, J.E., "Shareholder Buy-sell Agreements to Operate on the Winding-up of a Trust" (1991) 39 Can. Tax J. 983.

PART XI: PRACTICE & PROCEDURE

CHAPTER 23 — AUDITS, OBJECTIONS, APPEALS, AND INVESTIGATIONS

I. — General Comment

One of the basic features of the Canadian income tax system is that it relies heavily on taxpayers to self-assess their income on an annual basis on a prescribed form and in a pre-scribed manner. Filing requirements depend on a taxpayer's status. Thus, voluntary compliance and self-assessment are the foundation of the administrative structure of the Act. Of course, the tax system does not rely exclusively upon voluntary compliance. It has persuasive inducements to encourage taxpayers to disclose their income. The Minister can impose penalties, make third-party demands, garnish income, seize property, and prosecute through the criminal process. Indeed, as we see in this chapter, the Canada Revenue Agency's powers exceed those of most other government agencies and are subject to fewer legislative and judicial controls.

II. — Income Tax Returns

1. — Who Must File

Not all taxpayers must file tax returns every year: filing requirements vary according to the taxpayer's status, type of income earned, and tax credits claimed. The following, however, must file income tax returns:[1]

- Corporations (other than registered charities);

- Individuals, if they are taxable in the year;

- Individuals who have taxable capital gains or have disposed of capital property in the year; and

- Individuals who owe an amount under the Home Buyer's Plan or Lifelong Learning Plan.

In addition to income tax returns, some taxpayers must also file various information returns that report income paid to other taxpayers.

2. — Filing Deadlines

Tax returns are filed on prescribed forms. Each return is in respect of a "taxation year"[2] in accordance with the following filing times:

---

[1]Subs. 150(1); IC 71-14R3, "The Tax Audit" (June 18, 1984).

[2]S. 249.

Taxpayer	Time Limit	Form
Individuals	April 30 of the following year	T1
Deceased Persons	6 months after death*	T1
Corporations (whether or not year-end tax is payable)	6 months after fiscal year-end	T2
Trusts and estates (if tax is payable in respect of the year)	90 days from end of estate's or trust's taxation year	T3
Registered charities (Info. returns)	6 months after year-end	T3010

Notes:

*   This rule applies for individuals who die between November 1 and the normal filing date. Where an individual dies between January 1 and October 31, the normal filing date (April 30) applies.

For individuals in business, the Act extends the deadline for filing from April 30 to June 15.[3]

3. — Individuals

An individual must file an income tax return in respect of a taxation year if the individual is taxable in the year.[4] An individual may, however, voluntarily file a return even though he or she is not taxable in a particular year. Voluntary filing a nil return even if there is no tax payable triggers the limitation period within which the individual may be reassessed in respect of the return.[5]

It is generally prudent for an individual to file annual tax returns regardless of whether or not the individual believes that tax is payable for the particular year. Otherwise the indivi-

---

[3]Para. 150(1)(d).

[4]Para. 150(1)(d); 150(1.1)(b).

[5]Subs. 152(4). The prescribed form for individuals is Form T1 General. Taxpayers filing simple tax returns may in certain circumstances use Form T1 Special.

dual may be subject to penalties if it is later established that he or she was liable for tax in respect of that year.[6]

4. — Corporations

A corporation (other than a corporation registered as a charity) must file an income tax return within six months from the end of its taxation year.[7] The return, accompanied by financial statements and supporting schedules, must be filed whether or not the corporation is taxable.

5. — Trusts and Estates

A trust or estate must file a return in respect of each taxation year for *which taxes are payable* within 90 days from the end of its taxation year.[8]

A trustee in bankruptcy, liquidator, receiver, or agent acting on behalf of a person who has not filed a return must file a return on behalf of that person within the relevant time limit.[9]

6. — Deceased Persons

The legal representative of a person who has died without filing an income tax return must file the deceased's return within six months from the day of death,[10] if the taxpayer dies between November 1 and the normal filing date. Where the individual dies between January 1 and October 31, the normal filing date applies.

7. — Designated Persons

Where a person who is required to file an income tax return fails to do so, the Minister may designate another person to file the return within a stipulated time.[11]

---

[6]S. 162.

[7]Para. 150(1)(a).

[8]Para. 150(1)(c).

[9]Subs. 150(3).

[10]Para. 150(1)(b).

[11]Para. 150(1)(e).

8. — Non-Resident Taxpayers

A non-resident who is employed in Canada, carries on business in Canada, or disposes of taxable Canadian property is taxable on his or her Canadian source income. Non-residents must file income tax returns in the same manner as resident taxpayers.[12] Non-resident taxpayers carrying on business in Canada are exempt from withholding tax on any income that is otherwise taxable under Part I of the Act.[13]

9. — Receipt of Documents

The Act deems a document mailed by first class mail (or its equivalent) to have been received by the person to whom it was sent on the day when it was mailed.[14] Courier services are generally equivalent to first class mail service. The onus rests on the taxpayer to establish the facts.[15]

III. — Amended Tax Returns

1. — General Rule

A taxpayer does not generally have a statutory right to amend his or her tax return in respect of a taxation year. As a matter of practice, however, the Minister will usually accept a taxpayer's amended income tax return or supplementary information and reassess the taxpayer.

2. — Voluntary Disclosure

To encourage self-assessment and voluntary disclosure of tax information, the Agency accepts voluntary disclosures of undeclared income. The Agency's policy in respect of voluntary disclosure is set out in its Information Circular:[16]

> If a taxpayer has never filed tax returns, and the returns are then voluntarily filed, the taxpayer
> will be required to pay only the tax owing on the reported incomes, with interest. If a taxpayer

---

[12]Subs. 2(3).

[13]Subs. 215(4); Reg. 805.

[14]Para. 248(7)(a).

[15]*Erroca Ent. Ltd. v. M.N.R.*, [1986] 2 C.T.C. 2425, 86 D.T.C. 1821 (T.C.C.). See also: *VIH Logging Ltd. v. R.* (2003), [2004] 2 C.T.C. 2149, 2004 D.T.C. 2090 (T.C.C. [General Procedure]); affirmed [2005] 1 C.T.C. 387 (F.C.A.) (notice sent when courier picked up mail).

[16]IC 85-1R2, "Voluntary Disclosures" (October 23, 1992) (IC 5-IR2 has been cancelled and replaced by IC 00-1R "Voluntary Disclosures Program" (September 30, 2002)).

has given incomplete information in a return and subsequently submits the missing information, the taxpayer will be required to pay only the tax owing on the adjusted income, with interest. No prosecution will be undertaken, nor will any civil penalties, including late filing penalties, be imposed, on any amounts included in such voluntary disclosures. The identity of anyone making a voluntary disclosure will be held in confidence, as in the case with all taxpayer information.

This policy applies to corporations and individuals making voluntary disclosures if the following requirements are met:

(a) *Voluntary Disclosure* — The taxpayer has to initiate the voluntary disclosure. A disclosure is not considered to be voluntary if it arises when the CRA has begun audit or enforcement action.

(b) *Verification* — Each voluntary disclosure should include enough details to allow the facts to be verified.

(c) *Incomplete Disclosure* — If a disclosure is voluntary but incomplete, the disclosed information will be considered voluntary. However, the taxpayer will be subject to penalties, prosecution, or both, relating to any substantial undisclosed amounts.

(d) *Payment* — The taxpayer must pay the total amount of any taxes and interest owing, or make acceptable arrangements for paying such amounts.

(e) *Procedure* — A person can make a voluntary disclosure by contacting the CRA. That person will not need to make a detailed submission of the first contact. However, the taxpayer must do so within a period of time that is mutually agreed upon. The initial contact will be considered to be the date of the voluntary disclosure.

3. — Statutory Right to Amend Return

A taxpayer can carry back a deduction from one tax year to a preceding year and file an amended return in the following circumstances:[17]

Deduction	References
Capital losses in year of death and immediately preceding year may be carried back and deducted from other income	subs. 111(2)
Three-year carryback of listed personal property losses	s. 41
Carryback of gifts made in the year of death	s. 118.1

---

[17]Subs. 152(6).

Deduction	References
Three-year carryback of unused foreign tax credits	subs. 126(2)
Three-year carryback of non-capital, net capital, restricted farm and farm losses	subs. 111(1)
Three-year carryback of investment tax credits to immediately preceding year	subs. 127(5)
Three-year carryback of unused Part VI tax credits	s. 125.2
Carryback of RRSP premium	para. 60(i), 146
Election upon disposition of property by legal representative of deceased taxpayer	subs. 164(6)

Taxpayers can also file amended tax returns to adjust income in a preceding taxation year where the adjustment arises as a consequence of exercising an option contract.[18]

IV. — Withholding Taxes

Certain types of payments are subject to withholding taxes. For example, a person who makes a compensatory payment to a taxpayer must withhold an amount on account of the payee's potential tax liability.[19] Withheld taxes must be remitted to the Receiver General of Canada.[20]

A person may also be required to file an information return. For example, every person who pays a dividend or makes an interest or royalty payment to a resident taxpayer must file a Return of Investment Income (Form T5).[21] Similarly, a person who pays to a non-resident

---

[18]Subs. 49(4); see Chapter 11, "Capital Gains and Losses".

[19]Subs. 153(1); Regs. 100–108 (withholding and remittance).

[20]See subs. 227(9) (failure to remit on time can result in penalty); *Electrocan Systems Ltd. v. M.N.R.*, [1986] 1 C.T.C. 269, (sub nom. *Electrocan Systems Ltd. v. The Queen*) 86 D.T.C. 6089 (F.C.T.D.); affd 89 D.T.C. 5079, [1989] 1 C.T.C. 244 (Fed. C.A.) (penalty payable even if taxpayer remits arrears before assessment issued).

[21]Reg. 201.

an amount in respect of dividends, interest, rents, royalties, management fees, or support payments must also file an information return outlining the details of the payment.

A person who controls or receives income, gains, or profits in a fiduciary capacity is required to file a Trust Information Return.[22]

V. — Demand To File Return

The Minister can demand that a person file a tax return in prescribed form and disclose prescribed information, regardless of whether the taxpayer has already filed a return or is liable for tax.[23] The Minister must serve such a demand personally on the taxpayer or send it by registered mail.[24]

VI. — Failure To File Return

1. — Voluntary System

The income tax system relies heavily upon "voluntary" self-assessment of taxes. There are, however, severe penalties for failure to voluntarily file and conform. The system is "voluntary" only in the sense that a taxpayer must file income tax returns without being called upon to do so by the Minister. Failure to file a return, or to respond to a demand for a return, within the time limits can trigger various penalties, interest charges and even criminal prosecution.

2. — Penalties

There is a two-tier penalty for failure to file a tax return.

---

[22]Reg. 204; Form T3.

[23]Subs. 150(2).

[24]See, generally, subs. 220(1); see also subss. 244(5), (6) (procedure for proof of service).

(a) — First Offence

On the first offence, the penalty is calculated by reference to the amount of tax unpaid at the time when the return should have been filed. This penalty is equal to the aggregate of:[25]

- 5 per cent of the tax that was unpaid at the time when the return was required to be filed; and

- 1 per cent of the unpaid tax for each complete month (not exceeding a total of 12 months) between the date on which the return was required to be filed and the date on which it was actually filed.

Thus, the maximum late-filing penalty is 17 per cent of the amount of tax unpaid at the time when the return was required to be filed.

(b) — Subsequent Offences

On a second or subsequent offence, the penalty is equal to the sum of 10 per cent of the unpaid tax plus 2 per cent of the unpaid tax per month (not exceeding 20 months) of default.[26]

This penalty applies if the taxpayer, at the time of the subsequent failure to file a return, was previously assessed a penalty for failure to file within the preceding three-year period and the Minister has demanded a return under subsection 150(2).

(c) — Criminal Sanctions

Failure to file an income tax return as required by the Act is also a criminal offence that carries a minimum fine of $1,000.[27] A taxpayer can be liable for both the civil and criminal penalties for failure to file a return but only if the civil penalty is assessed *before* the complaint giving rise to the criminal conviction is laid.[28]

---

[25] Subs. 162(1).

[26] Subs. 162(2).

[27] Subs. 238(1).

[28] Subs. 238(3).

(d) — Trustees

A trustee or other fiduciary who fails to file a return on behalf of a person for whom the trustee is acting is liable to a penalty of $10 for each day of default,[29] subject to a maximum penalty of $50.

VII. — Failure To Provide Information

In addition to providing information on income tax returns, taxpayers may also have an obligation to provide further and supplementary information to the Minister. This information is used to monitor the tax system and as a check on other taxpayers. Failure to provide the supplementary information that is required of taxpayers gives rise to civil, and in some cases criminal, penalties.

1. — Failure to Complete Ownership Certificate

Where a non-resident person pays a Canadian resident interest or dividends by means of a bearer coupon or dividend warrant, the resident payee must complete an ownership certificate in prescribed form.[30]

The bank at which the coupon or dividend warrant is cashed must obtain the ownership certificate from the payee and file it with the Minister on or before the 15th day of the month following the cashing of the cheque or warrant.[31]

A taxpayer who fails to complete or deliver the ownership certificate is liable to a penalty of $50 per failure.[32]

2. — Failure to Provide Social Insurance or Business Number

An individual must provide his or her social insurance number ("SIN") or business number when requested to do so by a person who must file an information return in respect of that individual. An individual who fails to provide his or her SIN or business number when required to do so is subject to a penalty of $100.[33]

---

[29]Subs. 162(3).

[30]S. 234.

[31]Subs. 234(2); Reg. 207.

[32]Subs. 162(4).

[33]Subs. 162(6).

The penalty does not apply where the individual applies for a number within 15 days of the request for the number and then subsequently provides the information within 15 days of its receipt.

The person or partnership who must supply the SIN or business number on an information return is also liable to a penalty of $100 for failure to supply the information.[34] The penalty does not apply if:

- The person or partnership made a reasonable effort to obtain the number from the individual; or

- The individual had applied for, but had not received, the number at the time when the information return was filed.

3. — Failure to File Information Returns

Taxpayers are sometimes obliged to file information returns in respect of their own and other people's affairs. A taxpayer who fails to provide the information as and when required by the Act or Regulations may be penalized.

The penalty depends upon the nature of the offence. Where the Act sets out a specific penalty, that penalty applies to the offence. If the Act does not specify a penalty, a general penalty equal to the *greater* of $100 and $25 per day (not exceeding 100 days) of default applies.[35]

4. — Failure to File Partnership Information

Partnerships also have an obligation to file information returns. The penalty for failure to file, which is *in addition* to the general penalty for non-compliance with the Act or Regulations, is targeted at repeat offenders. The partnership penalties apply where:[36]

- The general penalty for failure to file information has been assessed;

- A demand for the information has been made; and

- A general penalty was imposed in respect of the partnership for a similar offence in any of the three preceding fiscal years.

The penalty is $100 per member for each month or part of a month (not exceeding 24 months) during which the failure continues.

---

[34]Subs. 162(5).

[35]Subs. 162(7).

[36]Subss. 162(8), (7.1) and (8.1).

(a) — Tax Shelter Information

A promoter of a tax shelter must obtain an identification number for the shelter from the Minister before the promoter begins selling the shelter to the general public. This number must be provided to all purchasers who acquire an interest in the tax shelter.[37] A taxpayer who purchases an interest in a tax shelter cannot claim a deduction or a credit in respect of the shelter unless the taxpayer has an identification number.

The promoter must also file an information return that discloses:

- The name, address, and social insurance number of each person who acquires an interest in the shelter;

- The amount paid by each investor; and

- Such other information as is required by the prescribed form.

A promoter who files false or misleading information in respect of the promotion of a tax shelter is liable to a penalty.

A person who sells or accepts an investor's contribution for the purchase of a tax shelter without an officially-issued identification number is also guilty of an offence and subject to penalties. The penalty is equal to the *greater* of:

- $500; and

- 25 per cent of the total of all amounts each of which is the consideration received or receivable from a person in respect of the tax shelter before the correct information is filed with the Minister or the identification number is issued, as the case may be.

5. — Failure to Furnish Foreign-Based Information

Individuals, corporations, partnerships and trusts resident or carrying on business in Canada must file information returns for the year. The return, which must disclose prescribed information regarding transactions with non-resident, non-arm's length persons, must be filed within six months from the end of the corporation's fiscal year.[38]

A separate information return must be filed in respect of each non-resident person with whom the corporation had non-arm's length dealings at any time in the year. Certain non-arm's length non-residents are exempt where the total FMV of transactions does not exceed $1,000,000.

---

[37]Subs. 237.1(7.4).

[38]Subs. 162(10); ss. 233.1 and 233.4.

A corporation that fails to provide information in respect of its non-arm's length transactions with non-resident persons within the stipulated time of a demand for the information is liable to a penalty.

VIII. — Calculation Of Tax Liability

1. — Self-Assessment Procedure

A taxpayer is responsible for determining his or her own income tax liability.[39] As already noted, there are penalties for failure to file a return or to fully disclose income. There are, however, no sanctions for incorrectly calculating the amount of tax that is payable if all relevant information is fully disclosed.

2. — Interest

A taxpayer who incorrectly underestimates his or her tax liability is liable for interest on the difference between the taxpayer's estimate and the amount of tax that the Minister assesses.[40] The sting of the penalty is that late payment interest charges are not deductible as an expense for tax purposes.

IX. — Assessments

1. — General Check

Income tax returns are initially computer-processed and checked for mathematical accuracy. Agency officials also examine returns to ensure that information filed with the return conforms to the requirements of the Act. We refer to this process of agency return verification and information as an "assessment".[41]

---

[39]S. 151.

[40]Subs. 161(1).

[41]*Pure Spring Co. v. M.N.R.*, [1946] C.T.C. 169, 2 D.T.C. 844 (Ex. Ct.), *per* Thorson P. ("assessment" defined as "the summation of all the factors representing tax liability, ascertained in a variety of ways, and the fixation of the total after the necessary computations have been made").

2. — *Quick Assessment*

The Minister must examine *with all due dispatch* all income tax returns and assess the tax and penalties payable.[42] The Minister must also notify the taxpayer of the assessment by means of a notice sent to the address shown on the return.[43]

The initial assessment (sometimes called a "quick assessment")[44] is essentially a check of mathematical accuracy and verification of supplementary documentary evidence. The quick assessment procedure, which can take between eight and 12 weeks from the date that the return is filed, results in a Notice of Assessment.

3. — *Ministerial Delay*

Unfortunately, the phrase "with all due dispatch" lacks clarity and precision. As Fournier J. said in *Jolicoeur*:[45]

> There is no doubt that the Minister is bound by time limits when they are imposed by the statute, but, in my view, the words "with all due dispatch" are not to be interpreted as meaning a fixed period of time. The "with all due dispatch" time limit purports a discretion of the Minister to be exercised, for the good administration of the Act, with reason, justice and legal principles.

The courts tolerate, perhaps even excessively, Ministerial delays, up to 15 months in some cases.[46] They appear, however, to draw the line at 22 months.[47]

---

[42]Subs. 152(1).

[43]Subs. 152(2); *Scott v. M.N.R.*, [1960] C.T.C. 402, 60 D.T.C. 1273 (Ex. Ct.) (notice of assessment mailed to taxpayer's solicitor not proper notice); *Charron v. The Queen*, [1984] C.T.C. 237, 84 D.T.C. 6241 (F.C.T.D.) (no obligation on Minister to serve assessment or send it by registered mail); see also s. 166 (effect of irregularity in complying with Act).

[44]The "quick assessment" triggers the limitation periods for reassessments under subs. 152(4).

[45]*Jolicoeur v. M.N.R.*, [1960] C.T.C. 346 at 358, 60 D.T.C. 1254 at 1261 (Ex. Ct.).

[46]*Hutterian Brethren Church of Wilson v. The Queen*, [1979] C.T.C. 1, 79 D.T.C. 5052; affd. [1980] C.T.C. 1, 79 D.T.C. 5474, 31 NR 426 (F.C.A.) (delay allowed where original assessments did not say that no tax payable; unusual circumstances; colony owed $37,000,000 in 96 actions); *Weih v. M.N.R.*, [1988] 2 C.T.C. 2013, 88 D.T.C. 1379 (T.C.C.) (reassessment at last possible date within four-year period allowed).

[47]*M.N.R. v. Appleby*, [1964] C.T.C. 323, 64 D.T.C. 5199 (Ex. Ct.) (where misrepresentation or fraud, court will extend time limit); *J. Stollar Const. Ltd. v. M.N.R.*, [1989] 1 C.T.C. 2171, 89 D.T.C. 134 (T.C.C.) (delay of seven years invalidated assessment, not made with "all due dispatch").

4. — Subsequent Changes

A "quick assessment" is valid even if the Minister subsequently changes it. As Thorson P. said in *Provincial Paper*:[48]

> The Minister may, therefore, properly decide to accept a taxpayer's income tax return as a correct statement of his taxable income and merely check the computations of tax in it and without any further examination or investigation fix his tax liability accordingly. If he does so it cannot be said that he has not made an assessment.

> It may happen that it will subsequently appear that an assessment so made is inaccurate and that a reassessment is desirable. But there is a vast difference between an assessment that has turned out to be erroneous and an act that is not an assessment at all. It is for the Minister to decide in each case what he shall do. Indeed, in the vast majority of cases he accepts the taxpayer's statement of taxable income as correct and fixes his liability accordingly. It would be fantastic to say that in such cases he has not made an assessment at all. In my opinion, he has plainly done so.

5. — Deemed Valid

The presumption of validity of an assessment is the single most significant rule for taxpayers. The Act *deems* an assessment to be valid and binding on the taxpayer even if it contains an error or defect or has been incorrectly calculated or improperly issued.[49]

The taxpayer's only recourse to an assessment is to file a Notice of Objection and ask that a court or the Agency vary it.[50] The burden of proof rests squarely on the taxpayer to show that the assessment is wrong. Thus, a taxpayer is liable unless he or she can prove otherwise. This rule, from which flows the Minister's ultimate power over taxpayers, is an aberration in Anglo-Canadian law and unique to tax law. The rule places an intolerable burden on taxpayers, particularly those who cannot afford high professional fees to fight the Minister over an extended period of time. The rule effectively denies most individual taxpayers access to justice in tax disputes.

---

[48]*Prov. Paper Ltd. v. M.N.R.*, [1954] C.T.C. 367 at 374, 54 D.T.C. 1199 at 1202 (Ex. Ct.).

[49]Subs. 152(8).

[50]Subs. 152(8); s. 165.

6. — No Judicial Review

A taxpayer can appeal an assessment, but only pursuant to the procedures set out in the *Income Tax Act*.[51] The Federal Court does not have the authority to otherwise quash, review, or restrain an assessment under section 18 of the *Federal Court Act*.[52]

7. — Net Worth Assessments

The Minister is not bound to accept the taxpayer's income tax return. The Minister may assess the amount of tax payable using whatever method is appropriate in the circumstances.[53] The Minister may even issue an "arbitrary" or "net worth" assessment.

(a) — When Used

The Minister generally uses an arbitrary assessment where the taxpayer refuses to file a tax return, files a return that is grossly inaccurate, or does not furnish any evidentiary support or documentation to allow verification of the return.[54] Notwithstanding that an assessment is "arbitrary", the Minister must disclose the basis on which it is formulated.[55]

(b) — Method Applied

The Minister is not statutorily constrained in the manner in which the Minister issues an arbitrary assessment. In most cases, however, the Minister uses the "net worth" method. This method involves determining the taxpayer's worth at the beginning and at the end of the taxation years in question. Income for the period is calculated by adding the taxpayer's

---

[51]See s. 169.

[52]R.S.C. 1985, c. F-7; *The Queen v. Parsons*, [1984] C.T.C. 352, (sub nom. *M.N.R. v. Parsons*) 84 D.T.C. 6345 (F.C.A.) ("legal authority" of Minister challengeable only on specific grounds of "quantum" and "liability"); *Gibbs v. M.N.R.*, [1984] C.T.C. 434, 84 D.T.C. 6418 (F.C.T.D.) (motion to quash assessment dismissed).

[53]Subs. 152(7); *Dezura v. M.N.R.*, [1947] C.T.C. 375, 3 D.T.C. 1101 (Ex. Ct.); *Commercial Hotel Ltd. v. M.N.R.* (1947), 3 D.T.C. 1119 (Ex. Ct.).

[54]*Johnston v. M.N.R.*, [1948] S.C.R. 486, [1948] C.T.C. 195, 3 D.T.C. 1182 (S.C.C.). See also *Hsu v. R.*, [2001] 4 C.T.C. 1, 2001 D.T.C. 5459 (Fed. C.A.); leave to appeal refused (2002), 293 N.R. 328 (note) (S.C.C.); *Cheung v. R.*, [2005] 2 C.T.C. 2098, 2005 D.T.C. 269 (Eng.) (T.C.C. [Informal Procedure]).

[55]See *Kerr v. Can.*, [1989] 2 C.T.C. 112, (sub nom. *Kerr v. The Queen*) 89 D.T.C. 5348 (F.C.T.D.) (income from earnings as prostitute and living off avails of other prostitutes assessed on net worth basis).

non-deductible expenditures to the increase in the taxpayer's "net worth" and deducting therefrom any appreciation in the value of the taxpayer's capital assets. Having determined the total increase in the taxpayer's "net worth" between two points in time, the Minister allocates the estimated net income between the taxation years in question.

Example		
Assume:		
	YEAR 1	YEAR 2
Assets	$ 100,000	$ 200,000
Liabilities	$ 40,000	$ 60,000
Personal expenditures	$ 30,000	
Appreciation in capital value of assets between YEAR 1 and YEAR 2	$ 20,000	

Then:

Income = NW (YEAR 2) - NW (YEAR 1) + Personal expenditures - Appreciation in assets

= $140,000–60,000 + 30,000–20,000

Income = $90,000

(c) — Deemed Valid

By its very nature, an arbitrary assessment is an estimate. The Minister assesses the taxpayer on the best evidence available. Unless the taxpayer can show that the assessment is incorrect, it is valid and binding.[56] The burden of proof in the appeal of an assessment rests with

---

[56]See, e.g., *Dezura v. M.N.R.*, [1947] C.T.C. at 380, 3 D.T.C. 1101 at 1102 (Ex. Ct.) *per* Thorson P. (presumption of validity of Minister's assessment: when Minister invokes subs. 152(7), the tax so determined subject to review by court under its appellate jurisdiction; if, on appeal, court finds that amount determined by Minister is incorrect in fact, appeal must be allowed to extent of error; if court not satisfied on evidence that there has been error in amount, then appeal must be dismissed; onus of proof of error in amount of determination rests on appellant).

the taxpayer. This is so whether or not the Minister imposes a penalty based on the assessment.[57] As the Supreme Court of Canada said in *Anderson Logging*:[58]

> First, as to the contention of the point of onus. If, on an appeal to the judge of the Court of Revision, it appears that, on the true facts, the application of the pertinent enactment is doubtful, it would, on principle, seem that the Crown must fail. That seems to be necessarily involved in the principle according to which statutes imposing a burden upon the subject have, by inveterate practice, been interpreted and administered. But, as concerns the inquiry into the facts, the appellant is in the same position as any other appellant. He must show that the impeached assessment is an assessment which ought not to have been made; that is to say, he must establish facts upon which it can be affirmatively asserted that the assessment was not authorized by the taxing statute, or which bring the matter into such a state of doubt that, on the principles alluded to, the liability of the appellant must be negatived. The true facts may be established, of course, by direct evidence or by probable inference. The appellant may adduce facts constituting a *prima facie* case which remains unanswered; but in considering whether this has been done it is important not to forget, if it be so, that the facts are, in a special degree if not exclusively, within the appellant's cognizance, although this last is a consideration which, for obvious reasons, must not be pressed too far.

8. — Determination of Losses

A taxpayer can ask the Minister to determine the amount of his non-capital losses, net capital losses, limited partnership losses, restricted farm losses, or farm losses for a year.[59] The Minister must make the calculations and send the taxpayer a notice of the determined amount. Thus, the taxpayer has an option in respect of disputes concerning his or her losses: the taxpayer can either have the amount of the loss determined immediately or wait until such time as the amount of the loss has an effect upon his or her tax liability in another year. As we shall see, the limitation periods applicable to these two alternatives may be quite different.[60]

9. — Non-Residents

Non-residents who are employed in Canada, carry on business in Canada, or dispose of taxable Canadian property are taxable in Canada on their Canadian source income and are

---

[57]*The Queen v. Taylor*, [1984] C.T.C. 436, 84 D.T.C. 6459 (F.C.T.D.) (since burden of proof is on taxpayer, taxpayer must start by adducing evidence).

[58]*The King v. Anderson Logging Co.*, [1925] S.C.R. 45 at 50, [1917–27] C.G.T.C. 198 at 201, 52 D.T.C. 1209 at 1211; affd. [1926] A.C. 140, [1917–27] C.T.C. 210, 52 D.T.C. 1215 (P.C.).

[59]Subs. 152(1.1).

[60]See subs. 152(4).

subject to the normal assessment procedures applicable to residents. Assessments arising from the withholding tax obligations and the liability for Part XIV tax on branch profits are, with appropriate modifications, also subject to the same procedures as those applicable to residents.[61]

X. — Reassessments

The Minister can also reassess a taxpayer's income. Unlike the timetable for "quick assessments", however, the power to reassess is subject to stringent limitation periods.

The limitation periods run from the date of *mailing* of the notice of original assessment. Within the prescribed limitation period the Minister may issue as many reassessments as the circumstances require.[62] Two criteria determine the limitation period:

1. The type of taxpayer; and

2. The nature of the transaction that triggers the reassessment.

1. — General Rule

In the absence of fraud or misrepresentation, the Minister may normally reassess an individual's return for a particular taxation year within three years from the date of mailing of the original notice of assessment for the year.[63] During this three-year period, the Minister may reconsider *any* fact considered relevant to the calculation of the taxpayer's liability, interest, or penalties.

2. — Losses, Gifts, and Tax Credits

The limitation period extends to six years in respect of claims that arise from:[64]

• An individual's death, in respect of allowable capital losses for the year immediately preceding death;

• Listed personal property losses in computing net gains from dispositions of such property for the preceding three taxation years;

---

[61]Subs. 219(3).

[62]*Abrahams v. M.N.R.*, [1966] C.T.C. 690, 66 D.T.C. 5451 (Ex. Ct.).

[63]Subs. 152(4).

[64]Para. 152(4)(b) and subs. 152(6).

- Gifts made by an individual in the year of death, carried back to the preceding taxation year;

- Non-capital, net capital, restricted farm, and farm losses that are carried back to the preceding three taxation years;

- Unused business foreign tax credits to be carried back to the preceding three taxation years;

- Investment tax credits in respect of property acquired in a year that may be carried back to the preceding three taxation years;

- Carrybacks arising from an election by an individual's estate to treat capital losses incurred by the estate in its first taxation year as losses deductible by the deceased taxpayer incurred in the year of death;

- Transactions involving a taxpayer and a non-resident person with whom the taxpayer was not dealing at arm's length;

- Carryback of RRSP premiums; or

- Transactions involving additional income tax payments to, or reimbursements from, the government of a foreign country.

A reassessment issued within the six-year limitation period may be made only on the basis of adjustments that may reasonably be regarded as relating to the deduction or credit that is to be carried back to a previous taxation year.

3. — Corporations

Special rules apply to corporations: the limitation period during which the Minister can assess a corporation depends on the nature of the corporation.

(a) — Canadian-Controlled Private Corporations ("CCPCs")

A CCPC can be reassessed only during the "normal reassessment period", that is, three years after the day of mailing of the original Notice of Assessment.

(b) — Large Corporations and Mutual Funds

The limitation period for mutual funds and corporations other than CCCPs is four years from the mailing of the original assessment.[65]

---

[65]Para. 152(3.1)(a).

4. — Method of Giving Notice

(a) — Mail

Most, but not all, notices of assessment and reassessment are sent by mail. We presume a Notice of Assessment to have been mailed on the date appearing on its face. The presumption may be challenged by the submission of evidence to establish otherwise.[66] The Act also deems a Notice of Assessment to have been *made* on the day when it was mailed.[67]

(b) — Any Other Method

The Minister can send a notice to a taxpayer by any method. For example, in the event of postal disruptions, the notice may be hand-delivered. The Act merely requires that the Minister *send* the notice of assessment within the stipulated limitation periods.[68] There is no specific requirement that the taxpayer receive the assessment. Hence, a notice that is properly mailed to the taxpayer's correct address is valid even if it is lost in the mail.

5. — Fraud or Misrepresentation

(a) — No Limitation

There is no limitation period where the taxpayer makes a misrepresentation that is attributable to neglect, carelessness or wilful default, or where the taxpayer commits a fraud in connection with his or her tax return.[69]

The Minister has the onus to prove that the usual limitation period should not apply because of the taxpayer's neglect, carelessness, wilful default, or fraud.

---

[66]Subs. 244(14).

[67]Subs. 244(15).

[68]*Flanagan v. The Queen*, [1987] 2 C.T.C. 167, 87 D.T.C. 5390 (F.C.A.) (only dispatch required, not receipt, in this case notice of assessment not sent since retained by the CRA); *Bhatti v. M.N.R.*, [1981] C.T.C. 2555, 81 D.T.C. 506 (F.C.T.D.) (notice sent to taxpayer's previous address invalid where taxpayer had notified Minister of change of address).

[69]Para. 152(4)(a).

(b) — Burden of Proof

"Fraud" means a false representation that is made knowingly or without belief in its truth, or recklessly, or without care as to whether it is true or false.[70]

If the Minister discharges the burden of proof and has the limitation period set aside, the onus reverts to the taxpayer to show that the reassessment is incorrect.[71]

Even where the Minister proves that the normal reassessment period does not apply, the reassessment may be made only in respect of amounts that the taxpayer failed to include in income *as a result* of neglect, carelessness, wilful default, or fraud. The Minister may not reassess any amounts that are beyond the three-year limitation period and are not attributable to the neglect, carelessness, wilful default, or fraud.[72]

(c) — "Neglect, Carelessness, or Wilful Default"

What constitutes neglect, carelessness, or wilful default? Every error of fact is, in a sense, a misrepresentation of fact. But not every misrepresentation of fact is sufficient to set aside the statutory limitation period. The Minister must go further and show on a balance of probabilities that the misrepresentation is attributable to the taxpayer's neglect, carelessness, or wilful default. Thus, the Minister must show something more than mere error: the Minister must establish culpable negligence.

(i) — Culpable Negligence

Culpable negligence implies fault. The "misrepresentation" does not have to be fraudulent: innocent misrepresentation is sufficient to extend the limitation period if the misrepresenta-

---

[70]*Derry v. Peek* (1889), 14 App. Cas. 337 at 374 (H.L.).

[71]Subs. 152(4); IT-241, "Reassessment Made after the Four-Year Limit" (August 11, 1975); IC 75-7R3, "Reassessment of a Return of Income" (July 9, 1984) (archived); see also *M.N.R. v. Taylor*, [1961] C.T.C. 211, 61 D.T.C. 1139 (Ex. Ct.) (Minister must establish misrepresentation or fraud on balance of probabilities); *M.N.R. v. Foot*, [1964] C.T.C. 317, 64 D.T.C. 5196 (Ex. Ct.) (statutory time limit set aside where misrepresentation in reported income); *M.N.R. v. Appleby*, [1964] C.T.C. 323, 64 D.T.C. 5199 (Ex. Ct.) (Minister must establish beyond a reasonable doubt that there has been a misrepresentation on the part of the taxpayer); *Roselawn Invt. Ltd. v. M.N.R.*, [1980] C.T.C. 2316, 80 D.T.C. 1271 (T.R.B.) (onus on Minister to establish misrepresentation or fraud in any appeal from an assessment made beyond the four-year period).

[72]Subs. 152(4.01).

tion is attributable to the taxpayer's neglect, carelessness, or wilful default. In *Bisson*, for example:[73]

> ... any fraud necessarily presupposes a "misrepresentation", and if the latter word covered every type of inaccurate representation, the reference to fraud in [subpara. 152(4)(a)(i)] would be totally unnecessary. In my view, the fact that the legislator referred not only to "misrepresentation" but to "fraud" indicates that, by the first word, he meant innocent misrepresentations which, without being fraudulent, are still culpable in the sense that they would not have been made if the person committing them had not been negligent. I therefore conclude that a taxpayer who, without any negligence on his part, commits an error in declaring his income, does not make a misrepresentation within the meaning of [subpara. 152(4)(a)(i)]. When the Minister seeks to rely on this provision to proceed with a re-assessment after four years, he must therefore not only show that the taxpayer committed an error in declaring his income but also that error is attributable to negligence on his part.

(ii) — Standard of Care

The test for culpability is whether the taxpayer exercised a standard of care that a wise and prudent person would in comparable circumstances. But "wisdom is not infallibility and prudence is not perfection."[74] The Minister must show more than that the taxpayer committed an error of fact. The Minister must also show that the error was attributable to an unacceptable standard of care; in other words, that the taxpayer was negligent in that he or she did not exercise reasonable care:[75]

> For the Minister to show the taxpayer has not exercised reasonable care requires, in my view, something more than simply submitting evidence that the taxpayer has made deposits to his bank accounts in amounts greater than his employment income and advising the court that he ... does not accept the taxpayer's explanation of the source of funds. ... It is not enough to suggest misrepresentation or fraud.

A taxpayer may be negligent in misstating income because of negligence in maintaining, or failing to maintain, records. A person who does not act with sufficient care, or exercise the care of a "reasonable person", is negligent.

It is important to note, however, that a finding of "negligence" sufficient to empower the Minister to reassess beyond the normal limitation period in subsection 152(4) is not, *per se*, enough to justify the imposition of a penalty under subsection 163(2). The latter provision requires a finding of "gross negligence".

---

[73]*M.N.R. v. Bisson*, [1972] C.T.C. 446 at 454, 72 D.T.C. 6374 at 6380 (F.C.T.D.).

[74]*Reilly v. R.*, [1984] C.T.C. 21 at 42, 84 D.T.C. 6001 at 6018 (F.C.T.D.), *per* Muldoon J.

[75]*Markakis v. M.N.R.*, [1986] 1 C.T.C. 2318 at 2321, 86 D.T.C. 1237 at 1239 (T.C.C.); see also *Venne v. The Queen*, [1984] C.T.C. 223, 84 D.T.C. 6247 (F.C.T.D.) (taxpayer who did not read tax returns prior to signing them did not exercise reasonable care).

Gross negligence involves a very high degree of negligence: indifference as to whether the law is obeyed or not.[76] In *Venne*,[77] for example:

> Gross negligence must be taken to involve greater neglect than simply a failure to use reasonable care. It must involve a high degree of negligence tantamount to intentional acting, an indifference as to whether the law is complied with or not.

(iii) — Burden of Proof

The onus rests initially on the Minister to establish that the taxpayer's misrepresentation is attributable to neglect, carelessness or wilful default, or that the taxpayer has committed a fraud. If the Minister successfully discharges the burden, the onus shifts to the taxpayer to establish that the reassessment is incorrect.

Where the appropriate treatment of a transaction or event is in doubt or susceptible to alternative interpretations, the taxpayer is entitled to select the interpretation that is most favourable to the taxpayer. The taxpayer does not have to adopt the interpretation that is more favourable to the revenue authorities. This is so even if a similar or identical transaction is under dispute with the Agency.[78]

6. — Waiver of Limitation Period

The Minister may ask a taxpayer to waive the normal limitation period so that the parties can adduce information or make representations in respect of a taxation year that, in the absence of the waiver, will become time-barred. Without a waiver, the Minister would feel compelled to reassess the taxpayer, who would then have to pay the tax demanded pending resolution of the dispute.[79]

The limitation period does not apply where the taxpayer files a waiver with the Agency.[80] A taxpayer may, however, restrict the scope of the waiver and, by doing so, restrict the scope of matters that the Minister can reassess.[81] The taxpayer can also revoke the waiver by giving the Minister six months notice of the revocation.[82]

---

[76]*Honig v. Canada*, [1991] 2 C.T.C. 279, (sub nom. *Honig v. The Queen*) 91 D.T.C. 5612 (F.C.T.D.).

[77]*Venne v. The Queen*, [1984] C.T.C. 223 at 234, 84 D.T.C. 6247 at 6256 (F.C.T.D.).

[78]See, e.g., *Regina Shoppers Mall Ltd. v. Canada*, [1991] 1 C.T.C. 297, 91 D.T.C. 5101 (F.C.A.).

[79]S. 158.

[80]Subpara. 152(4)(a)(ii).

[81]Subs. 152(4.01).

[82]Subs. 152(4.1); Form T652.

XI. — Payment Of Tax

1. — Payable When Due

A taxpayer must pay forthwith the full amount of assessed taxes, together with any interest and penalties thereon. The amount outstanding must be paid whether or not the taxpayer has filed a Notice of Objection to, or appeal from, the assessment.[83] The Minister may, however, accept security for payment of taxes or any other amount payable under the Act.[84]

The Minister's powers go further: the Minister can demand payment of taxes even *before they are due* if it is suspected that the taxpayer is about to leave Canada.[85] The Minister may not commence collection procedures, however, until 90 days after the assessment is issued.

2. — Judgment

Where a taxpayer fails to pay his or her taxes within the requisite time, the Minister may have the debt certified and registered in the Federal Court. Upon registration, the certificate can be used as a judgment under which execution can be issued for the amount unpaid.[86] The Minister can also use the judgment to garnish any debts due to the taxpayer by a third party,[87] or to seize the taxpayer's goods and chattels.[88] As already noted, the Minister may, in his or her discretion, accept security for unpaid taxes.[89]

---

[83] S. 158; see also *Interpretation Act*, R.S.C. 1985, c. I-21, subs. 27(2) (number of days calculated by excluding first day of notice and including last day).

[84] Subs. 220(4).

[85] Subs. 226(1); IC 98-1R, "Collections Policies" (September 15, 2000).

[86] S. 223.

[87] S. 224.

[88] S. 225; *Morgan Trust Co. v. Dellelce*, [1985] 2 C.T.C. 370, 85 D.T.C. 5492 (Ont. H.C.) (under *Execution Act*, R.S.O. 1980, c. 146, s. 18, sheriff can seize judgment debtor's equitable or beneficial interest in property, i.e., registered retirement savings plan); *Nat. Trust Co. v. Lorenzetti* (1983), 41 O.R. (2d) 772 (H.C.).

[89] Subs. 220(4).

3. — Collection Procedure

(a) — Normal Procedures

As a general rule, the Minister cannot "collect" on an amount assessed against a taxpayer for a period of at least 90 days after the Notice of Assessment is issued.[90] Where a taxpayer objects to a Notice of Assessment, the Minister cannot collect the tax payable until 90 days after the day on which the Minister mails the notice that confirms or varies the assessment.[91] If the taxpayer files a Notice of Appeal to a court, the Minister cannot collect any taxes under the reassessment until the court pronounces judgment.[92]

(b) — Limitation Periods for Collection

In *Markevich v. Canada*,[93] the Supreme Court of Canada held that since the *Income Tax Act* did not provide for limitation periods within its collection provisions, it is subject to the limitation provisions of general application found in s. 32 of the *Crown Liability and Proceedings Act*,[94] which limit the collection of federal debts to six years.

The Court also held that the Minister, in its role as an agent of a province, is also subject to the *provincial* limitations acts with respect to debts that arise under the *provincial* income tax acts. However, the Court made it clear that tax debts created under the federal *Income Tax Act* were not subject to provincial limitation periods.[95] In response to the Supreme Court's decision in *Markevich*, the Act has a 10-year limitation period for the collection of federal tax debts.[96]

---

[90]Subs. 225.1(1.1).

[91]Subs. 225.1(2).

[92]Subs. 225.1(3) (once a Tax Court decision has been reached against the taxpayer, the CRA can enforce collection even if the case is further appealed to the Federal Court of Appeal).

[93]*Markevich v. Canada*, [2003] 1 S.C.R. 94, [2003] 2 C.T.C. 83, 2003 D.T.C. 5185 (S.C.C.).

[94]*Crown Liability and Proceedings Act*, R.S.C. 1985, c. C-50.

[95]*Markevich v. Canada*, [2003] 1 S.C.R. 94, [2003] 2 C.T.C. 83, 2003 D.T.C. 5185 (S.C.C.); and *Kirkwood v. R.* (2003), [2004] 2 C.T.C. 30, 2004 D.T.C. 6035 (F.C.A.).

[96]Subs. 222(4).

(c) — Collection in Jeopardy

The Minister may collect an account immediately where there are reasonable grounds to believe that a delay would jeopardize collection.[97] To do so, however, the Minister must apply to a judge for permission to proceed. The Minister can apply *ex parte*.

The determination as to whether delay will jeopardize the collection of taxes from a taxpayer is made on a balance of probabilities. The Minister has the burden of proof, and must show that there is a real risk that the taxpayer will dissipate his or her property if collection is delayed because of the appeal process. As McNair J. said in *Danielson*:[98]

> ... the issue goes to the matter of collection jeopardy by reason of the delay normally attributable to the appeal process. The wording of [subs. 225.2(2)] would seem to indicate that *it is necessary to show that because of the passage of time involved to an appeal the taxpayer would become less able to pay the amount assessed.*
>
> In my opinion, the fact that the taxpayer was unable to pay the amount assessed at the time of the direction would not, by itself, be conclusive or determinative. Moreover, the mere suspicion or concern, that delay may jeopardize collection would not be sufficient per se. *The test of "whether it may reasonably be considered" is susceptible of being reasonably translated into the test of whether the evidence on balance of probability is sufficient to lead to the conclusion that it is more likely than not that collection would be jeopardized by delay.* [Emphasis added.]

4. — Fleeing Taxpayer

Where the Minister suspects that a taxpayer is about to leave Canada without settling his or her tax account, the Minister may demand *immediate* payment of all amounts that are payable by the taxpayer. The demand is made by serving, either personally or by registered letter, a notice on the taxpayer demanding payment of all outstanding taxes, interest, and penalties thereon for which the taxpayer is liable. In these circumstances, the Minister does not have to wait for the taxpayer to act after the notice has been served; the Minister may *immediately* seize the taxpayer's goods and chattels through summary execution.[99]

---

[97] Subs. 225.2(2).

[98] *Danielson v. Dep A.G., Canada*, [1986] 2 C.T.C. 380 at 381, 86 D.T.C. 6518 at 6519 (F.C.T.D.); see also *1853-9049 Que. Inc. v. The Queen*, [1987] 1 C.T.C. 137, 87 D.T.C. 5093 (F.C.T.D.) (mere suspicion not sufficient).

[99] S. 226.

XII. — Notice Of Objection

1. — *Limitation Periods*

A taxpayer who objects to a Notice of Assessment or reassessment may file a "Notice of Objection" with the Minister. The notice triggers the appeal process, which is divided into two segments, administrative and legal. The limitation periods for filing the Notice of Objection are as follows:[100]

- Individuals and testamentary trusts: within 90 days of the date of mailing of the Notice of Assessment or within one year of taxpayer's "filing due date", whichever is later.

- All other taxpayers: within 90 days of the date of mailing of the Notice of Assessment.

2. — *Procedure*

The procedure for filing a Notice of Objection is straightforward: the Notice must be in writing, delivered or mailed to the Chief of Appeals in a CRA Tax Services Office. The Notice must set out the reasons for the objection. The Minister retains discretion, however, to accept a Notice that is not served in the proper manner.

A taxpayer's rights of appeal depends upon the Notice being filed within the time limit. Failure to comply with the limitation period can substantially prejudice a taxpayer's rights. The CRA almost always stands on its strict and technical legal rights.[101]

Failure to meet the time limit can deprive the taxpayer of all legal rights in respect of objecting to the Notice of Assessment. A taxpayer can apply for an extension of time to file the Notice,[102] but there is no assurance that it will be granted.

3. — *Extension of Time to File*

(a) — *"Just and Equitable"*

The Minister has discretion to extend the time for filing a Notice of Objection in limited circumstances.

---

[100]Subs. 165(1); Form T400A; IC 98-1R, "Collection Policies" (September 15, 2000); see also s. 169.

[101]See, e.g., *Can. Marconi Co. v. Canada*, [1989] 2 C.T.C. 128, 89 D.T.C. 5370; revd. [1991] 2 C.T.C. 352, 91 D.T.C. 5626; leave to appeal to S.C.C. refused (1992), 90 D.L.R. (4th) viii.

[102]Subs. 166.1.

The first condition is that the Minister must consider the extension "just and equitable" in the circumstances.[103] The words "just and equitable" conjure up an impression of "soft law and palm tree justice". In fact, the courts are quite reluctant to grant extensions of time. As the Chairman of the Tax Review Board said in *Savary Beach*:[104]

> This Board takes the position that the granting of an extension in time under section 166.1 will be the exception rather than the rule. Human frailty will no doubt give rise on occasion to unusual circumstances, such as those before the Board this morning, wherein it is fair and reasonable to grant such an extension. However, to simply grant such extensions and imply that all applications — where the breach is but a few days — will be granted, is to make a mockery of the period of limitations set down in the Act.

> Therefore this Board will, in all cases, regardless of the time that passes between the limitation period in the Act and the filing of the application for extension of time, require exceptional circumstances before any such application will receive approval.

(b) — "Exceptional Circumstances"

The second condition is that there must be "exceptional circumstances". This is a question of fact. The following examples illustrate some of the circumstances that are taken into account:

Extension Granted	
Bourdon v. M.N.R., [1984] C.T.C. 2654, 84 D.T.C. 1411 (T.C.C.)	Taxpayer's accountant filed Notice 42 days late.
Caouette v. M.N.R., [1984] C.T.C. 2447, 84 D.T.C. 1413 (T.C.C.)	Notice of Objection filed on 91st day after assessment.
The Queen v. Tohms, [1985] 2 C.T.C. 130, 85 D.T.C. 5286 (F.C.A.)	Taxpayer's mental and physical condition justified extension.
Batey v. M.N.R., [1986] 1 C.T.C. 2439, 86 D.T.C. 1294 (T.C.C.)	Mix-up caused by incorrect application and address. Court found circumstances "just and equitable" without giving any clear reasons.

---

[103]Subs. 166.1(7).

[104]*Savary Beach Lands Ltd. v. M.N.R.*, [1972] C.T.C. 2608 at 2609, 72 D.T.C. 1497 at 1498 (T.R.B.); but see *Thody v. M.N.R.*, [1983] C.T.C. 2741, 83 D.T.C. 641 (T.C.C.) (extension granted where delay explained and no "culpable negligence" on part of taxpayer); *Ramos v. M.N.R.*, [1983] C.T.C. 2744, 83 D.T.C. 643 (T.C.C.) (extension granted where taxpayer was out of country); *Graphic Specialties Ltd. v. M.N.R.*, [1983] C.T.C. 2743, 83 D.T.C. 644 (T.C.C.) (extension granted where delay attributable to taxpayer's accountants).

Extension Denied	
Morasutti v. M.N.R., [1984] C.T.C. 2401, 84 D.T.C. 1374 (T.C.C.)	Taxpayer's solicitor became aware of need to file Notice of Objection two weeks after expiry of 90-day period.
Tanaka v. M.N.R., [1985] 1 C.T.C. 2333, 85 D.T.C. 305 (T.C.C.)	Notice of Objection filed late by accountant, who then appeared on behalf of client arguing that taxpayer should not be penalized for his mistake. Court commented on accountant's conflict of interest.
Harris v. M.N.R., [1985] 1 C.T.C. 2363, 85 D.T.C. 302 (T.C.C.)	Notice filed 14 days late. Application for extension not brought for six months. Court attributed delay to accountant's negligence.
Extension Denied	
McGill v. M.N.R., [1985] 2 C.T.C. 209, 85 D.T.C. 5439 (F.C.A.)	Taxpayer wholly indifferent to proper manner of exercising his legal rights. Ignorance of law may be proper excuse in certain circumstances, but not in this case.
Aspinall v. M.N.R., [1986] 1 C.T.C. 2355, 86 D.T.C. 1284 (T.C.C.)	Application for extension delayed for seven months; not brought as soon as circumstances permitted.
The Queen v. Pennington, [1987] 1 C.T.C. 235, 87 D.T.C. 5107 (*sub nom. Pennington v. M.N.R.*) (F.C.A.)	Notice of Objection filed three days late and application for extension filed 359 days after expiry of limitation period. Taxpayer not acting as soon as possible in filing application, but simply passing matter on to accountant.

(c) — Additional Requirements

The Minister's discretion to dispense just and equitable relief is also restricted by the following additional requirements:

- The application for the extension of time for filing the Notice of Objection must be made no later than one year after the expiry of the original time limit;[105]

---

[105]Para. 166.1(7)(a).

- The taxpayer must have been unable to act within the limitation period or had a *bona fide* intention to object to the assessment;[106] and

- The application must be brought as soon as circumstances permit.[107]

In other words, the taxpayer must have a plausible case for objecting to the assessment and act quickly and prudently to protect his or her interests.

There are two separate requirements in respect of the time limits for an extension to file a Notice of Objection: the application must be brought "as soon as circumstances permit" *and*, at the very latest, no later than one year after the expiration of the original date for filing the Notice. The two time periods are conjunctive and the taxpayer must satisfy each independently of the other. Thus, the taxpayer should not wait to see if negotiations with the CRA will prove successful and then file for an extension of time if they are not. The better course is to file the application for extension immediately upon becoming aware of the expiration of the initial deadline and to continue negotiations with the CRA on a parallel track.

Pennington[108] illustrates the problems that can arise by not bringing an application for extension of time at the earliest possible opportunity. The taxpayer filed a Notice of Objection three days after the 90-day limitation period. The CRA rejected the notice and sent the taxpayer a letter telling him that he could apply for an extension of time, and that the application must be made "as soon as possible and not later than one year" from the 90-day limit. The taxpayer took up the matter with his accountant and asked him to attempt to negotiate a settlement of the matter in issue. When it became clear some time later that a satisfactory settlement was unlikely, the taxpayer applied for an extension of the limitation period. The Federal Court of Appeal refused the extension on the basis that the taxpayer did not act "as soon as possible" to file his application and it was not a sufficient excuse in law that he had passed the matter on to his accountant for settlement. Thurlow C.J.F.C. said:[109]

> What the statute appears to me to require is that the taxpayer make his application as early as, under the particular circumstances, he could *reasonably be expected to get an application ready and presented*. [Emphasis added.]

The phrase "as soon as circumstances permit" is strictly construed, and should not be confused with the maximum time limit of one year prescribed in the statute.

---

[106]Subpara. 166.1(7)(b)(i); see also *Reid v. M.N.R.*, [1985] 2 C.T.C. 2396, 85 D.T.C. 695 (T.C.C.).

[107]Subpara. 166.1(7)(b)(iii).

[108]*The Queen v. Pennington*, [1987] 1 C.T.C. 235, 87 D.T.C. 5107 (F.C.A.).

[109]*The Queen v. Pennington*, [1987] 1 C.T.C. 235 at 237, 87 D.T.C. 5107 at 5109 (F.C.A.).

4. — Appeal

A taxpayer can appeal the Minister's refusal to grant an extension of time to file a Notice of Objection.[110] The appeal is to the Tax Court of Canada, which has the power to grant the application on such terms as it considers just. The taxpayer must, however, satisfy all of the conditions in subsection 166.2(5), which places the same limits on the court's discretion as those placed on the Minister.[111] The courts generally adopt a more flexible approach to extensions upon appeals.[112]

5. — Disposition

The Minister must consider the Notice of Objection and either confirm, vacate, or vary the assessment to which objection is made.[113] Where the Minister does not confirm, vacate, or vary the assessment within 90 days of service of the Notice,[114] the taxpayer may appeal to the Tax Court without further delay.[115]

6. — Refund of Taxes

A taxpayer who files a Notice of Objection or launches an appeal against an assessment can apply for a refund of the tax paid in respect thereof if another taxpayer has successfully challenged a similar assessment in court. The Minister is not obliged to make the refund, but may refund the tax paid if the Minister is satisfied that it would be "just and equitable" to do so.[116]

XIII. — Withholding Taxes

Taxpayers who make certain types of payments must deduct tax at source. The types of payments that require withholding at source are generally payments of a compensatory na-

---

[110]S. 166.2.

[111]Subs. 166.1(7).

[112]See *Carew v. M.N.R.*, [1993] 1 C.T.C. 1, 92 D.T.C. 6608 (F.C.A.) (as a matter of principle, courts are loath to let procedural technicalities stand in the way of a case being decided on its merits).

[113]Subs. 165(3).

[114]*Jolicoeur v. M.N.R.*, [1960] C.T.C. 346, 60 D.T.C. 1254 (Ex. Ct.) (although taxpayer may appeal to Tax Court if Minister does not respond within 90 days, no time limit imposed on Minister to reply).

[115]S. 169.

[116]Subs. 164(4.1).

ture, payments out of deferred income plans, and payments to non-residents.[117] The taxpayer must remit taxes withheld at source to the Receiver General of Canada. Failure to remit taxes is a strict liability offence.[118]

1. — Failure to Withhold

A person who fails to withhold taxes when required to do so may be penalized. The penalty is determined in two tiers:[119]

1. The first failure to withhold is penalized at 10 per cent of the amount not deducted or withheld; and

2. A second (or subsequent) failure made knowingly or under circumstances amounting to gross negligence in the same calendar year is penalized at 20 per cent.

The penalty applies if the tax is remitted after the due date, regardless whether the taxpayer pays the withheld taxes before the Minister issues a penalty assessment.[120]

Where a corporation fails to deduct, withhold or remit taxes in accordance with the Act, its directors may be *personally* liable for the taxes, together with interest and penalties thereon.[121] Failure to withhold taxes on account of certain payments[122] to non-residents renders the payer and the non-resident jointly and severally liable for the interest payable on the penalty.[123]

---

[117]Subs. 153(1); s. 215; Regs. 100–110.

[118]*The Queen v. Swendson*, [1987] 2 C.T.C. 199, 87 D.T.C. 5335 (Alta. Q.B.).

[119]Subs. 227(8).

[120]*Electrocan Systems Ltd. v. Canada*, [1989] 1 C.T.C. 244, 89 D.T.C. 5079 (F.C.A.).

[121]S. 227.1; see *Barnett v. M.N.R.*, [1985] 2 C.T.C. 2336, 85 D.T.C. 619 (T.C.C.) (director/sole shareholder liable for unremitted deductions); *Beutler v. M.N.R.*, [1988] 1 C.T.C. 2414, 88 D.T.C. 1286 (T.C.C.) (director/taxpayer did not exercise due care, skill and diligence to prevent failure to remit taxes); *Fraser Estate (Trustee) v. M.N.R.*, [1987] 1 C.T.C. 2311, 87 D.T.C. 250 (T.C.C.) (minority shareholder/director may be liable even if others could have prevented default).

[122]S. 215.

[123]Subs. 227(8.1).

2. — *Criminal Sanctions*

Where a corporation fails to remit taxes, its directors and officers become criminally liable if they acquiesced or participated in the offence. But to be criminally liable for corporate acts, the directors and officers must have the *mens rea* to participate in the offence.

XIV. — Instalment Payments

1. — *General Comment*

As noted above, compensatory payments to employees are subject to withholding of tax at source. The employee must file an income tax return by April 30 of the year following receipt of payment and make up any deficiency in the tax payable. Where the amount withheld at source exceeds the taxpayer's liability for taxes, the employee is entitled to a refund of the excess.[124]

2. — *Individuals*

Individuals (other than those whose chief source of income is farming or fishing) may be required to make quarterly instalments if either no source deductions or an insufficient amount of such deductions have been taken from the taxpayer's income. The individual settles any deficiency in the amount payable by April 30 of the following year.[125]

The first four instalments are payable on March 15, June 15, September 15 and December 15 in each taxation year. The amount of each instalment is 25 per cent of:

- The *estimated* tax payable for the year; or

- The taxpayer's "instalment base" for the immediately preceding taxation year.

The final instalment is payable by April 30 of the following year.

The CRA also uses a third method — "the no-calculation method" — to calculate instalments: the first instalment base for the first two quarterly payments and the second instalment base for the last two instalments. There are no penalties or interest if the taxpayer complies with this method.

A taxpayer's "instalment base" for the immediately preceding taxation year is, in essence, the amount of tax that was payable under Part I of the Act for that preceding year.[126]

---

[124]Subs. 153(1), s. 164.

[125]Subs. 156(1).

[126]Subs. 156(3), Reg. 5300(1).

To relieve individuals from the obligation to make quarterly payments where the tax payable is insignificant, the Act exempts individuals from making instalment payments where the federal tax payable in the year, or for each of the two preceding years, is $2,000 or less.[127] In these circumstances, the individual may pay his or her entire tax liability by April 30 of the following year.

3. — Corporations

(a) — Estimated Payments

A corporation must make monthly instalments of its Part I tax over a 14 or 15 month period: one instalment on the last day of each month of its taxation year, and the final instalment, for the balance of the tax payable, by the last day of the second or third month following the end of the taxation year.[128]

We determine a corporation's monthly instalments in one of three ways:

1. Each instalment can be 1/12 of the tax on its *estimated* taxable income for the year;

2. Each instalment can be 1/12 of its "first instalment base"; or

3. The first two instalments can be 1/12 of its "second instalment base" and the next 10 instalments can be 1/10 of its first instalment base minus the first two payments.

A corporation's "first instalment base" is its tax payable under Part I for the immediately preceding taxation year; its "second instalment base" is its tax payable under Part I for the second preceding taxation year.[129]

(b) — Balance Payable

The balance of any Part I tax payable is due on or before the end of the third month following its year-end, if the corporation is a Canadian-controlled private corporation throughout the current year and claimed the small business deduction in the current or preceding year.[130] For other corporations, the balance is payable within two months after the year-end.[131]

---

[127]Subs. 156.1(1).

[128]Subs. 157(1).

[129]Reg. 5301.

[130]Subpara. 157(1)(b)(i) and subs. 248(1)"balance-due day".

[131]Subpara. 157(1)(b)(ii) and subs. 248(1)"balance-due day".

(c) — Exemption

A corporation need not make tax instalments for a taxation year if its federal tax payable or first instalment base is $1,000 or less.[132]

(d) — Failure to Remit

Failure to remit the full amount of its instalment payments on the dates due renders the corporation liable to interest at a prescribed rate on the deficiency.[133] Hence, a corporation that makes instalment payments calculated by reference to its previous year's income may be liable for interest on deficient instalments as a consequence of a subsequent reassessment of that income.[134] Subsection 161(4.1), however, absolves the corporation of interest on deficient instalments if it uses one of the prescribed methods that produces the least amount of instalments for the year.[135]

(e) — Short Fiscal Periods

Special rules apply in respect of tax instalments payable by corporations with short fiscal periods. In these circumstances instalments are required only on the last day of each complete month in the short taxation year; the remainder is due on the balance due date. The instalment base is calculated by grossing up the tax payable by the ratio that 365 is of the actual number of days in the year.

XV. — Books And Records

1. — Form and Content

Every person who carries on a business or is obliged to pay, or withhold, taxes from payments made to others must keep books and records of accounts at a place of business or residence in Canada.[136] The books and records should be kept in a manner that allows the

---

[132]Subs. 157(2.1).

[133]Subs. 161(2). Interest is calculated from the date when the payment was due to the date when payment was made.

[134]*No. 384 v. M.N.R.* (1957), 16 Tax A.B.C. 300, 57 D.T.C. 67.

[135]See: *I.G. (Rockies) Corp. v. R.*, [2005] 2 C.T.C. 2052, 2005 D.T.C. 289 (Eng.) (T.C.C. [Informal Procedure).

[136]S. 230; IC 78-10R4 (June 2005), "Books and Records Retention/Destruction" (October 5, 1998). The Minister can also designate the place where the books and records are to be kept.

Minister to determine the tax payable or the tax withheld. The Minister can also specify the books and records to be maintained in any particular case.

A taxpayer is not required to keep his or her accounts in any particular form or adhere to any particular bookkeeping system. The taxpayer need only maintain accounts sufficient to determine the amount of income that is taxable and the amount of tax that is owing.[137] There are, however, special rules in respect of record keeping requirements applicable to registered charities, amateur athletic associations, and contributions to federal political parties and candidates.[138]

2. — Retention

A taxpayer must maintain general records, books of accounts, and supporting vouchers for a period of at least six years following the taxation year to which the records and documents relate.[139] The "permanent" records of a corporation (such as minutes of directors' and shareholders' meetings, share ledgers, general ledgers and special contracts and agreements) must be maintained for a period of at least two years after the corporation is dissolved.

Similarly, the "permanent" records of a registered charity or registered Canadian amateur athletic association must be maintained for a period of at least two years after the registration of the charity or amateur athletic association is revoked.

Records in respect of political contributions and expenditures must be maintained for a period of at least two years following the calendar year to which the records relate.

A taxpayer who objects to or appeals from a Notice of Assessment must maintain his or her books and records until such time as the objection or appeal is resolved or the time period for a further appeal has elapsed.[140]

3. — Minister's Discretion

The statutory time periods in respect of the maintenance of books and records are all subject to the discretion of the Minister, who may require a taxpayer to maintain such books and records (together with supporting documents) for whatever length of time the Minister con-

---

[137]*Labbé v. M.N.R.*, [1967] Tax A.B.C. 697, 67 D.T.C. 483 (Can. Tax. App. Bd.); see also *Freitag v. M.N.R.* (1951), 5 Tax A.B.C. 54, 51 D.T.C. 350; *P.X. Cossette & Fils Inc. v. M.N.R.* (1959), 23 Tax A.B.C. 65, 59 D.T.C. 551.

[138]Subs. 230(2); s. 230.1.

[139]Reg. 5800 and para. 230(4)(b).

[140]Subs. 230(6).

siders necessary for the administration of the Act.[141] The taxpayer must obtain permission from the Minister to destroy any records or books of account prior to the prescribed time.[142]

Failure to comply with the requirements in respect of the maintenance of books and records is a criminal offence carrying a monetary penalty of between $1,000 and $25,000 and possible imprisonment for a term of up to 12 months.[143]

XVI. — Directors' Liability For Corporate Taxes

A corporation is a taxpayer in its own right. Thus, with few exceptions, we tax a corporation as a separate legal entity and it is responsible for the payment of its taxes. There are circumstances, however, when the Act pierces the corporate veil and holds shareholders and directors personally liable for corporate acts.

There are two categories of circumstances in which directors may be personally liable for corporate taxes: (1) improper payment of dividends, and (2) failure to remit withheld taxes.

1. — Improper Dividends

Directors who declare dividends that render the corporation unable to pay its taxes may be liable *to the corporation* for the amount of the improper payment.[144] Thus, directors can end up liable for the corporation's Part I tax liability.

2. — Failure to Withhold or Remit Taxes

A director may also be personally liable for corporate acts if:

- The corporation fails to withhold taxes as required or fails to remit withheld taxes;[145]

- In his or her capacity as an executor or administrator, the director fails to obtain a clearance certificate before distributing corporate property;[146] or

---

[141]Subs. 230(7).

[142]Subs. 230(8).

[143]Subs. 238(1).

[144]See, e.g., *Canada Business Corporations Act*, R.S.C. 1985, c. C-44, s. 42; para. 118(2)(c).

[145]*Income Tax Act*, s. 227.1; IC 89-2R, "Director's Liability — Section 227.1 of the *Income Tax Act* and Section 323 of the *Excise Tax Act*" (June 27, 1997).

[146]Subs. 159(3).

• The director authorizes or acquiesces in the commission of an offence by the corporation.[147]

Corporate directors are jointly and severally liable with the corporation if the corporation fails to deduct, withhold, or remit income tax the Act requires.[148]

(a) — Withholding Taxes

(i) — Compensatory Payments

A corporation must withhold income tax at source when it pays salary, wages, and certain other types of compensatory payments.[149] We determine the amount to be withheld in accordance with rules prescribed under Part I of the Regulations. A corporation may be civilly or criminally liable for failure to deduct or withhold income tax at source.[150]

(ii) — Payments to Non-Residents

A resident corporation that pays or credits an amount to a non-resident person must withhold tax on behalf of the non-resident.[151] Failure to withhold renders the corporation liable for the entire amount that should have been withheld.

(iii) — Trust Funds

A corporation must remit all withheld taxes to the Receiver General of Canada. Pending remittance, the moneys are held in trust for the benefit of the Crown, and are not available for the satisfaction of judgment creditors.[152] The rights of the Crown are further protected under the *Bankruptcy and Insolvency Act*.[153] The Act purports to protect from legal action

---

[147]S. 242.

[148]Subs. 227.1; *Barnett v. M.N.R.*, [1985] 2 C.T.C. 2336, 85 D.T.C. 619 (T.C.C.) (director liable for payroll deductions; corporation obliged to hold funds in trust for the Crown separate and apart from its own funds).

[149]Subs. 153(1).

[150]Subs. 238(1).

[151]S. 215.

[152]Subss. 227(4), (5).

[153]R.S.C. 1985, c. B-3 ss. 86, 87. These sections effectively create a deemed trust for provable Crown claims that arise as legislated obligations.

any person who withholds or deducts tax at source in compliance, or *intended* compliance, with the withholding provisions.[154]

(b) — Personal Liability

The directors of a corporation that does not comply with the withholding requirements can be held personally liable for the amount due by the corporation, together with interest and penalties thereon.[155]

(c) — Limitations

A director cannot, however, be held personally liable unless:[156]

- A certificate for the amount of the corporate tax liability has been registered in the Federal Court and execution thereof has been partially or wholly unsatisfied;

- The corporation has commenced proceedings for liquidation or dissolution and a claim for the amount of the corporate tax liability is proved within six months after commencement of such proceedings; or

- The corporation has made an assignment (or had a bankruptcy order made against it) under the *Bankruptcy and Insolvency Act* and a claim for the amount of the corporate tax liability is proved within six months after the date of the assignment or bankruptcy order.[157]

A director of a corporation is immune from personal liability unless the Minister commences proceedings against him within two years from the time when the director last ceased to be a director of the corporation.[158] To use this defence, a person must have legally ceased being a director.[159]

---

[154]Subs. 227(1). This provision raises the constitutional question as to whether the federal government has the power to withdraw a taxpayer's right of legal action.

[155]Subs. 227.1(1).

[156]Subs. 227.1(2).

[157]*Bankruptcy and Insolvency Act*, R.S.C. 1985, c. B-3.

[158]Subs. 227.1(4).

[159]It is insufficient to simply lose control of the corporation due to its being put into receivership or liquidation. *Kalef v. Canada*, [1996] 2 C.T.C. 1, 96 D.T.C. 6132 (F.C.A.); *Drover v. Canada*, [1998] G.S.T.C. 45, 98 D.T.C. 6378 (F.C.A.).

(d) — Defence of "Due Diligence"

A director of a corporation is not personally liable for the corporation's failure to withhold or remit taxes where the director has exercised "the degree of care, diligence and skill to prevent the failure that a reasonably prudent person would have exercised in comparable circumstances."[160] What constitutes the degree of care and skill that would be exercised by a reasonably prudent person in comparable circumstances is a question of fact.

(i) — Objective Test

In common law, a director must demonstrate the degree of care, skill, and diligence that could reasonably be expected from him or her, *having regard to the director's knowledge and experience.*[161] The test under the Act goes one step beyond the common law: it is objective. Thus, the obligation of directors to exercise due care and skill in supervising the corporation's responsibilities to withhold and remit taxes to the Crown falls somewhere between the subjective standard applied in common law and the more stringent obligation imposed upon professionals. Corporate directors need exercise only the degree of care, diligence, and skill that a *reasonably prudent individual* would have exercised in comparable circumstances.

The rather low expectation of corporate directors stems from the judicial perception of the qualifications necessary to become a director. The description in *Brazilian Rubber Plantations* reflects the expectations of directors:[162]

> The directors of the company, Sir Arthur Aylmer, Bart., Henry William Tugwell, Edward Barber, and Edward Henry Hancock, were all induced to become directors by Harbord or persons acting with him in the promotion of the company. Sir Arthur Aylmer was absolutely ignorant of business. He only consented to act because he was told the office would give him a little pleasant employment without his incurring any responsibility. H.W. Tugwell was partner

---

[160]Subs. 227.1(3).

[161]*Re City Equitable Fire Ins. Co.*, [1925] 1 Ch. 407 (C.A.), *per* Romer J.:

> ... [a] director need not exhibit in the performance of his duties a greater degree of skill than may reasonably be expected from a person of his knowledge and experience. A director of a life insurance company, for instance, does not guarantee that he has the skill of an actuary or of a physician. In the words of Lindley M.R.: 'If directors act within their powers, if they act with such care as is reasonably to be expected from them, having regard to their knowledge and experience, and if they act honestly for the benefit of the company they represent, they discharge both their equitable as well as their legal duty to the company'. ... It is perhaps only another way of stating the same proposition to say that directors are not liable for mere errors of judgment.

[162]*Re Brazilian Rubber Plantations & Estates Ltd.*, [1911] 1 Ch. 425 at 427; subsequent proceedings 103 LT 882 (C.A.).

in a firm of bankers in a good position in Bath; he was seventy-five years of age and very deaf; he was induced to join the board by representations made to him in January, 1906. Barber was a rubber broker and was told that all he would have to do would be to give an opinion as to the value of rubber when it arrived in England. Hancock was a man of business who said he was induced to join by seeing the names of Tugwell and Barber, whom he considered good men.

(ii) — Standard of Care

What constitutes an adequate standard of care, diligence, and skill on the part of a director is a question of fact in each case. A director is not bound to give continuous attention to the affairs of the corporation.[163] It is also clear that a director is entitled to rely upon the officials of the corporation to keep him or her informed on corporate developments. In the absence of grounds for suspicion, a director is justified in trusting his or her officials to execute their duties according to corporate policies.[164]

At the very least, however, a director is expected to take positive action to ensure compliance with the remittance provisions of the Act. Passive reliance on the other directors or officers of the corporation is not sufficient to discharge the standard of care expected of directors.[165] Thus, we expect the directors of a corporation to:

- Establish corporate policies in respect of accounting for income taxes, both under Part I of the Act in respect of the corporation's own tax liabilities and in respect of withholding from employees and payments to non-residents;

- Call upon the financial officers of the corporation to report upon compliance with established corporate policies;

- Obtain undertakings from senior corporate officials that corporate policies in respect of income tax and other financial matters have in fact been complied with during the relevant period;

- Wherever prudent, maintain a separate trust account for payroll deductions; and

---

[163]*Re City Equitable Fire Ins. Co.*, ante, at 429.

[164]*Re City Equitable Fire Ins. Co.*, ante, at 429.

[165]*Fraser Estate (Trustee) v. M.N.R.*, [1987] 1 C.T.C. 2311, 87 D.T.C. 250 (T.C.C.) (minority shareholder/director in corporation's manufacturing operations liable for failure to remit taxes); *Beutler v. M.N.R.*, [1988] 1 C.T.C. 2414, 88 D.T.C. 1286 (T.C.C.) (failure to deposit payroll deductions in separate trust account suggested absence of "due diligence").

- Exercise independent judgment and not simply rely on the other directors or officers of the corporation.[166]

Corporate directors cannot be expected to do much more.[167]

A director who is called upon to satisfy a claim in respect of corporate tax liabilities is entitled to claim contribution from fellow directors who are also liable under the claim.[168]

(iii) — Accounting Systems

Each corporate director is responsible for ensuring that the corporation uses a proper and acceptable accounting system to control the withholding and remittance of source deductions.[169] Further, the director should be aware of current practices and systems in the corpo-

---

[166]*Fraser Estate (Trustee) v. M.N.R.*, *ante*; *Quantz v. M.N.R.*, [1988] 1 C.T.C. 2276, 88 D.T.C. 1201 (T.C.C.).

[167]*Re Nat. Bank of Wales Ltd.*, [1899] 2 Ch. 629 at 673 (C.A.):

Was it his duty to test the accuracy or completeness of what he was told by the general manager and the managing director? This is a question on which opinions may differ, but we are not prepared to say that he failed in his legal duty. Business cannot be carried on upon principles of distrust. Men in responsible positions must be trusted by those above them, as well as by those below them, until there is reason to distrust them. We agree that care and prudence do not involve distrust; but for a director acting honestly himself to be held legally liable for negligence, in trusting the officers under him not to conceal from what they ought to report to him, appears to us to be laying too heavy a burden on honest businessmen.,

; affd. *(sub nom. Dovey v. Cory)* [1901] A.C. 477 (H.L.), *per* Lord Davey:

I think the respondent was bound to give his attention to and exercise his judgment as a man of business on the matters which were brought before the board at the meetings which he attended, and it is not proved that he did not do so. But I think he was entitled to rely upon the judgment, information and advice, of the chairman and general manager, as to whose integrity, skill and competence he had no reason for suspicion.

See also *Polsinelli v. R.*, 2004 TCC 186, 2004 G.T.C. 237 (T.C.C. [General Procedure]); additional reasons at (2004), 2004 TCC 720 (T.C.C. [General Procedure]) (Director not liable since he had taken all reasonable measures to ensure the company complied with the *Excise Tax Act*, including the hiring of a bookkeeper and a chartered accountant to handle the company's finances.).

[168]Subs. 227.1(7). It is questionable whether the *Income Tax Act* can constitutionally confer the power on a director to claim contribution from her fellow directors. In any event, the common law would recognize such a right.

[169]*Barnett v. M.N.R.*, *ante*; *Quantz v. M.N.R.*, *ante*; *Moore v. M.N.R.*, [1988] 2 C.T.C. 2191, 88 D.T.C. 1537 (T.C.C.) (director personally liable for unremitted payroll deductions as he did not exercise the required degree of care, diligence and skill); *Merson v. M.N.R.*, [1989] 1 C.T.C. 2074, 89 D.T.C. 22

ration.[170] We do not expect a director to be an accounting expert or a controller. He or she may rely upon competent professional advice and the guidance of those who are experts in accounting and control systems. A director is not expected to personally verify the collection and remittance of all source deductions, but the failure to segregate withheld deductions may indicate a lack of prudence.[171]

(iv) — Trust Accounts

Taxes withheld at source are trust funds. Thus, although not absolutely necessary, it is prudent to maintain a separate trust account for collecting and remitting corporate source deductions.

Although a director is a fiduciary to the corporation, the director cannot use trust funds that belong to the government of Canada to assist the corporation in overcoming a cash shortage or financial embarrassment.[172]

(v) — Passive Directors

The personal liability of directors for corporate source deductions applies equally to "passive" and "nominee" directors as to those who are actively involved in the corporation's management. As a matter of administrative practice, the CRA does not distinguish between active, passive, inside, and outside directors.[173]

A corporate director is not entitled to delegate responsibility, and cannot claim diminished responsibility by virtue of non-involvement in the corporation's management and affairs. In this context, there is no difference between directors of large public corporations and small private corporations: they all carry the same burden of responsibility to ensure that source deductions are properly accounted for and remitted to the Receiver General.

(T.C.C.) (director not personally responsible for unremitted source deductions as he exercised the required degree of care and diligence and the corporation did not benefit).

[170]*Fraser Estate (Trustee) v. M.N.R.*, *ante*.

[171]*Barnett v. M.N.R.*, *ante*; *Beutler v. M.N.R.*, *ante*.

[172]*Pilling v. M.N.R.*, [1989] 2 C.T.C. 2037, 89 D.T.C. 327 (T.C.C.).

[173]CRA Directive CA87-67 (October 6, 1987), obtainable under *Privacy Act*, R.S.C. 1985, c. P-21. See also CRA's response to Question 81 at the 1987 Annual Canadian Tax Conference Round Table; and para. 9 of IC89-2R (Directors who relinquish their responsibilities to co-directors, officers or employees may be held liable).

(vi) — Administrative Policies

Information Circular 89-2R sets out the CRA's practices in respect of assessing directors personally for source deductions:[174]

- The CRA will write to directors who may be liable to inform them that an assessment is being considered and to request an explanation of all actions taken to ensure that the corporation deducted, withheld, remitted, or paid all prescribed amounts.

- A director who does not respond to the CRA's information request within the time limits set out may be assessed without further notice.

- Department of Justice lawyers will be consulted only where a due diligence defence has been raised by the director. Otherwise, a decision to issue the assessment against the director will be made by the Collections Division.

3. — Clearance Certificates

A legal representative must obtain a clearance certificate from the Minister before distributing any property under his possession or control.[175] The certificate should certify that all taxes, interest and penalties chargeable against or payable out of the property that is to be distributed have been paid. This requirement does *not* extend to a director of a corporation if the director is acting *qua* director and not *qua* executor, assignee, liquidator, or administrator.[176]

---

[174]IC 89-2R, "Directors' Liability — Section 227.1 of the *Income Tax Act* and Section 323 of the *Excise Tax Act*" (June 27, 1997).

[175]Subs. 159(2); see also IC82-16R4 (Dec. 22, 2005).

[176]*Parsons v. M.N.R.*, [1983] C.T.C. 321 at 330-31, 83 D.T.C. 5329 at 5337; revd. on other grounds [1984] C.T.C. 352, 84 D.T.C. 6345 (F.C.A.) (roles of the various fiduciaries mentioned in subs. 159(2) described by court as follows: "An assignee is a person to whom an assignment is made and assignment means that property is transferred to another. The assignee is the recipient of that property. A liquidator is a person appointed to carry out the winding up of a company whose duty is to get in and realize the property of the company, to pay its debts and to distribute the surplus (if any) among the shareholders. An executor is the person to whom the execution of a will is entrusted by a testator ... an executor is bound to satisfy all claims on the estate before distributing it among the legatees and other beneficiaries. An administrator is the person to whom the property of a person dying intestate is committed for administration and whose duties with respect thereto correspond with those of an executor.").

4. — *Participation in Offences Committed by the Corporation*

A director of a corporation may be held to be a party to, and guilty of, an offence committed by the corporation if the director directs, authorizes, assents to, acquiesces in, or participates in an offence committed by the corporation. The director can be held liable even though the corporation itself is not prosecuted or convicted for the offence.[177]

There are two elements to a director's personal liability for corporate offences:[178]

    1. The corporation is guilty of an offence under the Act; and

    2. The director participated in some way in the commission of the offence.

Thus, mere proof that a corporation was convicted of the offence is not sufficient by itself to convict a director; the corporation must be shown to have been guilty of, and not merely to have been convicted of, the offence.[179] A director may be criminally convicted in his or her personal capacity only if he or she had the *mens rea* to commit the offence.[180]

XVII. — Penalties For False Statements Or Omissions

Subsection 163(2) of the Act authorizes the Minister to impose a penalty on a person who has either

- "knowingly", or

- "under circumstances amounting to gross negligence,"

made, participated, assented, or acquiesced in the making of a false statement or omission in an income tax return.

1. — *"Knowingly"*

There are three degrees of knowledge: (1) actual knowledge; (2) deliberate refraining from making inquiries; and (3) constructive knowledge.

In the first category, the taxpayer must have *actual* knowledge of the misstatement or omission on the return. The second category deals with a situation where a person *deliberately* shuts his or her eyes to an obvious means of knowledge — in other words, deliberately refrains from making inquiries the result of which the taxpayer might not care to know. The

---

[177]S. 242.

[178]*Hartmann v. The Queen*, [1971] C.T.C. 396, 70 D.T.C. 6219 (Sask. Dist. Ct.).

[179]*The Queen v. Anisman*, [1969] 1 O.R. 397, 69 D.T.C. 5199 (Ont. H.C.).

[180]*The Queen v. Swendson*, [1987] 2 C.T.C. 199, 87 D.T.C. 5335 (Alta. Q.B.).

third category, generally referred to as "constructive knowledge", is concerned with what a taxpayer "ought to have known."[181]

2. — *Gross Negligence*

Negligence is a failure to use reasonable care. "Gross negligence" involves something greater or worse or more reckless than simply a failure to use reasonable care. "Gross negligence" requires a greater degree of culpability or errant behaviour on the taxpayer's part than one might expect in a case of "ordinary" negligence. For example, in *Venne*:[182]

> ... "gross negligence" ... must involve a high degree of negligence tantamount to intentional acting, an indifference as to whether the law is complied with or not. ... To be sure, the plaintiff did not exercise the care of a reasonable man, and ... should have at least reviewed his tax returns before signing them. A reasonable man in doing so, having regard to other information available to him, would have been led to believe that something was amiss and would have pursued the matter further with his bookkeeper.

But the mere failure to exercise the care of a reasonable person is not enough to constitute *gross* negligence.

3. — *"Has Made"*

The penalty under subsection 163(2) can be imposed only on a taxpayer who "has made" or participated in, assented to, or acquiesced in the grossly negligent misstatement or omission. In other words, a taxpayer is liable only if he or she is grossly negligent or the gross negligence of the taxpayer's agent can be directly attributed to the taxpayer. In *Udell*:[183]

> In my view the use of the verb "made" in the context in which it is used also involves a deliberate and intentional consciousness on the part of the principal to the act done. ...

Any doubt, ambiguity or uncertainty as to whether there was deliberate or intentional consciousness on the taxpayer's part should be resolved in the taxpayer's favour:[184]

> I take it to be a clear rule of construction that in the imposition of a tax or a duty, and still more of a penalty if there be any fair and reasonable doubt the statute is to be construed so as to give the party sought to be charged the benefit of the doubt.

---

[181]See *Taylor's Central Garages (Exeter) Ltd. v. Roper*, [1951] 2 T.L.R. 284 (Div. Ct.), in particular *per* Devlin J. at 288-89.

[182]*Venne v. The Queen*, [1984] C.T.C. 223 at 234, 84 D.T.C. 6247 at 6256 (F.C.T.D.) *per* Strayer J.

[183]*Udell v. M.N.R.*, [1969] C.T.C. 704, 70 D.T.C. 6019 (Ex. Ct.) at 714 [C.T.C.] and 6025 [D.T.C.] *per* Cattanach J.

[184]*Udell v. M.N.R..*, *ibid.*, at 714 [C.T.C.] and 6026 [D.T.C.].

If the words of a penal section are capable of two interpretations, one that imposes liability and one that does not inflict a penalty, the latter interpretation should prevail.[185]

Thus, subsection 163(2) applies in two main circumstances:

1. The taxpayer is grossly negligent or knowingly makes a misstatement or omission on his or her return for the year; or

2. The taxpayer's agent is grossly negligent or knowingly makes a misstatement *and* the agent's action or knowledge can be directly attributed to the taxpayer.

The second alternative has two separate requirements: (1) the taxpayer's advisers must be grossly negligent in the preparation of the tax return; and (2) the taxpayer must have been privy, in one of the three senses of "knowingly", to the gross negligence and in fact acquiesced or participated in the false statement or omission.

4. — Penalties for Tax Advisors and Promoters

Section 163.2 also provides civil penalties against those who knowingly, or in circumstances amounting to gross negligence, make false statements or omissions in respect of *another person's* tax matters. This provision is a result of recommendations from the Auditor General, the House of Commons Public Accounts Committee, and the Mintz Committee.[186]

(a) — Tax Shelter and other Tax Planning Arrangements

A penalty applies to an individual who plans, promotes, or sells an arrangement that the person knows or would have known, but for circumstances amounting to gross negligence, includes a statement or omission that may be used in an arrangement.[187] This provision also applies to a person who provides false information for use in an arrangement. This penalty will be the greater of $1,000 and 100 per cent of the gross revenue derived by the person in respect of the arrangement. This provision applies to situations where, for example, an asset is purchased at an allegedly inflated price to circumvent GAAR. The rules are particularly strict on valuation and deem them to have been false if the value stated is not within prescribed limits.

---

[185]*Tuck & Sons v. Priester* (1887), 19 Q.B.D. 629.

[186]See generally IC 01-1 "Third-Party Civil Penalties" (Dec. 18, 2002) for CRA's views, and Income Tax Technical News #22 (July 15, 2005).

[187]Subs. 163.2(3) and 237.1(7.4).

5. — Onus of Proof

(a) — Burden

The burden of proof rests squarely on the Minister to establish that the taxpayer acted knowingly or with gross negligence in the misstatement on the income tax return. The Minister must show that the taxpayer acted in circumstances amounting to gross negligence on the particular facts.[188]

(b) — Omissions

A mere omission or misstatement of income on a return is not *in and of itself* sufficient to establish gross negligence. Subsection 163(2) requires proof of the omission or misstatement *in circumstances of conduct* that are tantamount to gross negligence. Thus, there must be an act of omission or misstatement by the taxpayer or his or her agent, and a state of mind or conduct that justifies a finding of *gross* negligence. The courts are hesitant to attribute the knowledge and conduct of accountants to their clients.[189]

XVIII. — Third-Party Penalties

1. — Criminal Penalties

A tax advisor may be held criminally liable for actions that amount to tax evasion.[190] For example, any person who intentionally participates in the filing of a false return — such as an accountant who deducts a non-deductible expense on his client's tax return — may be subject to criminal sanctions.

In practice, the CRA invokes the criminal penalty provisions only in the most "extraordinary circumstances" since pursuing criminal penalties for all cases of egregious behaviour on the part of tax advisors is administratively difficult.[191] Not only does it take considerable time

---

[188]*James v. M.N.R.*, [1993] 1 C.T.C. 2126, 93 D.T.C. 161 (T.C.C.) (Minister failed to discharge the onus of proving that the penalties were appropriate). See also, subs. 163(3), which establishes the reverse onus for penalties under subs. 163(2) and s. 163.2.

[189]See, e.g., *Udell v. M.N.R.*, *ante*; *M.N.R. v. Weeks*, [1972] C.T.C. 60, 72 D.T.C. 6001 (F.C.T.D.); affd. 70 D.T.C. 1431 (Can. Tax. App. Bd.); *Oudot v. M.N.R.*, [1970] Tax A.B.C. 915, 70 D.T.C. 1599; *Apex Auto-Matic Centres Ltd. v. M.N.R.*, [1971] Tax A.B.C. 751, 71 D.T.C. 480; *Joris v. M.N.R.*, [1981] C.T.C. 2596, 81 D.T.C. 470 (T.R.B.) (accountant's errors in tax returns not gross negligence on the part of the taxpayer).

[190]S. 239.

[191]Roch Martin, "Recent Income Tax Developments" (2002) 40:1 Alta. L. Rev. 19. 16.

and expense to pursue criminal penalties, but it is difficult to satisfy the burden of proof ("beyond a reasonable doubt") without compelling evidence.

2. — Civil Penalties

The third-party civil penalties are far more of a concern to tax advisors than the criminal penalties. Not only is the burden of proof much lower — the Crown need only prove its case on a balance of probabilities — but the financial penalties are significant.

Prior to the introduction of the third-party civil penalties, civil penalties extended only to taxpayers. Tax advisors and lawyers, on the other hand, could only be pursued under the criminal provisions. Apart from these criminal sanctions, professional bodies were wholly responsible for governing the ethical behaviour of their members. Professional bodies are not generally inclined to pursue disciplinary actions on complex tax matters that require considerable technical expertise.

Following the failure of professional bodies to regulate the ethical behaviour of their members, the government introduced third-party civil penalties. The catalyst for the establishment of third-party civil penalties was *Global Communications Limited v. The Queen*.[192] The taxpayer, a reputable Canadian corporation, and certain promoters, members of major law firms, structured an aggressive tax scheme that they should have known would fail. In the wake of *Global*, the Auditor General, the House of Commons Standing Committee on Public Accounts, and the Technical Committee on Business Taxation (the "Mintz Committee") all recommended the creation of civil penalties for tax advisors.

(a) — The Provisions

The recommendations of the Mintz Committee were eventually enacted in subsections 163.2(2) and 163.2(4) of the Act. These provisions, which came into force June 29, 2000, are aimed primarily at two types of abuse. The first involves tax planners who create transactions that are unsupported by the *Income Tax Act* and result in unwarranted claims for deductions (subsection 163.2(2)). The second type of abuse involves tax preparers who create or acquiesce in the creation of unsupportable deductions in the preparation of returns (subsection 163.2(4)).

---

[192] [1997] 3 C.T.C. 2527, 97 D.T.C. 1496 (T.C.C.), affd. 99 D.T.C. 5377, [1999] 4 C.T.C. 53 (F.C.A.).

(b) — The Penalties

The planner penalty in subsection 163.2(3) is the greater of $1,000, and the person's "gross entitlements". The preparer penalty in subsection 163.2(5) is the greater of either $1,000, or the lesser of:

- the penalty the other person would be liable to under subsection 163(2), and

- $100,000 plus the advisor's gross compensation.

To apply the penalties the CRA must show that on a balance of probabilities that the taxpayer engaged in "culpable conduct".

Culpable conduct is active conduct or a failure to act that:

(a) is tantamount to intentional conduct;

(b) shows an indifference as to whether the tax legislation is complied with; or

(c) shows a wilful, a reckless, or wanton disregard for the law.

These criteria are subjective and, given the onus of proof in tax cases, difficult to defend against.

(c) — Good Faith Exception

In response to the concerns about the definition of "culpable conduct" and the eventual application of section 163.2, the Department of Finance built a few exceptions into the third-party civil penalty provisions. For example, subsection 163.2(6) provides for a "good faith" exception, which exculpates a tax preparer or advisor who, in good faith, relies on information provided by another person, or because of such reliance, fails to verify, investigate, or correct the information.[193]

Thus, if a client gives false information to his or her tax preparer and there is no obvious reason for the tax preparer to question its legitimacy, the tax preparer will not be penalized for relying on this information in the preparation of the client's tax return. Likewise, a tax advisor who relies on false information supplied by a client and provides advice on structuring a transaction to minimize tax should not be subject to these penalties.

(d) — Penalty Assessment Process

In 2001 the CRA created the Third-Party Penalty Review Committee to further alleviate concerns that the new civil penalties might be used abusively or inconsistently by tax offi-

---

[193]The "good faith" defence is not available where the activity is an "excluded activity" under subs. 163.2(1).

cials. A field auditor who encounters a situation in which civil penalties might apply must first consult with a senior audit manager before implementing a third-party penalty audit. If the auditor recommends a penalty, the Committee reviews the facts, including the third party's representations, before endorsing or rejecting the recommendation.[194]

XIX. — Transfers Of Property

1. — Tax Liability

Generally, when an individual transfers property to a spouse or to a person under 18 years of age, the transferor and transferee become *jointly and severally* liable for any tax payable by the transferor at the time of transfer. The purpose of the joint and several liability rules is to enable the tax authorities to take their share of any tax payable to them. But the rules go further: they also apply to transfers between unrelated persons who do not deal with each other at arm's length.

The first two categories of transferees (spouses and persons under 18 years of age) are readily identifiable. Transfers to the third category (transferees not at arm's length with the transferor), however, contain hidden traps.

2. — Non-Arm's Length

The Act does not define "arm's length". The question as to whether taxpayers are dealing with each other at arm's length is sometimes a question of law and sometimes a question of fact. Persons who are married or related to each other are generally considered not to be dealing with each other at arm's length. Persons may, however, also be considered not to be at arm's length with each other as a matter of fact.

Unrelated persons who do not deal with each other in an independent manner may act in concert. If they do, they are not at arm's length with each other. The question is one of fact and, as with many questions of fact, depends upon the credibility of the taxpayer's testimony.[195] The onus is on the taxpayer to establish the nature of the relationship between the parties.

The joint and several liability of the parties is equal to the shortfall between the value of the property transferred and any consideration received by the transferor. Any subsequent payments by the transferor first reduce the transferor's personal liability in respect of his or her other tax debts. It is only when those other tax debts are fully paid that further payments

---

[194]Canadian Tax Foundation, *Canadian Tax Highlights* 10:10 (24 October 2002), available online at: <http://www.ctf.ca/articles/News.asp?article_ID=1832> [February 3, 2003].

[195]*Lindsay v. M.N.R.*, [1990] 1 C.T.C. 2245, 90 D.T.C. 1085 (T.C.C.).

reduce the joint and several liability. Hence, the non-arm's length transferee can remain liable for taxes long after the transfer of property.

XX. — Investigations

1. — Ministerial Powers

The income tax system relies on self-assessment. The Minister does, however, have considerable audit powers to ensure that taxpayers do not use self-assessment to evade income taxes. The administrative requirements in respect of the maintenance of books and records, filing of tax and information returns, payments of taxes, interest and penalties are all directed towards persuading taxpayers to remain on the "straight and narrow" path.

The Agency also has extensive powers to conduct investigations into a taxpayer's financial affairs.[196] The scope of these powers is broad, sometimes frighteningly so in a free society. The powers are not, however, without limit: the Canadian *Charter of Rights and Freedoms* provides some restraint on the Minister's statutory powers.

The Agency's investigative powers are intended to prevent tax evasion and fraud. The scope of the powers is, however, disproportionate to the problem. As Lord Denning M.R. said:[197]

> In the tax evasion pool, there are some big fish who do not stop at tax avoidance. They resort to frauds on a large scale. I can well see that if the legislation were confined, or could be confined, to people of that sort, it would be supported by all honest citizens. Those who defraud the Revenue in this way are parasites who suck out the life-blood of our society. The trouble is that the legislation is drawn so widely that in some hands it might be an instrument of oppression. It may be said that "honest people need not fear; that it will never be used against them; that tax inspectors can be trusted only to use it in the case of the big, bad frauds". This is an attractive argument, but I would reject it. Once great power is granted, there is a danger of it being abused. Rather than risk such abuse, it is, as I see it, the duty of the courts so to construe the statute as to see that it encroaches as little as possible on the liberties of the people. ...

2. — Audit and Examination

(a) — Audits vs. Investigations

The income tax system relies primarily upon self-assessment by taxpayers and "voluntary" reporting of tax liabilities. The taxpayer initially determines his or her liability and submits the tax return to the CRA. The CRA checks the mathematical accuracy of the return, reviews

---

[196]IC 71-14R3, "The Tax Audit" (June 18, 1984).

[197]*R. v. I.R.C.*, [1979] 3 All E.R. 385 at 399; revd. [1980] 1 All E.R. 80 (H.L.).

supporting documents, performs perfunctory cross checks, and issues a "quick assessment" within approximately 12 weeks of filing. Mercifully for most taxpayers, particularly employees who have income and payroll taxes withheld at source, that is the end of their annual ritual with the tax authorities.

But that is not the end of the tax process. Although the tax system relies on self-assessment, the CRA has substantial audit and investigative powers to ensure compliance with the Act. These powers are of two types: civil audits and criminal investigations. However, the line between the Agency's regulatory audit and criminal investigative powers is not always clear, which causes procedural disputes and litigation.

A civil audit is an examination for the purpose of verifying the accuracy of the taxpayer's self-assessed income. Such an audit under the CRA's regulatory powers is simply a routine process for verifying the taxpayer's financial information and examining relevant supporting documents. The purpose of the audit is to ensure regulatory compliance, mathematical accuracy and supporting data. If the Agency disagrees with the taxpayer's self-assessed income, it will reassess the taxpayer and charge interest on any deficiency in taxes paid.

The CRA also has the power to impose civil penalties in circumstances where it can show egregious conduct by the taxpayer in preparing his or her return. Civil penalties can add up to an additional 50 per cent (plus interest) of the tax deficiency to the final bill.[198]

The Act confers broad audit powers on the CRA in sections 231.1 (access to records on business premises) and 231.2 (demand for information). The law allows the tax authorities considerable latitude under these provisions and taxpayer constitutional rights are only minimally protected. In contrast, a tax investigation is essentially a criminal examination and, therefore, subject to the tighter control that the *Charter* extends to criminal matters.

Civil audits and investigations are both relationships of opposing interests. There is, however, an important difference between the nature of the parties' interests in an audit or investigation. Although all audits between taxpayers and the CRA are adversarial, the intensity of the adversarial relationship increases exponentially where the Agency is looking to lay criminal charges against the taxpayer. In an investigation "the state is pitted against the individual in an attempt to establish culpability."[199] The adversarial relationship escalates because the liberty of the subject is at stake.

In an investigation the Agency must look to section 231.3 (warrant for search and seizure),[200] which deals with serious offences against the Act. For example, for the purpose

---

[198]Subsec. 163(2)

[199]*R. v. Jarvis*, [2002] 3 S.C.R. 757, [2003] 1 C.T.C. 135, 2002 D.T.C. 7547 (S.C.C.) at headnote [S.C.R.].

[200]*R. v. Jarvis*, *ibid.*, at paras. 78-84 and 99.

of investigating penal liability, section 231.3 sets out an application process for an *ex parte* search warrant similar to that found in section 487 of the *Criminal Code*.

Of course, an examination that starts out as a routine civil audit can turn into a criminal investigation. If this happens, the nature of the relationship between the CRA and the taxpayer also changes and the Agency's powers become subject to *Charter* restrictions. Nevertheless, the CRA may still be able to use any information that it procures during the proper exercise of its audit function in a subsequent penal investigation. The use of such information for criminal purposes does not offend either section 7 (the principles against self-incrimination) or section 8 (reasonable expectation of privacy) of the *Charter*.[201]

Under section 7 of the *Charter* there are competing principles of fundamental justice. In inquiries in income tax matters, the principle that relevant evidence should be available to the trier of fact outweighs the principle against self-incrimination.

Similarly, individuals have few privacy interests under section 8 of the *Charter* in materials and records that they are obliged to keep and produce for the purposes of the *Income Tax Act*.[202] Once an auditor has inspected or compelled the production of a document or information, the taxpayer cannot be said to have a reasonable expectation that the auditor will guard its confidentiality. Given the taxpayer's diminished expectation of privacy, the State's interest to intrude on the individual's privacy in order to advance its goals of law enforcement outweighs the individual's privacy interest in his or her materials and records.

The CRA may also conduct an audit and an investigation concurrently. However, once the Agency begins its investigation, it can use *further* information that it obtains under its concurrent audit powers[203] only for the purposes of the audit and not for the purposes of the investigation.

It is not easy in practice to distinguish the divergence in powers and obligations related to civil audits and investigations. An inquiry becomes an investigation when its *predominant purpose* is to determine penal liability. However, there is no bright line test for determining the predominant purpose of an inquiry or when it changes. However, the following factors are relevant and provide some guidance:[204]

> (a) Did the authorities have reasonable grounds to lay charges? Does it appear from the record that a decision to proceed with a criminal investigation could have been made?

> (b) Was the general conduct of the authorities such that it was consistent with the pursuit of a criminal investigation?

---

[201] *R. v. Jarvis*, [2002] 3 S.C.R. 757, [2003] 1 C.T.C. 135, 2002 D.T.C. 7547 (S.C.C.).

[202] *R. v. Jarvis, ibid.*

[203] Ss. 231.1 and 231.2

[204] *R. v. Jarvis*, [2002] 3 S.C.R. 757, [2003] 1 C.T.C. 135, 2002 D.T.C. 7547 (S.C.C.) at para. 94.

(c) Had the auditor transferred his or her files and materials to the investigators?

(d) Was the conduct of the auditor such that he or she was effectively acting as an agent for the investigators?

(e) Does it appear that the investigators intended to use the auditor as their agent-in the collection of evidence?

(f) Is the evidence sought relevant to taxpayer liability generally? Or, as is the case with evidence as to the taxpayer's *mens rea*, is the evidence relevant only to the taxpayer's penal liability?

(g) Are there any other circumstances or factors that can lead the trial judge to the conclusion that the compliance audit had in reality become a criminal investigation?

This list of relevant considerations is not exhaustive and, apart from a clear decision to pursue a criminal investigation, no single factor is determinative in every circumstance. Hence, a court has considerable latitude in its decision to admit evidence. In arriving at its decision, the court should consider the totality of the circumstances to determine whether the inquiry sufficiently engages the adversarial relationship between the State and the taxpayer to warrant *Charter* protection.

(b) — Business Premises

Under section 231.1 an "authorized person"[205] is entitled to audit or examine a taxpayer's books, records or property for the purposes of an audit.[206] Such a person can enter into a taxpayer's business premises and, upon gaining entry, audit and examine all of the books, records, accounts, vouchers, letters, and any other documents which may, or should, relate to the amount of tax payable under the Act.

An auditor is entitled to reasonable assistance from the owner or manager of the property or business and *any* other person on the premises. The auditor can demand written or oral answers in respect of any question relating to the audit or examination, and can require the owner or manager of the premises to attend at the premises.[207]

The auditor's right to obtain answers to questions is not restricted to questioning employees of the taxpayer. The auditor may question *any* person who is on the premises, and in certain circumstances may even question members of the taxpayer's family who are not involved in the business.

---

[205]S. 231 ("authorized person" means a person authorized by the Minister).

[206]Paras. 231.1(1)(a), (b); *R. v. Jarvis*, [2002] 3 S.C.R. 757, [2003] 1 C.T.C. 135, 2002 D.T.C. 7547 (S.C.C.).

[207]Para. 231.1(1)(d).

Thus, tax auditors have unfettered and unrestricted power to disrupt a business for an unlimited period of time. Other than restricting entry to a reasonable time, there are no statutory limitations on the auditor's right to scrutinize the taxpayer's books, records or documents or to question the taxpayer, the employees and members of the taxpayer's family.

The courts have not restrained the Minister's powers of examination. As Martland J. said in *Western Minerals*:[208]

> ... it is not for the Court or anyone else to prescribe what the intensity of the examination of a taxpayer's return in any given case should be. That is exclusively a matter for the Minister, acting through his appropriate officers, to decide... There is no standard in the Act or elsewhere, either express or implied, fixing the essential requirements of an assessment. It is exclusively for the Minister to decide how he should, in any given case, ascertain and fix the liability of a taxpayer. The extent of the investigation he should make, if any, is for him to decide.

An auditor can demand entry to a taxpayer's business premises for the purpose of conducting an audit (not an investigation), and only at a reasonable time, that is, during normal business hours. There is no limitation upon the number of times that a tax auditor can enter onto a taxpayer's premises for the purposes of the examination.

(c) — Dwelling-House

An auditor may not enter into a taxpayer's "dwelling-house"[209] without the taxpayer's consent or the authority of a search warrant.[210] A search warrant may be issued on the Minister's *ex parte* application if there are reasonable grounds for believing that entry into the dwelling-house is necessary for administrative purposes.[211]

---

[208]*Western Minerals Ltd. v. M.N.R.*, [1962] S.C.R. 592, [1962] C.T.C. 270 at 273, 62 D.T.C. 1163 at 1165 (S.C.C.), referring to the headnote of *Provincial Paper Ltd. v. M.N.R.*, [1954] C.T.C. 367, 54 D.T.C. 1199 (Ex. Ct.).

[209]S. 231"dwelling-house".

[210]Subs. 231.1(2).

[211]Subs. 231.1(3).

(d) — Search Warrants

(i) — Application

Section 231.3 allows the Minister to make an *ex parte* application to a judge for a search warrant to enter into a taxpayer's dwelling-house. The CRA can also apply for a search warrant under the *Criminal Code*,[212] which is now the Agency's standard practice.[213]

The judge may[214] issue the warrant if the judge is satisfied that there are reasonable grounds to believe that an offence has been committed under the Act and that evidence of the offence is likely to be found on the premises.[215]

(ii) — Scope

The warrant must be "reasonably specific" as to its scope, and must specify the documents to be searched for and seized.[216] Typically, a CRA investigator will prepare an information setting out the details of a *prima facie* offence under section 239 of the Act. The auditor is, however, allowed to seize not only the documents or things referred to in the search warrant but also any other document or thing which the auditor believes, on reasonable grounds, affords evidence of the commission of an offence under the Act.[217] Thus, in effect, the Minister has virtually unlimited powers[218] of search and seizure if entry is obtained on the authority of a search warrant. This is so even if the warrant is of limited scope.[219]

(iii) — Custody of Seized Documents

---

[212]*Criminal Code*, R.S.C. 1985, c. C-46, s. 487.

[213]*The Queen v. 282109 Canada Inc.*, [1995] G.S.T.C. 67 (N.B.C.A.).

[214]The judge retains a discretion as to whether he or she will issue the warrant.

[215]Subs. 231.3(3).

[216]Subs. 231.3(4).

[217]Subs. 231.3(5).

[218]An earlier version of section 231.3, which did not give the judge any discretion over the issuance of the warrant, was ruled unconstitutional under section 8 of the *Charter* in *Baron v. Canada*, [1993] 1 S.C.R. 416, [1993] 1 C.T.C. 111, 93 D.T.C. 5018 (S.C.C.).

[219]See subs. 231.3(7) (in certain circumstances, such as non-compliance with warrant, judge may order documents returned to taxpayer).

The Minister must report the list of documents seized from the taxpayer to the judge, but is entitled to retain the seized items that are the subject of the investigation.[220] The Act is quite clear that the judge "shall" order retention of the seized items unless the Minister waives the right to retain the seized items. Thus, there is very limited judicial control over the Minister and the Ministry's agents.

3. — Demand for Information

(a) — Minister's Power

Under section 231.2 the Minister may demand from *any* person *any* information for *any* purpose related to the administration or enforcement of the Act. Although on the face of it this provision appears to have very broad application, in *R. v. Jarvis*,[221] the Supreme Court held that this section may be used only for the purpose of an audit and not for the purposes of an investigation. The Minister may also demand production of any books, letters, accounts, invoices, statements, or other documents from any person. The person from whom the demand is made must respond within such "reasonable time" as is stipulated in the Notice of Demand.[222]

(b) — Defences

A taxpayer can challenge a demand for information on the basis that:

- The documents demanded are not germane or relevant to the issues between the parties;

- The Minister is on a "fishing expedition" and not on a specific inquiry as to some taxpayer's liability;

- The taxpayer has not been given a reasonable time to produce the documents; or

- The documents are privileged.

---

[220]Subs. 231.3(6).

[221]*R. v. Jarvis*, [2002] 3 S.C.R. 757, [2003] 1 C.T.C. 135, 2002 D.T.C. 7547 (S.C.C.).

[222]Subs. 231.2(1); *Tower v. Minister of National Revenue* (2003), [2004] 1 F.C.R. 183, [2003] 4 C.T.C. 263, (sub nom. *Minister of National Revenue v. Kitsch*) 2003 D.T.C. 5540 (F.C.A.) (S. 231.2(1) permits the Minister to demand responses to questions; also, tax-accountant privilege should not be recognized); *Joseph v. M.N.R.*, [1985] 2 C.T.C. 164, 85 D.T.C. 5391 (Ont. H.C.) (in case of lawyer, period of less than seven to ten days would usually not be "reasonable").

A demand for information constitutes a seizure, but not an unreasonable one within section 8 of the *Charter*.[223]

(c) — *Named Persons*

The Minister can make the demand only in respect of information relating to named persons and for a purpose related to the administration or enforcement of the Act.[224] The test is objective and is determined on the basis of the particular facts.

It is not necessary that the person from whom the information is sought be the person whose tax liability is under investigation. The fact that the giving of the information may disclose private transactions involving persons who are not under investigation and may not be liable for tax does not invalidate an otherwise valid demand for information.

(d) — *"Fishing Expeditions"*

The demand for information must be a genuine and serious inquiry into the tax liability of some *specific* person or persons. The Minister cannot be on a "fishing expedition" into the affairs of an unknown group of taxpayers. For example, a taxpayer cannot be compelled to provide a random sample as a check on the general compliance of some unidentified class of taxpayers.[225]

(e) — *Reasonable Time to Respond*

What constitutes a "reasonable time" within which information must be supplied is also a question of fact. The Minister usually stipulates a time or date in the Notice of Demand for Information. Whether the stipulated period of time is reasonable depends upon the volume

---

[223] *Can. v. McKinlay Tpt. Ltd.*, [1990] 1 S.C.R. 627, [1990] 2 C.T.C. 103, 90 D.T.C. 6243 (S.C.C.); affirming (1987), [1988] 1 C.T.C. 426, 88 D.T.C. 6314 (Ont. C.A.).

[224] Subs. 231.2(2).

[225] Subs. 231.2(2) (amendment to conform to decision of Supreme Court of Canada in *Richardson, post*); *James Richardson & Sons Ltd. v. M.N.R.*, [1984] 1 S.C.R. 614, [1984] C.T.C. 345, 84 D.T.C. ·6325 (S.C.C.) (a demand can only be made for information relevant to the tax liability of a person or persons if a genuine and serious inquiry into their tax liability is being conducted).

and complexity of the information demanded and the ease with which the taxpayer can obtain the information. As the Federal Court observed in *Richardson*:[226]

> The purpose of the statutory provision is to ensure that the person from whom the information is required will have a reasonable time (which will vary considerably depending on the amount of information, the time required to collect and compile it, and other circumstances) to comply, and that he will comply within that reasonable time. The words "without delay" do not comply strictly with the statute, but in the sense of "within a reasonable time", which is the meaning courts have frequently held to be the correct meaning, and which in my opinion is the right meaning in the circumstances of this case, they afford the Applicant all the protection intended by the statute. A reasonable time is not exact, as is a stated period or a terminating date, but it can be ascertained for the circumstances of a particular case. If in the present case, the information is not forthcoming and legal proceedings are begun, the Minister will have to satisfy the Court that a reasonable period of time for compliance with the requirement elapsed before the proceedings were started.

(f) — Unnamed Persons

The Minister may demand information in respect of unnamed persons, but only pursuant to a court order authorizing the "fishing expedition".[227] The Minister may obtain the order on the basis of an *ex parte* application. The judge must be satisfied that:[228]

- The unnamed person or group of persons is ascertainable; and

- The demand is made for the purpose of compliance with the Act.

The party from whom the information is demanded may seek a review of the order within 15 days after its service.[229]

(g) — Multiple Demands

Since the purpose of the subsection is not to penalize criminal conduct but to enforce compliance with the Act, the purpose would be defeated if the Minister's power were exhausted

---

[226]*James Richardson & Sons Ltd. v. M.N.R.*, [1981] C.T.C. 229 at 249, 81 D.T.C. 5232 at 5246 (F.C.T.D.); affd. [1982] C.T.C. 239, 82 D.T.C. 6204 (F.C.A.); revd. on other grounds [1984] 1 S.C.R. 614, [1984] C.T.C. 345, 84 D.T.C. 6325 (S.C.C.).

[227]Subss. 231.2(2), (3).

[228]Subs. 231.2(3).

[229]Subs. 231.2(5); see also *Redeemer Foundation v. Minister of National Revenue* (2005), [2006] 1 C.T.C. 7, 2005 D.T.C. 5617 (Eng.) (F.C.) (on appeal to the F.C.A.).

after a single demand and conviction.[230] Thus, the Minister can make multiple demands for the same information. Failure to comply with multiple demands in respect of the same information can lead to multiple convictions.[231]

XXI. — Inquiry

In addition to the power to audit a taxpayer's books of account and general records, the Minister can also conduct an inquiry or private hearing into the taxpayer's affairs:[232]

> This procedure is used in Special Investigations cases where persons who are considered able to give evidence concerning transactions or practices constituting tax evasion are reluctant to furnish voluntary explanations or are so closely related to the taxpayer under examination, by family relationship or business association, that they will not, for fear of recriminations or financial loss, give information unless compelled to do so.

An inquiry or hearing under section 231.4 does not violate sections 7 or 8 of the *Charter*.[233]

1. — Hearing Officer

The Minister must apply to the Tax Court for an order appointing a hearing officer to conduct the inquiry.[234] For the purposes of the inquiry, the hearing officer has all the powers of a commissioner under the *Inquiries Act*,[235] including the right to summon witnesses, to require evidence on oath, to compel the attendance of witnesses, to engage technical specialists (accountants, engineers, etc.) and to deputize technical advisors to inquire into matters within the scope of the commission.[236] A hearing officer does not have the power to punish any person unless the officer obtains the approval of a judge of a superior court and the person to be punished is given 24 hours' notice, or such shorter time as the judge deems reasonable.[237]

---

[230]*The Queen v. Grimwood*, [1987] 2 S.C.R. 755, [1988] 1 C.T.C. 44, 88 D.T.C. 6001 (S.C.C.).

[231]Subs. 238(1).

[232]S. 231.4; IC 73-10R3, "Tax Evasion" (February 13, 1987), para. 25.

[233]*Del Zotto v. Canada*, [1999] 1 S.C.R. 3, [1999] 1 C.T.C. 113, 99 D.T.C. 5029 (S.C.C.).

[234]Subs. 231.4(2).

[235]*Inquiries Act*, R.S.C. 1985, c. I-11; *Income Tax Act*, subs. 231.4(3).

[236]*Income Tax Act*, subs. 231.4(3); *Inquiries Act*, R.S.C. 1985, c. I-11, s. 11.

[237]Subs. 231.4(4).

2. — *Exclusion From Hearing*

A person whose affairs are being investigated in the course of an inquiry is entitled to be present and represented by counsel *unless* the person is excluded by the hearing officer. The basis for excluding a taxpayer and his or her counsel from an inquiry is that the taxpayer's presence would be prejudicial to the conduct of the inquiry.[238] It does not appear to matter that removing the taxpayer's legal counsel from the inquiry might be prejudicial to the taxpayer! In contrast, a person who attends as a witness in an inquiry is always entitled to be represented by legal counsel and to receive a transcript of the evidence given by him or her.[239]

XXII. — Advance Rulings

An advance ruling is a written statement/opinion from the Agency as to how it will interpret specific provisions in the context of specific proposed transactions.

The formal advance rulings procedure was initiated in 1970. Unlike Interpretation Bulletins and Information Circulars that are issued for use by the general public, Advance Rulings are issued by the CRA directly to the taxpayer who applies for the ruling. An Advance Ruling on a complex transaction provides certainty for the taxpayer, but obtaining one can be a frustrating bureaucratic process.

1. — *Procedure*

A ruling is issued on the basis of specific facts set out in the taxpayer's application. Requests for income tax rulings must be forwarded in duplicate to the applicable directorate, and should identify the taxpayer and the relevant Tax Services Office.

A ruling request should contain a clear statement of relevant facts, copies of all pertinent documents, and a statement of the purpose of the transaction. It is also useful to include an interpretation of the relevant statutory provisions upon which the taxpayer is relying, citations to Interpretation Bulletins and, where relevant, any case law on point. The request should also contain a statement confirming that none of the issues are being currently considered by a Tax Services Office in respect of a return which has already been filed by the taxpayer. The CRA will only rule on prospective, not completed, transactions.

---

[238]Subs. 231.4(6).

[239]Subs. 231.4(5).

2. — Fee for Service

The advance ruling mechanism is organized on the basis of a fee for service.

3. — Conference with the Canada Revenue Agency

A taxpayer may request a conference with the Agency at the time that an Advance Ruling request is filed. Although the CRA's official policy (IC 70-6R5) indicates that a taxpayer is entitled to only one conference as a matter of right, the Agency is generally prepared to grant further conferences if the taxpayer so requests. In fact, the Agency will usually accede to as many conferences as are needed in the circumstances.

4. — Rejection of Request at Initial Stage

An Advance Ruling request may be rejected on policy grounds at the time when it is filed. For example, where the request clearly falls within one of the categories listed in IC 70-6R5, the request will be returned without a ruling. The CRA will not issue an Advance Ruling where:

- The central issue involves a matter that is before the courts;

- The request for a ruling contains alternative courses of action on the part of the taxpayer;

- The major issue is whether a sale or purchase of property should be viewed as of an income nature or as a capital transaction;

- The matter involved is a determination of fair market value of property; or

- A ruling would require an opinion as to generally-accepted accounting or commercial practices in certain circumstances.

5. — Discretion

The CRA is not bound to issue a ruling on any proposed transactions. It will issue a ruling only in circumstances when it is comfortable with the facts and the nature of the transaction that is the subject of the ruling. It is entirely in the CRA's domain to determine whether it considers a proposed transaction to be "offensive" or "abusive" in the sense that it has no business purpose, is improper tax avoidance, or constitutes unlawful tax mitigation.

6. — Appeals

There is no formal appeal procedure for taxpayers who are dissatisfied with the Agency's ruling. A taxpayer may, however, request a reconsideration of the ruling. The CRA will entertain such a request only where the taxpayer has new information or can show that the ruling was based on a misunderstanding of the information previously submitted. In most cases, the taxpayer may meet with the Agency to discuss the ruling. The Agency usually contacts the taxpayer before it issues an unfavourable ruling. A taxpayer who is unable to resolve outstanding contentious issues with the CRA may withdraw the ruling request prior to the issuance of an unfavourable ruling.

7. — Delayed Rulings

There is no particular timetable for the issuance of a ruling. In routine matters the ruling may be issued quite quickly (three to four months). In more contentious circumstances, however, the CRA may take longer (eight to 12 months) to issue a ruling. In extreme cases the Agency may simply refuse to issue a ruling even though the taxpayer's request for a ruling is based on perfectly legal grounds.

The Agency will usually not issue a ruling if it is offended by the underlying tenor of the proposed transaction. This is so even if the ruling is based on perfectly legal interpretations. There is also a danger in such cases that the CRA may use the delay to persuade the Department of Finance to amend the law to block transactions similar to the one proposed in the ruling request.

8. — Status of Rulings

Advance Rulings are not binding in law. They are issued at the sole discretion of the CRA so that business transactions may proceed in an environment of certainty. The Advance Ruling mechanism is entirely an administrative creation, not an expression of legislative authority. As a matter of practice, however, the CRA generally considers itself to be bound in respect of both the taxpayer requesting the ruling and the issues ruled upon. The Agency rarely revokes an issued ruling, but it can do so. Although it is arguable that the revocation of an issued ruling would constitute an abuse of power, it would be fairly difficult to establish.[240]

The CRA does not consider itself to be bound by its rulings in the following circumstances:

* Where there is a material omission or misrepresentation in the statement of relevant facts or disclosure of purpose submitted by the taxpayer;

---

[240]*R. v. IRC, ex parte Matrix-Securities Ltd.*, [1994] B.T.C. 85 (H.L.) (the revocation would need to result in clearly manifested injustice).

- Where the advanced ruling was based on an interpretation of the law which has since been changed as a result of a judicial decision;

- Where the transaction in respect of which an Advance Ruling was given has not been substantially completed within the time limits specified in the ruling; or

- Where there has been a change in the law upon which the Advance Ruling was based.

9. — Publication of Rulings

The CRA does not have a coherent policy on publishing its rulings. It is torn between its concern for transparency and its fear of disclosing innovative schemes that other taxpayers may use to advantage.

Between June 1974 and December 8, 1980, for example, the Agency published a total of 101 rulings. In 1983 the Agency announced that it would no longer publish Advance Rulings and that previously-published rulings should not be relied upon as a reflection of the CRA's policy.

The Agency's decision to stop publishing rulings met with considerable opposition. For example, the CBA/CICA Joint Committee commented:

> It is the Committee's view that the publication of rulings was a good way to publicize Revenue Canada's position in matters affecting large numbers of taxpayers.

The Agency eventually relented and began to issue a second series of Advance Tax Rulings in 1986. The CRA has said that it will reissue previously issued rulings where the issues raised in the published rulings are still relevant.

For a while, the Agency did not publish all of its rulings. Indeed, it was very selective in its publication of rulings, a policy that attracted adverse comment from the Auditor General in its review of the CRA's procedures. Between 1985 and 1993, for example, the Agency published only 58 Advance Rulings out of an estimated 4,300 that were issued. Most of the rulings were published at least two years after they were issued.

Since then, the CRA has decided to publish all its rulings, but in substantially severed form, to the public through private on-line tax publishers, such as Carswell and CCH. The downside, however, is that there is a cost for the rulings and they are substantially edited, which limits their value as a source of relevant information. Thus, the tension between full disclosure of relevant information and the privacy rights of taxpayers continues.

XXIII. — Search And Seizure

1. — The Power

The Minister can enter and search *any* building or place and seize therefrom *any* document or thing that *may* afford evidence as to the commission of an offence under the Act. However, the Minister's power of search and seizure can be exercised only on the basis of a search warrant issued by a superior court or Federal Court judge.[241]

2. — "Seizure"

"Seizure" is the forcible taking of possession of property. Not all seizures violate section 8 of the *Charter*, only unreasonable ones. Hence, the questions in each case are: (1) has there been a "seizure"? and (2) if so, was it reasonable in the circumstances?[242]

A demand for information constitutes a "seizure", but not an unreasonable one in the context of the administrative and regulatory scheme of the Act. On the other hand, the transmission of information by the Minister to the Tax Court pursuant to subsection 176(1) is an unreasonable seizure that is protected by section 8 of the *Charter*![243]

3. — The Warrant

(a) — Ex Parte Application

The Minister may make an *ex parte* application for the issuance of a search warrant. Any document or thing that is seized pursuant to the search must be brought before the judge. The Minister's application for the search warrant must be supported by information on oath establishing the facts on which the application is based.[244]

---

[241]Subs. 231.3(1).

[242]*Hunter v. Southam Inc.*, [1984] 2 S.C.R. 145, 84 D.T.C. 6467 (S.C.C.); *Thomson Newspapers Ltd. v. Dir. of Investigation & Research, Combines Investigation Branch* (1986), 57 O.R. (2d) 257 (Ont. C.A.); affd [1990] 1 S.C.R. 425 (S.C.C.); *The Queen v. McKinlay Tpt. Ltd.*, [1990] 1 S.C.R. 627, [1990] 2 C.T.C. 103, 90 D.T.C. 6243 (S.C.C.); affirming (1987), [1988] 1 C.T.C. 426, 88 D.T.C. 6314 (Ont. C.A.).

[243]*Gernhart v. Canada* (1999), [2000] 1 C.T.C. 192, 99 D.T.C. 5749 (F.C.A.); revd. [1997] 2 C.T.C. 23, 97 D.T.C. 5038 (F.C.T.D.).

[244]Subs. 231.3(2).

The decision to apply for a search warrant is an administrative decision that is not subject to judicial review.[245]

A judge may issue a search warrant if the judge is satisfied that there are reasonable grounds to believe that:[246]

- An income tax offence has been committed;

- A document or thing that *may* afford evidence of the commission of the offence is *likely* to be found; and

- The building or place to be searched is *likely* to contain the evidence.

(b) — Contents

The warrant must refer to the offence for which it is issued, identify the building or place to be searched and the person who allegedly committed the offence, and be reasonably specific as to the document or thing that is the object of the search.[247]

The authority of the warrant, however, extends beyond the itemized list for which it is issued. Thus, the Minister may also seize any other document or thing not specified in the warrant if the Minister believes that it affords evidence of the commission of an income tax offence.[248] All documents or things that are seized by the Minister must be brought before the judge who issued the warrant or, if that judge is not available, before another judge of the same court.

(c) — Not Reviewable

A judge's decision to issue a warrant on an *ex parte* application is not reviewable by an appellate court.[249]

---

[245]Subs. 231.3(3). *F.K. Clayton Group Ltd. v. M.N.R.*, [1989] 1 C.T.C. 82, 89 D.T.C. 5186 (F.C.T.D.) (Minister's decision to apply for warrant is purely a procedural step).

[246]Subs. 231.3(3).

[247]Subs. 231.3(4).

[248]Subs. 231.3(5).

[249]*Knox Contracting Ltd. v. The Queen*, [1989] 1 C.T.C. 174, 89 D.T.C. 5074 (N.B. C.A.); affd. [1990] 2 S.C.R. 338, [1990] 2 C.T.C. 262, 90 D.T.C. 6447 (S.C.C.).

4. — Return of Documents

A judge may, on his or her own motion or on application by a third party, order that a document or thing seized be returned to its owner. To issue such an order for return of documents or things, the judge must be satisfied that the document or thing:[250]

- Will not be required for an investigation or a criminal proceeding; or

- Was not seized in accordance with the warrant or the rules described in section 231.3.

5. — Access to Seized Information

The person from whom the documents have been seized has the right to obtain one copy of all the seized documents.[251] The photocopies are to be supplied at the Minister's expense. In addition, the owner of the documents is entitled to have access to the documents at all reasonable times and subject to such reasonable conditions as may be imposed by the Minister. The items to be searched for and seized do not have to be described with specific particularity in the application for the warrant. Indeed, given the nature of income tax offences which lead to search and seizure, it is probably impossible to describe in detail all of the documents sought in a search.

6. — Material in "Plain View"

(a) — Common Law Rule

The common law recognizes the "plain view" doctrine. Thus, where, during the course of executing a legal warrant, an officer locates anything which he or she reasonably believes is evidence of the commission of a crime, the officer has the legal power to seize it.[252] Hence, an official may seize a document without a warrant for that specific document.

---

[250]Subs. 231.3(7).

[251]Subs. 231.3(8).

[252]*Ghani v. Jones*, [1970] 1 Q.B. 693 (C.A.) at 706, *per* Lord Denning M.R.; *Chic Fashions (West Wales) Ltd. v. Jones*, [1968] 2 Q.B. 299 (C.A.) at 313, *per* Diplock L.J.; *Reynolds v. Metro. Police Commr.*, [1984] 3 All E.R. 649 (C.A.) at 653, 659, 662; *The Queen v. Shea* (1983), 1 C.C.C. (3d) 316 (Ont. H.C.) at 321-22; *Texas v. Brown* (1983), 75 L. Ed. (2d) 502; *The Queen v. Longtin* (1983), 5 C.C.C. (3d) 12 (Ont. C.A.) at 16.

(b) — Criminal Code

The CRA also has the power to seize any material falling in "plain view" that affords evidence of any income tax offence. Section 489 of the *Criminal Code*[253] enables a person executing a warrant to seize, in addition to the material that affords evidence of an offence for which the warrant was issued, any other documentary material that he or she believes on reasonable grounds to afford evidence of any other offence under the Act. Since the Minister has the power to seize "plain view" material, the material has the same status as any other materials seized pursuant to the warrant.

The Minister's power may, however, depend upon the jurisdiction in which the warrant is obtained. In *Knox Contracting*,[254] for example, the New Brunswick court held that a warrant issued under what is now section 487 of the *Criminal Code* could not be used for the purpose of any other statute. Presumably, the limitation would also apply, in New Brunswick, to any "plain view" material seized under section 489.

7. — The Raid

The manner in which a search and seizure is carried out can be a formidable experience. The following excerpt from the reasons for judgment of Lord Denning M.R. in *I.R.C.*[255] describes the logistics of a tax raid:

> It was a military style operation. It was carried out by officers of the Inland Revenue in their war against tax frauds. Zero hour was fixed for 7 am on Friday, 13th July 1979. Everything was highly secret. The other side must not be forewarned. There was a briefing session beforehand. Some 70 officers or more of the Inland Revenue attended. They were given detailed instructions. They were divided into teams each with a leader. Each team had an objective allotted to it. It was to search a particular house or office, marked, I expect, on a map: and to seize any incriminating documents found therein. Each team leader was on the day to be handed a search warrant authorising him and his team to enter the house or office. It would be empowered to use force if need be. Each team was to be accompanied by a police officer. Sometimes more than one. The role of the police was presumably to be silent witnesses: or may be to let it be known that this was all done with the authority of the law: and that the householder had better not resist — or else!

> Everything went according to plan. On Thursday, 12th July, Mr. Quinlan, the senior inspector of the Inland Revenue, went to the Central Criminal Court: and put before a circuit judge, the Commons Sargeant, the suspicions which the Revenue held. The circuit judge signed the warrants. The officers made photographs of the warrants, and distributed them to the team leaders.

---

[253]*Criminal Code*, R.S.C. 1985, c. C-46.

[254]*Knox Contr. v. The Queen*, [1986] 2 C.T.C. 194, 86 D.T.C. 6417 (N.B.Q.B.); see also *Purdy v. The Queen* (1972), 28 D.L.R. (3d) 720 (N.B.C.A.).

[255]*The Queen v. I.R.C.*, [1979] 3 All E.R. 385 at 396; revd. [1980] 1 All E.R. 80 (H.L.).

Then in the early morning of Friday, 13th July, the next day, each team started off at first light. Each reached its objective. Some in London. Others in the Home Counties. At 7 am there was a knock on each door. One was the home in Kensington of Mr. Ronald Anthony Plummer, a chartered accountant. It was opened by his daughter aged 11. He came downstairs in his dressing-gown. The officers of the Inland Revenue were at the door accompanied by a detective inspector. The house-holder Mr. Plummer put up no resistance. He let them in. They went to his filing cabinet and removed a large number of files. They went to the safe and took building society passbooks, his children's cheque books and passports. They took his daughter's school report. They went to his bedroom, opened a suitcase, and removed a bundle of papers belonging to his mother. They searched the house. They took personal papers of his wife.

Another house was the home near Maidstone of Mr. Roy Clifford Tucker, a fellow in the Institute of Chartered Accountants. He was away on business in Guernsey. So his wife opened the door. The officers of the Inland Revenue produced the search warrant. She let them in. She did not know what to do. She telephoned her husband in Guernsey. She told him that they were going through the house taking all the documents they could find. They took envelopes addressed to students who were tenants. They went up to the attic and took papers stored there belonging to Mr. Tucker's brother. They took Mr. Tucker's passport.

The main attack was reserved for the offices at 1 Hanover Square of the Rossminster group of companies of which Mr. Plummer and Mr. Tucker were directors. They were let in by one of the employees. Many officers of the Inland Revenue went in accompanied by police officers. It was a big set of offices with many rooms full of files, papers and documents of all kinds. They took large quantities of them, pushed them into plastic bags, carried them down in the lift, and loaded them into a van. They carried them off to the offices of the Inland Revenue at Melbourne House in Aldwych. Twelve van loads. They cleared out Mr. Tucker's office completely: and other rooms too. They spent the whole day on it from 7am until 6:30 at night. They did examine some of the documents carefully, but there were so many documents and so many files that they could not examine them all. They simply put a number on each file, included it in a list, and put it into the plastic bag. Against each file they noted the time they did it. It looks as if they averaged one file a minute. They did not stop at files. They took the shorthand notebooks of the typists; I do not suppose they could read them. They took some of the financial newspapers in a bundle. In one case the "top half" of a drawer was taken in the first instalment and the balance of the drawer was taken in the second.

Another set of offices was next door in St. Georges Street, I think along the same corridor. It was the office of AJR Financial Services Limited. The director Mr. Hallas was not there, of course, at 7 o'clock. He arrived at 9:10 am. He found the officers of the Inland Revenue packing the company's files into bags for removal. He said that it amounted to several hundreds of documents. Police officers were in attendance there too.

At no point did any of the householders make any resistance. They did the only thing open to them. They went off to their solicitors. They saw counsel. They acted very quickly. By the evening they had gone to a judge of the Chancery Division, Walton, J., and asked for and obtained an injunction to stop any trespassing on the premises. They telephoned the injunction through the Hanover Square at about a quarter to six at night. The officers therefore brought the search and seizure to an end. They had, however, by this time practically completed it. So the injunction made very little difference. ...

So end the facts. As far as my knowledge of history goes, there has been no search like it, and no seizure like it, in England since that Saturday, 30 April 1763, when the Secretary of State issued a general warrant by which he authorised the King's messengers to arrest John Wilkes and seize all his books and papers. They took everything, all his manuscripts and all papers whatsoever. His pocket-book filled up the mouth of the sack. He applied to the courts. Pratt, C.J. struck down the general warrant. You will find it all set out in *R v Wilkes* (1763), 2 Wils 151, *Huckle v Money* (1763), 2 Wils 205 and *Entick v. Carrington* (1763), 2 Wils 275. Pratt CJ said:

> To enter a man's house by virtue of a nameless warrant, in order to procure evidence, is worse than the Spanish inquisition; a law under which no Englishman would wish to live an hour: it was a most daring public attack made upon the liberty of the subject [2 Wils 205 at 207].

8. — *Constitutional Restrictions*

(a) — *Section 8 of the Charter*

Three provisions of the *Charter* determine whether, and how, constitutionally-tainted evidence may be used against a taxpayer. We must answer four separate questions:

1. Has there been a seizure?

2. Was the seizure unreasonable?

3. Should the court provide relief against the unreasonable seizure? and

4. Should the constitutionally-tainted evidence be excluded?

Section 8 of the *Charter* reads as follows:

8. Everyone has the right to be secure against unreasonable search or seizure.

The operative word in section 8 is "unreasonable". There is no personal security against search and seizure *per se*. The only security is that the state's search or seizure cannot be unreasonable in the particular circumstances.[256]

---

[256]*Kourtessis v. M.N.R.* (1988), [1989] 1 C.T.C. 56, 89 D.T.C. 5214 (B.C. S.C.); affd. (1989), [1990] 1 C.T.C. 241, 89 D.T.C. 5464 (B.C. C.A.); revd. [1993] 2 S.C.R. 53, [1993] 1 C.T.C. 301, 93 D.T.C. 5137 (S.C.C.).

A "seizure" is a forcible taking of possession of property.[257] However, not every taking is a seizure for the purposes of section 8. In Justice Grange's words:[258]

> It is not necessary to formulate a general rule as to what constitutes a seizure; it is sufficient to say that the s. 8 prohibition does not encompass an order requiring the production of documents so long as the section authorizing the order (or the law apart from that section) gives the person required to produce a reasonable opportunity to dispute the order and prevent the surrender of the documents.

The determination as to what is a "reasonable" search or seizure is made in the context of section 231.3 of the *Income Tax Act*. The judge who issues the warrant must be satisfied that the Minister has reasonable grounds to believe that an offence has been committed, and the executing officer must have reasonable grounds for believing that the documents seized afford evidence of the commission of an offence. These two safeguards render a properly executed search and seizure "reasonable" in the context of section 8 of the *Charter*.[259] Pratte J. explained the scope of section 8 as follows:[260]

> Searches and seizures are intrusions into the private domain of the individual. They cannot be tolerated unless circumstances justify them. A search or seizure is unreasonable if it is unjustified in the circumstance. Section 8 does not merely prohibit unreasonable searches and seizures. It goes further and guarantees the right to be secure against unreasonable search and seizure. That is to say that section 8 of the Charter will be offended, not only by an unreasonable search or seizure or by a statute authorizing expressly a search or seizure without justification, but also by a statute conferring on an authority so wide a power of search and seizure that it leaves the individual without any protection against searches and seizures.

The underlying value that is protected by section 8 of the *Charter* is the taxpayer's interest in privacy. However, section 8 provides protection only from an *unreasonable* search and seizure, not from all seizures.

What constitutes a "reasonable" search and seizure? The test is fluid: it depends upon the type of intrusion into the taxpayer's privacy (for example, demand for information vs. physical seizure of documents), the type of taxpayer (for example, individual vs. corporate), the location where the seizure is executed (for example, business premises vs. personal resi-

---

[257]*Thomson Newspapers Ltd. v. Dir. of Investigation & Research, Combines Investigation Branch*, *ante*, at 267.

[258]*Thomson Newspapers Ltd. v. Dir. of Investigation & Research, Combines Investigation Branch*, *ante*, at 269.

[259]*Solvent Petroleums Extraction Inc. v. M.N.R.*, [1988] 1 C.T.C. 325, 88 D.T.C. 6224 (Fed. T.D.); affd. [1989] 2 C.T.C. 177, 89 D.T.C. 5381 (Fed. C.A.); application for leave to SCC dismissed (1989), 105 N.R. 159 (note) (S.C.C.); reconsideration refused (July 9, 1992), Doc. 21556 (S.C.C.)

[260]*M.N.R. v. Kruger Inc.*, [1984] C.T.C. 506, 84 D.T.C. 6478 (F.C.A.) at 512 [C.T.C.] and 6483 [D.T.C.].

dence), and the context (for example, criminal vs. regulatory/administrative). As Dickson C.J.C. said in *Hunter*:[261]

> It is clear that the meaning of "unreasonable" cannot be determined by recourse to a diction-ary, nor for that matter, by reference to the rules of statutory construction. The task of ex-pounding a constitution is crucially different from that of construing a statute. A statute de-fines present rights and obligations. It is easily enacted and as easily repealed. A constitution, by contrast, is drafted with an eye to the future. Its function is to provide a continuing frame-work for the legitimate exercise of governmental power and, when joined by a Bill or a Char-ter of Rights, for the unremitting protection of individual rights and liberties.

Three tests determine whether a search and seizure is reasonable:[262]

    1. Was the search authorized by law?

    2. Is the law itself reasonable? and

    3. Was the manner in which the search was carried out reasonable?

If the answer to all three questions is affirmative, the seizure is reasonable and does not impugn section 8 of the *Charter*.

The burden of proof for adducing evidence that *Charter* rights have been infringed or denied depends upon the nature of the search. If the search and seizure was conducted pursuant to a warrant, the burden rests initially with the person making the allegation of infringement, namely, the taxpayer. The burden is discharged on a balance of probabilities.[263] Where, however, the search was conducted without the authority of a warrant, the onus is on the Minister to show that the search was, on a balance of probabilities, reasonable in the circumstances.[264]

(b) — Section 24 of the Charter

Prior to the *Charter*, the traditional remedies to protect taxpayers were sparse. Typically, and almost invariably, Canadian courts followed the English, as opposed to American, tradi-tion, and allowed illegally obtained evidence to be used against taxpayers and citizens.[265]

---

[261]*Hunter v. Southam Inc.*, [1984] 2 S.C.R. 145, 84 D.T.C. 6467 (S.C.C.) at 155 [S.C.R.] and 6471-72 [D.T.C.].

[262]*The Queen v. Collins*, [1987] 1 S.C.R. 265 (S.C.C.).

[263]*The Queen v. Collins, ante.*

[264]*Hunter v. Southam Inc., ante*, at 161; see also *The Queen v. Collins, ante.*

[265]See, e.g., *The Queen v. Wray*, [1971] S.C.R. 272 (S.C.C.); for criticisms see Weinberg, "The Judi-cial Discretion to Exclude Relevant Evidence" (1975) 21 McGill L.J. 1, at 4-5; Sheppard, "Restricting

If it is determined that a particular search and seizure was conducted in an "unreasonable" manner, what is to be done with any evidence that is seized as a result of the illegal search? Two provisions of the *Charter* bear on this question.

Subsection 24(1) provides as follows:

> 24. (1) Anyone whose rights or freedoms, as guaranteed by this Charter, have been infringed or denied may apply to a court of competent jurisdiction to obtain such remedy as the court considers appropriate and just in the circumstances.

This is a remedial provision which allows a court considerable, though not unlimited, latitude in devising a remedy. There is no suggestion that this provision is the exclusive remedy for *Charter* violations, but it appears to be the one that is most frequently invoked in tax cases.

Although subsection 24(1) of the *Charter* confers broad discretionary power on a court to provide relief from illegal conduct, it does not mandate the court to exclude the evidence from judicial proceedings.[266] The court *may* exclude evidence from a trial, but only if it is satisfied that the test in subsection 24(2) of the *Charter* is met. That subsection reads as follows:

> (2) Where, in proceedings under subsection (1), a court concludes that evidence was obtained in a manner that infringed or denied any rights or freedoms guaranteed by this Charter, the evidence shall be excluded *if* it is established that, having regard to all the circumstances, the admission of it in the proceedings would bring the administration of justice into disrepute.

Unlike subsection 24(1) of the *Charter*, subsection 24(2) does not confer a discretion on the judge. The judge is under a duty to admit or exclude the tainted evidence.[267] Tainted evidence is *prima facie* admissible. Here too the burden of persuasion rests on the taxpayer to show that the admission of the evidence *would* bring the administration of justice into disrepute.

The focus of subsection 24(2) is on the effect that the admission of the evidence would have on the reputation of the administration of justice. The principal focus of this test is not on the misconduct of the authorities during the course of their investigative process, but on the effect that admission of the evidence would have on the administration of justice. Investigative misconduct goes to the question whether the search and seizure was "unreasonable" and contrary to section 8 of the *Charter* in the first place. To be sure, the nature of the misconduct may colour the decision to admit the evidence, for example, if the conduct is outrageously scandalous.

---

the Discretion to Exclude Admissible Evidence: An Examination of Regina v. Wray" (1972), 14 Cr. L.Q. 335, at 342–47.

[266] *The Queen v. Therens*, [1985] 1 S.C.R. 613 (S.C.C.).

[267] See, *The Queen v. Collins, ante.*

The interpretation of subsection 24(2) is complicated by the substantial difference in the language of the English and French versions of the text. The English text uses the words "*would* bring the administration of justice into disrepute". The French version provides "*est susceptible de* déconsidérer l'administration de la justice." The difference between "would" in the English text and "could" in the French text has the effect of lowering the threshold level for excluding evidence. The Supreme Court of Canada has said that the less onerous French text better serves the purpose of the *Charter*.[268]

By what yardstick do we measure the effect of admitting or excluding evidence? By whose standards and values do we determine the likelihood that inclusion of tainted evidence could bring the administration of justice into disrepute? It is easy enough to articulate an objective "reasonable person" test. To use Professor Yves-Marie Morissette's test:[269] "Would the admission of the evidence bring the administration of justice into disrepute in the eyes of the reasonable man, dispassionate and fully apprised of the circumstances of the case?" The reasonable person test, long familiar to those who have followed the career of "the man on the Clapham omnibus," requires time for maturation before the interpretation of subsection 24(2) becomes more certain. For present purposes, the test is to be read as an objective test that involves an assessment of community views on the administration of justice.

Professor Hogg has alluded to the irony of subsection 24(2), which calls for the exclusion of evidence if its admission could taint the reputation of the administration of justice. There is some impressionistic evidence to suggest that the exclusion of incriminating evidence tends to tarnish the reputation of the administration of justice in the eyes of the community. In Professor Hogg's words:[270]

> As has been frequently pointed out, there is something irrationale about allowing a guilty person to go free (usually the result when reliable evidence is excluded), because another person (usually a police officer) has committed a wrong.

It is the long-term effect of the admission of evidence on the reputation of the administration of justice that is to be weighed in determining whether to exclude tainted evidence.[271]

The difficulty with the "community values" test is that such values usually reflect the views of the majority, whereas the thrust of the *Charter* is to protect the minority. As the Supreme

---

[268]*The Queen v. Collins, ante.*

[269]Yves-Marie Morissette, "The Exclusion of Evidence under the *Canadian Charter of Rights and Freedoms*: What to Do and What Not to Do" (1984) 29 McGill L.J. 521, at p. 538, cited with approval by the Supreme Court of Canada in *The Queen v. Collins, ante.*

[270]Hogg, *Constitutional Law of Canada*, 2nd ed. (Toronto: Carswell, 1985), at 699.

[271]*The Queen v. Collins, ante.*

Court of Canada has said, "The *Charter* is designed to protect the accused from the majority, so the enforcement of the *Charter* must not be left to that majority."[272]

To summarize: evidence that is constitutionally tainted as the result of an unreasonable search and seizure may be excluded if its admission *could* bring the administration of justice into disrepute. The issue is determined by an objective standard of the "reasonable person" in the community, but only when that community's mood is reasonable. The court must look at the long-term effect that the admission or exclusion of the evidence would have on the reputation of the justice system.

XXIV. — Privilege

1. — General Comment

Certain types of communication between a taxpayer and his or her legal advisors are privileged from disclosure. In common law, communications made by a person to legal counsel in that counsel's professional capacity are privileged, and, subject to a few exceptions, neither counsel nor the client can be compelled to disclose the contents of such communications where they were intended to be confidential.[273]

Privilege has been described as follows:[274]

> A client (whether party or stranger) cannot be compelled, and a legal adviser (whether barrister, solicitor, the clerk or intermediate agent of either, or an interpreter) will not be allowed without the express consent of his client, to disclose oral or documentary communications passing between them in professional confidence.

The claim of privilege of a communication is no longer confined to communications made in contemplation, or conduct, of litigation. Where available, it extends to all professional communications made in confidence in a professional capacity with the intent that they be kept secret.[275]

---

[272]*The Queen v. Collins, ante.*

[273]See, generally, *Greenough v. Gaskell* (1833), 39 E.R. 618 (L.C.); *Clergue v. McKay* (1902), 3 O.L.R. 478 (Ont. Div. Ct.); *Butler v. Bd. of Trade*, [1971] 1 Ch. 680; *The Queen v. Bencardino* (1973), 15 C.C.C. (2d) 342 (Ont. C.A.); *Wigmore on Evidence*, McNaughton revision, vol. 8 (Boston: Little, Brown & Co., 1961) paras. 2290–2329, at 541–641; *McCormick on Evidence*, 2nd ed. (St. Paul: West Publishing Co., 1972) at 175 *et seq.*; Radin, "The Privilege of Confidential Communication between Lawyer and Client" (1928) 16 Calif. L. Rev. 487; Kahrl, "The Attorney-Client Privilege" (1979) 40 Ohio State L.J. 699, at 701-702; Pye, "Fundamentals of the Attorney-Client Privilege" (1969) 15 Prac. Law 15, at 16.

[274]*Phipson on Evidence*, 10th ed. (London: Sweet & Maxwell, 1963) at 251, para. 585.

[275]*Alcan-Colony Contr. Ltd. v. M.N.R.*, [1971] 2 O.R. 365, 71 D.T.C. 5082 (Ont. H.C.).

2. — Rationale

The rationale for holding legal communications to be privileged from disclosure is to permit legal advice to be given untrammelled by any apprehension of disclosure. As Brougham L.C. said:[276]

> The foundation of this rule is not difficult to discover. It is not (as has sometimes been said) on account of any particular importance which the law attributes to the business of legal professors, or any particular disposition to afford them protection, though certainly it may not be very easy to discover why a like privilege has been refused to others, and especially to medical advisers.
>
> But it is out of regard to the interests of justice, which cannot be upholden, and to the administration of justice, which cannot go on, without the aid of men skilled in jurisprudence. ... If the privilege did not exist at all, every one would be thrown upon his own legal resources; deprived of all professional assistance, a man would not venture to consult any skillful person, or would only dare to tell his counsellor half his case.

Solicitor-client privilege is an evidentiary rule. The rule was stated as follows by Munroe J. in *Canada Safeway*:[277]

> This application raises a question of importance, namely, does s. 10 of the *Combines Investigation Act* abrogate the common law solicitor-and-client privilege, a privilege established three centuries ago upon grounds of public policy designed to ensure that members of the public may receive the benefit of legal assistance uninhibited by fear of any breach of their confidence.
>
> That rule as to the non-production of communications between solicitor and client says that where (as here) there has been no waiver by the client and no suggestion is made, of fraud, crime, evasion or civil wrong on his part, the client cannot be compelled and the lawyer will not be allowed without the consent of the client to disclose oral or documentary communications passing between them in professional confidence, whether or not litigation is pending.

3. — Waiver by Client

The solicitor-client privilege to withhold or conceal confidential communications belongs to the *client*. The privilege is granted to protect the interests of the client, *not* the interests of

---

[276]*Greenough v. Gaskell, ante,* at 620-21. See, however, *Bindal* (Nov. 15, 2005) (the lawyer received funds as part of an abusive scheme to remove funds from a RRSP on a tax-free basis. Federal Court ordered the release of documents notwithstanding claim of privilege).

[277]*Dir. of Investigation & Research v. Can. Safeway Ltd.* (1972), 26 D.L.R. (3d) 745 at 746 (B.C.S.C.).

the solicitor. As such, the client can always renounce the claim for privilege. Privilege can also be waived through voluntary disclosure.[278]

4. — Statutory Definition

For tax purposes, "privilege" means the right that a person has to refuse to disclose an oral or documentary communication on the ground that the communication is one passing between client and lawyer in a professional confidence.[279]

In general terms, the following types of documents are covered by solicitor-client privilege:

- Correspondence between a solicitor and client;
- Opinion letters; and
- Tax plans, reorganizations, agreements of purchase and sale and other agreements.

The Act deems a lawyer's accounting record (including supporting vouchers and cheques) not to be a confidential communication. A solicitor's statement of account is, however, not considered an "accounting record", and is subject to solicitor-client privilege.[280] We determine solicitor-client privilege by reference to the law of the province in which the matter arises.[281]

A lawyer's accounting records are specifically deemed not to be confidential communications eligible for the claim of privilege. Without this exception, it would be difficult for the CRA to conduct a thorough audit of the lawyer's own income tax returns. A detailed statement of account and computerized dockets can provide a clear trail to an auditor as to the underlying nature of a tax plan and the areas of concern. Hence, the tax lawyer's dilemma: provide detailed accounting to keep the client informed and leave a road map showing the auditor the path to areas of concern to the lawyer.

---

[278]*Visser v. M.N.R.*, [1989] 1 C.T.C. 192, 89 D.T.C. 5172 (P.E.I. S.C.).

[279]Subs. 232(1)"solicitor-client privilege".

[280]*Mut. Life Assur. Co. of Can. v. Dep. A.G. Can.*, [1984] C.T.C. 155, 84 D.T.C. 6177 (Ont. H.C.).

[281]*Dep. A.G. Can. v. Brown*, [1964] C.T.C. 483 at 486, 64 D.T.C. 483 (S.C.C. [B.C.]) (extent of privilege depends upon law of province in which document situated); see also *In re W.W. Kask et al.*, [1966] C.T.C. 659, 66 D.T.C. 5374 (B.C.S.C.) ("communication" given common law meaning); *Herman v. Dep. A.G. Can.* (1979), 79 D.T.C. 5372 (Ont. C.A.) (decision of judge in respect of solicitor-client privilege for documents not subject to appeal).

Whether a document constitutes "an accounting record" is a question of fact. Solicitors' charge sheets[282] and statements of accounts[283] are not accounting records, and therefore may be the subject of a claim of privilege. Accounting records such as ledgers, books of accounts and supporting documents cannot be privileged. Although the matter is not free from doubt, the better view is that a lawyer's trust accounts ledger is a privileged document that is not to be revealed without the client's consent.[284]

5. — *Procedure*

Privilege is invoked by the solicitor on behalf of his or her client. Thus, where an official seeks to examine or seize a document *in the possession of a lawyer*, the lawyer may invoke the privilege on behalf of a *named* client.[285] Unlike the common law, where privilege may extend to the identity of a lawyer's clients, the Act specifically requires disclosure of the name of the client on whose behalf solicitor-client privilege is claimed.

Where a lawyer claims that a document is covered by solicitor-client privilege, the tax officer must place the document in a package without inspecting, examining, or making copies of it. The package must be sealed and deposited either with the sheriff of the district or county in which the seizure is made or with a custodian acceptable to both parties.[286] Where the privilege is claimed in respect of a document that the tax officer is about to inspect or examine, the lawyer must place the document in a package, seal the package, and retain it until the matter is adjudicated by a judge.[287]

Within 14 days from the placing of the sealed package in the custody of the sheriff (or other custodian), either the client or the client's lawyer may apply to a court to have the question of privilege adjudicated. The application to determine the existence of privilege is heard in *camera*.[288] The judge decides the matter summarily, and will either return the document to the lawyer or give it to the CRA.[289]

---

[282]*Re Evans* (1968), 68 D.T.C. 5277 (B.C.S.C.).

[283]*Mut. Life Assur. Co. of Can. v. Dep. A.G. Can., ante*.

[284]*Cox v. A.G. Can.*, [1988] 2 C.T.C. 365, 88 D.T.C. 6494 (B.C.S.C.).

[285]Subs. 232(3).

[286]Paras. 232(3)(a), (b).

[287]Subs. 232(3.1).

[288]S. 179.

[289]Subss. 232(4), (5).

A lawyer who claims privilege on behalf of a client must disclose to the Minister the last known address of the client, so that the client can be approached and afforded the opportunity to waive the privilege.[290]

6. — Defence to Prosecution

We have seen that the Minister can examine and audit a taxpayer's business records and, where authorized, can seize any documents and records which may be required as evidence in a subsequent proceeding. Obstruction of a tax audit is a criminal offence carrying a financial penalty and the possibility of imprisonment. A lawyer who makes a good faith claim for solicitor-client privilege on behalf of a named client cannot be convicted for refusing to disclose information sought by the Minister as part of a tax audit.[291]

7. — Fraud and Crimes

Since the rationale for solicitor-client privilege is to promote the administration of justice through full and frank disclosure of all relevant information, it would be perverse to allow privilege to assist in the perpetration of a fraudulent or criminal act.

There is a distinction between a communication made to commit a fraud or crime and a communication made in seeking advice on the defence of past crimes or fraudulent conduct. As *McCormick on Evidence* states:[292]

> It is settled under modern authority that the privilege does not extend to communications between attorney and client where the client's purpose is the furtherance of a future intended crime or fraud. Advice secured in aid of a legitimate defence by the client against a charge of past crimes or past misconduct, even though he is guilty, stands on a different footing and such consultations are privileged. If the privilege is to be denied on the ground of unlawful purpose, the client's guilty intention is controlling, though the attorney may have acted innocently and in good faith.

Thus, privilege can be lost if it is shown that the privileged relationship exists for the purpose of perpetrating a fraud or crime.

Privilege is not set aside merely by alleging fraud. The Minister must make out a *prima facie* case of fraud and lead some evidence to support the allegation. Further, the allegation must be supported by first hand knowledge; it cannot rest solely on affidavit evidence based on

---

[290]Subs. 232(14).

[291]Subs. 232(2).

[292]*McCormick on Evidence*, 2nd ed. (St. Paul: West Publishing Co., 1972) at 199-200.

information and belief of unspecified and ill-defined inquiries.[293] There must be an intelligible and specific allegation of fraud supported by sufficient evidence to establish at least a *prima facie* case.

Even where fraud is established and the privilege lost, solicitor-client privilege may be claimed in respect of communications between the solicitor and client on advice given *after* the fraudulent act.[294]

8. — *Third-Party Communications*

Third-party communications (communications by a person other than the solicitor or the client) may also be privileged in certain circumstances. Clearly, where a lawyer retains another lawyer to act as his or her agent, the communications of the agent lawyer are privileged.[295] Communications by a third party acting on behalf of a client are also privileged communications if the third party is retained as the lawyer's agent.[296] Jackett P. explained the status of third-party communications as follows:[297]

> ... that no communication, statement or other material made or prepared by an accountant as such for a business man falls within the privilege *unless* it was prepared by the accountant as a result of a request by the business man's lawyer to be used in connection with litigation, existing or apprehended; and that, where an accountant is used as a representative, or one of a group of representatives, for the purpose of placing a factual situation or a problem before a lawyer to obtain legal advice or legal assistance, the fact that he is an accountant, or that he uses his knowledge and skill as an accountant in carrying out such task, does not make the communications that he makes, or participates in making, as such a representative, any the less communications from the principal, who is the client, to the lawyer and similarly, communications received by such a representative from a lawyer whose advice has been so sought are none the less communications from the lawyer to the client.

But not all third-party documents are privileged. In certain circumstances, environmental audit reports and appraisal reports have been held not to be privileged even when prepared at the solicitor's request.[298]

---

[293] *Re Romeo's Place Victoria Ltd.*, [1981] C.T.C. 380, 81 D.T.C. 5295 (F.C.T.D.).

[294] *Re Hoyle Indust. Ltd.*, [1980] C.T.C. 501, 80 D.T.C. 6363 (F.C.T.D.).

[295] *Klassen-Bronze Ltd. v. M.N.R.* (1970), 70 D.T.C. 6361 (Ont. H.C.).

[296] *Re Sokolov*, [1968] C.T.C. 414, 68 D.T.C. 5266 (Man. Q.B.).

[297] *Susan Hosiery Ltd. v. M.N.R.*, [1969] C.T.C. 353, 69 D.T.C. 5278 at 5283 (Ex. Ct.).

[298] *Gregory v. M.N.R.*, [1992] 2 C.T.C. 250, 92 D.T.C. 6518 (F.C.T.D.).

9. — Accountants' Communications

The general rule is that communications between an accountant and client are not privileged.[299] Thus, an accountant's audit working papers and tax files cannot be the subject of a claim for privilege. As noted above, however, where the accountant is retained as an agent of the client's solicitor, papers prepared as part of the agency contract are in effect the solicitor's papers, and are privileged communications.[300]

XXV. — Appeals

1. — General Comment

The income tax system operates on the basis that a taxpayer initially assesses their own tax liability in respect of a taxation year. The tax return is then examined by the Minister, who may assess, or reassess, the taxpayer in respect of the taxpayer's self-assessed liability. A taxpayer who is assessed by the Minister may appeal the assessment.

Once issued, the Minister's assessment may be challenged only through an appeal. It cannot be challenged by a writ of *certiorari*.[301]

2. — Notice of Objection

The first formal legal step in the appeal process is the filing of a Notice of Objection.[302] Although a taxpayer may negotiate with the Agency prior to filing a Notice of Objection, *all* of the taxpayer's statutory legal rights in respect of an appeal hinge upon the timely filing of the objection — that is, within the 90-day period from the *date of mailing* of the notice of assessment or within one year of the "filing due date". The 90-day time limit is quite strictly enforced, and is extended only in exceptional circumstances.[303]

---

[299]*Tower v. Minister of National Revenue* (2003), [2004] 1 F.C.R. 138, [2003] 4 C.T.C. 263, (sub nom. *Minister of National Revenue v. Kitsch*) 2003 D.T.C. 5540 (F.C.A.).

[300]See, e.g., *Mut. Life Assur. Co. of Can. v. Dep. A.G. Can.*, [1984] C.T.C. 155, 84 D.T.C. 6177 (Ont. H.C.) (letter from solicitors containing professional correspondence between solicitors and chartered accountants with respect to tax matters was privileged).

[301]*Federal Court Act*, R.S.C. 1985, c. F-7; see *The Queen v. Parsons*, [1984] C.T.C. 352, 84 D.T.C. 6345 (F.C.A.) (Minister's assessments not to be reviewed, restrained or set aside by court in exercise of its discretion under ss. 18 and 28 of *Federal Court Act*, R.S.C. 1970, c. 10 (2nd Supp.)).

[302]S. 165; IC 98-1R, "Collection Policies" (Sept. 15, 2000).

[303]Ss. 166.1, 166.2; see, e.g., *Morasutti v. M.N.R.*, [1984] C.T.C. 2401, 84 D.T.C. 1374 (T.C.C.) (leave refused where taxpayer's solicitor became aware of necessity to file within two weeks of expiry

3. — Administrative Appeals

An "administrative appeal" involves discussion with, and representations to, the Agency to determine whether the matters raised in the Notice of Objection can be resolved on an informal basis. At this stage of the dispute, the taxpayer (or the taxpayer's representative) may be asked to supply further information by way of explanation or supplementary documentation.

Failing resolution of disputed items, the next step for the taxpayer is to proceed to the more formal administrative process before the Appeals Branch of the CRA. The Appeals Branch is theoretically "independent" of the auditing and assessing sections of the Agency. It is supposed to take a fresh and independent view of the facts and the law and render a decision on an objective basis. It is, however, important to bear in mind that the staff of the Appeals Branch are recruited from the audit and assessing sections of the Agency and they return to their assessing responsibilities upon completion of their tour of duty with the Appeals Branch. Therefore, their approach to appeals may be influenced both by their past association with the assessing and audit divisions and the knowledge that they will return to their peers in those divisions upon completion of their assignment in Appeals.

4. — Appeal to Tax Court

Where a taxpayer fails to resolve a dispute with the Agency at an administrative level, he or she may launch an appeal to the Tax Court. An appeal lies to the Tax Court where the Minister has confirmed the assessment or 90 days have elapsed from the date of service of the Notice of Objection.[304]

---

of 90-day period); *Wright v. M.N.R.*, [1983] C.T.C. 2493, 83 D.T.C. 447 (T.R.B.) (leave refused where taxpayer missed limitation period because he would not pay his lawyer's retainer); *Horton v. M.N.R.* (1969), 69 D.T.C. 821 (T.A.B.) (taxpayer served notice of objection 92 days after date of assessment after learning only on last day that he had to file such notice; board rejected argument and dismissed appeal); see also *Gregg v. M.N.R.*, [1969] Tax A.B.C. 782, 69 D.T.C. 559; *Brady-Browne v. M.N.R.* (1969), 69 D.T.C. 797 (T.A.B.); *Grenier v. M.N.R.* (1970), 70 D.T.C. 1299 (T.A.B.); *Vineland Quarries & Crushed Stone Ltd. v. M.N.R.*, [1971] C.T.C. 501, 71 D.T.C. 5269 (F.C.T.D.); varied as to costs [1971] C.T.C. 635, 71 D.T.C. 5372 (F.C.T.D.); *Paletta v. M.N.R.*, [1977] C.T.C. 2285, 77 D.T.C. 203 (T.R.B.).

[304]Subs. 169(1).

(a) — General Comment

The Tax Court of Canada has the sole power initially to hear appeals under the *Income Tax Act*. The court has two different tracks: informal and general. A taxpayer can use the Informal Procedure for appeals in three circumstances:[305]

1. Where the aggregate of all tax amounts (other than interest or provincial tax) in issue does not exceed $12,000;

2. Where the amount of the loss in issue does not exceed $24,000; or

3. Where the only amount in issue is the amount of interest assessed under the Act.

Where the disputed amounts exceed the threshold limits, the taxpayer can elect to restrict the appeal to the limits and forego any claim for the excess.

(b) — Informal Procedure

A taxpayer must elect to have the Informal Procedure apply. Decisions of the Tax Court under the Informal Procedure cannot be appealed, but may be "judicially reviewed" by the Federal Court of Appeal. The limit of $12,000 for the informal track is intended to provide taxpayers with a quick and inexpensive route for the settlement of tax disputes. Since approximately 70 per cent of income tax appeals involve amounts of less than $12,000, this procedure is intended to facilitate the processing of tax disputes in an expeditious and inexpensive manner.

The following procedures apply to informal appeals:[306]

• The appeal must be submitted in writing.

• The appeal should set out the reasons for the appeal and the relevant facts.

• The Minister is generally required to submit a reply within 60 days from the time when the notice of appeal is filed.

• The appeal must be heard within 180 days of the Minister's reply.

• Judgment must be issued within 90 days of the hearing of the appeal.

Thus, the entire appeal process is usually completed within eleven months from the date that the taxpayer files the Notice of Appeal and chooses to have the case heard through the Informal Procedure. The taxpayer can represent him- or herself or be represented by an agent. The agent may be a person other than a lawyer.

---

[305]*Tax Court of Canada Act*, R.S.C. 1985, T-2, subs. 18(1).

[306]See http://www.tcc-cci.gc.ca.

(c) — General Procedure

The general appeal to the Tax Court of Canada is more formal and strictly controlled by rules that are similar to the rules of the Federal Court of Canada. Generally, the General Procedure is more expensive and is used where the appeal in question involves federal tax for a taxation year in excess of $12,000.

A taxpayer can represent him or herself in a formal appeal or be represented by a lawyer. Non-lawyer agents are not allowed to appear before the Tax Court of Canada in a formal appeal.

The General Procedure is governed by the formal rules of evidence and any decisions of the Tax Court following such an appeal are considered precedents.

In contrast with the informal procedure, there is no pre-determined time frame for completion of the appeal in the general process. Thus, cases involving a formal appeal may extend over three to four years. The following chart gives a brief overview of the general and informal procedures.

	General	**Informal**
Representation	By self or lawyer	By self, lawyer or agent
Procedure	Similar to procedures now existing in most courts	No formal procedure required except for filing the appeal in writing
Evidence	Strict rules apply	Rules are flexible
Appeals	To the Federal Court of Appeal	Review by Federal Court of Appeal on questions of law and jurisdiction
Precedential value of case decisions	Yes	No
Time frame	No mandatory time frame for completion of an appeal	Explicit time deadlines for the CRA and the court Maximum of: — 60 days between filing of appeal and reply — 180 days between reply and hearing — 90 days between hearing and decision

5. — Settlements

A taxpayer who enters into a settlement with the Agency is generally bound by the terms of the settlement, and may not appeal the same assessment. In *Smerchanski*,[307] the taxpayer, faced with the possibility of criminal proceedings on the grounds of income tax evasion, entered into a settlement just prior to the time when the right of prosecution would otherwise have been outlawed by the passage of time. Later, the taxpayer challenged the assessment which was the basis of the settlement on the grounds that it had been obtained by duress and threat of prosecution. The Supreme Court of Canada unanimously upheld the settlement. Laskin C.J.C. stated:[308]

> Since it is not contested that a taxpayer may validly waive his rights of appeal against a tax assessment and that no question of public policy is involved to preclude such a waiver, the only issue of importance in this appeal is whether the tax authorities, seriously contemplating prosecution, and by indictment as in the present case, are entitled to exact a waiver of rights of appeal as a binding term of settling a clear tax liability when overtures for settlement are made by the taxpayer and, in consequence, to abandon their intention to prosecute.

> The threat of prosecution underlies every tax return if a false statement is knowingly made in it and, indeed, this is inscribed on the face of the tax form. It cannot be that the tax authorities must proceed to prosecution when faced with a dispute on whether there is a wilful tax evasion rather than being amenable to a settlement, be it a compromise or an uncompromising agreement for payment of what is claimed. Here there was not even such a dispute but an acknowledgement of evasion and the taxpayer's position cannot be stronger when he is a confessed evader than when he has disputed wilful evasion.

> I leave to one side situations where the tax authorities, having no substantial case against a taxpayer, nonetheless importune and harass him with the threat of prosecution in order to exact an unjustified settlement.

6. — Disposition of Appeal by Tax Court

The Tax Court can dispose of an appeal in one of four ways. It may:[309]

1. Dismiss the appeal;

2. Vacate the assessment;

3. Vary the assessment; or

4. Refer the assessment back to the Minister for further reconsideration and reassessment.

---

[307] *Smerchanski v. M.N.R.* (1976), [1977] 2 S.C.R. 23, [1976] C.T.C. 488, 76 D.T.C. 6247 (S.C.C.).

[308] *Smerchanski v. M.N.R.*, *ibid.*, at 494 [C.T.C.] and 6251 [D.T.C.]. See subs. 165(1.2) and 169(2.2).

[309] Subs. 171(1).

7. — Appeal to the Federal Court of Appeal

Decisions of the Tax Court of Canada rendered under the General Procedure may be appealed to the Federal Court of Appeal pursuant to the rules of the *Federal Courts Act*.[310] Decisions under the informal procedure may be eligible for judicial review by the Federal Court of Appeal.

(a) — Procedure

An appeal to the Federal Court of Appeal must be instituted within 30 days from the judgment of the Tax Court. The appeal is commenced by filing a Notice of Appeal with the Federal Court Registry and by serving all parties who are directly affected by the appeal with a true copy of the Notice.

Evidence of service must also be filed with the registry of the court.[311] The Federal Court of Appeal hears appeals with a panel of three judges.[312]

(b) — Direct References

The taxpayer may appeal directly to the Federal Court of Appeal where the Minister:[313]

* Refuses to grant registration as a charitable organization, private or public foundation or Canadian amateur athletic association;

* Gives notice that it is proposed to revoke the registration of one of the above-listed organizations;

* Refuses to register a retirement savings plan;

* Refuses to register a profit-sharing plan;

* Revokes the registration of a profit-sharing plan;

* Refuses to issue a certificate of exemption under subsection 212(14) of the Act;

* Refuses to accept the registration of an education savings plan;

* Revokes the registration of an education savings plan;

---

[310]R.S.C. 1985, c. F-7, subs. 27(1.1).

[311]*Federal Courts Act*, subss. 27(2), (3).

[312]*Federal Courts Act*, subs. 16(1).

[313]Subs. 172(3).

- Refuses to accept the registration of a retirement income fund;

- Refuses to register a pension plan;

- Revokes the registration of a pension plan; or

- Refuses to accept an amendment to a registered pension plan.

The Act deems the Minister to have refused the registration, acceptance or issuance, as the case may be, in any of the situations listed above if the Minister does not notify the applicant within 180 days after the filing of the application.[314]

The appeal must be instituted within a period of 30 days from the date of the Minister's decision refusing the application for registration, issuance of a certificate of exemption, or revocation of the registration.[315] The Federal Court of Appeal may grant an extension of time beyond the 30-day period.[316]

8. — Appeal to the Supreme Court of Canada

A decision of the Federal Court of Appeal may be appealed, but only with leave, to the Supreme Court of Canada. Leave to appeal may be granted either by the Federal Court of Appeal or by the Supreme Court of Canada. There is no automatic right of appeal to the Supreme Court of Canada. Leave to appeal is granted only if the court is satisfied that the question being appealed involves a matter of public importance or is one which, in its opinion, it should hear for any other reason.

The Supreme Court receives approximately 600 applications for leave to appeal each year of which it grants approximately 12 per cent. The probability of having the Supreme Court hear a tax appeal is low — in the order of 0.2 to 0.5 per cent. A panel of three judges usually decides leave applications.

An appeal to the Supreme Court of Canada must usually be brought within 30 days from the pronouncement of the judgment by the Federal Court of Appeal, or within such further time as a judge of the Federal Court of Appeal allows.

A copy of the Notice of Appeal must be filed with the Registrar of the Supreme Court, and all parties directly affected by the appeal must be served with a copy of the Notice. Evidence of service of the Notice must also be filed with the registrar of the Supreme Court.

---

[314]Subs. 172(4).

[315]Subs. 180(1).

[316]Subs. 180(1).

Selected Bibliography to Chapter 23

General

Beaubier, David W., "The Tax Court of Canada: An Outline of Informal Procedure and General Procedure", in *Proceedings of 41st Tax Conf.* 41:1 (Can. Tax Foundation, 1989).

Beaufry, John, "Taxing Matters" (1991) 15 Can. Lawyer No. 4 23.

Brooks, Neil and Anthony N. Doob, *Making Taxpayer Compliance Easier: Preliminary Findings of a Canadian Survey* (1990).

Canadian Tax Foundation, *Canadian Tax Highlights* 10:10 (24 October 2002). <http://www.ctf.ca/articles/News.asp?article_ID=1832> [3 February 2003].

Colley, Geoffrey M., "Tax Affairs Aren't Just an April Filing" (1989) 122 CA Magazine 46.

Dealing with Revenue Canada: Audits, Appeals, Instalments, Collections (Toronto: Canadian Institute, 1993).

Duncan, Deborah, "A Review of Recent Administrative Positions" in *Proceedings of 45th Tax Conf.* 47:1 (Can. Tax Foundation, 1993).

Gaignery, Gillis P., "Access to Revenue Canada Taxation Files", *Corp. Mgmt. Tax Conf.* 7:1 (Can. Tax Foundation, 1988).

Harris, Edwin C., "Curl Penalties Under the *Income Tax Act*", *Corp. Mgmt. Tax Conf.* 9:1 (Can. Tax Foundation, 1988).

Hickey, Paul B., "Administrative Issues Arising From Tax Reform", *Corp. Mgmt. Tax Conf.* 3:1 (Can. Tax Foundation, 1988).

Huggett, D.R., "Administration" (1985) 13 Can. Tax News 103.

Lefebvre, Wilfrid, and Marie-Claire Lalonde, "Recent Issues in Tax Collection", in *Proceedings of 38th Tax Conf.* (Can. Tax Foundation, 1986).

Martin, Roch "Recent Income Tax Developments" (2002) 40:1 Alta L. Rev. 19.

McKie, A.B., "No Accounting for Tax Audits" (1987) 2:1 Can. Current Tax C-1.

Nazzer, Eric G., "Section 174, Procedural Simplicity or Procedural Unfairness" (1992) 3 Can. Current Tax A11.

Orvoine, Alaine, "Dealing with Revenue Canada: An Accountant's Perspective" in *Proceedings of 45th Tax Conf.* 11:1 (Can. Tax Foundation, 1993).

Pitfield, Ian H., "Dealing with Revenue Canada: A Lawyer's Perspective" in *Proceedings of 45th Tax Conf.* 10:1 (Can. Tax Foundation, 1993).

Pitfield, Ian H., "Tax Collection Practices and Procedures", in *Proceedings of 37th Tax Conf.* 28:1 (Can. Tax Foundation, 1985).

Richards, Gabrielle M.R., "No Relief for Revenue Canada's Carelessness: *City Centre Properties v. The Queen*, Federal Court — Trial Division" (1994) 4 Can. Current Tax J53.

Sanford, Cedric, Michael Goldwin and Peter Hardwick, *Administrative and Compliance Costs of Taxation* (Bath: Fiscal Publications, 1989).

Scheuermann, Scott L., "Interest on Underpaid and Overpaid Amounts", *Corp. Mgmt. Tax Conf.* 10:1 (Can. Tax Foundation, 1988).

Westmacott, Ernie "The 'Big Stick' Becomes Law" *The Scrivener* 9:3 (October 2000). http://www.notaries.bc.ca/article.php3?214> [3 February 2003].

Slutsky, Samuel, *Tax Administration Reports* (Toronto: Richard De Boo, 1986).

Income Tax Returns

Tremblay, Richard G., "Information Reporting: Transactions with Non-Residents: Revenue Canada Extends its Reach" (1989) 2 Can. Current Tax P-57.

Withholding Taxes

Broadhurst, David G., "Issues in Withholding", *Corp. Mgmt. Tax Conf.* 11:1 (Can. Tax Foundation, 1988).

Calculation of Tax Liability

Smith, David W., "Recent Decisions Underline Taxpayers' Liabilities" (1987) 14:6 Nat. (C.B.A.) 28.

Assessments

Role of the Department of Justice Counsel in Tax Disputes, Audio Archives of Canada, 1984.

Reassessments

Gibson, "An Overview of Income Tax Litigation", in *Proceedings of 35th Tax Conf.* 967 (Can. Tax Foundation, 1983).

Krishna, Vern, "Reassessments Bases on Fraud or Misrepresentation" (1992) 3 Can. Current Tax A25.

Ledoux, Georges, "Tax Audits" in *Proceedings of 45th Tax Conf.* 47:1 (Can. Tax Foundation, 1993).

Role of the Department of Justice Counsel in Tax Disputes, Audio Archives of Canada, 1984.

Power, Mary V., "Do Statutes Have Limitations?" (1989) 122 CA Magazine 44.

Smith, David W., "Reassessments, Waivers: Amended Returns and Refunds", *Corp. Mgmt. Tax Conf.* 8:1 (Can. Tax Foundation, 1988).

Payment of Tax

Bartlett, R., "Judicial Review in Taxation: A Modern Perspective" (1987) Br. Tax Rev. 10.

Bowman, Stephen W., "Collections in the Insolvency Context", *Corp. Mgmt. Tax Conf.* 12:1 (Can. Tax Foundation, 1988).

Bowman, Stephen W., "Subsection 224(12) Supergarnishment: Constitutionality" (1992) 40 Can. Tax J. 395.

Lalonde, Phil and Kathleen Marta, "Revenue Canada's Super Garnishee: Secured Creditors Beware!" (1991) 8 Nat. Bank. and Insolvency Rev. 65.

Potvin, Jean, "'Superpriority' Garnishment Provision: Subsection 224(12)" in *Proceedings of 44th Tax Conf.* 5:54 (Can. Tax Foundation, 1992).

Robertson, Ronald N. and Edmond F.B. Lamek, "Tax Collection and Insolvency: An Update" in *Proceedings of 45th Tax Conf.* 8:1 (Can. Tax Foundation, 1993).

Skulski, B.J., "Tax Collection in Recessionary Times" in *Proceedings of 44th Tax Conf.* 9:1 (Can. Tax Foundation, 1992).

Notice of Objection

Bartlett, R., "Judicial Review in Taxation: A Modern Perspective" (1987) Br. Tax Rev. 10.

Dixon, Gordon D., "Just and Equitable Considerations for Applications for the Extension of Notice of Objections" (1990) 28 Alta. L. Rev. 762.

Krishna, Vern, "Obtaining Extension of Time to File Notice of Objection: The Palm Tree Withers" (1987) 2 Can. Current Tax A-1.

McDonnell, T.E., "Leave to Late File Notice of Objection Granted" (1992) 40 Can. Tax J. 703.

Power, Mary V., "Do Statutes Have Limitations?" (1989) 122 CA Magazine 44.

Instalment Payments

Carr, Brian R. and Karen Yull, "Tax on the Instalment Plan" (1994) 127 CA Mag. No. 6 35.

Drache, A.B.C., "Instalment Payments Clarified" (1991) 13 Can. Taxpayer 185.

Drache, A.B.C., "Retroactivity Upheld Still Again" (1991) 13 Can. Taxpayer 191.

Speiss, Terry J., "New Rules for Income Tax Instalments" (1990) 3:2 Can. Current Tax T-5.

Liability of Directors for Corporate Taxes

Bowman, S.W., "Director's Liability: Deficiencies in Notices of Assessments" (1991) 39 Can. Tax J. 1324.

Bowman, S.W., "Director's Liability — The Outsider" (1990) 38 Can. Tax J. 1242.

Brahmst, Oliver C., "Revenue Canada's Administration of Section 227.1 and the Application of Subsection 15(1) of the Charter" (1991) 3 Can. Current Tax P25.

Campbell, R. Lynn, "Director Liability for Unremitted Employee Deductions" (1992) 25 U.B.C.L. Rev. 211.

Fien, Cy M., "Directors' Liability and Indemnifications, Section 160 Assessments, and Ordinary Course of Business Provisions" in *Proceedings of 44th Tax Conf.* 53:1 (Can. Tax Foundation, 1992).

Fien, Cy M., "Liability of a Corporation for Acts of Corporate Officials in the Tax Field and Liability of Corporate Officials for Acts of a Corporation", *Corp. Mgmt. Tax Conf.* 177 (Can. Tax Foundation, 1983).

Fulcher, J.E., "Section 227.1 of the *Income Tax Act* and the Director's Duty of Care in BCA Jurisdictions: Some Lessons from the Corporate Governance Debate of the Last Twenty-five Years" (1992) 5 Can. Petro. Tax J. No. 1 17.

Gottlieb, Dan, "Corporations Have No Privilege Against Self-Incrimination" (1986) 6:13 Lawyers Weekly 13.

Krishna, Vern, "Liability of Shareholders for Corporate Taxes" (1993) 4 Can. Current Tax A11.

Krishna, Vern, "Personal Liability for Shareholders for Unpaid Corporate Taxes" (1991) 3 Can. Current Tax C81.

Kroft, Edwin G., "The Liability of Directors for Unpaid Canadian Taxes", in *Proceedings of 37th Tax Conf.* 30 (Can. Tax Foundation, 1985).

MacKnight, Robin J., "Indemnities for Officers and Directors: Adding Insult to Injury" (1991) 3 Can. Current Tax P41.

Muskowitz, Evelyn P., "Directors' Liability: An Update" in *Proceedings of 43rd Tax Conf.* 47:1 (Can. Tax Foundation, 1991).

Muskowitz, Evelyn P., "Directors' Liability Under Income Tax Legislation and Other Related Statutes" (1990) 38 Can. Tax J. 537.

Nicholl, John I.S., "Director's and Officer's Liability Insurance" (1985) 3 Can. J. Ins. L. 42.

Investigations

Corn, George, "Illegal Search and Seizure and Application of Charter of Rights and Freedoms" (1986) 1 Can. Current Tax J-123.

Dellinger, "Of Rights and Remedies: The Constitution as a Sword" (1972) 85 Harvard L. Rev. 1532.

Gauthier, E.H., "Audit Function in Revenue Canada Taxation" in *Proceedings of 44th Tax Conf.* 9:1 (Can. Tax Foundation, 1992).

Gibson, "Overview of Income Tax Litigation (An)", in *Proceedings of 35th Tax Conf.* 967 (Can. Tax Foundation, 1983).

Gibson, "Shocking the Public" (1983) 13 Man. L.J. 495.

Kafka, Gerald A., "Taxpayer Bill of Rights Expands Safeguards and Civil Remedies" (January 1989) 70 J. Taxation 4.

Kellough, Howard J., "Emerging Income Tax Issues: Section 231.2 Requirement Letters, Uses and Abuses of Trusts, and Interest Deductibility" in *Proceedings of 45th Tax Conf.* 2:1 (Can. Tax Foundation, 1993).

Krishna, Vern, "Investigative Powers Under the *Income Tax Act*" (1986) 1 Can. Current Tax 1161.

Lefebvre, Wilfrid, and Marie-Claire Lalonde, "Recent Issues in Tax Collection", in *Proceedings of 38th Tax Conf.* 41 (Can. Tax Foundation, 1986).

Levy, "The Invocation of Remedies under the Charter" (1983) 13 Man. L.J. 523.

Lorinc, John, "The Tax Man Cometh" (1994) 127 CA Mag. No. 4 28.

Martinez, Leo P., "Tax Collection and Populist Rhetoric: Shifting the Burden of Proof in Tax Cases" (1988) 39 Hastings L.J. 239.

McKie, A.B., "Tax Inquisitors" (1991) 3 Can. Current Tax C85.

McLellan and Elman, "The Enforcement of the Charter" (1983) 21 Alta. L. Rev. 205.

Roberts, Robert A., "Demand for Information under Section 231.1 of the *Income Tax Act*" (1993) 4 Can. Current Tax P11.

Role of the Department of Justice Counsel in Tax Disputes, Audio Archives of Canada, 1984.

Smith, David W., "Time Must be Allowed to Produce Documents" (1985) 12:11 Nat. (C.B.A.) 29.

"Some New Reporting Requirements and Penalties" (1988) 16 Can. Tax News 14.

Inquiry

Corn, George, "Illegal Search and Seizure and Application of Charter of Rights and Freedoms" (1986) 1 Can. Current Tax J-123.

Dellinger, "Of Rights and Remedies: The Constitution as a Sword" (1972) 85 Harvard L. Rev. 1532.

Search and Seizure

Butler, Alison Scott, "Making Charter Arguments in Civil Tax Cases: Can the Courts Help Taxpayers?" (1993) 41 Can. Tax J. 847.

Corn, George, "Illegal Search and Seizure and Application of Charter of Rights and Freedoms" (1986) 1 Can. Current Tax J-123.

Corr, George, "Search and Seizure: Validity of Section 231.3" (1993) 4 Can. Current Tax J1.

Dellinger, "Of Rights and Remedies: The Constitution as a Sword" (1972) 85 Harvard L. Rev. 1532.

Deschamps, J. Michel, "Crown Priorities and Tax Collection: An Overview", in *Proceedings of 37th Tax Conf.* 29:1 (Can. Tax Foundation, 1985).

Fairley, "Enforcing the Charter" (1982) 4 S.C.L. Rev. 217.

FISS, *The Civil Rights Injunction* (1978).

Gibson, "Determining Disrepute: Opinion Polls and the Charter" (1983) 61 Can. Bar Rev. 377.

Gibson, *Law of the Charter (The): General Principles* (Calgary: Carswell, 1986).

Gibson, "Overview of Income Tax Litigation (An)", in *Proceedings of 35th Tax Conf.* 967 (Can. Tax Foundation, 1983).

Gibson, "Shocking the Public" (1983) 13 Man. L.J. 495.

Goodman, Wolfe D., "Search and Seizure, Evasion, Records and Tax Opinions", (1986) Special Lectures LSUC 207.

Grossman, B.K., "Search and Seizure under the *Income Tax Act*: A Constitutional Assessment of the Bill C-84 Amendments to the *Income Tax Act*" (1987) 35 Can. Tax J. 1349.

Hill, "Constitutional Remedies" (1969) 69 Columbia L. Rev. 1109.

Kafka, Gerald A., "Taxpayer Bill of Rights Expands Safeguards and Civil Remedies" (January 1989) 70 J. Taxation 4.

Krishna, Vern, "Investigative Powers Under the *Income Tax Act*" (1986) 1 Can. Current Tax 1161.

Lefebvre, Wilfrid, and Marie-Claire Lalonde, "Recent Issues in Tax Collection", in *Proceedings of 38th Tax Conf.* 41 (Can. Tax Foundation, 1986).

Levy, "The Invocation of Remedies under the Charter" (1983) 13 Man. L.J. 523.

Martinez, Leo P., "Tax Collection and Populist Rhetoric: Shifting the Burden of Proof in Tax Cases" (1988) 39 Hastings L.J. 239.

McDowall, *Equity and the Constitution* (1982).

McLellan and Elman, "The Enforcement of the Charter" (1983) 21 Alta. L. Rev. 205.

Morisette, "The Exclusion of Evidence under the *Canadian Charter of Rights and Freedoms* — What to Do and What Not to Do" (1984) 29 McGill L.J. 521.

Paciocco, D., "*The Proposed Canada Evidence Act* and the 'Wray Formula': Perpetuating An Inadequate Discretion" (1983) 29 McGill L.J. 141.

Peiris, "The Admissibility of Evidence Obtained Illegally: A Comparative Analysis" (1981) 13 Ottawa L. Rev. 309.

Pilkington, "Damages as a Remedy for Infringement of Charter" (1984) 62 Can. Bar Rev. 517.

Pound, Richard W., "Audit, Inquiry, Search and Seizure", in *Proceedings of 37th Tax Conf.* 27:1 (Can. Tax Foundation, 1985).

Role of the Department of Justice Counsel in Tax Disputes, Audio Archives of Canada, 1984.

"Some New Reporting Requirements and Penalties" (1988) 16 Can. Tax News 14.

Templeton, W., "Search and Seizure" (1985) 13 Can. Current Tax 98.

Vita, Peter A., "Collection Remedies of the Crown", (1988) Special Lectures LSUC 411.

Ward, David A., and John M. Ulmer, "Corporate Taxation: Search and Seizure Update" (1985) 4 Legal Alert 142.

Watchuk, Jeanne, "Search and Seizure Provisions Contravene Charter" (1991) 39 Can. Tax J. 644.

Privilege

Ivankovich, Ivan F., "A Question of Privilege: Confidential Communications and the Public Accountant" (1994) 23 Can. Bus. L. J. 201.

MacKnight, Robin J., "Privileges of the Taxpayer" (1991) 3 Can. Current Tax P27.

Nathanson, David C., "The Fairness Package, the Long Reach of Section 160, and Solicitor — Client Privilege" in *Proceedings of 43rd Tax Conf.* 49:1 (Can. Tax Foundation, 1991).

Perry, John Lilburn, "The *Income Tax Act*: Solicitor — Client Privilege and Solicitor — Client Confidentiality" (1994) 52 Advocate 405.

Roberts, Robert A. and Russell W. Watson, "Solicitor — Client Privilege from a Tax Perspective" (1993) 4 Can. Current Tax T5.

"Some New Reporting Requirements and Penalties" (1988) 16 Can. Tax News 14.

Watson, Russ, "Next Case, Please: Case-by-case Privilege Offers Some Hope for Non-lawyer Advisors (1993) 4 Can. Current Tax P23.

Appeals

Boyle, Patrick, *Canadian Tax Objection and Appeal Procedures* (Don Mills, Ont.: CCH Canadian, 1991).

Broadhurst, David G., "Late-Filed Elections and U.K. Advance Corporation Tax Refunds" (1986) 34 Can. Tax J. 165.

Drache, Arthur B.C., "Hazarding an Appeal" (1995) 17 Can. Taxpayer 78.

Festeryga, Paul, "The Onus Issue: Who Carries the Burden of Proof in an Income Tax Appeal?" (1992) 125 CA Mag. No. 7 34.

Huggett, D.R., "Administration" (1985) 13 Can. Tax News 103.

Krishna, Vern, "Appealing Tax Assessments" (1987) 21 CGA Magazine 42.

Krishna, Vern, "Obtaining Extension of Time to File Notice of Objection: The Palm Tree Withers" (1987) 2 Can. Current Tax A-1.

Lefebvre, Wilfrid, and Deen Olsen, "The Tax Litigation Process: An Update", in *Proceedings of 39th Tax Conf.* 50:1 (Can. Tax Foundation, 1987).

McDonnell, Thomas E., "Administrative Matters and Appeals", (1986) Special Lectures L.S.U.C. 181.

McMechan, Robert and Gordon Bourgard, *Tax Court Practice 1995* (Scarborough, Ont.: Carswell, 1995).

Ontario Tax Appeals: Practices and Procedures (Revised) (Toronto: Ontario Ministry of Revenue, 1988).

Quigley, Michael G., "Dealing with Expert Evidence in Tax Cases" (1993) 41 Can. Tax J. 1071.

Smith, David W., "Time Must be Allowed to Produce Documents" (1985) 12:11 Nat. (C.B.A.) 29.

"Some New Reporting Requirements and Penalties" (1988) 16 Can. Tax News 14. *Your Right to Appeal Ontario Taxes* (Revised) (Toronto: Ontario Ministry of Revenue, 1988).

Other

Bartlett, R., "Judicial Review in Taxation: A Modern Perspective" (1987) Br. Tax Rev. 10.

Corn, George, "Dismissal of Action for Want of Prosecution" (1993) 4 Can. Current Tax A1.

Corn, George, "Interpretation of the 'Fairness Package'" (1994) 4 Can. Current Tax A19.

Corn, George, "Restriction on Collection of Taxes and Whether Collection in Jeopardy" (1987) 2 Can. Current Tax A-5.

Fridman, G.H.L., "No Justice for Taxpayers: The Paucity of Restitution" (1990) 19 Man. L. J. 303.

Fulcher, J.E., "Is the 'New' Tax Court of Canada Absolutely Bound by Decisions of Federal Court — Trial Division? (1992) 40 Can. Tax J. 99.

Hsu, Berry F.C., "The Politics in the Canadian Judicial Decision Making Process: Economic Analysis of Tax Litigation" (1994) 32 Alta. L. Rev. 741.

King, Bruce, "A Fix for Frustration!" (1991) 124 CA Mag. No. 4 30.

Lanthier, Allan R., "Emerging Income Tax Issues: Public Service 2000, International Finance, and U.S. Limited Liability Companies" in *Proceedings of 45th Tax Conf.* 3:1 (Can. Tax Foundation 1993).

Lefebvre, Denis, "Recent Revenue Canada Initiatives" in *Proceedings of 45th Tax Conf.* 6:1 (Can. Tax Foundation, 1993).

McDonnell, T.E., "Ministry Refused Leave to Late File Report" (1992) 40 Can. Tax J. 716.

Mitchell, Robert E., "From Advisor to Business Partner" (1994) 127 CA Mag. No. 2 42.

Nathanson on Tax Litigation (Montreal: Federated Press, 1992).

Pateras, Bruno J., "Tax Evasion after the Charter" (1990), *Meredith Mem. Lectures* 435.

Peterson, Shirley D., "International Enforcement of Canadian and U.S. Tax Laws" in *Corp. Mgmt. Tax Conf.* (Can. Tax Foundation, 1993).

Pound, Richard, "Remedial Tax Planning: How to Fix It when It's Broke" in *Proceedings of 45th Tax Conf.* 9:1 (Can. Tax Foundation, 1993).

Read, Robert J.L., "The Income Tax Advance Rulings Service" in *Proceedings of 44th Tax Conf.* 6:1 (Can. Tax Foundation, 1992).

Roy, Robert, "The Tax Avoidance Program" in *Proceedings of 45th Tax Conf.* 7:1 (Can. Tax Foundation, 1993).

Sherman, H. Arnold and Jeffrey D. Sherman, "Income Tax Remission Orders: The Tax Planner's Least Resort or the Ultimate Weapon?" (1986) 34 Can. Tax J. 801.

Shultis, Elizabeth and Stephen Smith, "Valuation by Compromise in the Tax Courts: Myth or Reality?" (1992) 40 Can. Tax J. 1253.

Tax Litigation: Effective Preparation and Conduct (Mississauga, Ont.: Insight, 1991).

Webber, Philip B., "In the Clear with or without a Clearance Certificate: But Trustees Beware!" (1992) 40 Can. Tax J. 706.

Wise, Richard M., "Tax Evasion and Mens Rea Forensic Accounting" (1990) Meredith Mem. Lectures 405.

CHAPTER 24 — TAX AVOIDANCE

"Lawyers use the law as shoemakers use leather: rubbing it, pressing it, and stretching it with their teeth, all to the end of making it fit for their purposes."

(Louis XII of France)

I. — General Comment

It is a fundamental principle of Anglo-Canadian tax law that a taxpayer is *entitled* to arrange his or her affairs to minimize tax. Parliament has endorsed this principle — generally known as the *Westminster* principle — as a legitimate and accepted part of Canadian tax law.[1] Tax avoidance implies the reduction of tax payable by lawful means. Thus, we start with the premise that the avoidance of tax is perfectly legitimate, and indeed, even moral. A government should intervene in the economy only if it must deliver essential services or can deliver services at a cost or price that is lower than equivalent private sector comparables. As Justice Learned Hand said:[2]

> Over and over again courts have said that there is nothing sinister in so arranging one's affairs as to keep taxes as low as possible. Everybody does so, rich or poor; and all do right, for nobody owes any public duty to pay more than the law demands: taxes are enforced exactions, not voluntary contributions. To demand more in the name of morals is mere cant.

As world economies interlink, cross-border transactions increase, and tax rates take an increasing slice of income, tax planning becomes increasingly important, both in domestic and

---

[1] See Explanatory Notes (1988) to GAAR tabled with the legislation at 464, quoted per curiam in *Canada Trustco Mortgage Co. v. R.*, [2005] 5 C.T.C. 215 (S.C.C.) at 227.

[2] *C.I.R. v. Newman* (1947), 159 Fed. (2d) 848 at 850-851.

international contexts. At the same time, governments focus on methods to curtail abusive tax avoidance. Countries respond to tax avoidance in different ways. Some enact highly specific domestic legislative provisions; others resort to broad anti-abuse rules. Canada has both types in domestic law and in its tax treaties.

The regulation and control of tax avoidance is more complicated on the international front. There is no rule of international law that forbids double taxation — the imposition of taxes in two jurisdictions on the same taxpayer in respect of the same income. However, since double taxation harms economic growth, countries attempt to promote the exchange of goods and services and the movement of capital and persons by eliminating international double taxation through treaties. Tax treaties are, however, bilateral agreements and their terms must be individually negotiated. Hence, there is no uniformity in international tax avoidance rules.

We start with the premise that tax avoidance is legitimate and legally acceptable. That, however, is only the beginning. Statutory restrictions on tax avoidance narrow the scope of legitimate tax planning. Having said that tax avoidance is legitimate, one must distinguish between acceptable tax mitigation and "abusive" tax avoidance. The fact that tax avoidance is legal does not necessarily imply that it is always successful. Success depends upon whether the avoidance transactions achieve their desired goal of tax minimization.

Tax avoidance falls into two categories: (1) Tax mitigation[3] and (2) Abusive avoidance. In the former case, transactions achieve the desired result of tax minimization and, therefore, are effective. In the latter case, abusive transactions may be ignored for tax purposes and do not achieve the desired goal of tax minimization. What is not always clear, however, is the line between the two: When does lawful tax mitigation cross over and become abusive tax avoidance? What if a general anti-avoidance rule conflicts with a specific permissive rule? How far may a taxpayer go in reducing tax before the Canada Revenue Agency (CRA) intervenes to disallow the benefits of tax planning? How innovative and creative can one be in arranging or rearranging one's affairs to reduce taxes? What measures are available to the CRA in restraining tax avoidance?

The short history of Canadian taxation is replete with statutory measures and judicial doctrines intended to control and curtail tax avoidance. The history is a tug-of-war between the taxpayer, anxious to preserve his earnings, and the CRA, with its apparently insatiable appetite for revenues to support public sector spending.

The measures to control tax avoidance vary in scope and intensity. Some are narrow and specific to certain types of transactions; others are broad and stated as general principles. The General Anti-Avoidance Rule ("GAAR"), a broadly stated statement of principle of statutory construction that affects both domestic and international tax planning, is at the apex of all anti-avoidance measures.

---

[3]See, *C.I.R. v. Challenge Corporation Ltd.*, [1986] N.Z.T.C. 5219 (P.C.).

GAAR shifts fiscal control away from the judicial process to the hidden and discretionary administrative processes of the CRA. Commercial transactions and tax planning now depend more than ever before on administrative advance rulings, which the CRA issues on a discretionary basis. Thus, GAAR places taxpayers at the mercy of administrative discretion. The large accounting and law firms lure CRA officials with large salaries to exploit their insider information.

GAAR is a fertile source for tax opinions and rulings. The rule gives the CRA the ultimate weapon with which to control tax avoidance: The Agency applies its administrative discretion behind closed doors. By exercising its discretion to issue or withhold advance rulings on specific transactions and through its statements in circulars and public pronouncements, the CRA's administrative practices shape the application of the rule. Thus, the rule shifts the power base of control into the hands of bureaucrats not directly accountable to taxpayers.

The law says that no person is under any legal obligation to abstain from arranging her affairs to reduce the tax bite. To be sure, a person is *entitled* to arrange her affairs so as to reduce tax. This right, however, is subject to a proviso that the arrangement must constitute lawful tax mitigation. Thus, the question becomes: What constitutes lawful tax mitigation? The answer to this seemingly simple question is fraught with uncertainty. By definition, all tax planning involves tax minimization. But at what point does one cross over from acceptable tax mitigation to unacceptable tax avoidance?

Tax mitigation that is not subject to GAAR is "lawful" avoidance. Tax avoidance that is caught by GAAR is considered "unlawful" in the sense that it is not in accordance with the law, as it is subsequently determined. The distinction, however, between what is "lawful" and "unlawful" depends upon the purpose of the transaction, the rationale of the particular provision(s) and the Act read as a whole. Thus, the tax adviser must exercise judgment and distinguish between minimization schemes that will withstand GAAR and tax avoidance arrangements that will not. That is not always an easy task. How far can one go in tax planning without running into GAAR? What are the limits of the rule? The answer is that the boundaries are not marked. One must proceed with caution. To employ the analogy of Mr. Justice Brandeis:[4]

> If you are walking along a precipice, no human being can tell you how near you can go to that precipice without falling over, because you may stumble on a loose stone, you may slip, and go over; but anybody can tell you where you can walk perfectly safely within convenient distance of that precipice.

GAAR is a loose stone that lies near the line between lawful tax mitigation and unlawful tax avoidance. We see this in the first two decisions of the Supreme Court — both handed down

---

[4]Brandeis, Mason, *A Free Man's Life* (1946), at 352.

on October 19, 2005 — *Canada Trustco*[5] and *Mathew*,[6] in which the Court applied GAAR in one case and not the other. To be sure, the CRA will always rule on "safe" tax plans. However, the tax adviser's task is to give legal opinions on whether GAAR applies to arrangements that are closer to the precipice and more vulnerable to loose stones.

II. — Judicial Doctrines

Tax planning is not a new phenomenon: It is as old as civilization itself and has always provided stimulus for innovative and creative schemes. It appeared 6,000 years ago in Mesopotamia when a king imposed fines on his citizens who swam across the local river to avoid the toll tax on the local ferry. The king responded by making swimming across the river illegal.

The containment of tax planning within acceptable boundaries is both a legislative and judicial function. Thus, some control mechanisms have been developed judicially, while others are in the statute. Although GAAR falls into the latter category, we understand its design and structure better in the context of earlier judge-made doctrines.

1. — Taxpayers' Rights

It is well settled that one is entitled to arrange one's affairs so as to attract the minimum amount of tax. We usually identify this principle with the decision of the House of Lords in *I.R.C. v. Duke of Westminster*, where Lord Tomlin said:[7]

> ... Every man is entitled, if he can, to order his affairs so that the tax attaching under the appropriate Acts is less than it otherwise would be. If he succeeds in ordering them so as to secure this result ... he cannot be compelled to pay an increased tax.

In fact, the House of Lords identified the principle ten years earlier in *Fisher's Executors*:[8]

> [M]y Lords, the highest authorities have always recognized that the subject is entitled so to arrange his affairs as not to attract tax imposed by the Crown, so far as he can do so within the law, and that he may legitimately claim the advantage of any express terms or any omissions that he can find in his favour in taxing Acts. In so doing he neither comes under liability nor incurs blame.

---

[5] *Canada Trustco Mortgage Co. v. R.*, [2005] 5 C.T.C. 215 (S.C.C.).

[6] *Mathew v. R.*, [2005] 5 C.T.C. 244 (S.C.C.).

[7] *I.R.C. v. Duke of Westminster*, [1936] A.C. 1 at 19-20, 19 T.C. 490 at 520 (H.L.). See also *Neuman v. Canada*, [1998] 1 S.C.R. 770.

[8] *I.R.C. v. Fisher's Executors*, [1926] A.C. 395 at 412 (H.L.) (taxpayer may reduce taxes by distributing profits to shareholders in the form of debenture stocks).

And, in *Ayrshire Pullman Motor Service v. C.I.R.*:[9]

> ... [N]o man in this country is under the smallest obligation, moral or other, so to arrange his legal relations to his business or to his property as to enable the Inland Revenue to put the largest possible shovel into his stores. The Inland Revenue is not slow — and quite rightly — to take every advantage which is open to it under the taxing statutes for the purpose of depleting the taxpayer's pocket. And the taxpayer is, in like manner, entitled to be astute to prevent, so far as he honestly can, the depletion of his means by the Revenue. ...

The *Westminster* principle is also well entrenched in American tax jurisprudence. As Justice Holmes said:[10]

> We do not speak of evasion, because, when the law draws a line, a case is on one side of it or the other, and if on the safe side is none the worse legally than a party that has availed himself to the full of what the law permits. When an act is condemned as an evasion, what is meant is that it is on the wrong side of the line indicated by the policy if not by the mere letter of the law.

These speeches reflect the high watermark of judicial tolerance towards tax planning. The phrase "... every man is entitled to arrange his affairs to minimize tax ..." is probably the best known and most frequently cited maxim of tax law. Taken at its face value, however, the maxim is deceptive. How far can a taxpayer actually go in arranging affairs so as to minimize tax? What are the acceptable limits of tax planning? In fact, the courts through judicial doctrines, and the legislature through statutory provisions, severely curtail the limit of tax avoidance.

(a) — Tax Mitigation

As with any maxim, the danger with the *Westminster* principle is that blanket reliance upon it can mislead taxpayers into believing that all tax plans are sound. The maxim invites taxpayers to believe that they need attend only to the specific words of the Act without concern for the underlying policies of tax law.

To be sure, a taxpayer is entitled to arrange her affairs so as to mitigate tax if it is done in an acceptable and lawful manner. Thus, tax planning is not an open arena: It is circumscribed by judicial doctrines and legislative restraints. Tax arrangements must withstand the scrutiny of anti-avoidance doctrines that constrain the freedom to tax plan.

Four judicial doctrines warrant close attention:

    1. The "sham transactions" doctrine;

---

[9]*Ayrshire Pullman Motor Service v. C.I.R.* (1929), 14 Tax Cas. 754 at 763-64 (Scot.) (taxpayer may arrange his/her affairs so as to reduce taxes, however, the transaction is not effectual prior to the dates on which it was executed).

[10]*Bullen v. Wisconsin* (1916), 240 U.S.R. 625 at 630-31.

2. The "ineffectual transactions" doctrine;

3. The "substance over form" doctrine; and

4. The "business purpose" test.

These doctrines hover over all tax planning and one must carefully consider them in structuring tax arrangements.

(b) — Judicial Attitudes

Judicial attitudes towards tax planning shift to reflect social, political, and economic values. The case law reflects the ebb and flow of judicial tolerance towards tax avoidance: The tolerance of the *Westminster* principle in the heyday of *laissez-faire* economics; the hardening of attitudes after the Second World War and a lessening tolerance towards tax arrangements that threaten to curtail public revenues. For example, we see the beginning of the change in sentiment towards tax avoidance in Lord Greene's speech in *Lord Howard de Walden v. C.I.R.*:[11]

> For years a battle of manoeuvre has been waged between the Legislature and those who are minded to throw the burden of taxation off their own shoulders on to those of their fellow-subjects. In that battle the Legislature has often been worsted by the skill, determination and resourcefulness of its opponents, of whom the present appellant has not been the least successful. It would not shock us in the least to find that the Legislature has determined to put an end to the struggle by imposing the severest of penalties. It scarcely lies in the mouth of the taxpayer who plays with fire to complain of burnt fingers.

And in Viscount Simon's speech in *Latilla*:[12]

> [T]here is, of course, no doubt that they are within their legal rights, but that is no reason why their efforts, or those of the professional gentlemen who assist them in the matter, should be regarded as a commendable exercise of ingenuity or as a discharge of the duties of good citizenship.

And, later, in Lord Denning's characteristically terse admonition: "The avoidance of tax may be lawful, but it is not yet a virtue."[13]

---

[11]*Lord Howard de Walden v. C.I.R.*, [1942] 1 K.B. 389 at 397 (C.A.) (taxpayer who transferred assets to a foreign Canadian company liable for income tax and surtax as he had the "power to enjoy" these assets within the meaning of the *Finance Act*).

[12]*Latilla v. I.R.C.*, [1943] A.C. 377 at 381 (H.L.) (taxpayer unsuccessfully attempted to reduce British income tax by transferring profit to capital; transaction within s. 18 of the *Finance Act*).

[13]*Re Weston's Settlements; Weston v. Weston*, [1969] 1 Ch. 223 at 245 (C.A.) (in making a determination whether to vary trusts for the purpose of avoiding or reducing tax, court may consider the expediency of such a scheme and the interests of the beneficiaries).

As we will see shortly, the judicial approach to controlling tax avoidance depends upon the depth and detail of statutory anti-avoidance provisions. The greater the detail of statutory anti-avoidance rules, the greater the reluctance of the judiciary to add further gloss to the rules. Thus, if Parliament speaks, it should do so with certainty.

2. — Evasion, Avoidance and Mitigation

The law distinguishes between evasion, avoidance, and lawful tax mitigation. The distinction between these three concepts lies at the core of effective tax planning, both from a substantive and evidentiary perspective.

Tax evasion is the commission of an act knowingly *with the intent to deceive* so that the tax reported by the taxpayer is less than the tax payable under the law. This may occur through a deliberate omission of revenue, the fraudulent claiming of expenses or allowances, or the deliberate misrepresentation, concealment or withholding of material facts.[14]

Tax evasion is a *mens rea* criminal offence. The Crown carries the burden to prove the offence beyond a reasonable doubt. Similarly, the prosecution of tax evasion is governed by the procedural rules of criminal law.

Tax avoidance is concerned with the minimization of tax. It can be "lawful" or "unlawful" either because of the manner or the motive with which one executes it.

Lawful tax planning is the mitigation of taxes that would otherwise be payable in the absence of the plan.

Tax avoidance is unlawful, but only where it offends established judicial doctrines or prescriptive legislation such as GAAR. Otherwise, it is lawful. In a civil tax dispute the taxpayer has the burden to prove, on a balance of probabilities, that the Minister's assessment is incorrect. An assessment is presumed to be valid until the taxpayer demonstrates otherwise.

---

[14]See IC 73-10R3, "Tax Evasion" (February 13, 1987); see also *The Queen v. Myers*, [1977] C.T.C. 507, 77 D.T.C. 5278 (Alta. Dist. Ct.); *The Queen v. Baker* (1973), 6 N.S.R. (2d) 38 (Co. Ct.); *The Queen v. Paveley*, [1976] C.T.C. 477, 76 D.T.C. 6415 (Sask. C.A.); *The Queen v. Nicholson* (1974), 75 D.T.C. 5095 (Ont. Prov. Ct.); *The Queen v. Thistle*, [1974] C.T.C. 798, 74 D.T.C. 6632 (Ont. Co. Ct.); *The Queen v. Regehr*, [1968] C.T.C. 122, 68 D.T.C. 5078 (Y.T. C.A.); *Branch v. The Queen*, [1976] C.T.C. 193, 76 D.T.C. 6112 (Alta. Dist. Ct.).

3. — Motive

It used to be the general rule that the motive with which a taxpayer entered into an avoidance transaction was irrelevant to the legitimacy of the transaction. As Viscount Dilhorne said:[15]

> ... [A] trading transaction does not cease to be such merely because it is entered into in the confident hope that ... some fiscal advantage will result.

Similarly, *per* Justice Learned Hand:[16]

> ... [T]he rights resulting from a legal transaction otherwise valid, are not different vis-à-vis taxation, because it has been undertaken to escape taxation. That is a doctrine essential to industry and commerce in a society like our own, in which, and so far as possible, business is always shaped to the form best suited to keep down taxes.

However, motive is now an important component of the statutory rules to control tax avoidance. Motive, for example, determines whether a transaction constitutes an "avoidance transaction" under GAAR.

4. — Sham Transactions

We determine the legal effect of an arrangement by the rights and obligations that it *actually* creates and not merely by the wording of documentation. An arrangement that does not, in fact, create the legal rights and obligations that it purports to create is a "sham".

(a) — Meaning of "Sham"

A "sham" is a fiction: an apparition of rights and obligations that do not really exist.[17] A sham transaction is one in which acts committed or documents executed by the parties to the

---

[15]*F.A. & A.B. Ltd. v. Lupton*, [1971] 3 All E.R. 948 (U.K. H.L.). (transactions of the taxpayers clearly joint ventures guised as share-dealing transactions intended to result in tax minimization; transactions fail).

[16]*C.I.R. v. Nat. Carbide Corp.* (1948), 167 Fed. (2d) 304 at 306 (creation of wholly-owned subsidiaries not necessarily invalid due to underlying motive to avoid taxation).

[17]*Snook v. London & West Riding Invt. Ltd.*, [1967] 2 Q.B. 786, [1967] 1 All E.R. 518 (Eng. C.A.) (to have a sham transaction all parties must be in common agreement that the acts and documents do not create the legal rights and obligations that they appear to create); see also *C.I.R. v. Challenge Corp.*, [1986] S.T.C. 548 (P.C.) ("sham is transaction constructed to create false impression in eyes of tax authority"); *Susan Hosiery Ltd. v. M.N.R.*, [1969] C.T.C. 533, 69 D.T.C. 5346 (Ex. Ct.); *M.N.R. v. Cameron* (1972), [1974] S.C.R. 1062, [1972] C.T.C. 380, 72 D.T.C. 6325 (S.C.C.); *Richardson Terminals Ltd. v. M.N.R.*, [1971] C.T.C. 42, 71 D.T.C. 5028; affirmed [1972] C.T.C. 528, 72 D.T.C. 6431 (S.C.C.); *Malka v. The Queen*, [1978] C.T.C. 219, 78 D.T.C. 6144 (F.C.T.D.); *Dom. Bridge Co.*

transaction attempt to give to third parties the appearance of having created between the parties, legal rights and obligations that are different from those which the parties actually intended to create.[18] The definition implies that the parties to the transaction have deliberately set out to misrepresent the actual state of affairs.

A sham may exist despite documentary appearance.[19] A sham requires an intention that the rights and obligations created by the documentary evidence be different from the actual rights and obligations contemplated by the parties to the transaction. In the words of Lord Diplock:[20]

> I apprehend that, if it has any meaning in law, it means acts done or documents executed by the parties to the "sham" which are intended by them to give to third parties or to the court the appearance of creating between the parties legal rights and obligations different from the actual legal rights and obligations (if any) which the parties intend to create. One thing I think, however, is clear in legal principle, morality and the authorities ... that for acts or documents to be a "sham," with whatever legal consequences follow from this, all the parties thereto must have a common intention that the acts or documents are not to create the legal rights and obligations which they give the appearance of creating. No unexpressed intentions of a "shammer" affect the rights of a party whom he deceived.

(b) — Development of Doctrine

(i) — Uncertainty

The CRA sometimes uses the term "sham" to attack transactions based on the general aroma (the "smell test") of a scheme that cannot otherwise be struck down on other grounds.[21] At other times, the doctrine is confused with the "ineffectual transactions" doctrine and the "business purpose" test. In *Spur Oil*,[22] for example, the court said that sham transactions "...

---

v. The Queen, [1975] C.T.C. 263, 75 D.T.C. 5150; affirmed [1977] C.T.C. 554, 77 D.T.C. 5367 (F.C.A.).

[18]This definition was adopted by the Supreme Court of Canada in *M.N.R. v. Cameron* (1972), [1974] S.C.R. 1062, [1972] C.T.C. 380, 72 D.T.C. 6325 (S.C.C.).

[19]*The Queen v. Redpath Industries*, [1984] C.T.C. 483, 84 D.T.C. 6349 (Que. C.S.P.) (must be *prima facie* evidence that tax was undisputably payable before the court will decide tax has been eroded and a sham has occurred).

[20]*Snook v. London & West Riding Invt. Ltd.*, [1967] 2 Q.B. 786, [1967] 1 All E.R. 518 (Eng. C.A.) at 528 [E.R.].

[21]See, for example, *Stubart Investments Ltd. v. The Queen*, [1984] 1 S.C.R. 536, [1984] C.T.C. 294, 84 D.T.C. 6305 (S.C.C.).

[22]*Spur Oil Ltd. v. R.*, [1980] C.T.C. 170, 80 D.T.C. 6105 (F.C.T.D.); reversed [1981] C.T.C. 336, 81 D.T.C. 5168 (F.C.A.); leave to appeal to S.C.C. refused 39 NR 406 (purchase of oil from an offshore

appear to be transactions in which the taxpayer has used various technicalities or devices for the purpose of tax avoidance."[23] This argument is circular and not at all helpful. Tax avoidance is lawful if the arrangement is not a sham and does not otherwise offend GAAR.

(ii) — Clarification

The decision of the Supreme Court of Canada in *Stubart*[24] removed some of the confusion previously associated with the sham transactions doctrine by substantially limiting its application to the circumstances contemplated by Lord Diplock in *Snook*.[25] As Mr. Justice Estey said:[26]

> ... sham transaction: This expression comes to us from decisions in the United Kingdom, and it has been generally taken to mean (but not without ambiguity) a transaction conducted with an element of deceit so as to create an illusion calculated to lead the tax collector away from the taxpayer or the true nature of the transaction; or, simple deception whereby the taxpayer creates a façade of reality quite different from the disguised reality. ... With respect to the courts below, it seems to me that there may have been an unwitting confusion between the incomplete transaction test and the sham test. ... The courts have thus far not extended the concept of sham to a transaction otherwise valid but entered into between parties not at arm's length. The reversibility of the transaction by reason of common ownership likewise has never been found, in any case drawn to the Court's attention, to be an element qualifying or disqualifying the transaction as a sham.

Mr. Justice Estey's use of the word "deceit" in his description of "sham" did not likely narrow Lord Diplock's interpretation of the doctrine. A transaction that purports to put forward the appearance of legal rights and obligations that are different from those actually created is "deceitful" according to the common understanding of that term. Any more technical or legal interpretation of "deceit" that involves a significant redefinition of an established doctrine would require a more explicit judicial statement.

---

affiliated company at a price below market value not a sham despite the fact that the oil could have been obtained for less).

[23]*Spur Oil Ltd. v. R., ibid.*, at 170 [C.T.C.].

[24]*Stubart Investments Ltd. v. The Queen*, [1984] 1 S.C.R. 536, [1984] C.T.C. 294, 84 D.T.C. 6305 (S.C.C.).

[25]*Snook v. London & West Riding Invt. Ltd.*, [1967] 2 Q.B. 786, [1967] 1 All E.R. 518 (Eng. C.A.).

[26]*Stubart Invt. Ltd. v. The Queen*, [1984] C.T.C. 294, 84 D.T.C. 6305 (S.C.C.) at 298 [C.T.C.] and 6308, 6320 [D.T.C.].

(iii) — More Uncertainty

Only three years after *Stubart*, the Supreme Court clouded the doctrine again. In *Bronfman Trust*,[27] the taxpayer financed a capital payment through a bank loan. The CRA disallowed a deduction for the interest expense on the loan on the basis that it was a payment on account of capital. The taxpayer argued that the expense would have been deductible if it had re-structured the borrowing to make the interest payable on account of business income. For example, the trust could have:

- Sold its portfolio securities to raise cash;

- Made its capital expenditure with the cash;

- Borrowed an equal amount from the bank; and

- Used the borrowed funds to repurchase the portfolio of securities.

Had the trust executed each of these four steps in sequence, it would *actually* have created the legal rights and obligations that it purported to create, namely, borrowing to purchase income bearing securities. Each of the individual steps would have been a legitimate and valid commercial transaction and, hence, outside of the definition of "sham." The Supreme Court, albeit in *obiter*, observed that the restructured arrangement *might* be considered a sham. The Chief Justice said:[28]

> If, for example, the trust had sold a particular income-producing asset, made the capital alloca-tion to the beneficiary and repurchased the same asset, all within a brief interval of time, the courts might well consider the sale and repurchase to constitute a formality or a sham designed to conceal the essence of the transaction, namely that money was borrowed and used to fund a capital allocation to the beneficiary.

In *Singleton v. R.*, [29] the CRA refers to the *obiter* in an attempt to attack the Singleton structure of borrowing. The Supreme Court, however, tactfully deflects the attempt by char-acterizing the Bronfman comments as "more musing than jurisprudence." In *Shell*, the Su-preme Court finally retreats from this approach and, once again, restores the legitimacy of tax planning.[30]

---

[27]*The Queen v. Bronfman Trust*, [1984] 1 S.C.R. 32, [1987] 1 C.T.C. 117, 87 D.T.C. 5059 (S.C.C.). See, however, *Shell Canada Ltd. v. Canada*, [1999] 3 S.C.R. 622, [1999] 4 C.T.C. 313, 99 D.T.C. 5669 (S.C.C.), which retreats from this approach towards tax planning.

[28]*The Queen v. Bronfman Trust*, *ibid.*, at 55 [S.C.R.] and 129 [C.T.C.].

[29][2001] 2 S.C.R. 1046 (S.C.C.).

[30]*Shell Canada Ltd. v. Canada*, [1999] 3 S.C.R. 622, [1999] 4 C.T.C. 313, 99 D.T.C. 5669 (S.C.C.).

5. — Ineffectual Transactions

A taxpayer is entitled to arrange his affairs to minimize tax. To be effective, however, the plan must be completely and fully implemented according to the relevant law. Tax reduction schemes in particular tend to attract close scrutiny and should be meticulously documented.[31] In *Atinco Paper Prod. v. The Queen*, for example, Urie J. cautioned:[32]

> I do not think that I should leave this appeal without expressing my views on the general question of transactions undertaken purportedly for the purpose of estate planning and tax avoidance. It is trite law to say that every taxpayer is entitled to so arrange his affairs as to minimize his tax liability. No one has ever suggested that this is contrary to public policy. It is equally true that this court is not the watch dog of the Minister of National Revenue. Nonetheless, it is the duty of the Court to carefully scrutinize everything that a taxpayer has done to ensure that everything which appears to have been done, in fact, has been done in accordance with applicable law. It is not sufficient to employ devices to achieve a desired result without ensuring that those devices are not simply cosmetically correct, that is correct in form, but, in fact, are in all respects legally correct, real transactions. ... The only course for the Court to take is to apply the law as the Court sees it to the facts as found in the particular transaction. If the transaction can withstand that scrutiny, then it will, of course, be supported. If it cannot, it will fall.

Thus, tax mitigation arrangements should be *bona fide* and properly executed. They must be real. As Viscount Simon said in *I.R.C. v. Wesleyan & Gen. Assur. Soc.*:[33]

> [I]t may be well to repeat two propositions which are well established in the application of the law relating to Income Tax. First, the name given to a transaction by the parties concerned does not necessarily decide the nature of the transaction. ... The question always is what is the real character of the payment, not what the parties call it. Secondly, a transaction which, on its true construction, is of a kind that would escape tax, is not taxable on the ground that the same result could be brought about by a transaction in another form which would attract tax.

---

[31]See, for example, *The Queen v. Daly*, [1981] C.T.C. 270 at 279 (F.C.A.):

> In a case of this kind, where it is acknowledged that what is sought by a certain course of action is a tax advantage, it is the duty of the court to examine all of the evidence relating to the transaction in order to satisfy itself that what was done resulted in a valid, completed transaction.

See also *Kingsdale Securities Co. v. M.N.R.*, [1975] C.T.C. 10, 74 D.T.C. 6674 (F.C.A.); *Richardson Terminals Ltd. v. M.N.R.*, [1971] C.T.C. 427, 71 D.T.C. 5028; affirmed [1972] C.T.C. 528, 72 D.T.C. 6431 (S.C.C.).

[32]*Atinco Paper Prod. v. The Queen*, [1978] C.T.C. 566 at 577-78, 78 D.T.C. 6387 (F.C.A.); leave to appeal to S.C.C. refused 25 N.R. 603 (ineffectual trust; only legal partners to the business were corporations; unsuccessful attempt to income split).

[33]*I.R.C. v. Wesleyan & Gen. Assur. Soc.* (1948), 30 Tax Cas. 11 at 25 (H.L.) (taxpayer not taxable on amount given to employee on account of a loan).

6. — Substance vs. Form

The substance versus form argument is the single most difficult and uncertain aspect of statutory interpretation. There is only one inviolate rule of tax planning: substance prevails over form except in those circumstances that form prevails over substance.

It is sometimes said that the substance of a transaction determines its legal and tax consequences. This doctrine has intuitive appeal and is easy to state. It is not, however, quite so easy to define. The difficulty with the doctrine is that, despite its intuitive appeal, it does not offer any objective criteria or parameters by which particular facts may be measured against. Hence, it is an unpredictable doctrine of varying scope. Lord Tomlin referred to it as the "so-called doctrine" in *I.R.C. v. Duke of Westminster*:[34]

> ... it is said that in revenue cases there is a doctrine that the Court may ignore the legal position and regard what is called "the substance of the matter". ... This supposed doctrine (upon which the Commissioners apparently acted) seems to rest for its support upon a misunderstanding of language used in some earlier cases. The sooner this misunderstanding is dispelled, and the supposed doctrine given its quietus, the better it will be for all concerned, for the doctrine seems to involve substituting "the uncertain and crooked cord of discretion" for "the golden and straight metwand of the law". ... Every man is entitled if he can to order his affairs so as that the tax attaching under the appropriate Acts is less than it otherwise would be. ... This so-called doctrine of "the substance" seems to me to be nothing more than an attempt to make a man pay and notwithstanding that he has so ordered his affairs that the amount of tax sought from him is not legally claimable.

The doctrine of substance over form is often used to attack tax plans that the Agency sees as "offensive" in some vague and unarticulated sense but that are otherwise in technical compliance with the Act. Used in this manner, the doctrine becomes a camouflage for applying a motive test to tax mitigation arrangements.

III. — The General Anti-Avoidance Rule

"Kings and government ought to shear, not skin their sheep." (Robert Herrick)

1. — Background

There are two broad categories of tax avoidance:

(1) Tax mitigation;[35] and

---

[34]*I.R.C. v. Duke of Westminster*, [1936] A.C. 1 at 19-20 (H.L.) (employer's annual payments, under covenant, to servants not payments of salary and wages; taxpayer may arrange his affairs so as to minimize taxes).

[35]See, *C.I.R. v. Challenge Corporation Ltd.*, [1986] N.Z.T.C. 5219 (P.C.).

(2) Abusive tax avoidance.

Tax minimization is legal and acceptable; abusive tax avoidance is not. Unfortunately, it is not always easy to draw the line between these two forms of tax avoidance. The distinction, however, is important for taxpayers and requires a careful evaluation of tax plans. Aggressive tax planning can have substantial downside costs if the CRA reassesses the taxpayer and adds interest and penalties to his or her tax.

The *Westminster* principle allows taxpayers to mitigate their taxes by arranging their affairs in any lawful manner. Under the principle, tax transactions and arrangements do not require a business or economic purpose. Tax saving is, in and of itself, sufficient justification to structure a transaction in a particular manner. The principle does not require that tax transactions and arrangements should have a business or economic purpose. As Mr. Justice Noel said:[36]

> There is indeed no provision in the *Income Tax Act* which provides that, where it appears that the main purpose, or one of the purposes for which any transaction or transactions was or were effected was the avoidance or reduction of liability to income tax, the court may, if it thinks fit, direct that such adjustments shall be made as respects liability to income tax, as it considers appropriate so as to counteract the avoidance or reduction of liability to income tax which would otherwise be effected by the transaction or transactions.

After some initial uncertainty, the Supreme Court of Canada finally struck down the business purpose doctrine in *Stubart*.[37] The taxpayer had transferred its profitable business to a sister corporation with accumulated tax losses. The *sole* objective of the arrangement was to marry the profits and the losses in the sister corporation. The taxpayer continued to operate the business, but now only as an agent of its sister corporation. Since an agent's profits belong to the principal, the arrangement allowed the taxpayer to use the accumulated losses to offset the profits. The transfer had no other business purpose. The sole purpose of the transaction was tax mitigation through the utilization of tax losses in the sister corporation.

The question before the Court was simple: Was the arrangement invalid because it lacked a business purpose? The Court rejected the necessity of a business purpose:[38]

> I would therefore reject the proposition that a transaction may be disregarded for tax purposes solely on the basis that it was entered into by a taxpayer without an independent or *bona fide* business purpose.

---

[36]*Foreign Power Securities Corp. Ltd. v. M.N.R.*, [1966] C.T.C. 23, 66 D.T.C. 5012 at 5027 (Ex. Ct.); affirmed [1967] S.C.R. 295, [1967] C.T.C. 116, 67 D.T.C. 5084 (S.C.C.) (profits from the sale of shares was capital gain rather then business income, despite parent company's involvement).

[37]*Stubart Investments Ltd. v. The Queen*, [1984] 1 S.C.R. 536, [1984] C.T.C. 294, 84 D.T.C. 6305 (S.C.C.).

[38]*Ibid., per* Estey J., at 575 [S.C.R.], 314 [C.T.C.].

Reading a business purpose test into Canadian tax law might deter taxpayers from participating in the very activities that the Act sought to promote:[39]

> Without the inducement offered by the statute, the activity may not be undertaken by the taxpayer for whom the induced action would otherwise have no *bona fide* business purpose. Thus, by imposing a positive requirement that there be such a *bona fide* business purpose, a taxpayer might be barred from undertaking the very activity Parliament wishes to encourage. At minimum, a business purpose requirement might inhibit the taxpayer from undertaking the specified activity which Parliament has invited in order to attain economic and perhaps social policy goals.

Thus, by 1984, the business purpose test ceased to exist as a separate judicial doctrine to control tax avoidance. However, within four years, Parliament introduced section 245 of the *Income Tax Act*, a general anti-avoidance rule ("GAAR"), to restrict tax planning and curtail the *Westminster* principle by requiring a business type of purpose in certain circumstances. Thus, the question is: To what extent does GAAR curtail the *Westminster* principle?

It is not clear whether Canada needed GAAR to counteract tax avoidance. The Supreme Court in *Stubart* outlined the "object and spirit" test for reading tax legislation. Does GAAR add any greater certainty?

Clearly, the specific statutory provisions in place prior to the introduction of GAAR were not sufficient to counter the proliferation of tax schemes that spawned each year. The frenzy of legislative activity between 1972 and 1987 was directed in substantial measure at the ever expanding inventory of tax planning schemes. As quickly as the Legislature blocked one avenue of fiscal escape, innovative tax planners burrowed another hole in the statutory patchwork. The Department was, and continues to be, a victim of its own verbosity. Particularization of the statute breeds more, not less, avoidance. The more words it used, the more loopholes it opened. But the Department cannot contain itself. Its frustration is reflected in its testimony before the House Committee on Finance and Economic Affairs: "... we no sooner get the stuff out and the ink gets dry than there is a new way to beat the rules."[40] Canadian legislators began to realize, as their American counterparts had done much earlier,[41] that when they closed the dike in one place, they often opened up a hole right next to it.

To be sure, the income tax system relies in varying degrees on specific statutory anti-avoidance provisions targeted at "offensive" tax activities or transactions. Some of these anti-avoidance rules are detailed and specific and apply only to a particular provision or type of transaction; others are of a more general nature and apply to a wider area, for example, the

---

[39]*Ibid., per* Estey J., at 576 [S.C.R.], 315 [C.T.C.].

[40]Minutes of the Commons Standing Committee on Finance and Economic Affairs, June 29, 1987, *per* Jim Wilson.

[41]*Gregory v. Helvering, C.I.R.* (1935), 293 U.S. 465, 69 F (2d) 809.

computation of capital gains.[42] The number of specific anti-avoidance provisions has increased in proportion to the size of the Act. Particularization of the statute, however, breeds loopholes; loopholes invite ever more detailed provisions to block avenues of escape; detail causes complexity, and complexity provides the tax planner with the opportunity to ferret out more loopholes and slip through gaps in the legislation.

The specific anti-avoidance rules do not always work well and are unpredictable. The General Counsel of the Department of Finance testified before the Commons Standing Committee on Finance and Economic Affairs:[43]

> It is apparent, from looking at the kind of activity that gave rise to very specific anti-avoidance rules over the last couple of years that taxpayers are becoming a bit more aggressive than they have been historically. And that is reflected, I think in a number of ways. Obviously the proliferation of fairly well publicized tax-avoidance schemes is evidence, I think, of the willingness of taxpayers and their advisers to undertake fairly aggressive tax planning. They do that because they examine, presumably, as advisers do, the limits that exist on tax avoidance, statutory or judicial, and they feel comfortable that within those limits they can still advise taxpayers to proceed. The result of that I think has been the proliferation of legislation, which we have seen over the last couple of years, to deal with it on a case-by-case or specific basis.

The Department of Finance saw three difficulties with the specific anti-avoidance rules. First, specific rules targeted at specific transactions close the barn door only after the horses have bolted. Moreover, in most cases, newly introduced specific rules that address a particular abuse usually exempt any completed or partially completed transactions. Thus, the most innovative and aggressive tax planners usually escape.

Second, specific provisions add tremendous complexity to the statute by attempting to anticipate every conceivable permutation and combination of potential tax abuse that might arise in commercial transactions.

Third, the tax avoidance industry is far more productive, both in terms of intellectual energy and efficiency, than tax collectors and policy advisors. Given the formidable intellectual talent engaged in the tax avoidance industry in Canada's legal and accounting firms, the Department of Finance wanted a more powerful weapon to equalize the battle against an increasingly aggressive group of tax lawyers and accountants.

The Department's testimony before the House Committee captured its frustration:[44]

> You could wait until [the] courts develop more sophisticated judicial limits along the lines of what the courts have done in the United States. The difficulty with that, though, is that the Supreme Court of Canada, in one case at least [the *Stubart* decision], looked at the existing

---

[42]See, e.g., subss. 110.6(6), (7) and (8) which govern the capital gains exemption.

[43]Minutes of the Commons Standing Committee on Finance and Economic Affairs, June 29, 1987, *per* Jim Wilson.

[44]*Ibid.*

Canadian Act, looked at the question of whether there should be a judicially introduced tax-avoidance test, and said no, there exists in the Canadian *Income Tax Act* already a general anti-avoidance rule and it is therefore inappropriate for the courts to develop such a rule.

In reviewing the existing provisions of the Act, particularly the one referred to by the Supreme Court, our view is that it is not of broad enough application, as I think has been amply demonstrated over the last couple of years. If taxpayers thought the rule was that effective, we would not have had nearly the need for the kind of legislation we have introduced over the last couple of years. Obviously taxpayers are not intimidated. ...

GAAR is an amalgam of the business-purpose test in the United States and the step transactions doctrine in the United Kingdom. In effect, GAAR is a statutory business type purpose test that looks through all of the steps of a transaction or series of transactions. The rule attempts to fill the vacuum that *Stubart* created.[45] Parliament wrote GAAR because it was dissatisfied with the Supreme Court's decision in *Stubart*, which rejected both the literal interpretation of the Act and the business purpose test. Unlike its American and British counterparts, however, the Minister's discretion in applying GAAR extends well beyond the constructs of traditional fiscal legislation.

2. — Purpose

If not the taxpaying public or the fisc, who ultimately benefits from this approach? The only unequivocal beneficiary is the tax bar. The heavier the layers of judicial divination superimposed on the Internal Revenue Code, the richer tax lawyers are apt to get. The development of an exquisite set of intuitions about what kinds of transactions the courts "like" and "don't like" has become a large part of what tax lawyers sell.

> (Joseph Isenbergh, "Musings on Form and Substance in Taxation" (1982), 49 Univ. of Chicago LR 859 at 883.)

GAAR draws a line between legitimate tax minimization and abusive tax avoidance. It is not, however, a bright line that one can easily identify and apply in a complex world with evolving business structures — both domestic and international. As the Supreme Court acknowledged in *Canada Trustco*: "But what precisely constitutes abusive tax avoidance remains the subject of debate."[46]

The Act defines abusive tax avoidance as *any* transaction, or series of transactions, that gives rise to a tax benefit.[47] A "tax benefit" is any reduction, avoidance or deferral of tax or other amount payable under the Act, regulations, ITARs and tax treaties or an increase in a

---

[45]*Stubart Investments Ltd. v. The Queen*, [1984] 1 S.C.R. 536, [1984] C.T.C. 294, 84 D.T.C. 6305 (S.C.C.).

[46]*Canada Trustco Mortgage Co. v. R.*, [2005] 5 C.T.C. 215 (S.C.C.) at 224.

[47]Subs. 245(3)

refund of tax or other amount under the Act.[48] Thus, without more, these rules would catch most commercial transactions and virtually negate all tax planning. Since the tax benefit does *not* have to be significant, *any* tax benefit is sufficient to trigger the rule. Thus, the CRA has virtually unlimited discretion to apply the rule. There are, however, two important limitations to GAAR that constrain the doctrine.[49]

The purpose of GAAR is to prevent "abusive" tax avoidance transactions or arrangements. The rule is extremely broad. The Technical Notes (June 30, 1988) explain the rationale of the rule as follows:

> ... [S]ection 245 of the Act is a general anti-avoidance rule which is intended to prevent abusive tax avoidance transactions or arrangements but at the same time is not intended to interfere with legitimate commercial and family transactions. Consequently, the new rule seeks to distinguish between legitimate tax planning and abusive tax avoidance and to establish a reasonable balance between the protection of the tax base and the need for certainty for taxpayers in planning their affairs.

Thus, GAAR is a supplementary rule to catch abusive tax avoidance where the other, more specific, anti-avoidance rules fail. As the Supreme Court said in *Canada Trustco*: "The GAAR was enacted as a provision of last resort in order to address abusive tax avoidance, it was not intended to introduce uncertainty in tax planning." To be sure, a noble sentiment, but we shall wait to see how the CRA applies the rule in practice.

The key question is: What is the distinction between lawful tax mitigation and "abusive" tax planning? GAAR does not catch transactions that comply with the policy of statutory provisions in the context of the Act read as a whole. The Technical Notes focus on the "object and spirit" of the Act:

> Transactions that comply with the object and spirit of other provisions of the Act read as a whole will not be affected by the application of this general anti-avoidance rule. For example, a transaction that qualifies for a tax-free rollover under an explicit provision of the Act, and that is carried out in accordance, not only with the letter of that provision but also with the spirit of the Act read as a whole, will not be subject to new section 245. However, where the transaction is part of a series of transactions designed to avoid tax and results in a misuse or abuse of the provision that allows a tax-free rollover, the rule may apply. If for example, a taxpayer, for the purpose of converting an income gain on a sale of property into a capital gain, transfers the property on a rollover basis to a shell corporation in exchange for shares in a situation where new section 54.2 of the Act does not apply and subsequently sells the shares, the new section could be expected to apply.

A transaction is not an avoidance transaction if the taxpayer undertakes it *primarily* for *bona fide* purposes *other than* obtaining the tax benefit. Thus, to avoid GAAR, a taxpayer should

---

[48]Subs. 245(1).

[49]See below at 6 — Immunity from GAAR.

have substantial commercial, family or philanthropic reasons to support the transaction and tax savings should be ancillary in the overall plan.[50]

One determines the "primary purpose" of tax arrangements or transactions in an objective manner.[51] This requires a careful examination of the evidence — financial evidence, estimated tax benefits, cost of implementation, risk of loss, and probability of success — when the taxpayer was arranging the transaction. This is essentially a facts and circumstances test. It is not permissible to introduce hindsight evidence of intention or purpose. The determination of primary purpose is a prospective analysis from the vantage point of the taxpayer at the time he, she, or it was arranging and negotiating the transaction.[52]

The CRA uses the Minister's Technical Notes and Parliamentary debates to determine the legislative intention underlying provisions of the Act.[53] Thus, the starting point in determining whether a transaction or arrangement constitutes lawful tax mitigation or tax avoidance is to ascertain the purpose of the statutory provisions used to implement the tax plan. The purpose of individual provisions must be read in the context of the Act read as a whole. In determining the context of the Act, however, one must also consider the specific provisions. GAAR cannot simply override specific provisions of the Act without reference to statutory context and legislative purpose.

GAAR does not apply to *any* transaction (whether an avoidance transaction or otherwise) that does not misuse the provisions of the Act or abuse the provisions of the Act, regulations, ITARs or treaties when read as a whole.[54] This limitation is a significant constraint on what would otherwise be a boundless rule.

GAAR analysis is a multi-step process:

1. A factual finding whether the taxpayer engaged in a transaction (usually obvious) or series of transactions (less obvious).

2. A factual finding that the taxpayer derived a "tax benefit" from the transaction or series of transactions through a reduction, avoidance, or deferral of tax.

---

[50]*Canadian Pacific Ltd. v. Canada* (2001), [2002] 2 C.T.C. 197, [2001] F.C.J. No. 1946, 2001 CarswellNat 2916 (F.C.A.); reconsideration refused 2002 CarswellNat 555, 2002 FCA 98, [2002] 2 C.T.C. 150, (sub nom. *Minister of National Revenue v. Canadian Pacific Ltd.*) 289 N.R. 159 (Fed. C.A.).

[51]*OSFC Holdings Ltd. v. Canada*, 2001 FCA 260, [2001] 4 C.T.C. 82, 2001 D.T.C. 5471 (F.C.A.), ¶46.

[52]*OSFC Holdings Ltd. v. Canada, ibid.*

[53]See, for example, Technical Interpretation (October 24, 1990).

[54]Subs. 245(4).

3. A factual finding whether the taxpayer arranged the transaction or series of transactions that gave rise to the benefit *primarily* for tax or non-tax purposes.

4. If the taxpayer derived a tax benefit from a transaction arranged primarily for tax purposes, an analysis whether the transaction (or series of transactions) misused any provisions of the Act.

5. GAAR applies if the transaction (or series of transactions) misuses a provision of the Act or abuses the provisions read as a whole.

6. The burden of establishing misuse or abuse of statutory transactions is on the Minister. The benefit of any doubt goes to the taxpayer.[55]

The first three steps — existence of a transaction or series of transactions, determination of tax benefit and the primary purpose of a transaction (or series of transactions) — are essentially questions of fact. Hence, the taxpayer carries the burden to refute the facts. The determination as to whether the transaction (or series of transactions) constitute a misuse of a specific provision or an abuse of the provisions of the Act read as a whole are questions of law and tax policy.

3. — The Charging Provision

Subsection 245(2) reads as follows:

> Where a transaction is an avoidance transaction, the tax consequences to a person shall be determined as is reasonable in the circumstances in order to deny a tax benefit that, but for this section, would result, directly or indirectly, from that transaction or from a series of transactions that includes that transaction.

The key terms in the charging provision are: "tax benefit," "tax consequences," and "transaction." The Act defines these terms in subsection 245(1):

- "Tax benefits" means a reduction, avoidance or deferral of tax or other amount payable or an increase in a refund of tax or other amount;

- "Tax consequences" to a person means the amount of income, taxable income, or taxable income earned in Canada, of tax or other amount payable by, or refundable to the person under this Act, or any other amount that is relevant for the purposes of computing that amount; and

- "Transaction" includes an arrangement or event.

The existence of a tax benefit is a question of fact for the Tax Court. The amount of the benefit is not relevant.

---

[55]See *Canada Trustco Mortgage Co. v. R.*, [2005] 5 C.T.C. 215 (S.C.C.) at 236 (The Minister is in a better position than the taxpayer to make submissions on legislative intent).

(a) — Legislative Intention

The Technical Notes explain the scope of GAAR as follows:

> Generally, for the purposes of section 245, a transaction, to be an avoidance transaction, must result in a "tax benefit". This expression is defined as a reduction, avoidance or deferral of tax or other amount payable under the Act or an increase in a refund of tax or other amount under the Act. The references in this definition to "other amount payable under this Act" and "other amount under this Act" are intended to cover interest, penalties, the remittance of source deductions, and other amounts that do not constitute tax.

> Where a transaction is an avoidance transaction, new subsection 245(2) provides that the tax consequences to any person shall be determined as is reasonable in the circumstances in order to deny the tax benefit that would otherwise result from that transaction. The expression "tax consequences" is defined in such a way as to permit an adjustment to the income, taxable income, or taxable income earned in Canada of, tax or other amount payable by, or amount refundable to, any person under the Act as well as any other amount, such as the adjusted cost base of a property or the paid-up capital of a share, that is relevant for the purposes of the computation of the income or other above-mentioned amount.

> The term "transaction" is defined to include an arrangement or event.

(b) — Recharacterization of Transactions

A taxpayer is entitled to mitigate his or her taxes provided that the mitigation does not result in abusive tax avoidance. The Agency can recharacterize the tax consequences of abusive "avoidance transactions" by ignoring any tax benefits derived from the particular transaction. In other words, the Agency can redetermine the tax consequences of an avoidance transaction "as is reasonable in the circumstances." According to the Minister's Technical Notes:

> Subsection 245(2) of the Act provides that where a transaction is an avoidance transaction, the tax consequences to a person ... are to be determined as is reasonable in the circumstances in order to deny the tax benefit of that transaction. ...

> Where subsection 245(2) applies, the tax consequences to a person are to be determined so as to deny the tax benefit on a basis that is reasonable in the circumstances. New subsection 245(5) provides a non-exhaustive list of what may be done to achieve that result. In many cases the manner in which this should be accomplished will be obvious or will be provided for in the Act. However, the "reasonable basis" approach adopted in subsection 245(2) recognizes that it is not possible to exhaustively prescribe the appropriate tax consequences for the range of avoidance transactions to which the rule might apply.

Therein lies the formidable power of GAAR: The rule empowers the Minister to ignore and set aside a taxpayer's arrangements and substitute an alternative tax cost in lieu thereof.

It is important to note, however, that the Minister does *not* have the power to recharacterize a transaction for the purpose of determining that it is an "avoidance transaction." The Minister can recharacterize the consequences of a transaction only *after* he determines that it constitutes an "avoidance transaction." Thus, within the parameters of the rule, a taxpayer may still arrange his or her affairs to mitigate tax. The Technical Notes explain as follows:

> Subsection 245(3) does not permit the "recharacterization" of a transaction for the purposes of determining whether or not it is an avoidance transaction. In other words, it does not permit a transaction to be considered to be an avoidance transaction because some alternative transaction that might have achieved an equivalent result would have resulted in higher taxes. It is recognized that tax planning — arranging one's affairs so as to attract the least amount of tax — is a legitimate and accepted part of Canadian tax law. If a taxpayer selects a transaction that minimizes his tax liability and this transaction is not carried out primarily to obtain a tax benefit, he should not be taxed as if he had engaged in other transactions that would have resulted in higher taxes.

Thus, in the face of a GAAR assessment, a taxpayer must demonstrate that his or her tax plan or arrangement is lawful tax mitigation in the sense that it constitutes avoidance, but avoidance that is not "abusive" of the Act read as a whole. The taxpayer carries the burden to show that his or her plan does not offend the underlying policy of the statute. An arrangement that complies with the express and specific language of the statute cannot be abusive of its underlying policy. For example, an individual who contributes to his RRSP solely to avoid current taxation does not violate GAAR because the Act specifically authorizes the deduction. Similarly, an individual who contributes to his or her spouse's RRSP for the sole purpose of income splitting and tax deferral is within the purpose of the statutory structure.

(c) — "Reasonable in the Circumstances"

What is "reasonable in the circumstances" is a question of fact. The language is broad enough to allow the Minister to keep open the list of transactions that he may consider abusive in the future, and allows the CRA considerable administrative flexibility in coping with new circumstances as they arise. The Agency can ignore the offensive component or steps of an avoidance transaction and determine its tax consequences as if that component or step had not occurred.

GAAR legislatively implements what the House of Lords did judicially in *Furniss v. Dawson:*[56]

> [T]he fiscal consequences of a preordained series of transactions, intended to operate as such, are generally to be ascertained by considering the result of the series as a whole, and not by dissecting the scheme and considering each individual transaction separately.

Thus, GAAR empowers the Minister to ignore certain steps in a series of commercial transactions and recalculate the resulting tax liability without regard to those steps.

---

[56] *Furniss (Inspector of Taxes) v. Dawson*, [1984] 1 All E.R. 530 (U.K. H.L.) at 532, *per* Lord Fraser of Tullybelton.

In a sense, however, GAAR goes further than the step transactions doctrine in *Furniss v. Dawson*. GAAR looks at the "object and spirit" of the Act read as a whole. This makes its potential reach longer than that of its English counterpart.

4. — *Avoidance Transactions*

An "avoidance transaction" is:[57]

> ... any transaction

>> (a) that ... would result, directly or indirectly, in a tax benefit, unless the transaction may reasonably be considered to have been undertaken or arranged primarily for bona fide purposes other than to obtain the tax benefit; or

>> (b) that is part of a series of transactions, which ... would result, directly or indirectly, in a tax benefit, unless the transaction may reasonably be considered to have been undertaken or arranged primarily for bona fide purposes other than to obtain the tax benefit.

Thus, an "avoidance transaction" is any transaction, or series of transactions, that gives rise to *any* tax benefit unless the transaction may reasonably be considered to have been undertaken *primarily* for *bona fide* purposes other than obtaining the tax benefit. In order for a transaction not to be considered an "avoidance transaction," it must be supported by substantial reasons other than the tax benefit or savings that result from the transaction. The non-tax purpose must be primary. This is a factual inquiry.

Given the broad definition of "tax benefit," however, it is difficult to characterize any financial transaction that one can implement through alternative strategies — and on which one takes professional advice — as other than tax driven. All exchanges of goods, services and intellectual property — domestic or international — involve tax consequences. Where there is a choice, an informed taxpayer will usually seek the least costly tax route that meshes with his overall business objectives. The tax benefit of the transaction does *not* have to be "significant." *Any* tax benefit is sufficient. This allows the CRA virtually unlimited discretionary latitude to apply the rule as it sees fit.

(a) — *Contextual Interpretation*

One must consider an arrangement in its entire context in order to determine whether it constitutes an avoidance transaction for tax purposes. Where an arrangement is implemented through a series of transactions or steps, one should look at the entire series to determine

---

[57]Subs. 245(3).

whether or not the resulting transactions constitute tax avoidance.[58] In *OSFC Holdings*, Rothstein J.A. held that:[59]

> Once it is determined that a series of transactions results in a tax benefit, any transaction that is part of the series may be found to be an avoidance transaction. The question is the primary purpose of each of the transactions in the series. If the primary purpose of any transaction is to obtain the tax benefit, it is an avoidance transaction.

(b) — Legislative Intention

The June 30, 1988 Technical Explanatory Notes explain the meaning of an "avoidance transaction" as follows:

> ... if a transaction is an avoidance transaction, the tax consequences to any person are determined as is reasonable in the circumstances in order to deny the tax benefit resulting from the circumstances.

> ... a transaction that, but for section 245, would result, directly or indirectly, in a tax benefit is considered to be an avoidance transaction unless the transaction may reasonably be considered to have been undertaken or arranged primarily for bona fide purposes other than for the purposes of obtaining the tax benefit.

> New paragraph 245(3)(a) refers to "bona fide purpose other than to obtain the tax benefit" rather than to "bona fide business purposes" as originally proposed, because the latter expression might be found not to apply to transactions which are not carried out in the context of a business, narrowly construed. The vast majority of business, family or investment transactions will not be affected by proposed section 245 since they will have bona fide non-tax purposes.

> Where a transaction is carried out for a combination of bona fide non-tax purposes and tax avoidance, the primary purposes of the transaction must be determined. This will likely involve weighing and balancing the tax and non-tax purposes of the transaction. If, having regard to the circumstances, a transaction is determined to meet this non-tax purposes test, it will not be considered to be an avoidance transaction. Thus a transaction will not be considered to be an avoidance transaction because, incidentally, it results in a tax benefit or because tax considerations were a significant, but not the primary, purpose for carrying out the transaction.

> Ordinarily, transitory arrangements would not be considered to have been carried out primarily for bona fide purposes other than the obtaining of a tax benefit. Such transitory arrangements might include an issue of shares that are immediately redeemed or the establishment of an entity, such as a corporation or a partnership, followed within a short period by its elimination.

---

[58] *OSFC Holdings Ltd. v. Canada*, 2001 FCA 260, [2001] 4 C.T.C. 82, 2001 D.T.C. 5471 (F.C.A.), at para. 46.

[59] *OSFC Holdings Ltd. v. Canada*, *ibid.*, at para. 45.

New paragraph 245(3)(b) recognizes that one step in a series of transactions may not by itself result in a tax benefit. Thus, where a taxpayer, in carrying out a series of transactions, inserts a transaction that is not carried out primarily for bona fide non-tax purposes and the series results in a tax benefit, that tax benefit may be denied under subsection 245(2). This is accomplished by expressly defining an avoidance transaction in paragraph 245(3)(b) as including a step transaction (a step transaction being one that is part of a series of transactions) in a series that, but for new section 245, would result directly or indirectly in a tax benefit, unless that transaction has primary non-tax purposes. For that purpose, reference may be made to existing subsection 248(10) of the Act which provides that a series of transactions includes any related transactions or events completed in contemplation of the series.

Thus, where a series of transactions would result in a tax benefit, that tax benefit will be denied unless the primary objective of each transaction in the series is to achieve some legitimate non-tax purposes. Therefore, in order not to fall within the definition of "avoidance transaction" in subsection 245(3), each step in such a series must be carried out primarily for bona fide non-tax purposes.

(c) — Business Purpose

A transaction need not satisfy a business purpose test. An arrangement without a business purpose is a valid transaction for tax purposes if it is undertaken *primarily* for *bona fide* purposes *other than* obtaining a tax benefit or saving. Thus, non-business reasons can support a commercial transaction. For example, family and financial security reasons can justify the structure of transactions. Thus, an offshore asset protection trust set up to protect one's assets is not *per se* an avoidance transaction even if it has incidental tax benefits.

It is for the trier of fact to weigh the evidence and objectively determine the taxpayer's primary purpose. The taxpayer carries the burden of showing his purpose.

(d) — Summary

We can summarize the scope of GAAR as follows:

- An avoidance transaction is a transaction that one enters into for the purposes of obtaining a tax benefit or advantage;

- An arrangement predicated primarily (though not exclusively) on *bona fide* non-tax purposes is not an avoidance transaction;

- GAAR applies only to "abusive" tax avoidance; it does *not* apply to lawful tax mitigation;

- Transactions that do not misuse specific provisions of the Act or the statute read as a whole are not abusive tax avoidance;

- The use of specific provisions of the Act is lawful tax mitigation;

- In determining whether an arrangement or event is an avoidance transaction or lawful tax mitigation, the Minister may take into account not only the transaction itself, but also all other transactions that are part of the same series of transactions or events;

- Once it is determined that a series of transactions results in a tax benefit, any transaction that is part of the series may be found to be an avoidance transaction.

- The Minister may recharacterize the tax consequences only of an "abusive" avoidance transaction;

- The Minister's recharacterization must be reasonable and he carries the burden to show that it is so.

5. — Purpose of Transaction

Subsection 245(3) exculpates a transaction (or series of transactions) if it may reasonably be considered to have been undertaken or arranged primarily for *bona fide* purposes other than to obtain a tax benefit.

To determine the taxpayer's "purpose" where there is more than one transaction, the entire series of related transactions must be considered and not just the one transaction that gave rise to the benefit.

The taxpayer's purpose in undertaking a transaction or series of transactions is to be determined *objectively*. Thus, the focus is on the relevant facts and circumstances and not on statements of intention. In addition, the purpose is to be determined at the time the transactions took place. The court will not attempt to make an assessment in hindsight.[60]

The words "reasonably be considered" simply mean that the determination of purpose is tested against the circumstances surrounding the transaction and the nature of the evidence. A taxpayer's "purpose" is her intention in, or reason for, engaging in a transaction or series of transactions. The law cannot enter into a taxpayer's mind to determine her purpose or intention. It can, however, evaluate assertions of intention and purpose in an objective manner to determine whether the asserted purpose is plausible in the circumstances.

In the absence of any other external evidence to support a transaction, the taxpayer's credibility may be the only basis for explanation of the transaction. Thus, uncorroborated but credible testimony can be sufficient proof of taxpayer intention.

---

[60] *OSFC Holdings Ltd. v. Canada*, 2001 FCA 260, [2001] 4 C.T.C. 82, 2001 D.T.C. 5471 (F.C.A.), at para. 46.

(a) — Primary Purpose

An "avoidance transaction" is a transaction that a person undertakes for tax purposes. A transaction or series of transactions undertaken *primarily* for non-tax purposes is not an avoidance transaction.

A transaction undertaken for both tax and non-tax reasons must be carefully scrutinized to determine its *primary* purpose. This is not an easy task and requires careful evaluation of both tax and non-tax considerations to determine which dominates the transaction. What if the tax and non-tax reasons are equal considerations?

6. — Immunity from GAAR

GAAR applies to all avoidance transactions except those that do not misuse or abuse the Act.

Thus, tax-driven transactions constitute lawful tax mitigation if they do not violate the underlying policy of the Act, Regulations, ITARs or tax treaties. This subsection is the single most significant limitation on the Rule.

(a) — Legislative Intention

The Technical Notes explain subsection 245(4) as follows:

> Even where a transaction results, directly or indirectly, in a tax benefit and has been carried out primarily for tax purposes, section 245 will not apply if it may reasonably be considered that the transaction would not result directly or indirectly in a misuse of the provisions of the Act or an abuse having regard to the provisions of the Act read as a whole. This measure is intended to apply where a taxpayer establishes that a transaction carried out primarily for tax purposes does not, nonetheless, constitute an abuse of the Act.

> Subsection 245(4) recognizes that the provisions of the Act are intended to apply to transactions with real economic substance, not to transactions intended to exploit, misuse or frustrate the Act to avoid tax. It also recognizes, however, that a number of provisions of the Act either contemplate or encourage transactions that may seem to be primarily tax-motivated. The so-called "butterfly" reorganization is a good example of such transactions. It is not intended that section 245 will apply to deny the tax benefits that results from these transactions as long as they are carried out within the object and spirit of the provisions of the Act read as a whole. Nor is it intended that tax incentives expressly provided for in the legislation would be neutralized by this section.

> Where a taxpayer carries out transactions primarily in order to obtain, through the application of specific provisions of the Act, a tax benefit that is not intended by such provisions and by the Act read as a whole, section 245 should apply. This would be the case even though the strict words of the relevant specific provisions may support the tax result sought by the tax-

payer. Thus, where applicable, section 245 will override other provisions of the Act since, otherwise, its object and purpose would be defeated.

Subsection 245(4) draws on the doctrine of "abuse of rights" which applies in some jurisdictions to defeat schemes intended to abuse the tax legislation. It refers to an abuse having regard to the provisions of the Act read as a whole as well as to a misuse of some specific provisions. For instance, a transaction structured to take advantage of technical provisions of the Act but which would be inconsistent with the overall purpose of these provisions would be seen as a misuse of these provisions. On the other hand, a transaction may be abusive having regard to the Act read as a whole even where it might be argued, on a narrow interpretation, that it does not constitute a misuse of a specific provision. Thus, in reading the Act as a whole, specific provisions will be read in the context of and in harmony with the other provisions of the Act in order to achieve a result which is consistent with the general scheme of the Act.

Therefore, the application of new subsection 245 must be determined by reference to the facts in a particular case in the context of the scheme of the Act. For example, the attribution provisions of the Act set out detailed rules that seek to prevent a taxpayer from transferring property by way of a gift and thereby transferring income to a spouse or minor children. A review of the scheme of these provisions indicates that income splitting is of concern in relation to gifts of property only where the transfer is to a spouse or child under 18 years of age. The attribution rules are not intended to apply to gifts to adult children. This can be discerned from a review of the scheme of the Act, its relevant provisions and permissible extrinsic aids. Thus a straightforward gift from a parent to his adult child will not be within the scope of section 245 either because it is made primarily for non-tax purposes or because it may reasonably be regarded as not being an abuse of the provisions of the Act. If however, the gift is made so that the adult child acquires an investment and, through a series of transactions, disposes of it and subsequently transfers the proceeds, including any income therefrom, to the parent, proposed section 245 should apply where the purpose of the transaction is the reduction, avoidance or deferral of tax. As another example, "estate freezing" transactions whereby a taxpayer transfers future growth in the value of assets to his children or grandchildren will not ordinarily be avoidance transactions to which the proposed rules would apply despite the fact that they may result in a deferral, avoidance or reduction of tax. Apart from the fact that many of these transactions may be considered to be primarily motivated by non-tax considerations, it would be reasonable to consider that such transactions do not ordinarily result in a misuse or abuse given the scheme of the Act and the recent enactment of subsection 74.4(4) of the Act to accommodate estate freezes.

Another example involves the transfer of income or deductions within a related group of corporations. There are a number of provisions in the Act that limit the claim by a taxpayer of losses, deductions and credits incurred or earned by unrelated taxpayers, particularly corporations.

The loss limitation rules contained in subsections 111(4) to (5.2) of the Act that apply on a change of control of a corporation represent an important example. These rules are generally restricted to the claiming of losses, deductions and other amounts by unrelated parties. There are explicit exceptions intended to apply with respect to transactions that would allow losses, deductions or credits earned by one corporation to be claimed by related Canadian corporations. In fact, the scheme of the Act as a whole, and the expressed object and spirit of the corporate loss limitation rules, clearly permit such transactions between related corporations where these transactions are otherwise legally effective and comply with the letter and spirit of these exceptions. Therefore, even if these transactions may appear to be primarily tax-motivated, they ordinarily do not fall within the scope of section 245 since they usually do not result in a misuse or abuse.

However, not all inter-company transactions within a related corporate group will necessarily be outside the scope of the anti-avoidance rule. There may be circumstances where new section 245 would apply, for example:

- where the transaction results in the deduction of the same amount twice,

- where the transactions are entered into to make two or more corporations related only for the purpose of avoiding a loss limitation, or

- where the transaction otherwise attempts to abuse the loss limitation rules.

(b) — Abusive Transactions

GAAR does not apply to any transaction that does not misuse or abuse the Act. A "misuse" of the Act depends upon the policy of the particular provision under scrutiny. What constitutes an "abuse" of the Act as a whole is a broader question that requires contextual examination of the inter-relationship of the relevant statutory provisions. It is clear that the Minister would prefer not to be constrained by the statutory language of specific provisions. This is quite clear in the Ministerial Technical Notes:

> Where a taxpayer carries out transactions primarily in order to obtain, through the application of specific provisions of the Act, a tax benefit that is not *intended* by such provisions and by the Act read as a whole, section 245 should apply. This would be the case even though the strict words of the relevant specific provisions may support the tax result sought by the taxpayer. Thus, where applicable, section 245 will override other provisions of the Act since, otherwise, its object and purpose would be defeated.

Fiscal legislation, however, must be interpreted according to the clear and unambiguous meaning of the language used.[61] Thus, clear language should have a clear effect. For example, paying bonuses to reduce a private corporation's active business income to its business limit is often purely tax driven. However, paying a bonus to reduce income is not abusive *per se* because it clearly complies with the statute. The transaction may be tax motivated, but it falls within the clear and unambiguous language of the statute that allows one to deduct reasonable salaries and bonuses.[62]

---

[61] *Jabs Construction Ltd. v. Canada*, [1999] 3 C.T.C. 2556, 99 D.T.C. 729 (T.C.C.).

[62] Ss. 9 and 67.

The terms "misuse" and "abuse" essentially refer to the legislative rationale that underlies specific or interrelated provisions of the Act. The Department of Finance explains these terms as follows:[63]

> ... the application of subsection 245(4) should involve an analysis of the object and spirit of the provisions of the Act read as a whole in the context of each particular case. An attempt to define the object and spirit of the provisions, far from being a 'meaningless platitude', as once suggested, will be the key to a coherent solution of those cases where it is uncertain whether the proposed rule will apply.

Determining whether there has been misuse or abuse involves two steps. First, one must identify the relevant policies of the particular provisions of the Act and of the Act read as a whole. The second step is to assess the facts to determine whether the avoidance transaction constituted a misuse or abuse having regard to the identified policies.[64]

The court will determine the relevant policies. However, given the complexity of the Act and the fact that the Minister is in the best position to determine its underlying policies, the Minister should assist the court by setting out the relevant policies. Where there is no evidence of a "clear and unambiguous" policy, the court cannot make a factual finding of misuse or abuse.[65]

(i) — Misuse of a Provision

An avoidance transaction that offends the underlying *purpose* of a *specific* rule is a misuse of the rule that attracts GAAR. An avoidance transaction that does not misuse a provision used to implement it may, nevertheless, be caught by GAAR if it is part of a transaction that abuses the Act as a whole.

It is important to distinguish between the *purpose* of a particular provision and its effect. A taxpayer can use a provision to mitigate taxes (the *Westminster* principle) if she does not offend *its purpose*. A transaction that is expressly permitted by the Act cannot, *in and of itself*, constitute misuse of the Act. For example, a transaction that takes advantage of a specific authorization to claim a deduction or offset a loss is not normally subject to GAAR.

The exclusionary rule requires an examination of the "object and spirit" of the provision under review to determine whether the taxpayer has misused its purpose in the particular

---

[63]David A. Dodge, "A New More Coherent Approach to Tax Avoidance" (1988), 36 Can. Tax J. 1–22 at 21; see also IC 88-2, "General Anti-Avoidance Rule — Section 245 of the *Income Tax Act*" (October 21, 1988), para. 5 and IC 88-2, "General Anti-Avoidance Rule: Supplement 1" (July 13, 1990).

[64]*OSFC Holdings Ltd. v. Canada*, 2001 FCA 260, [2001] 4 C.T.C. 82, 2001 D.T.C. 5471 (F.C.A.), at para. 67.

[65]*OSFC Holdings Ltd. v. Canada, ibid.*, at paras. 68-70.

circumstances. Thus, in a sense, the rule implicitly applies the *Stubart* guidelines to test the validity of tax-driven transactions.

Example
A corporation that holds publicly traded shares with unrealized gains rolls over the shares at cost (under section 85) to its wholly-owned subsidiary. The shares are then immediately repurchased by the corporation at their fair market value. The subsidiary has sufficient deductions available to offset the gain from the sale of the shares to its parent corporation.   The Agency says that it *will* not apply GAAR in these circumstances.* Section 85 specifically allows a taxpayer to rollover property at its cost amount and the cumulative effect of the series of transaction does not offend the underlying premise of the provision. Query: Is the effective result of the series of transactions to allow a consolidation of income and losses between related corporations? What if the subsidiary had losses, which were about to expire, that were used to offset the gain from the sale of the shares?

Notes:

*   Memorandum dated February 23, 1990, Financial Industries Division; see also IC 88-2, "General Anti-Avoidance Rule — Section 245 of the *Income Tax Act*" (October 21, 1988), examples 8 and 9; see also ATR-44, "Utilization of Deductions within a Related Corporate Group" (February 17, 1992) (archived).

The "misuse" test in subsection 245(4) is essentially a restatement of the "object and spirit" test prior to the introduction of GAAR. Hence, a transaction that was not offensive or abusive of the object and spirit of a particular provision before GAAR is not a misuse of the provision after the enactment of GAAR. The Agency has stated that:[66]

> Since the principles of statutory interpretation that Revenue Canada will follow will be similar to those followed to date, transactions that before the enactment of the general anti-avoidance rule were seen to comply with the Act in the sense mentioned will not now be seen to constitute a misuse of the provisions of the Act or an abuse of the Act read as a whole. Therefore the vast majority of transactions undertaken primarily to obtain a tax benefit that were seen to be consistent with the intention of Parliament before the amendment of section 245 will continue to be acceptable.

---

[66]Michael Hiltz, "Section 245 of the *Income Tax Act*", in *Proceedings of 40th Tax Conf.* 7:1, (Can. Tax Foundation, 1988), at 7:3.

But, as we see below, the misuse test is not as clear-cut as the Agency suggests. They also say that:[67]

> ... transactions that rely on specific provisions, whether incentive provisions or otherwise, for their tax consequences, or on general rules of the Act can be negated if these consequences are *so inconsistent* with the general scheme of the Act that they cannot have been within the contemplation of Parliament.

How do we determine the object and spirit of a provision? Through the use of extrinsic evidence, including legislative history and Ministerial technical notes:[68]

> In determining the intention of Parliament, Revenue Canada will take into account the words and context of any relevant provisions of the Act and the scheme of the Act read as a whole and any legislative history including the comments and examples contained in the Explanatory Notes to Legislation Relating to Income Tax issued by the Minister of Finance on June 30, 1988.

The Agency does not usually invoke GAAR where a transaction or series of transactions clearly comes within the technical ambit of clearly specific provisions.[69]

Example
A taxpayer disposes of a capital property to trigger a capital loss to offset realized capital gains. The taxpayer then reacquires an identical property 31 days after the disposition. The acquisition of the property on the 31st day after its disposition is intended to avoid the "superficial loss" rules in subparagraph 40(2)(g)(i) [acquisition prior to 31 days would deem the loss to be nil]. The sale and reacquisition of the property clearly constitute avoidance transactions. They are not caught by GAAR, however, because they clearly fall outside of a definite and stipulated time limit.* Thus, the transactions circumvent GAAR because they do not misuse subparagraph 40(2)(g)(i), even though they avoid the underlying policy of the superficial loss rules.

Notes:

*   Revenue Canada Round Table, in *Proceedings of 41st Tax Conf.* (Can. Tax Foundation, 1989), Question 41 45:24.

---

[67]IC 88-2, "General Anti-Avoidance Rule — Section 245 of the *Income Tax Act*" (October 21, 1988), para. 5.

[68]Michael Hiltz, "Section 245 of the *Income Tax Act*", in *Proceedings of 40th Tax Conf.* 7:1 (Can. Tax Foundation, 1988), at 7:3.

[69]See, e.g., ATR-57, "Transfer of Property for Estate Planning Purposes" (May 28, 1993).

Example

An individual (who has utilized her capital gains exemption) gives shares of a family farm corporation to her children. Subsection 73(4) allows the taxpayer to rollover the shares without triggering a capital gain. Immediately thereafter, the children sell the shares in an arm's length transaction and claim a capital gains exemption of $500,000. The purpose of the transactions is to multiply the capital gains exemption.

The CRA states that GAAR does not apply to the transaction because:

- Subsection 73(4) specifically provides for a rollover in the circumstances; and
- Subsection 110.6(2) allows for the capital gains exemption for shares of a family farm corporation without stipulating a minimum holding period for the shares.[*]

Since both provisions are permissive, the series of transactions does not misuse either. The Act allows each individual a capital gains exemption of $500,000 in respect of farm property. The transactions merely take advantage of specifically permitted deductions.

Notes:

[*]   Revenue Canada Round Table, in *Proceedings of 41st Tax Conf.* (Can. Tax Foundation, 1989), Question 44 at 45:26.

Example

An individual, concerned that the exemption of $500,000 in respect of capital gains on QSBC shares might be reduced or eliminated, transfers his shares in an operating company ("Opco") to his holding company ("Holdco") in exchange for new shares. The aggregate paid-up capital of the new shares is equal to the paid-up capital of his old shares in Opco. By electing an appropriate amount under subsection 85(1), the individual triggers a capital gain of $500,000 on the Opco shares. The gain is eligible for the exemption under subsection 110.6(2.1) and the adjusted cost base of the Opco shares is increased by the amount of the capital gain. Holdco acquires the Opco shares at a stepped-up cost base, which will, in effect, reduce the ultimate capital gain on a subsequent disposition of the shares. Thus, the individual has crystallized his accrued capital gain in the Opco shares and is protected from any subsequent elimination or reduction of the exemption. GAAR does not apply to the crystallization transaction even though it is clearly intended to avoid tax.[*] Section 85 specifically allows a taxpayer to elect an amount as proceeds of disposition and to trigger or defer a gain as appropriate in the circumstances. Subsection 110.6(2.1) specifically exempts from tax certain amounts of capital gains from the disposition of QSBC shares. The combined effect of the two transactions does not offend the object and spirit of either provision, individually or collectively. The transactions come within the *Westminster* principle of lawful tax mitigation.

Notes:

[*]   Revenue Canada Round Table, in *Proceedings of 41st Tax Conf.* (Can. Tax Foundation, 1989), at 53:9.

The above examples illustrate that the CRA interprets "misuse of the Act" in a fairly narrow and technical manner. The Agency does not, however, have any philosophical commitment to its interpretative techniques: Each case is decided on its own facts and is subject to the exercise of administrative discretion. Thus, the Agency's view can change without notice.

(ii) — Abuse of the Act

GAAR does not apply to avoidance transactions consummated primarily for tax purposes if the transaction does not constitute an abuse of the Act read as a whole. "Abuse of law," essentially a civil law concept incorporated into GAAR, can be used to defeat an otherwise lawful tax arrangement that is considered offensive in terms of policy.

Immunity from GAAR is only available if the avoidance transaction does not fall within *either* the "misuse" and "abuse" tests.[70] A transaction which misuses a particular provision but does not abuse the Act read as a whole is caught by GAAR. Conversely, a transaction which complies with the literal and technical words of particular statutory provisions may, nevertheless, be subject to GAAR if its composite effect abuses the Act as a whole.

The abuse test in subsection 245(4) is probably the most controversial aspect of GAAR. A taxpayer must evaluate the statutory purpose of several, sometimes conflicting, provisions with no clear-cut or articulated rationale. This aspect of the Rule also gives the Agency its broadest discretionary power, particularly in the context of its advance rulings procedures. Since the CRA does not rule on questions of fact, it can quash virtually any GAAR ruling request by simply refusing to rule. The only small comfort that one can derive is from the Agency's public pronouncement: "... Transactions that before the enactment of the general anti-avoidance rule were seen to comply with the Act ... will not now be seen to constitute a misuse of the provisions of the Act or an abuse of the Act read as a whole."[71] Apart from this statement, however, the Agency does not provide any interpretational guidance to tax-payers. Thus, one obtains guidance as to the scope of subsection 245(4) by deducing its meaning from *ad hoc* advance rulings.

(iii) — Burden of Proof

The burden of proof for establishing the application of GAAR depends upon whether one is interpreting a factual or legal issue. Determining whether a transaction involves a tax benefit or is an avoidance transaction is a question of fact in each case. Hence, the taxpayer carries the burden of proof to refute the Minister's factual assumptions. This accords with the gen-

---

[70]Subs. 245(4).

[71]Michael Hiltz, "Section 245 of the *Income Tax Act*", in *Proceedings of 40th Tax Conf.* 7:1 (Can. Tax Foundation, 1988), at 7:3.

eral rule in tax law regarding the burden of proof: see *Hickman Motors Ltd. v. R.* (1997), [1997] 2 S.C.R. 336, [1998] 1 C.T.C. 213 (S.C.C.).

Subsection 245(4) clearly excludes certain types of transactions from the category of "abusive" avoidance. Since the subsection derogates from the thrust of the charging provision, it is, in effect, a relieving provision. At least that was the intention of the Department of Finance that tabled the legislation. As David A. Dodge, Senior Assistant Deputy Minister, said:[72]

> Subsection 245(4) is intended to be a relieving provision. Where a transaction does not have primarily non-tax purposes, it nonetheless escapes the application of the proposed section 245 if, on a normal construction of the Act read as a whole, it may reasonably be concluded that the transaction does not represent a misuse of the provisions of the Act or an abuse of the Act read as a whole.

"Abuse" and "misuse" of the Act are questions of law and policy. Hence, the Minister carries the burden of proof on these issues. The Minister must identify the object, spirit or purposes of the underlying provisions in order to apply GAAR to avoidance transactions. The theory is that on questions of legislative intent the Minister is in a better position to make submissions on the statutory scheme underlying the provisions under review.[73] He must discharge the burden on a balance of probabilities.

7. — Determining the Policy of the Statute

The purpose of GAAR is to control only *abusive* tax avoidance. The Act defines tax avoidance as any transaction that results in a tax benefit, unless the taxpayer undertakes the transaction *primarily* for *bona fide* non-tax purposes. Using this test, GAAR would catch all commercial transactions with any significant element of tax planning. This would emasculate the right of a taxpayer to plan his or her affairs to minimize tax. To avoid this absurd state of affairs, the Act exempts from GAAR transactions that do not directly or indirectly misuse its provisions or abuse the provisions of the statute read as a whole. The difficulty with these exemptions is that the first is too broad and the second too obscure. Thus, GAAR can catch virtually everything or nothing.

It is trite law that a taxpayer can plan his or her business affairs to minimize taxes. As Judge Learned Hand said: "There is nothing sinister in arranging one's affairs to keep taxes as low as possible". The general anti-avoidance rule, however, states that the Minister can ignore a taxpayer's avoidance transactions if the taxpayer misuses the provisions of the *Income Tax Act* or abuses the provisions of the Act read as a whole. Thus, GAAR allows the Minister to recharacterize the taxpayer's tax minimization arrangements. Clearly, in the most egregious

---

[72]David A. Dodge, "A New and More Coherent Approach to Tax Avoidance" (1988), 36 Can. Tax J. 1.

[73]*Canada Trustco Mortgage Co. v. R.*, [2005] 5 C.T.C. 215 (S.C.C.) at 236.

cases, the statutory rule overrides the common law. But what is egregious? Does a taxpayer who implements a transaction to reduce his or her taxes in a manner that the Act *specifically* authorizes misuse the statute? For example, does a taxpayer who contributes to a spouse's RRSP solely to minimize taxes and income split, not to plan for retirement, misuse the provision specifically authorizing the deduction for contributions to spousal plans? Which of the two statutory provisions prevails: the specific authorization or the general anti-avoidance rule?

GAAR is an extreme sanction and taxpayers are entitled to a clear understanding of the scope of the rule. A taxpayer who uses the specific statutory language of the *Income Tax Act* to his or her advantage cannot violate GAAR merely because he or she minimizes taxes.

A taxpayer who relies on subsection 245(4) carries the burden of establishing that the transactions in question do not offend the underlying policy of a particular provision or involve an abuse of the Act read as a whole. This is not an easy task. In many, if not most, cases it is quite difficult to obtain an authoritative reading of the "object and spirit" of particular provisions. It is only since 1982 that Canada began tabling Technical Notes to explain amendments to the *Income Tax Act*. Until that time, the Department of Finance jealously guarded its legislative intentions from the public. Thus, it is not easy to determine what constitutes an abuse of the Act "read as a whole" for provisions enacted before 1982.

It is important to distinguish between the rule of statutory construction that requires an ambiguous provision to be interpreted according to its "object and spirit" (the purpose rule) and the application of subsection 245(4), which limits the scope of GAAR to avoidance transactions that do not offend the policy of the Act. The rule of statutory construction is that clear and unequivocal words are to be given their ordinary, grammatical meaning in the context in which they appear. Thus, it is not necessary to determine the object and spirit of a clear and unambiguous statutory provision. The statute is read as it is written.

Subsection 245(4), however, only exempts an "avoidance transaction" from GAAR if it does not misuse the particular provision or abuse the statute read as a whole. Thus, compliance with the literal language of the Act, even where that language is clear and unequivocal, is not by itself enough to immunize a transaction from GAAR. The Technical Notes (June 30, 1988) make this quite clear:

> ... a transaction structured to take advantage of technical provisions of the Act but which would be inconsistent with the overall purpose of these provisions would be seen as a misuse of these provisions. On the other hand, a transaction may be abusive having regard to the Act read as a whole even where it might be argued, on a narrow interpretation, that it does not constitute a misuse of a specific provision. Thus, in reading the Act as a whole, specific provisions will be read in the context of and in harmony with the other provisions of the Act in order to achieve a result which is consistent with the general scheme of the Act.

When is it appropriate to overlook clear and unambiguous statutory language and apply GAAR? The answer must surely be: Only when the overall purpose and policy of the particular provisions is equally clear and unequivocal.

To summarize: An avoidance transaction or arrangement is legally acceptable if it is:

1. Arranged primarily for *bona fide* non-tax purposes; or

2. Carried out primarily for tax purposes but does not misuse specific provisions of the Act or abuse the statute read as a whole.

Thus, GAAR applies only if the transaction or arrangement clearly offends the underlying policy or purpose of the statute. The analysis of subsection 245(4) is a mixed question of fact and law. Purposive analysis is a question of law; applying a provision to particular facts is a question of fact. Absent palpable and overriding error, an appeal court should not over-rule Tax Court findings.[74] In determining the policy of the statute, one must look at both the language of the provision and extrinsic evidence. Absent cogent evidence, in the face of clear and unambiguous statutory language, one must apply the statute as it is written by the legislature.[75]

---

[74]*Canada Trustco, ibid.*, at 231.

[75]The following are the results of some GAAR cases (GAAR was applied in the first two cases only):

OSFC Holdings Ltd. v. Canada, 2001 FCA 260, [2001] 4 C.T.C. 82, 2001 D.T.C. 5471 (F.C.A.); leave to appeal refused [2001] S.C.C.A. No. 522 (S.C.C.) (An insolvent corporation ("Standard Trust") entered into a series of transactions that resulted in the transfer of its non-capital losses to another arm's length corporation ("OSFC"). The Court held that these were avoidance transactions that, in light of the Act's general policy against the transfer of losses between corporations, resulted in an abuse of the Act as a whole and applied GAAR to deny OSFC's tax deductions.).

Water's Edge Village Estates (Phase II) Ltd. v. Canada, 2002 FCA 291, [2002] 4 C.T.C. 1, 2002 D.T.C. 7172 (F.C.A.); leave to appeal refused [2002] S.C.C.A. No. 386 (S.C.C.) (On December 20, 1991 several taxpayers bought into a partnership for $320,000 in order to gain access to an unrealized capital loss of $4,441,390, which was crystallized on December 31 in the form of a terminal loss. The Court held that these avoidance transactions resulted in a misuse of the relevant provisions. Moreover, since they were contrary to the scheme of the capital cost allowance system generally, they also resulted in an abuse of the Act as a whole. GAAR applied to deny the tax deductions.).

Donahue Forest Products Inc. v. Canada, 2002 FCA 422, [2003] 3 C.T.C. 160, 2003 D.T.C. 5471 (F.C.A.) (Donahue completed a series of transactions to transfer virtually all of the equity in its subsidiary ("DMI") to a new subsidiary, while maintaining the $62,210,000 adjusted cost base of its shares in DMI. Donahue then sold its DMI shares to an unrelated third party for $2 creating an ABIL of $46,675,499 (75 per cent of recorded loss). The Court held that these avoidance transactions did not misuse the provisions. Moreover, since there was no clear and unambiguous policy to which they were contrary, there was no abuse of the Act as a whole. Thus, GAAR not applicable.).

Loyens v. R., 2003 TCC 214, [2003] 3 C.T.C. 2381, 2003 D.T.C. 355 (T.C.C. [General Procedure]) Taxpayers (land developers) agreed to sell a piece of land they held as inventory. With the use of section 85 and 97 rollover provisions, the taxpayers transferred the land at cost to a part-

Michelin Tires[76] ("Michelin") is an example of clearly abusive tax planning. Michelin, a Canadian corporation was in the business of manufacturing and distributing motor vehicle tires. It sold its inventory of imported tires to Uniroyal Goodrich ("Goodrich"), an affiliated Canadian corporation in the same business.

Michelin imported tires and remitted federal sales tax (FST) at the then applicable rate of 13.5 per cent. As a result of the transition from the FST to the goods and services tax (GST), the federal government granted licensed manufacturers inventory rebates of only 8.1 per cent. This meant that Michelin would not obtain the full refund of FST that it paid on the purchase of its imported tires.

To obtain the higher rebate of 13.5 per cent, Michelin entered into an agreement to sell its entire inventory of imported tires to Uniroyal in the expectation that such a transaction would entitle it to the full refund rather than the 8.1 per cent inventory rebate. The tax differential was approximately $800,000.

To implement the scheme, Uniroyal expanded its manufacturer's license to be considered the manufacturer of tires marketed under Michelin's brand name and to be able to import or purchase these tires on an FST-exempt basis. The imported tires were held at Michelin's warehouses at a cost of $30,000 per week.

Uniroyal then entered into another agreement with Michelin and sold the imported tires back to Michelin as of the opening of business on January 2, 1991. Uniroyal and Michelin filed a joint election under subsection 156(2) of the *Excise Tax Act* and the taxable supply made between them was deemed to have been made for no consideration. Hence, the government did not collect any GST on the sale of the imported tires from Uniroyal to Michelin.

The sole purpose of the transactions was to allow Michelin to obtain a full refund of the FST paid on the imported tires. There was absolutely no *bona fide* business purpose to the transactions. The transactions lacked any economic substance other than the benefit from the refund.

---

nership, and then transferred their partnership interest to a related corporation which had unused losses. The corporation sold the land at market value and the resulting gain (income) was almost completely offset by the corporation's losses. The Court held that these were avoidance transactions, however since there was no misuse of the rollover provisions or abuse of the Act, GAAR was not applicable.).

Imperial Oil Ltd. v. R., 2004 FCA 36, [2004] 2 C.T.C. 190, 2004 D.T.C. 6044 (F.C.A.) (In order to reduce its capital for the purposes of the large corporations tax (LCT), just before Imperial Oil's fiscal year end it made three short term loans totalling $500 million. The company loaned the money to wholly-owned subsidiaries of chartered banks, which the banks guaranteed. This entitled *Imperial Oil* to an investment allowance deduction in determining its LCT. The Court held that these were avoidance transactions, but since there was no misuse of the provisions or abuse of the Act as a whole, GAAR was not applicable.).

[76]*Michelin v. Canada*, [1995] G.S.T.C. 17; affirmed [2000] G.S.T.C. 17 (F.C.T.D.).

Section 68.2 of the *Excise Tax Act* permitted refunds of the FST in order to avoid the duplication of taxes that would otherwise have transpired with the introduction of the GST. The section provided for refunds where a manufacturer, wholesaler or importer, who had paid the FST on the purchase of certain goods, subsequently sold those goods under tax-exempt circumstances. The transactions misused section 68.2 of the *Excise Tax Act*. The impugned transactions were clearly abusive of the underlying policy of the legislation, which was to prevent the duplication of the FST and the GST.

McNichol[77] is a more difficult case. Here, four taxpayers, partners in a law firm, owned equally shares of a company B Inc., which owned the office building in which they practised law. The partners had disagreements because some received rent indirectly and others did not. The taxpayers decided to sell the building in which they practiced. On March 29, 1989, the taxpayers entered into an agreement to sell their shares of B Inc. to H Ltd. for $300,000. At the time of the agreement, B Inc.'s assets comprised only cash and an RDTOH account. H Ltd. borrowed the $300,000 purchase price by way of a bank loan secured by B Inc.'s assets. On April 15, 1989, B Inc. amalgamated with H Ltd. In their 1989 tax returns, the taxpayers reported the proceeds of disposition from the sale of shares as a capital gain and claimed the capital gains exemption.[78] The Minister ignored the capital gains and reassessed the taxpayers *as if* they received taxable dividends of $75,000 each.

The taxpayers had two choices: They could have distributed B Inc.'s accumulated surplus as liquidating dividends, which would have been taxable or they could sell its shares. The taxpayers chose the latter option because it was cheaper in tax terms. They clearly benefited choosing the cheaper tax option. The Act specifically exempted capital gains. On the other hand, the Act treats corporate distributions to shareholders as income. The transaction was a classic example of surplus stripping by opting to liquidate an investment through capital gains. The Act invites surplus stripping by taxing dividends and exempting capital gains. The taxpayers responded to the differential tax costs by using B Inc.'s surplus to fund the purchase price of the shares. The Tax Court considered the transaction abusive even though the taxpayers were within the clear language of the capital gains exemption.[79]

In contrast, in *Jabs Construction*,[80] the Tax Court did not apply GAAR to a tax plan in which the taxpayer opted for the option with the lowest tax cost. Jabs, a successful businessman, was the shareholder of a corporation (Jabs Construction) that owned and operated commercial real estate. Following the settlement of complex litigation between Jabs Construction and a third party, Callahan.

---

[77]*McNichol v. Canada*, [1997] 2 C.T.C. 2088, 97 D.T.C. 111 (T.C.C.).

[78]See former subs. 110.6(3)

[79]See also *RMM Canadian Enterprises Inc. v. Canada* (1997), [1998] 1 C.T.C. 2300, 97 D.T.C. 302; additional reasons at 1997 CarswellNat 734, [1997] 3 C.T.C. 2103, 97 D.T.C. 420 (T.C.C.).

[80]*Jabs Construction Limited v. The Queen*, [1999] 3 C.T.C. 2556, 99 D.T.C. 729 (T.C.C.).

The taxpayer had two choices. It could simply transfer the properties directly to Callahan and recognize the accrued capital gain on the properties or arrange for a less expensive indirect transfer of the property. Not surprisingly, the taxpayer chose the less expensive tax option. Jabs and his wife registered a private charitable foundation (Felsen) and, together with their adult children, became its directors. The corporate taxpayer then donated its interest in the properties to Felsen at their cost base. The Act allows a corporation that donates capital property to a charity to elect as its proceeds of disposition any value between the adjusted cost base and the fair market value of the property.[81] The corporation uses the elected amount to calculate its capital gain and its deduction for charitable donations. This rule, which applies to both to arm's length and non-arm's length donations, specifically allows corporations to avoid capital gains by donating their properties at cost. Motive is not a part of the provision. When Felsen immediately sold the properties to Callahan at their fair market value, the resulting capital gain was not taxable because the Act specifically exempts charities from tax.

Taken individually, each of the transactions was genuine and proper. Nevertheless, as a composite, the transactions clearly lacked any business purpose. Their sole purpose was tax avoidance. The corporate taxpayer used a specific provision of the Act to avoid triggering capital gains on the initial transfer to the charity. It then used another specific provision to exempt the capital gain from tax. Thus, the taxpayer combined two separate provisions of the Act to minimize the tax that it would otherwise have had to pay by transferring the property directly to Callahan. It executed each step in the series of transactions under the authority of a specific provision of the Act.

To be sure, the transactions lacked economic substance. Did the taxpayer do wrong by choosing the lower cost alternative that reduced its taxes? Should the taxpayer have opted for the more expensive tax route and paid more in taxes than it was obliged to pay under the Act? The Minister thought so. The Minister characterized the transactions as an elaborate and sinister form of tax avoidance, applied GAAR, and recharacterized the charity's capital gain from the sale of the interests in the properties as Jab Construction's income. Thus, the Minister completely ignored the taxpayer's actual transactions and reconstructed them as if subsection 110.1(3) of the Act, which authorized the initial election to transfer at cost, did not exist. In effect, the Minister would have the taxpayer opt for the more expensive tax route and ignore the clear and unambiguous language of section 110.1(3).

Canadian tax law does not have a doctrine of economic substance. Instead, we control tax avoidance through specific statutory provisions. Parliament makes this choice in determining the structure of the Act. Where Parliament considers it appropriate, it includes purpose as part of the specific provisions.[82]

---

[81] Subs. 110.1(3)

[82] See, for example, subs. 256(2.1).

Section 245 is an extreme sanction that the Minister should use with reluctance in the face of clear and unambiguous statutory language. We should not penalize taxpayers for using the statute within its legislated ambit. Where Parliament legislates explicit language that permits a rollover of capital property at its cost base, a taxpayer is within its rights to utilize the provision to save taxes. Parliament has the power to legislate a clear doctrine of economic substance if that is in the best interests of the system. Until then, the courts should apply the clear and unambiguous language of the statute. Where there is a conflict between specifically legislated and general provisions, taxpayers are entitled to the benefit of specific provisions.

8. — Extrinsic Evidence

Extrinsic evidence is admissible to determine the "object and spirit" of specific tax provisions. Indeed, *Stubart* requires ambiguous provisions to be determined according to their "object and spirit" and this can only be done through the admission of extrinsic evidence to determine the purpose of tax provisions.

(a) — The Initial Proposal

The first version of GAAR (December 16, 1987) would have admitted, as evidence of the legislative intention underlying the rule, extrinsic evidence in the form of the Minister's technical notes. Subsection 245(10) (as originally proposed) lent support to the new judicial tendency to admit extrinsic evidence in tax cases. The proposed subsection specifically authorized the introduction of certain forms of extrinsic evidence in the interpretation of GAAR. For example, in applying the purpose, scope, and application of GAAR to a particular set of circumstances, a court would have been allowed to take into account the explanatory notes published in the *Canada Gazette*.

Subsection 245(10) (as proposed) would not, in effect, have substantially changed the rules of statutory interpretation. The specific authorization to admit a particular source of extrinsic evidence would not, *per se*, have precluded the admission of other sources of extrinsic evidence in the interpretation of GAAR. The subsection would merely have reinforced the evidentiary rule that all *relevant* extrinsic evidence is admissible in interpreting the Act.

The importance of the subsection lay not in what it would have admitted as evidence of abusive tax avoidance, but in what it would have precluded from the ambit of GAAR. For example, the Technical Notes say that the rule will not ordinarily apply to "estate freezing" transactions in which a taxpayer transfers future growth in the value of any assets to his children. This explanation permits a certain degree of certainty in arranging family transactions. Subsection 245(10) (as proposed) would have permitted the introduction of such statements to immunize certain routine tax driven transactions from attack by GAAR.

Subsection 245(10) was, however, vehemently opposed by the Joint Committee of the Canadian Bar Association and the Canadian Institute of Chartered Accountants (CBA/CICA). The Department of Finance retreated, as it is inclined to do in the face of opposition from the CBA/CICA, and dropped the subsection.

It is arguable that the withdrawal of subsection 245(10) as proposed reflected a legislative intention to preclude the admission of extrinsic evidence in the interpretation of GAAR. Any such argument should, however, be rejected. The intervention of the CBA/CICA Joint Committee was not intended to preclude extrinsic evidence or stem the new trend of legislative interpretation. It was merely a narrow and technical response driven more by a sense of panic than by analysis of the extrinsic evidence rule.

(b) — Documentation of Transactions

The importance of proper documentation in implementing business transactions cannot be overemphasized. A taxpayer should be prepared to carry the full burden of proving that the primary purpose of a transaction, or series of transactions, was *bona fide* and not primarily tax-driven.

In the event that a transaction is tax motivated, the taxpayer must establish that the transaction does not offend the object and spirit of the specific provisions used in its implementation *and* that it does not offend the object and spirit of the provisions of the Act read as a whole. Thus, tax plans must not only be technically sound, but must also comply with the purpose and philosophy of the provisions used and the general structure of the Act. According to the Technical Notes (June 30, 1988):

> Transactions that comply with the object and spirit of other provisions of the Act read as a whole will not be affected by the application of this general anti-avoidance rule. For example, a transaction that qualifies for a tax-free rollover under an explicit provision of the Act, and that is carried out in accordance not only with the letter of that provision but also with the spirit of the Act read as a whole, will not be subject to new section 245. However, where the transaction is part of a series of transactions designed to avoid tax and result in a misuse or abuse of the provision that allows a tax-free rollover, the rule may apply. If, for example, a taxpayer, for the purpose of converting an income gain on sale of property into a capital gain, transfers the property to a shell corporation in exchange for shares and subsequently sells the shares, the proposed section would ordinarily apply.

9. — Redetermination of Tax Liability

Subsection 245(5) allows the Minister to ignore the tax benefits of a transaction to which GAAR applies.

(a) — Legislative History

The Technical Notes explain subsection 245(5) as follows:

> Where new subsection 245(2) applies, the tax consequences to a person are to be determined so as to deny the tax benefit on a basis that is reasonable in the circumstances. For that purpose, by virtue of new subsection 245(5), among other things:
>
> - all or part of any deduction in computing income, taxable income, taxable income earned in Canada or tax payable may be disallowed,
>
> - all or part of any deduction, income, loss or other amount may be allocated to any person,
>
> - a payment or other amount may be recharacterized, or
>
> - the tax effects that would otherwise result from the application of other provisions of the Act may be ignored.

For example, payments under an agreement that are, in legal form, a lease, may be characterized as proceeds of disposition of property where, having regard to the agreement as a whole, it would be reasonable to establish the tax results of that transaction as if it were a sale.

As another example, assume that, in contemplation of an arm's length sale, a taxpayer transfers an asset on a tax-free basis, under a rollover provision of the Act, to a related corporation, which subsequently sells the shares. New subsection 245(2) could be applied if the sale to the related corporation is found to be an avoidance transaction. The appropriate tax treatment might be to treat the taxpayer as having sold the property *directly* to the ultimate purchaser. Further, it might be appropriate in this situation for the Minister to approve, through a determination under subsection 152(1.11), an increase in the cost base of the shares of the related corporation in order to prevent the double taxation of the sale proceeds, once when the property is sold and again when the taxpayer disposes of the shares. Thus, the effect of the rollover provision would be ignored in order to allow this increased cost base.

A taxpayer has the right to dispute, through the ordinary notice of objection and appeal procedures, not only a Ministerial determination that a transaction is an avoidance transaction, but also the reasonable determination of the appropriate tax consequences.

(b) — Reasonable Redetermination

The Minister can redetermine a taxpayer's liability under GAAR "as is reasonable in the circumstances" in order to deny him the tax benefits of the avoidance transaction. What is "reasonable in the circumstances" is a question of fact in each case. Among other things, the Minister may:

- Disallow all or part of any deduction, exemption or exclusion in computing income, taxable income, taxable income earned in Canada or tax payable; or

- Allocate all or part of any deduction, exemption or exclusion, income, loss or other amount to any person, recharacterize a payment or other amount, or ignore the tax effects that would otherwise result from the application of other provisions of the Act.

The taxpayer is then liable for the redetermined tax payable after the recharacterization of the offensive payments, deductions, etc. The taxpayer may dispute the reconstruction of her tax liability in accordance with the usual objection and appeal procedures.

10. — Third Parties

Where the reconstruction of a taxpayer's income tax liability affects a third party, the third party may request an adjustment to his tax liability, taking into account the amended and redetermined amounts. Subsection 245(6) reads as follows:

> Where with respect to a transaction
>
> > (a) a notice of assessment, reassessment or additional assessment involving the application of subsection (2) with respect to the transaction has been sent to a person, or
> >
> > (b) a notice of determination pursuant to subsection 152(1.11) has been sent to a person with respect to the transaction
>
> any person (other than a person referred to in paragraph (a) or (b)) shall be entitled, within 180 days after the day of mailing of the notice, to request in writing that the Minister make an assessment, reassessment or additional assessment applying subsection 245 (2) or make a determination applying subsection 152(1.11) with respect to that transaction.

(a) — Legislative History

The Technical Notes explain the structure of subsection 245(6):

> Under new subsection 245(6), where proposed subsection 245(2) applies with respect to a transaction and, consequently, a taxpayer has been assessed or reassessed or a determination has been made under proposed subsection 152(1.11) with respect to that person, another person is entitled to request that the Minister apply subsection 245(2) in his case in order to make adjustments of a relieving nature with respect to the same transaction.
>
> A request for adjustment may be made by that other person within 180 days after the day of mailing to the taxpayer of a notice of assessment, reassessment or determination, as the case may be.
>
> Amendments to section 245 of the Act allow that other person to make an application to the Tax Court of Canada for a time extension in the circumstances considered in existing subsection 167(5).
>
> Subsection 245(6) does not apply to a taxpayer who has already been assessed or in respect of whom a determination pursuant to subsection 152(1.11) has been made by the Minister of National Revenue under section 245, because this taxpayer is in a position to request the ap-

propriate adjustments through the objection and appeal mechanisms provided by other provisions of the Act.

The request for adjustments must be made within 180 days after the day of mailing to the taxpayer of the notice of assessment, reassessment or redetermination.

(b) — Redetermination vs. Recharacterization

It is important to distinguish between redetermination of the taxpayer's liability in the light of adjustments made because of an avoidance transaction and recharacterization of a transaction for the purposes of determining the tax consequences of an avoidance transaction. Subsection 245(3) does not permit the CRA to recharacterize a transaction to determine whether it is an avoidance transaction. Either the transaction is an avoidance transaction on its facts or it is not. Merely because the taxpayer could have rearranged his affairs to achieve an equivalent result at a higher tax cost does not mean that the transaction is *per se* an avoidance transaction. A taxpayer is entitled to mitigate his taxes if tax mitigation is not the primary motivation for the transaction or the Act is not misused or abused in the process of the taxpayer's planning. It is for the trier of fact to evaluate the evidence to determine whether the transaction was primarily tax or non-tax driven.

IV. — Series Of Transactions

"I am at one with those of your Lordships who find the complicated and stylised antics of the tax avoidance industry both unedifying and unattractive but I entirely dissent from the proposition that because there is present ... the element of a desire to mitigate or postpone the respondents' tax burdens, this fact alone demands from your Lordships a predisposition to expand the scope of the doctrine of Ramsey and of *Furniss v. Dawson* beyond its rational basis in order to strike down a transaction which would not otherwise realistically fall within it."(Lord Oliver)

(*Craven. v. White*, [1988] 3 WLR 423 at 463-64.)

1. — General Comment

GAAR applies to avoidance transactions, whether undertaken individually or as part of a series of transactions. Thus, in any fact situation involving more than a single transaction, one needs to determine whether the particular transactions constitutes a "series". Where a sequence of events is a series of transactions, one must then determine whether GAAR applies to the entire series as a composite.

The *Income Tax Act* does not define or illustrate the meaning of the expression "series of transactions". The expressin is unclear but essential to the doctrine controlling tax avoidance. The House of Lords developed the meaning of the expression in a number of cases —

most notably *Craven v. White* (1988), [1989] A.C. 398 (U.K. H.L.); *W.T. Ramsay Ltd. v. Inland Revenue Commissioners*, [1981] 1 All E.R. 865 (U.K. H.L.); and *Furniss v. Dawson*, [1984] 1 All E.R. 530 (U.K. H.L.). The *Canadian Act*, however, adds a further gloss to the expression.[83]

Whether a sequence of transactions constitutes a "series" or independent transactions requires an analysis of the taxpayer's intentions and conduct. The essential question is: Are the individual steps or transactions sufficiently tied or linked to constitute a series?

The *Shorter Oxford English Dictionary* defines series as "a number of things of one kind following one another in temporal succession...". In the context of GAAR, it is clear that the term "series" is not merely a sequence of events in a temporal sense. It is trite to observe that all events occur in a sequence. As Lord Oliver said in *Craven v. White*:[84]

> ... a series means no more than a succession of related matters — a description that applies to virtually every human activity embarked upon with a view to producing any rational result.

A series of transactions constitutes a composite when its individual components are linked or glued together through firm arrangements or understandings that each component will be completed. In other words, it is "well understood" by the parties that the entire sequence will be carried to completion.

"Series of transactions" refers to the integration of individual and separate steps into a composite transaction. The linkage of the separate steps into a "series" results from their interdependence and the manner in which the transactions are structured. Thus, we must determine: When is a sequence of events (e.g., A to B, then B to C) considered a single composite transaction, such as A to C?

2. — The Common Law

(a) — Floor v. Davis

We can trace the origins of the step transactions doctrine in the U.K. to the dissenting judgment of Eveleigh L.J., in *Floor v. Davis*.[85] The taxpayers, who were shareholders in a corporation (A), agreed in principle to sell their shares to another corporation (B). With a view to reducing or avoiding capital gains tax that would otherwise be payable on a direct sale of the shares, the taxpayers incorporated a new corporation, (C), with which they exchanged their shares in A. Corporation C, now the owner of the A shares, then sold the shares for cash to the ultimate purchaser, Corporation B. C, the new corporation, was then wound up.

---

[83]See subs. 248(10), discussed *infra*.

[84]*Craven v. White*, [1988] 3 W.L.R. 423 (H.L.) at 452.

[85]*Floor v. Davis*, [1980] A.C. 695; affirming [1978] 1 Ch 295.

As a result of the reorganization of its capital, C passed on the cash that it received from B to an offshore corporation. The taxpayers would not be liable for capital gains tax if it could be shown that they had not disposed of their shares directly for cash to the ultimate purchaser of the shares.

The majority of the Court of Appeal held that each step in the sequence of transactions was properly executed and represented a genuine transaction. Eveleigh L.J. dissented: The taxpayer had, in effect, disposed of his shares to the ultimate purchaser even though they were transmitted through the medium of an intermediary corporation. His Lordship considered the series of events as one composite transaction.

(b) — The Ramsey Principle

In *Ramsey*,[86] the taxpayer, a farming corporation, realized a substantial capital gain on the sale of farmland which would have been subject to capital gains tax. To avoid the tax that would otherwise have been payable, the taxpayer embarked upon a "scheme" to create a paper capital loss to offset the capital gain on the farmland. The essence of the capital loss scheme was as follows:

- The taxpayer purchased the shares of a company and loaned it two equal amounts at a rate of 11 per cent;

- The loans were made on the basis that the interest on one loan could be increased provided that there was a corresponding decrease in the interest rate charged on the other loan;

- The taxpayer reduced the interest rate on one loan to zero and increased the interest rate on the other loan to 22 per cent;

- The zero interest loan was then paid in full and, as a result, the taxpayer sustained a loss in the value of the shares of the corporation;

- The loss was equal to the gain realized on the other loan.

Thus, the decreasing asset was sold to create a loss; the increasing asset was sold to create a tax-exempt gain. The scheme had neither commercial justification nor business purpose. The sole purpose of the transactions was to produce a paper loss equal in amount to the capital gain that the taxpayer realized.

---

[86]*W.T. Ramsey v. I.R.C.*, [1981] W.L.R. 449 (H.L.).

(i) — Circular Transactions

Ramsey involved a circular transaction. The arrangements were, in Lord Oliver's words:[87]

> An artificially contrived concatenation of individual transactions linked together for the purpose of producing an end result entirely different from that which, on the face of it, would have been achieved by each successive link. ...

The entire arrangement constituted two transactions of a self-cancelling nature which returned the taxpayer to his starting position. In the process, however, the taxable capital gain was eliminated by offsetting it against a paper capital loss. Lord Wilberforce described the scheme as follows:[88]

> ... In each case two assets appear, like "particles" in a gas chamber with opposite charges, one of which is used to create the loss, the other of which gives rise to an equivalent gain which prevents the taxpayer from supporting any real loss, and which gain is intended not to be taxable. Like the particles, these assets have a very short life. Having served their purpose they cancel each other out and disappear. At the end of the series of operations, the taxpayer's financial position is precisely as it was at the beginning, except that he has paid a fee, and certain expenses, to the promoter of the scheme.

Every step of the transactions was genuinely carried through and every transaction was exactly what it purported to be: No part of the scheme was a sham. Although there was no binding arrangement that each step would be followed by the next planned step, it was *well understood* that the entire sequence of events would be carried through to completion. Otherwise the scheme had no value.

The composite effect of the two transactions was that the taxpayer made neither a gain nor a loss. The transactions *taken together* were nothing more than a scheme to avoid taxes and the House of Lords treated it as such. Lord Wilberforce said:[89]

> To force the courts to adopt, in relation to closely integrated situations, a step by step, dissecting, approach which the parties themselves may have negated, would be a denial rather than an affirmation of the true judicial process.

(ii) — Effect on Westminster Principle

Ramsey does not overrule the *Westminster* principle: It merely limits it to genuine cases of tax mitigation. The principle does not apply where it is plain that a particular transaction is

---

[87]*Craven v. White*, [1988] 3 W.L.R. 423 (H.L.) at 452.

[88]*W.T. Ramsey v. I.R.C.*, [1982] A.C. 300 (H.L.) at 322.

[89]*W.T. Ramsey Ltd. v. I.R.C.*, *ibid.*, at 326.

but one step in a connected series of interdependent steps designed to produce a *single* composite overall result. Lord Wilberforce said of the principle:[90]

> While obliging the court to accept documents or transactions, found to be genuine, as such, it does not compel the court to look at a document or a transaction in blinkers, isolated from any context to which it properly belongs. If it can be seen that a document or transaction was intended to have effect as part of a nexus or series of transactions, or as an ingredient of a wider transaction intended as a whole, there is nothing in the doctrine to prevent it being so regarded; to do so is not to prefer form to substance, or substance to form. It is the task of the court to ascertain the legal nature of any transaction to which it is sought to attach a tax or a tax consequence and if that emerges from a series or a combination of transactions, intended to operate as such, it is that series or combination which may be regarded.

(iii) — Integrated Transactions

In what circumstances can one aggregate separate transactions into a composite transaction? What, in effect, constitutes a "series of transactions"? The facts in *Ramsey* provide a clue to the answer: The transactions were circular, could not stand alone, were not intended to do so, and it was well understood that all of the steps had to be completed in order for the tax plan to work. In Lord Oliver's words:[91]

> But the fact was, as was plain to see, that those transactions not only were not intended to be interrupted or to stand in isolation but could not in fact have done so in the real world. They were totally dependent upon and integrated with other transactions whose purpose, and whose only purpose, was to nullify their effects and to leave the taxpayer in exactly the same position as they were before. In the one case there was actually a contractual obligation to carry the steps through to the end; in the other there was the confident expectation that they would be carried through to the end and no likelihood whatever that they would not.

But *Ramsey* did not imply that all sequential steps must necessarily be aggregated into a composite transaction. A sequence is only a "series" if the component transactions cannot have an independent existence and are not intended to do so. As Lord Oliver said:[92]

> What the case does demonstrate, as it seems to me, is that the underlying problem is simply one of the construction of the relevant statute and an analysis of the transaction or transactions which are claimed to give rise to the liability or the tax exemption. But it does not follow that because the court, when confronted with a number of factually separate but sequential steps, is not compelled, in the face of the facts, to treat them as if each of them had been effected in isolation, that all sequential steps must invariably be treated as integrated, interdependent and without individual legal effect.

---

[90]*W.T. Ramsey Ltd. v. I.R.C.*, *ibid.*, at 323.

[91]*Craven v. White*, [1988] 3 W.L.R. 423 (H.L.) at 454.

[92]*Ibid.*

(c) — Burmah Oil

The House of Lords reaffirmed the *Ramsey* principle in *Burmah Oil*,[93] and clarified the *Westminster* doctrine. Lord Diplock said:[94]

> It would be disingenuous to suggest, and dangerous on the part of those who advise on elaborate tax avoidance schemes to assume, that *Ramsey*'s case did not mark a significant change in the approach adopted by this House in its judicial role to a preordained series of transactions (whether or not they include the achievement of a legitimate commercial end) into which there are inserted steps that have no commercial purpose apart from the avoidance of a liability to tax which in the absence of those particular steps would have been payable. The difference is in approach. It does not necessitate the overruling of any earlier decisions of this House; but it does involve recognizing that Lord Tomlin's oft quoted dictum in *I.R.C. v. Duke of Westminster...*" Every man is entitled, if he can, to order his affairs so that the tax attaching under the appropriate Acts is less than it otherwise would be", tells us little or nothing as to what methods of ordering one's affairs will be recognized by the courts as effective to lessen the tax that would attach to them if business transactions were conducted in a straightforward way.

Lord Scarman went even further:[95]

> First, it is of the utmost importance that the business community (and others, including their advisers) should appreciate ... that *Ramsey*'s case marks "a significant change in the approach adopted by this House in its judicial role" towards tax avoidance schemes. Secondly, it is now crucial when considering any such scheme to take the analysis far enough to determine where the profit, gain or loss is really to be found.

Thus, "circular" tax planning schemes solely intended to produce self-cancelling consequences do not constitute legitimate tax mitigation. But what of schemes that are not self-cancelling but have enduring consequences?

(d) — Furniss v. Dawson

Furniss v. Dawson[96] involved a tax scheme intended to mitigate the capital gains tax that would have been payable by the taxpayer had he disposed of the shares of his corporation in an open-market transaction directly to the intended ultimate purchaser. To avoid the capital gains tax, the taxpayer exchanged his shares for shares of an offshore investment corporation that he owned. The offshore investment corporation then sold the shares to the ultimate purchaser, who was unconnected to the taxpayer. Under the U.K. *Finance Act, 1965*, the first disposition by way of share exchange to the offshore investment corporation was not a

---

[93]*I.R.C. v. Burmah Oil Co. Ltd.* (1981), 82 B.T.C. 56 (H.L.).

[94]*I.R.C. v. Burmah Oil Co. Ltd., ibid.*, at 58.

[95]*I.R.C. v. Burmah Oil Co. Ltd., ibid.*, at 64–65.

[96]*Furniss (Inspector of Taxes) v. Dawson*, [1984] 1 All E.R. 530 (U.K. H.L.).

disposition or acquisition for capital gains tax purposes. Further, there would be no capital gains tax liability on the sale of the shares by the offshore investment corporation until such time as the taxpayers disposed of their shares in the investment corporation. Thus, *Furniss* involved a "linear" as opposed to a "circular" transaction.

The House of Lords applied the *Ramsey* principle, not only to self-cancelling transactions, but also to those which have "enduring legal consequences." (The offshore investment corporation was not wound up after it had disposed of the corporation's shares to the ultimate purchaser, but continued in existence.) Lord Brightman's speech captures the essence of the decision:[97]

> My Lords, in my opinion the rationale of the new approach is this: in a pre-planned tax-saving scheme, no distinction is to be drawn for fiscal purposes, because none exists in reality, between (i) a series of steps which are followed through by virtue of an arrangement which falls short of a binding contract, and (ii) a like series of steps which are followed through because the participants are contractually bound to take each step *seriatim*. In a contractual case the fiscal consequences will naturally fall to be assessed in the light of the contractually agreed results. ... The day is not saved for the taxpayer because the arrangement is unsigned or contains the words 'this is not a binding contract'.

(e) — Summary of the Common Law

The English common law judicial doctrine determines the existence of a series by looking at two distinct aspects of transactions: preordination of the sequence of events and existence of a commercial or business purpose. First, there must be a preordained series of transactions that constitute a composite transaction. Second, there must be steps inserted in the sequence that have no commercial purpose other than to reduce tax payable.[98]

3. — Section 245

Under the Act, a series of transactions constitutes a composite whole when its individual components are linked or glued together through "firm" arrangements or understandings that each component will be completed. In other words, it is "well understood" that the entire sequence will be completed in a preordained sequence. This is the first leg of the two-pronged English test.

How "firm" must the understanding be in order to provide the linkage between individual transactions? Must the arrangements be "preordained" in a legal sense in order to constitute a series of transactions? The answer is clearly "No." There is no distinction between tax

---

[97]*Furniss (Inspector of Taxes) v. Dawson, ibid.,* at 542-43.

[98]See, for example, *Craven v. White*, [1988] 3 All E.R. 495, [1989] A.C. 398, 62 T.C. 151 (U.K. H.L.).

schemes comprised of a series of steps that are followed through by virtue of an arrangement that falls short of a binding contract and schemes that are followed through because the participants are contractually bound to take each step *seriatim*. Preordination does not depend upon strict contractual rights, but on a practical certainty that transactions will be completed as planned.

Under the statutory test a sequence of transactions is considered a "series" or composite if, at the time when the intermediate transaction is entered into:[99]

- The sequence is preordained to produce a given result;

- There is no practical likelihood that the planned events will not take place in the order ordained, so that the intermediate transaction is not even contemplated practically as having an independent life; and

- The preordained events do in fact take place.

In these circumstances, the first transaction can be linked to the last and the linked group is considered a single composite whole. Preordination of transactions implies, at the very least, an orchestrated sequence with a degree of certainty and control over the end result at the time that the intermediate steps are taken. It does not require absolute certainty as to every detail, but there should be no practical or substantial likelihood or risk that the transaction will not take place. Thus, a series of transactions is preordained, so as to constitute a single composite transaction, if there is a practical certainty when the first transaction takes place that the subsequent transactions will also take place.[100]

A composite transaction is one in which, when the first transaction is implemented, all of the *essential features* (not just the general nature) of the second transaction are determined by persons who have the firm *intention and ability* to implement the second transaction. For example, in a sale from A to B and from B to C, at the time that A sells to B, C is identified as prospective purchaser and *all the main terms* of the sale are agreed to in principle. There does not have to be a pre-existing contract when the scheme begins; it is sufficient that there is a practical certainty that all the steps of the various transactions will be carried through to completion.

Thus, for the purpose of determining whether a particular sequence of transactions is a series or composite under section 245, it is not necessary to satisfy the second prong of the English common law test, namely, the existence of a commercial purpose for the transactions.[101] For Canadian tax purposes, the commercial purpose test is a separate and distinct test.

---

[99]*Craven v. White*, [1988] 3 W.L.R. 423 (U.K. H.L.) at 462-63.

[100]*Hatton v. I.R.C.*, [1992] B.T.C. 8024 (Ch. Div.).

[101]See *Canutilities Holdings Ltd. v. R.*, [2004] F.C.J. No. 1070, 2004 FCA 234, 2004 CarswellNat 3336, 2004 CarswellNat 1882, [2004] 4 C.T.C. 210, 2004 D.T.C. 6475 (F.C.A.); leave to appeal refused (2005), 2005 CarswellNat 554, 2005 CarswellNat 555 (S.C.C.) (June 18, 2004).

(a) — Subsection 248(10)

The expression "series of transactions" generally refers to a number of transactions that are pre-ordained to produce a given result. The Act then expands the common law concept of "series of transactions" to also include any *related* transactions or events completed in *contemplation* of the series.[102] In *OSFC*,[103] for example, the court included within a series subsequent related events by a third party that occurred two years later in an arm's length transaction.

The facts in OSFC are complex:

1. Standard Trust Company (Standard) was a company in the business of lending money on the security of mortgages of real property. Because of the downturn in the real estate market in the late 1980's and early 1990's, Standard became insolvent.

2. On May 2, 1991, the Ontario Court of Justice ordered Standard wound-up and appointed Ernst & Young (E&Y) as liquidator of the company.

3. As liquidator, E&Y sought to maximize the recovery from disposing of Standard's assets.

4. To do so, E&Y devised a plan designed to sell Standard's non-performing mortgage portfolio to investors in a way that would make maximize recovery in a tax efficient manner — that is, through a loss trading arrangement.

5. Standard did not want to sell its portfolio of mortgages directly to an arm's length purchaser because that would trigger a loss.

6. Since Standard was not profitable and, therefore, not taxable, it could not utilize the loss to reduce its taxes.

7. E&Y could better accomplish its objectives if it could preserve Standard's loss and then structure the plan so that a third party could utilize the loss to reduce its income tax.

8. The plan was that:

   • Standard would incorporate a wholly-owned subsidiary;

   • Standard and the subsidiary would form a partnership with Standard having a 99 per cent interest and the subsidiary a 1 per cent interest;

---

[102]Subs. 248(10): "For the purposes of this Act, where there is a reference to a series of transactions or events, the series shall be deemed to include any *related* transactions or events completed in *contemplation* of the series."

[103]*OSFC Holdings Ltd. v. Canada*, 2001 FCA 260, [2001] 4 C.T.C. 82, 2001 D.T.C. 5471 (F.C.A.); leave to appeal refused [2001] S.C.C.A. No. 522 (S.C.C.).

- Standard would transfer the portfolio to the partnership as its contribution to the capital of the partnership and would lend the subsidiary sufficient cash to make its share of capital contribution;

- For tax purposes, the partnership would acquire the portfolio at Standard's cost ($85,368,872) notwithstanding the then current market value (approximately $33,262,000) was much less;[104]

- At the end of its first fiscal year, the partnership would incur a net loss for income tax purposes of some $52 million, because of the sale of properties for proceeds much less than Standard's original investment and the write-down of the remaining properties from Standard's original investment to their fair market value.

- Prior to the end of the partnership's first fiscal year, Standard would sell its interest in the partnership to an arm's length purchaser who could claim 99 per cent of the tax loss.

9. On May 31, 1993, two years after the initial planning for the sale of Standard's assets, the taxpayer, OSFC, purchased Standard's 99 per cent interest in the partnership.

10. The taxpayer did not intend to retain its 99 per cent interest in the partnership. In transactions pre-arranged before the closing of its purchase of the partnership interest, the taxpayer disposed of 76 per cent of its interest for a loss of $12,572,274.

11. The taxpayer sought to deduct the loss against its other income in 1993, 1994 and future years.

12. The Minister disallowed the taxpayer's deduction for the non-capital loss.

The taxpayer knew of the prior series of transactions to which it was not a party. Because the taxpayer knew of the series, it took them into account in arranging their own transaction. Thus, the taxpayer's knowledge of the history of the prior series was sufficient, to contaminate its own transaction even though they were not a part of the original series.

A literal reading of subsection 248(10) extends the meaning of the expression "series of transactions" beyond *Furniss v. Dawson*. It is not entirely clear, however, how far the subsection goes in expanding the expression. Certainly, the Department of Finance was not entirely candid about its legislative intention when it enacted the subsection. The Technical Notes to the amending bill state that the legislative intention underlying the subsection — introduced in 1986, two years before the enactment of GAAR — was to "clarify" the meaning of "series of transactions".[105] In speeches by senior departmental officials, the government confirmed that it fully accepted the concept of series as developed in *Furniss v. Daw-*

---

[104]Subs. 18(13).

[105]See Bill C-84; S.C. 1986, c. 6, s. 126(6):

son. For example, Michael Hiltz, Director, Reorganizations and Non-Residents Division, Specialty Rulings Directorate, CRA, stated:[106]

> The series itself would include a preliminary and a subsequent transaction only if, at the time the preliminary transaction is carried out, all important elements of the subsequent transaction are settled, and the subsequent transaction is eventually carried out.

Similarly, David A. Dodge, then Senior Assistant Deputy Minister of the Department of Finance, in an article entitled "A New and More Coherent Approach to Tax Avoidance" ((1988) 36 Can. Tax J. 1), stated at page 15:

> The step transaction doctrine, however, when completed by the business purpose test as suggested in *Burmah* and *Furniss v. Dawson*, represents a coherent and orthodox approach. For that reason, this doctrine has been included in proposed section 245 in the form suggested by these cases.

Under this approach, a sequence would be a "series" only if at the time of the preliminary transaction, all the important elements of subsequent transactions were settled and eventually carried out. The language of subsection 248(10), however goes beyond the *Furniss v. Dawson* interpretation of the expression "series of transactions". In *OSFC*, for example, the taxpayer was not even on the horizon when E&Y hatched its plan to maximize the recovery from disposing of the assets of the Standard Trust Company. Thus, as the Federal Court of Appeal found, the taxpayer was not a part of the original series under the judicial doctrine of *Furniss v. Dawson*. However, the court clearly went further in holding that subsection 248(10) more than clarifies the meaning of "series of transactions"; it extends the concept to include all related transactions that the taxpayer contemplates in structuring its own arrangements.

The fatal flaw for the taxpayer in *OSFC* was that it disclosed its knowledge of the prior series of transactions in the "whereas" clauses of its subsequent agreement. It was the unnecessary "whereas" components of the agreement, which add little, if anything, to an agreement, that pulled the rug from under the taxpayer's feet. Thus, lawyers drafting agreements should curtail their proclivity to include unnecessarily long preamble clauses as a part of their agreements.

In *Canada Trustco*, however, the Supreme Court appears to amend the broad reading of subsection 248(10) that Justice Rothstein gave the provision in *OSFC*. In its *per curiam* decision the Supreme Court says that "in contemplation" should not be read in the sense of actual knowledge but in the broader sense of "because of " or "in relation to" the series.

> New subsection 248(10) of the Act clarifies that a reference in the Act to a series of transactions or events includes any related transaction or event completed in contemplation of the series.

[106] At page 7:7 of "Section 245 of the *Income Tax Act*" in *1988 Conference Report: Proceedings of the Fortieth Tax Conference* (Toronto: Canadian Tax Foundation, 1988).

Thus, the phrase can be applied to events either before or after the basic avoidance transaction.

(4) — The Westminster Principle

Where does the series of transactions doctrine leave the dictum in the *Duke of Westminster*? The dictum is accurate so far as tax mitigation is concerned. It does not apply to abusive tax avoidance, whether implemented through a single transaction or a series of transactions.[107] As Lord Diplock candidly declared in *Burmah Oil Co.*, the principle that every taxpayer is entitled to order her affairs to minimize tax "... tells us little or nothing as to what methods of ordering one's affairs will be recognized by the courts. ..."[108]

Tax arrangements that are not shams or artificial and that are effectively implemented can be structured to mitigate tax. Tax mitigation, in and of itself, is neither abusive nor offensive. The manner in which it is executed, however, determines whether it is effective. As Lord Oliver put it:[109]

> I am at one with those of your Lordships who find the complicated and stylized antics of the tax avoidance industry both unedifying and unattractive but I entirely dissent from the proposition that because there is present ... the element of a desire to mitigate or postpone the respondents' tax burden, this fact alone demands from your Lordships a predisposition to expand the scope of the doctrine of *Ramsey* and of *Furniss v. Dawson* beyond its rational basis in order to strike down a transaction which would not otherwise realistically fall within it.

His Lordship distanced himself, however, from Lord Scarman's suggestion that abusive tax avoidance schemes constitute "tax evasion":[110]

> [T]here appears to be introduced in the speech of Lord Scarman at least, a moral dimension by which the court is to identify what he described as "unacceptable tax evasion". On the face of it this might be taken to suggest that the long accepted distinction between tax avoidance and tax evasion is to be elided and that the fiscal effect of a transaction is no longer to be judged, as *Ramsay* and *Burmah*, by the criterion of what the taxpayer has actually done, but by whether what he has done is "acceptable". It may be doubted whether this was indeed what Lord Scarman intended to suggest, but if it was, he was, I think, alone in expressing this view.

Subsection 245(3) states that transactions that are primarily non-tax driven are not subject to GAAR. The expression "non-tax purpose" refers to business, family, investment or security arrangements. If, however, even one transaction that is part of a series of transactions is

---

[107]*Ensign Tankers (Leasing) Ltd. v. Stokes (Inspector of Taxes)*, [1992] S.T.C. 226 (H.L.).

[108]*I.R.C. v. Burmah Oil Co. Ltd.* (1981), 82 B.T.C. (H.L.), at 64-65.

[109]*Craven v. White*, [1988] 3 W.L.R. 423 (H.L.) at 463-64.

[110]*Craven v. White, ibid.*, at 467–68.

primarily tax driven, the entire series becomes an avoidance transaction. The inquiry then proceeds to the next step — does the avoidance transaction misuse or abuse the Act?

V. — Administration

The administrative responsibility for GAAR lies with the CRA. Unlike other income tax matters, however, where tax returns and assessments are administered by the tax services offices of the CRA through normal audit procedures, the administration of GAAR is centred in Ottawa. The GAAR Committee in Ottawa clears tax assessments that might invoke the Rule so as to provide a more consistent basis of application.

1. — Assessments

The assessment and appeal procedure in respect of GAAR is, with one exception, essentially the same as that which applies to other income tax assessments under section 152 of the Act. Subsection 245(7) provides as follows:

> Notwithstanding any other provision of this Act, the tax consequences to any person, following the application of this section, shall only be determined through a Notice of Assessment, reassessment, additional assessment or determination pursuant to subsection 152(1.11) involving the application of this section.

Thus, notwithstanding the application of GAAR to a taxpayer's income tax return, the usual assessment procedures of section 152 apply.[111]

The purpose of subsection 245(7) is explained in the Technical Notes as follows:

> New subsection 245(7) of the Act provides that a person may not rely on subsection 245(2) in order to determine his income, taxable income, or taxable income earned in Canada of, tax or other amount payable by, or amount refundable to, any person under the Act as well as any other amount under the Act which is relevant for the purposes of the computation of the foregoing, except through a request for adjustment under subsection 245(6). This prevents a person from using the provisions of subsection 245(2) in order to adjust his income, or any of the above-mentioned amounts, without requesting that adjustment following the procedure set out in subsection 245(6).

2. — Request for Adjustment

Where the rule is used to assess a taxpayer and that assessment has consequential effects on another taxpayer, the second taxpayer may request an adjustment to her return. The request

---

[111]*Michelin Tire v. Canada*, [1995] G.S.T.C. 17; affd. [2000] G.S.T.C. 17 (F.C.T.D.).

for the adjustment must be made within a period of 180 days after the Notice of Assessment or Reassessment has been mailed.

Where a taxpayer asks the Minister to adjust his or her income tax liability because of another taxpayer's assessment under GAAR, the Minister must make the necessary adjustments. Subsection 245(8) provides as follows:

> Upon receipt of a request by a person under subsection (6), the Minister shall, with all due dispatch, consider the request *and notwithstanding subsection 152(4)* assess, reassess or make an additional assessment or determination pursuant to subsection 152(1.11) with respect to that person, except that an assessment, additional assessment or determination may be made under this subsection only to the extent that it may reasonably be regarded as relating to the transaction referred to in subsection (6). [Emphasis added.]

The Minister's obligation to reassess or make the necessary adjustments only extends to matters that may reasonably be regarded as relating to transactions affected by subsection 245(6).

Where a taxpayer makes a request in respect of a matter raised pursuant to a third-party assessment, the Minister must consider the request and is obliged to assess the taxpayer even though the relevant statutory limitation period may have expired. Note, however, that the Minister's obligation to make an adjustment or issue a reassessment only extends to matters that may reasonably be regarded as relating to a transaction under subsection 245(6). In the event that the Minister rejects the request, the Minister must notify the taxpayer in writing.

Subsection 152(1.11) allows the Minister to readjust or reassess amounts affected because of the application of GAAR. For example, the application of GAAR to one taxpayer may well affect the adjusted cost base of property or the paid-up capital of shares of another taxpayer. The Minister's authority to make a determination under subsection 152(1.11) is restricted to those cases where there has been a request for an adjustment of amounts under subsection 245(6). In the absence of such a request, the Minister is entitled to wait until he can assess a person to determine that individual's tax circumstances under subsection 245(2). For example, an avoidance transaction can result in an inappropriate increase in the capital cost of a depreciable property. In these circumstances, the Minister has two options:

> 1. If a request for an adjustment has been made, the Minister can rely on subsection 152(1.11) to make a determination of the undepreciated capital cost of the class of property to which that property belongs; or

> 2. If no request for a determination has been made, the Minister can wait until the taxpayer claims capital cost allowance in respect of the class and issue an assessment either denying all or a part of that claim.

3. — Administrative Structure

The head office of the CRA in Ottawa reviews assessments involving GAAR. The office has an informal committee (the "GAAR Committee"), which is made up of officials from the Rulings and Audit Divisions of the CRA and representatives from the Departments of Justice and Finance. The Committee reviews files that are referred to it from the Audit and Rulings divisions. It also handles any relevant GAAR matters that are referred to it from the various tax services offices.

The GAAR Committee has enormous administrative power, both in respect of its power to issue GAAR related assessments and its power to issue or deny requests for advance rulings. The administrative perception of what is "abusive" or "offensive" determines the disposition of most proposed transactions. Although, in theory, the power of the Committee is neither greater nor less than the power of the Rulings Division to "bless or kill" proposed transactions, it actually has a far greater influence in respect of GAAR. A Committee decision to turn down a request for a GAAR ruling has a chilling effect on the proposed transaction. As IC 88-2 states:[112]

> Transactions that rely on specific provisions, whether incentive provisions or otherwise, for their tax consequences, or on general rules of the Act can be negated if these consequences are so inconsistent with the general scheme of the Act that they cannot have been within the contemplation of Parliament. On the other hand, a transaction that is consistent with the object and spirit of provisions of the Act is not to be affected. Revenue Canada will follow this principle in interpreting section 245 of the Act.

The "object and spirit" of a provision or of a series of provisions can result in the application of GAAR and places the burden of proof on the taxpayer to establish that the transaction is not "offensive."

VI. — Administrative Interpretation

We have seen that a taxpayer's right to arrange his affairs to mitigate taxes is not an unfettered right. Section 245 of the Act curtails the *Westminster* principle in that a taxpayer is only entitled to arrange affairs in a tax efficient manner if his arrangements are not "abusive" or "offensive" to the underlying purpose of the Act.

---

[112]IC 88-2, "General Anti-Avoidance Rule — Section 245 of the *Income Tax Act*" (October 21, 1988).

1. — Discretionary Power

The explanatory notes to GAAR are the foundation upon which the CRA administratively interprets the rule. In the Department of Finance's words:[113]

> It is recognized that the introduction of the new Rule will inevitably carry with it a degree of uncertainty that in some cases can only be clarified through judicial interpretation of specific cases. To minimize this uncertainty to the maximum extent possible, the detailed explanatory notes ... describe the rule in some detail and how it is intended to deal with artificial tax avoidance arrangements.

Although useful as explanatory policy statements, the Technical Notes are of limited value in applying the rule to specific situations. To be sure, expository statements that the rule is not intended to apply to certain types of transactions provide tax practitioners with some comfort in arranging business transactions. The Notes are, however, qualified by several *caveats* and, as such, must be read closely if they are to be relied upon. The Technical Notes explain:

> ... transactions that comply with the object and spirit of other provisions of the Act read as a whole will not be affected by the application of this General Anti-Avoidance Rule. For example, a transaction that qualifies for a tax-free rollover under an explicit provision of the Act, *and that is carried out in accordance not only with the letter of that provision but also with the spirit of the Act read as a whole, will not be subject to new section 245.* [Emphasis added.]

The CRA is responsible for administering the *Income Tax Act* and it assumes the primary role in the interpretation of GAAR. Although the Agency's role in administering the rule is not, at least in theory, any different from its general administrative responsibility for the Act, it has a substantially enhanced role to play in the context of the rule. The rule depends upon two factors: (1) the taxpayer's primary motive in undertaking a transaction, and (2) an interpretation as to what constitutes an "abusive" or "offensive" transaction. The determination of both of these elements requires the exercise of administrative discretion.

The potential for abuse of discretionary power concerned the Joint Committee of the CBA/CICA:

> The potential for abuse of power, while inherent in the administration by government of any legislation, is writ large in the context of GAAR because of the breadth of section 245. We therefore applaud the sensitivity to this problem displayed by the Department of National Revenue, Taxation, in deciding, as indicated in Information Circular No. 88-2, to review proposed assessments involving GAAR at Head Office in order to ensure application of GAAR in a consistent manner. ... For so long as GAAR remains with us, much administrative effort will have to be expended with a view to making it work from a practical point of view. ... If nothing else, the Circular illustrates the extent to which the whole exercise of interpreting and applying GAAR is fact-oriented and involves subjective elements.

---

[113]Canada, Department of Finance, *Tax Reform 1987: Income Tax Reform* (Ottawa: June 18, 1987), at 130.

Information Circular 88-2 is of interest, but of limited value, to tax practitioners. The circular does very little, if anything, to contribute to an understanding of the development of policy in the interpretation of the rule. Indeed, it is somewhat of a paradox that the circular, which focuses on the "object and spirit" of the Act, does very little to contribute to the development of principles or the interpretation of tax policy. The circular is little more than an aggregation of factual examples supplemented by terse, sometimes single sentence, statements that the rule does or does not apply to particular facts. The circular may be helpful to those who have transactions involving factual circumstances that are virtually identical to those described, but it is of limited value to those who must base their professional advice on facts that are not "on all fours" with those described in the circular.

2. — *Purposive Approach*

The purpose underlying GAAR is set out in the testimony of Mr. Jim Wilson (General Counsel/General Director, Department of Finance) speaking on the need for an anti-avoidance rule in Canada and the experience of other jurisdictions in similar matters:

> The main rule we saw when we looked at the United States experience was the business-purpose doctrine. ... They do have a business-purpose test. They have had one for 50 years. It was developed by the courts, and it is a very simple doctrine and one that is quite compelling. Their courts looked at the tax code in the States and they said it is drafted to deal with business or commercial transactions; therefore, when you have in front of you a transaction that lacks any business purpose whatsoever, it is not unreasonable to treat it differently from transactions that have a business purpose and come within the general intention or purpose of the tax code. So we looked at the U.S. experience.

> We also looked at the U.K. experience, and they recently, like Canada, took a very strict or literalistic approach to tax interpretation. ... Recently, however, the U.K. courts looked at the U.S. experience and struck down a number of transactions that had no business purpose, that were effectively step transactions designed to create paper losses. The Courts looked at them, looked at the U.S. experience and I think, frankly, said enough is enough; the strict literal approach to tax interpretation is no longer appropriate.

> With the proposed General Anti-Avoidance Rule the underlying premises are really two. First, specific rules do not work in every case ... second — and I think the second premise is as important — Canada is out of line with other jurisdictions and it is time it was brought into line.

> . . . . .

> *I think the rule is aimed at transactions that use provisions of the Act inappropriately or avoid provisions of the Act inappropriately.* [Emphasis added.]

The clear inference is that the interpretation of what constitutes an "avoidance transaction" must be made in the context of the policy rationale of the Act as a whole to determine whether its provisions have been used appropriately or inappropriately.

The purposive approach to statutory interpretation is simple to state: Since legislation has a purpose, it should be interpreted in such a manner as best enhances the attainment of that purpose. As Justice Frankfurter said:[114]

> Legislation has an aim; it seeks to obviate some mischief, to supply an inadequacy, to effect a change of policy, to formulate a plan of government. That aim, that policy is not drawn, like nitrogen, out of the air; it is evinced in the language of the statute, as read in the light of other external manifestations of purpose.

The question is: How do we get at the purpose, "object and spirit" or intention of particular statutory provisions or of the Act as a whole? The answer to this question is of as much, if not more, concern to tax planners as it is to litigation counsel.

If the courts are to apply the purposive approach to statutory construction, they must admit all relevant evidence in determining the legislative intention underlying particular provisions. There is no useful purpose to be served by setting up *a priori* rules of exclusion. The trier of fact can always assess the reliability of the evidence and the weight that should be attached to it:[115]

> Unhappily, there is no table of logarthims for statutory construction. No item of evidence has a fixed or even average weight. One or another may be decisive in one set of circumstances, while of little value elsewhere. A painstaking, detailed report by a Senate Committee bearing directly on the immediate question may settle the matter. A loose statement even by a chairman of a committee, made impromptu in the heat of debate, less informing in cold type than when heard on the floor, will hardly be accorded the weight of an encyclical.

3. — *Avoidance Transactions*

An avoidance transaction is a single transaction carried out *primarily* to obtain a tax benefit. A "tax benefit" means a reduction, avoidance, or deferral of tax or any other amount payable or an increase in a refund of tax or any other amount under the Act or a Tax Treaty.[116]

An "avoidance transaction" includes a transaction that is primarily tax-motivated but forms part of a series of transactions carried out primarily for non-tax purposes. In the CRA's view, the fact that the *series* of transactions has *bona fide* non-tax purposes does not preclude one of its components from being considered an avoidance transaction. Hence, in effect, a single tax-motivated transaction can upset a multi-part scheme or business arrangement that is not *per se* tax driven.

---

[114]Felix Frankfurter, "Some Reflections on the Reading of Statutes" (1947) 47:4 Columbia L. R. 527 at 538-539.

[115]*Ibid.* at 543.

[116]Subs. 245(1).

(a) — Determination of Purpose

We determine a taxpayer's purpose for undertaking a transaction in a particular manner, not only from the taxpayer's statement of intention, but also from all of the circumstances that surround the transaction(s). The taxpayer's declared statement of intention is not necessarily determinative in any case.

It is important to distinguish between the purpose and the effect of a transaction. An "avoidance transaction" is one that is carried out primarily for tax purposes. Thus, even though a transaction has a business, investment, family or other non-tax effect, it may nevertheless be an "avoidance transaction" if its *primary* purpose is to obtain a tax benefit.

(b) — Misuse or Abuse of the Act, Regulations and Treaties

A tax motivated transaction that complies with the specific provisions of the Act may, nevertheless, be considered to be an "avoidance transaction" if it results in consequences that "... are so inconsistent with the general scheme of the Act that they cannot have been within the contemplation of Parliament."[117]

In respect of the determination of both the purpose of a transaction and whether the transaction offends the general scheme of the Act and Treaties, etc., the MNR, in effect, carries the burden of proof to demonstrate that the transaction is not an avoidance transaction.

Determining whether a particular provision of the Act has been misused, or whether the Act read as a whole or a Treaty has been abused, requires an examination of the purpose ("object and spirit") of the particular provision or scheme of provisions. It is not sufficient merely to rely on the technical language of the particular provision or scheme of provisions to determine whether there has been a misuse of the Act or an abuse of the Act read as a whole. This is quite clear in the Technical Notes:

> Where a taxpayer carries out transactions primarily in order to obtain, through the application of specific provisions of the Act, a tax benefit that is not *intended* by such provisions and by the Act read as a whole, section 245 should apply. This would be the case even though the strict words of the relevant specific provisions may support the tax result sought by the taxpayer. Thus, where applicable, section 245 will override other provisions of the Act since, otherwise, its object and purpose would be defeated. [Emphasis added.]

VII. — Interpretations And Rulings

The general theme running through the CRA's Information Circular 88-2 is that a taxpayer is not entitled to arrange her affairs to reduce tax if such an arrangement permits her to do indirectly what the spirit of the Act would not permit directly. Time and again, the CRA

---

[117]IC 88-2, "General Anti-Avoidance Rule — Section 245 of the *Income Tax Act*", para. 5.

indicates in its Circular that it will apply the General Anti-Avoidance Rule in circumstances where the taxpayer implements an arrangement or transaction by utilizing two or more provisions of the Act to circumvent a specific provision. We see this in the examples discussed below. Where the Act contains, whether specifically or by inference, a prohibition against a deduction or characterization of a receipt, a multiple-step arrangement that bypasses the prohibition can trigger GAAR. Thus, the concept of "abuse of the Act read as a whole" is very wide indeed and, probably, more extensive in its reach than comparable anti-avoidance doctrines in other jurisdictions.

1. — Form of Business Organization

The choice of form of a business organization can depend upon several factors: legal restrictions, considerations of limiting legal liability, sources of financing, and income tax considerations. Most small businesses face a real choice at the time that the business is started. This choice is usually between a sole proprietorship and a limited liability corporation.

If it is anticipated that a business will suffer losses in its start-up period, it is generally preferable to conduct a business as a sole proprietorship so that the owner's business losses can be offset against income from other sources. Later, when the business becomes successful, the sole proprietorship can be converted, on a tax-free basis, into a limited liability corporation. It is generally preferable to conduct a successful business through a Canadian-controlled private corporation because of the low income tax rate chargeable on active business income earned by such corporations.

The CRA's view is that there is nothing offensive about incorporating a sole proprietorship through a transfer of business assets on a tax-free basis under section 85. Even though the incorporation of the proprietorship may be motivated by income tax considerations, the rollover of the business does not offend the scheme of the Act in general and is not contrary to the object and spirit of any particular provisions. The Act clearly contemplates a choice of form of business organization. Hence, the incorporation of a sole proprietorship is not subject to the Rule.[118]

2. — Consolidation of Profits and Losses in a Corporate Group

A corporation is a separate legal entity and a taxpayer in its own right. A related group of corporations cannot consolidate the group's income for tax purposes. Each separate corporation within a related group of corporations must file an income tax return based on its own income or loss for its fiscal period.

---

[118]IC 88-2, "General Anti-Avoidance Rule — Section 245 of the *Income Tax Act*" (October 21, 1988), para. 11.

A corporation may, however, transfer property that it uses in its business to a related corporation so that the transferee corporation can deduct its non-capital losses against the income generated from the property. Thus, related corporations can sometimes obtain the economic effect of consolidated tax returns by transferring assets within the group in order to offset income from profitable assets against accumulated business losses.

The CRA does not consider a transfer of property between related or affiliated corporations to be an abusive "avoidance transaction" where all of the shares of the transferor and transferee corporations have been owned by the same taxpayer during the period in which the losses were incurred. Such a transfer is "consistent with the scheme of the Act." Therefore, subsection 245(2) will not apply.[119]

A transfer of property between related corporations may, however, be "abusive" where there has been a change of control by an arm's length person. If the transfer of property is undertaken to avoid a specific rule, such as a rule designed to preclude the deduction of losses after the acquisition of control of a corporation by an arm's length person, the transfer would constitute a misuse of the provisions of the Act and, therefore, be subject to GAAR.

3. — Purifying a Corporation

Where a taxpayer disposes of shares of a "qualified small business corporation" ("QSBC") as defined in subsection 110.6(1), any capital gain resulting from the disposition of the shares may be eligible for the capital gains exemption of $500,000. Thus, there is a substantial tax advantage to a QSBC. One of the requirements to qualify is that *all or substantially all* of the assets of the corporation are used in an active business carried on primarily in Canada. A corporation that is off-side this requirement can, however, be reorganized and "purified" for the purposes of the capital gains exemption.

A fairly typical scheme to "purify" a corporation is to have the shareholders of the non-qualifying corporation ("Opco") incorporate a corporation ("Newco"). The shareholders can transfer to Newco sufficient shares of Opco with a fair market value equal to the market value of the assets that are not used in the active business of Opco. Opco can then purchase its common shares from Newco and pay for the shares by transferring its non-business assets to Newco.

The CRA does not consider the formation of Newco and the transfer of Opco's shares to it to be an abuse of the Act. Section 85 specifically permits a transfer of capital property to a taxable Canadian corporation on a tax-free basis. Nor does the CRA consider the distribution of Opco's non-business assets prior to the sale of its shares to constitute an abuse of the Act read as a whole. The definition of a small business corporation does not require that all or substantially all of the assets of the corporation be used in carrying on an active business

---

[119]See ATR-44, "Utilization of Deductions within a Related Corporate Group" (February 17, 1992); Income Tax Technical News #9 (Feb 10, 1997).

in Canada for a particular period of time prior to the sale of the shares. Hence, the series of transactions to "purify" Opco are in accordance with the scheme of the Act and, as such, do not constitute an abusive "avoidance transaction" under GAAR. (Note, however, that the transactions described may generate a tax liability to Opco when it disposes of its non-business assets to Newco, and that Newco may be subject to subsection 55(2) if the gain on the purchased shares is attributable to something other than income earned or realized by Opco.)[120]

4. — Services Rendered to a Corporation

Where an individual renders services to a corporation, the manner of payment for the services can depend upon the relationship between the individual and the corporation.

(a) — Non-Payment of Salary

Where an individual provides services to a corporation with which he does not deal at arm's length, the parties may agree that the corporation is not under an obligation to pay the individual a salary for services rendered because payment of a salary would increase the corporation's loss for the year. Since there is no provision in the Act requiring payment of a salary for services rendered, the failure to do so is not considered to be contrary to the scheme of the Act read as a whole. Hence, the CRA will not apply subsection 245(2) to deem a salary to have been paid by the corporation to the individual. Note, however, that the situation would be different if there were a legal obligation to pay the salary and if the individual were to waive payment of the amount.

(b) — Salary/Bonus Mix

A Canadian-controlled private corporation is taxable at a special low rate on the first $300,000 of its active business income earned in a year. Hence, where an owner/manager of a Canadian-controlled private corporation is taxable at a higher rate than the corporation, it is usually advantageous to reduce the corporation's income to $300,000 for the year through, for example, payment of a salary/bonus to the owner/manager. Provided that the amount of the salary/bonus is not in excess of a reasonable amount, the CRA will not use GAAR to

---

[120]See ATR-53, "Purification of a Small Business Corporation" (April 8, 1993); see also IC 88-2, "General Anti-Avoidance Rule — Section 245 of the *Income Tax Act*" (October 21, 1988), para. 15 and IC 88-2, "General Anti-Avoidance Rule: Supplement 1" (July 13, 1990), paras. 3 and 4. *Granite Bay Charters Ltd. v. R.*, [2001] 3 C.T.C. 2516, 2001 D.T.C. 615 (T.C.C. [General Procedure]) (purification transfer ran afoul of subs. 55(2) — identity of subsequent purchaser not fatal to concept of series of transactions); Income Tax Technical News #22 (January 11, 2002).

deny a deduction for the payment since the Act permits the deductibility of reasonable business expenses.

(c) — Unpaid Amounts

Where a corporation owes an amount for services rendered to it, any amount accrued for payment is deductible to the corporation in the year in which the service is rendered. If the amount accrued is not paid, however, the person who renders the services is not taxable on the accrued amount. This misalignment between the deduction to the corporation and the non-inclusion to the individual allows the corporate taxpayer the advantage of the deduction and the individual the benefit of tax deferral until receipt.

To prevent taxpayers from taking undue advantage of this imbalance between deduction and inclusion, section 78 provides that either the corporation or the individual entitled to the payment must include the amount in income in the third taxation year following the year in which the expense is incurred. Thus, the Act specifically contemplates that limited tax deferral is acceptable: The "object and spirit" of subsection 78(1) is to permit such a deferral. Hence, subsection 245(2) does not apply in these circumstances, even though the arrangement is patently tax motivated.

5. — Conversion of Salary into Capital Gain

Salaries and bonuses are taxable as employment income and, as such, are potentially subject to higher rates of tax. In contrast, a capital gain may either be completely non-taxable or, if taxable, subject to a low effective rate of tax. Hence, it is usually to an employee's benefit to be compensated through capital gains rather than through salary or bonus payments. Thus, it will usually be advantageous to convert potential salary payments into capital gains.[121]

Where an employee of a private corporation wishes to receive a portion of a salary or bonus as a capital gain, she can subscribe for the employer's preferred shares, redeemable at a premium that reflects the relevant portion of the employee's annual salary or bonus payment. Prior to the redemption of the preferred shares, a corporation related to the employer corporation can purchase the shares, thereby allowing the employee to receive a distribution of surplus as a capital gain. In these circumstances, since the acquisition of the preferred shares is part of an arrangement designed to avoid tax that would otherwise have been paid had the income been received as a salary or bonus, the transactions would be considered to be "avoidance transactions." In the CRA's view, the transaction results in an abuse of the Act as a whole.

---

[121] See IC-88-2.

Presumably, if the initial arrangement with the employee was structured so that he would be compensated on the basis of salary/bonus and equity participation in preferred shares *and* the arrangement was primarily driven by non-tax considerations, the arrangement would not constitute an "avoidance transaction" and the question of abuse of the Act as a whole would not arise. In other words, where an arrangement does not constitute an "avoidance transaction" in that it is undertaken *primarily* for non-tax purposes, it does not matter that the arrangement may circumvent specific provisions of the Act or be tantamount to an abuse of the Act read as a whole.

Provided that an arrangement has been sanctified by having been undertaken primarily for non-tax purposes, it does not matter that it runs counter to the "object and spirit" of the Act. Non-tax motivated transactions need only comply with the technical requirements of the Act. Hence, the principal focus of tax planning should be to ensure that business and family transactions are undertaken primarily for non-tax purposes. It is only if transactions are undertaken primarily for tax purposes that it is necessary to ensure they do not offend either the scheme of the Act read as a whole or any particular provisions.

6. — Interest Expense

Paragraph 20(1)(c) limits the deductibility of interest expenses to, *inter alia*, borrowing incurred for the purpose of gaining or producing income from business or property. This restriction on the deductibility of interest can cause difficulties for a related group of corporations where one of the corporations is profitable and the other sustains losses and needs additional capital to carry on its operations. In these circumstances, although the unprofitable corporation can borrow money, it cannot use the tax saving by deducting its interest expense. If the profitable corporation borrows the money from its bank and subscribes for common shares in the non-profitable corporation, it can reduce its net income by deducting the interest expense. The non-profitable corporation can use the money received from the sale of shares to gain or produce income from its business. The borrowing by the profitable corporation is for the purpose of gaining or producing income and, therefore, subsection 245(2) would not apply.

The above example illustrates the vulnerability of taxpayers to the administrative discretion of the CRA. The Agency issues terse statements that an arrangement is or is not an "avoidance transaction" or that it does or does not abuse the Act read as a whole. In this case, compliance with paragraph 20(1)(c) of the Act is considered sufficient reason not to classify the transaction as an "avoidance transaction." In other circumstances, however, compliance with the technical statutory requirements of a provision(s) may not *per se* be sufficient to avoid characterizing a transaction as an "avoidance transaction."

Without explanation or elaboration, the Agency has stated that borrowing by one corporation for the purposes of financing the business activities of another related corporation is deductible because the transaction conforms with the technical wording of the statute.[122]

The statement provides comfort for the particular transaction described. It is, however, quite dangerous to extrapolate from this statement that technical compliance with the requirements of the statute will, in all cases, be sufficient to avoid the rule. Clearly this is not the case.

The CRA also indicates that borrowing from one corporation to finance the purchase of shares of another corporation, followed by an amalgamation of the purchaser with its subsidiary will not trigger the rule in respect of the deductibility of interest expense.[123] For example, where a taxable Canadian corporation has agreed to purchase all of the shares of an operating corporation, which is also a taxable Canadian corporation, the purchaser can incorporate a holding corporation (Holdco) which borrows the purchase price and pays the vendor for the shares. Holdco and the operating corporation amalgamate so that the interest payable on the monies borrowed to acquire the shares can be deducted in computing the income from the business of the amalgamated corporation. The Agency's position is that the borrowing by the holding corporation and the amalgamation are not abusive and that subsection 245(2) does not apply to the borrowing by the holding corporation.

7. — Section 85 Rollover to Related and Affiliated Corporations

Suppose an individual has property with an unrealized capital gain that she wishes to sell to a third party. The individual also has an affiliated corporation with net capital loss. If she sold the property directly to a third party, she would realize a capital gain. To avoid the gain, the property is transferred to the individual's affiliated corporation on a tax-deferred basis under subsection 85(1). The affiliated corporation then sells the property to the third party and offsets the resulting taxable capital gain against its net capital loss.

It is clear that such a transaction is tax motivated and, without more, would be an avoidance transaction. The CRA does not, however, consider a transfer of property to an affiliated corporation on a tax-deferred basis to contravene the object and spirit of the Act. Since subsection 69(11) does not permit a person to transfer property to an *unrelated* corporation on a tax-deferred basis where it is intended that the unrelated corporation will sell the property and reduce the amount of the gain by amounts of losses or similar deductions which it

---

[122]IC 88-2, "General Anti-Avoidance Rule — Section 245 of the *Income Tax Act*" (October 21, 1988), para. 19: The borrowing by the parent corporation is for the purpose of gaining or producing income as required by para. 20(1)(c) of the Act, and subs. 245(2) would, therefore, not apply.

[123]The Agency accepts that the jurisprudence supports interest deduction in these circumstances, which makes the GAAR issue moot — see IT-533, para. 21.

may claim, the Agency reasons that "... by implication, the subsection does permit a transfer to a *related* corporation on a tax-deferred basis."[124]

The Agency does not specifically address the broader question of whether the grouping of income and losses of an affiliated corporate group is within the general scheme of the Act with respect to consolidated income reporting for tax purposes. This may suggest that in applying GAAR, the CRA is less likely to be concerned with the general scheme of the Act read as a whole and more concerned with the misuse of specific statutory provisions.

8. — Estate Freezes

Generally, estate freezing is a technique whereby an individual organizes or, more usually, reorganizes property with a view to "freezing" the value of that property for the purposes of minimizing the tax payable on accrued capital gains at death. Subsection 70(5) deems a taxpayer to have disposed of all capital property immediately before her death. Hence, where a taxpayer dies with unrealized capital gains, this subsection will trigger the capital gains by deeming the property to have been disposed of at fair market value. To curtail the amount of gain that may be realized on a deemed disposition of property, a taxpayer may rearrange her affairs and freeze the value of the estate. Most, if not all, estate freezes are tax motivated transactions.[125]

(a) — Holding Company Freeze

A typical estate freeze might operate as follows: a parent who owns shares of an operating company ("Opco") which have appreciated in value, may transfer the shares to a newly formed corporation ("Holdco") in exchange for Holdco's shares and/or debt. The transfer can be made under subsection 85(1) on a tax-deferred basis so that the parent does not realize any capital gain on the transfer of Opco's shares to Holdco. The consideration for the transfer is usually made up of preferred shares that are retractable at the option of the parent for an amount equal to the fair market value of the Opco shares transferred. The preference shares carry voting control. A trust for the parent's minor children can subscribe for Holdco's common shares for a nominal amount. Properly executed, the value of the preferred shares taken back by the parent should be frozen at their value as at the date of the reorganization.

---

[124]ITTN #9, "Loss Consolidation within a Corporate Group" (February 10, 1997).

[125]See ATR-25, "Estate Freeze" (October 9, 1987); ATR-47, "Transfer of Assets to Realtyco" (February 24, 1992); ATR-57, "Transfer of Property for Estate Planning Purposes" (May 28, 1993).

The CRA's position on estate freezes is that, *generally*, they will not ordinarily result in a misuse or abuse of the Act. The Technical Notes state:

> ... "Estate freezing" transactions whereby a taxpayer transfers future growth in the value of assets to his children or grandchildren will not ordinarily be avoidance transactions to which the proposed rules would apply despite the fact that they may result in a deferral, avoidance or reduction of tax. Apart from the fact that many of these transactions may be considered to be primarily motivated by non-tax considerations, it would be reasonable to consider that such transactions do not ordinarily result in a misuse or abuse given the scheme of the Act and the recent enactment of subsection 74.4(4) of the Act to accommodate estate freezes.

(b) — Income Splitting

Section 74.4 deals with income splitting and may apply to estate freeze transactions. Under this section, an amount may be deemed to be received as interest by an individual who loans or transfers property to a corporation where one of the main purposes of such a loan or transfer may reasonably be considered the reduction in income of the individual, and the benefit of a designated person.

A designated person is the individual's spouse, common-law partner, or a person under 18 who does not deal with the individual at arm's length, or who is the individual's niece or nephew.[126]

There are several exceptions to the attribution rules. For example, they do not apply in respect of loans or transfers of property to a small business corporation; and they do not apply where the only interest which the designated person has in the corporation is a beneficial interest in the shares of the corporation which are held through a trust, and the terms of the trust provide that person may not obtain the use of any income or capital of the trust while he is the designated person.[127]

These rules and their exceptions facilitate estate freezing transactions. The Agency's view is that subsection 245(2) does not apply to a transfer of shares to a corporation where subsection 74.4(2) applies to deem the parent to receive an amount as interest. Similarly, subsection 245(2) does not apply where subsection 74.4(2) does not apply to deem the parent to receive an amount as interest.[128]

---

[126]Subss. 74.4(1) and 74.5(5).

[127]Subs. 74.4(4).

[128]See IC 88-2, para. 10.

(c) — Reorganization of Capital

Similar considerations apply to an estate freeze executed under section 86 of the Act, which allows a corporation to reorganize its capital.[129] For example, a taxpayer may wish to dispose of the common shares of an operating company in exchange for shares that are structured so as to freeze their value at their fair market value as of the date of reorganization. In Advance Income Tax Ruling ATR-22R, "Estate Freeze Using Share Exchange" (April 14, 1989) the Agency confirmed that it would not apply subsection 245(2) to an estate freeze using a share exchange under subsection 86(1).

9. — Avoidance of Part IV Tax on Taxable Dividends

The Part IV tax applies to private corporations.[130] It is a special tax intended to prevent tax deferral through the use of holding companies. The tax is also used to integrate personal and corporate taxes insofar as private corporations are concerned. The Part IV tax places an individual who owns portfolio investments through a holding company in the same position as a person who holds portfolio investments directly.

The critical factor in determining the liability of a corporation for the Part IV tax is its relationship with the corporation from which it receives a dividend. If the payor and recipient corporations are not connected with each other, the recipient is liable for the tax on taxable dividends it receives from the payor. If the corporations are connected, the recipient is only liable for the tax if the payor corporation obtains a refund by paying the dividend. Thus, in certain circumstances, there is an incentive to connect corporations which might otherwise not be connected.

For example, assume that each of two private corporations owns less than 10 per cent of the common shares of a payor corporation required to pay a substantial taxable dividend which would otherwise be subject to Part IV tax, and that none of the corporations are related to each other. The payor corporation will not be entitled to a dividend refund on the payment of the dividend. To avoid the Part IV tax, each of the two corporations then transfers its shareholdings to a new holding corporation ("Newco") in exchange for common shares of Newco. The parties elect under subsection 85(1) to execute the transfer on a tax-deferred basis. Following the transfer of the payor corporation's shares to Newco, it will be connected with the payor corporation. The dividend is then paid. Since the corporations are now connected to each other, the dividend can flow through Newco to the two private corporations without any Part IV tax liability. Newco then pays the same amount to the private corporations as a dividend, also free of Part IV tax. The primary purpose for the transfer of the shares is to avoid the Part IV tax which would otherwise be payable if the dividend was paid directly to the private corporations.

---

[129]See Chapter 27, "Share-for-Share Acquisitions."

[130]See Chapter 19, "Corporate Investment Income."

The CRA has indicated that in these circumstances, the transfer of the shares to Newco would be an "avoidance transaction." The Agency has also indicated, but without elaboration or explanation, that "... the transfer of the shares would be a misuse of a provision of the Act *or* an abuse of the Act as a whole ...".[131] Whether the transactions constitute a misuse of the specific Part IV provisions *or* an abuse of the Act as a whole is not clarified in the circular.

10. — Change of Fiscal Periods

Generally, a corporation is entitled to select its fiscal year end, provided that the fiscal period of the corporation is not more than 53 weeks. A corporation cannot change its usual and accepted fiscal period without the concurrence of the Minister.[132]

Where a corporation amalgamates with another corporation to form a new corporation, the Act deems the taxation year of the "old" corporation to end immediately before the amalgamation, and the newly created amalgamated corporation commences its fiscal period.[133]

Where an operating corporation amalgamates with a shell corporation pursuant to subsection 87(1), and the merger is undertaken solely for the purpose of terminating the taxation year of the operating company immediately before the amalgamation, the transaction is considered an "avoidance transaction" to which GAAR applies.[134]

11. — Indirect Transfer of Land Inventory

Subsection 85(1) allows a taxpayer to transfer property to a taxable Canadian corporation on a tax-deferred basis. An important exception to this rule is that a taxpayer is not permitted to transfer land inventory on a tax-deferred basis to a corporation. There is, however, no explicit prohibition against transferring land inventory on a tax-deferred basis to a Canadian partnership. Hence, where a taxpayer wants to transfer land inventory to a corporation on a tax-deferred basis, she can proceed in two stages. First, the taxpayer can form a partnership with the prospective purchaser of the property and transfer the land to the partnership, electing under subsection 97(2) to defer the gain on the transfer. The purchaser can contribute a nominal amount of cash for the partnership interest. Second, the vendor can transfer his partnership interest to the purchaser corporation in consideration for shares with a fair market value equal to the value of the partnership interest, and the parties may then elect under

---

[131]IC 88-2, "General Anti-Avoidance Rule — Section 245 of the *Income Tax Act*" (October 21, 1988).

[132]See IT-179R, "Change of Fiscal Period" (May 28, 1993) and subs. 249.1(7).

[133]Para. 87(2)(a).

[134]IC 88-2, "General Anti-Avoidance Rule — Section 245 of the *Income Tax Act*" (October 21, 1988), paras. 21 and IC 88-2, "General Anti-Avoidance Rule: Supplement 1" (July 13, 1990), para.9.

subsection 85(1) in respect of the transfer. On the acquisition by the purchaser corporation of the taxpayer's partnership interest, the partnership ceases to exist and subsection 98(5) applies to deem the purchaser to have acquired the land at an amount equal to the taxpayer's cost amount for the land.[135]

As a consequence of this two-step arrangement, the purchaser corporation acquires the land inventory and the taxpayer avoids the recognition of any gain on the transfer of the property. The purpose of the transactions is to circumvent the prohibition in subsection 85(1) against the transfer of land inventory to a taxable Canadian corporation. Hence, the transactions misuse the subsection and GAAR applies: the transfer of the land to the partnership is contrary to the scheme of the Act read as a whole.

In other words, the CRA appears to take the position that it will invoke section 245 where a taxpayer does indirectly what he cannot do directly. Stated another way, a taxpayer does not have *carte blanche* to arrange his affairs so as to minimize a tax burden through technically correct arrangements. A taxpayer is only entitled to mitigate tax if the arrangements undertaken in this respect comply with the spirit of the *Act read as a whole*.[136]

12. — *Indirect Disposition of Property Through a Partnership*

Generally, the disposition of a property triggers an income gain (loss) or a capital gain (loss). But a taxpayer who owns property which, if it were disposed of in a straightforward manner, would result in the immediate realization of an income or capital gain, may proceed by a more circuitous route. For example, the taxpayer and the prospective purchaser of the property can form a partnership. The taxpayer can then transfer the property into the partnership and elect under subsection 97(2) to defer recognition of any gain which would otherwise arise. The purchaser may contribute cash into the partnership in an amount equal to the

---

[135]IC 88-2, "General Anti-Avoidance Rule — Section 245 of the *Income Tax Act*" (October 21, 1988), paras. 12 and 22.

[136]But see *Loyens v. R.*, 2003 TCC 214, [2003] 3 C.T.C. 2381, 2003 D.T.C. 355 (T.C.C.) where GAAR was not applied in a similar fact situation (Taxpayers agreed to sell a piece of land they held as inventory. With the use of the section 85 and 97 rollover provisions, the vendors transferred the land at cost to their partnership, and then transferred their partnership interest to their corporation which had unused losses. The corporation sold the land at market value and the resulting gain (income) was almost completely offset by the corporation's losses. The Court found that these transactions were avoidance transactions, but that GAAR did not apply. The policy behind the real property inventory restriction in subsection 85(1) is to prevent the conversion of income into capital gains by a real property trader. In this case, there was no conversion of income into capital gains. Both the transfer of the partnership interest to the corporation and the sale of the land inventory by the corporation resulted in the reporting of taxable business income. Thus, the avoidance transactions did not offend the policy behind the restriction in subsection 85(1). Hence, there was no misuse of the rollover provisions or abuse of the Act as a whole. GAAR not applicable.).

fair market value of the property. The taxpayer then withdraws all of the cash from the partnership and, because of such withdrawal, her share of the income and loss of the partnership is correspondingly reduced. The partnership continues to carry on business and the purchaser, in effect, acquires the property. The CRA considers such an arrangement as an attempt to circumvent provisions which provide that the proceeds of disposition of property are to be accounted for at the time of their receipt. Hence, it views the entire arrangement as one that is "... contrary to the scheme of the Act read as a whole ..." and will apply GAAR to such arrangements.[137]

13. — Conversion of Income Gains into Dividends

Generally, where a taxpayer disposes of depreciable property, any proceeds of disposition over the undepreciated capital cost (but not in excess of capital cost) of the property are included in income as recapture of capital cost allowance. Recaptured capital cost allowance is taxable as ordinary income. Proceeds that exceed the capital cost of the property are considered capital gains.

A corporation that is resident in Canada and that owns depreciable property, may wish to circumvent the potential recapture of capital cost allowance as follows:

- The taxpayer can sell the property to an arm's length taxable Canadian corporation in consideration for redeemable shares having a redemption amount equal to the fair market value of the property sold.

- The taxpayer and the purchaser can elect under subsection 85(1), in respect of the property, to defer recognition of the profit which would otherwise have been realized on a direct sale of the property.

- The shares have a paid-up capital equal to the amount elected so that, on their redemption, the amount received in excess of paid-up capital is characterized as a taxable dividend deductible under subsection 112(1) of the Act.

The CRA has stated that it will apply GAAR to this type of transaction. Since the taxpayer would normally have been taxable on the excess of the proceeds of disposition over the undepreciated capital cost of the property as ordinary income, the two-step transaction converting ordinary income into a non-taxable dividend is offensive in that it circumvents the scheme of the Act. The taxpayer's right, then, to arrange his affairs to mitigate tax, is curtailed by GAAR.[138]

---

[137]*Ibid.*

[138]*Ibid.* at para. 13.

14. — Reserves for Future Proceeds

Generally, where a taxpayer realizes a gain on the sale of property, the amount of the gain must be taken into income in the year of disposition. Where, however, a taxpayer does not receive the full amount of the proceeds of disposition, she is entitled to claim a reserve in respect of proceeds to be received at a later date. Hence, subject to certain limiting rules, a taxpayer is entitled to defer recognition of a gain on the disposition of property to the extent that the proceeds of disposition from its sale have not been realized.

A taxpayer who does not wish to recognize sale proceeds from a cash sale to an arm's length purchaser may sell the property to an intermediary corporation and defer receipt of the proceeds of disposition for more than two years after the date of the sale. The intermediary corporation can then sell the property to the arm's length purchaser for cash. The vendor can receive interest from the intermediary corporation in respect of the moneys received by the corporation from the third party purchaser.

The CRA's view is that if the interposition of the intermediary is made solely to enable the owner of the property to defer recognition of the gain from the sale of the real property, the transaction is subject to GAAR. Although the Agency does not give any explicit reason for applying the rule, it appears reasonable to presume that they interpret the transaction as contravening the general rule that a reserve may only be claimed in respect of proceeds that have not actually been received. Thus, in the above example, the CRA, by inference, considers the owner of the real property and any intermediary corporation to be, in effect, one taxpayer for the purposes of the reserve rules.[139] With the introduction of paragragph 20(8)(c), the GAAR argument becomes less important.

15. — Conversion of Dividend Income into Capital Gains

As a general rule, the effective income tax rate on dividend income should be approximately equal to that on capital gains for taxpayers in the highest marginal tax bracket. In fact, the two rates can vary quite substantially because of adjustments to one rate — generally capital gains — without corresponding adjustments to the other. There is, however, one important difference between the tax burden on dividend income and capital gains, namely an individual is entitled to receive a certain amount ($100,000 or $500,000 depending upon the type of property sold) of capital gains on a tax-free basis. This makes it attractive for taxpayers to utilize their capital gains exemption instead of receiving taxable dividends.

Where a private corporation wishes to provide an annual dividend payment to its individual shareholders as tax-free capital gains, it may arrange to pay a stock dividend instead of a cash dividend. The shares received as part of a stock dividend have a low paid-up capital and a high fair market value. As a part of the same arrangement, the shares are purchased by a corporation related to the issuing corporation (or by a third party broker or dealer) and the

---

[139]*Ibid.* at para. 24.

purchase price of the shares is funded by the issuing corporation. Since the payment and the repurchase of the stock dividend shares is part of an arrangement to avoid the shareholder tax which would normally be required to be paid on taxable cash dividends, the payment and repurchase of the shares is considered to be a misuse of a provision of the Act *or* an abuse of the Act as a whole, and GAAR applies.[140]

---

[140]*Ibid.* at para. 26; see also *McNichol v. Canada*, [1997] 2 C.T.C. 2088, 97 D.T.C. 111 (T.C.C.) and *RMM Canadian Enterprises Inc. v. Canada* (1997), [1998] 1 C.T.C. 2300, 97 D.T.C. 302 (T.C.C.); additional reasons at [1997] 3 C.T.C. 2103 (T.C.C.).

Bibliography by Country and Subsection

Canada

I. — General Comment

Barbeau, "Tax Opinions: The Dilemma" (1963) 6 Can. B.J. 328.

Canada Tax Service, Stikeman Analysis, 245, Tax Avoidance (July 30, 2005).

Carlyle, W.M., "Section 138A Should Be Repealed" (1968) 11 Can. Bar J. 212.

Clarke, Timothy W., "The GAAR [general anti-avoidance rule]: the pendulum swings in favour of the taxpayer" (2001) 49 Can. Tax J. 713–720.

David Sherman's Analysis, 274, General Anti-Avoidance Rule (November 15, 2002).

Flatters, Michael J./McCarthy Tétrault Calgary, Alberta, "General Anti-Avoidance Rule Update" (1999) 12, No. 1 Canadian Petroleum Tax Journals 10.

Krishna, Vern, "The Scope of GAAR [general anti-avoidance rule]" (2000) 19 Lawyers Wkly. No. 44, 4(2).

McKie, A.B., "Tax Compliance — A Fine (or penalty) State of Affairs" (1988) 2 Can. Current Tax C-69.

Maclean, Alexandra & Paul Festeryga, "GAAR [general anti-avoidance rule]: it's alive!" (2001) 48 Can. Tax. J. 372–375.

McNair, Arnold, et al., ed., *Materials of Canadian Income Tax*, 8th ed. (Don Mills, Ontario: DeBoo Publishers, 1989) 148.

Nichols, Brian S., "GAAR [general anti-avoidance rule] and more" (2002) Ont. Tax Conf. (Tab 1) 1–42.

Nitikman, Joel A., "The Onus of Proof in Tax Litigation and Other Litigation Matters Affecting GAAR," in *Report of Proceedings of the Forty-Ninth Tax Conference*, 1997 Conference Report (Toronto: Canadian Tax Foundation, 1997), 7:1–37.

Lynch, Paul, "GAAR [general anti-avoidance rule] 2001: an update from the CCRA [Canada Customs and Revenue Agency]" (2001) 14 Can. Petro. Tax J. 165–169.

Thomas, Richard, "GAAR [general anti-avoidance rule] update" (2003) 51 Can. Tax J. 1301–1305.

Van Der Hout, Susan, "Tax Court decision restricts ambit for Minister's use of GAAR [general anti-avoidance rule] (2003) 23 Lawyers Wkly. No. 13, 15(2).

Ward, David A., "Has Revenue Canada Become 'Big Brother'?/Revenue Canada, est-il tout-puissant?" (1984) 117:4 CA Magazine 22.

II. — Judicial Doctrines?

1. Taxpayers' Rights (994)?

Adamson, Edith and Jane McEwan, *For Conscience Sake* (Victoria, B.C.: Conscience Canada, 1991).

Batty, Trevor, "Singleton, Ludco, the Supreme Court and GAAR" (2003) 66 Sask. L. Rev. 337.

Beach, Don, "Anti-Avoidance Rules are an End Run Around the Courts" (1987) Financial Times 25.

Chisholm, Patricia, "U.S. Tax Doesn't Affect Evasion Here" (1985) 4:23 Ont. Lawyers Weekly 6.

Corn, G. "Right to Arrange One's Affairs to Avoid Taxation" — Lack of Business Purpose — Sham Transactions" (1984) 1 Can. Current Tax 131.

Felesky, Brian A. & Cindy L. Rajan, "Judicial Anti-Avoidance: Where Are We?" (1996) 9, No. 2 Canadian Petroleum Tax Journals 1.

Hellerstein, Jerome R., "Judicial Approaches to Tax Avoidance", in *Proceedings of 18th Tax Conf.* 62 (Can. Tax Foundation, 1964).

Harris, R.G., "Tax Planning: The Practitioner's Viewpoint" (1970) 96 Can. Chart. Acc. 156.

Hogg, Peter W. *et al.*, *Principles of Canadian Income Tax Law*, 5th ed. (Toronto: Carswell, 2005) 20.2.

Lefebvre, Wilfrid & Patrick-James Blaine, "GAAR [general anti-avoidance rule]: un peu plus de clarté?: En attente des tribunaux d'appeals" (2000-2001) 22 Rev. plan. fisc. & success. 691–702.

2. Evasion, Avoidance and Mitigation (996)

Avey, T., and M. Quigley, "A Case of Tax Evasion: An Accountant's Day in Court" (1984) 117:9 CA Magazine 58.

Avey, Tedd & Michael Quigley, "A Case of Tax Evasion: An Accountant's Day in Court" (September 1984), 117 *CA Magazine* 58–66.

Bergh, Colin S. *Effective Tax Avoidance* (Toronto: Carswell, 1965).

Bouvet, Y., "Analyse des mesures anti-évitement relatives a l'exoneration du gain en capital", 9 RPFS 357.

Corporate Crime in Canada (Toronto: Law Society of Upper Canada, Dpt. of Education, 1988).

Davison, G. Kent, CA, "Avoidance, Evasion, and the Problem Client", in *Report of Proceedings of the Fiftieth Tax Conference*, 1998 Conference Report (Toronto: Canadian Tax Foundation, 1998), 7:1–20.

Dodge, David A., "A New and More Coherent Approach to Tax Avoidance" (1988) 36 Can. Tax J. 1.

Dodge, David A., "A New and More Coherent Approach to Tax Avoidance" (1988) vol. 36, no. 1 *Canadian Tax Journal* 1–22.

Drache, A.B.C., "Anti-avoidance Proposal Goes Too Far" (1987) 9 Can. Taxpayer 121.

Duval, G., "Acquisition et disposition d'une entreprise canadienne par un non-resident" (1987) 9 RPFS 413.

Fortin, Guy, "Abuse or Misuse", in *Report of Proceedings of the Forty-Ninth Tax Conference*, 1997 Conference Report (Toronto: Canadian Tax Foundation, 1998), 5:1–22.

Goodlet, W.E., "Tax Minimization: Avoiding or Planning" (1971) 98 Can. Chart. Acc. 195.

Goodman, W.D., "Search and Seizure, Evasion, Records and Tax Opinions" (1986) Special Lectures LSUC 207.

Gourlay, J.L. "Tax Abuse — a View from Revenue Canada" (1980) 87 Can. Taxation 82.

Gourlay, J.L. "Tax Planning or Tax Evasion" (1969) 95 Can. Chart. Acc. 250.

Greenspan, Edward L., "Tax Evasion is a Crime!", *Corporate Management Tax Conf.* 1:1 (Can. Tax Foundation, 1988).

Harris, R.G., "Tax Planning: The Practitioner's Viewpoint" (1970) 96 Can. Chart. Acc. 156.

Hasson, R., "Tax Evasion and Social Security Abuse — Some Tentative Observations" (1980) 2 Can. Taxation 98.

Hogg, Peter W. *et al.*, *Principles of Canadian Income Tax Law*, 5th ed. (Toronto: Carswell, 2005) 2.8.

Hogg, Peter W. *et al.*, *Principles of Canadian Income Tax Law*, 5th ed. (Toronto: Carswell, 2005) 20.1.

Huggett, Donald R., "With Cap in Hand" (1988) 16 Can. Tax News 9.

Huggett, Donald R., "Foul Balls" (1979) 7 Can. Tax News 17.

Illersic, A.R. Innes, W.I., "Tax Havens and Residence" (1982) 30 Can. Tax J. 52.

Kellough, Howard J., "The Legal Efficacy of Unwinding or Negating a Transaction in Whole or in Part", in *Proceedings of 37th Tax Conf.* 9:1 (Can. Tax Foundation, 1985).

Krishna, Vern, "Deductibility of Legal and Accounting Fees in Defending Tax Evasion Charges (IT-99R3)" (1986) 1 Can. Current Tax C-129.

Labrie, F.E., "The Uncertainties of Tax Planning" (1960) 9 Chitty's L.J. 114; 146; 177.

Latimer, W.R., H.E. Crate and Jacques Barbeau, "Crimes under the Income Tax", in *Proceedings of 14th Conf.* 53 (Can. Tax Foundation, 1961).

McBarnet, Doreen, "Legitimate Rackets: Tax Evasion, Tax Avoidance, and the Boundaries of Legality" (1992) 3 J. of Hum. Justice No. 2 56.

McCracken, Gerald H., "Preventing Tax Evasion Through Enforcement: The Government Perspective", *Corp. Management Tax Conference* 2:1 (Can. Tax Foundation, 1988).

McDonnell, Thomas E., "The GAAR [general anti-avoidance rule]: avoidance transaction" real issue avoided" (2004) 52 Can. Tax J. 555–563.

McKie, A.B., "Tax Havens — Health Bulletin" (1982) 89:1 Can. Bank 62.

McKie, A.B., "Tax Tellers" (1982) 89:2 Can. Bank 28.

McKie, A.B., "Info-Intertax" (1980) 87 Can. Bank 69.

McKie, A.B., "Offshore Banking — or Laundering?" (1983) 90:5 Can. Bank 18.

McKie, A.B., "Oversight of Tax Havens" (1980) 87:3 Can. Bank 50.

McKie, A.B., "Tax Sparing — Some Thoughts" (1985) 1:1 Can. Bank 62.

McKie., A.B., "Tax Avoidance, Handle with Care" (1978) 85:4 Can. Bank 37.

Pateras Bruno J., "Tax Evasion after the Charter" (1990) Meredith Mem. Lect. 435.

Potvin, Jean, "Tax Evasion in Canada" (1977) 25 Can. Tax J. 229.

Robert C. Strother, "Avoidance and Evasion: The World Beyond *Stubart*", in *Report of Proceedings of the Thirty-Sixth Tax Conference*, 1984 Conference Report (Toronto: Canadian Tax Foundation, 1985), 105–47.

Robert McMechan, "Canada Trustco is Hardly a Sanction for Tax Avoidance" (2005) 24 Tax Times 1.

Robertson, J.R., "The Use of Tax Evasion and Tax Avoidance by Multinational Companies: A Canadian View" (1977) 25 Can. Tax J. 513.

Rochon, M., "Évasion fiscale" (1978) 9 R. Gen. 438.

Roseman, Ellen, "Anti-Avoidance Law Irks Tax Planners," *The Globe and Mail* (November 28, 1988) B1.

Rosemarie Wertschek, "The Tax Adviser and Commercial Law: Some Issues", in *Report of Proceedings of the Forty-Fifth Tax Conference*, 1993 Conference Report (Toronto: Canadian Tax Foundation, 1994), 24:1–39.

Roy, Robert, "The Tax Avoidance Program", in *Proceedings of 45th Tax Conf.* 7:1 (Can. Tax Found., 1993).

Savage, H.B., *Tax Saving* (Montreal: 1952).

Schwartz, Alan M., "Tax Avoidance", in *Proceedings of 33rd Tax Conf.* 922 (Can. Tax Foundation, 1981).

Sherbaniuk, "Tax Avoidance — Recent Developments", in *Proceedings of 21st Tax Conf.* 430 (Can. Tax Foundation, 1968).

Silver, S., "Surplus Stripping: A Practitioner's View" (1974) 22 Can. Tax J. 430.

Sossin, Lorne, "Welfare State Crime in Canada: The Politics of Tax Evasion in the 1980s" (1992) 12 Windsor Y.B. Access Justice 98.

Strother, Robert C., "Avoidance and Evasion: The World Beyond Stubart", in *Proceedings of 36th Tax Conf.* 89 (Can. Tax Foundation, 1984).

"Tax and Social Security Abuse: Panel Discussion" (1980) 2 Can. Taxation 109.

Thornsteinsson, P.M., "Precautionary Considerations on Tax Haven Companies" (1966) 2 UBC Law Rev. 491.

Vercheres, B., "Tax Havens: Myth or Reality", (1969) RJT 23.

Wise, Richard M., "Tax Evasion and Mens Rea in Forensic Accounting", (1990) Meredith Mem. Lectures 405.

"With Cap in Hand" (June/July 1988) 16:2 Can. Tax News 9.

3. *Motive*

4. *Sham Transactions (998)*

Bowman, S. W., "Willful Evasion — Nature of Offence — Relevance of Sham Arguments — Use of Offshore Companies [Case Comment: *R. v. Redpath Industries Ltd.*, [1984] C.T.C. 483, 84 D.T.C. 6349 (Que. S.C.)]" (1984) 32 Can. Tax J. 906.

Creighton, G.D., "*Stubart Investments Ltd. v. The Queen*, [1984] C.T.C. 294, 84 D.T.C. 6305" (1984) 1 Business and Law 42.

Edwards, Stanley E., "Planning After the Stubart Decision", in *Proceedings of 36th Tax Conf.* 78 (Can. Tax Foundation, 1984).

Freisen, R.A. and D.Y. Timbrell, "Shams and Simulacra II — The Capital Gains Aspect" (1979) 27 Can. Tax J. 135.

Harris, E.C., "Intercompany Cross-Border Transactions: A Growing Concern for Revenue Canada/Les opérations intersociétés par delà les frontières inquiétent Revenue Canada" (1985) 118:6 CA Magazine 22.

McDonnell, Thomas E. "Developments Relating to Sham, Benefits and Business Purpose", in *Proceedings of 29th Tax Conf.* 89 (Can. Tax Foundation, 1977).

Nichols, Neil W., "Tax Planning After Stubart: Consolidated Bathurst and Other Interpretations", in *Proceedings of 37th Tax Conf.* 39:1 (Can. Tax Foundation, 1985).

Roy, J.P., "L'interprétation des lois fiscales dans la foulée de l'arrêt Stubart" (1986) 9 RPFS 207.

Stanley, Edward, "Planning After the Stubart Decision", in *Proceedings of 36th Tax Conf.* 78 (Can. Tax Foundation, 1984).

Timbrell, D.Y., "Of Shams and Simulacra" (1973) 21 Can. Tax J. 529.

Wilkie, "The Stubart Decision: An Act of Reason", in *Can. Tax Letter* (1985), No. 351 (De Boo, 1985).

Yakisch, M.M., "Captive Insurance Company — *Stubart Investments Ltd.* Applied [Case Comment: *Consolidated Bathurst Ltd. v. R.*, [1985] 1 C.T.C. 142 (Fed. TD)]" (1985) 33 Can. Tax. J. 333.

5. Ineffectual Transactions

6. Substance vs. Form

Baille, W.J., "Form or Substance — Where Are We?" (1980) 18 Alta. L. Rev. 237.

III. — The General Anti-Avoidance Rule

1. Background

Allgood and Ahmed, "The Modified General Anti-Avoidance Rule", in *Recent Tax Changes Including the Tax Reform Proposals: Proceedings of a Conference of the Law Society of Upper Canada and the Canadian Bar Association — Ontario* (Toronto: Department of Education, Law Society of Upper Canada and Canadian Bar Association — Ontario, 1988) C-1.

Ahmed, Firoz, "Certain Guesses as to the Application of GAAR", in *Ontario Tax Conf.* Tab 13 (Toronto: Canadian Tax Foundation, 1988).

"Anti-Avoidance" (1987) 15:6 Can. Tax News 100.

"Anti-Avoidance Proposal Goes Too Far" (1987) 9:16 Can. Taxpayer 121.

"Anti-Avoidance Remains Central Theme of Tax Legislation" (1988) 10:9 Can. Taxpayer 65.

"Anti-Avoidance Rule Guidelines" (1988) 16:4 Can. Tax News 46.

"Anti-Avoidance Rules" (1987) 15:2 Can. Tax News 22.

Arnold, Brian J. and James R. Wilson, "The General Anti-Avoidance Rule — Part I" (1988) 36 Can. Tax J. 829.

Arnold, Brian J. and James R. Wilson, "The General Anti-Avoidance Rule — Part II" (1988) 36 Can. Tax J. 1123.

Arnold, Brian J. and James R. Wilson, "The General Anti-Avoidance Rule — Part III" (1988) 36 Can. Tax J. 1369.

Birnie, David A.G., "Living with GAAR: The Effect on Tax Practice", *Corporate Management Tax Conf.* 5:1 (Can. Tax Foundation, 1988).

Boyle, Patrick, et al., "The GAAR [general anti-avoidance rule] committee: myth and reality" (2002) Can. Tax Found. 10:1–10:20.

Brown, Robert D., "Revenue Canada's New View of Tax Avoidance Activities", in *Proceedings of 44th Tax Conf.* 5:2 (Can. Tax Found., 1992).

Brown, Robert D., et. al., "GAAR and Tax Practice: More Questions Than Answers", in *Proceedings of 41st Tax Conf.* 11:1 (Can. Tax Foundation, 1989).

CICA, *General Anti-Avoidance Rules*, August 1989.

Clow, John M., "The Great GAAR Guessing Game" (1989) 63 CMA 58.

Colley, Geoffrey M., "Anti-Avoidance Rules Under Tax Reform Too Broad" (1987) 120 CA Magazine 44.

Colley, Geoffrey M., "What You See is What You Get: Or Is It? (New Anti-Avoidance Income Tax Provisions)" (1989) 122:1 CA Magazine 50.

Dodge, David A., "Tax Reform and the Anti-Avoidance Proposal", in *B.C. Tax Conf.* Tab 4 (Can. Tax Foundation, 1987).

Fryers, Clifford H., "Tax Planning and the New General Anti-Avoidance Rule", in *Prairie Provinces Tax Conf.* Tab 10 (Can. Tax Foundation, 1989).

Fuke, J.M., "Can Tax Advisers Successfully Serve Two Masters? Les conseillers fiscaux peuvent-ils servir deux maîtres à la fois?" (1985) 118:3 CA Magazine 32.

"GAAR Circular Released" (1982) 10:21 Can. Taxpayer 161.

"GAAR Supplement Issued" (1990) 12:17 Can. Taxpayer 130.

"General Anti-Avoidance Provisions Promised" (1987) 9:11 Can. Taxpayer 82.

"General Anti-Avoidance Rule", *Can. Tax Handbook* 1988-89 (Toronto: Carswell, 1989) at 8.

"General Anti-Avoidance Rule" (1988) 17:2 Tax Profile 113.

Glover, Paul, "The General Anti-Avoidance Provisions" (September 1988) 62 CMA Magazine 44.

Goodman, W.D., "What has Canada to Gain from the Proposed General Anti-Avoidance Rule?", *Insight: Tax Reform 1987 — The New Regime*, L'hotel (Toronto), July 22, 1987, Tab VI.

Hiltz, Michael, "Section 245(1) of the ITA", in *Proceedings of 40th Tax Conf.* 7:1 (Can. Tax Foundation, 1988).

Hobson, William J.A., "New Guidelines from the Supreme Court of Canada and Other Canadian Courts: A Broad Interpretation of Subsection 245(1), the Interpretation Test, and Clearer Lines of Demarcation for Tax Avoidance and Tax Evasion", in *Proceedings of 36th Tax Conf.* 148 (Can. Tax Foundation, 1984).

Income Tax Technical News, No. 22, (January 11, 2002).

"International Tax Planning — Stubart: What the Courts did Next" (1987) 35 Can. Tax J. 155.

Kellough, H.J., "A Discussion of the White Paper's Proposed General Anti-Avoidance Rule", in *B.C. Tax Conf.* Tab 6 (Can. Tax Foundation, 1987).

Kellough, Howard J., "A Review and Analysis of the Redrafted General Anti-Avoidance Rule" (1988) 36 Can. Tax J. 23.

Kellough, H.J., "The Pre White Paper Anti-Avoidance Regime", *Insight: Tax Reform 1987 — The New Regime*, L'hotel (Toronto), July 22, 1987, Tab VII.

Krishna, Vern, "GAAR: The Ultimate Tax Avoidance Weapon" (1988) 2:16 Can. Current Tax C-75.

Krishna, Vern, "General Anti-Avoidance Rule: An Attempt to Control Tax Abuses" (1988) CGA Magazine 16.

Lavrey, J., Michael and Karen Watson, "Is It or Is It Not, Canadian Tax Reform?" (1987) 3 The Journal of Strategy in Int'l. Taxation 264.

Lindsay, Robert F., "The General Anti-Avoidance Rule: Points to Consider", in *Proceedings of 40th Tax Conf.* 5:1 (Can. Tax Foundation, 1989).

McDonnell, Thomas E., "Legislative Anti-Avoidance: The Interaction of the New General Rule and Representative Specific Rules", in *Proceedings of 40th Tax Conf.* 6:1 (Can. Tax Foundation, 1988).

McDonnell, Thomas E. and R.B. Thomas, "GAAR and Pre-September 13, 1988 Tax Planning: Part 2 — The Commodity Straddles Issues" (1989) 37 Can. Tax J. 728.

Morgan, Vivien, "Stubart: What the Courts did Next" (1987) 35 Can. Tax J. 155.

Nitikman, Joel, "Is GAAR Void for Vagueness?" (1989) 37 Can. Tax J. 1409.

"No, We're Not Happy", 9:14 Can. Taxpayer 101.

Sasseville, J., "Implementation of the Anti-Avoidance Rule", *Corporate Management Tax Conf.* 4:1 (Can. Tax Foundation, 1988).

Sasseville, J., "La règle générale anti-évitement" (1988) 10 RPFS 221.

Schmitz, Cristin, "Lawyers Find Flaws with Proposed Tax Avoidance Rule" (July 17, 1987) 17:2 Lawyers Weekly 12.

Stikeman, Elliott, *Tax Reform '87: An Analysis* (Toronto: De Boo, July 17, 1987).

Stikeman, H., "Tax Reform '87 — An Analysis", (July 17, 1987) *Can. Tax Service* 231.

Sturrock, Craig, C., "Tax Reform and the Anti-Avoidance Proposals", in *B.C. Tax Conf.* Tab 7 (Can. Tax Foundation, 1987).

"Tax Legislation: The Latest Media Event", *Can. Tax Letter* (February 27, 1987) 1.

"Tax Reform", *Explanatory Notes for April 13th Draft Income Tax Amendments Special Release* (April 21, 1988) 240.

"Tax Reform '87 — An Analysis" (July 9, 1987) Can. Tax Reports 106.

"Tax Reform — Some Comments" (August/September 1988) 16:3 Can. Tax News 31.

Technical Notes, 245(4), (December 2004).

"The Proposed Anti-Avoidance Provision: Mark II" (1988) 10:2 Can. Taxpayer 9.

Tilak, Hemant & Matthew Peters, "GAAR [general anti-avoidance rule] revisited by the Federal Court of Appeal" (2004) 14 Can. Current Tax 61–65.

Watson, Russ, "GAAR (General Anti-avoidance Rule)" (1992) 3. Can. Current Tax P51.

"Whither GAAR?" (1990) 12:9 Can. Taxpayer 70.

World According to GAAR (Toronto: Canadian Bar Association — Ontario, Continuing Legal Education, 1990).

2. Purpose

3. The Charging Provision

4. Avoidance Transactions

Armstrong, George H., *Hart System of Effective Tax Avoidance* (Winnipeg: A & A Pub., 1990).

Fraser, Rodney, "Tax-Planning Strategies in the World According to GAAR", (January 9, 1989) *Financial Times* 17.

Gourlay, J.L., "Enforcement Provisions: Offences and Tax Avoidance" (1968) Pitblado Lect. 110.

Huggett, Donald R., "Tax Avoidance — Recent Developments", in *Proceedings of 21st Tax Conf.* 452 (Can. Tax Foundation, 1968).

International Fiscal Association, "Seminar on Recent International Developments to Counter Tax Avoidance and Evasion: Texts of Seminar Papers Presented February 18, 1982" (Don Mills, Ontario: Richard De Boo, 1982).

Labrie, F.E., "Fraudulent Tax Transactions" (1964) 3 Western L. Rev. 48.

Labrie, F.E., "The Role of the Courts in Tax Avoidance" (1955) 3 Can. Tax. J. 326; (1955-56) 11 UTLJ 128.

Lawlor, William R.G., "Surplus Stripping and Other Planning Opportunities With the New $500,000 Capital Gains Exemption", in *Proceedings of 37th Tax. Conf.* 8:1 (Can. Tax Foundation, 1985).

Lefebvre, Wilfred, "Tax Avoidance: An Update", (1990) Meredith Mem. Lectures 389.

McDonnell, T.E., "Tax Avoidance: Section 137(2) as a Charging Section" (1968) 16 Can. Tax. J. 281.

Ward, David A. "Tax Avoidance and Compliance", *Insight: Tax Reform 1987 — The New Regime*, L'hotel (Toronto), July 22, 1987, Tab VIII.

Ward, David A., "Tax Avoidance: Judicial and Legislative Approaches in Other Jurisdictions", in *Proceedings of 39th Tax Conf.* 45:1 (Can. Tax Foundation, 1987).

Ward, David A., "The Judicial Approach to Tax Avoidance", in *Proceedings of 25th Tax Conf.* 408 (Can. Tax Foundation, 1973).

5. Purpose of Transaction

Arnold, Brian J., "In Praise of the Business Purpose Test", in *Proceedings of 39th Tax Conf.* 10:1 (Can. Tax Foundation, 1987).

Gideon, Kenneth W., and Ruth E. Kent, "Mrs. Gregory's Northern Tour: Canadian Proposals to Adopt the Business Purpose Rule and the Step Transaction Doctrine", in *Proceedings of 39th Tax Conf.* 7:1 (Can. Tax Foundation, 1987).

Hanly, K.S.M., "Management Companies — Business Purpose Test [Case Comment: *R. v. Parsons*, [1984] C.T.C. 354, 84 D.T.C. 6447; *R. v. Vivian* (1984), 84 D.T.C. 6452 (Fed. CA)" (1984) 32 Can. Tax J. 891.

Krishna, Vern, "The Demise of the Business Purpose Test?" (1984) 1 Can. Current Tax C-43.

Lemon, K.W., "Artificial Transactions: Business Purpose" (1978) 43 Bus. Q. 4:5.

McDonnell, Thomas E., and R.B. Thomas, "The Supreme Court and Business Purpose: Is There Life After Stubart [*Stubart Investments Ltd. v. The Queen*, 84 D.T.C. 6305]?" (1984) 32 Can. Tax. J. 853.

McGregor, G., "Dividend Stripping: The Business Purpose Test" (1968) 16 Can. Tax J. 16.

McGregor, G., "The Business Purpose Test" (1984) 6 Can. Taxpayer 5.

Nathanson, David C., "General Anti-Avoidance Rule and Tax Reform: The Business Purpose Test — Proposed Section 245" Paper Presented at Insight Conference, November 14, 1988.

O'Keefe, M.J., "The Business Purpose Test — Who Needs It?" (1977) 25 Can. Tax J. 139.

Stikeman, H., "Is the Business Purpose Test Dead? Its Life After Stubart" (1985) Cambridge Lect. 197.

Thomas, R.B., "The Business Purpose Test — Not in Canada, Thank You! (Case Comment) *Stubart Investments Ltd. v. R.*, [1984] C.T.C. 294 (SCC)", 32 Can. Tax. J. 529.

Timbrell, D.Y, "Planning after the Stubart Decision: The Business Purpose Test", in *Proceedings of 36th Tax Conf.* 89 (Can. Tax Foundation, 1984).

Ward, David A. and Maurice C. Cullity, "Abuse of Rights and the Business Purpose Test as Applied to Taxing Statutes" (1981) 29 Can. Tax J. 451.

Ware, "The Business Purpose Test and Sham Transactions", in *Proceedings of 28th Tax Conf.* 602 (Can. Tax Foundation, 1976).

6. Immunity from GAAR

7. Determining the Policy of the Statute

Cherneski, Valerie-Ann, "GAAR [general anti-avoidance rule] survives Charter challenge" (2002) 12 Can. Current Tax 105–110.

8. Extrinsic Evidence

9. Redetermination of Tax Liability

10. Third Parties

IV. — Series of Transactions

1. General Comment

Adams, L.D., "Craven v. White: U.K. Step-Transaction Doctrine Evolves — Canadian Planners Beware" (1988) 2:13 Can. Current Tax C-57.

Forgie, Jeremy, "Series of Acquisitions and Dispositions Found not to Constitute Tax Avoidance" (1993) 1 RRSP Plan. 13.

Hiltz, Michael, "Subsection 247(1) and the 1985 Amendments to the *Income Tax Act*", in *Proceedings of 39th Tax Conf.* 7:1 (Can. Tax Foundation, 1987).

Krishna, Vern, "Step Transactions and the General Anti-Avoidance Rule — Part I" (July 1990) 24 CGA Magazine 34.

Krishna, Vern, "Step Transactions and the General Anti-Avoidance Rule — Part II" (August 1990) 24 CGA Magazine 25.

Krishna, Vern, "Step Transactions: An Emerging Doctrine or an Extension of the Business Purpose Test?" (1984) 1 Can. Current Tax C-15.

Newcombe, Janet, "Section 84.1 [of the *Income Tax Act*] and GAAR [general anti-avoidance rule]" (2005) 2 T. Hyperion No. 5, 1(3).

Tiley, John, "Series Transactions" in *Proceedings of 40th Tax Conf.* 8:1 (Can. Tax Foundation, 1988).

2. The Common Law

Colden, Julie A., "Recent GAAR [general anti-avoidance rule] jurisprudence" (2001) 11 Can. Current Tax 97–104.

Crerar, David, "Interpretations of GAAR: Before and Beyond McNichol and RMM" (1997) 23 Queen's L.J. 231.

Meredith, Mark, "GAAR in Quotes: Section 245 Cases from the Past 12 Months", in *Report of Proceedings of the Fifty-Fifth Tax Conference*, 2003 Conference Report (Toronto: Canadian Tax Foundation, 2003), 2:1–19.

Richards, Gabrielle, M.R., "OSFC Holdings Limited: first GAAR [general anti-avoidance rule] appeal" (2001) 12 Can. Current Tax No. 1, 6–10.

Shafer, J., "*Furniss v. Dawson*, [1984] 1 All ER 530" (1984) Inc. Tax Aspects 47.

Stikeman, H., "*Furniss v. Dawson*: The Canadian Approach" (1986) 7 Fiscal Studies 82.

Thomas, Richard, "The Focus of GAAR [general anti-avoidance rule] is sharpened" (2000) 48 Can. Tax J. 1861–1868.

V. — Administration

1. Assessments

Bowman, Stephen W., "Collections under the *Income Tax Act*" in *Proceedings of 42nd Tax Conf.* 22:1 (Can. Tax Found., 1990).

Boyd, C.W., "The Enforcement of Tax Compliance: Some Theoretical Issues" (1986) 34 Can. Tax J. 588.

Cameron, D.B., "Tax Evasion by Non-payment of Assessments", (1969) Pitbaldo Lect. 101.

Canada Department of Finance, "Explanatory Notes to Legislation Relating to Income Tax", in *Can. Tax Reports*, Special Report No. 851, extra ed. (Don Mills, Ont.: CCH Canadian, June 30, 1988) 315.

Canada Department of Finance, "Supplementary Information Relating to Tax Reform Measures" (Ottawa: The Department, December 16, 1987).

Canada Department of Finance, "Tax Reform 1987: Income Tax Reform" (Ottawa: the Department, June 18, 1987).

Canada Department of Finance, "Tax Reform 1987: Proposed Legislative and Regulatory Amendments" (Ottawa: the Department, December 16, 1987).

Canada, House of Commons, "The Standing Committee on Finance and Economic Affairs Report of the White Paper on Tax Reform (Stage I)" (Ottawa: Queen's Printer, November 1987).

Canada, "Report of the Royal Commission on Taxation", Vol. 3 (Ottawa: Queen's Printer, 1966), 537.

Harris, D.C., "Nonfiling and Underreporting of Income Taxes in the United States" (1980) 2 Can. Taxation 88.

Information Circular 70-6R5, "Advance Income Tax Rulings", May 17, 2002.

Information Circular 88-2, "General Anti-Avoidance Rule: Section 245 of the *Income Tax Act*", October 21, 1988.

Jones, McShane Devlin, "Reference to GAAR [general anti-avoidance rule] on notice of assessment" (2002) 50 Can. Tax J. 1141–1146.

Martin, Roch, "Recent Income Tax Developments" (2002) 40 Alta. L. Rev. 19–82.

Nathanson, David C., "The Reach for Information", in *Proceedings of 30th Tax Conf.* 299 (Can. Tax Foundation, 1978).

Patrick Boyle, Sharon Gulliver, Jerry Lalonde, Anne-Marie Levesque, and Paul Lynch, "The GAAR Committee: Myth and Reality" 2002 Conference Report, Report of Proceedings of the Fifty-Fourth Tax Conference (Toronto: Canadian Tax Foundation, 2002), 10:1–20.

Pitfield, I.H., "Search and Seizure and the *Income Tax Act*" (1981) 29 Can. Tax J. 30.

Pitfield, I. H., "Dealing with Revenue Canada: A Lawyer's Perspective", in *Report of Proceedings of the Forty-Fifth Tax Conference*, 1993 Conference Report (Toronto: Canadian Tax Foundation, 1994) 10:1–15.

Robert, J.L. Read, "The Income Tax Advance Rulings Service", in *Report of Proceedings of the Forty-Fourth Tax Conference*, 1992 Conference Report (Toronto: Canadian Tax Foundation, 1993), 6:1–26.

Roy, Robert, "The Tax Avoidance Program", in *Report of Proceedings of the Forty-Fifth Tax Conference*, 1993 Conference Report (Toronto: Canadian Tax Foundation, 1994), 7:1–16.

Stacey, John A., "Revenue Canada's Administration of the General Anti-Avoidance rule", in *Proceedings of 42nd Tax Conf.* 4:2 (Can. Tax Foundation, 1990).

Wayne Adams, "The General Anti-Avoidance Rule (GAAR) Committee", in *Report of Proceedings of the Forty-Seventh Tax Conference*, 1995 Conference Report (Toronto: Canadian Tax Foundation, 1996), 54:1–9.

2. Request for Adjustment

3. Administrative Structure

Bergh, Collin S., "Handling Tax Fraud Cases" (1963) 82 Can. Chart. Acc. 54.

Dymond, A. Christopher, Robert J. Reid, and Michael A. Cutran, *Income Tax Administration, Avoidance and Evasion* (Toronto: Butterworths, 1981).

VI. — Administrative Interpretation

Couzin, Robert, "Subsection 245(3): A Framework", in *Report of Proceedings of the Forty-Ninth Tax Conference*, 1997 Conference Report (Toronto: Canadian Tax Foundation, 1997), 4:1–15.

VII. — Interpretations and Rulings

1. Form of Business Organization

Haney, Mary-Ann, "GAAR [general anti-avoidance rule and the large corporations tax: the right result for the wrong reasons?" (2002) 50 Can. Tax J. 2098–2102.

Interpretation Bulletin IT-3007, "General Anti-Avoidance Rule and Inter-Provincial Anti-Avoidance", (October 2001).

Noble, W.R., "Some Tax Avoidance Aspects of Non-Resident Trusts" (1979) 5 EJQ 81.

Robison, I. Michael, "Personal Services Corporations: New Opportunities and Old Concerns", in *Corporate Management Tax Conf.* 165 (Can. Tax Foundation, 1985).

Rossiter, J., "The Application of Part 13 Non-Resident Withholding Tax to Deemed Payments" (1986) 34 Can. Tax J. 511.

2. Consolidation of Profits and Losses in a Corporate Group

Corn, G., "Disposition of Economic Interests and Attribution of Income on Issuance of Treasury Shares" (1991) 3 Can. Current Tax J-101.

Canada, Department of Finance, "Tax Changes Proposed for Mutual Fund Reorganizations", *Release* no. 94-068, July 21, 1994.

3. Purifying a Corporation

Krishna, Vern, "GAAR and the Purification of Corporations for the Capital Gains Exemption (Part I)" (1993) 4 Can. Current Tax A7.

4. Services Rendered to a Corporation

5. Conversion of Salary into Capital Gain

Templeton, Wendy, "Anti-Avoidance and the Capital Gains Exemption" (1986) 34 Can. Tax J. 203.

Templeton, Wendy, "Anti-Avoidance and the Capital Gains Exemption: Part Two" (1986) 34 Can. Tax J. 446.

6. Interest Expense

7. Section 85 Rollover to Related Corporations

Interpretation Bulletin IT-291R2, "Transfer of Property to a Corporation under Subsection 85(1)", (September 1994).

Tax Legislation Bulletin 93-3, "Inter-Provincial Asset Transfers", (December 2006).

8. Estate Freezing

CRA Views, Ruling 9903163, "Stock option transfer to trust, general anti-avoidance rule", (1999).

Cullity, M.C., "Trusts and Estates" (1981) Can. Taxation 773.

Fraser, Rodney, "You Can Still Do the Splits, But..." (1989) Financial Times 19.

Jack, Sandra E., "Neuman v. M.N.R.: The Supreme Court Allows Income Splitting" (1999) 26 Man. L.J. 257–266.

Hartkorn, D.N., "Income Splitting: the New Rules" (1985) 33 Can. Tax J. 1226.

McDonnell, T.E., "Tax Avoidance: Splitting Decision" (1991) 39 Can. Tax J. 637.

Zylberger, Frank, "GAAR and Estate Planning", in Proceedings of 42nd Tax Conf. 38:1 (Can. Tax Foundation, 1990).

9. Avoidance of Part IV Tax on Taxable Dividends

Jaques, Harold, "A Practical Overview of GAAR and the Parts IV.1 and VI.1 Dividend Taxes", in Prairie Provinces Tax Conf. Tab 13 (Can. Tax Foundation, 1988).

CRA Views, Tech Interp (internal) 2003-0029717, "Stock dividends", (August 12, 2003).

10. Change of Fiscal Periods

11. Indirect Transfer of Land Inventory

Goodman, W.D., "The Impact of Tax Reform on Estate Planning" (1988) 8 Estates and Trusts Quarterly 281.

12. Indirect Disposition of Property Through a Partnership

Sherman, H.A., "How to Kill a Mouse With an Elephant Gun, or, Foreign Accrual Property Income: Some Problem Areas" (1972) 20 Can. Tax J. 397.

13. Conversion of Income Gains into Dividends

14. Reserves for Future Proceeds

15. Conversion of Dividend Income into Capital Gains

Boutlebee, J.A., "Minimizing the Taxation Effects of Dividends", in Proceedings of 37th Tax Conf. 7:1 (Can. Tax Foundation, 1985).

CRA Views, 9525030, "Surplus strips," (October 12, 1995).

Australia

I. — General Comment

Burgess, P., "Lessons from the Bottom of the Harbour" (1984) NZLJ 16.

Cooper, Graeme S., Richard E. Krever and Richard J. Vann, *Income Taxation: Commentary and Materials* (Sydney: The Law Book Company, 1989).

Krever, Richard, ed., *Australian Taxation: Principles and Practice*, (Melbourne: Longman, 1987).

Krever, Richard E., "Tax Avoidance and Tax Reform: Who's to Blame and Who's to Repair?" (September 1987) 14 Brief 22.

Reicher, H. "Taxation" (1982) 10 Aust. Bus. Rev. 68.

II. — Judicial Doctrines

1. Taxpayers' Rights

Fayle, R.D., "Tax Planning and Current Thinking" (1983) 17 Tax. in Aust. 704.

Grantham, R.B., "John v. FCT: A New Direction in the Judicial Response to Tax Avoidance" (1989) 33:7 NZ Current Tax 161.

2. Evasion, Avoidance and Mitigation

Dalton, D.J., "Avoidance of Taxation: Section 260 and the *Income Tax Assessment Act*", 9 MULR 95.

Edstein, John V., "Superannuation: Anti-Avoidance Provisions and Judicial Approaches" (1989) 23 Tax. in Aust. 524.

Ferrers, A.O., "Tax Avoidance — What's in a Name?" (1982) NZLJ 412.

Forsyth, N.H.M., "Morality and Avoidance", 7 Brief 74–79, 82–87.

Grantham, R.B., "Fiscal Nullity Reconsidered" (1988) NZLJ 311.

Grantham, R.B., "John v. FCT: A New Direction in the Judicial Response to Tax Avoidance" (1989) 33:7 NZ Current Tax 161.

Greenwood, J.M., "Taxation Notes: New Zealand — Avoidance of Tax [*Haliwell v. C.I.R.* (1977), 3 NZTC 61208]" 30 Chartered Sec. 38.

Grbich, Y., "Problems of Tax Avoidance in Australia", *Taxation Issues of the 1980's* (Australian Tax Research Foundation: Sydney, 1983) 413.

Grbich, Y., "Section 260 Re-Examined: Posing Critical Questions About Tax Avoidance" (1975) 1 UNSWLJ 211.

Guild, W.G., "Fiscal Nullities and the Overruling of Curran's Case", (1989) AT 36017.

Harley, G.J., "Structural Inequities and Concepts of Tax Avoidance" (1983) 13 Victoria University of Wellington L. Rev. 38.

"The House of Lords and Tax Avoidance [*W.T. Ramsey Ltd. v. I.R.C.*, [1981] 2 WLR 449]" (1981) 55 ALJ 315.

"I Can Get It For You Tax Free! — The Ethics of Tax Avoidance", 11 Q. Law Soc. J. 411.

Kinross, Jeremy, "Applicability of 'Fiscal Nullity' Doctrine" (March 1988) CLQ 7.

Lucy Robb, "With all My Wordly Goods I Thee Endow: A Review of the Attorney-General's Proposed Reform of Bankruptcy Law" (September 2003) 25 Sydney L. Rev. 361 (QL).

MacLean, D.M., "Recent Developments in Fiscal Nullity" (1987) 16 Aust. Tax Rev. 166.

Maher, L.W., "Lawyers' Ethics and Tax Avoidance", 56 LIJ 515.

Pane, Tony, "The Relevance of Fiscal Nullity After John's Case" (1989) 1 J. Aust. Tax 34.

Prebble, J., "Tax Avoidance Arrangements that Comply With Section 104, *Income Tax Act 1976*", 8 NZULR 70.

Reicher, H., "Taxation [Tax Avoidance Schemes and the New Legislation]", 6 Aust. Bus. Rev. 177.

Reicher, H., "Tax Avoidance in 1977: The Decline and Fall of Section 260" (1978) 12 Tax. in Aust. 680.

Richardson, I.L.M., "Appellate Court Responsibilities and Tax Avoidance", 2:1 ATF 3.

Richard Krever, "Taming Complexity in Australian Income Tax" 25 Sydney L. Rev. 467 (QL).

Spry, I.C.F., "Fiscal Nullity in Australia" (1984) 13 Aust. Tax Rev. 150.

Spry, I.C.F., "The Use of Tax Shelters" (1981) 10 Aust. Tax Rev. 4.

Stone, Phillipa, and K. Powrie, "Taxation: The Fiscal Nullity Doctrine" (1989) 63 ALJ 622.

Slater, A.H., "A Ruse by Any Other Name Would Smell as Sweet [*FC of T. v. K. Porter & Co. Pty. Ltd.*]" (1974) 45:1 Chartered Acc. 30-1.

Spry, I.C.F., *"Arrangements for the Avoidance of Taxation* (Melbourne: Law Book Co., 1971).

Spry, I.C.F., "Arrangements for the Avoidance of Taxation", 46 LIJ 344-345.

Trebilcock, M.J., "Arrangement for the Avoidance of Taxation", 4 Adelaide L.R. 491.

Voumard, L.C., "Arrangement for the Avoidance of Taxation", 10 Law Soc. J. 131.

Wallschutzky, I., "Results of a Survey on Some Aspects of Tax Avoidance" (1985) 14 Aust. Tax Rev. 48.

Wallschutzky, I., "Towards a Definition of the Term Tax Avoidance" (1985) 14 Aust. Tax Rev. 48.

3. Motive

4. Sham Transactions

Guild, W.G., "Shams, Fiscal Nullities and Section 260 of the *Income Tax Assessment Act 1936* (Cth)", (1985) AT 36036.

Jenkin, P.J.H., "Tax Avoidance, Politics and Privy Councillors or: How Does One Mitigate the *Challenge* Decision?" (1988) NZLJ 305.

5. Ineffectual Transactions

6. Substance vs. Form

III. — The General Anti-Avoidance Rule

1. Background

Avery Jones, "Nothing Either Good or Bad, But Thinking Makes It So — The Mental Element in Anti-Avoidance Legislation — I", (1983) 1 British Tax Rev. 9.

Avery Jones, "Nothing Either Good or Bad, But Thinking Makes It So — The Mental Element in Anti-Avoidance Legislation — II", (1983) 2 British Tax Rev. 113.

Baxt, R., "The New Anti-Avoidance Provisions" (1981) 9 Aust. Bus. Rev. 284.

Grbich, Y., "Anti-Avoidance Discretions: The Continuing Battle to Control Tax Avoidance", 4 UNSWLJ 17.

Halkyard, Andrew, "Hong Kong: A Tax Haven Enacts Anti-Avoidance Legislation" (1986) 15 Aust. Tax Rev. 170.

Krever, Richard, "Tax Reform in Australia: Base-Broadening Down Under" (1986) 34 Can. Tax. J. 346.

Molloy, A.P., "Fiscal Fantasy" (1974) NZLJ 297.

New Zealand, Commissioner of Inland Revenue, "Policy Statement on Sec. 99" (June 1990) 44 Bull. Int'l. Fisc. Doc. 288.

Sweeney, C.A., ed., "Revenue Note" (1988) 62 ALJ 470.

Sweeney, C.A., ed., "Revenue Note — Revised Legislative Provisions Against Avoidance of Income Tax" (1981) 55 ALJ 887.

Sweeney, C.A., ed., "Revenue Note" (1985) 59 ALJ 346.

Sweeney, C.A., ed., "Revenue Note" (1987) 61 ALJ 148.

"Tax Avoidance Reform?", (January 1980) 17 Reform 107.

"Tax Avoidance: The Pursuit of Scapegoats" (1987) 16 Aust. Tax Rev. 3.

Wallace, E.W., "Government Moves on Stamp Duty Avoidance — *Stamp Duties Amendment Act 1980*", 3:1 Law Soc. Bull. 1.

Wallace, E.W., "Stamp Duty Amendments — Proposed Abolition of Death Duty and Sixth Schedule Rates, Anti-Avoidance" (1981) 19 Law Soc. J. 223.

2. Purpose (1006)

Davies, D.J., "'Purpose' in Section 26(A) and in Section 260" (1977) 6 Aust. Tax Rev. 32.

MacDonald, J.H.S., "The Principle of Certainty" 9:3 Brief 10.

3. The Charging Provision

4. Avoidance Transactions

5. Purpose of Transaction

6. Immunity from GAAR

7. Determining the Policy of the Statute

> Spry, I.C.F, "A Recent Privy Council Decision on Tax Avoidance" (1975) 4 Aust. Tax Rev. 220.

8. Extrinsic Evidence

9. Redetermination of Tax Liability

10. Third Parties

IV. — Series of Transactions

1. General

2. Common Law

> Briggs, Peter, "John v. Federal Commissioner of Taxation: The Uneasy Death of Curran (1989) ATC 1" (March 1990) 12 Syd. L.R. 584.
>
> Cooke, M.I., "Practical Issues Arising From the Gulland, Watson and Pincus Cases" (1986) 20 Tax. in Aust. 680.
>
> Dabner, Justin, "Tax Planning for Professional People — What Remains After the Unholy Trinity" (1987) 21 Tax. in Aust. 568.
>
> "Dr. Gulland, Pincus and Watson" (January 22, 1986) 7 Leg. Rep. 1.
>
> Ferrers, A.O., "Fiscal Nullity in the Nether World: The *Ramsay* Doctrine in Australia" (1988) NZLJ 315.
>
> *"The Gregrhon Investments Pty. Ltd. Appeal"* (1988) 17 Aust. Tax Rev. 1.
>
> Hambly, J.C., "The High Court's Decision in John's Case" (1989) 18 Aust. Tax Rev. 69 at 72.
>
> Mannix, E.F., "*Ramsay* in Australia", [1984] AT 36017.
>
> Krever, Richard, "*Furniss v. Dawson* — Tax Jurisprudence Re-Enters the Real World" (1984) 18 Tax. in Aust. 1057.
>
> Myers, A.J., "Federal Court Decides for Commissioner in Gregrhon Investments Case" (1988) 1 BWT Bull. 2.
>
> Myers, A.J., "The Federal Court Decision in the Gregrhon Investments Pty. Ltd. Case" (1988) 17 Aust. Tax Rev. 4.
>
> Norman, Peter J., "Gulland, Watson and Pincus in the High Court" (1986) 20 Tax. in Aust. 639.
>
> O'Connor, R.K., "Analysis and Implications of the Gulland, Watson and Pincus Cases on s.260" (January 21, 1986) 3 BWT Bull. 16.
>
> Sweeney, C.A., ed., "Revenue Note — Curran's Case Confined to Its Own Facts" (1987) 61 ALJ 742.

3. Section 245

4. Westminster Principle

> Beattie, C.N., *"Furniss v. Dawson* — The *Duke of Westminster* Doctrine and Lord Tomlin's Dictum" (March 2, 1984) 128 Solic. J. 139.
> Ferrers, A.O.,"Fair is Foul and Foul is Fair" (1989) 18 Aust. Tax Rev. 93.
> Russell, D.G., "Bury the Great Duke" (1984) 19 Tax. in Aust. 250.

V. — Administration

1. Assessments

2. Request for Adjustment

3. Administrative Structure

> Binh Tran-Nam, "Tax Reform and Tax Simplification: Some Conceptual Issues and a Preliminary Assessment" (September 1999) 21 Sydney L. Rev. 500 (QL).

VI. — Administrative Interpretation

1. Discretionary Power

> McKay, L., "Section 108 and the Issue of Legislative Property" (1976) NZLJ 238.
> McLaughlin, D.W., "Section 108: Further Problems for the Commissioner", 5 NZULR 72.

2. Purposive Approach

3. Avoidance Transactions

VII. — Interpretations and Rulings

1. Form of Business Organization

> Azzi, John, "Assignments of Partnership Income" (1989) 18 Aust. Tax Rev. 262 at 268.
> "Editorial" (1986) 14 Aust. Business Law Rep. 61.

2. Consolidation of Profits and Losses in a Corporate Group

3. Purifying a Corporation (1054)

4. Services Rendered to a Corporation

5. Conversion of Salary into Capital Gain

6. Interest Expense

7. Section 85 Rollover to Related Corporations

8. Estate Freezing

A.P.M., *"Gerard v. C.I.R.*, 75 ATC 6020 [Family Trusts]" (1973) NZLJ 152.

A.P.M., *"Wheelans v. C.I.R.: Ashton v. C.I.R.*, 73 ATC 6030 [Family Trusts]" (1973) NZLJ 151.

Bassett, J.G., "Estate Plans and Arrangements to Avoid Income Tax" (1978) 9 Victoria University of Wellington L. Rev. 217.

Challoner, N.E., "Income Splitting — S. 260 and Part IVA" (September 1986) 57 Chartered Acc. 69.

O'Connor, R.K., "Income Splitting by Professionals" (1986) 20 Tax. in Aust. 87.

Richardson, Jim, "Splitting Personal Income" (1990) 60 Aust. Acc. 43.

9. Avoidance of Part IV A Tax on Taxable Dividends

Binetter, Michael T.R., "A Reflection on Part IVA" (1987) 21 Tax. in Aust. 404.

Boucher, Trevor, "Section 260/Part IVA — The Doctors' Cases (1986) 20 Tax. in Aust. 633.

Challoner, N.E., "Section 260 — How Far Will the Resurgence Extend?" (June 1985) 55 Chartered Acc. 59.

Challoner, N.E., "Section 260 Now Clarified — Or Is It?" (March 1986) 55 Chartered Acc. 64; (April 1986) 56 Chartered Acc. 57.

Challoner, N.E., "The Taxpayer: Contract, Agreement or Arrangement Within s. 260" (March 1987) 57 Chartered Acc. 65.

"Correspondence — Part IVA" (1981) 15 Tax. in Aust. 387.

Dabner, Justing, "The First Part IVA Cases and Rulings — The Worst Fears Realized" (1990) 24 Tax. in Aust. 665.

Forsyth, N.H.M., "The General Structure of Part IVA" (1981) 10 Aust. Tax Rev. 133.

Hill, D.G., "A New Interpretation of s. 260 and Its Implications for Part IVA", *Tax Institute of Australia 7th National Convention Papers* 3.

Hulme, S.E.K., "The Place of Part IVA in the *Income Tax Assessment Act*" (1981) 10 Aust. Tax Rev. 121.

MacLean, D.M., "Section 260 and Tupicoff's Case", (1985) 14 Aust. Tax Rev. 5.

Madden, Bryan, "The Revival of Section 260: Implications for Part IVA" (1985) 19 Tax. in Aust. 709.

Richardson, R.J. and M. Ferrier, "Commissioner's Views on Section 260 and Part IVA" (August/September 1986) 38 Prof. Admin. 40.

"The New Approach by the High Court on Section 260" (1986) 15 Aust. Tax Rev. 1.

Somers, T.C., "Income Tax — Anti-Avoidance Provisions New Developments in Relation to S. 260 and Part IVA of the *Income Tax Act 1936* (as amended)" (1987) 17 Q. Law Soc. J. 417.

Speed, Robin, "The High Court and Part IVA" (1986) 15 Aust. Tax Rev. 156.

Spry, I.C.F., "A Further Decision on Section 260" (1978) 7 Aust. Tax Rev. 9.

Spry, I.C.F., "Discretionary Trusts and Section 260" (1971) 1 Aust. Tax Rev. 265

Spry, I.C.F., "Recent Decisions Concerning Section 260 [*Gerard v. C.I.R.; Wheelans v. C.I.R.*]" (1973) 2 Aust. Tax Rev. 170.

Spry, I.C.F., "Section 260 and Choices Presented to Taxpayers" (1971) 1 Aust. Tax Rev. 54.

Spry, I.C.F. "Section 260 of the *Income Tax Assessment Act*" (1984) 13 Aust. Tax Rev. 236.

Sweeney, C.A., ed., "Revenue Note — Section 260 Finds New Life" (1986) 60 ALJ 302.

Sweidan, Andre, "Section 260 of the *Income Tax Assessment Act* 1936 (Cth) Vendor Shareholders" (1988) 22 Tax. in Aust. 113.

"Tax Avoidance: Is Part IVA Really Necessary?" (August 1984) 54 Aust. Acc. 566.

Trebilcock, M.J., "Section 260: A Critical Examination" (1964) 38 ALJ 237.

Voumard, L.C. "New Zealand's Section 260 [*Gerard v. C.I.R.; Wheelans v. C.I.R.*]", 47 LIJ 230.

Wallschutzky, I. "A Further Decision on Section 260" (1978) 7 Aust. Tax Rev. 79.

10. Change of Fiscal Periods

11. Indirect Transfer of Land Inventory

12. Indirect Disposition of Property Through a Partnership

13. Conversion of Income Gains into Dividends

14. Reserves for Future Proceeds

15. Conversion of Dividend Income into Capital Gains

United Kingdom

I. — General Comment

Tiley, John, *Butterworth's U.K. Tax Guide 1989-90* (8th Ed.), (London: Butterworth, 1989) 4–17, 862–900.

Tiley, John and David Collison, *Butterworth's U.K. Tax Guide 2005-06* (23rd Ed.), (London: Butterworth, 2005) 143–225.

Tiley, John and David Collison, *Butterworth's U.K. Tax Guide 2004-05* (22nd Ed.), (London: Butterworth, 2004) 147–206.

Tiley, John and David Collison, *Butterworth's U.K. Tax Guide 2001-02* (19th Ed.), (London: Butterworth, 2001) 93–144.

Tiley, John and David Collison, *Butterworth's U.K. Tax Guide 1999-00* (17th Ed.), (London: Butterworth, 1999) 57–104.

Tax Law in the Melting Pot (London: The Law Society of England and Whales, 1985).

II. — Judicial Doctrines

Butterworths Corporate Law Update, *Copyright Reed Elsevier (UK) Ltd. Corp LS 2006.89*, (February 2006).

Tiley, John, "Judicial Ant-Avoidance Doctrines: Some Problem Areas"(1988) 3 British Tax Rev. 63.

Tiley, John, "Judicial Anti-Avoidance Doctrines: The U.S. Alternatives — Part I" (1987) 5 British Tax Rev. 180.

Tiley, John, "Judicial Anti-Avoidance Doctrines: The U.S. Alternatives — Part II" (1987() 6 British Tax Rev. 220.

Tiley, John and David Collison, *Butterworth's U.K. Tax Guide 2000-01* (20th Ed.), (London: Butterworth, 2002) 115–143.

Tiley, John and David Collison, *Butterworth's U.K. Tax Guide 2000-01* (21st Ed.), (London: Butterworth, 2003) 123–152.

Wheatcroft, G.S.A., "The Attitude of the Legislature and the Courts to Tax Avoidance" (1955) 18 Modern L.R. 209.

1. Taxpayer's Rights

2. Evasion, Avoidance and Mitigation

Avery Jones, J.F., "Noting Either Good or Bad, But Thinking Makes It So — The Mental Element in Anti-Avoidance Legislation — I" (1983) 1 British Tax Rev. 9.

Avery Jones, J.F., "Noting Either Good or Bad, But Thinking Makes It So — The Mental Element in Anti-Avoidance Legislation — II" (1983) 2 British Tax Rev. 113.

"Billions written off by tax clampdown" *Estates Gazette* (December 10, 2005), Finance pg. 39.

Deane, K.D., "Law, Morality and Tax Evasion" (1984) 13:1 Anglo-Am. L. Rev. 1.

Farnsworth, A., "Legal Evasion of Taxation" (1942) 6 Modern L. Rev. 243.

Foster, Hartley, "The right amount of tax" *Legal Week* (13 October 2005) online: Legal Week <http://news@legalweek.com>.

Hamersley, M, "Nick or cheat" *The Lawyer* (3 October 2005) Pg.23.

John Fortgang, "The A–Z of Legal Absurdities" (September 2005) 155 NLJ 1330 (QL).

Millett, Peter J., "Artificial Tax Avoidance: The English and American Approaches" (1986) British Tax Rev. 327.

Morse, G.K., "New Mythology of Tax Avoidance", (1983) 47 Conv. 11.

Morse, G.K., "Tax Avoidance: Mythology as Fact", (1984) 48 Conv. 296.

Paul Jayson, "Stamping out Tax Avoidance Schemes" (September 2005) 155 NLJ 1395 (QL).

Peta Dollar and Eli Hillman, "When Virtual becomes Real" *Estates Gazette* (October 8, 2005), Professional pg. 176 (QL).

Robert Brodrick, "Practice Points: Revenue Stalks the Matrimonial Home" (July 2005) 102.27(34) LSG (QL).

Thompson, A., "Some Thoughts on Tax Avoidance" (1978) 128 New L.J. 629.

Tiley, John, "Tax Enforcement, Avoidance and Evasion" (1985) Cambridge Lect. 211.

Tiley, John and David Collison, *Butterworth's U.K. Tax Guide 2000-01* (18th Ed.), (London: Butterworth, 2000) 61–86.

3. Motive

Kay, J.A., "The Economics of Tax Avoidance" (1979) 6 British Tax. Rev. 354.
Ryan Myint, "The Pre-Owned Assets Tax — What Options are still Available?" (June 2005) 12 ITCP 67 (QL).

4. Sham Transactions

Hartley Foster, "The Right amount of Tax" *Legal Week* (October 13, 2005), (QL). *mailto:news@legalweek.com>*,
Ward, David A., et al., "The Business Purpose Test and Abuse of Rights" (1985) 2 British Tax Rev. 68.

5. Ineffectual Transactions

6. Substance vs. Form

III. — The General Anti-Avoidance Rule

1. Background

Bruce Russel, "SCC on GAAR", (2005) 2, No. 11 Tax Hyperion.
"Current Notes: Bringing Forth More Mice" (1988) 10 British Tax Rev. 401.
"Current Notes: Taking Stock of the New Approach" (1988) 6 British Tax Rev. 209.
Hayton, D., "The Revenue's Trump Card Against Tax Avoidance" (1984) 43 Cambridge L.J. 259.
Mansfield, Graham, "The 'New Approach' to Tax Avoidance: First Circular, Then Linear, Now Narrower" (1989) 1 British Tax Rev. 5.
Milnett, Peter J., "A New Approach to Tax Avoidance Schemes" (1982) 98 Law Quarterly Rev. 209.
Ray, R.P., "Revenue Suffers Further Anti-Avoidance Setback" (June 30, 1989) Taxes 1.
Tiley, John, "Tax Avoidance — A Change in Rules" (1982) 41 Cambridge L.J. 50.
White, Roger, "The New Approach and the Views of the Law Society" (1986) 1 British Tax Rev. 18.
Whitehorse, Chris, "Reopening the Door to Tax Avoidance" (1988) 138 News L.J. 540.

2. Purpose

3. The Charging Provision

4. Avoidance Transactions

5. Purpose of Transaction

> Ward, David, A., et. al., "The Business Purpose Test and Abuse of Rights" (1985) 2 British Tax Rev. 68.

6. Immunity from GAAR

7. Determining the Policy of the Statute

8. Extrinsic Evidence

9. Redetermination of Tax Liability

10. Third Parties

IV. — Series of Transactions

1. General Comment

> Potter, D.C., "Retrospective Anti-Avoidance Legislation" (1978) British Tax Rev. 133.

2. The Common Law

> Adams, L.D., "*Craven v. White*: U.K. Step-Transaction Doctrine Evolves — Canadian Planners Beware" (1988) 2:13 Can. Current Tax C-75.
>
> Archambault, P., "La nouvelle disposition générale anti-évitement et l'expérience jurisprudentielle anglaise récent" (1987) 9 RPFS 501.
>
> Ashton, R.K., "The Ramsay and Burmah Decisions — A Reappraisal" (1983) 4 British Tax Rev. 221.
>
> Avery Jones, J.F., "The New Approach in U.K. Tax Law — Where Do We Stand?" (Octover 1987) Asian-Pacific Tax and Investment Bull. 414.
>
> Bartlett, R.T., "The Constitutionality of the Ramsay Principle" (1985) 6 British Tax Rev. 338.
>
> Beattie, C.N., "*Furniss v. Dawson* — I: The Duke of Westminster Doctrine and Lord Tomlin's Dictum" (1984) 128 Solic. J. 139.
>
> Beattie, C.N., "Notes of Cases *Furniss v. Dawson*" (1984) 2 British Tax Rev. 109.
>
> Bretten, G.R., and Fay Stockton, "The Ramsay Doctrine: An Interim Review" (1987) 8 British Tax Rev. 280.
>
> "The Boundaries of Ramsay" (1985) 4 British Tax Rev. 197.
>
> Cane, L., "*Furniss v. Dawson*, [1984] 2 WLR 226: Where Do We Go From Here?" (1984) New L.J. 597.
>
> "Development Land Tax: Tax Avoidance Scheme — Application of Ramsay Principle" (1986) 130 Solic. J. 15.
>
> Gammie, M.J., "After Dawson" (1984) 5:3 Fiscal Studies 23.
>
> Gammie, M.J., "The Implications of *Furniss v. Dawson*" (1985) 6:3 Fiscal Studies 51.
>
> Gammie, M.J., "Revenue Practice — A Suitable Case of Treatment" (1980) British Tax Rev. 304.

Goldsworth, John, "United Kingdom: Anti-Avoidance Cases Examined" (1989) 1 Tax Notes Int'l. 180.

Goldsworth, John, "United Kingdom: The Fiscal Motive — Not Enough to Invoke the Ramsay Principle" (1989) 1 Tax Notes Int'l. 294.

Kessler, James, "Notes of Cases: *Craven v. White*" (1987) 7 British Tax. Rev. 354.

Kessler, James, "Note of Case: *Kwok Chi Leung Karl v. Commissioner of Estate Duty*" (1989) 4 British Tax Rev. 130.

Lawton, P., "The Ramsay Doctrine" (April 1982) Taxation Practitioner 88.

MacDonald, E., "Reflections on Recent Leading Tax Cases" (1985) 129 Solic. J. 307.

MacDonald, G., "*Coates (Inspector of Taxes) v. Arndale Properties Ltd.*, [1982] STC 573 — Tax Avoidance, Trading Stock and Motive" (1982) British Tax Rev. 382.

Marsh, I.A., "*Magnavox Electronics Co. Ltd. (in liquidation v. Hall*, [1985] STC 260" (1985) British Tax Rev. 313.

Nicoll, David, "Notes of Cases: *IRC v. Challenge Corporation Ltd.* — Tax Mitigation" (1987) 3 British Tax Rev. 134.

Oliver, J.D.B., "Current Note: *Sherdley v. Sherdley or Furniss v. Dawson* Again" (1986) British Tax Rev. 249.

Oliver, J.D.B., "The Boundaries of Ramsay" (1985) 4 British Tax Rev. 197.

Oliver, Stephen, "The Ramsay/Dawson Doctrine — The Quest for the Relevant Transaction", in *Recent Tax Problems: Current Legal Problems* 1 (Stevens & Sons: London, 1985).

Shipwright, J., "Is Tax Planning Dead? — Burmah: A Case Note" (1982) 126 Solic. J. 144.

Stary, Erica, "*Furniss v. Dawson*: Revenue Guidelines" (1985) British Tax Rev. 1015.

Tax Law After Furniss v. Dawson (London: The Law Society of England and Wales, 1988).

Taylor, T.P.D., "Tax Planning and Tax Avoidance after Ramsay" (1982) Taxation 494.

Tiley, John, "An Academic Perspective on the Ramsay/Dawson Doctrine", in *Recent Tax Problems: Current Legal Problems* 19 (London: Stevens & Sons, 1985).

Tiley, John, "Note of Case" (1989) 1 British Tax Rev. 20.

3. Section 245

Ferrier, Ian, "The Meaning of the Statute: Mansfield on Tax Avoidance" (1981) British Tax Rev. 303.

4. The Westminster Principle

Monroe, H.H., "Fiscal Finesse: Tax Avoidance and the Duke of Westminster" (1982) British Tax Rev. 200.

Shipwright, J., "Play Based on Duke of Westminster? The Ramsay and Rawling Cases" (1981) 125 Solic. J. 227.

V. — Administration

1. Assessments

2. Request for Adjustment

3. Administrative Structure

VI. — Administrative Interpretation

1. Discretionary Power

> Goldberg, D., "O Brave New World That Hath Such Decisions in It: And Herein of the Separation of Powers" (1982) British Tax Rev. 13.

2. Purposive Approach

> Goldberg, D., "Mete Wands: How Gold and Straight?" (1981) British Tax Rev. 233.
> "Property: Landing a Hand" (April 2005) The Lawyer 18 (QL).

3. Avoidance Transactions

VII. — Interpretations and Rulings

1. Form of Business Organization

> Avery Jones, J.F., ed., *Tax Havens and Measures Against Tax Evasion and Avoidance in the EEC* (London: Associated Business Programmes, 1974).
> Chopin, L.F., "Taxation and Unremitted Partnership Income: A Vestige of Unchecked Tax Abuse" (1979) 42 Modern L. Rev. 342.
> Flanagan, T., "Tax Avoidance and the Legal Personality", (1979) 43 Conv. 195.
> Ray, R.P., "Deeds of Covenant — Revisited" (1984) 134 New L.J. 63.
> *Tax Havens and Measures Against Tax Evasion and Avoidance in the EEC*, ed., J.F. Avery Jones (London: Associated Business Programmes, 1974).

9. Avoidance of Part IV A on Taxable Dividends

> "Briefing" (May 2005) 19.5 T& E 3 (QL).

United States

I. — General Comment

> The Carter Commission Report, 3 *Report of the Royal Commission on Taxation: Taxation of Income* (Canada, 1966) 537.

II. — Judicial Doctrines

Bittker, Boris I., "Pervasive Judicial Doctrines in the Construction of the *Internal Revenue Code*" (1978) 21 Howard L.J. 693, 714.

Tiley, John, "Judicial Anti-Avoidance Doctrines: The U.S. Alternatives — Part I" (1987) 5 British Tax Rev. 180.

Tiley, John, "Judicial Anti-Avoidance Doctrines: The U.S. Alternatives — Part II" (1987) 6 British Tax Rev. 220.

Wolfman, Bernard, "The Supreme Court in the *Lyon's* Den: A Failure of Judicial Process" (1981) 66 Cornell L. Rev. 1075.

1. Taxpayer's Rights

2. Evasion, Avoidance and Mitigation

"American Ingenuity, Irish Residence" *The New York Times* (17 November 2005) A1.

Angell, Mongomery B., "Tax Evasion and Tax Avoidance" (1938) 38 Colum. L. Rev. 80.

Bailey, Jeff & Lynnley Browning, "KPMG May Dodge One Bullet, Only to Face Another" *The New York Times* (21 June 2005) C1.

Browning, Lynneley, "Bank One is Sued by Illinois Investors Over Tax Shelters" *The New York Times* (29 June 2005) C1.

Browning, Lynnley, "In Study, Most Companies Reported No Taxes" *The New York Times* (6 April 2004) C3.

David P. Hariton, "Kafka and the Tax Shelter" (Fall 2003) 57 Tax L. Rev. 1 (QL).

Gunn, A. "Tax Avoidance" (1978) 76 Mich. L. Rev. 733.

Griesel, L.W. and D. Beail, "Tax Planning: Problem or Solution?" (1984) 38 Wash. St. B. News 23.

Millett, Peter, "Artificial Tax Avoidance: The English and American Approach" (1986) 6 British Tax Rev. 327.

Richard Schmalbeck, "Reconsidering Private Foundation Investment Limitations" (Fall, 2004) 58 Tax L. Rev. 59 (QL).

3. Motive

Blum, Walter J., "Motive, Intent and Purpose in Federal Income Taxation" (1967) 34 University of Chicago Law Rev. 485.

Deborah A. Greier, "The Myth of the Matching Principle as a Tax Value" (Spring 1998) 15 Am. J. Tax Pol'y 17 (QL).

Waizer, Harry, "The Business Purpose Doctrine: The Effect of Motive on Federal Income Tax Liability" (1981) 49 Fordham L. Rev. 1078.

4. Sham Transactions

Carr Kelly, David, "Tax Motivated Divorce and the Sham Transaction Doctrine *Boyter v. Commissioner* (1982), 668 F. 2d 1382, 18 Wake Forest L. Rev. 881.

Gideon, Kenneth W. and Ruth E. Kent, "Mrs. Gregory's Northern Tour: Canadian Proposals to Adopt the Business Purpose Rule and the Step Transaction Doctrine", in *Proceedings of 39th Tax Conf.* 7:1 (Can. Tax Foundation, 1987).

Greiner, R.G., P.L. Behling and J.D. Moffett, "Assumption of Liabilities and the Improper Purpose — A Re-Examination of Section 357(b)", (1978) 32 Tax Lawyer 111.

Summers, Robert S., "A Critique of the Business Purpose Doctrine" (1961) 41 Or. L. Rev. 38.

Warren, A.C., "Requirement of Economic Profit in Tax Motivated Transactions" (1981) 59 Taxes 985.

9. Redetermination of Tax Liability

Paul, Randolph E., "Restatement of the Law of Tax Avoidance" (1937), in *Selected Studies in Federal Taxation* 9.

IV. — Series of Transactions

1. General Comment

Hobbet, "The Step Transaction Doctrine and Its Effect on Corporate Transactions" (1970) 19 Tul. Tax Inst. 102.

Mintz, S.S. and W.T. Plumb Jr., "Step Transactions in Corporate Reorganizations", in *Proceedings of New York University's 12th Annual Institute on Federal Taxation*, November 4–13, 1953 (New York: Matthew Bender, 1954) 247.

Murray Jr., Oliver C., "Step Transactions" (1969) 24 University of Miami Law Rev. 60.

Note, "Evolution of the Step Transaction Doctrine" (1971) 11 Washburn Law J. 84.

Paul, Randolf E. and Philip Zimet, "Step Transactions", in *Selected Studies in Federal Taxation* (2nd series, 1938) 200.

"Step Transactions" (1969) 24 U. Miami L. Rev. 60, 66.

Whitmire, R.L., "Bailing Out of Tax Shelters: Selected Techniques" (1978) 30 So. Calif. Tax Inst. 503.

2. The Common Law

Aidinoff, M.B., "*Furniss v. Dawson*: The U.S. Experience" (1985) 6:4 Fiscal Studies 76.

3. Section 245

4. The Westminster Principle

V. — Administration

1. Assessments

Jay A. Soled, "A Proposal to Lengthen the Tax Accounting Period" (Spring, 1997) 14 Am. J. Tax Pol'y 35 (QL).

Johnston, David Cay, "Ernst & Young Says it Faces Criminal Inquiry on Shelters" *The New York Times* (25 May 2004) C5.

VII. — Interpretations and Rulings

1. Form of Business Organization

Blum, Walter J., "*Knetch v. US.*: A Pronouncement on Tax Avoidance" (1962) 40 Taxes 296.

"Corporate Welfare Runs Amok" *The New York Times* (30 January 2005) p. 16.

"Corporate Tax Avoiders" *The New York Times* (21 September 2004) A5.

Ditkoff, J.H., "Intercorporate Dividends and Legitimate Tax Avoidance" (1977) 4 J. Corporate Taxation 5.

McMahon, "Defining the 'Acquisition' in Business Reorganizations Through the Step Transaction Doctrine" (1981) 67 Iowa Law Rev. 31.

Bittker, Boris I., *Federal Taxation of Income and Gifts*, 5th ed. (New York: Warren, Gorham & Lamont, 1985) 4:29.

2. Consolidation of Profits and Losses in a Corporate Group

Gissel, L.H., "Income Shifting Devices — What's Left?" (1986) 20 Inst. of Est. Plan. 14.1.

15. — Conversion of Dividend Income into Capital Gains

Ethan Yale, "When are Capitalization Exceptions Justified?" (Summer, 2004) 57 Tax L. Rev. 549 (QL).

Ireland

"American Ingenuity, Irish Residence" *The New York Times* (17 November 2005) A1.

Judge, Norman E., ed., *Tax Law: Principles and Practice* (Butterworth & Co. (Publishers) Ltd.).

Lavery, Brian, "Irish Financial Regulator Faces Its First Major Test" *The New York Times* (1 April 2005) C2.

2. Evasion, Avoidance and Mitigation

Bracewell-Milnes, Barry, *The Economics of International Tax Avoidance* (Deventer, the Netherlands: Kluwer).

James Loh Ching Yew, "Modern Trends in Tax Avoidance" (1993) 1 MLJ 65 (QL).

Low Chee Keong, "Labuan: South East Asia's International Offshore Financial Centre" (1996) 2 MLJA 129 (QL).

OECD, "International Tax Avoidance and Evasion", 31 Bull. Int'l. Fisc. Doc. 11.

OECD, *International Tax Avoidance and Evasion, Four Related Studies* (Paris: OECD, 1987).

OECD, "Work on Tax Avoidance and Evasion" (1980-81) Intertax 11.

"Russia's Big Trial" *The New York Times* (21 June 2004) A1.

Ward, David A., "Tax Avoidance: Judicial and Legislative Approaches in Other Jurisdictions", in *Proceedings of 39th Tax Conf.* 8:1 (Can. Tax Foundation, 1987).

Wisselink, M.A. and Barry Bracewell-Milnes, *International Tax Avoidance — Volume A*, pp. 128–134, 198–214 (Deventer, the Netherlands: Kluwer, 1979).

III. — The General Anti-Avoidance Rule

1. Background

Edwards, P.S.A., "Anti-Avoidance Provisions in Hong Kong" (1987) 3 The Journal of Strategy in Int'l. Taxation 247.

Halkyard, Andrew, "Hong Kong: A Tax Haven Enacts Anti-Avoidance Legislation" (1986) 15 Australian Tax Rev. 170.

Van Hoorne, J., "Problems, Possibilities and Limitations With Respect to Measures Against International Tax Avoidance and Evasion" (1978) 8 Ga. J. Int'l. & Comp. L. 763.

2. The Common Law

Garde, H.S., *Swedish National Reporter Tax Avoidance and Tax Evasion* (London: Sweet & Maxwell, 1982).

PART XII: CORPORATE RESTRUCTURING

CHAPTER 25 — TRANSFER OF PROPERTY TO A CORPORATION

I. — General Comment

As a rule, a taxpayer who disposes of property will receive or be *deemed* to have received proceeds of disposition from the property. Where a taxpayer disposes of property to a person with whom the taxpayer does not deal at arm's length, the Act deems the taxpayer to receive proceeds of disposition equal to the fair market value of the property.[1] These basic rules recognize the principle of taxation upon realization of income. Hence, in the absence of

---

[1] Para. 69(1)(b).

special rules, any reorganization of business affairs (e.g., transfer of proprietorship assets into a corporation) would be deemed to occur at fair market value and could trigger taxable gains.

The deemed disposition rule could have punitive consequences if it was applied every time a taxpayer reorganized his or her business. For example, a sole proprietor who transfers business assets to a corporation could face a substantial tax on any gains accrued on capital assets, eligible capital property, inventory and for recapture from depreciable property. Since the change would be merely in the legal form of the business rather than its economic substance, a deemed disposition with substantial tax consequences would be inappropriate in the circumstances. The general rule does not promote tax neutrality as between different forms of business organizations.

Section 85 provides a special rule to accommodate business reorganizations. The essence of section 85 is that it overrides the general rule in section 69 and allows a taxpayer to transfer property to a corporation on a tax-deferred basis. Thus, tax that would ordinarily be triggered from a disposition of assets is deferred to a later date when the assets are disposed of by the corporation without cover of a rollover.

Section 85 is an elective provision. It allows taxpayers to recognize transfers of assets at amounts other than their fair market value and to rollover the cost of their assets into other property. To prevent inappropriate use of the provision, however, the Act severely circumscribes the section with various rules, limits, and time constraints.

1. — Meaning of "Rollover"

We use the term "rollover" in tax law to describe transactions in which the tax cost of property disposed of is transferred or "rolled over" into the tax cost of property acquired in exchange for the disposition. This allows us to defer any gain accrued at the time of the rollover until such time as we subsequently sell the newly acquired property in an "unprotected" transaction.

The general thrust of rollovers is that, in stringently controlled circumstances, a taxpayer can dispose of property without recognizing any immediate gain or loss from the disposition. The property is rolled over at its cost amount to the transferee. The transferor's tax basis in the transferred property becomes the tax basis in the property taken back by the transferor as consideration. The rationale for permitting a taxpayer to rollover assets is that it is undesirable, and perhaps unfair, to impose a tax on transactions that do not involve a fundamental economic change in ownership, even though there may be a change in form or legal structure.

2. — *Types of Rollovers*

The general thrust of section 69 is to prevent manipulation of asset transfer prices between parties who are not dealing with each other on an economic arm's length basis. The "rollover" provisions of the Act are exceptions to section 69 and allow taxpayers to defer recognition of gains, and sometimes losses, until a subsequent date or event. Thus, the first question to consider in rearranging business or family affairs is whether it is desirable in the particular circumstances to realize any gain or loss accrued on the property.

If it is considered to be undesirable to trigger an accrued gain or loss at the particular time, the proposed disposition of assets should be evaluated in the light of one or more of the "rollover" provisions of the Act. For example, each of the following provisions of the Act permit rollovers in varied circumstances:

- s. 97(2) — Transfers of property to a partnership;

- s. 85 — Transfers of property to a corporation;

- s. 85.1 — Share for share exchanges;

- s. 86 — Reorganization of share capital of a corporation;

- s. 87 — Amalgamations;

- s. 88 — Winding-up of a corporation.

We must consider each provision on its own merits and applicability to the circumstances under review.

II. — Section 85

1. — *Uses*

Section 85 applies where:

- A taxpayer,

- Disposes of an eligible property,

- To a taxable Canadian corporation,[2]

- In exchange for consideration that includes shares of the corporation, and

- The parties elect to have the section apply to the disposition.

---

[2]Subs. 97(2) provides that the s. 85 rollover provision may also apply to transfers of property from an individual to a partnership, of which he or she is a member immediately after the transfer.

Under section 85, a taxpayer who transfers property to a taxable Canadian corporation may *elect* as proceeds of disposition an amount that is less than the fair market value of the property. In other words, section 85 specifically overrides the general rule in section 69 that deems dispositions of property to occur at fair market value. Hence, for example, a taxpayer can transfer property with an accrued gain to a taxable Canadian corporation, elect a transfer price equal to the *cost* of the transferred property, and avoid immediate recognition of the accrued gain for tax purposes.[3]

One can use section 85 to advantage in any of the following circumstances:

- Incorporation of a business carried on by a sole proprietor or by a partnership;

- Transfer of portfolio securities to a holding corporation;

- Transfer of business assets within related corporate groups;

- Transfer of business assets from a sole proprietorship to a partnership;[4]

- Transfer of a controlling interest in an operating company to a newly-created holding corporation as part of an estate freeze or an income splitting reorganization;

- Pooling of assets to form a joint venture corporation;

- Split-off of assets held by a joint venture corporation;

- Division of assets of a corporation among its shareholders (a "butterfly" reorganization);[5] and

- Share exchange in a take-over bid.[6]

Thus, section 85 is a versatile provision that one can use in a variety of familial and business reorganizations, estate planning, and commercial transactions that involve a disposition of assets between taxpayers. But the section is strictly controlled and may be used only in narrowly circumscribed circumstances.[7] The slightest deviation from the technical rules of the section can invalidate the rollover and trigger a deemed disposition at fair market value.

---

[3]Para. 85(1)(a); see also IT-291R3, "Transfer of Property to a Corporation under Subsection 85(1)" (January 12, 2004).

[4]Subs. 97(2).

[5]Para. 55(3)(b).

[6]A share-for-share exchange may also be implemented on a rollover basis under s. 85.1; see Chapter 27, "Share-for-Share Acquisitions".

[7]Some of these rules deal with the manner of electing and designating values; others deal with the time of filing returns.

(a) — Incorporation of Business

An individual may start a business enterprise as a sole proprietorship so that the individual can offset business losses against his or her income from other sources. Where a business is financially successful, however, it is generally advantageous to operate it as a corporation. A Canadian-owned private corporation, for example, can take advantage of the small business deduction and the low rate of tax levied on active business income. Section 85 can be used to transfer the assets of the proprietorship to the incorporated business without triggering any immediate tax liability.

(b) — Capital Gains Exemption

A taxpayer who disposes of shares of a qualified small business corporation may claim an exemption in respect of $500,000 of capital gains realized from the disposition.[8] This exemption is only available on a sale of shares; it is not available to sole proprietors. A sole proprietor may, however, incorporate his or her business and use section 85 in order to take advantage of this generous exemption.

(c) — Tax Deferral

A Canadian-owned private corporation can defer taxes by leaving its income in the corporation. Generally, the tax paid (approximately 18 per cent) by a Canadian-owned small business corporation is substantially lower than the tax payable by an individual in the top tax bracket. Hence, provided that the owner of a business is prepared to leave his or her income in the business, there is a substantial deferral of the tax that would otherwise be payable if the income flowed through to the owner either as salary or dividends. Section 85 can be used to incorporate a business on a tax deferred basis to take advantage of the low tax rate on active business income.

(d) — Incorporation of Portfolio

In certain circumstances, particularly for taxpayers in the top marginal tax brackets, there may be some tax deferral available in respect of an investment portfolio held in a corporation. The magnitude of the deferral depends upon the difference in tax paid by individuals and corporations on dividend income. Section 85 allows a taxpayer to incorporate his or her portfolio investments without triggering any immediate income tax liability.

---

[8]Subs. 110.6(2.1).

(e) — Removing Excess Cash from Corporation

Where an operating company ("Opco") generates cash in excess of its immediate needs, it may wish to utilize the excess cash for investment purposes. It is usually prudent for Opco to segregate its excess cash in a holding company ("Holdco"), which can then invest the funds in a portfolio of investments. In this way, the corporation's investments are not exposed to business risks and Opco can more easily retain its status as a corporation engaged primarily in active business. Section 85 can be used to restructure Opco by transferring its shares to Holdco. Opco then becomes a subsidiary of Holdco. Any excess cash can usually be paid to Holdco as a tax-free dividend.

(f) — Estate Planning and Income Splitting

A taxpayer who owns an operating company ("Opco") may wish to restructure to minimize the potential for death taxes and to reduce the burden of current income taxes. A reorganization to reduce the impact of death taxes can be implemented through an "estate freeze".

One technique of estate freezing is to transfer the shares of Opco to a holding company ("Holdco") in exchange for "preferred" or "special" shares that will not appreciate in value from the date of the freeze. The effect of such an exchange is that future growth in value is diverted to Holdco's "common" shares, which can be taken up by the taxpayer's children. We can implement such a transaction (referred to as a "holding company freeze") on a tax deferred basis under section 85.

Similarly, a taxpayer may wish to reorganize an operating business in order to minimize the amount of current taxes payable. One method is to reorganize the capital structure of the corporation so that its shares are held by the taxpayer and the members of the taxpayer's family. This allows the taxpayer to split the corporation's income into several parts and sprinkle it, through dividends, into the hands of the family. Section 85 permits such a reorganization on a tax deferred basis.[9]

(g) — Transfer of Assets Within a Corporate Group

In certain circumstances it may be advantageous to transfer assets within an affiliated corporate group. For example, where one of the corporations in an affiliated group has business losses that it cannot utilize, a profitable corporation in the same group can transfer a profitable asset into the loss corporation. The asset can generate income in the loss corporation that

---

[9]The CRA has challenged the legitimacy of these arrangements, but without success — see: *Ator v. Minister of National Revenue*, 99 D.T.C. 427, [1999] 2 C.T.C. 2369 (T.C.C.); *Korol v. Minister of National Revenue*, 99 D.T.C. 418, [1999] 2 C.T.C. 2332 (T.C.C.); *Rao v. Minister of National Revenue*, 99 D.T.C. 413, [1999] 2 C.T.C. 2783 (T.C.C.); *Sykes v. Minister of National Revenue*, 99 D.T.C. 423, [1999] 2 C.T.C. 2946 (T.C.C.).

can be sheltered by the losses. Thus, the group as a whole pays less tax. Section 85 can be used to transfer the profitable assets on a tax-free basis without any immediate income tax consequences to the transferor.

(h) — Butterfly Reorganizations

A "butterfly reorganization" is a method of splitting a corporation into two or more separate corporations. This may be necessary if the shareholders of a corporation wish to go their separate ways and to split up an existing corporation. For example, a family-owned business enterprise may require reorganization if the principal shareholders (husband and wife) separate or divorce. In these circumstances, family law legislation may require a sharing of the net value of business assets. A butterfly reorganization allows for the division of the corporation into two or more components on a tax deferred basis under section 85 without the adverse consequences of the anti-avoidance capital gains stripping rules of subsection 55(2).

2. — Example

The following illustrates a rollover involving the transfer of capital property to a corporation under section 85.

Example		
Assume:		
An individual owns a building (capital property) to which the following data applies:		
	Land	*Building*
Adjusted cost base	$ 150,000	—
Capital cost	—	$ 120,000
UCC	—	$ 75,000
Fair market value	(225,000)	(105,000)
Potential capital gain/recapture of CCA	$ 75,000	$ 30,000
without rollover		
The individual transfers the property to a taxable Canadian corporation and the parties elect proceeds of disposition as follows:		
Land		$ 150,000

Example		
Building		$ 75,000

Then:

	Land	Building
Deemed proceeds of disposition	$ 150,000	$ 75,000
Adjusted cost base	(150,000)	—
UCC	—	(75,000)
Capital gain/recapture of transfers	NIL	NIL
Deferred capital gain/recapture of CCA	$ 75,000	$ 30,000

3. — Partnerships

Subsection 85(1) deals with transfers by a taxpayer to a taxable Canadian corporation. There are other provisions that deal with comparable transfers of property by a partnership to a corporation.[10]

Subsection 97(2) provides that the section 85 rollover may be used where a taxpayer transfers property to a partnership.

4. — Election of Values

Section 85 is an elective provision. It allows a taxpayer who transfers property to a taxable Canadian corporation to *elect* as proceeds of disposition of the property an amount other than its fair market value or the value of the consideration received. The election is, however, subject to certain limits. The lower limit is generally the cost amount of the property. Stop-loss rules may prevent the transferor from claiming a loss on the property. The upper limit is usually the fair market value of the property transferred. Thus, a taxpayer who elects to use section 85 to transfer property to a taxable Canadian corporation has some latitude in determining the amount, if any, of the gain which the taxpayer will recognize at the time of the transfer.

---

[10]Subss. 85(2), (3).

III. — Who Can Use Subsection 85(1)?

1. — Transferors

Any taxpayer (whether resident or non-resident in Canada) who disposes of property to a taxable Canadian corporation can use the rollover. "Taxpayer" includes any person regardless of whether he or she is liable to pay tax.[11] Thus, the rollover can be used by individuals, trusts, and corporations. In addition, this rollover is also available to partnerships that transfer property to a taxable Canadian corporation.[12]

2. — Transferees

The transferee must be a *taxable* Canadian corporation. A "taxable Canadian corporation" is a Canadian corporation that is not exempt from tax under Part I of the Act.[13]

A "Canadian corporation" is a resident corporation that was either incorporated in Canada or resident in Canada *throughout* the period from June 18, 1971 to the relevant date, that is, the date of the transfer.[14] It is not generally possible to rollover property to a non-resident corporation.[15]

Section 85 is also available where a taxpayer transfers property to a partnership that qualifies as a Canadian partnership immediately after the property transfer.[16]

3. — Exclusion of Subsection 86(1)

Subsection 86(1) applies when a taxpayer exchanges *all* of his or her shares of one class for shares of another class of the same corporation as part of a reorganization of the corporation's capital. Subsection 86(1) does not apply to an exchange of shares if subsection 85(1) or (2) are applicable.[17]

Where a taxpayer transfers *all* of his or her shares in a taxable Canadian corporation in exchange for shares of another class in the *same* corporation, the Canada Revenue Agency

---

[11]Subs. 248(1)"taxpayer".

[12]Subs. 85(2).

[13]Subs. 89(1)"taxable Canadian corporation" except by reason of para. 149(1)(t).

[14]Subs. 89(1)"Canadian corporation".

[15]See, however, the foreign affiliate rollover in subsection 85.1(3).

[16]Subs. 97(2).

[17]Subs. 86(3).

(CRA) is of the view that subsection 85(1) applies; hence, subsection 86(1) cannot apply to such an exchange of shares.

IV. — Property Eligible For Rollover

1. — Types of Property

A taxpayer can rollover the following types of property:[18]

- Capital property (except for real or immovable property, or an interest therein, or an option in respect thereof, owned by a non-resident);

- Eligible capital property;

- Inventory,[19] except real property inventory, an interest in real property or an option in respect thereof;

- Accounts receivable in respect of which no election has been made;[20]

- Canadian resource properties;

- Foreign resource properties;

- Certain property used in an insurance or money lending business;

- Real property that is capital property and is used by a non-resident in the course of carrying on a business in Canada; and

- A NISA Fund No. 2.

Eligible property includes personal property that qualifies as capital property. It also includes debt owing to a corporation by another taxable Canadian corporation. The rollover is available for any capital property (depreciable or otherwise), regardless whether it is situated in Canada or in a foreign country.

---

[18]Subs. 85(1.1).

[19]Including a professional's work in progress; see definition of "inventory" in subsection 248(1).

[20]S. 22; see Chapter 30, "Purchase and Sale of a Business".

2. — Real Estate

(a) — Inventory

The exclusion of real property inventory from eligible property is intended to prevent a real estate trader from converting business income into a capital gain by selling inventory to a corporation and then selling the shares of the corporation for a capital gain. Such a transformation of business income into a capital gain would in any event probably fail.[21] Subsection 85(1), however, adds certainty through its outright prohibition of the use of the rollover for real property inventory.

The distinction between capital property and business inventory depends on the intention of the taxpayer who disposes of the property.[22] Therefore, it may be difficult to determine with certainty whether real estate does or does not qualify for the rollover under subsection 85(1). Since the characterization of real estate gains and losses depends on the factual circumstances surrounding its ownership, it is not possible to obtain an advance ruling on its status from the CRA.[23] In cases of doubt, it may be prudent not to transfer real property that may later be determined to constitute inventory.

(b) — Non-Residents

As a rule, a non-resident cannot rollover real property even if it constitutes capital property. This prohibition prevents non-residents from avoiding tax by transferring real estate that is capital property into a corporation, selling the shares of the corporation and then claiming the benefits of a bilateral treaty to exempt the gains from tax.

Canada's bilateral tax treaties generally allow Canada to tax capital gains from a non-resident's sale of shares only if the value of the shares is derived principally from Canadian real

---

[21]*Fraser v. M.N.R.*, [1964] S.C.R. 657, [1964] C.T.C. 372, 64 D.T.C. 5224 (S.C.C.) (profit realized from sale of shares of corporation is income from business where corporation is an alternative method chosen by the taxpayer to conduct real estate transactions); *Claude Belle-Isle v. M.N.R.*, [1966] S.C.R. 354, [1966] C.T.C. 85, 66 D.T.C. 5100 (S.C.C.) (sale of hotel to a corporation followed by the sale of the shares in that corporation generated business income); *Gibson Bros. Industries Ltd. v. M.N.R.*, [1972] C.T.C. 221, 72 D.T.C. 6190 (F.C.T.D.) (rather than selling assets directly to customer, parent sold assets to subsidiary and customer bought shares of subsidiary; sales of assets and shares treated as one transaction); *Burgess v. M.N.R.*, [1973] C.T.C. 58, 73 D.T.C. 5040 (F.C.T.D.) (sale of shares in a corporation with only one asset was an adventure in the nature of trade).

[22]IT-218R, "Profit, Capital Gains and Losses from the Sale of Real Estate, Including Farmland and Inherited Land and Conversion of Real Estate from Capital Property to Inventory and Vice Versa" (September 16, 1986).

[23]See IC 70-6R5, "Advance Income Tax Rulings" (May 17, 2002).

estate.[24] Since the prohibition does not generally apply to property used by a non-resident in the course of a business carried on in Canada, a non-resident might otherwise avoid the tax if the value of the shares could be substantially attributed to other assets.

(c) — Partnerships

An interest in a partnership is capital property and, as such, is eligible for the rollover under section 85. Thus, although real estate inventory cannot be rolled over under section 85, an interest in a partnerhip that owns real property inventory can be rolled over to a taxable Canadian corporation.[25] The CRA has indicated, however, that it considers such a double rollover to be an abusive form of tax avoidance and contrary to the General Anti-Avoidance Rule ("GAAR").[26]

3. — Receivables

We generally consider business accounts receivables to be capital property.[27] Hence, they are eligible to be rolled over to a corporation under subsection 85(1).

An election under section 22 allows the vendor to claim a deduction for the amount by which the consideration that the vendor receives for the receivables is less than their face value. Provided that the election is for the fair market value of the receivables sold, the election is binding upon all parties.[28]

4. — Eligible Capital Property

Eligible capital property generally refers to goodwill, customer lists, patents, trademarks and perpetual franchises.[29] It also includes "know how".[30]

---

[24]See, generally, Article XIII of Canada's tax treaties.

[25]See Question 48 — CRA Round Table, 36th Tax Conf., pp. 819-820 (Can. Tax Foundation, 1984).

[26]See IC 88-2, "General Anti-avoidance Rule — Section 245 of the *Income Tax Act*" (October 21, 1988), para. 22. See also, Chapter 24 and the *Loyens* case.

[27]*Doughty v. Commr. of Taxes*, [1927] A.C. 327 (P.C.); *Crompton v. Reynolds* (1952), 33 Tax Cas. 288 (H.L.).

[28]Subs. 22(2).

[29]Subs. 248(1)"eligible capital property"; s. 54"eligible capital property".

[30]See *Rapistan Canada Ltd. v. M.N.R.*, [1974] C.T.C. 495, 74 D.T.C. 6426 (F.C.A.).

A mere right to receive income without any interest in the property that generates the income does not constitute a capital property. An amount paid to acquire the right is not considered to be an eligible capital expenditure.

V. — Individual Asset Test

A section 85 rollover is implemented on an asset-by-asset basis. Technically, each property is the subject of a separate election even though the taxpayer can list several properties on a single election form. Thus, the transferor must specify a particular transfer price for each asset. Assets that are not listed on the form are disposed of at their fair market value.[31] However, it is possible to elect different amounts in respect of identical properties such as shares. Thus, a transferor can control the amount of capital gains to be recognized on the transfer. For example, if a taxpayer owns 100 shares with a cost base of $10 per share and fair market value of $100, the taxpayer might elect a transfer value of $10 for 50 shares and $80 for the other 50 shares.

VI. — The Election

1. — A Legal Fiction

The rollover is entirely optional: the transferor and the transferee must jointly elect to have subsection 85(1) apply and they must do so in prescribed form and within a certain period of time.[32] Once made, the election is irrevocable[33] and it may be amended only in very limited circumstances.[34]

The election is the centrepiece of the rollover under section 85 and requires careful consideration. It determines the amount that the transferor will recognize as the transferor's proceeds of disposition and the transferee's cost of acquisition. The transferee's consent to the election causes it to become liable for the tax liability deferred on the transfer of property. The elected amount is, in effect, a legal fiction to the extent that it varies from the contractually determined transaction price. Within certain constraints, however, the Act deems the elected

---

[31]S. 69.

[32]Subs. 85(6).

[33]*Walker (A.S.) Holdings Ltd. v. M.N.R.*, [1979] C.T.C. 2112, 79 D.T.C. 132 (T.R.B.); *Busch v. M.N.R.*, [1979] C.T.C. 2275, 79 D.T.C. 277 (T.R.B.); *One for Three Ltd. v. M.N.R.*, [1980] C.T.C. 2293, 80 D.T.C. 1244 (T.R.B.); *Deconinck v. The Queen*, [1988] 2 C.T.C. 213, 88 D.T.C. 6410 (F.C.T.D.); affd. [1990] 2 C.T.C. 464, 90 D.T.C. 6617 (F.C.A.).

[34]Subs. 85(7.1).

amount to be the proceeds of disposition and the acquisition cost of the property in respect of which the election is made.

2. — Individual Listing of Assets

Technically, a taxpayer is required to separately list *each* property that is transferred and provide a specific transfer amount for *each* asset. For the purpose of these rules, the CRA does not consider "nil" to be an amount.

An exception is made in respect of depreciable properties. Where *all* of a class of depreciable property is transferred to a corporation, the election need only show aggregate amounts for each class provided that the taxpayer retains supporting schedules showing the order of disposition of each of the properties in the class.[35] As a matter of practice, it is usually sufficient in a major transaction to list the type and class of asset on the election form.

3. — Late-Filed Elections

As a general rule, an election under section 85 is final and irrevocable as between the parties to the transaction. The Act does, however, permit a late, as opposed to an amended, election to be filed in certain limited circumstances.

(a) — Within Three Years

The transferor and the corporation must file the election by the date on which the income tax return for the year must be filed.[36] An election filed within three years of that date will, however, be accepted, subject to a late-filing penalty.[37] The taxpayer is liable for an amount equal to 1/4 of 1 per cent per month of the difference between the fair market value of the property transferred and the amount elected in respect of it. The maximum penalty is $8,000.[38]

---

[35]IC 76-19R3, "Transfer of Property to a Corporation under Section 85" (June 17, 1996).

[36]Subs. 85(6).

[37]Subss. 85(7), (8).

[38]Para. 85(8)(b).

(b) — Beyond Three Years

A taxpayer may file an election beyond the three year late filing period or may file an amended election where, in the opinion of the Minister, the circumstances are such that it would be "just and equitable" to accept the election.[39] The election must be accompanied by a written submission requesting its acceptance and it must set out the reasons why it is just and equitable that it should be accepted. The CRA is quite stringent in this matter and it will not usually accept an election that is not accompanied by the taxpayer's submission of reasons in support of the election.

The Agency generally accepts amended elections if the purpose of the amendment is to revise an agreed upon amount that would otherwise trigger unintended tax consequences for the parties involved. It will also usually accept an amended election in order to correct an error, omission, or oversight in the original election.

(c) — "Just and Equitable" Reasons

The Agency generally accepts amendments that:

- Result from an inaccurate valuation of the property that gives rise to unintended tax consequences;

- Reduce the agreed upon amount of transferred shares to the correct cost amount in circumstances where a transfer at cost was intended or certain dividends (e.g. subsection 83(1)) were omitted when calculating the adjusted cost base of the shares;

- Implement a correction where it is quite clear that the amount was entered in error (for example, an entry for depreciable capital property at its net book value instead of at its undepreciated capital cost);

- Correct other situations that give rise to unintended income tax consequences[40] when it is quite clear that the parties really intended to implement the rollover without any immediate income tax consequences but did not in fact do so effectively.

The Agency does not accept amended elections where the purpose of the election is:

- To implement retroactive tax planning;

- To take advantage of losses or tax credits that were not originally taken into account at the time the election was filed;

- To take advantage of amendments in the law that were enacted after the election was filed;

---

[39]Subs. 85(7.1).

[40]For example, the application of s. 84.1, subs. 15(1), or 84(1).

- To avoid or evade tax; or

- To increase the agreed amount in a statute-barred taxation year.

VII. — Price Adjustment Clauses

A taxpayer who wants to implement the terms of a price adjustment clause must file an amended election under subsection 85(7.l). The Agency's administrative position[41] is that it should be notified in advance of the existence of all agreements with price adjustment clauses. A "yes" answer on the rollover election form (T2057) to the question about the existence of a PAC constitutes acceptable notification.

VIII. — Filing Of Election

The joint election is a prerequisite to the rollover. The assets that are to be rolled over to the corporation must be listed; an estimate of the fair market value of each property must be disclosed. It is particularly important to list eligible capital property (such as goodwill) in the election, even if only at $1. In the event that goodwill is not listed (and it is quite easy to omit listing goodwill since it does not usually appear as an asset on financial statements), it is considered to have been transferred at its fair market value and may trigger an unexpected gain.

IX. — Sale Of Business As Going Concern

Where a business is sold as a going concern, it is prudent to include eligible capital property as an asset in the election. This is so even if the parties believe that there is no eligible capital property to be transferred. A successful business generating income usually has goodwill even if it does not show on the balance sheet. A sale of a business as a going concern includes its goodwill as one of the assets sold. The amount elected is usually set at a nominal $1. "Nil" is not an amount and should not be elected.[42]

---

[41]IT-169, "Price Adjustment Clauses" (August 6, 1974).

[42]IC 76-19R3, "Transfer of Property to a Corporation under Section 85" (June 17, 1996).

X. — Consideration Received

1. — *Share Consideration*

The rollover only applies if the transferor receives[43] share consideration of the transferee corporation in exchange for the property transferred. Even one share of the capital stock of the purchasing corporation is sufficient consideration. The purpose of this rule is to ensure that any tax deferred on the transfer of property will eventually be taxable on a subsequent disposition of the share consideration in an unprotected transaction.

The share consideration is allocated to each asset. Although subsection 85(1) speaks of "shares" in the plural, the vendor need take back only a single share in return for all of the property transferred to the corporation.[44] The agreement of purchase and sale can allocate some, even if only a fraction of the shares, to all of the assets that are the subject of the election. A more conservative approach is to allocate at least one share to each asset, or type of property, transferred to the corporation.

2. — *Boot*

The vendor may also take back non-share consideration (sometimes referred to as "boot") in exchange for the property sold. "Boot" consists of any consideration other than shares of the purchaser corporation. Examples include, cash, assets of the purchaser corporation, a promissory note of the purchaser, or assumption of the vendor's liabilities by the purchasing corporation.

3. — *Allocation*

Subject to certain constraints, the amount elected (referred to as the "agreed upon" amount) to be recognized as proceeds of disposition must be allocated between the non-share consideration (if any), preferred shares (if any), and common shares issued to the transferor. The allocation of cost to the share consideration must be made on a class-by-class basis[45] and may affect the cost of other identical properties owned by the transferor.[46]

---

[43]*Dale v. The Queen*, [1994] 1 C.T.C. 2303, 94 D.T.C. 1100 (T.C.C.); revd. [1997] 2 C.T.C. 286, 97 D.T.C. 5252 (Fed. C.A.) (shares do not have to be issued, but there must be a binding obligation to do so at the time of the transfer).

[44]See the *Interpretation Act*, R.S.C. 1985. c. I-21, subs. 33(2).

[45]Paras. 85(1)(g), (h).

[46]S. 47.

The allocation of the elected amount, rather than the contractually agreed upon transfer price, allows the transferor to defer recognizing any gain on the property transferred by electing the cost of the property transferred rather than its fair market value. To prevent taxpayers from misusing the rollover, however, the Act imposes four additional restrictions:

1. There are upper and lower limits on the amount that may be elected in respect of different types of property transferred and consideration received;

2. Subsection 84(1) may apply to deem a dividend if the paid-up capital of the shares received as consideration exceeds the fair market value of the property transferred to the corporation;

3. Subsection 85(2.1) may apply to reduce the paid-up capital of the shares received as consideration if the paid-up capital is higher than the tax cost of the asset transferred; and

4. Section 84.1 may deem a dividend in certain circumstances.[47]

The first three of these control devices are discussed below. Section 84.1 is considered in Chapter 26 "Non-Arm's Length Share Transfers".

XI. — Elected Amounts

As a general rule, the Act deems non-arm's length transfers to occur at fair market value.[48] Subsection 69(11) extends the fair market value rule to certain non-affiliated transactions.

The general scheme in subsection 85(1) is that both the vendor and the purchasing corporation can agree upon an amount other than fair market value in respect of *each* property transferred to the corporation. Within certain limits, the agreed upon amount in respect of each property becomes the vendor's deemed proceeds of disposition and the purchaser's cost of that property.[49]

The agreed upon or elected amount is also used to determine the cost base of the consideration paid to the vendor. Thus, within limits, the vendor can control the amount of the capital gain or recapture of capital cost allowance that will be recognized in the year of transfer.

---

[47]See Chapter 26, "Non-Arm's Length Share Transfers".

[48]Subs. 69(1).

[49]Para. 85(1)(a).

1. — General Limits

There are two general upper and lower limits on the amount that may be agreed upon by the vendor and the purchasing corporation.

(a) — Elected Amount Cannot Exceed Fair Market Value

First, the amount elected in respect of a property cannot exceed its fair market value; if it does, the Act *deems* the fair market value of the property to be the elected amount.[50] This places an upper limit on the election. The purpose of this rule is to prevent the vendor from artificially inflating capital gains on property in order to offset such gains against capital losses. The rule also prevents the purchaser from artificially stepping-up its cost base in the property.

Example	
Assume:	
ACB	$ 100
FMV	$ 200
Elected amount	$ 250
Then:	
Deemed POD	$ 200
ACB	(100)
Capital gain	$ 100

The fair market value of property transferred must be set out in the prescribed form. The Agency accepts a "reasonable estimate" of fair market value where the elected amount is not affected by the fair market value.

---

[50]Para. 85(1)(c).

(b) — Elected Amount Cannot be Less than Boot

Second, the elected amount cannot be less than the value of any *non-share consideration* ("boot") received from the purchaser corporation.[51] This places a lower limit on the election. Where the elected amount is less than the value of boot received, the Act *deems* the value of the boot to be the elected amount. The purpose of this limit is to prevent a taxpayer from actually realizing and extracting the economic value of a gain without, at the same time, recognizing the gain for tax purposes.

A corollary of this rule is that a taxpayer can extract boot from the corporation, at least up to the value of the cost in the asset, without triggering a capital gain.

Example

Assume:

ACB	$ 100
FMV	$ 200
"Boot" (promissory note)	$ 120
Elected amount	$ 100

Then:

Deemed POD	$ 120
ACB	(100)
Capital gain	$ 20

In the absence of this rule the taxpayer could have the promissory note paid off without recognizing the actual gain of $20.

With the exception of the upper limit rule noted above, the value of "boot" sets the floor of the range of amounts that may be elected. Thus, the election can range between the value of "boot" received from the purchaser corporation and the fair market value of the property sold to the corporation. In the above example, the taxpayer can extract up to $100 in boot without triggering a capital gain on the transfer of the asset.

---

[51] Para. 85(1)(b).

(c) — Fair Market Value Determines Upper Limit

A taxpayer cannot elect an amount in excess of the fair market value of the property transferred to the corporation: fair market value is the upper limit of electable amounts.

Where the value of "boot" exceeds the fair market value of the asset sold to the corporation, the fair market value of the asset determines the upper limit of the election range. Any excess of "boot" over the fair market value of the asset sold is a taxable shareholder benefit.[52] The amount of the benefit may be added to the cost base of the "boot" received from the corporation.[53]

Example

Assume:

	Case A	Case B
ACB	$ 100	$ 100
FMV	$ 200	$ 200
"Boot" (cash)	$ 250	$ 200
Elected amount	$ 225	$ 225

Then:

	Case A	Case B
Deemed POD	$ 200	$ 200
ACB	(100)	(100)
Capital gain	$ 100	$ 100
Shareholder benefit (subs. 15(1))	$ 50	—

---

[52] Subs. 15(1).

[53] Subs. 52(1). It is unclear what would happen if the "boot" takes the form of cash, i.e., if the value of the shareholder benefit is added to the cost of cash so that there is a capital loss on the disposition of the cash. The CRA's view is that money does not constitute "property" and, therefore, the cost adjustment rule in subs. 52(1) would not apply. Subs. 248(1) states that property includes money *unless* there is a contrary intention.

(d) — Liabilities are Boot

Liabilities assumed by the purchaser corporation constitute "boot". Where an asset that has a liability attached to it (e.g., mortgaged land) is sold, the excess of the liability over the cost of the asset is "boot" for the purposes of para. 85(1)(b).[54]

Example	
Assume:	
ACB of land	$ 100
FMV of land	$ 300
Mortgage on land ("boot")	$ 210
Elected amount	$ 100
Cost of other assets sold	$ 200
FMV of other assets	$ 170
Elected amount	$ 170
Then:	
1. Without allocation	
Deemed POD of land ("boot")	$ 210
ACB of land	(100)
Capital gain on land	$ 110
2. With allocation of boot	
To land: $100 of mortgage.	
To other assets: $110 of mortgage.	
Then:	
Deemed POD of land	$ 100
ACB of land	(100)
Capital gain	NIL

---

[54]See IT-291R3.

2. — Specific Limits

In addition to the general rules dealing with elected amounts, there are a number of special rules designed to prevent taxpayers from artificially avoiding tax.[55]

(a) — Inventory and Non-Depreciable Capital Property

Where the property transferred to a corporation is inventory or non-depreciable capital property, the elected amount cannot be less than the *lesser* of its fair market value and cost amount to the taxpayer.[56] This rule prevents the taxpayer from creating an artificial loss.

Example	
Assume the following applies to inventory or non-depreciable capital property:	
ACB/Cost amount	$ 100
FMV	$ 200
"Boot" (cash)	$ 90
Elected amount	$ 90
Then:	
Deemed POD	$ 100
ACB	(100)
Capital gain	NIL

Note, the general rule merely disallows an election at "boot".[57] This special rule, in effect, raises the election floor to the lower of the fair market value and cost amount of the property.

---

[55]Paras. 85(1)(c.1), (d), (e), (e.1), (e.2).

[56]Para. 85(1)(c.1).

[57]Para. 85(1)(b), para. 85(1)(e.3).

Example

Assume the following applies to inventory:

ACB	$ 100
FMV	$ 80
"Boot" (cash)	$ 70
Elected amount	$ 70

Then:

Deemed POD	$ 80
ACB	(100)
Capital loss	$ (20)

As the above example illustrates, this rule prevents a taxpayer from creating an *artificial* loss by electing an amount that is less than the fair market value of the property.

(b) — Eligible Capital Property

The amount elected in respect of eligible capital property sold to a corporation cannot be less than the *least* of the following amounts:[58]

- 4/3 the vendor's cumulative eligible capital in respect of the business immediately before the transfer;

- The cost of the property to the taxpayer; and

- The fair market value of the property at the time of its disposition.

The Act deems a taxpayer who elects a lesser amount to have elected the least of these three amounts.

Example

Assume:

Cost	$ 100
FMV	$ 200
"Boot" (cash)	$ 70
CEC (cumulative eligible capital)	$ 60

---

[58]Para. 85(1)(d).

Example	
Then:	
Deemed POD (4/3 × $60)	$ 80
CEC	$ 60
75% × $80	(60)
Balance CEC	NIL

Here too, the rationale of limiting the vendor to the least of the three amounts is to prevent the creation of an artificial loss on the disposition of eligible capital property.

A terminal loss in respect of eligible capital property may only be claimed where its actual value is less than the balance in the vendor's cumulative eligible account before the transfer of property.[59] Where an individual incorporates an existing business, however, he cannot claim the deduction, which flows through to the corporation (subsection 24(2)).

(c) — Depreciable Properties

(i) — General Rule

There are two rules in respect of dispositions of depreciable properties of a prescribed class. The general rule is that the amount agreed upon by the vendor and the purchaser corporation cannot be less than the *least* of:[60]

- The undepreciated capital cost (UCC) of all property of that class;

- The cost of the property to the taxpayer; and

- The fair market value of the property at the time of disposition.

The purpose of this rule is to prevent the vendor from claiming an artificial terminal loss by electing an unduly low amount. Thus, generally, a taxpayer may only claim a terminal loss where the fair market value of the depreciable property is *actually* less than its un-depreciated capital cost.

---

[59]Subs. 24(1).

[60]Para. 85(1)(e).

Example		
Assume:	*Case A*	*Case B*
Cost	$ 100	$ 100
UCC	$ 50	$ 60
FMV	$ 70	$ 40
"Boot" (cash)	$ 40	$ 40
Elected amount	$ 40	$ 40
Deemed POD	$ 50	$ 40
UCC	(50)	(60)
Terminal loss	NIL	$ (20)*

The elected amount of $40 in Case A would otherwise produce an artificial terminal loss since the fair market value of the property exceeds its UCC.

Notes:

*   The stop-loss rule in subsection 13(21.2) may apply if the transferor and the transferee corporation are affiliated.

(ii) — Company Cars

A taxpayer is restricted in the amount that he may deduct as capital cost allowance on passenger automobiles. Generally, a taxpayer may not claim capital cost allowance on more than $30,000 in respect of the capital cost of a passenger automobile.[61] This $30,000 limit is the prescribed amount after 2000 and will be increased from time to time as circumstances warrant.

The $30,000 rule effectively limits the maximum capital cost allowance permitted on passenger vehicles. To prevent taxpayers from circumventing the limit when a passenger vehicle is transferred to a corporation under section 85, a special anti-avoidance rule restricts the amount that may be elected in respect of the undepreciated capital cost of the vehicle immediately before its transfer to the corporation.[62] For the purposes of calculating the standby

---

[61]Para. 13(7)(g); Reg. 7307(1).

[62]Para. 85(1)(e.4).

charge,[63] however, the Act deems the cost of the automobile to the corporation to be its fair market value immediately before its transfer to the corporation.

(d) — Ordering of Dispositions

Where a taxpayer simultaneously transfers several items of depreciable property of the same class, or several eligible capital properties in respect of a business, he should designate the sequence of the dispositions so as to avoid recapture of capital cost allowance previously claimed on the properties.[64] Then each of the properties will be transferred separately in the designated order and the undepreciated capital cost of the class, or the cumulative eligible capital, will be reduced as each asset is transferred. In practice, the order in which properties are transferred is generally significant where the vendor receives non-share consideration (e.g., cash) as part of the purchase price. This is because the non-share consideration or "boot" acts as the floor for the taxpayer's election.

Example

Assume that a taxpayer transfers two Class 8 assets:

	Asset #1	Asset #2
Cost	$ 100	$ 500
FMV	$ 80	$ 400
Cash consideration	$ 80	NIL
UCC of Class	$ 300	

The taxpayer stipulates that the properties are to be transferred at their minimum allowable amounts and Asset #1 is transferred first, then:

UCC of class	$ 300
Amount elected (Asset #1)	(80)
UCC remaining	$ 220
Amount elected (Asset #2)	(220)
Recapture	NIL

---

[63]See Chapter 6, "Employment Income".

[64]Para. 85(1)(e.1).

Example

If the taxpayer had designated in the reverse order, i.e., Asset #2 before Asset #1, then:

UCC of class	$ 300
Amount elected (Asset #2)	(300)
UCC remaining	NIL
Amount elected (Boot for Asset #1)	80
Recapture of CCA	$ 80

As the above example illustrates, the designated order of dispositions is generally important if the taxpayer receives boot as part of the consideration for the transfer. The Minister may designate the order of disposition if the taxpayer fails to do so.

XII. — Conflict Between Rules

Given the numerous rules that limit the upper and lower values of the elected amounts, it is possible that one rule may dictate a result that is in conflict with the result produced by another rule. To resolve such conflicts, an overriding rule deems the order in which the individual rules are to apply.[65] In the event that the application of paragraph 85(1)(c.1),(d), or (e) produces a result that conflicts with the result obtained by applying paragraph 85(1)(b), the elected amount is deemed to be the *greater* of the two conflicting amounts. Hence, the elected amount cannot be less than "boot" received and can never be more than the fair market value of the property transferred.

Example		
Assume a capital property:		
	Case A	*Case B*
ACB	$ 60	$ 60
FMV	$ 100	$ 100
"Boot"	$ 40	$ 80
Elected amount	$ 30	$ 30

---

[65]Para. 85(1)(e.3).

Example		
Then:		
Result under para. 85(1)(b)	$ 40	$ 80
Result under para. 85(1)(c.1)	$ 60	$ 60
Deemed elected amount by para. 85(1)(e.3)	$ 60	$ 80

XIII. — Indirect Benefits Rule

1. — Purpose

Section 85 contains a specific anti-avoidance rule that is intended to prevent a taxpayer from disposing of property for inadequate consideration in order to benefit a related person. For example, an individual may dispose of property valued at $1 million to a corporation controlled by the individual's child in exchange for consideration valued at $400,000. The shortfall of $600,000 in the value of the consideration received would accrue to the benefit of the controlling shareholder, the transferor's child. Paragraph 85(1)(e.2) adds the value of the benefit conferred to the proceeds of disposition elected by the taxpayer.

Paragraph 85(1)(e.2) only applies where the consideration received by the taxpayer in exchange for property transferred to a corporation is less than the value of the property *and* it is reasonable to regard the difference as a benefit that the taxpayer desires to confer on a person related to him or her. In these circumstances the elected proceeds are increased by the value of the benefit.[66]

2. — Scope of Rule

More specifically, where the fair market value of property transferred to a corporation exceeds *both*:

- The fair market value of the consideration received from the corporation in exchange for the sale, *and*

- The amount agreed upon (subject to the various deeming provisions discussed above) in respect of the property,

---

[66]Para. 85(1)(e.2).

and it is reasonable to infer that any portion of the excess is intended to be a benefit conferred on a person related to the taxpayer, the "excess portion" is added to the elected proceeds of disposition and, as such, may trigger a capital gain on the property transferred.

In the absence of this rule, it would be possible for a taxpayer to dispose of assets to a corporation for less than their fair market value and take back a minimum number of shares in the corporation. This would effectively transfer the assets to the other shareholders of the corporation without triggering any tax on accrued capital gains.

Example

Assume:

Holdco is a family business owned by:

X	10%
X's spouse	50%
X's child	40%
	100%

X transfers land (capital property) with an ACB of $10,000 and FMV of $60,000 to *Holdco* in exchange for preferred shares with a fair market value of $1,000. The parties elect $10,000.

Then:

FMV of property of land		$ 60,000
Exceeds *greater* of:		
FMV of consideration	$ 1,000	
Elected amount	$ 10,000	
		(10,000)
Inadequate consideration		$ 50,000
Benefit conferred (90% of $50,000)		$ 45,000
Elected amount		10,000
Deemed elected amount		55,000
ACB of property		(10,000)
Capital gain realized		$ 45,000

Example		
Assume:		
Ownership of shares prior to transfer:		
Father	20	
Mother	45	
Child	35	
	100	
Property transferred by father:		
ACB	$ 15,000	
FMV	$ 75,000	
Elected amount		$ 15,000
Consideration: shares (PUC and FMV)		$ 15,000
Then:		
Inadequate consideration		$ 60,000
Indirect benefit (80% × 60,000)		$ 48,000
Deemed elected amount		$ 63,000
Gain to father		$ 48,000
ACB of property to corporation		$ 63,000
Father's ACB of shares taken back		$ 15,000

3. — Penal Provision

Paragraph 85(1)(e.2) operates as a penal provision. The amount of the indirect gift included in the transferor's proceeds of disposition is neither added to the adjusted cost base of the share consideration received in exchange for the property nor to the adjusted cost base of the shares of the shareholder who has benefited from the transfer.[67] Thus, the tax cost of the "indirect gift" results in a permanent loss that is not recoverable by any person at any time. The value of the indirect gift is, however, added to the cost of the asset transferred to the corporation.

---

[67]Paras. 85(1)(e.2) and 53(1)(c).

4. — Bump-Up

The bump-up to the amount elected by the transferor and the purchaser corporation in their election is made *after* applying all of the other rules in subsection 85(1) and not to the amount actually set out in their joint election.[68] In the above example, if X and *Holdco* had initially elected $1,000, the elected amount would have been bumped up to $10,000 (paragraph 85(1)(c.1)) which would then be bumped up by $45,000 (benefit conferred) to bring it up to $55,000.

5. — Related Persons

The rule only applies to transfers between related persons. Thus, the scope of this rule is similar to its counterpart provisions in other parts of the Act.[69] Of course, it is quite unlikely that a taxpayer would confer a benefit on a complete stranger.

6. — Post-Transfer Benefits

The indirect benefits rule is broad enough to catch a benefit conferred on a person who becomes a shareholder of the transferee corporation *after* the transfer of property to the corporation. Thus, where a taxpayer's children take up shares in the corporation to which he or she has transferred property in circumstances such that it may reasonably be regarded that they have benefited, the rule will apply to bump-up the taxpayer's proceeds of disposition.[70]

7. — Transfers Between Corporations

The rule also applies to any benefits conferred on the transferee corporation itself unless the corporation is a wholly-owned corporation of the transferor immediately after the disposition.

8. — Value of Transferred Property

The value of the property transferred and the consideration received in exchange is a question of fact in each case. The Agency takes the position that the fair market value of the

---

[68]Any other interpretation of para. 85(1)(e.2) would undermine its rationale and be contrary to the *Interpretation Act*, R.S.C. 1985, c. I-21, s. 12.

[69]See, e.g., subss. 86(2), 87(4) and para. 51(2)(c).

[70]Any other interpretation would clearly defeat the "object and spirit" of the provision and provide a gaping loophole.

transferred property is not reduced by the amount of the potential deferred tax liability on the asset in the hands of the transferee. For example, where a property with an adjusted cost base of $100 and a fair market value of $700 is transferred to a corporation under section 85, the deferred tax on the $600 potential gain cannot be taken into account in determining the value of the consideration paid to the transferor. In the event that such a deferred gain is taken into account, the reduced consideration received on the transfer will be used to determine the excess for the purposes of paragraph 85(1)(e.2).

XIV. — Cost Of Property To Corporation

1. — General Rule

The general rule is that a purchaser corporation acquires the property transferred to it at a cost equal to the amount agreed, or deemed to have been agreed, upon by the parties in their joint election.[71] Thus, the corporation stands in the shoes of the transferor in respect of properties transferred to it and is liable for any tax payable upon the eventual disposition of the property. Hence the rollover: the transferor's elected amount is, in effect, "rolled over" to the corporation.

2. — Pre-1972 Property

Special rules regulate the transfer of non-depreciable capital property owned by a taxpayer on June 19, 1971. Where a taxpayer who has not elected to use Valuation Day[72] values in respect of pre-1972 capital properties, transfers such property to a corporation with which the taxpayer does not deal at arm's length, the Act deems the corporation to have owned the capital property continuously since June 18, 1971. The Act deems the "actual cost" of the property to be equal to the cost of the property to the taxpayer.[73] In effect, the corporation steps into the taxpayer's shoes and calculates the cost of its pre-1972 capital property by applying the median rule under ITAR 26(3). Thus, the transferee corporation can take advantage of the tax-free or neutral zone of the property in calculating its gain or loss when it disposes of the property.[74]

---

[71]Para. 85(1)(a).

[72]ITAR 26(7). See Part XII of the Act.

[73]ITAR 26(5). Note also, a transfer of capital property under s. 85 is deemed not to be an arm's length transfer for the purposes of ITAR 26(5).

[74]ITAR 26(5)(c) provides for various adjustments to the cost of the property.

3. — Depreciable Properties

Another special rule applies in respect of depreciable property. Where the elected amount in respect of depreciable property is less than the transferor's cost of the property, for the purpose of calculating capital cost allowance and any recapture thereof, the Act deems the transferee corporation to:[75]

- Acquire the property for an amount equal to the capital cost of the property to the transferor, and

- Have claimed capital cost allowance in an amount equal to the difference between the vendor's capital cost and the elected amount.

In effect, the capital cost of the property to the transferor flows through to the purchaser corporation, as does any capital cost allowance previously claimed on the property by the transferor. Hence, on a subsequent disposition by the purchaser corporation, the corporation may be liable for recapture of capital cost allowance previously claimed by the transferor in respect of the property.

This rule only applies in respect of depreciable properties transferred pursuant to subsections 85(1) and (2) (transfer from partnership) and does not apply in respect of transfers of property to a corporation where the transfer has not been made under those subsections. If the purchaser corporation disposes of the depreciable property under subsection 85(1), the original capital cost will flow through once again to the new transferee and the potential for recapture will pass through to the new owner of the property.[76]

Example

Assume one depreciable property:

Capital cost	$ 200
FMV	$ 250
UCC	$ 150

---

[75]Subs. 85(5).

[76]Unrealized capital gains on depreciable property owned on V-Day that are the subject matter of a section 85 rollover are protected from tax upon their ultimate disposition by the purchaser: ITAR 20(1) and (1.2) (see above example).

Example	
Then:	
Deemed elected amount (para. 85(1)(e))	$ 150
Purchaser's capital cost (subs. 85(5))	$ 200 *
Deemed proceeds	(150)
CCA deemed claimed (potential recapture)	$ 50

Notes:

*   equals vendor's capital cost

Example	
Assume one depreciable property of a prescribed class:	
Capital cost	$ 100
V-Day	$ 200
UCC	$ 70
Sold by purchaser at FMV	$ 250
Then:	
(i) Deemed elected amount on transfer to corporation (para. 85(1)(e))	$ 70
(ii) Cost of property to purchaser	$ 100
CCA deemed claimed	(30)
UCC to purchaser (subs. 85(5))	$ 70
(iii) On sale by purchaser	
Recapture of CCA	$ 30
Capital gain (FMV — V-Day)	$ 50

One aspect of the cost flow-through rules warrants emphasis: subsection 85(5) only flows through the transferor's capital cost to the purchaser corporation for the purposes of calculating capital cost allowance and recapture thereof. The provision does not flow through such cost to the purchaser corporation for the purposes of calculating the corporation's capital gain or loss on a disposition of the property at a later date. Therefore, it is possible for the same amount (that is, the difference between the vendor's original cost and the agreed upon amount) to be subject to both recapture of capital cost allowance and taxed again as a capital gain. The argument against this view is that there is a general judicial understanding that fiscal statutes are to be interpreted so as to avoid double taxation of the same amount. Alternatively, it is also arguable that the mechanics of paragraph 39(1)(a) resolves the problem by deducting the portion of the gain — recapture of CCA — taxed elsewhere.

XV. — Cost of Consideration Received By The Transferor

Subsection 85(1) requires the transferor to take back share consideration from the purchaser corporation. The taxpayer may, of course, also take back non-share consideration. We determine the cost of the consideration received from the corporation by allocating the amount jointly elected (the agreed upon amount) by the transferor and the purchaser corporation to the various classes of consideration.[77] The agreed upon amount is allocated in the following sequence:

- First, to non-share consideration or "boot";

- Next, to preferred shares; and

- Finally, to common shares.

1. — Boot

The Act deems non-share consideration ("boot") paid to the transferor to have a cost equal to the lesser of its fair market value and the fair market value of the property transferred.[78] Where the transferor receives more than one property from the corporation, the Act deems the cost of *each* property to be the *lesser* of:[79]

- Its fair market value; and

- The proportion of the fair market value of all assets transferred to the corporation that the fair market value of the particular property bears to the fair market value of all "boot" received.

In effect, the cost of boot taken back from the corporation cannot exceed the fair market value of the property transferred to it.

---

[77]Paras. 85(1)(f), (g) and (h).

[78]Para. 85(1)(f).

[79]Para. 85(1)(f).

Example

Assume that property with a fair market value of $100,000 is transferred to a corporation in exchange for:

Cash	$ 5,000
Promissory note (FMV)	$65,000
Shares (FMV)	$30,000

Then:

Cost of promissory note is lesser of:

(i) $65,000 and

(ii) $\dfrac{65}{70} \times \$100,000 = \$92,857$

Lesser amount	$65,000

Example

Assume that an individual transfers a portfolio of shares with a value of $60,000 to a holding company in exchange for nominal share consideration and four properties valued as follows:

Property #1	$ 10,000
Property #2	15,000
Property #3	20,000
Property #4	55,000
	$100,000

Then, the cost of the four properties is determined as follows:

Property #1

$\dfrac{10 \times \$60,000}{100}$ $ 6,000

Property #2

$\dfrac{15 \times \$60,000}{100}$ 9,000

Example	
Property #3	
$\dfrac{20 \times \$60,000}{100}$	12,000
Property #4	
$\dfrac{55 \times \$60,000}{100}$	33,000
	$\$\ 60,000$

Where the transferor receives both shares and "boot" from the purchaser corporation, the cost base of the shares is determined as follows:

- First, calculate the amount to be allocated to the "boot";

- Second, determine the amount to be allocated to any preferred shares received as consideration;[80] and

- Finally, determine the cost to be allocated to any common shares of the purchaser corporation received as consideration in exchange for the transferred property.[81]

2. — *Preferred Shares*

In the simplest case, where the vendor receives only one class of preferred shares, the cost of each share is the *lesser* of:

- Its fair market value, and

- The difference between the agreed upon amount and the fair market value of "boot" received.

---

[80]Para. 85(1)(g). A "preferred share" is defined as a share other than a common share (subs. 248(1)"preferred share"). Although most new corporate statutes have moved away from the terminology of "preferred" and "common" shares, these concepts remain important for income tax purposes.

[81]Para. 85(1)(h).

Example

Assume that X transfers securities with a cost of $50,000 and fair market value of $120,000 to *Holdco Ltd.* in exchange for the following:

Consideration	FMV
Land	$ 50,000
Promissory note	40,000
Preferred shares	30,000
	$ 120,000

The agreed upon amount is $100,000.

Then:

Consideration	Cost Base to Transferor
Land	$ 50,000
Promissory note	40,000
Preferred shares	
($100,000–$90,000)	10,000
	$ 100,000

Where the transferor takes back more than one class of preferred shares, the cost of each class of preferred shares is deemed to be the *lesser* of:[82]

- Their fair market value; and

- That proportion of the excess of the agreed upon amount over the value of "boot" that the fair market value of the preferred shares of that class is of the fair market value of all preferred shares received as consideration.

In other words, the excess of the deemed proceeds of disposition (agreed upon amount) received by the transferor over the amount of "boot" paid is allocated to the preferred shares in proportion to their fair market value.

---

[82]Para. 85(1)(g).

Example

Assume that an individual transfers public securities with a cost of $50,000 and fair market value of $120,000 to *Holdco* in exchange for the following:

Consideration	FMV
Promissory note	$ 50,000
Class A preferred shares	40,000
Class B preferred shares	30,000
	$ 120,000

The parties elect $100,000 as the agreed upon amount.
Then:

Cost of Class A preferred shares
Lesser of:

FMV	$ 40,000	
(100,000 - 50,000) × 40/70 =	$ 28,571	
		$ 28,571

Cost of Class B preferred shares
Lesser of:

FMV	$ 30,000	
(100,000 - 50,000) × 30/70 =	$ 21,429	
		$ 21,429

Consideration	Cost Base to Transferor
Promissory note	$ 50,000
Class A preferred	28,571
Class B preferred	21,429
	$ 100,000

3. — *Common Shares*

The cost of any common shares received as consideration is simply the residual amount remaining after the deemed cost of "boot" and any preferred shares is deducted from the elected (or deemed elected) amount. Once again, in the simplest case, if the transferor takes back only one class of common shares from the purchaser corporation, the entire remaining balance, *if any*, is allocated to those shares.

Example	
Assume:	
Cost of property transferred	$ 100,000
FMV of property transferred	$ 180,000
Consideration received:	
Boot (FMV)	$ 100,000
Shares	?
Amount elected	$ 100,000
Then:	
Amount elected (POD)	$ 100,000
Cost of boot	(100,000)
Cost of shares received	NIL

Example	
Assume Y transfers property with a cost of $100,000 and fair market value of $150,000 to *Opco Ltd.* in exchange for the following:	
Consideration	*FMV*
Cash	$ 20,000
Class A preferred	80,000
Class B preferred	50,000
	$150,000
The agreed upon amount is $100,000	
Then:	
Proceeds of disposition	$100,000
Less: boot	(20,000)
Excess	$ 80,000
Cost of Class A preferred	

Example

$$\frac{80,000}{130,000} \times \$80,000$$
                                        $ 49,231

Cost of Class B preferred

$$\frac{50,000}{130,000} \times \$80,000$$
                                        $ 30,769

Consideration	*Cost Base to Transferor*
Cash	$ 20,000
Class A preferred	49,231
Class B preferred	30,769
	$100,000

Where the transferor receives more than one class of common shares from the purchaser corporation, the balance is allocated amongst the various classes of common shares in proportion to their fair market value.

Example

Assume Z transfers property with an adjusted cost base of $100,000 and fair market value of $180,000 to *Newco Ltd.* in exchange for the following:

Consideration	*FMV*
Cash	$ 20,000
Class A preferred	80,000
Class B preferred	50,000
Class C common	30,000
	$180,000

The agreed upon amount is $100,000

Then:

Proceeds of disposition	$100,000
Less: non-share consideration ("boot")	(20,000)
Excess	$ 80,000

Example

Cost of Class A preferred		
$\dfrac{80,000}{130,000} \times \$80,000$		$ 49,231
Cost of Class B preferred		
$\dfrac{50,000}{130,000} \times \$80,000$		$ 30,769
Cost of Class C common		NIL

Consideration	Cost Base to Transferor
Cash	$ 20,000
Class A preferred	49,231
Class B preferred	30,769
Common	NIL
	$100,000

XVI. — Paid-Up Capital Of Shares Issued By Purchaser Corporation

The concept of paid-up capital ("PUC") is fundamental to the corporate income tax system. Generally, a corporation can return paid-up capital to its shareholders on a tax-free basis. Hence, the tax system seeks to prevent artificial increases in the PUC of shares.

1. — In Excess of Fair Market Value of Property Acquired

The paid-up capital ("PUC") of shares issued to the vendor must not exceed the fair market value of the transferred property. To the extent that it does, the Act deems the vendor to have received a dividend under subsection 84(1).

Example

Assume:	
Cost of property transferred	$ 100,000
FMV of property transferred	$ 200,000

Example	
Consideration received:	
Boot	$ 60,000
PUC of preferred shares	40,000
PUC of common shares	120,000
	$ 220,000
FMV of property transferred	(200,000)
Deemed dividend	$ 20,000

Where the paid-up capital of shares issued by the purchaser corporation exceeds the fair market value of the property transferred to it, the Act deems *each* shareholder of the class of shares to receive a dividend.[83] Such a transaction may contravene the applicable corporate law. Under the *Canada Business Corporations Act*[84] a corporation may not add to the stated capital account of a class of shares an amount that is greater than the amount of the consideration it receives in exchange for the shares. The purpose of this rule is to prevent taxpayers from converting taxable surpluses into paid-up capital, which can then be returned to shareholders on a tax-free basis.

Example	
Assume:	
Adjusted cost base of capital property	$ 100
Fair market value of property	$ 400
Mortgage on property	$ 100
Consideration received:	
Paid-up capital/preferred shares	$ 200
Paid-up capital/common shares	130
	$ 330

---

[83]Subs. 84(1).

[84]R.S.C. 1985, c. C-44, subs. 26(4). See also, *Business Corporations Act*, R.S.O. 1990, c. B.16, subs. 24(4).

Example	
Then:	
Increase in paid-up capital	$ 330
Net increase in value of assets	(300)
Deemed dividend (subs. 84(1))	$ 30

The *pro rata* value of the dividend is added to the cost base of the shares on which the Act deems the dividend to have been paid.[85] Note, that *all* holders of shares of the particular class are affected by an improperly valued transfer of property to a corporation.

The stated capital of shares may be controlled through the use of an appropriate directors' resolution. The following is an example:

> BE IT RESOLVED THAT in accordance with Section # of the *Canada Business Corporations Act*, there be added to the stated capital account maintained for the First Preference shares in the capital of the Corporation, (state number) of which are being issued to the Vendor as consideration for the Property, an amount equal to the fair market value of the Property immediately before the completion of the purchase, which the directors of the Corporation have determined to be (state value); provided, however, that if hereafter the directors of the Corporation become satisfied that such fair market value of the Property was not (state value), then this addition to the said stated capital account shall be changed to such amount as the directors are satisfied is equal to such fair market value.

2. — Reduction of Paid-Up Capital of Shares

A special anti-avoidance rule in subsection 85(2.1) prevents the removal of taxable corporate surpluses as a tax-free capital gain in circumstances when other more particular provisions (such as sections 84.1 and 212.1) might not apply.

Where the paid-up capital of share consideration issued by the purchaser corporation exceeds the cost of property that it acquires less the value of "boot" paid, the paid-up capital of the shares is reduced by the amount of the excess.[86] The rule prevents misuse of the lifetime capital gains exemption. Note that this rule applies to arm's length and non-arm's length transfers, but it does not apply if either section 84.1 or 212.1 applies.

The formula for reducing the paid-up capital of the shares issued by the purchaser corporation (sometimes referred to as a "PUC grind") is as follows:[87]

---

[85]Para. 53(1)(b). Non-resident shareholders may be subject to withholding tax (subs. 212(2)).

[86]Subs. 85(2.1).

[87]Para. 85(2.1)(a).

$$(A - B) \times \frac{C}{A}$$

where:

    A   = the increase in the corporation's total paid-up capital for corporate purposes as a result of the acquisition;

    B   = excess of the cost of property to the corporation over "boot" paid;

    C   = the increase in the paid-up capital of the particular class of shares as a result of the acquisition.

The C/A part of the formula only applies if more than one class of shares is issued as consideration for the property transferred. It has no application if only one class of shares is issued.

Example

Property transferred to a corporation under subsection 85(1):

Adjusted cost base (ACB)	$ 100
Fair market value (FMV)	$ 300
Consideration received:	
Promissory note	$ 150
Common shares (PUC and FMV)	$ 150
Deemed elected amount	$ 150
ACB of common shares	NIL

Without subsection 85(2.1), the taxpayer could redeem the common shares at their fair market value ($150) for a potentially tax-exempt capital gain of $150. There would be no deemed dividend because the amount paid would be equal to the paid-up capital ($150) of the shares.

Subsection 85(2.1) prevents this from happening:

Stated capital for corporate purposes	$ 150
Less: PUC "grind"	
(A - B) × C/A	
(150 - 0) × 150/150	(150)
PUC for tax purposes	NIL

Now, on a redemption of the common shares at their FMV, the transferor is required to recognize a deemed dividend instead of a capital gain.

Example

Redemption price	$ 150
PUC of shares	NIL
Deemed dividend (subs. 84(3))	150
Cash received on redemption	$ 150
Less, deemed dividend	(150)
Proceeds of disposition (para. 54 "proceeds of disposition"(j))	NIL
ACB of shares	NIL
Capital gain	NIL

Thus, subsection 85(2.1) prevents the bump-up in the paid-up capital of the shares and thereby prevents the transferor from converting the potential deemed dividend upon redemption of the shares into a tax-free capital gain.

Example

Assume:

Mr. White transfers land to an operating corporation (*Opco*) in exchange for its Class A shares. The following data applies to the transaction:

Fair market value (FMV) of land	$ 140,000
Adjusted cost base (ACB) of land	$ 40,000
FMV and PUC of *Opco* shares issued in exchange for land	$ 140,000

Assume, alternatively, that the parties elect	
Case A	$ 40,000
Case B	$ 140,000

as the transfer price under subsection 85(1) and that the shares are subsequently redeemed when their fair market value is $140,000.

Then:		
Proceeds of disposition	$ 40,000	$ 140,000

Example		
ACB of land	(40,000)	(40,000)
Capital gain realized under subs. 85(1)	NIL	$ 100,000
Stated capital of *Opco* shares	$ 140,000	$ 140,000
Less, cost of property to *Opco*	(40,000)	(140,000)
PUC "grind"	$ 100,000	NIL
Stated capital of *Opco* shares	$ 140,000	$ 140,000
Subs. 85(2.1) reduction "grind"	(100,000)	(NIL)
PUC for tax purposes	$ 40,000	$ 140,000
Deemed dividend on redemption of shares (subs. 84(3))	$ 100,000	NIL

XVII. — Taxable Canadian Property

Where property transferred to a corporation constitutes "taxable Canadian property", the Act also deems shares of the purchaser corporation paid to the transferor to be taxable Canadian property in the transferor's hands.[88]

XVIII. — Identical Properties

A taxpayer who has acquired identical properties before and after Valuation Day must segregate the properties into two separate pools.[89] The average cost of each property is calculated separately within each pool. Upon disposition of any of the properties, the Act deems the taxpayer to have disposed of properties acquired prior to V-day first; when that pool is exhausted, the Act deems further dispositions to come out of the post V-day pool.[90]

---

[88]Para. 85(1)(i).

[89]Subs. 47(1) and ITAR 26(8).

[90]ITAR 26(8)(e).

XIX. — Potential For Double Taxation

As we have seen, subsection 85(1) is a relieving provision. It allows a taxpayer to rollover property to a taxable Canadian corporation, and defer the tax on any gain accrued on the property, in circumstances when the Act would otherwise deem a disposition to occur at fair market value. The section does, however, create problems of double taxation.

1. — The Problem

The rollover comes at a price. It exposes both the taxpayer and the purchaser corporation to the risk of double taxation on the deferred accrued gain: once, when the taxpayer disposes of the consideration which he or she receives from the purchaser corporation; and again when the purchaser corporation disposes of the transferred assets.

The double tax problem is an intrinsic part of every section 85 rollover because the elected amount determines the tax basis of *both* the consideration received from the corporation *and* the property transferred to it. Thus, the deferred accrued gain is a latent tax liability in the hands of both the transferor and the transferee corporation.

Example

Assume:

F owns land (capital property)

ACB	$ 200,000
FMV	$ 700,000

1. If F sold the land to *Holdco Ltd.* at its fair market value of $700,000, he would realize a capital gain of $500,000 and the corporation's ACB in the land would be $700,000.

2. F transfers the land to *Holdco Ltd.* and the parties elect $200,000 as the agreed-upon amount under subs. 85(1) and F receives the following consideration in exchange for the land:

Promissory note (boot)	$ 200,000
Preferred shares (FMV)	500,000
	$ 700,000

Example	
Then:	
• Consequences to F	
POD (elected amount)	$ 200,000
ACB	(200,000)
Capital gain	$ NIL
• Cost of preferred shares	
POD	$ 200,000
Less: "boot"	(200,000)
Cost of preferred shares	$ NIL
Potential capital gain on preferred shares	$ 500,000
• Potential consequences to *Holdco*	
Cost of land	$ 200,000
FMV of land	700,000
Potential capital gain on disposition of land	$ 500,000

Thus, the accrued capital gain of $500,000 has been doubled to potential gains of $1,000,000.

The severity of the double taxation problem will vary with the circumstances. The longer the intended holding period of the shares received from the purchaser corporation, the less severe is the problem. Where the holding period is long, the discounted present value of the tax deferred on the rollover will outweigh the disadvantage of double taxation. We must evaluate each case on its own facts to determine what, if any, further steps are necessary to solve the problem.

2. — The Cure

In certain circumstances, for example, when the section 85 rollover is used to implement an estate freeze, the double tax problem can be redressed through subsection 164(6) in the year following the taxpayer's death.[91] We can avoid the problem of double taxation if the taxpayer's life is insurable and the corporation takes out a policy to pay for the redemption of the shares.

---

[91]See, generally, Ronald G. Gravelle, "Estate Freezing Today" in *Special Lectures of the Law Society of Upper Canada* (Toronto: DeBoo, 1980) 249 at 270.

Subsection 164(6) is an elective provision that allows the legal representative of a deceased taxpayer to amend the deceased's terminal return and offset any net capital losses suffered by the estate in its first taxation year against gains reported in the terminal return.

Thus, the length of the estate's first taxation year has important implications. On the one hand, it is desirable for the taxation year to be as long as possible so as to trigger the maximum number of losses for carryback to the terminal return. On the other hand, a short taxation year allows one to offset the losses as quickly as possible and to trigger the refund of taxes previously paid or to minimize the interest on unpaid taxes.

Example

Assume that the following facts apply in 2006:

Mr. Black owns 50 per cent of the shares of *Holdco*, (a Canadian controlled private corporation) which he acquired in exchange for his *Opco* shares rolled over to *Holdco* under section 85. The following data applies to his shares:

ACB	$ 100
PUC	$ 100
FMV	$500,000

Black has entered into an agreement with *Holdco* that it will redeem his shares on his death. The redemption price is to be the fair market value of the shares at that time. Black's life is insured for $500,000 by *Holdco*. The tax consequences on Black's death will be as follows:

1. Death

Deemed proceeds of disposition (para. 70(5)(a))	$ 500,000
Adjusted cost base	(100)
Capital gain	$ 499,900

2. Corporate redemption of shares from estate

Redemption price	$ 500,000
Less: PUC of shares	(100)
Deemed dividend (subs. 84(3))	$ 499,900
Capital dividend (subs. 83(2))*	(499,900)
Taxable amount	NIL

Example	
3. Net result to estate	
Redemption price	$ 500,000
Less: deemed dividend	(499,900)
Proceeds of disposition	100
Less: deemed ACB of shares (para. 70(5)(c))	(500,000)
Capital loss**	$(499,900)

Notes:

*   elect to treat as capital dividend using the capital dividend account arising from the life insurance proceeds

**   may be used to offset taxable capital gain of equal amount per subsection 164(6). The stop-loss rules in subsections 40(3.4) and (3.6) will deny the capital losses if the estate and the corporation are affiliated immediately after the redemption. However, subsection 40(3.61) ensures that the stop-loss rules will not apply to losses that are the subject of an election under subsection 164(6).

XX. — Transfer Of Property By A Partnership

A partnership is not a taxpayer under the *Income Tax Act*. For certain purposes, however, a partnership is treated *as if* it were a taxpayer.[92] In the context of transfers of property to a corporation, subsection 85(2) treats a partnership *as if* it were a taxpayer resident in Canada. It is important to note that subsection 85(2) is only available on a transfer of partnership property by the partnership itself; it does not apply to taxpayers who have joint ownership of property but who are not in partnership with each other. Note also, the share consideration paid by the purchaser corporation must be paid directly to the partnership and not to the individual partners.

1. — Real Property

We distinguish a partnership's assets from the partnership interests: the assets belong to the partnership; the interests belong to the partners. An interest in a partnership is not considered to be an interest in its underlying assets. Hence, where a partnership owns an inventory of real property, the partnership interest itself is not real property inventory. Thus, a partnership

---

[92]See, e.g., s. 96.

interest of a partnership that owns real property inventory may be rolled over to a corporation under subsection 85(1).

2. — *Winding-Up*

A special rule applies where a partnership has transferred all of its property to a corporation and the partnership is then wound up within 60 days of the transfer. In these circumstances, the cost of the consideration received by the partnership from the purchaser corporation may be rolled over from the partnership to the partners.[93] Thus, in certain circumstances, share consideration issued by the purchaser corporation in exchange for assets transferred by the partnership may be rolled over to the members of the partnership.

The rollout of property from a partnership to its members is only available where:[94]

- Partnership property has been rolled over from the partnership to a taxable Canadian corporation;

- The affairs of the partnership are wound up within 60 days after the disposition of the property; and

- Immediately before the winding-up of the partnership, there was no partnership property other than money or property received from the purchaser corporation as consideration for the disposition under subsection 85(2).

In effect, these requirements prevent a rollout of partnership assets to individual members if property that does not qualify for a rollover is transferred by the partnership to the corporation. Nor is the rollout available unless all of the partnership's property has been transferred to the corporation.

There are several rules to determine the cost of consideration received by the members of the partnership. Thus:

- The cost of "boot" is its fair market value at the time of the winding-up;[95]

- The cost of the preferred shares distributed to a partner is the *lesser* of:[96]

    - The fair market value of the shares immediately after the wind-up, and

---

[93]Subs. 85(3).

[94]Subs. 85(3).

[95]Para. 85(3)(d).

[96]Para. 85(3)(e). When no common shares were receivable as consideration, the cost of the preferred shares is the adjusted cost base of a partnership interest immediately before the wind-up less the fair market value of any "boot" distributed to the partner (subpara. 85(3)(e)(ii)).

- The adjusted cost base of a partnership interest immediately before the wind-up less the fair market value of any "boot" distributed to the partner;

- The cost to a partner of any common shares is the adjusted cost base of the partnership interest less the fair market value of "boot" and the cost allocated to any preferred shares distributed to him or her.[97]

The Act deems each partner to receive proceeds from the disposition of the partnership interest equal to the cost of all of the share and non-share property that is received on the winding-up of the partnership.[98]

Comprehensive Examples

SECTION 85 ROLLOVER		
Assume: Hilda Rumpole is the sole proprietor of a business to which the following data applies:		
	Cost *Amount*	*FMV*
Portfolio securities	$ 37,500	$ 28,000
Accounts receivable	56,250	56,250
Inventory	112,500	115,000
Machinery & equipment*	65,625	96,250
Goodwill	—	67,750
Liabilities	(26,250)	(26,250)
	$ 245,625	$ 337,000
She transfers the assets and liabilities of her business to a newly formed taxable Canadian corporation in exchange for the following consideration:		
Promissory note	$ 175,000	
Preferred shares (FMV)	87,500	
Common shares (FMV)	74,500	
	$ 337,000	

---

[97]Para. 85(3)(f).

[98]Para. 85(3)(g).

SECTION 85 ROLLOVER

The corporation also assumes the liabilities of $26,250. Mrs. Rumpole and the corporation elect under subsection 85(1) to minimize taxes. The parties do *not* elect under section 22 in respect of the accounts receivable.

Then:

		Agreed Amount	*Gain (Loss)*
1.	Elected amounts		
	Portfolio securities	$ 28,000	$ (9,500)
	Accounts receivable (s. 22)	56,250	—
	Inventory	112,500	—
	Machinery & equipment	65,625	—
	Goodwill	1	—
		$ 262,376	$ (9,500)**

2.	Cost of consideration received by Mrs. Rumpole		
	Agreed upon amount		$ 262,376
	Cost of "boot":		
	Liabilities assumed	$ 26,250	
	Promissory note	175,000	(201,250)
	Cost allocated to preferred shares		$ 61,126
	Cost allocated to common shares		NIL

3.	PUC reduction under subs. 85(2.1).	
	Assuming that PUC of preferred is $87,500 and PUC of common is $74,500, the reduction is as follows:	
	Preferred PUC $87,500 - $54,484 =	$ 33,016
	Common PUC $74,500 - $46,390 =	$ 28,110
	Total	$ 61,126

Notes:

*   Capital cost of $120,000

** Loss deemed to be nil under subparagraph 40(2)(g)(i) as a superficial loss.

REDUCTION OF PAID-UP CAPITAL OF SHARES UNDER SUBSECTION 85(2.1)

Assume:

Mr. Black sells his shares in an operating company (*Opco*) to a company (*Newco*) in an arm's length transaction. The following data applies to the *Opco* shares:

Fair market value (FMV)	$ 500,000
Adjusted cost base (ACB)	$ 1,000
Paid-up capital (PUC)	$ 1,000
Newco pays Mr. Black the following amounts:	
Promissory note	$ 200,000
Shares (FMV and PUC)	300,000 *
Purchase price	$ 500,000

The parties elect $200,000 as the transfer price for the *Opco* shares. The consequences to Mr. Black are as follows:

1. Capital gain on *Opco* shares

Proceeds of disposition (para. 85(1)(a))	$ 200,000
ACB of shares	(1,000)
Capital gain	$ 199,000

2. Adjustment to PUC of *Newco's* shares

Legal PUC of shares		$ 300,000
Less: amount by which		
Cost of *Opco* shares to *Newco*	$ 200,000	
exceeds		
Non-share consideration	(200,000)	
PUC reduction		NIL
PUC of *Newco* shares		$ 300,000
Legal PUC		$ 300,000
Less: subs. 85(2.1) reduction		$ (300,000)
PUC for tax purposes		NIL

3. ACB of *Newco's* shares   NIL

REDUCTION OF PAID-UP CAPITAL OF SHARES UNDER SUBSECTION 85(2.1)

4. Upon redemption of shares by Newco	
Redemption price	$ 300,000
PUC for tax purposes	NIL
Deemed dividend (subs. 84(3))	$ 300,000
Redemption	$ 300,000
Less: deemed dividend	(300,000)
Proceeds of disposition	
(s. 54"proceeds of disposition"(j))	NIL
ACB of shares	NIL
Capital gain	NIL

Notes:

*   Redeemable at $300,000.

Without the section 85 election, there would have been a capital gain of $499,000.

Selected Bibliography to Chapter 25

General

Battye, George A., "Structuring Corporate Transactions", *British Columbia Tax Conf.* 65 (Can. Tax Foundation, 1981).

Bernstein, Jack, "Corporate Spin-Offs and Creditor Proofing", *Proceedings of 39th Tax Conf.* 30:1 (Can. Tax Foundation, 1987).

Bollefer, Stuart F. and Sheldon M. Rochkin, "The Wingless Butterfly" (January 1986) 119 CA Magazine 70.

Boultbee, Jack, "A Survey of the Use of Rollovers in Acquisitions and Mergers" (1980) 28 Can. Tax J. 504.

Brown, Robert D. and Thomas E. McDonnell, "Capital Gains Strips: A Critical Review of the New Provisions", in *Proceedings of 32nd Tax Conf.* 51 (Can. Tax Foundation, 1980).

"Butterflies: An Endangered Species?" (1990) 12:17 The Canadian Taxpayer 135.

Dart, Robert J., "Specific Uses of Companies in Tax Planning", in *Proceedings of 31st Tax Conf.* 117 (Can. Tax Foundation, 1979).

Dart, Robert J. and Howard J. Kellough, "The Butterfly Reorganization: A Descriptive Analysis", in *Proceedings of 41st Tax Conf.* 20:2 (Can. Tax Foundation, 1989).

Dolan, Claude, "Roulements", *Congres "79"*, Association Quebecoise de Planification Fiscale et Succesorale, 165.

Ewens, Douglas S., "The Butterfly Matures", in *Proceedings of the 36th Tax Conf.* 866 (Can. Tax Foundation, 1984).

Ewens, Douglas S., "The Capital Gains Exemption and the Butterfly" (1986) 34 Can. Tax J. 914.

Ewens, Douglas S., "Transfers to a Corporation Under Subsection 85(1)" (1984) 32 Can. Tax J. 378.

Ewens, Douglas S. and Sharon J. Hugo, "The Effect of Bill C-139 on Certain Corporate Reorganizations" (1988) 36 Can. Tax J. 1021.

Harris, E.C., "Rollovers — Some Practical Questions: Subsection 85(1)" (1981) Can. Taxation 1027–1049.

Hausman, James S., "US-Canada Cross-Border Reorganizations" (1990) 38 Can. Tax J. 678.

Hiltz, Michael A., "The Butterfly Reorganization: Revenue Canada's Approach", in *Proceedings of 41st Tax Conf.* 20:32 (Can. Tax Foundation, 1989).

Kellough, Howard J., "Splitting Up the Business of a Private Corporation", *Corporate Management Tax Conf.* 12 (Can. Tax Foundation, 1984).

Kellough, Howard J. and Peter E. McQuillan, "Taxation of Private Corporations and Their Shareholders", *Canadian Tax Paper No. 72* 395 (Can. Tax Foundation, 1983).

Middleton, David W., "Common Tax Problems and Pitfalls in Effecting Reorganizations of Private Corporations", in *Proceedings of 41st Tax Conf.* 13:1 (Can. Tax Foundation, 1989).

Muirson, Stephen R., "Transfers of Property Within a Corporate Group" (1986) 34 Can. Tax J. 646.

Pitfield, Ian H., "Section 85 Transfers Revisited" (1978) 12 CGA Magazine 27.

"Reorganizations — Reorganized" (1991) 13:2 The Canadian Taxpayer 13.

Rohde, Richard C., "Section 85 Transfers — Limitations and Pitfalls" (1988) 36 Can. Tax J. 1302.

Scwartz, Alan M., "Transferring Shares of Private Corporations Need Not Be So Taxing" (1980) 113 CA Magazine No. 5, 49.

Sider, Vance A., *Butterfly Reorganizations* (Don Mills, Ontario: CCH Canadian, 1989).

Singer, Paul, "The Rollover Provisions in Respect of Corporate Reorganizations Provided under the *Income Tax Act*: Efficiency and Equity as Policy Considerations" (1983) 31 Can. Tax J. 569.

Spindler, Robert J., "Butterflies Revisited" (1989) 37 Can. Tax J. 808.

Stacey, John A., "Transfer of Assets To and From a Corporation", in *Proceedings of 40th Tax Conf.* 14:1 (Can. Tax Foundation, 1988).

Thomas, James P., "Restructuring the Ownership of Property Within a Closely-Held Group", *Corp. Management Tax Conf.* 6:1 (Can. Tax Foundation, 1989).

Williamson, W.G., "Transfers of Assets To and From a Canadian Corporation", in *Proceedings of 38th Tax Conf.* 12:1 (Can. Tax Foundation, 1986).

Witterick, R.G., "Acquisitions of Shares of Private Corporations in Arms's Length Transactions", *Corporate Management Tax Conf.* 120 (Can. Tax Foundation, 1978).

Property Eligible for Rollover

Murison, Stephen A., "Transfers of Property Within a Corporate Group (Taxation)" (1986) 34 Can. Tax J. 646–660.

Spindler, Robert J., "Mutual Fund Reorganizations" (1987) 35 Can. Tax J. 736.

Consideration Received

Boultbee, Jack A., "Dividend Stop-Loss Rules" (1985) 33 Can. Tax J. 150.

Stein, Boris P., "Part Two: Canadian Case Law Concerning Shares Received on a Rollover", *The Journal of Business Valuation*, Canadian Assoc. of Business Valuators, Vol. 7, 1981, 95.

Elected Amounts

Beam, Robert E. and Stanley N. Laiken, "Changes in Use and Non-Arm's Length Transfers of Depreciable Property" (1987) 35 Can. Tax J. 461.

Boultbee, Jack A., "Gifts and Rollovers" (1983) 31 Can. Tax J. 84.

Ewens, Douglas S., "Retractable Preferred Shares" (1983) 31 Can. Tax J. 713.

Heller, Stephen, "Part One: Valuation of Preferred Shares Received on a Rollover Under the *Income Tax Act*", *The Journal of Business Valuation*, Canadian Assoc. of Business Valuators, Vol. 7, 1981, 71.

Peters, Steven, "The Effect of Amendments to Paragraph 85(1)(e.2) on Transfers To and Between Wholly-Owned Corporations" (1989), 2:32 Can. Current Tax J-139.

Stainsby, Joseph A., "Recent Developments in Capital Cost Allowance and Eligible Capital Expenditures", *Corporate Management Tax Conf.* 196 (Can. Tax Foundation, 1981).

Wise, Richard M., "Fair Market Value Determinations — A Few More Requirements" (1983) 31 Can. Tax J. 337.

Wise, Richard M., "Valuation and the *Income Tax Act*" (1981) 29 Can. Tax J. 626.

Wise, Richard M., "The Valuation of Preferred Shares Issued on a Section 85 Rollover" (1984) 32 Can. Tax J. 239.

Paid-Up Capital of Shares Issued by Purchaser Corporation

Roberts, David G.,"Determination of Paid-Up Capital" (1992) 40 Can. Tax J. 338.

Simpson, M.A., "Planning Around the New Paid-Up Capital Restrictions" (1986) 34 Can. Tax J. 631.

Potential for Double Taxation

Swiderski, Tony, "Transfers of United States Real Property Interests in Canadian Reorganizations: Opportunities, Limitations and Pitfalls" (1989) 37 Can. Tax J. 605.

Tremblay, Richard G., "Canada-United States Cross-Border Butterflies", in *Proceedings of 39th Tax Conf.* 22:1 (Can. Tax Foundation, 1987).

Estate Freezing and Subsection 85(1)

Barbacki, Richard, "Estate Freezing in the Light of Recent Income Tax Changes", in *Proceedings of 38th Tax Conf.* 36:1 (Can. Tax Foundation, 1986).

Bowden, Gregory, T.W., "Estate Freezing", *British Columbia Tax Conf.* 266 (Can. Tax Foundation, 1980).

Crawford, William E., "Corporate Freezes — Are You Getting Your Money's Worth?", in *Proceedings of 32nd Tax Conf.* 772 (Can. Tax Foundation, 1980).

Hart, Stephen D., "Estate Freezes, Part 1: Holding Companies" (1982) 115 CA Magazine No. 10, 54.

Morris, J.S.D., "Freezing Family Business Interests — Inflation and Other Concerns" (1981) 29 Can. Tax J. 211.

Promislow, Norm, "Estate Planning and Income Splitting: Recent Developments", *Prairie Provinces Tax Conf.* 371 (Can. Tax Foundation, 1983).

Rochwerg, Martin J., "Post-Mortem Estate Freezing" (1983) 31 Can. Tax J. 69.

Silver, Sheldon, "A Simple Case of Freezing" (1976) 24 Can. Tax J. 74.

Silver, Sheldon, "A Simple Case of Freezing — Part 2" (1976) 24 Can. Tax J. 171.

Silver, Sheldon, "Has the Dust Settled?" (1977) 25 Can. Tax J. 652.

Other

Colley, Geoffrey M., "Tax Planning Implications for New Business" (1980) 113 CA Magazine No. 12, 78.

Davidson, Barrie, "Inter Vivos Tax Planning" (1981) 15 CGA Magazine 2.

Gordon, Hugh A.,"Discussion by Hugh A. Gordon. C.A.", in *Proceedings of 33rd Tax Conf.* 370 (Can. Tax Foundation, 1981).

Hiltz, Michael A., "Section 55: An Update", *Corp. Management Tax Conf.* 40 (Can. Tax Foundation, 1984).

Hogg, R.D., "Stock Option Benefits in Canadian Controlled Private Corporations" (1978) 26 Can. Tax J. 85.

Lindsay, Robert F., "Canadian Holding Corporations for Canadian Subsidiaries of Non-resident Parent Corporations", *Corporate Management Tax Conf.* 347 (Can. Tax Foundation, 1980).

Mida, I.H., "More on Intra Group Transfers" (1986) 34 Can. Tax J. 1184.

Playfair, J.L., "Planning for the Successful Tax-Sheltered Investment" (1980) 28 Can. Tax J. 647.

Read, Robert J.L., "Section 55: A Review of Current Issues", in *Proceedings of 40th Tax Conf.* 18:1 (Can. Tax Foundation, 1988).

CHAPTER 26 — NON-ARM'S LENGTH SHARE TRANSFER

I. — General Comment

Generally, a taxpayer who disposes of capital property must recognize the proceeds of disposition in the year of the disposition. There are, however, several important exceptions to this rule. Chapter 25, "Transfer of Property to a Corporation" illustrates how a taxpayer can rollover capital property at its adjusted cost base into a taxable Canadian corporation under subsection 85(1). For example, a taxpayer can transfer shares of an operating company into a holding company without triggering a capital gain on the disposition. Although the Act allows taxpayers to rollover capital property to a corporation without triggering capital gains,[1] it prevents taxpayers from ultimately avoiding tax on the transfer. Two easy methods of avoiding tax are to convert a corporation's taxable surplus into tax exempt capital gains or to remove the taxable surplus of a corporation as a tax-free return of capital. Section 84.1 prevents the inappropriate tax-free removal of capital.

---

[1] Subs. 85(1).

II. — Purpose of Section 84.1

Section 84.1 is essentially an anti-avoidance rule. It prevents the removal of taxable corporate surplus as a tax-free return of capital or as a tax-exempt capital gain when an individual transfers shares to a corporation in a *non-arm's length* transaction.[2] The section applies only to a non-arm's length transfer of shares to a "connected" corporation.

Before looking at the details of section 84.1, it may be useful to consider the type of transactions against which the section safeguards. Consider the following example: Rodgers is the sole shareholder of an operating small business company ("Opco"). Her shares have a paid-up capital of $1,000, an adjusted cost base of $150,000 and a fair market value of $500,000, all of which is represented in cash. If Opco simply pays a cash dividend to Rodgers, she will be taxed on the dividend. If Opco redeems its shares at their fair market value, the Act will deem Rodgers to receive a taxable dividend of $499,000 and a capital loss of $149,999, which will be affected by the stop-loss rule in subsection 40(3.6). Thus, Rodgers will be taxed under either option if she extracts the corporation's surplus.

But what if Rodgers incorporates a new company ("Holdco") and sells her Opco shares to Holdco in exchange for a demand promissory note in the amount of $500,000? Assume that the gain of $350,000 on the sale of Opco's shares qualifies as a tax-exempt capital gain. If Opco and Holdco amalgamate after the sale, the amalgamated corporation could pay off its demand note to Rodgers without any tax cost to her. In effect, Rodgers could extract Opco's taxable surplus without any tax payable either on the proceeds of the disposition of the Opco shares or on the corporation's surplus. Section 84.1 is intended to prevent these types of surplus stripping transactions.[3]

III. — Non-Arm's Length Transactions

Section 84.1 is directed solely towards controlling "surplus stripping" in non-arm's length transactions; it does not have any effect whatsoever where a taxpayer sells shares in an arm's length transaction. Similar, though not identical, provisions deal with sales by a non-resident person of shares of any corporation resident in Canada to any other corporation resident in Canada.[4]

---

[2]S. 84.1.

[3]See following examples under the headings "Avoiding Reduction in Paid-up Capital" and "Avoiding a Deemed Dividend".

[4]See s. 212.1.

IV. — Application of Section 84.1

Section 84.1 applies to non-arm's length transfers of shares where the purchaser corporation and the subject corporation are "connected"[5] to each other immediately after the disposition of shares. It applies regardless of whether or not the share transfer is the subject of an election under section 85. The section applies when an individual, partnership or a trust resident in Canada disposes of shares to a corporation in the following circumstances:[6]

- The shares are capital property;

- The shares disposed of are the shares of a corporation resident in Canada;

- The vendor and the purchaser corporation do not deal with each other at arm's length; and

- Immediately after the disposition of the shares the corporation whose shares are disposed of (referred to as the "subject corporation") and the purchaser corporation are "connected" with each other.

Note: (1) the purchaser corporation does not have to reside in Canada for the section to apply; (2) the section applies both to pre-1972 and post-1971 shares; and (3) the section does not apply to dispositions of shares of non-resident corporations (for example, it does not apply to a disposition of shares in a foreign affiliate).

V. — "Non-Arm's Length" Relationships

Section 84.1 applies only where the vendor and the purchaser corporation do not deal with each other at "arm's length".[7] Although the statutory language is not entirely clear, it appears that the section applies if the parties are not at arm's length at the time of the disposition of the shares even if the parties are at arm's length after the transaction. This is consistent with CRA's position.

---

[5]See subs. 186(4).

[6]Subs. 84.1(1).

[7]S. 251.

1. — *Deemed Non-Arm's Length Relationships*

The Act deems the vendor and the purchaser corporation not to be dealing with each other at arm's length if:[8]

- Immediately before the disposition, the vendor was one of a group of less than six persons that controlled the "subject corporation";

- Immediately after the disposition, the vendor was part of a group of less than six persons who controlled the "purchaser corporation"; and

- Each member of the group that controlled the "purchaser corporation" was also a member of the group that controlled the "subject corporation".

The members of the group do not have to be related to each other for these rules to apply. If an individual was part of a group of less than six persons who controlled the subject corporation before, and the purchaser corporation after the disposition of the shares, the Act deems the individual not to be at arm's length with the purchaser corporation.

In determining whether a group of persons controls a corporation, "group" in respect of the corporation means any two or more persons each of whom owns shares of the corporation.[9]

2. — *Deemed Ownership of Shares*

For the purposes of determining whether or not the vendor and the purchaser corporation are at non-arm's length, the Act deems the vendor to own any shares of the corporation that are owned by:[10]

- A spouse or common-law partner;

- Children under 18 years of age;

- An *inter vivos* trust of which either the vendor or the vendor's spouse or common-law partner or children are beneficiaries;

- An *inter vivos* trust of which a controlled corporation is a beneficiary;

- A corporation that the vendor, the vendor's spouse or common-law partner or children under 18 years of age control; or

---

[8]Para. 84.1(2)(b).

[9]Para. 84.1(2.2)(b).

[10]Para. 84.1(2.2)(a).

- A corporation that is controlled by an *inter vivos* trust of which the vendor or the vendor's spouse or common-law partner or children under 18 years of age are beneficiaries.

For the purpose of these rules, "children" includes grandchildren, great-grandchildren and persons under the age of 18 who are wholly dependent on the taxpayer.[11]

VI. — "Connected" Corporations

Generally, a purchaser corporation and a subject corporation are connected to each other if the former, either alone or with other non-arm's length parties, controls the latter within the meaning of control in subsection 186(2).[12] They are also connected to each other if the purchaser corporation owns shares of the subject corporation that represent more than 10 per cent of the votes and fair market value of all the shares of the subject corporation.[13]

VII. — Dispositions By Trusts

A disposition of shares by a trust to a corporation will be considered to be non-arm's length if a beneficiary of a trust — or a person related to the beneficiary — controls the corporation.[14]

VIII. — Scope Of Section 84.1

Section 84.1 applies to share transfers regardless of whether the transferor has elected to rollover the shares under subsection 85(1). Indeed, the section can apply even if the purchaser corporation has not issued any shares as consideration for the transfer.

The section can have two effects: (1) it can deem a dividend to have been paid to the transferor of the subject shares; and (2) it can reduce the paid-up capital of any new shares issued as consideration for the subject shares. Hence, if the section applies to reduce the paid-up capital of shares, the paid-up capital of the shares can be different from their stated capital for corporate purposes. This can be an important consideration in the purchase and sale of shares.

---

[11]Para. 84.1(2.2)(a); subs. 70(10).

[12]Para. 186(4)(a).

[13]Subs. 186(4).

[14]Paras. 84.1(2)(d) and 251(2)(b) and *Hickman*, [2004] 4 C.T.C. 2557 (T.C.C. [General Procedure]).

Generally, the maximum tax free "safe amount" that a person who transfers shares to a corporation can receive from the corporation, either as "hard" consideration or as the paid-up capital of shares, is the *greater* of the paid-up capital and the modified adjusted cost base of the transferred shares. Any consideration in excess of the greater of these two amounts will trigger a dividend, either immediately or in the future, for the person who transferred the shares.

1. — Reduction in Paid-Up Capital of Shares

Where a purchaser corporation issues shares in exchange for other shares and the paid-up capital of the newly issued shares exceeds the excess (if any) of the *greater* of the paid-up capital and the adjusted cost base of the shares over the value of "hard" consideration, the excess amount reduces the paid-up capital of the new shares.

The paid-up capital of the newly issued shares is reduced by an amount determined by the following formula:[15]

$$(A - B) \times C / A$$

where, generally:

A   = paid-up capital of all new shares issued by purchaser corporation;

B   = excess of *greater* of paid-up capital and adjusted cost base of transferred shares over the value of "hard" consideration received; and

C   = increase in paid-up capital of particular class of new shares issued.

Hence, where the purchaser corporation issues only one class of shares in exchange for the transferred shares, the formula reduces to:

$$(A - B)$$

Where the amount determined by the formula is negative, the Act deems the negative amount to be nil.[16]

---

[15]Para. 84.1(1)(a).

[16]S. 257.

Example

Assume:	Case 1	Case 2	Case 3
PUC of purchaser corporation shares	$ 100	$ 100	$ 5,000
PUC of transferred shares	100	100	100
ACB of transferred shares	100	1,000	1,000
"Hard" consideration	NIL	1,100	NIL

Then, the reduction in paid-up capital is (A - B), determined as follows:

	Case 1	Case 2	Case 3
A. PUC of purchaser corporation shares	$ 100	$ 100	$ 5,000
B. Greater of:			
PUC and ACB of transferred shares	$ 100	$ 1,000	$ 1,000
Exceeds:			
"Hard" consideration	—	1,100	—
	$ 100	—	$ 1,000
PUC reduction (A–B)	NIL	$ 100	$ 4,000
PUC after reduction	$ 100	NIL	$ 1,000

Thus, one effect of section 84.1 is that redemption of the new shares for an amount in excess of their revised paid-up capital gives rise to a deemed dividend.

2. — Deemed Dividend

Section 84.1 can also trigger a deemed dividend to the transferor. The Act deems the purchaser corporation to have paid a dividend to the transferor where the aggregate of the increase in the paid-up capital of its shares and the value of any "hard" consideration that it issues exceeds the total of:[17]

- The *greater* of the adjusted cost base and the paid-up capital of the transferred shares; and

- The total paid-up capital reduction required in the purchaser corporation's shares.

---

[17]Para. 84.1(1)(b).

The amount of the deemed dividend is determined by the formula:

$$(A + D) - (E + F)$$

where, generally:

A   = paid-up capital of all new shares issued by purchaser corporation

D   = value of "hard" consideration

E   = greater of PUC and ACB of transferred shares

F   = reduction in paid-up capital of purchaser corporation by application of paragraph 84.1(1)(a)

Example

Assume:

PUC of purchaser corporation shares	$ 2,500
PUC of transferred shares	$ 100
ACB of transferred shares	$ 1,000
"Hard" consideration	$ 2,500

Then, the paid-up capital reduction is determined as follows:

A.	PUC of purchaser corporation shares	$ 2,500
B.	Greater of:	
	PUC ($100) and ACB ($1,000) of transferred shares	$ 1,000
	Exceeds: "Hard" consideration	(2,500)
		NIL
	PUC reduction (A–B)	$ 2,500 *
	PUC after reduction	NIL

The deemed dividend is determined as follows:

A.	PUC of purchaser corporation shares	$ 2,500
D.	"Hard" consideration	2,500
	A + D	$ 5,000

Example	
E. Greater of:	
PUC of transferred shares	$ 100
ACB of transferred shares	$ 1,000
Greater amount:	$ 1,000
F. PUC reduction	2,500 *
E + F	$ 3,500
Immediate dividend (A + D) - (E + F)	
$5,000 - $3,500	$ 1,500

APPLICATION ON SHARE TRANSFER							
	I	II	III	IV	V	VI	VII
				(dollars)			
A. Paid-up capital of shares of purchaser received for transferred shares (before s. 84.1 reduction)	100	100	100	5,000	4,000	2,500	—
B. Paid-up capital of transferred shares	100	100	100	100	100	100	100
C. Adjusted cost base of transferred shares	100	1,000	1,000	1,000	1,000	1,000	1,000
D. Non-share consideration received for transferred shares	—	900	1,000	—	1,000	2,500	1,500
Paid-Up Capital Reduction:							
1. Amount A	100	100	100	5,000	4,000	2,500	—
2. Amount by which greater of B and C exceeds D	100	100	—	1,000	—	—	—
3. E: Paid-up capital reduction	—	—	100	4,000	4,000	2,500	—
4. Paid-up capital after reduction	100	100	—	1,000	—	—	—
Immediate Dividend:							
1. Aggregate of A and D	100	1,000	1,100	5,000	5,000	5,000	1,500
2. Aggregate of the greater of B and C plus E	100	1,000	1,100	5,000	5,000	3,500	1,000
3. Immediate dividend	—	—	—	—	—	1,500	500

Example

Assume:

Mr. X owns all of the issued shares of X Ltd.

These shares have the following attributes:

PUC and original cost	$ 100
V-Day Value	$ 300,000
FMV	$ 1,000,000

The shares of X Ltd. are QSBC shares for the purposes of the $500,000 capital gains deduction.

Mr. X wishes to transfer these shares to his brother's corporation, Y Ltd., in consideration for $1,000,000 cash.

X Ltd. and Y Ltd. will be connected after this transaction.

Then:

1. The transaction would be caught by the provisions of s. 84.1.

    Mr. X would be deemed to receive a dividend equal to $1,000,000 cash–$100 PUC = $999,900.

    Mr. X could not claim his capital gains deduction to offset the dividend.

2. If Mr. X sold the shares of X Ltd. to his brother Y he would realize a capital gain of $700,000, which could be partially offset by his $500,000 capital gains deduction. Subsection 84.1 does not apply unless the disposition is to a corporation.

    If Mr. Y then transfers his X Ltd. shares to Y Ltd. he may receive only non-share consideration of $200,100 and shares with a nominal PUC. If the non-share consideration is greater he will realize a deemed dividend pursuant to para. 84.1(1)(b). If the PUC of the shares received from Y Ltd. is greater, it will be ground to a nominal amount by para. 84.1(1)(a).

    Mr. Y's ACB of Y Ltd. shares:

ACB otherwise determined		$ 1,000,000
Less: Excess of V-day	$ 300,000	
Over Cost	100	(299,900)
Less: CGE claimed by brother		(500,000)
Arm's length ACB		$ 200,100

    (See: Para. 84.1(2)(a.1))

IX. — Avoiding Reduction In Paid-Up Capital

The easiest way to avoid a reduction of paid-up capital under paragraph 84.1(1)(a) is to ensure that the fair market value of boot (non-share consideration) and the paid-up capital of the new shares does not exceed the *greater* of the adjusted cost base and the paid-up capital of the shares transferred to the corporation.

Example

Transferred shares:

PUC	$ 1,000
ACB	$ 150,000
FMV	$ 500,000

New shares:

PUC	$ 1,000
FMV	$ 351,000

Boot:	$ 149,000

There is no reduction in the paid-up capital of the new shares in these circumstances.

X. — Avoiding A Deemed Dividend

It is also possible to have a reduction in the paid-up capital of the purchaser corporation's shares without triggering a deemed dividend.

Example

AVOIDING DEEMED DIVIDEND UNDER SECTION 84.1

Assume:

Mr. Black owns the shares of *Blackco* to which the following data applies:

FMV	$ 500,000
ACB	$ 150,000
PUC	$ 1,000

Example

Black transfers the shares to a new corporation ("*Newco*") in exchange for the following consideration:

Promissory note	$ 150,000
Shares (PUC and FMV)	$ 350,000
	$ 500,000

Section 84.1 applies to the transaction.

Then:

1. PUC Reduction

Legal PUC of *Newco* shares	$ 350,000
S. 84.1 reduction	(350,000)
PUC for tax purposes	NIL
Potential dividend on redemption of shares	$ 350,000

2. Deemed dividend

Increase in PUC of *Newco*		$ 350,000
Non-share consideration		150,000
Total consideration		500,000
Less aggregate of:		
(i) Greater of PUC of *Blackco's* shares and ACB of $ 150,000		
Blackco's shares; and		
(ii) PUC reduction under s. 84.1	350,000	(500,000)
Deemed dividend		NIL

The safest way, however, to avoid problems under section 84.1 is to take back shares that have a paid-up capital equal to the paid-up capital of the shares transferred.[18]

---

[18]See Column I in "Application on Share Transfer" example, above.

XI. — Price Adjustment Clauses

1. — Purpose

A price adjustment clause is a term in a contract of purchase and sale that allows the parties to the contract to *retroactively* adjust the price of the subject matter of the sale. A price adjustment clause is usually used in contracts when the parties to the contract intend to transact at fair market value, but where the determination of value is difficult or uncertain in the particular circumstances.[19]

To appreciate the purpose served by a price adjustment clause, one should first look at subsection 69(1).

The Act deems a taxpayer who acquires property in a non-arm's length transaction at a price in excess of its fair market value to have acquired the property at its fair market value. Thus, for tax purposes, the cost of the property acquired is reduced to its fair market value. For example, the Act deems a taxpayer who pays $150,000 for an asset that has a fair market value of $100,000 to have acquired it for $100,000. The reduction in cost increases the purchaser's potential tax liability when he or she disposes of the property in the future. Note, however, that there is no concurrent adjustment to the seller's proceeds of disposition.

The Act *deems* a taxpayer who disposes of property at less than its fair market value in a non-arm's length transaction to receive proceeds of disposition equal to its fair market value. For example, we deem a taxpayer who sells an asset worth $100,000 for $75,000 to have received proceeds of $100,000. Hence, the gain or loss is calculated on the basis of the deemed, rather than actual, proceeds of disposition.[20] The purchaser calculates any subsequent gain on the basis of *actual* cost.

Thus, subsection 69(1) does not provide a mirror image of the same transaction from the purchaser's and the vendor's points of view. Consequently, taxpayers who do not deal at arm's length with each other may be financially penalized if they do not transact at fair market value. Subsection 69(1) is, and is intended to be, a penal provision: it does not allow a taxpayer who has paid less than fair market value for property to "bump-up" the cost base of the property.

The primary purpose of a price adjustment clause is to rectify the mismatch of costs and values. A price adjustment clause allows a taxpayer who purchases property in a non-arm's length transaction for less than its fair market value to *retroactively* "bump-up" the cost base of the property at a later date.

---

[19]See generally, Douglas Ewens, "Use of Adjustment Clauses in Non-Arm's Length Reorganizations" (1981) 20 Can. Tax J. 718.

[20]Para. 69(1)(b).

2. — Determination of Fair Market Value

A taxpayer who transfers property to a corporation usually receives consideration equal to the value of the property. If the consideration received is less than the value of the property transferred, there may be an indirect gift.[21] If the assets are transferred in exchange for too much consideration from the corporation, the taxpayer receives a shareholder benefit that is taxable as income.[22] Hence, the determination of the fair market value of property is a critical step in all non-arm's length transfers.

The calculation of fair market value, however, is a complex and uncertain process. Subsequent events may show that the values used in an agreement do not in fact reflect market values. The use of a price adjustment clause in an agreement of purchase and sale can alleviate the uncertainty. In the event that the estimate of fair market value set out in the agreement of purchase and sale subsequently proves to be incorrect, the parties to the contract can retroactively adjust the purchase price according to the price adjustment clause in order to reflect the revised figure.[23]

3. — Bona Fide Intention

The use of price adjustment clauses is subject to an important qualification. A price adjustment clause is only valid where it reflects the *bona fide* intention of the parties to contract at fair market value.[24] Thus, it is imperative that the parties make a good faith attempt to arrive, by some fair and reasonable valuation method, at the fair market value of the property transferred. A price adjustment clause may be ineffective for tax purposes in the absence of a good faith effort to determine the fair market value of the subject of the purchase and sale.[25]

4. — Administrative Interpretation

The Canada Revenue Agency (CRA) requires taxpayers who use price adjustment clauses in agreements of purchase and sale to notify the CRA of the existence of the clause. There is no legislative authority for this requirement. Notification to the CRA almost certainly "red-flags" the file and is an invitation to a valuation dispute. At the very least, it is a signal to the CRA that the parties to the transaction are uncertain about their valuation.

---

[21]Para. 85(1)(e.2); see Chapter 25, "Transfer of Property to a Corporation".

[22]Subs. 15(1).

[23]IT-169, "Price Adjustment Clauses" (August 6, 1974).

[24]*Guilder News Co. (1963) Ltd. v. M.N.R.*, [1973] C.T.C. 1, 73 D.T.C. 5048 (F.C.A.).

[25]IT-169, "Price Adjustment Clauses" (August 6, 1974).

XII. — Averaging Paid-Up Capital

The paid-up capital of a share of a class of capital stock of a corporation is the average paid-up capital of the entire class. For example, if a corporation issues 1,000 Class A shares at $1 per share and later issues 1,000 Class A shares at $20 per share, the paid-up capital of each Class A share is $10.50, that is, $21,000/2,000.

Paid-up capital adjustments under section 84.1 are similarly averaged. The paid up capital of the issued shares of a particular class of shares is the average of the entire class. Hence, an adjustment under section 84.1 that is triggered by a transaction with one shareholder of a class of shares also affects all other shareholders of the same class.

XIII. — Comprehensive Example

REDUCTION OF PAID-UP CAPITAL OF SHARES UNDER SECTION 84.1

Assume:

Mr. Green owns the shares of an operating company (*Opco*) to which the following data applies:

Fair market value (FMV)	$ 500,000
Adjusted cost base (ACB)	$ 1,000
Paid-up capital (PUC)	$ 1,000

Green transfers the shares to a holding company (*Holdco*) in exchange for the following consideration:

Promissory note	$ 400,000
Shares (PUC and FMV)	$ 100,000
Total consideration	$ 500,000

Green and *Holdco* are not at arm's length with each other.

Then:

1. The legal paid-up capital of the shares newly issued by *Holdco* (the "purchaser corporation") is reduced for tax purposes as follows:

Legal PUC of shares	$ 100,000
S. 84.1 reduction (see Note)	(100,000)
PUC for tax purposes	NIL

REDUCTION OF PAID-UP CAPITAL OF SHARES UNDER SECTION 84.1

Potential dividend on redemption of shares $ 100,000

Note:

$$\text{PUC reduction} = (A - B) \times (C / A)$$

where:

A = Increase in PUC of *all* new shares;

B = Amount by which greater of PUC and ACB of *Opco's* shares exceeds fair market value of non-share consideration; and

C = Increase in PUC of new shares of the *particular* class issued by *Holdco*.

= (100,000 - 0) × (100,000 / 100,000)

= $100,000

2. *Holdco* is deemed to have paid a dividend of $399,000 to Mr. Green. The amount of this deemed dividend is determined as follows:

Increase in PUC of *Holdco*		$ 100,000
Non-share consideration		400,000
Total consideration		500,000
Less, aggregate of		
(i) greater of PUC of *Opco's* shares		
($1,000) and ACB of *Opco's* shares		
($1,000), and	$ 1,000	
(ii) PUC reduction under s. 84.1	100,000	(101,000)
Deemed dividend		$ 399,000

3. Hence, a potential capital gain of $499,000 (that is, $500,000 - 1,000) is converted into:

Deemed dividend	$ 399,000
Capital gain on disposition of Opco shares	100,000 *
	$ 499,000

* Consideration for Opco shares	$ 500,000
Deemed dividend under s. 84.1	399,000
Proceeds of disposition	101,000
Less: ACB of Opco shares	1,000

REDUCTION OF PAID-UP CAPITAL OF SHARES UNDER SECTION 84.1

Capital gain	$ 100,000

If the new shares are redeemed, there will be a deemed dividend under subsection 84(3) of $100,000 and a corresponding capital loss — that may be affected by subsection 40(3.6) — of $100,000.

Selected Bibliography to Chapter 26

General

Couzin, Robert, "Of Arm's Length, and Not Dealing Threat" (1978) 26 Can. Tax. J. 271.

Cronkwright, Glen E., Robert J. Dart & Robert F. Lindsay, "Corporate Distributions and the 1977 Tax Changes", in *Proceedings of 29th Tax Conf.* 279 (Can. Tax Foundation, 1977).

Fryer, D.J., "84.1 and Two-Tier Tax Problems" (1980) 28 Can. Tax J. 208.

Gordon, Hugh A., "Discussion by Hugh A. Gordon, C.A.", in *Proceedings of 33rd Tax Conf.* 370 (Can. Tax Foundation, 1981).

Hart, Stephen D., "Estate Freezes, Part 1: Holding Companies" (1982) 115 CA Magazine No. 10, 54.

Holtz, D.E., "Transfer of a Small Family Business Corporation" (1980) 28 Can. Tax J. 357.

Kellough, Howard J., "Acquisition of Shares in a Non-Arm's Length Transaction", *Corporate Management Tax Conf.* 186 (Can. Tax Foundation, 1978).

Kellough, Howard J., "Formation, Operation, and Disposition of Closely Held Corporations", in *Proceedings of 30th Tax Conf.* 703 (Can. Tax Foundation, 1978).

Kellough, Howard J., "Selecting an Appropriate Share Capital Structure for Private Corporations", in *Proceedings of 33rd Tax Conf.* 49 (Can. Tax Foundation, 1981).

Laflamme, Pierre, "Planning an Estate Freeze" (1978) 111 CA Magazine No. 7, 57.

Laushway, Keith, "Documentation and Non-arm's Length Transactions" (1992) 3 Can. Current Tax P-55.

Lemmon, K.W., "Corporate Distributions" (1978) 43 Business Quarterly 90.

Lessard, Pierre, "Nouvelles dispositions des articles 84.1 et 84.2" (1978) 26 Can. Tax J. 466.

Little, L.M., "Further Tax Traps for the Unwary" (1978) 12 CGA Magazine No. 7, 7.

McQuillan, Peter, "Financing Corporate Acquisitions", *Tax Planning and Management*, Vol. 9, No. 32 of *Canadian Income Tax Revised* (Butterworth and Co. (Canada) Ltd., 1978).

Morris, J.S.D., "Freezing Family Business Interests — Inflation and Other Concerns" (1981) 29 Can. Tax J. 211.

Reid, Robert J., "Tax Aspects of Incorporation", *Tax Planning and Management*, Vol. 9, No. 38 of *Canadian Income Tax Revised* (Butterworth and Co. (Canada) Ltd., 1979).

Schwartz, Alan M., "Transferring Shares of Private Corporations Need Not Be So Taxing" (1980) 113 CA Magazine No. 5, 49.

Stein, Boris P., "Part Two: Canadian Case Law Concerning Shares Received on a Rollover", *The Journal of Business Valuation*, Canadian Association of Business Valuators, Vol. 7, 1981, 95.

Ward, David A., "Arm's Length Acquisitions Relating to Shares in a Public Corporation", *Corporate Management Tax Conf.* 108 (Can. Tax Foundation, 1978).

Ward, David A. and Neal Armstrong, "Corporate Taxation: Arm's Length Dealings" (1986) 5 Legal Alert 49.

Williamson, W. Gordon, "Transfers of Assets To and From a Canadian Corporation", in *Proceedings of 38th Tax Conf.* 12:1 (Can. Tax Foundation, 1986).

Witterick, R.G., "Acquisitions of Shares of Private Corporations in Arm's Length Transactions", *Corporate Management Tax Conf.* 120 (Can. Tax Foundation, 1978).

Application of Section 84.1

Birnie, David A.G., "The New Approach to Dividend Stripping and Its Implications for Share Acquisitions and Capital Reorganizations", in *Proceedings of 29th Tax Conf.* 537 (Can. Tax Foundation, 1977).

Brown, Robert D., "Last Gun-Fight at the Surplus-Stripping Corral", in *Proceedings of 30th Tax Conf.* 590 (Can. Tax Foundation, 1978).

Dixon, Gordon D., "Depreciable Property: Rules Affect Non-Arm's Length Transfers" (January 1988) 22 CGA Magazine 24.

Eng, Susan, "The Arm's-Length Rules", in *Proceedings of 40th Tax Conf.* 13:1 (Can. Tax Foundation, 1988).

Ewens, Douglas S., "New Considerations in Structuring Share-for-share Exchange Offers" (1988) 36 Can. Tax J. 449.

Moskowitz, Evelyn P., "Dealing at Arm's Length: A Question of Fact", in *Proceedings of 39th Tax Conf.* 33:1 (Can. Tax Foundation, 1987).

Rohde, Richard C., "Section 85 Transfers — Limitations and Pitfalls" (1988) 36 Can. Tax J. 1302 at 1315–1318.

Templeton, Wendy, "The Taxation of Corporate Reorganizations — Anti-Avoidance and the Capital Gains Exemption" (1986) 34 Can. Tax J. 203.

Price Adjustment Clauses

Ewens, Douglas, "Use of Adjustment Clauses in Non-Arm's Length Reorganizations" (1981) 29 Can. Tax J. 718.

Morris, J.S.D., "Freezing Family Business Interests — Inflation and Other Concerns" (1981) 29 Can. Tax J. 211.

Wise, Richard M., "Valuation and the *Income Tax Act*" (1981) 29 Can. Tax J. 626.

Averaging Paid-Up Capital

Sinclair, B.R., "Paid-up Capital" (1986) 34 Can. Tax J. 1483.

CHAPTER 27 — SHARE-FOR-SHARE ACQUISITIONS

I. — General Comment

1. — Purpose

The share-for-share exchange rules in section 85.1 facilitate share exchange transactions on a tax-deferred basis. The rules serve two principal purposes: (1) to allow Canadian corporations to finance takeover bids using share consideration; and (2) to allow for the reorganization of foreign affiliates.[1]

2. — Tax Deferral

Section 85.1 is a flexible provision. It allows shareholders who exchange shares of a taxable Canadian corporation for shares of a Canadian purchaser corporation in an arm's length transaction to defer taxes on the exchange. In effect, the tax cost of the shareholder's old shares is rolled over into the tax cost of the new shares. Thus, the shareholder can defer taxes on capital gains accrued on the old shares until he or she disposes of the shares.

3. — Not Elective

The share-for-share exchange provisions in section 85.1 do not require an election by the parties. Therefore, they are particularly suitable in arm's length transactions, such as take-

---

[1]See subs. 95(2).

over bids, where the shares are widely held and it would not be feasable to get an election from every shareholder. However, the rollover is not mandatory and the vendor may recognize any portion of the capital gain or loss for tax purposes simply by including the amount on his or her return for the year. The provision is somewhat unusual in that the acquiring corporation determines the cost of the shares acquired independently of the vendor's tax treatment.

II. — Conditions For Rollover

A taxpayer who disposes of shares in a taxable Canadian corporation ("old shares") in exchange for treasury shares of a Canadian corporation ("new shares") may rollover the cost of the old shares into the cost base of the new shares on a tax-free basis in the following circumstances:[2]

- The purchaser of the "old shares" is a Canadian corporation;[3]

- The vendor held the "old shares" as capital property;[4]

- The "old shares" are shares of a taxable Canadian corporation;[5]

- The purchaser corporation issues *its own* (i.e., treasury) shares to the vendor in exchange for the vendor's shares;[6]

- The only consideration the vendor receives for the shares is shares of *one* particular class of the purchaser corporation;[7]

- The vendor and the purchaser are at arm's length with each other immediately before the exchange of shares;[8]

- The vendor and purchaser do not elect for the rollover under subsection 85(1) or (2);[9]

---

[2]Para. 85.1(1)(a); see also IT-450R, "Share for Share Exchange" (April 8, 1993).

[3]Subs. 89(1)"Canadian corporation".

[4]The rollover is not available to a dealer in securities.

[5]Subs. 85.1(1).

[6]Subs. 85.1(1).

[7]Para. 85.1(2)(d); see also IT-450R, "Share-for-Share Exchange" (April 8, 1993).

[8]Para. 85.1(2)(a).

[9]Para. 85.1(2)(c).

- Immediately after the exchange, the purchaser corporation is not controlled directly, indirectly, or in any manner whatever by the vendor and/or persons with whom the vendor does not deal at arm's length;[10] and

- Immediately after the exchange, the vendor and/or persons with whom the vendor does not deal at arm's length do not beneficially own shares of the purchaser corporation that have a fair market value of more than 50 per cent of the fair market value of all of the purchaser corporation's issued shares.[11]

The rationale of this provision is to facilitate takeovers of corporations by Canadian corporations. However, non-resident purchaser corporations can also take advantage of section 85.1 by issuing as consideration shares of a Canadian subsidiary that are exchangeable for shares of the non-resident parent corporation.

The rollover is not available if the vendor acquires the purchaser's shares from any person other than the corporation; nor is the rollover available if the purchaser corporation gives the vendor shares other than its own shares in return for the shares of the vendor.

Thus, with one exception in respect of *de minimis* payments for fractional shares, the rollover is not available where the purchaser corporation issues non-share consideration for the vendor's shares. By administrative discretion, however, a vendor can receive up to $200 in cash in lieu of fractional shares without prejudicing the rollover.[12]

An option to acquire additional shares of the purchaser corporation at a later date precludes the rollover. Similarly, a collateral agreement that allows the vendor the right to "put"[13] newly acquired shares from the purchaser corporation to an associated or related corporation constitutes "other consideration" sufficient to cause the transaction to be outside subsection 85.1(1).[14]

III. — Piecemeal Dispositions

A taxpayer may sever his or her shareholdings into two or more distinct parts and dispose of each of the parts separately. For example, a taxpayer may dispose of one part in exchange for one class of shares of the purchaser corporation to obtain the benefit of the rollover and

---

[10]Subpara. 85.1(2)(b)(i).

[11]Subpara. 85.1(2)(b)(ii).

[12]IT-450R, "Share for Share Exchange" (April 8, 1993).

[13]A "put" is an option permitting its holder to sell a certain stock or commodity at a fixed price for a stated quantity and within a stated period of time.

[14]Unpublished CRA technical interpretation (February 11, 1991), Reorganizations and Non-Resident Division.

dispose of another part for cash. In these circumstances, the taxpayer should separately and clearly identify each disposition.[15]

Alternatively, a taxpayer can reorganize share capital into two distinct classes of shares and then dispose of each class separately. It is important to ensure that the different classes of shares are *in fact* different and not merely labelled as such.[16]

IV. — Effect Of Exchange On Vendor

The rollover applies automatically unless the vendor opts out of it.[17] Thus, in the absence of an indication on the return that the taxpayer is opting out of the rollover, the Act deems the taxpayer to have disposed of the shares for proceeds of disposition equal to their adjusted cost base.[18] Concurrently, the taxpayer is deemed to acquire the new shares from the purchaser corporation at a cost equal to the adjusted cost base of the old shares.[19]

Where the old shares are taxable Canadian property to the vendor, the new shares are also considered to be taxable Canadian property.[20]

Example		
Assume:		
X owns 100 shares of *Targetco* (a taxable Canadian corporation) that have a total ACB of $1,000. He exchanges his *Targetco* shares for 300 shares of *Hitco* (a Canadian corporation) that have a fair market value of $6,000.		
Then:	Under general rules	Under s. 85.1
Proceeds of disposition	$ 6,000	$ 1,000
ACB of old shares	(1,000)	(1,000)
Immediate capital gain	$ 5,000	$ NIL
ACB of new shares	$ 6,000	$ 1,000
FMV of new shares	6,000	6,000

---

[15]See paras. 7 and 8 of IT-450R, "Share for Share Exchange" (April 8, 1993).

[16]See, for example, *Champ v. The Queen*, [1983] C.T.C. 1, 83 D.T.C. 5029 (F.C.T.D.).

[17]Subs. 85.1(1).

[18]Subpara. 85.1(1)(a)(i).

[19]Subpara. 85.1(1)(a)(ii).

[20]Para. 85.1(1)(a).

Example		
Deferred capital gain	NIL	$ 5,000

V. — Effect Of Exchange On Purchaser

The cost of the shares to the purchaser corporation is the lesser of the fair market value of the shares and their paid-up capital immediately before the exchange.[21] Thus, section 85.1 is somewhat unusual in that we determine the purchaser corporation's cost of shares acquired independently of the vendor's tax treatment. In contrast, where the purchaser elects under subsection 85(1) for the share-for-share exchange, the tax cost of the shares to the purchasing corporation is the amount elected in respect of the shares.

Example		
Assume the same facts as in the above example and the following additional data:		
	PUC	FMV
Per *Targetco* share	$ 10	$ 60
Then, the deemed adjusted cost base of each *Targetco* share to *Hitco* equals the lesser of:		
PUC of shares	$ 10	
FMV of shares	$ 60	
ACB of *Targetco* shares	$ 10 /share	

VI. — Paid-Up Capital Of Purchaser's Shares

The paid-up capital of the purchaser corporation's shares that it issues to the vendor is reduced by the amount by which the total increase in the paid-up capital of the purchaser's shares exceeds the paid-up capital of the exchanged shares.[22] In other words, the paid-up capital of the new shares is reduced by any attempted step-up in their paid-up capital.

---

[21]Para. 85.1(1)(b).

[22]Subs. 85.1(2.1).

Example

Assume the same facts as in the first example with the following additional data:

	PUC/share	Total PUC
Targetco shares exchanged	$ 10	$ 1,000
Hitco shares exchanged	$ 20	$ 6,000

Then:

Corporate PUC of *Hitco* shares	$ 20	$ 6,000
Less, PUC of *Targetco* shares	(10)	(1,000)
PUC reduction	$ 10	$ 5,000
Tax PUC of *Hitco* shares	$ 10	$ 1,000

This rule prevents vendors in a share-for-share exchange from taking advantage of a step-up in the paid-up capital of the purchaser's shares, which could then be returned to shareholders on a tax-free basis. In the above example, the vendors of *Targetco* would be entitled to a return of $20 per *Hitco* share if there was no adjustment to the paid-up capital of *Hitco* shares. Following the adjustment to the paid-up capital of *Hitco* shares, only $10 per *Hitco* share may be returned on a tax-free basis. Thus, in effect, the paid-up capital of the exchanged shares is rolled over into the purchaser's shares issued to the vendors.

VII. — V-Day Value

The tax-free zone of a taxpayer who exchanges shares owned on December 31, 1971 is preserved[23] provided that he has not previously elected under ITAR 26(7) to use V-Day values.

---

[23]ITAR 26(26).

Selected Bibliography to Chapter 27

General

Singer, Paul, "The Rollover Provisions in Respect of Corporate Reorganizations Provided Under the *Income Tax Act*: Efficiency and Equity as Policy Considerations" (1983) 31 Can. Tax J. 569.

Taxation of Corporate Organization and Reorganization (Montreal: Federated Press, 1993).

Exchange for Shares of Canadian Corporation

Boultbee, Jack, "A Survey of the Use of Rollovers in Acquisitions and Mergers" (1980) 28 Can. Tax J. 504.

Boultbee, Jack, "Public Company Split-Ups", *Corporate Management Tax Conf.* 1 (Can. Tax Foundation, 1984).

Cronkwright, Glen E., "Amalgamations and Share-For-Share Exchanges", in *Proceedings of 26th Tax Conf.* 53 (Can. Tax Foundation, 1974).

Ewens, Douglas, "New Considerations in Structuring Share-for-Share Exchange Offers" (1988) 36 Can. Tax J. 449.

Ewens, Douglas, "Share-For-Share Exchanges" (1982) 30 Can. Tax J. 99.

McNair, D.K., "Share-For-Share Exchange: Section 85.1" (1981) Can. Taxation 1051.

Watkins, Donald H., "Income Tax Consequences of Reorganizations and Arrangements", in *Proceedings of 30th Tax Conf.* 452 (Can. Tax Foundation, 1978).

CHAPTER 28 — EXCHANGE OF SHARES IN A REORGANIZATION

I. — General Comment

A taxpayer entitled to receive "proceeds of disposition", whether in cash or kind, in respect of a property is considered to have disposed of the property.[1] Hence, a change in the share capital structure of a corporation can trigger a disposition of shares. For example, a shareholder of a corporation that amends its articles, amalgamates with another corporation, continues under the laws of another jurisdiction, or sells all or substantially all of its property is *entitled* to receive the "fair value" of the shares.[2] Such an event would be considered a disposition of the shares since the shareholder would be entitled to proceeds. There are, however, special rules in section 86 that allow for a rollover of capital gains when corporate share capital is restructured.

---

[1] S. 54"proceeds of disposition"; s. 248(1)"disposition".

[2] Under certain corporate statutes (see, for example, the *Canada Business Corporations Act*, R.S.C. 1985, c. C-44, s. 190; Ontario *Business Corporations Act*, R.S.O. 1990, c. B-16, s. 185).

II. — Uses Of Section 86

Section 86 is a versatile provision with many uses. Generally, the section can be used to restructure the share capital of a corporation in circumstances when it is necessary to change the rights, conditions, privileges or restrictions of its existing shares or to create new shares in order to accommodate shareholder needs. The section is particularly useful in estate planning and capital reorganizations to accommodate or restructure family shareholdings. For example, section 86 is often used to:

- Exchange common shares of a corporation for preferred shares with a fixed and predetermined value (an "estate freeze");

- Reorganize the capital of a corporation to allow for dividend sprinkling among family members or where new shareholders are introduced into the corporation;

- Fight off hostile takeovers by changing the characteristics and rights of existing shares into new weighted voting shares.

III. — Application Of Subsection 86(1)

Section 86 is deceptively straightforward. A taxpayer who exchanges *all* of his or her shares of a class of a corporation for new shares from the corporation may rollover the cost base of the old shares into the new shares if the exchange is a reorganization of the share capital of the corporation.

More specifically, the rollover is available where a taxpayer:[3]

- Disposes of all of the shares ("old shares") of a particular class of a corporation;

- In the course of a reorganization of share capital; and

- The exchange is for consideration from the corporation that includes "new shares" of the corporation.

An important point to note at the outset is that the rollover does not depend upon the nationality or residence of the corporation or upon the residence of the taxpayer who disposes of the shares.

Thus, there are four essential ingredients to the rollover:

1. There must be "a reorganization of the capital of a corporation";

2. The shareholder must "dispose" of the shares "in the course of" the reorganization;

---

[3]Subs. 86(1). See ATR-22R, "Estate Freeze Using Share Exchange" (April 14, 1989); ATR-25, "Estate Freeze" (October 9, 1987); ATR-33, "Exchange of Shares" (October 7, 1988); and ATR-36, "Estate Freeze" (November 4, 1988).

3. The "old shares" must have been the taxpayer's capital property prior to their disposition and exchange for the new shares; and

4. The disposition must be in respect of *all* of the shares of a class of the capital stock of the corporation.

The rollover is not available if the taxpayer utilizes the rollover under section 51 or 85.[4]

1. — *"Reorganization of Capital"*

The phrase "reorganization of capital" is determined according to the corporate law of the jurisdiction in which the reorganization occurs. The following types of transactions generally constitute a reorganization of capital:[5]

- An increase or decrease in authorized capital;

- A subdivision or reclassification of share capital;

- Reclassification or redesignation of shares from one class into shares of another class;

- A variation, deletion or addition to share conditions as described in the articles of incorporation; or

- The creation of a new class of shares.

Typically, a reorganization of capital requires an amendment to the corporation's articles of incorporation and approval of the amendment through a special resolution of shareholders. In effect, any amendment that *substantially* affects the rights, privileges, restrictions or conditions attached to shares qualifies as a reorganization of capital for corporate purposes.[6] The phrase "winding-up, discontinuance or reorganization" is interpreted broadly, and there is no reason to believe that the phrase "reorganization of capital" would not be similarly interpreted.

2. — *"In the Course of"*

Section 86 only applies if the exchange of shares is pursuant to and *"in the course of"* the reorganization of capital. The exchange of shares must occur concurrently with, or shortly after, the reorganization of the capital of the corporation. Thus, timing is the key. The longer the delay between the reorganization of capital and the exchange of shares, the greater the

---

[4]Subss. 51(4), 86(3).

[5]See, for example, *Canada Business Corporations Act*, R.S.C. 1985, c. C-44, s. 173.

[6]See, for example, *Smythe v. M.N.R.*, [1969] C.T.C. 558, 69 D.T.C. 5361 (S.C.C.).

risk that the exchange may not be seen as being *in the course of* the reorganization. This can cause some uncertainty in complex reorganizations that span an extended period of time.

3. — Disposition of Shares

The taxpayer must *dispose* of the shares. But a transaction that qualifies as a reorganization of capital does not necessarily imply a disposition of shares. For example, although from a corporate perspective, a stock split or consolidation involves a reorganization of the share capital of a corporation, it does not *per se* involve a disposition of shares.[7] Similarly, a reclassification of one class of shares into two separate inter-convertible classes which offers shareholders a choice between cash dividends and stock dividends is not considered a disposition of shares.[8]

"Disposition" involves more than a reorganization: it requires cessation, divestiture, alienation or transfer of the incidents of ownership of property. The divestment does not have to be in respect of all of the incidents of ownership, but it should involve an alienation of at least some of the substantive rights of share ownership. The essential question is whether or not the taxpayer alienates a sufficient bundle of rights and privileges in the shares. For example, in the simplest case, a reclassification of shares to alienate voting rights is sufficient to constitute a "disposition" even if all of the other rights (such as the right to dividends and the right to receive residual property) remain intact.[9] But a mere split in the number of shares outstanding does not affect any substantive rights and privileges in the shares.

The term "disposition" is broadly interpreted. For example:[10]

> The entire expression "disposed of, lost or destroyed" is apt to embrace every event by which property ceases to be available to the taxpayer for use for the purpose of producing assessable income, either because it ceases to be his, or because it ceases to be physically accessible to him, or because it ceases to exist ... the words "is disposed of" are wide enough to cover all forms of alienation ... and they should be understood as meaning no less than "becomes alienated from the taxpayer", whether it is by him or by another that the act of alienation is done.

---

[7]See IT-65, "Stock Splits and Consolidations" (September 8, 1972).

[8]IT-146R4, "Shares Entitling Shareholders to Choose Taxable or Capital Dividends" (September 6, 1991).

[9]See *Victory Hotels Ltd. v. M.N.R.*, [1962] C.T.C. 614, 62 D.T.C. 1378 (Ex. Ct.); *M.N.R. v. Wardean Drilling Ltd.*, [1969] C.T.C. 265, 69 D.T.C. 5194 (Ex. Ct.); *The Queen v. Cie Immobilière BCN Ltée*, [1979] C.T.C. 71, 79 D.T.C. 5068 (S.C.C.).

[10]*Henty House Pty. Ltd. v. Fed. Commr. of Taxation* (1953), 88 C.L.R. 141 at 151-152 (Aust. H.C.); see also, *Rose v. Fed. Commr. of Taxation* (1951), 84 C.L.R. 118 (Aust. H.C.); *Gorton v. Fed. Commr. of Taxation* (1965), 113 C.L.R. 604 (Aust. H.C.); *Lord Elgin Hotel Ltd. v. M.N.R.* (1964), 36 Tax A.B.C. 268, 64 D.T.C. 637 (Can. Tax App. Bd.).

The essential test is whether or not it is reasonable to regard the new or amended shares as being in substance the same property as the old shares. If they are, there is no disposition. If they are not, there is a disposition.

The following are some examples of changes in share conditions that the Canada Revenue Agency (CRA) normally considers to be a disposition:[11]

- A change in voting rights attached to shares that effects a change in the voting control of the corporation;

- A change in a defined entitlement (for example, a change in par value) to share in the assets of a corporation upon dissolution;

- The giving up or the addition of a priority right to share in the distribution of assets of the corporation upon dissolution;

- The addition or deletion of a right attaching to a class of share that provides for participation in dividend entitlements beyond a fixed preferential rate or amount; and

- A change from a cumulative to a non-cumulative right to dividends or *vice versa*.

The following are examples of changes in share conditions that the Agency does *not* consider as dispositions:

- The addition of the right to elect a majority of the directors of the corporation if, at that time, the shareholders of that class are already in a position to control the election of directors;

- A change in the number of votes per share, if the ability of any one shareholder to influence the day-to-day affairs of the corporation is neither enhanced nor impaired thereby;

- The giving up of contingent voting rights which, in the event they were exercised, would not have been of sufficient number to control the affairs of the corporation;

- Restrictions added or removed concerning transfer of shares;

- Stock splits or consolidations;

- A change of shares with par value to shares without par value or vice versa, provided that there is no change in any pre-set entitlements to dividends and/or distribution of assets upon dissolution;

- A change in ranking concerning preference features (e.g., 1st preference to 2nd preference); and

---

[11]IT-448, "Dispositions — Changes in Terms of Securities" (June 6, 1980) as amended by Special Release (June 21, 1982). See also Arnold and Ward, "Dispositions — A Critique of Revenue Canada's Interpretation" (1980) 28 Can. Tax J. 559.

- An increase or decrease in the amount or rate of a fixed dividend entitlement.

It is important to observe, however, that even if each of the above transactions in isolation does not constitute a disposition, a combination of changes taken together may well amount to a disposition.

4. — Capital Property

The rollover is available only in respect of shares that constitute capital property.[12] Generally, "capital property" includes shares, the gain or loss from the disposition of which would be a capital gain or loss. In certain circumstances, however, a taxpayer may elect to have Canadian securities deemed to be capital property.[13] This election is not available to a trader or dealer in securities.[14]

5. — Dispose of All Shares

The final requirement in respect of the rollover is that the taxpayer dispose of *all* of the shares of any particular class owned by the taxpayer. A partial disposition of share holdings of a class does not qualify for the rollover even if all of the other conditions are satisfied.[15]

IV. — Calculation Of Gain On "Old Shares"

Subsection 86(1) allows a taxpayer to defer the capital gain which the taxpayer might otherwise have been required to recognize on a disposition of shares with accrued gains.

The subsection involves three separate computations:

- The cost of any non-share consideration received from the corporation;

- The cost of the share consideration received from the corporation; and

- The proceeds of disposition of the "old shares".

---

[12]See s. 54"capital property"; Chapter 7, "The Meaning of Business Income, Investment Income, and Capital Gains".

[13]Subs. 39(4).

[14]Para. 39(5)(a); see also Chapter 9, "Deductions from Business and Investment Income".

[15]Subs. 86(1); see generally, ATR-25, "Estate Freeze" (October 9, 1987) and ATR-36, "Estate Freeze" (November 4, 1988).

The cost of non-share consideration received is its fair market value at the time of the disposition.[16]

The cost of share consideration is the difference between the adjusted cost base of the "old shares" and the fair market value of any non-share consideration received.[17] A taxpayer who receives more than one class of new shares is required to allocate the cost between the various classes of shares. The allocation is made on the basis of the relative fair market value of each class of new shares taken back from the corporation.

The proceeds of disposition of the old shares are deemed to be equal to the *cost* of the taxpayer's non-share consideration and the new shares.[18]

Hence, unless the taxpayer receives non-share consideration (for example, cash) in excess of the cost of the "old shares", the proceeds of disposition will always equal the adjusted cost base of the "old shares" and there can be no capital gain. Where the taxpayer receives excessive non-share consideration (that is, an amount in excess of the cost base of the old shares), the proceeds of disposition for the old shares will exceed their ACB and result in a capital gain.

Example

Assume:

Mr. S. exchanges his "old shares" in *S Ltd.* for debt and "new shares" in the corporation. The following data applies to the exchange:

"Old Shares"		Consideration Received	
		Debt	New Shares
Case A			
ACB	$ 100	$?	$?
FMV	$ 300	$ 80	$ 200
Case B			
ACB	$ 100	$?	$?
FMV	$ 300	$ 100	$ 190

Then:

	Case A	Case B
(1) ACB of "old shares"	$ 100	$ 100

---

[16]Para. 86(1)(a).

[17]Para. 86(1)(b).

[18]Para. 86(1)(c).

Example				
Cost of debt received (FMV)		(80)		(110)
ACB of "new shares"	$	20	$	NIL
Proceeds of disposition				
of "old shares"	$	100	$	110
ACB of "old shares"		(100)		(100)
Capital gain (immediate)		NIL	$	10
(2) FMV of "new shares"	$	220	$	190
ACB of "new shares"		20		NIL
Deferred capital gain	$	200	$	190

V. — Indirect Gifts

A special rule prevents taxpayers from avoiding tax by indirectly diluting the value of their shares in order to benefit related persons. In the absence of a rule to prevent indirect dilution of shares, a taxpayer could deplete the value of his or her shareholding and eliminate any capital gain that might otherwise be taxable to the taxpayer's estate on death.

The special rule is as follows: where, in a reorganization of capital, a taxpayer exchanges "old shares" in return for inadequate consideration, the amount by which the fair market value of the "old shares" exceeds the value of the consideration that the taxpayer receives from the corporation may be considered a "gift".

The shortfall in consideration is a gift if it can reasonably be considered a benefit which the taxpayer desired to confer on a person related to him or her.[19] In these circumstances, the taxpayer's proceeds of disposition are recalculated to be equal to the *lesser* of:[20]

- The aggregate of any non-share consideration taken back from the corporation *and* the amount of the "gift portion"; and

- The fair market value of the "old shares" immediately before the disposition.

Subsection 86(2) has two effects: (1) the amount of the indirect gift (i.e., the amount by which the share value is diluted) is added to the taxpayer's proceeds of disposition for the

---

[19]Subs. 86(2).

[20]Para. 86(2)(c).

purpose of calculating a capital gain from the disposition of the old shares; and (2) it affects the adjusted cost base of the new shares.

Example

Mr. T exchanges his "old shares" in *T Ltd.* for "new shares" in the corporation. Assume that the following data and subsection 86(2) apply to the exchange:

	"Old Shares"	"New Shares" Consideration Received	
		Case A	Case B
ACB	$100	$?	$?
FMV	$300	$ 250	$ 150

Then:

(1) POD of old shares is *lesser* of:			
Gift portion, and		$ 50	$ 150
FMV of old shares		$ 300	$ 300
Proceeds of disposition of old shares (lesser amount)		$ 50	$ 150
ACB of old shares		(100)	(100)
Capital gain or loss		NIL*	$ 50
(2) ACB of old shares		$ 100	$ 100
Exceeds: "gift portion"		50	(150)
ACB of new shares		$ 50	NIL
(3) FMV of new shares		$ 250	$ 150
ACB of new shares		(50)	NIL
Deferred capital gain		$ 200	$ 150

Notes:

*   deemed nil by para. 86(2)(d)

In the above example, the gift portion of $150 in Case B causes the proceeds of disposition of the old shares to exceed their ACB and trigger an immediate capital gain of $50. It also drops the ACB of the new shares to nil, thereby increasing the potential capital gain on the shares in the future.

VI. — Cost Base Of New Shares

The cost base of the taxpayer's "new shares" is the amount by which the adjusted cost base of the "old shares" exceeds the aggregate of:[21]

- Any non-share consideration received from the corporation on the exchange of shares, and

- The amount of the indirect gift (the "gift portion") conferred on a related person.

VII. — Deemed Dividends

A shareholder is deemed to receive a dividend if the paid-up capital of the new shares plus the amount of any non-share consideration received exceeds the paid-up capital of the old shares disposed of in the course of the reorganization of capital.[22]

VIII. — Capital Loss

The proceeds of disposition of the new shares and any non-share consideration can never be less than the adjusted cost base of the "old shares". Hence, it is not possible to recognize a capital loss on a disposition of shares under section 86.

IX. — Estate Freezing

Section 86 can be used to freeze the value of an individual's growth shares by exchanging the shares for fixed value preferred shares in the corporation. In a typical estate freeze, a parent exchanges growth common shares for fixed value preferred shares of equal value and the children acquire new common shares with future growth potential. Thus, the value of the parent's shares is frozen at their exchange value and future growth enures to the benefit of the children. The type of business carried on by the corporation is not a material factor and the CRA accepts that the shares of a corporation may be frozen regardless of the nature of its business activity.

---

[21]Para. 86(2)(e).

[22]See subss. 84(3), (5).

Section 86 can also be used to implement a reorganization of capital that is principally motivated by income splitting considerations. In this scenario, the shares of the reorganized corporation are distributed or sprinkled amongst various family members so that they can each participate in dividend distributions. The corporation's share capital is structured so that each class of shares is in substance a different type of property. Dividends may be paid to one class of shareholders to the exclusion of another class.

This type of selective dividend sprinkling through the use of discretionary dividends has been popular for a long time and continues to attract the CRA's ire. Although the Agency has had limited success in controlling income splitting through discretionary dividends, they are reluctant to approve of and further encourage such transactions by issuing favourable advance tax rulings. Thus, the CRA will not give an advance ruling on a section 86 reorganization of capital involving an estate freeze in favour of a spouse, because the Agency generally considers such arrangements to constitute income splitting.

The Agency's view is that a section 86 reorganization involves a transfer of property, and hence the attribution rules would normally apply to the transaction. The Agency will not usually issue a ruling in these circumstances unless the taxpayer can establish to its satisfaction that he or she has *bona fide* business reasons (other than income splitting) for including a spouse in the estate freeze. The rationale is that an estate freeze in favour of a spouse is not really necessary, since a taxpayer's capital property can be rolled over without any immediate tax consequences to the spouse or to a spouse trust.[23] Hence, the CRA may invoke subsection 15(1) (shareholder benefits), 56(2) (indirect payments), or 245(2) (GAAR) to attack such transactions.

The CRA is more disposed, however, towards estate freezing in favour of children and has taken the position that it will not normally invoke GAAR in such circumstances. For example, the Agency states that[24] "... estate freezes would not ordinarily result in misuse or abuse..." of the Act, including those provisions of the statute which deal with income attribution.

Where the freeze is in favour of minor children, however, the Agency takes the position that the shares which represent a child's interest must be held in trust and that dividends should not be paid to the trust until such time as the child reaches the age of 18. In other words, given that the Act generally circumscribes income splitting with minors, the Agency takes the position that an estate freeze to facilitate such splitting does not accord with the scheme of the Act. It remains unclear whether the Agency's reluctance to issue a favourable advance ruling in these circumstances means that they will invoke GAAR to attack the transaction on the theory that such an arrangement constitutes an "abuse of the Act read as a whole."

---

[23]See subs. 70(6).

[24]IC 88-2, "General Anti-Avoidance Rule — Section 245 of the *Income Tax Act*" (October 21, 1988), para. 10.

X. — Valuation Of Shares

The valuation of the "new shares" received as part of a section 86 rollover can give rise to several difficulties.

1. — Indirect Gifts

The indirect benefit rule in subsection 86(2) can trigger a deemed gift or benefit where the value of consideration received exceeds the value of the "old shares" disposed of by the freezor. The value of the benefit is the difference between the fair market value of the old shares disposed of and the aggregate fair market value of the consideration received in exchange. Subsection 86(2) applies only where the taxpayer confers a benefit on a related person. To be sure, in an arm's length transaction it is quite unlikely that the taxpayer would confer a benefit on a person who was not related to the taxpayer.

2. — Redeemable Shares

In order to freeze the value of preferred shares at a given amount, it is necessary to circumscribe their economic attributes so as to prevent any increase or decrease in their value. This may be achieved by setting their redemption value (the price at which the corporation may redeem its shares) and retractable value (the price at which a shareholder may cause the corporation to purchase the shares) at a pre-determined value. For example, in the simplest case, assume that an individual exchanges shares that have a value of $500,000 for new shares with a value of $100,000 and $400,000 cash. In order to ensure that the new shares remain frozen at a value of $100,000, the shares should be redeemable and retractable for $100,000. Absent any other considerations, this should be sufficient to "freeze" the value of the new shares at that amount.

The proposition that the value of shares can be frozen at their redemption and retraction amounts is both logical and defensible. Why would an arm's length purchaser pay more than $100,000 for the frozen shares if they can be redeemed by the corporation at any time for that amount? Why would the shareholder sell the shares for less than $100,000 if he or she can require the corporation to redeem its shares for the stipulated retraction amount? Thus, absent any special share characteristics or contractual conditions which might cause the value of the shares to deviate from their "frozen" value, the "new shares" should remain frozen at their contractually determined redemption and retraction value.

But what if the corporation is financially incapable of meeting its potential obligation to redeem the preferred shares? Do the preferred shares have to have some inherent minimum investment quality to be considered equal to the value of the common shares for which they are exchanged? The CRA does not have definite answers to these questions. There is a real risk that, in these circumstances, the value of the preferred shares will be considered to be less than the value of the common shares for which they are exchanged. If so, subsection 86(2) may trigger an indirect benefit to the freezor of the common shares.

3. — *Reasonable Dividends*

The dividend payable on a share can also affect its value. The Agency's general position is that preferred shares that are issued as part of an estate freeze should bear a *reasonable* dividend rate. It accepts, however, that the absence of a dividend does not, "in and of itself", reduce the value of the preferred shares.[25] Clearly, an excessive dividend rate can cause the value of the preferred shares to escalate and defeat the estate freeze.

COMPREHENSIVE EXAMPLE

Assume:

Ms. Jones owns all of the issued Class A shares of *Opco Ltd.*, a private corporation to which the following data applies:

	Per share
PUC	$ 100
ACB	$ 500
FMV	$ 1,000

- Pursuant to a reorganization of capital under section 86, Ms. Jones exchanges *each* Class A share for one Class B share plus $300 debt.

- Ms. Jones' children subscribe for new Class C shares which have a PUC, ACB and FMV of $100.

- Each Class B share has paid-up capital (PUC) of $100 and a FMV of $700.

- *Opco Ltd.* cancels the Class A shares previously held by Ms. Jones.

Then:

1. Cost of Class B shares:
   ACB of old shares $ 500

---

[25]See for example, Revenue Canada Round Table, in *Proceedings of 33rd Tax Conf.* (Can. Tax Foundation, 1981), Question 45 at 759.

COMPREHENSIVE EXAMPLE

Exceeds	
FMV of non-share consideration (debt)	(300)
Cost of Class B shares	$ 200

2. Calculation of capital gain:

Cost of Class B shares	$ 200
Cost of non-share consideration (debt)	300
POD of old shares	500
ACB of old shares	(500)
Capital gain	NIL

3. Deemed dividend on cancellation of old shares

Amount paid by debt	$ 300
PUC of Class B shares	100
Total amount paid	400
PUC of old shares	(100)
Deemed dividend [subs. 84(3)]	$ 300

Selected Bibliography to Chapter 28

General

Bennett, Sharon, "Phantom Income, Real Tax: Section 86 Reorganizations" (1990) 3:11 Canadian Current Tax P-21.

Boultbee, Jack A., "A Survey of the Use of Rollovers in Acquisitions and Mergers" (1980) 28 Can. Tax J. 504.

Boultbee, Jack A. and D.S. Ewens, "The Taxation of Corporate Reorganizations" (1986) 34 Can. Tax J. 203.

Deaves, Brian M.P., "Tax and Estate Planning with Section 86" (1982) 115 CA Magazine No. 2 79.

"Estate Planning in Canada" (1975) 23 Can. Tax J. 542 at 545.

Ewens, Douglas, "Retractable Preferred Shares" (1983) 31 Can. Tax. J. 713.

Kellough, "A Planning Update for Private Corporations — Corporate Reorganizations", *Prairie Provinces Tax Conf.* 131 (Can. Tax Foundation, 1981).

Lindsay, Robert F., "Winding-Up of Corporations: Changes in Capital Structure of Corporations", in *Proceedings of 26th Tax Conf.* 69 (Can. Tax Foundation, 1974).

McNair, D.K., "Exchange of Shares by Shareholder in the Course of a Reorganization of Capital: Section 86" (1981) Can. Taxation 1063.

McQuillan, P., et al., "Section 86 — Exchange of Shares Checklist", in *Purchase and Sale of a Business* 5–55 (Toronto: The Canadian Institute of Chartered Accountants, 1982).

Middleton, David W., "Common Tax Problems and Pitfalls in Effecting Reorganizations of Private Corporations", in *Proceedings of 41st Tax Conf.* 13:1 (Can. Tax Foundation, 1989).

Shannon, H., "Part 5: Reorganization of Corporate Share Capital", in *Income Taxation in Canada*, W.A. MacDonald and G.E. Cronkwright (Scarborough: Prentice-Hall Canada Inc., 1977), 63-040.

Stein, Boris P., "Part Two: Canadian Case Law Concerning Shares Received on a Rollover", *The Journal of Business Valuation*, Canadian Assoc. of Business Valuators, Vol. 7, 1981, 95.

Taxation of Corporate Organization and Reorganization (Montreal: Federated Press, 1993).

"The Taxation of Corporate Reorganizations — Section 86 Reorganizations" (1984) 32 Can. Tax J. 1165.

Ward, David A. and Brian J. Arnold, "Dispositions — A Critique of Revenue Canada's Interpretation" (1980) 28 Can. Tax J. 559.

Wilson, Ronald S., "Cost Adjustments in Corporate Reorganization Transactions: Policy and Practice", in *Proceedings of 38th Tax Conf.* 8:1 (Can. Tax Foundation, 1986).

Wise, Richard M., "Valuation and the *Income Tax Act*" (1981) 29 Can. Tax J. 626.

Witterick, R.G., "Estate Freezing through Corporate Reorganizations of Capital", *Tax Planning and Management*, Vol. 9, No. 24 of *Canadian Income Tax Revised* (Butterworth and Co. (Canada) Ltd., 1977).

Witterick, R.G., "Section 86: A Slumbering Giant" (1975) 23 Can. Tax J. 89.

Indirect Gifts

Boultbee, Jack, "Gifts and Rollovers" (1983) 31 Can. Tax J. 84.

Estate Freezing and Section 86

Barnett, James J., "Estate Planning and the Life Stages of the Business, Owner and the Business" (1991) 39 Can. Tax J. 1576.

Bowden, Gregory T.W., "Estate Freezing", *British Columbia Tax Conf.* 266 (Can. Tax Foundation, 1980).

Cadesky, Michael, "Succession of the Family Business" (1994) Estates and Trusts J. 219.

Crawford, William E., "Corporate Freezes — Are you Getting Your Money's Worth?", in *Proceedings of 32nd Tax Conf.* 772 (Can. Tax Foundation, 1980).

Drache, Arthur B.C., "The Flexible Freeze" (1995) Can. Taxpayer 21.

Krishna, Vern, "Administrative View on Estate Freezing", (1990–92) Can. Current Tax A21.

Louis, David, "Estate Freezing — The Next Generation" (1994) No. 377 Tax Notes 1.

Morris, J.S.D., "Freezing Family Business Interests — Inflation and Other Concerns" (1981) 29 Can. Tax J. 211.

Morrissette, Andre, "Unfreezing an Estate", in *Proceedings of 44th Tax Conf.* 15:1 (Can. Tax Foundation, 1992).

Rochwerg, Martin J., "Post-Mortem Estate Freezing" (1983) 31 Can. Tax J. 69.

Silver, Sheldon, "A Simple Case of Freezing — Part 2" (1976) 24 Can. Tax J. 171.

Silver, Sheldon, "Has the Dust Settled?" (1977) 25 Can. Tax J. 652.

Silver, Sheldon, "Unplanning an Estate — Part I" (1976) 24 Can. Tax J. 652.

Witterick, R.G., "Estate Freezing through a Reorganization of Capital under Section 86", in *Proceedings of 28th Tax Conf.* 732 (Can. Tax Foundation, 1976).

Other

Davidson, Barrie, "Inter Vivos Tax Planning" (1981) 15 CGA Magazine No. 1 2.

Heller, Stephen, "Part One: Valuation of Preferred Shares Received on a Rollover under the *Income Tax Act*", *The Journal of Business Valuation*, Canadian Assoc. of Business Valuators, Vol. 7, 1981, 71.

Sohmer, David H., "Partnerships and Corporations", (1991) Meredith Mem. Lect. 199.

PART XIII: MERGERS & ACQUISITIONS

CHAPTER 29 — AMALGAMATIONS AND WIND-UPS

I. — Amalgamations

1. — General Comment

A merger or an "amalgamation" is a form of acquisition that involves the fusion of two or more corporations into a new corporate entity. An amalgamation coalesces two or more corporations to create a homogeneous whole. An amalgamation is sometimes described by analogy as "a river formed by the confluence of two streams," or "the creation of a single rope through the intertwining of strands."[1] The amalgamated corporation acquires all of the assets and assumes all of the liabilities of the amalgamating corporations.[2] The shareholders and creditors of the predecessor corporations become the shareholders and creditors of the amalgamated corporation.

(a) — Distinguished from Other Acquisitions

An amalgamation is to be distinguished from an acquisition of the assets or shares of one corporation by another. Where a corporation purchases all of the assets and liabilities of another corporation, the vendor corporation continues its existence as a separate entity, *albeit* as a "shell" corporation. Where a corporation acquires all of the shares of another corporation, the vendor corporation becomes a subsidiary of the purchaser corporation. In contrast to these two forms of acquisition, an amalgamation involves a fusion of the amalgamated corporations into one corporation.[3] The new corporation is sometimes referred to as the "continuing" or "survivor" corporation.

---

[1] *The Queen v. Black & Decker Mfg. Co.*, [1975] 1 S.C.R. 411 at 420 (S.C.C.).

[2] See, e.g., *Canada Business Corporations Act* ("CBCA"), R.S.C. 1985, c. C-44, s. 186.

[3] *The Queen v. Black & Decker Mfg. Co., ante*, at 417 (amalgamated companies continue as one company; antithesis of notion that amalgamating corporations extinguished or continue in truncated state).

(b) — Type

There are three different types of amalgamations: "vertical", "horizontal" and "hybrid".

In a vertical amalgamation, a parent corporation is merged with one or more of its subsidiary corporations to form the new amalgamated corporation. Thus, a "vertical" amalgamation is similar in effect to the winding-up of a subsidiary into its parent corporation.

In a "horizontal" amalgamation, two or more corporations which do not own shares of each other are merged to form a new amalgamated corporation.

A "hybrid" amalgamation is a combination of a "vertical" and "horizontal" amalgamation.

"Amalgamation" is both a corporate and a tax concept. For the purposes of corporate law, an amalgamation is implemented according to the law of the relevant jurisdiction.[4] To qualify as an "amalgamation" for tax purposes, however, the merger must satisfy the specific requirements of subsection 87(1) of the Act.

(c) — Form Over Substance

It is important to emphasize at the outset that the income tax consequences of a corporate reorganization (such as an amalgamation) depend entirely on the form of the arrangement, rather than on the economic consequences that flow from the reorganization. Thus, choice of method and form of implementation, rather than the economic substance of the reorganization, dictate the tax consequences. For example, if Corporation B acquires the assets and liabilities of Corporation A and Corporation A is then wound up, the economic result is identical to that of an amalgamation of Corporations A and B into a new Corporation AB. In both cases, one corporation ends up with all of the assets and liabilities of the other. In both cases, the shareholders of Corporation A end up with shares which may be exchanged for cash, either by way of a liquidating dividend on winding-up or by disposition on the open market. The tax consequences of the two alternatives are, however, very different. A purchase and sale of assets triggers a gain or loss at the time of the disposition.[5] An amalgamation can be accomplished on a tax-free basis.

2. — Corporate Law

(a) — General Comment

Absent specific statutory authority, corporations may amalgamate only with other corporations governed by the same corporate statute. Corporations incorporated under the same cor-

---

[4]See, e.g., CBCA, ss. 181–86.

[5]Unless the disposition and purchase of assets is eligible for a rollover under, e.g., s. 85.

porate statute automatically come within the jurisdiction of that statute. Where one corporation is incorporated under one statute and another corporation is incorporated in some other jurisdiction, the two corporations cannot amalgamate unless one of the corporations is imported into the jurisdiction of the other. For example, assume that Corporation X is incorporated under the *Canada Business Corporations Act* and Corporation Y is incorporated under the Ontario *Business Corporations Act*.[6] For the two corporations to amalgamate, one of them must be imported into the jurisdiction of the other. Either Corporation Y can be continued under the *Canada Business Corporations Act*[7] or Corporation X can be continued under the Ontario *Business Corporations Act*.[8] The corporations may then amalgamate according to the corporate law of the jurisdiction in which they are both incorporated.

Where a corporation is continued from one jurisdiction to another, it is not considered to have disposed of its assets or its shares.[9]

(b) — Amalgamation Agreement

Two or more federal corporations (including holding and subsidiary corporations) may amalgamate and continue as one corporation. The first step in an amalgamation is for the corporations to enter into a proposed agreement to settle, *inter alia*, the following issues:[10]

- Corporate name, registered office, share capital structure, share transfer restrictions;

- Number of directors, and restrictions on business activities in respect of the amalgamated corporation;

- Name and address of each proposed director of the amalgamated corporation;

- Description of the method by which the shares of each of the amalgamating corporations is to be converted into the shares of the amalgamated corporation;

- Compensation to be paid to the holders of shares that are not converted into securities of the amalgamated corporation;

- By-laws of the amalgamated corporation, if they are different from those of the amalgamating corporations; and

---

[6]Ontario *Business Corporations Act*, R.S.O. 1990, c. B.16 ("OBCA").

[7]CBCA, s. 187.

[8]OBCA, s. 180.

[9]TR-1, "Exporting a Corporation — Whether a Disposition — Effect on Incorporation Date" (June 24, 1974); TR-37, "Amalgamations" (August 9, 1976); TR-49, "Sale of Assets — Amalgamations" (March 8, 1977).

[10]CBCA, subs. 182(1); see OBCA, subs. 175(1) (similar requirements set out).

- Details of arrangements necessary for the subsequent management and operation of the amalgamated corporation.

The proposed amalgamation agreement must be submitted to the shareholders of each of the amalgamating corporations for their approval.[11]

(c) — Voting

Each share of an amalgamating corporation carries the right to vote in respect of the amalgamation regardless of whether the share has voting rights in other circumstances.[12] Where the proposed amalgamation involves a change in the rights of a class of shares, the agreement requires the additional approval of the shareholders of the class voting separately as a class.[13]

An amalgamation agreement is adopted when the shareholders of each amalgamating corporation approve of the amalgamation by special resolutions.[14]

(d) — Effect

The Director of the Corporations Branch will issue a certificate of amalgamation upon receipt of the articles of amalgamation. The effect of the certificate is as follows:[15]

- The amalgamation of the amalgamating corporations and their continuance as one corporation is effective as of the date shown on the certificate;
- The property of each amalgamating corporation continues as the property of the amalgamated corporation;
- The amalgamated corporation continues to be liable for the obligations of each amalgamating corporation;
- Existing causes of action, claims or liabilities remain unaffected;
- Civil, criminal or administrative actions or proceedings pending by or against an amalgamating corporation may be continued to be prosecuted by or against the amalgamated corporation;

---

[11]CBCA, subs. 183(1).

[12]CBCA, subs. 183(3).

[13]CBCA, subs. 183(4).

[14]CBCA, subs. 183(5); subs. 2(1)"special resolution".

[15]CBCA, s. 186.

- A conviction against, or ruling, order or judgment in favour of or against, an amalgamating corporation may be enforced by or against the amalgamated corporation;

- The articles of amalgamation are deemed to be the articles of incorporation of the amalgamated corporation; and

- The certificate of amalgamation is deemed to be the certificate of incorporation of the amalgamated corporation.

(e) — "Short-Form" Amalgamation

A "short-form" amalgamation is an amalgamation implemented without shareholder approval. A holding corporation and one or more of its *wholly-owned* subsidiary corporations may amalgamate without shareholder approval if the amalgamation is approved by the directors of each corporation, the shares of each subsidiary corporation are cancelled without repayment of capital, and the amalgamated corporation does not issue new securities as part of the amalgamation.[16]

Similarly, two or more *wholly-owned* subsidiary corporations of the same holding corporation may amalgamate without shareholder approval upon resolution of the directors of each corporation if the shares of the amalgamating corporation are cancelled without repayment of capital.[17]

In both of the above cases, shareholder approval would serve little purpose, since the corporations are wholly-owned by the same corporation and the amalgamation does not involve any diminution in the share capital of the amalgamated corporations.

3. — "Amalgamation" for Tax Purposes

The amalgamation provisions of the Act allow amalgamated corporations to share tax attributes that they would not otherwise be able to share. Thus, the general rules of subsection 87(1) tie into corporate law and allow sharing of property and liabilities. This means that there are no dispositions of corporate assets or liabilities for tax purposes.

---

[16]CBCA, subs. 184(1) (this type of amalgamation is referred to as "vertical short-form" amalgamation).

[17]CBCA, subs. 184(2) (referred to as "horizontal short-form" amalgamation).

For income tax purposes, an amalgamation is a merger of two or more *taxable Canadian corporations* (the "predecessor corporations") into a new corporate entity (the "new corporation"), such that:[18]

- All of the properties of the predecessor corporations become property of the new corporation;

- All of the liabilities of the predecessor corporations become liabilities of the new corporation; and

- All of the shareholders of the predecessor corporations before the merger receive shares of the capital stock of the new corporation.

Inter-corporate accounts receivable, accounts payable and shareholdings are eliminated upon amalgamation.

A "short-form" amalgamation also qualifies as an amalgamation for income tax purposes even though no new shares of the amalgamated corporation are issued as a result of the amalgamation.[19]

The corporate entity created as a result of an amalgamation is considered to be a "new" corporation for certain purposes[20] and a continuation of the predecessor corporations for other purposes.[21] The account balances of the predecessor corporations generally pass through in aggregate to the new corporation. Shareholders of the predecessor corporations can usually exchange their old shares for shares in the new corporation on a tax-free basis.[22]

---

[18]Subs. 87(1).

[19]Subs. 87(1.1).

[20]Para. 87(2)(a).

[21]*The Queen v. Pan Ocean Oil Ltd.*, [1994] 2 C.T.C. 143, 94 D.T.C. 6412 (F.C.A.); *The Queen v. Guaranty Properties Ltd.*, [1990] 2 C.T.C. 94, 90 D.T.C. 6363 (F.C.A.); leave to appeal to S.C.C. refused; *The Queen v. Black & Decker Mfg. Co.*, [1975] 1 S.C.R. 411 (S.C.C.); *Witco Chemical Co. Can. v. Oakville (Town)*, [1975] 1 S.C.R. 273 (S.C.C.) (for corporate law purposes, new corporation considered to be continuation of old). See also subs. 87(1.2) (new corporation continuation of predecessor); para. 87(2)(l) (new corporation permitted to utilize unused scientific research expenditures of predecessor corporation by deeming new corporation to be continuation of its predecessors).

[22]Subs. 87(4).

4. — *The New Corporation*

(a) — *Taxation Year*

The first taxation year of the new corporation commences at the time of the amalgamation. Thus, the new corporation may adopt any fiscal period commencing from the date of the amalgamation, so long as the period does not exceed 53 weeks.[23]

(b) — *Tax Instalments*

Although the new corporation is deemed to have come into existence at the time of the amalgamation, the instalment bases of its predecessor corporations are added together and constitute the instalment base of the new corporation for the immediately preceding year. Thus, the new corporation must make instalment payments *as if* it had been in existence in the preceding taxation year.[24]

(c) — *Inventory*

As a general rule, inventory is valued at the lower of its cost or market value.[25]

A taxpayer must value its opening inventory on the same basis as its closing inventory for the preceding year.[26] Similarly, the closing inventories of the predecessor corporations become the opening inventory of the new corporation. The Act deems property that was included in the closing inventory of each predecessor corporation to have been acquired by the new corporation at the *commencement* of its first taxation year at the same value used by the predecessor corporations in computing their income for their last taxation year.[27] Thus, inventory values are carried over from the predecessor corporations to the new corporation without any loss of inventory basis.

Property that would have been included in the inventory of a predecessor corporation if it had followed the cash method of calculating income is deemed to have been acquired by the new corporation at an amount equal to the value specified in the predecessor's election.[28]

---

[23]Paras. 87(2)(a), 249(1)(a), s. 249.1; see also para. 87(2)(oo).

[24]Reg. 5301(4).

[25]See subs. 10(1); Regs. 1801, 1802 (special rules permitting *all* of taxpayer's inventory to be valued at fair market value).

[26]Subs. 10(2).

[27]Para. 87(2)(b).

[28]Para. 87(2)(b).

This amount will usually be nil where the predecessor corporation accounts for its inventory on a cash basis. It may, however, be equal to fair market value, in the case of livestock inventory.[29]

(d) — Depreciable Property

For the purposes of capital cost allowance and recapture, the Act deems the new corporation's depreciable property to have a capital cost equal to the capital cost of the property to its predecessor corporations. The undepreciated capital cost of depreciated property to the new corporation is, in effect, equal to the total of the undepreciated capital cost of property of that class owned by the predecessor corporations. Thus, on a disposition of the property by the new corporation, recapture of capital cost allowance is calculated by reference to the original capital cost of the property to the predecessor corporation.[30] The rules ensure that the depreciable property of each class can be separately identified and linked to the predecessor corporation.

Example

Assume:

	Predecessor Corporations		
	A	B	Total
Depreciable property (Class 8)			
Capital cost	$ 100,000	$ 68,000	$ 168,000
CCA claimed	(50,000)	(46,000)	(96,000)
UCC	$ 50,000	$ 22,000	$ 72,000

Corporations A and B amalgamate to form *AB Ltd.*

Then:

Capital cost of property to *Corp. A*	$ 100,000
Capital cost of property to *Corp. B*	68,000
Capital cost to *AB Ltd.*	168,000

---

[29]Subs. 28(1).

[30]Para. 87(2)(d); Reg. 1102(14).

Example

Add:

UCC of property acquired from *Corp. A*	50,000
UCC of property acquired from *Corp. B*	22,000
	240,000
Less:	
Capital cost to *AB Ltd.*	(168,000)
UCC of class to *AB Ltd.*	$ 72,000[*]

Notes:

[*]   This amount is in effect equal to the aggregate UCC of the predecessor corporations.

Example

Assume:

	Predecessor Corporations		
	C	D	Total
Depreciable property (Class 6)			
Capital cost	$ 150,000	$ 80,000	$ 230,000
CCA claimed	(50,000)	(40,000)	(90,000)
UCC	$ 100,000	$ 40,000	$ 140,000

Corporations C and D amalgamate to form *CD Ltd.*, which disposes of the building previously owned by *C. Ltd.* and acquires a new Class 6 building.

Proceeds of disposition of old building	$ 225,000
Cost of new Class 6 building	$ 300,000
Then (ignoring replacement property elections):	
Capital cost of property (*C Ltd.*)	$ 150,000
Capital cost of property (*D Ltd.*)	80,000
Capital cost of new property to *CD Ltd.*	300,000

Example	
	530,000
Add: UCC of class of predecessors	140,000
Less: Capital cost of class to predecessors	(230,000)
	440,000
Less: Proceeds of disposition	(150,000)*
UCC of class to *CD Ltd.*	$ 290,000

Notes:

*　　Being the lesser of the proceeds of disposition of the property ($225,000) and its capital cost ($150,000).

(e) — Non-Depreciable Capital Property

The Act deems the new corporation to acquire non-depreciable capital property (other than an interest in a partnership) from its predecessor corporations at an amount equal to the adjusted cost base of the property to its predecessors immediately before the amalgamation.[31] The tax-free zone of capital property owned by the predecessor corporations is preserved and passed on to the new corporation.[32]

(f) — Eligible Capital Property

Where the new corporation carries on the business of its predecessor corporation, the predecessor's cumulative eligible capital immediately before the amalgamation is added to the new corporation's cumulative eligible capital account. The new corporation calculates its cumulative eligible capital account by adding 75 per cent of its eligible capital expenditure, to any amount that it inherits from its predecessor corporations, less 75 per cent of its disposition proceeds on account of eligible capital properties.[33]

---

[31]Para. 87(2)(e).

[32]Subs. 251(3.1); ITAR 26(5).

[33]Para. 87(2)(f).

Example

Assume:

| | Predecessor Corporations | | New Corporation |
	C. Ltd.	D. Ltd.	CD Ltd.
Cumulative eligible capital	$ 130,000	$ 30,000	—
Eligible capital expenditures	—	—	$ 50,000
Proceeds of disposition of eligible capital property	—	—	$ 26,000
Then:			
Eligible capital expenditures (75% of $50,000)			$ 37,500
Inherited from C Ltd. and D Ltd.			160,000
			197,500
Dispositions (75% of $26,000)			(19,500)
			178,000
Less: maximum claim (7%)*			(12,460)
Cumulative eligible capital of CD Ltd.			$ 165,540

Notes:

* Prorated over 365 days if the amalgamated corporation has a short fiscal year.

(g) — Reserves

(i) — General Comment

A taxpayer may claim a reserve only if it is *specifically* authorized by the Act.[34] Under the statutory scheme in respect of reserves a taxpayer must include in income the amount of any reserve claimed by the taxpayer in the immediately preceding year, and may deduct an amount as a new reserve in the current year.

The Act *deems* a reserve claimed by a predecessor corporation in its final year to have been claimed by the new corporation, and is included in the new corporation's income in its first taxation year. Thus, the new corporation inherits the ongoing responsibility for reserves pre-

---

[34]Para. 18(1)(e).

viously claimed by its predecessor corporations.[35] The new corporation may claim a reserve in respect of its first taxation year in the usual manner.

Similarly, the Act deems the new corporation to have included in its income in its first taxation year any amounts receivable by it in future years that were included in the predecessor corporation's last taxation year. Here too, the new corporation steps into the shoes of the predecessor corporations and continues to claim the reserve.[36]

(ii) — Debts

The Act deems the predecessor corporation's debts, and debts which arose from loans made in the ordinary course of its business which included lending money, to be debts owing to the new corporation. The new corporation may deduct a reasonable amount as a reserve in respect of doubtful debts.[37]

(iii) — Capital Gains Reserve

Where an amount owing to a taxpayer in respect of a disposition of capital property is not due at the end of the taxation year, a portion of any gain resulting from the disposition may be claimed as a reserve.[38] A reserve claimed by a predecessor corporation in its last taxation year is included in the income of the new corporation for its first taxation year. The new corporation may claim a reserve in respect of any proceeds of disposition which remain due at the end of its first taxation year.[39]

(h) — Property Lost, Destroyed or Taken

Where a corporation's property is unlawfully taken, lost, destroyed or expropriated prior to its amalgamation, and the new corporation replaces the property within certain time limits, the new corporation can defer any recapture of capital cost allowance or capital gain that results from the disposition of the property. The rollover in respect of replacement properties

---

[35]Para. 87(2)(g).

[36]Para. 87(2)(i).

[37]Para. 87(2)(h).

[38]Para. 40(1)(a) (note that the critical test is whether the amount is "due", not whether the amount is outstanding).

[39]Para. 87(2)(m).

applies *as if* the new corporation was the same corporation as, and a continuation of, the predecessor corporation.[40]

(i) — Pre-Paid Expenses

Pre-paid expenses for services to be rendered after the end of the taxation year may be claimed as a deduction only in the year to which the expenditure relates.[41]

Pre-payments of interest, taxes, rent or royalty in respect of a period after the end of the year may be deducted only in the period to which the expense relates.

Following an amalgamation, the Act deems the new corporation to be the same corporation as, and a continuation of, each of its predecessor corporations.[42] Thus, the new corporation is subject to the same limitations in respect of its pre-paid expense deductions.

(j) — Options

Where an option issued by a corporation expires, the Act deems the corporation to have disposed of a capital property for proceeds equal to the option price.[43] If the option expires after the corporation has amalgamated with another corporation, it is deemed to have been issued by the new corporation. Thus, the Act deems option proceeds received by the predecessor to have been received by the new corporation.[44]

(k) — Attribution Rules

The attribution rules apply where an individual loans or transfers property to a corporation (other than a small business corporation) in which a spouse or a person under 18 years of age has an interest.[45] These rules continue to apply if the corporation amalgamates with another corporation. Thus, the new corporation is considered the same as, and a continuation of, its predecessor corporation.[46]

---

[40]Para. 87(2)(l.3).

[41]Subs. 18(9).

[42]Para. 87(2)(j.2).

[43]Subs. 49(2).

[44]Para. 87(2)(o).

[45]Ss. 74.4, 74.5; see also, Chapter 14, "Assignment and Attribution of Income".

[46]Para. 87(2)(j.7).

(l) — Partnership Interests

The new corporation's cost of a partnership interest held by its predecessor corporation depends upon the relationship between the corporations. If both the new and predecessor corporations were related[47] to each other, the new corporation's cost of the partnership interest is equal to its cost to the predecessor corporation.[48] The new corporation is treated in the same manner as its predecessor corporation in so far as the partnership interest is concerned. Thus, any adjustments to the adjusted cost base of the partnership interest flow through to the new corporation. Any negative adjusted cost base of a partnership interest held by the predecessor corporation is preserved on the amalgamation.[49]

Where the new corporation and its predecessor were not related to each other, the Act deems the predecessor corporation to have disposed of its partnership interests to the new corporation for proceeds equal to their adjusted cost base. The new corporation acquires the interests at the same amount. Thus, the predecessor is required to recognize any gain on the disposition of any interests with a negative adjusted cost base.[50]

(m) — "Stop-Loss" Rules

A corporation's loss on the sale of a share may be reduced by the amount of any tax-free dividends that it receives on the share. The loss is reduced if the share was owned for less than 365 days prior to the sale, or if the corporation owned more than 5 per cent of the shares on which the dividend is paid.[51] This rule, known as the "stop-loss" rule, also extends to taxable dividends received by the predecessor corporation. Such dividends are taken into account on a disposition of the share after the amalgamation.[52]

(n) — Other

The Act also deems the new corporation to be the same corporation as each predecessor corporation for the following purposes:

• Employee benefit plans	para. 87(2)(j.3)
• Lease cancellations	para. 87(2)(j.5)

---

[47]Subs. 251(3.1).

[48]Para. 87(2)(e.1).

[49]See Chapter 11, "Computation of Gains and Losses".

[50]Subs. 100(2.1); see also subs. 53(2).

[51]Subss. 112(3.01), 112(4.01).

[52]Para. 87(2)(x).

- Income accrual rules   para. 87(2)(j.4)
- Unused investment tax credits   para. 87(2)(qq)
- Repayments of inducements   para. 87(2)(j.6)
- Salary deferral arrangements   para. 87(2)(j.3)
- Deferred profit sharing plans   para. 87(2)(q)
- Scientific research and experimental development   para. 87(2)(l)

5. — Predecessor Corporations

The Act deems the taxation year of a corporation that amalgamates with another corporation to have ended immediately before the amalgamation.[53] The predecessor corporation must file an income tax return for the period up to the date of its amalgamation. Capital cost allowance in respect of the final taxation year is prorated if the amalgamation does not coincide with the predecessor corporation's taxation year.[54]

In corporate law, a corporation that amalgamates with another corporation does not terminate its existence.

The companies "are amalgamated and are continued as one company," which is the very antithesis of the notion that the amalgamating corporations are extinguished or that they continue in a truncated state.[55]

The status of predecessor corporations for tax purposes is unclear. The general scheme of the Act suggests that the predecessor corporations do not terminate their existence. At the very least, they are not deemed to have disposed of their assets upon amalgamation.

6. — Creditors of Predecessor Corporations

In order for a merger to qualify as an amalgamation for income tax purposes, the new corporation must assume *all* of the liabilities of the amalgamating corporations.[56] Creditors of the predecessor corporation may be entitled to rollover their receivables for new obligations from the new corporation.

Where a creditor of the predecessor corporation receives a debt obligation from the new corporation that has the same amount payable at maturity as was payable on the old obliga-

---

[53]Para. 87(2)(a).

[54]Reg. 1100(3); IT-474R, "Amalgamations of Canadian Corporations" (March 14, 1986).

[55]*The Queen v. Black & Decker Mfg. Co.*, [1975] 1 S.C.R. 411 (S.C.C.) at 417

[56]Other than inter-corporate accounts payable to the predecessor corporations.

tion, the Act deems the creditor to dispose of the old debt at its adjusted cost base and to acquire the new debt at a cost equal to the cost base of the old debt. In other words, the creditor can rollover the cost of the old debt into the new debt and defer the recognition of any gain on the instrument. This rollover is available only where the debt obligation is a capital property to the creditor of the predecessor corporation.[57]

Debt obligations of the predecessor corporation assumed by the new corporation are treated as if they were always debts of the new corporation. Thus, there is continuity of treatment in respect of such obligations. For example, the deduction for discounts on debts issued by the predecessor continues to be available to the new corporation.[58]

7. — Paid-Up Capital

A corporation must maintain a separate stated capital account for each class and series of shares that it issues.[59] The stated capital account of each class of shares is to be credited with the full amount of any consideration that it receives in respect of the particular shares.[60]

Where shares are issued pursuant to an amalgamation, however, the new corporation may, in certain circumstances, credit the stated capital account with *less* than the consideration that it receives for the shares.[61] The corporation cannot credit its stated capital account with more than it receives.[62]

The computation of the paid-up capital of the new corporation is particularly important for income tax purposes, because, as a general rule, paid-up capital can be returned to shareholders on a tax-free basis.[63] The paid-up capital of shares for income tax purposes is generally determined according to the corporate law concept of stated capital.[64]

For corporate purposes, the paid-up capital of the new corporation usually will not exceed the aggregate of the paid-up capital of its predecessor corporations less the amount eliminated as a result of the cancellation of inter-corporate shareholdings. There are circumstan-

---

[57]Subs. 87(6).

[58]Para. 20(1)(f).

[59]CBCA, subs. 26(1); see also Chapter 18, "Corporate Finance".

[60]CBCA, subs. 26(2).

[61]CBCA, para. 26(3)(b).

[62]CBCA, subs. 26(4).

[63]Subss. 84(2), (3).

[64]Subs. 89(1)"paid-up capital".

ces, however, where the paid-up capital of a corporation for tax purposes may be less than its stated capital for corporate purposes.[65]

In the absence of special rules, taxpayers might be inclined to increase the paid-up capital of the new corporation in order to later withdraw it on a tax-free basis. A special rule provides, however, that the paid-up capital of the new corporation is reduced to the extent that it exceeds the aggregate paid-up capital of all classes of shares of its predecessor corporations.[66] Any such reduction is allocated among *all* of the classes of shares of the new corporation in proportion to their respective paid-up capital amounts.

Example

Assume:	PUC of Predecessors		Legal (Stated) Capital New Corporation
	A Ltd.	*B Ltd.*	*AB Ltd.*
Class A	$70,000	$ 40,000	$ 150,000
Class B	25,000	—	—
Class C	—	15,000	—
Class D	—	—	50,000
	$95,000	$ 55,000	$ 200,000

A Ltd. and *B Ltd.* amalgamate to form *AB Ltd.*

Then:

The increase of $50,000 in the legal stated capital of *AB Ltd.* is allocated to the various classes of shares as follows:

Class A shares of *AB Ltd.*

Stated capital for corporate purposes		$ 150,000
Less:		
$150,000 × ($200,000 - 150,000)		
$200,000		(37,500)
PUC for tax purposes		$ 112,500

---

[65]For example, where s. 84.2 or s. 212.1 are applied to reduce the paid-up capital of the predecessor corporation.

[66]Para. 87(3)(a).

Example

Class D shares of *AB Ltd.*	
Stated capital for corporate purposes	$ 50,000
Less:	
$\dfrac{\$50,000 \times (\$200,000 - 150,000)}{\$200,000}$	(12,500)
PUC for tax purposes	$ 37,500
PUC of *AB Ltd.* for tax purposes	
Class A shares	$ 112,500
Class D shares	37,500
Total paid-up capital	$ 150,000

Note: a reduction in the paid-up capital of one class of shares of a corporation reduces the paid-up capital of *all* other classes of shares if the corporation amalgamates with another corporation. Thus, a reduction in paid-up capital can have a ripple effect on other shareholders of the corporation.

As a general rule, a shareholder who exchanges shares in a predecessor corporation for shares of the new corporation with a paid-up capital in excess of the paid-up capital of the old shares is not considered to have received a dividend.[67] If, however, the shares are redeemed or otherwise cancelled for an amount in excess of their paid-up capital, the Act deems the shareholder to receive a dividend.[68] To prevent double taxation of the proceeds, the amount of the dividend that is attributable to the previous reduction of paid-up capital is added back to the paid-up capital of the particular class of shares.[69]

Example

Assume:

	Predecessor Corporations		New Corporation	
	PUC	Legal Capital	PUC	Legal Capital

---

[67]IT-474R, "Amalgamations of Canadian Corporations" (March 14, 1986).

[68]Subss. 84(3), (4), (4.1).

[69]Para. 87(3)(b).

Example

Whiteco	$ 10,000	$ 10,000		
Blackco	40,000	50,000		
Newco/Class A	—	—	?	$ 20,000
Newco/Class B	—	—	?	40,000
Total	$ 50,000	$ 60,000		$ 60,000

Whiteco and *Blackco* amalgamate to form *Newco*, which issues 100 Class A and 400 Class B shares, for a total stated capital of $60,000. *Newco* redeems 60 of its Class A shares for $200 per share.

Then:

1. Reduction in *Newco*'s PUC

Legal capital for corporate purposes	$ 60,000
Less: Paid-up capital of predecessors	(50,000)
Amount by which *Newco*'s PUC is reduced for tax purposes (para. 87(3)(a))	$ 10,000

2. Allocation of reduction to *Newco*'s shares

Legal capital of Class A shares	$ 20,000
Less: $\dfrac{20,000 \times \$10,000}{60,000}$	(3,333)
PUC of Class A shares	$ 16,667
PUC per Class A share	$ 167
Legal capital of Class B shares	$ 40,000
Less: $\dfrac{40,000 \times \$10,000}{60,000}$	(6,667)
PUC of Class B shares	$ 33,337
PUC per Class B share	$ 83

3. Deemed dividend on redemption of 60 Class A shares

Redemption price ($200 × 60)	$ 12,000
PUC of shares redeemed ($167 × 60)	10,020
Deemed dividend (subs. 84(3))	$ 1,980
Deemed dividend per Class A share	$ 33

Example		
4. Revised computation of PUC of Class A shares		

Legal capital of remaining 40 Class A shares
(40% × $20,000) $ 8,000
Less: para. 87(3)(a) reduction (step 2 above)   (3,333)
                                                                                 $ 4,667

Add *lesser* of (i) and (ii)

(i)   subs. 84(3) deemed dividend $ 1,980
       exceeds
       deemed dividend *without* reduction
          in PUC under para. 87(3)(a)
          ($200 - $200)   (NIL)
                                                       $ 1,980

(ii)   para. 87(3)(a) reduction $ 3,333

Lesser amount
                                                                           1,980

Remaining PUC of 40 Class A shares $ 6,647

Remaining PUC *per* Class A share
$6,647
──── $ 166
  40

In effect, the deemed dividend of $1,980 under subs. 84(3) is added back to determine the remaining PUC of the Class A shares to avoid double taxation in the future. For example, if the remaining 40 Class A shares were redeemed for $200 per share, the amount taxable would be:

Redemption price (40 × $200) $ 8,000
PUC of shares redeemed   (6,646)
Deemed dividend $ 1,354
Deemed dividend per Class A share $ 34

Note that shareholders of *Whiteco* who received Class A shares from *Newco* are deemed to receive a dividend even though the PUC of *Whiteco* equals its legal capital prior to the amalgamation.

8. — Amalgamation Involving Issuance of Shares by Parent Corporation

For income tax purposes, an amalgamation is a merger of two or more taxable Canadian corporations in which, *inter alia*, all of the shareholders of the predecessor corporations receive shares of the new corporation as a result of the merger.[70]

One can also arrange an amalgamation by issuing shares of a corporation other than the new corporation (for example, shares of the parent of the new corporation) to the shareholders of the predecessor.[71]

Where two or more taxable Canadian corporations merge to form a new corporation that immediately after the merger is controlled by a taxable Canadian corporation (the "parent" corporation), the Act deems any shares issued by the parent corporation to be shares issued by the new corporation.[72] This type of amalgamation (referred to as a "triangular amalgamation") also qualifies for the flow-through provisions even though the shareholders of the predecessor corporation are not shareholders of the new corporation. Similarly, shareholders of the predecessor corporation may rollover their shares on a tax-free basis when they become shareholders of the new corporation's parent.

Here too, the Act controls the paid-up capital of the parent corporation's shares issued to the shareholders of the predecessor corporation. The paid-up capital of the parent corporation's shares is reduced by the amount that the paid-up capital of all the shares of the capital stock of the parent, immediately after the amalgamation, exceeds the aggregate of the paid-up capital of the parent corporation and each of its predecessor corporations immediately before the amalgamation. Thus, the parent corporation cannot increase the paid-up capital of its shares by an artificial amount.

The increase in the parent's paid-up capital is limited to the amount of the paid-up capital of the shares of its predecessor corporations for which they are issued.[73]

9. — Carryover of Losses

The new corporation may use the non-capital losses, net capital losses, limited partnership losses, restricted farm losses and farm losses of its predecessor corporations.[74] For the purposes of determining the type and amount of losses to be carried forward from the predecessor corporations to the new corporation, the Act deems the new corporation to be the same

---

[70]Para. 87(1)(c).

[71]CBCA, subs. 182(1).

[72]Para. 87(9)(a).

[73]Para. 87(9)(b).

[74]Subs. 87(2.1).

corporation as, and a continuation of, each predecessor corporation. Thus, the character of the predecessor's unused losses is carried through to the new corporation. Subject to certain restrictions, the losses may be used by the new corporation.

The Act deems the new corporation to be a continuation of each of its predecessor corporations only for the purpose of calculating the taxable income of, and tax payable by, the *new* corporation. Losses realized in the first taxation year of the new corporation may *not* generally be carried back to reduce the income, taxable income or tax payable by its predecessor corporations in previous years. There is a specific exemption in subsection 87(2.11) where a parent predecessor amalgamates with its wholly-owned subsidiary.

The Act deems the taxation year of a corporation that amalgamates with another corporation to have ended immediately before the amalgamation.[75] Hence, unless the amalgamation occurs at the predecessor corporation's year-end, the predecessor corporation will have a short taxation year, which will count towards the number of years available for the carryforward of losses.[76]

There are special rules which govern reorganizations implemented solely for the purpose of utilizing corporate losses. The general thrust of these rules is to restrict the availability of loss carryovers where corporate control changes as a result of an amalgamation.

Where, immediately following an amalgamation, the new corporation is controlled by a person (or group of persons) that did not control a particular predecessor corporation, control of the particular predecessor corporation is deemed to have changed unless the persons who control the new corporation are related to the persons who controlled the predecessor.[77] Where control of a predecessor corporation has changed, the corporation's net capital losses for taxation years preceding the change of control may not be carried forward.[78] Similarly, non-capital losses and farm losses may not be carried forward following a change of control unless the business in which the losses were incurred continues to be carried on for profit or with a reasonable expectation of profit, and then only to the extent of income from the particular business or a similar business.[79]

---

[75]Para. 87(2)(a).

[76]Subs. 111(1).

[77]Para. 256(7)(b).

[78]Subs. 111(4).

[79]Subs. 111(5); see also ATR-7, "Amalgamation Involving Losses and Control" (March 3, 1986); Chapter 15, "Taxable Income".

10. — Shareholders of Predecessor Corporations

(a) — General Comment

A taxpayer who disposes of shares in a corporation must recognize any capital gain or loss realized at that time.[80] A share converted into another share by virtue of an amalgamation or merger is a disposition of property.[81] Thus, in the absence of specific rules, a shareholder of a corporation that amalgamates with another corporation would be required to recognize a capital gain or loss at the time of the amalgamation.

There are, however, special rules which allow the shareholders and creditors of a corporation that has amalgamated with another corporation to exchange their shares or debt obligations for shares or debt obligations of the new corporation. The general thrust of these rules is that the cost of the shareholder's "old shares" becomes the cost of "new shares", and the shareholder is not required to recognize a capital gain or loss at the time of the amalgamation.[82]

This rollover is available only if:[83]

- The "old shares" constitute capital property; and

- The shareholder receives as consideration only the shares of the new corporation.

Where these conditions are satisfied, the Act deems the shareholder of the predecessor corporation to have:

- Disposed of the "old shares" for proceeds equal to the adjusted cost base immediately before the amalgamation;[84] and

- Acquired the new shares at a cost equal to the adjusted cost base of the old shares.[85]

Where a shareholder receives more than one class of shares of the new corporation, the adjusted cost base of the old shares is allocated among the various classes of the new shares. The allocation ratio is the fair market value of the new shares of the particular class to the fair market value of all of the shares received by the shareholder.

The shareholder of the predecessor corporation determines the proceeds of disposition from the total adjusted cost base of all of the shares of that class. The total adjusted cost base is

---

[80]Subs. 40(1) (shares presumed to be capital property of shareholder).

[81]Subs. 248(1)"disposition".

[82]Paras. 87(4)(a), (b).

[83]Para. 87(4)(a), IT-474R, "Amalgamations of Canadian Corporations" (March 14, 1986).

[84]Para. 87(4)(a).

[85]Para. 87(4)(b).

then allocated among the new shares, but on a class-by-class basis. Where a shareholder of the predecessor corporation holds shares of more than one class, a separate calculation is required for each class of old shares in order to allocate the adjusted cost base of these shares among the various classes of the new shares. The formula for allocation is as follows:

$$\begin{array}{ccc} \text{Cost of new shares} \\ \text{of particular class} \end{array} = \begin{array}{c} \text{ACB of all} \\ \text{old shares} \end{array} \times \dfrac{\text{FMV of new shares of the particular class}}{\text{FMV of all new shares of all classes}}$$

Example

Assume:

White owns common shares of *Alpha Ltd.*:

	No. of shares	ACB/share	Total ACB
	10	$10	$100

Alpha amalgamates with *Beta Ltd.* to form *Omega Ltd.*, and White receives the following new shares:

Type	No of shares	FMV/share	Total FMV
Class A	4	$ 25	$ 100
Class B	1	$ 100	100
			$ 200

Then:

Cost of Class A shares to White: $100 × $\dfrac{100}{200}$ = $50

Cost per Class A share: $\dfrac{\$50}{4}$ = $12.50

Cost of Class B shares to White: $100 × $\dfrac{100}{200}$ = $50

Cost per Class B share: $50

Summary:

Cost of new Class A shares ($12.50 × 4) $ 50

Example	
Cost of new Class B shares ($50.00 × 1)	50
Total cost of all new shares	$ 100

(b) — Indirect Gifts

A special anti-avoidance rule prevents taxpayers from using amalgamations to divert, or reduce the value of, their shareholdings while taking advantage of the rollover. Where a taxpayer exchanges old shares for new shares that have a lesser value, and it is reasonable to regard any portion of the difference between the two values as a gift that the taxpayer has conferred on a related person, the Act deems the taxpayer to have disposed of the old shares for an amount that is equal to the *lesser* of:[86]

- The aggregate of the adjusted cost bases of the old shares plus the "gift portion"; and

- The fair market value of the old shares.

The effect of this rule is that the taxpayer is compelled to recognize a capital gain upon the amalgamation. The taxpayer may not, however, recognize a capital loss on the disposition of the old shares.[87]

The capital gain is generally equal to the value of the "gift portion", that is, the value of the benefit conferred on the related person.

The cost base of the new shares is equal to the *lesser* of:[88]

- The aggregate of the adjusted cost bases of the old shares; and

- The aggregate of the fair market value of the new shares *and* any capital loss disallowed to the taxpayer on the disposition of the old shares.

Example	
Assume:	
Black owns all of the shares of *X Ltd.*, to which the following data applies:	
Number of shares	100

---

[86]Para. 87(4)(c).

[87]Para. 87(4)(d).

[88]Para. 87(4)(e).

Example

Total fair market value	$	200,000
Total adjusted cost base	$	100,000

X Ltd. amalgamates with Y Ltd., a corporation wholly owned by Black's son, to form XY Ltd. In exchange for his shares in X Ltd., Black receives Class A shares of XY Ltd. that have a fair market value of $140,000.

Then:

Proceeds of disposition are the *lesser* of:

(i) ACB of shares plus "gift portion"	$	100,000
		60,000
	$	160,000
(ii) FMV of shares	$	200,000
Lesser amount	$	160,000
ACB of shares		(100,000)
Capital gain to Black	$	60,000

II. — Winding-Up

1. — General Comment

Winding-up or dissolving a corporation refers to the termination or liquidation of corporate existence. The procedure on winding-up is governed by the appropriate corporate law. Consequently, the procedure varies between jurisdictions.

The tax consequences, however, are determined by section 88 of the Act, and are uniform. A corporation is wound up only when all of the corporate steps are completed.

The winding-up of a corporation and distribution of its assets to shareholders results in a deemed disposition of the assets.[89] The amount by which the value of the assets exceeds the paid-up capital of the corporation's shares is deemed to be a dividend to the shareholders.[90]

---

[89]Para. 69(5)(a).

[90]Subs. 84(2).

There are special rules, however, which permit a tax-free rollover of corporate assets when a parent corporation winds up a subsidiary of which it owns at least 90 per cent of the capital stock. In such circumstances, the Act deems the property distributed by the subsidiary corporation to the parent corporation to have been disposed of for proceeds of disposition that generally result in a tax-free rollover of the property.[91]

The rollover is not available where the special anti-avoidance rules in respect of partnerships apply.[92] These rules apply where a taxpayer transfers property with an accrued gain to an unaffiliated corporation or partnership on a tax-free basis so as to shelter the gain from tax upon a subsequent disposition.[93] Where the anti-avoidance rules apply, the property is treated as having been disposed of at its fair market value.

2. — Corporate Law

A corporation can be dissolved only under the authority of the jurisdiction in which it is incorporated.[94] A corporation may be dissolved by action of its shareholders, its directors, the Director of the Corporations Branch, or by court order.

(a) — Voluntary Dissolution

Under the *Canada Business Corporations Act*, a corporation may be dissolved voluntarily in several ways: if it has not issued any shares, it may be dissolved at any time by a resolution passed by all of its directors;[95] if it has issued shares but does not have any property or liabilities, it may be dissolved by a special resolution of its shareholders.[96]

---

[91] Subs. 88(1).

[92] *Ibid.*

[93] Subs. 69(11).

[94] See, generally, *Russian Commercial & Indust. Bank v. Comptoir d'Escompte de Mulhouse*, [1925] A.C. 112 (H.L.); *Banque Int. de Commerce de Petrograd v. Goukassow*, [1925] A.C. 150 (H.L.); *Employers' Liability Assur. Corp. v. Sedgwick, Collins & Co.*, [1927] A.C. 95 (H.L.); *Lazard Bros. & Co. v. Midland Bank*, [1933] A.C. 289 (H.L.); *Russian & Eng. Bank v. Baring Bros.*, [1936] A.C. 405 (H.L.); *Re Russian & Eng. Bank*, [1932] 1 Ch. 663; *Re Russian Bank for Foreign Trade*, [1933] Ch. 745; *Re Russo-Asiatic Bank*, [1934] Ch. 720. This rule applies whether the winding-up is voluntary or involuntary.

[95] CBCA, subs. 210(1).

[96] CBCA, subs. 210(2).

Where it has issued more than one class of shares, the special resolution must be passed by the holders of each class of shares, whether or not the shareholders of the class are otherwise entitled to vote.

A corporation with property or liabilities can be dissolved by a special resolution of the shareholders, if it discharges its liabilities prior to dissolution.[97] A parent corporation can, for example, assume its subsidiary's obligations.

Shareholders of a corporation can submit a proposal for dissolution at the annual meeting.[98] If the proposal is approved by a special resolution, a statement of intent to dissolve the corporation must be sent to the Director of the Corporations Branch.[99] The corporation must communicate its intention to dissolve to each known creditor of the corporation.[100]

Following the completion of the appropriate corporate steps, including the completion and filing of all outstanding income tax returns, the Director will issue a certificate of dissolution. The certificate terminates the existence of the corporation as of its date of issuance.[101]

(b) — Involuntary Dissolution

The Director of the Corporations Branch has the power to dissolve a corporation where the corporation:[102]

- Has not commenced business within three years after the date shown on its certificate of incorporation;

- Has not carried on its business for three consecutive years; or

- Is in default for a period of one year in filing its corporate documents and annual fees.

In these circumstances, the Director can dissolve the corporation by giving 120 days notice of intention to do so, followed by the issuance of a certificate of dissolution.

---

[97]CBCA, subs. 210(3).

[98]CBCA, subs. 211(1).

[99]CBCA, subs. 211(4).

[100]CBCA, subs. 211(7).

[101]CBCA, subs. 211(16).

[102]CBCA, s. 212.

(c) — Dissolution by Court Order

Any interested person (including the Director of the Corporations Branch) may apply to a court for an order to dissolve a corporation where the corporation:[103]

- Has failed for two or more consecutive years to comply with the requirements of the *Canada Business Corporations Act* with respect to the holding of annual meetings of shareholders;

- Is carrying on a business that is prohibited by its articles of incorporation;

- Does not make its records available to its shareholders and creditors as required;

- Procured any certificate under the *Canada Business Corporations Act* by misrepresentation;

- Fails to keep proper financial information available for inspection by its shareholders; or

- Fails to distribute its financial statements to its shareholders prior to its annual general meeting.

There are similar provisions under the various provincial statutes.

3. — Winding-Up a 90 per cent Subsidiary

For corporate purposes, a corporation is considered to have been wound up where it has followed the procedures for winding-up and dissolution in the relevant corporate statute. For income tax purposes, however, a corporation is "wound up" even though it has not completed all of the formalities in respect of winding-up, if there is substantial evidence that the corporation will be dissolved within a short period of time.[104] Thus, the timing of a winding-up may be different for tax purposes and corporate law purposes.

A taxable Canadian corporation that is at least 90 per cent owned by its parent corporation can be wound up into its parent on a tax-free basis. In these circumstances, the subsidiary is considered to have disposed of each of its assets (other than partnership interests) at its "cost amount" immediately before the winding-up, and the Act deems the parent corporation to acquire the assets at the same amount. Thus, in general terms, the assets and liabilities of a subsidiary are "rolled over" into its parent corporation without triggering any immediate

---

[103]CBCA, s. 213.

[104]IT-126R2, "Meaning of Winding-up'" (March 20, 1995)

capital gain or loss.[105] The rollover is not available in respect of assets transferred to minority shareholders.[106]

(a) — Eligibility for Rollover

The rollover applies if:[107]

- Both the subsidiary and the parent are taxable Canadian corporations;

- The parent owns at least 90 per cent of the issued shares *of each class* of the subsidiary; *and*

- All of the shares of the subsidiary that the parent does not own are owned by persons with whom the parent deals at arm's length.

The rollover is *not* elective: it applies automatically whenever the above conditions are satisfied.

(b) — Property of the Subsidiary Corporation

The general scheme of the rollover is that property of the subsidiary that is distributed to its parent corporation is transferred at its cost amount. Thus, there is no capital gain (or loss) or income recognized at the time of the winding-up. Note: the presumptions in subsection 88(1) do no more than establish the cost of property acquired by a parent on the winding-up of its subsidiary. It does not otherwise flow through the character of the property.[108]

The rollover is available only in respect of property distributed by a subsidiary to its parent corporation. The Act deems property distributed to minority shareholders to have been disposed at fair market value.[109] Thus, the subsidiary corporation has some flexibility in determining the assets on which it will realize or defer gains and losses.

---

[105]Subs. 88(1).

[106]Subs. 69(5).

[107]Subs. 88(1).

[108]*The Queen v. Mara Properties Ltd.*, [1995] 2 C.T.C. 86, 95 D.T.C. 5168 (F.C.A.); leave to appeal allowed (October 12, 1995), Doc. 24684 (S.C.C.); revd [1996] 2 S.C.R. 161, [1996] 2 C.T.C. 54, 96 D.T.C. 6309 (S.C.C.) (subsidiary's inventory did not retain character in parent's hands).

[109]Subpara. 69(5)(a).

(i) — Eligible Capital Property

The Act deems the subsidiary to have disposed of its eligible capital property for proceeds equal to its cost amount.[110] The "cost amount" of eligible capital property is 4/3 of the cumulative eligible capital multiplied by the proportion that the fair market value of the property is of all of the eligible capital property owned. Since the cumulative eligible capital account is reduced by 3/4 of the deemed proceeds, this formula provides for a complete rollover in respect of such property.

Example		
Assume:		
	Cumulative eligible capital (CEC) of subsidiary	$ 10,000
Then:		
	Proceeds of disposition: "cost amount" 4/3 × CEC	$ 13,333
	Eligible capital amount 3/4 × Proceeds of disposition	$ (10,000)
	Opening balance (CEC)	$ 10,000
	Less: Eligible capital amount	(10,000)
	Closing balance (CEC)	NIL

Any eligible capital property acquired by the subsidiary prior to 1972 has a cost amount equal to nil. Thus, the subsidiary is not required to include any amount in its income in respect of its pre-1972 eligible capital property.

(ii) — Non-Depreciable Capital Property

The Act deems a subsidiary's non-depreciable capital property to be distributed to its parent corporation for proceeds equal to the adjusted cost base of the property.[111]

(iii) — Depreciable Capital Property

---

[110]Subpara. 88(1)(a)(iii); subs. 248(1)"cost amount".

[111]Subpara. 88(1)(a)(iii).

The Act deems depreciable capital property to be disposed of at its undepreciated capital cost.[112] Hence, the subsidiary is not liable for recapture of capital cost allowance, and cannot recognize a terminal loss on the distribution of its depreciable property to its parent corporation.

The Act deems depreciable capital property acquired by the subsidiary prior to 1972 and owned continuously since December 31, 1971, to have been owned by the parent corporation prior to 1972. Thus, any capital gain accrued on the property prior to that date is not taxable to the parent corporation when it disposes of the property.[113]

(iv) — Accounts Receivable and Reserves

A subsidiary's accounts receivable are transferred to its parent corporation at their face amount. In computing its income, however, the subsidiary may claim a reserve for doubtful accounts as if it had not been wound up.[114]

The Act deems the parent corporation to have claimed the reserve actually claimed by the subsidiary in the year in which it was wound up. Thus, in the following year the parent must add back the reserve to its own income.[115]

(v) — Inventory

The Act deems the subsidiary's inventory to be distributed to its parent corporation at the lower of its cost and fair market value.[116] It is a question of fact, however, whether the inventory retains its character as such in the hands of the parent corporation.[117]

(vi) — Partnership Interests

---

[112]Subpara. 88(1)(a)(iii); subs. 248(1)"cost amount".

[113]ITAR 20(1.2).

[114]Para. 88(1)(e.1).

[115]Paras. 88(1)(e.2); 87(2)(g).

[116]Para. 88(1)(a), subs. 248(1)"cost amount"; s. 10.

[117]*The Queen v. Mara Properties Ltd.*, [1995] 2 C.T.C. 86, 95 D.T.C. 5168 (F.C.A.); leave to appeal allowed (October 12, 1995), Doc. 24684 (S.C.C.); revd [1996] 2 S.C.R. 161, [1996] 2 C.T.C. 54, 96 D.T.C. 6309 (S.C.C.).

The subsidiary's partnership interests distributed to its parent corporation are not considered to have been disposed of by the subsidiary.[118] Hence the transfer of a partnership interest with a negative cost base will not trigger a capital gain until such time as it is disposed of by the parent corporation.

(c) — Liabilities of the Subsidiary

(i) — Owing to the Parent Corporation

A prerequisite to the legal dissolution of a corporation is that it discharge its obligations to its creditors.[119] A subsidiary may discharge any indebtedness to its parent corporation either by payment in cash or by transferring assets of equivalent value to the parent. Note: the rollover under subsection 88(1) is available only in respect of assets transferred *pursuant* to the liquidation proceedings.

Where a debt payable by the subsidiary to its parent corporation is settled without payment, or by payment of a sum less than the principal amount of the amount payable, the parent can elect to assume the debt at its cost amount.[120] If the parent elects, the Act deems the subsidiary to have paid an amount equal to the cost amount of the debt to the parent. The "cost amount" of the debt is its adjusted cost base, if it constitutes capital property, and the lower of its cost and fair market value, if it is inventory.[121]

(ii) — Owing to Third Parties

Debts owing to third parties must also be settled before a subsidiary is wound up. Here too, the subsidiary may discharge its obligations either in cash or by transferring assets of an equivalent value to its creditors. A disposition of assets in satisfaction of a debt can give rise to capital gains, income or recapture of capital cost allowance.

A subsidiary's obligations to third parties that are assumed by its parent corporation are not considered to be a settlement of a debt if: (1) the indebtedness is assumed by the parent as part of the distribution of the subsidiary's assets on liquidation; and (2) the amount payable by the parent on maturity of the debt is the same as the amount payable by the subsidiary.[122]

---

[118]Para. 88(1)(a.2).

[119]See, e.g., CBCA, para. 211(7)(c).

[120]Subs. 80(3); IT-142R3, "Settlement of Debts on the Winding-up of a Corporation" (January 11, 1988).

[121]Subs. 248(1)"cost amount"; s. 10.

[122]Para. 88(1)(e.2); subs. 87(7).

For example, where a parent corporation acquires mortgaged real estate from its subsidiary, it can assume the mortgage together with the property as part of the liquidation distribution. The parent steps into the shoes of the subsidiary, and is considered to have issued the debt from the outset. Thus, the parent is entitled to any deduction for "deep" or "shallow" discounts to which its subsidiary was entitled.[123]

Third-party creditors can rollover debts owed to them by the subsidiary if the only consideration which they receive in exchange for the debts is new debts issued by the parent corporation and the amount payable on maturity of the new debts is the same as that payable on the old. The rollover is restricted to debts which constitute capital property to the creditor.[124]

(d) — Acquisition of Property by Parent Corporation

(i) — General Comment

The rules that govern the acquisition of property by a parent corporation from its subsidiary are the mirror image of the rules in respect of the subsidiary's disposition of the property. Generally, the Act deems the parent to receive each asset distributed to it at an amount that is equal to the proceeds of disposition deemed to have been received by the subsidiary.[125] Hence, the tax-free rollover to the parent: in effect, the parent corporation steps into the shoes of its subsidiary corporation by taking over its property at their tax values. These rules are set out below:

COST TO PARENT CORPORATION OF PROPERTIES		
Property	**Cost to Parent Corporation**	**Statutory Reference**
1. Accounts receivable	Face amount of receivables	para. 88(1)(c)
	Doubtful accounts deducted by subsidiary deemed deducted by parent in previous year	para. 88(1)(e.2)
2. Inventory (non-farming)	Lower of cost or market	para. 88(1)(c); s. 10
Farming inventory (cash basis)	NIL	s. 28
3. Eligible capital property	4/3 of subsidiary's cumulative eligible capital	para. 88(1)(c)

---

[123]Para. 20(1)(f); See Chapter 8, "Inclusions in Business and Investment Income".

[124]Para. 88(1)(e.2); subs. 87(6).

[125]Para. 88(1)(c).

COST TO PARENT CORPORATION OF PROPERTIES		
Property	**Cost to Parent Corporation**	**Statutory Reference**
4. Depreciable property	UCC (in proportion to capital cost)	para. 88(1)(c)
5. Non-depreciable capital property	ACB, with potential step-up in cost base	paras. 81(1)(c), (d)

(ii) — Non-Depreciable Capital Property

The parent acquires the subsidiary's non-depreciable capital property at its adjusted cost base. The tax-free zone in respect of any such property owned on June 18, 1971, flows through to the parent corporation.[126]

The cost base of the property can be stepped up by an amount equal to the difference between the cost base of the subsidiary's shares to the parent and the underlying *net* tax cost of the subsidiary's properties.[127] The amount of the step-up allocated to a particular capital property cannot exceed the difference between its fair market value at the time when the parent last acquired control of the subsidiary and the cost amount of the property to the subsidiary immediately before the winding-up. In effect, the amount of any step-up allocated to a property is limited to the *unrealized* gain in respect of the property at the time when the parent last acquired control of the subsidiary.[128]

In the case of partnership interests, the step-up is to the parent's cost of the interest — the cost of the partnership interest to the subsidiary corporation.[129]

The cost base of non-depreciable capital property may be stepped-up only where the property was owned by the subsidiary at the time when the parent last acquired control of it, *and* continuously thereafter until the time when it was distributed to the parent corporation.[130] Note: the election to step-up the cost base of capital property is not available in respect of property transferred in the course of a "butterfly" reorganization.[131]

---

[126]ITAR 26(5).

[127]Paras. 88(1)(c), (d).

[128]Subpara. 88(1)(d)(ii).

[129]Para. 88(1)(c).

[130]Para. 88(1)(c) and subs. 88(4) (for purposes of these rules, amalgamation does not give rise to change of control).

[131]See subs. 55(3) and subpara. 88(1)(c)(iv).

Specifically, the adjusted cost base of capital properties may be stepped-up by an amount equal to the excess of the adjusted cost base of the parent's shares in its subsidiary over the aggregate of:[132]

- The tax values of the subsidiary's *net* assets (that is, after deducting its liabilities and certain reserves) immediately before the winding-up; and

- Taxable dividends, capital dividends or life insurance capital dividends received by the parent corporation (or any other corporation with which the parent corporation does not deal at arm's length) on the subsidiary's shares.

Example

Assume:

On January 1, YEAR 1, *P Ltd.* purchased all of the issued shares of *S Ltd.* for $1,000,000. On December 31, YEAR 2, *S Ltd.* is liquidated and wound up; its assets are distributed to *P Ltd.* The following data applies to *S Ltd.*:

	January 1, Cost Amount	YEAR 1 FMV	December 31, Cost Amount	YEAR 2 FMV
Assets:				
Cash	$ 50,000	$ 50,000	$ 50,000	$ 50,000
Securities	80,000	125,000	80,000	175,000
Inventory	100,000	100,000	100,000	100,000
Land	200,000	350,000	200,000	400,000
Buildings	250,000	400,000	250,000	475,000
	$ 680,000	$1,025,000	$ 680,000	$ 1,200,000
Liabilities:				
Payables	$ 100,000	$ 100,000	$ 100,000	$ 100,000
Long-term debt	400,000	400,000	400,000	400,000
	$ 500,000	$ 500,000	$ 500,000	$ 500,000

Then:
1. Maximum designation under para. 88(1)(d):

Tax cost of *P Ltd.*'s investment in *S. Ltd.* $ 1,000,000

---

[132]Para. 88(1)(d).

Example		
Tax value of *S Ltd.*'s *net* assets		
($680,000–$500,000)		(180,000)
Maximum overall designation	$	820,000
2. Cost of *S Ltd.*'s assets to *P. Ltd.*:		
Cash	$	50,000
Inventory		100,000
Buildings		250,000
Land		
FMV at acquisition of control	$350,000	
ACB to *S. Ltd.*	(200,000)	
Maximum step-up in cost	$150,000	
Revised cost base	$	350,000
Securities		
FMV at acquisition of control	$125,000	
ACB to *S Ltd.*	(80,000)	
Maximum step-up in cost	$ 45,000	
Revised cost base	$	125,000

(e) — Disposition of Property to Minority Shareholders

As a general rule, the Act deems a shareholder who acquires property from a corporation on its winding-up to acquire the property at its fair market value immediately before the winding-up.[133] This is also the same value at which the subsidiary corporation is deemed to have sold its property.[134]

(f) — Disposition of Subsidiary's Shares by Parent Corporation

A parent corporation's shares in its subsidiary are cancelled when the subsidiary is wound up. The Act deems any payment of an amount in excess of the paid-up capital of the shares to be a dividend.

---

[133]Para. 69(5)(b).

[134]Para. 69(5)(a).

A special rule applies, however, where a 90 per cent-owned subsidiary is wound up into its parent corporation. In certain circumstances, the Act deems the parent to have disposed of its shares in its subsidiary for proceeds equal to the *greater* of:[135]

- The paid-up capital of the shares *or* the tax value of the subsidiary's net assets after deducting liabilities, *whichever* is the lesser; and

- The adjusted cost base of the shares immediately before the winding-up.

Thus, the parent corporation cannot realize a loss on the disposition of its subsidiary's shares. It may, however, realize a capital gain.

The difference between the fair market value of a subsidiary's *net* assets distributed to its parent and the paid-up capital of the parent's shares in the subsidiary at the time of the distribution is *not* considered a dividend.[136] Instead, the future liability for the dividend is passed on to the shareholders of the parent corporation.

Example		Case A	Case B
Assume:			
	PUC of parent's shares in subsidiary	$ 1,000	$ 1,000
	Tax value of subsidiary's *net* assets at dissolution	$ 10,000	$ 10,000
	ACB of subsidiary's shares to parent	$ 15,000	$ 500
Then:			
	Deemed POD	$ 15,000	$ 1,000
	ACB of shares	(15,000)	(500)
	Capital gain (loss)	NIL	$ 500

---

[135]Para. 88(1)(b).

[136]Para. 88(1)(d.1).

(g) — Losses

A parent corporation may use the non-capital, net capital, limited partnership, restricted farm, and farm losses accumulated by its subsidiary to reduce its taxable income or Part IV tax if:[137]

- Both the parent and its subsidiary are Canadian corporations;

- Immediately before the winding-up, the parent owns at least 90 per cent of the issued shares *of each class* of its subsidiary; and

- All of the remaining shares (maximum 10 per cent) of the subsidiary are owned by persons with whom the parent is dealing at arm's length.

A corporation is restricted in carrying forward its own accumulated losses when control of the corporation changes. Similarly, the losses of a subsidiary corporation which is wound up into its parent may not be available to the parent corporation where control of the parent or subsidiary changes. The purpose of these restrictions is to discourage artificial tax avoidance through "loss company" trading.

Following a change of control of a parent or a subsidiary corporation, the parent can use its subsidiary's non-capital or farm losses only if the business that incurred the losses has been carried on continuously by either the parent or the subsidiary following the change of control, for profit or with a reasonable expectation of profit.[138] The subsidiary's losses from property and allowable business investment losses before the acquisition of control cannot be carried forward and deducted by the parent after the change of control.

A subsidiary's net capital losses may also be carried over and utilized by its parent corporation, if control of the parent or subsidiary corporation has not been acquired by a person who did not control the parent or subsidiary at the end of the year *in which the net capital loss* was incurred.[139] Thus, a change of control of the parent corporation *after* the winding-up of its subsidiary precludes the parent from claiming the subsidiary's capital loss.

The Act does not define the term "control". It usually implies ownership of a sufficient number of shares to elect a majority of the board of directors of the corporation.[140] The power to wind-up a corporation may, however, confer control despite equality of voting

---

[137]Subss. 88(1.1), (1.2).

[138]Para. 88(1.1)(e).

[139]Subs. 88(1.2).

[140]*Buckerfield's Ltd. v. M.N.R.*, [1964] C.T.C. 504, 64 D.T.C. 5301 (Ex. Ct.); see, generally, *I.R.C. v. B.W. Noble Ltd.* (1926), 12 Tax Cas. 911 at 926; *Br. Amer. Tobacco Co. v. I.R.C.*, [1943] A.C. 335 (H.L.); *Vancouver Towing Co. v. M.N.R.*, [1947] C.T.C. 18, 2 D.T.C. 706 (Ex. Ct.); *M.N.R. v. Sheldon's Engr. Ltd.*, [1954] C.T.C. 241, 54 D.T.C. 1106 (Can. Ex. Ct.); affd. [1955] S.C.R. 637, [1955] C.T.C. 174, 55 D.T.C. 1110 (S.C.C.); *Forand Auto Ltée v. M.N.R.* (1966), 66 D.T.C. 184

power.[141] Note: the acquisition of shares of a corporation by a person who immediately before the acquisition was related to the corporation does not constitute a change of control.[142]

4. — Winding-Up of Other Canadian Corporations

The winding-up of a Canadian corporation *other than* a 90 per cent-owned subsidiary is governed by the usual rules in respect of dispositions of property. The Act deems the subsidiary to have sold each of its properties immediately before its liquidation for proceeds of disposition equal to the fair market value of its properties. Capital gains and losses, recapture of capital cost allowance, inventory gains and terminal losses are all taken into account in computing its income in its final year.[143] Note: the subsidiary can use capital losses resulting from a disposition of capital property in the course of its winding-up even if the property is distributed to its controlling shareholder. The stop-loss rules do not apply to property distributions by the winding-up of a Canadian corporation.[144]

(a) — Deemed Dividends

Distribution of a subsidiary's property to its parent corporation can give rise to a deemed dividend where the parent does not own at least 90 per cent of each class of shares of the subsidiary. The dividend is equal to the excess of the value of the property distributed over the reduction in the paid-up capital of the class of shares on which the distribution is made. The Act deems the dividend to have been received by each shareholder in proportion to the shareholdings.[145]

(T.A.B.); *Aaron's (Prince Albert) Ltd. v. M.N.R.*, [1966] C.T.C. 330, 66 D.T.C. 5244; affd. [1967] S.C.R. 223, [1967] C.T.C. 50, 67 D.T.C. 5035 (S.C.C.).

[141]*The Queen v. Imp. Gen. Properties Ltd.*, [1985] 2 S.C.R. 288, [1985] 2 C.T.C. 299 at 302, 85 D.T.C. 5500 (S.C.C.) (in determining control, court not limited to highly technical and narrow interpretation of legal rights attached to shares).

[142]Subs. 256(7).

[143]Para. 69(5)(a).

[144]Para. 69(5)(d).

[145]Subs. 84(2).

(b) — Proceeds of Disposition

Each shareholder of a corporation is considered to have disposed of the shares for proceeds of disposition equal to the value of the property received by the shareholder from the corporation. Where the corporation is a Canadian-resident corporation, the proceeds of disposition are reduced by the amount of any dividend deemed to have been paid to the shareholder.[146] Thus, a shareholder may realize a capital gain or loss upon the liquidation of the corporation.

Example

Assume:

In YEAR 1, Green subscribed for 100 shares of *White Ltd.* at a total cost of $1,000. In YEAR 7, Blue subscribed for 100 shares of *White Ltd.* for $5,000. These were the only share capital transactions. *White Ltd.* was wound up in YEAR 8, and Green received property valued at $4,000 from the corporation in exchange for his shares.

Then:

PUC of all shares ($1,000 + $5,000)	$ 6,000
PUC *per* share ($6,000 ÷ 200)	$ 30
PUC of Green's shares ($30 × 100)	$ 3,000
Value of property distributed on winding-up	(4,000)
Deemed dividend (subs. 84(2))	$ 1,000
Proceeds of disposition ($4,000 - $1,000)	$ 3,000
ACB of shares cancelled	(1,000)
Capital gain	$ 2,000

Summary:

Deemed dividend	$ 1,000
Capital gain	2,000
Increase in value of shares ($4,000 - $1,000)	$ 3,000

---

[146]S. 54"proceeds of disposition" (j).

5. — Non-Resident Corporations

The tax-free rollover of assets on the winding-up of a 90 per cent-owned subsidiary into its parent corporation is limited to taxable Canadian corporations.

The Act deems a non-resident corporation that is wound up to have sold its property at fair market value.[147] If the non-resident corporation is carrying on business in Canada or owns taxable Canadian property, it is deemed to have disposed of its property, and must take into account any income (loss) or capital gain (loss). The tax treatment of income or capital gains resulting from a deemed disposition may depend upon the relevant international tax treaty.

A winding-up distribution by a non-resident corporation does not give rise to a deemed dividend,[148] nor is any amount distributed to a shareholder by a non-resident corporation considered to be a shareholder benefit.[149] Instead, the entire amount distributed by a non-resident corporation to its resident shareholders is considered to be proceeds of disposition.

6. — Clearance Certificates

An assignee, liquidator or receiver is required to obtain a certificate from the Minister certifying that any taxes, interest or penalties payable out of property under his or her control have been paid or acceptable security has been provided in lieu of payment. A person acting in the capacity of a liquidator of a corporation, whether or not the liquidator has been formally appointed, must comply with this rule and obtain a clearance certificate.[150]

A non-resident who disposes of shares of a corporation that is wound up is obliged to obtain a clearance certificate from the Minister if the shares constitute "taxable Canadian property". The non-resident has two options: (1) to report the details of the *proposed* transaction to the Minister;[151] or (2) to complete the transaction and report the details thereof within 10 days.[152]

The information that is reported to the Minister must disclose the actual or estimated selling price of the property and its adjusted cost base. The Minister will issue a clearance certifi-

---

[147]Para. 69(5)(a).

[148]Subs. 84(2) applies only to a corporation resident in Canada.

[149]Subs. 15(1) does not apply to the winding-up of a corporation.

[150]Subs. 159(2).

[151]Subs. 116(1); see also Chapter 30, "Purchase and Sale of a Business".

[152]Subs. 116(3).

cate upon payment of 25 per cent of the amount by which the estimated or actual proceeds of disposition exceed the adjusted cost base of the property.[153]

A person who purchases property from a non-resident who has not obtained a clearance certificate is liable to pay tax *on behalf of* the non-resident vendor. The purchaser's liability is for 25 per cent of the *cost* of the property purchased. The purchaser is entitled to withhold that amount from the price paid to the non-resident vendor.[154]

7. — *Corporate Emigration*

In certain circumstances, a corporation incorporated in one jurisdiction may move out of, or be "exported" from, that jurisdiction and apply for continuance in another jurisdiction. Under the *Canada Business Corporations Act*, for example, a corporation may apply for export to another jurisdiction, and may request that it be continued *as if* it had been incorporated under the laws of that other jurisdiction.[155]

An application to continue a corporation from one jurisdiction to another must be supported by a special resolution of its shareholders.[156] *All* of the shareholders, whether or not they have voting rights, are entitled to vote in respect of the application to move.[157] Upon compliance with the applicable corporate provisions of the continuing jurisdiction, the Director of the Corporations Branch will issue a certificate of discontinuance to the corporation.[158]

The continuance of a corporation from one Canadian jurisdiction to another Canadian jurisdiction is not considered a disposition by the shareholders of their shares in the corporation.[159] Special statutory rules apply, however, where a corporation which is incorporated in Canada is granted Articles of Continuance in a foreign jurisdiction or becomes resident in a

---

[153]Subss. 116(2), (4).

[154]Subs. 116(5). It is questionable whether the federal government has constitutional power to affect property rights by allowing for the right of set-off through the *Income Tax Act*.

[155]CBCA, subs. 188(1).

[156]CBCA, subs. 188(5).

[157]CBCA, subs. 188(4).

[158]CBCA, subs. 188(7).

[159]TR-1, "Exporting a Corporation — Whether a Disposition — Effect on Incorporation Date" (June 24, 1974); TR-37, "Amalgamations" (August 9, 1976); TR-49, "Sale of Assets — Amalgamation" (March 8, 1977).

foreign jurisdiction and, as a consequence thereof, becomes exempt from Part I tax. In these circumstances the Act deems the corporation:[160]

- To have ended its taxation year *immediately before* it is continued under, or takes up residence in, the foreign jurisdiction;

- To have disposed of its property *immediately before* it is "exported", for proceeds equal to the fair market value of the property; and

- To have acquired its property *immediately after* its "export" at the fair market value of the property.

The effect of these rules is that the exported corporation is liable for any recapture of capital cost allowance, capital gains, inventory gains and any other income inclusions resulting from dispositions of property. Note: since the Act deems the corporation to dispose of its property immediately before it is exported, it cannot seek the protection of an international tax treaty to reduce its Canadian taxes payable. Thus, the tax payable by a corporation on its emigration is similar to the liability of an individual who gives up residence in Canada: the corporation is subject to a form of "departure tax".

Since the Act deems the corporation's taxation year to have ended immediately prior to its departure, it must file an income tax return within a period of six months after its deemed departure date.

A corporation that "emigrates" from Canada may remain a resident of Canada for tax purposes. This may occur, for example, where the corporation's "central management and control" remain in Canada.[161] In such circumstances, the corporation would continue to be taxable in Canada on its global income even though it had emigrated.

Paragraph 250(5.1)(b) deems a corporation that continues into a foreign jurisdiction to be incorporated in that jurisdiction from the moment of continuance.

An emigrating corporation is liable to pay 25 per cent on its "net surplus" at the date of emigration.[162] "Net surplus" is the difference between the fair market value of the corporation's assets and the aggregate of its paid-up capital and liabilities. This tax is in lieu of the withholding tax that would be payable had the corporation simply distributed its "net surplus" to non-resident shareholders.[163]

---

[160]Subs. 128.1(4).

[161]Subs. 250(4).

[162]S. 219.1.

[163]S. 212.

Selected Bibliography to Chapter 29

Amalgamations

General

Ahmed, Firoz and Sarah Gagan, "Amalgamations After Pan Ocean" (1994) 4 Can. Current Tax J71.

Birnie, David A.G., "Consolidation of Corporate Structures", in *Proceedings of 31st Tax Conf.* 177 (Can. Tax Foundation, 1979).

Boultbee, Jack A., "Public Company Split-Ups", in *Corp. Mgmt. Tax Conf.* 1 (Can. Tax Foundation, 1984).

Boultbee, Jack A., "Survey of the Use of Rollovers in Acquisitions and Mergers (A)" (1980) 28 Can. Tax J. 504.

Brown, Robert D., "Corporate Liquidations", in *Proceedings of 25th Tax Conf.* 52 (Can. Tax Foundation, 1973).

Cronkwright, Glen E., "Amalgamations and Share-for-Share Exchanges", in *Proceedings of 26th Tax Conf.* 53 (Can. Tax Foundation, 1974).

Dart, Robert J., "Specific Uses of Companies in Tax Planning", in *Proceedings of 31st Tax Conf.* 117 (Can. Tax Foundation, 1979).

Edwards, Stanley E., "Statutory Amalgamations and Recapitulations", in *Proceedings of 24th Tax Conf.* 401 (Can. Tax Foundation, 1972).

Ewens, Douglas S., "Amalgamations — Part I" (1980) 28 Can. Tax J. 661.

Ewens, Douglas S., "Corporate Dissolutions" (1985) 33 Can. Tax J. 1246.

Farwell, Peter M., "Statutory Amalgamations", *Corp. Mgmt. Tax Conf.* 82 (Can. Tax Foundation, 1972).

Harris, Edwin C., "New Sections 88.1 and 219.1 and Amendments to Sections 51, 85, 86, 87, 88, and 184", in *Proceedings of 32nd Tax Conf.* 92 (Can. Tax Foundation, 1980).

Hartkorn, D.N., "Income Splitting — The New Rules" (1985) 33 Can. Tax J. 1226.

Kellough, H.J., "A Planning Update for Private Corporations — Corporate Reorganizations", *Prairie Prov. Tax Conf.* 131 (Can. Tax Foundation, 1981).

Laflamme, Pierre, "Acquisition Strategies" in *Proceedings of 45th Tax Conf.* (Can. Tax Foundation, 1993) 13:1.

Levin, Jonathon A. *et al., Tax Features of Major Business Agreements: Effectively Structuring the Transactions* (Mississauga, Ont.: Insight, 1991).

Lindsay, Robert F., "Canadian Income Tax Considerations in the Consolidation of Business Operations", in *Proceedings of 27th Tax Conf.* 304 (Can. Tax Foundation, 1975).

Lindsay, Robert F., "Winding-Up of Corporations: Changes in Capital Structure of Corporations", in *Proceedings of 26th Tax Conf.* 69 (Can. Tax Foundation, 1974).

MacDonald, Nancy, "Amalgamations Following Guaranty Properties Limited" (1991) 39 Can. Tax J. 1399.

McCallum, J. Thomas, *Amalgamations and Wind-ups* (Vancouver: Certified General Accountants' Association of Canada, 1994).

Mintz, Jack M., *Policy Forum on Takeovers and Tax Policy* (Kingston, Ont.: Queen's University, John Deutsch Institute for the Study of Economic Policy, 1990).

O'Keefe, Michael J., "Liquidation of Corporations under the *Income Tax Act*" (1973) 102 CA Magazine No. 5, 28.

Palmer, J.S., "Amalgamation — Winding-Up", in *Proceedings of 30th Tax Conf.* 469 (Can. Tax Foundation, 1978).

Richler, Ronald, "Triangular Amalgamations" (1985) 33 Can. Tax J. 374.

Schwartz, Alan M., "Statutory Amalgamations, Arrangements, and Continuations: Tax and Corporate Law Considerations" in *Proceedings of 43rd Tax Conf.* (Can. Tax Foundation, 1991) 9:1.

Singer, Paul, "The Rollover Provisions in Respect of Corporate Reorganizations Provided Under the *Income Tax Act*: Efficiency and Equity as Policy Considerations" (1983) 31 Can. Tax J. 569.

Skingle, L.E., "Guaranty Properties Ltd. v. R." (1992) 5 Can. Petro. Tax J. 171.

Smith, D.W., "Amalgamations: Section 87" (1981) Can. Taxation 1079.

Smith, John G., "Winding Up", in *Proceedings of 23rd Tax Conf.* 53 (Can. Tax Foundation, 1972).

Spindler, Herbert O., "Mergers, Acquisitions and Divestitures" (1975) 107 CA Magazine No. 3, 65.

Turner, Graham, "Amalgamations and Continuations" (1988) 36 Can. Tax J. 1479.

Williamson, David M., "Checklists: Corporate Reorganizations, Amalgamations (Section 87) and Wind-Ups (Subsection 88(1))", in *Proceedings of 39th Tax Conf.* 29:1 (Can. Tax Foundation, 1987).

Wilson, Ronald S., "Cost Adjustments in Corporate Reorganization Transactions: Policy and Practice", in *Proceedings of 38th Tax Conf.* 8:1 (Can. Tax Foundation, 1986).

Williamson, W. Gordon, "Recent Developments Affecting Corporate Reorganizations" in *Proceedings of 42nd Tax Conf.* (Can. Tax Foundation, 1990) 13:1.

Federal Corporate Law

Hansen, Brian G., "Minority Squeeze-Outs", in *Proceedings of 30th Tax Conf.* 408 (Can. Tax Foundation, 1978).

Slutsky, Samuel, "Short-Form Amalgamations — Some Problems" (1984) 32 Can. Tax J. 595.

The New Corporation

Boultbee, Jack, "Amalgamations — Part III" (1981) 29 Can. Tax J. 83. "Mid-Year Amalgamations", *Can. Tax Letter*, January 20, 1978 (De Boo).

Thomas, James P., "Restructuring the Ownership of Property Within a Closely Held Group", *Corp. Mgmt. Tax Conf.* 6:1 (Can. Tax Foundation, 1989).

Wilson, Ronald S., "Cost Adjustments in Corporate Reorganization Transactions: Policy and Practice", in *Proceedings of 38th Tax Conf.* 8:1 at 8:37–8:39 (Can. Tax Foundation, 1986).

Predecessor Corporations

Birnie, David A.G., "Consolidation of Corporate Structures", in *Proceedings of 31st Tax Conf.* 177 (Can. Tax Foundation, 1979).

Boultbee, Jack, "Amalgamations — Part III" (1981) 29 Can. Tax J. 83.

Richler, Ronald, "Triangular Amalgamations" (1985) 33 Can. Tax J. 374.

Paid-Up Capital

Ewens, Douglas, "Amalgamations — Part II" (1980) 28 Can. Tax J. 826.

Sinclair, B.R., "Paid-Up Capital" (1986) 34 Can. Tax J. 1494.

Carryover of Losses

Arnold, Brian J., and David C. Poynton, "Tax Treatment of Losses on Amalgamation and Winding-up" (1978) 26 Can. Tax J. 444.

Cronkwright, Glen E., "The Utilization of Losses in Corporate Groups and Further Relief That Might be Taken", in *Proceedings of 31st Tax Conf.* 316 (Can. Tax Foundation, 1979).

Flynn, Gordon W., "Tax Planning for Corporations with Net Capital and Noncapital Losses", *Corp. Mgmt. Tax Conf.* 208 (Can. Tax Foundation, 1981).

Treharne, R., "Loss Carryforward Rollovers" (1977) 51 Cost & Mgmt. 45.

Shareholders of Predecessor Corporations

Cowan, R.I., "Amalgamations — Shareholders and Investors" (1977) 51 Cost & Mgmt. 46.

Richler, Ronald, "Triangular Amalgamations" (1985) 33 Can. Tax J. 374.

Winding-up

Winding-up of a 90 Per Cent Subsidiary

Alpert, Howard J., "Winding-Up under Section 88" (1974) 22 Can. Tax J. 98.

Arnold, Brian J., and David C. Poynton, "Tax Treatment of Losses on Amalgamation and Winding-Up" (1978) 26 Can. Tax J. 444.

Cronkwright, Glen E., "The Utilization of Losses in Corporate Groups and Further Relief That Might Be Taken", in *Proceedings of 31st Tax Conf.* 316 (Can. Tax Foundation, 1979).

Flynn, Gordon W., "Tax Planning for Corporations with Net Capital and Noncapital Losses", *Corp. Mgmt. Tax Conf.* 208 (Can. Tax Foundation, 1981).

Nitikman, Bert W., and G. David Eriks, "Macbeth and Subsection 88(1)" (1976) 24 Can. Tax J. 1.

Pister, Tom, "Paragraph 88(1)(d) Bump on the Winding Up of a Subsidiary — Part I" (1990) 38 Can. Tax J. 148.

Pister, Tom, "Paragraph 88(1)(d) Bump on the Winding Up of a Subsidiary — Part II" (1990) 38 Can. Tax J. 426.

Scace, Arthur R.A., "The Purchase and Sale of Shares: Section 88 Winding-Up", *Corp. Mgmt. Tax Conf.* 51 (Can. Tax Foundation, 1972).

Smith, D.W., "Winding-Up: Section 88" (1981) Can. Taxation 1141.

Swiderski, Tony, "Transfers of U.S. Real Property Interests in Canadian Reorganizations: Opportunities, Limitations and Pitfalls" (1989) 37 Can. Tax J. 605, at pp. 624-25.

Tinker, John B., "Rollovers on Winding Up Wholly-Owned Subsidiaries and Distributing Property of Trusts", in *Proceedings of 23rd Tax Conf.* 407 (Can. Tax Foundation, 1972).

Winding-up of Other Canadian Corporations

Ewens, Douglas S., "The Winding-Up of Corporations Otherwise than Under Section 88" (1973) 21 Can. Tax J. 1.

Ewens, Douglas S., "The Winding-Up of Corporations Otherwise than Under Section 88: An Update" (1975) 23 Can. Tax J. 352.

Corporate Emigration

Boultbee, J., "Change of Residence and Continuance" (1984) 32 Can. Tax J. 792.

Other

Lindsay, Robert F., "Purchase and Sale of a Canadian Business by a Non-resident of Canada", *Corp. Mgmt. Tax Conf.* 305 (Can. Tax Foundation, 1984).

Pooley, Joanne, and Terry Clark, "Comparison Between Canadian and U.S. Reorganizations — Part I" (1982) 30 Can. Tax J. 284.

Pooley, Joanne, and Terry Clark, "Comparison Between Canadian and U.S. Reorganizations — Part II" (1982) 30 Can. Tax J. 437.

"The Taxation of Corporate Reorganizations — Change of Residence and Continuance" (1984) 32 Can. Tax J. 792.

CHAPTER 30 — PURCHASE AND SALE OF A BUSINESS

I. — General Comment

We must make three principal decisions in a business acquisition:

1. Do we buy the business?

2. What do we buy? and

3. How do we pay for it?

The first of these decisions is essentially a business decision: is the business attractive in terms of its potential financial returns? Does it integrate with the purchaser's other businesses? Does the purchaser have the necessary expertise to run the new business? Will it ensure lines of supply or customers that will enhance the purchaser's existing businesses?

The next two decisions, however, are substantially influenced by tax law. Both the purchaser and the vendor have the same economic interests; namely, they want the best deal. The structure of an acquisition determines not only its price but also the manner of payment.

The method of financing a business depends upon both financial and tax considerations. Financial considerations concern the state of the debt and equity markets, the availability of funds and, most importantly, the cost of capital at the relevant time. The cost of capital and the available internal rate of return from the invested capital determine whether the acquisition is justifiable on a business basis.

From a tax perspective, the first important consideration is the dichotomy between debt and equity capital. The general rule is that the cost of debt capital is deductible for tax purposes, whereas equity capital is financed with after-tax dollars. Thus, taxpayers have an incentive to finance business acquisitions with debt capital. Given a choice between financing an acquisition with 10 per cent debt and 10 per cent preferred shares with equivalent protection, the taxpayer is better off issuing debt, which will have an after-tax cost of 5 to 7 per cent. The deductibility of interest expenses and the non-deductibility of dividends for tax purposes colours most business acquisitions and explains the enormous amount of debt financing in Canada. Thus, taxpayers almost invariably approach financing with the motive of tax avoidance.

The second structural characteristic of the tax system that influences financing decisions is that inter-corporate dividends generally flow on a tax-free basis. This means that equity or near-equity financing can be attractive to the lender if it is paid in the form of dividends. The avenues for after-tax financing are, however, substantially closed with the tightening of the rules in respect of taxable preferred shares.[1]

One of the early decisions to be made in the purchase and sale of a business is the manner in which the acquisition will be structured. This decision has an important effect on the ultimate purchase price of the business because it directly affects the net proceeds that the vendor receives from the sale.

Two common methods for the acquisition of a business are through the purchase of its assets or, in the case of a corporation, the purchase of its shares.

There are no absolute rules that indicate invariable preference of one method over the other. Each acquisition is influenced by facts that are unique to the particular business. In general terms, however, the purchaser and vendor should consider the following:

- The tax status of the purchaser, the target business ("Targetco"), and Targetco's shareholders. If Targetco is a Canadian-controlled private corporation ("CCPC"), there will be some integration of corporate and shareholder taxes for its shareholders who are Canadian residents.

- The tax rates of Targetco and its shareholders.

- The tax rate of the purchaser and its marginal cost of capital.

- The type of income that the sale of Targetco will generate. A sale of shares generally triggers capital gains. A sale of assets usually triggers a mixture of ordinary income and

---

[1]See Parts IV.1 and VI.1 of the Act.

capital gains. The relative amount of each of these types of income has a bearing on the net proceeds that Targetco's shareholders receive.

• The basis of Targetco's assets and its shares.

• The amount of "safe income" (after-tax retained earnings) on Targetco's books.

• The value of any tax deferrals under each of the alternatives, asset purchase and share purchase.

• The presence of accumulated losses in Targetco and the purchaser's prospects of utilizing the losses.

• The presence of tax free accounts, such as the "capital dividend account", that may be extracted at nil cost prior to the sale of the business.

• The business complexities of completing the transaction as an asset or share acquisition.

II. — Financial Statements

The decision to acquire a business, whether by purchasing its assets or shares, relies heavily on the accuracy of its financial statements. In an asset acquisition, the financial statements disclose valuable information about the cost and basis of assets, the face value of liabilities and shareholder loans. In a share purchase, the financial statements provide the underpinning of the purchase price, namely, the corporation's earning stream.

Despite their aura of exactitude and precision, financial statements have limitations. An audit of financial statements and the expression of an unqualified opinion on them provides some level of comfort in their accuracy. It cannot be overstated, however, that an audit opinion is merely an opinion. It simply expresses the view of the auditors that the financial statements "present fairly the results of operations in accordance with generally accepted accounting principles on a basis consistent with that of the preceding year." It is not a certification of accuracy of every detail of each asset or liability represented on the financial statement.

There are many versions of generally accepted accounting principles, each of which may be suitable in appropriate circumstances, which produce widely divergent results in the valuation of a business enterprise. Auditors are concerned only that the financial statements do not *materially* misstate the underlying financial picture of a business. Materiality is an elastic concept that will produce varied interpretations in the event of a dispute between the purchaser and the vendor. Hence, it is prudent to carefully consider the content and substance of the financial statements prior to executing the agreement of purchase and sale.

There are many aspects of financial statements that should be taken into account in the preparation of an agreement of purchase and sale of a business. For example:

- Financial statements are traditionally prepared on an historical cost assumption basis and do not reflect, in most cases, the market value of assets unless there is a permanent and substantial decline of market values below cost.

- Financial statements are prepared *as at* a particular date and their usefulness declines exponentially with their age.

- The historical cost of assets shown in the financial statements may not reflect their basis for tax purposes, particularly if they were acquired in non-arm's length transactions at values other than fair market value.

- The market value of accounts receivable depends upon their collectibility. The allowance for doubtful accounts on the balance sheet is only an estimate and reflects management's perception of the collectibility of the outstanding accounts. As with all the other values reflected on the financial statements, the estimate of uncollectible accounts is valid only as of the date at which the estimate was made. Subsequent events (for example, the insolvency of a major customer) may have an important effect on the value of the *net* accounts collectible.

- The valuation of inventory, particularly in a manufacturing enterprise, reflects many accounting assumptions. Inventory may be valued on the basis of any of several equally acceptable accounting principles, each of which produces different results. The value of inventory also reflects management's judgment as to the condition and viability of the inventory.

- Finally, and most importantly, historical cost financial statements do not reflect any value of what may be the enterprise's most valuable asset: Goodwill. A successful business is valued at a premium to the net fair market value of its assets. The premium, which in effect recognizes the enterprise's internally generated goodwill, is an important element in the determination of the ultimate purchase price.

To summarize: the financial statements of a business enterprise are a useful *starting* point in the determination of its value. They are, however, just that: a starting point. The purchaser must ensure that the tax values and basis of the business assets are fully and properly disclosed. Thus, the purchaser will want to confirm, and obtain representations on, the amount of tax losses, tax reserves, the capital dividend account balance, the amount of refundable dividend tax on hand, and the status of outstanding tax assessments.

III. — Mode Of Acquisition

Business acquisitions require an evaluation of:

- Choice of structure;

- Form of acquisition;

- Mode of financing;

- Location of acquiring structure;

- Securitization of assets and contracts;

- Valuation of assets and liabilities;

- Transfer of contracts and statutory relationships and obligations; and

- Tax considerations in respect of all of the above.

There are three broad categories of tax decisions in the acquisition of a domestic business as a going concern: (1) how to acquire the business? (2) the form of the business? and (3) how to finance the business? International acquisitions involve additional considerations such as the location of the acquiring entity and the effect of double tax treaties.

Business acquisitions typically occur through:

- A purchase of the assets of a going business;

- An acquisition of shares; or

- An amalgamation of corporations.

The method selected depends upon business and tax factors, the source of financing, and the significance of minority ownership interests.

We use the term "acquisition" in the present context to describe any transaction in which a buyer acquires all or substantially all of the assets and business of a seller or all or a control portion of the share capital of the seller in a voluntary transaction between a willing buyer and a willing seller. The term is not used here to describe a takeover in which the seller's management is an unwilling partner to the acquisition (for example, a hostile takeover).

Traditionally, the most popular methods of acquisitions are the purchase of assets and the purchase of shares. Each of these methods has certain business and tax advantages and disadvantages. Whether a particular method is more suitable than another depends upon the particular circumstances and the reasons for the acquisition.

Business acquisitions involve three different but inter-related considerations:

(1) Price;

(2) Form; and

(3) Financing.

The latter two almost invariably influence the former. The first decision is a business decision, while the second and third are "tax-driven".

1. — Assets vs. Shares

Having decided upon an acquisition, the next decision (if there is a choice) is on the form of the acquisition. Generally, if the business is incorporated, the seller will want to sell his or her shares in the corporation, in order to claim the gain as a capital gain. An asset acquisition generally involves a greater tax liability, because inventory gains and recaptured capital cost allowance are fully taxable as income.[2]

In contrast, the purchaser usually prefers to acquire assets in order to step up the "basis" of the assets acquired so that he or she can claim capital cost allowance on the stepped-up basis. A purchaser of assets also knows exactly what he or she is buying and is not exposed to the risk of assuming any hidden and contingent liabilities.

There are, however, circumstances where the purchaser may prefer to acquire the shares of a corporation rather than its assets. For example, a purchaser may prefer to purchase shares if he or she is interested in acquiring the corporation's losses and intends to continue operating the acquired business.

2. — Amalgamations

The third method of business acquisition is by way of amalgamation. An amalgamation involves a merger of two or more corporations to form a new corporation. In certain circumstances, corporate amalgamation is the preferred method of acquiring a business because of the availability of tax-free rollovers.[3]

IV. — Purchase And Sale Of Assets

1. — General Comment

One can acquire a business by purchasing its assets and liabilities *in toto*. The disposition of an *entire* business constitutes a capital transaction and the proceeds of sale are capital receipts to the vendor. Similarly, the acquisition of a business is usually considered a capital expenditure.[4]

---

[2]Subs. 13(1).

[3]S. 87.

[4]*Frankel Corp. v. M.N.R.*, [1959] S.C.R. 713, [1959] C.T.C. 244, 59 D.T.C. 1161 (S.C.C.) (sale of inventory is part of sale of taxpayer's business, proceeds not taxable as business income); *The Queen v. Farquhar Bethune Ins. Ltd.*, [1982] C.T.C. 282, 82 D.T.C. 6239 (F.C.A.) (purchase of customer lists and a covenant of non-competition constituted the acquisition of a capital asset); *Cumberland Invt. Ltd. v. The Queen*, [1975] C.T.C. 439, 75 D.T.C. 5309 (F.C.A.) (payment by insurance agency to competi-

There are, however, a multitude of provisions that vary these general rules, and we must consider each category and type of asset separately to determine the tax consequences that flow from its acquisition or disposition.

2. — Purchaser's Perspective

(a) — Advantages

There are several advantages to purchasing a business by acquiring its assets and liabilities *in toto*.

- *Elimination of minority interests:*

    If the business is carried on by a corporation, the purchaser is not encumbered with minority shareholdings from the acquired business. The minority shareholders are, however, entitled to dissent if the corporation sells all of its assets. If they do, they are entitled to be bought out at the fair value of their shares.[5]

- *Limitation of liability:*

    The purchaser acquires only the liabilities stipulated in the agreement of purchase and sale and, subject to "bulk sales" legislation, is not generally liable for the vendor's undisclosed liabilities.

- *Selective asset acquisition:*

    A purchaser can be more selective in an asset acquisition and exclude any assets that are not required.

- *Allocation of purchase price:*

    The purchaser can negotiate the allocation of the purchase price among the assets acquired. In an arm's length transaction, the negotiated allocation will usually determine the tax cost or the basis of the acquired assets.[6]

- *Step-up in cost base:*

    The fair market value of business assets will usually exceed their tax basis. By negotiating appropriate purchase price allocations, the purchaser can usually step-up the cost base of the depreciable assets acquired and obtain larger CCA write-

---

tor for latter's list of sub-agents, insurance policies and card index system was an acquisition of a capital asset).

[5]See, e.g., *Canada Business Corporations Act*, R.S.C. 1985, c. C-44, subss. 189(3), 190(1).

[6]See, however, s. 68.

offs in the future. Similarly, the purchaser can step-up the basis of non-depreciable and other assets and reduce the amount of capital gains that may ultimately be realized on disposition of the assets. This can be particularly important if the purchaser intends to divest any assets with accrued gains in the near future.

(b) — Disadvantages

There are also some disadvantages to asset acquisitions. For example:

- *Complexity:*

    An asset acquisition is a complex transaction, because it involves the transfer of individual assets, registration of title transfers and assignment of leases, contracts and franchises. It can also involve other taxes (e.g., land transfer taxes) on the transfer of certain assets.

- *Consents to transfers:*

    The seller may need consent to transfer non-assignable contracts such as leases, licence agreements and franchises. Obtaining the consent of third parties may be difficult and expensive.

- *Bulk sales laws:*

    To avoid liability to creditors, it is usually necessary to comply with the bulk sales laws of the jurisdiction in which the seller's assets are located.[7] The purpose of bulk sales legislation is to protect the creditors of the seller and to discourage a disposition of assets in bulk, leaving behind unpaid creditors. Non-compliance with the provisions of the relevant bulk sales legislation renders the sale voidable and the purchaser liable to the seller's creditors.

- *Contractual restrictions:*

    The seller's long term debt obligations may contain covenants which restrict the sale of assets that have been pledged as security to creditors.

- *Higher price:*

    Because of the increased tax basis available to the purchaser (and the resulting increased proceeds to the seller), the purchaser will generally have to pay a higher price to acquire assets than for shares. Thus, the purchase price for a business depends upon whether the purchase is structured as an asset or share acquisition.

---

[7]See, e.g., *Bulk Sales Act*, R.S.O. 1990, c. B.14.

3. — Seller's Perspective

The shareholders of a corporation generally prefer to sell their shares rather than the corporation's assets. This is demonstrated by the numerous advantages to the seller of a share sale.

(a) — Advantages

- A share sale usually triggers a capital gain for a shareholder. Since only 1/2 of a capital gain is subject to tax, shareholders usually prefer to dispose of their shares rather than the assets of the corporation. This consideration is that much more important if the shareholder can claim the $500,000 capital gains exemption on the sale of shares of a small business corporation.

- Purchase and sale of shares is generally a less complicated transaction than an asset sale. This is because a share sale does not require individual identification of every asset and allocation of the purchase price to each asset or group of assets. In any event, a sale of assets is simply not possible in the case of a large corporation with a diversified asset base spread over multiple locations in several jurisdictions.

- A sale of appreciated assets results in recaptured capital cost allowance and other income gains to the corporation. A further tax is payable on the distribution of income from the corporation to its shareholders. A share sale bypasses these problems of double taxation by eliminating any direct tax consequences to the corporation.

(b) — Disadvantages

- A share sale may not be advantageous if the corporation has accumulated tax losses. An asset sale may be more beneficial if gains from the sale of assets can be offset against corporate tax losses. In such circumstances, the shareholders may prefer to see the corporation's losses utilized to shelter any gains that result from the disposition of assets. This consideration is relevant if the shareholders do not withdraw funds from the corporation but reinvest their proceeds.

4. — Allocation of Purchase Price

The allocation of the purchase price among the assets purchased is one of the most significant tax issues in an asset acquisition. The allocation affects both the purchaser and the seller and will almost invariably influence the acquisition price of the assets.

The purchase price must be allocated on a reasonable basis among the assets acquired. The allocation should be part of the agreement of purchase and sale. In the absence of a written agreement, the Minister may challenge the allocation of the price between the parties. This can lead to valuation disputes and, in the absence of a satisfactory resolution of such problems, to protracted litigation regarding the fair market value of the assets purchased.

The allocation of the purchase price to the assets determines the proceeds of disposition of each property sold and the cost basis of each property acquired by the purchaser.

(a) — Purchaser's Perspective

From the purchaser's perspective, it is generally preferable to allocate the maximum amount possible to assets in the following sequence of priority:

1. Inventory;

2. Depreciable capital property;

3. Eligible capital property; and

4. Non-depreciable capital property.

The purchaser should allocate as much of the total purchase price as possible to the first two categories, inventory and depreciable capital property. Costs allocated to inventory will be fully deductible as cost of goods sold. Amounts allocated to depreciable capital property will form the basis of capital cost allowance claims in the future. The larger the cost base, the greater the write-off.

In contrast, only 3/4 of amounts allocated to goodwill and other eligible capital property are deductible on a declining balance basis at a rate of 7 per cent.

Amounts allocated to non-depreciable capital property cannot be deducted at all, but will reduce the amount of any capital gains that may be realized on the disposition of the property in the future.

(b) — Vendor's Perspective

The vendor should negotiate to allocate the global selling price with the opposite priorities. From the vendor's perspective, it is best to assign the highest amounts to assets in the following sequence:

1. Non-depreciable capital property;

2. Eligible capital property;

3. Depreciable capital property; and

4. Inventory.

Non-depreciable capital property triggers capital gains; depreciable property triggers recapture and capital gains; and inventory gains are fully taxable as income.

5. — Section 68

The purchaser and the vendor must allocate the purchase and sale price to the assets sold. The allocation must be on some reasonable basis, which is generally considered to be the fair market value of the assets at the time of the transaction. Where the seller and the purchaser are at arm's length and bargain with each other with opposing economic interests, the Canada Revenue Agency (CRA) will usually consider the negotiated allocation of the purchase price as fair and reasonable.

But even parties who are at arm's length with each other may not have truly opposing economic interests. For example, a non-taxable entity that sells its assets is unlikely to be concerned about potential recapture of capital cost allowance or inventory gains that may result from the sale. Similarly, a taxable entity with large accumulated losses may be prepared to agree to an allocation of convenience in exchange for a higher overall selling price for its assets.

The allocation of the total price by the seller and the purchaser in the agreement of purchase and sale is usually acceptable for income tax purposes.[8] Where the parties do not make the allocation, it may be necessary to obtain expert testimony supported by a valuation of the various assets.

To prevent manipulations of asset price allocations, section 68 of the Act allows the Minister to set aside an otherwise legal agreement, substitute reasonable amounts in lieu of the amounts allocated by the purchaser and seller, and bind both parties to the revised allocation.[9]

---

[8]See, generally, *Herb Payne Tpt. Ltd. v. M.N.R.*, [1963] C.T.C. 116, 63 D.T.C. 1075 (Ex. Ct.) (court arbitrated the values of the assets adopted by each party); *Klondike Helicopters Ltd. v. M.N.R.*, [1965] C.T.C. 427, 65 D.T.C. 5253 (Ex. Ct.); Ward, "Tax Considerations Relating to the Purchase of Assets of a Business", *Corp. Mgmt. Tax Conf.* 22 (Can. Tax Foundation, 1972).

[9]*The Queen v. Golden*, [1986] 1 S.C.R. 209, [1986] 1 C.T.C. 274, 86 D.T.C. 6138 (S.C.C.) (validity of s. 68 upheld); *Crawford Logging Co. v. M.N.R.* (1962), 29 Tax A.B.C. 436, 62 D.T.C. 421 (breakdown of consideration for sale of logging equipment disregarded as unrealistic); *Blackstone Hldg. Ltd. v. M.N.R.* (1966), 41 Tax A.B.C. 224, 66 D.T.C. 417 (valuations for hotel, land and goodwill set aside in favour of apportionment between land and building proportionate to municipal assessment values); *Can. Propane Gas & Oil Ltd. v. M.N.R.*, [1972] C.T.C. 566, 73 D.T.C. 5019 (F.C.T.D.) (Minister's apportionment preferred over taxpayer's in absence of any real bargaining between parties as to breakdown of price); *Clement's Drug Store (Brandon) Ltd. v. M.N.R.*, [1968] C.T.C. 53, 68 D.T.C. 5053 (Ex. Ct.) (in absence of sham or subterfuge, contract between arm's length parties should govern apportionment); *Klondike Helicopters Ltd. v. M.N.R.*, [1965] C.T.C. 427, 65 D.T.C. 5253 (Ex. Ct.) (price of $50,000 for depreciable property admittedly worth $71,300 upheld by court in absence of evidence of sham or subterfuge); *Kerim Bros. Ltd. v. M.N.R.*, [1967] Tax A.B.C. 438, 67 D.T.C. 326 (in arm's length sale of business, amount imputed by parties to depreciable property accepted over fair market value); *Co-op. Agricole de Granby v. M.N.R.*, [1970] Tax A.B.C. 969, 70 D.T.C. 1620 (consideration allotted by agreement unalterable by purchaser in light of appraisal subsequently obtained).

(a) — Land and Buildings

Some of the most difficult price allocation problems arise in the context of real property, particularly where land and buildings are sold to a person who is interested in acquiring only the land and not the buildings situated thereon. What happens, for example, if the purchaser demolishes the building immediately after purchasing the property? Can it be said that the seller actually received any proceeds of disposition in respect of the building? Should all of the proceeds be allocated to the land?

The general test used to determine the reasonableness of allocated values is to ask whether the building has economic value *to the seller* at the time of the sale of the property. Merely because the purchaser does not see any value in the building, and demolishes it immediately upon acquiring it, does not mean that the building does not have economic value to the seller. It means only that it has no value to the purchaser.[10] Where, however, the seller is really selling land, and does not receive any *additional* proceeds for the building, it is reasonable to allocate the entire proceeds to the land.[11]

(b) — Sale of Land Only

Where the purchaser is interested in acquiring only the land, and not the buildings situated on the land, the parties may agree to sell the property "clear of all buildings". Special rules apply, however, where buildings are demolished *prior* to their sale. In such circumstances, the proceeds of disposition of the demolished building are, in effect, determined *as if* it had been sold at its fair market value.[12] Thus, the vendor cannot avoid recapture of capital cost allowance by selling the property "clear of all buildings".

---

[10]*Stanley v. M.N.R.*, [1967] Tax A.B.C. 1048, 67 D.T.C. 700; affd. [1969] C.T.C. 430, 69 D.T.C. 5286; affd. [1972] C.T.C. 34, 72 D.T.C. 6004 (S.C.C.).

[11]*Moulds v. The Queen*, [1977] C.T.C. 126, 77 D.T.C. 5094; affd. [1978] C.T.C. 146, 78 D.T.C. 6068 (F.C.A.); see *Mora Bldg. Corp. v. M.N.R.*, [1967] Tax A.B.C. 365, 67 D.T.C. 275 (proceeds of disposition may be allocated on basis of municipal assessments); *Flanders Installation Ltd. v. M.N.R.*, [1967] Tax A.B.C. 1018, 68 D.T.C. 9 (reasonable apportionment between land and building based on expert evidence and municipal assessment); *Coulter v. M.N.R.*, [1968] Tax A.B.C. 369, 68 D.T.C. 335 (in absence of allocation in deed of sale, Minister's allocation on basis of municipal assessment upheld); *Samuel-Jay Invt. Ltd. v. M.N.R.*, [1968] Tax A.B.C. 552, 68 D.T.C. 439 (allocation based on municipal assessment); *Hamilton v. M.N.R.*, [1969] Tax A.B.C. 831, 69 D.T.C. 580 (apportionment based on municipal assessment in absence of first-hand evidence of land values).

[12]Subs. 13(21.1). This rule was introduced to reverse *Malloney's Studio Ltd. v. The Queen*, [1979] 2 S.C.R. 326, [1979] C.T.C. 206, 79 D.T.C. 5124 (S.C.C.) (taxpayer allowed to allocate entire proceeds of disposition to land where buildings on land had been demolished prior to sale).

Example

Assume that a taxpayer owns one building, to which the following data applies:

	Land	Building	Total
Adjusted cost base/capital cost	$ 200,000	$ 160,000	$ 360,000
Undepreciated capital cost (UCC)	—	$ 100,000	—
Fair market value to vendor	$ 240,000	$ 160,000	$ 400,000

The taxpayer tears down the building and sells the land for $400,000. *In the absence of the special rule* in subsection 13(21.1), the taxpayer would realize a capital gain of $200,000 and a terminal loss of $100,000. Under subsection 13(21.1), however, the proceeds of disposition of the demolished building are calculated as the *lesser* of:

(1) Aggregate proceeds of land and building

$ 400,000

    Exceeds *lesser* of:

      ACB of land $ 200,000

      FMV of land $ 240,000

                                       (200,000)

                                   $ 200,000 (1)

and

(2) *Greater* of:

      FMV of building $ 160,000

      UCC of building $ 100,000

                                   $ 160,000 (2)

Proceeds of disposition (lesser of (1) and (2)) $ 160,000

In effect, the taxpayer is forced to recognize his recapture of capital cost allowance of $60,000, which is the amount he would have had to recognize had he not demolished the building. The proceeds of disposition of the land are $240,000, which is also the amount fairly attributable to the land.

6. — Arm's Length Transactions

Subject to section 68, where the purchaser and the seller deal with each other at arm's length, the negotiated purchase price of assets determines the seller's proceeds of disposition and the purchaser's cost of the property. The price of each asset is usually specified in the agreement of purchase and sale. The purchaser can increase the price set out in the agreement by the amount of any transfer taxes, professional fees, commissions, finders fees, etc.[13]

7. — Non-Arm's Length Transactions

Where the purchaser and the seller are not dealing with each other at arm's length, we determine the seller's proceeds of disposition and the purchaser's acquisition costs as follows:

- Where the purchaser acquires a property at an amount in *excess* of its fair market value, the purchaser is deemed to have acquired the property at its fair market value and not at the higher amount stipulated in the agreement of purchase and sale.[14] The seller is taxed on the basis of the actual proceeds of sale and not upon the lower figure attributed to the purchaser.

- Where a taxpayer disposes of property for *less* than its fair market value, the taxpayer is deemed to have received proceeds of disposition equal to its fair market value.[15] We determine the purchaser's cost of acquisition by the amount actually paid for the property, and not by the seller's deemed proceeds of disposition.

8. — Accounts Receivable

(a) — General Rules

In computing income from a business or property, an accrual basis taxpayer may claim a reserve for doubtful accounts receivable which have been included in income.[16] An amount claimed as a reserve in one year is brought into income in the following year.[17] The taxpayer may then claim a new reserve based upon a new appraisal as to the collectibility of accounts receivable.

---

[13]See IT-285R2, "Capital Cost Allowance — General Comments" (March 31, 1994).

[14]Para. 69(1)(a).

[15]Para. 69(1)(b).

[16]Para. 20(1)(l).

[17]Para. 12(1)(d).

A bad debt (as opposed to one that is merely doubtful of collection) may be written off against income.[18] A bad debt is not brought back into income in the following year *unless* it is actually recovered.[19]

Accounts receivable are usually sold at a discount from their face value. The discount reflects the difficulty and expense of collecting accounts receivable.

The sale of accounts receivable at less than their face value generally gives rise to a capital loss.[20] Thus, the vendor, who previously included sales, which gave rise to the receivables, as income can offset the discount against the sales, but only as capital losses.

The seller cannot claim a reserve in the year of sale, since no debts will be owing at the end of the year.

A purchaser of accounts receivable acquires a capital asset.[21] Hence, any gain or loss on subsequent collection of the accounts is considered a capital gain or loss.

The purchaser cannot claim a reserve for doubtful accounts, since the receivables were not previously included in income.

Thus, both the vendor and the purchaser may be prejudiced when accounts receivable are sold as part of an asset acquisition. A special rule is necessary to relieve against hardship in these circumstances.

(b) — Section 22 Election

Where a taxpayer who has been carrying on a business sells all, or substantially all, of the property (including accounts receivable) used in the business to a purchaser who proposes to continue the business, the seller and the purchaser can elect jointly to have the full amount of any loss on the sale of receivables deducted from the seller's income and included in the purchaser's income for the year.[22]

(i) — Effect on Seller

In the absence of an election, a taxpayer who sells all of his or her accounts receivable may not claim a reserve in respect of doubtful debts in the year in which the receivables are sold.

---

[18]Para. 20(1)(p).

[19]Para. 12(1)(i); see IT-442R, "Bad Debts and Reserves for Doubtful Debts" (September 6, 1991).

[20]*Doughty v. Comm. of Taxes*, [1927] A.C. 327 (P.C.) [N.Z.].

[21]*Crompton v. Reynolds* (1952), 33 Tax Cas. 288 (H.L.).

[22]S. 22.

In addition, the taxpayer must bring into income any reserve for doubtful debts claimed in the preceding year.[23] Any discount on the sale of the receivables is considered a capital loss.

Where, however, the parties elect under section 22, the seller may claim a deduction from income for any discount, to the extent that the receivables have not been written off previously as a bad debt expense.[24] Thus, the effect of the election is to convert what would otherwise be a capital loss from the discount into a deduction from income.

Example

Assume that a taxpayer sells his accounts receivable on the following basis:

Face value	$ 100,000
Sale price	85,000
Bad debts written off	2,000
Reserve previously claimed	5,000

Then, assuming that the parties elect under subsection 22(1):

Face price	$ 100,000
Sale value	(85,000)
Discount on sale	15,000
Bad debts written off	(2,000)
Net deduction from income	$ 13,000

Thus, it is generally to the seller's advantage to elect under subsection 22(1) if the receivables are sold at a substantial discount. On the other hand, the seller will not usually benefit from the election if the receivables are sold at their face value.

(ii) — Effect on Purchaser

The election also requires the purchaser to include in income the amount that the seller deducts from income in that year.[25] In the above example, the purchaser must include $13,000 in income in the year in which he or she purchases the business assets. The overall

---

[23]Para. 12(1)(d).

[24]Para. 22(1)(a).

[25]Para. 22(1)(b).

result of the election to the purchaser and the vendor is to allow them to treat losses from accounts receivables as business losses rather than capital losses.

The advantage to the purchaser of making the election is that the purchaser can claim a deduction in respect of any of the receivables that later prove to be uncollectible. This is so even though the debts did not arise in the ordinary course of business.[26]

Hence, it is not usually to the purchaser's advantage to elect under section 22 if the receivables are purchased at a substantial discount, since the amount of the discount is fully taxable income.

The purchaser benefits from the election if the receivables are sold at face value, since it is possible that some of the accounts will not be collected. In such a case, the purchaser will want to claim a reserve for doubtful debts or a deduction for bad debts.

(iii) — Non-Arm's Length Sales

Although the election under section 22 is binding upon the vendor and the purchaser, it is not binding upon the Minister if the amount paid for the receivables is at variance with their fair market value and the parties do not deal with each other at arm's length.[27]

Example

Assume that in YEAR 2 S sold an unincorporated business to P on the following basis:

Face value of accounts receivable not previously written off as bad debts	$ 78,000
Reserve for doubtful accounts claimed by S (YEAR 1)	$ 4,000
Bad debts written off by S (YEAR 1)	$ 2,000
Purchase price allocated to receivables	$ 70,000
Bad debts recovered by P on account of receivables purchased (YEAR 2)	$ 500
Estimated reserve for doubtful accounts from receivables purchased (YEAR 2)	$ 3,000
Bad debts written off by P (YEAR 2)	$ 200

---

[26]Para. 22(1)(c).

[27]Subs. 22(2).

Example

S and P elect jointly under section 22.

Then, *effect on the seller (S):*

Face value of receivables not previously written off as bad debts	$ 78,000
Purchase price of receivables	(70,000)
Discount deductible from income	8,000
Reserve for doubtful accounts (YEAR 1)	(4,000)
Net deduction from income in YEAR 2	$ 4,000

Effect on the purchaser (P):

Face value of receivables purchased	$ 78,000
Purchase price paid for receivables	(70,000)
Discount included in income	8,000
Bad debts recovered	500
	8,500
Reserve for doubtful accounts (YEAR 2)	(3,000)
Bad debts written off	(200)
Net addition to income in YEAR 2	$ 5,300

---

9. — Inventory

In common law, where a business disposed of its entire inventory, any gain or loss from the disposition would be considered a capital gain or loss.[28]

The Act provides otherwise: section 23 deems a taxpayer who disposes of inventory in a bulk sale upon ceasing to carry on a business to have sold the inventory in the course of

---

[28]*Doughty v. Commr. of Taxes, ante*; *Frankel Corp. v. M.N.R., ante*; *M.N.R. v. McCord Street Sites Ltd.*, [1962] C.T.C. 387, 62 D.T.C. 1229 (Ex. Ct.) (sand sold with sand business resulted in capital receipt).

business, and the proceeds are considered to be normal sales.[29] Thus, what would have been a capital gain under general legal principles is considered to be business income for tax purposes.

As noted above, subject to sections 68 and 69, a purchaser will usually find it advantageous to allocate as much as possible to the cost of inventory, in order to reduce future profits on its sale.

10. — Depreciable Property

Depreciable capital property is capital property in respect of which the owner can claim capital cost allowance ("CCA"). We divide depreciable capital property into two broad categories: (1) assets with a fixed term (leaseholds, patents, etc.), and (2) assets of prescribed classes that are depreciated on a declining balance basis (buildings, automobiles, etc.). There are at least 50 classes of depreciable property.

(a) — General Rules

The cost of depreciable properties of each class is "pooled" and CCA is claimed as a percentage of each separate pool. The amount of CCA claimed on a class in a year is deducted from the balance in the pool. The balance in a pool of assets is referred to as the undepreciated capital cost (UCC) of the class.

When an asset is sold, the UCC of the class to which the asset belonged is reduced by the amount that the taxpayer receives as net proceeds from the disposition.

Net proceeds from dispositions of depreciable property are allocated to assets, either on an asset-by-asset or on a class-by-class basis, and credited towards the undepreciated capital cost of the relevant class. Net proceeds are the proceeds of disposition less any expenses incurred for the purpose of the disposition.

The maximum amount that may be credited to a class in respect of any property is its capital cost.[30] Proceeds in excess of the capital cost of assets trigger a capital gain.

Any credit (negative) balance in the undepreciated capital cost of a class as at the *end* of the taxation year is included in income as recapture of capital cost allowance.[31] A taxpayer can

---

[29]"Inventory" includes the inventory of a farmer who calculates income according to the cash method of accounting.

[30]Subs. 13(21)"undepreciated capital cost" (F).

[31]Subs. 13(1).

reduce or eliminate the effect of recapture of capital cost allowance by purchasing assets of the *same* class prior to the end of its taxation year.

Recapture of depreciation on assets used by a Canadian-controlled private corporation in active business is eligible for the small business deduction and, where appropriate, the manufacturing and processing credit.

A debit (positive) balance remaining in the class may be deducted from income as a terminal loss, provided that the taxpayer has disposed of *all* of the property in that class.[32]

Proceeds of disposition in excess of the capital cost of the property give rise to a capital gain. A disposition of depreciable property cannot give rise to a capital loss.[33]

The allocation of the purchase price of a business to assets is a crucial element in the negotiations leading to the acquisition. In particular, the allocation of amounts to depreciable property can have a significant effect on both the purchaser and the seller. From the purchaser's perspective, the amount allocated to depreciable property represents the basis against which future charges to income will be made. From the seller's perspective, amounts allocated to each pool of assets determine the amount of recaptured CCA and capital gains.

A purchaser will generally prefer a higher proportion of the total proceeds of disposition of depreciable property to be allocated to classes with high rates of depreciation. Indeed, one of the attractive aspects of an acquisition of a business through the purchase of its assets is that it allows the purchaser to step-up the cost base of the assets for purposes of future capital cost allowance claims. The vendor generally prefers to allocate a higher percentage of the price to those classes of depreciable property that trigger the least recapture of capital cost allowance.

(b) — Land and Buildings

As we saw earlier, where a taxpayer disposes of land and buildings together in a single transaction, the proceeds of disposition must be allocated between the two assets.[34]

The purchaser will usually want to allocate the highest amount possible to buildings, so as to be able to claim capital cost allowance on the stepped-up cost of the assets. Sometimes the

---

[32]Subs. 20(16).

[33]Para. 39(1)(b).

[34]S. 68; but see *Golden v. The Queen*, [1983] C.T.C. 112, 83 D.T.C. 5138 (Fed. C.A.); affd. [1986] 1 S.C.R. 209, [1986] 1 C.T.C. 274, 86 D.T.C. 6138 (S.C.C.).

very reason for the purchaser acquiring assets rather than shares is to step up the capital cost of the depreciable assets acquired.[35]

In contrast, it is usually to the seller's advantage to have as much as is reasonably possible allocated to the land and the least amount possible allocated to the buildings. This maximizes the capital gain and minimizes recapture of CCA.

A special rule applies, however, where a building is sold for less than its cost amount in order to create a tax loss.

Where a taxpayer[36] disposes of a building for less than its cost amount and, in the same year, disposes of the land subjacent or contiguous to the building, the proceeds of disposition from the two transactions can be reallocated from the land to the building.[37] In the simplest case, subsection 13(21.1) operates to deem the proceeds of disposition of the building to equal the cost amount (usually the UCC) of the building.

A reallocation can reduce the terminal loss that might otherwise have arisen on the disposition of the building, and may even involve recapture of capital cost allowance previously claimed by the seller. Thus, the loss on the sale of the building is reduced to the extent of any gain on the sale of the land.

Example

Assume: The following data applies to a sale of land and a building. The building, which has a capital cost of $150,000, is demolished *prior* to its sale.

	Land	Building	Total
ACB/UCC	$190,000	$ 100,000	$ 290,000
Fair market value to seller	$230,000	$ 70,000	$ 300,000
Allocation of proceeds on sale	$300,000	NIL	$ 300,000

Then, effect on seller:

	General Rules	Under para. 13(21.1)(a)

---

[35]But see Reg. 1102(1)(c) (taxpayer may claim CCA only on assets acquired for purpose of earning income from business or property).

[36]Or a person with whom the taxpayer is not dealing at arm's length.

[37]Subs. 13(21.1).

Example		
Building		
Proceeds of disposition	NIL	$ 100,000
UCC	(100,000)	(100,000)
Terminal loss	($100,000)	NIL
Land		
Proceeds of disposition	$ 300,000	$ 200,000
ACB	(190,000)	(190,000)
Capital gain	$ 110,000	$ 10,000
Taxable capital gain	$ 55,000	$ 5,000
Net increase (decrease) in income	$ (45,000)	$ 5,000

In effect, paragraph 13(21.1)(a) applies the terminal loss attributable to the building against the capital gain attributable to the land. The terminal loss of $100,000 reduces the capital gain on the disposition of land from $110,000 to $10,000.

The cost of the land to the purchaser is $300,000, and is not affected by the reallocation of proceeds in the seller's hands.

11. — *Capital Property*

A disposition of capital property can trigger a capital gain or capital loss. A capital gain results if the net proceeds of disposition exceed the adjusted cost base of the property. A capital loss results to the extent that the net proceeds of disposition are less than the adjusted cost base of the property.

Allowable capital losses may be carried back three years and applied against any taxable capital gains recognized in those years. Capital losses may be carried forward indefinitely,[38] but may be offset only against future taxable capital gains. Hence, it is important for the seller to determine the allocation of the purchase price so as to trigger the optimum amount of losses utilizable (if any) against capital and income. A seller will usually favour an alloca-

---

[38]Para. 111(1)(b).

tion of the purchase price so as to maximize losses on account of income rather than on account of capital.

From the purchaser's perspective, amounts allocated to capital property become the adjusted cost base of the property. These costs are recoverable by the purchaser only when the purchaser subsequently disposes of the property. Hence, in most cases, the purchaser usually prefers to allocate as little as possible to non-depreciable capital property since any amounts allocated to such property can only be recovered upon their eventual disposition.

12. — Eligible Capital Property

"Eligible capital property" refers to intangible capital assets with an unlimited life, such as goodwill, perpetual franchises, customer lists, non-competition clauses and licences.[39]

Goodwill normally encompasses the following:

- Reputation;
- Employee loyalty;
- Favourable commercial contracts;
- Trademarks or trade names;
- Favourable financial relationships;
- Management performance record; and
- Protected markets.

Expenditures on account of eligible capital property are classified as "eligible capital expenditures".[40]

Where a purchaser incurs eligible capital expenditures, 75 per cent of such expenditures go into the purchaser's cumulative eligible capital account. This account may be amortized at 7 per cent per year on a declining balance basis.[41]

A taxpayer who disposes of eligible capital property must reduce his or her cumulative eligible capital account by 75 per cent of the proceeds received in respect of such property. Any

---

[39]S. 54"eligible capital property".

[40]Subs. 14(5)"eligible capital expenditure".

[41]Subs. 14(5)"cumulative eligible capital", para. 20(1)(b) (only expenditures after 1971 qualify for amortization).

negative balance in the cumulative eligible capital account at the end of the taxation year is included in income for the year.[42]

Taxable proceeds from the sale of eligible capital property used to earn active business income qualify as "active business income" for purposes of the small business deduction.

A taxpayer who ceases to carry on a business may deduct from income any balance remaining in the cumulative eligible capital account in respect of that business.[43]

The terminal write-off of the cumulative eligible capital account may not be claimed if the terminated business is continued by the taxpayer's spouse, common-law spouse or by a corporation controlled directly or indirectly by the taxpayer.[44] Instead, the balance in the cumulative eligible capital account is transferred to the spouse, common-law spouse or to the corporation controlled by the taxpayer.

Where a taxpayer disposes of an eligible capital property and replaces the property within one year after the end of the year in which the proceeds of disposition become payable, the taxpayer can elect to defer recognition of recapture of any amortization.[45] In effect, 75 per cent of the cost of the replacement eligible capital property is *retroactively* added back to the taxpayer's cumulative eligible capital account to erase the negative balance which would otherwise be included in income.

Example

Assume that *Black Ltd.* acquires and disposes of eligible capital property in the following circumstances:

Balance in cumulative eligible capital ("CEC") (YEAR 1)	$ 60,000
Proceeds from disposition of perpetual franchise (YEAR 2)	$ 200,000
Acquisition of replacement perpetual franchise (YEAR 3)	$ 240,000

---

[42]Subs. 14(1).

[43]Subs. 24(1); IT-313R2, "Eligible Capital Property — Rules Where a Taxpayer Has Ceased Carrying on a Business or Has Died" (April 21, 1995).

[44]Subs. 24(2).

[45]Subss. 14(6),(7). Timing problems arise where the taxpayer files a return for the year in which the property is disposed of before acquiring the replacement property.

Example

Black Ltd.'s CEC is calculated as follows:

	General Rules	Subs. 14(6) Election
Opening balance in CEC (YEAR 1)	$ 60,000	$ 60,000
3/4 of proceeds of sale (YEAR 2)	(150,000)	(150,000)
3/4 of replacement property (YEAR 3)	—	180,000
Balance in CEC	(90,000)	90,000
Recapture under subs. 14(1)	90,000	—
	NIL	90,000
Maximum amortization (7%)	NIL	(6,300)
Closing balance	NIL	$ 83,700

13. — Instalment Payments

Interest expense on money borrowed to finance the acquisition of assets is deductible if the assets are acquired for the purpose of earning income from a business or property.[46] If the assets are depreciable property, the purchaser may elect to capitalize the interest expense into the capital cost of the property. Thus the purchaser can defer the immediate expense deduction and claim a larger capital cost allowance on the property.[47] Where the purchaser does elect to capitalize interest, it is necessary to allocate the portion of the interest expense that relates to the money borrowed to finance the depreciable property.

As a general rule, a taxpayer who disposes of property is neither required nor presumed to charge interest in respect of any portion of the consideration payable to the taxpayer on an instalment basis. The determination as to whether an instalment payment is a blend of capital and interest is entirely a question of fact.

(a) — Without Interest

Although it is usual in commercial dealings to charge interest on instalment sales, the absence of interest charges does not necessarily mean that the instalments represent a blend of income and capital. It is necessary to consider all of the surrounding circumstances of the

---

[46]Para. 20(1)(c).

[47]S. 21.

transaction to determine whether there is an interest component in the instalment payments. In *Vestey*, for example, the Court said:[48]

> It is necessary to decide whether we are bound to confine our attention to the words of the agreement and the related transfer of shares, and not to have regard for any surrounding circumstances. It appears clear to us on the authorities that we are not only entitled but are bound to consider such of the surrounding circumstances as are proved and admitted in evidence; not in order to vary the legal effect of the agreement and transfer nor to decide the matter by the doctrine (now exploded) of the "substance" of the matter, but in order to ascertain the true nature of the transaction comprised in the agreement. We have to look first at the legal effect of the agreement and then at the surrounding circumstances.

(b) — Blended Payments

Where instalment payments represent a blend of interest and capital, the interest component is taxable as income from property and is not considered to be a payment on account of capital.[49] The purchaser may deduct the interest component as an expense, provided that it relates to assets acquired for the purpose of earning income from business or property.[50]

The critical factor in determining whether a payment represents a blend of income and capital is the price paid for the property acquired. Where property is sold in an arm's length transaction at a price in excess of its fair market value, there is a strong inference that the price represents both income and capital. A persuasive argument is required to rebut the inference. As the Federal Court said:[51]

> It is well established that in similar cases the prime factor to be considered is whether or not the fair market value has been paid: if the price paid is in excess of fair market value, the excess is deemed interest; if the price reflects the fair market value, then there is no element of interest in the payment.

---

[48]*Vestey v. I.R.C.*, [1962] Ch. 861 at 865.

[49]Subs. 16(1).

[50]Para. 20(1)(c).

[51]*Rodmon Const. Inc. v. The Queen*, [1975] C.T.C. 73 at 75, 75 D.T.C. 5038 at 5039 (F.C.T.D.); IT-265R3 (archived), "Payments of Income and Capital Combined" (October 7, 1991); see also *Groulx v. M.N.R.*, [1967] C.T.C. 422, 67 D.T.C. 5284 (S.C.C.) (instalment payments represented blended payments of capital and interest).

14. — Pre-Paid Expenses

A "pre-paid expense" is an expenditure that one incurs in one fiscal period but relates to revenues to be realized in a subsequent period. Typical examples include amounts pre-paid as rent, insurance, taxes, and interest.

"Pre-paid expenses" are usually considered assets under generally-accepted accounting principles.[52] As such, they should be charged against revenues in the period to which they relate. As a matter of accounting practice, however, many accountants prefer to write off pre-paid expenses in the year in which they are incurred.

For tax purposes, expenses incurred for future services or in respect of specific types of periodic payments can be written off only when the services are actually rendered.[53] Thus, an amount paid by the purchaser to reimburse the vendor for pre-paid expenses may be deducted by the purchaser only in the year to which the expenses relate.

From the seller's perspective, any amounts allocated to pre-paid expenses are considered as on account of income.

15. — Reserves

A taxpayer who disposes of capital property in a year is entitled to claim a reserve in respect of proceeds of disposition which are not due until a subsequent year. A reserve claimed in one year must be brought into the taxpayer's income in the next year.[54] Thus, where a taxpayer disposes of all of his or her assets, capital gains reserves claimed in the preceding year must be included in income in the year in which the assets are sold.

A taxpayer is also entitled to deduct a reasonable amount as a reserve in respect of advance payments for goods and services which will be delivered or rendered after the end of the year.[55] Here too, a reserve claimed in one year is included in the taxpayer's income in the next year.[56]

---

[52]See *CICA Handbook*, s. 3040.01 ("Pre-paid expenses should be classified as current assets").

[53]Subs. 18(9).

[54]Para. 40(1)(a); subs. 40(1.1).

[55]Para. 20(1)(m).

[56]Para. 12(1)(e).

16. — Customer Lists

Customer lists acquired as part of, or ancillary to, the acquisition of a business as a going concern are considered eligible capital property, not operating expenses.

V. — Determination Of Purchase Price

The valuation of a business enterprise is an uncertain exercise, whether one is valuing assets or shares. The vendor and the purchaser will almost invariably view the business differently and each will have his or her own views on its earnings potential.

The determination of the purchase price of a business is a function of many variables, including, the perception of the owners and the purchasers as to future profitability, the reasons for the purchase and sale, the method of payment, the structure of the transaction and its tax consequences.

Assuming that the acquisition price of a group of assets is determined with the assistance of competent professionals, it is necessary to structure the transaction so as to maximize the advantages from a tax perspective.

The purchaser of assets is generally prepared to pay a higher price for the assets than in an equivalent share acquisition. This is because the purchaser can step-up the basis of the assets and thereby reduce tax through higher write-offs against future income.

Of course, the step-up in the basis of the assets that the purchaser acquires has a correlative detrimental effect on the seller, particularly if the step-up is heavily weighted towards highly depreciated property. The seller is subject to recapture of capital cost allowance, which will be taxable as ordinary income. Hence, the seller will generally demand a higher price for an asset sale than for an equivalent share sale.

An asset sale leaves the seller with a shell corporation with all of its hidden and contingent liabilities. At the same time, the seller cannot take advantage of the special rules in respect of the taxation of capital gains on shares.

Two principal components make up the purchase price of an asset acquisition:

    (1) Fair market value of the specific assets, and

    (2) Goodwill.

All assets are valued as of the closing of the transaction.

In a typical asset acquisition, the purchaser will pay an amount that exceeds the aggregate fair market value of the individual assets acquired. The excess amount represents the goodwill of the business, an asset that does not appear on the traditional historical cost balance sheet.

The agreement of purchase and sale of the assets should allocate the global purchase price to the specific assets conveyed. The allocation must be fair and the parties should be mindful of the potential application of section 68. Having said that, however, there is usually a reasonable amount of flexibility in allocating the purchase price to the various assets. Any excess that remains after allocation to the specific assets will be on account of goodwill, which will be considered an eligible capital expenditure in the hands of the purchaser.

VI. — Payment Of Purchase Price

One can pay the purchase price of a business in several ways:

- Cash;
- Issuance of debt;
- Assumption of the seller's debt;
- Exchange of property;
- Issuance of shares; or
- Some combination of the above.

Where the purchaser assumes the seller's debt, the purchase price of the acquisition is reduced by the face value of the debt assumed. If the debt carries interest, any interest paid by the purchaser on the debt is deductible[57] as an expense incurred for the purpose of earning income from a business or property.

1. — Deferred Payments

(a) — Purchaser's Perspective

The purchaser may pay the purchase price by issuing debt (promissory note) to the seller. The debt will be payable over a period of time upon agreed conditions.

Any interest payable on the debt is deductible by the purchaser as an expense incurred to earn income from the acquired business. Blended payments must be broken down into their interest and capital components.

---

[57]Para. 20(1)(c).

(b) — Reserves

Where the purchaser assumes the seller's debt, the seller will be considered to have disposed of the debt at its face amount.

Where the payment of the purchase price is deferred, the seller may be entitled to claim a reserve in respect of the payments to be made in the future. The amount and type of reserve depends upon the nature of the underlying asset sold.

(i) — Capital Property

The seller may claim a reserve in respect of that portion of the purchase price that is allocated to capital property. The reserve claimable is limited to the *lesser* of two amounts:[58]

1. A "reasonable amount"; and

2. An amount determined by reference to a formula.

The CRA accepts as "reasonable" a reserve that is calculated by reference to the following formula:

$$\frac{\text{Amount not payable until after the end of the year}}{\text{Total proceeds of sale}} \times \text{Capital gain}$$

In any event, regardless of what constitutes a "reasonable" reserve, the seller is required to recognize at least 20 per cent of the capital gain in each of the five consecutive years beginning with the year of sale.[59] In other words, the seller cannot claim a reserve that exceeds 80 per cent of the capital gain realized in the year that the capital property is sold.

(ii) — Inventory

A taxpayer who sells inventory is entitled to claim a reserve in respect of unpaid amounts that are not payable until some future date. In the case of inventory (other than land), the taxpayer may claim a reserve only if:[60]

• The proceeds from sale of the inventory were previously included in computing the taxpayer's income; and

---

[58]Subpara. 40(1)(a)(iii); IT-236R4 (archived), "Reserves — Disposition of Capital Property" (July 30, 1999).

[59]Cl. 40(1)(a)(iii)(D).

[60]Para. 20(1)(n).

- All or part of the amount payable at the end of the year is not due for at least two years after the time of sale.

In the case of land inventory the vendor may claim a reserve in respect of the profit from the sale of the property to the extent that the proceeds from the sale are payable after the end of the taxation year.

In either case, a reserve in respect of inventory may not be claimed in respect to the sale of property that occurred more than 36 months before the end of the year.[61]

VII. — Earn-Outs

One approach to the problem of uncertain valuation of a business is to structure the transaction so that the purchase price depends on the future profitability of the business. Thus, payment of the purchase price can be based on an "earn-out" or "reverse earn-out" arrangement.

In an earn-out arrangement, the purchase price may be increased in the event that the profits of the acquired business exceed a specified amount. In a reverse earn-out, the purchase price is subject to reduction in the event that the profits of the business do not attain a specified level.

Earn-outs and reverse earn-outs can be drafted in a variety of ways to accommodate the circumstances of the acquisition. By their very nature, however, earn-out agreements are complex. The parties need to specify the manner in which profits will be determined for the purposes of triggering the earn-out, the choice of accounting principles, depreciation methods, reserves, bonuses, provisions for contingencies, etc.

Having determined the manner in which profits are calculated, the parties must also resolve whether the step-up or step-down of the purchase price will be for the full variation from the threshold amount or for only some portion thereof.

1. — Vendor's Perspective

Earn-outs have serious tax consequences for the vendor. Paragraph 12(1)(g) provides that an amount paid that is dependent upon "the use of or production from property" is included in *income*, regardless whether the amount is an instalment payment on the purchase price of the property. This provision applies equally to the sale of individual assets and the sale of an entire business.[62] The vendor must include the gross amount of the earn-out payment in income, rather than only the gain on the sale of the business. Thus, paragraph 12(1)(g) con-

---

[61]Para. 20(8)(b).

[62]*Gault v. M.N.R.*, [1965] C.T.C. 261, 65 D.T.C. 5157 (Ex. Ct.).

verts what may otherwise have been a capital gain or a gain on eligible capital property (both of which would be taxable at reduced rates) into fully taxable income.

Paragraph 12(1)(g) applies to earn-out agreements that are contingent upon future earnings of the acquired business: only the variable portion of the purchase price is taxable as income, not the fixed component of the purchase price.

2. — Administrative Views

The CRA's views are set out in Interpretation Bulletin IT-462 (October 27, 1980). The Agency takes the position that:[63]

- Paragraph 12(1)(g) applies whether the sale price of the property depends upon gross income, on net income or on any other element that is related to production or use of the property.

- Where the payments under the earn-out agreement are all based on production or use, the vendor must bring into income all amounts that are received under the agreement.

- Where the agreement provides for payments based upon production or use plus a fixed sum, only the former need be taken into income under paragraph 12(1)(g) and the fixed amount may be treated as proceeds of disposition.

- Where the agreement provides for a fixed sum but with an additional amount payable upon production or use, the fixed amount is treated as proceeds of disposition and only the additional amount, if any, is brought into income under paragraph 12(1)(g).

The most difficult aspect of the Agency's position, however, is in respect of earn-out agreements that provide for both a minimum sale price and for payments based upon profitability. An earn-out agreement that provides for payments based on profitability but also stipulates that there is to be a minimum sale price will cause the payments based upon production or use to be brought into income regardless of whether they are less than or exceed the minimum sale price. In other words, the minimum sale price is not considered to be the floor of the earn-out agreement.

Paragraph 12(1)(g) does not apply to reverse earn-outs where the sale price of the business is originally set at a maximum amount that is equal to the fair market value of the assets. The portion of the fair price that is subsequently reduced if certain profitability conditions are not met is not subject to the paragraph. The entire proceeds are treated in the ordinary manner and the maximum amount is considered to be the sale price of the property. There must, however, be a reasonable expectation at the time of the disposition of the business that the profitability of the conditions will be met. If, subsequently, the conditions are not met, then

---

[63]IT-462, "Payments Based on Production or Use" (October 27, 1980).

an appropriate adjustment is made in the year in which the amount of the reduction in the sale price is known with certainty.

The purchaser of the business under a reverse earn-out agreement is not entitled to claim deductions in respect of the earn-out formula until such time as it is established with certainty that the purchaser has an absolute obligation to make the payment.[64]

VIII. — Purchase Of Shares

Where a business is operated by a corporation, a purchaser can acquire the business by buying the corporation's shares.

In most circumstances, a vendor of a business will prefer to sell the business by selling the corporation's shares. Share sales typically trigger capital gains to the vendor and only 50 per cent of capital gains are taxable as income. In contrast, an asset sale will usually trigger a mixture of ordinary income gains (recapture of depreciation, inventory) and gains that are taxable on a preferential basis (capital property and eligible capital property gains).

The determination of the share value of a corporation is a complex operation and will involve expert valuation. In a share purchase, the transaction price reflects the value of the business as a total entity, rather than the value of its individual assets. The price is usually determined by capitalizing the earnings of the business and setting as a floor the net realizable value of the business upon liquidation.

Share purchase agreements contain covenants, representations and warranties to ensure that the purchaser receives the value that was bargained for and does not take on the burden of substantial undisclosed liabilities. The representations and warranties in a share purchase agreement are critical because they go to the essence of the transaction, namely, the value bargained for in the share price.

Where the business qualifies as a "small business corporation", there is an added advantage to vendors who sell its shares rather than its assets. A gain on the sale of qualified small business corporation shares will be exempt on capital gains to a maximum of $500,000.[65]

To qualify for the capital gains exemption, the shares must satisfy three tests:[66]

1. The shares must qualify as shares of a "small business corporation" *at the time of the sale*;

---

[64]*Mandel v. The Queen*, [1980] 1 S.C.R. 318, [1980] C.T.C. 130, 80 D.T.C. 6148 (S.C.C.).

[65]See subs. 110.6(2.1).

[66]Subs. 110.6(1)"qualified small business corporation share".

2. Throughout the 24-month period prior to the sale, 50 per cent of the fair market value of the assets must be attributable to assets used in an active business carried on primarily in Canada; and

3. Throughout the 24-month period prior to the sale, the shares must not have been owned by anyone other than the vendor or a person or partnership related to the vendor.

Each of these requirements must be satisfied in order to take advantage of the exemption of capital gains.

In the event that the corporation does not qualify as a small business corporation, it can be "purified". Purification may involve a disposition of certain assets, generally through tax-free rollovers, to related corporations so as to qualify the corporation under the various percentage tests for asset use.

1. — Advantages to Purchaser

The advantages of share acquisitions are as follows:

- *Simplicity:*

    If the corporation to be acquired is a private corporation with a few shareholders, it is usually simpler to acquire the corporation's shares rather than its assets. The documentation required is an agreement and a transfer of the share certificates and an entry recording the transfer in the shareholder's register.[67]

- *Assignments:*

    A share acquisition involves a transfer of the entire corporate structure, with assets and liabilities intact. Thus, there are fewer problems with respect to the assignability of leases and other contracts; the consent of third parties is not usually required.

- *Speed:*

    The simplicity of the transfer of share certificates allows the acquisition to be accomplished in a short period of time.

- *Liabilities:*

    Since a corporation is a legal entity, its liabilities are not assumed directly by the purchaser. The corporate entity remains liable for its own liabilities and obligations; the purchaser does not become directly obligated with respect to the corporation's liabilities.

---

[67]See, for example, *Canada Business Corporations Act*, R.S.C. 1985, c. C-44, subss. 50(1), 51(1).

2. — Disadvantages to Purchaser

The disadvantages of a share acquisition include:

- *Hidden liabilities:*

    The corporation remains liable for unknown and contingent liabilities. The purchaser cannot limit liability to those specified in the acquisition contract. The purchaser may, however, obtain an indemnity for hidden and contingent liabilities.

- *Minority interests:*

    Where some shareholders of the vendor corporation refuse to sell their shares, the purchaser ends up with a corporation with outstanding minority interests.

- *Securities law:*

    An acquisition of shares may require the registration and clearance of a *prospectus* with the relevant Securities Commission.[68]

- *Compulsory acquisition of minority interests:*

    In certain jurisdictions, where a person acquires 90 per cent or more of a class of shares, the remaining shareholders of that class can require the corporation to acquire their shares.[69] This can involve a substantial cost and create cash flow problems.

3. — Timing of Acquisition

The timing of a share acquisition can be critical. The income tax status of a corporation and the tax treatment of its accounts depends sometimes upon the status of the corporation as at the *end* of the year and sometimes on its status *throughout* the year. For example:

- The small business deduction is available only to a corporation which is a Canadian-controlled private corporation *throughout* its taxation year.[70]

- The small business deduction is allocated amongst corporations that are associated with each other *at any time* in the year.[71]

---

[68]See, e.g., *Securities Act*, R.S.O. 1990, c. S.5, s. 53.

[69]See, for e.g., Ontario *Business Corporations Act*, R.S.O. 1990, c. B.16, s. 189.

[70]Subs. 125(1).

[71]Subs. 125(3).

- The Part IV tax on inter-corporate dividends is payable by a corporation that was a private corporation *at any time* in the taxation year.[72]

- Where a private corporation controlled directly or indirectly by non-resident persons becomes a Canadian-controlled private corporation, its capital dividend account is eliminated.[73]

4. — Cost Base of Shares Acquired

The adjusted cost base of the shares acquired is equal to the price paid for the shares.[74] The cost of the shares is a capital outlay and is not deductible against the future income of the corporation.

From the vendor's point of view, the sale price of the shares represents proceeds of disposition which will generally give rise to a capital gain. A vendor who is not entitled to his or her entire proceeds in the year of sale may claim a reserve against any capital gain resulting from the sale.[75] The reserve allows the seller to defer recognition of the capital gain.

5. — Covenants and Warranties

An agreement of purchase and sale of assets or shares is a contract between the purchaser and the vendor for the transmission of identified property at a determined or determinable price. Thus, the essence of the agreement is the proper identification of the parties, the property to be transferred, the manner in which the purchase price is determined or determinable, the method and timing of payments, and the manner in which undertakings and representations will be satisfied.

The purchase of a business implies reliance upon numerous facts, undertakings and assumptions as to the reliability of its financial and tax information. The purpose of representations, warranties and covenants is to ensure that the risk of non-compliance or the effect of inaccurate information is properly allocated between the purchaser and the vendor. In other words, who bears the loss when things go wrong?

To be sure, a representation, warranty or covenant is only as valuable as the financial strength and integrity of the person who makes it. It is useful in an agreement of purchase

---

[72]Subs. 186(1).

[73]Subs. 89(1.1).

[74]S. 54"adjusted cost base" (b).

[75]Para. 40(1)(a).

and sale, however, to anticipate where and how things can go wrong and to provide in advance for the allocation of responsibility for the essential terms of the agreement.

From a tax perspective, representations and warranties serve the same general purpose: they support the financial and tax assumptions on which the acquisition is premised and provide for an appropriate adjustment or remedy in the event of non-compliance or failure to meet contractual expectations.

A taxpayer must include in his income all amounts that he receives (or are receivable) on account of a restrictive covenant.[76] The Act defines "restrictive covenant" broadly. This rule does not apply if the taxpayer includes a non-competition payment in his employment income under sections 5 or 6. Payments in conjunction with a sale of shares may be taxable as on account of capital.

6. — Interest on Borrowed Money

Interest expense to finance a purchase of shares is generally deductible in computing the purchaser's income if the expense is incurred to earn business or property income.[77]

7. — Losses

A corporation is generally entitled to carry back and carry forward its net capital losses and non-capital losses to reduce its income in other periods. Non-capital losses may be carried back for three years and forward for ten years.[78] Net capital losses incurred may be carried back three years and carried forward indefinitely.[79]

(a) — Change of Control

The ability to carry forward corporate losses can be an important factor in a share acquisition. At its simplest level, the purchaser can put a profitable business into the corporation and utilize its accumulated losses to absorb the profits from the new business for the next seven years. There are, however, stringent and complex rules restricting the streaming of

---

[76]See subs. 56.4(2).

[77]Para. 20(1)(c); see subs. 248(1)"exempt income" (dividends on shares excluded from definition); *Ludco Enterprises v. Canada*, [1999] 3 C.T.C. 601, 99 D.T.C. 5153 (Eng.) (F.C.A.); leave to appeal allowed (2000), 225 N.R. 200 (note) (S.C.C.); revd. (2001), [2001] 2 S.C.R. 1082, [2002] 1 C.T.C. 95 (S.C.C.).

[78]Para. 111(1)(a) (rule applying to non-capital losses after 1982).

[79]Para. 111(1)(b).

losses upon a change of control of a corporation. The rationale for these rules is to discourage speculative trading in "loss corporations".

(i) — Timing

The timing of a share acquisition is an important determinant in the treatment of corporate losses.

Where control of a corporation changes, the Act deems the corporation to end its taxation year immediately before the change of control occurs.[80] This deemed year-end rule has important consequences for the corporation because it fixes the time at which the corporation's gains and losses must be accounted for and their subsequent treatment.

The Act deems the corporation to commence a new taxation year immediately after the acquisition of control. Since the corporation does not have a fiscal period before the deemed new year, it may adopt a new fiscal year-end without regard to any prior fiscal periods that may have been in effect at the time that control changed hands. The deemed change in year end rule does not apply to foreign affiliates.[81]

The Act deems the control of a corporation to have been acquired at the commencement of the day on which control is acquired, regardless of the actual time at which the transaction is finally consummated.[82]

(ii) — Control

The term "control" refers to *de jure* control and not *de facto* control.[83] Thus, control means the right of control that rests in ownership of such a number of shares of a corporation that ensures majority voting power. In most cases, ownership of the common shares of the corporation determines by whom the corporation is controlled. There are, however, circumstances where preferred shares may carry more votes than the common shares. In these circumstances, control may lie with the preferred shareholders and not with the common shareholders.

---

[80]Para. 249(4)(a).

[81]Subss. 249(4); 95(1)"taxation year".

[82]Subs. 256(9).

[83]See IT-302R3, "Losses of a Corporation — The Effect that Acquisition of Control, Amalgamations and Windings-up Have on their Deductibility — After 1987" (February 28, 1994).

The loss streaming rules are triggered upon an acquisition of control "by a person or group of persons."[84] The term "person" includes an individual, trustee, and another corporation.

The phrase "group of persons" is not defined for the purposes of these rules. It is, however, generally accepted by the CRA that in order to constitute a "group", the members must have a common link or interest, or act together to control the corporation.[85] The acquisition of a corporation through a management buy-out, for example, would constitute a change of control by a group of persons because the employees would be a clearly identifiable group with a common interest.

The loss streaming provisions apply only upon an *acquisition* of control and not upon a change of control. Hence, for example, a corporation that goes public does not usually trigger the loss streaming provisions because, although there may be a divestment of control by some shareholders, there is not an acquisition of control by a new group of persons. The new shareholders in a public offering are usually total strangers to each other and do not have any common link or interest. To constitute a group there must be a common link between persons.[86]

(iii) — Related Parties

Related-party transactions do not give rise to a change of control for the purposes of the loss streaming rules.[87]

(b) — Non-Capital Losses

Stringent loss streaming rules apply on the change of control of a corporation. The corporation's accumulated non-capital and farm losses are deductible from income, but only if the corporation carries on its business for profit, or with a reasonable expectation of profit, *throughout* the year in which the deduction is claimed.[88]

Non-capital and farm losses may be deducted only against income from the business that created the loss. If the business has sold, leased or rented its properties that were previously used in the business, its non-capital and farm losses are deductible against the income de-

---

[84]Subss. 111(4) and (5).

[85]See RCRT, 1988 Conference Report, 53:1–188, Question 40 and RCRT, *Report of Proceedings of the Thirty-Sixth Tax Conference*, 1984 Conference Report, 783–847, Question 42, at 816-17.

[86]*Silicon Graphics Ltd. v. R.*, [2002] 3 C.T.C. 527, 2002 D.T.C. 7112 (Fed. C.A.).

[87]Subs. 256(7).

[88]Subs. 111(5).

rived from the sale, lease or rental of the properties, if substantially all of the income is derived from such activities.

Thus, the loss business must be identified in order to determine whether non-capital losses can be applied against the business. Whether two or more operations of an enterprise constitute a single or separate businesses depends upon the degree of their interconnection, interlacing, and interdependence.[89] One looks to factors such as:

- Manufacturing processes,
- Product lines,
- Customer groups,
- Service lines,
- Common inventory,
- Employee groups, and
- Common use of machinery, plant and equipment.

Two or more operations that use the same physical premises, share common supplies, use an interchangeable labour force and a common administration are considered a single business.

Non-capital and farm losses may also be carried back three years and applied against the income of the corporation in those years. Where, however, there has been a change of control of a corporation, its non-capital or farm loss from carrying on a business is deductible in a year preceding the change of control only if, *throughout* the taxation year in which the loss arose and in the particular taxation year, the corporation carried on its business for profit or with a reasonable expectation of profit.[90]

(c) — Net Capital Losses

The rules in respect of net capital losses upon change of control are even more stringent: net capital losses from preceding years may not be carried forward[91] or carried back to reduce the income of taxation years subsequent or prior to the change of control.[92]

But capital losses incurred *in the year* in which control changes are not affected by this prohibition. Hence, a business should trigger capital gains in the year of change of control to

---

[89] IT-206R, "Separate Businesses" (October 29, 1979).

[90] Para. 111(5)(b).

[91] Para. 111(4)(a).

[92] Para. 111(4)(b).

utilize any capital losses. This is particularly important because the Act deems accrued capital losses or non-depreciable capital property to be realized in the year of change of control.[93]

8. — Prior Years' Taxes

The purchaser of shares should determine the tax assessment status of the vendor. The CRA has three years (longer, in some cases) from the date of its assessment within which it may reassess the taxpayer. The three-year period may be extended by waivers granted by the corporation. This potential liability should be taken into account in structuring the agreement of purchase and sale. The purchaser might use a right of set-off against the purchase price.

IX. — Anti-Avoidance Rules

1. — General Comment

A disposition of shares that constitute capital property gives rise to proceeds of disposition. The difference between the proceeds of disposition and the adjusted cost base of the shares is a capital gain.[94] In most cases, the vendor will want to minimize the amount of the taxable capital gain.

2. — "Capital Gains Strips"

The most obvious method of reducing what might otherwise be a taxable capital gain is to convert the proceeds of disposition into a non-taxable inter-corporate dividend.[95] For example, *in the absence of special anti-avoidance rules*, a corporate taxpayer that wanted to sell its shareholdings in another corporation might arrange to receive a tax-free dividend from the purchaser corporation in exchange for reducing the selling price of the shares sold by the amount of the dividend. The vendor corporation would reduce the proceeds of disposition on the sale of the shares and, as such, reduce its taxable capital gain.

Consider the following additional example. X and Y are shareholders of an operating corporation, ("Opco"). X would like to buy Y's shares; if X purchases the shares directly, Y will realize a capital gain. To avoid the gain, Y rolls over his or her shares to a holding corporation, ("Holdco"). Opco in turn purchases Y's shares for cancellation from Holdco. Any

---

[93]Para. 111(4)(c).

[94]Para. 39(1)(a).

[95]Subs. 112(1) (such transaction referred to as "capital gains strip", which is reverse of "dividend strip").

amount paid for the shares in excess of their paid-up capital is deemed to be a dividend. Since the dividend is paid by one corporation to another, it is non-taxable. In effect, Y would have converted what would otherwise have been a taxable capital gain on the disposition of his or her shares into a non-taxable inter-corporate dividend.

3. — Anti-Avoidance Measures

In certain circumstances, the Act deems a tax-free inter-corporate dividend to be a capital gain or proceeds of disposition.[96] This rule, which is directed squarely at preventing a "capital gains strip" of the type described above, applies where:[97]

1. The taxpayer is a corporation resident in Canada;

2. The taxpayer is in receipt of a taxable dividend in respect of which it is entitled to a deduction in respect of inter-corporate dividends;[98]

3. The dividend is part of a transaction, event or series of transactions or events *one* of the purposes of which was to significantly reduce the amount of capital gain that would otherwise have been recognized; and

4. The capital gain that would otherwise have been recognized is reasonably attributable to *anything* other than the corporation's post-1971 income.

In such circumstances, the Act deems the dividend not to be a dividend for most tax purposes. Instead, if the shares on which the dividend was paid have been disposed of, the amount of the dividend is added to the proceeds of disposition. If the shares have not been disposed of, the dividend is deemed to be a capital gain. This rule applies only to taxable dividends, whether received or deemed to have been received; it does not apply to non-taxable dividends paid out of the capital dividend account of a corporation.

The rule can apply even where the transaction or series of transactions is business motivated and not entered into for tax avoidance. Thus, the rule applies if *one* of the purposes of the transaction, event or series of transactions was to effect a significant reduction in the amount of the capital gain that would otherwise be realized. In other words, the taxpayer must show that *none* of the purposes of the transactions was to reduce the capital gain that would otherwise be realized.[99]

---

[96]Subs. 55(2).

[97]Subs. 55(2).

[98]See subs. 112(1).

[99]*Placer Dome Inc. v. R.* (1996), [1997] 1 C.T.C. 72, 96 D.T.C. 6562 (Fed. C.A.).

Where the taxable dividend is a deemed dividend under subsection 84(3), the rule applies if it can be shown that one of the *results* of the transaction, event or series of transactions was the reduction of the capital gain that would otherwise have been realized.

What constitutes a "significant reduction" of a capital gain is a question of fact. It may relate to the absolute dollar amount of the capital gain, or it may be determined by looking at the percentage reduction of the gain.[100]

The rule does not apply in respect of dividends paid out of post-1971 earnings, that is, out of "taxed retained earnings". This income is sometimes referred to as "safe income", and the dividend paid out of such income is referred to as a "safe dividend".

The anti-avoidance rule does not apply to rearrangements of shareholder interests where the parties are *not* related to each other (for example, in typical estate planning reorganizations), or dividends received in the course of a reorganization of capital intended to "demerge" a corporation by means of a "butterfly" transaction.[101]

4. — "Butterfly" Reorganizations

A "butterfly" reorganization describes a transaction in which two or more shareholders of a corporation undertake to dissolve their business relationship in a tax-free manner, such that each shareholder (or corporation) ends up with an undivided interest in the *pro rata* share of the assets previously owned by the corporation.[102] The "butterfly" is used to divide up corporate assets amongst shareholders who cannot resolve their differences and who wish to terminate their business relationship.

Typically, a "butterfly" reorganization involves four steps which are designed to allow a corporation to divest its assets to its shareholders in such a manner that the shareholders acquire their *pro rata* share of property from the distributing corporation on a tax-free basis.

Example

Assume:

Two shareholders, A and B, each own 50 per cent of the shares of an operating company ("Opco"). They would like to "splinter" Opco in a tax-efficient manner, so that they each end up with 50 per cent of its assets within their own corporations.

---

[100]The Agency appears to look at the absolute dollar amount of the reduction.

[101]Para. 55(3)(b).

[102]See, for example, TR-99, "Transfer of Shares to a Holding Company Followed by their Redemption" (May 23, 1980).

Example

Then:

Step 1:

A and B each incorporate a holding company, Holdco A and Holdco B, to which they transfer their respective shareholdings in Opco; they elect under subsection 85(1) so that the transfer occurs on a tax-free basis.

> Thus, Holdco A and Holdco B, each of which owns 50 per cent of Opco, become holding companies.

Step 2:

Opco transfers 1/2 of its assets to each of Holdco A and Holdco B in exchange for redeemable shares of the holding companies. Once again the transfers are executed on a tax-free basis under subsection 85(1). Typically, the redeemable shares of the holding companies have a paid-up capital that does not exceed the adjusted cost base of the shares to Opco.

> Now, Holdco A and Holdco B own the assets previously owned by Opco.
> Opco is reduced to a shell corporation that owns only redeemable shares in the holding companies.

Step 3:

The holding companies, Holdco A and Holdco B, redeem their shares from Opco at fair market value. The difference between the redemption price and the paid-up capital of the shares is deemed to be a dividend to Opco, and is received as a tax-free inter-corporate dividend. There is no capital gain.

> Now, Opco has only cash and no other assets.

Step 4:

Opco is wound up into the holding companies, Holdco A and Holdco B, and distributes its cash to the companies.

> Now, each of the holding companies of the individual shareholders, A and B respectively, owns one-half of the assets formerly owned by Opco. Since A owns all of the shares of Holdco A, and B owns all of the shares of Holdco B, they have achieved their objective.

The "butterfly" reorganization is an exception to the rules in respect of "capital gains strips". The importance of this is that a deemed dividend resulting from a redemption of shares or winding-up in the course of a butterfly is not considered a capital gain. Hence, it is fully deductible as an inter-corporate dividend.

There are other variations of the butterfly, but they all involve the same techniques: a divestment of assets into one or more new corporations under the protection of subsection 85(1) in return for redeemable shares that have a low paid-up capital and a high redemption value. The redemption of the shares gives rise to a deemed dividend which is not taxable;[103] the capital gain that would otherwise have been realized on a direct divestment of the assets to the individual shareholders is thereby avoided.

In addition to ensuring that each step in a butterfly reorganization conforms to the relevant corporate law, particular care must be taken to avoid running afoul of the following provisions:

- Subsection 15(1) (shareholder benefits);
- Subsection 56(2) (indirect payments);
- Paragraph 85(1)(e.2) (indirect gifts); and
- Section 245 (GAAR).

X. — Statutory Amalgamations

Another method of acquiring a business is by way of statutory amalgamation. In an amalgamation, two or more corporations are merged to become one. All of the assets and liabilities of the merged corporations are carried over into the newly-formed corporation.[104]

1. — Advantages

There are several advantages to statutory amalgamations:

- *Simplicity of title transfers:*

    The title to the assets of an amalgamated corporation passes to the new corporation by operation of law.

- *Elimination of minority interests:*

    Minority shareholders who object to an amalgamation have the right to dissent, and can be bought out at the fair value of their shares.

---

[103]Subs. 84(3).

[104]See, e.g., *Canada Business Corporations Act*, ss. 181, 186.

- *Tax-free rollover:*

  An amalgamation that conforms to the requirements of the Act can be implemented on a tax-free basis.[105]

2. — Disadvantages

There are also some disadvantages:

- *Assumption of liabilities:*

  The new corporation continues to be liable for all the debts and obligations of the
  amalgamated corporations, whether such debts have been disclosed or not and
  whether such debts are contingent or known.

- *Shareholders' meetings:*

  An amalgamation requires two shareholders' meetings; both the buyer and the
  seller corporations are generally required to approve the transaction.

- *Appraisal remedy:*

  Shareholders of the amalgamating corporations who object to the amalgamation
  are entitled to be paid in cash for the fair value of their shares. Where there are a
  substantial number of dissenting shareholders, the cash outflow to purchase their
  shares may be a drain on the new corporation. In addition, the determination of the
  fair value of shares can be troublesome.

XI. — Non-Residents

The residence of the vendor corporation and/or its shareholders are important tax considerations in the acquisition of a business.

Where the vendor is a non-resident of Canada, there are additional income tax requirements:

- The purchaser requires a section 116 clearance certificate from the vendor (in the case
  of an asset acquisition) or from the vendor's shareholders (in the case of a share
  acquisition);

- Tax must be withheld under Part XIII on payments of certain amounts (for example,
  interest) to non-residents;

- Payments to non-residents may be affected by double taxation treaties between Canada
  and the country of the vendor's residence.

---

[105]See s. 87.

1. — Section 116 Clearance Certificate

Section 116 of the Act is intended to ensure that the vendor discharges his or her Canadian income tax obligations that may arise from the sale of property. The section contemplates two mechanisms. A non-resident vendor who *proposes* to dispose of taxable Canadian property can pre-pay 25 per cent of the estimated value of the gain that will result from the proposed disposition of the property. The vendor can estimate the anticipated proceeds of disposition, determine the gain that will result from the disposition and disclose the name and address of the proposed purchaser of the property together with a description of the property itself. The Minister then issues a certificate of clearance on payment of 25 per cent of the estimated gain or upon the deposit of acceptable security in lieu thereof.

2. — Purchaser's Liability

Obtaining a clearance certificate under section 116 is, technically speaking, an optional procedure insofar as the vendor is concerned. Where the vendor does not obtain a clearance certificate, the Act provides for an alternative mechanism to collect the vendor's tax: the purchaser of the property becomes liable to pay. The amount of the purchaser's liability depends upon the nature of the property purchased.

The purchaser's liability in respect of non-depreciable capital property purchased from a non-resident is equal to 25 per cent of the *cost* of the property. This liability is reduced if the vendor obtains a clearance certificate in which case the purchaser is liable for 25 per cent of the amount by which the amount of the final consideration actually paid exceeds the amount estimated for the purposes of the certificate.

The Act purportedly empowers the purchaser to recover the full amount of the tax from the non-resident vendor. This may be a difficult provision to enforce and should not be relied upon as a substitute for proper withholding. In any event, it is a dubious proposition as to how the federal tax statute confers powers upon a purchaser that fall clearly within the property and civil rights jurisdiction of the provinces.[106]

Hence, it is clearly in the purchaser's interest to either withhold 25 per cent of the purchase price of non-depreciable taxable Canadian property until such time as the purchaser obtains a clearance certificate for the proper amount. Otherwise, the purchaser becomes liable to pay the tax (or shortfall in tax) within 30 days after the end of the month in which the property is acquired.[107]

---

[106]*Constitution Act, 1867* (U.K.), 30 & 31 Vict., c. 3, s. 92(13).

[107]Subs. 116(5).

The purchaser's liability for tax increases to 50 per cent of the purchase price in the case of depreciable taxable Canadian property.[108] The increase is justified on the basis that the tax liability on appreciated depreciable property will generally trigger not only a potential capital gain but also recapture of capital cost allowance.

Thus, the purchaser should determine the breakdown between depreciable and non-depreciable capital property in order to ascertain how much should be withheld from the proceeds. This will necessarily create some uncertainty because the allocation between depreciable and non-depreciable property and the classification of assets may be the subject of differing opinions and negotiation.

3. — Due Diligence

The purchaser is not liable to withhold any tax on behalf of the vendor if the purchaser is diligent and makes reasonable inquiries on the basis of which the purchaser comes to the conclusion that the vendor is resident in Canada. The CRA takes the view that "reasonable inquiry" requires the purchaser to at least enquire of the vendor's solicitor or agent as to the vendor's place of residence. A positive statement from the vendor that he or she is a Canadian resident is generally enough to satisfy the Agency that there was a sufficiently reasonable inquiry to relieve the purchaser of any withholding tax obligations in respect of the purchase.[109]

XII. — Third Party Liability For Taxes

Section 160 of the Act imposes potential liability on third parties who receive property from a person with whom they do not deal with at arm's length. The section renders the third party potentially liable for the vendor's taxes owing at the time that the property was sold. The liability is limited in amount to the shortfall between the consideration paid and the fair market value of the property purchased.

Section 160 has far reaching and enduring consequences for a non-arm's length purchaser because it can be triggered long after the date on which the property was purchased. The section does not have any limitation period. The Minister may reassess the vendor several years after the sale of the property and determine, retroactively, that the vendor was indeed liable for taxes at the date of the transfer of property.

Thus, the purchaser should obtain a representation that no taxes are owing by the vendor that have not been declared in the agreement of purchase and sale. The agreement should also

---

[108]Subs. 116(5.3).

[109]IC 72-17R5, "Procedures Concerning the Disposition of Taxable Canadian Property by Non-residents of Canada — Section 116" (March 15, 2005).

provide for indemnification (with or without holdbacks) of the purchaser if a subsequent assessment determines that the vendor is liable for back taxes as at the date that the property was transferred.

Selected Bibliography to Chapter 30

General

Ahmed, Firoz "Debt Forgiveness Rules and Share Purchase Transactions" (1995) 5 Can. Current Tax 58.

Ahmed, Firoz and Sarah Gagan, "Amalgamations after Pan Ocean", (1994) Can. Current Tax J71.

Albo, Wayne P., and Randal A. Henderson, *Mergers and Acquisitions of Privately Held Businesses*, 2nd ed. (Toronto: Can. Inst. of Chartered Accountants, 1989).

Bernstein, Jack, "Corporate Spin-Offs and Creditor Proofing", in *Proceedings of 39th Tax Conf.* 30:1 (Can. Tax Foundation, 1987).

Bernstein, Jack, "Sale of Businesses to Employees: The Leveraged Buy-Out", *Corp. Mgmt. Tax* Conf. 116 (Can. Tax Foundation, 1985).

Boultbee, Jack A., and Douglas S. Ewens, "The Taxation of Corporate Reorganizations" (1986) 24 Can. Tax J. 203.

Buying and Selling a Business — 1991 (Vancouver: Continuing Legal Education Society of British Columbia, 1991).

Cadesky, Michael, "Corporate Losses" in *Proceedings of 42nd Tax Conf.* 19:1 (Can. Tax Foundation, 1990).

Campbell, Ian R., "Valuation-related Issues: Tax Planning and Post-transaction Follow-ups" in *Proceedings of 45th Tax Conf.* (Can. Tax Foundation, 1993).

"Case Study", *Corp. Mgmt. Tax Conf.* 157 (Can. Tax Foundation, 1972).

Colley, Geoffrey M., "Assets or Shares: What does the Purchaser Want?" (1974) 104 CA Magazine 54.

Colley, Geoffrey M., "Tax Planning Implications for New Business" (1980) 113 CA Magazine 78.

Cooke, Philip J., and Jonathan Fox, *Effective Tax Strategies for Corporate Acquisitions* (Deventer, The Netherlands: Kluver, 1986).

Corn, George, "Acquisition of Unrealized Capital Losses — Tax Avoidance" (1995) 5 Can. Current Tax 53.

Dalsin, Derek J., "Dispositions of Property by Non-residents: Tax Deferral by Ministerial Discretion" (1991) Can. Tax J. 77.

Dancey, Kevin J., "Specific Expenditures: Timing and Deductibility", *Corp. Mgmt. Tax Conf.* 116 (Can. Tax Foundation, 1981).

Dart, Robert J., and David W. Smith, "Estate Planning: A New Era", (1986) 34 Can. Tax J. 1.

Ewens, Douglas S., "Debt-for-Debt Exchanges" (1991) 39 Can. Tax J. 1615.

Ewens, Douglas S., "New Consideration In Structuring Share-for-Share Exchange Offers" (1988) 36 Can. Tax J. 449.

Ewens, Douglas S., "Winding-Up of Corporations Otherwise than under Section 88 (The): An Update" (1975) 23 Can. Tax J. 352.

Forster, David, C.A., "The Purchase and Sale of Assets of a Business: Selected Tax Aspects", *Corp. Mgmt. Tax Conf.* 2:1 (Can. Tax Foundation, 1990).

Gordon, Donald M., "Intercompany Non-Arm's Length Transactions — Income Tax Consequences", in *Proceedings of 26th Tax Conf.* 69 (Can. Tax Foundation, 1974).

Grashuk, Harry S., "The Professional Corporation in Alberta" (1977) 25 Can. Tax J. 109.

Haney, K.S.M., "Current Cases — Allocation of Purchase Price" (1988) 36 Can. Tax J. 170.

Haney, M.A., "Current Cases — Non-Arm's Length — A Question of Fact" (1987) 35 Can. Tax J. 1256.

Haney, M.A., "Current Cases — Sale of Shares of a Corporation Formed for Land Development — Capital Gain or Income?" (1986) 34 Can. Tax J. 607.

Hanson, Suzanne I.R., "Planning for a Share Sale" in *Proceedings of 44th Tax Conf.* 27:1 (Can. Tax Foundation, 1992).

Hanson, Suzanne I.R., "Tax and Estate Planning for Specific Assets", in *Proceedings of 39th Tax Conf.* 40:1 (Can. Tax Foundation, 1987).

Hogg, Roy D., C.A., "Corporate Distributions: The Proposed Part II.1 Tax", in *Proceedings of 39th Tax Conf.* 31:1 (Can. Tax Foundation, 1987).

Houle, Louis, "Acquisition Agreements: Specific Tax Clauses" (1991) 39 Can. Tax J. 1245.

Howick, Wallace M., "Assets Versus Shares: An Approach to the Alternatives", *Corp. Mgmt. Tax Conf.* 1:1 (Can. Tax Foundation, 1990).

Kingson, Charles I., "Liquidations, Branches, and Losses: 1986 Changes in U.S. Tax Law", in *Proceedings of 38th Tax Conf.* 30:1 (Can. Tax Foundation, 1986).

Kroft, E.G., "Tax Clauses in Acquisition Agreements", *Corp. Mgmt. Tax Conf.* 9:1 (Can. Tax Foundation, 1990).

Jones, D. Alan, "Business Equity Valuations and Real Estate Appraisals in Revenue Canada" in *Proceedings of 45th Tax Conf.* 26:1 (Can. Tax Foundation, 1993).

Laflamme, Pierre, "Acquisition Strategies" in *Proceedings of 45th Tax Conf.* 13:1 (Can. Tax Foundation, 1993).

Lahmer, Craig, C.A., "Acquisition-of-Control Rules", *Corp. Mgmt. Tax Conf.* 4:1 (Can. Tax Foundation, 1990).

Larter, Ronald W., C.A., "Capital Cost Allowance and Eligible Capital Property: Tax Reform Implications", in *Proceedings of 40th Tax Conf.* 27:1 (Can. Tax Foundation, 1988).

Loveland, Norman C., "Acquisition of a US Business by Canadians: A US Perspective", *Corp. Mgmt. Tax Conf.* 11:1 (Can. Tax Foundation, 1990).

MacDonald, Nancy, "Amalgamations Following Guaranty Properties Limited" (1991) 39 Can. Tax J. 1399.

Mallin, Michael G., "Organizing and Reorganizing to Ensure 'Qualified Small Business Corporation Share' Status — Part 1: Preserving Existing 'Qualified Small Business Corporation' Share Status" (1990) 38 Can. Tax J. 745.

Mallin, Michael G., "Organizing and Reorganizing to Ensure 'Qualified Small Business Corporation Share' Status — Part 2: The Purification Transaction" (1990) 38 Can. Tax. J. 1026.

Mayo, Wayne, "Interest, Exempt Income and Inter-Corporate Dividends" (1987) 4 Australian Tax Forum 123–42.

McCallum, J. Thomas, *Amalgamations and Wind-ups* (Vancouver: Certified General Accountants' Association of Canada, 1994).

McCrodan, Andrew, "Tackling Tax-related Troubles" (1993) CA Magazine No. 4 45.

McDonnell, T.F., "Current Cases — Sale of a Business as a Going Concern — Whether Vendor's Gain Is Calculated By Reference to Total Package or Individual Assets" (1986) 34 Can. Tax J. 398.

Meghji, Al, "Collateralized Preferred Shares" (1987) 35 Can. Tax J. 467.

Mida, Israel H., C.A., "Goods and Services Tax (The) and Corporate Matters", in *Proceedings of 42nd Tax Conf.*, 14:1 (Can. Tax Foundation, 1990).

Mida, Israel H., C.A., "Goods and Services Tax (The) and Corporate Reorganizations — Part 1" (1990) 38 Can. Tax J. 1524.

Mida, Israel H., C.A., "Goods and Services Tax (The) and Corporate Reorganizations — Part 2" (1990) 38 Can. Tax J. 1524.

Mida, Israel H., C.A., "More on Intragroup Transfers" (1986) 34 Can. Tax J. 1184.

Middleton, David W., C.A., "Common Tax Problems and Pitfalls in Effecting Reorganizations of Private Corporations", in *Proceedings of 41st Tax Conf.* 13:1 (Can. Tax Foundation, 1989).

Mitchener, Donald G., "By Gosh! The Price May Not Be Right!" (1974) 104 CA Magazine 69.

Moore, D.H., "Current Cases — Non-Arm's Length in Fact" (1986) 34 Can. Tax J. 148.

Morrow, Robert G., "Purchasing and Selling a Business" (1973) 7 CGA Magazine 4.

Neville, Ralph J., "Acquisition of Control and Corporate Losses" in *Proceedings of 44th Tax Conf.* 25:5 (Can. Tax Foundation, 1992).

"New Strategies for Corporate Acquisitions", *Corp. Mgmt. Tax Conf.* (Can. Tax Foundation, 1978).

Novis, Derrick A., C.A., "Provisions That Restrict or Deny Losses and Corporate Attribution", in *Proceedings of 41st Tax Conf.* 14:1 (Can. Tax Foundation, 1989).

O'Brien, "Corporate Acquisitions and Amalgamations", (1972) Special Lectures LSUC 319.

O'Brien, "Sale of Assets: The Vendor's Position", *Corp. Mgmt. Tax Conf.* 1 (Can. Tax Foundation, 1972).

O'Keefe, Michael J., "Surplus Stripping After Tax Reform", in *Proceedings of 40th Tax Conf.* 17:1 (Can. Tax Foundation, 1988).

Perry, F. Brenton, "Capitalization and Asset Acquisitions for New Private Corporations" in *Proceedings of 45th Tax Conf.* 22:1 (Can. Tax Foundation, 1993).

Pister, Tom, "Paragraph 88(1)(d) Bump On The Winding Up of a Subsidiary — Part 1" (1990) 38 Can. Tax J. 148.

Pister, Tom, "Paragraph 88(1)(d) Bump On The Winding Up of a Subsidiary — Part 2" (1990) 38 Can. Tax J. 426.

Promislow, Norm, "Legal and Taxation Issues Affecting Estates With Certain Business Assets", in *Proceedings of 39th Tax Conf.* 41:1 (Can. Tax Foundation, 1987).

Pullen, K.T., and Howard J. Kellough, "Tax Treatment of Inter-corporate Dividends, Grandfathering Provisions, and the Use of Press Releases", *Corp. Mgmt. Tax Conf.* 3:1 (Can. Tax Foundation, 1987).

Read, Robert J.L., C.A., "Section 55: A Review of Current Issues", in *Proceedings of 40th Tax Conf.* 18:1 (Can. Tax Foundation, 1988).

Reid, Robert J., "Capital and Non-capital Losses" in *Proceedings of 42nd Tax Conf.* 20:1 (Can. Tax Foundation, 1990).

Resendes, Ray, Alan Smolal and Audrey Diamant, "Commodity Tax Implications of Corporate Reorganizations" (1989) 37 Can. Tax J. 171.

Richards, Gabrielle M.R., "No Relief for Revenue Canada's Carelessness: *City Centre Properties v. The Queen* Federal Court — Trial Division (1994) 4 Can. Current Tax J53.

Richardson, Douglas K., and Christopher H. Hanna, "US Tax Treatment of Cross-Border Acquisitive Reorganizations — Part 1" (1989) 37 Can. Tax J. 1074.

Richardson, Douglas K., and Christopher H. Hanna, "US Tax Treatment of Cross-Border Acquisitive Reorganizations — Part 2" (1989) 37 Can. Tax J. 1318.

Richardson, Elinore J., "Financing Business Acquisitions", *Corp. Mgmt. Tax Conf.* 7:1 (Can. Tax Foundation, 1990).

Richardson, Stephen R., "Purchase and Sale of a Business: Income Tax Aspects of Warranties, Price Adjustments, and Earn-outs", *Corp. Mgmt. Tax Conf.* 10:1 (Can. Tax Foundation, 1990).

Richter, Kirsten, "The Removal of Accrued Gains in Capital Stock Holdings through the Use of 'Safe Income'" (1991) 39 Can. Tax J. 1349.

Rohde, Richard C., "Section 85 Transfers — Limitations and Pitfalls" (1988) 36 Can. Tax J. 1302.

Rosenfeld, "Corporate Acquisitions", (1972) Special Lectures LSUC 367.

Sanderson, Anne C., "The Economics of Taxation" (1991) 39 Can. Tax J. 408.

Sanger, John H., "Tax Planning with Income Averaging Annuities" (1977) 110 CA Magazine 72.

Scace, Arthur, R.A., Q.C., "Tax Aspects of Some Takeover Defences", in *Proceedings of 38th Tax Conf.* 6:1 (Can. Tax Foundation, 1986).

Schwartz, Alan M., "Statutory Amalgamations, Arrangements, and Continuations: Tax and Corporate Law Considerations" in *Proceedings of 43rd Tax Conf.* 9:1 (Can. Tax Foundation, 1991).

Scobell, "Tax Treatment of Losses", *Corp. Mgmt. Tax Conf.* 119 (Can. Tax Foundation, 1975).

Segal, Brian D., "Disposition of Interests in and Options on Real Property and Shares by Non-residents of Canada" (1994) 42 Can. Tax J. 327.

"Selected Income Tax and Goods and Services Tax Aspects of the Purchase and Sale of a Business", *Corp. Mgmt. Tax Conf.* (Can. Tax Foundation, 1990).

"Shareholders' Agreements — Revisited" (1985) 33 Can. Tax J. 835.

Sider, Vance A., *Butterfly Reorganizations* (Don Mills, Ont.: CCH Can., 1989).

Sider, Vance A., "Corporate Restructuring Issues: Private Corporations", *Corp. Mgmt. Tax Conf.* 5:1 (Can. Tax Foundation, 1990).

Silver, "Surplus Stripping: A Practitioner's View" (1974) 21 Can. Tax J. 430.

Simpson, Muriel A., "Planning Around the New Paid-up Capital Restrictions" (1986) 34 Can. Tax J. 646.

Sinclair, B.R., "Paid-Up Capital" (1986) 34 Can. Tax J. 1483.

Sinclair, B.R., "Some Income Tax Aspects of Privatization" (1988) 36 Can. Tax J. 734.

Smith, David W., Q.C., "Corporate Restructuring Issues: Public Corporations", *Corp. Mgmt. Tax Conf.* 7:1 (Can. Tax Foundation, 1990).

Sohmer, David H., "Purchase and Sale of a Closely-Held Business (2)" (1979) 112 CA Magazine 70.

Spindler, Robert, "Mutual Fund Reorganizations" (1987) 35 Can. Tax J. 736.

Spindler, R.J., "New Part II.1 Tax (The)" (1987) 35 Can. Tax J. 1292.

Stacey, John A., "Transfer of Assets to and from a Corporation", in *Proceedings of 40th Tax Conf.* 14:1 (Can. Tax Foundation, 1988).

Stacey, John A., "Treatment of Losses (The)", in *Proceedings of 35th Tax Conf.* 29 (Can. Tax Foundation, 1983).

Steiss, Carl F., "Acquisition and Disposition of a Canadian Business by a Non-Resident", *Corp. Mgmt. Tax Conf.* 13:1 (Can. Tax Foundation, 1990).

Swiderski, Tony, "Transfer of US Real Property Interest in Canadian Reorganizations: Opportunities, Limitations, and Pitfalls" (1989) 37 Can. Tax J. 605.

Templeton, Wendy, "Anti-Avoidance and the Capital Gains Exemption: Part 2" (1986) 34 Can Tax J. 446.

Tillinghast, David R., "Acquisition of a US Business by Canadians: A US Perspective", *Corp. Mgmt. Tax Conf.* 12:1 (Can. Tax Foundation, 1990).

Vuketz, Michael C., "Structural Issues in Utilization of Domestic Loss Carryforward Pools" in *Proceedings of 45th Tax Conf.* 23:1 (Can. Tax Foundation, 1993).

Walker, "Acquisitions from Non-Residents: Section 116" (1972) 20 Can. Tax J. 131.

Ward, "Tax Considerations Relating to the Purchase of Assets of a Business", *Corp. Mgmt. Tax Conf.* 22 (Can. Tax Foundation, 1972).

Webb, "Escalator Clauses, Earn-outs and Reserves", in *Proceedings of 26th Tax Conf.* 555 (Can. Tax Foundation, 1974).

Wentzell, D.G., "Current Cases — Minister's Advantage (The) — Interest on Instalments" (1987) 35 Can. Tax J. 968.

Wentzell, D.G., "Current Cases — Section 68 — The Grave of a Paper Tiger" (1986) 34 Can. Tax J. 395.

Williamson, David M., C.A., "Checklists: Corporate Reorganizations, Amalgamations (Section 87), and Wind-Ups (Subsection 88(1))", in *Proceedings of 39th Tax Conf.* 29:1 (Can. Tax Foundation, 1987).

Williamson, Gordon W., C.A., "Recent Developments Affecting Corporate Reorganizations", in *Proceedings of 42nd Tax Conf.* 13:1 (Can. Tax Foundation, 1990).

Williamson, Gordon W., C.A., "Transfers of Assets to and from a Canadian Corporation", in *Proceedings of 38th Tax Conf.* 12:1 (Can. Tax Foundation, 1986).

Wilson, Ronald S., "Cost Adjustments in Corporate Reorganization Transactions: Policy and Practice", in *Proceedings of 38th Tax Conf.* 8:1 (Can. Tax Foundation, 1986).

Witterick on Corporate Acquisitions (Montreal: Federated Press, 1992).

Witterick, Robert G., Q.C., "Buy-Sell Agreements", in *Proceedings of 40th Tax Conf.* 16:1 (Can. Tax Foundation, 1988).

Witterick, Robert G., Q.C., "Syndicated Acquisitions and Financing of Businesses", *Corp. Mgmt. Tax Conf.* 3:1 (Can. Tax Foundation, 1990).

Woods, Judith M., "Dividend Access Shares" (1991) 39 Can. Tax J. 408.

Wright, J. Robert, "Remarks on Selected Securities Issues", *Corp. Mgmt. Tax Conf.* 14:1 (Can. Tax Foundation, 1990).

Butterfly Reorganizations

Ahmed, Firoz, "Proposed Rules Would Eliminate Purchase Burrerfly Transactions", (1994) Can. Current Tax P27.

Brown and McDonnell, "Capital Gains Strips", in *Proceedings of 32nd Tax Conf.* 51 (Can. Tax Foundation, 1980).

Dart, Robert J., F.C.A., and Howard J. Kellough, "The Butterfly Reorganization: A Descriptive Analysis", in *Proceedings of 41st Tax Conf.* 20:2 (Can. Tax Foundation, 1989).

Ewens, Douglas S., "The Capital Gains Exemption and the Butterfly" (1986) 34 Can. Tax J. 914.

Hiltz, Michael A., "The Butterfly Reorganization: Revenue Canada's Approach", in *Proceedings of 41st Tax Conf.* 20:32 (Can. Tax Foundation, 1989).

Lawlor, William R., "Surplus Stripping and Other Planning Opportunities with the New $500,000 Capital Gains Exemption" (1986) 34 Can. Tax J. 49.

Murison, Stephen R., "Transfers of Property Within a Corporate Group" (1986) 34 Can. Tax J. 646.

Potter, Christopher J., "Part IV Tax Complications in Butterfly Transactions" (1992) Can. Tax J. 992.

Richardson, Elinore, and Hillel Frankel, "Netting Canada's Elusive Cross-Border Butterfly" (1990) 2 Int. Tax Rev. 5.

Robertson, "Capital Gains Strips: A Revenue Canada Perspective on the Provisions of Section 55", in *Proceedings of 33rd Tax Conf.* 81 (Can. Tax Foundation, 1981).

Spindler, R.J., "Butterflies Revisited" (1989) 37 Can. Tax J. 605.

Storozuk, Leslie S., "An Examination of Section 55 and 1982 Proposed Amendments", *Prairie Prov. Tax Conf.* 341 (Can. Tax Foundation, 1983).

PART XIV: INTERNATIONAL ASPECTS

CHAPTER 31 — FOREIGN SOURCE INCOME

I. — General Comment

We saw in Chapter 3 that Canada imposes taxes based on taxpayer residence and on the source of income.[1] Hence, Canadian residents are taxed on their global income and non-residents only on their Canadian source income. Canadians who engage in outbound international transactions can be subjected to double (or multiple) taxation of the same income by two (or more) countries. In addition to the sophisticated and remarkably complex domestic tax structure for the taxation of income earned in foreign countries, Canada also has a comprehensive network of bilateral tax treaties designed to prevent double taxation and fiscal avoidance. Thus, Canada unilaterally provides relief from double taxation through its domestic tax credits and exemptions and shares taxing jurisdiction with its treaty partners to reduce the incidence of double taxation of income in international transactions.

The complexity of the international tax rules in the Act stem from several factors. First, the Act draws a substantial distinction between active business income and passive investment income. The rules in respect of foreign active business income, which permit tax deferral on earnings parked offshore, are generous. The theory permitting tax deferral is that it allows Canadian multinational companies to compete in international markets. In contrast, the rules in respect of passive income, which is sometimes taxable on a remittance basis and at other times on a current as-earned basis, are restrictive and punitive. Thus, taxpayers jockey to get on the right side of the distinctions to take advantage of the rules. Second, the distinction

---

[1]See Chapter 32, "Non-Residents".

between the two types of income requires exhaustive (and exhausting) definitions,[2] which in turn must be administratively and judicially interpreted. The definitions are long (some extend to seven pages in a single sentence), grammatically awkward, disjointed, circular, and ambiguous. These problems are likely to be exacerbated with the acceleration of electronic commerce.

II. — Repatriation Of Profits

1. — *General Comment*

The domestic rules in respect of the taxation of foreign-source income serve three broad purposes. They are intended to:

- Facilitate foreign investment;
- Prevent tax avoidance;[3] and
- Provide relief against double taxation of income.

The *Income Tax Act* balances these competing interests and attempts to provide a neutral tax environment that helps outbound foreign investment without encouraging tax avoidance. The rules, however, do not achieve "capital export neutrality" and, if anything, are biased in favour of foreign investment. To state it more starkly, it is sometimes more advantageous for a Canadian multinational to invest abroad rather than at home.

The domestic taxation of foreign-source income generally depends upon four principal factors:

- Type of income earned;
- Relationship between the foreign taxpayer and the Canadian resident;

---

[2]See the definition of "foreign accrual property income" in section 95.

[3]Prior to 1971, foreign corporations, trusts and partnerships were used to reduce Canadian tax on business and investment income earned outside Canada. By locating business investment operations in tax haven jurisdictions, Canadian taxpayers could substantially reduce, sometimes completely eliminate, and at other times indefinitely postpone, taxes that might otherwise have been payable in Canada. The foreign affiliate rules are the direct product of The CRA's frustrations in policing the foreign operations of resident Canadian taxpayers. In his Budget Speech on June 18, 1971, introducing the tax reform proposals, the Minister of Finance stated:

> [A] number of foreign countries impose taxes substantially lower than those in Canada, and investment income has been diverted to these countries to avoid Canadian tax. Rules ... will tax the investment income of foreign affiliates to the same extent as if it had been received in Canada.

- Timing of repatriation of foreign earnings to Canada; and

- Existence of a Canadian double taxation treaty with the source jurisdiction.

For tax purposes, we classify foreign-source income into four categories:

1. Business income;

2. Capital gains; and

3. Investment income,

    (a) "portfolio" dividends;

    (b) passive property income from "controlled foreign affiliates".

The tax rules in respect of foreign source income serve various purposes and, therefore, rely upon several variables such as the degree and extent of ownership that a resident taxpayer has in the foreign entity that gives rise to the income. We tax foreign source income on the basis of thresholds of ownership interest:

1. under 10 per cent;

2. 10-50 per cent; and

3. over 50 per cent.

We consider ownership of less than 10 per cent as a minimal interest and tax dividends from such investments on a remittance basis. Where a Canadian corporation owns at least 10 per cent of a foreign entity, the entity is a "foreign affiliate" (FA). Dividends from FAs are taxable in Canada subject to exemptions and tax credits depending upon their source and origin. An ownership interest of more than 50 per cent of a foreign affiliate makes the entity a "controlled foreign affiliate" (CFA). The income of a CFA is taxable in Canada either on a remittance or accrual basis depending upon the type of income and its source.

III. — Foreign Affiliates

We determine "foreign affiliate" (FA) status by reference to the relationship between a taxpayer resident in Canada and a non-resident corporation. A FA of a taxpayer resident in Canada means a non-resident corporation in which the resident taxpayer has:[4]

- A minimum equity percentage of 1 per cent, *and*

- A total equity percentage with any persons related to the taxpayer of at least 10 per cent.

---

[4]Subs. 95(1)"foreign affiliate".

A taxpayer's equity percentage is its direct and indirect equity percentages in the foreign entity.[5] The Act supplements the above definition with some anti-avoidance provisions that prevent companies from artificial arrangements to avoid tax.[6]

A foreign affiliate controlled by Canadian residents is a "controlled foreign affiliate" (CFA).[7] The distinction between a FA and a CFA is crucial to the structure of the taxation of business income and investment income.

Dividends from foreign corporations are generally taxable in Canada on a remittance basis,[8] but are eligible for tax relief for foreign taxes paid. Dividends from FAs are either exempted from income (the exemption method) or eligible for foreign tax credits (the credit method) depending upon the source of funds from which the dividend is paid and the nature of the Canadian investor. Dividends from non-FAs are not eligible for exemption. They may, however, be eligible for foreign tax credits.

Income from a CFA may be taxed in Canada either on a remittance or an accrual basis depending upon whether it is active or passive. A Canadian resident must recognize "passive" investment income from a CFA[9] in the year the income is *earned*, regardless whether the income is actually received in the year.[10] This requirement of "accrual basis" accounting prevents tax deferral that might otherwise be possible by delaying remittance of the income to Canada.

There are two steps in determining whether a non-resident entity is a FA of a Canadian resident taxpayer:

1. Characterize whether the foreign entity is a "corporation," and

2. Calculate the resident's "equity percentage" in the non-resident corporation.

---

[5]See *infra*.

[6]Subs. 95(6).

[7]Subs. 95(1)"foreign affiliate"; subs. 95(1)"controlled foreign affiliate". See *infra* for a detailed definition of "controlled foreign affiliate".

[8]Para. 12(1)(k).

[9]Subs. 95(1)"controlled foreign affiliate".

[10]Subs. 91(1).

1. — Characterization

(a) — Canadian Entities

The definition of a "foreign affiliate" is cast as the relationship between a non-resident *corporation* and a taxpayer resident in Canada.[11] Under Canadian law, a corporation is a legal entity created under the authority of a statute. It has a legal existence that is separate and distinct from those who create or own it. Thus, a corporation is a legal person that has the capacity to acquire rights and to assume liabilities on its own behalf. The rights and liabilities of a corporation are generally distinct from the rights and liabilities of those who have an ownership interest in the corporation.[12]

(b) — Foreign Entities

The status of a corporation in other legal systems depends upon the relevant law. Common law jurisdictions generally recognize a corporation as a separate legal entity. Other legal systems may have different interpretations. For the purpose of the foreign affiliate rules, however, the Canada Revenue Agency ("CRA") interprets "corporation" to include not only "joint stock" and "limited liability companies" as known to Canadian law, but also comparable entities organized under the laws of foreign jurisdictions.[13] Thus, for tax purposes, the Agency considers the following types of foreign associations as equivalent to a corporation:

Aksjeselskap (A/S or A.S.) (Norway)
Aktieselskab (A/S) (Denmark)
Aktiebolag (Sweden)
Aktiengesellschaft (A.G.)
Anpartsselskab (ApS) (Denmark)
Anstalt (Liechtenstein)
Besloten Vennootschap met beperkte aansprakelijkheid (B.V.) (Netherlands and possessions)
Compania Anonima
Gesellschaft mit beschrankter Haftung (G.m.b.H. or Ges m.b.H.)
Kabushiki Kaisha (K.K.) (Japan)
Limitada (Sociedade por quotas) (Portugal)
Naamloze Vennootschap (N.V.) (Netherlands and possessions)
Sharikat Al-Mossahamah (Saudi Arabia)

---

[11] Subs. 95(1)"foreign affiliate".

[12] See, e.g., *Canada Business Corporations Act*, R.S.C. 1985, c. C.44, subs. 15(1); Ontario *Business Corporations Act*, R.S.O. 1990, c. B.16, s. 15.

[13] IT-343R "Meaning of the Term Corporation" (September 26, 1977). See also, Technical News #20 (June 14, 2001) and #25 (October 30, 2002).

Sharikat Mussahama
Sherkat Sahami Aam (Iran)
Sherkat Sahami Khas (Iran)
Sociedad(e)(s) anoniam(s) (S.A.)
Sociedad(e)(s) (anonima) de responsabilid(e) (ad) limitada (por quotas)
   (S.L.)(S.A.R.L.) (SRL)
Société anonyme
Société de personnes a responsabilité limitée
Société a responsabilité limitée
Societa per Azioni (Italy)
Yugen Kaisha (Japan)

The characteristic that is common to these entities is that for most purposes they all have a separate identity and existence.

(c) — Partnerships

The characterization of foreign partnerships is a more difficult matter. Under Canadian law, a partnership is not a separate legal entity. Rather, a partnership is a *relationship* between persons carrying on business in common with a view to profit.[14] The members of a general partnership have joint and unlimited liability in respect of its debts and obligations. An interest in a partnership is a property right in and of itself distinguishable from the partnership's assets.

There is also a special type of partnership called a "limited partnership". A limited partnership is created under statutory authority[15] in which some, but not all, of the partners have limited liability. Generally, the limited partners are liable for the debts and obligations of the partnership, but only to the extent of their capital contributions to the partnership.[16] A limited partnership must have at least one general partner who has unlimited liability for partnership debts. Thus, a limited partnership stands somewhere between a general partnership with unlimited liability and a corporation with limited liability.

Under Canadian law, a partnership is not a separate legal entity. Some foreign jurisdictions[17] do, however, recognize partnerships as separate legal personalities. A foreign partnership that is considered to be a separate legal entity in its home jurisdiction may be considered a "corporation" for the purposes of the foreign affiliate rules. Thus, a foreign partnership may be a foreign affiliate of a Canadian resident taxpayer.

---

[14]See, e.g., *Partnerships Act*, R.S.O. 1990, c. P.5, s. 2.

[15]See, e.g., *Limited Partnerships Act*, R.S.O. 1990, c. L.16.

[16]See, e.g., *ibid.*, s. 9.

[17]For example, Scotland and France recognize partnerships as separate legal personalities.

(d) — Trusts

The rules in respect of the taxation of foreign affiliates also apply to certain non-resident trusts. The Act may deem a discretionary trust to be a person resident in Canada and subject to Canadian tax.[18]

2. — Equity Percentage

We determine a resident's "equity percentage" in a non-resident corporation by adding the resident's direct and indirect interests in the corporation.[19]

A resident's direct interest in a non-resident corporation (referred to as "direct equity percentage")[20] is the resident's *highest* percentage ownership of *any* class of shares issued by the non-resident corporation.

Example

Assume:

Canco, a Canadian resident corporation, owns the following percentages of shares in two non-resident corporations, *NR1* and *NR2*:

$$NR1 \quad — \quad 9\% \text{ Class A shares}$$
$$12\% \text{ Class B shares}$$

$$NR2 \quad — \quad 7\% \text{ Class C shares}$$
$$8\% \text{ Class D shares}$$

Then:

Canco's "direct equity percentage" is 12% in *NR1* and 8% in *NR2*.

A taxpayer has an indirect equity interest when the taxpayer owns shares in a corporation that owns shares in other corporations. The indirect equity interest is calculated by multiplying the taxpayer's direct equity percentage in the first corporation by the first corporation's

---

[18]Paras. 94(1)(c) and (d).

[19]Subs. 95(4)"equity percentage".

[20]Subs. 95(4)"direct equity percentage".

direct equity percentage in the second corporation, and so on.[21] Thus, a person's equity percentage in a particular corporation is his or her direct equity percentage in the corporation plus the product obtained when the person's equity percentage in any other corporation is multiplied by that corporation's direct equity percentage in the particular corporation.

Example

Assume:

- Canco, a resident corporation, owns 60% of the issued shares of *NR1* and 5% of the issued shares of *NR2*;
- *NR1* owns 30% of the issued shares of *NR2*;
- *NR2* owns 15% of the issued shares of *NR3*.
- *NR1*, *NR2* and *NR3* are all non-resident corporations.

Canco's equity percentage (being the sum of its direct and indirect interests) in *NR1*, *NR2* and *NR3* is calculated as follows:

In NR1	
Direct equity percentage	60%
In NR2	
Direct equity percentage	5%
Indirect interests (60% × 30%)	18%
	23%
In NR3	
Indirect interests (23% × 15%)	3.45%

Assuming that these are all of the relevant interests held, *NR1* is a controlled foreign affiliate of Canco; *NR2* is a foreign affiliate of Canco; and *NR3* is *not* a foreign affiliate of Canco.

For the purpose of determining FA status, it is irrelevant whether the shares on the basis of which equity percentages are calculated are voting or non-voting. Note also, for the purposes

---

[21] Subs. 95(4)"equity percentage", para. (b).

of the foreign affiliate rules, the Act deems an income bond or debenture[22] issued by a non-resident corporation to be a share unless the interest payable on the bond or debenture is deductible under the tax laws of the country in which the corporation is resident.[23]

IV. — Anti-Avoidance Rules

In addition to the numerical threshold tests, there are two anti-avoidance rules that are intended to prevent taxpayers from manipulating their equity percentages in non-resident corporations for the purpose of avoiding the foreign affiliate rules.

Where a taxpayer has a contractual right or option to acquire shares and *one* of the *main* reasons for the existence of the option or right may reasonably be considered to be the reduction or deferral of tax that might otherwise be payable, the Act deems the right or option to be shares owned by the taxpayer.[24] The test is objective and the Minister's discretion is reviewable in a judicial proceeding.

Where a taxpayer's foreign affiliate or a non-resident corporation controlled by the taxpayer issues shares and *one* of the *main* reasons for the issuance of the shares may reasonably be considered to be either a reduction in, or deferral of, tax that would otherwise be payable, the shares are deemed never to have been issued.[25] The control test applied to the taxpayer may be *de jure* or *de facto*, direct or indirect, and may apply to the taxpayer alone, or to a group related to the taxpayer.[26]

V. — Business Income

1. — General Comment

Canadian resident taxpayers are generally taxable on foreign dividend income on a remittance basis.[27] This rule applies both to individual and corporate taxpayers regardless of the status of the foreign corporation. There are, however, special rules for dividends from foreign affiliates. The tax treatment of dividends from FAs depends upon two factors:

    1. The type of income earned, and

---

[22]Para. 248(1)"income bond".

[23]Subs. 95(5); IT-388 "Income Bonds Issued by Foreign Corporations" (August 15, 1977) (archived).

[24]Para. 95(6)(a).

[25]Para. 95(6)(b).

[26]Subs. 256(5.1).

[27]Para. 12(1)(k) and s. 90.

2. The source of income.

Dividends from a FA that is resident and carrying on an active business in a designated treaty country are generally fully deductible in computing the resident corporation's income. A designated country is one with which Canada has a tax treaty in force. In other cases, the recipient may claim a credit for the FA's foreign tax paid in respect of its income (i.e., "underlying foreign tax") and any tax withheld on the dividend.

Dividends from a FA are presumed to be paid in sequence from one of three accounts as follows:[28]

- Exempt surplus;

- Taxable surplus; or

- Pre-acquisition surplus.

These three surplus accounts represent different types and sources of income and there are significant differences in the taxation of dividends paid out of the three accounts. A dividend from exempt surplus is, in effect, completely exempt from Canadian tax because the amount included in income is washed-out by the amount deducted in computing taxable income. This is the "exemption method" of preventing double taxation of income.[29]

In contrast, a dividend out of taxable surplus is included in income but eligible for a credit equal to the grossed-up value of the foreign affiliate's underlying foreign tax and any tax withheld on the dividend. The gross-up of the underlying foreign tax allows the taxpayer a credit that is equivalent to the rate at which the income would have been taxed in Canada if it had been earned in domestic operations. The gross-up factor is equal to:

$$[\frac{1}{\text{Canadian corporate tax rate}}] - 1 \times \text{foreign business tax}$$

Example			
Assume:			
FA with $1,000 in taxable earnings is subject to a foreign income tax rate of 27%			
Then:	27%	38%	42%
Taxable surplus ($1,000 - 270)	$730	$620	$580
Dividend included in income	730	620	580
Less deduction for UFBT:*	(441)	(620)	(685)

---

[28]Reg. 5901.

[29]See Article 23A *OECD Model Convention.*

Example

$$\$270 \times [(1/.38) - 1] =$$

Taxable income	289	nil	nil
Canadian tax at 38%	110	nil	nil
Total Canadian and foreign tax ($110 + 270)	380	380	420
Effective tax rate on foreign income	38%	38%	42%

Thus, the Canadian tax on the foreign income is reduced by the amount of the underlying foreign business tax charged on the income.

Notes:

*   Underlying Foreign Business Tax.

The deduction for foreign withholding taxes on dividends is calculated in a similar manner but with appropriate adjustments. The grossed-up value of the foreign dividend withholding tax is calculated according to the formula:

$$[\frac{1}{\text{Canadian corporate tax rate}}] \times \text{foreign withholding tax}$$

Example

Assume:

Dividend from FA of $730 subject to a withholding tax rate of 10% or $73.

Dividend included in income	$ 730
Less deduction for UFBT*	(441)
Less deduction for foreign withholding tax:	
$73 × (1/.38) =	(192)
Taxable income	$ 97
Canadian tax at 38%	$ 37
Total Canadian and foreign tax	
$37 + $270 + $73 =	$ 380
Effective tax rate	38%

Thus, the Canadian tax is reduced by the amount of the underlying foreign tax and the withholding tax on the dividend

Notes:

*   Underlying Foreign Business Tax.

(a) — Surplus Accounts

The technical mechanism for allowing a deduction for foreign taxes is quite complex and depends upon a detailed analysis of the payer corporation's surplus accounts. As noted above, there are three categories of surplus accounts: exempt surplus, taxable surplus, and pre-acquisition surplus. The deduction available depends upon the surplus pool from which the dividend is paid.

Dividends from a foreign affiliate may be entirely tax-free or included in income and subject to a credit for foreign taxes paid on the underlying income. The distinction between the exemption and credit methods of accounting for dividends from foreign affiliates depends upon two factors, type of income earned by the affiliate and its source.

A Canadian resident corporation that receives a dividend from its foreign affiliate can deduct:[30]

- The full amount of any dividend that it receives out of the foreign affiliate's "exempt surplus" (the "exemption method");

- A portion of the dividend that it receives that is paid out of the foreign affiliate's "taxable surplus" that represents its underlying foreign corporate tax and foreign withholding tax (the "credit method"); and,

- The amount of the dividend paid out of the foreign affiliate's "pre-acquisition" surpls.

The computation of the various surplus accounts lies at the core of the system for providing relief from double taxation of foreign source income. Each Canadian shareholder of a foreign affiliate must maintain surplus accounts for each affiliate. The account may be maintained in the currency of the country of the affiliate's residence or any other currency that is reasonable in the circumstances.[31] The accounting period commences on the first day of the taxation year of the foreign affiliate in which it became an affiliate and ends immediately before the dividend is paid. Each surplus account balance must be completed immediately before any dividend is paid. The characterization of the particular dividend and the effect on the surplus accounts depends upon the balances in the account at that time.

---

[30]Subs. 113(1).

[31]Reg. 5907(6).

(b) — Exempt Surplus

A Canadian resident corporation that receives a dividend from its foreign affiliate's exempt surplus must include the dividend in its income.[32] It may, however, deduct an equivalent amount in computing its taxable income.[33] Thus, in effect, dividends out of exempt surplus are completely tax-free.

In general terms, an affiliate's "exempt surplus" is its active business earnings from businesses carried on in a designated treaty country,[34] that is, countries with which Canada has signed a treaty that is in force.[35] The rationale for exempting dividends paid out of exempt surplus from Canadian tax is that the underlying income from which these dividends are paid is assumed to have already borne tax in the designated countries at rates that are approximately equivalent to Canadian tax rates. This assumption is generally valid because Canada does not enter into tax treaties with tax havens. It is, however, important to note that some countries with which Canada has treaties levy very low rates of tax on business income.[36] Active business income earned in these low tax countries (generally referred to as "treaty havens") are completely exempt from Canadian tax.

In general terms, the exempt surplus of a foreign affiliate resident in a listed country is the sum of:

- Its pre-1976 earnings from an active business, and

- Its post-1975 earnings from an active business carried on in a treaty country.

The main components of a foreign affiliate's exempt surplus (net of related foreign taxes) are:

- Net earnings from an active business that it carried on in any country before 1976;

- Net earnings from an active business that it carried on in Canada or a "designated treaty country" subsequent to 1975;

- the tax-free portion of most capital gains;

- taxable capital gains from dispositions of property used to earn active business income in treaty countries (e.g. excluded property);

- Certain amounts that it received from other foreign affiliates and related foreign corporations;

---

[32]S. 90.

[33]Para. 113(1)(a).

[34]Reg. 5907(1)"exempt surplus".

[35]Reg. 5907(11).

[36]For example, Cyprus, Malta, Ireland, and Barbados.

- Dividends that it received from the exempt surplus of other foreign affiliates;

- Dividends that would be deductible under section 112 if they had been received by the Canadian shareholder;

minus

- Dividends that it paid out of exempt surplus; and

- Losses from any of the above sources.

An "exempt deficit" arises when the deductions in the above list exceed the inclusions.

A foreign affiliate's net earnings[37] are calculated for each taxation year of the affiliate. Note, however, that only the exempt earnings (losses) of completed taxation years are taken into account in calculating the affiliate's exempt surplus or deficit at any particular time.

The calculation of net earnings (losses) takes into account four elements:[38]

- Capital gains and losses,

- Active business earnings carried on in treaty countries,

- Pre-1975 earnings and losses, and

- Earnings that qualify for tax-sparing because of an investment made or undertaken prior to 1976.

Post-1975 net earnings from an active business are included in earnings only if the affiliate is resident in a designated treaty country and the active business is carried on in a designated country or in Canada, or if a tax-sparing provision applies.[39]

"Net earnings" generally represent "earnings" net of applicable taxes.[40]

A foreign affiliate's "earnings" for a taxation year from an active business are its:[41]

- Income or profit from the business for the year computed in accordance with the income tax law of the country in which it is *resident* if it is required by such law to compute that profit or income;

---

[37]Technically referred to as "exempt earnings".

[38]Reg. 5907(1)"exempt earnings".

[39]Reg. 5907(10).

[40]Reg. 5907(1)"net earnings".

[41]Reg. 5907(1)"earnings" para. (a).

- Income or profit for the year computed in accordance with the income tax law of the country in which *the business is carried on* if it is required to calculate that income or profit according to such law; or,

- Income or profit for the year computed in accordance with the Canadian *Income Tax Act* on the assumption that the business was carried on in Canada and it was resident in Canada.

The Canadian tax rules in respect of calculating earnings apply only if neither the foreign affiliate's country of residence nor the country in which it carries on business provide specific computational rules.

To summarize:

1. Dividends from foreign affiliates resident and doing business in designated treaty countries are exempt from tax in Canada. Designated treaty countries are countries with which Canada has a tax treaty in force and effect for the particular taxation year of the foreign affiliate. The exemption is justified on the basis that these countries generally have relatively sophisticated tax regimes and tax rates that are comparable to Canadian corporate rates.

2. Some countries with which Canada has a tax treaty are "treaty havens" for corporations that earn certain types of income. For example, Barbados, Ireland, Malta, Cyprus, and Switzerland are considered "treaty havens" because of favourable tax rules for foreign corporations under their domestic regimes. Hence, Canadian corporations that arrange their foreign affiliate structure through treaty havens can earn income that is subject to little or no foreign income tax and that can be repatriated to Canada on a tax-free basis.

3. A foreign affiliate is considered to be resident in a designated treaty country for exempt surplus purposes only if it is resident in the country for purposes of the treaty. This replaces the old residence test that was based upon central management and control.[42]

4. Hybrid entities, such as LLCs are considered foreign affiliate corporations for Canadian tax purposes even though they may be treated as partnerships for U.S. tax purposes.

(c) — Taxable Surplus

Generally, a foreign affiliate's "taxable surplus" comprises its active business income earned in a non-designated country, that is, a country with which Canada does *not* have a tax treaty in force.

---

[42]Reg. 5907(11.2).

A Canadian resident corporation that receives a dividend from its FAs taxable surplus is taxable on the dividend. The corporation may, however, claim a deduction for any foreign income taxes that the affiliate paid on the income and for any tax withheld on the dividend.[43] The deduction is equal to the grossed-up amount of the underlying foreign income and withholding taxes paid to the foreign country. We determine the grossed-up amount of underlying foreign income taxes by multiplying the foreign income tax paid by the affiliate by the result of the "relevant tax factor" minus 1. We determine the grossed-up amount of the withholding tax by multiplying the withholding tax by the relevant tax factor.

(d) — Relevant Tax Factor

The "relevant tax factor" ("RTF") is a mathematical formula designed to permit a deduction for the *grossed-up* value of the foreign tax paid on foreign source income. The RTF is the reciprocal of the tax rate applicable to the taxpayer.[44]

The RTF for individuals is 2.2, which is premised on a marginal tax rate of 45.45 per cent.

The reciprocal of the corporate tax rate at 31 per cent is 3.23. The RTF is reduced by 1 to calculate the deduction for underlying foreign taxes levied on income paid out of taxable surplus of a foreign affiliate.[45] Hence, the factor applied to set the underlying corporate foreign tax is 2.23.

Example

Assume that *FA*, a foreign affiliate, earns $10,000 in an unlisted country, pays foreign corporate tax of $3,800 and remits $6,200 out of its taxable surplus to a Canadian resident corporation. Assume that there is no withholding tax.

Then:

A. Foreign Affiliate (FA)

Taxable income	$ 10,000
Tax @ 31%	3,100
Net available (paid as dividend)	$ 6,900

---

[43]Paras. 113(1)(b), 113(1)(c).

[44]Subs. 95(1)"relevant tax factor".

[45]Para. 123(1)(a) and subs. 95(1)"relevant tax factor"; subs. 123.4.

Example

B. Resident Corporation

Dividend income $ 6,900

Less: 2.23 x $3,100   6,900

Amount taxable in Canada   NIL

The factor of "minus 1" in the formula simply adjusts for the fact that the resident corporation has already included its foreign affiliate's *after-tax* earnings in income and that the foreign affiliate deducted one times the tax rate ($3,800 in the above example) in arriving at the amount that went into its taxable surplus account. No such adjustment is required for withholding taxes on dividends from a foreign affiliate because the resident corporation includes the *gross* amount of the dividend, without any reduction for withholding tax, in its income. The rationale for these mathematical rules in respect of taxable surplus dividends is to ensure that foreign earnings repatriated to Canada from non-treaty countries bear tax at a rate that is at least equal to the prevailing Canadian federal corporate tax rate.

As noted earlier, a foreign affiliate is presumed to pay dividends in the following order: first out of its exempt surplus (net of any taxable deficit); next, out of its taxable surplus (net of any exempt deficit); and, finally, out of pre-acquisition surplus.[46] It may, however, elect to reverse the order of the payments as between exempt surplus and taxable surplus.[47] This may be advantageous, for example, if the resident corporation needs to use up its loss carryovers or deductions.

A foreign affiliate's income from active business is included in its "taxable surplus" *unless*:[48]

- It is resident in a designated treaty country, *and*

- The income is earned from an active business that it carries on either in Canada or in a listed country.

Dividends out of "taxable surplus" are in effect taxed at a level equivalent to the Canadian tax rate on domestic earnings. This is achieved by including the dividend in income and providing a tax credit at the equivalent Canadian tax rate.

---

[46]Reg. 5901.

[47]Reg. 5900(2).

[48]Reg. 5907(1)"taxable surplus".

The main components of taxable surplus (net of related foreign taxes) are:[49]

- Net earnings from an active business that are not included in exempt srplus for the foreign affiliate's taxation years after 1975;

- FAPI for taxation years of the foreign affiliate ending after 1975;

- 1/2 of capital gains on certain "excluded property";

- Certain amounts received from other foreign affiliates and related foreign corporations;

- Dividends received from the taxable surplus of other foreign affiliates;

minus

- Dividends paid out of taxable surplus; and

- Losses from any of the above sources.

Income from an active business may sometimes be excluded from a foreign affiliate's exempt surplus and included in its taxable surplus. For example, where a foreign affiliate is resident in a designated treaty country, any active business income that it earns in a non-designated country is considered taxable surplus and not exempt surplus.

A resident Canadian corporation that receives a dividend from the taxable surplus of its foreign affiliate must include the full amount of the dividend in its income.[50] It may, however, deduct an amount on account of:[51]

- Any underlying foreign tax prescribed to be applicable to the dividend, and

- Any non-business-income tax paid by the corporation in respect of the dividend.

These two deductions reflect the foreign tax and non-business income tax applicable to the dividend and, in effect, equate the net tax payable with tax that would have been payable under a full foreign tax credit system.

The deduction is equal to the amount of the foreign tax that is attributable to the dividend paid out of taxable surplus multiplied by the result of the corporation's "relevant tax factor"[52] minus one. Given a basic Canadian federal corporate tax rate of 31 per cent, the multiplier is 2.23. The deduction cannot exceed the amount of the dividend included in the resident corporation's income.

---

[49] *Ibid.*

[50] S. 90.

[51] Paras. 113(1)(b) and (c).

[52] The "relevant tax factor" is defined in para. 95(1). For a corporate taxpayer, the factor is derived by dividing one by the corporate tax rate.

Example

Assume:

Alpha Ltd., a resident corporation, received a dividend of $30,000 in Year 1 out of the taxable surplus of its foreign affiliate, *Beta Ltd. Beta Ltd.* paid foreign tax of $4,000; in addition, *Beta Ltd.* was subject to a withholding tax of $2,400 on the dividend.

The tax payable on the dividend is calculated as follows:

Dividend income		$ 30,000
Less:		
Underlying foreign tax	$ 8,920	
$4,000 × [(1/0.31) - 1]		
Withholding tax	7,752	(16,672)
$2,400 × (1/0.31)		
Amount taxable		$ 13,328
Tax thereon at 31%		$ 4,132

The tax payable under the above credit system is equal to the tax that would have been payable on an equivalent amount of income under a system of full foreign tax credits.

Dividend income		$ 30,000
Add: underlying foreign tax		4,000
Amount taxable		$ 34,000
Tax thereon at 31%		$ 10,540
Less: foreign tax	$ 4,000	
withholding tax	2,400	(6,400)
Net tax (rounding error)		$ 4,140

Example
The system can over credit foreign tax if effective Canadian tax rates are higher than 31 per cent because of surtaxes or special taxes.

(e) — Pre-Acquisition Surplus

A dividend from a foreign affiliate greater than its exempt and taxable surpluses is presumed to come out of its "pre-acquisition surplus".[53] A foreign affiliate's pre-acquisition surplus is merely a notional account. Dividends are presumed to be paid out of pre-acquisition surplus only when an affiliate's exempt surplus and taxable surplus are exhausted.

A dividend from a foreign affiliate's pre-acquisition surplus is also deductible in computing taxable income,[54] but the cost base of the foreign affiliate's shares is reduced by the amount of the dividend less any withholding tax.[55] The Act deems the resident corporation to have realized a capital gain if the adjusted cost base of its foreign affiliate's shares becomes a negative amount.[56]

The Act does not define the term "pre-acquisition surplus". A dividend by a foreign affiliate is presumed to be paid out of its pre-acquisition surplus if it does not have any net exempt or net taxable surplus. In theory, the pre-acquisition surplus account represents the retained earnings and unrealized gains of the foreign affiliate as at January 1, 1972 or the date that the corporation became a foreign affiliate of a Canadian resident taxpayer. A dividend paid out of pre-acquisition surplus reduces the adjusted cost base of the shares of the foreign affiliate and, therefore, can lead to a capital gain if the adjusted cost base of the shares falls below zero.[57]

VI. — Holding Companies

An individual who invests directly in a foreign business is personally taxable on any dividends that he or she receives from the foreign corporation. Foreign dividends are not eligible for the dividend tax credit and, as such, are taxable at full rates. The personal tax rates vary

---

[53]Reg. 5901.

[54]Para. 113(1)(d).

[55]Para. 53(2)(b) and subs. 92(2).

[56]Subs. 40(3).

[57]Ibid.

between provinces, but at the top end of income brackets, the highest marginal rate is close to 50 per cent.

If a Canadian resident individual wishes to invest in a treaty country, it is generally advantageous to invest through a Canadian holding company rather than directly. The following example illustrates the comparative tax consequences of a direct investment in the United States versus an indirect investment through a holding company.

Example

Assume, alternatively, that an Ontario resident with a marginal rate of 50% invests in the U.S. either directly in a US corporation ("US Co") or through a Canadian holding company ("HOLDCO"). US Co is engaged in an active business and remits its after tax income to the individual or HOLDCO, as the case may be.

	Direct investment	Investment through HOLDCO
Host Country Tax		
Net Income earned by US Co	$ 100.00	$ 100.00
Host Country Tax	(34.00)	(34.00)
Net Income after tax	$ 66.00	$ 66.00
Dividend from US Co	$ 66.00	$ 66.00
Withholding Tax (15% or 5%)*	(9.90)	(3.30)
Net dividend to Canadian Investor	$ 56.10	$ 62.70
Canadian Tax		
Canadian Corporate Tax on Dividend	N/A	Nil (Exempt Surplus)
Canadian Personal Tax On:		
Foreign Source Dividend (50% × $66.00)	$ 33.00	
Domestic Source Dividend		$ 22.57
Foreign Non-Business Tax Credit	(9.90)	N/A

Example		
Net Canadian Personal Tax	$ 23.10	$ 22.57
Total Canadian & Foreign Tax	$ 67.00	$ 59.87
Net Cash Retained by Canadian Investor	$ 33.00	$ 40.13
Percentage increase in investment yield		22%

Notes:

*   See Article X, *Canada-U.S. Tax Treaty.*

VII. — Disposition Of Foreign Investment

1. — Foreign Subsidiary

Where a Canadian corporation disposes of its shares in its foreign subsidiary, it can elect under section 93 to treat all or part of the proceeds of sale as a dividend rather than as proceeds of disposition. This allows the Canadian parent corporation to receive the deemed dividends on a tax-free basis to the extent that the foreign subsidiary has a pool of active business income from which it can pay dividends. Thus, the subsidiary's exempt surplus pools and its underlying foreign taxes may be fully used by converting what would otherwise be a capital gain into a dividend. In certain cases, this election also allows the Canadian parent corporation to avoid foreign withholding taxes that might otherwise be payable on a dividend paid out of foreign profits before the sale of the shares.

Where a parent corporation disposes of its shares in its foreign subsidiary to a taxable Canadian corporation, it can defer Canadian tax payable on any gain on the shares if it takes back share consideration as part of the purchase price.[58]

Where the sale is to a foreign corporation, a rollover may be available under section 85.1. This rollover is available only if the Canadian parent corporation takes back shares from the purchaser corporation as consideration for the disposition.

2. — Foreign Affiliates

A taxpayer may rollover its shares of a FA to another corporation that also qualifies as its foreign affiliate. A taxpayer that disposes of its shares in a foreign affiliate to a corporation,

---

[58]S. 85.

which qualifies as his or her foreign affiliate immediately after the disposition, in exchange for consideration that includes shares of the acquiring foreign affiliate, may defer any capital gain or loss that arises by virtue of the disposition.[59] The rollover is, however, subject to anti-avoidance rules (discussed below).[60]

The rollover works as follows: the Act deems the vendor of the shares to receive proceeds of disposition equal to the *deemed* cost to the vendor of *all* of the consideration that he or she receives in exchange for the shares.[61] Thus, it defers recognition of any capital gains and losses that have accrued on the shares.

For these purposes, non-share consideration is valued at its fair market value.[62] The cost of share consideration received from the acquiring affiliate is simply the difference between the adjusted cost base of the shares disposed of by the vendor and the fair market value of non-share consideration received in exchange from the acquiring affiliate.[63] Thus, non-share consideration greater than the adjusted cost base of the shares disposed of triggers an immediate capital gain.

The acquiring affiliate acquires the vendor's shares at an amount equal to the vendor's deemed proceeds of disposition.[64] In effect, for tax purposes, the acquiring affiliate steps into the shoes of the vendor.

Example

Assume:

CR Ltd. (a Canadian corporation) has two foreign affiliates: *NR1 Ltd.* and *NR2 Ltd.* The adjusted cost base of *NR1 Ltd.'s* shares is $800. *CR Ltd.* reorganizes its shareholdings and sells its shares in *NR1 Ltd.* to NR2 Ltd. in exchange for the following consideration:

	Case A	Case B	Case C
Debt (FMV)	NIL	$ 200	$ 1,000
Shares of *NR2 Ltd.*	?	?	?

---

[59]Subs. 85.1(3).

[60]Subs. 85.1(4).

[61]Para. 85.1(3)(c)

[62]Para. 85.1(3)(a).

[63]Para. 85.1(3)(b).

[64]Para. 85.1(3)(d).

Example			
Then:			
ACB of shares sold	$ 800	$ 800	$ 800
FMV of debt	—	(200)	(1,000)
ACB of new shares of *NR2 Ltd.*	$ 800	$ 600	NIL
Deemed POD	$ 800	$ 800	$ 1,000
ACB of shares sold	(800)	(800)	(800)
Capital gain	NIL	NIL	$ 200
Cost of *NR1 Ltd.'s* shares to *NR2 Ltd.*:	$ 800	$ 800	$ 1,000

A rollover is also available where a taxpayer's foreign affiliate disposes of shares of another foreign affiliate of the taxpayer to a corporation that, immediately following the disposition, is also a foreign affiliate of the taxpayer.[65]

3. — Election to Treat Proceeds as Dividends

Where a Canadian resident corporation disposes of its shares of a foreign affiliate, it can elect to treat all, or any part, of its proceeds as a dividend rather than as proceeds of disposition.[66] The election is also available when a foreign affiliate of a Canadian resident corporation disposes of its shares of another of the resident corporation's foreign affiliates.

This election allows Canadian resident corporations to take advantage of the deductions available in respect of dividends received from foreign affiliates without having to actually pay a dividend and incur foreign tax.[67] As noted earlier, where a Canadian resident corporation receives a dividend from the exempt surplus of its foreign affiliates, the dividend is exempt from tax.[68] The election allows the resident corporation to take advantage of this rule if its foreign affiliate has an exempt surplus balance.

---

[65]Para. 95(2)(c).

[66]Subs. 93(1).

[67]See subs. 113(1).

[68]Para. 113(1)(a).

Where a foreign affiliate of a resident corporation disposes of shares of another foreign affiliate of the corporation and the shares are "excluded property",[69] the Act *deems* the resident corporation to have made the election in respect of each share disposed of and to have designated the prescribed amount.[70] "Excluded property" means shares in the capital of the other foreign affiliate where substantially all of the property of the affiliate is used or held in an active business.[71]

The amount deemed to have been designated is the lesser of the:[72]

- Capital gain otherwise determined in respect of the particular disposition, and

- Amount that would have been received on the share if the affiliate had paid dividends in an amount equal to its net surplus.

The amount elected is deducted from the corporation's proceeds of disposition. Thus, the corporation's capital gain is reduced by a corresponding amount.

Example

Assume:

CR Ltd. (a resident corporation) has a wholly-owned foreign affiliate, *FA Ltd.* The adjusted cost base of *FA Ltd.'s* shares to *CR Ltd.* is $50,000.

CR Ltd. sells its shares in *FA Ltd.* for $100,000. The following data applies to *FA Ltd.*:

Exempt surplus	$ 20,000
Taxable surplus	$ 30,000
Underlying foreign tax	$ 5,000

---

[69] Subs. 95(1)"excluded property".

[70] Subs. 93(1.1).

[71] Subs. 95(1)"excluded property".

[72] Reg. 5902(6).

Example		
Then:		
	Without election	With $50,000 Subs. 93(1) election
Proceeds of disposition	$ 100,000	$ 50,000
ACB	(50,000)	(50,000)
Capital gain	$ 50,000	NIL
Deemed dividend		$ 50,000
Less, aggregate of:		
(i) exempt surplus		
[para. 113(1)(a)]		(20,000)
(ii) underlying foreign tax × 2.23		
[para. 113(1)(b)]		(11,150)
Increase in taxable income ($50,000 × 1/2)	$ 25,000 *	$ 18,850

Notes:

*   Assuming a capital gains inclusion rate of 50%.

Special rules limit the amount of a capital loss that can be recognized on the disposition of shares of a foreign affiliate. The capital loss determined according to usual rules[73] is reduced by the amount of exempt dividends paid on the shares before their disposition.[74]

Where a resident taxpayer acquires shares in a FA because of a disposition of its shares in another of its foreign affiliates, the Act deems any capital loss resulting from the disposition to be nil and is added to the adjusted cost base of its newly acquired shares.[75]

---

[73]Subdivision c of Division B.

[74]Subs. 93(2).

[75]Subs. 93(4).

VIII. — Foreign Accrual Property Income (FAPI)

As noted earlier, Canada taxes income from a controlled foreign affiliate on a remittance or accrual basis depending upon whether the income is active or passive. A Canadian resident must recognize "passive" investment income (technically referred to as "foreign accrual property income") from a CFA in the year he or she earns the income, regardless whether he or she actually receives the income in the year. Thus, a taxpayer cannot generally defer taxes on FAPI.[76]

The conceptual framework of the FAPI rules is simple: they are intended to prevent taxpayers from deferring Canadian taxes by parking their investments in offshore corporations. For example, an individual could quite easily incorporate in a tax haven and put his or her entire portfolio in the corporation, which need never remit its portfolio income to Canada. Although we tolerate, and even encourage, such planning in respect of business income, the government does not condone such behavior for investment income. Hence, the dilemma: how to distinguish between business and passive income?

We saw in Chapter 7 that the Act distinguishes between income from property, income from business and income from capital gains. These concepts carry over to the definition of FAPI, but with considerably more complicated and badly drafted deeming provisions.

At its simplest level, the FAPI of a foreign affiliate is its income for the year from:

- Property;

- Businesses other than active businesses; and

- Certain taxable capital gains that have accrued after its 1975 taxation year.

Those said, however, subsections 95(1), (2) and (3) substantially redefine the underlying concept of investment income by enumerating numerous inclusions and exclusions in double and triple negatives.

The essence of FAPI, however, is to tax on a current basis foreign income from property and income from:

- An investment business;

- An adventure in the nature of trade;

- Trading or dealing in indebtedness; and

- Post 1975 taxable capital gains.

A long list of deeming provisions recharacterize various types of income and deem some business income to be inactive business income and some income that might be considered investment income into active business income.

---

[76]Subs. 91(1)

Although the Act does not explicitly specify, it appears that FAPI from property and businesses other than active businesses are generally to be calculated in accordance with Part I of the Act. For example, subsection 1102(3) of the Regulations provides that, except for the purposes of computing FAPI, a non-resident cannot claim capital cost allowance in respect of property outside of Canada. Similarly, subsection 95(1) provides that one must calculate an affiliate's income from property as if section 80 did not apply.

The starting point for determining FAPI is to identify "active business" income. This phrase has its ordinary meaning as in other parts of the Act. Thus, the jurisprudence applicable to section 125 in respect of Canadian-controlled private corporations and the small business deduction[77] also generally applies to the concept of active business as used in the FAPI rules.[78]

For the FAPI rules, however, the Act redefines an "active business" of a foreign affiliate as any business that the affiliate carries on *other than*:

- An investment business; or

- A business that subsection 95(2) *deems* to be a business other than an active business carried on by the affiliate.

The exclusions characterize income from these businesses as income from an inactive business (businesses other than active businesses).

Additionally, subsection 248(1), which includes an adventure or concern in the nature of trade in "business", excludes such activities from the meaning of business for the purpose of subsection 95(1). Thus, subsection 95(1) does not consider speculative activities, which do not constitute a business in the ordinary sense of the term but are only adventures in the nature of trade, as active businesses. Instead, gains from such activities are specifically included in the definition of income from property and are thereby included in FAPI.

---

[77]See Chapter 20, "Corporate Business Income".

[78]See, e.g., *Can. Marconi Company v. The Queen*, [1986] 2 S.C.R. 522, [1986] 2 C.T.C. 465, 86 D.T.C. 6526 (S.C.C.) (interest from an actively managed portfolio of short-term securities was active business income for the purpose of the manufacturing and processing profits); *Canada Trustco Mortgage Co. v. M.N.R.*, [1991] 2 C.T.C. 2728, 91 D.T.C. 1312 (T.C.C.) (interest income from a managed portfolio of mortgages was income from an active business carried on by a foreign affiliate of the taxpayer and was not FAPI). The deeming provision in para. 95(2)(a.3) overturns *Canada Trustco*.

IX. — Anti-Avoidance Rules

The rollover available to resident taxpayers who dispose of shares of one foreign affiliate to another foreign affiliate[79] is subject to an anti-avoidance rule. The rollover does not apply to dispositions of shares of foreign affiliates if:[80]

- All or substantially all of the affiliate's property is used to produce active business income, and

- The disposition is part of a transaction or series of transactions for the purpose of disposing of the shares to a person with whom the taxpayer is at arm's length.

---

[79]Subs. 85.1(3).

[80]Subs. 85.1(4).

Selected Bibliography to Chapter 31

Ahmed, Firoz, "Using LLCs to Finance Offshore Operations" (March 1996) 6 Can. Current Tax, 51.

Ahmed, Firoz, "The Investment Business Definition" (May 1996) 6 Can. Current Tax, 71.

Anderson, William D. and James J. Tobin, "Ownership and Financing of Overseas Operations of Canadian Companies: Conventional Wisdom of the 1980s Versus Realities of the 1990s" *Proceedings of the 45th Tax Conf.* 44:1 (Can. Tax Foundation, 1993).

Ansley, et al., "Taxation Considerations With Respect to Transactions in China" (1987) 35 Can. Tax J. 433.

Arnold, Brian, "The Canadian International Tax System: Review and Reform" (1995) 43 Can. Tax J. 1792.

Arnold, Brian J., "The Taxation of Controlled Foreign Corporations: An International Comparison", *Canadian Tax Paper No. 78* 237 (Can. Tax Foundation, 1986).

Arnold, Brian J., "The Taxation of Controlled Foreign Corporations: Defining and Designing Tax Havens" (1985) 33 Can. Tax J. 445.

Blessing, Peter H., "The Branch Tax in the U.S." (1986) 3 The Journal of Strategy in Int'l. Taxation 64.

Boidman, N., "Canadian Tax Proposals — Cross Border Effects (Part II)" (November 9, 1990) 19 Tax Management Int'l. J. 485.

Boidman, N., "The Canadian Approach to Offshore International Transactions" (1988) 40 The Tax Executive 283.

Boidman, N., *The Foreign Affiliate System: Canadian Taxation After 1982: A Structured Overview*, (Toronto: CCH Canadian Ltd., 1983).

Chapman, Larry F., "Emerging Tax Issues: Interpretation and Crown Forest Industries Ltd., Income of Financing Affiliates and the New FAPI Rules, Formation of Financing Affiliates by Non-residents-Owned Canadian Companies" *Proceedings of the 47th Tax Conf.* 6:1 (Can. Tax Foundation, 1995).

Conway, Wallace G., "The New Foreign Affiliate Provisions: The Department of Finance's Perspective" *Proceedings of the 47th Tax Conf.* 40:1 (Can. Tax Foundation, 1995).

Desjobert, Tatiana, "Legal and Tax Environment of Joint Ventures in the U.S.S.R." (1990) 1 Int'l. Business Law J. 557.

Dolan, D. Kevin and Carolyn M. Dupuy, "Engaged in U.S. Business — Permanent Establishment", *American Law Institute — American Bar Association Course of Study Materials: International Taxation* 67–90 (October 26-27, 1989, New York, New York).

Easson, Alex, "Reporting Offshore Assets" (May 1996) 6 *Can. Current Tax* 76.

Easson, A.J. and Li Jinyan, *Taxation of Foreign Investments in the People's Republic of China* (Deventer, the Netherlands: Kluwer, 1989).

Ensslin, Dankwart, "Taxation of Business Investment in the Federal Republic of Germany" (1988) 36 Can. Tax J. 176.

Fiszer, Janusz, "Poland: Taxation of Foreign Investment and Income Tax Treaties", [1991] 4 Intertax 221.

Kyres, Constantine, "The Use of Nonresident Trusts for Estate Planning and Asset Protection" (1995) 43 Can. Tax J. 314.

Kutzin, Michael S., "Canadian Limited Partner in U.S. Partnership has a U.S. Permanent Establishment Under Canada-U.S. Tax Treaty" (1990) 38 Can. Tax J. 1053.

Lahmer, Craig, "The Practical Application of the New Foreign Affiliate Provisions: Part I" *Proceedings of the 47th Tax Conf.* 36:1 (Can. Tax Foundation, 1995).

Lanthier, Allan R., "The Taxation of Foreign Affiliates" (1995) 43 Can. Tax J. 1603.

Li, Jinyan. "The Concept of Permanent Establishment in China's Tax Treaties." (1989) 7:120 International Tax and Business Lawyer 120.

Loveland, Norman C., "Acquisition of a U.S. Business by Canadians: A Canadian Perspective", *Corporate Management Tax Conf.* 11:1 (Can. Tax Foundation, 1990).

McAskile, C. Andrew, "Acquiring, Holding, and Financing US Businesses by Canadians: A Canadian Perspective" *Corp. Management Tax Conference* 17:1 (Can. Tax Foundation, 1996).

McLure, Charles E. Jr., "Economic Integration and European Taxation of Corporate Income — Some Lessons from the U.S. Experience" (1989) 29 European Taxation 243.

Meek, John H. "The Practical Application of the New Foreign Affiliate Provisions: Part 2" Proceedings of the 47th Tax Conf. 37:1 (Can. Tax Foundation, 1995).

Tremblay, Richard G., "'Active Business' Income in the FAPI Context: Recent Developments" (1987) 2:2 Canadian Current Tax C-4.

Tremblay, Richard and Susan Fisher, "Practice an Planning Tips: New Foreign Affiliate Reporting Rules" (April 1996) 6 Can. Current Tax 61.

Truster, Perry, "Offshore Tax Planning: A Practical Overview" *1996 Ontario Tax Conference*, Canadian Tax Foundation, TAB 6.

Ulmer, John M., "Canadian Acquisition of a Foreign Business: A Canadian Perspective", *Corp. Management Tax Conf.* 245 (Can. Tax Foundation, 1984).

CHAPTER 32 — NON-RESIDENTS

I. — General Comment

The taxation of non-residents raises important issues of a country's jurisdiction to tax income that has its source in the country. The traditional approach of most countries is that they exercise taxable jurisdiction over income sourced in the country but cede that jurisdiction (or part thereof) in certain circumstances through tax treaties to the country of residence. Thus, the law dealing with the taxation of non-residents is a balance between domestic and treaty law over taxable jurisdiction.

The *Income Tax Act* contains two distinct schemes for taxing non-residents and foreign persons. A non-resident who carries on business in Canada is taxable on his or her Canadian source business income under Part I of the Act.[1] We determine liability for Part I tax in the same manner as for residents of Canada except that the tax is limited to Canadian source income. A non-resident is also taxable under Part XIII of the Act on passive non-business Canadian source income. This tax is a flat withholding of 25 per cent on the gross amount of such income.[2] The rules in respect of the withholding tax reflect the difficulty of collecting taxes from persons who are neither physically present in Canada nor tied to the country by residence or business operations. Non-residents are also liable for provincial tax if they are employed or carry on business in a province.

---

[1]Subs. 2(3).

[2]Section 212. The 25 per cent rate is reduced in Canada's tax treaties.

A non-resident is taxable under Part I if the non-resident:

- is employed in Canada,

- carries on a business in Canada, or

- disposes of a taxable Canadian property,

at any time in the year or a previous year. Thus, a non-resident may be liable for Canadian tax on his or her earnings in a year even if the non-resident realizes the income in a subsequent year after he or she ceases employment or business.

Part XIII imposes a withholding tax on non-residents who derive certain forms of passive income from Canadian sources. The general rate of withholding is 25 per cent[3] on the gross amount[4] that a resident of Canada pays or credits to a non-resident.

II. — Tax Rates

1. — Individuals

A non-resident individual (other than a trust) is liable for Part I tax at the normal progressive rates on "taxable income" that he or she earns in Canada.[5] In lieu of the provincial tax, a non-resident is liable for an additional 48 per cent tax on any income that he or she does not earn in a province, for example, where the only source of Canadian income is capital gains.

2. — Corporations

Non-resident corporations are subject to federal tax at the normal corporate rate of 38 per cent on taxable income under Part I. The federal tax rate drops by 10 per cent on income attributable to a province.[6] Thus, the nominal federal rate on taxable income that a non-resident corporation earns in a province is 28 per cent. However, there is a surtax of 4 per cent on the federal tax and a general rate reduction of 7 per cent (2004). Thus in 2004, the effective federal rate is 22.12 per cent of taxable income under Part I (see Appendix D).

---

[3]This rate is typically reduced by treaty.

[4]Subs. 214(1); see also *PPG Industries Canada Ltd. v. MNR*, 78 D.T.C. 1062 (TRB).

[5]Subs. 117(2). See Appendix C for rates applicable.

[6]Subs. 124(1).

3. — Trusts

A non-resident testamentary trust is taxable under Part I at the same graduated rates as individuals.[7] A non-resident *inter vivos* trust,[8] however, is taxable at a flat rate of 29 per cent on taxable income.[9] This is equivalent to the highest marginal tax rate on individuals. Provincial taxes and surtaxes, if any, apply on top of the basic rate.

III. — Liability For Part I Tax

1. — Employed in Canada

A non-resident is taxable on his or her Canadian source employment income.[10] Employment in Canada is a question of fact. In addition, the Act deems the following non-resident persons to be employed in Canada:[11]

- Students in full-time attendance at post-secondary educational institutions in Canada;

- Persons who in a previous year ceased to reside in Canada in order to attend or teach at a post-secondary educational institution outside Canada;

- Persons who in a previous year ceased to reside in Canada in order to carry on research for which they received a research grant;[12]

- Individuals who in a previous year ceased to reside in Canada but who received remuneration in the current year in respect of an office or employment from a Canadian resident; and

- Individuals who received a "signing bonus" that is deductible for Canadian income tax purposes by the person who paid the bonus, if it can be shown that the payment was for services to be performed by the individuals in Canada.

A non-resident who is employed in Canada in the year must calculate his or her income from employment according to the usual rules.[13] Thus, salary and wages, employment bene-

---

[7]Subss. 117(2) and 104(2).

[8]Subs. 108(1)"*inter vivos* trust".

[9]Subs. 122(1).

[10]Para. 2(3)(a); see also paras. 248(1)"employed", "employment", and "office".

[11]Subs. 115(2); see also IT-161R3, "Non-residents — Exemption from Tax Deductions at Source on Employment Income" (October 8, 1982) (archived).

[12]Para. 56(1)(o).

[13]See Division B, subdivision a.

fits (including stock option benefits), taxable allowances, and directors' fees are all taxable as income. The non-resident may deduct related expenses.

A non-resident person deemed to be employed in Canada is taxable on remuneration received directly or indirectly from a Canadian resident. Canadian source scholarships, bursaries, research fellowships, education savings plan payments, and "signing bonuses" are also taxable as income.[14] Compensation for work performed outside Canada and subject to income tax in a foreign country, and payments in connection with the selling of property, the negotiating of contracts or the rendering of services in the ordinary course of a business that his or her employer carries on are not Canadian source income.[15]

(a) — The OECD Model Convention

Employment income typically includes the services of sales representatives, construction workers, engineers and employed consultants. The *OECD Model Convention*[16] varies the source rule of taxation depending upon the length of the employee's stay in a country and the source of payment. Article 15 of the *Model Convention* deals with the taxation of employment income other than pensions and government employment income. The purpose of Article 15 is to promote the mobility of qualified personnel employed by international concerns that are called upon to temporarily transfer personnel between operations in different countries. The *Model Convention* seeks to avoid double taxation and prevent tax avoidance through double exemptions of the same income.

Articles 15(1) and (2) state:

> 1. Subject to the provisions of Articles 16, 18 and 19, salaries, wages and other similar remuneration derived by a resident of a Contracting State in respect of an employment shall be taxable only in that State unless the employment is exercised in the other Contracting State. If the employment is so exercised, such remuneration as is derived therefrom may be taxed in that other State.

---

[14]Para. 115(2)(e).

[15]Subpara. 115(2)(e)(i); IT-161R3, "Non-residents — Exemption from Tax Deductions at Source on Employment Income" (October 8, 1982).

[16]Model Convention for the Avoidance of Double Taxation with respect to Taxes on Income and Capital, adopted by Organisation for Economic Co-operation and Development (OECD) on April 11, 1977, amended June 4, 1992.

2. Notwithstanding the provisions of paragraph 1, remuneration derived by a resident of a Contracting State in respect of an employment exercised in the other Contracting State shall be taxable only in the first-mentioned State if:

a) The recipient is present in the other State for a period or periods not exceeding in the aggregate 183 days in any twelve month period commencing or ending in the fiscal year concerned, and

b) The remuneration is paid by, or on behalf of, an employer who is not a resident of the other State, and

c) The remuneration is not borne by a permanent establishment or a fixed base, which the employer has in the other State. ...

As a rule, employment income is taxable in the source country but only if:

- The employee is in the country for an aggregate period exceeding 183 days in any 12 month period commencing or ending in the fiscal year,

- The employee is paid by, or on behalf of, an employer who resides in the source country, and

- The cost is borne by a permanent establishment or a fixed base maintained by the employer in the source country.

Otherwise, employment income is taxable by the employee's country of residence. Thus, a resident of a country who is sent on a temporary assignment to another country will generally be taxed only in his or her own country.

The "fiscal year" referred to in Article 15(2)(a) is the fiscal year of the country in which the employment activity occurs, not the fiscal year of the country in which the employee resides.

(b) — Canada-U.S. Treaty

Under domestic law, Canada has the right to tax a non-resident on his or her Canadian source employment income. Canada's tax treaties, however, often vary or restrict the domestic rule. The *Canada-U.S. Treaty* is an example.

Article XV — Dependent Personal Services

1. Subject to the provisions of Articles XVIII (Pensions and Annuities) and XIX (Government Service), salaries, wages and other similar remuneration derived by a resident of a Contracting State in respect of an employment shall be taxable only in the State unless the employment is exercised in the other Contracting State. If the employment is so exercised, such remuneration as is derived therefrom may be taxed in that other State.

2. Notwithstanding the provisions of paragraph 1, remuneration derived by a resident of a Contracting State in respect of an employment exercised in a calendar year in the other Contracting State shall be taxable only in the first-mentioned State if:

(a) Such remuneration does not exceed ten thousand dollars ($10,000) in the currency of that other State; or

(b) The recipient is present in the other Contracting State for a period or periods not exceeding in the aggregate 183 days in that year and the remuneration is not borne by an employer who is a resident of that other State or by a permanent establishment or a fixed base which the employer has in that other State.

3. Notwithstanding the provisions of paragraphs 1 and 2, remuneration derived by a resident of a Contracting State in respect of an employment regularly exercised in more than one State on a ship, aircraft, motor vehicle or train operated by a resident of that Contracting State shall be taxable only in that State.

The *Canada-U.S. Treaty* departs from the *OECD Model* in several aspects. The primary right to tax employee compensation rests with the residence country. The source country, however, may tax an individual's compensation if:

- The remuneration exceeds $10,000 in the source country's currency,

- The individual is present in the source country for more than 183 days during the taxable year, or

- A permanent establishment or fixed base in, or a resident of, the source country bears the cost of the compensation.

Bearing the cost of compensation means deducting the cost in computing taxable income. Thus, if a Canadian resident individual employed at the Canadian permanent establishment of a U.S. company, performs services in the United States, his or her income from such services is not exempt from U.S. tax if it exceeds $10,000 (U.S.) since the U.S. company is entitled to deduct such wages in computing its taxable income.

These exceptions do not apply to employees who work regularly on board ships, motor vehicles, trains or aircraft that operate in international traffic. Remuneration in respect of such employment is exempt from tax in the source country and is taxable by the country where the enterprise resides. The word "regularly" distinguishes crew members from persons who occasionally work on a ship, aircraft, motor vehicle, or train. This provision, however, is subject to the "saving clause" of paragraph 2 of Article XXIX (Miscellaneous Rules) of the *Canada-U.S. Treaty*, which permits the United States to tax its citizens.

(c) — Exemption from Source Country Taxation

(i) — The 183-Day Rule

An employee is exempt from source country taxation only if he or she is not physically present in the source country where the employee is employed for an aggregate period exceeding 183 days in the year. There is an important difference in the measure of "year" between the *OECD Model Convention* and the *Canada-U.S. Treaty*; namely, the *OECD Model* determines the aggregate of the days spent by the employee in any 12-month period commencing or ending in the particular fiscal year. In contrast, the *Canada-U.S. Treaty* counts only the number of days in the particular calendar year. The difference between the two methods is significant. It allows employees who move between Canada and the U.S. much greater flexibility to organise their stay to fall under the 183-day limit by timing their entry and exit into and out of each country.

Example
Assume that X, who ordinarily resides in the United States, is an employee of a U.S. corporation. He is temporarily assigned to his company's Canadian subsidiary from July 3, YEAR 1 to June 30, YEAR 2. If X stayed in Canada throughout the period, he would be physically present in Canada for 182 days in YEAR 1 and 181 days in YEAR 2 and would not be caught by the 183-day rule in either calendar year. Article 15(2)(a) of the Model Convention would however, have caught him because he would be present in the source country (Canada) in which he exercises employment for more than 183 days in a 12-month period ending in June YEAR 2.

The Canada Revenue Agency (CRA) accepts the double exemption in these circumstances. Indeed, the exemption would appear to be available even if X's employment arrangement continues year after year.

The number of days that the employee is physically present in the source country determines the 183-day period. One includes the following in calculating the number of days:

- Part of a day,
- Day of arrival,
- Day of departure,
- Saturdays and Sundays,
- National holidays,
- Vacation periods before, during and after the period of activity,
- Training periods, strikes, lock-outs,
- Days of inactivity because of delays in delivery of supplies, and
- Days of sickness (whether of the individual or the individual's family).

There is some flexibility insofar as holidays are concerned. Although holidays and vacations spent in the country of activity are normally included in the 183-day count, there appears to be some flexibility where the taxpayer can demonstrate that the holidays are clearly not related to employment.[17]

Illness in the middle of an employee's stay in the country of activity counts towards the 183 days; illness at the end of the employee's stay does not. The rationale for the difference between the two cases is that a delay caused by illness at the end of the employee's stay in the country of activity comes about after the employee's declared intention to leave and, as such, should not count towards his or her stay in the country. In the above example, X would qualify for the exemption in YEAR 2 even if he fell ill after June 30, YEAR 2 and was required to spend an additional two weeks in Canada as a result of his illness.

(ii) — Remuneration Not Paid by Resident of Source Country

The second condition for exemption from tax by the source country is that the employer who pays the remuneration is not a resident of the country in which the employment is exercised.[18]

The term "employer" is not defined in the *OECD Model Convention*. It is generally understood to mean the person who has the rights to the work produced and bears the risk and responsibility for its production. Substance prevails over form. One must examine each case to see whether the functions of "employer" are exercised and, if so, by whom. Where, for example, an individual comes to Canada and carries out employment duties for a Canadian corporation and the costs are borne, directly or indirectly, by the Canadian company, the Canadian company is presumed to be the "employer". The presumption, however, is rebuttable.

Article 15(2) gives rise to abuse in international hiring-out of labour arrangements. For example, a local employer who wants to employ foreign labour for a period of less than 183 days can recruit through an intermediary corporation established abroad, which purports to be the employer. Workers can be farmed out to the person in the country in which the employment is temporarily exercised and the employees can claim tax-exempt status if they otherwise satisfy the provisions of the Article.

The determination as to whether a user of services is an "employer" is essentially a question of fact. In determining whether the real employer is the user of the labour or the foreign intermediary corporation, one should consider the following circumstances:

- Does the hirer bear the responsibility and risk for the result produced by the employee's work?

- Who has the authority to provide the workers with instructions?

---

[17]*OECD Commentary.*

[18]Article 15(2)(b), *OECD Model Convention.*

- Is the work performed at a place that is under the control and responsibility of the user of the services?

- Is the remuneration to the hirer calculated on the basis of the time that the employee's services are utilised?

- Are the tools and materials utilised in the employment provided by the user of the services or by the foreign hirer? and

- Are the number and qualifications of the employees determined by the hirer or the user of the services?

(iii) — Remuneration Not Borne by Permanent Establishment

The third condition for the exemption is that the employee's remuneration is not borne by a permanent establishment or a fixed base that the employer may have in the source country where the employment is exercised. If the employer has a permanent establishment in the country in which the employment is exercised, the exemption is only available if the permanent establishment does not bear the cost of the employee's remuneration.

The terms "borne by" generally mean "allowable as a deduction in computing taxation income." For example, if a Canadian resident who is employed at the Canadian permanent establishment of a U.S. corporation performs services in the United States, his or her remuneration is not exempt from U.S. tax because the U.S. company is entitled to a deduction for the employee's wages in computing its taxable income. But there is some uncertainty associated with the phrase "not borne by" and the uncertainty is exacerbated by the use of the word "paid" in Article 15(2)(b) of the *OECD Model Convention* and its juxtaposition with "borne" in Article 15(2)(c). Are "borne" and "paid" intended to imply different meanings? It is also unclear what happens if an employer who is entitled to a deduction does not in fact take the deduction in the particular year.

(d) — International Transport Personnel

Remuneration from employment exercised aboard a ship or aircraft operated in international traffic, or aboard a boat engaged in inland waterways transport, may be taxed in the country where the enterprise is effectively managed. Article 15(3) of the *OECD Model Convention* provides as follows:

> 3. Notwithstanding the preceding provisions of this Article, remuneration derived in respect of an employment exercised aboard a ship or aircraft operated in international traffic, or aboard a boat engaged in inland waterways transport, may be taxed in the Contracting State in which the place of effective management of the enterprise is situated.

In many of Canada's bilateral treaties, however, the emphasis for taxation is on the country of residence and not on the place of effective management of the enterprise provided for in the *OECD Model*. For example, Article XV (3) of the *Canada-U.S. Treaty* states:

> ... remuneration derived by a resident of a Contracting State in respect of an employment regularly exercised in more than one State on a ship, aircraft, motor vehicle or train operated by a resident of that Contracting State shall be taxable only in that State.

Thus, under the *Canada-U.S. Treaty* a resident of one of the countries is exempt from tax in the other country in respect of employment income regularly exercised on a ship, aircraft, motor vehicle, or train operated by a resident of the taxpayer's country of residence.[19]

(e) — Stock Options

Canadian residents are generally taxable on stock option benefits as employment source income because they are, in substance, an alternative form of cash compensation.[20] A resident individual is taxable on the value of any benefit that he or she derives from the employer's stock option plan if the benefit is derived in respect of, in the course of, or by virtue of employment.[21]

A non-resident who exercises stock options that were granted while he or she was resident and employed in Canada is taxable in Canada on any benefit derived from the options. This is so regardless of whether the options are exercised within or outside Canada.

(i) — Options Exercised Outside Canada

What happens if a non-resident receives stock options from employment in Canada and later exercises the options when he or she has given up Canadian residence? Subsection 7(4) provides that a person who would otherwise come within the stock option rules continues to be subject to subsection 7(1) even though the person ceases to be an employee before exercising his or her options.

In *Hale*,[22] for example, the taxpayer had been employed in Canada and received stock options during his stay in Canada. He later moved to England where he exercised his rights under the stock option plan. The taxpayer was taxable on the value of his stock option bene-

---

[19]See also Article 15 in Canadian bilateral treaties with Australia, the Netherlands, Switzerland and Japan.

[20]Subs. 7(1) and 7(1.1).

[21]Subs. 7(5).

[22]*J. Hale v. Canada*, [1992] 2 C.T.C. 379, 92 D.T.C. 6473 (Eng.) (F.C.A.); leave to appeal refused (1993), 151 N.R. 159 (note) (S.C.C.).

fits by virtue of Article 15(1) of the *Canada-U.K. Treaty*. Since the taxpayer's employment was exercised in Canada, his benefits fell outside of the exemption in the *Treaty*. Tax treaties are negotiated primarily to prevent double taxation and they should be interpreted accordingly. Hale was not taxable on the value of his benefit in the United Kingdom and, consequently, was not subject to double taxation on the benefits. Giving the *Treaty* a large and liberal construction, the taxpayer was deemed to have exercised his employment in Canada and, as such, was taxable on the value of benefits derived from the Canadian stock option plan.

Thus, Article 15(1) should be interpreted by reference to the country where the employment, rather than the stock option, is exercised. That, however, is not always the case. In *Tedmon*,[23] for example, the taxpayer was liable for Canadian tax for stock option benefits exercised in Canada but in respect of employment exercised in the United States for a different employer. Notwithstanding that the taxpayer received the benefit in respect of employment exercised in the United States, he was subject to Canadian tax because he derived the benefit while he was resident in Canada.

Tedmon is clearly inconsistent with *Hale*. The Agency has not, however, revised its view and stands by its inconsistent positions.[24]

(ii) — Limited Presence in Canada

There are some exceptions to the source of employment rule in Article 15(1) of the *OECD Model*. Typically, an individual is not subject to Canadian tax in respect of stock option benefits exercised in Canada if the individual was not present in Canada for more than 183 days commencing or ending in the year and the remuneration was not borne by an employer resident in Canada or by a permanent establishment or fixed base of the employer in Canada. In the case of U.S. residents, there is a further exemption if the individual's total remuneration for employment exercised in Canada for the year in which the options were granted is less than $10,000.

2. — Carrying on a Business in Canada

A non-resident is subject to Part I tax if he or she carries on a business in Canada. The threshold test is whether the non-resident person conducts business in Canada. This is quite different from carrying on a business *with* Canada. The distinction between business and investment income is a mixed question of fact and law. Investment income is passive and derives from holding property. Thus, investment income is the yield on property. In contrast,

---

[23]*Tedmon v. M.N.R.*, [1991] 2 C.T.C. 2128, 91 D.T.C. 962 (T.C.C.).

[24]Technical Interpretation (November 26, 1992).

one derives business income by using property, a process that usually combines labor and capital.

Since the distinction between business and investment income depends essentially upon activity, it is sometimes difficult to distinguish between a passive business and actively managed investments. Although there is a refutable presumption that corporate income is business income,[25] the distinction between business and investment income is essentially one of facts and circumstances. We must answer two preliminary questions:

- Is the non-resident person carrying on a business? and

- If yes, is the non-resident carrying on the business in Canada?

(a) — "Business"

"Business" includes "a profession, calling, trade, manufacture, or undertaking of any kind whatever and — an adventure or concern in the nature of trade."[26] The phrase "carrying on business in Canada" also includes the solicitation of orders or the offering of anything for sale in Canada through an agent or servant. For this purpose, the location where the transaction is completed is irrelevant.[27]

By solicitation we mean that the non-resident seeks orders in Canada. The term "offer" has its ordinary meaning in contract law.[28] Thus, in the absence of treaty protection, a non-resident is liable for Canadian tax simply by soliciting orders or by offering goods for sale in Canada. Merely advertising a product for sale in Canada, however, is not an "offer" and is not, by itself, sufficient to characterize a business as being carried on in Canada.[29]

A "business" also includes an "adventure or concern in the nature of trade". Hence, even an isolated transaction can be a "business". The phrase "carrying on", however, implies contin-

---

[25]See e.g., *Canadian Marconi Co. v. The Queen*, [1986] 2 S.C.R. 522, [1986] 2 C.T.C. 465, 86 D.T.C. 6526 (S.C.C.); revg. [1984] C.T.C. 319, 84 D.T.C. 6267 (F.C.A.); *Anderson Logging Co. v. The King* (1924), [1925] S.C.R. 45, [1917-1927] C.T.C. 198, 52 D.T.C. 1209 (S.C.C.); affd. 52 D.T.C. 1215 (P.C.) (*raison d'etre* of a public company is to carry on business); *The Queen v. Rockmore Investments Ltd.*, [1976] C.T.C. 291, 76 D.T.C. 6156 (F.C.A.).

[26]Subs. 248(1)"business".

[27]Para. 253(b).

[28]*Sudden Valley Inc. v. The Queen*, [1976] C.T.C. 297 at 300, 76 D.T.C. 6178 at 6180 (F.C.T.D.); affd. [1976] C.T.C. 775, 76 D.T.C. 6448 (F.C.A.).

[29]*Sudden Valley Inc. v. The Queen*, [1976] C.T.C. 775, 76 D.T.C. 6448 (F.C.A.).

uing activity. Therefore, we cannot say that a non-resident person who engages in an isolated transaction carries on a business.[30]

There is no single criterion to decide whether a person is carrying on a business in Canada:[31]

> There is not, I think, any principle of law which lays down what carrying on trade is. There are a multitude of things which together make up the carrying on of trade, but I know no one distinguishing incident, for it is a compound fact made up of a variety of things.

The following factors determine whether a non-resident person is carrying on a business in Canada:

- The location of its contracts;

- The location where goods are delivered and payments are made;

- The location of its business assets;

- Whether it uses an agent or independent contractor;

- The location where it derives its profits;

- The nature of its activities;

- The location of its bank accounts, listed telephone numbers, and addresses;

- The location where it purchases its assets;

- The degree of supervisory or other activity in Canada;

- The substance of its transactions;

- Whether its activities in Canada are integral or merely ancillary to its main business; and

- Whether individuals in Canada help the business in its endeavours.

---

[30]*Tara Exploration & Dev. Co. v. M.N.R.*, [1970] C.T.C. 557 at 567, 70 D.T.C. 6370 at 6376 (Ex. Ct.).

> the better view is that the words 'carried on' are not words that can aptly be used with the word 'adventure'. To carry on something involves continuity of time or operations such as is involved in the ordinary sense of a 'business'. An adventure is an isolated happening. One has an adventure as opposed to *carrying on* a business.

[31]*Erichsen v. Last* (1881), IV T.C. 422 at 423 approved by Urie J. in *The Queen v. Gurd's Products Co.*, [1985] 2 C.T.C. 85 at 92, 85 D.T.C. 5314 at 5319 (F.C.A.); leave to appeal to S.C.C. refused 64 N.R. 156.

3. — Liability for Part I Tax under Treaty Law

Under domestic tax law, a non-resident person is taxable in Canada if the non-resident carries on business in Canada at any time in a taxation year.[32] The *Income Tax Act* defines business in the broadest possible terms in order to assert taxable jurisdiction over non-residents with minimal Canadian connections. This is harmful to international trade and business because it exposes non-residents to potential double taxation and considerable uncertainty. Hence, international tax treaties (at least those between developed countries) almost invariably provide an important exception to this domestic rule. International tax treaties usually restrict the source country's power to tax the business profits of a foreign enterprise to circumstances where the enterprise has a permanent establishment in the country.

Article 7(1) of the *OECD Model Convention*, for example, states:

> The profits of an enterprise of a Contracting State shall be taxable only in that State unless the enterprise carries on business in the other Contracting State through a permanent establishment situated therein. If the enterprise carries on business as aforesaid, the profits of the enterprise may be taxed in the other State but only so much of them as is attributable to that permanent establishment.

Article 7(1) states the general rule: an enterprise is taxable only in its country of residence.

The exception to this rule is that if an enterprise carries on business in another country, the other country may tax the enterprise if it is carrying on business through a permanent establishment situated therein. In that case, the enterprise's business profits may be taxed in the other country, but only to the extent that the profits are attributable to that permanent establishment. Article 7 raises the threshold for subjecting a non-resident enterprise to tax from the "solicitation and offering for sale" level[33] to the much higher "permanent establishment" test. A non-resident enterprise is not taxable in a treaty country merely because it concludes therein business contracts from which it derives profits. To be taxable by the country, it must have a permanent establishment in the country. Canada follows the *OECD Model Convention*. A non-resident person is taxable in Canada under Part I of the Act only if the non-resident carries on business in Canada through a permanent establishment in Canada.

A country should not tax foreign persons unless the foreign person becomes closely involved in the economic affairs of the country. The OECD states as follows:[34]

> ... it has come to be accepted in international fiscal matters that until an enterprise of one State sets up a permanent establishment in another State it should not properly be regarded as participating in the economic life of that other State to such an extent that it comes within the jurisdiction of that other State's taxing rights.

---

[32]Para. 2(3)(b).

[33]S. 253.

[34]Commentary, *OECD Model Convention*.

The theory underlying the permanent establishment concept is to distinguish between trading in a country and trading with a country. The concept of permanent establishment allocates taxable jurisdiction between source and residence countries over the business profits[35] of multinational enterprises. The source country assumes taxable jurisdiction if the non-resident enterprise has sufficient nexus with it. Otherwise, the residence country retains taxable jurisdiction over its enterprises.

The concept of permanent establishment provides a uniform measure of the depth of an enterprise's presence in a country. Thus, once we determine that a foreign enterprise has an economic presence in a country to render it taxable under its domestic law, we inquire whether the presence is sufficient to constitute a permanent establishment.

A permanent establishment is a "fixed" place of business. This generally implies that the business enterprise uses a particular building or physical location and that it is foreseeable that the use of the building or location will be more than temporary.[36] A "place of business" includes any premises, facilities, or installations that an enterprise uses to carry on business, regardless whether it uses the facilities exclusively for that purpose. An enterprise has a place of business even if it only has some space at its disposal. It is immaterial whether the enterprise owns or rents the premises, facilities or installations.[37] The OECD Commentaries give some examples:

> A place of business may thus be constituted by a pitch in a marketplace, or by a certain permanently used area in a customs depot. The place of business may be situated in the business facilities of another enterprise. This may be the case for instance where the foreign enterprise has at its constant disposal certain premises or a part of it owned by the other enterprise. ...
>
> Thus, in the normal way there has to be a link between the place of business and a specific geographical point. It is immaterial how long an enterprise of a Contracting State operates in the other Contracting State, if it does not do so at a distinct place, but this does not mean that the equipment constituting the place of business has to be actually fixed to the soil on which it stands. It is enough that the equipment remains on a particular site.

Article 7(1) of the *Model Convention* contains the four essential conditions for the taxation of a non-resident business enterprise:

1. The existence of an enterprise;

2. The carrying on of a business by the enterprise;

3. A place of business that is fixed; and

---

[35]The concept is also relevant for the purposes of determining the source of interest and royalty payments.

[36]See *OECD Commentaries* on Article 5 at paragraphs 4–8.

[37]See *OECD Commentaries* on Article 5 at paragraph 4.

4. A nexus between the enterprise and the fixed place of business.

A non-resident enterprise that meets these conditions is taxable on its business profits in the country where it conducts its business, but only to the extent that its profits are attributable to the permanent establishment in that country.

(a) — The Existence of an Enterprise

Article 7 applies only to an "enterprise of a Contracting State". The *OECD Model Convention* does not define the term "enterprise".[38] An enterprise generally refers to a business and a business implies activity. Thus, an enterprise is something more than a passive investment.[39] An enterprise's business activities refer to any independent activity other than the use of immovable property within the meaning of Article 6(3) and other independent personal services.

(b) — Carrying on a Business by the Enterprise

In the absence of any other evidence, the general rule is that a person carries on business in the place where it concludes its contracts and renders its services.[40] Both Canada and the U.S. require at least some minimal physical presence to characterize a foreign person as carrying on a business in the country. A foreign person is not carrying on business in Canada if its presence in the country is merely transient or insubstantial. In *Sudden Valley Inc.*,[41] for example, a U.S. company lured Canadians living on the west coast of Canada to the Seattle area, where its representative would then attempt to sell them land in the United States. The company took all of the offers to purchase and financial deposits in the United States. The U.S. company's only presence in Canada was a Vancouver office from which it invited Canadian residents to visit the United States. The company also conducted a sales campaign of advertisements in Canadian publications and television broadcasts from U.S. border stations. The advertising material, however, did not mention the offering of land for sale but merely referred to a "gracious invitation to Sudden Valley for a visit." They made no offer, and they offered nothing for sale, in Canada. The Federal Court held that "soliciting orders"

---

[38]See Article 3 *OECD Model Convention*.

[39]*Rutenberg v. M.N.R.*, [1979] C.T.C. 459, 79 D.T.C. 5394 (F.C.A.) (Passive investment in Canadian real estate by a New York diamond dealer was not sufficient to constitute a business activity of a United States enterprise and, therefore, did not qualify for exemption under the business profits article).

[40]*Geigy (Canada) Ltd. v. Commissioner, Social Services Tax*, [1969] C.T.C. 79 at 84.

[41]*Sudden Valley Inc. v. The Queen*, [1976] C.T.C. 297, 76 D.T.C. 6178 (F.C.T.D.); affd. [1976] C.T.C. 775, 76 D.T.C. 6448 (F.C.A.).

in section 253 does not include a mere "invitation to treat". The phrase "offered anything for sale in Canada" means an offer that, if accepted, will create a binding contract between the buyer and the seller. An invitation to treat is not a solicitation of orders. Thus, non-residents who merely canvass Canadian business are not liable to tax in Canada.[42]

What of a company's web page on the Internet? The key issue for a non-resident person from a country that does not have a treaty with Canada is whether a server used to store a sales catalogue and accept orders from Canadian residents is carrying on business in Canada. A web page is akin to an invitation to treat consumers. To be sure, the company may provide a comprehensive description of its products, prices, and delivery on the web page. Nevertheless, the information is surely no more detailed than that available in conventional catalogues which retail establishments routinely publish. Although the company may not have the same physical inventory constraints as a conventional retail establishment, it is difficult to characterize it as an offeror that is prepared to supply an unlimited quantity to all consumers worldwide.

Section 253 also requires that the solicitation for sale in Canada must occur through an agent or servant in the country. An agent is a person who can affect the legal relationships of his or her principal. A web page is an inanimate manifestation of graphics programmed to react in a particular sequence when it receives information. Although a web page eases interaction between the seller and the consumer, one can hardly consider a web page a "person" in law.

Similarly in the U.S., the mere solicitation of business is not sufficient to constitute "doing business" for the purposes of establishing taxable nexus. In *Piedras Negras*,[43] for example, a radio station that had previously broadcast from Texas moved over the Rio Grande to Mexico. Although all of its production facilities were in Mexico, it broadcast in English to a Texas audience and derived all of its revenues from advertisers in the United States. Other than the collection of payments from advertisers, the company did not employ any labour in the U.S. The foreign corporation was not subject to U.S. income tax on its income from the advertising contracts because it earned its income outside the United States.[44]

In North *Western States Portland Cement Co.*,[45] however, a U.S. court held solicitation plus an office in the U.S. to be sufficient taxable nexus for the purposes of state tax.

---

[42]*Grino v. Apthorpe*, 2 T.C. 182; *Granger & Son v. Gough* (1896), 3 T.C. 462.

[43]B.T.A. 297 (1941), affd. 127 F. 2nd 260 (5th Cir. 1942).

[44]The determination of being engaged in a trade or business is a matter of common law in the U.S. Solicitation per se does not create sufficient presence to be considered carrying on a trade or business.

[45]*North Western States Portland Cement Co. v. Minnesota* (1959), 358 U.S. 450.

Locating sales software on offshore servers that serve Canadians is not per se a taxable presence in Canada.[46]

(c) — A Fixed Place of Business

A permanent establishment implies stability, productivity, and dependence. An enterprise can establish a permanent establishment in a country by directly owning or controlling facilities, or by having a dependant agent act for it, in the country. In the first case, the permanent establishment is part of the same enterprise and a part of the legal entity. In the latter case, the agent is a separate legal entity but depends on the enterprise to such an extent that the agent becomes its permanent establishment.

A place of business is a permanent establishment only if it is fixed. This implies an establishment at a distinct place with a degree of permanence. "Permanent" means that the establishment is a stable one, and does have a temporary or tentative character. The OECD Commentary states:

> ... in the normal way there has to be a link between the place of business and a specific geographical point. It is immaterial how long an enterprise of a Contracting State operates in the other Contracting State if it does not do so at a distinct place, but this does not mean that the equipment constituting the place of business has to be actually fixed to the soil on which it stands. It is enough that the equipment remains on a particular site.

Is a server or web site a permanent establishment? If it is, where is it located? Income tax treaties do not provide easy answers to these questions because we developed the concept of permanent establishment in a non-digital era when transactions and commercial law dealt primarily with tangible property. Typically, however, tax treaties exclude from a fixed place of business any offices and facilities that one uses merely for promotional activities or for the storage, display, or delivery of goods and facilities.[47]

Where does a web site fit into this definitional structure of a permanent establishment? Is a web site a fixed place of business? If it is a fixed place of business, where is it located? Is it in the jurisdiction where the retailer itself is physically present or on the electronic server that serves the web site? Even if it is a fixed place of business in a taxable jurisdiction, is it

---

[46]See also Revenue Ruling 56-165 (1956-1 CB849), where the Internal Revenue Service ruled that regular and active solicitation in the United States was sufficient to cause a taxpayer to be engaged in a U.S. trade of business under the *U.S.-Swiss Treaty*. In this situation, however, the company had a physical presence in the United States beyond the mere solicitation of orders. The company brought logging equipment into the United States to display its products and generate orders that it filled in the country.

[47]Article 5(4)(a) *OECD Model Convention*. See, for example, Article 5(6)(a) of the *Canada-U.S. Treaty*.

arguable that the website is solely for the display, delivery, or advertising of goods or services? There are no absolute answers to these questions.

A "place of business" includes any premises, facilities, installations or space for the carrying on of the business. The enterprise may own or rent the space or otherwise have the space available to it. Thus, a place of business may even be situated in the business facilities of another enterprise.

The term "permanent" implies something more than a transitional or passing connection between an enterprise and a country. A "permanent establishment" requires more than transient business relations or connection between a geographical point and a place of business. There must be some fixed connection. Apart from that, however, the requirements for a fixed place of business are quite minimal. A hotel room or the living accommodation of a travelling salesman may qualify as a "permanent establishment". It is immaterial whether the enterprise rents or owns the premises. The Commentary to the *OECD Model*, for example, states:

> The place of business has to be a 'fixed' one. Thus, in the normal way there has to be a link between the place of business and a specific geographical point. It is immaterial how long an enterprise of a Contracting State operates in the other Contracting State if it does not do so at a distinct place, but this does not mean that the equipment constituting the place of business has to be actually fixed to the soil on which it stands. It is enough that the equipment remains on a particular site.

Although "permanent establishment" implies a degree of permanency, it does not necessarily mean that an establishment set up for a very short period of time cannot be a "permanent" place of business. One must look to the duration of time in the context of activities to determine whether it was "permanent" during its existence. Thus, a place of business that is set up at the outset for a short temporary purpose because of the nature of the enterprise's activity may, nevertheless, constitute a fixed place of business and a permanent establishment for treaty purposes.

Article 5(2) of the *OECD Model Convention* lists some examples of the types of presence that constitute a permanent establishment:

> The term "permanent establishment" includes especially:
>
> (a) A place of management;
>
> (b) A branch;
>
> (c) An office;
>
> (d) A factory;
>
> (e) A workshop, and
>
> (f) A mine, an oil or gas well, a quarry or any other place of extraction of natural resources.

We must read Article 5(2) in the context of Article 5(1). Notwithstanding the use of the words "includes especially" in Article 5(2), the Convention does not deem the types of places listed to be a permanent establishment. The listed places constitute only *prima facie* evidence of a permanent establishment. Thus, the types of places listed constitute permanent establishments *only if* they have a degree of permanence sufficient to be a fixed place of business.[48]

A special rule applies to construction projects. Article 5(3) of the *OECD Model* provides that:

> A building site or construction or installation project constitutes a permanent establishment only if it lasts more than twelve months.

Thus, a building site, construction or installation project can be a permanent establishment only if lasts more than 12 months. The time requirement is the *sine qua non* for qualification as a permanent establishment. The 12-month test applies to each individual site or construction project. Thus, one must consider each site as a self-contained project and only the time spent on that particular location counts for the purposes of determining whether or not the 12-month test is satisfied.

Article 5(4) deems certain types of facilities not to constitute a "permanent establishment":

> Notwithstanding the preceding provisions of this Article, the term "permanent establishment" shall be deemed not to include:
>
> a) the use of facilities solely for the purpose of storage, display or delivery of goods or merchandise belonging to the enterprise;
>
> b) the maintenance of a stock of goods or merchandise belonging to the enterprise solely for the purpose of storage, display or delivery;
>
> c) the maintenance of a stock of goods or merchandise belonging to the enterprise solely for the purpose of processing by another enterprise;
>
> d) the maintenance of a fixed place of business solely for the purpose of purchasing goods or merchandise or of collecting information, for the enterprise;
>
> e) the maintenance of a fixed place of business solely for the purpose of carrying on, for the enterprise, any other activity of a preparatory or auxiliary character;
>
> f) the maintenance of a fixed place of business solely for any combination of activities mentioned in sub-paragraphs a) to e), provided that the overall activity of the fixed place of business resulting from this combination is of a preparatory or auxiliary character.

The feature that is common to all these activities is that they are either preparatory or auxiliary in nature. The economic linkage of an enterprise that engages solely in auxiliary or

---

[48]See paragraph 12, *OECD Commentary* on Article 5(2): "This paragraph contains a list, by no means exhaustive, of examples, each of which can be regarded, *prima facie*, as constituting a permanent establishment."

preparatory activities in a country is not sufficiently firm to justify the taxation of business profits by the country. There is also a practical problem. It is extremely difficult to determine the business profits attributable to preparatory and auxiliary activities.

Since Article 5(4) is a deeming provision, it takes precedence over Articles 5(1), (2) and (3). There can be no permanent establishment if the enterprise's presence or facility qualifies under one of the exclusions. The exclusion applies even if the enterprise has a fixed place of business that it maintains solely for any combination of the listed activities, provided that the overall activity of the fixed place of business is of a preparatory or auxiliary character.

(i) — Dependent Agents

The *Model Convention* deems an enterprise to have a permanent establishment in a country if a dependent agent acts on its behalf in the country and the agent has, and habitually exercises, an authority to conclude contracts in the name of the enterprise. Article 5(5) of the *OECD Model Convention* states as follows:

> Notwithstanding the provisions of paragraphs 1 and 2, where a person other than an agent of an independent status to whom paragraph 6 applies is acting on behalf of an enterprise and has, and habitually exercises, in a Contracting State an authority to conclude contracts in the name of the enterprise, that enterprise shall be deemed to have a permanent establishment in that State in respect of any activities which that person undertakes for the enterprise, unless the activities of such person are limited to those mentioned in paragraph 4 which, if exercised through a fixed place of business, would not make this fixed place of business a permanent establishment under the provisions of that paragraph.

Thus, dependent agents with a power to contract, other than those who engage in activities of a preparatory or auxiliary character, can cause an enterprise to have a permanent establishment in a country. The dependent agent may be an individual, corporation, or other body or persons. A subsidiary corporation can also be a dependent agent with power to contract on behalf of its parent company.

An employee is a dependent agent of his or her employer when the employee acts within the scope of his or her authority. But not all employees have or exercise the power to contract on behalf of their employers. Article 5(5) applies only if the dependent agent has an authority to conclude contracts in the name of the enterprise that the dependent agent represents. "Authority" would appear to include "apparent" authority or authority by estoppel. Thus, it is the agent's actual behaviour that determines whether or not the agent has sufficient power to constitute a permanent establishment of his or her enterprise.

Further, it is not sufficient for the agent merely to have the authority to conclude contracts. The agent must, in fact, habitually exercise the authority on behalf of the enterprise. The term "habitually" implies a certain degree of continuity in the agent's activities.

(ii) — Independent Agents

The activities of an independent agent (for example, a broker or general commission agent) on behalf of an enterprise do not constitute a permanent establishment of the enterprise if the independent agent is acting in the ordinary course of business. The independent agent must be both legally and economically independent.

Article 5(6) of the *OECD Model Convention* provides that:

> An enterprise shall not be deemed to have a permanent establishment in a Contracting State merely because it carries on business in that State through a broker, general commission agent or any other agent of an independent status, provided that such persons are acting in the ordinary course of their business.

(iii) — Parent and Subsidiaries

A controlling interest held by a parent corporation in its subsidiary does not of itself constitute either corporate entity a permanent establishment of the other. Thus, tax treaties recognise the independence and separate legal status of corporations in much the same way as private law. Similarly, a one-person corporation and its sole shareholder do not constitute a permanent establishment for each other merely by virtue of the control relationship between them.

Article 5(7) of the *OECD Model Convention* provides as follows:

> The fact that a company which is a resident of a Contracting State controls or is controlled by a company which is a resident of the other Contracting State, or which carries on business in that other State (whether through a permanent establishment or otherwise), shall not of itself constitute either company a permanent establishment of the other.

(d) — Business through a Permanent Establishment

Article 7 requires that the enterprise carry on its business through a permanent establishment in the country if it is to be taxable in that country. Hence, it is necessary to look at an enterprise's activities and determine whether its activities are conducted through a particular location. Mere physical presence is not sufficient. For example, the rental of real estate located in a country does not by itself render the property a fixed place of business if the enterprise does not carry on its business on the real property.

(e) — Profits Attributable to Permanent Establishment

"Business profits" constitute the single most important category of economic activity in international trade. Thus, Article 7 (Business Profits) of the *OECD Model Convention* (and its counterpart in international double taxation treaties) is key to the formulation of international business structures.

The country in which an enterprise has a permanent establishment is entitled to tax its business profits, but only to the extent that the profits are attributable to the permanent establishment. Thus, the application of Article 7 depends upon the enterprise's business profits being economically connected to the permanent establishment in the taxing country. Hence, the Article requires an allocation between profits that result from the permanent establishment's activities and those that are attributable to other centres of the enterprise, for example, its head office. This rule provides incentive for enterprises to siphon off and allocate profits and losses between countries in order to minimise their overall international tax burden. There are, however, provisions to control such abuses.[49]

IV. — Forms Of Business Organizations

The selection of the appropriate form of organization or entity to conduct business is central to international tax planning. An enterprise must select the form of organization that is best suited to its business and that minimises tax or at least avoids double taxation. In most cases, it is the form of organization, and not its economic substance that controls the tax consequences of doing business in Canada. Thus, there is vast difference between a sole proprietorship and a wholly-owned private corporation.

A foreign enterprise can conduct its Canadian operations through:

- An agency,

- A branch, or

- A subsidiary corporation.

There are various forms of corporations, each of which attracts different tax consequences. It used to be that choice of entity involved a real choice between entities with substantially different characteristics. Increasingly, however, the choice of entity is based upon cosmetic differences that produce substantially different results.

1. — Agency

Agency is the relationship that exists between persons when one person (the "agent") is considered in law to represent the other (the "principal") so as to affect the principal's legal relations with third parties. Thus, the essence of agency is the power of an agent to affect legal relationships between the principal and third parties. Although the concept is easy to

---

[49]See, for example, Article 9, *OECD Model Convention*.

define, it is often difficult to identify. No word is more commonly and constantly abused than "agent".[50]

The existence of an agency relationship is a mixed question of fact and law. The determinative element is whether the person who acts in a representative capacity is acting on his or her own account and behalf or on behalf of the non-resident person. An agent can be independent of, or dependent upon, the principal for whom the agent conducts business. Traditionally, we use the term "agent" to refer to an independent agent and "servant" or "employee" to a dependent agent.

In law, a principal has the power to control the agent. It is a question of fact, however, whether a non-resident person has sufficient power or control over his or her representative to establish an agency relationship. One considers various factors. For example:

- The person with whom the goods are identified;

- The manner in which the representative fills orders, that is from existing inventory or upon receipt of a specific order;

- The representative's degree of control over the acceptance of orders and credit terms;

- The representative's degree of control over the price of goods sold and the terms and conditions of sale;

- The method of payment for goods and the name in which payment is received;

- The mode of compensation of the representative; and

- The manner of delivery of goods and the carriage of risk on inventory.

Agency is an attractive form of business because it is easy to set up and minimises operating costs. An agent conducts business on behalf of his or her principal, usually with minimal investment in financial or capital assets. The disadvantage of agency is that it denies the principal a formal presence in the country. The principal also has less than complete organizational control over business activities.

2. — Branch Operations

A non-resident corporation can do business in Canada through a branch. A branch is not a separate legal entity and there are no immediate tax consequences when it is created.

The decision to do business in Canada as a branch, rather than as a subsidiary, depends both upon business and tax considerations. Since a branch is not a separate legal entity, it does not insulate the non-resident corporation from full legal liability. The debts and obligations of the branch operation are the responsibility of the non-resident corporation.

---

[50]As Lord Herschell observed in *Kennedy v. DeTrafford*, [1897] A.C. 180.

We tax the business income of a branch in a manner similar to the income of domestic companies. In addition to the Part I tax, however, a branch is also liable for Part XIV tax (the "branch tax") on its net after-tax business profits to the extent that the branch repatriates its profits from Canada. This ensures that business profits bear the same amount of tax regardless of the legal form of organization through which one conducts the business. Thus, tax neutrality is the cornerstone of the branch tax. That said, however, it is important to note that there are substantial differences between the overall tax burden of a branch and a subsidiary. These differences result primarily because of differences in the timing of repatriation of profits or the manner in which one disposes of branch assets.

There are several advantages to conducting business through a branch in Canada:

- A branch operation is easy to set up with minimal start up costs and legal requirements.

- A branch is not a separate legal entity. Hence, its profits and losses are directly attributable to the non-resident corporation. This is an advantage if the home country does not permit consolidated financial reporting for tax purposes. Thus, the desirability of a branch structure can depend upon whether the non-resident corporation has sufficient income in the home country to offset foreign branch losses. This advantage diminishes if the home country permits consolidated reporting of corporate income for tax purposes.

- Some of Canada's tax treaties have a limited branch tax exemption, which reduces the tax on branches.[51] The *Canada-U.S. and the Canada-U.K. Treaties*, for example, exempt the first $500,000 (Cdn.) of branch profits from tax in the source country. Thus, one can use a branch to start up a business, use the $500,000 exemption, and then incorporate the branch into a subsidiary corporation.

- The thin capitalization rules[52] do not apply to branches.

- Branch start-up losses can be offset against the foreign corporation's income.

To summarize: a branch is usually cheaper to operate than a subsidiary, subject to less stringent rules of debt financing, and allows greater flexibility in loss utilization.

There are, however, some disadvantages of operating a branch:

- In addition to filing returns in the home jurisdiction, the branch must also file a return with respect to its Canadian source income.

- Allocation of income and expenses between a branch and its head office may be quite difficult in certain circumstances and invite audit disputes with the revenue authorities.

---

[51]The *Canada-U.S. Treaty*, for example, exempts the first $500,000 (Cdn.) of branch profits from the branch tax.

[52]Subs. 18(4).

(a) — Branch Tax

The principal purpose of the branch tax under Part XIV of the Act is to make the tax system neutral between branches and subsidiaries. The branch tax removes the incentive that would otherwise exist for foreign corporations to avoid Canadian withholding tax on dividends by carrying on their business in Canada through branch operations. Thus, the tax equalizes the tax burden between branch and subsidiary operations carrying on business in Canada. The tax base on which we impose the Part XIV tax, however, is somewhat different from the base upon which subsidiary corporations pay Part XIII withholding tax. Thus, the system is not completely neutral.

The branch tax applies to non-residents who carry on business in Canada at any time in a year through a branch operation.[53] The normal branch tax is 25 per cent on the branch's Canadian net after-tax income. This rate is lower in some of Canada's tax treaties. The *Canada-U.S. Treaty*, for example, exempts Canadian branches of U.S. corporations from the branch tax up to a maximum of $500,000 (Canadian) accumulative branch profits.

Part XIV reduces Canadian net after-tax income by the amount of any profits that the branch reinvests in qualifying Canadian property. This is an annual calculation. The amount by which the branch reduces its base in one year is added to its income in the following year. The branch can then claim a new allowance if it was carrying on business in Canada at the end of the year. Thus, the branch cannot claim the allowance for reinvested profits if it ceases to carry on business in a year. This is an important consideration in the timing of the decision to incorporate a branch into a subsidiary corporation.

In limited circumstances, one can defer the branch tax normally payable upon a transfer of assets to a subsidiary. The deferral is available, however, only if the entity that transfers the assets of the branch receives shares of a Canadian corporation with a low paid-up capital as consideration.[54] The requirement that the shares have a low paid-up capital ensures that the entity can extract the accumulated profits on which it defers the tax from Canada only as dividends and not by repatriating share capital. The dividends would then be subject to withholding tax. Further, the deferral is available only to the extent that the branch transfers certain qualified properties to a wholly-owned subsidiary corporation.

"Qualified property" is property that a branch uses immediately before the transfer for the purpose of earning income from a business that it carries on in Canada. The transferee corporation must be a Canadian corporation that becomes a wholly-owned subsidiary corporation immediately after the transfer. Thus, one can eliminate the branch tax if the paid-up capital of the shares that the transferee issues as consideration for qualified property does not exceed the elected amount of the property less the non-share consideration in the prior year's investment allowance.

---

[53]S. 219.

[54]Para. 219(1)(k).

(b) — Income Earned in Canada

The profits of a non-resident corporation carrying on business in Canada are taxable in Canada.[55] As noted earlier, Canadian double taxation treaties provide that the liability for Canadian tax arises only if the non-resident is carrying on business through a permanent establishment in Canada. Where a branch constitutes a permanent establishment, one must determine the portion of the profits of the non-resident enterprise attributable to the permanent establishment in Canada.

Article 7 of the *OECD Model Convention* states the general principles by which we attribute the business profits of an enterprise to a permanent establishment. The Article 7 states as follows:

> 1. The profits of an enterprise of a Country shall be taxable only in that State unless the enterprise carries on business in the other Country through a permanent establishment situated therein. If the enterprise carries on business as aforesaid, the profits of the enterprise may be taxed in the other State but only so much of them as is attributable to that permanent establishment.

> 2. Subject to the provisions of paragraph 3, where an enterprise of a Country carries on business in the other Country through a permanent establishment situated therein, there shall in each Country be attributed to that permanent establishment the profits which it might be expected to make if it were a distinct and separate enterprise engaged in the same or similar activities under the same or similar conditions and dealing wholly independently with the enterprise of which it is a permanent establishment.

> 3. In determining the profits of a permanent establishment, there shall be allowed as deductions expenses which are incurred for the purposes of the permanent establishment, including executive and general administrative expenses so incurred, whether in the State in which the permanent establishment is situated or elsewhere.

> 4. Insofar as it has been customary in a Country to determine the profits to be attributed to a permanent establishment on the basis of an apportionment of the total profits of the enterprise to its various parts, nothing in paragraph 2 shall preclude that Country from determining the profits to be taxed by such an apportionment as may be customary; the method of apportionment adopted shall, however, be such that the result shall be in accordance with the principles contained in this Article.

> 5. No profits shall be attributed to a permanent establishment by reason of the mere purchase by that permanent establishment of goods or merchandise for the enterprise.

> 6. For the purposes of the preceding paragraphs, the profits to be attributed to the permanent establishment shall be determined by the same method year by year unless there is good and sufficient reason to the contrary.

---

[55]Para. 2(3)(b).

7. Where profits include items of income which are dealt with separately in other Articles of this Convention, then the provisions of those Articles shall not be affected by the provisions of this Article.

The *Model Convention*, which Canada follows, restricts the right of the source country to tax the business profits of a non-resident enterprise. Only business profits generated through a permanent establishment and attributable to it are taxable by the source country. The principle is that an enterprise should not be regarded as participating in the economic life of the source country until such time as it has a direct and intimate involvement with the country. This approach permits simple and efficient administration of tax statutes and generally follows the way in which enterprises' organize and transact business.

"Business profits" are determined under the domestic law of the country in which the permanent establishment is located. The Act segregates income by source and calculates income from each source in a particular place as if:[56]

- There is no income or loss except from that source; and

- There are no deductions except those wholly applicable to that source.

Thus, one must allocate direct expenses such as the cost of goods sold, selling expenses, capital cost allowance on branch assets, and interest expense on specific borrowings for a branch asset directly to the branch. The allocation of indirect expenses to the branch, such as general and administrative expenses and interest on general borrowings, must be on some reasonable basis.

There is no set method for the allocation of indirect expenses. There are various allocation methods, all of which are somewhat arbitrary. For example, a business may allocate costs on the basis of sales, assets, gross income, number of employees, size of payroll or on some combination of these criteria.

Similarly, there are no hard and fast rules in respect of the sourcing of business income and expenses to a permanent establishment. One determines the source of business income and expenses by where the business:

- Makes its contracts;

- Makes its decisions to purchase and sell;

- Produces its goods;

- Delivers its goods;

- Performs its services;

- Makes its payments;

---

[56]S. 4.

- Locates its property; and

- Has its profit making operations.

3. — Subsidiary Corporations

A non-resident can also operate a business in Canada through a corporation. The corporation can be a Canadian subsidiary or a foreign subsidiary. A Canadian subsidiary is taxable as a resident corporation on its worldwide income.[57] A foreign subsidiary corporation that does not reside in Canada is taxable only on its Canadian source income.

There are several advantages to conducting business through a subsidiary corporation. For example:

- The subsidiary corporation is a separate legal entity. This means that the parent corporation limits its liability for the subsidiary's debts.

- Since the subsidiary corporation is a separate entity, it generally reports only its own activities without disclosure of its parent corporation's operations.

- Since the subsidiary is a separate entity, it is easier to account for its income and expenses and there are fewer expense allocation problems.

- Subsidiaries with substantial (at least 50 per cent) Canadian equity ownership may be eligible for tax incentives such as the small business deduction on the first $300,000 of active business income.

- It is generally easier to conduct business reorganizations of corporations than reorganizations of other entities or relationships.

There are, however, also some disadvantages:

- Since a subsidiary is a separate legal entity, its parent cannot directly utilize its losses for Canadian tax purposes.

- The thin capitalization rules apply to subsidiaries that are minimally financed with non-resident equity capital.

- A withholding tax of 25 per cent (subject to treaty reduction) applies to dividends from a Canadian subsidiary to its non-resident parent corporation.

- Subject to treaty exemptions, capital gains that a parent corporation realizes on an arm's length sale of its shares of a Canadian corporation are taxable in Canada.

---

[57]Subs. 2(1).

- A subsidiary corporation may be resident both in Canada and in its home country. This can create problems of double taxation for the subsidiary. Most Canadian double taxation treaties, however, contain "tie-breaker" rules that minimize this risk.

- The purchase and set-up of a subsidiary corporation is generally easier than the purchase of an unincorporated business.

4. — Conversion of a Branch to a Subsidiary

A taxpayer can convert a branch into a subsidiary corporation by transferring the assets of the branch to the corporation. In these circumstances and in the absence of special provisions, the Act deems the taxpayer to have disposed of its assets at their fair market value.[58] Section 85 allows a branch to rollover its assets to a taxable Canadian corporation without triggering any immediate tax consequences. Thus, a branch can defer accrued gains on assets such as inventory and capital property through the appropriate elections.

The rollover under section 85 is available only if the transferor of the assets receives some share consideration for the assets disposed of to the taxable Canadian corporation. The parties must jointly elect to determine the cost basis of the assets transferred to the corporation and the share consideration that it receives in exchange. Since the value of the assets will reflect in the shares, the taxpayer will ultimately realize any accrued gains from the transferred assets when he disposes of the shares.

The subsidiary corporation will also be liable for tax on any accrued gains on assets that it acquires. Thus, a rollover under section 85 almost inevitably creates a potential problem of double taxation in the long run. The penalty of double taxation, however, reduces with the passage of time as the value of the tax deferral outweighs the penalty.

Summary of Considerations in Canadian Business Structures		
Factors to Consider	Branch	Subsidiary
Separate legal entity	No	Yes
Containment of legal liability	No	Yes
Presence in Canada	Less	More
Business profits taxable in Canada on current basis	Yes	Yes
Offset start-up losses	Yes	No
Status in Canada	Non-resident	Resident

---

[58]S. 69.

Summary of Considerations in Canadian Business Structures		
Inter-company transactions	Branch allocation accounting	Transfer Pricing Rules
Thin capitalization rules	Less likely to apply	Apply
Repatriation of earnings	N/A Taxed on current basis	Withholding taxes under Part XIII on dividends
Branch tax	May apply, subject to treaty limits.	N/A
Rollover of assets to domestic corporation	Yes	Yes

5. — Holding Companies

We use holding companies for both business and tax reasons. A holding company isolates business risk in the operating company. Holding companies are also useful in acquiring and divesting Canadian corporate interests. The characterization of a distribution of funds from an operating company to its parent corporation depends upon its legal status.

A corporation can always return its paid-up capital (PUC) to its shareholders on a tax-free basis. The repatriation of PUC is a return of capital and, therefore, non-taxable. This allows foreign companies to finance their Canadian operations through equity capital and withdraw earnings as a return of PUC without withholding tax. This is in marked contrast to the U.S. rule, which considers distributions to come first out of earnings and profits and only upon their exhaustion out of capital.

The concept of PUC is the cornerstone of planning for inbound business investments by non-residents. Generally, PUC is the issue price of share capital.[59] In most cases, PUC is the equivalent of corporate stated capital. The Act does, however, adjust PUC in various circumstances. A corporation can return its PUC to shareholders without Canadian tax. Where the shareholder is a non-resident, the shareholder can also avoid, or at least defer, Canadian withholding taxes. Distributions in excess of PUC are dividends and subject to withholding tax.[60] Amounts that a corporation distributes as a reduction of PUC reduce the adjusted cost base (ACB) of the shares. A capital gain results if the ACB of shares becomes a negative amount.

In most cases, the PUC of shares of a successful business is significantly less than the current value of its shares. Where a foreign corporation purchases shares of a Canadian corpo-

---

[59]Subs. 89(1)"paid-up capital".

[60]Subs. 84(4).

ration for an amount that exceeds its PUC, the PUC remains at its historical amount. Thus, the foreign parent corporation cannot extract its full investment without withholding tax.

Example

Assume that a foreign corporation acquires a Canadian operating company (Opco) in the following circumstances:

PUC	=	$ 100
ACB	=	$ 1,000
FMV	=	$ 1,000

Opco can return only $100 tax-free to its parent corporation.

Example

Assume that the foreign parent interposes a Canadian holding company (Holdco) between itself and Opco and finances Holdco as follows:

PUC	=	$ 1000
ACB	=	$ 1,000
FMV	=	$ 1,000

Holdco then purchases Opco and finances it as follows:

PUC	=	$ 100
ACB	=	$ 1,000
FMV	=	$ 1,000

In this scenario, Opco can pay up its profits to Holdco as tax-free inter-corporate dividends.[*] This allows it to extract its profits and reduce its business risk. The foreign parent can withdraw up to $1000 from Holdco without incurring any Part I or Part XIII withholding tax.

Notes:

[*]   S. 112.

Thus, as a rule, a foreign corporation should use a Canadian holding company to acquire a Canadian company so that it can increase its PUC. Instead of buying Opco's shares directly, the foreign corporation invests the cash purchase price to Holdco in exchange for Holdco's shares. This creates PUC equal to the full cash purchase price of the investment.

6. — *Nova Scotia Unlimited Liability Companies*

A corporation is usually a separate legal entity that limits the liability of its shareholders for corporate debts. For tax purposes, the corporation and its shareholders are separate persons and taxpayers. Some jurisdictions, however, allow the incorporation of companies whose shareholders are liable on liquidation to satisfy the company's obligations in excess of corporate assets.[61] Others treat certain types of corporations as limited liability vehicles for corporate law purposes and as flow through conduits for their owners for tax purposes.[62] These vehicles are hybrids or entities that have characteristics of more than one entity. Also, such hybrids can be treated differently for tax purposes in different countries. Where that happens, taxpayers can sometimes utilize hybrids to their advantage for tax planning in both countries.

Canadian law does not generally recognize hybrid entities, either for corporate or tax law purposes. There are, however, exceptions. For example, the *Nova Scotia Companies Act* (NSCA),[63] which is modelled on the 1862 *English Companies Act*, permits the formation of companies:

- Limited by shares;

- Limited by guarantee; or

- With unlimited liability.

The third category, unlimited liability companies, are companies that do not have any limit on the liability of its members ("NSULC"). Section 9 of *the Nova Scotia Companies Act*[64] states:

> Any one or more persons ... may ... form an incorporated company, with or without liability, that is to say, ... (c) a company not having any limit on the liability of its members, in this Act termed an "unlimited company".

---

[61]For example, the United Kingdom and Ireland.

[62]For example, the limited liability company in several states of the United States.

[63]*Companies Act*, R.S.N.S. 1989, c. 81. For a general review of the corporate law of Nova Scotia see Paul W. Festeryga "Nova Scotia Unlimited Liability Companies: What are They and How Do They Work?" in 1998 Conference Report, Cdn. Tax Foundation, p. 17:1. Alberta also has ULCs.

[64]R.S.N.S. 1989, c. 81, as amended.

This facility arises from the historical antecedents of the Nova Scotia statute with the English statute.[65] There are, however, several countries (for example, United Kingdom, Ireland, Australia and India) that still have unlimited liability legislation on their books.

A Nova Scotia ULC is quite different from an LLC created in the United States. LLCs have limited liability. Although the members of a NSULC have unlimited joint and several liability for its debts to creditors, the NSULC is not a partnership. First, the members of the company cannot bind it in the manner that partners can bind a partnership. Second, unlike a partnership, the company's creditors must first establish their claim against the company. If the company cannot discharge its obligations, the creditors can pursue the shareholders by winding up the company and only then prosecute their claim directly against the shareholders. Third, a NSULC is a separate legal entity in Canada; a partnership has no separate corporate existence.

One forms a NSULC by filing a memorandum and articles of association with the Registrar of Companies. The solicitor will also file a declaration that the incorporation is appropriate together with a list of officers and directors. The company can use the word "company", "Co.", or "ULC" in its name. The company need not disclose in its name that it is an unlimited company.

A NSULC must have a registered office in Nova Scotia and keep in the office:

- Its register of members;
- Minutes of shareholder meetings;
- Its registers of directors, officers and managers; and
- Its register of debentures.

The law does not require the company to have Nova Scotian or Canadian directors. Further, there is no requirement that meetings be held in Nova Scotia. Hence, apart from some perfunctory statutory obligations, a NSULC is a flexible vehicle that foreign business enterprises can use with minimal inconvenience.

---

[65]The unlimited liability company is an archaic institution.

(a) — Canadian Tax Treatment

For Canadian tax purposes under subsection 248(1) of the Act,[66] NSULC and unlimited liability companies formed under the laws of foreign jurisdictions are "corporations". Thus, a NSULC is taxable as a corporation in Canada.[67]

(b) — U.S. Tax Treatment

Under U.S. federal tax law, a business entity with two or more members is either a corporation or a partnership. A business entity with only one owner is either a corporation or is "disregarded". If the entity is disregarded, the *Code* treats its activities in the same manner as a sole proprietorship, branch, or division of the owner. Thus, the first step is to determine whether a business entity is a corporation for federal tax purposes.

The term "corporation" means a business entity that is organized under a Federal or State incorporation statute.[68] Corporations are taxable under Subpart C of the *Code* as separate entities.[69] The term "partnership" means a business entity that is not a corporation and that has at least two members.

Under the *Code*, a C corporation is a taxpayer in its own right, separate and apart from its shareholders. The earnings and capital gains of such corporations are taxable twice, first at the corporate level and again, upon distribution, at the shareholder level. We refer to this form of double taxation as the "classical system" of corporate taxation. One can utilize the losses and deductions of C corporations only against corporate income and gains.

In contrast, a pass-through entity such as a partnership or sole proprietorship is tax exempt in its own right. Its current earnings and realized capital gains are taxable in the hands of its owners whether or not distributed as dividends. Thus, an owner of a pass-through entity can use its losses against his or her personal income from other sources.

Unincorporated business entities, however, are taxable according to an optional scheme. They can select their tax status by checking a box that, in effect, is an election of tax standing under the *Code*.[70] Under the "check the box" rules, a domestic U.S. unincorporated

---

[66]See, for example, Rev. Can. Document Nos. 9408195 (June 27, 1994) and 9129645 (March 23, 1992).

[67]See generally: Lessard, Kyres, Gagnon, *"Treaty Benefit Entitlements of Trusts, Partnerships, and Hybrid Entities,"* 1997 Conference Report, Canadian Tax Foundation, p.33:1.

[68]IRC Reg. Section 301.7701-2.

[69]See Reg. 301.7701-2(b)(1).

[70]Hence, the nickname "Check the Box" regulations.

business entity with multiple owners can choose its tax status either as a C corporation[71] or as a pass-through entity. Further, a pass-through entity can select to be a partnership under Subpart K or, if it qualifies, as an S corporation.

Similarly, a U.S. entity with a single owner can choose to be treated as a "disregarded entity" (sole proprietorship), an S corporation if it qualifies, or as a C corporation if it does not. These elections to be considered pass-through transparencies for tax purposes are not connected to the entity's statutory or structural similarity to a corporation. Likewise, any unincorporated entity can classify itself as a corporation whether or not it possesses any corporate characteristics.

Thus, tax status under the U.S. *Code* has little theoretical foundation and depends almost entirely on the taxpayer's election. This allows U.S. investors considerable choice and flexibility. For example, an investor may create a "real" C corporation or an unincorporated business entity that elects corporate status for tax purposes.

These differences in tax status have significant tax consequences for investors. Assume, for example, that an investor in the top marginal tax bracket in the U.S. (39.6%) starts a business that earns $1000, pays corporate tax at 34 per cent and distributes its earnings as dividends. The tax cost to the investor and the corporation is as follows:

Business income	$1,000
Corporate tax @ 34%	340
Net after tax	660
Paid as dividend	$660
Personal tax @ 39.6%	261
Net remaining	$399

In contrast, the same investor in a pass-through entity would retain $604 after paying tax of $396 on the $1,000 earnings at a rate of 39.6 per cent. Thus, in this example, the investor increases the rate of return by 51 per cent by selecting a pass-through entity for tax purposes.

The principal advantage of a NSULC derives from the differences between the manner in which Canada and the United States characterize unlimited liability companies for income tax purposes. The United States generally treats unlimited liability companies as flow through conduits. Specifically, the *Code* does not consider Canadian unlimited liability companies as corporations. In contrast, Canada treats such companies as corporate entities taxable in their own right. Thus, a NSULC can elect fiscally transparent status in the United States by checking the box.

United States investors can create a NSULC in Canada and qualify it as a partnership for taxation purposes under U.S. law. Thus, all of the NSULC's income and losses would flow

---

[71] That is, a corporation governed by Subpart C of the *Internal Revenue Code*.

through to the U.S. investors directly thereby avoiding U.S. corporate tax. This makes the NSULC equivalent to a branch for tax purposes even though it is a Canadian subsidiary for corporate purposes. Therefore, the NSULC can avoid Canadian branch tax. The U.S. investors can claim foreign tax credits on taxes that the NSULC pays in Canada. Similarly, the NSULC's losses pass through directly to U.S. investors.

Any gain from the sale of NSULC shares is treaty exempt unless the shares derive their value primarily from Canadian real estate. If a U.S. corporation owns more than 10 per cent of the shares of the NSULC, it can benefit from a reduced withholding tax of 5 per cent. Furthermore, an S corporation can acquire the shares of a NSULC, whereas it cannot acquire shares in an ordinary Canadian corporation.

Similarly, a U.S. resident who wants to acquire a Canadian company can use a NSULC for the acquisition. Upon acquisition, the Canadian target company can be wound up on a tax-free basis into the NSULC.[72] The NSULC might also step up the cost base of the target company's assets on its winding up.[73]

Since a NSULC exposes its U.S. shareholders to unlimited liability in Canada, the shareholders can minimize corporate risk by interposing a United States limited liability company (LLC), limited liability partnership (LLP) or a limited partnership (LP) between themselves and the Nova Scotia company. This provides the best of both worlds: flow through status in the U.S. through the LLC, LLP or LP and limited liability protection against lawsuits.

A start-up business may incorporate in Nova Scotia from the outset although it intends to conduct its business elsewhere in Canada or in a foreign country. Canadian corporate law merely requires compliance with extra-provincial registration rules in the province in which the NSULC conducts its business. Conversely, one can convert an existing Canadian business into a Nova Scotia ULC by re-domiciling the corporation into Nova Scotia and then amalgamating it with a NSULC. The NSULC then becomes the surviving corporation.

V. — Financing

1. — General Comment

The manner of financing a business depends upon several considerations. One must consider the availability of capital, the cost of financing in the host and home countries, foreign exchange risk and restrictions, debt-equity capital ratios and the anticipated cash flow from business operations to pay for borrowed capital.

---

[72]Subs. 88(1).

[73]Para. 88(1)(c).

One of the principal considerations in setting up a business operation in Canada is the form of organization. A subsidiary corporation is clearly an option. The choice of a subsidiary corporation inevitably raises the question as to whether one should finance it with debt or equity capital. The decision must take into account both business and tax considerations.

Part XIII of the Act imposes a withholding tax on payments of investment income to non-residents. The exceptions and exemptions from the withholding tax are, however, sometimes more important than the tax. The Act does not generally apply withholding tax on interest payments made by non-residents to other non-residents. The withholding tax on interest payments by a non-resident apply only if the non-resident:

- Carries on its business principally in Canada,

- Manufactures or processes goods in Canada, or

- Engages in certain resource-related activities in Canada.

A corporation carries on its business principally in Canada if it conducts more than 50 per cent of its activities in Canada.

The advantages of financing a Canadian business through debt capital are as follows:

- Interest expense on debt is deductible if one uses it for the purpose of earning income from a business provided that the amount is reasonable and is not incurred in the pursuit of exempt income.[74]

- Although interest paid to a non-resident person by a Canadian resident is generally subject to a withholding tax of 25 per cent (subject to treaty reduction) at source,[75] there are extensive exemptions from the tax.

- The non-resident can borrow either in a foreign currency or Canadian dollars without foreign exchange controls. Foreign exchange gains and losses will give rise to either income or capital depending upon the circumstances.

A foreign corporation can use debt to finance its Canadian operations in several ways. It can borrow and then:

- Lend money to its Canadian subsidiary;

- Invest in the equity of its Canadian subsidiary; or

- Allocate interest to its Canadian branch operations.

Each of these options has different tax consequences.

---

[74]Para. 20(1)(c).

[75]Para. 212(1)(b).

2. — Thin Capitalization

Debt financing is advantageous if one can deduct the cost of borrowing in computing income. In contrast, dividends on share capital are paid from after-tax dollars and usually subject to double taxation. Hence, it is usually advantageous to finance a Canadian subsidiary corporation through debt capital on which interest payments are fully deductible for Part I tax. A fully taxable Canadian subsidiary corporation that deducts its interest saves approximately 44 per cent Part I tax and pays a withholding tax of only 15 per cent (treaty rate) on interest payments to non-resident persons. Debt financing can also be set up to avoid even the withholding tax on interest.[76] To counter this type of manipulation, the Act contains special rules that deny the deduction of interest expense to a domestic corporation that is "thinly capitalized".

From the parent corporation's perspective also, it may be more advantageous to finance its subsidiary through equity capital rather than through debt. The return on equity capital is normally through dividends and dividends are often tax exempt to the recipient corporation or, if not exempt, subject to a lower rate of tax than that applicable to interest income from debt. The ultimate structure will depend upon the consolidated effects on the parent and subsidiary corporations.

The thin capitalization rules apply only to corporations that reside in Canada. They do not apply to non-resident corporations or partnerships.

Example

Assume:

Equity and surplus at start of year	$ 7,500,000
Debt outstanding from January 1st — December 30th of year	$15,000,000
Debt outstanding on December 31st	$16,000,000
Interest rate during year	10%

Interest payable:

$$\$15,000,000 \times 10\% = \$ 1,500,000$$

$$\frac{\$1,000,000 \times 10\%}{365} = 274$$

---

[76]See paragraph 212(1)(b).

Example	
Total Interest Paid	$ 1,500,274

Then the disallowed interest is $562,603 calculated as follows:

$$\$1,500,274 \quad \times \frac{\$16,000,000 - (2 \times \$7,500,000)}{\$16,000,000}$$

$$= \$562,603$$

(a) — Alternative Approaches

There are two broad approaches to attack thinly capitalized corporations: fixed formula denial of interest and anti-abuse legislation. Canada uses the fixed formula regime to control thin capitalization. The thin capitalization rules disallow the deduction of interest expense on indebtedness to a non-resident related party if debt exceeds two times the subsidiary's equity capital.[77] Subsection 18(4) provides that where a subsidiary corporation's debt to related party non-residents results in a debt to equity ratio in excess of 2:1, any interest on the excess portion of the loan over the maximum approved proportion is automatically disallowed for tax purposes. The formula is fixed and precise and the result is mathematically determinable.

The anti-abuse approach to thin capitalization has two principal variations. Under one variant, one looks to the circumstances to determine whether capital should be classified as debt or equity. Hence, for example, one looks at the substance of the financing over its form to see if the subsidiary corporation's capital should be regarded as debt or equity.

Under the second variant of the anti-abuse approach, one applies an arm's length yardstick to determine the amount of loan that would be made in a comparable commercial transaction where the parties were dealing with each other at arm's length. Under this approach, the debt to equity ratio would constitute one, but not necessarily the determinative, factor in asserting whether a corportion was thinly capitalized.

(b) — OECD Model Convention

The interpretation of a double tax treaty generally depends upon the domestic law of the particular country concerned. The *OECD Model Convention*, however, has an important role

---

[77]The government in its 2000 Budget proposed to reduce the ratio from 3:1 to 2:1.

to play in the interpretation of domestic law. The transfer pricing rules also play a vital role in non-arm's length transactions between corporations.

Article 9 of the *Model Convention* concerns associated enterprises (such as parent and subsidiary corporations) under common control. The Article allows for an adjustment in the computation of taxable profits when associated enterprises do not transact with each other on an arm's length basis. The Article does not have any effect where associated enterprises transact with each other on normal open market commercial terms.

Article 9 of the *Model Convention* reads as follows:

1. Where

a) an enterprise of a Country participates directly or indirectly in the management, control or capital of an enterprise of the other Country, or

b) the same persons participate directly or indirectly in the management, control or capital of an enterprise of a Country and an enterprise of the other Country,

and in either case conditions are made or imposed between the two enterprises in their commercial or financial relations which differ from those which would be made between independent enterprises, then any profits which would, but for those conditions, have accrued to one of the enterprises, but, by reason of those conditions, have not so accrued, may be included in the profits of that enterprise and taxed accordingly.

2. Where a Country includes in the profits of an enterprise of that State and taxes accordingly profits on which an enterprise of the other Country has been charged to tax in that other State and the profits so included are profits which would have accrued to the enterprise of the first-mentioned State if the conditions made between the two enterprises had been those which would have been made between independent enterprises, then that other State shall make an appropriate adjustment to the amount of the tax charged therein on those profits. In determining such adjustment, due regard shall be had to the other provisions of this Convention and the competent authorities of the Countries shall if necessary consult each other.

The purpose of Article 9 is to prevent economic double taxation of the same income. It achieves this result through a restrictive rule that prevents treaty countries that adopt the Article from unilaterally increasing the taxable profits of an enterprise to an amount higher than that which would be determined under an equivalent arm's length commercial transaction.

An enterprise is considered to be associated with another enterprise if one participates directly or indirectly in the management, control or capital of the other enterprise. Enterprises may also be associated with each other where the same persons participate directly or indirectly in the management, control or capital of the other enterprise.

The OECD Committee on Fiscal Affairs' Report on Thin Capitalization was of the view that the Article is relevant in the determination of whether the rate of interest in a loan contract is an arm's length rate. It is also pertinent to the determination as to whether capital is considered debt or equity.

As a rule, an enterprise's profits are taxable only by the Country in which the enterprise has its residence. The domestic law of the Country determines profits. For example, the thin capitalization rules apply to determine the amount of interest that is deductible for Canadian tax purposes. Article 9 permits an adjustment of the profits determined in accordance with domestic rules where associated enterprises do not transact with each other on an arm's length basis.

The application of the thin capitalization rules to a particular enterprise should not have the effect of increasing its taxable profits to more than the arm's length equivalent that would have been earned had it been transacting under normal commercial conditions. The application of a rigid statutory formula for the disallowance of interest in a thinly capitalized corporation may result in an increase in taxable income beyond the amount that would have been determined in an arm's length transaction. In these circumstances, the domestic rule would conflict with Article 9 of the *OECD Model Convention*.

The legal basis for making interest deduction adjustments to thinly capitalized corporations lies in domestic Canadian law, specifically, subsections 18(4)–(6) of the *Income Tax Act*. Article 9 of the *OECD Model Convention* (and its equivalents in double tax treaties) does not, by itself, permit a taxing authority to make an adjustment to the taxable profits of an enterprise. Domestic law must authorize the adjustment. Article 9 merely restricts the power of the domestic taxing authority so that it cannot make adjustments beyond the amounts that would be earned in equivalent arm's length commercial transactions.

Article 9 focuses on business enterprises that are factually and legally separate entities, but are in some way associated with each other. The underlying rationale of the Article is to prevent the manipulation of profits through transactions that artificially lower prices through the use of distorted "transfer pricing" techniques. Hence, the basic thrust of the Article is to adjust taxable profits to a level comparable to those that would have been achieved in open market transactions.

Article 9(2) deals with economic double taxation that may result from an upward adjustment of taxable profits in one country without an appropriate readjustment in the other country. In essence, the Article provides that where the taxable profits of a subsidiary are revised upwards in one Country, the other Country in which the artificially higher profits will have been earned should provide appropriate relief in order to avoid economic double taxation.

(c) — Disallowance of Interest Expense

The Act does not provide for a formal re-characterization of debt as equity. This is so even where the amount of non-arm's length debt exceeds the amount that could ordinarily be borrowed at commercial rates from arm's length lenders. The Act does, however, provide for a disallowance of interest expense to the extent that the amount claimed is unreasonable.[78]

Subsection 18(4) of the *Income Tax Act* disallows a deduction for interest expense paid to specified non-residents on that portion of debt that exceeds two times the borrowing company's equity.[79] For the purposes of this rule, debt means the greatest amount of interest-bearing debt that was outstanding to specified non-residents during the fiscal period.

We determine the greatest amount of outstanding debt during a fiscal period by aggregating all debts outstanding to specified non-residents. Similarly, we determine total interest expense payable for the year by aggregating all interest payable to specified non-residents. The restrictions on interest deductibility apply if the 2:1 ratio of debt to equity is exceeded at any time in the year. Thus, in the extreme case, interest-bearing debt that is outstanding for a period of even one day can result in a substantial restriction on the deductibility of interest expense for the year. In contrast, the borrower corporation's equity is the amount of its equity at the beginning of the year plus any increases in its paid-up capital during the year.

More specifically, where the amount of "outstanding debts to specified non-residents"[80] exceeds two times the "equity"[81] of the Canadian resident corporation, a *pro rata* portion of the interest paid or payable in the year to the non-residents may not be deducted in computing the income of the Canadian resident corporation.

The phrase "outstanding debts to specified non-residents" means debts, on which interest expense would otherwise be deductible, owing to a creditor who is a non-resident if the creditor and/or any other person with whom the creditor does not deal at arm's length owns 25 per cent or more of the issued shares of any class of the Canadian resident corporation.

Further, where the lender is a shareholder of the borrower corporation, any excess interest may be taxable as a dividend if it is considered to be an appropriation of profits. The dividend would be subject to withholding tax. The net effect of this approach may be the same as recharacterization of debt as equity for tax purposes.

The CRA is of the view that Canada's double taxation treaties do not modify the thin capitalization rules in subsection 18(4). Since double tax treaties are intended to protect the revenue base of signatory countries and thwart artificial transfers of profits through the manipulation of transfer prices, the thin capitalization rules do not violate the non-discrimination clauses in Canada's treaties. Indeed, it is arguable that the thin capitalization rules support the general principle encountered in double tax treaties that related parties should deal with each other at arm's length.

---

[78] Para. 20(1)(c).

[79] The ratio was reduced from 3:1 to 2:1 for taxation years that begin after 2000.

[80] Subs. 18(5) "outstanding debts to specified non-residents".

[81] Subpara. 18(4)(a)(ii).

(d) — Anti-Avoidance Rules

Apart from the General Anti-Avoidance Rule ("GAAR"),[82] there is a specific rule to prevent taxpayers from avoiding the thin capitalization rules by funnelling loans through third parties. Subsection 18(6) provides that where a specified non-resident loans money to a third party on the condition that the third party lend money to a Canadian corporation, any interest paid to the third party falls within the thin capitalization rules and is treated as if it had been paid directly by the Canadian corporation to a specified non-resident. For taxation years that begin after 2000, subsection 18(6) is expanded to deem indebtedness of a corporation to a third party that is guaranteed or secured by a specified non-resident to be debt owing by the corporation to the specified non-resident.

VI. — Capital Gains

Non-residents are liable for Part I income tax on taxable capital gains (net of allowable capital losses) from dispositions of "taxable Canadian property".[83] Capital gains from other types of capital property are not subject to Canadian tax.

"Taxable Canadian property" includes the following:[84]

- Real or immovable property situated in Canada;

- Capital property used in carrying on a business in Canada (other than a life insurance business);

- Where the non-resident is an insurer, capital property used by it in carrying on its insurance business in Canada;

- Shares of resident Canadian corporations other than public corporations;

- Shares in a public corporation if, at any time during the five years immediately preceding the disposition, the non-resident (or related persons) owned not less than 25 per cent of the issued shares of any class of the capital stock of the corporation;

- An interest in a partnership if, at any time during the 60 months immediately preceding the disposition, 50 per cent or more of the total fair market value of all partnership property consisted of property that is taxable Canadian property, an income interest in a trust resident in Canada, a Canadian resource property, or a timber resource property;

- A capital interest in a Canadian resident trust (other than a unit trust);

---

[82]S. 245.

[83]Para. 2(3)(c); subpara. 115(1)(a)(iii). This rule is also subject to any exemption provided for in an international tax treaty.

[84]Para. 115(1)(b) and subs. 248(1)"taxable Canadian property".

- A unit of a Canadian resident trust (other than a mutual fund trust);

- A unit of a mutual fund trust if, at any time during the five years immediately preceding the disposition, the non-resident (or related persons) owned not less than 25 per cent of the issued units of the trust; or

- Any property that is deemed to be "taxable Canadian property".[85]

An interest in any of the above listed properties is also considered "taxable Canadian property".

Shares of a public corporation do not constitute "taxable Canadian property". This would appear to be the case whether the corporation issuing the shares initially qualified as a public corporation or became a public corporation after originally starting out as a private corporation.

A non-resident's capital gain for a taxation year arises from a disposition of property that qualifies as a "taxable Canadian property". Hence, the status of the property at the time of the disposition determines whether the non-resident is liable for Canadian tax.

We generally calculate non-resident capital gains and losses according to the usual rules applicable to resident taxpayers.[86] There are, however, a few specific rules that apply only to non-residents. For example, a non-resident may not:

- Deduct a reserve in calculating capital gains;[87]

- Rollover capital property to a spouse or to a "spouse trust";[88] or

- Take full advantage of the principal residence exemption.[89]

Non-residents may deduct allowable capital losses from dispositions of taxable Canadian property against taxable capital gains.

---

[85]See, e.g., subss. 85.1(1) and 87(4).

[86]See, generally, Division B, subdivision c.

[87]Subpara. 40(2)(a)(i).

[88]Subss. 70(6) and 73(1).

[89]Para. 40(2)(b).

VII. — Taxable Income

In computing taxable income, a non-resident is entitled deductions in respect of:[90]

- Prospector's and grubstaker's shares;

- Amounts exempt by treaty;

- Workers' compensation;

- Amounts repaid under employment insurance;

- Stock option benefits from a Canadian controlled private corporation;

- Social assistance payments that are means-tested; and

- Inter-corporate taxable dividends.

Within the usual limits, non-residents may also offset Canadian source losses against Canadian source income.[91] Thus, a non-resident may claim non-capital losses, net capital losses, restricted farm losses, and farm losses that are reasonably attributable to his or her employment in Canada, a business carried on by the non-resident in Canada or to the disposition of taxable Canadian property.

In addition, where "all or substantially all" of the non-resident's income for a year is derived from Canadian sources, the non-resident may claim such other deductions as are reasonably considered to be wholly applicable to income.[92] It can be quite difficult to determine the portion of deductions that are wholly applicable to Canadian source income. In the simplest case, however, an allocation based upon the period of time that the non-resident was employed in Canada or was carrying on business in Canada is acceptable.[93] The Agency's view is that the phrase "all or substantially all" means 90 per cent or more.[94]

---

[90]Paras. 115(1)(d) and (e); IT-171R2, "Non-Resident Individuals — Computation of Taxable Income Earned in Canada and Non-Refundable Tax Credits" (March 30, 1992) (archived).

[91]Para. 115(1)(d); s. 111.

[92]Para. 115(1)(f).

[93]IT-171R2, "Non-Resident Individuals — Computation of Taxable Income Earned in Canada and Non-Refundable Tax Credits" (March 30, 1992) (archived).

[94]See IT-171R2, "Non-Resident Individuals — Computation of Taxable Income Earned in Canada and Non-Refundable Tax Credits (March 30, 1992) (archived).

VIII. — Withholding Tax

1. — General Comment

In addition to Part I tax on Canadian source business income, Part XIII of the Act also levies a tax on a non-resident's non-business (investment type) income.[95] Unlike the tax on business income, however, which requires the taxpayer to assess his or her own liability, the Part XIII tax is withheld at source of payment. A Canadian resident who pays or credits an amount to a non-resident must withhold 25 per cent of the gross amount.[96] Thus, Part XIII both imposes a tax and determines the manner in which it is collected. Withholding is the only feasible way to tax the income of non-residents who do not carry on business in Canada.

The withholding tax regime for passive income is a difficult compromise between two conflicting policy objectives. We want to tax non-residents fairly but without opening the door to tax evasion. The compromise is far from perfect. The withholding tax is essentially a prepaid tax. Since the non-resident may not have any business assets in Canada, the Canadian tax authorities may not be able to enforce payment of the tax. Withholding ensures that the non-resident will meet his or her tax obligations. Thus, once the non-resident (or the resident on the non-resident's behalf) pays the appropriate amount of withholding tax, the passive foreign investor has no further Canadian tax obligations. The Act levies the withholding tax at a flat rate on the gross amount of passive income that the non-resident earns from Canadian sources and designates the resident payer as the agent of the Canadian tax authorities. Since the Canadian agent cannot reasonably be expected to determine the non-resident's allocable expenses or the non-resident's appropriate tax bracket based on worldwide income, the tax is a flat rate based on the gross payment. This is a practical administrative solution, but not one that is always fair for the non-resident. For example, although one usually earns dividends and interest income without incurring much in expenses, this is not always the case. Indeed, in some cases the 25 per cent tax on gross income can exceed 100 per cent on net income. Assume, for example, that one borrows $100 to invest in bonds that yield 10 per cent. If the interest expense on the borrowing is 8 per cent, the non-resident will pay $2.50 tax on $10 of interest income without the benefit of deducting $8 interest expense. Similarly, the absence of a deduction for depreciation will often cause the 25 per cent on gross rents to exceed net income.

---

[95]See, generally, Part XIII, ss. 212–218. Canada's tax treaties reduce the 25 per cent withholding rate on most of the above payments.

[96]Subs. 214(1).

To resolve the conflict between administrative feasibility and fairness towards non-residents, we permit various deviations from the general scheme for the taxation of passive income. These include:

- Bilateral treaty adjustments that require Canada to reduce the withholding rate on certain forms of income such as dividends, interest, royalties, etc.;[97]

- Unilateral exemption of certain forms of interest from the withholding rules;[98] and

- Special elections that allow for net income taxation of rental income and other properties.[99]

These *ad hoc* adjustments blunt the harsher aspects of the withholding requirements.

2. — *Payments Subject to Withholding*

The withholding tax applies to the following types of passive income payments:[100]

- Dividends;

- Management fees;

- Interest;

- Income from estates and trusts;

- Rents, royalties and similar payments;

- Timber royalties;

- Patronage dividends;

- Pension benefits;

- Death benefits, employment insurance and payments on account of retirement compensation arrangements;

- Retiring allowances;

- Supplementary unemployment benefit plan payments;

- RRSP payments;

---

[97]See, for example, Article X (Dividends), XI (Interest) and XII (Royalties) in the *Canada-U.S. Treaty.*

[98]For example, the exceptions in para. 212(1)(b).

[99]See, for example, subs. 216(1).

[100]S. 215.

- Deferred profit sharing plan payments;

- Certain annuity payments;

- RRIF payments; and

- RESP payments.

There is also a limited withholding under Part I on the following:[101]

- Income from employment in Canada; and

- Fee for providing services (other than employment) in Canada.

Thus, in theory, a non-resident can be liable for tax under both Regulation 105 and Part XIII. This would occur, for example, where a non-resident renders services in Canada through facilities that are not a permanent establishment.[102] In practice, however, the CRA generally levies tax in these circumstances only under Part XIII.

Although the Act imposes the withholding tax on the non-resident who receives Canadian source "passive" income, it is the resident person who pays or credits the non-resident who is liable to withhold the tax. Failure to withhold and remit the tax renders the resident liable for the full amount of the tax, together with interest and penalties.[103] Interest is calculated by reference to a prescribed rate.

Tax at a rate of 25 per cent (reduced to 15 per cent under most Canadian treaties) is to be withheld at source[104] whenever a person resident in Canada pays or credits (or is deemed to pay or credit) a non-resident person an amount on account of one of the types of income enumerated in Part XIII of the Act.

(a) — Management Fees

A management or administration fee is an amount paid in respect of managerial services in connection with the direction or supervision of business activities. "Management and administration" includes:[105]

- Planning,

---

[101]Reg. 105.

[102]See, for example, subpara. 212(1)(d)(iii).

[103]Subs. 215(6). See also para. 227(8)(a). In certain circumstances, the directors of a corporation may be personally liable for taxes that have not been remitted: see s. 227.1.

[104]Subs. 212(1)

[105]IT-468R, "Management or Administration Fees Paid to Non-residents" (December 29, 1989).

- Direction,

- Control and co-ordination at a managerial level,

- Accounting,

- Financial and legal services,

- Electronic data processing,

- Employee relations,

- Management consultation,

- Labour negotiations, and

- Tax advice.

Management fees do not include reasonable payments for services where the parties are dealing with each other at arm's length[106] and the services were rendered in the ordinary course of the non-resident's business.[107] Reimbursed expenses actually incurred by the non-resident for services performed on behalf of the resident are not considered management fees.[108]

---

[106]On the meaning of arm's length see *M.N.R. v. Sheldon's Engineering Ltd.*, [1955] S.C.R. 637, [1955] C.T.C. 174, 55 D.T.C. 1110 (S.C.C.), *per* Locke, J. at 643 (SCC):

> The expression is one which is usually employed in cases in which transactions between trustees and *cestuis que trust*, guardians and wards, principals and agents or solicitors and clients are called into question. The reasons why transactions between persons standing in these relations to each other may be impeached are pointed out in the judgments of the Lord Chancellor and of Lord Blackburn in *MacPherson v. Watts* (1877), 3 App. Cas. 254.

See also *Swiss Bank Corp. v. M.N.R.*, 71 D.T.C. 5235 (Ex. Ct.), *per* Thurlow, C.J., at 5240-41:

> In my view, the basic premise on which this analysis is based is that, where the "mind" by which the bargaining is directed on behalf of one party to a contract is the same "mind" that directs the bargaining on behalf of the other party, it cannot be said that the parties are dealing at arm's length. In other words where the evidence reveals that the *same* person was "dictating" the "terms of the bargain" on behalf of *both* parties, it cannot be said that the parties were dealing at arm's length.

[107]Para. 212(4)(a). See *Windsor Plastic Products Ltd. v. The Queen*, [1986] 1 C.T.C. 331, 86 D.T.C. 6171 (Fed. T.D.).

[108]Para. 212(4)(b).

(b) — Interest

As a general rule, interest paid or credited to a non-resident person is subject to withholding tax of 25 per cent (reduced to 15 per cent in most Canadian treaties). There are, however, many exceptions to this rule. For example, there is no withholding tax on the following interest payments:[109]

- Interest on certain bonds issued or guaranteed by the Government of Canada;[110]

- Interest on certain obligations payable in a foreign currency to a person with whom the resident payer is dealing at arm's length;[111]

- Interest on a bond, debenture or similar debt obligation if the interest is payable to a non-resident person who has obtained a certificate of exemption from the Minister;[112]

- Interest payable by a life insurer on any obligation entered into in the course of carrying on a life insurance business in a foreign country, provided that the payer and the payee are dealing with each other at arm's length;[113]

- Interest paid by a corporation in respect of debt obligations issued after June 23, 1975 provided that the corporation and the creditor were dealing with each other at arm's length and not more than 25 per cent of the principal amount of the debt obligation was payable by the corporation within five years of the issue of the obligation;[114]

- Interest payable on a mortgage or similar obligation secured by real estate or to immovables situated outside Canada or a real right in any such immovable, except to the extent that the interest payable is deductible in computing the payer's income from a business carried on by the payer in Canada or from property other than real property situated outside Canada;[115]

---

[109]Para. 212(1)(b).

[110]Subpara. 212(1)(b)(ii).

[111]Subpara. 212(1)(b)(iii).

[112]Subpara. 212(1)(b)(iv) and subs. 212(14); the Minister can issue a certificate of exemption to a non-resident organization that would, *if* it were resident in Canada, be exempt from tax under the Act, e.g., a registered charity or a pension trust that qualifies under s. 149. Blended payments must be allocated as between principal and interest: subs. 214(2).

[113]Subpara. 212(1)(b)(v).

[114]Subpara. 212(1)(b)(vii); *General Electric Capital Equipment Finance Inc. v. R.* (2001), [2002] 1 C.T.C. 217, 2002 D.T.C. 6734 (Fed. C.A.).

[115]Subpara. 212(1)(b)(viii).

- Interest paid or credited in Canadian dollars by certain Canadian financial institutions in respect of Canadian dollar deposits in branches or offices outside Canada, if the depositor deals at arm's length with the Canadian financial institution;[116]

- Interest paid to a prescribed international organization,[117] or by a prescribed financial institution on an "eligible deposit";[118] and

- Interest payable under certain securities lending arrangements.[119]

The above listed interest payments are generally exempt from withholding tax. The exemption is lost, however, if the payment of interest is contingent on some other factor, for example, revenues, profits or dividends paid to shareholders. Thus, the exemption from withholding tax is only available in respect of payments that constitute interest, both in substance and in form.

In certain cases the Act deems payments to be on account of interest and other payments not to be interest. For example, interest computed by reference to revenue, profits, cash flow, commodity prices or any other similar criteria are deemed not to be interest for certain purposes.[120]

Where a non-resident person guarantees repayment of the principal amount of a debt obligation issued by a resident of Canada, the Act deems any amount paid or credited as consideration for the guarantee to be an interest payment on account of the debt. Similarly, the Act deems payments by a resident to a non-resident person on account of standby fees for funds made available by the non-resident to be a payment on account of interest.[121]

(c) — Estate or Trust Income

Trust and estate income is subject to withholding tax except to the extent that it is deemed to be a non-resident's taxable capital gain from the disposition of capital property.[122] Trust or estate income payable to a beneficiary is generally included in income whether or not it is actually paid in the year.[123] For withholding tax purposes, however, the Act deems the

---

[116]Subpara. 212(1)(b)(ix).

[117]Such as the Bank for International Settlements; Regs. 806 and 806.1.

[118]Subpara. 212(1)(b)(xi); s. 33.1.

[119]Subpara. 212(1)(b)(xii). See also, subpara. 212(1)(b)(iii).

[120]See the closing words of para. 212(1)(b).

[121]Subs. 214(15).

[122]Para. 212(1)(c), subs. 104(21).

[123]Subs. 104(13).

amount payable to the beneficiary to have been paid or credited to the beneficiary on the earlier of two dates:[124]

- The date of actual payment, and

- The 90th day after the end of the taxation year of the trust.

(d) — Rents and Royalties

Rents, royalties, and similar payments paid or credited to a non-resident by a resident of Canada are subject to withholding tax.[125] Payments for the use of the following types of properties are considered similar in character to rents and royalties and are also subject to withholding tax:

- Inventions,

- Trade names,

- Patents,

- Trademarks,

- Designs,

- Models,

- Plans,

- Secret formulas, and

- Processes.

Note that copyright royalties on literary, dramatic, musical, or artistic works are not subject to withholding tax.[126]

"Rent" includes not only payments for the use of real property, but also leases of personal property. As Thurlow, J. said in *United Geophysical Co.*:[127]

> It is, I think, apparent from the use in the section of the wording which follows the words 'rent' and 'royalty' that Parliament did not intend to limit the type of income referred to in the

---

[124]Para. 214(3)(f).

[125]Para. 212(1)(d).

[126]Subpara. 212(1)(d)(vi). See Richard G. Tremblay, "Canada-U.S. Cross Border Computer Software 'Fees'" (1986), 1 Cdn. Current Tax, C163.

[127]*United Geophysical Co. v. M.N.R.*, [1961] C.T.C. 134 at 145, 61 D.T.C. 1099 at 1105 (Ex.Ct.). See also *PPG Industries Can. Ltd. v. M.N.R.*, [1978] C.T.C. 2055, 78 D.T.C. 1062 (T.R.B.).

subsection to either what could strictly be called 'rent' or 'royalty' or to payments which had all of the strict legal characteristics of 'rent' or 'royalty'. Nor does the scope of the section appear to be restricted to payments of that nature in respect of real property for the word 'property' appears in the section and that word is defined in very broad terms in [s. 248(1), en. S.C. 1974-75-76, c. 26, subs. 125(5); am S.C. 1980-81-82-83, c. 140, subs. 128(9)] as including both real and personal property. It seems to me, therefore, that [s. 212(1)(d), as amended] includes any payment which is similar to rent but which is payable in respect of personal property. Moreover, in its ordinary usage, as opposed to its technical legal meaning, the word 'rent', besides referring to returns of that nature from real property, is broad enough to include a payment for the hire of personal property. ... Without attempting to determine just how wide the net of [s. 212(1)(d), as amended] may be, I am of the opinion that the subsection does refer to and include a fixed amount paid as rental for the use of personal property for a certain time.

Now it goes without saying that the mere use of the words 'rent' and 'rental' in the agreement between the [parent company] and the [subsidiary company] is not necessarily conclusive on the question whether the payment so provided for is in fact a rent or other payment of the kind referred to in [s. 212(1), as amended], but their use in the agreement, to my mind, affords some indication that the payment which was to be determined, having regard to reasonableness and the cost of each item to be 'rented', was to be a payment in the nature of rent for the equipment.

(e) — Pension Benefits

Pension and superannuation benefits are subject to withholding tax.[128] The following payments are, however, specifically excluded from the withholding tax:

- Certain exempt service pensions and allowances;

- Funds "rolled over" on behalf of the non-resident person to a registered pension fund or to a registered retirement savings plan under which the non-resident is the annuitant;

- Compensation payments that would have been deductible in computing the non-resident person's taxable income (or that of a spouse) if the non-resident had been resident in Canada throughout the year;[129] and

- Certain exempt payments under s. 57.

Pension payments that can reasonably be regarded as being attributable to services rendered by a non-resident person when he or she was neither resident in Canada nor more than occasionally employed in Canada are not subject to withholding tax.[130]

---

[128]Para. 212(1)(h).

[129]Para. 110(1)(f) sets out the types of payments that are deductible.

[130]Subparas. 212(1)(h)(v) and (vi).

(f) — Retiring Allowances

Generally, a retiring allowance paid to a non-resident is subject to withholding tax. A payment transferred on behalf of a non-resident person to a registered pension fund or to a registered retirement savings plan under which the non-resident person is the annuitant and that would be deductible in computing the non-resident's income if he or she were resident in Canada through the year is not subject to withholding tax.[131]

(g) — Registered Retirement Savings Plan Payments

A payment out of a registered retirement savings plan to a non-resident person is subject to withholding tax if such a payment would have been taxable to a person who was resident in Canada throughout the taxation year.[132] In other words, a non-resident is only subject to withholding tax in circumstances where a similar payment to a resident person would have been subject to Part I tax. Any portion of the registered retirement savings plan that is rolled over to another registered retirement savings plan under which the non-resident person is the annuitant is not subject to withholding tax.

(h) — Payments Out of Deferred Income Plans

A payment out of a deferred profit sharing plan,[133] registered education savings plan,[134] or a registered retirement income fund[135] to a non-resident person is subject to withholding tax if the payment would have been taxable had it been received by a person who was resident in Canada throughout the taxation year in which the payment is made.

---

[131]Para. 212(1)(j.1).

[132]Para. 212(1)(l).

[133]Para. 212(1)(m); s. 147.

[134]Para. 212(1)(r) and s. 146.1.

[135]Para. 212(1)(q); s. 146.3.

(i) — Dividends

A non-resident person is subject to withholding tax on dividends paid or credited, or deemed to have been paid or credited,[136] to the non-resident by a corporation resident in Canada that is on account of:[137]

- Taxable dividends,[138] or

- Capital dividends.[139]

Capital gains dividends paid by a mortgage investment corporation or a mutual fund corporation are not subject to withholding tax.[140]

(i) — Meaning of Dividend

The meaning of the term "dividend" can vary from country to country. Generally, a dividend implies an appropriation of corporate profits to the shareholder after income has been earned. Whether or not a payment constitutes a "dividend" is a matter for the domestic law of the source country.

Article 10(3) *OECD Model Convention* defines "dividends" as follows:

> The term 'dividends' ... means income from shares, 'jouissance' shares or 'jouissance' rights, mining shares, founders' shares or other rights, not being debt-claims, participating in profits as well as income from other corporate rights which is subjected to the same taxation treatment as income from shares by the laws of State of which the company making the distribution is a resident.

The above definition is neither complete nor exhaustive. The examples do, however, illustrate the types of payments that most OECD countries consider dividends. Thus, "dividends" generally imply the distribution of profits to the shareholders of a corporation limited by shares, limited partnerships with share capital, limited liability companies or other joint stock companies. Dividends are income from capital made available to a company by its shareholders and do not include debt claims that participate in profits.

---

[136]*Placements Serco Ltee v. The Queen*, [1988] 1 C.T.C. 42, 88 D.T.C. 6125 (F.C.A.) ("dividend" in subs. 212(2) includes any payment deemed to be a dividend).

[137]Subss. 212(2) and 212(2.1).

[138]Subs. 89(1)"taxable dividend".

[139]Subs. 83(2). The untaxed portion of capital gains accumulated by a private corporation may be distributed on a tax-free basis to Canadian shareholders.

[140]By virtue of the exclusions in para. 212(2)(a).

Partnership profit distributions are not considered to be dividends under Canadian domestic law. There are, however, certain countries in which partnerships are treated in a manner that is substantially similar to limited liability corporations.[141] Where a bilateral tax treaty does not specifically cover the matter, the determination as to what constitutes a "dividend" is made by reference to domestic law.

Economic double taxation of dividend income is an acute international economic problem. Under the classical system of taxation, dividend income is subject to taxation twice: first at the corporate level, then again at the shareholder level. The resulting tax burden on dividends can be significantly different from that on interest income depending upon the status of the payer corporation and the recipient.

An individual resident in Canada is taxable on dividends that he or she receives in the year.

Where a corporation resident in Canada pays the dividend, the individual is entitled to a dividend tax credit against his or her Canadian taxes.[142] Thus, the effective tax rate on Canadian source dividend income is reduced by virtue of the credit.

In contrast, foreign source dividends are fully taxable at their equivalent Canadian dollar value without any dividend tax credit for foreign corporate taxes. An individual may, however, be entitled to claim a foreign tax credit under section 126 for foreign withholding taxes.

(ii) — OECD Model Convention

Articles 10(1) and 10(2) of the *OECD Model Convention* provide:

Dividends that a company resident in a Contracting State pays to a resident of the other Contracting State may be taxed in that other State.

However, such dividends may also be taxed in the Contracting State of which the company paying the dividends is a resident and according to the laws of that State, but if the recipient is the beneficial owner of the dividend the tax so charged shall not exceed:

(a) 5 per cent of the gross amount of the dividend if the beneficial owner is a company (other than a partnership) which holds directly at least 25 per cent of the capital of the company paying the dividends;

(b) 15 per cent of the gross amount of the dividend in all other cases.

The competent authorities of the Contracting State shall by mutual agreement settle the mode of application of these limitations.

---

[141]For example, Belgium, Portugal, Spain and certain types of distributions in France.

[142]See para. 82(1)(b); s. 121.

> This paragraph shall not affect the taxation of the company in respect of the profits out of which the dividends are paid.

Hence, dividends may be taxable both in the recipient's country of residence and in the State in which the corporation that pays the dividend is resident. The *OECD Model* does not provide that dividends should be taxed exclusively either in the State of source or exclusively in the State of the shareholder's residence.

The term "paid" has a very wide meaning and implies the fulfilment of the obligation to put funds at the disposal of the shareholder in the manner required by contract or by custom.

Article 10(1) only deals with dividends that are paid by a company that is resident of a Contracting State to a resident of the other Contracting State. The Article does not apply to dividends paid by a company that resides in a third State. Nor does Article 10(1) apply to dividends paid by a resident company of a Contracting State that are attributable to a permanent establishment that a resident of that State has in the other Contracting State.[143]

(iii) — Appropriate Rate

A critical question in the context of dividends is: what is the appropriate rate of withholding tax to be applied by the source country to dividends? This question is particularly important in the context of dividends because of the different ways in which different countries tax dividends. The three basic models for the taxation of dividends are:

- The "classical" system;

- The "split rate" system; and

- The "imputation" system.

Under the "classical" system, a shareholder in a corporation suffers "economic" double taxation: the corporation pays tax on its income prior to the distribution of the income as dividends and the shareholder is taxed upon receipt of the dividend income. Thus, the rate of the withholding tax on dividends, which acts as a second tier tax, is central to the overall tax burden that is ultimately imposed on such income.

Some countries attempt to mitigate against the burden of economic double taxation by providing some relief either to the payer corporation or to the recipient shareholder. The relief generally takes one of two forms. Under a "split rate" system, undistributed profits are taxed at a higher rate than distributed earnings.

Under the "imputation" system, the tax paid by a corporation is notionally set-off against the tax liability of the recipient shareholder. This model can provide for either partial or com-

---

[143]See Article 21, *OECD Model Convention*.

plete relief from double taxation depending upon the rate of tax paid by the corporation and the rate at which those taxes are imputed to the recipient shareholder.

The *OECD Model Convention* allows both the payer country and the recipient's country to tax dividends; that is, dividends can be taxed by source and on the basis of residence.

Article 10(2) reserves a right to tax dividends to their source State, that is, to the State of which the corporation paying the dividends is a resident. The general rule in Article 10(2) is that the withholding tax on dividends is limited to 15 per cent of the gross value of the dividend. This is a withholding tax over and above any corporate tax, which the source State might have previously imposed on the corporation that pays the dividend.

Canadian tax treaties traditionally provide for a uniform maximum withholding tax rate limit of 15 per cent on the gross amount of the dividend paid or, in some cases, for 10 per cent in the case of significant (at least 25 per cent of share capital or 10 per cent of votes) share-holdings. More recently, however, Canada is negotiating a reduction in these rates. Effective January 1, 1993, for example, pursuant to *A Protocol to the Canada-Netherlands Treaty*, the withholding tax rate on dividends paid on significant shareholdings is 5 per cent, down from the previous 10 per cent. Similarly, in the *Protocol to Canada-U.S. Tax Convention*, the withholding tax on inter-corporate dividends in the case of significant shareholdings is 5 per cent.

Some countries seek to mitigate economic double taxation; others do not. A country can mitigate economic double taxation of dividend income in three principal ways:

- The corporate tax in respect of distributed profits can be charged at a lower rate than that on accumulated or retained profits (the "split rate" system);

- An individual may be allowed to offset a portion of the corporate tax paid on distributed profits against the individual's own personal tax ("imputation" of corporate tax against personal tax); or

- Distributed profits may not be taxed at all at the corporate level and only taxed at the recipient's level.

There is no consensus amongst the OECD countries as to the most appropriate method of providing relief from economic double taxation of corporate and dividend income. Canada uses the "imputation" system to provide relief for individuals who receive dividends from resident corporations.

It should be noted, however, that the Canadian method for providing relief against double taxation of dividend income is only a partial solution to the problem. The dividend tax credit is not a refundable credit and, as such, an individual does not receive any relief if the credit exceeds the indivdiual's personal tax. In this sense, the dividend tax credit is not an adjustment of the corporation's tax previously paid. Instead, it is a notional imputation of the corporate tax burden (whether or not the corporation actually paid the tax) to an individual resident in Canada.

Selected Bibliography to Chapter 32

Canadian Employment

Bacal, N. and R. Lewin, "The Taxation in Canada of Non-Resident Performing Artists and Behind-the-Camera Personnel" (1986) 34 Can. Tax J. 1287.

Boidman, N., "The Peripatetic Alien: His/Her Tax Problems in the U.S. and Abroad", in *Proceedings of the New York University Forty-Fourth Institute on Federal Taxation* 40-1 (New York: Matthew Bender, 1986).

Broley, J.A., "The Migrating Executive: Coming to and Transferring Within Canada", *Corp. Management Tax Conf.* 172 (Can. Tax Foundation, 1979).

Garcia, C.F. and J.H. Shividy, "Taxation of the U.S. Expatriate Living and Working in Canada" (1980) 26 Can. Tax J. 523.

Gray, Kerry, "U.S. Citizens Employed in Canada: An Update" (1986) 34 Can. Tax J. 1463.

Lowden, John H., "Employee Transfers: Moving To or From Canada on Foreign Assignment", in *Proceedings of 41st Tax Conf.* 34:1 (Can. Tax Foundation, 1989).

Miller, Donald, "Executive Transfers from the U.S. to Canada" (May 23, 1990) *Special Seminar on Current International Tax Issues* (DeBoo, 1990) 89.

Wray, D.G. and S.R. Barnard, "Taxation of Non-Resident Athletes and Entertainers Performing in Canada" (1986) 34 Can. Tax J. 1150.

Non-Resident Investments in Canada

Boidman, N. and Bruno Ducharme, *Taxation in Canada, Implications for Foreign Investment* (Netherlands: Kluwer, 1984).

Loveland, Norman C., "Non-Resident Investment in Canada: Earning Investment Returns Exempt from Canadian Taxation", in *Proceedings of 39th Tax Conf.* 20:1 (Can. Tax Foundation, 1987).

Perry, Harvey, "Federal Income Tax: Non-Residents", *Tax Paper No. 89* (Can. Tax Foundation, 1990).

Perry, Harvey, "Federal Income Tax: Foreign Income of Residents", *Tax Paper No. 89* (Can. Tax Foundation, 1990).

Canadian Real Estate

Atlas, Michael J., *Canadian Taxation of Real Estate*, 2nd ed., (CCH Canadian, 1989).

Atlas, Michael J., "Income Tax Issues in Real Estate Leasing", *Corp. Management Tax Conf.* 3:1 (Can. Tax Foundation, 1989).

Bernstein, Jack, "Real Estate Syndications", *Corp. Management Tax Conf.* 2:1 (Can. Tax Foundation, 1989).

Boidman, N., "Non-Resident Investment in Canadian Real Estate", *Corp. Management Tax Conf.* 371 (Can. Tax Foundation, 1983).

Boidman, N., "Tax Planning for Foreign Investment in Canadian Real Estate" (1988) 15 Tax Planning Int'l 12.

Dalsin, Derek T., "Dispositions of Property by Non-Residents: Tax Deferral by Ministerial Discretion" (1991) 39 Can. Tax J. 77.

Gauthier, Andre, "Investment in Canadian Real Estate by Non-Residents", *Corp. Management Tax Conf.* 195 (Can. Tax Foundation, 1978).

James, Larry W., "Disposing of Real Estate", *Corp. Management Tax Conf.* 5:1 (Can. Tax Foundation, 1989).

Lambe, Hugh B., "Foreign Investment in Canadian Real Estate Through a Netherlands Corporation" (1980) 28 Can. Tax J. 343.

Neville, Ralph T., "Tax Considerations in Real Estate Development and Construction", *Corp. Management Tax Conf.* 7:1 (Can. Tax Foundation, 1989).

Power, Mary, "The Taxation of Non-Resident Investment in Canadian Real Estate" (1989) 37 Can. Tax J. 1266.

Shagrie, Alan, "Taxation of Foreign Corporations Investing in Quebec Real Estate — Recent Developments" (1987) 16 Tax Management Int'l. J. 336.

Silver, Sheldon, "Vehicles for Acquiring and Holding Real Estate", *Corp. Management Tax Conf.* 4:1 (Can. Tax Foundation, 1989).

Ward, David A., "Foreign Investment in Canadian Real Estate", *Corp. Management Tax Conf.* 10:1 (Can. Tax Foundation, 1989).

CHAPTER 33 — OFFSHORE TRUSTS

I. — General Comment

Offshore trust planning is the legitimate arrangement of financial affairs in a foreign juris-diction for the purposes of risk and wealth management. The objectives of offshore planning are to:

- Attain business and/or personal and financial goals;
- Preserve and enhance capital;
- Secure assets; and
- Minimize tax.

A plan can implement some or all of the above objectives. Each offshore business plan should address each of these objectives in the context of the individual's particular personal and financial circumstances.

The phrase "offshore" is somewhat of a misnomer. Every jurisdiction is in a sense "off-shore" vis-a-vis the home country. Thus, a jurisdiction that is offshore for other countries will be onshore for its own residents. For example, the United Kingdom is "offshore" Can-ada and, indeed, even a "tax haven" for all persons except U.K. domiciles. Thus, it is a particularly attractive offshore jurisdiction for retirees. Although offshore planning requires a sophisticated understanding of two legal regimes, the home and the offshore location, the onshore advisor should be careful to confine his or her professional opinions to the jurisdiction where the advisor is licensed to practice.

An offshore trust should stand upon a clearly defined mission that allows the client and the client's professional advisor to assess its risks, costs, and financial returns in the context of the client's particular and specific circumstances. Generic solutions are rarely effective and sometimes cause financial harm. For example, an offshore plan that protects assets from prospective creditors (an Asset Protection Trust) is quite a different creature from one that minimizes tax for an immigrant or one that one uses to plan for an emigrant's retirement. Each plan must be specifically tailored to achieve the underlying purpose for which it is put into place.

There are three basic considerations in offshore planning:

- Form and structure;

- Location; and

- Administration and management.

Each of these factors should be evaluated in the context of the particular plan and its advantages weighed against the resulting savings and costs of administration. In addition, one must be sensitive to the reporting requirements of each plan.

Offshore jurisdictions are generally described either as International Financial Centres (IFCs) or Tax Havens. The former terminology deflects some of the odious implications of the latter. IFCs may be classified according to their:

- Scope of exemption from income taxes;

- Type of optimal user; and

- Scope and extent of anti-avoidance legislation.

We classify countries into three broad groups depending upon the extent of exemption from income tax:

1. No Income or Capital Tax;

2. Source Country Taxation; and

3. Treaty Havens.

1. — Jurisdictions With No Income Tax or Generous Tax Exemptions

The following countries — also known as "tax havens" — provide generous income tax exemptions:[1]

Andorra
Anguilla
Bahamas
Bermuda
Brunei
Cayman Islands
Cook Islands
French Polynesia
Grenada
Kuwait
Maldive Islands
Nauru
New Caledonia
Oman
Principality of Monaco
Turks & Caicos Islands
United Arab Emirates
Uruguay
Vanuatu

2. — Jurisdictions That Tax Only Domestic Source Income

The following countries tax only income originating within their jurisdiction and exempt all foreign income:

Costa Rica
Djibouti
Dominican Republic
Ecuador
Guatemala
Hong Kong
Ireland (non-resident companies only)
Jordan
Lebanon
Liberia

---

[1]See also: "Eliminating Harmful Tax Practices in Tax Havens: Defensive Measures in Major EU Countries and Tax Haven Reforms," Canadian Tax Journal, 2005 Vol. 53, No. 3, at 685-719.

Macau
Panama
Uruguay
Venezuela

3. — Treaty Havens

The term "Treaty Havens" generally applies to full tax system countries that have double taxation agreements and provide generous exemptions from domestic tax on income. This group includes:

Antilles
Barbados
Cyprus
Gibraltar
Guernsey (limited circumstances)
Ireland
Jersey (limited circumstances)
Luxembourg
Mauritius Islands
Netherlands
Switzerland

The form and structure of an offshore plan depends primarily upon the purpose for which we create it. Even at the simplest level, offshore investing requires careful planning. For example, an individual who wants to invest in foreign currencies can open an investment account with a bank or brokerage house in a full tax jurisdiction (e.g. the United States) or a tax haven for the purpose of building an offshore portfolio. The individual can retain complete legal ownership and control of his or her assets and be liable for the debts and taxes on any income from the investments. There are, however, tax considerations that must also be taken into account even for the simplest of structures. In the above example, there might be withholding taxes that depend upon the source and type of income, foreign tax credits, antiavoidance rules and foreign income reporting requirements.

At a more sophisticated level, an individual can use other vehicles for the purpose of offshore investments. Although trusts and corporations are the most commonly used tax planning vehicles, there are other forms of organizations, such as limited partnerships, foundations, Stiftungs, Anstalts, and the like. Each of these forms of organization serves different purposes. Some are more esoteric than others, but each has its use in particular circumstances and locations.

II. — Historical Background

The trust is one of the oldest forms of legal relationships known to common law. The trust was born in the branch of law known as Equity, which was originally administered through the Lord Chancellor's Court or the Court of Chancery. Conceived as a "use" in the Middle Ages, the trust was used primarily as a conveyancing vehicle that separated the legal title of real property from the benefits to be derived from it. Under feudal law, the King or a Lord was entitled to payment when an heir succeeded to the title or rights to feudal land. One could avoid these payments (the precursor to land transfer and succession taxes) if the land vested in another person for his use. Hence, there was an incentive to transfer the title of property to others for their use and enjoyment in order to reduce payments to the feudal lords.

Transferring the legal title of property to another person in order to minimize "tax" payments, however, rendered both the transferor and the person for whose benefit the property (beneficiary) was transferred vulnerable to the new owner who now had legal title to the property. Neither the transferor nor the beneficiary had any legal rights to the property under the common law because they did not have title to it. Thus, the "use", which was created as a vehicle for "tax" avoidance, brought in its wake another problem: both the transferor (the "settlor") and the person for whose benefit the property was transferred (the "beneficiary") were left without legal remedy in the common law courts, which did not recognize duality of property ownership. The common law had a simple approach to ownership: either you had title to property and could do anything with it or you did not have title and could do nothing. The common law did not recognize any intermediate category. Thus, without a remedy in common law, the settlor and the beneficiary could only appeal in good conscience to the Chancellor to have the legal owner of the property honour the terms and understandings upon which he received the property.

The Chancellor could not alter the fact that in law the transferee ("trustee") held the proper title to the property. By virtue of his ecclesiastical powers, however, he could in all good conscience compel the transferee to manage, administer and use it for the benefit of the beneficiary according to the terms of the transfer. Thus, the "use" would split the ownership of property from its enjoyment. A person could hold the legal title to property and yet be compelled to manage and administer it for the benefit of another person who had no title in the property. Although the use started as an occasional indulgence by the Chancellor dispensing justice according to the dictates of his conscience, it was later transformed into a formal and routine enforcement of uses.

The King, however, was not amused by these machinations. The King was deprived of his feudal "taxes" through the mechanism of the "use". The *Statute of Uses*, enacted in 1535, had the effect of causing the legal title of property to be transferred to the beneficiary for whose benefit the use was created. Thus, the *Statute of Uses* effectively eliminated the distinction between legal title and beneficial interests. This illustrates an early form of anti-avoidance tax legislation.

But as with all anti-avoidance legislation, the *Statute of Uses* stirred the creative juices of lawyers. Soon after its enactment, some lawyers began to circumvent the Statute through the creation of a second use. Instead of transferring property to a person to hold to the use of another person, lawyers conveyed the property to the use of another to the use of yet another person: the double-barrelled use. They executed the first use and conveyed title by operation of the *Statute of Uses*. The Statute was then exhausted. The Lord Chancellor then enforced the second use in the Courts of Equity for the benefit of the beneficiary. The second use came to be known as the trust.

III. — The Modern Day Trust

A trust divides the ownership of trust property into two components, legal and beneficial ownership. The advantage of divided ownership is that the *legal* title to trust property rests with the trustee and, if properly structured, is immune from claims by persons who are not claimants against the trust itself. Once one declares a trust and takes effect, one can deal with its property only according to the terms of its creation and for the benefit of its chosen or designated beneficiaries. Thus, the essence of a trust is that it permits the division of the legal ownership of property from its use and enjoyment. The pure trust is unique to Anglo-Saxon legal systems. As Maitland said:[2]

> If we were asked what is the greatest and most distinctive achievement performed by English-men in the field of jurisprudence, I cannot think that we should have any better answer to give than this, namely, the development from century to century of the trust idea.

In this context, a trust is the legal relationship governed by the principles of the English law of Equity. A trust does not include alien concepts such as the "Treuhanderschaft", "Stiftung", "Fidei Commissa", or the "Muslim Waqf".

1. — *Nature of a Trust*

A trust is a legal relationship created by a person (the settlor) whereby the settlor places assets (the trust fund) under the control of a person (the trustee) for the benefit of third parties (the beneficiaries). We can also create a trust for a *purpose*, for example, charitable purposes. The trustee may be a beneficiary and any beneficiary may enforce the trust's obligation.[3]

---

[2]Maitland, F.W., *Selected Essays* (1936).

[3]*Underhill's Law of Trusts and Trustees* (12th Ed.) 1970, p. 3 quoted with approval in *Andrews' Estate v. M.N.R.* (1966), 42 Tax A.B.C. 303 (TAB); and *Tobin Tractor (1957) Ltd. v. Western Surety Co.* (1963), 42 W.W.R. 532 (Sask. Q.B.).

An individual may create a trust either during his or her lifetime or upon death. Where a settlor transfers during his or her lifetime, the trust is an *inter vivos* or living trust. For private law purposes, a trust created upon the death of the settlor is a testamentary trust. Such a trust arises out of the settlor's last will and testament. For tax purposes, however, a "testamentary trust" is defined more restrictively.[4]

As a matter of private law, a trust is a *relationship*. A trust is not an equity. The relationship arises whenever a person is compelled in equity to hold property, whether real or personal, and whether by legal or equitable title, for the benefit of some other persons or objects permitted by law, in such a way that the real benefit of the property accrues, not to the trustee but to the beneficiaries or other objects of the trust.[5] We can create a trust quite easily and structure its terms to suit a variety of purposes. The ease with which we create a trust and its flexibility that it affords in business and family arrangements makes it particularly useful in tax planning for high wealth individuals. For tax purposes, however, a trust is a hybrid, taxable in its own right for some purposes and a conduit or flow-through vehicle for other purposes. Thus, in tax law a trust is a complex relationship.

We can also use a trust to protect assets from the reach of creditors. Many offshore financial centres (for example, Jersey, Bermuda, The Bahamas, and The Cayman Islands) have sophisticated legal systems with well developed trust laws. These centres are also generally "debtor friendly" countries with no income or capital taxes. Thus, they offer the advantages of well developed trust law, security of assets, and confidential banking arrangements. The use of these systems by Canadians, however, requires a clear understanding of the relevant commercial and tax rules.

2. — The Parties to a Trust

A trust is a *relationship* between the settlor and the trustee. The beneficiaries are strictly speaking not parties to the trust, but have a beneficial interest in its property. They do, however, have standing before a court to ensure that the trustee administers the trust according to its terms and for their beneficial interests.

Regardless of the manner in which one creates a trust, it necessarily implies splitting ownership of the trust fund into its legal and beneficial interests. The trustee acquires ownership and title to the fund and, therefore, can deal with it as its *legal* owner. The trustee may do so, however, only on the condition that he or she administers it according to the terms of the trust deed and the rules of common law and equity. Thus, the essence of a trust plan is that the settlor should trust the trustee to administer it effectively, efficiently, and legally.

---

[4]See subs. 108(1) [re-en. R.S.C. 1980-81-82-83, c. 140, subs. 63(2); am. R.S.C. 1985, c. 45, subs. 52(1)].

[5]Keeton, G.W., *The Laws of Trusts*, 9th ed. (1968), p. 5.

A settlor may also protect a trust by naming a protector in the trust deed. The role of a protector is to supervise (but not control) management of the trust and exercise supervisory powers in specified circumstances. Although not a party to the trust, the protector plays a key role in ensuring that the trustee administers it according to the settlor's wishes. Thus, the protector ensures the integrity of the trust, protects its interests, and gives added assurance to the settlor that the trustee will carry out the settlor's wishes.

The trust deed or will should set out the framework for the disposition and administration of the trust fund. It is here that we require careful planning and thought to implement the settlor's wishes, safeguard the beneficiaries' interests, and protect the trustee in the administration of the trust fund. The essence of a trust is that the trustee must control the trust. If the trustee is a mere nominee of the settlor, the alleged trust may be considered a sham. If it is a sham, the law considers the property to have remained with the settlor. Alternatively, the nominee "trustee" may be seen as an agent of the settlor, in which case the agent's acts are simply the acts of the principal.

(a) — The Settlor

A settlor creates the trust and transfers or settles assets on it by transferring title and ownership of the assets to the appointed trustees. The transfer of assets to the trustee is an act of faith. The settlor must be confident that a trustee with integrity and substance has been selected. Trust is the foundation of a trust.

A trust deed does not have to name a settlor. A trust may be created simply by a *Declaration of Trust* whereby the trustees declare that they hold property (usually a nominal sum of money) as the original trust fund. The settlor may then later transfer further assets to the trustees to be held as part of the trust fund.

The settlor may also attach a *Memorandum of Wishes* to the trust deed to make known his or her wishes as to how the trustees should administer the trust. Although a *Memorandum of Wishes* does not legally bind the trustee, it can be a key document in the administration of a trust in that it provides guidance as to the settlor's intentions. A *Memorandum of Wishes* usually covers critical issues, such as:

- The purpose of the trust;

- Investment policies; and

- Guidance in respect of the long term interests of the beneficiaries.

The trustee is not obliged to disclose the existence of the *Memorandum of Wishes* to the beneficiaries. The settlor may, however, transmit a copy of the *Memorandum* directly to the beneficiaries so that they are aware of its contents.

A trust may have more than one settlor if different people add assets to the trust fund. Where this occurs, it is important to ensure that there is a clear indication to whom the trust fund should revert in the event that the trust fails. It is also important to have a clear understanding as to the role of the *Memorandum of Wishes* insofar as the various beneficiaries are concerned and for the administration of trust funds.

(b) — The Trustee

The trustee is legally responsible for the administration of the trust. Thus, the trustee should fully understand the trust deed and have the ability to administer it according to its terms and the relevant law of the jurisdiction where it is situated. This involves obtaining a clear understanding of the local law of trusts and, in particular, any statutory variations of the common law.

An individual or a corporation may act as trustee. In the case of a trust with substantial assets, a trust company will usually have the administrative infrastructure to discharge the trustee's fiduciary obligations and properly account for the fund. A corporate trustee (with or without additional individual trustees) also ensures continuity in the administration of the trust and acts as its anchor so that it remains resident in the jurisdiction for tax purposes.

The trustee is initially appointed by the settlor under the terms of the trust deed. The duty of the trustee, however, is to act independently and exercise the trust powers as a fiduciary under the terms of the trust deed. The trustee must not simply act as a nominee or agent of the settlor. The fiduciary obligation applies not only to the exercise of administrative powers (such as the selection of investments), but also in the context of dispositive powers (such as, the allocation of income and capital between the beneficiaries). A trustee who acts as a mere nominee of the settlor risks being in breach of his or her fiduciary duties and liable to aggrieved beneficiaries for a breach of trust in the failure of its administration.[6]

It is not a defence to an action for breach of fiduciary duty that the trustee complied with the settlor's *Memorandum of Wishes*. The fiduciary must exercise his or her power independently. The trustee must balance the wishes of the settlor with the fiduciary obligations under the trust. The trustee should not be a mere rubber stamp for the settlor. On the other hand, the courts will look at the trustee's exercise of dispositive powers to ensure that the trustee exercises them in a responsible manner according to any expressed wishes[7] and may set aside trustee actions that are irrational, perverse or irrelevant to any sensible expectation of the settlor.[8] As long as the trustees take into account the *Memorandum of Wishes*, however, the ultimate decision to act in a particular manner is theirs and they can act contrary to the settlor's wishes.[9]

---

[6]*Bartlett v. Barclays Bank Trust Company Ltd. (No. 2)*, [1980] 2 All E.R. 92.

[7]*Re Hay's Settlements Trust*, [1981] 3 All E.R. 786.

[8]*Re Manisty's Settlement*, [1973] 2 All E.R. 1203.

[9]*Bank of Nova Scotia v. Borletta* (1994), 1 J.I.P. 35.

A trustee is not entitled to charge for his or her services unless there is an express power to do so in the trust. It is, therefore, important to ensure that the trust deed clearly specifies the method and the scale of fees by which the trustee is remunerated. This is particularly important where a trust has an extended term so that the professional fees can be adjusted to changing circumstances.

(c) — The Beneficiaries

The beneficiaries of a trust must either be clearly identified or identifiable with certainty. Thus, the trust deed should outline the class of beneficiaries and the nature and extent of their respective interests in the trust. Of course, a trust deed can empower the trustees to appoint additional beneficiaries or exclude beneficiaries already named. Where such a power is given, however, it is useful to stipulate when the power should be exercised. For example, the trustee may be empowered to change beneficiaries only with the prior written consent of the settlor or the protector of the trust. The inclusion of such a power in the trust deed should take into account the relevant local law and tax considerations.

A class of beneficiaries should not remain "open" for too long a period of time. For example, if the children of the settlor are to receive their beneficial entitlement at age 25, the trust would normally provide for the class to close when the first child attains the age of 25 years. Depending upon the jurisdiction and proper law of the trust, it may be important to preclude any possibility that the class of beneficiaries can close only after the end of the perpetuity period.

(d) — The Protector

The "protector" of a trust is a person (usually an individual) appointed for the purpose of providing a measure of control over the trustee(s) in circumstances where it is inadvisable or imprudent for the settlor to retain control of the trust assets. The protector is appointed under the terms of the trust deed and supervises the trust in respect of certain named matters concerning its administration. The appointment of a protector can relieve the settlor's anxiety about transferring the assets to a trustee who may be a complete stranger. Thus, in a sense, a settlor appoints a protector because he or she does not completely trust the trustee.

The protector should not, however, have too much power over the trust, particularly if the protector is resident in a high tax jurisdiction. An overzealous protector may be seen as a *de facto* trustee. If given too much power, the trust may be considered to reside in his or her jurisdiction. Thus, a Canadian resident should not control an offshore trust if the purpose of the trust is to minimize Canadian income tax. An offshore trust that is resident in Canada is taxable in Canada on its worldwide income.

The appointment of a protector is akin to taking out an insurance policy: one hopes that the insured event will not occur, but one is prepared for the contingency in the event that it does occur in adverse circumstances. The protector's powers depend entirely upon the settlor who determines the scope and extent of the "insurance cover" that the settlor requires or feels comfortable with in order to protect the trust. Obviously, the more confidence that the settlor has in the trustee(s), the less the need for supplementary protective powers.

Domestic trusts that are administered by close family members seldom use protectors because of the high level of confidence that the settlor usually has in the trustee. With offshore trusts, however, the settlor is typically far removed, both in distance and knowledge, from the trustee, which is likely to be a bank or trust company. In these circumstances, the settlor may appoint a close relative or friend to supervise the trustees in certain specified circumstances.

(e) — Powers

The appointment of a protector serves a different purpose from a *Memorandum of Wishes*. A *Memorandum of Wishes* communicates the settlor's intention and wishes to the trustee but without in fact exerting any legal control over the administration and supervision of the trust. Although a *Memorandum* offers some comfort to the settlor that his or her views as to the administration of the trust will receive appropriate consideration by the trustees, it is not akin to the appointment of a protector in that it has minimal legal status. The protector has a recognized status in law and the protector's powers should be incorporated into the trust deed so that they have the force and authority of the proper law by which the trust is governed.

The protector's powers will vary directly with the intensity of the settlor's angst. The trust deed should, however, address the following matters:

- The power to appoint and to remove trustees;

- The power to change the proper law of the trust;

- The power to physically relocate the administration of the trust to another jurisdiction;

- The power to consent to income distributions from the trust;

- Approval of capital payments to beneficiaries;

- Appointment of additional beneficiaries;

- Exclusion of named beneficiaries;

- Issuance of guarantees by the trust;

- Investment in unlimited liability companies; and

- The power to amend the terms of the trust.

(f) — Legal Status

A protector is a fiduciary. A fiduciary power is in essence a power that is conferred upon a person but to be exercised for the benefit of others rather than for the benefit of the holder of the power. Traditionally, trustees are held to an exceptionally high standard and their power, or more accurately the abuse thereof, is subject to strict judicial control. Although, absent special statutory provisions, protectors may not be subject to the same stringent standard as trustees, their power is certainly subject to judicial control and they cannot abuse or commit a fraud on the power. This applies to both administrative and dispositive powers. The exercise of a power is considered to be fraudulent when it is motivated to achieve a purpose that is beyond the scope of or not justified by the instrument that creates the power.[10]

To say that a protector is a fiduciary is not very helpful. To paraphrase Justice Cardozo, identifying a person as a fiduciary is merely the beginning of the analysis. Practising lawyers, academics and judges have not yet developed either a coherent or internally consistent theory of fiduciary relationships. The common lawyer's penchant for classification of forms of action into pigeon holes is frustrated when applied to the classification of fiduciary relationships and powers. Thus, one is left to wrestle with the meaning of and differences (if any) between "trust powers", "power coupled with a duty", "power coupled with a trust", "power in the nature of a trust", "beneficial powers" and "vicarious powers".[11]

One starts with the proposition that a fiduciary power is one that must be exercised for the benefit of some person other than the repository of the power. Thus, a protector's power must be exercised as a fiduciary if it is conferred for the benefit of either the settlor or the beneficiaries of the trust. The key is generally found in the settlor's intention in creating the trust and the reasons for conferring the power on the protector. It is a question of the proper construction of the instrument.

Professor Austin Scott[12] took the view that a settlor could confer powers to be held beneficially either with or without an accompanying fiduciary duty:[13]

> It is a question of interpretation of the trust instrument in the light of all the circumstances whether the power is conferred on him for his sole benefit or for the benefit of the beneficiaries of the trust. In determining this question the relationship of the holder of the power to the trust, as well as the nature of the power, is an important consideration.

---

[10]*Vatcher v. Paull*, [1915] A.C. 372 (P.C.).

[11]See, generally: *Fiduriacy Powers* (1976), 54 Can. Bar. Rev. 229.

[12]*Scott on Trusts*, Volume 2 (Third Edition).

[13]At pp. 227–9, cited with approval In The Matter of Star I (Revised) and Star II (Revised) Trusts, Supreme Court of Bermuda (Civil Jurisdiction), (1994). See also: *Rawson Trust v. Berlman* (April 25, 1990) (Supreme Court of Bahamas).

The powers conferred upon a protector can certainly be drafted in such a manner as to be interpreted as a fiduciary power exercisable for the benefit of either the settlor or the beneficiaries (or both) of the trust.

(g) — Tax Considerations

Where a trust confers powers upon the protector of a trust that are so far reaching that it makes the protector, in effect, the "mind and management" of the trust, there is a substantial risk that the residence of the trust will be determined by the residence of the protector and not that of the trustee. This risk is commensurately greater where the trust has only one trustee whose powers are effectively under the supervision of the protector. Hence, the appointment of an offshore protector is an additional safeguard that the residence of the trust will remain offshore, regardless of whether or not the protector exercises fiduciary powers.

The balance of power between the protector and the trustee is a delicate matter and must be carefully considered in the trust deed. The role of a protector is to allay the settlor's angst in transferring the assets to the legal control of the trustee. By appointing a protector, the settlor retains some residual influence over certain key actions of the trustee and provides for the trust's administration according to the settlor's wishes. If, however, the balance of power tilts too far in favour of the protector, the protector may become the *de facto* trustee. This raises serious tax concerns if the trust becomes resident in a high tax jurisdiction such as Canada. Thus, the sensible approach is to limit the protector's fiduciary powers and restrict the role to a supervisory function in respect of certain key elements, such as, adherence to the settlor's intentions as expressed in the non-binding *Memorandum of Wishes*.

As with a trustee, a protector is not entitled as of right to compensation for services. Hence, it is prudent to anticipate the method of compensation for the protector and base this on a flexible rate schedule that is adaptable to the circumstances of the trust over time.

IV. — Asset Protection

Asset protection planning is organizing one's financial affairs so as to safeguard assets against unforeseen risks. Thus, asset protection is a vaccine, not a cure. There are a variety of forms of planning for asset protection. Some are relatively straightforward and satisfy the objective at minimal cost; others require more complex structures and, necessarily, entail higher costs.

The concept of protecting one's assets against potential legal claims is not new. Individuals have always been concerned about protecting assets against creditor claims and the law provides various mechanisms that allow for such protection. The limited liability company, for example, is an asset protection vehicle to safeguard the personal assets of shareholders from claims by corporate creditors. Since the decision in *Salomon*,[14] the essence of a limited liability company is that its creditors are generally (though not invariably) restricted in their claims against the corporation's assets and may not reach through the corporation to attach the personal property of its shareholders. The principle of limited liability was then extended to inter-corporate shareholder protection. For example, the use of a holding company to own the shares of an operating company provides dual insulation and is the preferred method of protecting financial assets from operating creditors and personal assets from shareholders. In a bankruptcy, for example, the creditors of the operating company cannot easily reach through to the assets of the holding company.

1. — *Insurance*

Life insurance (particularly term insurance) is a simple form of asset protection. For example, life insurance may be used to protect a business against the unforeseen or untimely death of its key management and thereby reduce business risks. Personal term life insurance also protects one's estate. Similarly, where available, liability insurance in an adequate amount can be used to limit the exposure of a professional person (such as a lawyer, accountant, doctor, dentist, engineer) against malpractice claims. In certain cases, however, it may not be possible to obtain adequate insurance coverage at a reasonable cost. The accounting and legal professions, for example, beset with multi-million dollar claims from large public companies that threaten to put them into personal bankruptcy, can protect themselves through limited liability partnerships (LLPs).

2. — *Limited and Limited Liability Partnerships*

Limited partnerships (LPs) and limited liability partnerships (LLPs) can also be used to protect partners against the claims of creditors. The LP is a useful vehicle for limiting liability, particularly in the context of investor tax shelters. LLPs offer protection onshore but in more limited circumstances.

Tax shelter limited partnerships allow partnership costs and revenues to flow through to investors without exposing the investors to liability for the partnership's debts over and above beyond their capital contributions. Limited partnerships, however, have their limitations: the limited partners are protected from liability and the general partner is fully exposed to the partnership's liabilities. Thus, one can use a corporate general partner that itself has limited liability. Hence, one can use a LP in conjunction with a limited liability company to protect against unforeseen claims. A LP interest, however, is personal property that can be attached by creditors in order to satisfy their claims. Thus, a LP unit protects the partner from claims against the partnership itself, but does not protect the individual partner from

---

[14]*Salomon v. Salomon & Co.*, [1897] A.C. 22 (H.L.).

his or her personal creditors. A personal creditor need only attach the LP interest in satisfaction of a claim.

LPs and limited liability companies (LLCs) are useful vehicles when used in the context of domestic public investments and business operations. They do not, however, assist in protecting personal assets. An individual who transfers personal assets into a corporation takes back the shares of the corporation in exchange. Thus, the individual acquires assets (corporate shares) that have a value equal to the assets transferred into the corporation. In the event of a personal claim against the shareholders, the creditors may seize the corporate shares. If the shares represent a controlling interest, the creditors may dissolve the corporation and reach through to its assets.

In addition, the directors and shareholders may be held personally liable for certain corporate debts if they breach their statutory obligations. For example, corporate directors may be personally liable for the corporations's unpaid wages. Similarly, a corporate shareholder may be liable to the Canada Revenue Agency (CRA) for its unpaid taxes to the extent that it pays shareholder dividends when it owes taxes.

V. — Asset Protection Trusts

An asset protection trust (APT) is a trust whose principal purpose is to provide protection from *future unforeseen* creditors. The trust is probably the most versatile vehicle for asset and risk protection. Its creation involves a transfer of legal title of assets from a person to a trustee for the benefit of determined or determinable persons. A trust can be used for multiple purposes and is quite flexible, both insofar as structure and location. An added advantage is that a trust is a confidential relationship that is not open to scrutiny in any public registry or government records department. It is important to clearly identify the objectives of a trust at the outset of planning. The trust objectives will determine the manner in which it is created, its situs, the location of its assets, trustees and protectors. The structure and management of the trust will also determine how it is taxed.

The essence of an APT is that it protects individuals from *potential creditors and unforeseen liabilities* that may arise out of future events, such as:

- Damage awards from liability litigation;
- Forced heirship or succession rules;
- Personal liability of directors and shareholders of corporations;
- Forced property sharing under matrimonial property regimes; and
- Tax claims.

The underlying purpose of an APT is to ensure that the beneficiary of the trust is *legitimately* beyond the legal jurisdiction of any creditor who seeks to assert claims against him or her. Generally, in order to be an effective protective vehicle, an APT must not be within the *in rem* or *in personam* jurisdiction of a court that is likely to favour the creditor's claim over the debtor's defence in the place where the claim is asserted. A creditor's legal claim is only as good as the creditor's legal rights of enforcement and the debtor's legal requirement to satisfy the claim. Thus, just as, absent fraud, corporate creditors cannot generally attach the personal assets of shareholders, an APT can prevent creditors from reaching the assets of a debtor. In order to do so, however, the APT must be properly structured on the basis of the legal framework of the creditor's jurisdiction and the situs of the trust.

An APT offers protection only if it is not premised on a fraudulent conveyance to defraud a *present* creditor. An APT can protect only against future or subsequent creditors that have not appeared on the debtor's horizon at the time it is created. A conveyance in the face of a cause of action that has accrued or crystallized when the trust is created is fraudulent and can be set aside under common law or statutory rules. This means that timing is everything in the creation of an APT: the earlier the better. This is easier said than done. Most individuals prefer to wait until the horse has bolted before they close the barn door.

APTs should constitute a part of the financial planning of most high net worth individuals in order to legitimately protect their wealth and limit liability to potential legal claims. An APT is as intrinsic to financial planning as a corporation is to business planning. They each provide for orderly management of assets and risk. Having said that, however, there are a variety of ways in which these objectives can be satisfied. The overall objective is to build a protective wall around the debtor and to guard against future creditors that emerge in the form of business (liability suits against directors), professional (malpractice and negligence), personal (matrimonial settlements), or tax claims.

It is also important to ascertain at the outset whether it is intended to create a tax neutral or tax efficient APT. Generally, it is easier for Canadian residents to create a tax neutral APT than it is to create one that has tax savings as a dominant purpose. There are, however, tax planning opportunities in the case of non-residents, immigrants and emigrants, and inheritance trusts that can result in substantial savings.

Contrary to popular myth, APT planning is not about hiding assets in tax havens in a surreptitious manner. Nor should asset protection planning be viewed as a surrogate for income tax evasion by concealing money in secret offshore bank accounts. Proper asset protection planning involves the arrangement of one's affairs in such a manner that one derives legal confidentiality in the country in which the plan is located, but always subject to compliance with the laws concerning taxation and fraudulent conveyances in the country of the settlor's domicile and residence. This calls for careful planning taking into account both domestic and foreign laws.

1. — Offshore Trusts

An APT is usually established in a jurisdiction with specific legislation that is designed to protect trust assets from the claims of creditors and family members who might seek to set aside the trust. The objectives in setting up an APT are to:

- Protect the assets of the trust;

- Ensure complete compliance with domestic and foreign laws; and

- Provide efficient administration.

Thus, the essence of an APT is to create a vehicle that places an individual's assets outside of the legal reach of creditors.

A foreign situs APT may be used to:

- Replace or top-up professional liability insurance for directors and officers;

- Reduce domestic insurance coverage, particularly where large insurance coverage attracts litigation;

- Protect against risks unassociated with professional practice and which, therefore, are not covered by malpractice insurance;

- Remove assets from a high litigation jurisdiction (for example, the United States) to a low litigation country;

- Avoid forced heirship provisions in country of domicile;

- Reduce financial profile and increase financial privacy;

- Avoid or supplement pre-nuptial agreements;

- Protect retirement plan benefits; and

- Protect business assets.

2. — Creation of Trust

The first step is to "creditor proof" the settlor. This is done by transferring the legal ownership of the settlor's assets to a trust. Prior to setting up the trust, however, the professional advisor should ensure that the individual complies with the requirements of the various domestic anti-fraudulent conveyancing statutes in place at the relevant time. Generally, the transferor should be solvent, not a bankrupt, and should not be contemplating a transfer of assets that would render the transferor unable to meet his or her present and known creditors.

The particular structure selected for an individual will depend upon various personal, family, and financial circumstances. At the very least, however, one should be mindful of the following factors in setting up the structure:

- The structure should be at least "tax neutral", that is, the structure should not increase the individual's tax burden;

- The individual's estate planning needs should be considered and taken into account;

- Income and capital needs should be provided for now and into the future;

- The individual should be in a position to truthfully reveal his or her plan to any court of law and legally incapable of compliance with any court order so as not to be held in contempt of a court of competent jurisdiction;

- The trust should be administered by a truly independent trustee so that it is not considered a sham. The transferor (settlor) of the property into the trust should not legally control the trustee. For example, the trustee should not be a controlled foreign corporation;

- The trustee should be a person who is competent to ensure that the assets are safe and protected. The trustee should have a proven track record, be financially stable and subject to a strict supervisory regime in the jurisdiction where the trust is located;

- The trust arrangement should include a mechanism to change the trustees if required by subsequent events;

- The creation of the trust should be able to withstand scrutiny of the Canadian courts as a proper and validly created trust; and

- The transfer of assets into the trust should not contravene any of the domestic rules in respect of fraudulent conveyance of assets.

A trust that is illusory, constitutes a sham or pretense may be challenged. In each of these circumstances (and they are essentially variations of the same theory of legal liability), a court can look through the pretense and attach such terms and conditions as it considers appropriate to the real situation.

Similarly, a court can look through a trust on the basis of a theory of agency that the trust in substance is nothing more than the agent of the alleged settlor who in fact remains the principal. Thus, a settlor who retains too much control over the administration and management of the trust and retains too much of an interest in its property may be viewed as nothing more than the surrogate and agent of the settlor. Under this theory, a court may merge the interest of the two persons and consider them to be one and the same. Hence, unlike corporate law, which clearly contemplates that an individual may in respect of a corporation be its sole shareholder, director, employee and creditor, the law of trusts does not allow for the fusion of proprietary, management and economic interests between the settlor, the trustee, and the beneficiary.

3. — The Trust Agreement

The trust agreement will determine the integrity of the trust and whether it achieves its objective of asset protection. In most cases, the settlor of the trust will contribute most of its assets.

The following issues must be addressed in the trust deed:

- The trust should be irrevocable. There should be no mechanism to retrieve the assets once they have been settled upon the trust;

- The trustee should be permanently resident in the jurisdiction selected for the location of the trust. This almost inevitably requires that the trustee (or at least one of them) responsible for the administration of the trust should be a trust company that is resident in and licensed in the jurisdiction selected;

- The trust should be discretionary. It is imperative that the settlor should not have any power to control the trust. Distribution of income and capital should be solely within the discretion of the trustee;

- The beneficiaries of the trust may either be named or determinable from a named class. The beneficiaries can include the settlor, a spouse and children;

- The trustee should have complete discretion to accumulate or distribute income and capital amongst the beneficiaries. This will make it difficult for creditors to claim that the contributor has a vested and certain interest in the trust;

- The trust agreement should set out the powers of the trustee and the manner in which the trust is to be administered;

- A majority (if not all) of the trustees should be resident in the jurisdiction that it is intended to locate the trust. The trustee should not be within the legal jurisdiction of a Canadian court. If the trust is properly structured offshore, Canadian courts do not have any *in personam* jurisdiction because the trustee is outside the jurisdiction of the domestic courts. At the same time, Canadian courts will not have any *in rem* jurisdiction because the assets are offshore; and

- The trust agreement should be drafted by a lawyer who is qualified and licensed to practice in the jurisdiction selected for the trust's location.

In summary, the structure of the trust should ensure that Canadian courts do not have jurisdiction over the offshore trust to the extent that its assets are located outside Canada.

VI. — Location And Situs

One of the questions that must be resolved early in offshore planning is the situs or location of a prospective entity. Where should the entity be situated? The situs of a trust, for example, determines its "proper law", the forum for its administration and can have important domestic and foreign tax implications. Similarly, the place of incorporation or management (or both) may determine the domicile of a corporation. The placement of an entity in a particular location will determine many legal and tax questions and, therefore, should be evaluated carefully.

1. — Trusts

A Canadian trust is a trust that is set up and resident in Canada with Canadian trustees. Hence, a Canadian trust is within both the *in rem* and *in personam* jurisdiction of Canadian courts and subject to domestic laws in respect of conveyances, limitation periods, domestic statutes governing preferences, matrimonial claims, bankruptcy, and income tax laws. A foreign trust is one where a majority of its trustees reside outside Canada.

2. — Civil Law Jurisdictions

Many countries do not recognize the concept of a common law trust, that is, a relationship that divides the ownership of property into its legal and beneficial components. The trust as we know it is not a civil law or Islamic concept. Although some civil law jurisdictions have modified versions of the trust in their legal systems, the trust is not intrinsic to civil law. This can raise difficult issues of conflicts of laws where, for example, a trust in a common law jurisdiction owns property in a country that does not recognize the trust concept and can lead to challenges of the validity of the trust in the jurisdiction where the property is located.

Although the *Hague Convention* on the law of trusts (July 1, 1985) requires the signatories to the Convention to recognize trusts as a matter of private international law, the concept of the trust may be overridden by mandatory laws of the non-trust jurisdiction. Thus, despite the Convention, mandatory rules (for example, rules relating to the transfer of immoveable property, bankruptcy and succession) may completely override the trust concept.

3. — Common Law Jurisdictions

As noted earlier, the trust is quintessentially a common law (more accurately, an equitable) creation and, therefore, one would usually locate a trust within a common law jurisdiction. The advantage of locating a trust in a common law jurisdiction is the certainty that comes with a body of law that has developed over 600 years. As we shall see later, the law of trusts has been substantially modified by statute in many common law jurisdictions, particularly the offshore financial centres (a.k.a. "tax havens"). These modifications are often important considerations in choosing a trust's situs. As a practical matter, however, unless there is a compelling reason to locate a trust in a civil law jurisdiction, the obvious choice for the situs of a trust is a common law country.

Many common law offshore centres have substantially modified the common law of trusts through statutory amendments that modernize certain aspects of trusts and make them more amenable and flexible to offshore planning. For example, some countries have substantially extended the perpetuity period and others statutorily recognize the role of the protector and give the protector standing before their courts.

4. — Considerations in the Choice of Location

The choice of location necessarily depends upon the purpose for which the particular trust is created. The situs determines the "proper law" of the trust. The tax rules that apply to the trust, however, may be affected by foreign tax laws regardless of its situs. Hence, in the case of Canadian offshore planning, the selection of an appropriate situs to meet the purposes of the trust and comply with Canadian tax rules is central to the plan.

The location selected for the trust is also a critical element in the protection of its assets. Given the number (approximately 65) of jurisdictions that offer offshore financial services such as banking and trust administration, it is important to carefully evaluate their individual merits and advantages before making a final decision.

The selection of location should be made on the basis of the following criteria:

- The jurisdiction should have specific protective legislation for trusts and/or companies. Generally, this means that the jurisdiction should have statutory rules that override the *Statute of Elizabeth* and curtail the rights of the creditor that that statute conferred. For example, the statute that overrides the *Statute of Elizabeth* should generally place a high burden of proof on the creditor to establish his or her claim, impose a short limitation period in which the creditor can sue, and allow only creditors that exist at the time of the transfer to sue. Further, such legislation should generally provide that the creditor's claim will be determined in a new trial under the domestic fraudulent conveyancing law of the jurisdiction where the trust is located without protection for unknown future creditors.

- The local tax laws should exempt all income and capital from tax or, at the very least, exempt a certain category of trusts and companies (within which the trust would fall) from tax.

- There should be no foreign exchange controls so that income and capital can be moved in and out of the country in any currency and without restriction.

- The offshore financial centre should have a solid infrastructure for investments, management and custodial services.

- The jurisdiction should be easily accessible and, preferably, within the same time zones.

- The jurisdiction should have sophisticated communications facilities and be easily accessible through all electronic formats.

- Although most sophisticated financial centres can render their services in English, it is generally preferable to select a pure English speaking jurisdiction for two reasons: (1) most such jurisdictions also adopted the English common law and, therefore, have developed a sophisticated law of trusts (as amended by local statutes); (2) it is easier to communicate with one's professional advisors and trust officials about the technical matters of the trust and related documents if both sides have a clear and unfiltered understanding of the language.

- The jurisdiction should be politically stable with a history of established government and protection. Although one can always provide for transfers of trusts in the event of political instability, there is nothing more unsettling than a trust located in a jurisdiction that generates political controversy and is susceptible to erratic change in governance.

In summary, trusts require a stable and safe jurisdiction, competent professional services and a sophisticated infrastructure for the management of trust assets.

5. — Forced Succession Laws

Many jurisdictions have forced heirship or succession laws, that is, rules that specify the manner in which a deceased's estate must be distributed to the deceased's legal heirs. Forced succession laws restrict the freedom of an individual to dispose of property according to his or her wishes. For example, under Islamic law (of which there are many varieties), there are strict limitations on the manner in which an individual may dispose of property. An individual of the Sunni sect, for example, must leave at least 2/3 of the estate to his or her children and each son may receive a portion twice that which a daughter receives. Hence, in considering the situs of a trust, it is important to bear in mind not only the proper law of the trust itself, but also the law of any other jurisdiction that might apply to assets located therein. This is particularly important in the case of moveable property.

Some offshore financial centres and tax havens (for example, Jersey and Guernsey) have laws that specifically state that the forced succession laws of another jurisdiction do not apply and are not recognized. Although such laws may prevent an attack on the trust in the jurisdiction where it is located, they do not ensure immunity from attack in the settlor's home jurisdiction. Thus, in these circumstances, it is important to ensure that the settlor's home jurisdiction does not have either *in rem* or *in personam* jurisdiction over the trust.

6. — Asset Protection

Some countries are creditor friendly, others debtor friendly. Since Canada is essentially a creditor friendly country, a domestic APT can be attacked under a multitude of provincial and federal statutes (including the *Criminal Code*). Thus, although a domestic APT is useful in certain circumstances (for example, a spendthrift trust), it does not offer the protection of a foreign situs trust in a debtor friendly legislative regime.

Several offshore jurisdictions (including many common law countries) recognize the use of trusts to protect a settlor's assets against future and unforeseen creditors. These countries have laws that are generally considered to be debtor friendly and limit the rights of creditors to attack properly created trusts. The limitation of rights may be either in the form of restricted standing to sue to recover assets or in stringent limitation periods. The Bahamas, Bermuda, Cayman Islands, Cook Islands, Gibraltar, Belize, Cyprus, Mauritius and the Turks & Caicos Islands, for example, are generally friendly asset protection jurisdictions. Each of these jurisdictions, however, has its own peculiarities and idiosyncrasies of trust law. Thus, even within the group of debtor friendly countries, it is important to analyse each jurisdiction's strengths and weaknesses before deciding to locate a trust within a particular country.

A domestic APT where the settlor retains substantial control and has a substantial interest in the trust is vulnerable to attack by creditors and is less appealing than a foreign situated trust.

The advantage of a foreign situs trust domiciled and resident in a debtor friendly jurisdiction is the increased flexibility that the settlor has to retain benefit and control of the trust. Further, the fact of location in a foreign jurisdiction, together with confidentiality provisions, make a foreign situs trust less convenient to attack in litigation or by creditors. It is more cumbersome to litigate in a foreign jurisdiction, particularly one where the laws are specifically drafted to be friendly to debtors and foreign source trusts.

A foreign situs APT may be set up by a Canadian in a debtor friendly foreign jurisdiction pursuant to the laws of that jurisdiction. In most cases, the trustees are domiciled and resident in the jurisdiction where the trust is situated. The assets of the trust are also usually located offshore, although not necessarily in the same jurisdiction in which the trustee is domiciled or resident. If the trustees and assets are offshore, the APT should be outside the jurisdiction of Canadian courts. But care should be exercised if the settlor is domiciled and resident in Canada. Since a court of Equity can compel a person who is within its jurisdiction to act, or refrain from acting, in a particular manner in respect of property that is owned, it is imperative that the settlor should not have any legal power to control the trust. Otherwise, the settlor will be within the reach of a Canadian court with equitable jurisdiction. As a general rule, the less power that the settlor has to determine and control the trust's affairs, the better and stronger the trust against attack by creditors in Canadian courts. The more intrusive the settlor's powers into the affairs of the foreign APT, the greater the likelihood that it may be attacked by Canadian creditors, including the revenue authorities.

The analysis of a foreign situs APT requires consideration of three different sets of laws:

- The domestic law of the jurisdiction where the trust is to be located;

- The tax law of the foreign jurisdiction;

- The tax law of the settlor's home jurisdiction.

Foreign situs APTs can offer the best of both worlds: the common law of trusts and the statute based trust law of the foreign jurisdiction where the trust is located. Under the common law, trust assets are legally vested in the trustee and do not belong to the beneficiary. This is true even if the trustee is also a beneficiary of the trust. Thus, creditors cannot easily attack trust assets on account of claims against the beneficiary.

Trust assets must also be considered separately for the purposes of any claims made by the trustee's creditors against the trustee. This principle has been accepted and incorporated into the *Hague Convention*. Trust assets are also protected in the face of claims by creditors of the settlor. Hence, absent fraudulent conveyance, creditors cannot generally reach trust assets that have been properly and legally vested in a trust and that are in the trustee's name.

7. — Tax Considerations

(a) — General Comment

Income tax considerations can be important in the decision to locate a trust in a particular country. As a starting point, it is important to determine the residence of the trust. A trust that is resident in a particular jurisdiction may be taxable in that jurisdiction on its worldwide income. As a general rule, most common law countries consider a trust to be resident in the country if a majority of its trustees are resident therein. Canada, for example, considers a trust to be resident in Canada if a majority of its trustees are resident in and administer the trust in Canada. Hence, a Canadian resident trust is taxable on its worldwide income.

In determining the residence of a trust, the courts look not only at the residence of the trustees, but also where the trust is effectively administered. In other words, a court may ignore "rubber stamp" trustees if they do not perform their duties in a substantive and meaningful manner. This can lead to a trust being considered resident in a jurisdiction other than where a majority of its trustees are resident. In *Wensleydale*,[15] for example, a trust was supposedly administered from the Irish Republic and was resident there for income tax purposes. The English Inland Revenue argued successfully, however, that the trustees were in fact resident in the United Kingdom because all of the substantive decisions relating to the administration of the trust were made in the U.K. The Irish trustees acted as "rubber stamps" for decisions that had already been made by the English trustees. Hence, applying a *de facto* administration test, the trust was considered to be resident in the United Kingdom.

---

[15]*Re Wensleydale*, [1995] S.T.C. (S.C.D.) 196.

(b) — Residence for Canadian Tax Purposes

A trust is *not* a legal entity; it is a legal relationship. For tax purposes, however, a trust is deemed to be an individual.[16] Hence, a trust is taxable as a person separate and apart from its trustee.

The residence of a trust for tax purposes is essentially a question of fact and is determined according to the common law rules applicable to individuals. A trust is generally resident where its trustee resides.[17] Where a trust has more than one trustee, it is resident where a majority of its trustees reside, provided that the trust instrument permits majority decisions on all matters within the discretion of the trustees.[18] Canadian courts do not accept the notion that a trust can have a dual residence. In this respect, trusts are quite unlike individuals and corporations that can and often do, have dual residence.[19]

The problems of determining the residence of a trust are, however, exacerbated by the differences between the obligations of trustees and corporate directors. In the event that a trust has multiple trustees, some of whom are individuals and others corporations, it becomes necessary to determine the residence of each of the trustees according to the rules of residence. For example, an individual trustee's residence may be determined according to the common law factual tests and the residence of a corporate trustee determined by reference to statutory deeming provisions. The determination of a trust's residence becomes that much more complicated if its trustees are located in different jurisdictions, each with bilateral tax treaties with Canada.

Generally, a trust's residence is determined by the residence of its trustees and not by the residence of its beneficiaries or the residence of its settlor. Furthermore, the residence of a trust is not determined by the "central management and control" test because trustees cannot delegate any of the authority to co-trustees.

Given the uncertainty associated with determining the residency of a trust, it is crucial that non-resident trusts provide that a majority of the trustees are non-residents of Canada. Further, it is probably prudent that all meetings of the trustees are held outside of Canada and

---

[16]Subs. 104(2).

[17]*McLeod v. Min. of Customs & Excise*, [1917–27] C.T.C. 290, 1 D.T.C. 85 (S.C.C.) (taxation of accumulated income in hands of trustee); *M.N.R. v. Royal Trust Co.*, [1928–34] C.T.C. 74, 1 D.T.C. 217 (S.C.C.) (trust with non-resident beneficiaries but resident trustee taxable); *M.N.R. v. Holden*, [1928–34] C.T.C. 127, 1 D.T.C. 234; varied on other grounds [1928–34] C.T.C. 129, 1 D.T.C. 243 (P.C.) (trust taxed on undistributed income whether beneficiaries resident or not); *Williams v. Singer*, [1921] 1 A.C. 65 (H.L.) (trust not taxed on foreign dividends received for non-resident beneficiary); *I.R.C. v. Gull*, [1937] 4 All E.R. 290 (English charitable trust exempt where one Trustee non-resident).

[18]*Thibodeau v. The Queen*, [1978] C.T.C. 539, 78 D.T.C. 6376 (F.C.T.D.); see also IT-447, "Residence of a Trust or Estate" (May 30, 1980).

[19]IT-447, "Residence of a Trust or Estate" (May 30,1980).

that the majority of the trust's assets are invested outside Canada. In the event that a non-resident trust has a "protector", it is preferable that the protector should not be a Canadian resident. Further, the protector should not have the unrestricted power to appoint and remove trustees.

VII. — Administration And Management

1. — Relationship of the Trustee with the Settlor

The trustee owes his or her duty to the *trust* to hold and control the assets for the benefit of the beneficiaries in accordance with the terms of the trust deed. The trustee should advise the settlor of any potential or actual conflict of interest that may prevent the trustee from fairly administering the trust for the benefit of the beneficiaries.[20] The trust deed may permit a specific conflict of interest, but this is not generally advisable as the provision may be struck down as being contrary to public policy. A trustee is not under any obligation to engage in an illegal act.

2. — Compliance with Provisions of Trust Deed

The duty of a trustee is primarily to comply with the terms of the trust deed. This remains so even if the settlor has conferred a power on a protector to dismiss the trustees in certain circumstances.

Although a trustee is required to administer the trust in accordance with the terms and provisions of the trust deed, the trustee may obtain authorization from a court to vary its provisions. It is also possible in certain circumstances to obtain the consent of the beneficiaries to vary the terms of the trust deed. In the latter circumstances, however, all of the beneficiaries must be known and identified, in existence and of age and capacity at the time that they provide their consent. The consent must be "informed consent" and the trustee should make full disclosure of all of the facts to the beneficiaries prior to obtaining their written approval.

A trustee may always seek the approval of a court of competent jurisdiction to obtain a power to act under the terms of the trust for its benefit. For example, where trustees lack the power to make certain investments, they may seek the approval of the court for the power if they can establish that their conduct enures for the benefit of the trust.

---

[20]*Peyton v. Robinson* (1823), 1 L.J.O.S. Ch 191.

3. — Relationship of Trustees With the Beneficiaries

A trustee should be fully familiar with the terms of the trust deed and any other ancillary or supplementary documents such as a *Memorandum of Wishes*. Of course, the trustee must be fully apprised of the nature and extent of all assets that constitute the trust fund. All assets that constitute part of the trust fund should be transferred into the name of the trustee and should remain within the trustee's control.

4. — The Duty of Care

A trustee is bound to act as a "prudent businessperson". An unpaid trustee is expected to act with the due diligence and care that a businessperson of ordinary prudence and vigilance would exercise in comparable circumstances. As Lord Justice Lindley said:[21]

> A Trustee ought to conduct the business of the trust in the same manner that an ordinary prudent person of business would conduct his own, and that beyond that there is no liability or obligation on the Trustee. I accept this principle; but in applying it care must be taken not to lose sight of the fact that the business of the Trustee, and the business which the ordinary prudent man is supposed to be conducting for himself is the business of investing money for the benefit of persons who are to enjoy it at some future time, and not for the benefit of the person entitled to the present income. The duty of a Trustee is not to take such care only as a prudent man would take if he had only himself to consider; the duty rather is to take such care as an ordinary prudent man would take if he were minded to make an investment for the benefit of other people for whom he felt morally obliged to provide.

A professional trustee, however, is held to a higher standard than that applicable to an unpaid trustee. As Brightman J. said:[22]

> I am of opinion that a higher duty of care is plainly due from someone like a trust corporation which carries on a specialised business of trust management. A trust corporation holds itself out in its advertising literature as being above ordinary mortals with a specialist staff of trained trust officers and managers, with ready access to financial information and professional advice, dealing with and solving trust problems day after day, the trust corporation holds itself out, and rightly, as capable of providing expertise which it would be unrealistic to expect and unjust to demand from the ordinary prudent man or woman who accepts, probably unpaid and sometimes reluctantly from a sense of family duty, the burdens of a Trusteeship... I think that a professional corporate Trustee is liable for breach of trust if loss is caused to the trust fund because it neglects to exercise the special care and skill which it professes to have.

---

[21]*Learoyd v. Whitley* (1897), 12 Appeal Cases 727.

[22]*Bartlett v. Barclays Bank Trust Company Limited*, [1980] 1 All E.R. 139.

5. — *Limitation of Liability*

The trust deed may limit the liability of a trustee or reduce the duty of care in particular circumstances. This is essentially a matter of local law. The *Jersey Trust Act* (1984), for example, prohibits a trustee from limiting the liability for gross negligence. Some courts have also held that a clause that exonerates a trustee from liability is valid only if it was brought to the specific attention of the settlor at the time that the trust was created.[23] Even a clause brought to the attention of the settlor will be struck down if it is unreasonable in its effect. Thus, it is imperative that the settlor and the trustee should be independently advised on the terms of the trust and, in particular, on the effect of any clauses that exonerate the trustee's liability.

6. — *Investments*

A trustee may invest the trust's assets only in securities authorized by the trust deed or by the relevant statute. Thus, it is important to set out the powers of the trustee in respect of trust investments with some degree of particularity if the settlor intends to limit or restrain the trustee's powers. In the absence of clarity, the trustee may apply to a court for consent to make an investment for the benefit of trust fund. Such a process, however, necessarily involves time and expense.

A trustee is usually given wide investment powers so that he or she can manage the trust fund with the greatest degree of flexibility and in its best interest. Investments in any securities not authorized by the trust deed constitute a breach of trust and render the trustee liable for damages to the extent of any loss suffered by the trust. A trustee's general obligation is to invest the trust fund in a prudent manner. This implies that the trustee should diversify the trust's investments in an appropriate manner and minimize overall investment risk.

The trustee has a duty to act impartially between the different beneficiaries or classes of beneficiaries of the trust. This duty will affect the nature of the investments that the trustee can make and the risk associated with the trust fund's investments. For example, where the beneficiaries include individuals with income interests and others with capital interests, the trustee should not structure the portfolio in such a manner that it unfairly treats one class of beneficiaries by providing a very high income yield to the detriment of the capital interests. The trustee must achieve some balance between the income yield of the portfolio and the potential for capital appreciation which would enure for the benefit of the capital interests.

A trustee must exercise the care that "an ordinary prudent person" would take if he or she were investing for the benefit of some other person for whom the trustee felt morally bound to provide.[24] Thus, the trustee should normally seek advice on investment matters with

---

[23]*West v. Lazard Brothers*, [1993] J.L.R. 165.

[24]*Cowan v. Scargill*, [1985] Ch. 270.

which he or she is not fully familiar and conversant just as an ordinary prudent person would rely on professional advice. A trustee is not entitled to restrict the trust's investments to those that are "morally acceptable", unless such restrictions are specifically outlined in the trust deed.[25]

Any investments that are not authorized by the proper law of the trust must specifically be permitted by the terms of the trust deed. For example, the purchase of a property for the beneficiary to reside in or the purchase of property for use by the beneficiaries would require specific authorization in the trust deed.

The law is now more flexible in their attitude towards investments and the balancing of risk in a portfolio. As Megarry, LC, said in *Cowan v. Scargill*:

> In the case of a power of investment, ... the power must be exercised so as to yield the best return for the beneficiaries, judged in relation to the risks of the investments in question, and the prospects of the yield of income and capital appreciation both have to be considered in judging the return for the investments.

Thus, trustees acting within their investment powers are entitled to be judged by the standards of current portfolio theory, which emphasizes the risk level of the entire portfolio rather than the risk applicable to each investment in isolation.[26] But the issue is not completely free from doubt and the law is moving towards portfolio theory with caution.

In *Nestle*, for example, Leggart, LJ, said:

> The Trustee must also avoid all investments of that class that are attended by hazard. The power of investment must be exercised so as to yield the best return for the beneficiaries, judged in relation to the risks in question; and the prospects of the yield of income and capital appreciation both have to be considered in judging the return from the investment.

7. — Impartiality Between Beneficiaries

A trustee must be impartial between beneficiaries and the impartiality must be reflected in the management of the trust fund. It is not proper for a trustee to confer a benefit on one beneficiary to the detriment of another type or class of beneficiaries.

Where the trust is discretionary, however, and the trustees are allowed to choose in their absolute discretion between beneficiaries who are to receive distributions of income and capital, the trustee has much greater leeway in the manner in which the trustee exercises his or her discretion. Thus, in the absence of exceptional circumstances, a trustee with absolute discretionary power to select beneficiaries may allocate income and capital with considerable latitude. The beneficiaries of a discretionary trust do not have a legal right to any part of

---

[25]*Ibid.*

[26]See, for example, *Nestle v. National Westminster Bank*, [1994] 1 All E.R. 118.

the trust fund until such time as the discretion is exercised and they do not have the standing to complain that they have been excluded if the trustee exercises his or her discretion fairly and according to the terms of the trust deed.

The trustees are not required to reveal the reasons for the exercise of their discretion in deciding on distributions to the various beneficiaries of a discretionary trust. They are not obliged to explain their decision and the manner in which they have exercised their discretionary dispositive power relating to the distribution of trust monies.[27]

8. — *Accounting Records*

A trustee is obliged to keep clear and accurate accounts of the trust fund and to account to the beneficiaries at regular intervals. A trustee must also give full and accurate information relating to the trust fund, the nature of its assets and investments and expenses in relation to its administration. Of course, all trust funds should be kept segregated and accounted for on a separate basis from any other assets or funds under the administration of the trustee. The trustee is under no obligation to provide information in respect of the trust's accounts to persons who are not beneficiaries, for example, third party creditors of the beneficiary.

9. — *Duty to Reveal Information*

The beneficiaries of a trust generally have the right to see any trust related documents such as the books of account, receipts and vouchers, correspondence, and legal advice relating to the trust.[28]

A court will not generally force a trustee to reveal how the trustee has exercised his or her discretionary power unless the beneficiary can show that there is *prima facie* evidence that the discretion was exercised *mala fide*. A trustee may, of course, voluntarily disclose to the beneficiaries the reason behind a particular decision. In these circumstances, a court will, upon application, examine the reasons given to ensure that the trustees correctly exercised their discretionary power.[29] In ordinary circumstances, it is not prudent for trustees to volunteer the reasoning behind the exercise of any dispositive discretionary powers. Otherwise, it is possible that the decision may open the door to challenge or explanation in a judicial proceeding.

---

[27]*Wilson v. Law Debenture Trust Corporation Plc.*, [1995] 2 All E.R. 337.

[28]*Re Londonderry's Settlement*, [1965] Ch 198.

[29]*Re Londonderry's Settlement* at page 929.

10. — Duty to Apply Trust Funds Properly

The trustee should ensure that property of the Trust Fund is distributed to the person who is entitled to receive it. In particular, care should be taken when dealing with a class of beneficiaries to ensure that a person to whom payment is made is entitled to the payment as a member of the class. For example, if the trust is to be distributed equally between the settlor's grandchildren, it is necessary to check whether legitimate and illegitimate children are both within the class. This is a matter of the proper law of the trust. Some jurisdictions include illegitimate children within the class. Other jurisdictions (for example, the Cayman Islands) exclude illegitimate children unless a contrary intention is clearly indicated. If in doubt, the trustees should seek the guidance of a court in the particular jurisdiction. In the event that a mistake is made in the payout of the trust fund, the trustee will become liable for the erroneous payment.

11. — Secret Profits

A trustee is not entitled to deal with the trust fund to his or her own private advantage or to exploit it any manner for the trustee's own position. A trustee who acts inappropriately with the trust fund is personally liable to account, not only for any losses arising to the trust fund, but also for any profits that have been made. A trustee who makes a "secret profit" from the use of a trust fund (or from knowledge obtained as a trustee) is liable to be held to account as a constructive trustee of the profit that was made.[30] Further, a trustee cannot simply remove him- or herself from the trusteeship with a view of being free from the trustee obligations so as to make a profit from dealings with the trust fund or in transactions involving its assets.

VIII. — Fraudulent Conveyances

Canada has provincial and federal laws which are intended to protect creditors against transfers that are made with an intention to hinder, delay, or defraud them. Most of these laws have their beginning in the *Statute of Elizabeth* (13 Elizabeth Ch. 5 (1571)), which was the original British fraudulent conveyance law and the precursor to all common law fraudulent conveyance acts. The *Statute of Elizabeth* was a creditor friendly law that was intended to prevent the hiding of money during an era of rampant fraud. The Statute provided that 50 per cent of any amount recovered went to the defrauded creditor. Not surprisingly, the Statute also provided that the remaining 50 per cent went to the Queen, presumably as a form of user-pay fee in gratitude for the service rendered by Her agents. The debtor went to jail for six months and was not entitled to bail. Thus, it is clear that statutes intended to prevent fraudulent conveyances are inclined to be more creditor than debtor friendly.

---

[30]*Attorney General for Hong Kong v. Reid*, [1994] 1 A.C. 324.

A fraudulent conveyance may be attacked at common law if it is considered a "sham". For example, where a transferee (or alleged trustee) holds property merely as a nominee or agent of the transferor (or alleged settlor) and merely follows the transferor's instructions, the transferor is considered to own the property. Hence, allegedly settled assets may be available for execution or garnishment by the transferor's creditors or the trustee in bankruptcy.

The term "sham" must be carefully evaluated in the context of the circumstances surrounding the transfer. "Sham" is all too often loosely used to describe transactions that are perfectly proper, but which may legally defeat another's claims. In law, a sham transaction is one that gives rights to rights and obligations that are other than those actually created. In other words, a sham is a legal mirage. A legitimate and actual transfer of property to a person who is legally entitled to deal with the property is not a sham in law.

1. — Statutory Rules

The statutory rules are generally remedial in nature and protect against fraudulent conveyances. A fraudulent conveyance statute is a remedial statute and is quite different from common law fraud. The essence of fraudulent conveyance statutes is to unwind the conveyance and to place the creditor in a position as closely similar as possible to that which the creditor was in prior to the conveyance. Fraudulence conveyance statutes protect present and past creditors, but not future or potential creditors.

The common law generally favours alienability of property, but subject to the protection of creditors against fraud and fraudulent conveyances. Thus, under the common law, an individual is generally free to do whatever he or she wants with property. This right is, however, subject to the rights of *existing* creditors of the transferor.

2. — Provincial Legislation

Subsection 4(1) of the Ontario *Assignments and Preferences Act*[31] reads as follows:

> Subject to section 5, every gift, conveyance, assignment or transfer, delivery over or payment of goods, chattels or effects, or of bills, bonds, notes or securities, or of shares, dividends, premiums or bonus in any bank, company or corporation, or of any other property, real or personal, made by a person when insolvent or unable to pay the person's debts in full or when the person knows that he, she or it is on the eve of insolvency, with intent to defeat, hinder, delay or prejudice creditors, or any one or more of them, is void as against the creditor or creditors injured, delayed or prejudiced.

As noted above, the provision provides a remedy, not a sanction. It merely puts the creditor into the position that the creditor would have been in had the insolvent or potentially insol-

---

[31]R.S.O. 1990, c. A.33.

vent person not transferred the property to a third person. It is important to note that the provision only operates when the transferor has sufficient *mala fides* and an intention to defeat, hinder or otherwise prejudice creditors. Hence, absent *mala fides* and an intention to prejudice creditors, a transfer is valid against future creditors who may be prejudiced later in time by virtue of the transferor having rid him- or herself of assets.

3. — Federal Laws

Subsection 91(2) of the *Bankruptcy and Insolvency Act*[32] states:

> Any settlement of property made within the period beginning on the day that is five years before the date of the initial bankruptcy event in respect of the settlor and ending on the date that the settlor became bankrupt, both dates included, is void against . . . the trustee if the trustee can prove that the settlor was, at the time of making the settlement, unable to pay all the settlor's debts without the aid of the property that was the subject of the settlement or that the interest of the settlor in the property did not pass on the execution thereof.

A "settlement" includes a contract, covenant, transfer, gift and designation of beneficiary in an insurance contract, to the extent that the contract, covenant, transfer gift or designation is gratuitous or made for merely nominal consideration.[33]

Section 2 of the *Bankruptcy and Insolvency Act* defines an "insolvent person" as:

> A person who is not bankrupt and who resides, carries on business or has property in Canada, whose liabilities to creditors provable as claims under [the *Bankruptcy and Insolvency Act*] amount to one thousand dollars, and
>
> > (a) who is for any reason unable to meet his obligations as they generally become due,
> >
> > (b) who has ceased paying his current obligations in the ordinary course of business as they generally become due, or
> >
> > (c) the aggregate of whose property is not, at a fair valuation, sufficient, or if disposed of at a fairly conducted sale under legal process, would not be sufficient to enable payment of all his obligations, due and accruing due.

A trustee in bankruptcy is entitled to attack transactions that have been consummated if, for example, the settlor becomes bankrupt within one year after the date of the settlement. Similarly, a settlement of property is void against a trustee in bankruptcy if the settlor becomes bankrupt within five years after the date of settlement upon proof that the settlor was unable to pay all of his or her debts without the aid of the property settled at the time that the settlement was made. Settlements of property made before or in consideration of marriage or

---

[32]R.S.C. 1985, C.B-3.

[33]See section 2, *Bankruptcy and Insolvency Act*.

in good faith and for valuable consideration are exempt from attack by the trustee in bankruptcy.

In addition, a trustee can always apply to a court under section 100 of the *Bankruptcy Act* to review any transactions made within one year of bankruptcy between the bankrupt and a person with whom the trustee was not dealing with at arm's length.

4. — Criminal Statutes

In addition to the civil remedies available under provincial and federal law, a fraudulent transferor may also be subject to criminal sanctions. Section 392 of the *Criminal Code*[34] provides as follows:

> Every one who
>
> > (a) with intent to defraud his creditors,
> >
> > > (i) makes or causes to be made any gift, conveyance, assignment, sale, transfer or delivery of his property, or
> > >
> > > (ii) removes, conceals or disposes of any of his property, or
> >
> > (b) with intent that any one should defraud his creditors, receives any property by means of or in relation to which an offence has been committed under paragraph (a),
>
> is guilty of an indictable offence and liable to imprisonment for a term not exceeding two years.

Both the transferor and the transferee are potentially subject to criminal sanctions if they have with intent caused to be transferred or have received property with an intent to defraud the transferor's creditors.

Similarly, section 198 of the *Bankruptcy and Insolvency Act* provides:

> Any bankrupt who
>
> > (b) makes any fraudulent disposition of the bankrupt's property before or after the date of the initial bankruptcy event,
> >
> > . . . . .
> >
> > (g) after or within the one year immediately preceding the date of the initial bankruptcy event, hypothecates, pawns, pledges or disposes of any property that the bankrupt has obtained on credit and has not paid for, unless in the case of a trader the hypothecation, pawning, pledging or disposing is in the ordinary way of trade and unless the bankrupt had no intent to defraud,

---

[34]R.S.C. 1985, c. C-46.

is guilty of an offence and is liable, on summary conviction, to a fine not exceeding five thousand dollars or to imprisonment for a term not exceeding one year or to both, or on conviction on indictment, to a fine not exceeding ten thousand dollars, or to imprisonment for a term not exceeding three years or to both.

IX. — Other Methods Of Recovery

In addition to the statutory remedies which provide for recovery by setting aside fraudulent conveyances and providing criminal sanctions in respect of such transactions, the law also provides for recovery through other processes. Business corporation statutes modelled on the *Canada Business Corporations Act*,[35] for example, typically contain restrictions as to when a corporation may pay dividends or otherwise reduce its capital. These provisions are intended to protect corporate creditors against the stripping of corporate assets to the detriment of the creditor's claim.

Generally, a corporation that distributes its assets in the form of a dividend or pursuant to a reduction of capital may render its directors and shareholders liable to unsatisfied creditor claims. Thus, a corporation should only pay a dividend or reduce its capital if it is both solvent and liquid at the time that it makes the payment. A corporation is not considered to be liquid if it is unable to pay its liabilities as they come due. The test here is the ability to pay corporate debts on a timely basis and according to contractual or other legal requirements. For example, a corporation would be considered to be illiquid if it had a $1 million in real estate assets and a current and immediate income tax liability of $50,000 that it could not satisfy or meet on its due date. If the corporation paid a dividend when the income tax liability was outstanding, the CRA could later claim the amount paid as a dividend (to a maximum of $50,000) personally from the shareholders and directors of the corporation.

Creditors may also pierce the corporate veil and attach personal liability to shareholders and directors where a corporation pays a dividend or reduces its capital when it is insolvent. The test of solvency for these purposes is whether the dividend or reduction of capital causes the *realizable* value of the corporation's assets to be less than the aggregate of its liabilities and the stated capital of its shares. Thus, the test of solvency relies upon the market value of assets at the time that the dividend is paid or share capital reduced and not on the book value or cost of balance sheet assets. Hence, a corporation with assets that have a net realizable value lower than the cost of the assets should have its assets valued if there is any doubt that its dividend payment or reduction of capital may cause its directors and shareholders to become personally liable to creditors.

An intention to defeat, hinder, or delay the payment of creditors is a question of fact to be established by direct or circumstantial evidence. The following factors should be considered:

- Insolvency or impending insolvency;

---

[35]R.S.C. 1985, c. C-44.

- Insufficient consideration;

- The relationship between the transferor and the transferee, particularly where the consideration for the transfer is insufficient;

- The existence or threat of litigation;

- Departure from the usual and conventional methods of business;

- The removal of one's entire estate without further explanation;

- The retention of control by the transferor; and

- The transferor's continued use and possession of the transferred property.

X. — Due Diligence

A professional advisor should ensure that he or she undertakes the appropriate due diligence to satisfy him- or herself as to the financial position of the settlor as of the date that the assets are disposed of and put into the trust. At the very least, a professional advisor should obtain the following information:

- Full financial and net worth statements listing all assets, liabilities and estimated contingence liabilities.

- An affidavit from the settlor stating that there are no undisclosed liabilities, contingent liabilities and pending legal actions other than those disclosed in the financial statements.

Professional advisors will find themselves under considerable temptation to devise asset protection trusts and settle property without a full and complete review of the underlying circumstances. The temptation to accept such appointments should be resisted. The light is seldom worth the candle where the client seeks to protect him- or herself by transferring the risk to the professional advisor. Clients are generally quite willing, and sometimes enthusiastic, to throw their professional advisors to the lions when the structure unravels or unforeseen consequences emerge.

XI. — Deemed Residence

[Caution: The Department of Finance has been studying the non-resident and foreign entity rules since they were first announced in the 1999 Budget. The Department advises that it is on the "brink" of the final stages of announcing new rules.]

A trust that might not otherwise be considered resident in Canada by virtue of the common law tests may, nevertheless, be deemed to be a resident trust for tax purposes.

Generally, a non-resident discretionary trust with Canadian resident beneficial interests that acquires property from a Canadian resident is deemed to be resident in Canada.[36] This rule is intended to prevent tax minimization and tax deferral through the use of non-resident trusts. Such a trust (a section 94 trust) is taxable in Canada on its worldwide income, including FAPI.

There are two basic tests to determine whether a non-resident trust is deemed a Canadian resident for tax purposes:

- The "beneficiary test", and
- The "contribution test".

1. — *"Beneficiary Test"*

The beneficiary test is cast in broad terms. The Act speaks of a person "beneficially interested in a trust". A person is considered to be beneficially interested in a particular trust if the person has *any* right as a beneficiary under the trust to receive, whether directly or indirectly, any of its income or capital. The right may be immediate or future, absolute, contingent, conditional on or subject to the exercise of *any* discretionary power by *any* person.[37]

Hence, where the trustee has a discretionary power to allocate income or capital amongst a group of people named in the trust, the named persons are considered to be "beneficially interested" in the trust, even though in private law they would not be considered beneficiaries until such time as the discretion was exercised in their favour.

The beneficiary test is generally satisfied where a person (or a person related to him or her) who is resident in Canada benefits from an offshore trust. Thus, most foreign immigration trusts are caught by the "beneficiary test".

Clearly, the "beneficiary test" is easily met if the beneficiary is a Canadian resident. But the test is also satisfied when a person who is beneficially interested in the trust is:[38]

- A corporation or trust with which a resident does not deal at arm's length; or
- A controlled foreign affiliate of a resident person.

Note: the test is satisfied if *any* of the trust's beneficiaries meet *any* of the above conditions.

What happens if a discretionary trust is set up in an off-shore tax haven country and the only named potential beneficiaries are all non-residents of Canada, but the trustee has the power

---

[36]Subs. 94(1).

[37]Subs. 248(25).

[38]Para. 94(1)(a).

to add the names of Canadian residents as potential beneficiaries? The question arises as to whether such a trust is immediately caught by the "beneficiary test" in subsection 94(1) or whether the operation of the subsection is delayed until such time as the trustee exercises his or her discretionary power and adds a Canadian resident as a named beneficiary. In other words, are the unnamed and *potential* Canadian residents beneficially interested in the trust immediately upon the creation of the trust or only upon the naming of the Canadian residents as beneficiaries potential to the exercise of the discretionary power?

It is arguable that until such time as the trustee has exercised his or her discretionary power and named a Canadian resident as a beneficiary or potential beneficiary with some form of rights attached to the beneficial interest, the trust does not have any Canadian who is "beneficially interested in the trust". Any broader interpretation of subsection 94(1) might embrace clearly non-Canadian trusts with no Canadian beneficial interests and the subsection would attempt to reach beyond Canada's jurisdiction to tax.

2. — "Contribution Test"

The "contribution test" is made up of two parts:

- The source of the trust's property, and
- The source of the trust's interest.

The source of property test is concerned with the source from which the trust directly acquires its property.

The source of the trust interest test is concerned with indirect acquisitions of trust interests.

The "contribution test" is satisfied where the non-resident trust acquires property directly or indirectly in or before the taxation year of a trust from a person who was:[39]

- A beneficiary of the trust, a person related[40] to the beneficiary, or an uncle, aunt, nephew or niece of the beneficiary;
- A resident in Canada *at any time* in the 18 month period before the end of the trust's relevant taxation year; *and*
- Before the end of the particular year, resident in Canada for an *aggregate period of more than 60 months.*

These three requirements are cumulative and must all be satisfied in order for section 94 to apply.

---

[39]Subpara. 94(1)(b)(i).

[40]Subs. 251(2).

The test is also satisfied if the trust acquires property from another trust or corporation which in turn acquired its property from any of the above described persons with whom it did not deal at arm's length.[41]

The "contribution test" is strict. Even a token contribution by a relative who has been resident in Canada for more than 60 months invalidates the exemption. Thus, in order to preserve the 60 months exemption, it is imperative that only non-residents contribute to the trust.[42]

The "contribution test" is also satisfied where the beneficiary acquires any or all of the interest in the trust directly or indirectly by way of:[43]

- Purchase;

- Gift, bequest or inheritance from a related person; or

- Through the exercise of the power of appointment by a related person.

3. — Discretionary Trusts

A trust is considered to be a discretionary trust if the distribution of its income or capital to any beneficiary depends upon the exercise of (or failure to exercise) a discretionary power.

A discretionary trust usually gives trustees the freedom to determine who is to receive the income or capital of the trust, how much is to be received, and when the distribution is to be made. The power to select, add or delete beneficiaries from a class are discretionary powers. The scope of the discretion is usually determined by the settlor or testator of the trust. It would be unusual to create a trust that did not confer at least some discretionary powers on the trustee.

A resident trust is generally taxable on its worldwide income. The taxable income of a discretionary trust that is deemed to be resident in Canada by virtue of the "beneficiary" and "contribution" tests, however, is calculated according to special rules and is not based on its worldwide income. The taxable income for such a trust is its taxable income earned in Canada plus its foreign accrual property income for the year and its other foreign income *other than* active business income. Since such a trust's other income would not in any event have been taxable in Canada under the general rules applicable to non-residents, the essential focus of these rules is to render the trust taxable on its foreign accrual property income

---

[41]Cl. 94(1)(b)(i)(B).

[42]See *infra* for discussion of five year tax holiday for certain non-resident trusts.

[43]Subpara. 94(1)(b)(ii).

("FAPI").[44] The taxable income of the trust is reduced by the portion of the trust's FAPI that is payable to a beneficiary of the trust.[45]

4. — *Non-Discretionary Trusts*

A non-discretionary trust is deemed to be a corporation and the beneficiary is, in effect, considered to own a portion of its outstanding shares in proportion to the beneficial interest in the trust.

The Act deems a non-discretionary foreign trust to be a controlled foreign affiliate of each of its beneficiaries who have a beneficial interest of at least 10 per cent in the trust.[46] The 10 per cent is measured by reference to the aggregate fair market value of all of the beneficial interests of the trust. Thus, a Canadian resident beneficiary is taxable on a percentage share of the trust's income on an *accrual* basis at the time that the income is earned, regardless of when funds are remitted to the beneficiary.

XII. — Section 94

Section 94 is an anti-avoidance provision that is intended to prevent Canadian residents from parking their investments off-shore in trusts set up in tax havens. The section effectively taxes the passive income of certain non-resident trusts. But the provision also affords opportunities for tax planning in certain narrowly circumscribed circumstances.

1. — *Non-Resident Trusts*

Non-resident trusts can be structured so as not to attract any immediate Canadian tax liability.

A non-resident discretionary trust created and settled with property outside Canada is not resident in Canada for purposes of the Act if:

- All of its property is acquired from a non-resident settlor;

- It does not receive any financial assistance from any person resident in Canada at any time;

- Its non-resident trustees constitute a majority of the trustees; and

---

[44]Para. 94(1)(c).

[45]Subs. 94(3).

[46]Para. 94(1)(d).

- The non-resident trustees actively exercise their responsibilities as trustees.

If the above conditions are satisfied, section 94 of the Act does not apply and the Act does not deem the trust to be resident in Canada. Such a trust is not subject to Canadian tax on any of its income (including taxable capital gains) that the trustees accumulate offshore in each year.

Any income distributed to or for the benefit of a Canadian resident beneficiary (including taxable capital gains realized or deemed to be realized in any year) is taxable in the hands of the beneficiary. Distributions of capital, however, are not subject to Canadian tax. Thus, the trust can accumulate its income, add it to capital, and make capital distributions to Canadian resident beneficiaries, all without any tax liability.

The creation of a foreign immigration trust requires careful planning both for tax and non-tax purposes. A professional advisor must consider:

- The specific structure of the particular trust arrangement;
- The use of corporations;
- The source of funds for settlement of the trust;
- Selection of an appropriate tax haven;
- Appointment of trustees;
- Selection of a protector for the trust; and
- Set-up and administration fees.

The following is a summary of the steps that would generally be required to implement a foreign immigration trust structure for Canadian income tax purposes:

- The trust would be settled in a tax haven jurisdiction by way of a gift from non-residents of Canada;
- Non-resident trustees and, if necessary, a protector would be appointed;
- The trust would be irrevocable and would be discretionary;
- All investment decisions in respect of the trust and meetings of the trustees would occur outside of Canada in the tax haven jurisdiction or elsewhere; and
- The trust indenture would provide that the annual income of the trust be accumulated and that the trustees would have the discretionary power to make capital distributions to the beneficiaries.

2. — Five-Year Exemption

The "contribution test" in section 94 is satisfied if a trust acquires property (directly or indirectly) from an individual who has been resident in Canada for an aggregate period of more than 60 months. Where a trust acquires property from an individual who has been resident in Canada for less than 60 months, the "contribution test" does not apply and, therefore, the trust is not deemed to be resident in Canada. This effectively provides a five year tax holiday for qualifying non-resident trusts.

The five-year exemption for trusts was originally intended to allow foreign executives of multinational corporations who were temporarily transferred to Canada to leave their investments in offshore tax havens without attracting Canadian tax. But the exemption can also be used by immigrants who come to Canada on a permanent basis to structure their affairs on a tax efficient basis prior to taking up Canadian residence. The effect of the exemption in section 94 is that an immigrant can defer tax on foreign accrual property income for up to 60 months. This necessarily implies that some individuals who take up Canadian residence, but who subsequently relinquish their residence in less than five years, can completely escape tax on their offshore trust income.

3. — Indefinite Exemption

The 60 month clock does not begin to tick until such time as the settlor becomes a resident of Canada if the beneficiary acquires the beneficial interest as a gift, bequest, or inheritance.[47] Thus, the 60 month exemption can be extended if an individual who resides outside of Canada and who does not intend to settle in Canada establishes a trust for the benefit of Canadian residents. For example, a parent of a prospective immigrant may settle a non-resident trust with the prospective immigrant as its beneficiary. Such a trust would provide its Canadian resident beneficiaries with indefinite tax-free passive investment income beyond the 60 month exemption period.

The 60 month period does not have to comprise consecutive days or time spent in Canada. Any time spent in Canada as a resident is included in the calculation.

Where a trust is settled by an individual who then becomes a Canadian resident, it is in the best interests of the taxpayer to take up Canadian residence as early in the year as is possible. The offshore trust becomes taxable in the year in which the immigrant commences his or her 61st month of Canadian residency.

The 60 month exemption period commences from the time that *any* beneficiary (or related person) from whom the trust acquires property becomes a Canadian resident. Hence, it is important to ensure that the trust does not inadvertently acquire funds from a person related to the beneficiary who has been resident in Canada for more than 60 months.

---

[47]Para. 94(1)(b).

4. — Departing Residents

A Canadian resident who is about to leave Canada and take up residence in some other country can establish a non-resident trust for the benefit of Canadian relatives. If the departing resident (settlor) becomes a non-resident at any time in the 18 month period before the end of the trust's relevant taxation year, the non-resident trust is not subject to subsection 94(1). For example, if a Canadian resident settlor leaves Canada on June 30, YEAR 1 and sets up a trust in a tax haven, the trust will be deemed to be a Canadian resident trust during the YEAR 1 calendar year. When the settlor becomes a non-resident in YEAR 2, however, the non-resident trust will fall outside of subsection 94(1) because it would not have acquired property from a person who was resident in Canada at any time in the 18 months preceding December 31, YEAR 2. Hence, accumulations of income and capital gains after YEAR 1 will not be subject to Canadian income tax. Capital distributions to Canadian resident beneficiaries will not be taxable in Canada.

5. — Liability for Tax

A discretionary non-resident trust that is deemed to be resident in Canada under subsection 94(1) is taxable in Canada on its income and on its foreign accrual property income. Obviously, such a trust is outside of the physical reach of the Canadian tax authorities.

Subsection 94(2), however, renders any Canadian beneficiaries and contributors to the trust *jointly and severally* liable together with the trust for any taxes, interest and penalties due under the Act. The joint and several liability is restricted, however, to the extent that the Canadian resident beneficiaries and/or contributors to the trust actually receive an amount or are entitled to enforce payment of an amount, from the trust.

Thus, the primary liability for the non-resident trust's income tax rests with the trust itself. To the extent that the trust pays or otherwise entitles its Canadian resident beneficiaries to payment, the beneficiaries become jointly and severally liable with the trust for its liabilities.

Selected Bibliography to Chapter 33

Kyres, Constantine, "The Use of Non-resident Trusts for Estate Planning and Asset Protection" (1995) 43 Can. Tax J. 314.

Truster, Perry, "Offshore Tax Planning: A Practical Overview" *1996 Ontario Tax Conference*, Canadian Tax Foundation, TAB 6.

APPENDIX A

GLOSSARY OF TAX & FINANCIAL TERMS

NOTE: Some of the accounting definitions found in this Glossary are attributable to VentureLine and can be found, along with other accounting definitions, at http://www.ventureline.com/glossary.asp.

3% Rule

See Three Percent Rule.

4-4-5 Calendar

In budgeting and accounting, is the breakdown of each month into weeks by counting the number of times Friday occurs within each month, e.g., Jan = 4 weeks, Feb = 4 weeks, Mar = 5 weeks, Apr = 4 weeks, May = 4 weeks, Jun = 5 weeks ... etc. to total 52 weeks in a 12 month period. Every third month Friday will occur five times. All other months, Friday will occur 4 times. In the months where Friday occurs five times, it is considered a five week month. Whereas, the four Friday months will be considered as four-week months.

10-K

The audited annual report that most reporting companies file with the Securities Exchange Commission (SEC). It provides a comprehensive overview of the registrant's business. The report must be filed within 90 days after the end of the company's fiscal year.

10-Q

A report filed quarterly to the Securities Exchange Commission (SEC) by most reporting companies. It includes unaudited financial statements and provides a continuing view of the company's financial position during the year. The report must be filed for each of the first three fiscal quarters of the company's fiscal year and is due within 45 days of the close of the quarter.

13th Period

In the fiscal year is the period used for fiscal year-end adjusting entries (periods one-12 being the months in the fiscal year).

21-Year Deemed Disposition Rule

See Twenty-One-Year Deemed Disposition Rule.

A&E

A&E can mean either Appropriation & Expense or Analysis & Evaluation.

A&P

Administrative and Personnel.

ABA (Accredited Business Accountant or Accredited Business Advisor)

In the U.S., an ABA is a national credential conferred by the Accreditation Council for Accountancy and Taxation to professionals who specialize in supporting the financial needs of individuals and small to medium sized businesses. ABA is the only nationally recognized alternative to the CPA (Certified Public Accountant). Most accredited individuals do not perform audits. Generally, they are small business owners themselves. In addition to general accounting work, CPAs are also heavily schooled in performing audits; however, only a small fraction of America's businesses require an audit. In general, a CPA has majored in accounting, passed the CPA examination and is licensed to perform audits. An ABA has majored in accounting, passed the ABA comprehensive examination and in most states is not licensed to perform audits.

Abatement

In general, Abatement is the reduction or lessening of something. In law, it is the termination or suspension of a lawsuit. For example, an abatement of taxes is a tax decrease or rebate.

ABC

See Activity Based Costing.

ABM

See Activity Based Management.

Absorption Costing

The method under which all manufacturing costs, both variable and fixed, are treated as product costs with non-manufacturing costs, e.g. selling and administrative expenses, being treated as period costs.

Absorption Variance

The variance from budgeted absorption costing of manufactured product. See also Absorption Costing.

Abuse of Law

Sometimes referred to as "abus de droits" or "fraus legis", this concept is similar to the "Substance over Form" concept and provides that taxation cannot be avoided by legal structures which have no commercial basis.

ACAT (Accreditation Council for Accountancy and Taxation)

A national organization established in 1973 as a non-profit independent testing, accrediting and monitoring organization. The Council seeks to identify professionals in independent practice who specialize in providing financial, accounting and taxation services to individuals and small to mid-size businesses. Professionals receive accreditation through examination and/or coursework and maintain accreditation through commitment to a significant program of continuing professional education and adherence to the Council's Code of Ethics and Rules of Professional Conduct.

ACB

Normally refers to "adjusted cost base".

Accelerated Amortization

A method of allocating costs against income that records a greater portion of the total cost in the earlier years of an asset's life, and less in later years. For example, declining balance amortization allocates more in the earlier years than does the straight-line method.

Acceptance

A Drawee's promise to pay either a time draft or Sight Draft. Normally, the acceptor signs his/her name after writing "accepted" (or some other words indicating acceptance) on the bill along with the date. That "acceptance" effectively makes the bill a promissory note, i.e., the acceptor is the maker and the drawer is the endorser.

Accommodation Endorsement

(1) The guarantee given by one legal entity to induce a lender to grant a loan to another legal entity; (2) A banking practice where one bank endorses the acceptances of another bank, for a fee, qualifying them for purchase in the acceptance market.

Account

A record of an asset, liability, owners' equity, revenue, or expense, in which an enterprise records transactions, accruals, and adjustments, generally in the local currency of the country.

Account Aging

Usually refers to the methods of tracking past due accounts in accounts receivable based on the dates the charges were incurred. Account aging can also be used in accounts payable, to a lesser degree, to monitor payment history to suppliers.

Accountant

A person who performs accounting functions. Professional accountants are those who are granted designations by self-regulating bodies on the basis of special training and successful examination. For example: CA, or Chartered Accountant (Canada, the United Kingdom); CGA, or Certified General Accountant (Canada); CMA, or Certified Management Accountant (Canada, the United States); and CPA, or Certified Public Accountant (the United States).

Accountant's Opinion

A signed statement regarding the financial status of an entity from an independent public accountant after examination of that entity's records and accounts.

Accounting

"To account" is to provide a record, such as of funds paid or received for something. Being "accountable" is to be responsible for, as in to account for one's actions. These two ideas together describe the practice of accounting as the record keeping and reporting of an enterprise's performance and position in monetary terms. Management is responsible for the decisions made in an enterprise. Accounting provides the reports that summarize the economic results of these decisions for inside use and transmits them to outside, interested parties (such as investors, creditors, and regulatory agencies).

Accounting Concepts

The assumptions that underlying the preparation of financial statements, i.e., the basic assumptions of going concern, accruals, consistency and prudence.

Accounting Control

The practice of creating accounting records that provide expected quantities of important assets and liabilities and so improve the internal control over those assets. Used by most companies for cash, accounts receivable, sales taxes collected on behalf of governments and employee deductions, and by many companies for investments, inventories, property and equipment, and accounts payable.

Accounting Entity

The enterprise for which the accounting is being done. The entity may be a single legal corporation or other organization, an economic unit without legal standing (such as a proprietorship), or a group of corporations with connected ownership for which consolidated financial statements are prepared.

Accounting Entity Assumption

States that a business is a separate legal entity from the owner. In the accounts the business' monetary transactions are recorded only.

Accounting Equation

A mathematical expression used to describe the relationship between the assets, liabilities and owner's equity of the business model. The basic accounting equation states that assets equal liabilities plus owner's equity, but can be modified by operations applied to both sides of the equation, e.g., assets minus liabilities equal owner's equity.

Accounting Package/Software

Usually, a commercially available software program or suite that, with little customization, will satisfy the accounting system needs of the purchasing entity.

Accounting Period

The time period for which accounts are prepared, usually one year.

Accounting Policies

The accounting methods chosen by a company to recognize economic events on an accrual basis, and to report the financial position and results of operations. For examples, see the notes immediately following the financial statements of any company. The first such note is usually a summary of significant accounting policies.

Accounting Policy Choice

A decision among acceptable accounting policies is often needed because more than one acceptable policy exists in many areas.

Accounting Principles

See Generally Accepted Accounting Principles.

Accounting Research

The practice of studying accounting phenomena to determine their effects on other phenomena, such as share prices, and effects of those on accounting.

Accounting Standards

The recommending of particular accounting methods or policies by an authoritative body. In Canada this is done by the Accounting Standards Board of the Canadian Institute of Chartered Accountants, in the United States, by the Financial Accounting Standards Board.

Accounting Standards Board

The committee of the Canadian Institute of Chartered Accountants that is responsible for setting financial accounting standards in Canada.

Accounts Payable

Liabilities representing amounts owed to short-term trade creditors. (An account payable for the debtor is an account receivable for the creditor.)

Accounts Payable Period

The time between receipt of inventory and payment for it.

Accounts Payable-Trade

Open accounts and note obligations due to the trade.

Accounts Receivable

A current asset representing amounts owed by debtors (usually customers) for services performed or merchandise sold on credit.

Accounts Receivable Financing

A secured short-term loan that involves either the assignment or factoring of receivables.

Accounts Receivable Ledger

The bookkeeping ledger in which all accounts for which cash assets owed to an organization is maintained.

Accounts Receivable Period

The time between sale of inventory and collection of the account receivable.

Accretion

The adjustment of the difference between the price of a bond purchased at an original discount and the par value of the bond; or, asset growth through internal growth, expansion or natural causes, e.g., the aging of wine or growth of timber/trees.

Accrual Basis of Accounting (Accrual Accounting)

Wherein revenue and expenses are recorded in the period in which they are earned or incurred regardless of whether cash is received or disbursed in that period. (Contrast to the simpler cash basis of accounting.) This is the accounting basis that generally is required to be used in order to conform to Generally Accepted Accounting Principles (GAAP) in preparing financial statements for external users.

Accrual Concept

See Accrual Basis of Accounting.

Accrual Income

The result of subtracting expenses from revenue(s), when both kinds of accounts are calculated by accrual accounting.

Accrue

To enter amounts in the accounts to reflect events or estimates that are economically meaningful but that do not (at present) involve the exchange of cash. Examples would be recording interest that is building up on a debt prior to paying it or recording revenue from credit sales prior to receipt of cash from customers.

Accrued Assets

Assets from revenues earned but not yet received.

Accrued Expenses

Expenses incurred during an accounting period for which payment is postponed.

Accrued Income

Income earned during a fiscal period but not paid by the end of the period.

Accrued Interest

Interest earned but not yet received.

Accrued Inventory

Functions as a "clearing" account to establish a liability for inventory physically received into the warehouse, but for which a vendor invoice had not yet arrived.

Accrued Liability

Liabilities which are incurred, but for which payment is not yet made, during a given accounting period. Some examples in a manufacturing environment would be: wages, taxes, suppliers/vendors, etc.

Accumulated Amortization

The cumulative charges against the intangible assets of a company over the expected useful life of the assets.

Accumulated Amortization (Depreciation)

A balance sheet account that accumulates total amortization expense (for intangible assets) or depreciation expense (for fixed assets) over a number of years. The account balance is a credit and so is opposite to the debit-balance asset cost account. The difference between cost and accumulated amortization is the "book value" of the asset. See also Accumulated Amortization and Accumulated Depreciation.

Accumulated Depreciation

The cumulative charges against the fixed assets of a company for wear and tear or obsolescence.

Accumulated Foreign Currency Translation Adjustment

An account arising as a consequence of the method used to convert foreign operations' accounting figures into Canadian dollars for the purpose of combining them with the figures for Canadian operations. Because income statement accounts are generally converted at average foreign exchange rates and balance sheet accounts are generally converted at year-end or historical rates, converted accounts do not quite balance. The difference is put into equity as a separate item because it does not seem to fit anywhere else and it is part of the (converted) residual equity of the owners.

Acid-Test Ratio

See Quick Ratio.

ACMA

Associate Chartered Management Accountant.

Acquisition

One company taking over controlling interest in another company. See also Merger and Pooling of Interests.

Active Income

This term is used in comparison to Passive Income to reflect employment income, professional or trading income.

Activity Based Costing (ABC)

A costing system that identifies the various activities performed in a firm and uses multiple Cost Drivers (non-volume as well as the volume based cost drivers) to assign overhead costs (or indirect costs) to products. ABC recognizes the causal relationship of Cost Drivers with activities.

Activity Based Management (ABM)

Converts Activity Based Costing (ABC) into a system to manage an organization. Activity Based Management not only focuses on product, service, customer, and channel costing, it also emphasizes Cost Drivers (root cause analysis), action plans to improve and to achieve strategic objectives, and performance measures for activities and processes.

Activity Drivers

In Activity Based Costing (ABC), activity costs are assigned to outputs using activity drivers. Activity drivers assign activity costs to outputs based on individual outputs' consumption or demand for activities. For example, a driver may be the number of times an activity is performed (transaction driver) or the length of time an activity is performed (duration driver) see Duration Drivers, Intensity Drivers, Transaction Drivers.

Ad Hoc

Being concerned with a particular end or purpose, e.g., an *ad hoc committee* established to handle a specific subject.

Adjunct Account

An account that accumulates either additions or subtractions to another account. Thus the original account may retain its identity. Examples include premiums on bonds payable, which is a contra account to bonds payable; and accumulated depreciation, which is an off-set to the fixed asset.

Adjusted Book Value

Your MBA performs two types of adjusted book value analysis. Tangible Book Value and Economic Book Value (also known as Book Value at Market). Tangible Book Value is different than book value in that it deducts from asset value intangible assets, which are assets that are not hard (e.g., goodwill, patents, capitalized start-up expenses and deferred financing costs). Economic Book Value allows for a book value analysis that adjusts the assets to their market value. This valuation allows valuation of goodwill, real estate, inventories and other assets at their market value.

Adjusted Cost Base

The cost of an investment is used to calculate capital gains. Any additional purchases or reinvested income are averaged into the cost base, which is adjusted with each purchase or sale.

Adjusted Present Value (APV)

Base case net present value of a project's operating cash flows plus present value of any financing benefits.

Adjusted Trial Balance

The list of accounts prepared after all the accrual accounting adjustments and corrections have been made and so representing the final account balances used in preparing the financial statements.

Adjusting (journal) Entries

Special accounting entries that must be made when you close the books at the end of an accounting period. Adjusting entries are necessary to update your accounts for items that are not recorded in your daily transactions. For example, if there is no transaction to reveal the gradual wear and tear of a fixed asset, an adjusting entry must be made to recognize this depreciation.

Adjustment(s)

See Adjusting (journal) Entries.

Advising Bank

A bank in the exporter's country handling a letter of credit.

AFE

Dependent upon usage, is an acronym for Authorization for Expenditure or Average Funds Employed.

Affiliation Privilege

Where a company has a material interest, normally between 10% and 25%, of another resident or non-resident company, dividends receivable may be exempt from taxation in order to avoid economic double taxation of profits; this regime is described in many countries as the affiliation privilege.

After Hours Dealing

Dealing done at the end of the mandatory quote period. These are treated as dealings done on the following business day.

Agency Problem

The conflicts of interest between the stockholders and management of a firm.

Agent

A person who is party to a contract between that person and another, called the principal. The agent's role is to carry out the wishes of the principal as specified in the contract. Some examples of agents are managers, auditors, lawyers, and physicians, who are entrusted with acting on behalf of one or more others (the principals, such as owners, creditors, defendants, and patients). Agents have a stewardship responsibility to the principal.

Aggregation

Process by which smaller investment proposals of each of a firm's operational units are added up and treated as one big project.

Aggressive Accounting

Seeking out accounting methods and policy choices to meet management objectives for growth, financing, bonuses, or other purposes that seem to violate principles such as fairness and conservatism.

AGI (Annual Gross Income)

Annualized total income prior to exclusions and deductions.

Aging of Accounts Receivable

The process of classifying accounts receivable by the amount of time that has passed since the account came into existence. This classification is used as an aid to estimating the required allowance for doubtful accounts for the estimated amount of uncollectible accounts receivable.

Aging Schedule

A compilation of accounts receivable by the age of each account.

AICPA

The American Institute [of] Certified Public Accountants.

Air Waybill

A bill of lading and contract between the shipper and the airline for delivery of goods to a specified location, and sometimes with specified delivery date/time. Non-negotiable, but serves as a receipt from the airline to prove that goods were received.

Alien Resident

This term is generally used in the United States but can be used in other countries to describe a non-national or non-citizen of the particular country who happens to be resident there for tax purposes.

Allocating, Allocation

Spreading the impact of an event out over time, as in amortization of an asset's cost over its useful life or recognition of revenue for a long-term contract over several periods.

All Other Current Assets

Relates to any other current assets. Does not include prepaid items.

All Other Current Liabilities

Includes any other current liabilities, including bank overdrafts and accrued expenses.

All Other Expenses (Net)

Includes miscellaneous other income and expenses (net), such as interest expense, miscellaneous expenses not included in general and administrative expenses, netted against recoveries, interest income, dividends received and miscellaneous income.

All Other Non-Current Assets

Prepaid items and any other non-current assets.

All Other Non-Current Liabilities

Means any other non-current liabilities, including subordinated debt, and liability reserves.

Allowance for Doubtful Accounts

The estimated amount of accounts receivable that will not be collected (which are "doubtful"). The allowance, which is a contra account to accounts receivable, is used in order to recognize the bad debts expense related to such doubtful accounts but without removing those accounts from the books because the firm will still try to collect the amounts owing.

Alpha

The measurement of returns from an investment in excess of market returns. It represents the amount expected from fundamental causes, e.g., the growth rate in earnings per share. This contrasts with Beta, which is a measure of risk or volatility.

Alternative Minimum Tax (AMT)

A tax levied under the personal income tax to ensure that high-income Canadians claiming preferential tax deductions pay a reasonable amount of tax in any given year.

Altman Z-Score

By examining 85 public manufacturing companies, Edward Altman developed the "Altman Z-Score", which reliably predicts whether or not a company is likely to enter into bankruptcy within one or two years.

If the Z-Score is 3.0 or above — bankruptcy is not likely.

If the Z-Score is 1.8 or less — bankruptcy is likely.

A score between 1.8 and 3.0 is the grey area, i.e., a high degree of caution should be used.

Probabilities of bankruptcy within the above ranges are 95% within one year and 70% within two years; obviously, a higher Z-Score is desirable. It is best to assess each individual company's Z-Score against that of the industry. In low margin industries it is possible for Z-Scores to fall below the above. In such cases a trend comparison to the industry over consecutive time periods may be a better indicator.

Later, additional "Z-Scores" were developed for private manufacturing companies (Z-Score — Model A) and another for general/service firms (Z-Score — Model B). Venture-Line selects the "Z-Score" appropriate for each firm based upon the questionnaire input from the listing company.

Original "Z-Score" (for Public Manufacturer)

See above.

Model A "Z-Score" (for Private Manufacturer)

Appropriate for a private manufacturing firm; should not be applied to other companies. A Z-Score of 2.90 or above indicates that bankruptcy is not likely, but a Z-Score of 1.23 or below is a strong indicator that bankruptcy is likely. Probabilities of bankruptcy in the above ranges are 95% for one year and 70% within two years. Obviously, a higher Z-Score is desirable.

Model B "Z-Score" (for Private General Firm)

Appropriate for a privately owned non-manufacturing company; should not be applied to other companies. A Z-Score of 1.10 or lower indicates that bankruptcy is likely, while a score of 2.60 or above can be an indicator that bankruptcy is not likely. A score between the two is the grey area. Probabilities of bankruptcy in the above ranges are 95% for one year and 70% within two years. Again, obviously, a higher Z-Score is desirable.

It should be remembered that a Z-Score is only as valid as the data from which it was derived, i.e., if a company has altered or falsified their financial records/books, a Z-Score derived from those "cooked books" is of lesser use.

Amalgamations

Combinations of firms that have been joined by merger, consolidation, or acquisition.

American Institute of Certified Public Accountants (AICPA)

The national self-regulating body in the United States that sets and monitors the auditing and professional standards by which CPAs practice.

American Options

A call or put option that can be exercised on or before its expiration date.

Amortization

(1) The gradual reduction of a debt by means of equal periodic payments sufficient to meet current interest and liquidate the debt at maturity. When the debt involves real property, often the periodic payments include a sum sufficient to pay taxes and hazard insurance on the property; (2) The process of spreading the cost of an intangible asset over the expected useful life of the asset. For example: a company pays $100,000 for a patent, they amortize the cost over the 16 year useful life of the patent.

Amortization Expense

The expense recorded to recognize asset amortization.

Analysis, Analyze

The technique, common in accounting, of comparing information derived from different sources or methods in order to understand what has happened, identify errors, and answer questions about the effects of possible actions or events. See Reconciliation and "What-If" (Effects) Analysis. Also used to refer to the detailed study of accounting information, such as by using Ratios.

Angel Investor

A private wealthy individual that has no association with a venture capital firm, investment fund, etc. The "angel" invests private money into what he/she believes to be promising opportunities i.e., normally start-up companies.

Annualize

A statistical technique whereby figures covering a period of less than one year are extended to cover a 12-month period. The technique, to be accurate, must take seasonal variations into consideration.

Annual Percentage Rate (APR)

The interest rate charged per period multiplied by the number of periods per year.

Annual Report

The document provided annually to the shareholders by the officers of a company. It includes the financial statements, the notes to the financial statements, the auditor's report, supplementary financial information such as multi-year summaries, and reports from the company's board of directors and management.

Annuity

A level stream of cash flows for a fixed period of time.

Annuity Due

Annuity contract specification of payments at the beginning of each period.

APCIMS

Association of Private Client Investment Managers and Stockbrokers.

Applied Research

Designed to solve practical problems of the modern world, rather than to acquire knowledge for knowledge's sake.

Apportion

To divide and share out according to a plan.

Appreciation

The increase in the value of an asset in excess of its depreciable cost, which is due to economic, and other conditions, as distinguished from increases in value due to improvements or additions made to it.

Appropriation

Distribution of net income to various accounts and/or the allocation of retained earnings for a designated purpose, e.g., plant expansion.

Arbitrage

Buying securities in one country, currency or market and selling in another to take advantage of price differentials.

Argument in Accounting

Usually revolves around the premise that characterizes fair values of assets as being more relevant but less reliable than their historical costs, with fair value being ultimately more informative only if its increased relevance outweighs its reduced reliability.

Arm's Length

Arm's length generally refers to the proximity of the relationship between taxpayers. Persons who are related to each other are considered to be non-arm's length with each other. An arm's length price is a price charged in similar transactions between unrelated parties.

Arm's Length Principle

A fundamental principle of international tax law is that entities should transact with each other on open market terms even if they are related parties. The arm's length principle reflects this concept and is used in situations where two transacting parties are related by means of control through shareholding or other means. The arm's length principle is therefore used in transfer pricing adjustments and affects for example interest free loans, excessive payments of royalties or inadequate remuneration for services.

Arm's Length Transaction

A transaction that is conducted as though the parties were unrelated, thereby avoiding any semblance of conflict of interest.

ARR

An acronym for Accounting Rate of Return.

Articles of Association

Regulations for governing the rights and duties of the members of a company among themselves. Articles (also Bylaws in some jurisdictions) deal with internal matters such as general meetings, appointment of directors, issue and transfer of shares, dividends, accounts and audits.

Articulate, Articulation

Of the income statement, retained earnings statement, and balance sheet; refers to the fact that because these three statements are prepared from one set of balanced accounts, changes in anyone of the three normally affect the others. In particular, recognition of revenue and expense relies on the fact that a revenue causes a change in the balance sheet, as does an expense.

ASEAN (Association of Southeast Asian Nations)

A trading block of countries in SE Asia. Originally formed as an anti-communist military alliance, it is now focused on developing a free trade agreement among member nations.

Assessed Value

The estimated value of property used for tax purposes.

Asset

Anything owned by an individual or a business, which has commercial or exchange value. Assets may consist of specific property or claims against others, in contrast to obligations due others. See also Liabilities.

Asset Availability

The stated condition or availability of an asset for usability. The subject asset is not available if it is already in use, at capacity, undergoing maintenance, broken, etc.

Asset Earning Power

A common profitability measure used to determine the profitability of a business by taking its total earning before taxes and dividing that by total assets.

Asset Protection Trust

A trust to protect the settlor's assets against those who may attempt to make claims against them (e.g., creditors, former spouses and dependents) on death. The trust may be set up onshore or offshore. Some offshore jurisdictions provide protection from creditor claims against persons who have guaranteed bank loans.

Asset Revaluation Reserve

An accounting concept that represents a reassessment of the value of a capital asset at a particular date. The reserve is considered a category of the equity of the entity. An asset is originally recorded in the accounts at its cost and depreciated periodically over its estimated useful life as a measure of the amount of the asset's value consumed in that period. In practice, the actual useful life of an asset can be miscalculated or an event can cause a change to the useful life. Consequently, assets occasionally need to be revalued in order to reflect a more close approximation to their "worth" in the accounts. When the asset is revalued, the offsetting entry (in a double entry accounting system) would be either made to the profit or loss accounts or to the equity of the entity.

Assets Held for Sale

Those assets, primarily long-term assets, that an entity wishes to dispose of or liquidate through sale to others.

Asset Turnover Ratio

A general measure of a firm's ability to generate sales in relation to total assets. It should be used only to compare firms within specific industry groups and in conjunction with other operating ratios to determine the effective employment of assets.

Asset Valuation

Determination of the amounts to be used for assets on the balance sheet.

Associate

In business, is a person brought together with a company or another person into a relationship in any of various intangible ways.

Associated Enterprises

The concept of associated enterprises applies typically in tax treaties and encapsulates the arm's length principle. An enterprise of one contracting state may engage in commercial dealings with an enterprise of the other contracting state that is under common control, management or ownership. If the two enterprises deal under conditions that would not have been imposed on an independent enterprise, a contracting state may include as taxable profits of the enterprise amounts that would have been derived by the enterprise in an arm's length relationship.

Assumed Cost Flow

The practice in inventory accounting of determining the cost of inventories purchased at varying unit costs by assuming a specific order in which the inventory will be taken to have flowed into and out of the country.

Assumption

Generally, is one or more beliefs or unconfirmed facts that contribute to a conclusion. Specifically, it is the act of taking on the responsibility or assuming the liabilities of another.

Assurance

A broader word than "audit", encompassing auditing and similar procedures to confirm or verify reports or events as fair and proper and assure users of such reports that they may be relied upon.

AT

The total assets turnover ratio.

ATA (Accredited Tax Advisor)

In the U.S., is a national credential conferred by Accreditation Council for Accountancy and Taxation to professionals who handle sophisticated tax planning issues, including ownership of closely held businesses, qualified retirement plans and complicated estates.

ATP

An acronym for After Tax Profit, Accredited Tax Preparer, and possibly more.

ATP (Accredited Tax Preparer)

In the U.S., a national credential conferred by Accreditation Council for Accountancy and Taxation to professionals who have a thorough knowledge behind the existing tax code and tax preparation of individuals, corporate and partnership tax returns.

Attrition

A reduction in numbers usually as a result of resignation, retirement, or death.

Audit

The inspection of the accounting records and procedures of a business, government unit, or other reporting entity by a trained accountant for the purpose of verifying the accuracy and completeness of the records. It could be conducted by a member of the organization (internal audit) or by an outsider (independent audit). A CPA audit determines the overall validity of financial statements. A tax audit (IRS in the U.S.) determines whether the appropriate tax was paid. An internal audit generally determines whether the company's procedures are followed and whether embezzlement or other illegal activity occurred.

Audit Bureau of Circulation (ABC)

A third-party organization that verifies the circulation of print media through periodic audits.

Audit Committee

A committee of a corporation's Board of Directors, usually composed largely or entirely of directors not also having management positions, which reviews the company's accounting statements and communicates directly with the External Auditor.

Auditor

The person or firm who performs an Audit for the purpose of preparing a report on the credibility of the financial statements; also called the External Auditor.

Auditor's Report (or Auditors' Report)

The document accompanying the financial statements that expresses the auditor's opinion on the fairness of the financial statements. The auditor's report explains what the auditor did and states the auditor's opinion.

Audit Strategy

A game plan to attack audit issues before they are raised. Reasons and justifications for all positions must be understood and the foundation laid for taking the position.

Authorized Agent

A bank or trust company authorized by regulatory authorities to deal in foreign currency securities.

Authorized Dealer Bank

Banks permitted by their regulating authority to deal in precious metals and all foreign currencies.

Authoritative Standards

Written rules and guidance established by official accounting standard-setters such as the CICA in Canada and the FASB in the United States.

Auxiliary Journal

A journal in which accounting information is stored both before and after the transfer to the General Ledger.

Available Cost

The total dollar amount represented by the sum of beginning inventory and purchases during the period, and thus representing the total dollar cost of inventory available for sale or use during the period.

Average Accounting Return (AAR)

An investment's average net income divided by its average book value.

Average Age of Inventory

Calculated by the formula 365 / inventory turnover.

Average Cost (AVGE)

An inventory cost-flow assumption where the cost of an individual unit of inventory is the weighted average cost of the beginning inventory and subsequent purchases.

Average Interest Rate

An average calculated by dividing interest expense by total liabilities.

Average Settlement Period

Calculated: for Debtors = Trade Debtors × 365 days / Credit Sales for Creditors = Trade Creditors × 365 days / Credit Purchases.

Average Tax Rate

Total taxes paid divided by total taxable income. For example, someone who pays $10,000 in income tax on a taxable income of $50,000 would have an average tax rate of 20 per cent.

AVGE

See Average Cost and Weighted Average.

Backlog

Value of unfilled orders placed with a manufacturing company. Whether a firm's backlog is rising or falling is a clue to its future sales and earnings.

Back-to-Back Loan

This term describes a loan normally between related parties but which is channelled through an independent intermediary, and whose primary purpose is to obtain interest deductibility which would otherwise be unavailable due to a local restriction such as thin capitalization rules, or which may be used to hide the real source of funds. In typical situations, the lender would deposit funds in an offshore bank whose local branch would then advance the equivalent funds to the borrower.

Bad Debt

Is an open account balance or loan receivable that has proven to be uncollectible and is written off.

Bad Debts Expense

An expense account that results from the reduction in carrying value of those accounts receivable that have been projected to be uncollectible or doubtful.

Balance (an account total)

The net sum of the amounts added to and subtracted from an account since the account began. In financial accounting's double-entry system, the balance is expressed as a net debit (DR) or net credit (CR).

Balance (in the Balance Sheet or the Trial Balance)

Refers to the double-entry accounting requirement that the sum of the accounts with debit balances and the sum of those with credit balances be equal. In the balance sheet, this means that the sum of the assets equals the sum of the liabilities and equity.

Balanced Scorecard (BSC)

A strategic management system based upon measuring key performance indicators across all aspects and areas of an enterprise: Financial, Customer, Internal Process, and Learning and Growth.

Balance of Payments / Balance of Trade

The difference between a country's total export dollar value and its total import dollar value, generally or with respect to a particular trading partner. A positive balance means a net inflow of capital, while a negative means capital flows out of the country.

Balance Sheet

An itemized statement that lists the total assets and the total liabilities of a given business to portray its net worth at a given moment of time. The amounts shown on a balance sheet are generally the historic cost of items and not their current values. Also called a Statement of Financial Position.

Balance Sheet Equation

The double-entry arithmetic by which Assets = Liabilities + Owners' Equity.

Balance Sheet Gearing

The ratio of interest-bearing debt to equity.

Balance Sheet Valuation

Assigning numerical values to the balance sheet's assets, liabilities, and owners' equity accounts.

Banker's Acceptance

A short-term debt security issued by a non-financial company and guaranteed by the company's bank.

Bank Guarantee

An irrevocable commitment by a bank to pay a specified sum of money in the event that the party requesting the guarantee fails to perform the promise or discharge the liability to a third person in case of the requestor's default.

Bank Overdraft

A negative bank account balance (withdrawals exceeding deposits), which banks may allow as a *de facto* loan as long as it is temporary.

Bank Reconciliation

The practice of comparing the accounting records of the bank account with the information provided by the bank (such as in a monthly bank statement), to identify any errors in either record.

Bankruptcy

(1) A state of insolvency of an organization or individual, i.e. an inability to pay debts; (2) The usually involuntary termination of an enterprise due to its inability to pay its debts and continue in operation. Involves a legal proceeding for liquidating or reorganizing a business. Also, the transfer of some or all of a firm's assets to its creditors. Bankruptcy usually results in significant losses to both creditors and owners.

In the U.S., bankruptcy can take either one of three forms:

Chapter 7

> is involuntary liquidation forced by creditor(s). Some companies are so far in debt that they can't continue their business operations. They are likely to "liquidate" and are forced to file under Chapter 7. The courts take over and administers through a court appointed trustee. Their assets are sold for cash by a court appointed trustee. Administrative and legal expenses are paid first, and the remainder goes to creditors;

Chapter 11

> is voluntary by the debtor. Unless the court rules otherwise, the debtor stays in control of the enterprise. The U.S. Trustee, the bankruptcy arm of the Justice Department, will appoint one or more committees to represent the interests of creditors and stockholders in working with the company to develop a plan of reorganization to get out of debt; and,

Chapter 13

is where a debtor proposes a 3–5 year repayment plan to the creditors offering to pay off all or part of the debts from the debtor's future income. The amount to be repaid is determined by several factors including the debtor's disposable income. To file under this chapter you must have a "regular source of income" and have some disposable income. Like in a Chapter 7, corporations and partnerships may not file under this chapter.

Bare Trusts

Also known as dry, formal, naked, passive or simple trusts. These are trusts where the trustees have no duties to perform other than to convey the trust property to the beneficiary when called upon to do so.

BARS

An acronym for Base Accounts Receivable System.

Barter System

See Trade Exchange.

Base Companies

Such companies are normally in low tax countries or Tax Havens and are used for example as invoicing companies to related parties, or as a way of accumulating passive income to provide tax deferral until remittance.

Base Erosion Rule

This is a term which has been adopted primarily by the U.S. in its treaty arrangements to prevent treaty shopping, and reflects the payment of a significant percentage of income as deductible expenses to non-residents of the particular treaty country. For example, the U.S./Netherlands double tax treaty has a base erosion rule which prevents more than 50% of income from U.S. sources being paid by Dutch companies to non-Dutch residents as deductible expense.

Basic Earnings Power (BEP)

Useful for comparing firms in different tax situations and with different degrees of financial leverage. This ratio is often used as a measure of the effectiveness of operations. Basic Earning Power measures the basic profitability of assets because it excludes consideration of interest and tax. This ratio should be examined in conjunction with turnover ratios to help pinpoint potential problems regarding asset management.

Basic Tenets of Accounting

Four in number: (1) Assets = Liabilities + Owner's Equity; (2) Debits = Credits; (3) Assets are on the left (debit side); and (4) Liabilities and Equity are on the right (credit side).

Basis

That figure or value that is the starting point in computing gain or loss, depreciation, depletion, and amortization of a company.

Basis Points

The smallest measure used in quoting interest rates and yields on bills, notes and bonds. One basis point is equal to one one-hundredth of one percent. Basis points make for a handy way to state small differences in interest rates or yield. For example, if a bond's yield increased from 7.00% to 7.50%, it would have increased 50 basis points.

BAY

In business/accounting, means Buy Another Yearly.

Bear

An investor who has sold a security in the hope of buying it back at a lower price.

Bearer Form

Bond issued without record of the owner's name; payment is made to whoever holds the bond.

Bearer Share Certificate

A negotiable share certificate filled out in the name of "bearer" and not to a particular person or organization.

Bearer Stocks/Shares

Securities for which the company keeps no register of ownership. A bearer certificate has an intrinsic value. Dividends are not received automatically from the company but must be claimed by removing and returning 'coupons' attached to the certificate.

Bear Market

A market in which Bears prosper, that is, a falling market.

Bed and Breakfast Deal

Selling shares one day and buying them back the next for tax purposes at the end of the financial year.

"Belgian Dentist"

Stereotype of the traditional Eurobond investor as a professional who must report income, has a disdain for tax authorities, and likes to invest in foreign currencies.

Benchmark

A study to compare actual performance to a standard of typical competence; or, a standard for the basis of comparison as being above, below or comparable to.

Beneficial Owner

(1) The person who enjoys the benefits of ownership even though the title is in another name (often used in risk arbitrage). (2) The actual or economic owner of an offshore company as distinct from the registered or nominal owner.

Beneficiary

The person in whose favour a letter of credit is issued or a draft is drawn.

Benefit/Cost Ratio

The profitability index of an investment project.

Besloten Vennootschap ("B.V.")

This form of incorporation under Dutch company law is broadly comparable to the private limited liability company (PLC) in the United Kingdom.

Best Efforts Underwriting

Underwriter sells as much of the issue as possible, but can return any unsold shares to the issuer without financial responsibility.

Beta Coefficient

Amount of systematic risk present in a particular risky asset relative to an average risky asset.

Betterment

An expenditure to improve an asset's value to the business, more than just repairs and maintenance.

Bid

(1) The price at which a market maker will buy shares; (2) An approach made by one company wishing to purchase the entire share capital of another company.

Big Bang

27 October 1986, when the new London Stock Exchange introduced new regulations and the Automated Price Quotation System (SEAQ).

Big Bath

A way of manipulating reported income to show even poorer results in a poor year in order to enhance later years' results.

Billings

In accounting, is sales for which invoicing has been issued.

Bill of Exchange

See Draft.

Bill of Lading

The contract between the owner of the goods and the cargo carrier to move the goods to a specified destination. A clean bill of lading is issued by the carrier verifying receipt of the merchandise in apparent good condition (without visually apparent damage or defect). Bills of lading can sometimes be made to cover the whole trip, or separate bills of lading can be prepared for each carrier. Ocean shipments generally require two, an Inland Bill of Lading covering land transportation to the port and an Ocean Bill of Lading covering the ship portion. Bills of lading are negotiable while cargo is in transit.

Bill of Materials (BOM)

A listing of all the assemblies, sub-assemblies, parts, and raw materials that are needed to produce one unit of a finished product. Each finished product has its own bill of materials.

Bills Purchased

In trade finance, allows a seller to obtain financing and receive immediate funds in exchange for a sales document not drawn under a letter of credit. The bank will send the sales document to the buyer's bank on behalf of the seller.

Blind Trust

A trust in which the trustees are enjoined from providing any information to the beneficiaries about the administration of assets of the trust.

Blue Chip

Term for the most prestigious industrial shares. Originally an American term derived from the colour of the highest value poker chip.

Board of Directors

The senior level of management, representing and directly responsible to the owners (share-holders). Normally elected annually by the shareholders, the board is responsible for hiring and supervising the operating management (president, chief executive officer, etc.).

BOM

See Bill of Materials.

Bond, Bonded Debt

A debt security issued by a government or company. You receive regular interest payments at specified rates while you hold the bond and the face value when it matures. Short-term bonds mature in less than one year; medium-term bonds mature in two to 10 years; and long-term bonds mature in more than 10 years.

Bond Covenant

Agreements within a bond that can either be negative or positive in the view of the bond-holder, e.g., a negative bond covenant is a bond covenant that prevents certain activities unless agreed to by the bondholders.

Bonded Warehouse

A warehouse authorized by customs officials for the storage of goods on which payment of duty is deferred until the goods are removed.

Bonding

Generally used by service companies as a guarantee to their clients that they have the necessary ability and financial tracking to meet their obligations. Bonds are also used to guarantee payment of duty for U.S. Customs entry.

Bond Markets

Capital markets in which debt instruments (bonds and similar items), rather than shares, are traded.

Bond Refunding

The process of replacing all or part of an issue of outstanding bonds.

Bookbuild

A particular way of conducting a float where the price at which shares are sold is not fixed, but rather is determined following a process in which interested investors bid for shares. This is quite a common way of determining the price paid for shares by institutional investors (Funds Managers).

Book Cost

Normally, is the cost at the time an asset is purchased or realized, i.e., the total amount paid to acquire an asset.

Booking

In import/export, is an arrangement with a shipping company to load and carry a shipment.

Bookkeeping

The process of recording, classifying, and summarizing transactions in a business' books of account (accounting records).

Books

Colloquial term for the accounting records, including computerized records, left over from the time when the records were written in bound books.

Books of Original Entry

The journals in which transactions are first recorded.

Book-to-Market

The ratio of the firm's book equity to market equity.

Book Value

(1) The original purchase price of an investment; (2) An accounting term which usually refers to a business' historical cost of assets less liabilities. The book value of a stock is determined from a company's records by adding all assets (generally excluding such intangibles as goodwill), then deducting all debts and other liabilities, plus the liquidation price of any preferred stock issued. The sum arrived at is divided by the number of common shares outstanding and the result is the book value per common share. Book value of the assets of a company may have little or no significant relationship to market value. See also Tangible Book Value and Economic Book Value.

Book Value per Share

Total shareholders' equity divided by the number of shares issued.

Boot

The non-share consideration received by a vendor who sells property to a corporation under a section 85 rollover. It consists of any consideration other than shares of the purchaser corporation. Examples include cash, assets, a promissory note, or assumption of the vendor's liabilities.

Bottom Line

In accounting/finance, is specifically Net Income after taxes. In general, it is an expression as to the end results of something, e.g., the net worth of a corporation on a balance sheet, sales generated from a marketing campaign, or final decision on most any subject (often said: "give me the bottom line").

Bottom Up

A concept of analyzing a subject, such as costs or revenue, starting from the lowest level working towards the top.

Bought Deal

One underwriter buys securities from an issuing firm and sells them directly to a small number of investors.

Branch

A branch of an enterprise is a business carried on through a fixed place of business, which is also referred to as a permanent establishment. A branch is not separately incorporated.

Branch Level Tax

The majority of countries levy a withholding tax on the distribution of dividends by subsidiary companies to parents, particularly where they are not resident in the same country, with double tax treaties reducing the impact of such withholding taxes. However, the remittance of branch profits has often been exempt from further taxation after the primary level which creates an overall tax differential between the utilization of branches and subsidiary companies. Many countries are now rectifying this anomaly and impose a branch level tax on the remittance of branch profits to non-resident parents, normally at the same dividend withholding tax rate which again may be reduced by double tax treaty provisions.

Branch Profits Tax

The branch profits tax is a tax that may be imposed by the source State on that portion of the business profits of a foreign corporation that is attributable to a permanent establishment therein. The rate of the branch profits tax is determined by the *Income Tax Act* (Part XIV), but is often reduced in Canada's bilateral tax treaties.

Break-Even

For accounting purposes, the sales level that results in zero project net income.

Break-Even Analysis

An analysis method used to determine the number of jobs or products that need to be sold to reach a break-even point in a business.

Break-Even Point

The volume point at which revenues and costs are equal; a combination of sales and costs that will yield a no profit/no loss operation.

Broker/Dealer

A Stock Exchange member firm which provides advice and dealing services to the public and which can deal on its own account.

Budget

An itemized listing of the amount of all estimated revenue which a given business anticipates receiving, along with a listing of the amount of all estimated costs and expenses that will be incurred in obtaining the above mentioned income during a given period of time. A budget is typically for one business cycle, such as a year, or for several cycles (such as a five year capital budget).

Budget Control

Actions carried out according to a budget plan. Through the use of a budget as a standard, an organization ensures that managers are implementing its plans and objectives. Their actual performance is measured against budgeted performance.

Bull

An investor who has bought a security in the hope of selling it at a higher price.

Bull Market

One in which "Bulls" prosper, that is a rising market.

Burden Rate

When referring to personnel burden, is the sum of employer costs over and above salaries (including employer taxes, benefits, etc.). When referring to factory or manufacturing see Overhead.

Burn Rate

The rate at which a new company uses up its venture capital to finance overhead before generating positive cash flow from operations. It is the rate of negative cash flow, usually quoted as a monthly rate.

Business Combination

A merger of separate corporations or an acquisition of control of one corporation by another, in which the corporations become a single economic entity.

Business Entity

A selection of the legal form under which a business is to operate: sole proprietorship, general partnership, corporation, S corporation (in the U.S.), or, a limited liability company.

Business Matrix

Often used in business incubators, is where separate business entities join forces to advance the development of a start-up, e.g., one firm may offer offices, another marketing/sales assistance or manufacturing expertise, etc. Such a matrix may receive compensation in the form of equity from the start-up being assisted by that business matrix.

Business Plan

A description of a business (normally over a one to five year period). A basic business plan includes: product(s) and/or service(s), the market, competitor analysis, the key people involved, financing needs, and the financial rewards if the business plan is implemented successfully. A well-prepared business plan plays two important roles, firstly, it is a useful management tool that can help management plot a course for the company, and secondly, it is a vital sales tool that will impress funding sources, e.g., venture capitalists or the Board of Directors, with management's planning ability and general competence. Other things being equal, a well prepared business plan will increase a company's chances of obtaining a financial commitment to fund the business.

Business Publications Audit (BPA)

Similar to the Audit Bureau of Circulation; the BPA is a third-party organization that verifies the circulation of print media through periodic audits.

Business Risk

The equity risk that comes from the nature of the firm's operating activities.

Business Unit

Equivalent to a wholly owned subsidiary except that it is not treated as a separate legal entity. It is an organization within a firm that could operate separately because it has all support functions contained within the business unit. The internal financial reporting from a business unit to the corporate office is basically identical to a separate legal entity.

BVI

An acronym for British Virgin Islands (a major offshore banking and corporation player).

CA

Acronym for Chartered Accountant. See Canadian Institute of Chartered Accountants.

C.A.

Sometimes used to identify the Chief Accountant.

CAGR

See Compound Annual Growth Rate.

Call

The amount due to be paid to a company by the purchase of new or partly paid shares.

Call Account

A deposit account with a financial institution without a fixed maturity date. The deposit can be "called" (withdrawn) at any time. Call account deposits are usually one to seven day placements; however, two parties can agree on different maturities.

Call Option

The right to buy stock or shares at an agreed price at a future date. The opposite of a Put Option. See, generally, Option.

Call Premium

Amount by which the call price exceeds the par value of the bond.

Call Protected

Bond during period in which it cannot be redeemed by the issuer.

Call Provision

Agreement giving the corporation the option to repurchase the bond at a specified price before maturity.

Canada *Business Corporations Act* (CBCA)

The federal corporations act that provides the authority for the incorporation of federally incorporated companies in Canada and generally sets the requirements for their activities. It requires any such company to prepare annual financial statements.

Canada Plus Call

Call provision which compensates bond investors for interest differential making call unattractive for issuer.

Canada Yield Curve

A plot of the yields on Government of Canada bonds relative to maturity.

Canadian Certified General Accountants Association (CGA-Canada)

An association whose members (CGAs) have had training in accounting, taxation, auditing, and other areas of business and have passed qualifying exams. CGA-Canada and provincial associations of CGAs set and monitor standards by which CGAs practise. CGA-Canada is one of the three national professional accounting bodies.

Canadian Institute of Chartered Accountants (CICA)

A national, self-regulating association of chartered accountants who have met education and examination standards in Canada. The CICA and provincial institutes of CAs set and monitor the standards by which CAs practise. One of the three national professional accounting bodies.

C&F (Cost & Freight)

Includes all shipping costs except insurance. Generally used in statement of terms, stating cost and freight are paid by the exporter from his warehouse to a port in the importer's country. In this case, the buyer is responsible for insurance.

C&I (Cost & Insurance)

In a price that is quoted "C&I", means that the cost of the product and insurance are included in the quoted price. In this case, the cost of shipping would be borne by the buyer.

Capital

(1) In economics, can mean factories, machines, and other man-made inputs into a production process; (2) In finance, capital is money and other property of a corporation or other enterprise used in transacting the business; (3) The owner's contribution to or interest in a business (the equity); often used specifically to refer to the equity of unincorporated businesses (proprietor-ships and partnerships).

Capital Asset

A long-term asset that is not purchased or sold in the normal course of business. Generally, it includes fixed assets, e.g., land, buildings, furniture, equipment, fixtures and furniture.

Capital Budget

The estimated amount planned to be expended for capital items in a given fiscal period. Capital items are fixed assets such as facilities and equipment, the cost of which is normally written off over a number of fiscal periods. The capital budget, however, is limited to the expenditures that will be made within the fiscal year comparable to the related operating budgets.

Capital Budgeting

The process of planning and managing a firm's investment in fixed assets.

Capital Controls

Government restrictions on the acquisition of foreign assets or foreign liabilities by domestic citizens, or the acquisition of domestic assets or domestic liabilities by foreigners.

Capital Cost Allowance (CCA)

This term has been adopted by some countries, such as Canada, to describe a method of depreciation which is prescribed by law. The CCA method allows the government to categorize business-related property into classes and then control the rates at which the various classes are depreciated. Businesses can deduct up to a fixed percentage of the depreciated cost each year. CCA may differ from depreciation used for financial statement purposes. For example, in certain cases, the CCA rates at which assets can be written off against income may be faster than the rates used in companies' financial accounts.

Capital Expenditure

The amount used during a particular period to acquire or improve long-term assets such as property, plant or equipment.

Capital Gain (or Capital Loss)

The difference between the price you pay for an investment and the price you sell it for. When you sell an investment for more than you paid, you earn a capital gain. When you sell an investment for less than you paid, you earn a capital loss. For example, if a share is bought at $26 and sold at $30, there is a capital gain of $4.

Capital Gains Tax

A tax levied on the profits from the sale of capital assets or the deemed sale of capital assets. Usually only a portion (e.g. 50%) of the gain is taxable. In Canada, there is a $500,000 exemption for capital gains on small business shares and qualified farm property. A taxpayer's principal residence is not subject to capital gains taxation.

Capital Gains Yield

The dividend growth rate or the rate at which the value of an investment grows.

Capital Improvement

The increase in the total amount of money or other resources owned or capable of being used to acquire future income or benefits.

Capital Intensity Ratio

A firm's total assets divided by its sales, or the amount of assets needed to generate $1 in sales.

Capital Investment

See Capital Expenditure.

Capitalization

(1) The statement of capital within the firm — either in the form of money, common stock, long-term debt, or in some combination of all three. It is possible to have too much capital (in which case the firm is overcapitalized) or too little capital (in which case the firm is undercapitalized); (2) The recognition of an expenditure that may benefit a future period as an asset rather than as an expense of the period of its occurrence. Expenditures are capitalized if they are likely to lead to future benefits, and, thus, meet the criterion to be an asset.

Capitalization Rate ("Cap Rate")

The rate of return a property will produce on the owner's investment. It is stated as a rate of interest or discount rate used to convert a series of future payments into a single 'present value'. In real estate, the rate includes annual capital recovery in addition to interest.

Capitalization Issue

The process whereby money from a company's reserves is converted into issued capital and then distributed to shareholders as new shares, in proportion to their original holdings, also known as bonus or scrip issue.

Capitalize

To: a) convert a schedule of income into a principal amount, called *capitalized value*, by dividing by a rate of interest; b) record capital outlays as additions to asset accounts, not as expenses; c) convert a lease obligation to an asset/liability form of expression called a *capital lease*, i.e., to record a leased asset as an owned asset and the lease obligation as borrowed funds; or d) turn something to one's advantage economically, e.g., sell umbrellas on a rainy day.

Capitalized Costs

Costs that have been included with an asset on the balance sheet instead of being deducted as expenses on the income statement. This allows business expenses to be written off or deducted over a period of time through depreciation or amortization schedules.

Capital Lease

A lease obligation that has to be capitalized on the balance sheet. It is characterized by: it is non-cancellable; the life of lease is less than the life of the asset(s) being leased; and, the lessor does not pay for the upkeep, maintenance, or servicing costs of the asset(s) during the lease period. A capital lease has the economic character of asset ownership.

Capital Markets

Markets in which financial instruments such as shares and bonds are traded.

Capital Outlay

See Capital Expenditure.

Capital Rationing

The situation that exists if a firm has positive NPV projects but cannot find the necessary financing.

Capital Replacement (or Economic Depreciation)

The portion of the value of machinery and equipment, in addition to repairs, that is used up in the production of a particular commodity. It is based on the current value of the machinery. Capital replacement may be regarded as a discretionary expense in any particular year. It may be deferred when income is low but ultimately must be paid to maintain the capital stock so that over the long term, the operation remains in business.

Capital Reserve

A fund set aside for specific purposes, thereby cannot be distributed for other uses. See also Revenue Reserve.

Capital Stock

The ownership shares of a corporation authorized by its articles of incorporation, including preferred and common stock.

Capital Structure

The mix of debt and equity maintained by a firm.

Cap Rate

See Capitalization Rate.

Caps

An option-like contract for which the buyer pays a fee or premium, to obtain protection against a rise in a particular interest rate above a certain level. For example, an interest rate cap may cover a specified principal amount of a loan over a designated time period such as a calendar quarter. If the covered interest rate rises above the rate ceiling, the seller of the rate cap pays the purchaser an amount of money equal to the average rate differential times the principal amount times one quarter.

Captive Finance Company

Wholly owned subsidiary that handles credit extension and receivables financing through commercial paper.

Captive Insurance Company

A wholly owned or controlled subsidiary company established by a non-insurance parent for the purpose of participation in the insurance risks of the parent and its other affiliates or associates.

Carnet

A customs document which permits you to send or carry merchandise into a country duty and tax free for a short period, for use as samples or as display merchandise in a trade show, for example.

Carrying Value (or "Book Value")

A company's total assets minus intangible assets and liabilities, such as debt.

Case-Based Reimbursement

In healthcare, is a hospital payment system in which a hospital is reimbursed for each discharged inpatient at rates prospectively established for groups of cases with similar clinical profile and resource requirements.

Cash

Currency and coin on hand, balances in bank accounts, and other highly liquid assets.

Cash and Equivalents

Cash and near-cash assets minus near-cash liabilities: cash equivalent assets minus cash equivalent liabilities. Changes in cash and equivalents are explained by the cash flow statement (SCFP). Excludes sinking funds.

Cash Basis of Accounting

The accounting basis in which revenue and expenses are recorded in the period they are actually received or expended in cash. Use of the cash basis generally is not considered to be in conformity with Generally Accepted Accounting Principles (GAAP) and is therefore used only in selected situations, such as for very small businesses and (when permitted) for income tax reporting. See also Accrual Basis.

Cash Break-Even

The sales level where operating cash flow is equal to zero.

Cash Budget

A forecast of cash receipts and disbursements for the next planning period.

Cash Cycle

The time between cash disbursement and cash collection.

Cash Debt Coverage Ratio

The ratio of net cash provided by operating activities to average total liabilities, called the cash debt coverage ratio, is a cash-basis measure of solvency. This ratio indicates a company's ability to repay its liabilities from cash generated from operating activities without having to liquidate the assets used in operations.

Cash Disbursements

Cash payouts, by cheque, currency, or direct deductions from the bank account.

Cash Disbursements Journal

The record of cheques and other cash payments made.

Cash Discount

A discount given for a cash purchase.

Cash Equivalent Assets

A term used to describe cash plus very liquid bank deposits and similar assets that can be converted into cash on demand.

Cash Equivalent Liabilities

Liabilities that are payable on demand and so represent a reduction in the liquidity otherwise apparent from the amount of cash. Under current accounting standards, temporary bank overdrafts are the only common cash equivalent liabilities.

Cash Flow

The inflows of cash (cash receipts) and outflows of cash (cash disbursements) over a period. Information about cash flow is presented in the Cash Flow Statement.

Cash Flow Analysis

A method of accounting analysis directed at understanding the enterprise's cash inflows, outflows, and resulting balances. This analysis lies behind the Cash Flow Statement.

Cash Flow / Current Portion of Long Term Debt Ratio

A measure of the firm's ability to meet its obligations with internally generated cash.

Cash Flow from Assets

The total of cash flow to bondholders and cash flow to stockholders, consisting of the following: operating cash flow, capital spending, and additions to net working capital.

Cash Flow from Operations

The sum of all the individual operating activity cash flow line items, less cash realized from the sale of extraordinary items, e.g., fixed assets.

Cash Flow Statement

A statement that explains the changes in cash (and equivalent) balances during a fiscal period. Also referred to as "Statement of changes in financial position (SCFP)", "Funds statement", or "Statement of cash flows".

Cash Flow Time Line

Graphical representation of the operating cycle and the cash cycle.

Cash Flow to Creditors

A firm's interest payments to creditors less net new borrowings.

Cash Flow to Shareholders

Dividends paid out by a firm less net new equity raised.

Cash Flow to Total Assets

The ratio of Cash from Operations divided by total assets.

Cash from Financing

The sum of all the individual financing activity cash flow line items.

Cash from Investing

The sum of all the individual investing activity cash flow line items.

Cash from Operations

Cash generated by day-to-day business activities and highlighted as the first section in the Cash Flow Statement.

Cash in Advance

When full payment is due before the merchandise is shipped. Least risk to seller, most risk to buyer.

Cash Income

Cash receipts minus cash disbursements, or that subset of both that relates to day-to-day operations. The operating subset is roughly equivalent to the Cash Flow Statement's Cash from Operations figure.

Cash Payments

Payments by currency, cheque, or other bank withdrawal.

Cash Receipts

Cash inflows, by currency, others' cheques, or direct bank deposits.

Cash Receipts Journal

The record of customers' cheques and other cash received.

Cash Received Basis

Recognition of revenue only when the cash comes in.

Cash Transaction

The simplest kind of economic exchange routinely recorded by financial accounting, and an important starting point for the financial statements.

CCA

See Capital Cost Allowance.

CCA Tax Shield

Tax saving that results from the CCA deduction, calculated as depreciation multiplied by the corporate tax rate.

CEO

An acronym for Chief Executive Officer. The CEO is the principle individual responsible for the activities of a company.

Certificate of Inspection

Certification, generally by an independent third party, that the goods were in good condition at the time of shipment.

Certificate of Origin

A document that states where the goods were made. This document is legally required for many countries for the importation of merchandise.

Certified Financial Planner (CFP)

A financial planner who has received a licence from the Institute of Certified Financial Planners, indicating that he/she was trained in investments, budgeting, taxes, banking, estate planning and insurance. Some CFPs work on commission for the products they sell, and some work for a flat hourly fee.

Certified Financial Statements

Financial statements that have undergone a formal audit by a certified public accountant and usually contain statements of certification by the CPA.

CFM

In finance/accounting, means Certified in Financial Management.

CFO

Acronym for Chief Financial Officer. The CFO is the officer in a corporation responsible for handling funds, signing *cheques*, the keeping of financial records, and financial planning for the company.

CGA

Certified General Accountant.

C.G.A.

Acronym for Certified General Accountant.

Change Effects Analysis

Analysis of the effects on financial statements of economic or accounting policy changes.

Change in Cash

Demonstrating why cash changed as it did is the objective of the Cash Flow Statement's analysis. Cash income is part of this change.

Chapters or Subchapters

A legal corporate entity organized under the United States Federal *Tax Code* that allows Subchapter S Corporations to distribute all income/loss proportionately to its shareholders, who then claim that income/loss on their personal income taxes, thereby avoiding the payment of corporate taxes.

Chargeback

In the credit industry, occurs when a credit card processor "charges back" to the merchant the cost of returned items or incorrect orders that the customer claims were made to his or her credit card.

Chart of Accounts

A list of ledger account names and associated numbers arranged in the order in which they normally appear in the financial statements. The Chart of Accounts are customarily arranged in the following order: Assets, Liabilities, Owners' Equity (Stockholders' Equity for a corporation), Revenue, and Expenses.

Chattel Mortgage Contract

A credit contract used for the purchase of equipment where the purchaser receives title of the equipment upon delivery but the creditor holds a mortgage claim against it.

Cheque/Check

A draft drawn against a bank, payable upon demand to the person/entity named upon the draft. This is in effect a request by one party that their bank pay a specified amount to another party.

CIA

In accounting, is an acronym for Certified Internal Auditor; or, Cash in Advance.

CIBT

An acronym for Cash Income Before Taxes.

CICA Handbook

The authoritative source of financial accounting standards in Canada.

CIF (Cost, Insurance and Freight)

A shipment where all shipping costs are paid by the exporter, including insurance.

Circular Bid

Corporate takeover bid that is communicated to the stockholders by direct mail.

Classical System

The classical system as opposed to the imputation system of taxation allows economic double taxation of profits within a particular country by charging corporate income tax on the profits of a company plus personal income tax on the distribution of such profits to shareholders as dividends, without any credit being given for the corporate tax suffered.

Classification

Choice of where in the financial statements to place an account, such as whether an investment asset should be shown as a current asset or a non-current asset.

Classification Policies

Accounting policies covering where within a financial statement an account or description is to appear.

Classified Financial Statements

Financial statement with accounts organized under headings that clarify the accounts' meaning, done to increase the information value of the statements.

Clean Opinion

An external auditor's report which states the auditor's opinion that the financial statements are fairly presented. This is the kind of auditor's report that most companies receive because it indicates the auditor found no problems.

Clearing System

A mechanism for calculation of mutual positions within a group of participants with a view to facilitating the settlement of their mutual obligations on a net basis.

Clientele Effect

Stocks attract particular groups based on dividend yield and the resulting tax effects.

Close, Closing

Transfer(ring) the temporary accounts (revenues, expenses, and dividends declared) to retained earnings at the end of the fiscal period.

Closely Held

A description of a corporation whose voting stock is owned by a very small number of shareholders.

Closing Entry or Entries

Journal entries recorded at year-end to transfer the balances in temporary accounts (revenues, expenses, and dividends) to the balance sheet account retained earnings and set those balances to zero in preparation for entering the next year's transactions.

CMA

Certified Management Accountant.

C.M.O.

See Collateralized Mortgage Obligation.

COA

In accounting, means Chart of Accounts.

COGS

See Cost of Goods Sold.

COGS Expense

See Cost of Goods Sold Expense.

COGS (Cost of Goods) Ratio

Calculated as: COGS / Total Sales.

Collar

The simultaneous purchase of a cap and the sale of a floor with the aim of maintaining interest rates within a defined range. The premium income from the sale of the floor reduces or offsets the cost of buying the cap.

Collateral

Assets used as security for the extension of a loan.

Collateralized Mortgage Obligation (CMO)

Or, since 1986, a Real Estate Mortgage Investment Conduit (REMIC). CMOs and REMICs (terms which are often used interchangeably) are similar types of securities which allow cash flows to be directed so that different classes of securities with different maturities and coupons can be created. They may be collateralized by mortgage loans as well as securitized pools of loans.

Collection Papers

Those documents specified as necessary for payment to be made, such as the commercial invoice, certificate of inspection, and bill of lading.

Collection Period

Used to appraise accounts receivable (AR). This ratio measures the length of time it takes to convert your average sales into cash. This measurement defines the relationship between accounts receivable and cash flow. A longer average collection period requires a higher investment in accounts receivable. A higher investment in accounts receivable means less cash is available to cover cash outflows, such as paying bills. NOTE: Comparing the two Collection Period ratios (Period Average and Period End) suggests the direction in which AR collections are moving, thereby giving an indication as to potential impacts to cash flow.

Collection Policy

Procedures followed by a firm in collecting accounts receivable.

Collection Ratio

The ratio of accounts receivable to the daily sales, expressed in number of days' sales represented by accounts receivable. Also called Days' sales in receivables.

Collective Investment Scheme

Globally, is any arrangement for pooling several investors' funds so that the pooled fund can obtain economies of scale and a spread of investments beyond the reach of individual investors. It is usually called an investment company in the U.S.A.

Commercial Attaché

A business and trade expert on the staff of a consulate or embassy. They are responsible for promoting exports of their country's goods and are an excellent source of help.

Commercial Bank

A financial institution that provides commercial banking services. A commercial bank accepts deposits, gives business loans and provides other services to businesses.

Commercial Loan

A short-term business loan usually issued for a term of up to six months.

Commercial Paper

Short-term obligations with maturities ranging from two to 270 days issued by corporations, banks, or other borrowers to investors who have temporarily idle cash on hand. Commercial paper is usually unsecured and discounted.

Commission

The fee that a broker may charge clients for dealing on their behalf.

Committed Costs

Are costs, usually fixed costs, which the management of an organization has a long-term responsibility to pay. Examples include rent on a long-term lease and depreciation on an asset with an extended life.

Commodities

Bulk goods such as grains, metals and foods.

Commodity Options

A contract providing the purchaser the right but not the obligation to buy or sell a given quantity of a commodity at a strike price, on or before a given date.

Commodity Swaps

A transaction that allows an investor to exchange payment streams which are based on commodity prices. Commodity swaps involve swaps of payment streams only and are usually settled in cash. However, physical delivery may also occur. Commodity swaps enable producers and consumers to hedge commodity price risk.

Common-Base-Year Statement

A standardized financial statement presenting all items relative to a certain base year amount.

Common Share

A security that represents part ownership in a company. Common shares are the most frequently issued class of stock; usually they provide voting rights but are secondary to preferred stock in dividend and liquidation rights.

Common Size Analysis

As used in vertical analysis of financial statements, an item is used as a base value and all other accounts in the financial statement are compared to this base value. On the balance sheet, total assets equal 100% and each asset is stated as a percentage of total assets. Similarly, total liabilities and stockholder's equity are assigned 100%, with a given liability or equity account stated as a percentage of total liabilities and stockholder's equity. On the income statement, 100% is assigned to net sales, with all revenue and expense accounts then related to it in percentages. See Common Size Percentages.

Common-Size Financial Statements

A technique of analyzing financial statements in which income statement figures are expressed in percentages of revenue and balance sheet accounts are expressed in percentages of total assets.

Common Size Percentages

In the Income Statement, each "Common Size %" is the field amount expressed as a per cent of "Net Revenues". In the Balance Sheet, each "Common Size %" is the amount in the category as a per cent of "Total Assets". "Ratio Analysis" as prepared by VentureLine presents several standard "Key Ratios" to compare this firm to any of several standards. This firm's ratios may be compared to industry standards, to a single other firm of similar (or different) type, or to this firm's past or anticipated performance. In this analysis VentureLine uses industry data based upon the SIC Code of that particular listing (when available).

Common-Size Statement

A standardized financial statement presenting all items in percentage terms. Balance sheets are shown as a percentage of assets and income statements as a percentage of sales.

Common Stock

See Common Shares.

Company

See Corporation.

Company Limited by Guarantee

An incorporated entity without share capital.

Comparability

Information that enables users to identify similarities in and differences between two sets of economic phenomena, such as two different years of a company's financial statements. Comparability between companies and consistency of one company over time are major objectives of financial accounting.

Comparable Profit Interval

Another term recently adopted by the U.S., it is used in transfer pricing adjustments to ascertain "normal" profits within a certain industry for a transfer of similar rights products or services, by means of various criteria within a certain range, to see if the profits earned by the relevant associated enterprise fall within such range.

Compensating Balances

The funds a business might be required to keep in a deposit or reserve account to help offset what the bank perceives as risk. The lender might require that an amount based on the business' average account balance or a certain percentage of the face value of the loan be maintained in a deposit account.

Compensatory Tax

Where a country's tax system is based on the imputation system and provides for tax credits to be given in respect of dividend distributions, there has to be a mechanism whereby profits which have not been subject to local taxation either do not carry with them the available tax credit, or are subject to a further tax on distribution. This further tax on distribution, allowing the full tax credits to be available on all income, is known as a compensatory tax, e.g., the precompte in France. The ACT in the UK acts as both a compensatory tax and a tax credit.

Competent Authority

The competent authorities of a country are the persons responsible for its tax administration. Revenue Canada is the competent authority for the purposes of Canadian tax treaties. The competent authorities are responsible for resolving disputes and questions of treaty interpretation.

Compilation

The presentation of financial statement information by the entity without the accountant's assurance as to conformity with Generally Accepted Accounting Principles (GAAP). In performing this accounting service, the accountant must conform to the AICPA Statements on Standards for Accounting and Review Services (SSARS).

Completed Contract

A method of revenue recognition for long-term contracts in which the revenue is not reported on the income statement until the contract has been completed.

Compound Annual Growth Rate (CAGR)

The year over year growth rate applied to an investment or other part of a company's activities over a multiple-year period. The formula for calculating CAGR is (Current Value / Base Value) / # of years) — 1.

Compounding

The process of accumulating and reinvesting interest in an investment over time to earn even more interest.

Compound Interest

Interest earned on both the initial principal and the interest reinvested from prior periods.

Compound Journal Entry

A journal entry that involves more than one debit or more than one credit or both.

Compulsory Liquidation

The winding-up of a company by a court. A petition must be presented both at the court and the registered office of the company. Those by whom it may be presented include: the company, the directors, a creditor, an official receiver, and the Secretary of State for Trade and Industry. The grounds on which a company may be wound up by the court include: a special resolution of the company that it be wound up by the court; that the company is unable to pay its debts; that the number of members is reduced below two; or that the court is of the opinion that it would be just and equitable for the company to be wound up. The court may appoint a provisional liquidator after the winding-up petition has been presented; it may also appoint a special manager to manage the company's property. On the grant of the order for winding-up, the official receiver becomes the liquidator and continues in office until some other person is appointed, either by the creditors or the members.

Conditional Sale Contract

A form of borrowing whereby the title to an asset purchased on credit does not pass to the buyer until all the payments, usually plus interest, are made.

Conduit Companies

Conduit companies are intermediary companies which are used normally for tax treaty advantages. One can create intermediary licensing or finance companies, for example, as conduit vehicles to reduce the impact of foreign withholding taxes.

Conservatism, Conservative

A prudent reaction to uncertainty to ensure that risks inherent in business situations are adequately considered — often phrased as "anticipate possible losses but not possible gains". In situations where the accountant cannot decide on the superiority of one of two accounting treatments on the basis of accounting principles alone, being conservative means choosing the treatment that has the least favourable impact on the income of the current period.

Consideration

The money value of a transaction (number of shares multiplied by the price) before adding commission, stamp duty, etc.

Consignment

When goods are offered for sale on behalf of another without the seller actually purchasing or taking title to the goods. Only when there is a subsequent sale does the owner receive any payment.

Consistency

Treatment of like transactions in the same way in consecutive periods so that financial statements will be comparable. The reporting policy implying that procedures, once adopted, should be followed from period to period by a company.

Consistency Principle

Requires accountants to apply the same methods and procedures from period to period. When they change a method from one period to another they must explain the change clearly on the financial statements.

Consol

A perpetual bond.

Consolidated Entity

A user-defined combination of several consolidation units, grouped together for consolidation and reporting purposes.

Consolidated Financial Statements, Consolidation

Consolidation is a method of preparing financial statements for a group of corporations linked by ownership as if they were a single corporation. Consolidated financial statements recognize that the separate legal entities are components of one economic unit. They are distinguishable from the separate parent and subsidiary corporations' statements, and from combined statements of affiliated corporations.

Consolidated Goodwill

A form of Goodwill arising only when companies' financial statements are combined in Purchase Method consolidation.

Consolidated Revenue Fund

The general pool of all income of the federal government, such as tax, tariff, and licence fee income, and profits from Crown corporations. All money received by the federal government must be credited to this fund and be properly accounted for.

Consolidation

A merger in which an entirely new firm is created and both the acquired and acquiring firm cease to exist.

Constructive Dividends

These are normally payments to non-resident related parties which are not dividends declared in conformity to company law, but which nevertheless are hidden distributions of profit. Thus excessive interest or other payments which do not meet the arm's length principle in transfer pricing may be treated as constructive dividends, with the result that the expenses are disallowed for corporate income tax purposes, and withholding taxes may then be levied on such excessive payments as if they were dividends, subject to the provisions of any relevant double tax treaty.

Consular Declaration

A formal statement to the consul of a foreign country declaring the merchandise to be shipped.

Consummate

To bring to completion or fruition; conclude, e.g., consummate a business transaction.

Consumption Taxes

Taxes on consumption — purchases of goods and services — levied by both the federal and provincial governments. Federal consumption taxes consist mainly of GST and excise taxes on motor fuel, tobacco products and alcoholic beverages. Provincial consumption taxes consist mainly of retail sales taxes, and provincial taxes on motive fuel and tobacco products.

Continental Shelf

This describes the area outside of the territorial waters of a particular country, which is not regarded as part of the country's territory, but over which that country has certain rights, in particular with regard to the exploration and exploitation of natural resources.

Contingency

An economic event (especially a negative one) that is in the process of occurring and so is not yet resolved. Contingencies would include, but are not limited to, pending or threatened litigation, threat of expropriation of assets, guarantees of the indebtedness of others, and possible liabilities arising from discounted bills of exchange or promissory notes.

Contingency Planning

Taking into account the managerial options implicit in a project.

Contingent Liability

A liability that is dependent upon uncertain events that may occur in the future. In corporate reports, are pending lawsuits, judgments under appeal, disputed claims, and the like, representing potential financial liability.

Contra Account

Accounts established to accumulate certain deductions from an asset, liability, or owners' equity item. (1) The reduction to the gross cost of an asset to arrive at the net cost; also known as a *valuation allowance*; e.g., accumulated depreciation is a contra account to the original cost of a fixed asset to arrive at the book value; or (2) the reduction of a liability to arrive at its carrying value, e.g., bond discount, which is a reduction of bonds payable.

Contract

A contract is an oral or written agreement between or among parties, setting out each party's responsibilities and specifying actions agreed to and resulting payments or other settlements.

Contractee

The person or entity who will receive the goods or services under the provisions of the contract.

Contract Note

On the same day as a bargain takes place, a member of the firm must send the client a contract note detailing the transaction, including full title of the stock, price, consideration and stamp duty (if applicable).

Contractor

The person or entity who will provide the goods or services under the provisions of the contract.

Contract Revenues

The revenues recognized under percentage of completion method.

Contractual Allowance

In healthcare, is the difference between what hospitals bill and what they receive in payment from third party payers, most commonly government programs; also known as contractual adjustment.

Contributed Capital

See Paid-in-Capital.

Contributed Surplus

The difference between the legal Par value (or Stated value) of a share and the cash or other consideration received by the company when the share was issued. Also referred to with terms like "capital in excess of par value". Does not apply to No-par shares, which are the usual kind in Canada.

Contribution Margin (CM)

The difference between sales and the variable costs of the product or service, also called marginal income. It is the amount of money available to cover fixed costs and generate profits.

Contribution Margin Ratio

The computation showing Contribution Margin as a percentage of sales.

Control Account

An account used to contain the aggregate amounts of many detailed transactions and so help to prevent or detect errors in the detailed records. The accounts receivable control account, for example, should have the same total as the sum of all the individual customers' accounts receivable. Control accounts with detailed backup include cash, accounts receivable, inventory, accumulated amortization, accounts payable, sales tax due, employee deductions due, and share capital.

Control Block

An interest controlling 50 per cent of outstanding votes plus one; thereby it may decide the fate of the firm.

Controllable Expense

An expense that managers have the power to influence, e.g., salaries or travel & entertainment.

Controlled Foreign Affiliate

A controlled foreign affiliate is a foreign affiliate controlled by a domestic taxpayer. Control generally refers to a direct or indirect ownership interest of at least 50% of the shares.

Controlled Foreign Corporation

CFCs are now part of the anti-avoidance tax legislation of many countries and denotes foreign corporations, often resident in low tax countries, whose shares are more than 50%

owned by domestic shareholders. Base companies may often be CFCs depending upon their degree of ownership.

Controller

Usually an experienced accountant who directs internal accounting processes and procedures, including cost accounting.

Conversion Premium

Difference between the conversion price and the current stock price divided by the current stock price.

Conversion Price

The dollar amount of a bond's par value that is exchangeable for one share of stock.

Conversion Ratio

The number of shares per $1,000 bond received for conversion into stock.

Conversion Value

The value of a convertible bond if it was immediately converted into common stock.

Convertible

A bond or share that can be changed into another kind of security, usually a preferred share that can be converted into a common share.

Convertible Bond

A bond that can be exchanged for a fixed number of shares of stock for a specified amount of time.

Convertible Currency

Any national currency that can be easily exchanged for that of another country.

Convertible Debenture

A debenture that can be exchanged for common shares at a specified rate and date.

Convertible Debt

A debt instrument which can be exercised into the security of the debtor in accordance with the conditions set forth in the debt instrument.

Convertible Preferred Share

A share that can be exchanged for common shares at a specified rate and date.

COO

An acronym for Chief Operating Officer. The COO is responsible for the day-to-day management of a company. The COO usually reports to the CEO.

"Cooking the Books"

When a company fraudulently misrepresents the financial condition of a company by providing false or misleading information.

Cooperative Advertising

A joint advertising strategy under which costs are shared; e.g., by a manufacturer and another firm that distributes its products.

Copyright

A form of legal protection used to safeguard original literary works, performing arts, sound recordings, visual arts, original software code and renewals.

Core Process

A process is a set of related and interdependent activities that transform an input to a system to an output with added value to a customer. It is the transformation of people, money, materials or information that is the value-added work of the organization. The Core Processes are those by which the organization creates its most value-added and essential transformations for the customers.

Corporate Governance

Rules and practices relating to how corporations are governed by management, directors, and shareholders.

Corporate Group

A group of corporations linked by common or mutual ownership.

Corporate Tax

Tax on corporate income in Canada. In addition, Canadian corporations pay a variety of taxes and other levies to the various levels of government in Canada. These include capital and insurance premium taxes; payroll levies (e.g., health taxes, Unemployment Insurance, Canada Pension Plan, Quebec Pension Plan, Workers' Compensation); property taxes; and indirect taxes, such as sales and excise taxes, levied on business inputs.

Corporation

A legal entity with or without share capital, legally separate from those who own it or work as a part of it. It enjoys most of the rights and responsibilities of a person except for those that only an actual person can enjoy. Its main feature is limited liability; in other words, only the assets of the company can be claimed by creditors, not the assets of owners.

Corporation Tax

The tax payable by corporations.

Correspondent Bank

A bank having communications and business links with the seller's bank.

Corresponding Adjustment

Where a country considers certain payments to be excessive according to the arm's length principle, they will seek to adjust taxable profits by the disallowance of such excessive payments. However, the related or other party in a second country may have declared the original receipt of income on which tax may have been paid, and a corresponding adjustment would denote the reduction of such taxable profits to eliminate the excessive portion of income from tax.

Cost

The amount of money that must be paid to take ownership of something; expense or purchase price.

Cost Accounting

A managerial accounting activity designed to help managers identify, measure, and control operating costs.

Cost Allocation

Spreading the cost of an asset out over the periods in which it is useful.

Cost Avoidance

An action taken in the present designed to decrease costs in the future.

Cost Basis

In securities, is the purchase price after commissions or other expenses. It is used to calculate capital gains or losses when the security is eventually sold.

Cost-Benefit Analysis

The method of measuring the benefits anticipated from a decision by determining the cost of the decision, then deciding whether the benefit outweighs the cost of that decision.

Cost Center

A non-revenue-producing element of an organization, where costs are separately figured and allocated, and for which someone has formal organizational responsibility.

Cost Driver

Any activity or series of activities that takes place within an organization and causes costs to be incurred. Cost drivers are used in a system of activity-based costing to charge costs to products or services. Cost drivers are applied to cost pools, which relate to common activities. Cost drivers are not restricted to departments or sections, as more than one activity may be identified within a department.

Cost Flow Assumption

An assumption made about the order in which units of inventory move into and out of an enterprise, used to compute inventory asset value and cost of goods sold expense in cases where the order of flow is not or cannot be identified. Possible assumptions include FIFO, LIFO, and weighted average.

Cost Object

Any activity or item for which a separate measurement of cost is desired.

Cost of Capital

(1) The cost of raising debt or equity funds (e.g., the cost of borrowed funds is mostly the interest to be paid to the lender); (2) The rate of return that a business could earn if it so chose other investments with the equivalent risks. Also can be stated as *opportunity cost* of the funds used due to the investment decision.

Cost of Debt

The return that lenders require on the firm's debt.

Cost of Equity

The return that equity investors require on their investment in the firm.

Cost of Goods Sold (COGS)

A figure representing the cost of buying raw material and producing finished goods. Included are precise factors, i.e., material and factory labour; as well as others that are variable, such as factory overhead.

Cost-of-Living Lease

A lease where yearly increases are tied to the cost of living index.

Cost of Revenue

See Cost of Goods Sold.

Cost of Sales

See Cost of Goods Sold.

Cost per Thousand (CPM)

Advertising terminology used in buying media. CPM refers to the cost it takes to reach a thousand people within your target market.

Cost Plus Method

Where a company performs services in a particular country on behalf of a non-resident related party, the services should be charged according to the arm's length principle. In order to prevent transfer pricing adjustments, as well as to ensure that the profits of the foreign company are not treated as effectively connected to the local service company, an agreement may be reached with the tax administration to compute taxable profits of the service company according to a notional mark up based on expenses. Such a cost plus system of taxation may mean for example that taxable profits are computed at say between 5% and 25% of local expenses.

Cost Principle

The use of the historical cost of assets to value them on the balance sheet.

Cost Split

The breakdown of the costs associated with producing a product or providing a service. The makeup is dependent upon what costs are being analyzed, e.g., in manufacturing a company would track the cost split between materials, direct labour, and production overhead.

Counterparty

Second borrower in currency swap. Counterparty borrows funds in currency desired by principal.

Coupon

(1) On bearer stocks, the detachable part of the certificate exchangeable for dividends; (2) On bonds and debentures, the stated interest payments (e.g., 10 per cent coupon pays interest of 10 per cent per year).

Coupon Rate

The annual coupon divided by the face value of a bond.

Covenants

A promise by the firm, included in the debt contract, to perform certain acts. A restrictive covenant imposes constraints on the firm to protect the interests of the debt-holder.

Cover

The total net profit a company has available for distribution as dividend, divided by the amount paid, gives the number of times that the dividend is covered.

CP

An acronym with many possible meanings, e.g., Capacity Planning, Central Procurement, Change of Plan (insurance), Claims Procedure (insurance), Commercial Paper, Community Property, Consumer Products, Contingency Plan, Contract Price, Change Proposal, etc.

C.P.A.

Means Certified Public Accountant.

CPA Certified Public Accountant (a designation used especially in the United States)

See American Institute of Certified Public Accountants.

CPT

Cost per Thousand.

CR

In accounting, is an acronym for Credit Record.

CRAT

An acronym for Charitable Remainder Annuity Trust.

Creative Accounting

Slang for the concept of maintaining accounts giving possibly illegal or dubious benefits to the entity for which the accounts are maintained.

Credit (CR or Cr)

The right hand of double-entry accounting. The term credit can be used as a noun to refer to the right-hand side of a journal entry or account, or as a verb referring to the action of making an entry to the right-hand side of an account. Most accounts on the right-hand side of the balance sheets have credit balances (in other words, the credits to them exceed the debits to them). The term credit also refers to the right to buy or borrow on the promise of future payment. A credit journal entry to the liabilities and equity side of the balance sheet causes an increase in the account, while a credit to the assets side of the balance sheet causes a decrease.

Credit Analysis

The process of determining the probability that customers will or will not pay.

Credit Card

A card authorizing purchases on credit at a predetermined interest rate and payment conditions.

Credit Card Receipts

Sales revenue where payment has been made through the use of recognized/authorized credit cards versus cash or *cheque* receipts/payments.

Credit Cost Curve

Graphical representation of the sum of the carrying costs and the opportunity costs of a credit policy.

Credit Equivalent Value

Amount representing the credit risk exposure in off-balance sheet transactions. In the case of derivatives, credit equivalent value represents the potential cost at current market prices of replacing the contract's cash flows in the case of default by the counter-party.

Credit Instrument

The evidence of indebtedness.

Credit Method

The credit method provides relief from double taxation by allowing taxpayers a credit for foreign taxes paid by a Canadian resident.

Credit Notes

Issued to indicate a positive action within an account. Credit notes are issued for reasons such as overpayment, duplicate payment, damaged goods, returned merchandise, etc.

Creditor

One who extends credit (that is, gives someone the right to buy or borrow now in consideration of a promise to pay at a later date).

Creditors Turnover

Calculated as: Average creditors / (Credit Sales / 365).

Credit Period

The length of time that credit is granted.

Credit Risk

The risk that a counter-party to a transaction will fail to perform according to the terms and conditions of the contract, thus causing the holder of the claim to suffer a loss.

Credit Scoring

The process of quantifying the probability of default when granting consumer credit.

Credit Transaction

An economic exchange in which at least one party makes a promise to pay cash or other consideration later. This kind of transaction is recognized by most financial accounting systems, especially if it is a routine way of doing business.

Critical Event

A point in the revenue generation and collection process chosen to represent the earning of the revenue, and so the point at which the revenue is recognized in the accounts. This is a simplification: a common critical event is the point at which the customer takes delivery of the goods sold. Not all revenue is accounted for this way: some is allocated over more than one point in the process: long-term construction projects and franchise revenue are examples where the critical event simplification is generally not used.

Cross Border Transactions

Cross border transactions are those in which goods and/or services cross over national boundaries. Cross border transactions usually have international tax consequences.

Cross-Currency Interest Rate Swaps

A transaction involving the exchange of streams of interest rate payments (but not necessarily principal payments) in different currencies and often on different interest bases e.g., fixed Deutsche Mark against floating dollar, but also fixed Deutsche Mark against fixed dollar).

Cross-Currency Settlement Risk (or Herstatt Risk)

Risk relating to the settlement of foreign exchange contracts that arises when one of the parties to a contract pays out one currency prior to receiving payment of the other. Herstatt risk arises because the hours of operation of domestic interbank fund transfer systems often do not overlap due to time zone differences. In the interval between final settlements of each leg, counterparties are exposed to credit risk and market risk.

Cross-Hedging

Hedging an asset with contracts written on a closely related, but not identical, asset.

Cross-Rate

The implicit exchange rate between two currencies (usually non-U.S.) quoted in some third currency (usually the U.S. dollar).

Crown Corporation

A corporation that has been established by a nation's government.

CRUT

An acronym for Charitable Remainder Unitrust.

Cum

Latin for 'with', used in the abbreviations Cum Cap, Cum Div, Cum Rights and so on, to indicate that the buyer of a security is entitled to participate in the forthcoming capitalization issue, dividend or rights issue.

Cumulative Voting

Procedure where a shareholder may cast all votes for one member of the board of directors.

Currency Swaps

A transaction involving the exchange of cash flows and principal in one currency for those in another with an agreement to reverse the principal swap at a future date.

Current Assets

Cash and other assets such as temporary investments, inventory, receivables, and current prepayments that are realizable or will be consumed within the normal operating cycle of an enterprise (usually one year). See such current asset categories as Cash Equivalent Assets, Inventory, and Accounts receivable.

Current Cash Debt Ratio

Measures ability to pay current liabilities in given year with cash derived from operating activities. Calculated using net cash from operating activities divided by average current liabilities.

Current Cost Accounting

A system of accounting which adjusts for changing pricing.

Current Debt to Total Debt

Shows Current Liabilities as a per cent of Total Debt. Smaller firms carry proportionally higher level of current debt to total debt than larger firms.

Current Exposure Method

Term used in the Basle Capital Accord to denote a method of assessing credit risk in off-balance sheet transactions, consisting of adding the market-to-market replacement cost of all contracts with positive value and an add-on amount for potential credit exposure arising from future price or volatility changes.

Current Liabilities

Debts or estimated claims on the resources of a firm that are expected to be paid within the normal operating cycle of an enterprise (usually one year).

Current Maturities-L/T/D

That portion of long term obligations which is due within the next fiscal year.

Current Ratio

A comparison of current assets to current liabilities, is a commonly used measure of short-run solvency, i.e., the immediate ability of a firm to pay its current debts as they come due. Also called the Working Capital Ratio. Current Ratio is particularly important to a company thinking of borrowing money or getting credit from their suppliers. Potential creditors use this ratio to measure a company's liquidity or ability to pay off short-term debts. Though acceptable ratios may vary from industry to industry below 1.00 is not atypical for high quality companies with easy access to capital markets to finance unexpected cash requirements. Smaller companies, however, should have higher current ratios to meet unexpected cash requirements. The rule of thumb Current Ratio for small companies is 2:1, indicating the need for a level of safety in the ability to cover unforeseen cash needs from current assets. Current Ratio is best compared to the industry.

Current (or Market) Value

The estimated sale value of an asset, settlement value of a debt, or trading value of an equity share.

Current Value Accounting

A proposed accounting method that would use current or market values to value assets and liabilities and to calculate income.

Custodian Bank

The bank that acts as a custodian to a mutual fund. Does not manage anything, just holds the cash and securities and does the clerical.

Customs

The authorities charged with collecting duty and controlling the entry of merchandise into a country.

Customs Broker

An individual or firm licensed to process entry and clear goods into the country for another.

Cut Off

The end of a fiscal period and the procedures used to ensure accuracy in measuring phenomena up to that date.

Cut-Off Rate

The predetermined maximum rate and/or minimum rate at which the subject is still acceptable, but where a rate above the proscribed higher or below the proscribed lower rate is no longer acceptable.

Cut-Off Yield

In securities, is the yield at which or below which the bids are accepted.

Cycle Count

A partial count of a single inventory location as opposed to a Complete Count, i.e., a complete count of a single inventory location. An organization should not wait to do a complete count; usually once a year. The best way to ensure that a minimum of 97% accuracy is maintained in inventory on an ongoing basis is to continually count your products. That is, count part of your inventory every day, and count each item several times per year. This process is called "cycle counting".

DAC

In accounting, is an acronym for Deferred Acquisition Costs.

Date Draft

A payment option draft that matures in a specified number of days after the date issued.

Date of Payment

Date on the dividend cheques.

Date of Record

Date on which holders of record are designated to receive a dividend.

Days Inventory

Shows the average length of time items are in inventory, i.e., how many days a business could continue selling using only its existing inventory. The goal, in most cases, is to demonstrate efficiency through having a high turnover rate and therefore a low days' inventory. However, realize that this ratio can be unfavourable if either too high or too low. A company must balance the cost of carrying inventory with its unit and acquisition costs. The cost of carrying inventory can be 25% to 35%. These costs include warehousing, material handling, taxes, insurance, depreciation, interest and obsolescence.

Days' Sales in Receivables

The ratio of accounts receivable to the daily sales, expressed in number of days' sales represented by accounts receivable. Also called Collection Ratio.

Days Sales Outstanding (DSO)

The average collection period on accounts receivable for sales revenue.

DBA (Doing Business As)

A legal entity (sole proprietorship, partnership, corporation) conducting business under any chosen name for which a business licence has been issued.

DCF

See Discounted Cash Flows, another phrase for "present value" analysis of future cash flows.

Debenture

A form of Security taken by a creditor on a loan or bond, in which the creditor has a general ability to influence or direct management decisions if the debt payments are not made on schedule; not a claim on a specific asset as a Mortgage has.

Debenture

A loan raised by a company paying a fixed rate of interest, usually with a maturity of 10 years or more, and secured on the general, rather than specific, assets of the company. Being an unsecured debt instrument, it is somewhat riskier than a bond.

Debit (DR or Dr)

The left-hand side of double-entry accounting. The term debit can be used as a noun to refer to the left-hand side of a journal entry or account or as a verb referring to the action of making an entry on the left-hand side of an account. Most accounts (except contra accounts) on the left-hand side of the balance sheet have debit balances, which means the debits to them exceed the credits to them. A debit will increase the amounts on the asset side of the balance sheet, but decrease the amounts on the liabilities and equity side.

Debit Card

An automated teller machine card used at the point of purchase to avoid the use of cash. As this is not a credit card, money must be available in the user's bank account.

Debit Memorandum

Can be either a) a form or document given by the bank to a depositor to notify that the depositor's balance is being decreased due to some event other than the payment of depositor originated *cheque*, e.g., bank service charges; or b) a form of document used by a seller to notify a buyer that the seller is debiting (increasing) the amount of the buyer's accounts payable due to errors or other factors requiring adjustments.

Debit Notes

Issued to indicate a short payment.

Debt

An obligation to make a future payment in return for a benefit already received.

Debt Capacity

The ability to borrow to increase firm value.

Debt Covenant

One of many terms used to describe rules governing the loans that a company has outstanding. Other related phrases would be "loan terms" "credit agreement," "loan agreement".

Debt Financing

Raising money through selling bonds, notes, or mortgages or borrowing directly from financial institutions. You must repay borrowed money in full, usually in installments, with interest. A lender incurs risk and charges a corresponding rate of interest based on that risk. The lender usually assesses a variety of factors such as the strength of your business plan, management capabilities, financing, and your past personal credit history, to evaluate your company's chances of success.

Debt Ratio

Measures the per cent of total funds provided by creditors. Debt includes both current liabilities and long-term debt. Creditors prefer low debt ratios because the lower the ratio, the greater the cushion against creditor's losses in liquidation. Owners may seek high debt ratios, either to magnify earnings or because selling new stock would mean giving up control. Owners want control while "using someone else's money". Debt Ratio is best compared to industry data to determine if a company is possibly over or under leveraged. The right level of debt for a business depends on many factors. Some advantages of higher debt levels are:

- The deductibility of interest from business expenses can provide tax advantages.

- Returns on equity can be higher.

- Debt can provide a suitable source of capital to start or expand a business.

Some disadvantages can be:

- Sufficient cash flow is required to service a higher debt load. The need for this cash flow can place pressure on a business if income streams are erratic.

- Susceptibility to interest rate increases.

- Directing cash flow to service debt may starve expenditure in other areas such as development which can be detrimental to overall survival of the business.

Debt Security

When you invest in a debt security, you are lending your money to a government or company (the issuer) to help pay for their operations or major projects. In return for the use of your money, the issuer pays you interest plus the face value of the investment when it matures. Short-term debt securities include money market instruments such as treasury bills, bankers' acceptances and commercial paper. Long-term debt securities include fixed income investments such as government and corporate bonds, and mortgage-backed securities.

Debt to Assets Ratio

Total liabilities divided by total assets.

Debt to Equity Ratio

Total liabilities divided by total equity. Measures the risk of the firm's capital structure in terms of amounts of capital contributed by creditors and that contributed by owners. It expresses the protection provided by owners for the creditors. In addition, low Debt/Equity ratio implies ability to borrow. While using debt implies risk (required interest payments must be paid), it also introduces the potential for increased benefits to the firm's owners. When debt is used successfully (operating earnings exceeding interest charges) the returns to shareholders are magnified through financial leverage. Depending on the industry, different ratios are acceptable. The company should be compared to the industry, but, generally, a 3:1 ratio is a general benchmark. Should a company have debt-to-equity ratio that exceeds this number; it will be a major impediment to obtaining additional financing. If the ratio is suspect and you find the company's working capital, and current/quick ratios drastically low, this is a sign of *serious* financial weakness.

Debt to Total Assets Ratio

Measures the percentage of assets financed by all terms of debt, includes both current and long term debt.

Decelerated Amortization

The opposite of accelerated amortization or depreciation. Not acceptable for most enterprises.

Decision Relevance

An accounting objective: information should be available to the user at a time and in a form that is useful to the user's decision-making.

Declaration Date

Date on which the board of directors passes a resolution to pay a dividend.

Declining Balance Amortization

An accelerated amortization (depreciation) method in which the annual amortization (depreciation) expense is calculated as a fixed percentage of the book value of the asset, which declines over time as amortization is deducted.

Deemed Domicile

As for deemed settlor below, local tax legislation may deem an individual to have fiscal domicile locally for say inheritance tax purposes where, although not domiciled under legal provisions relating to domicile, the individual has been resident locally for a certain length of time.

Deemed Settlor

The settlor of a trust may nominally be an individual or company, but the real transferor of assets either initially through a back-to-back arrangement, or by reason of a subsequent transfer of assets, may be considered as the deemed settlor, or the *de facto* settlor.

Default Risk Premium

The portion of a nominal interest rate or bond yield that represents compensation for the possibility of default.

Defeasance Clause

The clause in a mortgage that permits the mortgagor to redeem his or her property upon the payment of the obligations to the mortgagee.

Deferral

Part of accrual accounting but often used as the opposite to an accrual. A deferral involves keeping a past cash receipt or payment on the balance sheet, in other words, putting it on the income statement as revenue or expense at a later time. An example is recognizing a deferred revenue liability resulting from a recent cash receipt, such as for a magazine subscription to be delivered later. (In contrast, accruals involve recording a revenue or expense before the cash receipt or payment occurs.)

Deferral Method

A way of accounting for future income tax expenses incurred by present activities, now largely replaced by future income tax liability estimates.

Deferred

In accounting, is any account where the asset or liability is not realized until a future date, e.g., annuities, charges, taxes, income, etc. The deferred item may be carried, dependent on type of deferral, as either an asset or liability.

Deferred Asset

An amount owed to an entity that is not expected to be received by that entity within one year from the date of the balance sheet.

Deferred Call

Call provision prohibiting the company from redeeming the bond before a certain date.

Deferred Charge

A non-current Prepaid expense, in which the costs of issuing bonds, incorporation costs, or other expenditures benefiting several future periods are shown as non-current assets and usually amortized to expense over several periods or otherwise charged to expenses in some future period.

Deferred Development Costs

The non-recognition of costs of development until some such condition(s) is satisfied.

Deferred Income Tax (Expense and Liability)

An expense account and corresponding liability intended to recognize the future tax consequences of income reported on the current income statement but not to be reported on the tax return until a future period. Now largely replaced by future income tax liability estimates.

Deferred Payment Credit

A type of a letter of credit where payment is made at a specified interval after collection papers are submitted.

Deferred Revenue

A liability account used for customer deposits or other cash receipts prior to the completion of the sale (for example, before delivery).

Deferred Taxes

A business accounting concept. Income for tax purposes must always be calculated and taxes paid in accordance with the rules set out in the *Income Tax Act*. However, businesses' methods of calculating their income for financial statement purposes often differ from those used for tax purposes, and thus companies' income for financial statement purposes will often differ from (and appear greater than) the income on which businesses actually have to pay taxes. In order to reconcile these two amounts in their books, businesses use the accounting concept of deferred taxes.

Deficit

Negative retained earnings and sometimes also used to refer to negative earnings.

Degree of Operating Leverage

The percentage change in operating cash flow relative to the percentage change in quantity sold.

Delinquency Ratio

The ratio of past-due loans to total number of loans serviced.

Delivery

The most common basis of recognizing revenue. Revenue is said to be earned when the product or service has been delivered to the customer.

Delta

In securities trading, is the relationship between an option price and the underlying futures contract or stock price. In general usage, it is the difference between two empirical data points, e.g., the *delta* between 4 and 6 is 2.

Deminimus

Root is '*De minimis non curat lex*' (Latin), a common law principle whereby judges will not sit in judgement of extremely minor transgressions of the law. It has been restated as "the law does not concern itself with trifles". It is commonly used to include a test of anyone judging conformance to accounting principles, regulations or rules.

Demographics

The attributes such as income, age, and occupation that best describe your target market.

Demutualization

The legal process of a life insurance company shifting from mutual ownership by policy-holders to shareholder ownership.

Departure Tax

Many countries levy an exit or departure tax when individuals, companies or trusts transfer their residence abroad. The departure tax would be based on the market value of assets held by the individual, company or trust, the cost of which assets would then be deducted to arrive at a notional capital gain on transfer of residence; capital gains at the appropriate rate would then be levied as the departure tax.

Dependent Agent

The term "dependent agent" is a tax treaty concept that refers to a person who acts on behalf of another person and who exercises contractual authority on behalf of that other person. The concept of dependent agent is important in determining whether a non-resident person has a permanent establishment in a country.

Depletion

An amortization (depreciation) method used for physically wasting assets such as natural resources.

Depository Account

Those accounts where assets, e.g., cash or securities, are placed on deposit in favour of the depositor.

Depreciated Historical Cost (DHC)

The method of valuation of certain assets at the actual cost of their acquisition and subsequent enhancement less a reduction for depreciation to date.

Depreciation

The recognition of the expense due to use of the economic value of fixed tangible assets (for example, trucks, building, or plant).

Depreciation

The amount of expense charged against earnings by a company to write off the cost of a plant or machine over its useful life, giving consideration to wear and tear, obsolescence, and salvage value. If the expense is assumed to be incurred in equal amounts in each business period over the life of the asset, the depreciation method used is straight line (SL). If the expense is assumed to be incurred in decreasing amounts in each business period over the life of the asset, the method used is said to be accelerated. Two commonly used variations of the accelerated method of depreciating an asset are the sum-of-years digits (SYD) and the double-declining balance (DDB) methods. Frequently, accelerated depreciation is chosen for a business' tax expense but straight line is chosen for its financial reporting purposes. Usage, at least in Canada, appears to be changing to replace the term depreciation with the more general term amortization.

Depreciation Tax Shield

See CCA Tax Shield.

Derivative

A transaction or contract whose value depends on or, as the name implies, derives from the value of underlying assets such as stock, bonds, mortgages, market indices, or foreign currencies. One party with exposure to unwanted risk can pass some or all of the risk to a second party. The first party can assume a different risk from a second party, pay the second party to assume the risk, or, as is often the case, create a combination. Derivatives are normally used to control exposure or risk.

Derivative Securities

Securities whose returns depend on the price of an underlying asset and that allow market participants to offset the exposure of their cash market positions.

Destination Principle

This principle applies to Value Added Taxation and under EC Directives requires VAT to be paid where goods are consumed, rather than in the exporting country.

Devaluation

In economics, is the lowering in value of one currency in relation to other currencies.

Development

Normally refers to a) improving a product or producing new types of products; or b) in real estate, process of placing improvements on or to a parcel of land.

Diluted Earnings per Share

Earnings per share, including common stock, preferred stock, unexercised stock options, and some convertible debt. Diluted earnings per share are usually a more accurate reflection of the company's real earning power.

Dilution

Loss in existing shareholders' value, in either ownership, market value, book value, or EPS.

Diminishing Balance

Another name for Declining Balance Amortization.

Direct Attribution

The most precise method of costing an output. It seeks to capture accurately the volume and cost of resources used by particular activities. This can be expensive unless the information is already available because it requires detailed measurement of actual costs. Such direct measurement is seldom justifiable solely to improve the accuracy of a cost system, but many institutions use this method to obtain efficiency gains and cost savings.

Direct Bankruptcy Costs

The costs that are directly associated with bankruptcy, such as legal and administrative expenses.

Direct Cost

That portion of cost that is directly expended in providing a product or service for sale and is included in the calculation of Cost of Goods Sold, e.g., labour and inventory (it can be traced to a given cost object in an economically feasible manner).

Direct Expense

That portion of expense that is directly expended in providing a product or service for sale and is included in the calculation of Cost of Goods Sold, e.g., labour and inventory.

Direct Method of Cash Flow Analysis

A method of preparing the Cash Flow Statement, especially the Cash from Operations section, using records of cash receipts and disbursements instead of the adjustments to net income used in the more traditional Indirect method of cash flow analysis.

Directors Valuation

A valuation that is not an independent valuation.

Direct Write-Off

Transferring the cost of an asset to an expense or loss account by removing the amount entirely from the asset account. Used in cases where there is no prior allowance for the expense or loss, so used when there is no Contra Account such as Accumulated Amortization or Allowance for Doubtful Accounts.

Disability Insurance

In the United States, is a payroll tax required in some states that is deducted from employee *paycheques* to insure income during periods where an employee is unable to work due to an injury or illness.

Disbursement

The paying out of money to satisfy a debt or an expense.

Disbursements

See Cash Disbursements.

Disclosure

Provision of information about economic events beyond that included in the financial statement figures. Usually given in the notes to the financial statements, but also provided outside the financial statements in press releases, speeches, and other announcements.

Disclosure Document Program

In the United States, is a form of legal protection that safeguards intellectual property while it is in its development stages.

Disclosure Principle

States that any and all information that affects the full understanding of a company's financial statements must be included with the financial statements. Some items may not affect the ledger accounts directly. These would be included in the form of accompanying notes. Examples of such items are outstanding lawsuits, tax disputes, and company takeovers.

Discontinued Operations

Portions of the business that the enterprise has decided not to keep going and/or to sell to others. It is good practice to separate the effects of discontinued operations from continuing operations when measuring income and cash flow.

Discount

(1) Calculate the present value of some future amount; (2) When the market price of a newly issued security is lower than the issue price. If it is higher, the difference is called the premium.

Discounted Cash Flow

A valuation method best used to evaluate a business established for the purpose of fulfilling a specific project, in certain startup and other companies where cash flow is more important than net income, and when a certain time frame is set where an investor wishes to see his investment returned over a specific period of time. In discounted cash flow, the present value of liabilities is subtracted from the combined present value of cash flow and tangible assets, which determines the value of the business.

Discounted Cash Flow (DCF) Valuation

The process of valuing an investment by discounting its future cash flows.

Discounted Earnings

Determines the value of a business based upon the present value of projected future earnings, discounted by the required rate of return (capitalization rate). Usually, the question is how well earnings are projected.

Discounted Payback Period

The length of time required for an investment's discounted cash flows to equal its initial cost.

Discount Note

Debt security that is sold at less than face value and matures at face value. A treasury bill is an example of a discount note.

Discount on Bonds

Arises when bonds are issued at a price below their legal face value, such as a $100 bond being issued for $95 cash, indicating a $5 discount.

Discount Rate

(1) The rate used to calculate the present value of future cash flows; (2) The interest rate that the Federal Reserve of the U.S. Government charges a U.S. bank to borrow funds when a bank is temporarily short of funds. Collateral is necessary to borrow, and such borrowing is quite limited because the Fed views it as a privilege to be used to meet short-term liquidity needs, and not a device to increase earnings.

Discount Swaps

Also called off-market swaps, in which the fixed payments are low market rates. At the end of the swap, the shortfall is made up by one large payment. The credit risk taken on by the fixed rate recipient (usually the bank) increases with the discount applied to interest rates.

Discrepancy

In import/export, is a situation relating to official documents that are presented that do not conform to what is required within the Letter of Credit.

Discretionary

Means it is not mandatory, it is up to the individual or company.

Discretionary Accrual

A non-mandatory expense/asset that is recorded within the accounting system that has yet to be realized. An example of this would be management 'bonus'.

Discretionary Expenses

Expenses that depend on management's discretion rather than on the necessities of producing, selling, or shipping goods and services. Examples might be donations, political contributions, some maintenance and warranty costs, and bonuses not specifically called for in employment contracts.

Discretionary Income

Means the amount of a company's income available for spending after the essentials have been met.

Discretionary Trust

The form of trust usually established offshore. The "discretions" are vested in the trustee who can usually decide which of the beneficiaries is to benefit, when and to what extent. Discretions are exercised under advice of, or suggestions from the settlor or protector.

Distributions

Payments from fund or corporate cash flow (e.g., payment of a mutual fund's income to its unit holders). May include dividends from earnings, capital gains from sale of portfolio holdings and return of capital. Fund distributions can be made by cheque or by investing in additional shares. Funds are required to distribute capital gains (if any) to shareholders at least once per year. Some corporations offer Dividend Reinvestment Plans (D.R.P.).

DIT

See Deferred Income Tax.

Diversification

Investment in more than one asset, whose returns do not move proportionally in the same direction at the same time thus reducing risk.

Dividend(s)

"Dividends" refer to income from shares or other corporate rights (other than debt-claims) that participate in profits. In general terms, dividend income must be attributable to the ownership of shares or other units of equity ownership carrying a right to participate in profits. Since this type of payment does not relate to the operating performance of the company, it is placed on the statement of retained earnings and not the income statement. Dividend payments are made either in the form of cash or stock.

Dividend Capitalization

Since most closely held companies do not pay dividends, when using dividend capitalization valuators must first determine dividend paying capacity of a business. Dividend paying capacity based on average net income and on average cash flow are used. To determine dividend paying capacity, near term capital needs, expansion plans, debt repayment, operation cushion, contractual requirements, past dividend paying history of a business and dividends of a comparable company should be investigated. After analyzing these factors, per cent of average net income and of average cash flow that can be used for the payment of dividends can be estimated. What also must be determined is the dividend yield, which can best be determined by analyzing comparable companies. As with the price earnings ratio method, this usually produces a subjective result.

Dividend Capture

A strategy in which an investor purchases securities to own them on the day of record and then quickly sells them; designed to attain dividends but avoid the risk of a lengthy hold.

Dividend Cover

See Dividend Payout Ratio.

Dividend Growth Model

Model that determines the current price of a stock as its dividend next period, divided by the discount rate less the dividend growth rate.

Dividend Payout Ratio

A measure of the percentage of earnings paid out in dividends; computed by dividing cash dividends by the net income available to each class of stock.

Dividend Stripping

This term basically denotes the payment of dividends out of retained earnings upon acquisition of a company. If the dividends are received tax free and are not offset against acquisition costs by the effect of anti-avoidance legislation, a high base cost is generated for capital gains tax purposes whilst the company is now stripped of reserves and is therefore valueless, thereby creating the ability to incur a capital loss to be offset against other capital gains.

Dividend Tax Credit

Tax formula that reduces the effective tax rate on dividends.

Dividend Yield

A stock's cash dividend divided by its current price.

Division

A self sufficient unit within a company. A division contains all the functions necessary to operate independently from the parent company.

Dock Receipt

A document issued by the ocean carrier of a shipment acknowledging receipt of the goods to be shipped.

Documentary Credit

An arrangement by banks for settling international business transactions. A letter of credit is a form of documentary credit.

Dollar Control Systems

Systems used in inventory management that reveal the cost and gross profit margin on individual inventory items.

Dollar-Cost-Averaging

Investing a fixed amount in a security at regular intervals. You buy more of the security when its price is low and less when its price is high. Over time, this usually results in a lower average cost.

Dollar Value LIFO

In the U.S., is a method of expressing the value of an inventory in monetary values rather than units. Each homogeneous group of inventory items is converted into base-year prices by using the appropriate price indices. The difference between opening and closing inventories is a measure in monetary terms of the change in the financial period.

Dollar-Weighted Rate of Return

Also called the internal rate of return, the interest rate that makes the present value of the cash flows from all the sub-periods in an evaluation period plus the terminal market value of the portfolio equal to the initial market value of the portfolio.

Domicile

Under English common law, one's domicile is his/her permanent home and the place to which he/she intends to return. Your domicile is the means by which you are connected with a certain system of law for certain legal purposes such as marriage, divorce, succession of estate and taxation. The English definition of "domicile" differs from the continental definitions of fiscal domicile, which may simply be where a person is resident for a particular tax year.

Doomsday Ratio

Related to the quick (acid test) ratio in that it is a conservative approach to debt coverage. The doomsday ratio only considers the cash on hand when evaluating if an entity can cover their current liabilities. The approach is that if the business were to go bankrupt today, would the business have enough cash on hand to cover current debts. The ratio is considered a good indicator of the cash cushion of safety. It may spot cash shortages, thereby assisting in avoiding a credit crisis. It is calculated: Cash divided by Current Liabilities.

Double Dipping

This term is frequently used for leasing arrangements where for example the lessor can claim tax deductions in one country, whilst a related lessee in another jurisdiction can also obtain depreciation or other deductions against taxable profits.

Double-Entry Accounting

A system of recording transactions in a way that maintains the equality of the accounting equation. The accounting technique records each transaction as both a credit and a debit. Double-entry bookkeeping (DEB) or accounting was developed during the fifteenth century and was first recorded in 1494 as a system by the Italian mathematician Luca Pacioli.

Double-Entry Bookkeeping

See Double-Entry Accounting.

Double Exit

Use of two passports for the purpose of confusion or convenience.

Dr

An ancient Italian abbreviation for the Italian word 'debare'; meaning 'debit' (not to be confused with the acronym DR with both letters in uppercase).

DR

In accounting, is an acronym for Debit Record.

Draft

In import/export, is a contract between buyer and seller that the buyer will pay a certain amount of money, within a specified period of time, for the goods purchased.

Draft, Demand or Sight

In import/export, is a draft payable upon presentation to the drawee. It may be used when the exporter wishes to retain control of the shipment for credit or title retention reasons. The buyer must pay the bank before receiving the documents to take custody of the goods. A COD shipment is similar.

Drawee

The buyer of a draft instrument.

DSO

In accounting, is an acronym that usually means 'Days Sales Outstanding'.

Dual Resident Companies

Companies may be resident in two or more countries according to local tax law definitions of residence. Thus a company incorporated in the U.S. will be a U.S. tax resident, whilst a company managed and controlled in the UK would be UK tax resident. This used to enable double dipping advantages to be obtained by the deduction of the same expense, commonly interest, against taxable profits in two jurisdictions, but local tax legislation and double tax treaty provisions attempt to clarify taxing rights within one country, and restrict the use of dual resident companies to obtain tax benefits.

Due Diligence

Usually refers to an internal audit of a target firm by an acquiring firm.

Dumping

The selling of merchandise in a foreign country at, or, below cost in order to seize market share.

Dun

When you importune (beg or are insistent upon) a debtor for payment: a dunning letter.

Dun & Bradstreet (D&B)

A United States based for profit agency that furnishes subscribers with marketing statistics and the financial standings and credit ratings of businesses.

"Du Pont Identity"

Popular expression breaking ROE into three parts: profit margin, total asset turnover, and financial leverage.

Duration Drivers

Represent the amount of time required to perform an activity.

Duty

A tax imposed by a customs authority on imported goods. Often used interchangeably with the term "tariff".

EA

Enrolled Agent.

E&OE

A British acronym that stands for "Errors and Omissions Excepted". E&OE is a legal disclaimer that notifies the reader that, without prejudice, that the content and/or validity of the subject data may change without notice.

Earned Income

That income realized by the provisioning of goods and services.

Earning Power

Earnings before interest and taxes (EBIT) divided by total assets.

Earnings

A common synonym for net income. A term that refers to the financial capacity of a corporation to make distributions to shareholders other than return of capital, e.g., dividends. See also Retained Earnings.

Earnings Management

Choosing accounting methods and/or making business deals with the specific objective of altering the size, trend, or interpretation of the company's earnings (net income). Usually frowned on as a form of Manipulation of accounting information.

Earnings per Share (EPS)

Net income minus any cash dividends to preferred stock, divided by the average number of common (voting) shares outstanding. This ratio is used to allow the owner of the shares to relate the corporation's earning power to the size of his or her investment. The calculation of EPS can be quite complex, so most public companies calculate it for the users (as required by generally accepted accounting principles for such corporations) and report it on their income statements.

Earnings Retention

The proportion of net income that is not paid in dividends. A firm earning $80 million after taxes and paying dividends of $20 million has a retention rate of $60 million/$80 million, or 75%. A high retention rate makes it more likely a firm's income and dividends will grow in future years.

EBITDA

Means Earnings Before Interest, Taxes, Depreciation and Amortization, but after all product/service, sales and overhead (SG&A) costs are accounted for. Sometimes referred to as Operating Profit.

EBITDARM

An acronym for Earnings Before Interest, Taxes, Depreciation, Amortization, Rent and Management fees.

E.C. (European Community or European Common Market)

A trading block of countries in Europe that have agreed on common regulations on cross-border trade.

E-Commerce

See Electronic Commerce.

Economically Feasible

Means that the benefit of tracing the cost (greater accuracy) outweighs the cost of doing so.

Economic Book Value

Allows for a book value analysis that adjusts the assets to their market value. This valuation allows valuation of goodwill, real estate, inventories and other assets at their market value.

Economic Double Taxation

Economic double taxation refers to the taxation of two different taxpayers with respect to the same income (or capital). Economic double taxation occurs, for example, when income earned by a corporation is taxed both to the corporation and to its shareholders when distributed as a dividend.

Economic Entity

The financial accounting definition of an enterprise, used to determine what is to be included in transactions and in the financial statements. Also used to refer to a group of companies considered to be under the same control and, so, constituting a larger economic group.

Economic Exposure

Long-term financial risk arising from permanent changes in prices or other economic fundamentals.

Economic Profits

The difference between the total revenue and the total opportunity costs.

Economic Value (EV)

The value of an asset deriving from its ability to generate income.

Economic Value Added (EVA)

Performance measure based on WACC.

Economic Value Added (EVA)

Measures the difference between the return on a company's capital and the cost of that capital. A positive EVA indicates that value has been created for shareholders; a negative EVA signifies value destruction.

Economies of Scale

Concept based upon the theory that the more you produce of a good, the less that it costs for each additional unit, i.e., efficiency. Specifically, it is the reduction of the costs of production of goods due to increasing the size of the producing entity and the share of the total market for the good/product.

ECU

European Currency Unit.

Effective Annual Rate (EAR)

The interest rate expressed as if it were compounded once per year.

Effective Income Tax Rate

The income tax rate the company appears to incur, as deduced from the financial statements. Differs from the statutory or legal rate because of many possible tax incentives, varying rates across jurisdictions, etc. Can be estimated as the company's income tax expense divided by income before income tax, both from the income statement.

Effective Interest Rate

The cost of credit on a yearly basis expressed as a percentage. Includes up-front costs paid to obtain the loan, and is, therefore, usually a higher amount than the interest rate stipulated in the note.

Effectively Connected Income

This is a U.S. term which connects the income of non-resident individuals or companies to a trade or business carried on within the U.S., and therefore subjects such income to U.S. tax.

Effects Analysis

See "What If" (Effects) Analysis.

Efficiency (of information use, or informational efficiency)

Refers to a market's prices quickly and appropriately changing to reflect new information.

Efficient Capital Market

A theoretical description of a capital market whose prices respond quickly and appropriately to information, and thus one in which security prices reflect all available information.

Efficient Market Hypothesis

The proposal that capital markets actually are "efficient", responding quickly, smoothly, and appropriately to information. Within this theory, investors who adhere to it believe it to be highly improbable that market movement can be predicted, i.e., using darts to chose stocks are just as effective as stock or market analysis.

Electronic Commerce

Also called e-commerce, this is the conduct of financial transactions, and much of the business transactions behind them, over electronic media such as telecommunication lines or the Web.

Electronic Funds Transfer (EFT)

Transfer of money between a buyer's bank account and the seller's bank account without need to write cheques or make deposits. EFT is what is happening if a customer uses a bank card to pay for groceries in the supermarket and the amount is automatically deducted from the customer's bank account.

EMC (Export Management Company)

A private company that serves as the export agent for manufacturers, being paid by commission or retainer. Merchandise is not normally purchased by the EMC.

Employee Deductions

Amounts an employer is required to deduct from an employee's pay and remit to someone else on behalf of the employee. Such deductions include income tax, pension contributions, union dues, and many other amounts the employee wants to or has to pay before receiving the net pay that is left over.

Employer-Provided Health and Dental Benefits

The cost of benefits paid by employers on behalf of employees under employer-sponsored health and dental care plans. Such benefits are not included in the employee's employment income.

Encumbered

When an asset is owned by one party subject to the legal claims of another party. One example is a homeowner that owns a home that is subject to (encumbered by) the claims of the mortgage holder.

Encumbrance

(1) A right or interest in land owned by someone other than the owner of the land itself; examples include easements, leases, mortgages, and restrictive covenants; or (2) in government accounting, an encumbrance is an anticipated expenditure, or funds restricted for anticipated expenditures, such as for outstanding purchase orders.

End-User (Swap Market)

In contrast to a swap-trading institution, a counterparty which engages in a swap to change its interest rate or currency exposure. End-users may be non-financial corporations, financial institutions or governments.

Enterprise Value (EV)

A measure of a company's value. Enterprise value is calculated by: market capitalization plus debt and preferred shares minus cash and cash equivalents. In effect, enterprise value is the theoretical takeover price, i.e., in the event of a buyout an acquirer would have to take on the company's debt but would pocket its cash.

Enterprise Zone

A depressed neighbourhood, usually in an urban area, where businesses are given tax incentives and are not subject to some government regulations. These advantages are designed to attract new business in the zone.

Entity

In business, is a separate or self-contained existence that provides goods or services. See also Accounting Entity, Business Entity, Consolidated Entity, Economic Entity, Legal Entity, Reporting Entity, and Social Entity.

Entity Assumption

The assumption that financial statements are prepared for an entity that is separate and distinct from its owners.

Entity Concept

The concept that financial accounting and reporting relates only to the activities of a specific business entity and not to the activities of the owners of that entity.

Entrepreneur

The person who assumes the financial risk of the initiation, operation and management of a given business or undertaking. He/She is primarily a financial and/or professional risk taker almost to the extreme.

Entry

See Journal Entry.

EPS

See Earnings per Share.

Equipment Loan

A loan used for the purchase of capital equipment.

Equity(-ies)

Normally, ownership or percentage of ownership in a company or items of value. Equity equals the net assets or residual interest of an owner or shareholder (Assets = Liabilities + Equity, or restated as Equity = Assets - Liabilities). See also Equity Capital and Equity Security.

Equity Accounting

The practice of showing in a company's accounts the share of undistributed profits of another company in which it holds equity ownership (usually below 50%). The share of profit shown is usually equal to its share of the equity in the other company. The profit may not actually be paid over, but the equity holding company has a right to this share of the undistributed profit.

Equity Basis

A method of accounting for intercorporate investments usually used when a company owns between 20% and 50% of another company. The investment is carried at cost, and any profit or loss, multiplied by the percentage ownership of the owned company, is added to or deducted from the investment. Any dividends received are deducted from the investment.

Equity Capital

Capital raised by an entity through the sale of common shares.

Equity Financing

A method of an entity obtaining funds by issuing either common or preferred stock, or both. Receipts can be through cash, services, or property. It is in the entities best interest to issue shares when the market price for the stock is at its highest.

Equity Kicker

As with a lot of international tax jargon, this term is also from the U.S. and describes the additional amount of interest payable on a loan over and above the basic rate, which is normally a percentage of the profit made by the debtor company from the investment of the loan monies.

Equity Method

A method of accounting for investments in *associated companies*. See Equity Accounting.

Equity Multiplier (EM)

Shows the amount of assets owned by the firm for each equivalent monetary unit owner claims held by stockholders, i.e., the equity multiplier measures how many dollars of assets an institution supports with each dollar of capital. If a firm is totally financed by equity, the equity multiplier will equal 1.00, while the larger the number the more highly leveraged is the firm. EM compares assets with equity: large values indicate a large amount of debt financing relative to equity. EM, thus, measures financial leverage and represents both profit and risk measurement. EM affects a firm's profit because it has a multiplier impact on Return on Assets (ROA) to determine the firm's Return on Equity (ROE). EM is also a risk measure because it reflects how many assets can go into default before a company becomes insolvent. The EM ratio is best compared to industry averages.

Equity Options

Encompass a class of options giving the purchaser the right but not the obligation to buy or sell an individual share, a basket of shares, or an equity index at a predetermined price on or before a fixed date.

Equity Security

An investment that gives you part ownership in a company. Equity securities include common and preferred shares, convertible preferred shares, rights and warrants.

Equity Share Capital

See Equity Capital.

Equity Swaps

A transaction that allows an investor to exchange the rate of return (or a component thereof) on an equity investment (an individual share, a basket or index) for the rate of return on another non-equity or equity investment.

Equity-to-Asset Ratio

Expresses the proportion of total assets financed by the owner's equity capital. It is the reciprocal of the debt-to-asset ratio.

Equivalent Annual Cost (EAC)

The present value of a project's costs calculated on an annual basis.

Erosion

The cash flows of a new project that come at the expense of a firm's existing projects.

ERP

Can mean either Enterprise Resource Planning or Early Retirement Program.

Estate

The entire group of assets owned by an individual at the time of his or her death. The estate includes all funds, personal effects, interests in business enterprises, titles to property-real estate and chattels, and evidences of ownership such as stocks, bonds and mortgages owned, notes receivable, etc. All claims against an estate must be duly filed with the Executor or Administrator of the estate, and approved by the court of law under which the will is being probated or the line of heritage is being determined before the indebtedness may be satisfied.

Estate Taxes

The Federal taxes levied on the transfer of property from the deceased to his or her heirs, legatees or devisees.

ETC (Export Trading Company)

A private company that usually purchases items from domestic manufacturers, then sells them to foreign markets. The difference between an EMC and an ETC is sometimes insignificant, i.e., an EMC may occasionally take title of goods, while an ETC may sometimes work strictly on commission without purchasing the goods. The difference is what the company *normally* does.

Eurobanks

Banks that make loans and accept deposits in foreign currencies.

Eurobond

International bonds issued in multiple countries but denominated in a single currency (usually the issuer's currency).

Eurocurrency

Money deposited in a financial centre outside of the country whose currency is involved.

EV (Economic Value)

The value of an asset deriving from its ability to generate income.

Event Risk

The risk that the ability of an issuer to make interest and principal payments will change because of rare, discontinuous, and very large, unanticipated changes in the market environment such as (1) a natural or industrial accident or some regulatory change, or (2) a takeover or corporate restructuring.

Ex

Latin for 'without', the opposite of Cum. Used to indicate that the buyer is not entitled to participate in whatever forthcoming event is specified, for example, Ex Cap, Ex Dividend, and Ex Rights.

Excess of Revenue over Expenses

The not-for-profit sector. There is a common misconception that not-for-profit organizations are not allowed to have a financial cushion as they are "not-for-profit". In this context it is useful to remember that not-for-profit organizations are also "not-for-loss" organizations. An organization cannot sustain losses over the long term without ceasing to operate or going bankrupt. Excess of revenue over expenses is the planned financial position that there will always be a sufficient amount of funds on hand to continue to run the not-for-profit entity for some period without additional funding, usually 3-4 months.

Exchange

A transfer of goods, services, or money between two parties. In financial accounting, the most significant kind of exchange is external, that is, between the enterprise and parties it deals with, such as customers, suppliers, owners, employees, and creditors.

Exchange Control or Restrictions

Limits on free dealings in foreign exchange or on free transfers of funds into other currencies and other countries.

Exchange of Information

Tax administrations may voluntarily or on request supply information to the tax administration of another jurisdiction with which they have entered into a double tax treaty, one of whose provisions provides for the exchange of information.

Exchange Rate

The price of one country's currency expressed in another country's currency.

Exchange Rate Risk

The risk related to having international operations in a world where relative currency values vary.

Excise Tax

A tax imposed by federal, state, and local governments on an act, occupation, privilege, manufacture, sale, or consumption that is not deductible (e.g., tobacco, gasoline and spirits). This term is in increasing usage to describe almost every tax other than income tax and property tax.

Ex-Dividend Date

Date before the date of record, establishing those individuals entitled to a dividend.

Executor

A legal entity, frequently an individual, known before death to a testator, who is named in the testator's will to carry out the desires of the deceased after his death as designated in the will. Executors must be approved by the court of law probating the will. An executor pays all indebtedness as claimed by creditors of the estate, with the approval of the court of law, and then carries out or executes the will according to the terms set forth by the testator.

Exemption Method

The exemption method provides relief from double taxation by exempting income that is subject to tax in the State of source from tax in the State of residence. The exemption method refers to the amount of income that is subject to tax. Hence, a taxpayer can be affected by the difference in tax rates between the State of source and the State of residence.

Exemption with Progression

Under the exemption with progression method, the State of residence provides an exemption from its tax for income earned in the State of source, but the residence State retains for itself the right to take the exempt income into account for the purposes of determining the marginal rate at which the taxpayer's non-exempt income is subject to tax. The exemption with progression method prevents a taxpayer from taking advantage of a lower tax bracket in the State of residence by earning income abroad.

Exercise Price

The fixed price at which an option holder has the right to buy, in the case of a call option, or to sell, in the case of a put option, the financial instrument covered by the option.

Exercising the Option

The act of buying or selling the underlying asset via the option contract.

Ex-Factory

Where a seller's responsibility ends when the buyer at point of origin, i.e., factory, accepts merchandise. This can also be written as ex-warehouse, ex-works, etc.

Existing Use Value (EUV)

The price at which a property can be sold on the open market assuming that it can only be used for the existing use for the foreseeable future.

Expatriation

The removal of one's legal residence or citizenship from one country to another in anticipation of future restrictions on capital movements or to avoid estate taxes.

Expected Annual Capacity

The planned activity levels or output for a given year taking into account efficiency and idle capacity.

Expected Return

Return on a risky asset expected in the future.

Expected Value of Perfect Information (EVPI)

The difference between the expected value with (additional) perfect information and the expected value with current information. The expected value of perfect information is the maximum amount a decision maker should pay for additional information that gives a perfect signal as to the state of nature.

Expendable Trust Fund

A governmental fiduciary fund held in a trustee capacity by a governmental agency that accounts for assets and activities restricted to a specific purpose in accordance to formal intent. The principal of the fund can be expended towards only the activity specified, e.g., Unemployment Compensation Fund, Employee Benefits Fund, etc.

Expenditure

The term can mean any Cash payment, but usually spending on non-current assets or debts is meant. Also used instead of the word Expense for governments and other non-business organizations that may not use full accrual accounting and therefore do not have expenses as accountants usually mean them.

Expense

The cost of assets used and/or obligations created in generating revenue, whether or not paid for in cash in the period they appear on the Income statement.

Expense Recognition

Incorporating measures of expenses incurred into the measurement of income by entering into the accounts the amount of expense determined, according to the firm's accounting policies, to be attributable to the current period.

Expensing

Classifying an expenditure or promised expenditure (accrual) as an expense rather than an asset. Opposite of Capitalization.

Expiration Date

The last day on which an option can be exercised.

Exploratory Research

A method used when gathering primary information for a market survey where targeted consumers/customers are asked very general questions geared toward eliciting a lengthy answer.

Export Broker

An entity that brings together foreign buyers with domestic manufacturers for a fee, generally providing little other services. An EMC, who is also a middleman, often provides extensive services to complete the transaction as well.

Export Declaration

The official paperwork required of exporters so trade transactions and goods can be tracked.

Export Development Corporation (EDC)

Canadian Federal Crown corporation that promotes exports by making loans to foreign purchasers.

Export Licence

The governmentally issued legal permit to export merchandise. In the U.S., it is either a general licence requiring no additional paperwork or a validated licence for certain federally controlled items.

Ex Rights

Period when stock is selling without a recently declared right, normally beginning four business days before the holder-of-record date.

External Audit

The audit conducted by an External Auditor.

External Auditor

An independent outside auditor appointed to review the financial statements.

Extraordinary Items

Gains and losses that arise out of situations that are not normal to the operations of a firm, not under the control of management, and not expected to recur regularly in the future. These nonrecurring items must be explained to shareholders in an annual or quarterly report of financial or operational results.

Face Value

The principal amount of a bond that is repaid at the end of the term. The expression "par value" is often used interchangeably.

Factoring

The practice of buying debt at a discount, e.g., if somebody owes you $10,000 payable within a year, a factoring lender may pay you $9,000 for the debt. You receive $9,000 cash quickly, but at the cost of the $1,000 discount.

Fair Labour Standards Act

A U.S. federal law that enforces a group of minimum standards that employers must abide by when hiring employees.

Fair Market Value

A value or price determined by an unrelated buyer and seller who are separate and acting rationally in his or her own self-interest. The value is considered more meaningful if established in an actual transaction than if estimated hypothetically. Historical cost is assumed to have been the fair market value of an asset when it was acquired. See also Open Market Value (OMV).

Fairness

Because of all the estimations, judgments, and policy choices that go into preparing financial statements, there is no one correct set of figures or disclosures. Instead, there is the idea of fairness, which means playing by the rules and preparing statements honestly, without any intent to deceive or to present any particular view. The opinion paragraph of the auditor's report states that the financial statements "present fairly ... in accordance with generally accepted accounting principles". Attention to fairness in the application of accounting principles requires care and judgment in distinguishing the substance from the form of a transaction and identifying the accepted principles and practices.

Fair Value

An estimate of the fair market values of assets and liabilities of an acquired company used in the purchase method of consolidation accounting.

Family Income

For income tax purposes, the combined incomes of both spouses. Family income does not include income of children living at home.

Family Trusts

Family trust arrangements allow property to be held by a trust for the benefit of beneficiaries under the trust. Trusts are used for many purposes, including succession planning for businesses and dealing with the needs of beneficiaries in special circumstances, such as age and disability. The 1995 budget proposed changes to the taxation of family trusts to ensure that they do not provide any undue tax advantages.

F.A.S. (Free Along Side)

E.g. "*F.A.S. New York*", means that, for instance, if goods are shipped from the State of Nevada in the U.S. to Madrid, Spain, no charges for shipment are made to the importer until the goods are "free alongside the vessel" in New York. After this point, charges may be applied to the importer.

FASB

See Financial Accounting Standards Board.

FBWT

In finance, is Fund Balance with Treasury.

FCIA (*Foreign Credit Insurance Act*)

An ExImBank program that offers credit insurance against losses due to political conflict or buyer default.

Federal *Unemployment Tax Act* (FUTA)

A U.S. federal law providing guidelines for the unemployment compensation system. A Federal tax is paid by all liable employers to fund the administration of Federal and State unemployment insurance programs and the extended benefits program. FUTA provides for payments of unemployment compensation to workers who have lost their jobs. Most employers pay both a federal and a state unemployment tax.

FFO (Funds from Operations)

Used by real estate and other investment trusts to present the cash flow from trust operations, i.e., earnings plus depreciation and amortization.

FIBV

World Federation of Stock Exchanges.

FICA (Federal *Insurance Contributions Act*)

The U.S. law requiring U.S. employers to match the amount of Social Security tax deducted from an employee's *paycheque*.

Fictitious Name

Often referred to as a DBA, "Doing Business As", a fictitious name is frequently used by sole proprietors or partnerships to provide a name, other than those of the owners or partners, under which the business will operate.

Fiduciary Account

An amount typically deposited with a Swiss Bank which will redeposit the sum with a third party bank outside Switzerland in its own name (to overcome Swiss withholding tax on interest).

FIFO (First-In, First-Out)

An inventory cost flow whereby the first goods purchased are assumed to be the first goods sold so that the ending inventory consists of the most recently purchased goods. In a period of inflation, FIFO usually creates a smaller Cost of Goods Sold and higher income and ending inventory asset value than LIFO or Weighted average.

Final Dividend

The dividend paid by a company at the end of its financial year, recommended by the directors not authorized by the shareholders at the Company's Annual General Meeting.

Financial Accounting

The reporting in Financial Statements of the Financial Position and performance of a firm to users external to the firm on a regular, periodic basis.

Financial Accounting Standards Board (FASB)

A U.S. body responsible for setting the standards that financial reporting must follow. The Canadian counterpart is the Canadian Institute of Chartered Accountants.

Financial Analysis

Analysis of a company's financial statement, usually by accountants or financial analysts.

Financial Assets

Near-cash assets such as traded shares, bonds, some kinds of loans, and accounts receivable, especially as would be held by financial institutions such as banks. Part of the general category of Financial instruments.

Financial Break-Even

The sales level that results in a zero NPV.

Financial Distress Costs

The direct and indirect costs associated with going bankrupt or experiencing financial distress.

Financial Engineering

Creation of new securities or financial processes.

Financial Instruments

Debts, shares, foreign exchange contracts, and other financial obligations and assets, many of which are traded on Stock markets and other Capital markets.

Financial Lease

Typically, a longer-term, fully amortized lease under which the lessee is responsible for upkeep. Usually not cancellable without penalty.

Financial Leverage

See Leverage.

Financial Performance

The enterprise's ability to generate new resources from day-to-day operations over a period of time, via dealing with customers, employees, and suppliers. Measured by the Net income figure in the Income statement and the Cash from operations figure in the Cash flow statement, as well as by the details of both statements.

Financial Position

The enterprise's set of assets, liabilities, and owners' equity at a point in time. Measured by the Balance sheet, also called the Statement of financial position.

Financial Ratios

Relationships determined from a firm's financial information and used for comparison purposes.

Financial Reporting

Use of Financial statements and Disclosure to report to people outside the enterprise on its Financial performance and Financial position.

Financial Reporting Release (FRR)

In the U.S., is the policy releases and pronouncements from the SEC (Securities Exchange Commission).

Financial Results

Usually refers to the summary financial results provided in compliance to the GAAP guidelines. They can cover any period(s), but usually cover either single month, quarter, or annual periods.

Financial Risk

The equity risk that comes from the financial policy (i.e., capital structure) of the firm.

Financial Schedule

Contained in an audited annual report, summarizes the audited financial position of the audited entity. Other application of the term is the scheduling of amounts, not necessarily by date, of major financial events by any given category as to projected receipts, payments, costs, etc.

Financial Statements

The reports, for people external to the enterprise but also of interest to management, referred to in the definition of Accounting, which generally comprise a Balance sheet, Income statement, Statement of retained earnings, Cash flow statement, and the Notes to these statements.

Financial Statements Analysis

Use of the financial statements to develop summary measures (ratios) and interpretive comments about an enterprise's financial performance and position.

Financing Activities

The category of the Cash flow statement that describes the cash obtained or used in connection with non-current debt and equity.

Firm Commitment Underwriting

Underwriter buys the entire issue, assuming full financial responsibility for any unsold shares.

First-In, First-Out

See FIFO.

Fiscal Period

The period (usually a year, a quarter, or a month) over which performance (net income) is measured and at the end of which the corporation's position (balance sheet) is determined. See also Fiscal Year.

Fiscal Transparency

Besides the limited partnerships, trusts and other similar entities, corporate entities may also be fiscally transparent, i.e., their shareholders are subject to primary level tax on the corporate profits, without any tax being levied on the corporation itself.

Fiscal Year

The declared accounting year for a company, but it is not necessarily in conformance to a calendar year (January through December). However, it does cover twelve months, 52 weeks, 365 days. For example, the U.S. government fiscal year ends September 30, i.e., October 1 through September 30 is their fiscal or accounting year.

Fisher Effect

Relationship between nominal returns, real returns, and inflation.

Five Cs of Credit

The following five basic credit factors to be evaluated: character, capacity, capital, collateral, and conditions.

Fixed Assets

Those assets of a permanent nature required for the normal conduct of a business, and which will not normally be converted into cash during the ensuing fiscal period. For example, furniture, fixtures, land, and buildings are all fixed assets. However, accounts receivable and inventory are not. Sometimes called Plant.

Fixed Assets (Net)

All property, plant, Leasehold Improvements and equipment, net of accumulated depreciation or depletion.

Fixed Assets (Net)/Net Worth

Measures liquidity by comparing "fixed" assets with "fixed" capital. A lower ratio indicates proportionately smaller investment and a better "cushion" for creditors in case of liquidation. This may be important if the fixed assets are not easily used in other businesses. The presence of substantial leased fixed assets (not shown on the balance sheet) may deceptively lower this ratio. Therefore smaller is better, i.e., greater than .75 (75%) should merit caution.

Fixed Asset Turnover

Measures management's ability to generate revenues from investments in fixed assets. FAT considers only the firm's investment in property, plant and equipment and is extremely important in high asset firms such as manufactures and telecommunications companies. Generally, the higher this ratio:

- the smaller the investment required to generate sales, thus the more profitable the firm.

- indicates the firm has less money tied up in fixed assets for each dollar of sales revenue.

A declining ratio may indicate that the firm has over-invested in plant, equipment, or other fixed assets.

Fixed Charge

Those expenses incurred each time a batch of product is produced. Primarily consists of ordering cost for the raw material, engineering costs for machine setup and preparation for the production run, and work order processing cost; also known as Setup Cost.

Fixed Charge Ratio

Calculated as: total fixed costs/total expenses.

Fixed Costs

Costs that do not change when the quantity of output changes during a particular time period. For example, rent, property taxes, and interest expense. Contrast to Variable Costs.

Fixed Expenses

In the operation of a business are those expenses that remain the same regardless of production or sales volume, i.e., do not fluctuate with sales volume. Contrast with Variable Expenses.

Fixed Fee

A set price for the completion of a project. It is easier for the customer to budget, but provides higher risk for the contractor due to cost overruns.

Fixed Interest

Loans issued by a company, the government or local authority, where the amount of interest to be paid each year is set on issue. Usually the date of repayment is also included in the title.

Fixed Overhead

Those costs like rent, utilities, basic telephone, loan payments, etc., that stay the same whether sales go up or down. Variable overhead, on the other hand, are those costs which vary directly with production.

Flag of Convenience

A flag of convenience is a shipping term and describes the registration of a ship in a jurisdiction chosen for its advantageous legal and tax regime, as opposed to a place where the ship is conducting its activities, or where its owners are resident.

Flat Interest

Refers to charging interest on the full original loan amount, rather than on the declining balance. With group based loans, for example, a common "interest rate" is "3% per month, flat, for four months". This means that a $100 principal amount lent is multiplied by 3%, and then by four months to come up with $12 in interest. Thus, $112 would be repaid over four months in equal installments.

Flat Lease

A lease where the cost is fixed for a specific period of time.

Flat Tax

A tax levied at the same rate on all income for all individual taxpayers, usually on a broadly defined income base with only a limited number of deductions.

Flexible Budget

Based upon different levels of activity. It is a very useful tool for comparing actual costs experienced to the cost allowable for the activity level achieved, i.e., it is dynamic in nature as compared to static. A series of budgets can be readily developed to fit any activity level. Flexible budgeting distinguishes between fixed and variable cost, thereby allowing for a budget that can be automatically adjusted to the level of activity actually attained.

Flight Capital

The movement of large sums of money from one country to another to escape political or economic turmoil, aggressive taxation or to seek higher rates of interest.

Float

(1) The time between the deposit of *cheques* in a bank and when the amount is truly accessible; (2) The amount of funds represented by *cheques* that have been written but not yet presented for payment. Some entities will 'play the float' by writing *cheques* although there are

insufficient funds actually on deposit to cover the *cheques*; and (3) To issue new securities through an underwriter.

Floor

A contract whereby the seller agrees to pay to the purchaser in return for the payment of a premium, the difference between current interest rates and an agreed (strike) rate times the notional amount should interest rates fall below the agreed rate. A floor contract is effectively a string of interest rate guarantees.

Flotation (Initial Public Offering or IPO)

The occasion on which a company's shares are offered on the market for the first time.

Flow-through Share

A flow-through share is available to mining and petroleum companies to facilitate financing their exploration and development activities. Resource companies issue these equity shares to new investors. Investors receive an equity interest in the company and income tax deductions associated with new expenditures incurred by the company on exploration and development. Flow-through shares are available to all mining and petroleum companies, but are of greater benefit to non-taxpaying junior exploration companies. These companies are unable to utilize income tax deductions for exploration and development against their corporate income and are willing to forgo the deduction to new investors.

F.O.B. (Free on Board)

E.g., "*F.O.B New York*", is where the importer would pay all costs for shipping from one point (New York) on to the final destination.

Footing

In accounting, is the sum of a column of figures.

F.O.R. (Free on Railroad)

Where goods will be delivered by the exporter to a railway station. The importer is responsible from this point on.

Force of Attraction

A foreign company with activities in a particular country, normally carried on through a permanent establishment, may find that its own profits are subjected to tax in the relevant country even though those profits should not be attributable to the permanent establishment. This force of attraction principle is specifically prevented under double tax treaty provisions. However, another example of the force of attraction principle which is accepted in international law, is where a foreign company has a permanent establishment in a particular country which it then closes; income subsequently received by the foreign company which no longer has a local permanent establishment may nevertheless be subject to local taxation under the force of attraction principle, particularly where the income is earned in the same fiscal year.

Foreign Accrual Property Income

This is a Canadian term and refers to income earned by CFCs which may be attributed to the Canadian shareholders under anti-avoidance legislation.

Foreign Affiliate

A non-resident corporation in which a taxpayer resident in Canada has a significant interest (an equity percentage of not less than 10 per cent). A controlled foreign affiliate is generally a foreign affiliate in which the taxpayer has or participates in a controlling interest.

Foreign Bond

International bonds issued in a single country, usually denominated in that country's currency.

Foreign Currency Account

An account maintained in a foreign bank in the currency of the country in which the bank is located. Foreign currency accounts are also maintained for depositors by banks in the United States. Such accounts usually represent that portion of the carrying bank's foreign currency account that exceeds its contractual requirements.

Foreign Currency Translation, Foreign Currency Translation Adjustment

The conversion of foreign monies into domestic monies at a specific date — either a transaction date, if translating a single transaction, or a financial statement date, if translating a foreign operation for consolidation purposes. This process normally produces an adjustment to make the accounts balance, shown in the Equity section of the balance sheet.

Foreign Exchange Market

The market where one country's currency is traded for another's.

Foreign Sales Agent or Representative

An entity that works to sell your merchandise in a foreign country. Equivalent to the "Manufacturer's Representative" in the U.S.

Foreign Trusts

A foreign trust is an entity organized outside Canada that is set up to hold and administer funds or property on behalf of beneficiaries. For example, a Canadian taxpayer may transfer funds or property to a foreign trust for the benefit of his children living abroad. However, such arrangements can also be set up for the purpose of reducing income from property for Canadian tax purposes. The *Income Tax Act* contains provisions designed to prevent the avoidance of tax in such cases. In order to facilitate the enforcement of such provisions. There are reporting requirements in respect of foreign investments held by Canadians and, in particular, in respect of foreign trusts.

Forensic Accounting

Provides for an accounting analysis that is suitable to a court of law which will form the basis for discussion, debate and ultimately dispute resolution. Forensic accounting encompasses investigative accounting and litigation support. Forensic accountants utilize accounting, auditing and investigative skills when conducting an investigation. Equally critical is the ability to respond immediately and to communicate financial information clearly and concisely in a courtroom setting.

Forward Contract

An agreement to buy or sell an asset at the current price on a specified date.

Forward Contract

A legally binding agreement between two parties calling for the sale of an asset or product in the future at a price agreed upon today.

Forward Exchange Rate

The agreed-on exchange rate to be used in a forward trade.

Forward Trade

Agreement to exchange currency at some time in the future.

Franchising

A franchisor sells the right to use the franchisor's name, products, or other economic goods to a franchisee.

Franked Income

Income is deemed to be franked when tax has already been incurred and further taxation would result in economic double taxation of the same profits.

Free Cash Flow

Net income plus non-cash charges to income, specifically depreciation and amortization less capital expenditures, to sustain the basic business. Free cash flow is another name for cash flow from assets.

Free Trade Agreement

An agreement between countries that will result, over an agreed period of time, in an elimination of duties for goods flowing between the signatories.

Free Trade Zone (FTZ)

An area, usually a port of entry, designated by the country for duty-free entry of goods. As long as the goods do not go into the country from the FTZ, no duty is assessed. While in the FTZ, goods may be processed, packaged, serviced or displayed.

Freight Forwarder

An individual or firm that provides for the packing and shipping of merchandise. Generally they also assist with export and other documentation.

Frequency

In advertising, is the number of times you hope to reach your target audience through your advertising campaign.

FRF

An acronym for French Francs.

FRR

See Financial Reporting Release.

FSA

Has several possible meanings, e.g., Flexible Spending Account (employee benefit offered by some companies) or Funding Standard Account.

FSC (Foreign Sales Corporations)

A corporation that provides U.S. businesses that export with tax benefits. Exporters can establish a Foreign Sales Corporation ("FSC") in a specially designated foreign country, or one of several designated U.S. possessions. The statute providing for the establishment of FSCs was part of the *Deficit Reduction Act of 1984*.

FT 30

Index Owned and calculated by the Financial Times, this index is based on the prices of 30 leading industrial and commercial shares and is calculated hourly during the day with a closing index at 4:30 pm.

FT-SE 100

Share Index Popularly known as the 'Footsie', this is an index of 100 leading shares listed on the London Stock Exchange. It provides a minute-by-minute picture of how share prices are moving and is the basis of futures and traded options listed on the London International Financial Futures and Options Exchange (LIFFE).

FT-SE Actuaries All-Share Index

The principal index for UK portfolio performance — covering large, medium and smaller companies.

FT-SE Eurotrack 200

Index Denominated in ECUs, this comprises the stocks on the FT-SE 100 Share Index plus the constituents of the FT-SE Eurotrack 100 Index. The UK component is weighted to ensure that the 200 index clearly tracks the major benchmark indices.

FT-SE Mid 250

The real-time benchmark for medium-sized companies consisting of the 250 next largest companies after those on the FT-SE 100. The FT-SE Actuaries 350 is a combination of the FT-SE 100 and the Mid 250 indices — this is an index of the more actively traded shares in large and medium sized UK companies. The FT-SE SmallCap, launched in January 1993 provides investors with a daily measure of the performance of around 500 smaller companies.

Full Disclosure

Generally, is the requirement to disclose all relevant or material facts to a transaction.

Fully Paid

Applied to new issues when the total amount payable in relation to the new shares has been paid to the company.

Fund Accounting

A kind of accounting used by governments and other non-business organizations to segregate groups of assets, liabilities, some forms of equity, revenues, and expenditures, in accordance with the purpose for which the funds were obtained. For example, donations received might be segregated from research grants received so that each kind of money is put to the use intended when it was obtained.

Fundamental Analysis

A method used to evaluate the worth of a security by studying the financial data of the issuer. Performing fundamental analysis will teach you a lot about a company, but virtually nothing about how it will perform in the stock market. Apply this analysis to two competing companies and it becomes clearer which the better investment choice is.

Funds Statement

See Cash Flow Statement.

FUTA

See Federal *Unemployment Tax Act*.

Future Income Tax

Income tax expected to be paid in future years based on business events and income tax calculations done up to the present. The liability and associated expense are calculated by the Liability method, which estimates the likely future tax payments directly, and which has recently replaced the Deferral method and its Deferred Income Tax.

Futures

Securities or goods bought or sold for future delivery. There may be no intention to take them up but to rely upon price changes in order to sell at a profit before delivery.

Futures Contract

An agreement to buy or sell an asset at a specified price on a specified date. The price is set through a futures exchange.

Future Value

The amount of money that an investment made today (the Present Value) will grow to by some future date. Since money has time value, we naturally expect the future value to be greater than the present value. The difference between the two depends on the number of compounding periods involved and the going interest rate.

FX Account (Foreign Exchange Account)

A trading account usually based in foreign currencies.

GAAP

See Generally Accepted Accounting Principles.

GAAS

See Generally Accepted Auditing Standards.

GAI

Guaranteed Annual Income.

Gain(s)

Usually refers to the profit (proceeds minus book value) obtained from the disposition of assets (or liabilities) not normally disposed of in the daily course of business, such as from selling land, buildings, or other non-current assets, or from refinancing debt. These are considered non-operating items and so, if material, are segregated from normal revenues and expenses on the income statement and the cash flows involved are included in the investing or financing sections of the cash flow statement.

Gain (Loss) on Sale

A gain on sale occurs when a company receives a larger amount of proceeds for an asset than its book value. An income statement account is then credited with the difference. A loss on sale occurs when the asset's book value is more than the proceeds received from the sale. An income statement account is then debited with the difference.

G&A

Usually refers to the indirect overhead costs contained within the General and Administrative expense/cost categories. See also SG&A.

GASB

The Governmental Accounting Standards Board.

GATT (General Agreement on Tariffs and Trade)

A multilateral treaty that aims to reduce trade barriers and increase trade. The GATT was an interim treaty process that has now culminated in the World Trade Organization (WTO).

Gearing

A company's debts expressed as a percentage of its equity capital. High gearing means that debts are high in relation to assets.

Gearing

The proportion of the *capital employed* of a company that is financed by lenders rather than shareholders.

Gearing Ratio

Measures the percentage of capital employed that is financed by debt and long term financing. The higher the gearing, the higher the dependence on borrowing and long term financing. Whereas, the lower the gearing ratio, the higher the dependence on equity financing. Traditionally, the higher the level of gearing, the higher the level of financial risk due to the increased volatility of profits. Financial managers face a difficult dilemma. Most businesses require long term debt in order to finance growth, as equity financing is rarely sufficient, on the other hand, the introduction of debt and gearing increases financial risk. A high gearing ratio is positive; a large amount of debt will give higher return on capital employed but the company dependent on equity financing alone is unable to sustain growth. Gearing can be quite high for small businesses trying to become established, but in general they should not be higher than 50%. Shareholders benefit from gearing to the extent that the return on the borrowed money exceeds the interest cost so that the market value of their shares rise.

GEMMs

Gilt-Edged Markets Makers.

General Journal

An accounting record used mainly to record accrual adjustments (journal entries) not provided for in separate specialized journals.

General Ledger

A collection of individual accounts that summarizes the entire financial accounting system of an enterprise.

Generally Accepted Accounting Principles (GAAP)

Principles and methods of accounting that have the general support of standard-setting bodies, general practice, texts, and other sources. These are the common set of standards and procedures by which financial statements should be prepared.

Generally Accepted Auditing Standards (GAAS)

In the U.S., are the broad rules and guidelines set down by the Auditing Standards Board of the American Institute of Certified Public Accountants (AICPA). In carrying out work for a client, a certified public accountant would apply the generally accepted accounting principles (GAAP); if they fail to do so, they can be held to be in violation of the AICPA's code of professional ethics.

General Partnership

One or more partners who are jointly and severally responsible or liable for the debts of the partnership.

Gilts or Gilt Edged Securities

Loans issued on behalf of the British and Irish governments to fund their spending. 'Longs' have a redemption date greater than 15 years, 'mediums' between seven to 15 years and 'shorts' within seven years.

Global Custody

A term used within the investment banking industry in defining securities/monetary instruments that are traded internationally by Global Custodians. Those securities would be held in "Global Custody". Chase Bank originated the concept of providing Global Custody trading services for institutional investors trading in foreign markets in 1974. Banks recognized as Global Custodians provide their customers with Global Custody services in respect to securities traded and settled not only in the country in which the Global Custodian is located but also in numerous other countries throughout the world.

Global Depository Receipts

Receipts evidencing ownership in the underlying shares of a foreign company. Generally, U.S. banks and trusts issue American depository receipts (ADR) and American depository shares (ADS). They hold the foreign company securities underlying the receipts in their vaults. In addition to the underlying securities, the receipts entitle the shareholder to all dividends and capital gains. The bank or trust company issuing the receipts may have denominated the receipts in a currency other than the currency underlying the foreign security. U.S. and European banks and trust companies usually issue global depository receipts (GDR), which are receipts in the shares of global offering of a foreign issuer who has issued two securities simultaneously in two markets, usually publicly in non-U.S. markets and privately in the U.S. market. European banks and trust companies generally issue European depository receipts (EDR), sometimes called continental depository receipts (CDR) when issued in bearer form, which evidence ownership in foreign securities.

GMBH (Ger. Gesellschaft mit Beschrankter Haftung)

In Germany, Switzerland and Austria, a limited liability company in which the liability of the members is limited to amounts of agreed contributions or as stipulated in the Articles of Association.

GMROI

An acronym for Gross Margin Return On Investment (retail).

Goal

The milestone the organization aims to achieve that evolves from the strategic issues. They transform strategic issues into specific performance targets that impact the entire organization. They can be qualitative or quantitative. Dependent upon usage, Goals are general in nature, while Objectives are specific, measurable and time-based. In some organizations, the meanings for Goal and Objective are reversed.

Going Concern

A fundamental assumption in financial accounting that a firm will be financially viable and remain in business long enough to see all of its current plans carried out. If a firm is not a going concern, normal accounting principles do not apply.

Going-Private Transactions

All publicly owned stock in a firm is replaced with complete equity ownership by a private group.

Golden Hello

A golden hello is similar to a golden handshake, except that a payment is made prior to the commencement of an employment rather than on its termination, and often before an individual becomes resident in the country where he is to be employed.

Goods and Services Tax (GST)

The GST is a 7 per cent value-added tax applied to the vast majority of goods and services sold in Canada for domestic consumption. The GST does not apply to basic groceries, most medical services and devices, prescription drugs, residential rents and exports. Businesses must collect the GST on most of their revenue and remit it to the government after deducting any GST the businesses paid on their own purchases. See also GST Rebates.

Goodwill

The difference between the price paid for a group of assets and the sum of their apparent fair (market) values. Arises when a bundle of assets or a whole company is acquired and when the difference is positive. ("Badwill," a negative difference, is not recognized.) Goodwill is that intangible possession which enables a business to continue to earn a profit that is in excess of the normal or basic rate of profit earned by other businesses of similar type. The goodwill of a business may be due to a particularly favourable location, its reputation in the community, or the quality of its employer and employees. The evidence that goodwill exists is the proven ability to earn excess profits. Goodwill is created on the books of a newly purchased company to the extent that the purchase price of the company is greater than the value of its net tangible assets. See also Negative Goodwill.

Goodwill Arising on Consolidation

Goodwill existing only in Consolidated Financial Statements accounted for using the Purchase Method, indicating that the "parent" corporation paid more for its investment in a "subsidiary" corporation included in the consolidated statements than the fair values of the subsidiary's assets.

Governmental Accounting

Accounting procedures, usually different, from GAAP for businesses but in recent years becoming more like GAAP, used to account for governments and their agencies.

Grandfather Clause

Where there is a change in tax law, but the status quo of existing arrangements are to be left unaffected, the legislation may provide for the new system to apply only on transactions from that date; this provision is referred to as a grandfather clause.

Grantee

The person or entity to whom property or assets are transferred.

Grantor

The person or entity who transfers property or assets.

Grantor Trust

Under U.S. tax law, income of the trust is taxed as the income of the grantor.

Greenmail

A targeted stock repurchase where payments are made to potential bidders to eliminate unfriendly takeover attempts.

Gross

Before deduction of tax.

Gross Contribution

The starting amount prior to any relevant deductions have been made to the gross amount, e.g., *Gross Contribution to Margin.*

Grossing Up

(1) Calculating the amount that would be required in the case of an investment subject to tax, to equal the income from that investment as if it were not subject to tax; (2) Tax credits are normally given by deduction from tax that is calculated on the amount of income received grossed up for underlying tax, or the tax credit itself. For example, in Canada, the federal Dividend Tax Credit provides a tax credit based on the grossed-up value of the dividend (i.e., the dividend received × 125%).

Gross Margin or Gross Profit

Revenue minus cost of goods sold expense (i.e., net sales minus cost of sales). See also Gross Profit Margin on Sales.

Gross Margin Ratio or Gross Profit Ratio

Equals (revenue — cost of goods sold expense) / revenue.

Gross Profit

See Gross Margin.

Gross Profit Margin on Sales (GPM)

One of the key performance indicators. The gross profit margin gives an indication on whether the average markup on goods and services is sufficient to cover expenses and make a profit. GPM shows the relationship between sales and the direct cost of products/services sold. It measures the ability of both to control costs and to pass along price increases through sales to customers. The gross profit margin should be stable over time. A persistent gradual decrease is likely to indicate that productivity needs to be increased to return profitability back to previous levels.

Gross Receipts

The total amount received prior to the deduction of any allowances, discounts, credits, etc.

Gross Sales

The total revenue at invoice value prior to any discounts or allowances.

Gross Weight

The weight of a shipment including packing material.

Group

A number of individual companies assembled together; often having some unifying relationship.

Group Accounts

The financial statements of a group of companies. These are usually presented in the form of consolidated accounts.

Growing Annuity

A finite number of growing annual cash flows.

Growing Perpetuity

A constant stream of cash flows without end that is expected to rise indefinitely.

GST

See Goods and Services Tax.

GST Rebates

Taxable (including zero-rated) sales by all sectors are eligible for full rebate of tax paid on associated inputs through the input tax credit mechanism. However, certain sectors are also eligible for rebates of a portion of the GST paid on inputs into exempt sales. These rebates go to qualifying public sector bodies such as municipalities, universities, schools and hospitals (MUSH), as well as to qualifying public service organizations such as charities and non-profit organizations. GST rebates to these institutions minimize the impact of the GST on the cost of providing exempt public services. Other GST rebates include a rebate to foreign tourists for GST paid on hotel accommodation in Canada and goods taken out of the country, as well as a rebate of a portion of the GST paid on the purchase of a new home (excluding rental properties).

Guarantee

See Warranty.

Half-Year Rule

CRA's requirement to figure CCA on only one half of an asset's installed cost for its first year of use.

Hard Costs

The purchase price of actual assets. For example, the purchase price of a new printing press would be the hard cost. The soft costs are additional fees for items like factoring-invoiced installation, prepaid and extended warranties, or service contracts for the new equipment.

Hard Currency

The term "hard currency" is a carry-over from the days when sound currency was freely convertible into "hard" metal, i.e., gold. It is used today to describe a currency that is sufficiently sound so that it is generally accepted internationally at face value.

Hard Rationing

The situation that occurs when a business cannot raise financing for a project under any circumstances.

Harmonization

The movement toward making countries' accounting standards the same as those of other countries, and that would strengthen the internationalization of accounting standards. The term harmonization is also used to refer to the stated desire of tax bureaucrats in Brussels to see every European country with the same tax laws.

Harmonized System

An internationally agreed upon classification system for trade. It provides code numbers to specify a goods classification, thereby making customs duty determination more predictable.

Headcount

The act of counting people in a certain way or in a particular group.

Head of Household

A U.S. income tax filing status that can be used by an unmarried person who maintains a home for a dependent (or nondependent relative) during the tax year.

Hedge(-ing)

A protective manoeuvre (transaction) intended to reduce the risk of loss from price fluctuations.

Hedge Funds

Speculative funds managing investments for private investors.

HIPs

TSE 100 Index participation units. HIPs allow you to buy the companies in the TSE 100 Index in a single security.

Historical Cost

The dollar value of a transaction on the date it happens, normally maintained in the accounting records from then on because of accounting's reliance on transactions as the basis for recording events. The cost, or historical cost, of an asset is therefore the dollar amount paid for it or promised to be paid as of the date the asset was acquired.

Historical Cost Accounting

An accounting principle requiring all financial statement items to be based on original cost. It is usually based upon the dollar amount originally exchanged in an arm's-length transaction; an amount assumed to reflect the fair market value of an item at the transaction date.

Holder-of-Record Date

The date on which existing shareholders on company records are designated as the recipients of stock rights. Also the date of record.

Holding Company

A company which owns or controls other companies. (Control can occur through the ownership of 50 per cent or more of the voting rights or through the exercise of a dominant influence.)

Homemade Dividends

Idea that individual investors can undo corporate dividend policy by reinvesting dividends or selling shares of stock.

Homemade Leverage

The use of personal borrowing to change the overall amount of financial leverage to which the individual is exposed.

Horizontal Financial Analysis

Allows comparison of one company's ratios to the ratios of other companies as well as to average industrial ratios and internal industrial deviation of these ratios.

Hot Money

(1) Large quantities of money that move quickly in international currency exchanges due to speculative activity; (2) Foreign funds temporarily transferred to a financial centre and subject to withdrawal at any moment.

HST

Harmonized sales tax.

Hurdle Rate

A term used in the budgeting of capital expenditures meaning the Required Rate of Return in a Discounted Cash Flow analysis. If the *expected rate of return* on an investment is below the hurdle rate, the project is not undertaken. The hurdle rate should be equal to the Incremental Cost of Capital.

Hybrid Instrument

A package containing two or more different kinds of risk management instruments that are usually interactive.

Hypothecation

In securities, is the pledging of securities to brokers as collateral for loans made to cover short sales or purchase securities. In banking, it is the pledging of property to secure a loan.

IASC

See International Accounting Standards Committee.

Identifiable Assets and Liabilities

Those assets and liabilities of a business that can be disposed of without disposing of the entire business. It includes both tangible and intangible assets.

IMA

In accounting, refers to the Institute of Management Accountants.

Impaired Assets

In banking, applies to all problem assets which banks hold, and is not limited to problem loans. In addition to loans, it also captures off-balance sheet exposures and assets which have come onto banks balance sheets through enforcement of security conditions.

Imprest

See Petty Cash.

Imputation System

The imputation system as opposed to the classical system provides for a tax credit to be given to restrict the impact of economic double taxation of profits. This tax credit is given against the personal income tax due by shareholders on dividends received which have been grossed up to reflect the credit, and on which the relevant personal income tax rates are computed prior to deduction of the tax credit.

Imputed Costs

Refer to the cost of an asset, service, or company that is not physically recorded in any accounts but is implicit in the product.

Imputed Value

The logical or implicit value that is not recorded in any accounts, e.g., in the projection of annual figures, values are imputed for months for which the actual values are not yet known.

IN(ATI)

The after-tax overall interest rate paid by an enterprise on its liabilities. Used in the Scott formula.

Income

The money and other benefits net of certain expenses flowing to individuals, firms and other groups in the economy. For purposes of the Income Tax, income is specifically defined to exclude certain types of benefits, such as a capital gain on sale of a principal residence. In the context of a business, (net) income is the residual after deducting expenses from revenues; also referred to as profit or earnings.

Income before (income) Tax

An amount equal to revenue plus other income minus all other ordinary expenses except income tax. Appears quite low down on the income statement. Some non-taxed or special items, such as Extraordinary items, are placed after Income Tax has been deducted, and are therefore not part of income before Income Tax.

Income Capitalization

First you must determine the capitalization rate — a rate of return required to take on the risk of operating the business (the riskier the business, the higher the required return). Earnings are then divided by that capitalization rate. The earnings figure to be capitalized should be one that reflects the true nature of the business, such as the last three years average, current year or projected year. When determining a capitalization rate you should compare with rates available to similarly risky investments.

Income from Continuing Operations

Income after deducting Income Tax but before adding gains or deducting losses from Discontinued Operations.

Income Gearing Ratio

Interest Expense / Operating Profit.

Income Measurement

A phrase used to describe financial accounting's way of calculating (net) income as shown on the income statement. The phrase is also used to describe the general problem of determining what income is and considering alternatives to the usual Accrual accounting basis.

Income Smoothing

The "manipulation" of net income so that the year-to-year variations in reported income are reduced.

Income Statement

See Profit and Loss Statement.

Income Tax

Tax assessed on income, according to laws about the computation of income for Income Tax purposes.

Income Tax Allocation

The attempt to allocate Income Tax expense to the appropriate year or activity to which it applies even if it is paid in another year or in aggregate across activities.

Income Tax Expense

An estimate of the current and future Income Tax arising from the income as computed on the income statement and matched to the revenues and expenses shown on the statement.

Income Tax(es) Payable

Income taxes due including current portion of deferred taxes. This is the liability for the amount of Income Tax due on the year's income, calculated according to the income tax law whether or not that matches the Income Tax Expense.

Income Testing

A reduction in the level of a benefit based on the recipient's income level.

Incremental Cash Flows

The difference between a firm's future cash flows with a project and without the project.

Incremental Cost of Capital

The weighted cost of the additional capital raised in a given period. Weighted cost of capital, also called *composite cost of capital*, is the weighted average of costs applicable to the issues of debt and classes of equity that compose the firm's capital structure. Also called *marginal cost of capital*.

Incur

Acquiring or getting into something undesirable. In business it usually is referencing a liability, e.g., incurring a loss or to incur a debt.

Indenture

A contract signed by a borrower and lender under which the borrower undertakes to meet certain conditions, such as keeping the working capital ratio above a specified amount, violation of which would give the lender the right to ask for immediate repayment of the loan or to take other action.

Indenture

An agreement between lender and borrower which details specific terms of the bond issuance. Specifies legal obligations of bond issuer and rights of bondholders. There is usually a indenture document spelling out the specific terms of a bond as well as the rights and responsibilities of both the issuer of the security and the holder.

Independence

Having no financial or other interest that could influence one's decisions. External auditors are expected to be independent of the enterprises they audit, and so can hold no shares, nor management positions, etc.

Index

A statistical measure of a market based on the performance of a sample of securities in that market. Examples are the TSE 300 Composite Index, the Standard & Poor's 500 Stock Price Index and the Scotia Capital Markets Universe Bond Index.

Index Linked Gilt

Gilt, the interest and capital of which change in line with the Retail Price index.

Indirect Bankruptcy Costs

The difficulties of running a business that is experiencing financial distress.

Indirect Cost

That portion of cost that is indirectly expended in providing a product or service for sale (cannot be traced to a given cost object in an economically feasible manner) and is included in the calculation of Cost of Goods Sold, e.g., rent, utilities, equipment maintenance, etc.

Indirect Method of Cash Flow Analysis

The traditional method of deriving the Cash flow statement, especially the Cash from operations section, by adjusting net income for non-cash items.

Industrial Revenue Bond (I.R.B.)

A bond issued by local government agencies in favour of corporations.

Inflation

An increase in the general price level of goods and services; alternatively, a decrease in the purchasing power of the dollar or other currency.

Inflation Accounting

A system of accounting which, unlike *historical cost accounting*, takes into account changing prices.

Inflation Premium

The portion of a nominal interest rate that represents compensation for expected future inflation.

Information Content Effect

The market's reaction to a change in corporate dividend payout.

Information System

An organized and systematic way of providing information to decision makers. Accounting is an information system.

Infrastructure

The resources (personnel, buildings, or equipment) required for an activity.

Initial Public Offering (IPO)

A company's first equity issue made available to the public. Also an unseasoned new issue.

Initiate

To get going by taking the first step, e.g., initiate contract negotiations.

Input Market Value

The market value of an asset calculated as the amount it would cost to replace or reproduce it.

Input Tax Credits

The input tax credit mechanism under the GST effectively provides a refund to registered businesses of all GST paid on inputs involved in the production and sale of taxable goods and services. In this manner, the input tax credit minimizes the amount of indirect tax embedded in the price of Canadian-produced goods and services, making them more competitive internationally and in the domestic market.

Insider Dealing

A criminal offence involving the purchase or sale of shares by someone who possesses "inside" information about a company's performance and prospects which is not yet available to the market as a whole, and which if available might affect the share price.

Insolvency

Occurs when a business is unable to pay debts as they fall due.

Instalment Receipts

Shares that you can pay for by instalment instead of in one lump sum.

Instalment Sale

Selling property and receiving the sales price over a series of payments, instead of all at once at the close of the sale, is an instalment sale. Unless you elect out, you will report the gain on that transaction as you receive it through the series of payments.

Institutional Net Settlement (INS) Service

A central service for institutional investors, which enables them to make or receive one net payment each day to the London Stock Exchange for, settled transactions and other cash distributions.

Intangible Asset

An asset that is not physical in nature. Examples are things like copyrights, patents, intellectual property, or goodwill. An intangible asset is the opposite of tangible asset.

Intangibles (Net)

Intangible assets, including goodwill, trademarks, patents, catalogues, brands, copyrights, formulas, franchises, and mailing lists, net of accumulated amortization.

Intensity Drivers

Used to directly charge for the resources used each time an activity is performed.

Interbank Rate of Exchange

The rate at which banks deal with each other in the market.

Intercorporate Investments

Investments by one corporation in other corporations.

Interest

The amount charged by a lender for the use of borrowed money.

Interest Coverage Ratio

Usually calculated as (income before interest expense + Income Tax) / interest expense.

Interest Expense

The cost of borrowing funds in the current period. It is shown as a financial expense item within the income statement.

Interest on Interest

Interest earned on the reinvestment of previous interest payments. See Compound Interest.

Interest Rate Parity (IRP)

The condition stating that the interest rate differential between two countries is equal to the difference between the forward exchange rate and the spot exchange rate.

Interest Rate Risk Premium

The compensation investors demand for bearing interest rate risk.

Interest Rate Swap

A transaction in which two counterparties exchange interest payment streams of differing character based on an underlying notional principal amount. The three main types are coupon swaps (fixed rate to floating rate in the same currency), basis swaps (one floating rate index to another floating rate index in the same currency), and cross-currency interest rate swaps (fixed rate in one currency to floating rate in another).

Interest Tax Shield

The tax saving attained by a firm from interest expense.

Interim Dividend

A dividend declared part way through a company's financial year, authorized solely by the directors.

Intermediary (Swap Market)

A counter party who enters into a swap in order to earn fees or trading profits. Most intermediaries or swap dealers are major U.S. money-centre banks, major U.S. and UK investment and merchant banks and major Japanese securities companies.

Internal Auditor

An auditor who works for the enterprise and thus verifies information for management's use and to help the enterprise perform better.

Internal Control

Methods of providing physical security and management control over an enterprise's cash, inventories, and other assets.

Internal Growth Rate

The growth rate a firm can maintain with only internal financing.

Internal Rate of Return (IRR)

Also called the dollar-weighted rate of return; the interest rate that makes the present value of the cash flows from all the sub-periods in an evaluation period plus the terminal market value of the portfolio equal to the initial market value of the portfolio.

International Accounting Standards Committee (IASC)

A committee made up of representatives of more than 50 countries that sets international accounting standards.

International Business Company ("IBC")

A term used to define a variety of offshore corporate structures. Common to all IBC's are its dedication to business use outside the incorporating jurisdiction, rapid formation, secrecy, broad powers, low cost, low to zero taxation and minimal filing and reporting requirements. An increasing number of offshore jurisdictions are permitting the use of bearer shares, nominee shareholders, directors and officers. See also Offshore Company.

International Fisher Effect (IFE)

The theory that real interest rates are equal across countries.

Interperiod Tax Allocation

Allocating the enterprise's income tax expenses over several years to match the expenses to the incomes shown in the income statement. Necessitated by timing differences between GAAP and the income tax law in the recognition of various revenues and expenses.

Intraperiod Tax Allocation

The attempt to match income tax expense to the various items in the income statement, especially separating general income tax expense from that due to special items below that expense on the income statement, such as Extraordinary Items and Discontinued Operations.

Intrinsic Value

The lower bound of an option's value, or what the option would be worth if it were about to expire.

Inventory(ies)

The goods purchased or manufactured by a company for sale, resale, or further use in operations, including finished goods, goods in process, raw materials, and supplies. In the context of the securities industry, it is the securities bought and held by a broker or dealer for resale.

Inventory Costing

Comprises various methods of determining the cost of inventory for balance sheet valuation purposes and of valuing cost of goods sold. The more common methods are FIFO, LIFO, and Weighted average.

Inventory Loan

A loan that is extended based upon the, usually, discounted/factored value of a business' inventory.

Inventory Period

The time it takes to acquire and sell inventory.

Inventory Turnover

A ratio that shows how many times the inventory of a firm is sold and replaced over a specific period. Calculated as the Cost of Goods Sold expense / average inventory assets.

Inventory Turns (period average)

Measures the *average* efficiency of the firm in managing and selling inventories during the last period, i.e., how many inventory turns the company has per period and whether that is getting better or worse. It is imperative to compare a company's inventory turns to the industry average. A company turning their inventory much slower than the industry average might be an indication that there is excessive old inventory on hand which would tie up their cash. The faster the inventory turns, the more efficiently the company manages their assets. However, if the company is in financial trouble, on the verge of bankruptcy, a sudden increase in inventory turns might indicate they are not able to get product from their suppliers, i.e., they are not carrying the correct level of inventory and may not have the product on hand to make their sales. If looking at a quarterly statement, there probably are more or less turns than an annual statement due to seasonality, i.e., their inventory levels will be higher just before the busy season than just after the busy season. This does not mean they are managing their inventory any differently; the ratio is just skewed because of seasonality. NOTE: Comparing the two Inventory Turns (Period Average and Period End) suggests the direction in which inventories are moving, thereby allowing an analysis of efficiency improvements and/or potential burgeoning inventory problems.

Inventory Turns (period end)

Measures the *ending* efficiency of the firm in managing and selling inventories during the last period, i.e., how many inventory turns the company has per period and whether that is getting better or worse. It is imperative to compare a company's inventory turns to the industry average. A company turning their inventory much slower than the industry average might be an indication that there is excessive old inventory on hand which would tie up their cash. The faster the inventory turns, the more efficiently the company manages their assets. However, if the company is in financial trouble, on the verge of bankruptcy, a sudden increase in inventory turns might indicate they are not able to get product from their suppliers, i.e., they are not carrying the correct level of inventory and may not have the product on hand to make their sales. If looking at a quarterly statement, there probably are more or less turns than an annual statement due to seasonality, i.e., their inventory levels will be higher just before the busy season than just after the busy season. This does not mean they are managing their inventory any differently; the ratio is just skewed because of seasonality. NOTE: Comparing the two Inventory Turns (Period Average and Period End) suggests the direction in which inventories are moving, thereby allowing an analysis of efficiency improvements and/or potential burgeoning inventory problems.

Inventory Valuation

The process of determining the amount at which inventory is shown on the balance sheet, normally the Lower of cost or market.

Investing Activities

The category of the Cash Flow Statement that describes the cash used to acquire, or obtained by disposing of, non-current assets.

Investment(s)

Usually refers to such assets as shares or bonds held for their financial return (interest or dividends), rather than for their use in the enterprise's operations. See also Securities.

Investment

The purchase of real property, stocks, bonds, collectible annuities, mutual fund shares, etc, with the expectation of realizing income or capital gain, or both, in the future. Investment is longer term and usually less risky than speculation.

Investment Centre

The responsibility centre within an organization that has control over revenue, cost, and investment funds. It is a profit centre whose performance is evaluated on the basis of the return earned on invested capital, e.g. corporate headquarters or a division of a large decentralized organization.

Investment Income

The income received from investment in securities and property. It includes rent from property, dividends from shares in corporations, and interest from bonds, guaranteed-investment certificates, bank accounts, certificates of deposit, treasury bills, and other financial securities.

Investment Tax Credit

A tax credit available for investments in scientific research and experimental development in certain regions. In the U.S., is a tax credit that allows businesses to write-off a portion of the cost of purchasing equipment for business use.

Investment Trust

A company whose sole business consists of buying, selling and holding shares.

Investment Turnover

A profitability measure used to calculate the number of times per year an investment or assets revolve.

Investors

People who own Investments and who, because of their interest in the value of those shares or bonds, are interested in information about the enterprises issuing such shares and bonds.

Invoice

Bill for goods or services provided by the seller to the purchaser. It usually includes an itemized list of the goods shipped/services provided, the price and the terms of sale.

Invoice, Commercial

A legal document that functions internationally as a bill of sale. It usually contains the exporting company, contents of the shipment, amount charged, name of carrying vessel, order number and payment terms.

Invoice, Consular

An invoice stamped or endorsed by the consulate of the country requiring such.

IOSCO

International Organisation of Securities Commissions.

IPO (Initial Public Offering)

The first or primary offering of stock to the public.

Issue

In securities, is stock or bonds sold by a corporation or a government; or, the selling of new securities by a corporation or government through an underwriter or private placement.

Issuing House

An organization, usually a merchant bank, which arranges the details of an issue of stocks and shares and the necessary compliance with the London Stock Exchange regulations on connection with the listing of that issue.

Jeopardy Assessment

Where it is unlikely that tax legitimately due from a taxpayer will be collected, the tax administration may raise a jeopardy assessment ensuring that there is legal authority for seizing (often) the box office receipts of travelling entertainers.

Job Costing

The allocation of all time, material and expenses to an individual project or job.

Joint Return

A U.S. income tax filing status that can be used by a married couple. The married couple must be married as of the last day of their tax year in order to qualify for this filing status. A married couple can also elect to file as married, filing separate returns.

Joint Stock Company

A company that has some features of a corporation and some features of a partnership. This type of company has access to the liquidity and financial reserves of stock markets as a corporation, however, as in a partnership; the stockholders are liable for company debts and have additional restrictions of a partnership.

Joint Venture

A business arrangement between corporations that is like a corporate partnership.

Joint Ventures & Investments

The total of investments and equity in joint ventures.

Journal

In accounting transactions, is where transactions are recorded as they occur.

Journal Entry

A record of a transaction or accrual adjustment that lists the accounts affected and in which the total of the debits equals the total of the credits.

Journals

Records in which accounting transactions of a similar nature are permanently recorded.

Juridical Double Taxation

Juridical double taxation refers to circumstances where a taxpayer is subject to tax on the same income (or capital) in more than one jurisdiction. For example, a resident of Canada who is also considered to be a resident of the United States would be potentially subject to concurrent full taxation in both countries. Bilateral tax treaties generally tend to eliminate (or at least reduce) the possibility of juridical double taxation.

Just-in-Time Inventory (JIT)

A management philosophy that strives to eliminate sources of manufacturing waste by producing the right part in the right place at the right time. Parts, raw materials, and other work-in-process are delivered exactly as needed for production to minimize inventory.

Keogh

A pension plan in the United States that allows a business to contribute a portion of profits into a tax-sheltered account.

Keynesian Growth Models

Models in which a long run growth path for an economy is traced out by the relations between saving, investing and the level of output.

Keynesian Macroeconomics

The theory that shows how a market-based capitalist economy may reach equilibrium with large scale unemployment and how government spending may be used to raise it out of this to a new equilibrium at the full-employment level of output.

Kiting

When used in the context of banking, refers to the practice of depositing and drawing cheques at two or more banks and taking advantage of the time it takes for the second bank to collect funds from the first bank. Can also refer to illegally increasing the face value of a cheque by changing the printed amount of the cheque. When used in the context of securities, it refers to the manipulation and inflation of stock prices.

Labour-Sponsored Venture Capital Corporations (LSVCCs)

Funds set up by labour organizations in which individuals pool their money to invest in small businesses. Individuals who purchase national LSVCC shares receive a 20 per cent federal tax credit based on the cost of acquiring these shares, which in most cases is subject to a clawback if sold within a specified time period (e.g., before then end of five years from date of purchase). These shares may also be contributed to an RRSP.

Land

In terms of accounting, is the value of real estate less the value of improvements, e.g., buildings.

Large-Cap

A stock with a level of capitalization of at least $5 billion market value.

Large Corporations Tax (LCT)

A tax levied on the amount by which a corporation's taxable capital employed in Canada exceeds $50 million. The 2003 Canadian Federal Budget announced the gradual elimination of the LCT over five years.

Last-In, First-Out

See LIFO.

Laundering

Laundering is the process of cleaning illicitly gained money so that it appears to others to have come from, or to be going to a legitimate source.

LCL

See Less than Container Load.

L/E

Total liabilities / total equity, the debt-equity ratio used in the Scott formula.

Lease

A contract requiring the user of an asset to pay the owner of the asset a predetermined fee for the use of the asset.

Leasehold Improvements

Those repairs and/or improvements, usually prior to occupancy, made to a leased facility by the lessee. The cost is then added to fixed assets and amortized over the life of the lease.

Ledger

Any book or electronic record that summarizes the transactions from the "books of original entry" in the form of accounts.

Legal Entity

A person or organization that has the legal standing to enter into contracts and may be sued for failure to perform as agreed in the contract, e.g., a child under legal age is not a legal entity, while a corporation is a legal entity since it is a person in the eyes of the law.

Lehman Formula

A compensation formula originally developed by investment bankers Lehman Brothers for investment banking services:

- 5% of the first million dollars involved in the transaction for services rendered
- 4% of the second million
- 3% of the third million
- 2% of the fourth million
- 1% of everything thereafter (above $4 million)

NOTE: Most investment bankers now require an additional multiplier to offset inflation.

Lessee

The user of an asset in a leasing agreement. Lessee makes payments to lessor.

Lessor

The owner of an asset in a leasing agreement. Lessor receives payments from the lessee.

Less than Container Load (LCL)

A shipment in which the freight does not completely fill the container; or a particular consignor's freight when combined with others to produce a full container load.

Letterbox Company

This term refers to a locally incorporated company which has its registered office at a particular address but no activities of any nature are carried out normally within the country of incorporation, and indeed the very existence of the company is often for a specific transaction carried out by the company's shareholders. Normally there are hundreds of companies whose registered offices are all at the same address.

Letter of Credit

A legal document issued by a buyer's bank that upon presentation of required documents payment would be made. Usually confirmed by the seller's bank, protection is given to the seller that payment will be made if the goods are shipped correctly, and protection is given to the seller that the goods will be shipped before payment is made.

Letter of Credit, Confirmed

A letter of credit that is guaranteed by a bank that is acceptable to a seller (usually a local bank), regardless of the buyer's bank.

Letter of Credit, Irrevocable

A letter of credit where payment is guaranteed as long as the seller meets all conditions stipulated. A revocable letter of credit can be cancelled or altered by the buyer without permission of the seller.

Letter of Renunciation

This applies to a rights issue and is the form attached to an allotment letter, which is completed, should the original holder wish to pass his entitlement to someone else, or to renounce his rights absolutely.

Letter of Wishes/Memorandum of Wishes

A document prepared by the settlor or grantor of a trust providing guidance on how trustees should exercise their discretions.

Letter to the Shareholders

Part of the Annual report, it is a letter from senior management to the shareholders, summarizing major decisions and strategies, commenting on the company's performance for the year and usually looking ahead to future performance.

Leverage

Value of property rising or falling at a proportionally greater amount than comparable investments. For example, an option is said to have high leverage relative to the underlying stock because a small price change in the stock may result in a relatively large increase or decrease in the value of the option. In general, in finance, leverage is the use of debt financing. Leverage, within a corporation, is the use of borrowed money to increase the return on investment. For leverage to be positive, the rate of return on the investment must be higher than the cost of the money borrowed.

Leverage Analysis

Study of the financial statements and corporate financial structure in order to determine how, and how well, the company is making use of Leverage.

Leveraged Buyouts (LBO)

Going-private transactions in which a large percentage of the money used to buy the stock is borrowed through the use of bank loans and bonds. Because of the large amount of debt relative to equity in the new corporation, the bonds are typically rated below investment grade, properly referred to as high-yield bonds or junk bonds. Investors can participate in an LBO through either the purchase of the debt (i.e., purchase of the bonds or participation in the bank loan) or the purchase of equity through an LBO fund that specializes in such investments.

Leveraged Lease

A financial lease where the Lessor borrows a substantial fraction of the cost of the leased asset.

Leverage Potential

The difference between Operating Return (Return on Assets) and borrowing cost, which produces Leverage when multiplied by the degree of borrowing in the Scott formula.

Leverage Ratios

Measures the relative contribution of stockholders and creditors, and of the firm's ability to pay financing charges. Value of firm's debt to the total value of the firm.

Leverage Return

The portion of the return on equity that is due to earning more return on borrowed funds than it costs in interest to borrow them.

Liability

(1) In accounting, a loan, expense, or any other form of claim on the assets of an entity that must be paid or otherwise honoured by that entity. The debt may be legally existing or estimated via accrual accounting techniques; (2) In insurance, a term used when analyzing insurance risks that describes possible areas of financial exposure/loss. Presently, there are three forms of liability coverage that insurers will underwrite. The first is general liability, which covers any kind of bodily injury to non-employees except that caused by automobiles and professional malpractice. The second is product liability, which covers injury to customers arising as a direct result of goods purchased from a business. The third is public liability, which covers injury to the public while they are on the premises of the insured.

Liability Method

A method of Income Tax Allocation in which the impact of Future Income Tax is estimated according to what is expected to be paid rather than according to past timing differences as done in the former Deferred Income Tax accounting. The liability method is common in other countries, and Canada has recently adopted it too.

LIBOR

See London Interbank Offered Rate.

LIFFE

London International Financial Futures and Options Exchange.

LIFO (Last-In, First-Out)

A cost flow assumption that is the opposite of FIFO. "Last in, first out" assumes that the units sold are from the most recent purchases and thus bases cost of goods sold on the most recent purchases and ending inventory on the oldest purchases. Because of this, in a period of inflation the LIFO cost of goods sold figure is usually the highest of the inventory costing methods, and the inventory value on the balance sheet is usually the lowest.

LIFO Liquidation

A reduction in the reported value of inventory below levels established in prior years under the LIFO method; arises when purchases for the period are not sufficient to offset the sale of inventory in the period.

LIFO Reserve

The difference between the ending inventory under LIFO and FIFO (or other method that might be chosen).

Like Kind

In taxes, refers to property that is similar to another for which it has been exchanged: real estate exchanged for real estate, for instance. The definitions of like kind properties can be found in the U.S. *Tax Code* at Section 1031.

Limit

In relation to dealing instructions, a restriction set on an order to buy or sell, specifying the minimum selling or buying price.

Limitation

In contracts, is a certain period limited by statute after which actions, suits, or prosecutions cannot be brought in the courts.

Limitations of Benefits

Treaty benefits are generally available only to residents of a Contracting State, which, in the case of corporations, includes corporations incorporated in the Contracting State. Hence, corporations can engage in "treaty-shopping" by incorporating in a convenient State merely for the purpose of deriving treaty benefits. A Limitation on Benefits article in a treaty generally limits the ability of third-country residents to shop for a favourable treaty.

Limited Partner

A partner in a venture who has no management authority and whose liability is restricted to the amount of his or her investment.

Line Item Budget

A budget initiated by government entities in which budgeted financial statement elements are grouped by administrative entities and object. These budget item groups are usually presented in an incremental fashion that is in comparison to previous time periods. Line item budgets are also used in private industry for comparison and budgeting of selected object groups and their previous and future expenditure levels within an organization.

Line of Credit

An agreement whereby a financial institution promises to lend up to a certain amount without the need to file another loan application. The borrower is required to reduce the debt whenever the limit of the full amount of credit has been reached.

Liquidating Dividends

Dividends paid by a corporation that is in the process of liquidation/bankruptcy. Liquidating Dividends are paid from the capital of the corporation as opposed to earnings. Recipients of Liquidating Dividends are typically shareholders, bond holders and/or creditors. In the U.S. such dividends are generally non-taxable under the *Internal Revenue Code*.

Liquidation

Termination of the firm as a going concern.

Liquidation Value

A type of valuation similar to an adjusted book value analysis. Liquidation value is different than book value in that it uses the value of the assets at liquidation, which is often less than market and sometimes book. Liabilities are deducted from the liquidation value of the assets to determine the liquidation value of the business. Liquidation value can be used to determine the bare bottom benchmark value of a business, since this should be the funds the business may bring upon valuation.

Liquidity

A company's ability to meet current obligations with cash or other assets that can be quickly converted to cash.

Liquidity Premium

The portion of a nominal interest rate or bond yield that represents compensation for lack of liquidity.

Listed Company

A company that has obtained permission for its shares to be admitted to the Stock Exchange's Official List. See also Public Company.

Listed Investments

Those investments which are listed or quoted on a stock exchange.

Listing

A written contract between an agent and a principal giving authorization to the agent to perform services for the principal involving the principal's property; or, a record of a property for sale by a broker who has been authorized by the owner of the property to be sold.

Listing Particulars

The details a company must publish about itself and any securities it issues before these can be listed on the Official List. Often called a prospectus in North America.

LMA

Among others, is an acronym for Lease Management Agreement, Local Marketing Agreement or Legal Marketing Association.

Loaded Labour Rate

The employee hourly rate plus employee benefits, capital expenses, and other overhead.

Loan Covenant

A legally enforceable promise or restriction in a mortgage. For example, the borrower may covenant to keep the property in good repair and adequately insured against fire and other casualties. A breach of covenant in a mortgage usually creates a default, defined by the mortgage, and can be the basis for foreclosure.

Loans from Shareholder(s)

Informal loans to the corporation by shareholders(s), who therefore act as creditors as well as owners. It is most common in private company corporations.

Loan Stock

Stock bearing a fixed interest rate. Unlike a debenture, loan stocks may be unsecured.

Lockboxes

Special post office boxes set up to intercept and speed up accounts receivable payments.

London Interbank Offered Rate (LIBOR)

The rate that the most creditworthy international banks that deal in Eurodollars charge each other for large loans. It is equivalent to the federal funds rate in the U.S.

Long-Lived Assets

Usually those assets that are not consumed during the normal course of business, e.g., land, buildings and equipment, etc.

Long-Term Debt

All senior debt, including bonds, debentures, bank debt, mortgages, deferred portions of long term debt, and capital lease obligations.

Long-Term Debt to Equity Ratio

Calculated as (long-term loans + mortgages + bonds + similar long-term debts) / total equity. This ration expresses the relationship between long-term capital contributions of creditors as related to that contributed by owners (investors). As opposed to Debt to Equity, Long-Term Debt to Equity expresses the degree of protection provided by the owners for the *long-term* creditors. A company with a high long-term debt to equity is considered to be highly leveraged. But, generally, companies are considered to carry comfortable amounts of debt at ratios of 0.35 to 0.50, or \$0.35 to \$0.50 of debt to every \$1.00 of book value (shareholders equity). These could be considered to be well-managed companies with a low debt exposure. It is best to compare the ratio with industry averages.

Long-Term Liabilities

Liabilities of a business that are due in more than one year. An example of a long-term liability would be a mortgage payable.

Loss(es)

(1) Usually refers to the case of a negative return (proceeds being less than book value) obtained from the disposition of assets (or liabilities) not normally disposed of in the daily course of business, such as from selling land, buildings or other non-current assets, or from refinancing debt. These are considered non-operating items and so if material are segregated from normal revenues and expenses on the income statement and the cash flows involved are included in the investing or financing sections of the cash flow statement; (2) In finance, is when expenses exceed sales or revenues, i.e., goods or services are sold for less than their cost.

Loss Carry-Forward, Carry-Back

Using a year's Capital Losses to offset Capital Gains in past or future years.

Loss Carry-Overs

Business or investment losses that are incurred in one year that may be used as a deduction from taxable income in another year.

Loss on Sale

Selling a non-current asset for less than its Book Value.

Lower of Cost or Market

A method of valuing items of inventory, temporary investments, or other current assets, under which losses inherent in declines of the market prices of items held below their costs are recognized in the period in which such declines become apparent. Gains from market increases above cost are not recognized until the items are sold. Lower of cost or market is a conservative procedure.

Managed Bank

An offshore bank also known as a Class "B" or Cubicle Bank. The Managed Bank is not required to maintain a physical presence in the licensing jurisdiction. Its presence in the licensing jurisdiction is passive with nominee directors and officers provided by a managing trust company with a physical presence. The Managed Bank is not permitted to transact business within the licensing jurisdiction but may maintain its books, records, etc., to assure secrecy of operations.

Management

The people (managers) who run the day-to-day operations of an enterprise or other organization, in contrast to the shareholders (investors), members, and voters who own or legally control the enterprise.

Management Accounting

Accounting information designed to aid management in its operation and control of the firm, and in its general decision-making. It is different from Financial Accounting, which is aimed primarily at users external to the firm.

Management and Control

Management and control of a company's business refers to that applied by the directors, rather than shareholder control, and is one of the principal concepts of corporate residence.

Management Control System

Essentially a strategic tool for holding managers accountable and responsible for their performance. Existence of such a system also provides feedback for managers to know how they perform, in which direction the organization is heading, and what type of course correction may be required to stay on course.

Management Discussion and Analysis (MD&A)

A section of a company's annual report in which management reviews the results for the year and explains what happened in some detail. The MD&A is used by many analysts to supplement ratios and other forms of analysis.

Management Information System (MIS)

A well-developed data management system that provides uniform organizational information from all areas of the entity within a database. Information within the database is manipulated to help management reach accurate and rapid organizational decisions.

Management of Corporate Financial Disclosure

Steps taken by management to manage the outward flow of information about an enterprise, much as other aspects of the enterprise are managed.

Managerial Accounting

A system using financial accounting records as basic data to enable better business decisions in the areas of planning and control.

Managerial Options

Opportunities that managers can exploit if certain things happen in the future.

Managers

See Management.

Mandatory Quote Period

Time of the day during which market makers in equities are obliged to quote prices under London Stock Exchange rules: SEAQ 8.30am–4.30pm; SEAQ International 9.30am–4.00pm.

Mandatory Transfers

Transfers from the current (operating) fund group to other fund groups arising out of binding legal agreements related to the financing, e.g., in education: debt retirement, interest, and grant agreements with federal agencies and other organizations to match gifts and grants. Whereas non-mandatory transfers would be transfers from the current (operating) fund group to other fund groups made at the discretion of management to serve various objectives, e.g., additions to loan funds, endowment funds, plant additions, and voluntary renewal and replacement of plant.

M&M Proposition I

The value of the firm is independent of its capital structure.

M&M Proposition 11

A firm's cost of equity capital is a positive linear function of its capital structure.

Manipulation

The accusation that management, in choosing its accounting and disclosure policies, attempts to make the performance and position measures suit its wishes.

Man of Straw

Effectively a nominee settlor or grantor who creates an offshore trust but often has no further connection with the trust once it is created.

Manual Tag System

An inventory tracking system used in inventory management that tracks inventory using tags removed at the point of purchase.

Manufacturing Account

an accounting statement that is an integral part of the final accounts of a manufacturing organization. For any particular period, it indicates, among other things, prime cost of manufacturing, manufacturing overhead, the total manufacturing cost, and the manufacturing costs of finished goods.

Manufacturing and Processing (M&P) Tax Credit

A federal tax reduction is provided on Canadian manufacturing and processing income not subject to the small business deduction. This credit has the effect of lowering the tax rate on M&P income from the general federal rate of 28 per cent to 21 per cent. This reduction became redundant in 2004 when the general rate reduction was raised to 7 per cent, thereby lowering the general federal rate 21 per cent.

Manufacturing Concern

an entity that derives its products for sale, thereby revenue, through the direct manufacture of those products.

Manufacturing Statement

See Manufacturing Account.

Margin (stocks)

Allows investors to buy securities/assets by borrowing money from a broker/banker. The margin is the difference between the market value of a stock/asset and the loan a broker/banker makes.

Margin Account (stocks)

A leverageable account in which stocks can be purchased for a combination of cash and a loan. The loan in the margin account is collateralized by the stock and, if the value of the stock drops sufficiently, the owner will be asked to either put in more cash, or sell a portion of the stock. Margin rules are federally regulated, but margin requirements and interest may vary among broker/dealers.

Marginal Analysis

Focusing on revenues or expenses that change between two alternatives, rather than including all revenues and expenses, so as to highlight effects.

Marginal (or Incremental) Cost

A calculation showing the change in total cost as a result of a change in volume, e.g., if one more item of output increases the total cost by $25, the marginal cost is $25. It is usually useful to determine marginal cost because it can aid in determining if the rate of production should be altered.

Marginal Tax Rate

The ratio of the increase in tax to the increase in the tax base (i.e., the tax rate on each additional dollar of income). For example, in the case of an individual facing a marginal income tax rate of 29 per cent, each additional dollar of income would be subject to an income tax of 29 cents.

Margin Call (stocks)

A demand for additional funds because of adverse price movement is a stock.

Marine Insurance

Insurance coverage protecting against loss or damage of goods transported by sea.

Marketable Securities

Investments having a ready market for resale and held as a way of earning a return from temporarily unneeded cash.

Market Capitalization

The total dollar value of all outstanding shares. It is calculated by multiplying the number of shares times the current market price. The term is commonly referred to as "market cap".

Marketing Lever

Anything that provides positional advantage or power to act effectively. Potential levers may be price, brand name, corporate image, broad distribution, effective advertising, etc.

Market Maker

An Exchange member firm that is obliged to make a continuous two-way price, that is to offer to buy and sell securities in which it is registered throughout the Mandatory Quote Period.

Market Multiple

See Price/Earnings Ratio.

Market Risk Premium

Slope of the SML, the difference between the expected return on a market portfolio and the risk-free rate.

Market to Market

Daily settlement of obligations on futures positions.

Market Value

See Fair Market Value. See also Open Market Value (OMV).

Markup

The difference between the enterprise's selling prices for its products and the unit costs it incurs for those products, often a function of a specific decision to add a profit margin to the cost incurred.

Matching Concept

The accounting principle that requires the recognition of all costs that are directly associated with the realization of the revenue reported within the income statement.

Matching Credit

Where foreign income has been relieved from foreign taxation by way of a tax holiday, the double tax relief provisions of unilateral law or the relevant double tax treaty may have no foreign tax which may be credited against domestic tax; without a matching credit, domestic tax would be levied in full thereby negating the benefits of any foreign tax holiday. There-fore, the domestic tax administration may allow a notional foreign tax credit equivalent to the amount of foreign tax that would have been applied, had there not been a tax holiday, and this notional tax is referred to as the matching credit. Tax sparing credits and pioneer relief are similar terms (see below).

Matching Principle

See Matching Concept.

Material, Materiality

In accounting, material means that the magnitude of an omission or misstatement of ac-counting information makes it probable that, in the light of surrounding circumstances, the judgment of a reasonable person relying on the information would have been changed or influenced by the omission or misstatement. Materiality and Decision relevance are both defined in terms of what influences, or what makes a difference to, a decision maker. A decision not to disclose certain information may be made because it is believed that inves-tors or other users have no need for that kind of information (it is not relevant) or that the amounts involved are too small to make a difference (it is not material).

Materials

Physical goods (and their cost) used in the manufacture of a product, often separated into Direct Material (that which goes directly into the product such as cream into ice cream, or steel into cars) and Indirect Material (that which is used in maintaining the manufacturing environment such as cleaning fluids or oil for lubrication of manufacturing equipment). Indi-rect materials are usually part of the overhead component of cost. The term material, when used without the direct or indirect qualifier, usually refers to direct materials.

Material Weakness

A condition that could potentially result in the material misstatement of the financial statements.

Matrix Organization

Where a company superimposes a group or interdisciplinary team of project specialists on a functional organizational design. In a matrix organization the members have dual allegiances, i.e., to that particular assignment or project as well as their normal organizational department.

Maturity Factoring

Short-term financing in which the factor purchases all of a firm's receivables and forwards the proceeds to the seller as soon as they are collected.

Maturity Specified

Date at which the principal amount of a bond is paid.

MD&A

See Management Discussion and Analysis.

Mean

The measure of central tendency; also called the 'average'. It is calculated by the sum of the data points divided by the number of data points.

Measurement, Measuring

The attachment of dollar figures to assets, liabilities, revenues, and expenses in order to produce the figures (values) on the balance sheet and to enable the computation of income (revenues minus expenses) and equity (assets minus liabilities).

Median

The value of the midpoint variable when the data are arranged in ascending or descending order.

Media Plan

In advertising, is the plan that details the usage of media in an advertising campaign including costs, running dates, markets, reach, frequency, rationales, and strategies.

Member Firm

A trading firm of the London Stock Exchange may act as an agency broker on behalf of clients or on behalf of the firm itself.

Memorandum of Association

The charter of a company which indicates nationality, the nature of it's business and the share capital it is authorized to issue. It is a statutory document that effectively governs the company's relations with the outside world.

MER (Management Expense Ratio)

The percentage of the assets that were spent to run a mutual fund. It includes things like management and advisory fees, travel costs and 12b-1 fees. The expense ratio does not include brokerage costs for trading the portfolio. Also referred to as the expense ratio.

Merchant Bank

A European form of an investment bank.

Merger

The joining together of two corporations such that the owners of both become the owners of the combined corporation. Usually both corporations are approximately equal contributors to the combination. The merged companies, product lines, etc. may or may or may not lose their individual identities, however usually one company is completely absorbed by the other such that the acquiring firm retains its identity while the acquired ceases to exist as a separate entity.

Mid-Cap

A stock with a capitalization, total equity value, between $500 million and $5 billion.

Middle Market Company

See Mid-Cap.

Mid Price

The price half-way between the two prices shown in the London Stock Exchange's Official List under 'Quotation' or the average of both buying and selling prices offered by the market makers. The prices found in newspapers are normally estimates of the mid price.

Millage

A rate (as of taxation) expressed in mills per dollar.

Minimum Quote Size

The minimum number of shares in which market makers are obliged to display prices on SEAQ for securities in which they are registered.

Minimum Wage

The lowest compensation you are allowed to pay an employee for hourly work. It is defined by Federal, state, and sometimes local laws. State or local laws may be more restrictive than Federal law, and certainly may differ.

Mini-Trust

A short (usually pre-printed) form of trust, often used as a confidentiality enhancer, to bridge the ownership and management of an International Business Company. The Mini-Trust is intended only to pass assets on the death of the settlor, i.e., a will substitute.

Minority Interest

The interest or percentage ownership of a group of stockholders who, in total, own less than 50% of the shares in the corporation.

MIS

See Management Information System.

Miscellaneous Income

That income realized that is not directly related to the sale of standard products and services.

Mixer Company

One of the functions of a foreign holding company may be to receive dividends from high tax and low tax subsidiaries, which are then merged into one dividend payable to its parent company, whose income would normally be taxed on a dividend by dividend basis creating additional tax on profits from the low tax subsidiaries. The foreign taxes are thereby aggregated so that the average foreign tax on all dividends may be offset against domestic tax on the grossed up dividend from the mixer company.

Modified Accelerated Cost Recovery System (MACRS)

A system used in accounting to define the rate and method under which a fixed asset will be depreciated for tax purposes.

Modified Accrual Basis

Accounting is a mixture of the cash and accrual basis. The modified accrual basis should be used for governmental funds. To be recognized as a revenue or expenditure, the actual receipt or disbursal of cash must occur soon enough after a transaction or event has occurred to have an impact on current spendable resources. In other words, revenues must be both measurable and available to pay for the current period's liabilities. Revenues are considered available when collectible either during the current period or after the end of the current period but in time to pay year-end liabilities. Expenditures are recognized when a transaction or event is expected to draw upon current spendable resources rather than future resources.

Monetary

Anything pertaining to or having to do with money, money creation, money supply, and the government management of money.

Money Market Instruments

Short-term debt securities maturing in one year or less. These include treasury bills, bankers' acceptances, commercial paper, discount notes and guaranteed investment certificates.

Money Markets

Financial markets where short-term debt securities are bought and sold.

Money Measurement Concept

Stipulates that all business transactions must be expressed in money terms, i.e., if something cannot be measured in money; it will not be included in accounting books.

Mortgage

A form of Security on a loan in which the lender has a direct claim on title to property specified in the mortgage. Usually used to finance the acquisition of that property.

Mortgage-Backed Security (MBS)

A debt security that gives you a share of a pool of mortgages. An MBS pays monthly income, which is a combination of interest and a portion of the principal of the underlying mortgages.

Moving Average Cost, Moving Weighted Average

See AVGE and Average cost.

Multiple

Same as Price/Earnings Ratio.

Multiple Discriminant Analysis (MDA)

Statistical technique for distinguishing between two samples on the basis of their observed characteristics.

Multiple Rates of Return

One potential problem in using the IRR method if more than one discount rate makes the NPV of an investment zero.

Mutual Legal Assistance Treaty

A treaty that provides for mutual legal assistance, including the exchange of information, etc., in cases where criminal offences have been committed.

Mutually Exclusive Investment Decisions

One potential problem in using the IRR method if the acceptance of one project excludes that of another.

Naamloze Vennootschap (N.V.)

In Dutch Company law, the N.V. is the form of incorporation favoured by larger companies, similar to the American corporation.

Natural Business Year

A fiscal year based on the cycle of the given business rather than a calendar year. The year ends with inventories and activities at a low level, e.g., after winter shipments for a ski manufacturer.

Natural Classification (of costs)

Focuses on the nature of the cost item. In this classification structure, the total operating costs of an activity can be classified into manufacturing costs and commercial costs. Manufacturing costs include all direct materials and direct labour, as well as, factory overhead. Such factory overhead costs include indirect materials (such as factory supplies & lubricants), indirect labour (such as supervision and inspection) and other indirect costs (such as rent, insurance, and utilities). Commercial expenses include marketing expenses (such as advertising, printing, and sales salaries) and administrative (general and administrative (G&A)) expenses (such as administrative office salaries, rent, and legal expenses).

Negative Goodwill

Arises where the net assets at the date of acquisition, fairly valued, exceed the cost of acquisition. It is reflected on the balance sheet net of other intangible assets. Negative goodwill is recognized as income as follows:

- To the extent that negative goodwill relates to expected future losses and expenses, it is recognized in the income statement when the future losses and expenses are recognized.

- The amount of negative goodwill relating to identifiable non-monetary assets (not exceeding the fair values of such acquired assets), is recognized as income on a systematic basis over the remaining useful lives of the identifiable acquired depreciable/amortizable assets with a maximum of 20 years.

- The amount of the negative goodwill in excess of the fair values of the acquired identifiable non-monetary assets is recognized as income immediately.

- The amount of the negative goodwill relating to monetary assets is recognized as income immediately.

NOTE: Intangible assets are not revalued.

Negotiable Instrument

An unconditional order or promise to pay an amount of money; it is easily transferable from one person to another, e.g., a cheque, promissory note, bearer bond, and draft (bill of exchange).

Net

In general, is the figure remaining after all relevant deductions have been made from the starting, or gross, amount. In accounting, net means the residual after one quantity is subtracted from another. Examples are Net book value, Net income, Net-of-tax analysis, and Net realizable value.

Net Acquisitions

Total installed cost of capital acquisitions minus adjusted cost of any disposals within an asset pool.

Net Advantage to Leasing (NAL)

The NPV of the decision to lease an asset instead of buying it.

Net Asset Value (NAV)

In securities, except money market funds which always have a NAV of $1.00, represents the market value or price of one fund share. It is calculated by the total value of the fund's portfolio less liabilities divided by the number of shares; or, in corporate valuations, it is the book value of all corporate assets less liabilities.

Net Book Value

The cost of an asset minus any accumulated depreciation, amortization, allowance for doubtful accounts, and so on.

Net Change in Cash

Calculated by adding cash from operating, investing, and financing activities and foreign exchange effects from the Statement of Cash Flows.

Net Contribution

The amount remaining after all relevant deductions have been made to the gross amount, e.g., Net Contribution to Margin.

Net Income

The difference between a business's total revenue and its total expenses. This caption and amount is usually found at the bottom of a company's Profit and Loss statement. Also called Net Profit.

Net Leases

Typically, there are three net leases: net lease, double-net lease, and triple-net lease. A net lease is a base rent plus an additional charge for taxes. A double-net lease is a base rent plus an additional charge for taxes and insurance. A triple-net lease is base rent plus an additional charge for taxes, insurance, and common area expenses.

Net Loss

Negative Net Income.

Net-of-Tax Analysis

A method of determining the impact of management decisions or accounting changes in which the effects of Income Tax are included to produce the net after-tax effect of the decision or change.

Net Operating Income (NOI)

Income after deducting for operating expenses but before deducting for Income Taxes and interest.

Net Operating Loss (NOL)

Experienced by a business when business deductions exceed business income for the fiscal year. For income tax purposes, a net operating loss can be used to offset income in a prior year, or a taxpayer can elect to forego the carry back and carry the net operating loss forward.

Net Present Value (NPV)

The difference between the discounted value of an investment's market value and its cost. This is a method used in evaluating investments, whereby the net present value of all cash outflows (such as the cost of the investment) and cash inflows (returns) is calculated using a given discount rate, usually Required Rate of Return. An investment is acceptable if the NPV is positive. In capital budgeting, the discount rate used is called the Hurdle Rate and is usually equal to the Incremental Cost of Capital.

Net Present Value Profile

A graphical representation of the relationship between an investment's NPVs and various discount rates.

Net Profit

See Net Income.

Net Profit Margin (NPM after Tax)

Measures profitability as a percentage of revenues after consideration of all revenue and expense, including interest expenses, non-operating items, and income taxes. For a business to be viable in the long term profits must be generated; making the net profit margin ratio one of the key performance indicators for any business. It is important to analyze the ratio over time. A variation in the ratio from year-to-year may be due to abnormal conditions or expenses which need to be addressed. A decline in the ratio over time may indicate a margin squeeze suggesting that productivity improvements may need to be initiated. In some cases, the costs of such improvements may lead to a further drop in the ratio or even losses before increased profitability is achieved.

Net Profit Margin (NPM pre-Tax)

Incorporates all of the expenses associated with ordinary business (excluding taxes) thus is a measure of the overall operating efficiency of the firm prior to any tax considerations which may mask performance. For a business to be viable in the long term profits must be generated; making the net profit margin ratio one of the key performance indicators for any business. It is important to analyze the ratio over time. A variation in the ratio from year-to-year may be due to abnormal conditions or expenses which need to be addressed. A decline in the ratio over time may indicate a margin squeeze suggesting that productivity improvements may need to be initiated. In some cases, the costs of such improvements may lead to a further drop in the ratio or even losses before increased profitability is achieved.

Net Purchases

Those items purchased less returns, discounts and allowances on those purchases.

Net Realizable Value

The fair market value that an asset will bring if it is sold through the usual product market minus any completion or disposal costs.

Net Receivables

A company's accounts receivable (money owed to the company) minus any provisions for bad debts.

Net Revenue

Gross Revenue less discounts, allowances, sales returns, freight out, etc.

Net Sales

Gross sales less discounts, allowances, sales returns, freight out, etc.

Net Sales to Gross Sales

Shows the per cent of all transactions that may be considered as "good" net transactions. Differences may arise from returns, bad product, or other sales concessions.

Net 10, 30, etc.

usually refers to payment terms on an invoice, e.g., 'Net 10 2%, 30', would mean that if a purchaser pays the invoice within 10 days a 2% reduction in invoice amount may be enjoyed, but full invoice amount is due within 30 days.

Net Worth

The difference between Total Liabilities and Total Assets. Minority interest is included here.

Neutrality

An objective of preparing financial accounting information in which the information should represent phenomena neutrally, without attention to the particular interests of any party or parties.

New Issue

A company coming to the market for the first time or issuing additional shares.

New Shares

Shares newly issued by a company; these shares can usually be transferred on renounceable documents.

Nexus

The sufficient presence within the jurisdiction of a taxing authority. The taxable income of a multistate corporation may be apportioned to a specific state only if the corporation has a sufficient nexus in the state. The nexus for state sales tax requires a physical presence in the state, whereas the nexus for state income tax purposes requires more than just solicitations of sales.

Nil Paid

A new issue of shares, usually as the result of a rights issue on which no payment to the company has yet been made.

Nominal Rate of Interest

The stated rate of interest applied to your investment.

Nominee Company

A company formed for the express purpose of holding securities and other assets in its name or to provide nominee directors and/or officers on behalf of clients of its parent bank or trust company.

Nominee Director

A director whose function is passive in nature. The director receives a fee for lending his or her name to the organization. Nominee directors are subject to director responsibilities.

Nominee Name

Name in which security is registered and held in trust on behalf of the beneficial owner.

Non-Active Company

A company which is either in voluntary liquidation or wishes to protect a name which includes the word bank or trust company in it even though the company is not carrying on any banking or trust business.

Non-Cash Items

Expenses charged against revenues that do not directly affect cash flow, such as depreciation.

Non-Controlling Interest

The portion of a subsidiary corporation included in consolidated financial statements that is not owned by the controlling (majority) owners of the parent corporation.

Non-Current Assets

Assets expected to bring benefit for more than one fiscal year. Includes PPE (property, plant and equipment) as opposed to current assets which include cash, cash equivalents (e.g., securities, short-term notes, etc.), inventory and accounts receivable.

Non-Current Liabilities

Liabilities expected to be repaid or otherwise removed more than one year in the future.

Non-Discretionary

Means it is mandatory, not up to the individual or company.

Non-Discretionary Accrual

A mandatory expense/asset that is recorded within the accounting system that has yet to be realized. An example of this would be payroll taxes.

Non-Discrimination

A non discrimination Article in a double tax treaty prevents a country from treating a foreign taxpayer in a more disadvantageous way than a local taxpayer in respect of the same taxable item and in the same circumstances.

Non-Operating Cash Flows

Cash inflows and outflows related to non-current investments, financing, and usually dividends, and so separate from the cash flows resulting from day-to-day operations.

Non-Resident

A non-resident is a person who does not have a sufficiently close connection with a country to be subject to full tax liability on his or her worldwide income in the country. Non-residents are usually taxable only on their source income from the country.

No-Par (shares)

Shares having no legal minimum issue price (Par value) and so the proceeds of which are simply added to share capital at whatever price is obtained in each issue.

NOPAT (Net Operating Profit After Tax)

A company's potential cash earnings if its capitalization was unleveraged. NOPAT is commonly used in EVA calculations.

Normal Distribution

Asymmetric, bell-shaped frequency distribution that can be defined by its mean and standard deviation.

Normal Market Size

The SEAQ classification system that replaced the old alpha, beta, gamma system. NMS is a value expressed as a number of shares used to calculate that minimum quote size for each security.

Nostro Account

An account held by a bank in a foreign country in the currency of that country e.g., a German bank with an account in New York will call the record in its own books of its New York account a nostro account.

Note

See Promissory Note.

Note Issuance Facility (NIF)

Large borrowers issue notes up to one year in maturity in the Euromarket. Banks underwrite or sell notes.

Notes Payable

Accounts payable that are supported by signed contracts or other agreements and usually carrying interest. Often used to describe financing obtained from banks and other financial institutions used to provide operating funds OL funds for construction prior to completion of projects and obtaining of more secured financing like a Mortgage.

Notes Payable-Short Term

All short term note obligations, including bank and commercial paper. Does not include trade notes payable.

Notes Receivable

Accounts receivable supported by signed contracts or other agreements specifying repayment terms, interest rate, and other conditions.

Notes to the Financial Statements

A detailed set of notes immediately following the financial statements contained in the annual report that expands upon and/or explains in some depth the information contained in the financial statements.

Not-for-Profit Accounting

Procedures used to account for non-business, non-government entities. These procedures increasingly follow GAAP.

NPV

An acronym for Net Present Value.

NRGT (Non-Resettable Grand Total)

A concept used in retail point of sale (POS) terminals that does not allow the Grand Total to be reset, but does allow adjustments to be entered, e.g., errors, overwriting, etc. Improved security and control is provided for independent retail and chain operations with a Non-Resettable Grand Total (NRGT). Updated by all sales, this valuable audit figure may be selected by programmability to print on the Daily Business Report.

Objective

A statement that is written in terms of specific measurable time-based and verifiable outcomes that challenge the organization to be more responsive to the environment to achieve the desired goals. Dependent upon usage, Goals are general in nature, while Objectives are specific, measurable and time-based. In some organizations, the meanings for Goal and Objective are reversed.

Objectivity

The notion that the information in financial statements must be as free from bias as possible, in order that all user groups can have confidence in it. An accountant attempts to record and report data that are based on objective sources to make the data more acceptable to outside parties. Because completed arm's length transactions are supported by documents that can be verified by any interested observer, these constitute the preferred basis of measurement.

OCOR

See Opportunity Cost of Revenue.

OECD Commentary

The Commentary to the OECD Model Treaty is the official explanation of the Model Treaty by the OECD.

Off-Balance-Sheet Financing

Methods of obtaining financing that avoid having to record the sources as liabilities or equity.

Official List

The London Stock Exchange's Official List features listed securities and the prices of transactions published each specified period.

Offset Account

An account that is setup for elimination of a long or short position by making an opposite transaction.

Offshore Banking

By popular usage, the establishment and operation of U.S. or foreign banks in such offshore "tax havens" as the Bahamas and the Cayman Islands.

Offshore Banking Unit ("OBU")

A bank in Cyprus, or any other financial centre with similar organizations; not allowed to conduct business in the domestic market, only with other OBUs or with foreign persons.

Offshore Booking Centres

An offshore financial centre used by international banks as a location for "shell branches" to book certain deposits and loans. Such offshore bookings are often utilized to avoid regulatory restrictions and taxes.

Offshore Company

Although an offshore company is generally thought of as a tax haven or low tax entity, they are in fact companies registered in one country but whose activities are carried on elsewhere. Contrary to popular understanding, they may be entirely respectable and heavily controlled, such as offshore banking units or captive insurance companies. See also International Business Company.

Offshore Dollars

Same as Eurodollars, but encompassing such deposits held in banks and branches anywhere outside the United States, including Europe.

Offshore Financial Centres

A country or jurisdiction where an intentional attempt has been made to attract foreign business by deliberate government policy such as the enactment of secrecy laws and tax incentives.

Offshore Group of Banking Supervisors ("OGBS")

Established in October 1980 at the instigation of the Basel Committee on Banking Supervision with which the Group maintains close contact. The primary objective of OGBS is to promote the effective supervision of banks in their jurisdictions and to further international co-operation in the supervision between the Offshore Banking Supervisors band between them and Basel Committee member nations and other banking supervisors. Current OGBS members are Aruba, Bahamas, Bahrain, Barbados, Bermuda, Cayman Islands, Cyprus, Gibraltar, Guernsey, Hong Kong, Isle of Man, Jersey, Lebanon, Malta, Mauritius, Netherlands Antilles, Panama, Singapore and Vanuatu.

Offshore Limited Partnership

A partnership, the general partner of which is an offshore company, but the limited partners may be onshore entities.

Offshore Profit Centres

Branches of major international banks and multinational corporations located in a low tax financial centre that are established for the purpose of lowering taxes.

Offshore Trust

The quality that differentiates an offshore trust from an onshore trust is portability. The offshore trust can be transferred to additional jurisdictions to maintain confidentiality and to take advantage of desirable facets of the new jurisdictions laws.

One-Write System

(Also known as Pegboard System.) A useful system for small and home-based businesses. It captures information at the time the transaction takes place. These One-Write Systems are efficient because they eliminate the need for recopying the data and are compatible with electronic data processing if you should decide to computerize. Many small businesses rely totally on the One-Write System for simplicity and versatility. With only two pieces of paper, a cheque and a ledger, you get all the benefits of sound bookkeeping: accuracy, money distribution, cheque control, audit trail, running bank balance, and instant review.

Ontario Securities Commission (OSC)

The securities-trading regulator for Ontario and the leading such regulator in Canada.

Open Account

A non-guaranteed payment arrangement, e.g., similar to department store credit. Goods are purchased and delivered without payment. Future payment for delivered goods is dependent on the good faith of the purchaser.

Open Inflation

Means that prices are rising on consumer goods and services.

Open Market Value (OMV)

An opinion of the best price at which the sale of an interest in an asset would have been completed unconditionally for cash consideration on the date of valuation, assuming:

- a willing seller;

- that, prior to the date of valuation, there had been a reasonable period (having regard to the nature of the asset and state of the market) for the proper marketing of the interest, for the agreement of price and terms and for the completion of the sale;

- that the state of the market, level of values and other circumstances were, on any earlier assumed date of exchange of contracts, the same as on the date of valuation;

- that no account is taken of any additional bid by a purchaser with a special interest; and

- that both parties to the transaction had acted knowledgeably, prudently and without compulsion.

Open to Buy

The dollar amount budgeted by a business for inventory purchases for a specific time period.

Operating Activities

See Cash from Operations.

Operating Allowance

An advance/reimbursement against certain costs/expenses and/or a reduction in amount payable to cover those certain costs/expenses.

Operating Cash Flow

Cash generated from a firm's normal business activities.

Operating Cycle

The time period between the acquisition of inventory and when cash is collected from receivables.

Operating Expenditures

The amount used during a particular period directly in support of day-to-day operations such as wages, maintenance, office supplies, etc.

Operating Expenses

All selling and general and administrative expenses. Includes depreciation, but not interest expense.

Operating Expense to Sales

Reports the operating expenses as a per cent of Net Revenues. This then is a measure of the total overhead employed in the firm per Net Sales Revenue Dollar; thereby giving an indication of the efficiency of the cost structure of the company. It gives an indication of the ability of a business to convert income into profit. Generally, businesses with low ratios will generate more profit than others. In general business operations with larger and more stable cash flows can sustain higher ratios than smaller and less stable operations. Scale and income stability are important considerations though it is up to the management of a business to monitor costs in an appropriate manner whatever its size.

Operating Income

Revenue less cost of goods sold and related operating expenses that are applied to the day-to-day operating activities of the company. It excludes financial related items (i.e., interest income, dividend income, and interest expense), extraordinary items, and taxes.

Operating Lease

Usually a shorter-term lease where the lessor is responsible for insurance, taxes, and upkeep. Often cancellable on short notice.

Operating Leverage

The degree to which a firm or project relies on fixed costs.

Operating Loan

Loan negotiated with banks, usually by small business, for day-to-day operations.

Operating Profit

Gross Profit minus Operating Expenses.

Operating Profit to Sales

A useful ratio when evaluating value of a firm. It discounts the effect of varying tax rates and benefits to give a more accurate indication of the return associated with the firm.

Operating Return

The return earned by an enterprise before considering the cost of financing and usually also before considering nonrecurring items.

Opportunity Cost

Widely used in business planning in evaluating capital investment. A company measures the projected return against the anticipated return it would receive on a highest yielding alternative investment that contains a similar risk profile.

Opportunity Cost of Revenue (OCOR)

Where revenue/money held now may be invested to produce more money — thus we consider opportunity cost a return or more revenue.

Opportunity Loss

See Opportunity Cost.

Option

A contract that gives its owner the right (but not the obligation) to buy (Call Option) or sell (Put Option) some asset at a fixed price on or before a given date. For that right, the option holder (or buyer) pays the option writer (or seller) a Premium. If the option holder does not exercise her option by the specified date, it will expire and she will lose the Premium.

Order of Liquidity

When items on a balance sheet are listed in order of liquidity. After cash, the other current assets are listed in order of liquidity or nearness to cash (i.e., Accounts Receivable first, then Inventory...).

Order of Permanence

Where fixed assets are entered in the balance sheet in descending order of permanence (i.e., land first, then buildings, then equipment ...).

Ordinary Residence

This is a term used in the United Kingdom and Ireland to differentiate between people who are fiscally resident for a particular tax year, and those who are ordinarily resident for continuous fiscal years; certain types of income are subject to tax only where a person is ordinarily resident.

Ordinary Shares

The most common form of share. Holders receive dividends, which vary in amount in accordance with the profitability of the company and recommendations of the directors. The holders of the ordinary shares are the owners of the company.

Organization Cost

Amounts spent to begin a business entity, e.g., business filing fees, franchise acquisition, and legal fees. In the United States, costs associated with a corporation issuing or selling shares or other securities are capitalized and not tax deductible. Other organization expenses may be capitalized and amortized over a period of sixty (60) months or more; thereby providing possible tax relief through organization cost deductions.

Original Issue Discount

When a long-term debt instrument is issued at a price that is lower than its stated redemption value; the difference is called Original Issue Discount (OID).

OSC

See Ontario Securities Commission.

OSHA (*Occupational Safety and Health Act*)

A federal law in the United States that requires employers to provide employees with a workplace that is relatively free of hazardous conditions.

Other Assets

A catch-all category used for non-current (and occasionally current) assets that do not fit into other categories, are not material individually but aggregate to a material total.

Output Market Value

The market value of an asset if sold.

Outstanding Shares

The number of shares that are currently owned by all investors. It also includes restricted shares (shares owned by officers and insiders of the company) as well as shares held by the public. Shares that the company has repurchased or retired are not considered outstanding stock.

Overdraft

See Bank Overdraft.

Overhead Costs

The costs associated with providing and maintaining a manufacturing or working environment. For example: renting the building, heating and lighting the work area, supervision costs and maintenance of the facilities. Includes indirect labour and indirect material.

Overleveraged

A balance sheet condition where the entity is incapable of servicing its debt load (interest payments) with available capital sources. Simply put, the entity is carrying too much debt.

Oversubscription Privilege

Allows shareholders to purchase unsubscribed shares in a rights offering at the subscription price.

Overtrading

In securities, is: (a) excessive buying and selling by a broker in a discretionary account, or (b) practice of a member of an underwriting group inducing a brokerage client to buy a portion of a new issue by purchasing other securities from the client at a premium. In finance, overtrading is when a firm expands sales beyond a level that can be financed with normal working capital.

Owners

Parties who have contributed resources in return for the right to dividends and any residual value (equity) of the enterprise.

Owner's Capital

The owner's equity of the proprietor of an unincorporated business.

Owner's Draw

See Proprietor's Draw.

Owners' Equity

See Equity, Shareholders' Equity.

Own Work Capitalized

Represents the value of work performed for own purposes and capitalized as part of fixed assets.

Pacioli Luca

Pacioli's *Suma* is the first known book describing double-entry bookkeeping. It was published in 1494 and quickly became influential in the development of accounting and business in Europe.

Packing Slip

A document accompanying a shipment that describes the shipment's contents and can be used to verify the supplier's invoice for the cost of the shipment.

Paid-in-Capital

Capital received from investors for stock, equal to capital stock plus paid-in capital, NOT that capital received from earnings or donations. Also called contributed capital.

P&L

See Profit and Loss Statement.

Par

The nominal value of a security.

Parent

The dominant corporation in a corporate group linked by ownership, the name of which is usually used in the consolidated financial statements.

Participation Exemption

The Dutch participation exemption is well known, but this term applies in Luxembourg, Belgium, Austria and other holding company jurisdictions. It describes the exemption from tax on dividends receivable, and capital gains derived, from resident and non-resident companies in which the recipient has a substantial interest. Often this substantial interest may be 10% or 25%, but it may be 5% in Holland and some countries do not even require a minimum percentage holding. However, the important aspect is that the recipient participates in the share capital of the other companies, and has some business connection therewith, rather than holding the shares merely as a portfolio interest.

Partners' Capital

The owners' equity section of a partnership's balance sheet.

Partnership

An unincorporated business formed by two or more co-owners in a relationship with a view to profit. Like a sole proprietorship, this form of business does not have the privilege of limited liability. However, it is different from a sole proprietorship in that a sole proprietorship can have only one owner.

Par Value

A value set as the legal minimum amount for which a corporation's shares may be issued. Used in earlier years to prevent "watering the stock" and other frauds in which managers sold shares cheaply to themselves or their friends and then outvoted more legitimate shareholders. With the protection to shareholders provided by greater regulation and scrutiny of companies' affairs in the present time, Canadian companies typically have No-par shares instead, but par value is still used in many other jurisdictions, including some in the United States.

Passive Activity

Defined in the U.S. *Tax Code* as one or more trades, business or rental activity, that the taxpayer does not materially participate in managing or running. All income and losses from passive activities are grouped together on an income tax return and, generally, loss deductions are limited or suspended until the passive activity that generated them is disposed of in its entirety.

Passive Income

This term is used in comparison to Active Income to reflect income from dividends, interest, royalties, etc.

Patent

A legal form of protection that provides a person or legal entity with exclusive rights to exclude others from making, using, or selling a concept or invention for the duration of the patent. There are three types of patents available: design, plant, and utility.

Payable through Account

A correspondent banking account relationship established by a foreign bank with a U.S. bank, for the purpose of clearing U.S. dollar denominated cheques drawn on the foreign bank by its demand deposit customers.

Payback Period

In capital budgeting, is the length of time needed to recoup the cost of Capital Investment. The payback period is the ratio of the initial investment (cash outlay, regardless of the source of the cash) to the annual cash inflows for the recovery period. The major shortcoming for the payback period method is that it does not take into account cash flows after the payback period and is therefore not a measure of the profitability of an investment project. For this reason, analysts generally prefer the Discounted Cash Flow methods of capital budgeting; primarily, the Internal Rate of Return and the Net Present Value methods.

Payment

The satisfaction of a debt or claim; primarily money paid to fulfill an obligation.

Payoff Profile

A plot showing the gains and losses that will occur on a contract as the result of unexpected price changes.

Payout Ratio

Dividends paid divided by company earnings over some period of time, expressed as a percentage.

Payroll Burden

In the U.S., includes the cost of your payroll administration, FICA, FUTA, SUTA, workers' compensation, etc., based on each $100.00 of payroll. For example: $100.00 of payroll earned + $37.56 payroll burden = $137.56 total payroll.

Pegboard System

See One-Write System.

Pending

Usually refers to either: (1) Not yet decided; or (2) Being in continuance.

Pension Maximization

A controversial strategy, often espoused by life insurance agents, of using insurance to augment a company benefit plan. Under this arrangement, a retiree takes pension payments for his or her own life only and buys life insurance to provide for a surviving spouse. Also known as pension max.

PE Ratio

See Price-Earnings Ratio.

Percentage Lease

A type of lease where the landlord charges a base rent plus an additional percentage of any profits realized by the business tenant.

Percentage of Completion Method of Accounting

Instituted if your revenues exceed $10,000,000 (3-year average) or your contracts will not be completed within a two-year period, you are generally required to use the percentage of completion accounting for contracts. This method is generally used for long-term construction contracts, franchise revenue, and similar multi-period revenues. There are many advantages to using the percentage of completion method including:

- It is the best measurement of income.

- Percentage of completion normally needs to be computed for financial statement purposes eliminating confusing timing differences from tax to financial statements.

- There is no increase in alternative minimum taxable income.

- Losses can be recognized on contracts before the job is complete.

- It is useful in leveling taxable income, permitting use of lower tax brackets each year.

- When using the percentage of completion method, it is important to carefully compute the per cent complete, for it may have a great impact on your taxable income.

- Estimated costs to complete the contract, a component of calculating the per cent to complete, determine what your taxable income will be. Also, carefully reviewing the over-head allocation may result in lower tax.

Percentage of Sales Approach

Financial planning method in which accounts are projected depending on a firm's predicted sales level.

Per Country Limitation

Reference may be made to the mixer company where it is stated that some countries levy tax on a dividend by dividend basis; this prevents excess foreign tax credits from one source to be offset against additional tax payable on income derived from another source. The country therefore limits double tax relief on a source by source basis, hence the term 'per country limitation'.

Performance Indicators

Those empirical data points that indicate how well, or poorly, an entity is performing against preset goals and objectives. Normally, in business or strategic planning, a company will set targets over a specified period that the business believes are attainable and track performance over time to those targets or objectives.

Period Expenses

Expenses that are related to the passage of time rather than to the level of sales volume or other activities. Examples are interest, many salaries, and portions of some Overhead costs such as heat, light, and property taxes.

Periodic Inventory Control Method

A method of calculating inventory that uses data on beginning inventory, additions to inventory, and an end-of-period count to deduce the cost of goods sold.

Periodicity Concept

The concept that each accounting period has an economic activity associated with it, and that the activity can be measured, accounted for, and reported upon.

Periodic Reporting

A basic convention of financial accounting that holds that accounting information must be assembled and presented to users at regular intervals (at least yearly and often quarterly or monthly).

Permanence

The quality or state of being permanent; primarily judged by durability and useful life. See Order of Permanence.

Permanent Establishment

A permanent establishment is a fixed place of business through which an enterprise carries on its business in whole or in part. The concept of permanent establishment applies when a State determines that, under its domestic law, the business profits of a resident of another State may be taxable. Tax treaties generally provide that the business profits of an enterprise of one Contracting State derived from activities or sources in the other Contracting State are not taxable by the source State unless they are attributable to a permanent establishment therein.

Perpetual Inventory Control Method

A method of controlling inventory that maintains continuous records on the flow of units of inventory. Thus, there are figures on record for beginning inventory, each unit added to inventory, and each unit removed from inventory for sale. From this, an ending inventory figure can be determined and checked against the figure from a physical count. This method provides better internal control than the periodic inventory method, but it is also more costly to maintain the extra records.

Perpetual Succession

One of the legal distinctions between a business and a company. A company has perpetual succession meaning that a change in the membership does not affect the existence of the company whereas a business does not enjoy this perpetual succession. For example, in the case of a partnership, which is one form of business registration, a change in the membership affects the partnership.

Perpetuity

An annuity in which the cash flows continue forever.

Personal Guarantees

Additional Security on loans, often taken by banks lending to private corporations, in which some or all shareholders sign agreements to contribute personal assets if the corporation does not repay the loans or pay interest on schedule.

Personal Loan

A short-term loan that is extended based on the personal integrity of the borrower.

Personal Tax

Tax on personal income in Canada including both personal income taxes and the employee portion of social security contributions (in Canada these are primarily unemployment insurance premiums and Canada/Quebec Pension Plan contributions).

Petty Cash

A small fund of cash kept on hand by an employee for paying small expenses such as postage, minor supplies, and courier charges.

Phantom Profit

Hypothetical profit, i.e., no cash flow is generated. Appreciation on any asset, e.g., stock, is considered phantom profit unless or until the asset is sold, thereby generating cash flow.

Pioneer Relief

Similar to a matching credit, double tax treaties particularly with developing countries allow for tax holidays to be preserved through a distribution of income by means of a notional tax that would otherwise have been levied being creditable against domestic tax on receipt of the income.

PITI

An acronym for Principal, Interest, Taxes and Insurance when dealing with property mortgages.

Place of Incorporation Test

A rule that considers a corporation to be resident in the country in which it is incorporated. See, for example, subsection 250(4) of the *Income Tax Act*.

Planning Horizon

The long-range time period the financial planning process focuses on, usually the next two to five years.

Plowback Ratio

See Retention Ratio.

Plug

The double-entry system requires that debits equal credits. If adding up all the debits and the credits does not produce two equal figures, the statements must be adjusted so that a balance occurs. The amount of adjustment needed is often called a "plug". This would only be needed if there had been an error somewhere, though sometimes the word plug is used in criticism of accrual, consolidation, or other adjustments that produce amounts the critic does not like.

Point of Sale

Often used to refer to the point in time when a sale has been completed and the product or service has been delivered to the customer, which is the most common point of recognizing revenue.

Points

Additional fee paid to a lender. Points are generally stated as a per cent of the total amount borrowed and are in essence prepaid interest. Points paid can be deducted over the life of the loan.

Poison Pill

A financial device designed to make unfriendly takeover attempts unappealing, if not impossible.

Political Risk

Risk related to changes in value that arise because of political actions.

Pooling of Interests

In the U.S., is the method of accounting used in a business combination in which the acquiring company has issued voting common stock in exchange for voting common stock of the acquired company. The features of the method are that the acquired company's net assets are brought forward at book value, retained earnings and paid-in capital are brought forward, the net income is recognized for the full financial year regardless of the date of acquisition, and the expenses of pooling are immediately charged against earnings. In order to use the method there are a number of criteria to be met concerning the prior independence of the companies and the nature and timing of the acquisition.

Portfolio

A collection of securities held by an investor.

Portfolio Investments

Debt or equity investments in a corporation that do not provide the investor with substantial ownership or influence in the management of the corporation. Typically, equity ownership of less than 10% of a corporation is considered to be a portfolio investment.

Portfolio Weight

Percentage of a portfolio's total value in a particular asset.

Post(ed)(ing)

Transfer, transferring, or having transferred, journal entries to ledger accounts and thereby making them permanent. The only way to fix a mistake is to use an adjusting or correcting entry and post that.

Post-Closing Accounts

The accounts as they exist after the revenues, expenses, and dividends accounts have been transferred to retained earnings ("closed").

Post-Closing Trial Balance

A trial balance of the post-closing accounts.

PR

An acronym for, among others, 'payroll' and 'purchase request'.

Practical Capacity

Where the cost of production is based on the 'practical capacity' of production facilities. Therefore, the proportion of overheads allocated to a unit of production is not to be increased as consequence of idle capacity of the plant.

Precautionary Motive

The need to hold cash as a safety margin to act as a financial reserve.

Predictor Ratios

Most ratios are descriptive in nature; that is, they describe the firm as it is now. Predictor ratios provide suggestions about likely future conditions for the firm. Two industry standard predictor ratios are: (1) The Altman "Z-Score" (a valid predictor of bankruptcy); and (2) Sustainable Growth Rate (showing the degree to which a company can grow using retained earnings to fund growth).

Preference Share Capital

Capital raised by an entity through the sale of preferred shares.

Preference Shares

See Preferred Shares.

Preferential Form

The London Stock Exchange allows companies offering shares to the public to set aside up to 10 per cent of the issues for applications from employees and where a parent company is floating off a subsidiary, from shareholders of the parent company. Separate application forms, usually pink in colour, (hence the name pink forms) are used for this.

Preferred Shares

Usually, non-voting shares that pay dividends at a specified rate and have preference over common shares (but not over debentures and loans) in the payment of dividends and the liquidation of assets.

Preferred Stock

See Preferred Shares.

Premium

(1) If the market price of a new security is higher than the issue price, the difference is the premium. If it is lower, the difference is called the discount; (2) The cost of purchasing a traded option.

Premium on Bonds

Arises when bonds are issued at a price above their legal face value, such as a $100 bond being issued for $105 cash, indicating a $5 premium.

Prepaid Expenses

Amounts that are paid in advance to a vender or creditor for goods and services. Typically, insurance premiums are paid in advance of the coverage contained in the policy. Prepaid Expenses is a Current Asset for your business. This is because you have paid for something and someone owes you the service or the goods for which you prepaid.

Preparers

Managers and accountants who produce financial statements.

Present Value

The current value of one or more future cash payments, discounted at some appropriate interest rate.

Present Value Analysis

Analysis of future cash flows done by removing the presumed interest components of those flows.

Price Earnings Multiple

See Price Earnings Ratio.

Price-Earnings Ratio

The current share price divided by the last published earnings per share, where earnings per share is net profit divided by the number of ordinary shares. The P/E ratio is a measure of the level of confidence investors have in a company. Generally the higher the figure the higher the confidence. The P/E ratio is a performance benchmark that can be used as a comparison against other companies or within the stock's own historical performance. For instance, if a stock has historically run at a P/E of 35 and the current P/E is 12, you may want to explore the reasons for the drastic change. If you believe that the ratio is too low, you may want to buy the stock. You will generally find a P/E ratio based on either the prior reporting year's earnings, or the earnings of the prior four quarters added together (LTM or Latest Twelve Months). The P/E ratio is also used in one of the methods of valuing a business: (P/E ratio) × (net income of the business) = value of the business. If the business has no income, there is no valuation. If the common stock is not publicly traded, valuation of the stock is purely subjective. This may not be the best method, but can provide a benchmark valuation.

Price Elasticity

The degree to which customers respond to price changes. Calculated by dividing the per cent change in quantity by the per cent change in price. A value greater than 1 = customers exhibit a good sensitivity to price. A value less than 1 = customers are insensitive to price. Price Elasticity is if a small change in price is accompanied by a large change in quantity demanded, the product is said to be 'elastic' (or responsive to price changes). A product is 'inelastic' if a large change in price is accompanied by a small amount of change in demand.

Price-Level — Adjusted Historical Cost

A rarely used asset valuation method in which the historical cost of each asset is revalued for inflation.

Price to Book

A financial ratio that is derived by dividing a stock's capitalization by its Book Value. Also called Market-to-Book.

Price to Earnings Ratio (P/E)

See Price-Earnings Ratio.

Price to Revenue

A financial ratio derived by dividing current stock price by revenue per share (adjusted for stock splits).

Primary Dealer

A designation given by the Federal Reserve System to commercial banks or broker/dealers who meet specific criteria, including capital requirements and participation in Treasury auctions. A primary dealer is entitled and obligated to purchase and sell government securities with the Federal Reserve directly. They serve as the conduits for Federal Reserve open market activities. There are approximately 30–40 such dealers.

Primary Market

The first sale of a newly issued security. Those securities are purchased in the primary market. All subsequent trading of those securities is done in the secondary market.

Prime Brokers

Providers of back-office administration and stock lending for hedge funds.

Prime Cost

Equal to the sum of Direct Material plus Direct Labour.

Principal

(1) In interest calculations, the principal is the amount of money initially borrowed, lent, or invested and on which interest is calculated; (2) In some kinds of Contracts, the principal is the person to whom the Agent is responsible.

Principle of Diversification

Principle stating that spreading an investment across a number of assets eliminates some, but not all, of the risk.

Prior-Period Adjustment

A method formerly used in Canada but not recommended any more by Accounting standards, in which accounting is done separately for a gain or loss specifically identified with and directly related to the activities of particular prior periods, but not attributable to economic events occurring subsequent to those periods (so net income of those later periods is not increased or decreased because doing so could cause a distortion in the later results).

Private Company

A company that does not have a listing on the Exchange and is barred from offering its shares to the general public.

Private Placement

An issue that is offered to a single or a few investors as opposed to being publicly offered.

Private Trustee Company

A company incorporated in certain offshore jurisdictions, such as Bermuda, to act as a trustee for a limited class or group of trusts. Private trustee companies are not permitted to offer trustee services to the public generally.

Privatization

Conversion of a state run company into a public company, often accompanied by a sale of its shares to the general public.

Probate Price (UK)

The price used to assess the value of shares for inheritance tax purposes. Calculated on the 'quarter up' principle. That is instead of taking the mid price in the Official List, the difference between the two prices (bid and offer) given under 'quotation' is divided by four and the result added to the lower of the two prices.

Process Costing

A method of cost accounting applied to production carried out by a series of chemical or operational stages or processes. Its characteristics are that costs are accumulated for the whole production process and that average unit costs of production are computed at each stage.

Productivity

A measured relationship of the quantity and quality of units produced and the labour required per unit of time.

Productivity Ratio

The ratio of outputs to inputs. The closer the ratio is to 1.0, the higher the productivity; the closer the ratio is to 0.0, the lower the productivity. Productivity is important because it relates to an organization's ability to compete, and to the overall wealth and standard of living of a nation. Productivity is affected by work methods, capital, quality, technology, and management.

Professional Ethics

Codes of conduct to guide professionals in applying their professional judgment and that are conducive to their professional activities.

Professionalism

Acting according to the levels of competence, ethics, independence, etc., expected of professionals.

Professional Judgment

The judgment of professionals about problems in their domain, for example, that of accountants or auditors about financial accounting matters.

Profit

See Net Income.

Profitability

A company's ability to generate revenues in excess of the costs incurred in producing those revenues.

Profitability Index (PI)

The present value of an investment's future cash flows divided by its initial cost. Also benefit/cost ratio.

Profitability Ratios

Measures of performance showing how much the firm is earning compared to its sales, assets or equity.

Profit after Tax (PAT)

The net profit earned by the company after deducting all expenses like interest, depreciation and tax. PAT can be fully retained by a company to be used in the business. Dividends, if declared, are paid to the shareholders from this residue.

Profit and Loss Statement (P&L)

Shows your business revenue and expenses for a specific period of time. The difference between the total revenue and the total expense is your business net income. A key element of this statement, and one that distinguishes it from a balance sheet, is that the amounts shown on the statement represent transactions over a period of time while the items represented on the balance sheet show information as of a specific date (or point in time). Sometimes referred to as "Income Statement", "Statement of Earnings", "Statement of Operations", or "Statement of Income".

Profit before Taxes

Operating profit minus all other expenses (net).

Profit Centre

A section of an organization that is responsible for producing profit, e.g., a division of a corporation that is not a stand-alone entity but is required to produce profits within the corporation.

Profit Margin

See Sales Return Ratio, Ratios.

Profit Margin on Sales

A profitability ratio calculated by dividing Net Income by Average Total Assets.

Profit Multiple

Profit and sales multiples are the most widely used valuation benchmarks used in valuing a business. The information needed includes pre-tax profits and a market multiplier, which may be 1, 2, 3, or 4 and usually a ceiling of 5. The market multiplier can be found in various financial publications, as well as analyzing the sale of comparable businesses. This method is easy to understand and use. The profit multiple is often used as the valuation ceiling benchmark.

Pro-Forma

To provide in advance to a prescribed form or to describe items, e.g., *pro forma* financial statement or *pro forma* invoice.

Pro Forma Financial Statements

Financial statements projecting future years' operations.

Pro-Forma Invoice

A price quote. It is written as an invoice, and, in effect, says: 'This is the purchase price and terms we are offering'.

Progress Billings

Interim billings for construction work or government contract work. The entry is to debit progress billings receivable and credit progress billings on construction in progress. Progress billings is a contra account to Construction-in-Progress.

Progressive Tax

An income tax system to where the more income that is made the higher the tax percentage that must be paid.

Promises for the Future

Not a standard term, but is sometimes used in contracts to delineate what orders/commitments may exist in the future. Dependent upon the contractual language, it may or may not be binding.

Promissory Note

Usually just called a 'note', is a Negotiable Instrument wherein the maker agrees to pay a specific sum at a definite time. Usually an unsecured debt with a maturity under 10 years.

Proper Law

The body of law which governs the validity and interpretation of a contract or trust deed.

Proprietary Asset

Usually, any asset that is considered in the realm of intellectual property that should not be disclosed, e.g., all information having to do with clients/customers, including but not limited to names, addresses, telephone numbers and other contact information, as well as any other personal or business related information, as it may exist from time to time is a valuable, and unique proprietary asset to a company. Proprietary assets would also include trade secrets and undisclosed inventions.

Proprietor's Draw

When a business proprietor draws money for personal needs, but is taxed on business results (at marginal rate for individuals) regardless of drawings.

Proprietorship

A firm that is neither a corporation nor a partnership but is under the sole control of one individual. Such a firm is not legally separate from that individual.

ProShare

An independent organization set up to promote share ownership among individual investors including employees.

Prospective Payment System (PPS)

In healthcare, a Medicare administered payment plan where providers are paid a predetermined sum for caring for a given number of consumers. The built in incentive is for providers to control costs, theoretically leading to more cost effective care.

Prospective Reimbursement

In healthcare, a reimbursement method where the third party payer set the amount of money for a particular service to be delivered to clients in agreement with the organization before the service is delivered.

Prospectus

A formal document that includes detailed financial information, which is required by law when a company invites the public to subscribe to its securities. Compare to Red Herring.

Protective Covenant

Part of the indenture limiting certain transactions that can be taken during the term of the loan, usually to protect the lender's interest.

Protector

A person appointed by the settlor/grantor of a trust, who has limited powers to control the trustee, and usually has the right to change trustees.

Protocol

A protocol is normally known in international tax circles as a subsidiary document to the main double tax treaty agreed at a later date by the negotiators which clarifies or modifies the provisions of the double tax treaty.

Provision

Another phrase for a usually non-current accrual such as for future pension costs or warranties. Particularly common when the liability is created to anticipate losses or major expenses involved in discontinuing a business line, refinancing debts, or disposing of major assets.

Proximo

(Usually abbreviated to 'PROX'.) Means of or in the following month.

Proxy

Grant of authority by shareholder allowing for another individual to vote his or her shares.

Proxy Contests

Attempts to gain control of a firm by soliciting a sufficient number of stockholder votes to replace existing management.

Prudence

Having foresight and caution along with discretion, and to not act recklessly.

Prudence Concept

Otherwise known as conservatism, says that whenever there are alternative procedures or values, the accountant will choose the one that results in a lower profit, a lower asset value and a higher liability value.

PST

Provincial sales tax.

Public Accounting, Public Accounting Firms

Offering auditing, accounting, tax, consulting, and related services to the public on a professional basis. Some of these firms are very large, with thousands of professionals and staff, while others are very small one-person offices.

Public Bank Licence

The Bank is permitted to carry on banking business with members of the general public.

Public Company

A Corporation whose shares and related securities are sold widely, to members of the public and other investors, and whose securities are traded on Stock exchanges and other capital markets. See also Listed Company.

Public Corporation

A corporation formed by federal, state or local governments for specific public purposes.

Public File

The file available at the Company Registry for inspection on request.

Public Limited Company (PLC)

A public company limited by shares or by guarantee and having share capital and which may offer shares for purchase by the general public. Only PLCs may qualify for listing on the London Stock Exchange.

Public Ownership

Either: (1) Government ownership and operation of a productive facility for the purposes of providing some goods or services to citizens; or (2) In investments, portion of a corporations stock that is publicly traded and owned in the open market.

Purchase Method

A type of accounting for business combinations (compare with the Pooling of interests method). Under this method, which is the overwhelmingly dominant method of determining consolidated financial statement figures, the assets and liabilities of the acquired company are added to those of the parent at fair values and any difference between the portion of the sum of fair values acquired by the parent and the total price paid is accounted for as goodwill.

Purchase Money Interest

That interest associated with the purchase money mortgage.

Purchase Money Mortgage (PMM)

Seller financing as a part of the purchase price.

Purchase Order

A document used when a formal request to buy products or services is made. It is a written authorization for a vendor to supply goods or services at a specified price over a specified time period. Acceptance of the purchase order constitutes a purchase contract and is legally binding on all parties.

Purchasing Power Parity (PPP)

The idea that the exchange rate adjusts to keep purchasing power constant among currencies.

Pure Play Approach

Use of a WACC that is unique to a particular project.

Pure Research

Motivated exclusively by the search for knowledge for its own sake.

Purpose Trust

A trust created for an express purpose without any individually ascertained or ascertainable beneficiaries. A purpose trust is typically used in circumstances where the trust would not be exclusively charitable.

Put Option

The right to sell stock at an agreed price at or within a stated future time. The opposite of a Call Option. See, generally, Option.

Put Warrant

A security that, in contrast to a conventional warrant, gives the holder the right to sell the underlying or to receive a cash payment that increases as the value of the underlying declines. Put warrants, like their call warrant counterparts, generally have an initial term of more than one year.

PV

See Present Value.

Qualified Domestic Relations Order (QDRO)

When a state court allocates an interest in a qualified retirement plan to a former spouse through a qualified domestic relations order. Payments made to a former spouse as the result of a QDRO will not result in the taxpayer being assessed a penalty for early withdrawal from the plan; the former spouse will be taxed on the benefits when received, or the benefits can be rolled over tax free into an IRS or another qualified retirement plan.

Qualified Opinion

The auditor's opinion accompanying a financial statement that calls attention to limitations in the audit or exceptions the auditor has taken with the audit of the statements.

Qualitative Information

Information that is descriptive in nature, relating to, or involving quality or kind.

Quantitative Information

Information relating to, or expressible in, terms of quantity.

Quick Ratio (or Acid Test Ratio)

A more rigorous test than the Current Ratio of short-run solvency, the current ability of a firm to pay its current debts as they come due. This ratio is calculated by dividing total liquid assets (i.e., the most liquid forms of current assets, which include ONLY cash, marketable securities (cash equivalents) and accounts receivable) by current liabilities. A Quick Ratio less than 1.0 implies "dependency" on inventory and other current assets to liquidate short-term debt.

Quoted

Securities admitted to the Official List of the London Stock Exchange.

Rabbi Trust

A nonqualified deferred compensation plan whereby an employer and employee agree to defer payment for the employee's services until a specified future date. The rabbi trust features an irrevocable grantor trust that is set up by the employer to hold the contributions set aside for the employee. While this provides the employee some degree of safety that the money will be available when desired, the terms of the trust must be such that exposes the trust assets to the claims of the employer's creditors.

R&D

Research and development activities, a controversial accounting problem because the activities are intended to lead to future benefits and thus their costs may be considered to be assets, yet GAAP require that generally such costs be charged to expense as incurred.

Rate of Return

The gain or loss for a security in a particular period, consisting of income plus capital gains relative to investment, usually quoted as a percentage. The real rate of return is the annual return realized on that investment, adjusted for changes in the price due to inflation.

Ratios, Ratio Analysis

Numbers produced by dividing one financial statement figure by another figure; for example, the working capital ratio is the total current assets figure divided by the total current liabilities figure. Standard ratios are used to assess aspects of a firm, particularly profitability, solvency, and liquidity. These ratios allow comparisons to be made between one business and another (or collection of others) regardless of how similar or dissimilar the businesses are in terms of size or business type.

Reach

In advertising, the total number of people within a target market that will be reached through an advertising campaign.

Real Interest Rate

The nominal interest rate minus the rate of inflation.

Realization Principle

That revenue should be recognized at the time goods are sold and services are rendered.

Realized

Used as a synonym of received, or collected. Revenue is recognized when earned, but that is usually before it is collected, or realized.

Realized Capital Gains

The increase in value of an investment converted to cash.

Realized Income

The return or profit that is actually earned or collected over a given time period.

Real Option

An option with payoffs in real goods.

Reasonable Certainty

The degree of certainty that would be found to be in existence by a reasonable person.

Reasonable Person

A phrase to denote a hypothetical person who exercises qualities of attention, knowledge, intelligence, and judgment that society requires of its members for the protection of their interest and the interest of others.

Recapitalization

It is dependent upon how you use the term. The term recapitalization in itself is, depending upon the scenario, simply an adjustment of the relationships between the debt and equity that funds a firms assets. However, it can become quite complex depending upon under what conditions or reasons the firm is being recapitalized. This is specially true if recapitalization is being pursued to ward off a hostile takeover.

Recaptured Depreciation

The taxable difference between adjusted proceeds of disposal and UCC when UCC is greater.

Receivable

Funds expected to be collected by the enterprise. The usual kind is trade Accounts receivable but other kinds include taxes receivable, employee expense advances receivable, and Notes receivable.

Receiver

A court appointed person who takes possession of, but not title to, the assets and affairs of a business or estate that is in a form of bankruptcy called Receivership. The receiver collects rents and other income and generally manages the affairs of the entity until a disposition is made by the court.

Receiver General for Canada

The chief financial officer of the federal government, who receives all revenues from the government and deposits them in the Consolidated Revenue Fund.

Receivership

An equitable remedy whereby a court orders property placed under the control of a Receiver so that it may be preserved for the benefit of affected parties. A failing company may be placed in receivership in an action brought by its creditors. The business is often continued but is subject to the receiver's control. See also Bankruptcy.

Reclassification (entry)

A journal entry or repositioning of an account that changes the location of the account within the balance sheet or within the income statement but does not affect income.

Reclassified Account

An account moved to a different place within a financial statement without changing income or equity.

Recognition

Giving effect in the accounts to revenue believed to be earned, or expenses believed to be incurred, before (or after) the cash is collected or paid.

Recognized

Revenues or expenses (usually), entered into the accounts or given effect in the accounts.

Reconciliation

The adjusting of the difference between two items (e.g., balances, amounts, statements, or accounts) so that the figures are in agreement. Often the reasons for the differences must be explained. One example would be reconciling a chequing account (bringing the chequing ledger and bank balance statement into agreement).

Record Keeping

The bookkeeping and other methods used to create the underlying records on which accounting information is based.

Recourse

In finance, is the right to demand payment from the maker or endorser of a negotiable instrument (as a check).

Redeemable

A feature of an investment security (e.g., shares or bonds) which gives the issuer (company) the right to buy the investment back from the holder at a specified price during a specified period prior to maturity. Contrast to Retractable.

Redemption Date

The date on which a security (usually fixed interest stock) is due to be repaid by the issuer at its full face value. The year is included in the title of the security, the actual redemption date being that on which the last interest is due to be paid.

Red Herring

A preliminary Prospectus describing the issue (the IPO) and prospects of the company that must be filed with the SEC or provincial securities commission. There is no price or issue size stated in the red herring. Red Herrings are sometimes updated several times before it is called the final Prospectus. It is known as a red herring because it contains a statement typed in red that the company is not attempting to sell their shares before the registration is approved by the SEC.

Re-Domiciliation Corporations

Some offshore jurisdictions allow corporations incorporated in other jurisdictions to re-incorporate in their own at will.

Refined ROA

A version of the Return on assets ratio.

Refundable Tax Credit

Where a tax credit is refundable, a portion of the credit that is not needed to reduce a taxpayer's tax liability (because it is already zero) may be paid to the taxpayer. An example is the refundable investment tax credit.

Register

In accounting, is a formal or official recording of items within a book or register, e.g., Fixed Asset Register.

Registered Form

Registrar of company records ownership of each bond; payment is made directly to the owner of record.

Registered Investment Advisor (RIA)

An investment advisor registered with the SEC. No certification is required.

Regressive Tax

A tax system to where the more income that is realized the lower the tax rate becomes.

Regular Cash Dividend

Cash payment made by a firm to its owners in the normal course of business, usually made four times a year.

Regular Underwriting

The purchase of securities from the issuing company by an investment banker for resale to the public.

Regulatory Dialectic

The pressures financial institutions and regulatory bodies exert on each other.

Reimbursement

To pay back to someone, e.g., to pay an employee for travel expenses that was paid by the employee out of that employee's own personal funds.

REIT

Real Estate Investment Trust. A REIT is a trust that manages a portfolio of real estate to earn a profit for investors.

Related Party Transaction

An interaction between two parties, one of whom can exercise control or significant influence over the operating policies of the other. A special relationship may exist, e.g., a corporation and a major shareholder.

Relevance

The capacity of information to make a difference in a decision by helping users to form predictions about the outcomes of past, present, and future events, or to confirm or correct prior expectations.

Reliability

A characteristic of information that is represented faithfully and is free from bias and verifiable.

Remittance Basis

The United Kingdom and Ireland have the concept of domicile (see above) which allows non domiciled individuals to earn income on a tax free basis provided that the income is not remitted to the UK or Ireland; they are therefore subject to tax on a remittance basis.

Remitting Bank

A bank that sends a draft to the overseas bank for collection.

Renounceable Documents

Temporary evidence of ownership of which there are four main types. When a company offered shares to the public, it sends an Allotment Letter to its shareholders, or in the case of a capitalization issue, a renounceable certificate. All of these are in effect bearer securities and are valuable.

Reorganization

Financial restructuring of a firm to attempt to continue operations as a going concern or in a new structure.

Replacement Cost (of an asset)

The price that will have to be paid in order to replace an existing asset with a similar asset. This is likely to be a different amount than that of Fair Market Value or Net Realizable Value.

Replacement Value (of a business)

A valuation similar to an adjusted book value analysis. Replacement value is different than liquidation value in that it uses the value of the replacement value of assets, which is usually higher than book value. Liabilities are deducted from the replacement value of the assets to determine the replacement value of the business.

Reportable Condition

A matter coming to the auditor's attention relating to Significant Deficiencies in the design or operation of the entity's internal control that could Adversely Affect an entity's ability to fulfill future obligations with customers and/or the satisfaction of liabilities.

Reporting Entity

The legal entity for which financial reports are prepared and made available.

Reporting Period

See Accounting Period.

Repurchase

Another method used to pay out a firm's earnings to its owners, which provides more preferable tax treatment than dividends.

Required Rate of Return

See Hurdle Rate.

Reserve

An accounting entry that properly reflects contingent liabilities.

Reserve Accounts

Generally, are those accounts where retained earnings are set aside to satisfy dividends, improvements, contingencies, retirement of preferred stock, etc.

Resident

A resident is a person who has a sufficiently close connection or nexus with a country to be liable for tax on his or her worldwide income (full tax liability) in the country.

Resident Company

A bank, trust company or holding company permitted to deal only in local currency. The appropriate regulatory authority must approve foreign currency transactions.

Residual Claim

A claim to a share of earnings after debt obligations have been satisfied.

Residual Dividend Approach

Policy where a firm pays dividends only after meeting its investment needs while maintaining a desired debt-to-equity ratio.

Residual Value

(1) Realizable value of a fixed asset after deducting costs associated with its sale; (2) Scrap value or the value to a junk dealer; or (3) The amount remaining after all depreciation has been deducted from the original cost of a depreciable asset.

Resource Allowance

The resource allowance, which was first introduced in 1976, provides an annual deduction to mining and oil and gas producers. It is calculated as 25 per cent of a taxpayer's annual resource profits, computed after operating costs and capital cost allowances, but before the deduction of exploration expenses, development expenses, earned depletion and interest expenses. The resource allowance was introduced in 1976 after Crown royalties, mining taxes and other charges related to oil and gas or mining production were made non-deductible in calculating taxable income. The resource allowance measure effectively allows the provincial governments room to impose royalties or mining taxes on the production of natural resources. The non-deductibility of these charges coupled with the resource allowance means that these provincial charges no longer affect the level of federal income taxes payable as they did when these charges were deductible. The 2003 Budget announced a change in the resource allowance regime which involves the phasing out of the resource allowance and the phasing in of deductions for provincial and Crown charges over a five year period (2003–2007).

Resources

In financial accounting, the recognized assets of the enterprise as shown on the balance sheet.

Responsibility Accounting

The collection, summarization, and reporting of financial information about various decision centres throughout an organization; can also be called profitability accounting or activity accounting. It tracks costs, revenues, or profits to the individual managers who are responsible for making the decisions about costs, revenues, or profits and taking action about them.

Restricted Assets

Assets/resources which are restricted by legal or contractual requirements for use under specific circumstances or purposes.

Restricted Bank and/or Trust Licence

Is one that permits the holder to carry on business with certain specified persons whose names are usually in the licence.

Retail Inventory Control Method

Providing internal control and deducing inventory amounts for financial statements by using ratios of cost to selling price; for example, deducing cost of goods sold from sales revenue minus the mark up on cost. Ending inventory cost can be determined by measuring inventory at retail prices minus mark up.

Retained Earnings

Earnings not yet distributed to owners; the sum of net incomes earned over the life of a company, less distributions (dividends declared) to owners.

Retained Earnings Statement

See Statement of Retained Earnings.

Retention Ratio

Retained earnings divided by net income. Also called the plowback ratio.

Retractable

A feature of an investment security (e.g., shares or bonds) which gives the holder the right to sell (put) the investment back to the issuer at a specified price during a specified period prior to maturity. Contrast to Redeemable.

Retrospective Reimbursement

In healthcare, where reimbursement came after medical care was delivered.

Return

Some amount of gain (income or performance) usually measured in relation to the amount invested to get the return.

Return of Capital

The distribution of cash that resulted from tax savings on depreciation, sale of a capital asset or securities, or any other sources unrelated to retained earnings.

Return on Assets (ROA or ROA(ATI))

Net income, before considering interest expense or the tax saving provided by interest expense, divided by total assets. This measures the Operating return before the cost of financing.

Return on Assets (ROA)

Shows the after tax earnings of assets. Return on assets is an indicator of how profitable a company is. Use this ratio annually to compare a business' performance to the industry norms: the higher the ratio the greater the return on assets. However this has to be balanced against such factors as risk, sustainability and reinvestment in the business through development costs.

Return on Capital

The distribution of cash from depreciation tax savings, the sale of a capital asset or securities, or, any other transaction not related to retained earnings.

Return on Capital Employed (ROCE)

A measure of how effectively the company is using its capital. The formula to measures the return on all the assets the company is using: Profit before interest and tax (PBIT) / (total assets — current liabilities).

Return on Equity (ROE)

Net income after interest and taxes divided by average common shareholders' equity. Measures the overall efficiency of the firm in managing its total investments in assets and in generating a return to stockholders. It is the primary measure of how well management is running the company. ROE allows you to quickly gauge whether a company is a value creator or a cash consumer. By relating the earnings generated to the shareholders' equity, you can see how much cash is created from the existing assets. Clearly, all things being equal, the higher a company's ROE, the better the company.

Return on Investment (ROI)

A profitability measure that evaluates the performance of a business. ROI can be calculated in various ways. The most common method is Net Income as a percentage of Net Book Value (total assets minus intangible assets and liabilities).

Revenue

The amount of benefit received or promised from the sale of goods or services, before any deductions for the cost of providing the goods or services.

Revenue Bonds

A type of municipal bond where principal and interest are secured by revenues such as charges or rents paid by users of the facility built with the proceeds of the bond issue. Projects financed by revenue bonds include highways, airports, and not-for-profit health care and other facilities.

Revenue Contract

A binding agreement between a governmental body and another party that defines the terms under which revenue will be received. A contract can be distinguished from a customer purchase order by the fact that a contract will contain the signatures of both parties, while a purchase order will contain only the signature of the customer.

Revenue Expenditure

An outlay that only benefits the current business year. It is treated as an expense that is matched against revenues.

Revenue Recognition

The entering into the accounts of the amount of revenue determined, according to the firm's accounting policies, to be attributable to the current period.

Revenue Reserve

A fund that is not a Capital Reserve, i.e., the funds are distributable.

Reverse Split

Procedure where a firm's number of shares outstanding is reduced. The opposite of a Stock Split.

Reversing Entry

A debit or credit bookkeeping entry made to reverse a prior bookkeeping entry.

Review

A report prepared on an enterprise's financial statements by a Public accounting firm that is less than an Audit but more than a Compilation; the accounting firm studies the statements' contents and compliance with GAAP to determine if there are any apparent problems but does not verify individual accounts or the underlying records. This is done to providing some assurance to the Board of Directors and interested parties as to the reliability of financial data.

Revolving Collateral

Accounts receivable or inventory which change from day to day.

Revolving Financing

Financing secured by collateral.

Revolving Fund

Money that is renewed as it is used.

Revolving Line of Credit

In commercial banking is a contractual agreement between a bank and, usually, a company where the bank agrees to provide loans up to a specified maximum over a specified period, usually a year or more. In consumer banking, it is a loan account requiring monthly payments less than the full amount of the loan, and the balance is carried forward with a finance charge on that balance.

Revolving Loan

A loan that is automatically renewed upon maturity.

RIE

Recognised Investment Exchange. The status required by Securities and Investment Board for exchanges in the UK.

Right

A temporary privilege allowing investors who already own common shares to purchase additional shares directly from the company at a specified price.

Rights Issue

An invitation to existing shareholders to acquire additional shares in the company in proportion to the number of shares they already own — usually at a preferential price.

Ring Fence

Tax law often needs to separate a particular transaction whose profits or losses should not be aggregated with those of other transactions; a ring fence is the term used to contain these transactions to be taxed entirely separately from others.

Risk

The probable variability in possible future outcomes above and below the expected level of outcomes (for example, returns), but especially below. Risk and return go hand in hand, because a high risk should mean a higher potential return and vice versa.

Risk Adjusted Return

When we subtract from the rate of return on an asset a rate of return from another asset that has similar risk. This gives an abnormal rate of return that shows how the asset performed over and above a benchmark asset with the same risk. We can also use the beta against the benchmark to calculate an alpha which is also risk adjusted performance.

Risk Premium

The excess return required from an investment in a risky asset over a risk-free investment.

Risk Profile

A plot showing how the value of the firm is affected by changes in prices or rates.

RNS

Regulatory New Service. A service operated by the Exchange in its role as Competent Authority for Listing, which ensures that information required from listed companies in line with their continuing obligations is collected and distributed to all RNS subscribers at the same time.

ROA

See Return on Assets.

ROA(ATI)

See Refined ROA and Return on Assets.

ROCC

An acronym for Return on Committed Capital.

ROG

In business, an acronym meaning "Receipt of Goods".

ROI

See Return on Investment.

Rolling Settlement

A modification to the Talisman system, which brought to an end the two-week account cycle. Instead, settlement takes place on any business day 10 days after the trade date.

Roll-over Relief

Capital gains tax referral may be achieved, particularly on transactions between related parties, or typically on replacement of business assets, by transferring the initial cost of acquisition of the assets disposed of or transferred to the new assets or transferee; on subsequent sale of the assets, the capital gain is the sale proceeds less the historic cost of the original assets. Such capital gains tax deferral is referred to as roll-over relief, or in certain situations hold-over relief.

Royalty(ies)

The term "royalties" generally refers to amounts paid for the use of personal property (usually, but not always, intangible property), such as industrial, commercial, scientific, or artistic property. Payments for technical assistance are sometimes considered royalties if the technical assistance is related or ancillary to other royalty generating rights.

Running Rate

A sustained constant rate, often the only important single rate except for zero observed under a given schedule (as in some ratio performances); also known as *stream rate*.

Run Rate

In finance, is how the financial performance of a company would look if you were to extrapolate current results out over a certain period of time. In accounting, it is the average annual dilution from stock option grants at a company over the most recent three year period reported in the annual report.

SAEF

The SEAQ Automated Execution Facility. This enables trade in UK shares to be executed automatically at a computer terminal instead of being executed over the telephone.

Safe Harbour

Where a tax administration gives general guidelines on the interpretation of tax laws, these may state that transactions falling within a certain range will be permitted. For example, debt to equity ratios, or the deductibility of interest at certain rates, may have prescribed limits, and these limits are referred to as a safe harbour, or the guidelines as safe haven rules.

Sale and Leaseback

A financial lease in which the lessee sells an asset to the lessor and then leases it back.

Sales Contract

See Sales Order.

Sales Invoice

A document containing the details of a sale of goods or services from a *vendor* to a *customer*.

Sales Journal

A record of sales made, used to produce the Revenue data in the accounts.

Sales Multiple

The most widely used valuation benchmark used in the valuation of a business. The information needed includes annual sales and an industry multiplier, which is usually a range of .25 to 1 or higher. The industry multiplier can be found in various financial publications, as well as analyzing sales of comparable businesses. This method is easy to understand and use. The sales multiple is often used as the valuation benchmark.

Sales Order

Also known as Sales Contract, is a contract by which buyer and seller agree to the terms and conditions of a sale.

Sales/Receivables (Receivables Turnover)

A ratio that measures the number of times trade Receivables turn over during the year. Generally, the higher the turnover of receivables, the shorter the time between sale and cash collection. It indicates how fast the company is getting paid for goods and services. Receivables turnover is best compared to the industry in order to determine if the company should improve their collection rate. The faster the receivables turnover, the better cash flow will look. Slow or below par turnover can be an indication of systemic problems within the company. It is best to compare receivables turnover with that of industry averages.

Sales Return

The ratio of net income to revenue.

Sales Taxes

Taxes the enterprise must charge its customers and remit to the government.

Salvage Value

(1) Realizable value of a fixed asset after deducting costs associated with its sale; (2) Scrap value or the value to a junk dealer; or (3) The amount remaining after all depreciation has been deducted from the original cost of a depreciable asset.

Same Day Value

Bank makes proceeds of cheques deposited available the same day before cheques clear.

Same Store Sales

Used when analyzing the retail industry. It compares sales in stores which have been open for a year or more.

SAP

An integrated enterprise resource planning (ERP) system that seamlessly integrates most activities of a company.

Scenario Analysis

The determination of what happens to NPV estimates when we ask what-if questions.

SCFP (Statement of Changes in Financial Position)

See Cash Flow Statement.

Scientific Research and Experimental Development Investment Tax Credit (SR&RD)

There are currently two rates of tax credit for SR&RD a general rate of 20 per cent and an enhanced rate of 35 per cent for certain small businesses. SR&RD tax credits may be used to reduce federal income taxes otherwise payable or to obtain cash refunds.

Scott Formula

A financial analysis technique for studying leverage effects by combining a group of ratios into a more comprehensive explanation of performance. The formula separates Return on equity into Operating return and Leverage return.

SEC

See Securities and Exchange Commission.

Secondary Withholding Tax

Withholding tax may be levied on the distribution of dividends, interest, royalty and other expenses, particularly where these are paid to non resident entities. Where such non-resident entities then pay third parties such income which has a source in the original country of distribution, the tax administration may seek to impose a secondary withholding tax on the onward distributions, even though these are not made by a resident entity.

Secured Liability

A liability that has a degree of protection towards satisfaction if unpaid because the debtor has pledged personal/company assets towards satisfaction of that liability; e.g., a property mortgage is a secured liability because the mortgage holder has a guarantee through a lien on the property.

Securities

Shares, bonds, and other financial instruments issued by corporations and governments and usually traded on Capital markets.

Securities and Exchange Commission (SEC)

An agency of the U.S. government that supervises the registration of security issues, prosecutes fraudulent stock manipulations, and regulates securities transactions in the United States.

Securitization

The process of creating a pass-through, such as the mortgage pass-through security, by which the pooled assets become standard securities backed by those assets. Also, refers to the replacement of non-marketable loans and/or cash flows provided by financial intermediaries with negotiable securities issued in the public capital markets.

Security

(1) Singular of Securities; (2) Protection to a lender or other creditor in which the lender is given rights to specific assets (as in a Mortgage), more general rights to monitor the borrower (Debenture or Indenture), or other promises (such as Personal Guarantees).

Security Market Line (SML)

Positively sloped straight line displaying the relationship between expected return and beta.

Segmented Information

Financial statement information desegregated by geographical or economic area of activity in order to provide greater insight into financial performance and position. Segmented information is usually placed at the end of the notes to the financial statements.

Segregation of Duties

An internal control technique whereby tasks involved in sensitive assets such as cash, accounts receivable, or inventories are divided up so that no one both handles the asset and keeps the records of the asset.

Self-Constructed Assets

The costs incurred to build it yourself (e.g. a company builds a building rather than buying one). All costs of self-constructing the asset should be capitalized, subject to a ceiling amount (the fair value of the asset). The portion of the fixed overhead (e.g., salaries) necessary to construct the building should be allocated to the construction.

Senior Debt/Note

Loans or debt securities that have a claim prior to junior obligations and equity on a corporation's assets in the event of a liquidation.

Sensitivity Analysis

Investigation of what happens to NPV when only one variable is changed.

Setoff

The discharge of a debt by setting against it a distinct claim in favour of the debtor.

Settlement

The process of exchanging money and shares for shares.

Setup Cost

See Fixed Charge.

SFA

The Securities and Futures Authority — the Self Regulating Organization responsible for regulating the conduct of brokers and dealers in securities options and futures, including most member firms of the Exchange.

SG&A

Refers to the indirect overhead costs contained within the Sales, General and Administrative expense/cost categories.

Share Application Money

That money received by a company during an IPO. Payments received for a subscription of stock is normally received over the IPO life. For example: Widgets Limited has been registered with an authorized capital of $2,00,000 divided into 2,000 shares of $100 each of which, 1,000 shares were offered for public subscription at a premium of $5 per share, payable as:

on application	$ 10	
on allotment	$ 25	(including premium)
on first call	$ 40	
on final call	$ 30	
for a total of	$ 105	per share

The amounts received would be carried as a current liability until such time as the stock is issued, then it would be considered as part of equity.

Share Capital

The portion of a corporation's equity obtained by issuing shares in return for cash or other considerations.

Share for Share Exchanges

This term reflects the tax position where an individual or company exchanges its shares in one entity for those in another, and many countries will allow this to be effected on a non-recognition basis. As for roll-over relief, the original cost of acquisition of the shares exchanged will be taken as the base cost for capital gains tax purposes of the shares received. The term paper for paper is often used to describe share for share exchanges.

Shareholder(s)

The holders of a corporation's Share Capital, and so the owners of the corporation.

Shareholder Rights Plan

Provisions allowing existing shareholders to purchase stock at some fixed price should an outside takeover bid take place, discouraging hostile takeover attempts.

Shareholder's Equity

The sums of shareholders' direct investment (share capital) and indirect investment (retained earnings). Calculated as total assets minus total liabilities. It is the same as Equity, Net Worth and stockholder's equity.

Share Premium

The difference between the higher price paid for a share of stock and the stocks face amount when it was issued.

Shares (stock)

Units of Share capital, evidenced by certificates and, for Public companies, traded on Capital markets with other Securities.

Share Split

See Stock Split.

Shortage Costs

Costs that fall with increases in the level of investment in current assets.

Short Term Asset

An asset expected to be converted into cash within the normal operating cycle (usually one year), e.g., accounts receivable and inventory.

Short Term Liability

A liability that will come due within one year or less.

SIB

The Securities and Investments Board. The agency appointed by the government under the *Financial Services Act* to oversee the regulation of the investment industry, including the SROs, RIEs and clearing houses.

SIC (Standard Industrial Classification)

A U.S. Government numerical coding system used in the U.S. to group and classify basically all products and services existing within the U.S. economy.

Sight Draft

A draft which is payable on demand.

Signature Loan

A loan secured by the borrower with nothing more than the signature of that borrower.

Significant Accounting Policies

The main choices among possible accounting methods made by the enterprise in preparing
its financial statements. These policies are usually summarized in the first note to the financial statements.

Significant Influence

An investment in another corporation that is not large enough for voting control but is large
enough to influence how that corporation does business.

Simple Interest

Interest earned only on the original principal amount invested. Does not include interest on
the interest. Compare to Compound Interest.

Simple Journal Entry

A journal entry that involves only one debit and one credit in the transaction.

Simulation Analysis

A combination of scenario and sensitivity analyses.

Sinking Fund

A sum set apart periodically from the income of a government or a business and allowed to accumulate in order ultimately to pay off a debt. A preferred investment for a sinking fund is the purchase of the government's or firm's bonds that are to be paid off. Usually the fund is administered by a trustee.

SIPS

An acronym for Secure Internet Payment Service (Cybercash).

SKU

An acronym for Stock Keeping Unit. It is usually used to identify an item carried in inventory or stock.

SLR

An acronym with several possible meanings, e.g., Stock Level Report, Stock Level Requirement, System Level Requirement(s).

Small Business Deduction (SBD)

Corporations that are Canadian-controlled private corporations (CCPCs) are eligible for a small business tax rate reduction known as the small business deduction. This deduction lowers the basic federal tax rate on the first $300,000 (2005 et. seq.) of active business income of CCPCs by 16 percentage points — from 28 per cent to 12 per cent. Some large CCPCs are ineligible for the small business deduction.

Small-Cap

A stock with a capitalization, meaning a total equity value, of less than $500 million.

Smart Card

Much like an automated teller machine card; one use is within corporations to control access to information by employees.

Social Entity

The separate existence of an organization that is perceived to exist, by its members and the public at large, as a 'given', i.e., something that exists before and outside of them.

Society of Management Accountants of Canada (SMA-Canada)

A society whose members have had training in tax, accounting, internal audit, and other related areas, with a particular focus on internal management accounting, and have passed qualifying exams. It is one of the three national, professional accounting bodies.

SOES (Small Order Execution System)

Trading is an electronic method of day trading the NASD market. At present, SOES trading is at the centre of controversy between the NASD, SEC, individual traders, and the courts. SOES is changing the way trading is done on the NASD, and it may rewrite the rules of the game for trading. Bandits is just a term being used for the individuals using the SOES system for day trading.

Soft Costs

Those extraneous costs that are not readily foreseen or budgeted for, e.g., legal fees, loan fees and interest, etc.

Soft Rationing

The situation that occurs when units in a business are allocated a certain amount of financing for capital budgeting.

Sole Proprietor

An individual that owns a business as opposed to stock in a corporation. A sole proprietor pays individual income tax rather than corporate income tax on his business income, and has unlimited liability for his/her business debts and obligations.

Sole Proprietorship

A form of business organization. The distinguishing characteristics of a sole proprietorship include: only one owner for the business (hence, "sole") and the business is unincorporated.

Solvency

The condition of being able to meet all debts and obligations.

Source Documents

The evidence required to record a Transaction.

Sources

The right-hand side of the balance sheet (liabilities and equity) are the sources of the enterprise's assets.

Sources of Cash

A firm's activities that generate cash.

Specialized Ledgers

Ledgers used to keep track of particular assets, liabilities, or equities, such as accounts receivable, fixed assets, or share capital.

Special Journal

Contains records of original entry other than the general journal that are designed for recording specific types of transactions of similar nature, e.g., Sales Journal, Purchase Journal, Cash Receipts Journal, Cash Disbursements Journal, and Payroll Journal.

Specific Identification

Accounting for inventories according to the specific cost of the items, which therefore requires some sort of identification of the items, such as by serial number.

Specific Research

A method used when gathering primary information for a market survey where targeted customers/consumers are asked very specific and in-depth questions geared toward resolving problems found through prior exploratory research.

Speculative Motive

The need to hold cash to take advantage of additional investment opportunities, such as bargain purchases.

Spontaneous Assets

Assets that arise automatically, in the course of operating a company day-to-day, when a company purchases assets and they are delivered.

Spontaneous Liabilities

Obligations that are realized automatically, in the course of operating a company day-to-day, when a company buys goods and services on credit.

Spot Commodity

A commodity traded with the expectation that it will actually be delivered to the buyer, as contrasted with to a Futures Contract that will usually expire without any physical delivery actually taking place. Spot commodities are traded in the Spot Market.

Spot Exchange Rate

The exchange rate on a spot trade.

Spot Trade

An agreement to trade currencies based on the exchange rate today for settlement in two days.

Spread

(1) The gap between the interest rate a bank pays on deposits and the rate it charges on loans; (2) Compensation to the underwriter, determined by the difference between the underwriter's buying price and offering price.

Spreadsheet

(1) A multi-column sheet of paper used for performing numeric work, especially accounting and business related weekly or monthly summaries; (2) A computer application program that supports a user in numeric manipulation, especially in column/row format.

SR(ATI)

See Sales Return.

SRO

Self-Regulating Organization — an organization recognized by the SIB and responsible for monitoring the conduct of business and capital adequacy of investment firms.

Stag

One who applied for a new issue in the hope of being able to sell the shares allotted to him at a profit as soon as dealing starts.

Stakeholder

Anyone who potentially has a claim on a firm.

Stamp Duty

A UK tax currently levied on the purchase of shares.

Stand-Alone Principle

Evaluation of a project based on the project's incremental cash flows.

Standard & Poor's Depository Receipts (SPDRs)

SPDRs allow you to buy the companies in the S&P 500 Index in a single security.

Standard Cost

Production or operating cost that is carefully predetermined. A standard cost is a target cost that *should be attained*. The standard cost is compared with the actual cost in order to measure the performance of a given costing department or operation. See Standard Cost System.

Standard Cost System

An accounting system designed to properly allocate costs of direct labour, indirect labour, materials, overhead, and selling/general/administrative accounts on a unit basis for the purpose of accurately costing products and the subsequent control of those costs in managing the production, marketing, purchasing, and administrative functions of the business.

Standard Deviation

The positive square root of the variance.

Standard Rate and Data Service (SRDS)

In advertising, a company that produces a directory for each different type of media, normally listing: rates, circulation, contacts, markets serviced, etc.

Standby Fee

Amount paid to underwriter participating in standby underwriting agreement.

Standby Underwriting

Agreement where the underwriter agrees to purchase the unsubscribed portion of the issue.

Stated Capital

The declared total amount of money or other resources owned or used to acquire future income or benefits.

Stated or Quoted Interest Rate

The interest rate expressed in terms of the interest payment made each period. Also quoted interest rate.

Stated Value

A value provided to shares that is similar to Par Value but less legally binding.

Statement of Cash Flows

See Cash Flow Statement.

Statement of Changes in Financial Position (SCFP)

See Cash Flow Statement.

Statement of Financial Position

A synonym for Balance Sheet.

Statement of Retained Earnings

A financial statement that summarizes the changes in retained earnings for the year. Change in retained earnings equals Net income minus Dividends plus or minus any retained earnings adjustments.

Statement of Source and Application of Cash

See Cash Flow Statement.

Static Theory of Capital Structure

Theory that a firm borrows up to the point where the tax benefit from an extra dollar in debt is exactly equal to the cost that comes from the increased probability of financial distress.

Statutory Account

An involuntary account, which is created by law rather than by business need. An example of a statutory account would be taxes.

Statutory Lien

An involuntary lien, which is created by law rather than by contract. Statutory liens include tax liens, judgment liens, mechanic's liens, etc.

Steamship Conference

An agreement between multiple shipping companies to provide common freight rates. Some shipping lines will state that they are "non-conference", i.e., they charge an independent and likely lower rate.

Step Lease

A type of lease that outlines or stipulates the expected annual increases in the tenant's base rent based on an approximation of what the landlord believes what the landlord's expenses may be.

Stewardship

The concept that some persons (for example, management) are responsible for looking after the assets and interests of other persons (for example, shareholders), and that reports should be prepared that will be suitable to allow the "stewards" to be held accountable for the actions taken on behalf of the other persons.

Stock Dividend

A Dividend paid by issuing more shares to existing shareholders rather than paying them cash. This dilutes the value of each share.

Stock Exchange

A place where Shares and other Securities are traded.

Stock Exchange Bid

Corporate takeover bid communicated to the stockholders through a stock exchange.

Stockholder

An alternative term for Shareholder, particularly used in the United States.

Stock Market

A Capital market in which equity shares are traded. Often used as a generic term for stock exchanges and capital markets.

Stock Option(s)

Promises, usually made to senior managers, to issue shares to them at specified prices. The prices are usually set to be higher than present prices but lower than expected future prices, to provide an incentive to work to increase those future prices.

Stocks

Usually used to mean Shares, but also used to mean Inventories, as in "stocktaking" for counting inventories.

Stock Split

An increase in a firm's shares outstanding without any change in owner's equity. This involves reissuing shares in which the number of new shares is some multiple of the previous number. For example, a two for one split results in an existing shareholder owning twice as many shares as before. Because there has been only a change in the number of shares but not in the underlying value of the corporation, the share price should fall in accordance with the split (e.g., the new shares above should have a share price about half the previous price). A company will often introduce a stock split when the price per share has climbed too high and it wants to reduce the price in order to facilitate open-market trading of the stock.

Stocktaking

The process of counting and evaluating stock-in-trade, usually at an organization's year end in order to value the total stock for preparation of the accounts. In more sophisticated organizations, in which permanent stock records are maintained, stock is counted on a random basis throughout the year to compare quantities counted with the quantities that appear in the, usually, computerized records.

Stock Turnover Period

Calculated as: (Long Term Disabilities × 100%) / Cost of Sales.

Straight Bond Value

The value of a convertible bond if it could not be converted into common stock.

Straight-Line Amortization (Depreciation)

A method of computing amortization (depreciation) simply by dividing the difference between the asset's cost and its expected salvage value by the number of years the asset is expected to be used. It is the most common amortization method used in Canada.

Straight Voting

Procedure where a shareholder may cast all votes for each member of the board of directors.

Stranded Plant

A cost that has been incurred, but cannot be reversed. Usually referred to as a sunk cost.

Strategic Options

Options for future, related business products or strategies.

Strategic Planning

The activity of defining what you want to accomplish in your business and then identifying the path that will allow you to reach your goal in the most efficient and sensible manner.

Straw Man

A weak or imaginary opposition (as an argument or adversary) set up only to be easily confuted. Often done to create an environment for brainstorming from a certain starting point.

Strike Price

The fixed price in the option contract at which the holder can buy or sell the underlying asset. Also the exercise price or striking price.

Stripped Bond

A bond that has been separated into its component parts (namely the principle and the Coupons) and each part sold separately at a large discount. The investor's profit is derived entirely from the discount (the difference between the purchase price and the maturity value); there are no interest (Coupon) payments. Compare to Zero Coupon Bonds.

Stripped Common Shares

Common stock on which dividends and capital gains are repackaged and sold separately.

Subchapters

A legal corporate entity organized under the United States Federal *Tax Code* that allows Subchapter S Corporations to distribute all income/loss proportionately to its shareholders, who then claim that income/loss on their personal income taxes; thereby avoiding the payment of corporate taxes.

Subledger

For the purpose of organizing revenue and expense transaction for only one account, e.g., For an individual salesperson, like a general ledger, the subledger has different default account types, each from a salesperson's perspective, not a company perspective. Thus, Due is due to the salesperson and Payable is payable by the salesperson.

Sublet

In real estate, refers to the leasing of space within a leased facility by the original lessee.

Subordinated Debt

Where there is a pecking order determining the sequence in which a company will pay off its debt instruments, subordinate (or junior) issues will not be repaid until unsubordinated (or senior) debt has been repaid in full.

Subsidiary

A company a majority of whose voting shares are owned by another company (the Parent).

Subsidiary Ledgers

See Specialized Ledgers.

Substance over Form

There has been a general trend away from technically legal structures to avoid tax towards those that have commercial reality. This is generally referred to as the substance over form principle, so that the substance of structural arrangements or certain transactions achieves the desired tax savings.

Subvention

The provision of assistance or financial support such as an endowment or a subsidy from a government or foundation.

Sum-of-the-Years'-Digits

An accelerated method of computing amortization (depreciation) that produces a declining annual expense, which is used in the United States but rare in Canada.

Sundry Account

An account where miscellaneous items are recorded, e.g., Sundry Receivables represent miscellaneous receivables.

Sunk Cost

A cost that has already been incurred and cannot be removed and therefore should not be considered in an investment decision.

Super Royalty

This term was introduced by the 1986 U.S. *Tax Reform Act* and denotes that part of royalty payments which the IRS deems to be in excess of an arm's length royalty.

Suppressed Inflation

Means that a situation exists in which prices would rise — if government regulations did not establish artificial limits on prices, wages, etc.

Surplus

Generally means any excess amount, but in finance it is the remainder of a fund appropriated for a particular purpose. In a corporation, surplus means assets left after liabilities and debt, including capital stock, have been subtracted.

Surtax

An additional tax levied as a percentage of an income tax amount. Thus, a surtax is a tax on tax. Both individuals and corporations pay surtaxes in addition to their base amount of federal tax. Some provinces also levy surtaxes on provincial taxes payable.

Suspense Account

In accounting, is an account that is used on a temporary basis for receipts, disbursements, or discrepancies until such time as the analysis is complete and they can be properly classified.

Sustainable Growth Rate (SGR)

Shows how fast a company can grow using internally generated assets without issuing additional debt or equity. SGR provides a useful benchmark for judging a company's appropriate rate of growth. A company with a low sustainable growth rate but lots of opportunities for expansion will have to fund that growth via outside sources, which could lower profits and perhaps strain the company's finances. Growth can be a major dilemma because with growth comes a spontaneously generated need for increased working capital. VentureLine calculates a Sustainable Growth Rate from the data entered into the Income Statement and Balance Sheet. The Sustainable Growth Rate is the rate at which the firm may grow the Stockholder's Equity Account (Net Worth) using only increases in Retained Earnings (Net Profit's contribution to retained earnings) to fund the growth. Growth beyond this amount will force the firm to obtain additional financing from external sources to finance growth.

Swap Contract

An agreement by two parties to exchange, or swap, specified cash flows at specified intervals in the future.

Swaps

Agreements to exchange two securities or currencies.

Sweeteners or Equity Kickers

A feature included in the terms of a new issue of debt or preferred shares to make the issue more attractive to initial investors.

SWOT Analysis

One of the most used forms of business analysis. A SWOT examines and assesses the impacts of internal strengths and weaknesses, and external opportunities and threats, on the success of the "subject" of analysis. An important part of a SWOT analysis involves listing and evaluating the firm's strengths, weaknesses, opportunities, and threats. Each of these elements is described:

Strengths:

> Strengths are those factors that make an organization more competitive than its marketplace peers. Strengths are what the company has a distinctive advantage at doing or what resources it has that is strategic to the competition. Strengths are, in effect, resources, capabilities and core competencies that the organization holds that can be used effectively to achieve its performance objectives.

Weaknesses:

> A weakness is a limitation, fault, or defect within the organization that will keep it from achieving its objectives; it is what an organization does poorly or where it has inferior capabilities or resources as compared to the competition.

Opportunities:

> Opportunities include any favourable current prospective situation in the organization's environment, such as a trend, market, change or overlooked need that supports the demand for a product or service and permits the organization to enhance its competitive position.

Threats:

> A threat includes any unfavourable situation, trend or impending change in an organization's environment that is currently or potentially damaging or threatening to its ability to compete. It may be a barrier, constraint, or anything that might inflict problems, damages, harm or injury to the organization.

A firm's strengths and weaknesses (i.e., its internal environment) are made up of factors over which it has greater relative control. These factors include the firm's resources, culture, systems, staffing practices, and the personal values of the firm's managers. Meanwhile, an organization's opportunities and threats (i.e., its external environment) are made up of those factors over which the organization has lesser relative control. These factors include, among others, overall demand, the degree of market saturation, government policies, economic condition, social, cultural, and ethical developments, technological developments, ecological developments, and the factors making up Porter's Five Forces (i.e., intensity of rivalry, threat of new entrants, threat of substitute products, bargaining power of buyers, and bargaining power of suppliers).

Syndicate

A group of underwriters formed to reduce the risk and help to sell an issue.

Synergy

The positive incremental net gain associated with the combination of two firms through a merger or acquisition.

Synoptic

A bookkeeping record listing cash transactions of the business.

Systematic Risk

A risk that influences a large number of assets. Also market risk.

Systematic Risk Principle

Principle stating that the expected return on a risky asset depends only on that asset's systematic risk.

T-Account

A T-shaped representation of a ledger account used in analysis or demonstration.

Talisman

The Exchange's computerized settlement system that acts as a central clearing for transactions in equities.

T&E

An acronym for Travel & Entertainment.

T&R

Among others, can mean: Technical & Research or Termination & Recoupment.

Tangible

Normally refers to assets that can be held or seen and that are capable of being appraised at an actual or approximate value (e.g., inventory, land & buildings, etc.).

Tangible Assets

See Fixed Assets.

Tangible Book Value

Is different than book value in that it deducts from asset value intangible assets, which are assets that are not hard (e.g., goodwill, patents, capitalized start-up expenses and deferred financing costs).

Tap Stocks

Government stocks which the Government Broker (an official of the Bank of England) supply at a given price. The price chosen provides a means of influencing interest rates in general.

Tare Weight

The weight of packing container and packaging material without the weight of the goods contained therein.

Target Cash Balance

A firm's desired cash level as determined by the trade-off between carrying costs and shortage costs.

Target Payout Ratio

A firm's Ion a term desired dividend to-earnings ratio.

Tariff

Usually, a country's tax on imports. May sometimes refer to the rate of tax; and, is used interchangeably with the term "duty".

Tariff, Ad Val Orem

A tariff determined as a percentage of the value of the goods.

Taxable Income

Income calculated according to income tax law (e.g., net income minus certain allowable deductions) and used as the basis for computing income tax payable.

Tax Base

The amount on which a tax rate is applied. In the case of personal or corporate income tax, for example, the tax base is taxable income; if some kinds of income are excluded from the definition of taxable income (such as a portion of capital gains, or certain types of benefits), they are said to be excluded from the tax base. In the case of sales taxes, the tax base is the value of items that are subject to tax; basic groceries, for example, are not part of the tax base of the GST. When economists speak of the tax base being broadened, they mean a wider range of goods, services, income, etc., has been made subject to a tax.

Tax Collection Agreement

An agreement that enables different governments to have access to a tax field through a single administration and collection agency. For example, the federal government collects personal income taxes on behalf of all provinces (except Québec) under a tax collection agreement.

Tax Credit

An amount deducted directly from income tax otherwise payable. Examples include the disability credit and the married credit for individuals, and the scientific research and experimental development investment tax credit for corporations.

Tax Deduction

An amount deducted in computing income for tax purposes. Examples include the childcare expense deduction and the capital cost allowance.

Tax Deferral

A deferral of income taxes from the current year to a later taxation year through the use of provisions such as deductions for RRSP contributions.

Tax Equivalent Yield

The yield that must be offered before factoring in taxes so that an investment pays off a certain after-tax yield. This measure is often necessary to compare taxable and tax-free investments, since tax-free issues tend to have lower pre-tax yields due to the fact that the investment's proceeds will not be reduced by taxes. Tax equivalent yield is equal to required after-tax yield divided by (1 minus the tax rate).

Tax-Exempt Goods and Services

Some types of goods and services are exempt under the GST. This means that tax is not applied to these sales. However, vendors of exempt products are not entitled to claim input tax credits to recover the GST they paid on their inputs to these products. Examples of tax-exempt goods and services include long-term residential rents, most health and dental care services, day care services, most sales by charities, most domestic financial services, municipal transit and legal aid services.

Tax Expenditure

Foregone tax revenues, due to special exemptions, deductions, credits and deferrals that reduce the amount of tax that would otherwise be payable. Examples of tax expenditures include deductions for pension and RRSP contributions, credits for charitable donations, and incentives for firms to invest in research and development. As these examples indicate, tax expenditures are often designed to encourage certain kinds of activities. They may also serve other objectives, such as providing assistance to lower income or elderly Canadians (e.g., the pension and age credits, the GST credit and the child tax benefit).

Tax Haven

A country (offshore jurisdiction) that provides generous tax exemptions. Compare to Treaty Haven.

Tax Holiday

A term used to denote a tax free period sometimes of five years or 10 years during which income may be earned without local taxation.

Tax Loss Carry Forward/Backward

A tax benefit that lets a company or individual deduct losses in order to reduce a tax liability.

Tax-Oriented Lease

A financial lease in which the lessor is the owner for tax purposes. Also called a true lease or a tax lease.

Tax Shelter

Any investment sold on the basis that the investor can receive accelerated deductions and/or credits. An example is flow-through shares.

Tax Sparing (Credit)

Tax sparing refers to the allowance of a credit to a domestic taxpayer for the amount of foreign taxes that were not actually paid, but that would otherwise be levied were it not for the provisions of a tax holiday or a relevant double tax treaty.

Temporary Differences

Differences between accounting calculations of income and calculations required for income tax purposes that will eventually net out to zero. These affect income tax expense calculations.

Temporary Investments

Investments made for a short term, often used as a place to put temporarily excess cash to work.

Tender Offer

In an offer by tender, buyers of shares specify the price at which they are willing to buy.

Term Debt

As in term bonds, is debt that matures in one lump sum at a specified future date. Term debt is usually carried as one type of long-term debt.

Term Deposit

Debt security issued by a bank with terms ranging from several weeks to several years.

Terminal Loss

The difference between UCC and adjusted proceeds of disposal when UCC is greater.

Term Loans

Direct business loans of, typically, one to five years.

Term Preferred Shares

Preferred Shares issued with a fixed term and dividend rate, and therefore having some of the characteristics of debt.

Terms of Sale

Conditions on which a firm sells its goods and services for cash or credit.

Term Structure of Interest Rates

The relationship between nominal interest rates on default-free, pure discount securities and time to maturity; that is, the pure time value of money.

Territoriality Principle

Many countries impose taxation on a worldwide basis, so that profits will be subject to local tax wherever earned. There are some countries, however, which restrict their taxation to sources within the particular country, and such systems work on the territoriality principle.

Testimony

Evidence given by a competent witness under oath.

Thin Capitalization

Thin capitalization refers to the ratio of debt to equity. Where a corporation is heavily capitalized by debt claims, it is considered to be thinly capitalized. In certain circumstances, a corporation that is thinly capitalized by non-residents may not be entitled to a full deduction of its interest expense.

Three Percent (3%) Rule

A rule used in vesting pension plan benefits. The participant's accrued benefit must be at least equal to 3% of the participant's normal projected retirement benefit for each year of participation, with a maximum of 100% after 33 $\frac{1}{3}$ years of participation.

TI

An acronym that could mean, among others, Total Income or Tenant Improvements.

Time Draft

A draft which is payable at a specified point in the future, or under certain circumstances. It matures either a certain number of days after acceptance or a certain number of days after the date of the draft. Compare Date Draft and Sight Draft.

Timeliness

Timely information is usable because it relates to present decision needs. Information received late may be too late to be usable, since decisions pass it by.

Times Interest Earned (TIE)

Measures the extent to which operating income can decline before the firm is unable to meet its annual interest costs. The TIE ratio is used by bankers to assess a firm's ability to pay their liabilities. TIE determines how many times during the year the company has earned the annual interest costs associated with servicing its debt. Normally, a banker will be looking for a TIE ratio to be 2.0 or greater, showing that a business is earning the interest charges two or more times each year. A value of 1.0 or less suggests that the firm is not earning sufficient amounts to cover interest charges.

Time Value of Money

Money can earn interest, so money received in the future is worth less in "present value" terms because the lower amount can be invested to grow to the future amount. Money has a time value because interest accrues over time.

Top Down

A concept of analyzing a subject, such as costs or revenue, starting from the highest level working towards the bottom.

Top Slicing Relief

A taxpayer may find that in one particular year he is subject to tax at the highest marginal rates on an exceptional item of income. Top slicing relief is the term used to denote relief given by averaging such exceptional income over a period of years in order to limit the rate of marginal taxation imposed on such income.

Toronto Stock Exchange

The leading Stock Exchange in Canada.

Total Assets

The total of all assets; both current and fixed.

Total Asset Turnover

Measures management's efficiency in managing all of a firm's assets — specifically the generation of revenues from the firm's total investments in assets. This ratio is extremely important in high asset firms such as manufactures and telecommunications companies. Generally, the higher this ratio as compared to like companies or the industry:

- the smaller the investment required to generate sales, thus the more profitable the firm.
- indicates the firm has less money tied up in fixed assets for each dollar of sales revenue.

Total Current Assets

Total of cash and equivalents, trade receivables, inventory and all other current assets.

Total Current Liabilities

The total of notes payable-short term, current maturities-LTD, trade payables, income taxes payable, and all other current liabilities.

Total Income

For income tax purposes, the sum of all income that is potentially subject to tax.

Totalization Agreement

This is an agreement entered into between many countries to limit the social security taxing rights of a country to which an individual becomes temporarily resident during a period of employment abroad.

Total Liabilities & Net Worth

The sum of all liability items and Net Worth.

Touch

The best buying and selling prices available for a stock from market makers as quoted in SEAQ and SEAQ International.

Traceable

In accounting, is to discover by going backward over the transactions (evidence) step by step establishing a "paper-trail" for a transaction. Non-traceable is where the "paper-trail" of a transaction is broken or non-existent.

Trade Discount

A producer discount given to retail trade members to assist them in increasing sales of the producer's product.

Traded Options

Transferable options with the right to buy and sell a standardized amount of a security at a fixed price within a specified period.

Trade Exchange

A barter system where people or companies trade goods and services without the use of money. In the U.S., income from barter transactions is considered taxable.

Trade Name

A distinctive name used to identify a product or company and build recognition. Many corporations; e.g., Coca Cola, Ford, IBM, etc., aggressively protect their trade names within the market.

Trade Payable

Also known as an account payable, is an amount owed to a creditor for goods and services received.

Trade Receivables

These are Accounts Receivable arising in the normal course of business with customers.

Trade Receivables (Net)

All accounts from trade, net of allowance for doubtful accounts.

Trading Concern

An entity that derives its products for sale, thereby revenue, through purchasing products for sale from other producers/manufacturers for resale to their customer base.

Trading Profit

That profit earned from the short-term trading of securities that were held for less than one year. Such profit is usually subject to tax at regular income tax rates.

Trading Range

Price range between highest and lowest prices at which a stock is traded.

Trading Trust

A trustee vehicle that carries on a trade via its trustee. Often used to circumvent accounting disclosure requirements as offshore trusts do not generally file accounts.

Tranches

Related securities that are offered at the same time but have different risk, reward, and/or maturity.

Transaction

An accounting transaction is the basis of bookkeeping.

Transaction Base

The idea that financial accounting is substantially defined by the use of the Transaction as the fundamental record keeping basis underlying the accounting data.

Transaction Drivers

Used to count the frequency of an activity, i.e., the number of times an activity is performed.

Transaction Motive

The need to hold cash to satisfy normal disbursement and collection activities associated with a firm's ongoing operations.

Transactions Exposure

Short-run financial risk arising from the need to buy or sell at uncertain prices or rates in the near future.

Transfer Form

The form signed by the seller of a security authorizing the company to remove his name from the register and substitute that of the buyer.

Transfer Price

The price charged by an individual entity in a multi-entity corporation on transactions among the entities involved.

Transfer Pricing

Another buzz word in international tax planning is transfer pricing, which seeks to adjust taxable profits between related entities in different countries to reflect arm's length pricing policies and thereby yield a fair return to each taxing authority.

Transnational

A term used to describe any transactions that may encounter laws of more than one country.

Treasury Bill (T-Bill)

Short-term debt security issued by federal or provincial governments. T-bills are sold at less than face value (at a discount) and mature at their face value. The difference is the investor's profit.

Treasury Shares (Stock)

Share capital issued and then reacquired by the firm that issued the shares. The result is a reduction of shareholders' equity because resources have been used to reduce the actual amount of outstanding equity.

Treaty Haven

A term adopted by the IFS Group to distinguish low tax countries commonly known as Tax Havens, such as Panama, Liberia, etc., and those whose double tax treaties make them especially useful in international tax planning for businesses, such as Cyprus, Malta, Madeira etc.

Treaty Shopping

Where a national or resident of a third country seeks to obtain the benefit of a double tax agreement between two other countries by interposing a company or other entity in one or the other of them.

Trial Balance

A list of all the general ledger accounts and their balances. The sum of the accounts with debit balances should equal the sum of those with credit balances. This is contrasted with the Chart of Accounts, which lists only the account names.

True and Fair View

One of the most prominent principles of accounting. It suggests that an enterprise should provide a true and fair view about its financial conditions and operating results. The concept of true and fair view does not mean absolute truth about enterprises. Financial statements are a product of management's judgments and estimates. The principle of true and fair view requires comparative truth about the enterprise's picture. True and fair view is rather defined operationally; it is thought to be accomplished by complying with all other lower accounting principles.

True Value

The amount that a buyer is finally willing to pay.

Trust(s)

An arrangement under which money or other property is held by one person, often a trust company, for the benefit of another person or persons. These assets are administered according to the terms of the trust agreement. Each province has a trustee act, which regulates the kinds of investments that can be made by the trustees of a trust fund.

Trust Deed

An instrument of conveyance of title to property wherein the transferee will be holding the title to the property on behalf of another person.

Trustee Status

Used with reference to ordinary shares of those companies that meet the requirements of 'wider range' investments as defined by the *Trustee Investment Act 1961*.

Trust Fund

A fiduciary relationship calling for a trustee to hold the title to assets, usually monetary, for the benefit of the beneficiary.

Trust Receipt

An instrument acknowledging that the borrower holds certain goods in trust for the lender.

TSE

The Toronto Stock Exchange.

T/T

A payment or financial transaction designation meaning "Telegraphic Transfer" of funds.

Turnover

In U.S. accounting, is the number of times an asset is replaced during a financial period; often used in terms of inventory turnover or accounts receivable turnover. In securities, for either a portfolio or exchange, Turnover is the number of shares traded for a period as a percentage of the total shares. In Great Britain, Turnover means sales.

Twenty-One-Year Deemed Disposition Rule

A rule requiring that trust assets be treated for tax purposes as if they were disposed of every 21 years. This measure accompanied the introduction of capital gains taxation in 1972 to prevent trusts from being used to avoid the taxation of capital gains on death.

Unadjusted Trial Balance

The Trial balance of the accounts prior to making various accrual adjustments in preparation for the financial statements.

Unallocated Costs

Represents corporate costs not associated either directly or indirectly in providing a product or service for sale. Unallocated costs are not included in the calculation of Cost of Goods Sold.

Unbiased Forward Rates (UFR)

The condition stating that the current forward rate is an unbiased predictor of the future exchange rate.

Uncovered Interest Parity (UIP)

The condition stating that the expected percentage change in the exchange rate is equal to the difference in interest rates.

Underlying

The security, cash commodity, forward, futures contract, swap, or other contract or instrument that is the subject of a derivative contract or instrument.

Underlying Tax Credit

(After-tax) dividends from a non-resident subsidiary may be subject to additional domestic taxation in the hands of the parent company. Relief from this double taxation may be available under either the domestic law or a tax treaty with the source country. The double tax relief would take into account secondary taxation (withholding taxes), and may also take into account the primary taxation levied on profits out of which dividends have been declared, known as underlying tax. The underlying tax credit may be available for all companies in which a substantial interest exists, and for many tiers of ownership, or alternatively be restricted to immediate subsidiaries or say direct and first tier subsidiaries.

Underwriting

An arrangement by which a company is guaranteed that an issue of shares will raise a given amount of cash because the underwriters for a commission agree to subscribe for any of the issue not taken up by the public.

Undistributed Earnings

See Retained Earnings.

Unearned Revenue/Income

Represents money that you have received in advance of providing the goods or services to your customer. Unearned revenue is a liability of your business until you provide the goods or services you agreed to provide to the customer.

UNICAP

See Uniform Capitalization Rules.

Uniform Capitalization Rules (UNICAP)

In the U.S., is a method of valuing inventory for tax purposes that requires capitalization of direct costs, e.g., material and labour, and an allocable portion of indirect costs that benefit or are incurred because of production or resale activities. Certain expenses must be included in the basis of the property or in inventory costs rather than currently deducted. These costs are then recovered through depreciation or amortization or as cost of goods sold.

Unitary Taxation

A system of taxation under which the worldwide profits and losses of multi-national enterprises are allocated amongst its component parts in different countries in accordance with a formula based upon multiple factors, such as sales, assets and payroll in each country.

Unit-Control System

An accounting system used in inventory management that tracks inventory using bin tickets and physical inventory checks.

Units-of-Production Amortization

An amortization (depreciation) method in which the annual amortization expense varies directly with the year's production volume.

Unit Trusts

A form of collective investment vehicles. The beneficial rights to the trust assets are divided into a number of units and these units are offered for sale to the public. The unit trust vehicle can either be a trust or corporate entity.

Unlevered Cost of Capital

The cost of capital of a firm that has no debt.

Appendix A

Unrealized Income ("paper profit")

Profit which has been made but not yet realized or collected through a transaction, such as a stock which has risen in value but is still being held. Also called unrealized gain or unrealized profit or paper gain or book profit.

Unrealized Loss

A term that commonly refers to the write-down of an investment portfolio resulting from applying the lower of cost or market value on an aggregate basis. On a short-term portfolio, the unrealized loss is shown on the income statement. On a long-term portfolio, the unrealized loss is presented as a separate item in the stockholder's equity section of the balance sheet.

Unrestricted Assets

Assets/resources which are not restricted for use by legal or contractual requirements and may be used for any purpose.

Unsystematic Risk

A risk that affects at most a small number of assets. Also unique or asset-specific risks.

Unusual Items

Unusual revenues or expenses that are large enough to be worth identifying separately in the income statement.

Upstream Loan

Subsidiary companies may distribute dividends to their parent companies, in which case such income would be subject to taxation or otherwise depending upon local laws of exemption or double tax relief. However, monies may be loaned by the subsidiaries to the parent without such potential taxation, and such loans are referred to as upstream loans.

Users

People who use financial statements to assist them in deciding whether to invest in the enterprise, lend it money, or take other action involving financial information.

Uses of Cash

A firm's activities in which cash is spent. Also applications of cash.

VAD

In business, can mean: Value of Annual Demand, Value-Added Data, Value-Added Dealer, or, Value-Added Distributor.

Valuation

Determining the amounts at which assets, liabilities, and equity should be shown in the balance sheet.

Valuation Date

The date when the value of a fund is calculated for a purchase exchange or redemption.

Value

A term that defines the worth of a thing. The term is usually preceded by the word, or words such as "Fair" or "Fair Market", and it is usually defined in the document where it is found. Not all value for an item is the same, i.e., value is usually perceived.

Value for Money

Is in the perception of the buyer or receiver of goods and/or services. Proof of good value for money is in believing or concluding that the goods/services received was worth the price paid. Examples of the types of factors that may be considered are suitability, quality, skills, price, whole of life costs and other criteria. The mix of these and other factors and the relevant importance of each will vary on a case by case basis.

Value in Use

The value of an asset determined by the future cash flows it brings in, or the future expenses that will be avoided by owning the asset.

VAR

An acronym for Value-Added Reseller (usually of technology products); or, in finance, Value at Risk.

Variable Costs

Costs that change when the quantity of output changes. For example, the direct material or labour required to complete the build or manufacturing of a product. Contrast with Fixed Costs.

Variable Expenses

Those business expenses that usually fluctuate dependent upon production or sales volume. Contrast with Fixed Expenses.

Variance

In accounting, is the difference between a projected number and the actual number, e.g., (1) a budget variance is spending either more or less from the amount that was budgeted; and (2) a cost variance is the difference between actual cost and standard cost in the categories of direct material, direct labour, and direct overhead.

VAT (Value Added Tax)

A consumption tax where taxes are levied at each step of a manufacturing process where value is added to that product at that point in the manufacturing cycle; as well as at the point where the consumer purchases the end product.

Venture Capital

Capital committed to an unproven venture. The initial, start-up money is referred to as "seed money" and entails the greatest risk. If the project gets off the ground it may require additional financing at additional "rounds" or the "mezzanine level" before the company is finally brought to the market and the venture capitalist can enjoy handsome rewards. Experienced investors in venture capital situations typically plan on turning away a minimum of nine out of every 10 proposals which are brought to them, and then they expect as many failures as successes from their selected investments.

Verifiability

Ability to trace an accounting entry or figure back to the underlying evidence of its occurrence and validity.

Vertical Financial Analysis

Allows comparison of the financial ratios of a company in time — past, present and future.

Wage

Actual remuneration paid to an employee for services rendered. Minimum wages, in the U.S.A., are established by the federal *Fair Labour Standards Act*.

Warrant

(1) In government accounting, an order drawn authorizing payment to a designated payee; (2) In securities, it is a security entitling the holder to buy a proportionate amount of stock at some specified future date at a specified price, usually one higher than current market. This "warrant" is then traded as a security, the price of which reflects the value of the underlying stock. Warrants are issued by corporations and often used as a "sweetener" bundled with another class of security to enhance the marketability of the latter. Warrants are like call options, but with much longer time spans — sometimes years. In addition, warrants are offered by corporations whereas exchange traded call options are not issued by firms.

Warranty

A guarantee given to a buyer from a seller that the goods or services purchased will perform as promised, or a refund will be given, repair will be done at no charge, or an exchange made.

Water's Edge

This term was developed in the U.S. to describe the limitation of unitary tax to corporations conducting activities in the U.S., so that it would not be necessary to take into account turnover, payroll and assets of the relevant corporation outside of the United States, i.e., the water's edge.

Wealth Tax

Tax imposed either annually (annual net wealth tax) or at death (gift and inheritance or estate tax) on the net value of assets. Property taxes levied by provincial or municipal governments are a form of wealth taxation in Canada. With the general exception of a taxpayer's principal residence, capital gains tax is assessed on the increase in value of assets upon the death of a taxpayer.

Weighted Average

One in which different data in the data set are given different "weights". Varying subjective assumptions are derived for determining the level of importance for each data category. For example, many teachers will use a "weighted average" when calculating a student's grade in a course. A teacher might determine the final grade for the course by calculating that the test average is 60% of the grade, quiz average is 30% of the grade, and a single project is 10% of the grade.

Weighted Average Cost of Capital (WACC)

The weighted average of the costs of debt and equity.

Weighted Cost of Capital

The expected return on a portfolio of all a firm's securities. Used as a hurdle rate for capital investment.

"What If" (Effects) Analysis

Analyzing potential business decisions or accounting policies by determining their effects on income, cash flow, or other important items.

White Knight

A company that rescues another which is in financial difficulty, especially one that saves a company from an unwelcome takeover bid.

White Paper

(1) In a technological industry, is an informational brief offering an overview of a technology, product, issue, standard, policy, or solution — its importance, use and implementation, and business benefits. White Papers have emerged as the standard way of communicating more in-depth information to business decision-makers in terms of problems solved and markets addressed; or (2) a White Paper can be an official government report of an investigation into a public event that received a great deal of publicity and notoriety; it indicates the official government position on a particular public issue.

Wholly Owned Subsidiary

An entity whose parent owns virtually 100% of its common stock.

Window Dressing

The act or an instance of making something appear deceptively attractive or favourable. Usually using something, e.g., inflated sales projections, to create a deceptively favourable or attractive impression.

WIP

An acronym for Work in Process/Progress. Usually refers to inventory that has value added from labour or additional processing. When considered for inventory value, the value of the raw material plus the value added component is accounted for in determining the value of that inventory at that point in the process.

Withholding Tax

(1) In international tax law, a withholding tax is a tax levied by the country in which income arises (the source country) at a flat rate on the gross amount of the income paid by a resident of the country to a non-resident. The tax is usually collected by the resident taxpayer and remitted to the government on behalf of the non-resident person; (2) In domestic tax law, withholding tax usually refers to those taxes that are withheld from an employee's compensation to account for that individual's tax liability on his/her compensation.

Work Centre

Normally, is an individual production area or sub-process of an overall manufacturing process.

Workers' Compensation

Usually, a state or privately managed insurance fund in the United States that reimburses employees for injuries suffered on the job.

Working Capital (WC)

(The difference between current assets and current liabilities) measures the margin of protection for current creditors. It reflects the ability to finance current operations.

Working Capital Management

Planning and managing the firm's current assets and liabilities.

Working Capital Ratio

See Current Ratio.

Working Capital Turnover (WCT)

Shows how efficiently Working Capital (WC) is employed, i.e., it measures how efficiently the business is using its available assets. WCT measures the amount of Net Revenue generated per monetary unit of Working Capital. It varies widely by industry; therefore it is best to compare WCT to industry averages.

Work Order

A document specifying the components and assembly or other work to be done to provide a product ordered by a customer.

World Trade Organization (WTO)

Is the international trade body formed by the agreement of member nations. The WTO is an evolution of the GATT process designed to resolve trade disputes and work for the lowering of tariff and non-tariff trade barriers.

Wrap Account

At its most basic is an alternative form of commission arrangement between a securities firm and its client. Wrap accounts generally charge the client an annual fee based on assets in the account in lieu of a per transaction commission structure. In other words, the firm "wraps" together all the costs and charges them off as a "management fee". Firms often add further features to wrap accounts such as investment management, custodial services, and enhanced reporting.

Write-Off

To decrease the value of an item, e.g., a tax write-off decreases tax liability, a vehicle involved in an accident can be declared a write-off if the cost to repair is in excess of the value of the vehicle.

Write-Up

The increase in value of an asset, but it is seldom used and is not allowed in GAAP (Generally Accepted Accounting Principles).

X-Inefficiency

The failure to minimize costs or maximize returns. (Sometimes referred to as X-efficiency, but carrying the same meaning.)

Yankee Bond

A dollar bond issued by a non-U.S. borrower in the United States.

Yen

The currency of Japan. Its subdivisions are 100 sen and 1000 rin.

Yield

The annual income from an investment expressed as a percentage of the investment's current value. There are three factors that affect an investment's yield: its current value, its term to maturity, and its income stream. If an investment is purchased at "par" (i.e., its face value), the yield will be equal to the income stream. For example, a one year bond that has a current value of $1,000 and pays $100 in interest has a yield of 10%. If an investment instrument is purchased at a discount (i.e., a price lower than its face value), the benefit of the discount will increase the yield. For example, a one year bond that has a current value of $960 and pays $100 in interest has a yield of 14%. If an investment instrument is purchased at a premium (i.e., a price higher than its face value), the premium paid will lower the yield of the investment. For example, a one year bond that has a current value of $1,040 and pays $100 in interest has a yield of 6%.

Yield to Maturity (YTM)

See Yield.

Zero-Balance Account

A chequing account in which a zero balance is maintained by transfers of funds from a master account in an amount only large enough to cover cheques presented.

Zero Based Budget

Where the expenses or costs of the prior year are not taken into consideration when establishing expense or budgetary levels looking forward. Each expense category starts from zero. All expenses or cost levels within the budget must be justified or re-justified as being necessary; thus "zero-base".

Zero Coupon Bonds

Bonds priced at a large discount from face value. The bonds mature at full face value so the difference between the original issue price and the face value represents interest income. The issuer of the zero coupon bond saves on cash flow since the interest isn't paid out until the end of the bond holding period. Sometimes called Stripped Bonds.

Zero Coupon Convertible Debenture/Security

A Zero Coupon Bond that is convertible into the common stock of the issuing company after the common stock reaches a certain price.

Zero-Rated Goods and Services

Under the GST, certain categories of goods and services are considered taxable at a "zero" rate, rather than at the general rate of 7 per cent. Vendors do not charge GST on their sales of zero-rated goods and services. However, vendors are entitled to claim input tax credits to recover any GST they paid on inputs used to produce zero-rated products. As a result, zero-rated goods and services are tax-free. Major categories of zero-rated sales include basic groceries, prescription drugs, medical devices, and most agricultural and fishing industry inputs.

"Z-Score"

See Altman "Z-Score".

APPENDIX B

INCOME STATISTICS 2005 (BASED ON 2003 TAX YEAR)

	Taxable Returns	% of Total	Non-Taxable Returns	% of Total	Total Returns	% of Total	Total Income (000 $)	% of Total	Total Tax (000 $)	% of Total
Loss and Nil	880	0.0	959,470	13.1	960,350	4.1	(1,463,654)	-0.2	943	0.0
$1-$10 K	524,210	3.3	3,972,750	54.4	4,496,960	19.4	24,691,371	3.3	133,524	0.1
$10-$15 K	1,227,140	7.7	1,612,810	22.1	2,839,950	12.3	35,541,630	4.7	778,085	0.6
$15-$20 K	1,771,330	11.2	488,210	6.7	2,259,540	9.8	39,165,398	5.2	2,070,616	1.6
$20-$25 K	1,650,970	10.4	128,120	1.8	1,779,090	7.7	39,911,060	5.3	3,751,054	3.0
$25-$30 K	1,563,270	9.9	54,490	0.8	1,619,760	7.0	44,493,896	5.9	4,601,828	3.7
$30-$35 K	1,517,100	9.6	31,590	0.4	1,548,690	6.7	50,208,528	6.6	5,872,474	4.7
$35-$40 K	1,308,080	8.3	17,670	0.2	1,325,750	5.7	49,603,779	6.5	6,588,411	5.3
$40-$50 K	2,011,480	12.7	15,960	0.2	2,027,440	8.8	90,547,152	11.9	13,714,778	11.0
Sub Total	11,574,460	73.1	7,283,070	99.8	18,857,530	81.5	372,699,160	49.2	37,511,713	30.0
$50-$100 K	3,528,040	22.3	15,650	0.2	3,543,690	15.3	236,400,893	31.1	44,830,089	35.8
$100-$150 K	444,440	2.8	2,010	0.0	446,450	1.9	52,849,236	6.9	12,729,675	10.2
$150-$250 K	179,030	1.1	1,180	0.0	180,210	0.8	33,979,469	4.5	9,421,025	7.5
$250K-over	110,110	0.7	310	0.0	110,420	0.5	63,188,236	8.3	20,646,417	16.5
Total	15,836,080	100.0	7,302,220	100.0	23,138,300	100.0	759,116,994	100.0	125,138,919	100.0

Notes:

Source: Canada Revenue Agency's *Income Statistics: 2005 Edition of Interim Statistics* (Ottawa: CRA), available online at http://www.cra-arc.gc.ca/agency/stats/menu-e.html.

APPENDIX C

PERSONAL FEDERAL INCOME TAX RATES

2005	
Percentage Rate	**Income Between**
15	$0-$35,595
22	$35,596-$71,190
26	$71,191-$115,739
29	Over $115,740

2006	
Percentage Rate	**Income Between**
15/15.5[1]	$0-$36,378
22	$36,379-$72,756
26	$72,757-$118,285
29	Over $118,285

Notes:

1   Based on May 2, 2006 budget. 15% rate applicable to June 30, 2006. 15.5% rate effective July 1, 2006. Average for 2006 is 15.25%.

APPENDIX D.1

2005 FEDERAL CORPORATE TAX RATES (%)

Rates for 12-month taxation years ended December 31. Prorate for taxation years that straddle the effective date.

General	Basic Rate[1]		38.00
	Less: Provincial abatement[2]		10.00
	Basic rate after abatement		28.00
	Plus: federal surtax (4% of 28%)[3]		1.12
	General federal rate (before reduction)		29.12
	Less: general rate reduction[4,5]		7.00
	General federal rate		*22.12*
Manufacturing & Processing (M & P) Income	General federal rate (before reduction)		29.12
	Less: M & P reduction[6]		7.00
	M & P rate		*22.12*
Canadian-Controlled Private Corporations (CCPCs)	*Active business income up to $300,000*[7]	General federal rate (before reduction)	29.12
		Less: small business deduction[8]	16.00
		CCPC small business rate[9]	*13.12*
	Investment income	General federal rate (before reduction)	29.12
		Additional refundable tax[10]	6.67
		CCPC investment income rate	*35.79*

Notes:

1   S. 123(1).

2   S. 124.

3   S. 123.2. Proposed reduction to 20.5% in 2008, 20.0% in 2009, and 19.0% in 2010.

4   S. 123.4(2); a 7% general rate reduction applies from January 1, 2004.

5   The general rate reduction does not apply to income benefiting from the small business deduction, manufacturing and processing income, resource income (for 2005 and 2006 only), investment companies benefiting from the refundable tax provisions and mutual

fund and investment corporations. Note that the resource income rule is repealed, beginning with 2007.

6   S. 125.1(1).

7   Up to $400,000 for 2007.

8   S. 125(1); the small business deduction applies on active business income up to the "business limit" (see s. 125(2)), earned in Canada, of associated CCPCs. The 2006 budget increased the budget limit from $300,000 to 400,000, beginning in 2007. The business limit is phased out when taxable capital employed in Canada in the preceding year is between $10 million and $15 million. There is a proposed increase to 16.5% for 2008 and to 17.0% for 2009 and 2010.

9   Proposed reduction to 11.5% for 2008 and 11.0% for 2009. The surtax will not apply after 2007.

10   S. 123.3; there is an additional 6.67% refundable tax on investment income. The tax applies to investment income (other than deductible dividends) of CCPCs. It is refundable through the refundable dividend tax on hand (RDTOH) mechanism.

APPENDIX D.2

2005 FEDERAL CORPORATE TAX RATES (%)
(AS ANNOUNCED TO JUNE 21, 2004)

Rates for 12-month taxation years ended December 31. Prorate for taxation years that straddle the effective date.

General	Basic Rate[1]		38.00
	Less: Provincial abatement[2]		10.00
	Basic rate after abatement		28.00
	Plus: federal surtax (4% of 28%)[3]		1.12
	General federal rate (before reduction)		29.12
	Less: general rate reduction[4,5]		7.00
	General federal rate		*22.12*
Manufacturing & Processing (M & P) Income	General federal rate (before reduction)		29.12
	Less: M & P reduction[6]		7.00
	M & P rate		*22.12*
Canadian-Controlled Private Corporations (CCPCs)	*Active business income up to $300,000*	General federal rate (before reduction)	29.12
		Less: small business deduction[7]	16.00
		CCPC small business rate	*13.12*
	Investment income	General federal rate (before reduction)	29.12
		Additional refundable tax[8]	6.67
		CCPC investment income rate	*35.79*

Notes:

1 S. 123(1).

2 S. 124.

3 S. 123.3.

4 S. 123.4(2); a 7% general rate reduction applies from January 1, 2004.

5 The general rate reduction does not apply to income benefiting from the small business deduction or the CCPC rate reduction, manufacturing and processing income, resource

income, investment companies benefiting from the refundable tax provisions and mutual fund and investment corporations.

6   S. 125.1(1).

7   S. 125(1); the small business deduction applies on active business income up to the "business limit" (see s. 125(2)), earned in Canada, of associated CCPCs. The 2003 Budget increased the business limit from $200,000 to $300,000; it was phased in as follows: $225,000 for 2003, $250,000 for 2004, and $300,000 for 2005. The business limit is reduced when the associated group's taxable capital employed in Canada in the preceding year exceeds $10 million.

8   S. 123.3; there is an additional 6.67% refundable tax on investment income. The tax applies to investment income (other than deductible dividends) of CCPCs. It is refundable through the refundable dividend tax on hand (RDTOH) mechanism.

APPENDIX E

2005 TOP PERSONAL MARGINAL TAX RATES (%)

Jurisdiction Income	Tax on Top Rate	Tax on Tax Surtax*	Provincial Income	2005 Combined Top Marginal Rates		
				Regular	Dividend	Capital
Federal	29.00	—	—	—	—	—
B.C.	14.70	—	—	43.70	31.58	21.85
Alta.	10.00	—	—	39.00	24.08	19.50
Sask.	15.00	—	—	44.00	28.33	22.00
Man.	17.40	—	—	46.40	35.08	23.20
Ont.	11.16	—	20/36	46.41	31.34	23.20
Que.	24.00	—	—	48.22	32.81	24.11
N.B.	17.84	—	—	46.84	37.26	23.42
N.S.	17.50	—	10	48.25	33.06	24.13
P.E.I.	16.70	—	10	47.37	31.96	23.69
Nfld./Lab.	18.02	—	9	48.64	37.32	24.32
Yukon	12.76	—	5	42.40	28.64	21.20
N.W.T.	14.05	—	—	43.05	29.65	21.53
Nunavut	11.50	—	—	40.50	28.96	20.25
Non-Resident	—	48.00	—	42.92	—	21.46

Notes:

* A surtax is a tax on tax. The surtax is applied to the portion of provincial/territorial taxes payable that exceed a specified threshold. For example, in Ontario, there is a 20% surtax on provincial taxes in excess of $3,929 and a 36% surtax on provincial taxes in excess of $4,957.

APPENDIX F

2005/2006 CORPORATE INCOME TAX RATES (%)
(BASED ON RATES AS ANNOUNCED TO MAY 2, 2006)

| Jurisdiction | Canadian Controlled Private Corporations (CCPCs) | | | Other Corporations | |
| | Active Business Income (ABI) | | | | |
	Rate	Income Limit ($)	Investment Income (%)	Manufacturing & Processing (%)	Other (%)
Federal	13.12	300K[1]	35.8	22.1	22.1
B.C.	4.50	400K	12.0[2]	13.5/12.0	13.5/12.0
Alta.	3.00	400K	11.5/10.0[3]	11.5/10.0	11.5/10.0
Sask.	5.00	300/400K[4]	17.0/14.0[5]	10.0	17.0/14.0
Man.	5.0/4.5[6]	400K	15.0/14.5[7]	15.0/14.5	15.0/14.5
Ont.	5.50	400K	14.0	12.0	14.0
Que.	8.9/8.5/8.0[8]	0/400K[9]	16.2	8.9/9.9[10]	8.9/9.9
N.B.	2.5/2.0/1.5[11]	425K-475K[12]	13.0	13.0	13.0
N.S.	5.00	350K-400K[13]	16.0	16.0	16.0
P.E.I.	7.5/6.5/5.4[14]	300K	16.0	7.5/16.0[15]	16.0
Nfld./Lab.	5.00	300K	14.0	5.0	14.0
Yukon	4.00	300K	15.0	2.5	15.0
N.W.T.	4.00	300K	14.0/11.5[16]	14.0/11.5	14.0/11.5
Nunavut	4.00	300K	12.0	12.0	12.0

Notes:

1   Proposed to be increased to $400,000 January 1, 2007.

2   Decrease from 13.5% to 12.0% effective July 1, 2005.

3   Decrease from 11.5% to 10.0% effective April 1, 2006.

4   Increases to $400, 000 effective July 1, 2006.

5   Decreases to 14.0% as of July 1, 2006.

6   Decreases to 4.5% effective January 1, 2006.

7   Decreases to 14.5% effective January 1, 2006.

8   8.5% effective January 1, 2006 drops to 8.0% March 24, 2006.

9    $400,000 limit begins January 1, 2006.

10   Rate increase to 9.9% is effective January 1, 2006.

11   2.0% rate effective July 1, 2005 dropping to 1.5% July 1, 2006.

12   $425,000 limit increasing to $450,000 effective July 1, 2005 and to $475,000 July 1, 2006.

13   $250,000 limit increasing to $350,000 April 1, 2005 and to $400,000 April 1, 2006.

14   7.5% rate decreasing to 6.5% April 1, 2005 and to 5.4% April 1, 2006.

15   Rate reduction for M&P to be eliminated effective April 1, 2005.

16   Decrease from 14.0% to 11.5% effective July 1, 2006.

APPENDIX G

2005 & 2006 TOP CORPORATE RATES (%)
(BASED ON RATES AS ANNOUNCED TO MAY 2, 2006)

Province	General	Manufacturing & Processing	Small Business
B.C.	35.6/34.1[1]	35.6/34.1	17.6
Alta.	33.6/32.1[2]	33.6/32.1	16.1
Sask.	39.1/36.1[3]	32.1	18.1
Man.	37.1/36.6[4]	37.1/36.6	18.1/17.6[5]
Ont.	36.1	34.1	18.6
Que.	31.0/32.0[6]	31.0/32.0	22.0/21.6/21.1[7]
N.B.	35.1	35.1	15.6/15.1/14.6[8]
N.S.	38.1	38.1	18.1
P.E.I.	38.1	29.6/38.1[9]	20.6/19.6/18.5[10]
Nfld./Lab.	36.1	27.1	18.1
Yukon	37.1	24.6	17.1
N.W.T.	36.1/33.6[11]	36.1/33.6	17.1
Nunavut	34.1	34.1	17.1

Notes:

1   Decrease effective July 1, 2005.

2   Decrease effective July 1, 2005.

3   Decrease effective July 1, 2006.

4   Decrease effective January 1, 2006.

5   Decrease effective January 1, 2006.

6   Rate increase effective January 1, 2006.

7   Rate decrease to 21.6% effective January 1, 2006 and a decrease to 21.1% effective March 24, 2006.

8   Rate decrease to 15.1% effective July 1, 2005 and a decrease to 14.6% effective July 1, 2006.

9   Previous M&P reduction repealed April 1, 2005.

10   Rate decrease to 19.6% effective April 1, 2005 and a decrease to 18.5% effective April 1, 2006.

11   Decrease effective July 1, 2006.

APPENDIX H

BUSINESS INCOME INTEGRATION (BASED ON RATES AS ANNOUNCED TO MAY 2, 2006)

| Province | Corporate Tax Rates on Active Business Income | | Comparison of Tax Rates on Active Income | | |
| | Small Business Rate (%) | General Corporate Rate (%) | Business or Salary Income Earned Personally (%) | Active Income Earned in Corp. and Net Income Paid Out as a Dividend | |
				With SBD (%)	Without SBD (%)
B.C.	17.6	35.6/34.1[1]	43.7	43.62	55.94/54.91
Alta.	16.1	33.6/32.1[2]	39.0	36.30	49.59/48.45
Sask.	18.1	39.1/36.1[3]	44.0	41.30	56.35/54.20
Man.	18.1/17.6[4]	37.1/36.6[5]	46.4	46.83/46.51	59.16/58.84
Ont.	18.6	36.1	46.4	44.11	56.13
Que.	22.0/21.6/21.1[6]	31.0/32.0[7]	48.2	47.59/47.32/46.99	53.64/54.31
N.B.	15.6/15.1/14.6[8]	35.1	46.8	47.04/46.73/46.42	59.28
N.S.	18.1	38.1	48.3	45.18	58.56
P.E.I.	20.6/19.6/18.5[9]	38.1	47.4	45.98/45.30/44.55	57.88
Nfld./Lab.	18.1	36.1	48.6	48.66	59.95
Yukon	17.1	37.1	42.4	40.84	55.11
N.W.T.	17.1	36.1/33.6[10]	43.1	41.68	55.05/53.29
Nunavut	17.1	34.1	40.5	41.11	53.18

All rates shown are the combined Federal and provincial rate.

Corporate rates used are as of May 2, 2006.

Assumes individual is in the top personal bracket.

Notes:

1   Decrease effective July 1, 2005.

2   Decrease effective July 1, 2005.

3   Decrease effective July 1, 2006.

4   Decrease effective January 1, 2006.

5   Decrease effective January 1, 2006.

6   Rate decrease to 21.6% effective January 1, 2006 and a decrease to 21.1% effective March 24, 2006.

7   Rate increase effective January 1, 2006.

8   Rate decrease to 15.1% effective July 1, 2005 and a decrease to 14.6% effective July 1, 2006.

9   Rate decrease to 19.6% effective April 1, 2005 and a decrease to 18.5% effective April 1, 2006.

10   Decrease effective July 1, 2006.

APPENDIX I

2005 DIVIDEND TAX CREDITS

Jurisdiction	As a % of Federal "Gross Up"	As a % of Dividend	Federal/Provincial Income Tax Act References
Federal	66.7	13.3	*Income Tax Act* s. 121 R.S.C. 1985, c. 1 (5th Supp.)
B.C.	25.5	5.1	*Income Tax Act* s. 4.69, R.S.B.C. 1996, c. 215
Alta.	32.0	6.4	*Alberta Personal Income Tax Act*, s. 21, R.S.A. 2000, c. A-35.03
Sask.	40.0	8.0	*Income Tax Act*, s. 32, R.S.S. 2000, c. I-2.01
Man.	25.0	5.0	*Income Tax Act*, s. 4.7(1), C.C.S.M., c. I10
Ont.	25.7	5.1	*Income Tax Act*, s. 4(3.4.1), R.S.O., c. I.2 (Calculated as the federal dividend gross up multiplied by the highest provincial rate of 11.16%/highest federal rate of 29.0%)
Que.	54.2	10.8	*Taxation Act*, s. 767, R.S.Q., c. I.3
N.B.	18.5	3.7	*New Brunswick Income Tax Act*, s. 35, S.N.B. 2000, c. N-6.001
N.S.	38.5	7.7	*Income Tax Act*, s. 21, R.S.N.S. 1989, c. 217
P.E.I.	38.5	7.7	*Income Tax Act*, s. 20, R.S.P.E.I. 1988, c. I-1
Nfld./Lab.	25.0	5.0	*Income Tax Act*, s. 20, R.S.N.L. 2000, c. I-1.1
Yukon	29.3	5.9	*Income Tax Act*, s. 6(39), R.S.Y. 2002, c. 118
N.W.T.	30.0	6.0	*Income Tax Act*, s. 2.32, R.S.N.W.T. 1988, c.I-1
Nunavut	20.0	4.0	*Income Tax Act*, s. 2.32, R.S.N.W.T. 1988, c.I-1 (as duplicated for Nunavut by s. 29 of the Nunavut Act, S.C. 1993, c. 28).

The "gross-up" amount is equal to 25% of the dividend received by the taxpayer (Federal *Income Tax Act*, s. 82(1)(b)).

APPENDIX J

SUMMARY OF TAX RATES ON SOURCES OF INCOME

Source of Income	Taxpayer			
	Individual	CCPC	Private Canadian Corporation	Public Corporation
Active Business Income	Profit taxed at relevant marginal rate (see Appendix C)	Federal rate: $0 - $300,000: 13.12%	General Federal rate of 22.12%	General Federal rate of 22.12%
Manufacturing & Processing Income	Profit taxed relevant marginal rate (see Appendix C)		General Federal rate of 22.12%	General Federal rate of 22.12%
Capital Gains	50% to be included in income as taxable $500,000 exemption for Qualified Small Business Shares	50% to be included in income as taxable Non-taxable income added to the Capital Dividend Account (CDA)	50% to be included in income as taxable Non-taxable income added to the Capital Dividend Account (CDA)	50% to be included in income as taxable Note: Capital Dividend Account not applicable
Dividends	Gross-up by 25% to calculate taxable amount Federal tax credit of 2/3 of gross-up applied against tax payable (dividend tax credits offered by all provinces)	Tax free if paid by connected corporation unless payer received a dividend refund 33.3% Part IV tax if paid by unconnected corporation Part IV tax added to the RDTOH account for refund when the dividend is paid out.	Tax free if paid by connected corporation unless payer received a dividend 33.3% Part IV tax if paid by unconnected corporation Part IV tax added to the RDTOH account for refund when the dividend is paid out.	Inter-corporate dividends not subject to Part IV tax unless the corporation is a subject corporation
Investment Income Including Taxable Capital Gains, Interest, and Property Income.	Included in income and taxed at relevant marginal rate.	Federal rate of 35.8%	General Federal rate of 22.12%	General Federal rate of 22.12%

APPENDIX K

SUMMARY OF SUBSECTION 85(1) AND SECTIONS 85.1 AND 86

	Section 85(1)	Section 85.1	Section 86
Rollover	Transfer of property to a corporation	Share for share exchange	Exchange of shares in a reorganization
When used	(1) Incorporating a business owned by a sole proprietor or partnership; (2) Transfer of securities from a holding corporation; (3) Transfer of business assets within related groups; (4) Transfer of a controlling interest in an operating company to a new holding company; (5) Pooling or splitting assets held in a joint venture corporation; (6) Butterfly reorganizations; (7) Share exchange in a take-over bid.	Arm's length transaction, such as a buy-out or a take-over, where vendor will not hold more than 50% of the purchasing corporation's issued shares. May elect piecemeal dispositions to exchange portions of the old shares for different classes of of the new shares.	(1) Exchange common shares for preferred shares in an estate freeze; (2) Reorganize capital for dividend splitting; (3) Fight off take-over bid.
Eligible Property	(1) Capital property, Property excluding real property held by non-residents (2) Eligible capital property (3) Inventory unless it is real property held as inventory (4) Accounts receivable (5) Canadian resource property (6) Foreign resource property (7) Real property used by non-residents in the course of business in Canada.	Shares of a taxable Canadian corporation.	All vendor's shares of a particular class in the course of a reorganization of share capital.

	Section 85(1)	Section 85.1	Section 86
Consideration	Consideration must include shares.	Consideration must not include any non-share consideration, and all shares received must be of one particular class.	Consideration must include shares.
Purchaser Qualifications	Purchaser must be a taxable Canadian corporation.	Purchaser must be be a Canadian corporation, and the shares being transferred must be of a Canadian corporation.	Corporation does not need to be Canadian.
Vendor Qualifications		Vendor must hold shares as capital property.	Vendor must hold shares as capital property.
Transfer price To vendor	Parties agree to a designated transfer price for tax purposes but the transferee still receives the consideration for the FMV.		Cost base price of the new shares is the ACB of the old shares less FMV of boot and indirect gifts.
Transfer price To purchaser	Elected amount cannot be less than boot or more than the FMV of transferred property.	Transfer price to purchaser deemed to be the lesser of FMV and PUC of acquired shares.	
Exclusion	Cannot create a loss by electing at less than the tax cost of transferred property.	Will not apply if election is made under ss. 85(1) or 85(2).	Will not apply if election is made under ss. 51 or 85.
Election	Both parties must file an election: T2057 within three years.	Rollover applies automatically unless the vendor opts out.	No election necessary.

Index